BARRON'S

Military Flight Aptitude Tests

4th Edition

Terry L. Duran

All photographs, illustrations, and diagrams in this book either are the property of the author or have been released for public use.

Barron's Educational Series, Inc. is not affiliated with the Department of Defense or any military service. Use of military insignia, logos, and/or graphics identifying specific services, departments, or programs, as well as images released for public use by the Department of Defense, are for educational and informational use only and do not constitute endorsement by, or connection with, the Department of Defense or any military service.

All inquiries should be addressed to:
Barron's Educational Series, Inc.
250 Wireless Boulevard
Hauppauge, New York 11788
www.barronseduc.com

ISBN: 978-1-4380-1104-2

Library of Congress Control Number: 2018935777

PRINTED IN THE UNITED STATES OF AMERICA
9 8 7 6 5 4 3 2 1

10%
POST-CONSUMER WASTE
Paper contains a minimum of 10% post-consumer waste (PCW). Paper used in this book was derived from certified, sustainable forestlands.

This book is dedicated to the glory of God
and in honor of my wonderful, loving, supportive family—
my angelic, beautiful, brilliant, talented, wise, witty, and wonderful wife, June;
our awesome children and their spouses; and our delightful grandchildren—
without whom I am nothing,

and

in memory of the fallen:

Captain Charles K. "Kelly" Castleberry '82, U.S. Marine Corps
Marine Fighter Attack Squadron 312
RIP 23 September 1986

1st Lieutenant Robert J. "Bobby" Cox '82, U.S. Marine Corps
Marine All-Weather Attack Squadron 533
RIP 17 January 1987

Captain John E. Nisbet, Jr. '82, U.S. Marine Corps
Marine Medium Helicopter Squadron 262
RIP 11 May 1988

and

Senior Master Sergeant (Retired) Travis C. Duran, U.S. Air Force
RIP 23 October 2013
Thanks, Dad

Softly call the Muster,
Let comrade answer, "Here!"
Their spirits hover 'round us
As if to bring us cheer.

Mark them "present" in our hearts.
We'll meet some other day
There is no death, but life etern'
For old friends such as they!

from "Roll Call for the Absent"
Dr. John Ashton '06

Contents

PART I: AVIATION AND THE ALL-VOLUNTEER AMERICAN MILITARY

PART II: TESTING FORMATS AND REVIEW INFORMATION

PART III: FLIGHT APTITUDE PRACTICE TESTS

PART I
Aviation and the All-Volunteer American Military

Officers and Aviators, Professionals All

1

"We only have those rights we can defend."

THE ROLE OF THE AMERICAN MILITARY IN TODAY'S WORLD

You've decided that you want to be a military aviator. Now you just have to figure out how to get there.

"Great things are not done by impulse, but by a series of small things brought together." —Vincent van Gogh (1853–1890)

That's commendable—military aviation is a noble, worthwhile, and even exciting profession, and you have shown good initiative and judgment by choosing this book to improve your chances for selection.

You may already be a member of the U.S. military, or you may just be considering your options. Either way, you need to know the bigger picture. You will have to study hard and prepare thoroughly to be selected as a military aviator—and then you will have to successfully complete long periods of challenging training, just to get started.

Can you measure up? The answer is *Yes*—if you prepare the right way. This book will help.

The American military exists (as you know, if you are already a service member) to protect and defend the people and freedoms of the United States of America. Its establishment is provided for in the Constitution, it is drawn from the nation it represents, and today's all-volunteer military ultimately reflects the best of the nation it defends—those who are willing to sacrifice or subordinate their own desires and comfort for the benefit and protection of all.

"If a man hasn't discovered something that he will die for, he isn't fit to live." —Dr. Martin Luther King, Jr. (1929–1968)

Today's American military is the world's largest "meritocracy," where rewards are primarily based on demonstrated merit and performance—not on an individual's background, social or economic status, race, ethnicity, connections, or other unearned factors. It is, on average, somewhat better educated than the country it represents—maybe because it emphasizes the value of education and self-improvement—and it includes every possible race, religion, ethnicity, and the like . . . even non-U.S. citizens who believe that our principles and way of life are worth fighting for. It's not perfect, and it definitely isn't easy—but it's better than anything else out there.

The U.S. military is one of the most respected American institutions, steeped in tradition and service and bound together by principles of honor, courage, and loyalty found nowhere else. It is by no means perfect—no human institution can be—but it holds itself and its members accountable and strives to become better.

And make no mistake, the United States is still at war *with those who declared war on us* years before September 11, 2001. More than a decade and a half of struggle and sacrifice have not been enough to finish the war against those who hate our liberties and want to either dictate how we think, act, and believe . . . or kill us. We have made tremendous inroads and huge progress, but we are not yet done—the mission is not yet complete.

"The true soldier fights not because he hates what is before him, but because he loves what is behind him."
—G. K. Chesterton (1874–1936)

It is precisely because of our freedoms and the blessings of our human and natural resources that we are able to fight a war against an enemy thousands of miles away and not have rationing and shortages at home . . . where war news is given far less play than entertainment and business news . . . and where only one percent of the population has seen military service.

If you are reading this, you are to be commended for considering how you can become part of that one percent.

The Cold War lasted 46 years, from the end of World War II in 1945 to the fall of the Soviet Union and its satellite dictatorships in 1991. Anyone who thinks that the current war against terror and violent extremism is less of a generational war—that it can be solved by just packing up and coming home—is sadly mistaken. Just because we as a nation, as a culture, are willing to "live and let live" *does not mean that other people think the same way.* This is a hard truth, but one that needs and deserves understanding.

"The country must have a large and efficient army, one capable of meeting the enemy abroad, or they must expect to meet him at home."
—British Field Marshal Arthur Wellesley, 1st Duke of Wellington (1769–1852)

The War on Terror fought by the United States and its allies since September 11, 2001, has been waged not only by the active, full-time component of all the services, but also by the Reserves of all the services, and by Army and Air National Guard units from all 54 states and territories. Active duty unit deployments that lasted a year or more—sometimes with a year or less in between—have given way to deployments of nine months or less overseas for ground troops (less for Air Force and Navy units). National Guard and Reserve units now have one to four years between deployments.

Regardless of whether the U.S. military is scheduled to grow or shrink in any given year (and it does go back and forth), all the services have a critical need for a steady stream of the highest-quality applicants, especially those who want to become aviators. Even during times when there is a pilot shortage, the services can't afford to lower their standards, and they won't.

Only the best will be chosen—will that be you?

It can be. Read and apply what's in this book—then it's up to you.

Military aviation is a vital part of the U.S. air, sea, and land forces that defend our nation and our way of life. Aviation units are integrated into the Army, Marine Corps, and Navy—and they are, of course, present in a "purer" sense in the most air-oriented branch of the military, the Air Force.

AMERICAN MILITARY AVIATION

The following information is meant to give you some context and background about how the American military, and especially American military aviation, is organized. **This is primarily because all three services' flight aptitude tests include problems and questions that require some understanding of the overall organization besides just surface-level math and reading skills, or even scientific or technical knowledge.** Other information will focus more on helping you understand what it takes to be an American military officer, rather than just focusing specifically on aviation. That's because, in all the services, you have to qualify to be an officer or a warrant officer first, and then to be an aviator.

The aircraft of the Air Force, Army, Navy, and Marine Corps are versatile, hard-hitting forces that can be employed swiftly anywhere in the world. These forces can quickly gain and maintain air superiority over regional aggressors and provide close air support for U.S. ground forces, permitting rapid air attacks on enemy targets while providing security and support for ground forces to conduct logistics, mission command, intelligence, and other functions.

Fighter/attack aircraft, operating from both land bases and aircraft carriers, oppose enemy fighters and attack ground and ship targets. Conventional bombers provide a worldwide capability to strike surface targets on short notice. Specialized aircraft supporting conventional operations perform functions such as airborne early warning and control, suppression of enemy air defenses, reconnaissance, surveillance, and combat search and rescue. In addition, the U.S. military operates a variety of transport planes, aerial-refueling aircraft, helicopters, and other support aircraft.

The role of unmanned aerial vehicles (UAVs) in both reconnaissance and attack missions is growing in all the services. Technological advances are enabling more and more capabilities to be placed on increasingly smaller airframes.

The ability of these forces to have an immediate impact on a conflict by precision attacks on selected enemy targets has expanded dramatically as an increasing proportion of "smart" munitions has been deployed.

Special operations aviation forces contribute to all phases of military operations. Some of their most important missions are insertion, support, and extraction of special operations forces; suppression of enemy air defenses; and aerial reconnaissance and surveillance.

Coast Guard aviation elements work in conjunction with ship- and shore-based units to perform their missions of coastal security and rescue and law enforcement. Their aircraft are specially adapted to the needs of their missions; in wartime they provide an important contribution to homeland defense, in addition to their other duties.

Roles, Duties, and Opportunities of Military Officers

If you are going to be an American military aviator or pilot, you will also generally be a commissioned or warrant officer. An *officer,* in the broadest sense of the term, is someone in an organization who has both the authority and the obligation to *lead*—to exert influence over others to accomplish the mission . . . to get the job done.

Aviation units have proportionately more officers than other units, in all the services, simply because almost all pilots are either commissioned or warrant officers. Military flying is a very technical *and* a very physical business. The educational, age, and other requirements have evolved based on studies of the types of people who have been successful in pilot training and beyond.

"Leadership is the art of getting someone else to do something you want done because he wants to do it." —Dwight D. Eisenhower (1890–1969), General of the Army, 34th president of the United States

Military Rank Structure, Pay, and Benefits

There are three types of officers in the U.S. military: commissioned officers, warrant officers, and noncommissioned officers. The remaining service members are known as "enlisted personnel." Every *rank,* officer or not, has a *pay grade* associated with it. Many times the rank and the pay grade are used interchangeably, but not always. Even though they do have leadership responsibilities, noncommissioned officers ("NCOs" for short) are also enlisted; the jump from the "just enlisted" lower ranks to NCO occurs at pay grade E-4 or E-5, depending on the service. The pay grades for enlisted members run from E-1 to E-9, for warrant officers from W-1 to W-5, and for commissioned officers from O-1 to O-10; you can see more detail in the charts that follow, beginning on page 7.

Pay grades can also be useful for comparison purposes among the services due to rank titles that are sometimes confusing. For example, an Air Force staff sergeant is an E-5, whereas an Army or Marine staff sergeant is an E-6. Likewise, an Army or Marine captain is an O-3, but a Navy or Coast Guard captain is an O-6.

The bottom line is that the same pay grade with the same number of years of service will get paid the same base pay, no matter which service they are in or what position they are currently assigned. Aviators, however, frequently get extra pay on top of this—but more about that shortly.

A few other technicalities: the Navy and Coast Guard call their NCOs *petty officers*; the Air Force doesn't have any warrant officers; the commander of a Navy or Coast Guard ship is commonly called *captain* regardless of pay grade or rank, and the Navy and Coast Guard use the term *rate* instead of *rank* when referring to enlisted personnel. Here, though, we are going to use only the term *rank* to avoid confusion, and *captain* will be a rank unless it's specified to be the commander of a ship.

When people refer to "officers" as such, they are usually talking about commissioned officers: those who have a *commission* at the direction of the president of the United States to act on his behalf (the military falls under the executive branch of government). Sometimes, though, they are talking about commissioned officers *and* warrant officers. Warrant officers have a *warrant* from the Secretary (head civilian official) of their service to perform special technical or staff functions.

The military values experience, as demonstrated by the fact that they pay more for it. Even though the newest second lieutenant or ensign (an O-1 in either case) technically outranks a senior NCO with possibly decades of experience, woe be unto that new officer if he or she doesn't take into account the wisdom and counsel of that experienced NCO!

"If your actions inspire others to dream more, learn more, do more, and become more, you are a leader." —John Quincy Adams (1767–1848), American statesman, diplomat, U.S. representative and senator from Massachusetts, and 6th president of the United States

And, yes, officers get paid more than the other pay grades. That's because they usually have more responsibility than the other pay grades—significantly more, in many cases. Even if an officer is not in a command position, his or her action (or inaction) can have a significant effect on service members and units, for either better or worse.

And, because of the "special trust and confidence in the patriotism, valor, fidelity, and abilities" placed in officers, there's a higher price to pay for failure. Not only could service members be hurt or killed (which is bad enough) because an officer did something stupid or wrong, but the officer can be relieved and discharged from the service, as opposed to an enlisted member, who might be fined or reduced one or more pay grades but allowed to stay in the military.

Some other benefits to military service regardless of pay grade include structured pay raises within pay grades over time (something you will seldom see in the civilian world); the potential for nontaxable allowances for subsistence (meals) and housing, depending on your situation; the opportunity for all of your basic pay to be tax free during those periods you are deployed to a combat zone; medical care; and special pays such as flight pay, sea pay, parachutist pay (commonly known as "jump pay"), combat zone pay, and so on.

The U.S. military usually gets at least a small pay raise once a year, usually in January, but this depends on Congress—there are no guarantees. The latest full pay table is available at *http://www.dfas.mil/militarymembers/payentitlements/military-pay-charts.html.*

In addition, military aviators are eligible for some special pays:

Aviation Career Incentive Pay (ACIP) is a financial incentive for officers to serve as military aviators throughout a military career. Payments range from $125 to $1,000 per month, determined by the needs of the service and the individual's years of service.

Aviation Continuation Pay (ACP) is a financial incentive designed to retain qualified, experienced officer aviators who have completed their Active Duty Service Obligation (ADSO) if they remain on active duty for a specified period of additional service. Services may pay thousands of dollars for each year of a qualified aviator's service agreement.

COMMISSIONED OFFICER RANK

Pay Grade	Army/Air Force/Marines	Navy/Coast Guard
O-1	Second Lieutenant (gold)	Ensign
O-2	First Lieutenant	Lieutenant Junior Grade
O-3	Captain	Lieutenant
O-4	Major (gold)	Lieutenant Commander
O-5	Lieutenant Colonel	Commander
O-6	Colonel	Captain
O-7	Brigadier General	Rear Admiral (lower half)
O-8	Major General	Rear Admiral (upper half)
O-9	Lieutenant General	Vice Admiral
O-10	General	Admiral

Note: The Navy also uses Air Force/Army/Marine style rank on the collar of uniforms that do not use shoulder boards.

Note: Army, Air Force, and Marine officer rank insignia is silver unless otherwise noted; Navy shoulder board insignia is gold on black, and Coast Guard shoulder boards are gold on blue.

WARRANT OFFICER RANK

	Army	Marines	Navy/Coast Guard
W-1	Warrant Officer 1 (black on silver)	Warrant Officer (red on gold)	The grade of Warrant Officer (W-1) is no longer used by the Navy and Coast Guard.
W-2	Chief Warrant Officer 2 (black on silver)	Chief Warrant Officer 2 (red on gold)	Chief Warrant Officer 2 (blue on gold)
W-3	Chief Warrant Officer 3 (black on silver)	Chief Warrant Officer 3 (red on gold)	Chief Warrant Officer 3 (blue on silver)
W-4	Chief Warrant Officer 4 (black on silver)	Chief Warrant Officer 4 (red on gold)	Chief Warrant Officer 4 (red on silver)
W-5	Chief Warrant Officer 5 (black on silver)	Chief Warrant Officer 5 (red on gold)	Chief Warrant Officer 5 (red on silver) (Navy only)

Note: The Air Force does not have warrant officers.

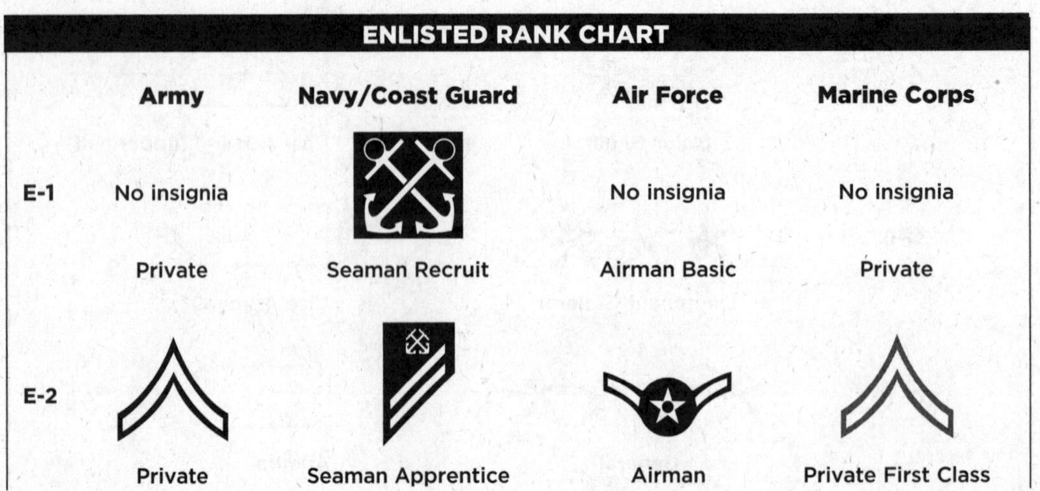

ENLISTED RANK CHART

	Army	Navy/Coast Guard	Air Force	Marine Corps
E-1	No insignia Private	Seaman Recruit	No insignia Airman Basic	No insignia Private
E-2	Private	Seaman Apprentice	Airman	Private First Class

Army
Navy/Coast Guard
Air Force
Marine Corps
E-3
Private First Class
Seaman
Airman First Class
Lance Corporal
E-4
Corporal
Specialist
Petty Officer Third Class
Senior Airman
Corporal
E-5
Sergeant
Petty Officer Second Class
Staff Sergeant
Sergeant
E-6
Staff Sergeant
Petty Officer First Class
Technical Sergeant
Staff Sergeant
E-7
Sergeant First Class
Chief Petty Officer
Master Sergeant
Gunnery Sergeant
First Sergeant (Master Sergeant)

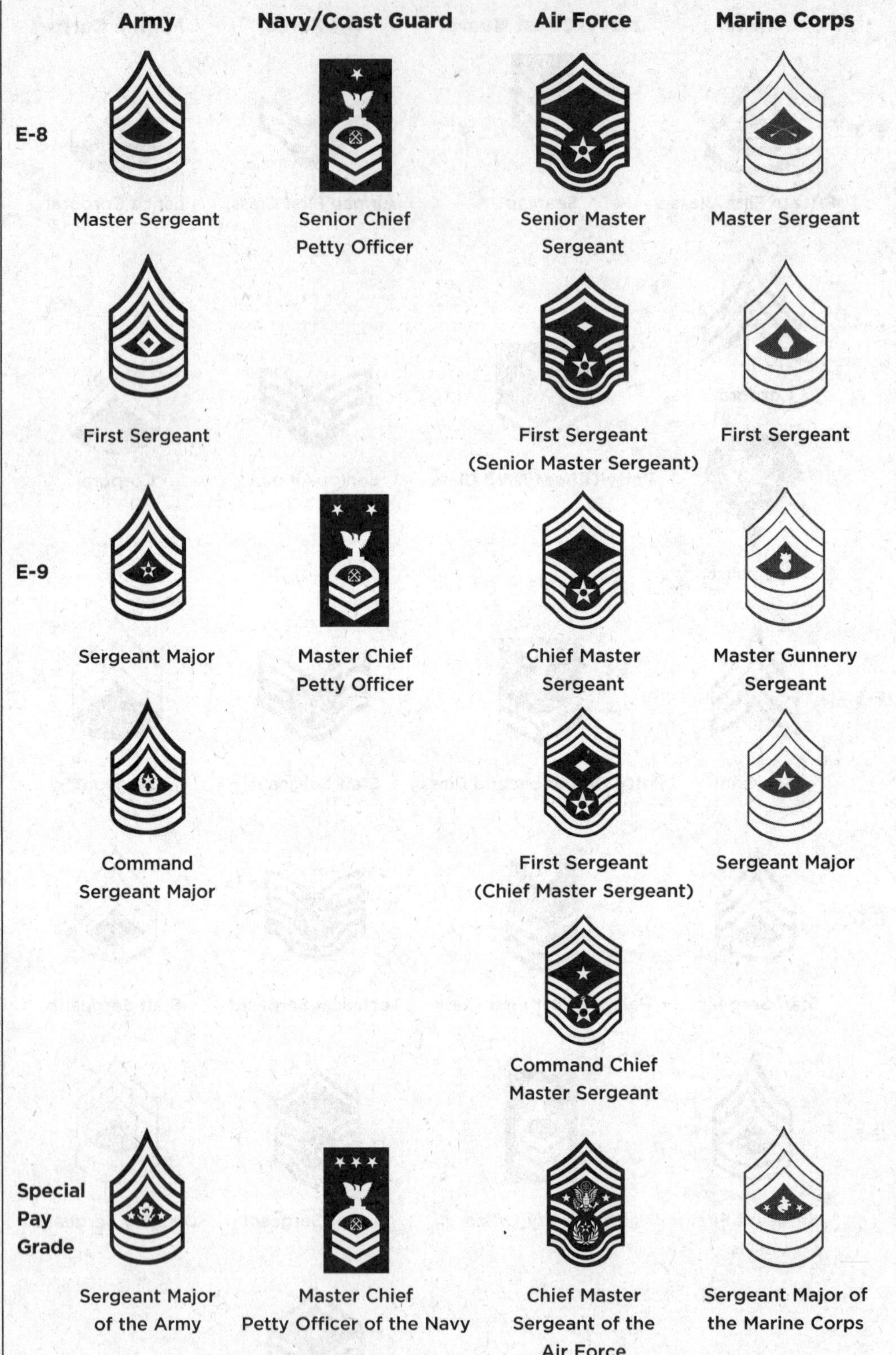
Army
Navy/Coast Guard
Air Force
Marine Corps
E-8
Master Sergeant
Senior Chief Petty Officer
Senior Master Sergeant
Master Sergeant
First Sergeant
First Sergeant (Senior Master Sergeant)
First Sergeant
E-9
Sergeant Major
Master Chief Petty Officer
Chief Master Sergeant
Master Gunnery Sergeant
Command Sergeant Major
First Sergeant (Chief Master Sergeant)
Sergeant Major
Command Chief Master Sergeant
Special Pay Grade
Sergeant Major of the Army
Master Chief Petty Officer of the Navy
Chief Master Sergeant of the Air Force
Sergeant Major of the Marine Corps

REQUIREMENTS FOR BECOMING AN OFFICER AND AVIATOR

"Once you have tasted flight, you will forever walk the earth with your eyes turned skyward, for there you have been, and there you will always long to return." —Leonardo da Vinci (1452–1519)

The Air Force, Army, Navy, and Coast Guard each have three main sources of commissioned officers: their service academy, their officer candidate or training school, and college-level Reserve Officer Training Corps (ROTC). As part of the Department of the Navy, potential officers of the U.S. Marine Corps attend the U.S. Naval Academy at Annapolis, Maryland, and participate in Naval ROTC, but they have their own Officer Candidate Course, separate from the Navy. Requirements for the service academies include being between 17 and 23 at the time of enrollment, outstanding high school records and test results, and a nomination from a member of Congress or the Executive Branch. Requirements for commissioning and for pilot/aviator training selection are similar among the services, with some benchmarks set by law and others by the services, based on their needs at that time.

U.S. Air Force

The U.S. Air Force has three pathways to becoming an officer first, after which you may be selected to become a pilot: the U.S. Air Force Academy (USAFA) at Colorado Springs, Colorado; Air Force Reserve Officer Training Corps (AFROTC), offered at more than 1,100 colleges and universities throughout the country; and Officer Training School (OTS), where current enlisted Air Force, Air Force Reserve, and Air National Guard members can be selected to undergo training and evaluations that can result in their commissioning as an officer.

The U.S. Air Force Academy at Colorado Springs, established in 1954, is the premier source of Air Force officers, graduating more than 800 second lieutenants each year. Applicants compete based on their overall high school record, college entrance test scores, physical fitness scores, and military test scores. USAFA cadets are paid during their four years of attendance and incur a mandatory service obligation upon their graduation and commissioning as second lieutenants.

There are two primary routes to an Air Force commission through AFROTC—the four-year program and the two-year program. Students in both programs attend AFROTC classes along with other college courses and normally receive elective academic credit. Cadets who successfully complete all requirements are commissioned as Air Force officers with a four-year active duty service commitment. Those selected as pilots, combat systems officers, and air battle managers have longer commitments upon completion of specialized training. If you want to be a pilot, you must be commissioned before you reach 29 years of age; you also have to meet Air Force height and weight requirements and pass a physical fitness test.

The Air Force conducts its Officer Training School (OTS) at Maxwell Air Force Base (AFB), Alabama, for current Air Force enlisted members who already have a bachelor's degree, meet physical and age requirements, have their commander's recommendation, and are chosen by a selection board. OTS is a demanding nine-week course that graduates a varying number of officers each year based on the needs of the total Air Force, which includes the Air Force Reserve and the Air National Guard. Upon graduation, candidates are commissioned as Air Force second lieutenants and proceed to technical training for their officer specialty.

Regardless of commissioning source, prospective Air Force pilots are assessed against a Pilot Candidate Selection Method (PCSM) index that measures a candidate's aptitude for pilot training. The PCSM takes into account the Pilot composite score on the Air Force Officer

Qualifying Test (AFOQT), the Test of Basic Aviation Skills (TBAS), and any previous flying hours (such as if you already have a private pilot's license).

A new version of the AFOQT, known as the "Form T," was introduced in 2014. The changes in Form T were based on feedback from an Air Force–wide survey where current officers identified the most important abilities and aptitudes needed for effectiveness as an officer. Form T changes include:

- Updated test questions throughout
- Elimination of the Rotated Blocks and Hidden Figures subtests
- Addition of new Reading Comprehension and Situational Judgment subtests
- Updated graphics in the Instrument Comprehension subtest and an increase in the number of questions from 20 to 25
- An increase in the number of questions on the Block Counting subtest (from 20 to 30 questions)
- Revised General Science subtest, with a focus on the physical sciences and renamed as the "Physical Science" subtest

The Reading Comprehension subtest contributes to the AFOQT Verbal and Academic aptitude composites and incorporates the types of written information used in Air Force officer professional military education. The Situational Judgment subtest contributes to a new composite that measures judgment and decision-making when responding to the types of interpersonal situations often encountered by junior USAF officers.

We'll go over both the AFOQT and the TBAS in much more detail in Chapter 3.

U.S. Army

The U.S. Army also has three primary sources of commissioned officers: the U.S. Military Academy (USMA) at West Point, New York; Army Reserve Officer Training Corps (ROTC), offered at more than 900 colleges and universities nationwide; and Officer Candidate School (OCS), where current enlisted soldiers can be selected to undergo training and assessments that can see them being commissioned as officers.

In the Army, aviators are either commissioned or warrant officers. Both have an aviation "branch," but this is not to be confused with *branches of service* (Army, Navy, etc.). Warrant officers fly more over the course of time, but they also spend less time in leadership positions within aviation units—although, as warrant officers, they are expected to be unparalleled subject matter experts on flying.

The USMA, established in 1802, is the premier source of officers for the Army, graduating more than 900 highly trained second lieutenants a year. Applicants compete based on their overall high school record, college entrance exams, demonstrated leadership abilities, physical fitness scores, and military test scores. USMA cadets are paid during their four years of attendance, and incur a five-year mandatory service obligation upon their graduation and commissioning.

Army ROTC commissions about 4,000 new second lieutenants a year—well over half the active Army's requirement. Students in Army ROTC attend military science classes along with other college courses and normally receive elective academic credit. Cadets who successfully complete all requirements are commissioned as Army officers with an eight-year total commitment, at least six of which must be in an active, Reserve, or National Guard unit. If you want to be a pilot, you must be commissioned before you reach 29 years of age, and you must enter flight school no later than your 30th birthday.

The Army conducts OCS at Fort Benning, Georgia, for the active Army, the U.S. Army Reserve, and selected members of the Army National Guard. Army OCS at Fort Benning is an intensive 12-week course whose graduates are commissioned in one of 16 basic branches. Army National Guard OCS is also conducted by most of the 54 states and territories under the accreditation and approved curriculum of the U.S. Army Infantry School at Fort Benning, just as is the federal OCS. Upon graduation, candidates are commissioned as Army second lieutenants and proceed to the Basic Officer Leader Course (BOLC) for their branch. Army aviator requirements for OCS graduates are the same as for ROTC.

Warrant Officer Candidate School (WOCS) is an intensive six-week course conducted at Fort Rucker, Alabama. Only candidates preselected for follow-on aviator duty can enter WOCS without significant prior military experience in a particular field (e.g., logistics, personnel, ordnance, etc.). Graduates are appointed a Warrant Officer One and proceed to their warrant officer basic course.

Army flight training, both basic and advanced, is conducted for both commissioned and warrant officers at Fort Rucker. Initial training of an Army aviator, whether commissioned or warrant officer, can take up to a year before assignment to an operational unit.

U.S. Navy and Marine Corps

There are four pathways to becoming a Naval or Marine officer: the U.S. Naval Academy (USNA), Naval ROTC, Navy OCS, and the Marine Corps' Platoon Leaders' Course (PLC) and Officer Candidate Course (OCC).

Like the other services, the U.S. Navy operates its own service academy, this one at Annapolis, Maryland, established in 1845. USNA midshipmen include prospective Marine officers, since the Marine Corps is part of the Department of the Navy. The Naval Academy provides the Navy and Marine Corps with more than a thousand new officers annually.

Likewise, Navy ROTC is offered at more than 150 colleges and universities nationwide. It is organized much as the other services' programs, with the exception that Marine Option cadets normally have extra training activities. NROTC is the largest single source of Navy and Marine Corps officers.

Navy OCS is one of five officer training schools located at Naval Station Newport in Rhode Island. The 12-week course not only assesses candidates to see if they have what it takes, but gives them a working knowledge of the Navy afloat and ashore, preparing them to assume the responsibilities of a naval officer. Graduates of Navy OCS are commissioned as ensigns and attend technical training before reporting to their first fleet assignment.

The Marine Corps' PLC is designed for college students who have not yet received their degree, splitting up their training into two six-week summer training courses. OCC candidates have already received their bachelor's degree, and so undergo a rigorous 10-week training and evaluation that focuses on military and leadership tasks, rapid absorption of military knowledge, physical training, and functioning under sleep deprivation. Graduates of both courses are commissioned as Marine second lieutenants and attend another six months of demanding instruction at The Basic School (TBS), where (regardless of their eventual specialty) they will learn to become Marine infantry platoon commanders. After completion of TBS, they proceed to technical schools for their particular specialty, and from there to the field and fleet.

To become a naval or Marine aviator, you must be between the ages of 19 and 27 at the time you apply for flight training. Waivers of up to 24 months can be made on a month-for-month basis for those with prior active duty military service, up to a maximum age of 29. The standards are the same for naval flight officers (such as Radar Intercept Officers or RIOs), except NFOs may be granted a waiver of up to 48 months for active duty served before their 27th birthday—again on a month-for-month basis—to a maximum age of 31.

Naval flight officers in both the Navy and Marine Corps are not pilots, but they undergo much of the same training. They perform many "copilot" functions in aircraft with multi-person crews, specializing in airborne weapons and sensor systems. They are by no means "second fiddle," however—they can serve as tactical mission commanders (although the pilot in command, regardless of rank, is always responsible for the safe piloting of the aircraft) of single or multiple air assets during a particular mission.

The pilot training program for new naval aviators takes 18 months altogether to complete. All students undergo common training at Naval Air Station (NAS) Pensacola, where they are screened for one of three primary pipelines: helicopters, multi-engine propeller aircraft, or strike warfare (jets). Upon completion of training at Pensacola, Student Naval Aviators (SNAs) enter their primary training pipelines, where they learn the basics of flying.

U.S. Coast Guard

Coast Guard officers receive their commissions as ensigns from either the U.S. Coast Guard Academy or Coast Guard OCS, both of which are located in New London, Connecticut. The Coast Guard also has the College Student Pre-Commissioning Initiative (CSPI) available to students at about 400 campuses that are classified as historically black colleges and universities; Hispanic-serving institutions; and tribal colleges or universities; plus six campuses in Hawaii, Alaska, and Guam. This is essentially a scholarship for the last two years of the participant's college time, with active duty E-3 pay, full tuition, some fees, and some book costs, but it also requires completion of Coast Guard basic training and participation in various training events during that period. After graduation comes Coast Guard OCS and then commissioning.

Regardless of commissioning source, newly commissioned Coast Guard ensigns are then integrated into the Navy's flight training program as appropriate for the kind of aircraft they will fly for the Coast Guard. The Coast Guard also directly commissions people with prior Department of Defense (DoD) flight experience in its Direct Commission Aviator program.

American Military Aviation

2

Military aircraft exist to perform one or more of four basic functions: *transporting* people and/or things from one place to another; *bombing* enemy forces or facilities on the ground, or ships at sea; *shooting*, either at enemy aircraft in the air or at enemies on the surface; or *observing* enemy actions and reporting them to other friendly forces.

In most cases, military aircraft operate at some level in support of surface (ground or sea) forces, since the only way to control what's happening on the surface for more than a short time is to *be* there. Or, said another way, ground units and air units often work together to accomplish the mission at hand.

Military aircraft can be divided into two general categories: *fixed-wing* aircraft, commonly referred to as *airplanes*; and *rotary-wing* aircraft, usually referred to as *helicopters*.

OVERVIEW OF FIXED-WING AIRCRAFT

Fixed-wing aircraft are just that—their wings are "fixed," meaning that they don't move. These aircraft get their ability to fly (a quality called *lift*) from air passing over their wings, and are usually either pulled through the air by a corkscrew-type propeller or pushed through the air by the thrust from one or more jet engines.

American fixed-wing military aircraft are referred to by an alphanumeric system that consists of three parts and a given name. The first part, which consists of one or two letters, refers to the function of the airplane. If there are two letters, the first letter indicates a modification of the aircraft's basic mission, which is indicated by the second letter. Here are some of the most common designators:

A—Attack
B—Bomber
C—Cargo/transport
AC—Cargo plane modified to perform an attack mission
KC—Cargo plane modified to perform an aerial refueling mission
E—Special electronics
F—Fighter
F/A—Fighter/attack
O—Observation
P—Patrol (maritime)
Q—Unmanned aerial vehicle
R—Reconnaissance
S—Antisubmarine
T—Trainer
U—Utility
V—Vertical takeoff and/or landing
X—Experimental/test

The second part of the designation is the model or sequence number, which, in combination with the functional designation, gives you the series designation. A letter that follows the sequence number denotes the exact model or version; successive letters designate upgrades, modifications, or improvements. Thus, we can tell that an F/A-18C is a fighter of the F/A-18 series, and that it is a later or modified (or at least different) version from an F/A-18A.

For ease of reference (and it doesn't hurt crew morale, either), American military aircraft are also given a name of some sort, usually one that relates to its mission, warlike qualities, or special characteristics. Thus, we have the F-117 Nighthawk, a stealthy fighter named after a bird of prey; the heavily armed B-52 Stratofortress; the EA-6B Prowler reconnaissance plane—even the A-10 Thunderbolt II, nicknamed the "Warthog," not much to look at, but without question rugged and powerful.

OVERVIEW OF ROTARY-WING AIRCRAFT

Rotary-wing aircraft don't have wings in the same sense as fixed-wing aircraft. They get their lift from air passing over rotor blades that are spun around at high speed in a circle by an engine; the tilt of the rotors relative to the helicopter's body or fuselage governs the aircraft's movement forward and backward, left and right, up and down. A notable difference between rotary- and fixed-wing aircraft is that rotary-wing craft can *hover*—stay aloft over just one spot.

The inside joke at some rotary-wing aviator schools is, "A helicopter doesn't fly—it beats the air into submission." A helicopter does not have the same stable tendencies while in flight that a well-designed conventional airplane does. It maintains its altitude and flight by a variety of forces and controls that are actually working in opposition to each other; the pilot's job is to balance (or nearly balance) these forces for the helicopter to go where he wants it to go.

By worldwide convention, helicopters are categorized by maximum gross weight (aircraft, fuel, crew, equipment, weapons, and so on—the most weight with which the aircraft can take off under normal conditions): "light," "medium lift," and "heavy lift." Light helicopters are generally considered to be those below 12,000 lbs. Medium-lift helicopters are those that weigh from about 14,000 to 45,000 lbs., and heavy-lift helicopters are usually considered to be those that weigh more than 50,000 lbs. Some in the field reserve the *heavy-lift* term for the very largest copters—above 80,000 lbs. The exact amount of load a helicopter can carry depends on the model, the fuel on board, the exact distance to be flown, and atmospheric conditions.

U.S. military helicopters are designated by a system that has three alphanumeric parts and a given name. The first part, which consists of letters, refers to the function of the helicopter. Here are some of the most common designations:

- AH—attack helicopter
- CH—cargo helicopter
- HH—heavy-lift and large rescue helicopters not otherwise classified
- MH—modified for special operations
- OH—observation, reconnaissance, and courier
- SH—antisubmarine warfare (ASW) helicopter
- UH—utility/general purpose; can move internal or external ("sling") loads

The second part of the designation is the model or sequence number, which, when put together with the functional designation, yields the series designation. A letter that follows the sequence number denotes the exact model or version; successive letters designate upgrades, modifications, and/or improvements. Thus, we can tell that a UH-60L is a utility helicopter of the UH-60 series, and that it is a later or modified version following a UH-60A.

Most Army helicopters are named after Native American tribes (such as Blackhawk, Apache, and Iroquois). Most Navy and Marine Corps helicopters have a maritime reference in their names, such as Sea Hawk, Sea Knight, and so on.

U.S. MILITARY AIRCRAFT SUMMARIES

This section will acquaint you with some of the most common aircraft used by the U.S. military today. There are many more types and variations of U.S. military aircraft than what can be included in this book. This section will give you an idea of the most common U.S. military aircraft types, capabilities, and missions—*which will prepare you with context and background for the Aviation Information subtests in all three services' flight aptitude tests.* See the section titled "Aviation Information" in Chapter 7 for more technical information.

Attack Aircraft

A-10 THUNDERBOLT II

USAF

The A-10 Thunderbolt II is the first USAF aircraft to be specifically designed for providing close air support to ground forces. It has excellent maneuverability at low speeds and low altitude and is a rugged, highly accurate weapons platform. It can remain near battle areas for extended time periods and operate in low visibility and bad weather conditions. The pilot and parts of the flight control system are protected by titanium armor that can take direct hits from armor-piercing and high-explosive projectiles. Its 30 mm seven-barrel Gatling gun, mounted in the fuselage and protruding under the nose, has given it a well-deserved reputation as a premier tank buster.

The Thunderbolt II—lovingly nicknamed the "Warthog"—has received many small and large upgrades since it was first introduced in 1975; the entire fleet is now designated as the A-10C. It has come close to being retired more than once, but the lack of a replacement with truly equivalent capabilities has kept it in the USAF inventory. Current plans call for it to remain in service until at least 2021.

AC-130U SPOOKY

USAF

The primary missions for the AC-130U Spooky gunship are close air support, air interdiction, and armed reconnaissance. Close air support missions include supporting ground troops in contact with the enemy, convoy escort/overwatch, and point air defense. Air interdiction missions are conducted against preplanned targets or targets of opportunity and include strike coordination, reconnaissance, and armed overwatch missions.

The heavily armed AC-130U incorporates side-firing heavy weapons integrated with sophisticated sensor, navigation, and fire control systems to provide surgically accurate firepower on a particular point or saturation of a larger area, even over extended periods, at night, and in bad weather.

A-10C THUNDERBOLT II ("WARTHOG")

Description	Low/straight-wing, twin tail, two-engine jet
Mission/users	Close air support, airborne forward air control, combat search-and-rescue support; USAF
Crew	One
Length	53 ft., 4 in. (16.16 m)
Height	14 ft., 8 in. (4.42 m)
Wingspan	57 ft., 6 in. (17.42 m)
Empty weight	29,000 lbs. (13,154 kg)
Max. gross weight	51,000 lbs. (22,950 kg)
Maximum speed	518 mph (450 knots)
Maximum altitude	45,000 ft. (13,636 m)
Maximum range	2,580 miles (2,240 nautical miles)
Powerplant(s)	Two General Electric TF34-GE-100 turbofans
Payload capacity	16,000 lbs. (7,257 kg)
Armament	One 30 mm GAU-8/A seven-barrel Gatling gun; up to 16,000 lbs. (7,200 kg) of mixed ordnance on eight under-wing and three under-fuselage pylon stations
Manufacturer	Fairchild Republic Co.
Variants	N/A

AC-130U SPOOKY

Description	Four-engine high-wing turboprop
Mission/users	Close air support, air interdiction, force protection; USAF
Crew	Five officers (pilot, copilot, navigator, fire control officer, electronic warfare officer) and eight enlisted (flight engineer, TV operator, infrared detection set operator, loadmaster, four aerial gunners)
Length	97 ft., 9 in. (29.8 m)
Height	38 ft., 6 in. (11.7 m)
Wingspan	132 ft., 7 in. (40.4 m)
Empty weight	79,469 lbs. (35,797 kg)
Max. gross weight	155,000 lbs. (69,750 kg)
Maximum speed	300 mph (261 knots)
Cruising speed	300 mph (261 knots) maximum
Maximum altitude	25,000 ft. (7,576 m)
Maximum range	Approx. 1,495 miles (2,411 km); limited only by crew endurance with aerial refueling
Powerplant(s)	Four Allison T56-A-15 turboprop engines, each generating 4,910 shaft hp
Payload capacity	N/A
Armament	40 mm and 105 mm cannons plus 25 mm Gatling gun
Manufacturer	Lockheed/Boeing Corp.
Variants	AC-130H Spectre, MC-130W Combat Spear/Stinger

AV-8B HARRIER II	
Description	Vertical/short takeoff and landing single-engine jet
Mission/users	Attack and destroy surface and air targets, escort helicopters; USMC, Italy, Spain
Crew	One (pilot)
Length	46 ft., 4 in. (14.12 m)
Height	11 ft., 8 in. (3.55 m)
Wingspan	30 ft., 4 in. (9.25 m)
Empty weight	13,086 lbs. (5,936 kg)
Max. gross weight	31,000 lbs. (14,091 kg)
Maximum speed	668 mph (580 knots)
Maximum altitude	Over 50,000 ft. (15,240 m)
Maximum range	1,496 miles (1,230 nautical miles)
Powerplant(s)	One Rolls Royce Pegasus F402-RR-402-406A turbofan engine generating 20,280 lbs. of thrust
Payload capacity	Can carry up to 17,000 lbs. of bombs or rockets
Armament	• One fuselage-mounted 25 mm gun system • Standard air-to-ground load: six Mk 82; 500-lb. bombs • Standard air-to-air load: four AIM-9L/M Sidewinder missiles
Manufacturer	Airframe prime contractor: McDonnell Douglas (now Boeing North America); engine prime contractor: Rolls Royce
Variants	TAV-8B (trainer), AV-8B Harrier II+

AV-8B HARRIER II

USMC

The AV-8B Harrier V/STOL (Vertical/Short Takeoff and Landing) strike aircraft has unique capabilities that allow it to operate from a variety of places inaccessible to other fixed-wing aircraft—such as amphibious ships, rapidly constructed expeditionary airfields, roads, forward area refueling points (FARPs), and damaged conventional airfields—while also being able to operate from aircraft carriers and conventional land-based airfields.

Bombers

B-1B LANCER

USAF

The B-1B is a stealthy, multi-role, swing-wing, long-range supersonic bomber, capable of flying a variety of conventional missions for intercontinental distances without refueling, penetrating both present and predicted enemy air defenses. Although smaller than the B-52 it was designed to replace, it carries more weapons and has only one-tenth the radar signature. The B-1B's electronic jamming equipment, infrared countermeasures, and radar warning systems add to its low-radar cross-section to greatly increase its survivability.

Although originally designed as a nuclear-capable bomber, the "New START" (Strategic Arms Reduction Treaty) agreement with Russia in 2011 called for the attachment points and the control electronics for nuclear weapons to be uninstalled. Once a year, Russian officials are granted access to the appropriate USAF bases for an inspection to ensure that the Air Force's fastest bomber is still unable to carry nuclear weapons. Even so, carrying the largest conventional payload of either guided or unguided weapons in the Air Force inventory, the B-1B Lancer is currently expected to remain in service until at least 2040.

USAF

B-2 SPIRIT

The B-2 Spirit is a multi-role stealth bomber capable of delivering conventional (including precision-guided standoff) and nuclear munitions. The combination of low-observable technologies with high aerodynamic efficiency and a large payload capacity gives the B-2 important advantages over other existing bombers. Its unique design and construction gives the B-2 its "stealth"—very low observability by sight, hearing, radar, or infrared sensors.

USAF

B-52H STRATOFORTRESS

The B-52 series "BUFF" (translated in polite company as "Big Ugly Fat Fellow") is a long-range heavy bomber that can perform a variety of missions. Capable of high subsonic speeds at up to 50,000 ft. (15,240 m), it can conduct aerial refueling and carry nuclear or precision-guided conventional ordnance worldwide.

B-1B LANCER	
Description	Swing-wing four-engine heavy bomber
Mission/users	Long-range, multi-role, heavy bomber; USAF
Crew	Four (aircraft commander, copilot, two weapons systems officers)
Length	146 ft. (44.5 m)
Height	34 ft. (10.4 m)
Wingspan	137 ft. (41.8 m) extended forward, 79 ft. (24.1 m) swept aft
Empty weight	Approximately 190,000 lbs. (86,183 kg)
Max. gross weight	477,000 lbs. (216,364 kg)
Maximum speed	900-plus mph (Mach 1.2 at sea level; 782 knots)
Maximum altitude	Over 30,000 ft. (9,144 m)
Maximum range	Intercontinental, unrefueled (more than 7,000 miles)
Powerplant(s)	Four General Electric F-101-GE-102 turbofan engines with afterburner, generating 30,000-plus lbs. of thrust each
Payload capacity	75,000 lbs. (34,019 kg)
Armament	500- to 2,000-lb. bombs, naval mines, cluster munitions, Joint Direct Attack Munitions, and/or air-to-surface missiles
Manufacturer	Boeing North America
Variants	N/A

B-2 SPIRIT

Description	Stealthy "flying wing" heavy bomber
Mission/users	Multi-role stealth heavy bomber; USAF
Crew	Two pilots
Length	69 ft. (20.9 m)
Height	17 ft. (5.1 m)
Wingspan	172 ft. (52.12 m)
Empty weight	160,000 lbs. (72,575 kg)
Max. gross weight	336,500 lbs. (152,635 kg)
Maximum speed	High subsonic
Maximum altitude	50,000 ft. (15,240 m)
Maximum range	Approximately 6,000 miles, unrefueled
Powerplant(s)	Four General Electric F-118-GE-100 engines, each generating 17,300 lbs. of thrust
Payload capacity	Up to 40,000 lbs. (18,144 kg)
Armament	Variety of conventional, precision, and/or nuclear munitions
Manufacturer	Northrop Grumman Corp.
Variants	N/A

B-52H STRATOFORTRESS

Description	High-wing eight-engine jet heavy bomber
Mission/users	Conventional and nuclear bomber; USAF
Crew	Five: aircraft commander, pilot, radar navigator, navigator, electronic warfare officer
Length	159 ft., 4 in. (48.5 m)
Height	40 ft., 8 in. (12.4 m)
Wingspan	185 ft. (56.4 m)
Empty weight	Approximately 185,000 lbs. (83,250 kg)
Max. gross weight	488,000 lbs. (219,600 kg)
Maximum speed	650 mph (Mach 0.86)
Maximum altitude	50,000 ft. (15,240 m)
Maximum range	8,800 miles unrefueled (7,652 nautical miles)
Powerplant(s)	Eight Pratt & Whitney engines TF33-P-3/103 turbofans generating up to 17,000 lbs. of thrust each
Payload capacity	Up to 70,000 lbs. (31,500 kg)
Armament	Mixed ordnance consisting of bombs, missiles, and/or mines; modified to carry air-launched cruise missiles
Manufacturer	Boeing Military Airplane Co.
Variants	Only the B-52H is still in the USAF inventory.

Cargo Aircraft

USN

C-2A GREYHOUND

The C-2A Greyhound, a twin-engine cargo aircraft designed to land on aircraft carriers, provides critical onboard delivery of passengers and cargo to the Navy's aircraft carriers. The cabin can readily accommodate cargo, passengers, or both; it is also equipped to accept litter patients for medical evacuation missions.

USAF

C-17 GLOBEMASTER III

The C-17 is capable of rapid strategic delivery of troops and all types of cargo to main operating bases or directly to forward bases in theater. It is also able to perform tactical airlift and airdrop missions (up to 102 troops), and it can transport 36 litters and 54 ambulatory patients with attendants during aeromedical evacuations. When configured with palletized airliner-style seats, it can carry up to 188 passengers. Alternatively, the C-17 can carry one M1-series Abrams tank, up to three Bradley armored vehicles, up to three Stryker infantry fighting vehicles, or two UH-60 Blackhawk helicopters.

USAF

C-130 HERCULES

The C-130 Hercules' primary role is the intratheater (within theater) portion of the Air Force's airlift mission. The "Herc" or "Herky Bird" can operate from rough dirt strips and is the prime transport for dropping or airlanding parachute troops and equipment into hostile areas. Basic and specialized versions accomplish a wide range of missions, including cargo and passenger airlift, Antarctic ice mission resupply, aeromedical missions, aerial spray missions, and firefighting duties for the U.S. Forest Service.

Although the C-130A began service in 1956, upgrades to engines, avionics, and propellers, along with added external fuel tanks, have kept successive B, E, H, and J models as familiar sights to U.S. forces around the world. The USAF, the USN, and the USMC are well on their way to replacing their C-130Es and C-130Hs with J models, including some of the C-130J-30 "stretch" variants with a 15-foot fuselage extension and the resulting additional payload capacity.

C-2A GREYHOUND

Description	Twin-engine turboprop cargo aircraft capable of landing on aircraft carriers
Mission/users	Carrier onboard cargo and passenger delivery; USN
Crew	Three: pilot, copilot, and flight engineer
Length	56 ft., 8 in. (17.3 m)
Height	15 ft., 2 in. (4.62 m)
Wingspan	80 ft., 7 in. (24.6 m)
Empty weight	31,250 lbs. (14,175 kg)
Max. gross weight	54,382 lbs. (24,667 kg)
Maximum speed	352 mph (306 knots)
Maximum altitude	33,500 ft. (10,210 m)
Maximum range	1,200 miles (1,043 nautical miles/1,931 km)
Powerplant(s)	Two Allison T-56-A-425 turboprop engines, developing 4,600 shaft horsepower each
Payload capacity	10,000 lbs. (5,546 kg); can be configured for cargo, 26 passengers, 12 litter patients, or a combination thereof
Armament	N/A
Manufacturer	Grumman Aerospace Corp.
Variants	N/A

C-17 GLOBEMASTER III

Description	High-wing, four-engined jet cargo aircraft with rear loading ramp
Mission/users	Cargo and troop transport; USAF, Australia, Canada, India, Kuwait, NATO, Qatar, United Arab Emirates (UAE), United Kingdom (UK)
Crew	Three: pilot, copilot, loadmaster
Length	174 ft. (53 m)
Height	55 ft., 1 in. (16.8 m)
Wingspan	169 ft., 10 in. (to winglet tips) (51.75 m)
Empty weight	269,363 lbs. (122,181 kg)
Max. gross weight	585,000 lbs. (265,352 kg) (peacetime)
Maximum speed	More than 517 mph/450 knots
Maximum altitude	45,000 ft. (13,716 m) at cruising speed
Maximum range	2,800 miles (4,506.16 km) unrefueled; unlimited with in-flight refueling
Powerplant(s)	Four Pratt & Whitney F117-PW-100 turbofan engines producing 40,440 lbs. (18,343 kg) of thrust each
Payload capacity	102 troops/paratroops; 48 litter and 54 ambulatory patients and attendants; 170,900 lbs. (77,519 kg) of cargo
Armament	N/A
Manufacturer	Boeing Company
Variants	N/A

C-130J HERCULES

Description	High-wing four-engined turboprop cargo aircraft
Mission/users	Airlift of cargo, passengers, or paratroops; USAF, USMC, USN, USCG, other government agencies, Australia, Canada, Denmark, France, India, Italy, Norway, Qatar, UK
Crew	C-130E/H: Five—two pilots, a navigator, a flight engineer, and a loadmaster C-130J: Three—two pilots and a loadmaster. More specialized crew members may be added as needed for airdrop or medevac missions.
Length	C-130E/H/J: 97 ft., 9 in. (29.3 m); C-130J-30: 112 ft., 9 in. (34.69 m)
Height	38 ft., 10 in. (11.9 m)
Wingspan	132 ft., 7 in. (39.7 m)
Empty weight	76,469 lbs. (34,686 kg)
Max. gross weight	155,000 lbs. (69,750 kg)
Maximum speed	417 mph at 22,000 ft. (6,706 m)
Maximum altitude	28,000 ft. (8,615 m) with 42,000 lbs. (19,051 kg) of payload
Maximum range	2,071 miles (1,800 nautical miles) (varies with payload)
Powerplant(s)	Four Rolls-Royce AE 2100D3 turboprops generating 4,700 shaft hp each
Payload capacity	Up to 45,000 lbs. (20,412 kg) of cargo; up to 92 troops, 64 paratroops, or 74 litter patients
Armament	N/A
Manufacturer	Lockheed-Martin Aeronautics
Variants	—HC-130J Combat King II extended-range version used by USAF for all-weather personnel recovery operations —KC-130Fs used by USN and KC-130F/J/R/Ts used by USMC for aerial refueling or fuel transport —HC-130H used by USCG to carry or drop rescue and oil pollution gear as well as to conduct maritime search and surveillance —C-130J-30 stretch version has a 15-foot fuselage extension —EC-130H Compass Call is a heavily modified USAF version used for electronic attack, disrupting enemy communications and suppressing air defense systems

Fighter Aircraft

F-15 EAGLE

USAF

The F-15 Eagle is an extremely maneuverable all-weather tactical fighter designed to gain and maintain aerial combat superiority through a combination of superior maneuverability, acceleration, range, weapons, and avionics. Although originally designed as a pure air superiority fighter, the F-15's superior performance characteristics resulted in the development of a ground attack variant, the Strike Eagle. Continuing upgrades of engines, avionics, radar, pilot interface systems, electronic countermeasures, fuel capacity, and munitions racks have kept the Eagle in production since it first entered service in 1976, and they are expected to keep the Eagle relevant and ready through about 2040.

F-16 FIGHTING FALCON

USAF

The F-16 Fighting Falcon, also known as the "Viper" by its pilots, is a relatively small, highly maneuverable multi-role fighter proven in both air-to-air and air-to-surface roles. In its air combat role, the F-16 can locate targets in all weather conditions and sort out low-flying aircraft from radar ground clutter. In its air-to-surface role, the F-16 can fly more than 500 miles (860 km), deliver its munitions with superior accuracy under any weather conditions, defend itself against enemy aircraft, and return to its starting point.

F-15 EAGLE	
Description	Two-engine, high-wing, twin-tail jet fighter
Mission/users	Tactical/air superiority fighter; USAF, Israel, Japan, Qatar, Saudi Arabia, Singapore, South Korea
Crew	F-15C: one pilot; F-15D: two pilots; F-15E: pilot and weapons systems officer (WSO)
Length	63 ft., 9 in. (19.4 m)
Height	18 ft., 6 in. (5.6 m)
Wingspan	42 ft., 10 in. (13.1 m)
Empty weight	31,700 lbs. (14,379 kg)
Max. gross weight	68,000 lbs. (30,600 kg) (C/D models)
Maximum speed	1,875 mph (Mach 2.5-plus) at 45,000 ft. (13,716 m)
Maximum altitude	65,000 ft. (19,812 m)
Maximum range	3,450 miles (3,000 nautical miles) ferry range with conformal fuel tanks and three external fuel tanks
Powerplant(s)	Two Pratt & Whitney F100-PW-100 turbofan engines with afterburners generating 23,450 lbs. of thrust each
Payload capacity	Varies based on model and mission
Armament	Internal 20 mm multibarrel gun, up to eight missiles under wings and on fuselage corners; F-15E bomb load 8,000 lbs. (3,636 kg)
Manufacturer	Boeing Company
Variants	F-15C, F-15D (two-seat trainer), F-15E Strike Eagle

F-16 FIGHTING FALCON

Description	Single-engine jet fighter
Mission/users	Multi-role fighter; USAF, USN (for adversary training), Bahrain, Belgium, Chile, Denmark, Egypt, Greece, Indonesia, Israel, Italy, Jordan, Morocco, Netherlands, Oman, Pakistan, Poland, Portugal, Singapore, South Korea, Taiwan, Thailand, Turkey, UAE
Crew	One or two, depending on model
Length	49 ft., 5 in. (14.8 m)
Height	16 ft. (4.8 m)
Wingspan	32 ft., 8 in. (9.8 m)
Empty weight	19,700 lbs. (8,936 kg)
Max. gross weight	37,500 lbs. (16,875 kg)
Maximum speed	1,500 mph (Mach 2 at altitude)
Maximum altitude	Above 50,000 ft. (15,152 m)
Maximum range	Over 2,002 miles (3,222 km) ferry range
Powerplant(s)	F-16C/D: one Pratt & Whitney F100-PW-200/220/229 or GE F110-GE-100/129 engine generating 27,000 lbs. (12,247 kg) of thrust
Payload capacity	Varies based on model
Armament	One internal 20 mm multibarrel gun; up to six air-to-air missiles, conventional air-to-air and air-to-surface munitions, and electronic countermeasure pods
Manufacturer	Lockheed Martin Corp.
Variants	A/C models single-seat multi-role; B/D models two-seat; CJ/DJ models one- and two-place Suppression of Enemy Air Defense (SEAD) versions

USN

USMC

F/A-18 HORNET/SUPER HORNET

The F/A-18 Hornet/Super Hornet series is a twin-engine, twin-tail, midwing, all-weather fighter and attack aircraft used by the U.S. Navy and Marine Corps. It can perform traditional strike missions, such as interdiction and close air support, without compromising its fighter capabilities. In its fighter role, the F/A-18 is used primarily for fleet air defense and fighter escort; in its attack role, it is used for interdiction, force protection, and close and deep air support missions.

The Navy is far along with replacing its F/A-18C and D model Hornets with the larger and more capable Super Hornet, while the Marine Corps has begun replacing its Hornets with the Short Take-off and Vertical Landing (STOVL) F-35B Lightning II. However, since this will take years to accomplish, the USMC plans to keep using F/A-18C and D model Hornets well into the 2020s.

USAF

F-22 RAPTOR

The F-22 Raptor is the U.S. Air Force's newest air superiority fighter. The fifth-generation aircraft's stealth, maneuverability, advanced sensors, supercruise capability (sustained supersonic flight without using afterburners), integrated avionics, and improved supportability are on the leading edge of warfighting capabilities worldwide. It is designed to penetrate enemy airspace and achieve a "first-look, first-kill" dominance against multiple targets.

FIFTH-GENERATION AIRCRAFT

Jet fighters are currently classified in five generations. The first generation consisted of early subsonic jets from World War II through the Korean War; the second incorporated lessons learned from the first and was capable of supersonic flight. Third-generation fighters were mostly shaped by Cold War competition with the Soviet Union and Vietnam combat experience and included increased use of air-to-air missiles and ground-to-air missile defense. Many fourth-generation fighters are still in service around the world, although recent upgrades of some aircraft are so improved that they are often called "generation 4.5."

Fifth-generation fighters are characterized by their inherent stealth; advanced airframe, maneuverability, avionics, and propulsion; and compatibility with a network-centric operational approach. Fifth-generation aircraft can direct strikes by any air, ground, or seagoing assets within range of a target, vastly increasing the effectiveness of military forces in an operational area.

F/A-18 SUPER HORNET

Description	Multi-role, midwing, two-engine, twin-tailed jet fighter/attack aircraft
Mission/users	Fighter/attack (strike) carrier-capable aircraft; USN, Australia, Canada, Finland, Kuwait, Malaysia, Spain, Switzerland
Crew	A/C/E models: one; B/D/F models: two
Length	Hornet: 56 ft. (17.07 m) Super Hornet: 60 ft., 4 in. (18.39 m)
Height	Hornet: 15 ft., 3.5 in. (4.66 m) Super Hornet: 15 ft., 10 in. (4.83 m)
Wingspan	Hornet: 37 ft., 6 in. (11.43 m) Super Hornet: 44 ft., 8.5 in. (13.63 m)
Empty weight	Hornet: 23,050 lbs. (10,455 kg) Super Hornet: 30,500 lbs. (13,835 kg)
Max. gross weight	Hornet: 51,900 lbs. (23,541 kg) Super Hornet: 66,000 lbs. (29,937 kg)
Maximum speed	Mach 1.7+
Maximum altitude	50,000+ ft. (15,240 m)
Maximum range	Combat: 1,089 nautical miles (1,253 miles/2,017 km)
Powerplant(s)	Hornet: Two F404-GE-402 turbofans generating 17,700 lbs. thrust each Super Hornet: Two F414-GE-400 turbofans generating 22,000 lbs. thrust each
Payload capacity	Hornet: up to 17,000 lbs. (7,711 kg) of bombs, missiles, rockets, and drop tanks Super Hornet: up to 17,750 lbs. (8,051 kg) of bombs, missiles, rockets, and drop tanks
Armament	One M61A1/A2 20 mm Vulcan cannon; can carry a combination of AIM-9 Sidewinder, AIM-7 Sparrow, AIM-120 AMRAAM, Harpoon, Harm, Shrike, SLAM, SLAM-ER, Walleye, Maverick missiles; Joint Stand-Off Weapon (JSOW); Joint Direct Attack Munition (JDAM); various general purpose bombs, mines, or rockets
Manufacturer	McDonnell-Douglas (now Boeing)
Variants	EA-18G Growler to detect, identify, locate, and jam or attack hostile emitters

F-22 RAPTOR	
Description	Single-seat, two-engine, twin-tailed fighter
Mission/users	Air superiority fighter; USAF
Crew	One pilot
Length	62 ft., 1 in. (18.9 m)
Height	16 ft., 8 in. (5.1 m)
Wingspan	44 ft., 6 in. (13.6 m)
Empty weight	43,340 lbs. (19,700 kg)
Max. gross weight	83,500 lbs. (38,000 kg)
Maximum speed	Mach 2+
Maximum altitude	Above 50,000 ft. (15,152 m)
Maximum range	More than 1,850 miles (29,800 km) with two external wing fuel tanks
Powerplant(s)	Two Pratt & Whitney F119-PW-100 turbofans generating 35,000 lbs. of thrust each
Payload capacity	(Not released)
Armament	One M61A2 20 mm cannon; side weapon bays can carry two AIM-9 infrared air-to-air missiles and main weapon bays can carry (air-to-air loadout) six AIM-120 radar-guided air-to-air missiles or (air-to-ground loadout) two 1,000-lb. GBU-32 JDAMs and two AIM-120 radar-guided air-to-air missiles
Manufacturer	Lockheed-Martin/Boeing/Pratt & Whitney
Variants	N/A

USAF

F-35 LIGHTNING II

The F-35 Lightning II is a family of fifth-generation, single-seat, single-engine, stealth multirole fighters. Unlike most aircraft, from which successive versions evolve over time, the F-35 was initially designed with three versions to meet the needs of the U.S. Air Force, Navy, and Marine Corps. Unlike the F-22 Raptor, the F-35 was intended from the beginning to be available for export to close U.S. allies and partners.

USN

USMC

All three versions have the same fuselage and internal weapons bay, common outer lines with similar structural geometry, an identical angle of wing sweep, and comparable tail shapes. The avionics, radar, ejection system, and most subsystems are common to all versions, as is the core engine.

The F-35A is the USAF version, designed for conventional takeoff and landing; it is the only version with an internal cannon. Although still an advanced fifth-generation fighter, it is the smallest and lightest of the three, as well as the least complex, in that it does not require hover or aircraft carrier launching and landing capability.

The F-35B is the STOVL variant designed for the USMC. It sacrifices some of the F-35A's fuel capacity to accommodate a vertical flight system that swivels an exhaust nozzle, directing thrust downward. Although this makes it useable aboard Navy aircraft carriers, it is not equipped for conventional carrier catapult launches or arresting hook landings.

The F-35C is the Navy's carrier-capable version, featuring larger wings with foldable wingtip sections; larger wing and tail control surfaces for improved low-speed control; stronger landing gear to withstand carrier arresting hook landings; and a tailhook designed for use with a carrier's arrestor cables. The larger wing area increases range and payload while allowing lower landing speeds.

F-35 LIGHTNING II

Description	Stealthy, supersonic, single-engine STOVL strike fighter
Mission/users	Multi-role (strike) fighter; USAF, USN, USMC, Australia, Canada, Denmark, Israel, Italy, Netherlands, Norway, Turkey, UK
Crew	One pilot
Length	A/B models: 51 ft., 2 in. (15.6 m) C model: 51 ft., 6 in. (15.7 m)
Height	A/B models: 15 ft., 1 in. (4.6 m) C model: 15 ft., 6 in. (4.7 m)
Wingspan	A/B models: 35 ft. (10.7 m) C model: 43 ft. (13.1 m) unfolded; 29 ft., 10 in. (9.1 m) folded
Empty weight	A model: 22,500–26,500 lbs. (10,206–12,020 kg) B model: 23,500–30,000 lbs. (10,659–13,608 kg) C model: 24,000–30,000 lbs. (10,886–13,608 kg)
Max. gross weight	A model: 50,000–60,000 lbs. (22,680–27,216 kg) B model: Approx. 60,000 lbs. (27,216 kg) C model: Approx. 60,000 lbs. (27,216 kg)
Maximum speed	Mach 1.8+
Maximum altitude	Above 65,000 ft. (19,812 m)
Maximum range	A model: 1,381 miles (1,200 nm/2,223 km) B model: 1,038 miles (902 nm/1,671 km) C model: 1,611 miles (1,400 nm/2,593 km)
Powerplant(s)	One Pratt & Whitney F135-PW-100 turbofan
Payload capacity	Varies depending on model
Armament	Both internal weapons bays are capable of carrying one 2,000-lb. (907.19 kg) class weapon and one AMRAAM each. Seven external stations provide an assortment of air-to-air and air-to-ground weapons, including the full range of "smart" (precision-guided) munitions
Manufacturer	Lockheed Martin/Northrop Grumman/British Aerospace
Variants	F-35A (air-to-ground/air superiority); F-35B (STOVL); F-35C (carrier capable)

Special Purpose Aircraft

USN

E-2C HAWKEYE

The E-2C Hawkeye is the U.S. Navy's all-weather, carrier-based tactical airborne warning and control system platform. It provides all-weather airborne early warning and command and control functions for the carrier battle group. Additional missions include surface surveillance coordination, strike and interceptor control, search and rescue guidance, and communications relay.

USAF

E-3 SENTRY (AWACS)

The E-3 Sentry is an airborne warning and control system (AWACS) aircraft that provides all-weather surveillance, command, control, and communications for commanders. It is the premier air battle command and control aircraft in the world today.

USN

USMC

EA-6B PROWLER

The EA-6B Prowler provides a long-range, all-weather umbrella of advanced electronic countermeasures over strike aircraft, ground troops, and ships by jamming enemy radar, electronic data links, and communications.

E-2C HAWKEYE	
Description	High-wing, two-engine, propeller-driven aircraft
Mission/users	Carrier-based all-weather airborne early-warning and control aircraft—provides early warning of approaching enemy aircraft and vectors (guides) interceptors into attack position; USN, Egypt, France, Japan, Mexico, Singapore, Taiwan
Crew	Crew of five: two pilots and three operators/controllers
Length	58 ft. (17.5 m)
Height	18 ft., 5 in. (5.6 m)
Wingspan	81 ft. (24.6 m)
Empty weight	39,290 lbs. (17,859 kg)
Max. gross weight	51,597 lbs. (23,453 kg)
Maximum speed	389 mph (338 knots)
Cruising speed	298 mph (259 knots)
Maximum altitude	37,200 ft. (11,275 m)
Maximum range	1,725 miles (1,500 nautical miles)
Powerplant(s)	Two Allison T56-A-427 turboprop engines, each generating approximately 5,100 hp
Payload capacity	N/A
Armament	N/A
Manufacturer	Prime contractor Northrop Grumman; Westinghouse, Lockheed Martin
Variants	Hawkeye 2000: upgraded engines, radar, propellers, and avionics E-2D Advanced Hawkeye: new avionics, air-to-air refueling; upgraded radar communications

E-3 SENTRY (AWACS)

Description	Four-engine jet with large rotating radome mounted above fuselage
Mission/users	Airborne surveillance, command, control, and communications; USAF, France, NATO, Saudi Arabia, UK
Crew	Flight crew of four plus mission crew of 13–19 specialists
Length	145 ft., 6 in. (44 m)
Height	41 ft., 4 in. (12.5 m)
Wingspan	130 ft., 10 in. (39.7 m)
Rotodome	Diameter: 30 ft. (9.1 m) thickness: 6 ft. (1.8 m); mounted 11 ft. (3.33 m) above fuselage
Empty weight	162,000 lbs. (73,480 kg)
Max. gross weight	347,000 lbs. (156,150 kg)
Maximum speed	530 mph (353 knots)
Maximum altitude	Above 29,000 ft. (8,788 m)
Maximum range	1,000 miles (1,610 km)
Powerplant(s)	Four Pratt & Whitney TF33-PW-100A turbofan engines, each generating 21,000 lbs. of thrust
Payload capacity	N/A
Armament	N/A
Manufacturer	Prime contractor Boeing Aerospace Co.; radar contractor Northrop Grumman
Variants	N/A

EA-6B PROWLER

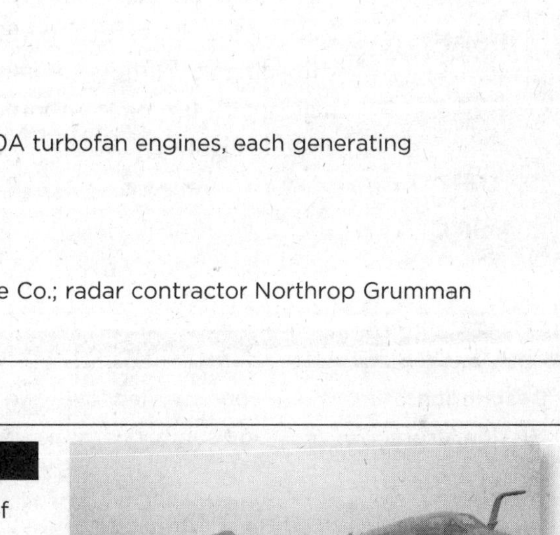

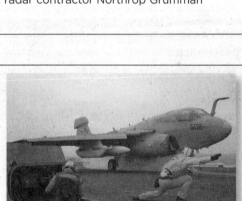

Description	Twin-engine, midwing jet; variant of A-6 Intruder attack plane
Mission/users	Electronic countermeasures; USMC
Crew	Four: pilot and three electronic countermeasures officers
Length	59 ft., 10 in. (17.7 m)
Height	16 ft., 8 in. (4.9 m)
Wingspan	53 ft. (15.9 m)
Empty weight	33,600 lbs. (15,273 kg)
Max. gross weight	61,500 lbs. (27,921 kg)
Maximum speed	Over 500 knots (575 mph, 920 kph)
Maximum altitude	40,000 ft. (12,192 m)
Maximum range	1,150 m (1,000 nautical miles, 1,840 km)
Powerplant(s)	Two Pratt & Whitney J52-P408 turbofan engines, generating 10,400 lbs. (4,767 kg) of thrust per engine
Armament	AGM-88A HARM missile
Manufacturer	Northrup Grumman Aerospace Corporation

USN

P-3 ORION

The P-3C Orion is a land-based, long-range antisubmarine warfare (ASW) patrol aircraft. The avionics system integrates all tactical displays and monitors, coordinates navigation information, and accepts sensor inputs for tactical display and storage; it can also automatically launch ordnance and provide flight information to the pilots.

USN

P-8A POSEIDON

The P-8A Poseidon, based on Boeing's 737 airframe, is the Navy's newest maritime patrol and reconnaissance aircraft, a multi-mission replacement in the process of replacing the P-3 Orion. Its open-architecture mission system facilitates planned upgrades, its accomplishment of anti-submarine and anti-surface warfare missions, and its intelligence, surveillance, and reconnaissance (ISR) efforts.

USAF

USN

USMC

V-22 OSPREY

The V-22 Osprey is a multi-service, multi-role combat aircraft that uses tilt-rotor technology to combine the vertical performance of a helicopter with the speed and range of a fixed-wing aircraft. With its rotors in the vertical position, it can take off, land, and hover like a helicopter—but once airborne, it can convert to a turboprop airplane for high-speed, high-altitude flight.

P-3 ORION	
Description	Four-engined low-wing turboprop
Mission/users	Antisubmarine/antisurface warfare (ASW/ASUW); USN, Argentina, Australia, Canada, Chile, Germany, Greece, Japan, New Zealand, Norway, Pakistan, Portugal, South Korea, Spain, Thailand
Crew	5 minimum flight crew; 11 normal crew; 21 max
Length	117 ft., 6 in. (35.6 m)
Height	33 ft., 11 in. (10.3 m)
Wingspan	100 ft., 3 in. (30.4 m)
Empty weight	61,360 lbs. (27,890 kg)
Max. gross weight	139,760 lbs. (63,527 kg)
Maximum speed	374 mph (411 knots)
Maximum altitude	28,500 ft. (8,625 m)
Maximum range	1,536 miles (1,690 nautical miles)
Powerplant(s)	Four T56-A-14 Allison turboprops generating 4,600 hp each
Armament	Up to approx. 20,000 lbs. (9,072 kg) internal and external loads of torpedoes, mines, depth bombs, missiles, sonobuoys, etc.
Manufacturer	Lockheed
Variants	EP-3 electronic surveillance

P-8A POSEIDON

Description	Low-wing, two-engine jet
Mission/users	Land-based anti-submarine warfare, anti-surface warfare, and ISR; USN, Australia, India
Crew	Nine (command pilot, two pilots, tactical coordinator, tactical coordinator/navigator, three sensor operators, and an inflight technician)
Length	129 ft., 6 in. (39.5 m)
Height	42 ft., 2 in. (12.8 m)
Wingspan	123 ft., 6 in. (37.6 m)
Empty weight	138,300 lbs. (62,732 kg)
Max. gross weight	189,200 lbs. (85,820 kg)
Maximum speed	564 mph (490 knots)
Maximum altitude	41,000 ft. (12,497 m)
Maximum range	1,200 nm radius with four hours on station
Powerplant(s)	Two CFM56-7B engines, each generating 27,300 lbs. thrust
Payload capacity	51,100 lbs. (23,179 kg)
Armament	Torpedoes, cruise missiles
Manufacturer	Boeing
Variants	N/A

V-22 OSPREY

Description	High-wing, two-engine tilt-rotor turboprop
Mission/users	Combat search and rescue, special warfare support, fleet logistics support; USMC, USAF, Japan
Crew	Two or three, depending on Service version
Length	57 ft., 4 in. (17.5 m)
Height	Nacelles vertical: 22 ft., 1 in. (6.7 m)
Rotor diameter	38 ft., 1 in. (11.6 m)
Max. gross weight	52,600 lbs. (23,859 kg)
Max. cruising speed	310 mph (269 knots/500 kph)
Maximum altitude	24,000 ft. (7,315 m)
Powerplant(s)	Two Rolls-Royce AE1107C generating 6,150 shp each
Payload capacity	20,000 lbs. (9,072 kg) internal cargo/15,000 lbs. (6,804 kg) external cargo/24 combat troops/9 litters with medical personnel and equipment
Armament	N/A
Manufacturer	Bell Helicopter/Boeing
Variants	MV-22B amphibious assault (USMC), CV-22 long-range/special operations (USAF/USSOCOM), HV-22 combat search and rescue and fleet logistics support (USN)

Tanker Aircraft

USAF

KC-10 EXTENDER

The USAF KC-10 Extender tanker/cargo aircraft is a modified DC-10 commercial airliner, providing increased mobility for U.S. forces in contingency operations, without dependence on overseas bases and without depleting critical fuel supplies overseas. The KC-10 fleet provides in-flight refueling worldwide to aircraft from all branches of the U.S. armed forces, as well as those of other coalition forces. Equipped with its own refueling receptacle, the KC-10A can support deployment of fighters, fighter support aircraft, and cargo aircraft from U.S. bases to any area in the world.

USAF

KC-135 STRATOTANKER

The USAF KC-135 Stratotanker not only refuels long-range bombers, but also provides aerial refueling support to Air Force, Navy, Marine Corps, and allied/coalition aircraft. Nearly all internal fuel can be pumped through the tanker's flying boom, the KC-135's primary fuel transfer method.

Attack Helicopters

USMC

AH-1W SUPER COBRA AND AH-1Z VIPER

The Marine Corps' AH-1W Super Cobra provides close-in all-weather fire support in aerial and ground escort operations during amphibious ship-to-shore movements and subsequent

KC-10 EXTENDER	
Description	Three-engine aerial refueler based on commercial DC-10
Mission/users	Aerial refueling and transport; USAF, Netherlands
Crew	Four (aircraft commander, pilot, flight engineer, and boom operator)
Length	181 ft., 7 in. (54.4 m)
Height	58 ft., 1 in. (17.4 m)
Wingspan	165 ft., 4½ in. (50 m)
Empty weight	240,026 lbs. (108,874 kg)
Max. gross weight	590,000 lbs. (265,500 kg)
Maximum speed	619 mph (Mach 0.825)
Maximum altitude	42,000 ft. (12,727 m)
Maximum range	4,400 miles (3,800 nautical miles) with cargo; 11,500 miles (10,000 nautical miles) without cargo
Powerplant(s)	Three General Electric CF-6-50C2 turbofans
Payload capacity	342,000 lbs. (155,129 kg) of fuel, all useable or transferable via either boom or probe and drogue refueling; some aircraft are modified with two wing-mounted air refueling pods, which allow simultaneous operations with probe-equipped aircraft
Armament	N/A
Manufacturer	McDonnell Douglas Aircraft Co.
Variants	N/A

KC-135 STRATOTANKER

Description	Four-engine intercontinental jet tanker
Mission/users	Aerial refueling; USAF, France, Singapore, Turkey
Crew	Four or five; up to 80 passengers
Length	136 ft., 3 in. (40.8 m)
Height	38 ft., 4 in. (11.5 m)
Wingspan	130 ft., 10 in. (39.2 m)
Empty weight	119,231 lbs. (53,654 kg)
Max. gross weight	322,500 lbs. (145,125 kg)
Maximum speed	Maximum speed at 30,000 ft. (9,144 m): 610 mph (Mach 0.93)
Maximum altitude	50,000 ft. (15,152 m)
Maximum range	11,192 miles (9,732 nautical miles) with 120,000 lbs. (54,000 kg) of transfer fuel
Powerplant(s)	Four CFM International F108-CF-100 turbojets producing 22,224 lbs. (10,081 kg) of thrust each
Payload capacity	Up to 83,000 lbs. (37,350 kg), depending on configuration
Armament	N/A
Manufacturer	Boeing Military Airplanes
Variants	KC-135E (new engines)

AH-1W COBRA

Description	Twin-engine tandem-seat attack helicopter, skid mounted
Mission/users	Close-in all-weather fire support for aerial and ground escort; USMC, Taiwan
Crew	Two in tandem: copilot/gunner in front, pilot elevated in rear
Length	Overall: 57 ft., 11 in. (17.7 m); fuselage: 45 ft., 5 in. (13.9 m)
Height	14 ft., 6 in. (4.4 m)
Rotor diameter	47 ft., 11 in. (14.6 m)
Empty weight	10,283 lbs. (4,634 kg)
Max. gross weight	14,845 lbs. (6,690 kg)
Maximum speed	195 mph (170 knots); climb rate: 1,925 ft. (586.74 km) per minute
Maximum altitude	More than 14,750 ft. (4,540 m)
Maximum range	365 miles (317 nautical miles/598 km) (without drop tanks)
Powerplant(s)	Two GE T700-GE-401 turboshaft engines producing 1,690 hp each
Payload capacity	931 lbs. (2,065 kg)
Armament	One M197 three-barrel 20 mm gun mounted in chin turret; under-wing attachments for four TOW missiles, eight Hellfire missiles, or one AIM-9L Sidewinder missile; can also be equipped with Zuni rocket launchers
Manufacturer	Bell Helicopter Textron

shore operations within the objective area. Additional missions include direct air support, antitank, armed escort, and air-to-air combat. The AH-1W is a two-place, tandem-seat, twin-engine helicopter capable of land- or sea-based operations.

Additional improvements in rotor blades, cockpit configuration, and other features continue to be planned and executed to upgrade the AH-1W to the AH-1Z Viper so that it can continue to serve the Marine Corps and the United States in the Global War on Terror and in its worldwide commitments.

USA

AH-6J/MH-6J LITTLE BIRD

The OH-6A was originally designed for use as a scout helicopter during the Vietnam War, but since the 1980s upgraded (and often armed) versions have seen extensive use by the U.S. special operations community.

AH-6J/MH-6J LITTLE BIRD	
Description	Single-engine light attack/special operations helicopter, 4–5 bladed main rotor
Mission/users	Fire support/personnel insertion for special operations; USA
Crew	One or two pilots
Length	Overall: 32 ft., 1 in. (9.8 m); fuselage: 23 ft., 11 in. (7.3 m)
Height	11 ft., 2 in. (3.4 m)
Rotor diameter	26 ft., 4 in. (8 m)
Empty weight	1,971 lbs. (896 kg)
Max. gross weight	3,542 lbs. (1,610 kg)
Maximum speed	170 mph (282 kph); climb rate: 2,063 ft. per minute
Maximum altitude	16,000 ft. (4,875 m)
Maximum range	288 miles (250 nautical miles/472 km)
Powerplant(s)	One 425-hp Allison 250-C30 turboshaft
Payload capacity	External load of 1,219 lbs. (550 kg); transports two or three service members or equivalent cargo internally, or six on external platforms in lieu of weapons
Armament	Combinations of: ■ two M134 7.62 mm six-barrel Gatling-type MG pods ■ two M260 2.75-in. Hydra 70 rocket pods (7 or 12 each) ■ two .50 cal MG pods ■ two M75 40 mm grenade launchers ■ two MK19 40 mm grenade launchers ■ two TOW missile pods (2 each) ■ two Hellfire antitank guided missiles ■ two Stinger air-to-air missiles
Manufacturer	McDonnell Douglas
Variants	AH-6J, MH-6J, OH-6A

USA

AH-64 APACHE

The AH-64 Apache is the Army's primary attack helicopter. It is a twin-engine, four-bladed, multi-mission attack helicopter that can fight in any weather, day or night, to destroy, disrupt, or delay enemy forces. The principal mission of the Apache is the destruction of high value targets with the Hellfire missile. It is also capable of using its 30 mm chain gun and 2.75-inch rockets against a wide variety of targets. The Apache can withstand hits from rounds up to 23 mm in critical areas.

AH-64 APACHE	
Description	Twin-engine, four-bladed, multi-mission attack helicopter
Mission/users	Close air support of ground forces; USA, Egypt, Greece, Israel, Japan, Kuwait, Netherlands, Saudi Arabia, Singapore, Taiwan, UAE
Crew	Two: copilot/gunner in front, pilot in back, elevated
Length	58 ft., 2 in. (17.7 m)
Height	A model: 15 ft., 3 in. (4.6 m); D model: 13 ft., 4 in. (4.1 m)
Rotor diameter	48 ft. (14.6 m)
Empty weight	11,800 lbs. (5,364 kg)
Max. gross weight	A model: 15,075 lbs. (6,838 kg); D model: 16,600 lbs. (7,530 kg)
Maximum speed	A model: 170 mph (279 kph); D model: 167 mph (273 kph)
Maximum altitude	20,500 ft. (6,248 m)
Maximum range	300 miles (483 km) on internal fuel
Powerplant(s)	Two T700-GE-701C engines generating 1,890 shp each
Payload capacity	Up to 16 Hellfire antitank missiles or 76 2.75-in. rockets
Armament	M230 33 mm automatic cannon 70 mm (2.75-in.) Hydra-70 folding-fin aerial rockets AGM-114 Hellfire antitank missiles AGM-122 Sidearm antiradar missile AIM-9 Sidewinder air-to-air missiles
Manufacturer	Boeing/McDonnell Douglas Helicopter Systems, General Electric, Martin Marietta
Variants	AH-64D Apache Longbow

Cargo Helicopters

USA

CH-47 CHINOOK

The CH-47 is a twin-engine, tandem-rotor helicopter designed for transportation of cargo, troops, and weapons during all conditions. Development of the medium-lift Boeing Vertol CH-47 Series Chinook began in 1956. Since then the effectiveness of the Chinook has been continually upgraded by successive product improvements—the CH-47A, CH-47B, CH-47C, and CH-47D, and now the MH-47E.

USA

USMC

CH-53E SEA STALLION

The CH-53E Sea Stallion transports equipment, supplies, and personnel during the assault phase of a Marine amphibious operation, as well as follow-on operations ashore. Capable of carrying supplies both internally and externally, the CH-53E is compatible with shipboard operations and can operate in adverse weather conditions day and night.

CH-47 CHINOOK	
Description	Twin-engine, three-bladed (per engine) tandem-rotor cargo helicopter
Mission/users	Cargo/assault; USA, Egypt, Greece, Iran,* Italy, Japan, Libya,** Morocco, Netherlands
Crew	Four to five, depending on mission: two pilots, one flight engineer, and one or two crew chiefs
Length	Fuselage: 51 ft. (15.3 m); 100 ft. (30.5 m) from leading tip of forward rotor sweep to rear of aft rotor sweep
Height	18 ft., 8 in. (5.7 m)
Rotor diameter	60 ft. (18.3 m)
Empty weight	23,401 lbs. (10,637 kg)
Max. gross weight	50,000 lbs. (22,727 kg)
Maximum speed	163 mph (142 knots); max rate of climb 1,522 ft. per min.
Maximum altitude	8,500 ft. (2,591 m)
Maximum range	1,279 miles (2,058.35 km)
Powerplant(s)	Two Textron Lycoming T55-L712 engines
Payload capacity	33 troop seats, 24 litters, 26,000 lbs. (11,793 kg) of external cargo
Armament	N/A
Manufacturer	Boeing

*CH-47Cs sold to Iran prior to 1979 or variants reverse engineered and illegally manufactured by Iran since then

**CH-47Cs sold to Libya in 1976 by an Italian manufacturer under a license from Boeing

CH-53E SEA STALLION	
Description	Three-engine heavy-lift helicopter w/seven-bladed rotor
Mission/users	Shipboard and onshore transport of supplies and personnel; USMC, USAF, USN, Germany, Israel, Mexico
Crew	Six: two pilots, two flight engineers, two aerial gunners
Length	99 ft., ½ in. (30.2 m)
Height	28 ft., 4 in. (8.7 m)
Rotor diameter	79 ft. (24.1 m)
Empty weight	33,226 lbs. (16,613 kg)
Max. gross weight	73,500 lbs. (33,409 kg)
Maximum speed	173 mph (150 knots)
Maximum altitude	18,500 ft. (5,640 m)
Maximum range	552 miles (480 nautical miles)
Powerplant(s)	Three General Electric T64-GE-416/416A turboshaft engines generating 4,380 shp each
Payload capacity	Normal configuration: 37 passengers; 55 passengers with centerline seats installed; can be configured for up to 14 litters; cargo payload up to 32,000 lbs. (14,545 kg)
Armament	Three 7.62 mm miniguns
Manufacturer	Prime: Sikorsky; engines: General Electric
Variants	MH-53E Sea Dragon; MH-53J Pave Low III

Utility Helicopters

UH-1 HUEY

USAF

The "Huey" helicopter, a legendary workhorse since the Vietnam War, has been produced in greater numbers than any aircraft since World War II; it is still operated by about 50 air forces around the world for command and control purposes, including the USAF.

UH-60 BLACK HAWK

USA

The UH-60 Black Hawk is the U.S. Army's frontline utility helicopter used for air assault, transportation, air cavalry, and aeromedical evacuation missions; variants are also used for electronic countermeasures, command and control, and special operations missions. The Black Hawk is designed to carry up to 11 combat-loaded air assault troops, and it is capable of slingloading a 105 mm howitzer as well as 30 rounds of artillery ammunition.

UH-1 HUEY (IROQUOIS)

Description	Two-bladed single-engine transport/assault utility helicopter
Mission/users	Utility transport; USAF, USMC, 35 other countries*
Crew	Up to five: pilot, copilot, crew chief, one or two gunners or medics
Length	57 ft., 1 in. with rotors (17.4 m)
Height	14 ft., 5 in. (4.4 m)
Rotor diameter	48 ft. (14.6 m)
Empty weight	5,215 lbs. (2,365 kg)
Max. gross weight	9,500 lbs. (4,318 kg)
Maximum speed	135 mph (220 km/hr)
Maximum altitude	12,700 ft. (4,097 m)
Maximum range	777 miles (1,275 km)
Powerplant(s)	One 1,400-hp Lycoming T53 turboshaft engine
Payload capacity	2,200 lbs. (990 kg)
Armament	Up to four 7.62 mm machine guns, two 40 mm grenade launchers, or six TOW antitank missiles
Manufacturer	Bell Helicopter
Variants	Medevac, gunship

*Afghanistan, Argentina, Bolivia, Bosnia-Herzegovina, Brazil, Cambodia, Chile, Colombia, Dominican Republic, El Salvador, Ethiopia, Georgia, Germany, Greece, Guatemala, Honduras, Iraq, Japan, Jordan, Laos, Lebanon, New Zealand, Pakistan, Papua New Guinea, Paraguay, Philippines, Senegal, Singapore, South Korea, Spain, Taiwan, Thailand, Tunisia, Turkey, Uruguay

UH-60 BLACK HAWK

Description	Twin-engine, medium-lift, four-bladed utility helicopter
Mission/users	Air assault, utility airlift, aeromedevac, command and control; USA, USAF, USN, Bahrain, Colombia, Israel, Japan, Jordan, Philippines, Saudi Arabia, South Korea, UAE
Crew	Up to four: pilot, copilot, crew chief/flight engineer, door gunner
Length	64 ft., 10 in. (19.7 m)
Height	16 ft., 10 in. (5.1 m)
Rotor diameter	53 ft., 8 in. (16.3 m)
Empty weight	11,516 lbs. (5,234.5 kg)
Max. gross weight	22,000 lbs. (10,000 kg)
Maximum speed	Up to 165 mph (150 knots)
Maximum altitude	Up to 11,125 ft. (3,400 m)
Maximum range	362 miles (315 nautical miles)
Powerplant(s)	Two GE T700-GE-701C turboshafts generating 2,000+ shp each
Payload capacity	9,000 lbs. (4,090 kg)
Armament	Two M60D 7.62 mm machine guns
Manufacturer	Sikorsky Aircraft Corp.
Variants	UH-60L (attack), UH-60Q (aeromedevac), MH-60G Pave Hawk (USAF special operations), MH-60K (Army special operations), SH-60 Seahawk

USA

UH-72A LAKOTA

The UH-72A Lakota is a light utility helicopter based on a Eurocopter design used by the U.S. Army for logistics and support missions, as well as by the Army National Guard for disaster response, medical evacuation, and homeland security requirements. Although it is based on a Eurocopter design, it is built in the United States.

Active matrix liquid crystal cockpit displays simplify flight and airframe information, increasing the crew's situational awareness and reducing the pilot's workload. The main and tail rotors are set high to allow fast but safe loading and unloading through both main and rear doors, even while the rotors are still turning. For medical missions the Lakota's cabin can accommodate two stretchers plus one medical attendant and a crew chief to operate the external electric hoist. Otherwise, foldup cabin seats can accommodate eight troops or passengers.

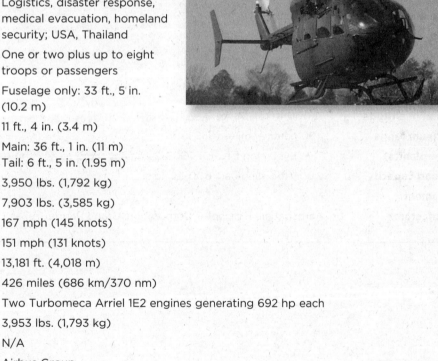

UH-72A LAKOTA	
Description	Twin-engine light utility helicopter
Mission/users	Logistics, disaster response, medical evacuation, homeland security; USA, Thailand
Crew	One or two plus up to eight troops or passengers
Length	Fuselage only: 33 ft., 5 in. (10.2 m)
Height	11 ft., 4 in. (3.4 m)
Rotor diameter	Main: 36 ft., 1 in. (11 m) Tail: 6 ft., 5 in. (1.95 m)
Empty weight	3,950 lbs. (1,792 kg)
Max. gross weight	7,903 lbs. (3,585 kg)
Maximum speed	167 mph (145 knots)
Cruising speed	151 mph (131 knots)
Maximum altitude	13,181 ft. (4,018 m)
Maximum range	426 miles (686 km/370 nm)
Powerplant(s)	Two Turbomeca Arriel 1E2 engines generating 692 hp each
Payload capacity	3,953 lbs. (1,793 kg)
Armament	N/A
Manufacturer	Airbus Group
Variants	N/A

USCG

HH-65A DOLPHIN

The U.S. Coast Guard's twin-engine HH-65A Dolphin helicopters operate up to 150 miles offshore and can fly comfortably at 120 knots for up to three hours. Though normally stationed ashore, Dolphins can be carried on board medium- and high-endurance Coast Guard cutters. They assist in search and rescue, drug interdiction, polar ice breaking, marine environmental protection, and military readiness operations. They also airlift supplies to ships and villages isolated by winter.

HH-65A DOLPHIN	
Description	Short-range recovery
Mission/users	Twin-engine rescue/ transport helicopter; USCG
Crew	Three: pilot, copilot, crew chief
Length	38 ft. (12.3 m)
Height	13 ft. (4.2 m)
Rotor diameter	39 ft. (12.6 m)
Empty weight	6,092 lbs. (2,769 kg)
Max. gross weight	9,200 lbs. (4,182 kg)
Maximum speed	165 knots (190 mph)
Cruising speed	120 knots (138 mph)
Maximum altitude	12,000 ft. (3,658 m)
Maximum range	400 nautical miles (655 km)
Powerplant(s)	Two Lycoming LTS-101-750B-2 engines rated at 742 shp each
Payload capacity	2,000 lbs. slingload, 600-lb. hoist
Armament	N/A
Manufacturer	Aerospatiale Helicopter Corporation, Grand Prairie, Texas

PART II

Testing Formats and Review Information

3 Test Information

TEST FORMATS

Air Force Officer Qualifying Test (AFOQT)

The Air Force Officer Qualifying Test (AFOQT) measures aptitudes used by the U.S. Air Force to select candidates for officer commissioning programs and specific officer training programs. Last revised in 2014, it consists of 12 timed subtests. The scores from the individual subtests are combined in different ways to generate seven composite scores used to help predict success in selected USAF training programs.

The AFOQT Form T incorporates several significant changes from the previous version, based on feedback from an Air Force–wide survey where officers identified abilities and aptitudes they considered critical for effectiveness as an officer. These changes included:

- Adding the Reading Comprehension subtest, which contributes to the test-taker's Verbal and Academic Aptitude composite scores. This subtest uses the type of information test-takers will see in USAF professional military education courses
- Adding the Situational Judgment subtest to evaluate the test-taker's judgment when responding to the types of situations often encountered by officers
- Renaming the General Science subtest the "Physical Science" subtest, with a correspondingly revised focus
- Updating the graphics on the Instrument Comprehension subtest and increasing the number of questions from 20 to 25
- Deleting the Rotated Blocks and Hidden Figures subtests
- Increasing the number of questions on the Block Counting subtest from 20 to 30
- Updating test questions throughout the AFOQT

The seven composite scores and the kinds of abilities and knowledge they measure are as follows:

1. **PILOT** This composite score measures some of the knowledge and abilities the Air Force considers necessary for successful completion of manned and unmanned pilot training. The Pilot composite includes subtests that measure quantitative ability, aeronautical concepts knowledge, ability to determine aircraft attitude from instruments, and perceptual speed (how fast the test-taker can figure things out). This composite score is used in combination with results from the Test of Basic Aviation Skills (TBAS) and any previous flying hours to determine your overall Pilot Candidate Selection Method (PCSM) score.
2. **COMBAT SYSTEMS OFFICER (CSO)** This composite score (previously called "Navigator-Technical") measures some of the abilities and knowledge considered necessary for

successful completion of CSO training. It shares some subtests with the Pilot composite, but tests that measure aeronautical knowledge and the ability to determine aircraft attitude from instruments are not included. However, additional subtests measure verbal aptitude and spatial abilities.

3. **AIR BATTLE MANAGER (ABM)** This composite measures some of the knowledge and abilities considered necessary for successful completion of ABM training. It shares some subtests with the Pilot composite, including measures of the ability to determine aircraft attitude, knowledge of aeronautical concepts, perceptual speed, and quantitative ability. However, like the CSO composite, it also includes subtests that measure verbal aptitude and spatial abilities.
4. **ACADEMIC APTITUDE** The Academic Aptitude composite measures verbal and quantitative abilities and knowledge. It is derived from all the subtests that make up the Verbal and Quantitative composites.
5. **VERBAL** The Verbal composite measures verbal knowledge and abilities using subtests that measure the ability to reason, make inferences (conclusions), recognize relationships between words, and understand synonyms and antonyms.
6. **QUANTITATIVE** This composite measures math-related abilities and knowledge. It shares subtests with the CSO composite and includes subtests that measure the test-taker's ability to understand and reason with mathematical relationships, as well as using mathematical terms, formulas, and relationships.
7. **SITUATIONAL JUDGMENT** This composite measures judgment and decision-making abilities when responding to the types of interpersonal situations often encountered by junior USAF officers. Test questions are based on real scenarios experienced by junior officers and require core competencies of integrity and professionalism, leadership, resource management, communication, innovation, and mentoring. Test questions are selected based on statistical score relationships to cadets' results in USAF Basic Officer Training and Field Training. Answers are scored based on the consensus judgment of a sample of identified high-potential USAF officers.

Sequence of Subtests

Subtest Name	Number of Questions	Time Limit	Pilot	CSO	ABM
Verbal Analogies	25	8 mins			X
Arithmetic Reasoning	25	29 mins			
Word Knowledge	25	5 mins		X	
Math Knowledge	25	22 mins	X	X	X
Reading Comprehension	25	38 mins			
Situational Judgment	50	35 mins			
Self-Description Inventory	240	45 mins			
Physical Science	20	10 mins			
Table Reading	40	7 mins	X	X	X
Instrument Comprehension	25	5 mins	X		X
Block Counting	30	4.5 mins		X	X
Aviation Information	20	8 mins	X		X

As you can see, that's a lot of time in the testing facility. When you count the time scheduled for administrative instructions, passing out materials, collecting materials, and so on, you will be there for almost five hours. Don't worry—there are two breaks totaling 25 minutes, so it's nothing you can't handle. However, as you can see, some of the subtests don't allow you much time, so you will have to know your stuff before you go in. That's where this book will help, if you study the subjects thoroughly and take the practice tests seriously.

Everyone who wants to become an Air Force officer of any type must take the AFOQT. The three USAF commissioning sources—the U.S. Air Force Academy, Air Force Reserve Officer Training Corps (AFROTC), and Officer Training School (OTS)—initially consider only the applicant's Verbal and Quantitative composite scores, so you could say that these parts of the AFOQT are the first gateway through which a prospective Air Force officer must pass. The three commissioning sources maintain their own standards for entry, which can and do change based on the needs of the Air Force at that time. It is only after an applicant gains entry to a commissioning program that further evaluation of other AFOQT composite scores determines the candidate's eligibility for Pilot, CSO, ABM, or other nonflying specialty areas.

It's important to achieve the best initial score possible on the AFOQT because the scores are valid for life and applicants may only take the test twice (one original and one retest at least 180 days later). Additional retests are sometimes allowed, but they require a waiver which is not guaranteed. Only the latest scores—not necessarily the highest—are used in selection consideration.

The TBAS is a computerized "psychomotor" test (eye/hand coordination and mental skills) used in conjunction with the AFOQT to predict levels of potential success in basic pilot training. It consists of nine subtests that either introduce a new skill area or test a combination of previous skill areas. The TBAS subtests are:

DIRECTIONAL ORIENTATION TEST

This 48-question subtest measures spatial orientation abilities. You must determine the position of an unmanned aerial vehicle (UAV) relative to a target. The computer screen displays a "tracker map" showing the UAV's direction of travel (heading) and location; it also shows another display representing what a fixed, forward-facing UAV camera would "see" when pointed at a single building surrounded by four parking lots. What you have to do is click on the correct parking lot based on computer-generated voice instructions. The trick is that, while the tracker map is always oriented with north at the top, the UAV camera view may not be. Your score is based on both the accuracy and speed of your responses.

3-DIGIT AND 5-DIGIT LISTENING TESTS

Through headphones, you will hear a series of letters and numbers, and you must then squeeze the trigger when you hear any of three or five specified numbers. Each test lasts about three minutes.

HORIZONTAL TRACKING TEST (HTT)

Using foot pedals resembling an airplane's rudder pedals, your task is to keep a box on the computer screen superimposed over an airplane symbol as it moves horizontally along the bottom of the screen. The airplane moves at a constant speed and changes direction when it reaches the side of the screen or if you successfully target it for a certain number of seconds.

The task lasts three minutes and the speed of the airplane (and therefore the level of difficulty) increases as the subtest goes on.

AIRPLANE TRACKING TEST (ATT)

Using a joystick, your task here is to keep the gunsight crosshairs on an airplane symbol as it moves around the computer screen at a constant speed. The airplane randomly changes direction when it reaches the side of the screen or if the test-taker successfully targets it for a certain number of seconds.

AIRPLANE AND HORIZONTAL TRACKING TEST

This subtest requires you to perform two previously tested tasks at the same time. First, you have to track an airplane using foot pedals as it moves horizontally along a strip at the bottom of the screen (as in the HTT). At the same time, though, you must track another airplane moving in two dimensions, as you did in the ATT.

ATT, HTT, AND LISTENING TESTS

This test requires you to perform three previously tested tasks simultaneously. First, you must track an airplane moving horizontally as you did in the HTT. Second, you simultaneously track an airplane moving in two dimensions as you did in the ATT. Third, while performing the first two tasks, you press the joystick trigger when you hear any of the three or five specified target numbers (one test using three numbers, and the next using five numbers).

EMERGENCY SCENARIO TEST

Simultaneously, you perform the horizontal tracking task and the airplane tracking task—then you are presented with three emergency scenarios (one at a time) that you have to cancel out by typing a code on the keyboard. You'll have eight minutes to read the instructions and memorize the three emergency situations and the correct response code for each of the three situations. Your test starts with both a verbal announcement in your headphones and the word *emergency* moving along the top of the screen. The difficulty of this subtest increases with the number of times you get it right. Approximate duration is three minutes.

Army Selection Instrument for Flight Training (SIFT)

The Selection Instrument for Flight Training (SIFT) is a battery of seven computerized tests measuring multiple aptitudes; it replaced the Army Flight Aptitude Selection Test (AFAST) in 2013. It is not an intelligence test. Unlike the AFAST, there is no paper version; the SIFT is only available on the Automated Pilot Exam (APEX.NET) platform—a web-based format operated on a secure server that's monitored and controlled.

Also, two of the seven subtests are adaptive. We'll talk more about that shortly.

Your SIFT score is your ticket to Army Aviation training. You are only allowed to take the SIFT twice in your lifetime, and the first time you achieve a passing SIFT score, you're done—there is no chance to take it over and try to improve your score. If you fail the SIFT twice, you will not be able to take the test again. This book will help you ensure that your SIFT score is the best it can be the first time.

The SIFT assesses math skills and abilities, the ability to understand the meaning of written passages, familiarity with mechanical concepts and simple machines, the ability to perform mental rotations of a depicted object, and the ability to quickly recognize patterns. The SIFT also measures the test-taker's knowledge of aviation terminology, familiarity with aircraft components and functions, knowledge of basic aerodynamic principles, and knowledge of basic flight rules and regulations. Since most Army aviation is rotary-wing (i.e., helicopters), you need to be just as familiar with helicopters as you are with airplanes.

All the SIFT components have already proven to be excellent predictors of flight training performance. The SIFT identifies individuals who already have a high level of the mental "right stuff" as well as some background knowledge of aviation concepts—those are the people most likely to make it through flight training.

The total time needed to take the SIFT will vary for different test-takers, but usually runs about two and a half hours, including registration and a 15-minute break.

This is how the SIFT is organized:

Sequence of Subtests

Subtest Name	Abbrev.	Number of Questions	Time Limit
Simple Drawings	SD	100	2 mins
Hidden Figures	HF	50	5 mins
Army Aviation Information Test	AAIT	40	30 mins
Spatial Apperception Test	SAT	25	10 mins
Reading Comprehension Test	RCT	20	30 mins
Math Skills Test	MST	Varies	40 mins
Mechanical Comprehension Test	MCT	Varies	15 mins

Because the subtests are different, there are different strategies and techniques needed to do your best:

SIMPLE DRAWINGS (SD)
HIDDEN FIGURES (HF)

Recommendation: **Work quickly and don't guess.** The SD and HF scores are taken from the number of problems you answered correctly, with incorrect answers deducted from your score. Most of the time, test-takers will not be able to get through all the questions. Answering as quickly and as accurately as possible—without randomly guessing as time is about to expire—is usually the best technique.

Time yourself when you practice these subtests in this book. It will not only help get you into the rhythm of these kinds of problems, but it will also give you some pretest confidence.

ARMY AVIATION INFORMATION TEST (AAIT)
SPATIAL APPERCEPTION TEST (SAT)
READING COMPREHENSION TEST (RCT)

Recommendation: **Work quickly and guess on questions you haven't reached if time is about to run out.** The AAIT, SAT, and RCT include a fixed number of questions for each subtest. On these subtests, any questions left unanswered will be graded as incorrect. Therefore, if time is about to expire, it's in your best interest to rule out poor answer choices on the remaining questions and make educated guesses.

Again, it will be helpful to you to practice these subtests in this book while timing yourself—and you can definitely improve your AAIT score by studying the Aviation Information section in Chapter 7.

MATH SKILLS TEST (MST)
MECHANICAL COMPREHENSION TEST (MCT)

Recommendation: **Work quickly and don't guess.** Both of these subtests are *adaptive*, which means the computer program tailors questions to the ability level of each examinee. In a paper test (and in the first five SIFT subtests, even though they are on the computer), all test-takers answer the same questions; this has the advantage of measuring everyone with the same yardstick, but there is no flexibility in that yardstick.

In an adaptive test, your first question will be in the middle range of difficulty. If you answer it correctly, the next question will be more difficult. Answer that one correctly, and the questions will get harder until you miss one, at which time it will ask you a less challenging question. If you don't answer the first question correctly, however, the next item will be less difficult. The test continues in this way until your proficiency level is determined in each area. You answer questions that are appropriate for your ability level, so you don't waste time answering questions that are either too easy or too hard—therefore, there are fewer questions and less time needed in each section.

Due to the nature of adaptive tests, there is a lower limit to the validity of the test when too few questions get answered—so test-takers who don't answer enough questions on either of the SIFT's adaptive subtests before time runs out may have a penalty applied to their scores. Therefore, examinees need to work as quickly as possible without losing accuracy. The size of the penalty will increase as the number of questions answered decreases, but there will not be a penalty if the test ends automatically before time has expired.

Many test-takers find that they need to put special emphasis on reviewing their math knowledge and skills before taking any of the services' flight aptitude tests. Unless you were a whiz in physics in school (and even if you were), you will benefit a lot from reviewing the Mechanical Comprehension section in Chapter 8.

"Don't let your speed affect your accuracy." —Major General Lee Henry

On the adaptive subtests, it's not a good idea to start randomly guessing as time is about to run out. The time limits for each subtest have been established to allow as many examinees as possible to finish the test. If you have worked diligently and quickly on a particular subtest, random guessing will in most cases be worse for your score than the penalty you might get for not finishing the entire test.

The advantages of adaptive tests are that they take less time and you don't have to wait to go on to the next subtest—even on the subtests that are not adaptive, you should be able to go to the next subtest when you are ready, and not have to wait on everyone else. Since the overall test is computerized, you will get your scores as soon as you finish the entire SIFT—but you can't skip around, and you can't go back to a question you already answered.

SIFT SCORES AND SCORING

Your pass/fail results will be generated as soon as you finish the SIFT. You will be instructed to see the Test Control Officer (TCO) or Test Examiner (TE) to get your score letter, which must be signed by the TCO or TE to be valid.

If you pass the SIFT, you are not authorized to retake it. If you don't make the cut score on your first try, you can retake the SIFT, but only once—and you have to wait at least 180 days (six months). You only get ONE retest. Let me say that again: you get a *maximum* of two chances to take the SIFT. That's it.

As of this writing, the minimum qualifying score to apply for the Army's Aviation Program is 40. Possible scores range from 20 to 80; 50 is considered an "average" score. The cutoff score may change to match the needs of the Army's Aviation Branch and Recruiting Command. The education center on an active duty post ought to be able to give you up-to-date information if there are any changes.

Here's something else to think about: if you barely pass the SIFT, that's passing, it's true—but it's a score that will be compared with other test-takers, and frequently those with higher scores have more options and more opportunities, such as which kind of aircraft, first choice for schooling or assignments, and so on.

The formulas and algorithms used to compute SIFT scores are not published by the Army, so unlike some other military tests, there's no breakdown of how each subtest contributes to your score. However, Army officials have stated that the formula used to calculate the SIFT score is compensatory, meaning that poor performance on one subtest may often be offset by high performance on another. What this really means is that you need to do as well as you can on all the subtests.

SIFT TESTING LOCATIONS

Since the SIFT is administered on a secure server platform, you can only take it at certain locations:

- Active duty Army post education centers
- Military Entrance Processing Stations (MEPS)
- Military academies
- Army Reserve Officer Training Corps (ROTC) programs at colleges and universities

You will need to schedule your SIFT exam at the location where you intend to test—you can't just walk in. Current military service members should contact their closest Army post education center. Warrant Officer Flight Training (WOFT) applicants should contact a recruiter for help with scheduling the SIFT.

ON THE DAY OF THE TEST

Bring some form of photo identification (driver's license, military ID card, passport, etc.) and verification of your Social Security number (preferably your Social Security card). You won't be able to bring in any electronic devices (phone, smartphone, camera, calculator, etc.) into the testing room, so you'll probably want to leave them in your car; if not, the test proctor should be able to store them outside the testing room for you. Likewise, personal belongings such as book bags and purses are not allowed in the testing room. Even pencils and scratch paper for calculations will be furnished at the testing facility.

And yes, that's right, no calculators—the SIFT math problems are designed to be completed without using a calculator. Whatever formulas you might need will be provided. Again, you will be given scratch paper to do calculations by hand as needed.

Navy/Marine Corps/Coast Guard Aviation Selection Test Battery (ASTB-E)

The Aviation Selection Test Battery (ASTB-E) is used by the Navy, Marine Corps, and Coast Guard as one factor in the selection of pilot and flight officer candidates; it is designed to predict a test-taker's potential performance during the beginning phases of aviation training. Aviation officer candidates and Navy intelligence officer applicants take the entire test, but all other Navy Officer Candidate School (OCS) candidates and Coast Guard officer candidates take just the first three sections of the exam (math skills, reading comprehension, and mechanical comprehension).

The current version of the ASTB, the ASTB-E, hit the streets in December 2013. It consists of seven subtests.

Sequence of Subtests

Subtest Name	Abbrev.	Number of Questions	Time Limit
Math Skills Test	MST	20–30	Up to 40 mins
Reading Comprehension Test	RCT	20–30	Up to 30 mins
Mechanical Comprehension Test	MCT	20–30	Up to 15 mins
Aviation and Nautical Information Test	ANIT	Up to 30	Up to 15 mins
Naval Aviation Trait Facet Inventory	NATFI	88	N/A
Performance-Based Measures	PBM	Six sections	N/A
Biographical Inventory with Response Verification	BI-RV	Varies based on individual	Not timed or proctored

Unless you are deployed aboard a ship, the ASTB-E is administered on a secure web-based testing platform known as Automated Pilot Examination (APEX); APEX platforms are also equipped with headphones and a video-game-like joystick. If you are deployed aboard your ship at sea, there are paper testing options, but you will need to contact your ship's testing or education officer to get details on what is available in your situation.

The first four ASTB-E subtests are all adaptive, in the same way as explained earlier in the SIFT section. The PBM is an interactive multimedia test that assesses motor skills, spatial ability, reaction time, and multitasking abilities. The BI-RV may be taken on any web-enabled computer by an examinee using a user name and password provided by the examiner. This may be (but is not required to be) an APEX-equipped workstation.

In an adaptive test, your first question will be in the middle range of difficulty. If you answer it correctly, the next question will be harder. Answer that one correctly, and the questions will keep getting harder (or at least stay at the max level of difficulty) until you miss one, at which time you will get a less challenging question. If you don't answer the first question correctly, however, the next one will be less difficult. The test continues in this way until your proficiency level is determined.

The advantages of adaptive tests are that they take less time and you don't have to wait to go on to the next subtest—but you can't go back to a previous question, and you can't skip around.

The four adaptive subtests of the ASTB-E (MST, RCT, MCT, and ANIT) will consist of a minimum of 20 multiple-choice questions and a maximum of 30, all from a test-specific item bank. Which questions you will see will depend a little bit on chance and mostly on your responses.

The Navy calculates six score components from weighted combinations of the ASTB-E subtests: the Academic Qualifications Rating (AQR), Pilot Flight Aptitude Rating (PFAR), Flight Officer Flight Aptitude Rating (FOFAR), Pilot Aviation Fit (PAF) Score, Flight Officer Aviation Fit (FOAF) Score, and Officer Aptitude Rating (OAR). The OAR score, derived from the MST, RCT, and MCT subtests only, is used for selecting nonaviation officer candidates.

It's important to point out that you can definitely study and raise your scores for the first four subtests (MST, RCT, MCT, and ANIT). We'll go over what the PBM consists of and how it's set up to help you prepare for it. The NATFI and BI-RV are questions about you, your attitudes, and your experience; you already know these answers, and they will be customized to you.

You can take some of the subtests at different times, but an ASTB-E score will not be generated until all subtests (including the BI-RV) are completed and merged together—and all the tests must be taken within a 90-day window. If any of the tests fall outside the 90-day window, the test-taker won't get any score but his or her OAR, and it will count against his or her lifetime three-test limit. AQR, PFAR, and FOFAR scores will not be generated until all ASTB-E subtests have been completed.

No one is permitted to take the ASTB-E more than three times in his or her lifetime—unless he or she previously took a nonadaptive version using a previous ASTB-E paper form, which won't count against the three-test limit. The online APEX ASTB-E is delivered in adaptive format, presenting a different combination of questions to test-takers each time. After three attempts, the individual is ineligible for further ASTB-E testing. Applicants must wait at least 90 calendar days between ASTB-E attempts.

If for some reason an individual manages to repeat the same form of a nonadaptive test, no score will be generated and the attempt will be declared an "illegal" test; it will also count against the three-time lifetime limit. Applicants who have taken the entire ASTB-E and are being retested must take the entire ASTB-E again, even though they may be happy with their previous performance on parts of it.

An applicant's official ASTB-E score will come from his or her most recent legal test. A retest found to be illegal due to insufficient time between tests or improper form usage will not replace legal recorded scores, but it will count against the three-time lifetime limit.

ON THE DAY OF THE TEST

Bring some form of photo identification (driver's license, military ID card, passport, etc.) and verification of your Social Security number (preferably your Social Security card). You won't be able to bring in any electronic devices (phone, smartphone, camera, calculator, watch with calculator, etc.) into the testing room, so you'll probably want to leave them in your car; if not, the test proctor should be able to store them outside the testing room for you. Likewise, personal belongings such as book bags and purses are not allowed in the testing room.

And yes, that's right, no calculators—the ASTB-E math problems are designed to be completed without using a calculator. Whatever formulas you might need will be provided, and you will be given pencils and scratch paper to do calculations by hand as needed.

The total time required to take the ASTB-E will vary from one person and one location to another. Completing all the subtests except the BI-RV will take from two to possibly as much as three and a half hours. If you are only taking the OAR subtests (the first three), the APEX version will take from 90 minutes to 2 hours and the paper version will take potentially a little longer.

The BI-RV portion of the ASTB-E can take anywhere from 45 minutes to 2 hours to complete, and does not have to be completed in one administration session. The Navy recommends taking the BI-RV first (before coming to the testing location), since it can be completed on any web-based computer.

Possibly because most ASTB-E test-takers are non-DoD personnel—as opposed to those who are already service members—only those who have achieved qualifying ASTB-E scores will progress to flight surgeons or aviation medical examiners for flight physical examinations.

Math Skills Test (MST)

The MST measures your basic arithmetic, algebra, and geometry skills and knowledge, and there is the potential for you to see problems dealing with statistics, probability, and exponents (including negative and fractional). Some will be word problems, and some will be equations. There will also be questions that require solving for variables, time/rate/distance calculations, fractions, square roots, and the calculation of geometric shapes' areas, angles, and perimeters.

Remember, on an adaptive test, the questions keep getting harder when you get them right, and you will keep going until the test module has determined your skill level. You can't skip and you can't go back, but on the computerized version you should work through the problems without too much regard for how long you are taking—what counts is the questions you get right and their level of difficulty.

You won't be allowed to use a calculator for either the paper or computerized version of the MST, but you won't be working with hugely complicated numbers, either. Test-takers have reported that you will be provided a list of general math equations, but it will still be up to you to know which ones to use and how to use them—you will need to be quick and confident with basic arithmetic and order of operations, and really understand the problems that you practice.

Reading Comprehension Test (RCT)

Reading comprehension items require ASTB-E examinees to understand the meaning of selected passages of text. Each item requires the test-taker to decide which of the possible answers can be inferred from the text in the passage. The questions will present you with a short passage to read, and you will then have to select the answer choice that can be deduced or inferred from the information given in the passage. This can be a little tricky because more than one of the answer choices may in fact be true or correct in some way—but if the information that backs that up is not in the passage, it won't be the right answer, no matter how true it is.

The difficulty and length of the passages will increase as you answer correctly, and many of the harder passages will deal with military-specific subjects. Therefore, it's important for you to become familiar with as much contextual or background information as possible—the Aviation and Nautical Information sections in Chapter 7 will help you with that.

Mechanical Comprehension Test (MCT)

Questions in the Mechanical Comprehension section of the ASTB-E include topics that would typically be found in a high school general physics course. The questions measure test-takers' knowledge of scientific principles dealing with gases and liquids, as well as their understanding of how these properties affect pressure, volume, and velocity. The subtest can also include questions about the components and performance of engines; potential and kinetic energy; principles of electricity, gears, and weight distribution; and the operation of simple machines, such as levers, fulcrums, and pulleys.

Aviation and Nautical Information Test (ANIT)

The ANIT measures an examinee's knowledge of aviation history, nautical terminology and procedures, and aviation-related concepts such as aircraft components, aerodynamic principles, and flight rules and regulations. Of all the ASTB-E subtests, ANIT scores are the most easily improved by studying because this subtest is primarily a test of knowledge instead of aptitude. Examinees can prepare for this subtest by reviewing Chapter 7 in this book, Federal Aviation Administration (FAA) and civilian aviation books, and handbooks and manuals about basic piloting, navigation, and seamanship.

Naval Aviation Trait Facet Inventory (NATFI)

The NATFI is a *forced choice* computer-adaptive personality inventory consisting of 88 questions. "Forced choice" means that you have to pick one of the pairs of alternatives offered as being more applicable to you—what you like, what you would do, how you are. The actual questions are not released by the Navy.

Although you can't study for the NATFI—and experience shows that you can't "game" it and give the answers you think the Navy wants—you should be prepared for some (or even most) of the choices presented to be between two alternatives that don't seem to apply, don't seem positive, or don't appear to relate to each other.

Reportedly, an example of this kind of "no good choice" question might go something like this:

A. I get nervous when I am under pressure.
B. I try not to drive at night because I am not confident in my driving ability.

The best strategy here is not to agonize over the choices—just pick the one that seems closest to being correct (or even just least incorrect) and drive on.

Performance-Based Measures (PBM)

The PBM is a set of interactive, multimedia, performance-based tests that are similar to some video games. It tests your motor skills, spatial abilities (how well you think in three dimensions), reaction time, ability to concentrate despite distractions, multitasking abilities, physical dexterity, and hand-eye coordination.

The point is not to see if you know how to fly an airplane, but to see how well you can perform certain relatively simple tasks while other things are going on that are intended to distract you. Unfortunately, you won't be able to study in the conventional sense for this subtest—but what follows is a preview of what you will experience.

Tests within the PBM include Dichotic Listening, Digit Cancellation, Multi-Tracking, Vertical Tracking, Airplane Tracking, and Emergency Scenarios.

When taking the PBM, you will use a joystick and throttle combination (sometimes known as a "hands-on throttle and stick" setup) similar to Figure 3.1, as well as some garden variety headphones. All these will be provided to you by the test site.

Each section is preceded by a practice session. Make the most out of the practice and take some time to understand what you are supposed to do, as well as to get comfortable with the joystick and throttle setup.

Another thing to keep in mind is that the PBM test session is layered, meaning that you get a single task, then another, and then you have to do both simultaneously. Then the test adds on another task, and so on. This makes the practice before each session even more important.

Figure 3.1 Examples of PBM Equipment

In the first section, you see a "north up" map and a symbol that shows which way you are facing. Then, from a point of view as if you were in the air looking down at the ground, you see a picture of a building with four parking lots—one on each side—and you are asked which cardinal direction a certain lot is from the building. This is repeated several times, with the direction you are facing and the parking lot concerned changing each time. This section requires both speed and accuracy; you may want to make some flash cards to practice.

In the next section, you will hear instructions in your headphones that tell you which ear to listen to; then you will be told to press a button on the joystick if you hear an odd number in that ear, and to click a button on the throttle if you hear an even number in that ear. Then, you will hear numbers and letters in both ears, and your task is to focus on the ear you were told to listen to and respond to even and odd numbers you hear by pressing the appropriate button.

In the following section, the screen has a narrow track on the left with an aircraft symbol in it. The symbol moves up and down, and your task is to use the throttle to keep your "pipper" (gunsight) superimposed on the symbol.

Next, the aircraft symbol moves over the entire screen, and your task is to use your joystick to keep your pipper on the aircraft symbol. This task then combines with the previous one, and you use both joystick and throttle to try to line up on the aircraft symbol as it moves randomly over the screen.

Based on reports from those who have recently taken the ASTB-E, the operative word here seems to be *try*—so do your best and don't get frustrated. Also, reportedly, you will only have to use one button on your joystick, but you may have to use more than one button on the throttle. Pay attention to the directions you get at the time and you will come out okay.

The next iteration adds in the numbers and letters in your headphones while you are chasing the aircraft symbol across the screen with your stick and throttle.

Eventually you will be given certain buttons to push (or other actions to take) as "emergency procedures." Then, during an on-screen flight, you are given "warnings" that require you to take the emergency procedure you were briefed on; both your accuracy and reaction time are graded on this part of the PBM.

Again, you won't be able to directly practice these events because the Navy wants to see how your "first-time" reaction stacks up against its standards. Even so, you will be better off now because you know a little about what is coming. However, you may find it useful to solve mental rotation problems like those in Chapter 9 and on the AFOQT.

Biographical Inventory with Response Verification (BI-RV)

The Biographical Inventory with Response Verification (BI-RV) is an unproctored (unsupervised) subtest taken outside of the APEX environment as a separate testing session from the ASTB-E. It can take anywhere from 45 minutes to two hours to complete in total, and it does not have to be completed in a single session. The Navy actually recommends that you get it done before you take the rest of the ASTB-E if you can; your recruiter can help you with this.

The BI-RV only assesses background experiences—things you have done—such as academic achievements and extracurricular activities in high school and college. However, it is a powerful predictor of whether you will finish pilot training or not because the questions it asks all have something to do with how you might deal with a demanding, fast-paced aviation instructional program.

When you take the BI-RV, you will be asked to provide verification information for some responses. For example, if you indicate that you played on a sports team in college, you will be required to manually type in the type of sport, position played, the name of the college or university, and the year(s) you played. Falsifying information on this test is grounds for disqualification for service as an aviator, even if you have already started training—and even if you have completed it.

What a shame it would be to finish pilot training but not be allowed to fly! Honesty really is the best policy here, as it is elsewhere in life.

ASTB-E TEST SCORES

Examinees who take the entire test receive four scores resulting from different combinations of the seven subtests. Examinees who only take the first three subtests receive only one score, the Officer Aptitude Rating (OAR). The four scores given to examinees taking the entire test are:

The **Academic Qualifications Rating (AQR)** is used to predict academic performance in aviation preflight instruction and the primary phase of ground school. This score is affected by the examinee's performance on all the subtests, but the strongest influence is made by his or her score on the Math Skills Test. Scoring ranges from 1 to 9; the minimum score to become a Navy pilot or flight officer is a 3.

The **Pilot Flight Aptitude Rating (PFAR)** ranges from 1 to 9 and is used to predict primary flight performance for student naval aviators. This score is affected by performance on all subtests, but the greatest contribution is made by scores on the Aviation and Nautical Information and Performance-Based Measures subtests. The current minimum score to qualify as a Navy pilot is a 4.

The **Flight Officer Flight Aptitude Rating (FOFAR)**, again ranging from 1 through 9, is used to predict primary phase flight school performance for student naval flight officers. This score is affected by performance on all subtests, but the strongest influence is from the Math Skills Test. The current minimum score to qualify as a Navy flight officer is a 4.

The **Officer Aptitude Rating (OAR)** is used by the Navy to predict academic performance in Navy Officer Candidate School. This score comes from performance on the first three subtests. This score ranges from a minimum of 20 through a maximum of 80, with a current average score of about 50.

Test-takers will get immediate ASTB-E scores as soon as all seven subtests are complete. If they are taking the OAR through APEX, scores will be generated upon completion. Those taking the paper version of the OAR have to wait until their tests are scored by the Navy. Recruiters and other test administrators are not able to provide unofficial scores for paper tests.

If you take the paper version of the OAR (the first three subtests), you are not allowed to take the other ASTB-E subtests until the Navy has processed the answer sheet. A paper OAR test will only generate an OAR score. If you complete the paper OAR and later need a full set of ASTB-E scores, you will have to complete the remaining subtests at an APEX-enabled testing site within 90 days of completing the paper test.

Test-Taking Strategies, Tips, and Techniques

4

"If you don't know where you are going, any path will take you there."

—Native American proverb

"Plan the work, then work the plan."

—A senior NCO

EFFECTIVE STUDYING

Many people hold two incorrect beliefs about test taking. First, they believe that the amount of time spent studying is the most important—or maybe even the only—factor in improving their test results. Likewise, many people believe that last-minute studying (commonly referred to as "cramming") will get the job done. Neither of these ideas is correct.

The proven truth is that *efficient* studying *ahead of time* is by far the best method, and the *only* really effective way to get significantly better results on whatever test you're preparing for. Although it *is* true that any time spent studying is better than none, the question you have to ask yourself is this: *Am I getting the most benefit possible out of the time I am spending studying?*

Because time is a finite resource—you're never going to have 25 hours in a day, nor 61 minutes in an hour—it makes sense to use it as wisely and as efficiently as possible. Remember that you have the same number of minutes in an hour and hours in a day that Aristotle, Leonardo da Vinci, Michelangelo, Benjamin Franklin, Thomas Edison, and the Wright brothers did—and you have vastly more resources at your fingertips than they ever did!

To make the time you *do* have count for as much as possible, *plan* your studying, and do it as far ahead of time as possible. This will make the time you spend studying more effective, instead of just time spent reading (there's a difference). Although the amount of time you spend studying is important, the amount of time you spend studying *effectively* is even more important—and it's what will help you get improved results on your test. So, you need to develop a system.

Spending an hour a day in uninterrupted studying in a quiet, nondistracting place will pay off far more than spending twice that time in 15–20 minute segments, especially if you are in a place where there are distractions or interruptions. Contrary to what many people today think, studying with the TV on is *not* the most effective way to study; *any* distraction is, well . . . distracting. If it takes away from your focus on what you're studying, it's bad. If you can start studying a week, two weeks, or more before your test—or, if not, as far ahead as possible—it will give your brain and memory time to shift the material from your short-term memory (think of a temporary file on your computer desktop) to your long-term memory (think of a file permanently saved on your hard drive), where you will be able to access it more easily.

STUDYING TIPS

Establish a study schedule and stick to it.

Don't put off studying until it's convenient, or for some time when you have nothing else to do. If the test is important enough for you to take, it's important enough to invest the time in it to do as well as you can. Make studying a priority, equal in importance at least to your social life or watching television. How many movies or concerts or music stars or actors have any chance at all to improve your future? Those celebrities are not going to take your test for you (and even if they did, you probably wouldn't like the results). Schedule your study time and make every effort not to let anything else interfere with that schedule.

Concentrate your study efforts in your weakest areas.

Chances are you already have an idea of the general areas where you are weak, strong, or just so-so. The first practice test for your service will give you some more focused insight about the kinds of questions you do well on, as well as the ones where you need some work—but don't neglect your stronger areas and let them become your new "need work" categories! Go back and review information in the specific areas where you realize that you need help; if some area is still not clear to you, do further research in a library or on the Internet. If you're in college, find a classmate who is strong in that area and ask for help, or go find a professor or graduate assistant in that subject and explain your goal; chances are they will make time to help you. Even if you're not enrolled in a college or university right now, you can still pick up the phone and call an expert in the field (maybe at that local college you're not enrolled in) and ask for suggestions on sources appropriate to your level and the time you have available.

When you're ready to take the second test, look back at how many questions in each section you got right and wrong, and decide that you are going to get every question right on the second practice test. Then take the second practice test for your preferred service and do what's necessary from there.

Study without interruption or stopping for at least 30 minutes at a time.

Set up your schedule so that you can study for an uninterrupted period of at least 30 minutes. If you have set aside a couple of hours, for instance, take a short break (maybe five, no more than 10 minutes) after 30–45 minutes—get a drink, go to the restroom, stretch briefly—but don't lose your focus! It's easy to get distracted during this time, so stay away from the TV, don't make any phone calls, don't start organizing your closet—don't do anything that's going to keep you from diving right back into your studying. BUT, when you are taking a practice test, do the complete examination in one sitting, just as you will have to do when it comes time to actually take the test.

Make sure you understand the correct meaning of every word you read or hear.

Your ability to grasp and comprehend what you read is the key to doing well on the test—after all, it *is* a *written* test, right? If it was a test on making baskets from the free-throw line, would you practice more on dribbling and passing or on what you were going to be tested on? Remember (and you already know this), the flight aptitude test you're preparing for is not just a test to earn a numerical grade on a report card; it's a test to see if you have what it takes to take advantage of a whole wealth of opportunities . . . or not. So, starting now, every time you see a word whose meaning you aren't completely sure of (whether you're studying at that moment or not), make the effort to look it up. If you can't look it up right then, write it down and look it up when you can. This will require self discipline, but you will get the benefit not only on the test, but also in your daily life.

"Knowledge of things and knowledge of words for them grow together. If you do not know the words, you can hardly know the thing."
—Henry Hazlitt (1894–1993)

Keep a list of the words you didn't know and had to look up.

Then go back and review them periodically. Try to use them in conversation when it's appropriate—not to make yourself sound like an egghead, but to be able to express yourself more precisely and concisely. Stretch your mental muscles by doing crossword puzzles.

Write it down.

It is a well-proven fact that you retain things that you write down better and longer than those things that you just hear, even if you say them—so take the time and effort to write down the word and its definition, not on a computer, but *longhand.* Okay, print it in block letters if you want, but *write it down.* Then write a sentence using that word as it might be used in a real conversation or in an imaginary term paper. The mental and physiological effort you expend to write that word or concept down significantly reinforces your memory of it far above just hearing or even saying it. Even if you never see those notes again—and you *should* review them—you will still retain the material better.

Simulate test conditions when studying—and *especially* when taking practice tests!

To the extent that you can, reproduce the same conditions you will encounter when you are taking the actual test. The more you do this when you are "just" studying—not to mention when you are taking a practice test—the more you will be used to this kind of environment when it comes time for the test that counts. If you have other people in the household, tell them that you are taking a practice test and ask for their support by not disturbing you; chances are they will be happy to comply.

Time yourself when taking practice tests.

Running out of time on a multiple-choice test is a tragedy that you can avoid. Learn through practice how much time is reasonable to spend on any particular question, and then stick to it.

Exercise regularly and stay in good physical shape.

It's hard to remember sometimes that life is supposed to be about balance, especially when you have too many things to do and nowhere near enough time to do even half of them. However, the bottom line here is that if your body isn't in at least decent shape, you will not do as well as you could on the test. Do at least 20–30 *uninterrupted* minutes of aerobic exercise (something that makes you breathe hard) at least two to three times a week, and preferably more. Strength training (lifting some kind of weights) is good, but balance the amount of weight you can lift with how many repetitions you can do, and don't overdo things to the extent that you risk injury. Even a temporary injury is a distraction you don't need.

Practice, practice, practice—stay in good mental shape, too.

After you take both practice tests for your preferred service, look at the sections in the other services' tests that are similar to the areas where you still need work. Even if you think vocabulary is a strong point for you, for instance, don't rest on your laurels; get everything out of this book that you can by looking at the language-related sections in the other tests. Look on the Internet for practice questions for your service's test. Look at practice SAT, ACT, and GRE tests that are available to you, even if they are older versions available in the library—the meaning of *indubitably* won't change, nor will the formula for the area of a circle.

GUIDELINES FOR MULTIPLE-CHOICE TESTS

This section lays out specific test-taking techniques that will help you on multiple-choice tests. Learn and then practice these techniques so that they are second nature to you by the time you take the test.

Read the directions.

Don't assume that you know what the directions are for a specific section, or for the test overall, without reading them. Make sure you read them thoroughly as if it was the first time you had seen them, and make sure you understand them fully. This is not *spending* time so much as *investing* it—and why take a chance on canceling out all the effort you've spent studying and otherwise preparing? Besides, the test monitor or proctor won't let you start until everyone has had plenty of time to read the directions—they may read them aloud, too—so there's no reason *not* to read the directions. Pay special attention to whether there are different directions from one section of the test to another.

Be careful when you mark your answers on paper tests.

Make sure that you mark your answers in accordance with the instructions on the answer sheet. Pay special attention to make sure that you do the following:

- **Make *sure* you are marking the numbered answer for the question you think you are answering.** Although this may seem pretty obvious (and it is), lots of test-takers have failed because of this kind of carelessness. All it takes is getting off track on one question. You probably won't notice it right away, so you'll continue being off for even more questions. Fortunately, this is not an issue with computerized tests.
- **Don't make any extra or stray marks on your answer sheet;** most tests are machine graded, and it's not going to help you to confuse the scanner or optical character reader.
- **Completely fill in the allotted space** (circle, oval, rectangle) for the answer you choose.
- **Erase *completely*** any answers you want to change. This goes back to your preparation, in that you need to bring a good, fresh eraser that works.

For Paper and Computerized Tests

- **Skip questions that are giving you too much trouble.** Don't dwell on any one question too long on your first trip through that section or subtest. If you've read the question twice, tried to eliminate any obviously incorrect answers, and still have no clue between three or four choices, it's time to go to the next question and come back when you get to the end of that section. There are two options on how to handle the question you're skipping. First, you can just plain skip it if you're reasonably certain you're going to get to the end of the subsection with time to spare; the trick here is to make sure that you leave that answer totally blank on your answer sheet and don't fill in the blank for the question that you skipped with the answer to the question *after* the one you skipped.

The second option is to go ahead and fill in an answer for one of the choices you think might be right so that you stay in sequence, and also to hedge your bets in case you don't get to the end of the test with time enough to go back to questions that you skipped. Either way, if you are allowed to mark in your test booklet, or if you have scratch paper, circle the number of the question you skipped or write it down on the scratch paper.

- **Go back to the questions you skipped within a subtest after you get to the end.** Once you have answered all the questions you were at least reasonably sure of in a section or subtest, check to see how much time you have remaining. If you can, go back to the questions you skipped and reread the question and the choices. Sometimes a subsequent question will have jarred loose something in your memory and you will be able to make a good choice. If you read the question again and you still are having trouble, make the best guess you can, following the guidelines outlined here.
- **Make sure you understand what the question is really asking.** Read carefully the *root* or *stem* of the question—the part before the answer choices—to make sure you know what the question really is. Don't be in such a galloping hurry that you slam through it and miss a *not* or *except* or some other small but important indicator. If none of the choices seem correct after the first time you look at them, read the question again.
- **Read all the choices before you choose an answer.** Don't fall into the trap of thinking that the best distractor—a plausible but still incorrect answer—is it because it's first and oh, boy, it seems right, and let's get on to the next question!
- **Know the key "tipoff" words that often signal a wrong answer.** Absolute words such as *never, nobody, nothing, always, all, only, any, everyone, everybody,* and the like are often clues that this answer is too broad and therefore wrong.
- **Know the key words that often signal a *possibly* correct answer.** Limiting words such as *usually, generally, sometimes, possible, many, some, occasionally, often,* and the like often signal a choice that at least *could* be correct—but read it carefully to be sure!
- **Look at how the meaning of the choices compare with each other.** If two choices have a conflicting or opposite meaning, chances are high that one of them is correct. If two choices are very close in meaning, chances are pretty good that *neither* of them is correct.
- **NEVER make a choice based on the frequency of lettered answer choices.** This is the same thing as rolling dice—the odds are stacked against you. If this is what you think will work, please just mail your money to the casino and don't waste time and taxpayer money taking the test.
- **Eliminate choices you recognize as being incorrect.** This is the most important guideline to success on any multiple-choice test. As you read through the choices, eliminate any choice you know is wrong. If you can eliminate all the choices except one, there's your answer! Read the choice one more time to make sure you haven't missed anything, and then mark that answer on your answer sheet and move on to the next question. If you can eliminate only one or two of the possible choices, read through the question and the remaining choices once more. Many times the right answer will become apparent; if not—even if you have to flat-out guess between two or three possible choices that you think *could* be right—you will have significantly increased your odds of answering that question correctly.
- **Don't reconsider answer choices that you have already eliminated.** If you thought it was wrong the first time through, you were probably correct. Focus on the ones that could be right.

- **Be very reluctant to change answers.** Unless you have an *excellent* reason, *don't* change an answer you have already marked in the belief that it was correct. Studies have shown again and again and again that if you are still unsure and are just trying to use the really dependable intuition that has helped you so much up to this point (yes, that's sarcasm), you are far more likely to change a right answer to a wrong one than the other way around.

ON THE DAY OF THE TEST

First, **get a good night's sleep** the night before the test. If you've established a plan and followed it, you won't be up until the wee hours cramming; if you haven't—well, good luck. Even better, try to get an adequate amount of sleep for several days before the test, and don't neglect an appropriate amount of physical exercise (and then keep that good habit *after* you take the test); this will help you sleep better at night, and you'll be more relaxed and have better stamina and resistance to stress during the day.

Organize your morning before you take the test for success. Lay out your clothes and test-taking materials the night before. Wake up early enough so that you can avoid rushing through your morning routine. Eat a good breakfast, but go easy on the carbs—some are okay, but just say "no" to that second stack of pancakes or second helping of hash browns. Your body won't realize that you need that blood to your brain, and it will be trying to divert more blood to your digestive system than you can afford during the test. Drink plenty of water early on, but not so much that you are guaranteed to need a restroom break after the first 15 minutes of the test.

If you have a choice, **wear comfortable clothes** to the test. If you are wearing a uniform, make sure you are wearing a fresh one, have a fresh haircut and shave, and generally look as if you are ready to be inspected by the local general or admiral. No one will give you points on the test for concluding from your rumpled, haggard appearance that you have been up studying nonstop for days—but *you* will feel more confident (and will therefore be mentally sharper) if you look squared away and you know it. This applies whether you are wearing a uniform or not.

Take a light jacket or sweater that you can put on or take off easily. It might be cold in the testing area, and why subject yourself to an avoidable distraction?

Take a stopwatch or digital watch with a timer. Some proctors may give you a heads-up when your time for a certain section has almost elapsed, but most won't—the proctors for the ASTB-E are actually instructed *not* to give any warnings. If you only have a few remaining questions, you can probably eliminate at least one or two wrong answer choices and guess between the ones that look plausible.

Get to the test location early. If you think it will take you 15 minutes to get there, allow 30. If you've been there a hundred times before and it's never taken longer than 30 minutes, allow an hour; this is the one day there will be road construction or a traffic jam in your way. If it's somewhere local but you haven't been there before, try to do a reconnaissance of the location, to include the room itself, in the week before you take the test. The one time that you get bad directions off the "always reliable" map-generating Internet site on your smartphone will be the time you need them, badly, to get to the test site on time. If you have to rush into the test site frustrated and out of breath, you are not setting yourself up for success—and in some circumstances, if you get there late, you'll be out of luck. If nothing else, get there with enough time to go to the restroom before you start the test, and to find a seat with a chair that doesn't make a distracting noise every time you move. Put yourself on Lombardi time: If you're not there early, you're late.

5 Language Review

"The limits of my language are the limits of my world."

—Ludwig Wittgenstein, 1889–1951, Austrian–British professor and philosopher in logic, mathematics, reasoning, and language

For officers to *lead*—which is, regardless of service or specialty, an officer's primary function—they must be able to *communicate* with the people they are trying to lead. The best plan in the world is worthless if the people who are supposed to execute it can't understand what they're supposed to do. If you want to be an officer in any service, you must be able to communicate at least reasonably well both orally and in writing—and, because officers are normally held to a higher standard, that "reasonably well" rating may be something at which you have to work.

This chapter reviews a wide array of language-related topics that help measure whether you can read and understand information presented to you. The flight aptitude tests evaluate this by a variety of multiple-choice questions dealing with synonyms and antonyms, analogies, and vocabulary—all of which add up to answering the question, *Can you comprehend what you read?*

Much of this information will hopefully already be familiar to you, but going over it won't hurt you any—and chances are you will learn or reinforce something that will help you.

SYNONYMS AND ANTONYMS

A *synonym* is a word that has the same or almost the same meaning as another word. An *antonym* is a word that has the opposite or nearly opposite meaning of another word. A desk-size dictionary (not just a paperback version) will give you insight on some synonyms and maybe some antonyms; a thesaurus will give you the full range of both.

In determining whether a word has a similar or opposite meaning to another word, it's helpful to understand the root of a word, as well as any prefixes or suffixes it may have. Go over the common roots, suffixes, and prefixes later in this chapter.

VERBAL ANALOGIES

The Air Force is the only service that tests flight aptitude test-takers on verbal analogies, but they are useful analytical tools for anyone. Verbal analogies test your ability to determine the relationships between words. To do that, though, you not only need to know what the words mean, you'll also have to apply logic to determine the relationships between the words in consideration.

There are two format types for verbal analogies on the AFOQT. The first type of analogy question contains three capitalized words in the stem, followed by five one-word choices.

The first two of the three words will give you the base analogy (THIS is to THAT); your task then is to choose which of the five choices has the same relationship to the third word as is established in the base analogy.

Here's an example:

CAT is to KITTEN as WOLF is to

(A) dog
(B) cub
(C) lion
(D) puppy
(E) cougar

The correct answer is **(B) cub**. A baby cat is a kitten, and a baby wolf is a cub. Therefore, the relationship between the second capitalized word is the infant or baby form of the first capitalized word. A wolf's offspring are called cubs, and that represents the same relationship to the wolf as the kitten has to the cat.

The second type of verbal analogy on the AFOQT involves only two capitalized words—the first pair—in the stem of the question. Your task is then to choose which of the five pairs of words presented most closely resembles the same relationship as in the first pair.

Here's a re-do of the first question recast in this format:

CAT is to KITTEN as

(A) puppy is to dog
(B) wolf is to cub
(C) lion is to lioness
(D) puppy is to kitten
(E) cougar is to panther

In this example, the only choice that represents the same relationship that CAT has to KITTEN is **(B) wolf is to cub**. Be careful to note that, in the base analogy, the adult form of the animal is listed first, so don't be thrown off by choice (A) puppy is to dog, which is wrong because the younger form of the animal is listed first.

The most important part of correctly answering these analogy questions is to determine what kind of relationship exists between the first and second word in the first, or base, analogy, and then find a choice that closely reproduces that relationship between the two words used as the second analogy. There's no way to list every possible relationship that could exist, but here are examples of the most common types of analogies.

Part to whole (correct): ROOM is to HOUSE as CABIN is to SHIP.

A room is an integral part of a house in the same way that a cabin is part of a ship.

Part to whole (incorrect): ROOM is to HOUSE as CABIN is to DECK.

The cabin and the deck are both parts of the ship; neither is a "whole" that the other is part of.

Part to whole (correct): GIRDER is to BUILDING as KEEL is to SHIP.

The girder and the keel are both structural components of the building and ship, respectively.

Part to whole (incorrect): GIRDER is to BUILDING as CABIN is to SHIP.

The girder is a structural component of the building; the cabin, although a component of the ship, is not so much the same kind of component—doesn't have the same relationship—as the girder is to the building.

Cause to effect (correct): SPARK is to FIRE as HURRICANE is to FLOOD.

The fire is the direct result of the spark, just as the flood is the direct result of the hurricane.

Cause to effect (incorrect): SPARK is to FIRE as HURRICANE is to DESTRUCTION.

The fire is the direct result of the spark, but the destruction is a result of the hurricane's wind or flooding, and not so much a direct result of the hurricane itself.

Source to product (correct): TREE is to ORANGE as FACTORY is to PRODUCT.

Source to product (incorrect): TREE is to BRANCH as FACTORY is to PRODUCT.

The branch is a part of the tree, but is not a product of it in the same way that a tree produces an orange or a factory produces its product.

Example to category (correct): CAR is to AUTOMOBILE as HOUSE is to DWELLING.

The first item is one of multiple items in the second item, which is the "next level up" category; trucks and vans are automobiles just like cars are, and caves and houseboats are dwellings in the same way that a house is.

Example to category (incorrect): CAR is to TRUCK as HOUSE is to DWELLING.

The car and the truck are both members of the same category—you could call this a "peer to peer" analogy—but the HOUSE is to DWELLING analogy is still an example-to-category exercise.

Example to category (incorrect): CAR is to AUTOMOBILE as HOUSE is to STRUCTURE.

This incorrect example is a little more subtle; STRUCTURE is a much broader, more inclusive category than DWELLING, including as it does structures that cannot be lived in as a house or a barn or a cave could, such as bridges, statues, gazebos, reviewing stands, and so on.

General to specific (correct): SHAPE is to TRIANGLE as PASTRY is to CROISSANT.

This could also be thought of as a "category to example" analogy, merely the mirror image of the previous example.

Object to function (correct): SHIELD is to PROTECT as CONTAINER is to HOLD.

Be sure the function word (almost certainly a verb) is the primary and definitive function of the noun/object that makes up the other word of the pair. If the function word is a minor or uncommon function of the object rather than a defining, typical function of the object, watch out!

Object to function (incorrect): WHEEL is to ROLL as SHIELD is to CARRY.

User to tool (correct): MECHANIC is to WRENCH as CARPENTER is to SAW.

Usually the tool mentioned in this kind of analogy is a defining or typical tool for the kind of user described, as it is in this example.

User to tool (incorrect): MECHANIC is to WRENCH as CARPENTER is to TROWEL.

A stonemason might use a trowel, but a carpenter would not normally do so.

Doer to action (correct): FARMER is to PLANTING as DOCTOR is to HEALING.

Again, make sure that the action word or verb associated with the doer is something that is a typical or defining task for the doer. If not, then the relationship is something else!

TIP

When one word of the pair is a verb, make sure that the verb tense (present, past, past participle, etc.) is the same for both word pairs. The same goes for the number of nouns—if one word pair mentions a singular object, chances are the correctly matching second pair will not have a plural noun for its object.

Doer to action (incorrect): FARMER is to HARVEST as DOCTOR is to HEALING.

Numerical (correct): ONE is to TEN as FIVE is to FIFTY.

> Note: The base analogy takes the first number and multiplies it by ten, so the second pair does the same thing.

Numerical (incorrect): ONE is to TEN as FIVE is to TEN.

Grammatical (correct): HOLD is to HELD as STOP is to STOPPED.

Grammatical (correct): DOG is to DOGS as CAT is to CATS.

The concept to watch out for here is nothing more difficult than identifying which choice has the analogy with the same grammatical relationship as the base analogy. Also, watch out for different tenses of the correct verb!

Grammatical (correct): RUN is to RAN as SING is to SANG.

Grammatical (incorrect): RUN is to RAN as SING is to SUNG.

Here, the base analogy is present/past, and the incorrectly matching analogy is present/past participle.

Geographic (correct): TEXAS is to OKLAHOMA as FLORIDA is to GEORGIA.

In both cases, the first of the pair is a U.S. state and the second is the state north of and adjacent to it.

Geographic (correct): AUSTIN is to TEXAS as MONTGOMERY is to ALABAMA.

Geographic (correct): BERLIN is to GERMANY as KABUL is to AFGHANISTAN.

Here we have the capital city of some U.S. states and some other nations, respectively. Sometimes you will have to bring other knowledge to bear to correctly match these analogies.

Geographic (incorrect): GEORGIA is to ALABAMA as MEXICO is to PARIS.

Geographic (incorrect): PARIS is to FRANCE as GERMANY is to MUNICH.

Here we have the base analogy with the capital of a country. The order of the countries is incorrectly matched, and a noncapital city is matched with Germany. This is wrong on two accounts: relationship and order.

Descriptive (correct): CANDY is to SWEET as ICE is to COLD.

In this case, the second, descriptive term is something that defines the first word; sweetness and cold are inherent qualities of candy and ice, respectively.

Descriptive (incorrect): CANDY is to SWEET as TURKEY is to COLD.

Because a turkey can be any temperature, COLD is not a defining or frequently associated description of TURKEY, so this is not a valid analogy match.

Age (correct): CHILD is to ADULT as SEEDLING is to TREE.

Age (correct): PUPPY is to DOG as TADPOLE is to FROG.

Again, make sure the order (younger/older or older/younger) is the same for the second pair of words as for the first.

Age (incorrect): CHILD is to ADULT as MAN is to WOMAN.

Age (incorrect): CALF is to COW as CATERPILLAR is to WORM.

Some other analogy relationships with single examples:

Type of Analogy	Example
Synonyms (same meaning)	HATE is to DESPISE
Antonyms (opposite meaning)	LOVE is to HATE
Homonyms (sound the same)	THERE is to THEIR
Measurement (time, distance, weight, volume, etc.)	MILE is to KILOMETER, MILLIMETER is to METER
Gender (one sex to the other)	COW is to BULL, GOOSE is to GANDER
Larger to smaller	LAKE is to POND
Degree/amount	COOL is to COLD, OLD is to ANCIENT AMUSING is to HILARIOUS

Remember, these categories are only examples to help you see the overall way that analogies are done, as well as for your convenience in studying and practice. The people who design the tests aren't bound by these categories! If the analogy you see on the test does not seem to fit into one of these categories, just remember these examples and guidelines, figure out what kind of relationship the base analogy demonstrates, and follow the lead of the base analogy.

READING COMPREHENSION

Understanding what you read involves being able to recognize the main idea, remember details, make conclusions or inferences, identify and understand factual relationships, and paraphrase or summarize. All three tests will directly test you on these specific skills.

The *main idea* is the most important point or concept that the writer wants the reader to know or understand. Sometimes the writer states the main idea clearly and directly; sometimes the main idea is implied or has to be inferred from what the passage *does* say. When a main idea is generalized across the entire passage, essay, book, and so on, it is known as the *theme.*

Whenever you are trying to determine a paragraph's main idea, it's a good idea to check the first (opening) and last (closing) sentences of the paragraph. Writers frequently use a *topic sentence* (often either at the beginning or end of a paragraph or essay, although they can be anywhere) that concisely addresses the main idea.

To help you find the main idea in reading a passage or paragraph, ask these questions:

1. **Who or what is this paragraph about?**
2. **What specific aspect or facet of this subject is the writer discussing?**
3. **What point is the writer trying to make about this subject or this particular aspect of it?**

Look at this example paragraph:

> Making any of the eight errors common to transformation efforts can have serious consequences. In slowing down the new initiatives, creating unnecessary resistance, frustrating employees endlessly, and sometimes completely stifling needed change, any of these errors could cause an organization to fail to offer the products or services people want at prices they can afford. Budgets are then squeezed, people are laid off, and those who remain are put under great stress. The impact on families and communities can be devastating.

In this paragraph, the main idea is stated in the first sentence. You can tell that the paragraph will be about what happens when an organization makes any of the "eight errors common to transformation." In the same way as a headline or title, the topic sentence introduces the rest of the paragraph, setting the stage and getting you thinking about what's going to follow.

> During the latter years of the American Revolution, a government structured under the Articles of Confederation was formed. This government, which gave the states more power than the central national government, suffered severely and had many problems. The states distrusted each other and allowed the national or federal government to exercise very little authority. The Articles of Confederation produced a government that could not effectively raise money from taxes, prevent or stop Indian raids, or force the British out of the United States.

Can you identify the topic sentence in the paragraph above? Yes, the paragraph *is* about the Articles of Confederation. However, is the main idea in the first sentence, the second, or somewhere else? In this example, the *second* sentence does the best job of giving you an overall understanding of this paragraph: The lack of centralized authority under the Articles of Confederation caused lots of problems. The first sentence really just tells us *when* the items in the paragraph happened—it doesn't explain anything about what happened, much less the overarching idea. The sentences that follow give more details about this idea; they give you some of the reasons why the topic sentence was true. It's not a good idea to assume that the topic sentence is always the first sentence.

> With its smaller population and more agriculturally centered (and therefore manpower-intensive) economy, the Confederacy had fewer men available as soldiers. Less than one-third of the railroads and even fewer prewar United States industries were in the South. For most of the war, the ports and coastlines of Confederate states were blockaded by the Union Navy. It is considered in many circles a tribute to Confederate leadership and Southern courage that the rebels were not defeated sooner.

In this case, you can see that the passage builds up to its main point, which is in the last sentence.

And, as mentioned before, you may also find that the main idea is not stated directly at all, but can only be inferred or deduced from the whole passage or paragraph.

Finding Details

In developing the main idea of a paragraph or passage, the writer usually makes statements or shows action to support his or her point. They may give examples to illustrate the main idea, or they may mention facts or statistics to support it. The writer may give reasons why the main idea statement is true or correct; they might offer arguments for or against the position or idea that the main idea states. The writer can also define a complex term, cite different characteristics of a complex system or organization, classify objects within a larger category, or use descriptive details to develop an idea and help the reader understand or envision the situation. Also, the writer may *compare* two ideas, objects, or processes, to show how they are alike or similar, or the writer may *contrast* them—show how they are different.

Read how the writer of the following paragraph uses supporting details:

> My most hyperactive year was from June 1944 to June 1945. Arriving in England just in time for the invasion, my first mission as a new pilot in the 353rd Fighter Squadron was flying top cover over the invasion, combined with emptying my guns—strafing anything that moved in front of the Allied troops fighting for a secure beachhead. The reality of war became more complete on D+10 (June 16) when I landed our first P-51 at airstrip A2 at Criqueville, France. The reality of war meant being fired on during takeoff and landing. It seemed questionable to me to risk planes and pilots so close to the front; the rationale was more missions per plane per day, in addition to the advantage of avoiding the "London fog" weather of England, but France turned out to be just as bad. Our mission was to patrol the skies above and in front of the Third Army, keeping the Luftwaffe at bay, dive-bombing before each patrol and strafing afterward. We also flew escort for B-17, B-26, and B-25 bombers.

To help you understand what was "hyperactive" about the year from June 1944 to June 1945, the writer gives supporting details, detailing not only the amount of work or effort that went into his activities, but also some clues about the pace of the operations and the pilots' concerns about enemy fire.

When the test requires you to answer a question about some detail or details in the passage, you have to find words or phrases in the passage that specifically answer the question.

In other words, considering the previous passage, the test will *not* ask you about what kind of plane the writer flew before coming to Europe; the passage doesn't address that. Instead, it might ask you what kind of plane the writer flew when landing in France (P-51, fighter), when the writer landed in France (June 16, 1944), or who the writer's unit was up against (the Luftwaffe or German Air Force).

Try the following techniques when a test asks you a specific question about details of the passage:

1. **Look for key words (nouns and verbs) in the question stem and answer choices.**
2. **Read rapidly through the passage, looking for those key words or their synonyms.**
3. **Reread the part of the passage that contains the key word(s) or synonyms.**

Understanding the Passage's Organization

Questions about a reading passage will also test your ability to understand the organization of the ideas in the passage and their relationship to each other. Writers usually organize their information in fairly predictable, logical ways to make it easier for the reader to understand. Recognizing common organizational patterns improves your understanding, memory, and reading speed—as well as helping you choose the right answer on the test.

SEQUENTIAL ORGANIZATION

A *sequence* is a series of events or steps where the order is important. If the sequence is *chronological* (time based), the events are described or listed in the order in which they occurred. Clues to help you spot sequential organization include ordinal numbers (*first, second, third,* etc.), cardinal numbers (*1, 2, 3,* etc.), transition words or phrases (*then, next, later, finally, ultimately*), and dates or other information referring to time (*this year, last month, in 1982, four days later,* and so on).

> If you are stung by a bee, the first thing you need to do is remove the stinger. Next, make a paste of baking soda and water and apply it to the sting site. Then, apply ice or cold water to help reduce the pain and minimize swelling. If the pain is severe or if you are allergic to the insect, find medical help immediately.

PHYSICAL OR SPATIAL ORGANIZATION

When the organization of a passage is physical or spatial, it describes the physical arrangement or situation of a place or object. Clues can include such words as *above, below, to the right of, to the left of, behind, in front of, next to,* and so on.

> Taste buds are distributed across the tongue, but the distribution is uneven, and certain areas of the tongue are more sensitive to certain basic tastes than other areas. The tip of the tongue is most sensitive to sweetness, but the area just behind the tip is the most sensitive to salty tastes. Only the sides of the tongue are very sensitive to sour tastes, and the back area specializes in bitter tastes.

Cause and Effect

A passage may include a description of a particular thing that happened, the reasons why it happened, and/or the results that came after the occurrence. For instance, a history passage may list the events that led up to a technological innovation, a social or political change, or a war; a scientific passage may explain tectonic plate shifts and how they affect mountain formation and earthquakes. Often, the relationship is presented as a chain of events, with one or more events leading to or resulting in one or more other events. Clues include words like *resulted in, because, consequently, since, therefore, thus,* and so on.

> By the year 2020, there will be approximately one retired American for every two working Americans. In these disproportionately large numbers, older Americans will therefore become an increasingly large and powerful political force, and political issues of concern to senior citizens and elderly people such as housing, medical benefits, and reduced employment levels will be taken more seriously by elected officials.

Comparing and Contrasting Ideas

A passage may present the similarities or differences between ideas, people, places, or other things. In a *comparison,* the passage will focus on similarities; clue words can include *like, likewise, also, in like manner, similarly,* and the like. The passage may instead focus on differences, presenting a *contrast*; clues for contrasting include *but, unlike, however, in contrast, on the other hand, versus,* and *nevertheless.*

> The American farm problem often centers on supply exceeding demand and farm policies that encourage surplus production. This is not true in most other parts of the world, however, where countries cannot produce enough food to support their own populations and have to import food or else face famine.

Solution to a Problem

The writer may present the reader with a problem or describe a situation that is causing difficulty, and then present or suggest a solution or a remedy. Clue words include *problem, cause, effects, consequences, answers, solutions,* and *remedy* or *remedies.*

> Students who lived in dormitories near an area in which earthquakes happened frequently, one study says, often just dealt with their problems by denying the seriousness of the situation and the potential danger they were in.

(In this case, the solution—although an unrealistic and ineffective one—was simply to ignore the problem.)

Drawing a Conclusion or Making an Inference

A conclusion is a logical inference based on information that is presented or implied. If you read a passage critically (which, in this case, doesn't mean *negatively,* but rather just *carefully*), you follow the writer's train of thought and arrive at logical conclusions. The writer may expect the readers to draw the conclusion by themselves, or the writer may explicitly state it, often using clue words such as *therefore, thus, hence,* or *in conclusion.*

The sample passage that follows is about Americans with disabilities. The reader can conclude that legislation has made progress in moving people with disabilities into society's mainstream, although the writer doesn't say so directly. Incidentally, note the sequence pattern in this passage.

> A major goal for the disabled is easier access to the mainstream of society. The 1973 Rehabilitation Act has moved them toward this goal, as has the Education for All Handicapped Children Act of 1975, which mandates that all children, however severe their disability, receive a free, appropriate education. Before the legislation, one million handicapped children were receiving no education and another three million were getting an inappropriate one (as in the case of a blind child who is not taught Braille or is not provided with instructional materials in Braille). In 1987, Congress enacted the Employment Opportunities for Disabled Americans Act, which allows disabled individuals to earn a moderate income without losing their Medicaid health coverage.

THE PARTS OF A WORD

When you first learned how to drive, you had to learn the parts of an automobile and what they did, from the hood to the wheels to the engine to the controls and instruments to the trunk. Now you can use that automobile to transport yourself from one place to another.

In much the same way, if you want to transport your message to your listener, words are your vehicle—and the more you understand about how words are built, the better work they will do for you. You can (and should) flip this around, too: **For you to understand the test you are preparing to take, you have to be able to understand the words the writers use.** This is not just for the part of the test dealing with language skills. The whole test is written, which means that you have to be able to read and understand it. You may be the world's best math whiz, but if you can't read the directions to a problem, you will never get a chance to demonstrate that skill.

The most important part of any word is the *root.* It may be a word in itself (for example, *flex*), or a word element from which other words are formed (*aud,* for instance). Knowing a large number of word roots is one way of multiplying your vocabulary's strength, because each root can lead you to the understanding of several words.

A *prefix* is a syllable or group of syllables added to the beginning of a word that changes its meaning. Let's go back to the previous example, *flex.* By itself, it means "to bend or contract"; we'll say that the context is the human body, so you can flex a muscle, an arm, or the like. If you add the prefix *re* to the root word *flex,* you get a new word, *reflex,* with a new meaning: *reflex* describes an action you can't control, such as a sneeze.

We can further change the meaning of the root word *flex* by adding a suffix. A suffix is a syllable or group of syllables added to the end of a word that changes its meaning. If you add the suffix *ible* to the end of the root, you get another new word, *flexible,* with a new meaning: *flexible* means *able to bend without breaking* or, in a more general sense, *able to adjust to change.*

You can also add *both* a prefix and a suffix to a root and get still another word. If, for example, you add both the prefix *in* (meaning *not*) and the suffix *ible,* you get another word, *inflexible,* which means *unbending*—or, in a broader sense, *stubborn, unable to adapt to change.*

To extend the example, let's look at some more of the *flex* "family" of words. It's helpful to know in this case that *flect* is another form of *flex*; however, even though similar-sounding words often have the same root, don't be fooled that it is always the case—because it's not.

flexibility	**deflect**	**inflection**
circumflex	**genuflect**	**reflection**

If you're not sure of the exact meaning of some of these words, look them up—the effort you expend in doing so will help the meanings stick in your memory.

Following is a list of prefixes frequently used in English. Write down at least one word that uses the prefix and then check your dictionary to verify that you have used the prefix and the root word correctly.

Prefix	Meaning	Complete Word(s)
a	not, no, without	
ab	not, away from	
acro	top, tip	
ad	to	
aero	air, gas	
amphi/ambi	both, around	
an	not	
ana	again, thoroughly	
andro/anthropo	man	
ante	before, prior to	
anti	against, not	
apo	away	
baro	weight	
be	completely	
bi	two	
biblio	book	
cent	hundred	
circum	around	
contra	against	
cosmo	universe	
cyto	cell	
dactylo	finger	
de	from, away	
dec/deca	ten	
dermo/dermato	skin	
di	two	
dia	across	
ergo	work	
eth/ethno	race, nation	
eu	well	
ex	out of	
extra	beyond	
fore	before, on the front	
gastro	stomach	
geronto	old age	
hema	blood	

Prefix	Meaning	Complete Word(s)
hemi	half	
hepta	seven	
hex/hexa	six	
hyper	above	
hypo	under, below	
in	into	
in	not	
inter	between	
intra	within	
kilo	thousand	
meso	middle	
meta	beyond, after, changed	
metro	measure	
mill	thousand	
milli	one-thousandth; very small	
mis	wrong, incorrect	
mono	one	
necro	dead, dead body	
non/nona	nine	
ob	against	
oct/octa	eight	
osteo	bone	
out	from, beyond	
over	above, too much	
para	beside, close, partial	
penta	five	
peri	around	
pneumo	lung, air	
poly	many	
post	after	
pre	before	
pro	forward or in favor of	
quadr	four	
quint	five	
re	back, do again	
retro	back	
se	apart	
semi	half	
sep/sept	seven	
sex	six	
sub	under	
super	above, beyond	
syn	together, with	
tetra	four	
tox/toxico	poison	
trans	across	
tri	three	
ultra	beyond	
un	not	

Prefix	Meaning	Complete Word(s)
under	below	
uni	one	
xeno	foreign	
zoo	living	
zygo	double	

Following is a list of frequently used root words. Write down at least one word using each listed root, then check your result. Try to combine the root with one of the prefixes listed earlier.

Root	Meaning	Complete Word(s)
ac/acr	sharp, bitter	
act	do	
amb	walk, go	
anim	life, spirit, breath	
ann/annu	year	
anthro	man	
aqua	water	
aud	hear	
bene	good, well	
cap/capit	head	
card/cord	heart	
carn	flesh	
cas	fall	
ced/cede	go	
chrom	color	
chron	time	
cid/cide	kill	
cor	heart	
corp	body	
cred	believe	
curr	run	
dem	people	
demi	one-tenth	
dic/dict	say	
do/don	give	
duc/duct	lead	
fac/fact	make	
fer	carry, move	
fin	end	
flect/flex	bend	
flu/flux	flow	
fract	break	
frater	brother, brotherly	
graph	write	
gress	walk	
hetero	different	
homo	same	
hydr/hydro	water	

Root	Meaning	Complete Word(s)
ject	throw	
jur/jure	swear	
litera	letter	
lith	stone	
logo/logos	thought, study	
mag/magn	large, powerful	
mal	evil, incorrect	
man/manu	hand	
mar	sea	
mater	mother	
ment	mind	
met/meter	measure, measurement	
micro	very small	
mit	send	
mono	one	
mort	death	
mot	move	
multi	many	
norm	rule	
nov	new	
ortho	right, correct	
pan	all	
pater	father	
path	suffer, feel	
ped	foot, base	
pend	hang	
phil	like	
phon	sound	
psych	mind	
pug/pugn	fight	
rupt	break	
sci	know	
scrib	write	
sec/sect	cut	
sol	alone	
spec/spect	look	
struc/struct	build	
tele	far	
temp	time	
tract	draw	
vad	go	
ven/vent	come	
vert	turn	
vic/vict	conquer	
vis	see	
voc/voke	call	
volv	turn	

Following is a list of frequently used suffixes. Write down at least one word using each listed root, then check your result. Try to combine the root with one of the prefixes listed earlier.

Suffix	**Meaning**	**Complete Word(s)**
androus	man	
archy	rule, government	
biosis	life	
cephalic/cephalous	head	
chrome	color	
cidal/cide	kill	
cracy/crat	rule, government	
derm	skin	
emia	blood	
fugal/fuge	run away from	
gamy	marriage	
gnosis	knowledge	
grade	walking	
gram/graph/graphy	writing	
hedral/hedron	sided	
iasis	disease	
iatrics, iatry	medical treatment	
itis	inflammation	
lepsy	seizure, fit	
lith	stone	
logy	science of, list	
machy	battle, fight	
mancy/mantic	foretelling	
mania/maniac	craving, strong desire	
meter/metry	measure	
morphic/morphous	shape	
nomy	science of, law of	
odont	tooth	
opsis	appearance	
pathy	suffering, disease	
phage/phagous	eating	
phany	manifestation	
phobe/phobia	fear	
phone/phony	sound	
plasm	matter	
rrhagia/rrhagic/rrhea	flow	
saur	lizard	
scope/scopy	observation	
soma/some	body	
taxis/taxy	order	
vorous	eating	

VOCABULARY

Mark Twain is supposed to have said, "The difference between the right word and the almost right word is the difference between lightning and the lightning bug." Military officers, who are responsible for the lives of the people they lead—not to mention accomplishing the missions they are assigned—must be able to choose words that communicate the message they want to transmit. They have to be able to do it all the time, even in humdrum peacetime situations, so that they will be used to doing it all the time—and therefore will be able to do it under pressure, or even under fire.

Additionally, a wide variety of studies have found that a good vocabulary is one of the most common characteristics that successful people in all professions share. This doesn't mean that you will automatically be successful if you have a good vocabulary, but it does suggest that it can help.

What's more, the AFOQT will test you directly on your knowledge of what certain words mean. All three tests will indirectly measure if you know what words mean by your ability to follow their directions.

Since words are the building blocks or bricks of language, you need to be sure you have enough of the right kind of bricks to construct your message to do its job well. The bigger your vocabulary, the more ideas you can express accurately. To help you build your vocabulary, this section has hundreds of words you ought to know and be able to use correctly—especially if you want to have the credibility to lead other people.

Don't forget, though, that the absolute best way to improve your vocabulary is to *read*. Read a newspaper, read magazines, read books—read about things you're interested in, read about things you find you need to know about, but *read*! Don't worry about reading things that are way above your level; read things that are slightly *above* your level, and that level will go up.

The other half of this equation is that you have to *write*. No one said you have to write for publication—no one's demanding that you win the Pulitzer Prize—but, in order for you to be able to apply what you're learning by reading, you need to write, go through it yourself after it's cooled off, and then have someone who is skilled and experienced in writing look at it and give you some pointers. It's the only way you will learn what you need to know, and it's the only way you will be able to significantly improve your vocabulary.

These words presented for your review are grouped into nouns, verbs, and adjectives. For each word, you'll find today's most common or widely used definition; however, that meaning may be a long way from the word's original or literal meaning. Some words have an alternate meaning that will be useful for you to know. It would be a good idea to study other meanings of the words, as well as to practice using them in sentences; this will help you remember the words and be able to use them correctly when you really need them.

Nouns

aberration—a deviation from the standard; not typical

access—a means of approach or admittance (e.g., to an area or organization)

accord—agreement

adage—wise proverb or saying (e.g., "Too soon old, too late smart")

adversary—enemy, opponent

advocate—one who speaks in favor of or on behalf of another

affluence—wealth or abundance

agenda—list of items to discuss or to accomplish

alacrity—cheerful willingness or ready response

alias—an assumed name or pseudodym, used for purposes of deception, as a pen name, or the like

allusion—an indirect reference to something else, especially in literature; a hint

amity—friendship

anarchy—lawlessness, disorder; a lack of government control or effectiveness

anecdote—a brief, entertaining story

animosity—bitter hostility or open hatred

anomaly—an abnormality or irregularity

anthology—collection of writings, songs, or other creative works

apathy—indifference or lack of caring

apex—highest point (e.g., of a triangle)

arbiter—one who decides; a judge

atlas—book of maps

audacity—boldness

avarice—greed, desire for wealth

awe—deep feeling of respect and wonder

bastion—stronghold, fortress, fortified place against opposition

beacon—a guiding light to show the way or mark a spot

benediction—blessing; often a benediction is given at the end of an event, ceremony, or religious service

bias—prejudice or tendency in a certain direction; literally, a slant or tilt

bigot—a person who is prejudiced against someone else because of the person's race, skin color, religion, gender, and so forth; also, a person who is intolerant of others with different opinions or beliefs

blasphemy—an insult to something held sacred

blemish—defect, stain, or flaw that takes away from the quality of the rest of the area or item

bondage—slavery

boon—benefit or gift

brawl—a noisy fight

brevity—shortness, conciseness

brochure—pamphlet

bulwark—strong protection or barrier to enemy attacks

cacophony—a harsh or unpleasant mixture of sounds, voices, or words

caliber—literally refers to size; the caliber or size of a bullet is referred to in hundredths of an inch, so a ".50 caliber" bullet is half an inch in diameter at the base, and a ".45 caliber" bullet is 45/100 of an inch across at the base; also used figuratively when referring to the *quality* of something or someone (British spelling: *calibre*)

camouflage—something that conceals people or things from the enemy by making them blend into their surroundings

TIP

You may look at these words and think that you already know them, but take the time to go through them and make *sure*. Many times the meaning you have deduced from seeing the word in context may not be quite right, or it may even be quite wrong. Remember another useful adage from Mark Twain: "It's not what we don't know; it's what we do know that ain't so."

caste—social class or category

catastrophe—sudden disaster

chagrin—embarassment or disappointment

chronicle—historical record or listing, usually in sequential, chronological order

chronology—an order or listing of events, either written or spoken, in the order in which they happened

clamor—uproar

clemency—mercy (e.g., on a prisoner or criminal)

condolence—expression of sympathy to one who has suffered a loss

connoisseur—an expert judge of the best of something, such as wine, food, paintings, etc.

consensus—general or group agreement

context—the words or ideas surrounding one particular word or idea that give clues or contribute depth to the word's meaning

conundrum—a perplexing puzzle or riddle

criterion—standard of judgment or comparison

crux—the essential point or central part

cynic—one who mocks or disbelieves the good intentions or values of others; one who believes people are motivated only by selfishness

data—facts or information

dearth—scarcity or lack of something

debacle—large-scale defeat or complete failure

debut—first appearance, especially before an audience

deference—conceding to another's desire or will; respect or courtesy

deluge—great flood or overwhelming inflow

depot—warehouse, large storage place

depravity—moral corruption

destiny—predetermined fate

detriment—damage, loss, or disadvantage

diagnosis—analysis or determination of the cause of a disease or problem

diction—the way in which words are used by a speaker

discernment—insight, ability to see things clearly

disdain—arrogant scorn or contempt

dilemma—situation requiring a choice between two or more deeply held values, or between two or more possibly unpleasant courses of action

din—loud, pervasive, continuous noise

directive—a general order or instruction

discord—disagreement, often noisy

discrepancy—inconsistency or error

discretion—freedom of choice; also refers to a judicious reserve in one's speech or behavior

dissent—difference of opinion, especially from a widely held opinion

drought—long period of dry weather or conditions

effluvium—a disagreeable or bad-smelling vapor or gas

egotist—self-centered person

elite—a part of the whole that is considered to be at or near the top. In society, *elite* usually refers to the wealthiest or best-educated group; in the military, *elite* usually refers to units who have special training and/or equipment, and are therefore capable of accomplishing particularly difficult missions

enigma—mystery, puzzling circumstance

enterprise—an important project or self-sufficient organization

environment—general surroundings, either physical or referring to influences

epitome—a top-level representation of a quality, usually a virtue (e.g., "June is the *epitome* of beauty and wisdom.")

epoch—a particular period of history, especially one regarded in some way as remarkable or significant

era—a period of time, usually of significant length, identified by particular conditions, events, or the influence of a person or group

essence—basic nature

etiquette—generally accepted rules of social behavior and manners

excerpt—passage quoted from a book or other document

exodus—departure, usually referring to a group or large numbers

exposition—an explanation or expounding

facet—a side or aspect of a problem or situation; also refers to a particular angled cut of a diamond or other precious stone

facsimile—exact copy or representation

fallacy—mistaken or erroneous idea, assumption, or conclusion

fantasy—imagined scenario or situation

fervor—passion or enthusiasm

feud—long-term disagreement or open hatred between individuals or groups

fiasco—disaster or complete failure

fiend—cruel, hateful person

finale—the last part of a performance

flair—natural-seeming talent or style

flaw—defect or imperfection

focus—central point

foe—enemy, adversary, opponent

format—arrangement, especially of a document, book, or audiovisual presentation

forte (pronounced *fort* or *fortay*)—an area in which a person excels

fortitude—steady courage or strength

forum—a gathering or place where ideas or situations are discussed

foyer—the entrance hall to a building or dwelling

fraud—deliberate deception, especially an illegal one

friction—the surface of one object rubbing against another

function—the purpose served by a person, object, or organization

furor—an outburst of excitement or disagreement

gamut—an entire range or spectrum of possible outcomes or conditions

genesis—beginning or origin

genre (pronounced *jhan-ruh*)—a class or category, especially when referring to arts or entertainment

gist—essential content, central idea

glutton—one who overeats or indulges in anything to excess

grievance—a complaint made against an individual or an organization; also a grudge held over a period of time

guile—cunning, deceit, duplicity

havoc—great damage, destruction, or confusion (often used in the phrase "wreak havoc")

hazard—danger or risk of injury

heresy—an opinion directly opposed to established beliefs, especially in a religious sense

heritage—historical family, cultural, or organizational set of traditions, customs, and/or values; also can refer to an inheritance of either real property or traditions

hindrance—obstacle or delaying obstruction

hoax—deliberate attempt to trick someone, either as a joke or seriously

horde—multitude, great mass of people

horizon—farthest limit, usually referring to vision, knowledge, or experience

hue—shade of color

hysteria—excessive or uncontrollable fear or other strong emotion

idiom—a regional or group jargon, dialect, or manner of speech; can also mean a phrase or expression that has a different meaning than the literal meaning of the words that make it up

illusion—an idea or impression that differs from reality

image—the likeness or reflected or interpreted impression of a person, object, or locale; can also refer to the general group of perceptions surrounding a person

impetus—moving force or starting idea

incentive—motivation or benefit to doing something

incumbent—present holder of an office or position

incursion—a hostile invasion

indolence—laziness

infirmity—physical disease, injury, or defect

influx—a flowing in of a substance, as of a wave or a flood

infraction—violation of a rule, regulation, or law

initiative—desire, idea, or ability to take the first step in carrying out some action

innovation—a new or improved way of doing something

integrity—moral and intellectual honesty and forthrightness; also refers to the quality of a structure or object to hold together

interim—a period of time between one event, process, or period and another

interlude—a short feature or period of time coming between two other, longer events (such as acts of a play or movements of an opera) or time periods

intrigue—secret plot or scheme

intuition—knowledge or conclusion obtained through instinct or feeling rather than conscious thought

invective—insulting or abusive speech

iota—a very small amount or piece

irony—a significant and often unexpected difference between what might be expected and what actually occurs; also, the conscious use of words to convey the opposite of their literal meaning

itinerary—agenda or schedule of events or places visited during a trip

jeopardy—risk of danger or harm

keynote—main theme or idea, usually referring to the main speech at a convention or the like

larceny—theft, usually small

layman—a "regular" person who is not a member of a particular professional or technical specialty

legacy—material or spiritual inheritance or heritage; can also refer to the historical perceptions of someone after they have left their office or position of responsibility

legend—unverified stories handed down from earlier times; can also refer to a person of great fame or reputation

legion—a large number of people; sometimes historically used as a designation of a military or paramilitary unit (e.g., French Foreign Legion)

lethargy—sluggishness, laziness, drowsiness

levee—a raised embankment designed to prevent flooding from a river or other body of water

levity—lightness, frivolity

liaison—contact or coordination between two or more individuals or groups

litigation—legal proceedings

lore—body of traditional or historical knowledge

malady—disease or illness

maneuver—movement of a unit or individual to achieve a goal

mania—abnormal concentration on or enthusiasm for something

marathon—a cross-country footrace of 26 miles, 385 yards named in commemoration of the messenger who ran that distance to bring news to Athens of the Greek victory over the Persians in 490 B.C. at Marathon; any contest or enterprise requiring unusual endurance or stamina

maverick—a person who acts independently instead of in conformance with common organizational or expected behavior

maxim—an adage or proverb prescribing a rule or method of conduct, as in, "Measure twice, cut once."

medium—means of communication of presentation (e.g., radio, telephone, television, etc.); plural is *media*

memento—object that commemorates or reminds someone of a past event

metropolis—a very large city

milieu—surroundings, environment

morale—the state of mind or attitude of an individual or group, usually in reference to how that attitude will either positively or negatively affect the future actions or success of that person or group

mores—established customs or values of a group or segment of society

multitude—large number of something

myriad—a vast number or great multitude of something, usually implying wide variations within that group

myth—a traditional story, usually attempting to explain a natural condition or occurrence, often involving supernatural influences

negligence—carelessness

neophyte—a beginner

niche—literally, a recess in a wall for holding a statue or other ornament; figuratively, an appropriate activity or situation that is especially well suited to a person's abilities or character

nomad—wanderer

nostalgia—desire to return to a past experience or situation

oasis—an isolated place or area of comfort surrounded by desolation or barrenness

objective—a goal

oblivion—a condition of complete ignorance, forgetfulness, or unawareness

obscure—unclear, clouded, partially hidden

odyssey—a long journey, usually involving significant challenges or obstacles; derived from the mythic ten-year journey home of Odysseus after the Trojan War chronicled in Homer's epic Greek poem "The Odyssey"

omen—a sign or event believed to foretell the future

optimum—the best possible condition or combination of factors

ovation—applause of an audience, or any enthusiastically positive reception accompanied by applause

oversight—an omission through error or carelessness; also can refer to a situation where one person or group supervises the activities of another, usually loosely

overture—first step, usually one that is intended to lead to others in action or discussion

panacea—a cure for all problems or diseases

panorama—an unobstructed view of a wide area

paradox—a statement that contradicts or appears to contradict itself

parsimony—stinginess or overzealous desire to be thrifty

partisan—one who supports a particular cause, person, or idea; in a country occupied by an enemy, a *partisan* is one who opposes the occupying enemy by acts of defiance or sabotage

pastime—a way of spending leisure time

pathology—the science of diseases; any deviation from a normal, healthy condition

paucity—scarcity of a resource or condition

pauper—a very poor person

pedagogue—a strict, overly academic teacher or speaker

peer—an equal in age, social standing, professional rank, or ability

phenomenon—an unusual, noticeable, or outstanding occurrence that is directly perceived by the senses or by results

philanthropy—love of mankind, usually exemplified by donations to charitable causes

phobia—an unreasonable fear of something

physique—the build or physical condition of a human body

pilgrimage—long journey to some place or condition worthy of respect or devotion

pinnacle—highest point

pitfall—trap or obstacle for the unwary

pittance—very small amount, usually referring to money

plateau—an elevated, relatively level expanse of land; also can refer to a leveling-off of progress or results

plight—an unfavorable condition or situation

poise—calm and controlled behavior

populace—the people living in a certain area

posterity—future descendants or generations

precedent—event or law that serves as an example for later action

predecessor—someone or something that came before another

predicament—unpleasant problem or situation, usually one that is difficult to escape

preface—introductory statement or passage to a book, speech, or other communication

prelude—something that is preliminary to some act or event that is more important

premise—a statement or assumption from which a conclusion is drawn

premium—best quality; can also refer to an amount added to the usual price or payment

prestige—respect or status achieved through achievement or rank

pretext—a reason given as a cover-up for the real purpose for an action

priority—something that comes before others in significance or importance

probity—integrity, uprightness, honesty

process—a system or design for accomplishing a goal or objective

prodigy—an extremely talented or gifted child

propinquity—nearness

propriety—good manners, appropriately respectful and reserved behavior

prospect—possibility for the future

proviso—a requirement that something specific is done, usually in writing

prowess—strength or superior ability

proximity—nearness

pseudonym—an assumed name, usually a "pen name" taken by an author (e.g., Mark Twain was the *pseudonym* used by Samuel Clemens.)

pun—a play on words that depends on two or more different meanings or sounds of the same word or phrase

pundit—a knowledgeable person in a particular field; can also refer to a commentator who publicizes his opinions, whether or not he is actually an expert in that field

quagmire—literally, a bog or swamp that impedes movement or in which people or vehicles could be stuck or mired; figuratively, a difficult or dangerous situation from which there is limited hope of escape

qualm—doubt or unease about some action or situation

quandary—deep uncertainty or indecision about a choice between two or more courses of action; a dilemma

query—a question or request for information

rampart—a fortification; bulwark or defense against attack

rapport—a harmonious or mutually trusting relationship

rarity—something that is infrequent or not commonly encountered

refuge—a place to which one can go for protection or separation from difficulty

remnant—remaining or left-over part of something

remorse—regret or guilt

renaissance (also **renascence**)—a rebirth or revival; a "Renaissance man" is one who is skilled in many different areas of learning

rendezvous—a meeting or location for a meeting

renown—fame or wide acclaim, especially for accomplishments or skill

replica—an exact copy or facsimile of something, although it may only be proportionate and not the same size

reprimand—severe scolding or rebuke, usually from a superior to a subordinate

reprisal—retaliation for real or perceived injuries; often implies giving back more than was originally received

reprobate—a wicked, sinful, depraved person

reserve(s)—a fighting force kept uncommitted until the need arises

residue—the remainder of something after removal of a part; usually implies a small amount left, perhaps in a container, after the majority is removed

resources—assets that are available for use, either material or spiritual

respite—a temporary break, usually one that brings relief

résumé—a written summary of work, education, and accomplishments, usually compiled for purposes of getting a particular job

reverence—a feeling of great respect, usually religious in nature

roster—list of names (e.g., of organization members, students in a class, etc.)

sabotage—deliberate damage to facilities or equipment belonging to an enemy, usually performed by spies or an underground movement within an occupied country

saga—a long story or tale, usually involving heroic deeds

salutation—a written or spoken greeting; also can refer to a person's title, such as *Dr.*, *Mr.*, *Mrs.*, etc.

sanction—approval, usually by a higher authority; can also mean a penalty for breaking a law or rule

sarcasm—cutting or insulting ironic remarks

satire—criticism of someone or something by seeming approval cast in a light or taken to an extreme that makes the subject appear ridiculous

scapegoat—someone who is blamed, usually unjustly, for the mistakes or misdeeds of others

scent—distinctive aroma or smell

scope—the complete area or extent of action or thought

scroll—a roll of paper or parchment with writing

sect—a group of people having the same beliefs, usually religious; often has a slight to severe negative connotation

semblance—outward appearance

sequel—something that follows from what has happened before (e.g., a novel or movie)

sham—a false imitation; in slang, refers to avoiding work, sometimes by pretense

sheaf—a bundle, usually either of papers or grain

sheen—shine or luster (e.g., of polished furniture)

silhouette—the outline of a person or object, usually without observable details because of low lighting

site—a location

slander—spoken untruth that damages one's reputation

slogan—motto or saying that sums up an individual or group's attitude

slope—the angle of a surface that is neither vertical nor horizontal; measured between 0 and 90 degrees

snare—trap

solace—comfort after loss or disappointment

sponsor—one who supports and approves of a person or activity; implies that the sponsor is at a higher level of status or authority than the sponsored person or group

stagnation—motionlessness or inactivity

stamina—endurance; physical or mental ability to withstand fatigue

stanza—a section of a poem or song; a verse

stature—a height, measured either physically or in respect

status—social or professional standing or level

stigma—mark or perception of disgrace or bad reputation

stimulus—an encouragement to act or react

strategy—planning and coordination aimed at achieving a goal or objective; a way to get something done

strife—conflict, disagreement, contention

summit—the highest point (e.g., of a mountain or a career)

supplement—an amount added to complete something

survey—a general study of a topic or issue

suspense—tenseness brought on by uncertainty about an outcome; can also refer to a deadline

sycophant—one who flatters a superior in hope of getting preferential treatment

symbol—a design or insignia that represents something, usually a value, action, or group identity

symptom—indication of a problem, usually referring to a disease or illness

synopsis—brief summary

synthesis—the combining of parts to form a whole, especially referring to ideas or procedures

tacit—silent or unspoken (e.g., "His brief grin constituted his *tacit* approval."); implied

tact—the ability to communicate a message without causing offense, especially an unpleasant message

tactics—specific actions used to achieve a purpose or accomplish an objective; in military terms, maneuvers by small or lower-level units in contact with the enemy

tally—a record of an account or score; any list that involves counting or enumeration

technique—a method or specific way of doing something

temerity—recklessness, audacity; boldness verging on foolhardiness

temperament—overall attitude, disposition, or character

tempo—the pace or speed of an activity or series of activities

tension—mental or emotional strain, usually brought on by perceived or actual problems or conflicts

theme—the main topic, as of a written work, movie, show, speech, etc.

threshold—the starting point of an activity; literally, the line that separates one area (such as a room or house) from another

thrift—an ability or desire to spend money wisely, to get the most value possible

timbre—the quality of a sound, independent of pitch and volume

tint—a shade of a color

token—a sign or object that signifies a greater feeling or whole (e.g., "a *token* of respect")

tradition—customs and beliefs common to a group that are passed down through time

trait—characteristic or distinguishing feature

transition—movement from one condition or situation to another; implies some degree of change or transformation

trepidation—fear, apprehension

tribunal—a place of judgment, usually legal in nature

tribute—a demonstration of respect or gratitude

turmoil—disturbance or upheaval

turpitude—shameful wickedness or depravity

tutor—a private teacher, often for a student who needs extra or specialized help in a particular academic area

tycoon—a very wealthy and powerful business leader

ultimatum—a final demand or condition (e.g., "Get the dog out of the house or I'm leaving!")

upheaval—conflict or disturbance, usually characterized by changes in group membership, leadership, or goals

utensil—an implement or tool to help the user accomplish something

utopia—an ideal place or society, usually regarded as unachievable

valor—courage, heroism

venture—a project or enterprise, usually one involving some degree of risk, although not necessarily physical risk

vicinity—local area

victor—winner

vigor—vitality or energy

visionary—one with lofty, revolutionary, or sometimes impractical goals or ideas about the future

volition—will or conscious choice

vow—solemn pledge or promise

wager—bet

welter—confused mass; commotion or turmoil

whim—impulsive idea or desire, usually not thought out

woe—great trouble or sorrow

wrath—intense anger or fury

zeal—eager desire or enthusiasm

zenith—highest point

zest—enthusiasm

Verbs

acquiesce—to give in; to agree

alleviate—to lessen or relieve discomfort or a bad situation, even if only temporarily

amass—to accumulate

ameliorate—to make better or more tolerable

appease—to soothe; to pacify by giving in

assuage—to soothe or comfort; to lessen the pain of

atrophy—to waste away from lack of use

augment—to add to or increase

authorize—to give permission

belittle—to insult or degrade

censor—to limit communication to prevent the loss of secret information

censure—to condemn severely for inappropriate or rule-breaking behavior

coalesce—to come together as one; to unite

condescend—to patronize; to stoop to someone else's level in an offensive way

condone—to approve of or allow to happen

denounce—to speak out against or condemn

deride—to ridicule or laugh at contemptuously

desecrate—to profane a holy place

deter—to prevent or stop someone from doing something

digress—to veer off the main topic

discriminate—to differentiate or make a distinction based on some quality; in recent times, usually has the connotation of unfair racial, ethnic, or gender bias

disparage—to belittle or say uncomplimentary things about in an indirect way

divert—to change the course or direction of

drone—to talk on and on in a dull way

efface—to erase or rub away the features of

emulate—to imitate as a role model

engender—to create or produce

enhance—to make better or improve

enthrall—to hold spellbound; to captivate or charm completely

exemplify—to serve as an example or representative of

expedite—to make faster or easier

extol—to praise

facilitate—to make easier

heed—to listen to and obey

innovate—to create a new or better way of doing something

instigate—to provoke or stir up a controversy

languish—to become listless, hopeless, or depressed

meander—to wander slowly or aimlessly

mitigate—to lessen the severity of something, such as a punishment or injury

nullify—to cancel out or make very unimportant, as if nonexistent

preclude—to prevent or make impossible

refute—to disprove

rejuvenate—to give new energy or strength to, as if made young again

repress—to hold down

reproach—to scold or rebuke

repudiate—to reject or deny

rescind—to repeal, to take back formally

retract—to take back or withdraw

revere—to worship or respect very deeply

scrutinize—to examine closely

solicit—to ask for, to seek

squander—to waste

vacillate—to waver between alternatives; to be indecisive

veer—to turn aside or swerve away from a course, direction, or purpose

venerate—to revere or treat as something or someone holy

vilify—to cast as a villain; to defame

Adjectives

abstract—theoretical or lacking substance; can also mean a brief summary of a scholarly article or paper

acute—sharp, shrewd; also, an angle of less than 90 degrees

aesthetic—having to do with art or artistic beauty or sensibility; not to be confused with *ascetic*

ambiguous—unclear in meaning; confusing; able to be interpreted in more than one way

ambivalent—undecided; wavering between alternatives

ambulatory—able to walk

amiable—friendly, pleasant

animated—alive, lively
apocryphal—of doubtful or uncertain origin
apprehensive—worried, anxious
arrogant—feeling superior to others and not hiding your high opinion of yourself
articulate—well-spoken, having a good command of the language
ascetic—austere, self-denying
astute—perceptive, intelligent
auspicious—favorable, seeming to point toward good results
austere—unadorned, forbiddingly bare
authentic—real, genuine
banal—unoriginal, ordinary to a fault, boring
belligerent—combative, quarrelsome
benevolent—kind, generous
benign—gentle; not harmful
blithe—carefree, cheerful
candid—honest, forthright, frank
caustic—like acid or corrosive; also, a very sharp or cutting insult or comment
complacent—smug, self-satisfied, content with the current situation
compliant—yielding, submissive
conciliatory—peacemaking
concise—succinct; brief and direct
congenial—agreeably pleasant
conspicuous—obvious, standing out, very noticeable
contrite—genuinely and deeply apologetic or remorseful
credulous—believing something outrageous; gullible
cryptic—mysterious, hard to understand
didactic—instructive
diffident—timid; lacking in self-confidence
diligent—hardworking
disparate—different, varied; often with a connotation of incompatible
dispassionate—without emotion; neutral
diverse—varied
dogmatic—arrogantly or overconfidently claiming the truth of unproven ideas, or claiming that a belief system is beyond dispute
dubious—doubtful or uncertain
eccentric—unconventional, irregular
elaborate—a result of great effort and attention to detail; intricate
elusive—hard to capture or pin down; can mean evasive
ephemeral—short-lived, fleeting, temporary
esoteric—hard to understand, cryptic
exemplary—setting a superior example; outstanding
exhaustive—very thorough and complete, with great attention to detail

expedient—meeting an immediate need; also, self-serving or granting immediate advantage
extraneous—irrelevant, extra, unnecessary
fallacious—false
fanatical—extremely devoted to or passionate about a cause or idea
fastidious—meticulous; insistent on attention to detail
fickle—not faithful or consistent; unpredictable
flagrant—shocking or outrageous violation of a custom, expectation, rule, or law
fortuitous—luckily coincidental; accidentally advantageous
frivolous—not serious; with levity; inconsequential
furtive—secretive, trying to remain hidden
futile—hopeless, without effect or result
gullible—overly trusting; willing to believe anything
hackneyed—overused, trite
hedonistic—pleasure seeking, overly indulgent
hypothetical—unproven; used as a theoretical example for the purpose of discussion
immutable—unchangeable, permanent
impartial—fair, unbiased, neutral
inadvertent—accidental
incessant—unceasing, never-ending; usually implies an unpleasant condition
incoherent—jumbled, hard to understand
incongruous—inconsistent or inappropriate
indifferent—not caring one way or the other; can also mean "mediocre"
indulgent—lenient, giving in to momentary desires or whims
inevitable—unavoidable, especially when referring to a result of a course of action or decision
infamous—having a bad reputation; disgraceful
innate—inborn, inherent
innocuous—harmless, insignificant
insipid—dull, meaningless, empty
irascible—irritable
ironic—marked by an unexpected difference between what might be expected and what acutally happens; using words so as to convey the opposite of their literal meaning; satiric
laudable—worthy of praise
lax—careless, negligent, not diligent
lucid—clear, easily understandable
marred—damaged or scarred
novel—new or original
objective—without bias, analyzing logically based on facts (opposite: *subjective*)
obscure—unclear, clouded, partially hidden; hard to understand
orthodox—conventional, adhering to established principles or practices, especially in religious matters
pedestrian—common, ordinary
peripheral—unimportant, of little consequence

pervasive—a quality of being present throughout; permeating

pious—reverent or devout; depending on context, can also mean *falsely* devout

pivotal—crucial, result changing

pragmatic—practical, based on experience rather than theory

pretentious—pompous, self-important

prodigal—extravagant, rebellious, wasteful

prodigious—enormous, of extraordinary size

profound—deep, insightful

profuse—extravagant, free-flowing

prosaic—dull, unimaginative

provincial—limited in outlook to one's own small area; narrow; implies that the *provincial* person also thinks that the rest of the world is just like his or her limited experience

provocative—exciting; attracting attention or sparking controversy

prudent—careful, wisely cautious

recalcitrant—stubbornly defiant of authority or control

redundant—repetitive, unnecessary

relevant—important to the matter at hand; pertinent

reprehensible—worthy of blame; disgraceful

resolute—firm, determined, unwavering in the face of challenges or obstacles

reticent—restrained, uncommunicative

rigorous—strict, harsh, severe

saccharine—overly sweet or flattering

sage—wise or knowledgeable, usually from experience

scanty—inadequate, minimal

scrupulous—strict or careful in an ethical sense

servile—submissive and subservient

skeptical—doubting

solemn—grave, serious

static—stationary or unmoving

stoic—outwardly indifferent to circumstances, especially to bad or challenging times

stringent—strict or restrictive

subtle—not obvious; also, able to make fine distinctions

supercilious—haughty, insultingly patronizing

superficial—on the surface only; shallow; not thorough

taciturn—untalkative by nature

tangible—touchable, not imagined or figurative

tedious—boring, overly detailed for no reason

temperate—moderate or restrained

tenacious—dogged or determined in the pursuit of an objective

tentative—temporary; uncertain; experimental

timid—shy, afraid of attention

uniform—consistent throughout; the same for everyone or in every situation

unprecedented—happening for the first time; never seen before

vehement—strong, urgent, passionate

verbose—wordy, overly talkative

virulent—malignant, malicious, full of hate

volatile—highly unstable, explosive

voluminous—very large, spacious

willful—deliberate, obstinate, insistent on having one's own way

zealous—enthusiastically devoted to a cause or idea

Abbreviations

Technical language for any given field often contains many abbreviations, and the military is a prime example. Fortunately, your flight aptitude test won't require you to learn all the military's abbreviations and acronyms (a word taken from the first letter or letters of a phrase; for instance, the term *scuba* is actually an acronym that stands for Self-Contained Underwater Breathing Apparatus). You will, however, need to be able to correctly use the most common abbreviations in everyday, official, and academic language—abbreviations that are often misused, misunderstood, or both.

A.D. (often seen in small capitals as A.D. or AD) is an abbreviation for the Latin phrase *anno Domini,* "in the year of our Lord"; measures time after the birth of Christ as established in the Middle Ages.

ASAP As Soon As Possible

B.C. (often seen in small capitals as B.C. or BC), "before Christ"

B.C.E. (often seen in small capitals as B.C.E. or BCE), "before Christian era" or "before common era"

e.g. is an abbreviation for the Latin phrase *exempli gratia,* which means "for example." This is the abbreviation you use when you want to give an example of a group of items or ideas, as in, "Not all Christmas tree decorations are expensive—e.g., candy canes—but they can all become family heirlooms."

etc. is an abbreviation for the Latin phrase *et cetera* which means "and so on"—or, literally, "and other things." You should use etc. only after a series of at least two or three things, as in, "We unpacked the Christmas tree lights, ornaments, tinsel, etc."

ibid. is short for the Latin term *ibidem,* meaning "in the same place."

i.e. is an abbreviation for the Latin phrase *id est,* "in other words." (This is the most misused abbreviation of the ones presented here.)

op. cit. is short for the Latin phrase *opere citato,* "in the work cited."

USS in front of a ship's name means it is a U.S. Navy vessel, a "United States Ship."

Mathematics Review 6

"Mathematics is a more powerful instrument of knowledge than any other that has been bequeathed to us by human agency."

—René Descartes, 1596–1650, French philosopher, mathematician, and scientist

This section reviews basic math terms and problem-solving methods taught in high school and basic college courses. You will find samples of math problems most often encountered in the various flight aptitude tests for the different services, with an explanation of how to solve each. You may find that you know one or more other ways to solve these problems, also—the more complex a math problem, the more chance that there's more than one way to solve it.

Although there is a fair amount of basic concept review here, the chapter's purpose is not to *teach* the concepts to you for the first time, but instead to remind you of "what right looks like." If you are completely unfamiliar with any of the concepts addressed in this chapter, you will probably want to do some special-emphasis math studying or get some math-focused tutoring.

Here's something else to consider: Most of us are so accustomed to using calculators that doing some pencil-and-paper calculations would be worthwhile to knock off the mental rust. Yes, it's a pain in the neck, and sure, you used to know how to do it—but why risk having a brain cramp during the test because you haven't done long division in a long time? Practice like it's game time and do it on paper—you won't have a calculator on the test!

Before you study the information in this section, consider these suggestions for effective math problem solving (and this includes those pesky word problems!):

1. Develop the habit of reading the problem carefully. Look for answers to these questions:
   - **a.** What are the facts given in the problem?
   - **b.** What is the unknown quantity or amount that the problem asks you to find? In what terms or units is it to be expressed (pure numbers, miles, square feet, number of children in the audience, etc.)?
   - **c.** What method should you use to solve the problem? What is the best method or series of steps?
2. Pay close attention to each word, number, and symbol. In math, directions and operations are usually compressed into a few words or symbols. The key to the problem or the principal direction can sometimes be expressed as a symbol.
3. How does one fact or idea lead to another? Which facts or ideas are connected, and which facts don't really contribute to the solution of the problem?

MATHEMATICS LAWS AND OPERATIONS

The numbers 0, 1, and 2 are *whole numbers.* So are 3, 4, 5, and so on; in comparison, $\frac{1}{3}$ is a *fraction*, and $5\frac{1}{2}$ is a *mixed number*—a whole number plus a fraction. Mathematically speaking, when we combine two or more whole numbers, we call it performing an *operation* on them. Officially, there are two basic operations, *addition* and *multiplication*; *subtraction* is the opposite, or *inverse*, of addition, and *division* is the inverse of multiplication.

In addition, we combine two or more individual numbers (24 + 2, for instance) to produce an answer called the *sum.* In multiplication, we combine groups of numbers to produce an answer called the *product.* An example of multiplication would be "eight times two" (8 × 2), which simply means eight groups of two, or counting two items eight times; the answer, or product, is 16.

Subtraction and *division*, as mentioned earlier, are really opposite or inverse operations of addition and multiplication, respectively. Subtraction is performed to undo addition, and division is performed to undo multiplication. The answer in subtraction is called the *difference*; in division, it's called the *quotient.* In both cases, we're going to presume that you know how to perform these basic mathematics operations and move on to make sure you're ready for your flight aptitude test.

Use of Parentheses: Order of Operations

Sometimes, math problems use parentheses to indicate which operation is supposed to be done first. For example, in the problem 3 + (5 × 2), you would first multiply 5 × 2, and then add 3. Look at the different results you get when you work without the parentheses and then with them.

$$3 + 5 \times 2 = \quad 8 \times 2 = 16$$

$$3 + (5 \times 2) = \quad 3 + 10 = 13$$

Even though we read a problem from left to right, there is an order in which we must perform arithmetic operations:

1. First, do all the operations within parentheses.
2. Next, do all multiplications and divisions. Do these in left-to-right order.
3. Finally, do additions and subtractions.

In the following example, notice the order in which arithmetic operations are carried out.

$(10 - 6) \times 5 - (15 \div 5)$	=	(first do operations inside the parentheses)
$4 \times 5 - 3$	=	(next do multiplication)
$20 - 3$	= 17	(then do subtraction)

Rounding Off Numbers

Sometimes, a problem will call for you to round off the answer to the nearest ten, hundred, thousand, etc. We do this in everyday conversation when we say that a steak dinner listed on the menu at $21.95 costs "about $20," or that a laptop computer advertised at $695.99 was "about $700." *Rounding off, estimating,* and *approximating* all mean the same thing: You are making a statement about the approximate value of a number.

When rounding off numbers, the first thing to do is to look at the way the number is constructed or organized, and the second thing to do is to determine the level of accuracy at which you want to express or talk about that number.

Look at the way the number 282,535,321 is written below.

282, 535, 321

Here we can see that the whole nine-digit number is divided up into three-number segments that are more easily dealt with—"eating the elephant one bite at a time," so to speak. But let's break this number down into its most understandable form:

Hundreds of millions	2	200,000,000 (two hundred million)
Tens of millions	8	80,000,000 (eighty million)
Millions	2	2,000,000 (two million)
Hundreds of thousands	5	500,000 (five hundred thousand)
Tens of thousands	3	30,000 (thirty thousand)
Thousands	5	5,000 (five thousand)
Hundreds	3	300 (three hundred)
Tens	2	20 (twenty)
Ones	1	1 (one)

If you need to round off 282,535,321 to the nearest hundred, you would first find the number in the "hundreds" row (3), and then look at the number to its right (2). If the number to the right is 5, 6, 7, 8, or 9, you round off the hundreds to the next higher number (4) and replace the 21 with 00. By the same token, if it's *less* than 5, you would round *down*, as we do in this case—so we can say that 321 is *about* 300. Your answer would then be 282,535,300.

This same method works regardless of whether you go higher or lower within this particular number—and it works with any number, no matter how large or small. For instance, if we wanted to round 282,535,321 off to the nearest *million*, following the same procedure, since the first number to the right of the million is 5 or larger, we would round *up* the last "millions" number and replace everything to its right with zeros, giving us 283,000,000.

Suppose your original amount was 763,219,846 and you needed to round this number to the nearest ten thousand. In this case, when you break down the number to its components, you find a 1 in the "ten thousands" position, and a 9 to its immediate right. Therefore, to round the complete number to the nearest ten thousand, we increase the 1 to a 2 and replace all numbers to its right with zeros, giving us 763,220,000.

Prime and Composite Numbers

Whole numbers are classified as either *prime* or *composite* numbers. A prime number is a number greater than one that can be divided evenly by two numbers, itself and 1, but not by any other whole number.

EXAMPLES

2, 3, 5, 7, 11, 13

A composite number is one that can be divided evenly by itself, by 1, and by at least one other whole number.

EXAMPLES

4, 6, 10, 15, 27, 82

Note: The number 1 is neither prime nor composite.

Factors

When a whole number has other divisors besides 1 and itself, these other divisors are called *factors.* In other words, factors are numbers we use to multiply to form a composite (whole) number. Sometimes you will be asked to "factor" a number—for example, 6. The factors of 6 are the numbers that you multiply to produce 6. Since 3 times 2 equals 6, the factors of 6 are 3 and 2.

Exponents

The short way of writing *repeated factors* in multiplication—i.e., when a given number is multiplied by itself a certain number of times—is called using *exponents.* For example, you can write 5×5 as 5^2 or "five times five equals five squared." The smaller 2 written to the right of and slightly above the 5 is called an *exponent*; it tells us that 5 is used twice as a factor. You can read 5^2 as either "5 to the second power" or "5 squared." Note that 5^2 does *not* represent "five times two" (5×2). The expression 2^3 is read as "2 to the third power," "2 to the power of 3," or "2 cubed," and represents $2 \times 2 \times 2$.

n Factorial

Don't confuse exponents (expressions of repeated factors) with the term *factorial.* When you see "5 factorial," for example, it means "find the product of every number between 1 and 5 multiplied together." Thus, "5 factorial" means $5 \times 4 \times 3 \times 2 \times 1$. The symbol for 5 factorial is "5!"

Reciprocal

You may also need to find the *reciprocal* of a number. To find the reciprocal of 4, for instance, look for the number that you multiply by 4 to get 1. The easiest way to calculate this is to divide 1 by 4. You can express the answer either as $\frac{1}{4}$ or as 0.25 (see the following sections on fractions and decimals). Remember that the product of a number and its reciprocal is always 1: the reciprocal of $\frac{1}{4}$ is 4; the reciprocal of $\frac{2}{4}$ is 2.

Series and Sequences

A frequently asked type of test question involves a *series* or *sequence* of numbers. You are given several numbers arranged in a pattern, and are then asked to find the number that comes next. The way to solve this is to figure out the pattern; i.e., figure out what the relationship is between the first and second number, second and third, and so on. Try the following two examples:

(A) 2, 4, 6, 8, ?
(B) 3, 9, 4, 8, ?

Each number in Series **(A)** is 2 higher than the previous number. Thus, the next term in the series is 10. By testing the relationships between numbers in Series **(B)**, you find the following pattern:

$3\ (+\ 6) = 9$	The first step is "add 6."
$9\ (-5) = 4$	The next step is "subtract 5."
$4\ (+\ 4) = 8$	The next step is "add 4."

To continue the pattern, the next step will have to be "subtract 3." Therefore, the next number in the series is 5.

FRACTIONS

Many problems in arithmetic have to do with fractions. (Decimals and percents are really just different ways of writing fractions.) There are at least four ways to think about fractions.

1. A fraction is a part or fragment of a whole. The fraction $\frac{2}{3}$ means that something has been divided into three parts, and we are working with two of those parts. The number written above the fraction line (2) is the *numerator*, and the number below it (3) is called the *denominator*.
2. A fraction can be the result of a multiplication operation. The fraction $\frac{3}{4}$ means 3 times $\frac{1}{4}$.
3. A fraction is an expression of division. Thus $\frac{2}{5}$ is the quotient (result) when 2 is divided by 5. This can also be written as $2 \div 5$.
4. A fraction is an expression of a ratio, which is a comparison between two quantities. For example, the ratio of 6 inches to 1 foot is $\frac{6}{12}$, since there are 12 inches in a foot.

Performing Mathematical Operations with Fractions

There are some special rules—and some shortcuts, too—for multiplying, dividing, adding, and subtracting fractions and mixed numbers. Remember, a *mixed number* is one that is made up of a whole number and a fraction—for example, $5\frac{1}{2}$.

MULTIPLYING FRACTIONS

The general rule for multiplying two or more fractions is to multiply the numerators by each other, and then multiply the denominators by each other.

EXAMPLE

$$\frac{1}{2} \times \frac{3}{4} \times \frac{5}{8} = \frac{15}{64} \quad \frac{\text{(numerators)}}{\text{(denominators)}}$$

EXPLANATION: $1 \times 3 \times 5 = 15$; $2 \times 4 \times 8 = 64$

Sometimes, the product you get when you multiply two fractions can be expressed in simpler terms than what originally results from your calculations. When you express a fraction in its *lowest terms*, you put it in a form in which the numerator and denominator no longer have a common factor by which they can be divided.

➡ EXAMPLE

Reduce $\frac{24}{36}$ to lowest terms.

STEP 1 Find a number that is a factor of both 24 and 36. Result: Both numbers can be divided by 4.

STEP 2 Divide 24 by 4 and then divide 36 by 4.

$24 \div 4 = 6$

$36 \div 4 = 9$

Therefore, $\frac{24}{36} = \frac{6}{9}$

STEP 3 Check again. Is there a number that is a factor of both 6 and 9? Yes, both numbers can be divided by 3. Divide 6 and then 9 by 3.

$6 \div 3 = 2$

$9 \div 3 = 3$

Therefore, $\frac{6}{9} = \frac{2}{3}$

ANSWER: $\frac{24}{36}$ can be reduced to the lowest terms of $\frac{2}{3}$.

CHANGING IMPROPER FRACTIONS TO MIXED NUMBERS

When the numerator of a fraction is larger than its denominator, it is called an *improper fraction.* An improper fraction can be changed to a mixed number.

➡ EXAMPLE

Change $\frac{37}{5}$ to a mixed number.

Because a fraction is also another way to express division, $\frac{37}{5}$ means $37 \div 5$. If 37 is divided by 5, the quotient is 7, and the remainder is 2—or, expressed another way, $\frac{37}{5} = 7\frac{2}{5}$.

CHANGING MIXED NUMBERS TO IMPROPER FRACTIONS

To multiply or divide mixed numbers, it is necessary to change them into improper fractions.

EXAMPLE: Change $8\frac{3}{5}$ to an improper fraction.

Convert the whole number, 8, to fifths: $8 = \frac{40}{5}$

$\frac{40}{5} + \frac{3}{5} = \frac{43}{5}$, an improper fraction. A shortcut for changing a number from a mixed number to an improper fraction is to multiply the whole part of the mixed number by the fraction's denominator, and then add the result to the original numerator.

Therefore, $8\frac{3}{5} = \frac{8 \times 5 + 3}{5} = \frac{43}{5}$.

MULTIPLYING MIXED NUMBERS

When multiplying or dividing with a mixed number, change the mixed number to an improper fraction before working out the problem.

$$2\frac{2}{3} \times \frac{5}{7} = \frac{8}{3} \times \frac{5}{7} = \frac{40}{21} = 1\frac{19}{21}$$

CANCELLATION

Cancellation is a shortcut you can use when you're multiplying or dividing fractions. For example, if you are going to multiply $\frac{8}{9}$ times $\frac{3}{16}$, you first multiply the numerators by each other, and then the denominators by each other; this gives you an answer you have to reduce to lowest terms.

$$\frac{8}{9} \times \frac{3}{16} = \frac{24}{144} = \frac{1}{6}$$

There's an easier way to solve this problem: See if there is a number you can divide evenly into both a numerator and a denominator of the original problem. In this example, there is such a number: You can divide 8 into both itself and 16.

STEP 1 $\frac{\overset{1}{\cancel{8}}}{9} \times \frac{3}{\underset{2}{\cancel{16}}} =$

You can also divide 3 into the numerator 3 and the denominator 9. Having found this, solve the problem by multiplying the new numerators and then the new denominators.

STEP 2 $\frac{\overset{1}{\cancel{8}}}{\underset{3}{\cancel{9}}} \times \frac{\overset{1}{\cancel{3}}}{\underset{2}{\cancel{16}}} = \frac{1}{6}$

DIVIDING FRACTIONS

Dividing fractions looks a lot like multiplying them, but there is an important extra consideration that we can use to manipulate the fractions in an equation: Dividing something by a number is the same as multiplying that something by 1 over that number. Therefore we can convert the division problem $\frac{1}{2} \div \frac{3}{1}$ into the multiplication problem $\frac{1}{2} \times \frac{1}{3}$.

To divide with fractions, you have to *invert* the second fraction (turn it upside down), and then change the division sign to a multiplication sign and solve as a multiplication of fractions. This is also called multiplying the first fraction by the *reciprocal* of the second fraction. Remember: Any whole number can be written as that number over 1; i.e., the number 5 can be written as $\frac{5}{1}$, 3 can be written as $\frac{3}{1}$.

$$\frac{1}{5} \div 4 = \frac{1}{5} \div \frac{4}{1} = \frac{1}{5} \times \frac{1}{4} = \frac{1}{20}$$

ADDING AND SUBTRACTING SIMPLE FRACTIONS

There are some basic rules for adding and subtracting fractions:

1. Add or subtract only those fractions that have the same denominator.
2. Add or subtract only the numerators of the fractions, keeping the same denominator.
3. If two fractions you want to combine by adding or subtracting do not have the same denominator (a *common denominator*), find a way to change them so that both denominators are the same.

This last operation is easy if one of the denominators divides evenly into the other. To add $\frac{2}{3}$ and $\frac{3}{6}$, for instance, you can work with the fact that 3 goes into 6 evenly. You can change the $\frac{2}{3}$ to $\frac{4}{6}$, a fraction with the same value, and then work with the two fractions on an equitable basis.

If you can't divide one of the denominators into the other, then you have to find a number that both denominators will go into evenly. If you are working with three fractions or even more, you have to find a number that all the denominators can divide into evenly.

For instance, if you need to add $\frac{1}{4}$, $\frac{1}{5}$, and $\frac{1}{6}$, you need to find a common denominator that all three fractions can divide into evenly. One technique for finding a common denominator between several fractions is to take the largest denominator and start multiplying it by 2, 3, and so on, until you find a number that the other denominators will also divide into evenly. In this case, 6 is the largest denominator; multiply 6 times 2 and you get 12, a number that 5 does not divide into evenly. You have to keep trying until you reach 60, which is the first product that all three denominators divide into evenly.

Don't forget—to convert a fraction expressed with one denominator, you have to multiply the numerator by the same number used to multiply the denominator.

Let's look at this example:

$$\frac{1}{4} = \frac{15}{60} \qquad \frac{1}{5} = \frac{12}{60} \qquad \frac{1}{6} = \frac{10}{60}$$

Now add the converted fractions:

$$\frac{15+12+10}{60} = \frac{37}{60}$$

ADDING AND SUBTRACTING MIXED NUMBERS

To add mixed numbers $\left(\text{numbers consisting of whole numbers and fractions, such as } 1\frac{2}{3}\right)$, follow these steps:

1. Add the whole numbers.
2. Add the fractions. (Make sure that the denominator is the same!) If the sum of these is an improper fraction, change the sum to a mixed number.
3. Add the sum of the whole numbers to the sum of the fractions.

EXAMPLE

$3\frac{2}{3} + 12\frac{2}{3}$

STEP 1 $3 + 12 = 15$

STEP 2 $\frac{2}{3} + \frac{2}{3} = \frac{4}{3} = 1\frac{1}{3}$

STEP 3 $15 + 1\frac{1}{3} = 16\frac{1}{3}$

The principles are the same when you subtract mixed numbers, but there are some additional wrinkles to watch out for. When you subtract mixed numbers, you may have to "borrow" in the same way that you do when you subtract whole numbers. For example, if you want to subtract $4\frac{3}{4}$ from $8\frac{1}{4}$, you realize you cannot take $\frac{3}{4}$ from $\frac{1}{4}$. (Kind of difficult to get $.75 out of a quarter!) Therefore, you have to borrow 1 $\left(\text{expressed in this case as } \frac{4}{4}\right)$ from 8, and rewrite the problem.

$$\begin{array}{ll} 8\frac{1}{4} = 7\frac{4}{4} + \frac{1}{4} & = 7\frac{5}{4} \\ -4\frac{3}{4} = & -4\frac{3}{4} \\ \hline & 3\frac{2}{4} = 3\frac{1}{2} \end{array}$$

DECIMAL FRACTIONS

Decimal fractions are special fractions whose denominators are powers (multiples) of ten. The *exponent* (smaller number to the upper right) tells you how many zeros there are in the power of ten. For instance:

$10^1 = 10 \quad = 10 \times 1$
$10^2 = 100 \quad = 10 \times 10$
$10^3 = 1{,}000 \quad = 10 \times 10 \times 10$
$10^4 = 10{,}000 \quad = 10 \times 10 \times 10 \times 10$

You can tell what the denominator of a decimal fraction is by counting the places (not just the zeros) in the number to the right of its decimal point. When it is written as a fraction, the denominator has the same number of zeros as this number of places; that is, it has the same power of ten. For example:

$0.7 = \frac{7}{10^1}$ *or* $\frac{7}{10}$ (seven tenths)

$0.07 = \frac{7}{10^2}$ *or* $\frac{7}{100}$ (seven hundredths)

$0.007 = \frac{7}{10^3}$ *or* $\frac{7}{1{,}000}$ (seven thousandths)

CHANGING FRACTIONS TO DECIMALS

To change a fraction to a decimal, divide the numerator by the denominator. Place a decimal point to the right of the numerator, and add a zero for each decimal place you want to show in your answer. For example:

$$\frac{2}{5} = 5\overset{0.4}{\overline{)2.0}}$$

We can see that $\frac{2}{5} = 0.4$ after we change the fraction to a decimal.

CHANGING DECIMALS TO FRACTIONS

Every decimal is really a fraction whose denominator is a power of ten. For example:

$$0.01228 = \frac{1,228}{100,000} = \frac{307}{25,000}$$

$$0.50 = \frac{50}{100} = \frac{1}{2}$$

$$6.1 = \frac{61}{10}$$

DIVIDING DECIMALS BY POWERS OF 10

To divide a decimal by a power of ten, count the number of zeros in the power of ten, then move that many places to the left of the decimal.

EXAMPLES

$182.7 \div 10^1 = 182.7 \div 10 = 18.27$

$.47 \div 10^2 = .47 \div 100 = .0047$

DECIMALS

ADDING AND SUBTRACTING DECIMALS

To add or subtract decimals, line up the numbers so that the decimal points are directly under one another, then add or subtract in the same way that you would with whole numbers. Write zeros at the end of decimals if you find it easier to work with placeholders to keep things lined up.

EXAMPLE

Add the numbers 5.14, 11.7, 798.1, and 0.0327, and then subtract their sum from 2,790.59. Remember to include the decimal point in the answers.

$$\begin{array}{r} 5.14 \\ 11.7 \\ 798.1 \\ +\ 0.0327 \\ \hline 814.9727 \end{array} \quad \text{OR} \quad \begin{array}{r} 5.1400 \\ 11.7000 \\ 798.1000 \\ +\ 0.0327 \\ \hline 814.9727 \end{array}$$

$$\begin{array}{r} 2790.59 \\ -\ 814.9727 \\ \hline 1975.6173 \end{array}$$

MULTIPLYING DECIMALS

To multiply two decimals, line them up from the right as though they were whole numbers, regardless of how many digits there are to the right of the decimal in either number. Count the number of places to the right of the decimal in each number, and then add them together. From right to left, count the same number of places in the answer as you got when you added the places together from the two numbers you multiplied—then insert a decimal point in the answer at that point.

$$
\begin{array}{r l}
\boxed{1\,2\,3\,4} & \\
17.8592 & \\
\times \quad 2.3 & \leftarrow \boxed{1} \\
\hline
41.07616 & \\
\boxed{5\,4\,3\,2\,1} &
\end{array}
$$

DIVIDING DECIMALS

To divide a decimal by a whole number, divide the numbers as though they were both whole numbers. Then place a decimal point in the answer directly above the decimal in the problem and solve the problem. Add zeros to the right of the dividend (the number inside the division sign) if you need to in order to finish the problem.

$$
\begin{array}{r}
7.0615 \\
2\overline{)14.1230} \\
-14 \\
\hline
0\;12 \\
-0\;12 \\
\hline
03 \\
-02 \\
\hline
10 \\
-10 \\
\hline
0
\end{array}
$$

To divide one decimal by another, begin by making the divisor a whole number. To do this, move the decimal to the far right of the number, and count the number of places that you move it. Then move the decimal in the dividend (the other number) the same number of places (in the same direction, of course!). For example:

$$\frac{3.6}{0.3} = \frac{36}{3} = 12$$

ROUNDING OFF DECIMALS

Many math problems require a process called *rounding off* to reach an answer, where one or more numbers are made shorter and therefore usually easier to deal with. The idea of rounding off also has to do with the accuracy or precision of the number or measurement—the longer the number (i.e., the more places used to the right of the decimal point), the more accurate or precise the number is considered to be.

Let's consider a measurement of 3.6 meters. Is this closer to 3 meters or to 4 meters? $3.6 = 3\frac{6}{10}$, which is closer to 4 meters than it is to 3 meters. But what about 3.5 meters? This is exactly midway between 3 and 4 meters. The common, widely accepted method of rounding off a number of this type is that anything that is halfway or more between one level or amount and another is rounded up to the higher level; anything lower than half is rounded down. This means that 3.5 and 3.6 are rounded *up* to 4, but that 3.3 and 3.4 are rounded *down* to 3, simply because they are closer.

This rounding principle works in the same way regardless of where you are looking at a number relative to the decimal point. Thus,

0.35 meters rounded to the nearest tenth of a meter is 0.4 meters (four-tenths of a meter)
3.6 meters rounded to the nearest meter is 4 meters
37 meters rounded to the nearest 10 meters is 40 meters
380 meters rounded to the nearest hundred meters is 400 meters

Also, when you have long numbers, it's important to remember to do your rounding off from *right to left*. Look at the first number to the right of the position you must round to, and any number of 5 or higher elevates the number to its left, whereas any number of less than 5 is dropped, along with any further numbers to the right. For example:

3.39 meters rounded to the nearest tenth of a meter is 3.4 meters
3.49 meters rounded to the nearest tenth of a meter is 3.5 meters
3.49 meters rounded to the nearest meter is 3 meters
3.267919 meters rounded to the nearest tenth of a meter is 3.3 meters
3.9847769034 meters rounded to the nearest hundredth of a meter is 3.98 meters

PERCENTAGES

A *percent* is a way to express a fraction that simply means a certain amount expressed in hundredths. To use a percent figure when solving a problem, change it to a fraction or a decimal. To change a percent to a fraction, drop the percent sign and multiply by $\frac{1}{100}$.

7% is the same as $7 \times \frac{1}{100}$ or $\frac{7}{100}$

25% is the same as $25 \times \frac{1}{100}$ or $\frac{25}{100} = \frac{1}{4}$

100% is the same as $100 \times \frac{1}{100}$ or $\frac{100}{100} = 1$

Changing a Percent to a Decimal

To change a percent figure to a decimal figure, drop the percent sign and move the decimal point two places to the left. Add extra zeros, if needed, to fill out the correct number of places. If the percent is given as a fraction, first change the fraction to a decimal. For example:

4% = .04	1.7% = .017
55% = .55	1/5% = .20% = .002
17% = .17	100% = 1.00 (or 1)

Changing a Decimal to a Percentage

To change a decimal to a percent, move the decimal point two places to the right and add the percent sign. For instance:

$0.47 = 47\%$ $\quad$ $0.03 = 3\%$

$0.008 = .8\%$ $\quad$ $3.27 = 327\%$

Percentages over 100% are often used to talk about an increase of twice as much or more.

SQUARE ROOTS

The square root of a number is one of the two equal factors (numbers) that, when multiplied together, result in that number. In other words, to find a square root, ask yourself, "What number multiplied by itself (squared) will yield the original number?"

For instance, the square root of 9 is 3, because $3 \times 3 = 9$, and the square root of 25 is 5, since $5 \times 5 = 25$.

The square root of a number is indicated by using a radical sign ($\sqrt{\ }$). For example, $\sqrt{64}$ means "the square root of 64," or $\sqrt{64} = 8$. In the same way, $\sqrt{36} = 6$, $\sqrt{49} = 7$, and so on.

Square roots are often complex in the sense that they may be very long numerically, and may, in fact, not be able to be expressed completely as a decimal number. Numbers that have *exact* square roots are called *perfect squares*. The perfect squares with which you are probably most familiar are 1, 4, 9, 16, 25, 36, 49, 64, 81, and 100. Also, it's worth remembering that a "gross" of something is a dozen dozens, or 144—so the square root of 144 is 12.

Finding the Square Root of a Number

You may be asked to find the square root of a number that is not a perfect square, giving your answer rounded off to the nearest tenth, for example. You can use a trial-and-error method to find a square root to the nearest decimal place that the problem asks you for. For example, suppose you are asked to find $\sqrt{28}$ to the nearest tenth: $\sqrt{28}$ is between $\sqrt{25}$, which we know is 5, and $\sqrt{36}$, which we know is 6. We can infer that $\sqrt{28}$ is closer to $\sqrt{25}$ than it is to $\sqrt{36}$. So, to start, make an estimate (yes, a guess, but an informed, reasonable guess) that 5.2 is $\sqrt{28}$ to the nearest tenth, and then see how close you are by multiplying 5.2×5.2 and seeing that the result is 27.04—less than our goal of 28. Because that was too low, we can multiply 5.3×5.3 and see that the result is 28.09, which is pretty close but a little more than our goal of 28.

Because we now have a "bracket" of 28—one set of factors on each side, one more and one less—we know that the square root of 28 is between 5.2 and 5.3.

Further, we know that the actual exact $\sqrt{28}$ is closer to 5.3 than 5.2, so, since our objective was to find $\sqrt{28}$ rounded off to the nearest tenth, our job is done: The answer is 5.3.

ALGEBRA

Algebra is a way to express a problem or mathematical relationship with a small set of symbols used to substitute for actual numbers. This is because we don't know what all the actual values are, or because the same relationship may apply to different sets of numbers.

Let's look at an example. We know that if a jacket is priced at $20, we have to pay $20 to buy one. If we want three jackets, we pay three times that amount, or $60. How do we find that answer of $60? We multiply two numbers together to find a third number. Using the style of algebra, we can express this operation briefly. Let p equal the price of one jacket, and let c (the "unknown") equal the cost of three jackets. This is the algebraic expression for how we find c:

$$c = 3 \times p \quad \text{or} \quad c = 3p$$

In this equation, the letters c and p are called *variables,* meaning that the numbers they stand for can change. In other words, if the price of the jacket is discounted to $18, then p will equal $18, and c will equal $54.

Arithmetic Operations in Algebra

All four arithmetic operations are possible in algebra: both basic operations (addition and multiplication) and both inverse operations (subtraction and division). We can express these operations algebraically:

1. The sum of two numbers x and y is $x + y$
2. The difference between two numbers x and y is $x - y$
3. The product of two numbers, x and y, is $(x) \times (y)$ or $x \cdot y$ or xy
4. The quotient of two numbers x and y is $x \div y$ or $\frac{x}{y}$

Equations

An *equation* is a statement that two quantities are equal. This is easily understandable and obvious when the quantities are expressed in numbers, such as these:

$$2 + 3 = 5$$
$$8 \times 2 = 16$$
$$24 - 7 = 17$$
$$99 \div 11 = 9$$

In algebra, however, equations will include *variables* (a letter or sign that can stand for more than one value) or *unknowns* (a letter or sign that stands for a quantity or idea that we don't know yet). Usually, you will be asked to *solve the equation* by finding or *solving for* the unknown number value, often represented as the letter *x*. In this sense, the *solution* to an equation is the number that proves that the equation is true, and you show that it's true by substituting the number for the variable. But how do you find the number?

Suppose you heard somebody say, "I can't afford to pay cash to buy a car for $9,000; that would leave me with only $500 to pay my bills for the rest of the month." What we don't know here is how much that person had originally; the other numbers are provided or given to us. How would we express his statement algebraically? (Remember, the "unknown" is the unstated amount x now in the bank account.) Here's one way of writing the expression:

$$x - \$9{,}000 = \$500$$

Now, how do we solve for x, the unknown?

STEP 1 Think about what the expression now means: A certain number minus \$9,000 equals \$500.

STEP 2 Decide how you want to express the solution: In this case, we have decided that x = the amount originally in the bank before we do any car buying or bill paying.

STEP 3 For your solution, think about how to get the unknown x by itself on one side of the equal sign. This means you will have to manipulate the entire equation by performing the same operations on both sides of the equal sign to get x by itself. How do we clear the \$9,000 from the side that shows x? Notice that the sign in front of \$9,000 is a minus sign. Saying "x – \$9,000" is the same as saying "x + (–\$9,000)," otherwise known as adding a negative number to a positive number. So, if you *add* \$9,000 to the left side of the equation, the two \$9,000s will cancel each other out. However, remember that, because it's an *equation*, everything has to stay equal or balanced; this means that whatever you do to the left side of the equation you have to do to the right side—otherwise it wouldn't be an equation. If you add \$9,000 to the left, you have to add it to the right. This, then, is how it looks:

$$x - \$9{,}000 = \$500$$
$$x - \$9{,}000 + \$9{,}000 = \$500 + \$9{,}000$$
$$x = \$9{,}500 \text{ (amount originally in the bank)}$$

How did we solve this equation? By performing an inverse operation on both sides of the equation. To solve for x, we went through three steps:

STEP 1 We decided to solve for x by removing all other operations from the side of the equation where x is—we have to isolate x, or get x "by itself."

STEP 2 We removed an operation (in this case, adding negative \$9,000) from one side of the equal sign by performing its inverse or opposite operation (adding a positive \$9,000) on the same side.

STEP 3 We then performed the same operation on the other side of the equal sign. This resulted in isolating x on one side of the equation, which tells us that x equals \$9,500.

This, then, is generally how we solve equations: We perform operations to both sides of the equation that will result in the unknown being "alone" on one side of the equation—and the other side of the equal sign shows us the answer.

OPERATIONS WITH MORE COMPLEX EQUATIONS

Sometimes, an equation shows x as part of more than one operation. There may also be negative terms (terms with a minus sign). The same basic steps are involved in finding the solution, but may have to be repeated. Remember, the goal is always to isolate x on one side of the equation. Here's an example:

$$3x + 7 = -11$$

STEP 1 Perform the inverse operation of + 7.

$$3x + 7 - 7 = -11 - 7$$
$$3x = -18$$

STEP 2 Perform the inverse operation of $3x$, which can also be expressed as $(3 \cdot x)$; using the dot $(\cdot)$ instead of the multiplication sign $(\times)$ can sometimes help reduce confusion by reducing the number of xs in the equation.

$$\frac{3x}{3} = \frac{-18}{3}$$

$$x = -6$$

Remember, in multiplication and division, if the signs of both terms are plus or minus (positive or negative), the answer has a plus or positive sign. If the two terms are different, the answer has a minus or negative sign.

Sometimes, x appears on both sides of the original equation. In that case, the first step is to remove or factor out x from one side (also known as "collecting all xs on one side") of the equal sign.

Algebraic Expressions

An *algebraic expression* is any collection of numbers and variables. This collection may have more than one variable. For example, $2x + 3y$ is an algebraic expression meaning, "2 times one unknown number (x) plus 3 times another unknown number (y)."

Arithmetic Operations with Algebraic Expressions

To add or subtract algebraic expressions, remember that only *similar* or *"like"* terms can be combined. Terms are similar if they have the same variable, raised to the same power. For instance, we can subtract $3x$ from $5x$ to get $2x$, but we cannot get x^3 by adding x and x^2, or get $9zh$ from adding $4z$ and $5h$. For example, simplify the following series of terms:

$$3x + 2y - 4z + 2x - 5y$$

Start by arranging like terms together and combining them.

$$3x + 2x = 5x \text{ (first partial sum)}$$
$$2y - 5y = -3y \text{ (second partial sum)}$$

Therefore, the simplified expression is $5x - 3y - 4z$.

To multiply algebraic expressions, first multiply the numbers of similar terms, then multiply the variables (letters) of similar terms. When you multiply one power of x by another power of x, just add the exponents together. For instance:

$$(3x^2)\ (4x^3)$$

$$3 \times 4 = 12 \text{ (first partial product)}$$
$$x^2 \cdot x^3 = x^5 \text{ (second partial product)}$$

Therefore, the product is $12x^5$.

The rules for multiplying more complex algebraic equations are basically the same—just take things step by step and stay organized. In the expression $x^2y(2x - 3y)$, the parentheses mean that x^2y is the multiplier for both $2x$ and $-3y$, so we work out the expression like this:

$$x^2y(2x - 3y)$$

$$x^2y(2x) + x^2y(-3y)$$

$x^2y(2x)$	+	$x^2y(-3y)$
$1 \cdot 2 = 2$	(first partial product)	$1 \cdot -3 = -3$
$x^2 \cdot x = x^3$	(second partial product)	$x^2 \cdot 1 = x^2$
$y \cdot 1 = y$	(third partial product)	$y \cdot y = y^2$

Therefore, the simplified expression is $2x^3y - 3x^2y^2$.

Evaluating Algebraic Expressions

To *evaluate* an algebraic expression means to replace the variables with numbers (usually given to you), and then simplify the expression by adding, multiplying, and so on. For instance, evaluate the expression $(x + 2a)$ if $x = 3$ and $a = 2$.

$$x + 2a = 3 + 2(2) = 3 + 4 = 7$$

Factoring in Algebra

Sometimes, you are given the answer to an algebraic multiplication problem and are then asked to find the original multipliers; this is called *factoring*. These kinds of problems can be of different types:

Type 1: Factor the Highest Common Factor

The highest common factor of an algebraic expression is the highest expression that will divide into every one of the terms of the expression.

EXAMPLE

$6x^2 + 3xy$

STEP 1 The highest number that will divide into the numerical coefficients, 6 and 3, is 3.

STEP 2 The highest literal factor that will divide into x^2 and xy is x. Notice that y is not contained in the first term at all.

STEP 3 Divide the highest common factor, $3x$, into $6x^2 + 3xy$ to find the remaining factor. When we do this, we find that the factors are $3x(2x + y)$.

Type 2: Factor the Difference of Two Squares

This type of problem contains the square of one number minus the square of another number. Remember, the square of a number is the product that you get when you multiply a number by itself, and the square root of a number is the number that was multiplied by itself to get the square or original number. For example:

Find the difference of two squares for $x^2 - 9$.

STEP 1 Find the square root of x^2 and place it to the left within each of two shell or empty parentheses you've set up for this purpose. The square root of x^2, of course, is x.

$$(x \quad)\,(x \quad)$$

STEP 2 Find the square root of 9 and place it on the right within each of the two parentheses you've set up. The square root of 9 is 3.

$$(x \quad 3)\,(x \quad 3)$$

STEP 3 Put a plus sign between one pair of terms, and a minus sign between the other pair of terms.

$$(x + 3)\,(x - 3)$$

The factors of $x^2 - 9$ are $(x + 3)$, $(x - 3)$.

Type 3: Factor a Quadratic Trinomial

A quadratic trinomial is an algebraic expression of the form $ax^2 + bx + c$, where a, b, and c are numbers and a does not equal zero. Its factors are always two pairs of terms. The terms in each pair are separated by a plus or minus sign.

EXAMPLE

Factor $x^2 - 11x + 30$.

STEP 1 Set up your two shell sets of parentheses, then find the factors of the first term in the trinomial; again, the factors of x^2 are x and x.

$$(x \quad)\,(x \quad)$$

STEP 2 Look at the last term in the trinomial, which in this case has a plus sign. We now have to find the factors of the third term; because it is positive, we know that the factors are either both positive or both negative. Because the middle term is negative, we know that the factors must both be negative.

$$(x - \quad)\,(x - \quad)$$

STEP 3 Find factors of the last term that will also add to get the number of the second term. In this case, although we know that 30 has several factors, only the factors 5 and 6 also add up to 11, which is the numerical part of the second term. We already know that both factors have to be negative, so the factors of 30 we are looking for are actually –5 and –6.

$$(x - 5)\,(x - 6)$$

Therefore, for our solution, the factors of $x^2 - 11x + 30$ are $(x - 5)$, $(x - 6)$.

Solving Quadratic Equations

A *quadratic equation* is an equation that contains a term with the square of the unknown quantity and has no term with a higher power of the unknown. In a quadratic equation, the exponent is never higher than 2 (x^2, b^2, c^2, etc.). Examples of quadratic equations include the following:

$$x^2 + x - 5 = 0$$
$$2x^2 = 3x - 5$$
$$x^2 - 3 = 0$$
$$81 = x^2$$

To solve equations like this, factor them, and then set each factor equal to zero. After that, it's easy to solve for x. Let's take it step by step.

Solve: $x^2 = 3x + 10$

STEP 1 Move all the terms onto one side of the equal sign so that the equation on that side is equal to nothing on the other side—in other words, zero. Don't forget inverse operations.

$$x^2 - 3x - 10 = 0$$

STEP 2 Factor the equation.

$$(x - 5)(x + 2) = 0$$

STEP 3 Set each factor equal to zero, then solve the resulting equations.

$$x - 5 = 0 \qquad x + 2 = 0$$
$$x = +5 \qquad x = -2$$

STEP 4 To check the accuracy of the answer, substitute each answer in the original equation.

$$x^2 = 3x + 10 \qquad x^2 = 3x + 10$$
$$(5)^2 = 3(5) + 10 \qquad (-2)^2 = 3(-2) + 10$$
$$25 = 15 + 10 \qquad 4 = -6 + 10$$
$$25 = 25 \text{ (proof)} \qquad 4 = 4 \text{ (proof)}$$

The solution of the quadratic equation is proven to be $x = 5, -2$.

GEOMETRY

Geometry is a useful tool in our world. Geometry problems require knowledge of both the principles and application of arithmetic and algebra to arrive at the correct solution. Many geometry problems require you to make or infer some kind of measurement; they also use familiar terms such as *line, angle,* and *point.*

Lines

A *line* is made up of *points*; it can have a definite length, or it can be infinitely long. For the purposes of our geometry problems, a line has no particular width. *Parallel lines* are lines that are equidistant (the same distance) from each other at every point along both lines so that, even if they were infinitely long, they would never touch.

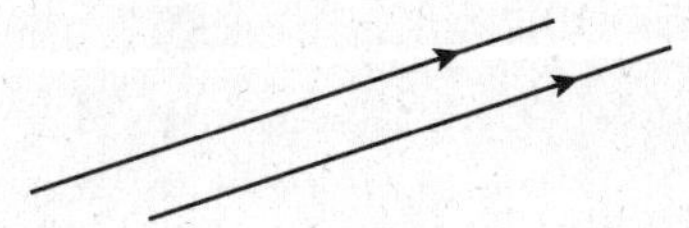

Perpendicular lines are lines that meet to form a right angle (90 degrees).

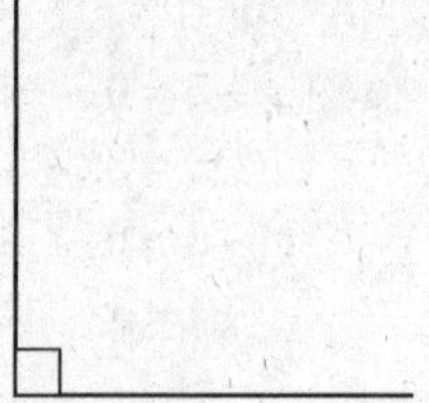

Angles

When two lines meet at a point, they form an *angle*. The point where the lines meet is called the *vertex* of the angle. Angles can be named or designated in one of three ways:

1. For the point at the vertex (in this case, angle Y).

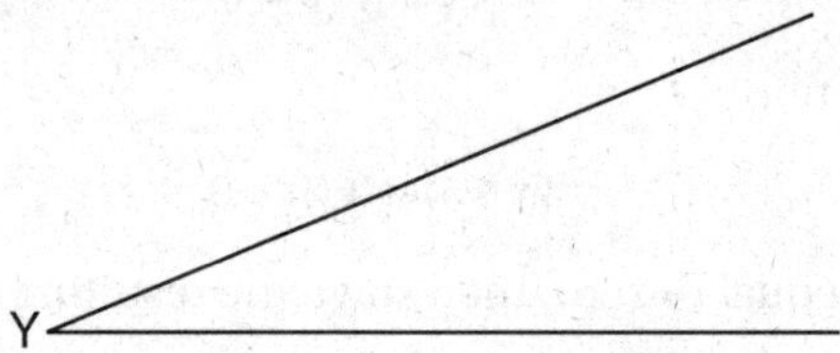

2. For the letter names of the lines that meet to form the angle, with the vertex in the middle (in this example, angle XYZ).

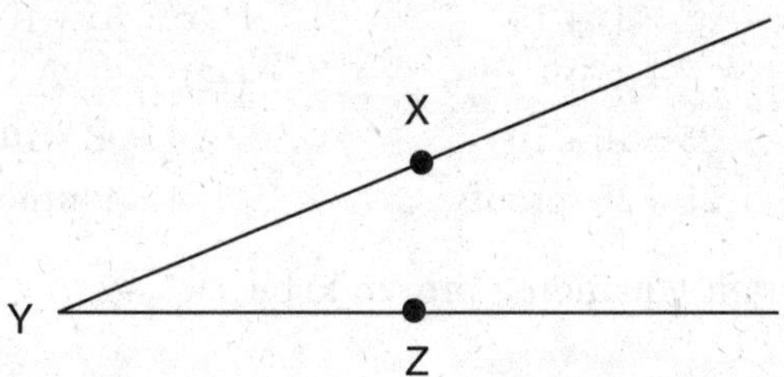

3. For a number written or displayed inside the angle (in the diagram below, angle #3).

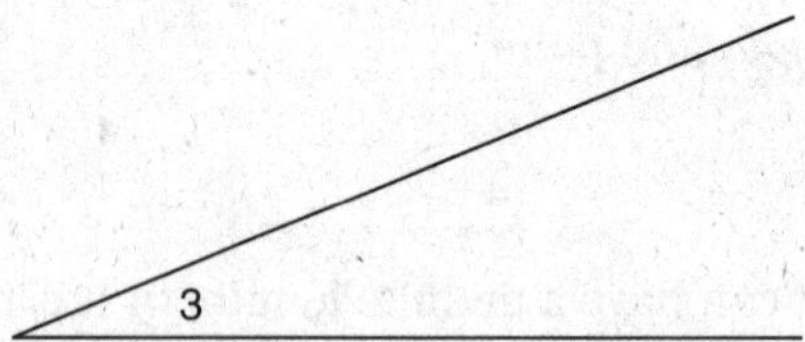

Measuring Angles

The best way to measure an angle is with a *protractor.* Angles are measured in *degrees,* up to 180°. Remember that a circle has 360°, and that half of that circle would be a semicircle with its bottom edge going from edge to edge through the middle of the circle. So we see that two lines joined at a "180° angle" would be no angle at all, but instead just one line joined to the other as a straight-out continuation.

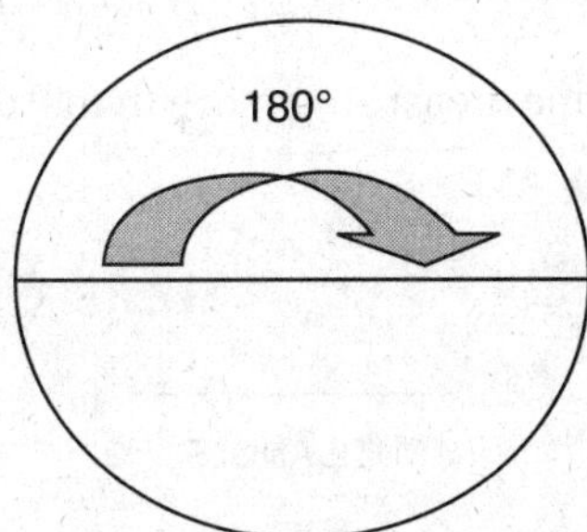

So, as we see the possible measures of an angle from 0° to 180°, we need to know that each degree is divided into 60 minutes (designated by a tick mark like this ′), and each minute of a degree is further divided into 60 seconds of arc (designated by a double tick mark ″).

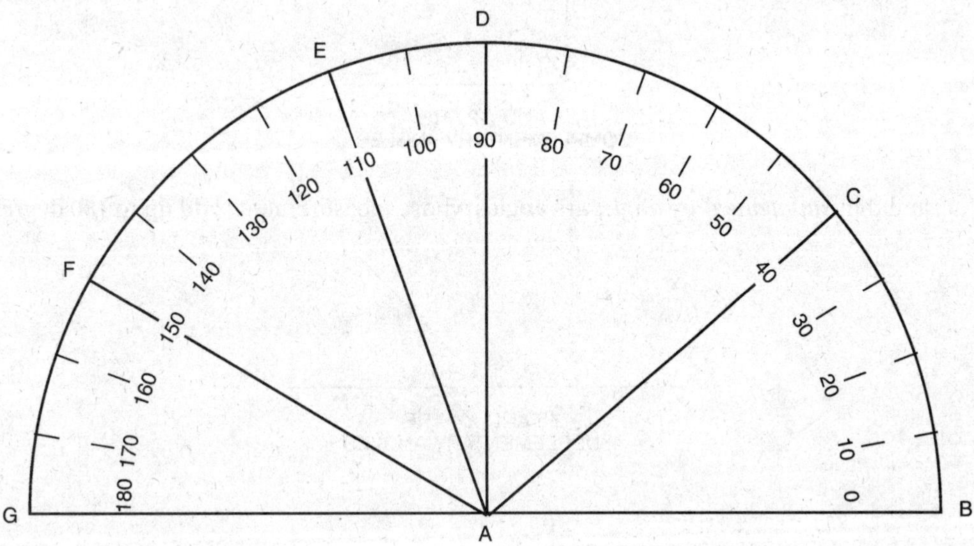

Further, we need to remember that a *right angle* is an angle of 90 degrees.

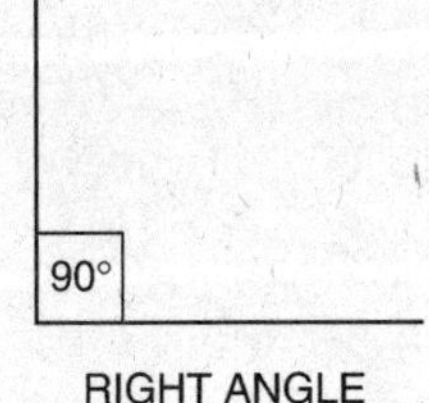

RIGHT ANGLE

Next, we need to remember that an *obtuse angle* is an angle measuring more than 90 degrees but less than 180 degrees . . .

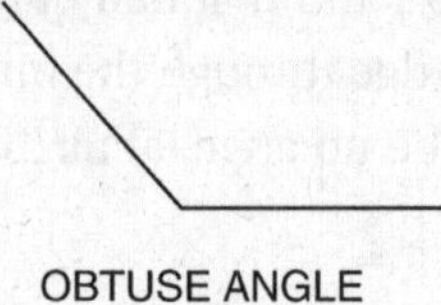

OBTUSE ANGLE

. . . and that an *acute angle* is one measuring more than 0 degrees but less than 90 degrees.

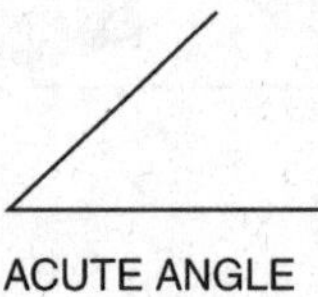

ACUTE ANGLE

We also need to remember that *complementary angles* are two angles that have measurements that add up to 90 degrees (a right angle) . . .

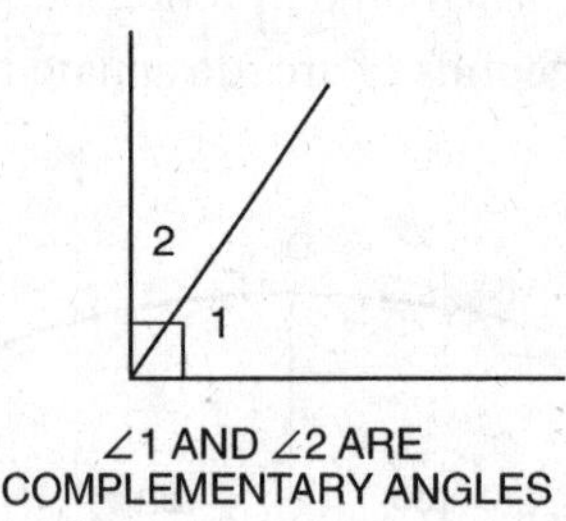

∠1 AND ∠2 ARE
COMPLEMENTARY ANGLES

. . . and that *supplementary angles* are angles whose measurements add up to 180 degrees.

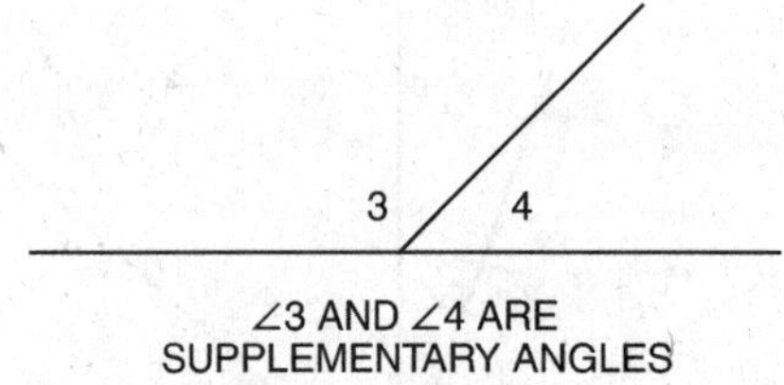

∠3 AND ∠4 ARE
SUPPLEMENTARY ANGLES

Polygons

A *polygon* is made up of three or more lines that are connected so that an area is enclosed. There are, technically, an infinite number of different types of polygons; here are some of the most common:

1. A *triangle* has three sides.
2. A *quadrilateral* has four sides.
3. A *pentagon* has five sides.
4. A *hexagon* has six sides.
5. An *octagon* has eight sides.
6. A *decagon* has ten sides.

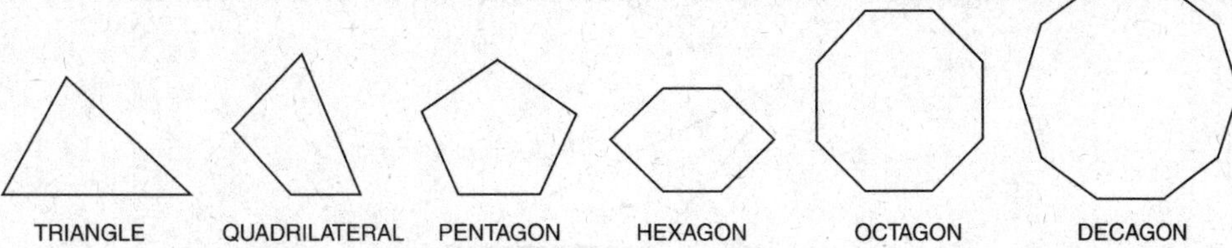

TRIANGLES

A *triangle* is a polygon with three straight sides. There are several ways to categorize triangles, but all triangles have three angles, and their measurements add up to 180 degrees.

1. An *equilateral triangle* is one where all three sides are of equal length, and whose angles are also equal at 60 degrees each.

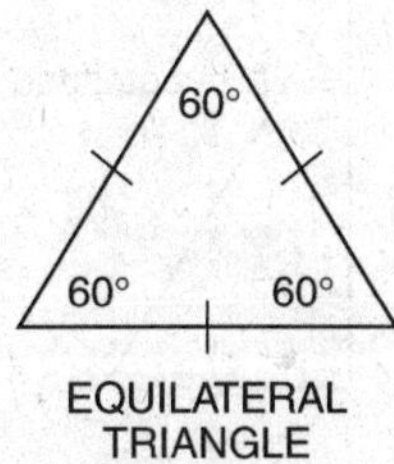

EQUILATERAL TRIANGLE

2. An *isosceles triangle* is one in which only two sides are equal; this results in the angles opposite those sides also being equal.

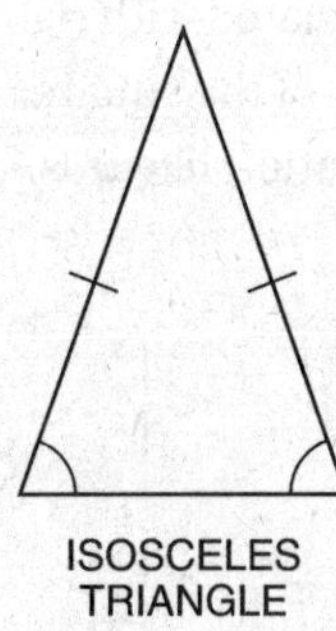
ISOSCELES TRIANGLE

3. A *scalene triangle* is one in which all three sides (and therefore all three angles) are *un*equal.

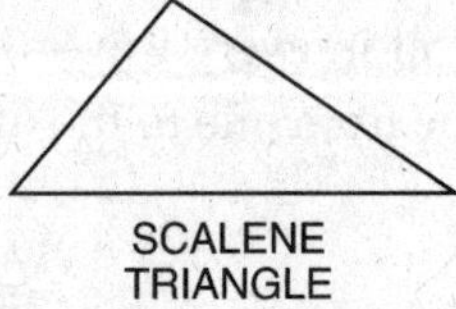
SCALENE TRIANGLE

4. An *acute triangle* is one in which all three angles are less than 90 degrees.

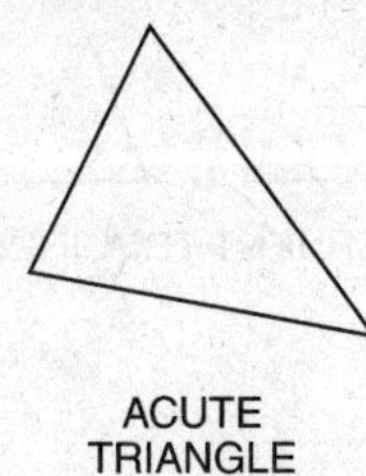
ACUTE TRIANGLE

5. An *obtuse triangle* is one where one angle is obtuse (more than 90 degrees).

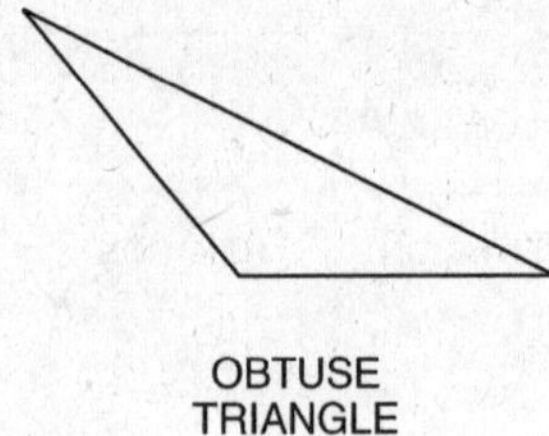

OBTUSE TRIANGLE

6. A *right triangle* is one that includes one angle of exactly 90 degrees. The longest side of a right triangle is called the *hypotenuse*; it is always the side opposite the right angle. The other two sides of a right triangle are called *legs.*

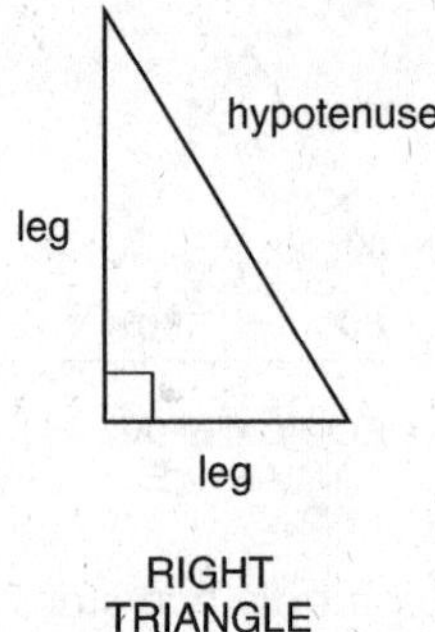

RIGHT TRIANGLE

A very important, useful concept associated with right triangles is the *Pythagorean Theorem.* This says that in a right triangle, the sum of the squares of the legs is equal to the square of the hypotenuse. This is expressed in an equation like this:

$$a^2 + b^2 = c^2$$

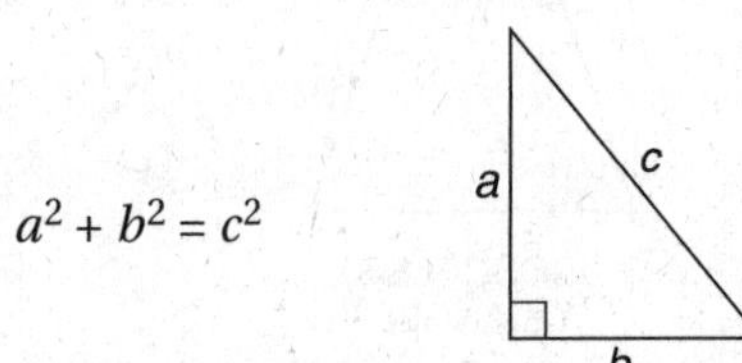

7. *Congruent triangles* are identical in every way—their sides are the same length, and their angles are exactly the same from one to the other.

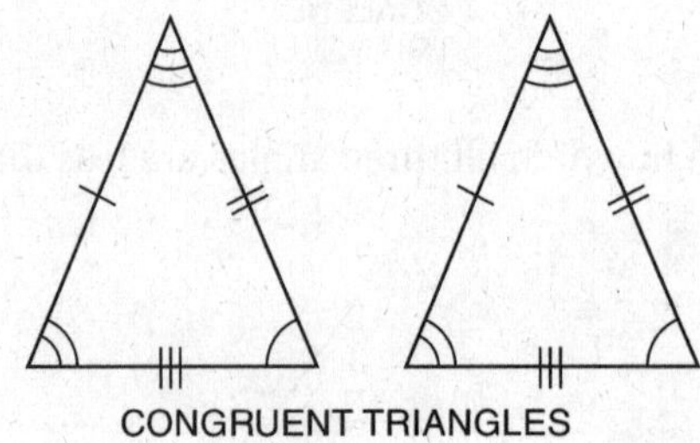

CONGRUENT TRIANGLES

8. *Similar triangles* are triangles with the same shape—whose sides are proportionate, but not the same measurement. The angles of similar triangles are identical.

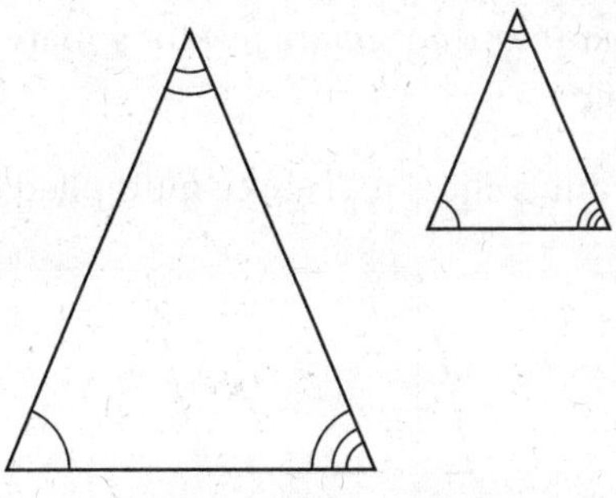

SIMILAR TRIANGLES

9. A special way to work with triangles is to calculate an *altitude*. In the diagram below, *BD* is an altitude . . .

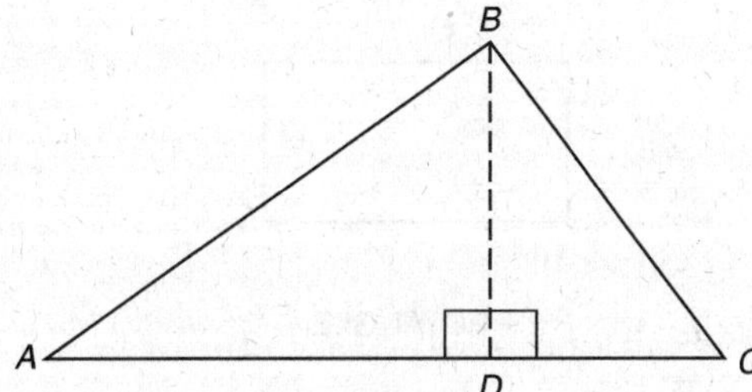

. . . and in this one, *CD* is an altitude, also. Notice that side *AB* has to be extended for the perpendicular *CD* to meet it at a right angle.

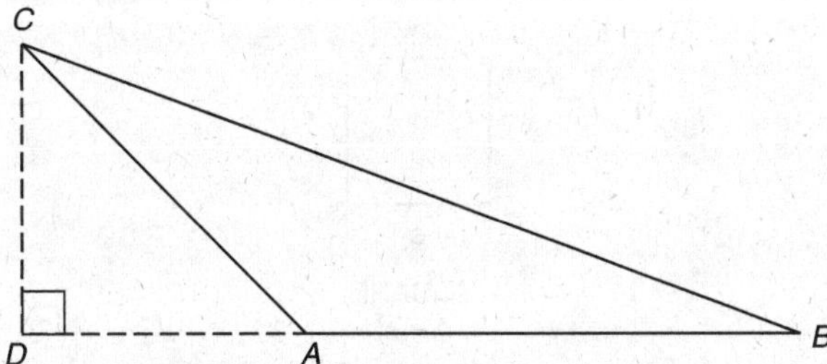

QUADRILATERALS

There are several types of quadrilaterals, but all of them have four sides and the measurements of their interior angles add up to 360 degrees.

1. A *parallelogram* has its opposite sides parallel; opposite sides and angles are also equal.
2. A *rectangle* is a parallelogram whose angles are all right angles.
3. A *square* is a rectangle that has four equal sides.
4. A *rhombus* is a parallelogram whose angles are not right angles (i.e., it's not a square), but whose sides are all equal.
5. A *trapezoid* is a quadrilateral with two sides that are parallel and two sides that are not.

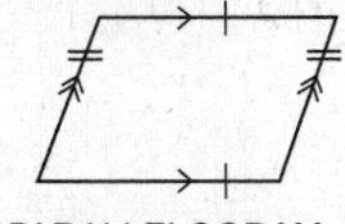

PARALLELOGRAM

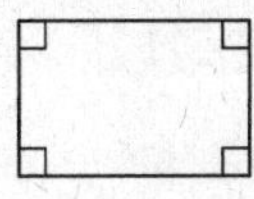

RECTANGLE

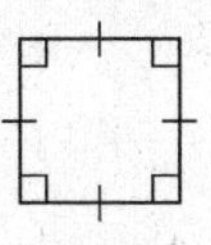

SQUARE

RHOMBUS

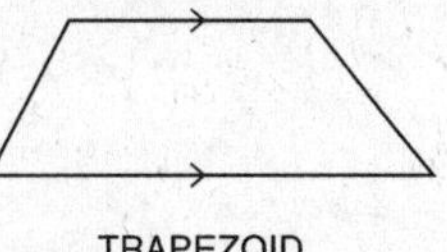

TRAPEZOID

Perimeter and Area Measurements of Polygons

The *perimeter* of a polygon is the sum of all its sides. The *area* of a polygon is the space enclosed by its sides and is expressed in *square feet* (or square inches, square yards, square meters, square centimeters, etc.)

1. The area of a parallelogram is equal to its base multiplied by its height.

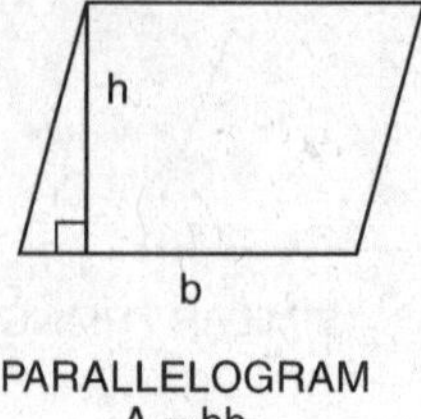

PARALLELOGRAM
A = bh

2. The area of a rectangle is equal to its length multiplied by its width.

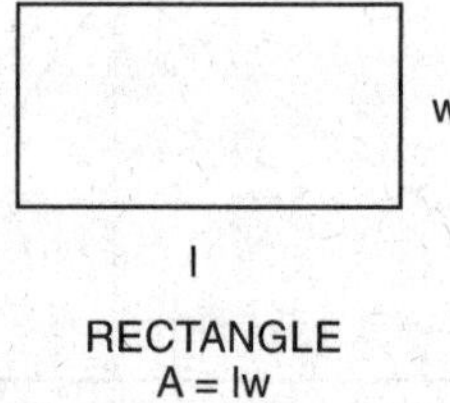

RECTANGLE
A = lw

3. The area of a square can be found by methods 1 or 2 above, or by simply multiplying the length of one side by itself (*squaring* it); if you take a moment, you will see that all three methods are the same for a square, because of its four equal sides.

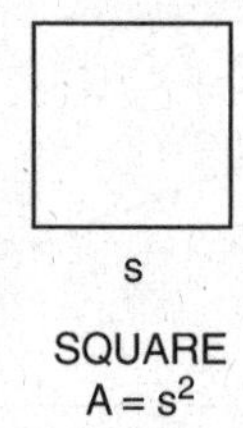

SQUARE
$A = s^2$

4. The area of a triangle is half the measurement of its base multiplied by its height.

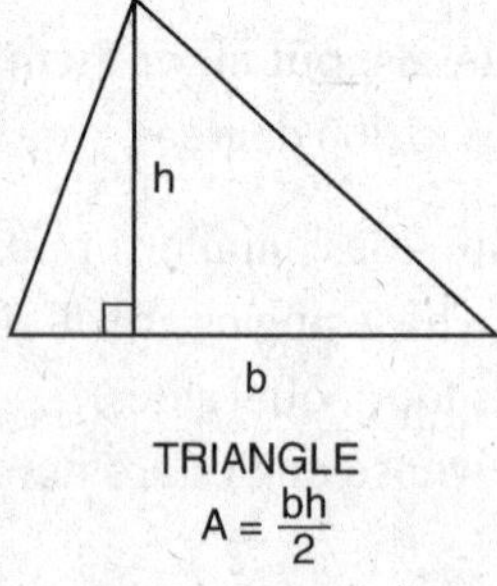

TRIANGLE
$A = \frac{bh}{2}$

Circles

A *circle* is a closed curved line, all of whose points are equidistant from the center. A circle is divided into 360 degrees; its *circumference* is the equivalent of the perimeter of a polygon. The *radius* of a circle is a line drawn from its center to any point on the circumference. The circle's *diameter* is a line from one point on the circumference that passes through the circle's center; it is equal to twice the length of the radius.

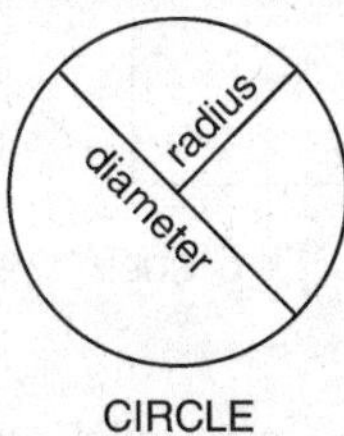

CIRCLE

Perimeter and Area Measurements of a Circle

To find the circumference of a circle, we need to use a new concept, the number π (pronounced "pi"), which is usually approximated as the fraction $\frac{22}{7}$. In geometry π expresses the unchanging relationship between the circumference of a circle and its diameter. Because the diameter is twice the length of the radius, we can also say that the circumference of a circle is π times twice the radius. Expressed mathematically it looks like this:

$C = \pi d$ (the circumference is equal to pi times the diameter)
$C = \pi 2r$ (the circumference is equal to pi times twice the radius)

Because π is an infinite, nonrepeating decimal, we can either approximate π's value by rounding it to 3.1415926 or even 3.14 for most problems. If a fraction is more appropriate, then we use the approximation $\frac{22}{7}$.

The area of a circle also has an unchanging relationship to π: The area of a circle equals π multiplied by the square of the radius, or

$$A = \pi(r^2)$$

Volume

Volume is the total, three-dimensional space occupied by a solid object, which has (for our mathematical purposes) flat sides of *length, width,* and *depth.* Volume measurements are expressed in *cubic* units. Therefore, the equation for the volume of a rectangular object is

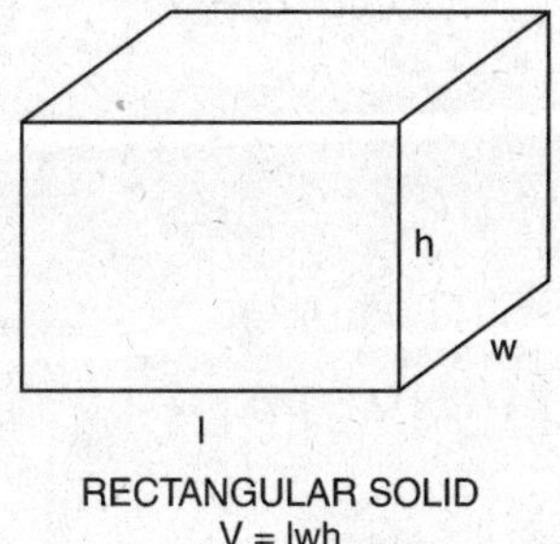

RECTANGULAR SOLID
V = lwh

A *cube* is a solid whose length, width, and height are all the same—a three-dimensional square. The volume of a cube is one side raised to the third power, i.e., one side multiplied by itself, then the result multiplied by itself again.

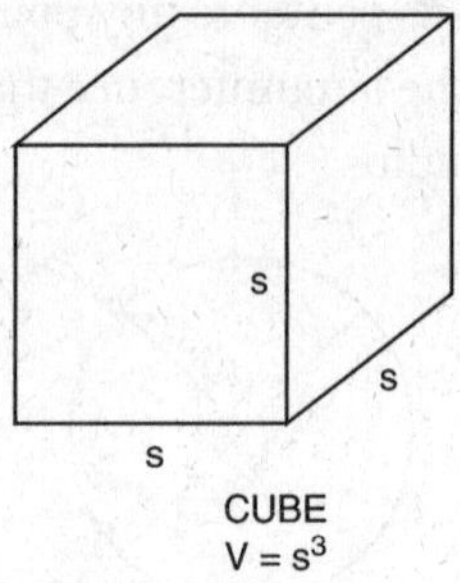

CUBE
$V = s^3$

A solid where both bases are circles in parallel planes is called a *cylinder*. The volume of a cylinder is the area of its base (which is a circle) multiplied by its height, or, expressed mathematically:

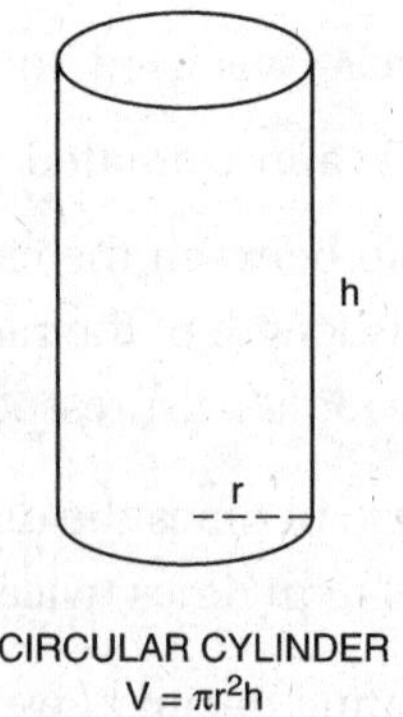

CIRCULAR CYLINDER
$V = \pi r^2 h$

A *sphere* is a perfectly round, three-dimensional object (e.g., a round ball). The volume of a sphere is found by multiplying $\frac{4}{3}$ times π times the cube of the radius.

$$V = \frac{4}{3}\pi r^3$$

Technical Knowledge 7

This chapter will provide you with information on aviation basics and nautical knowledge. This will help you on the AFOQT's Instrument Comprehension and Aviation Information subtests; the SIFT's Army Aviation Information subtest; and the ASTB-E's Aviation and Nautical Information subtest. It will also give you important background and context specific to U.S. military aviation to help you understand questions in many of the other subtests.

AVIATION INFORMATION

To do well on any of the aviation sections of these tests, you should have some basic knowledge of how airplanes and helicopters fly. It's a good idea, after you do some basic research of your own at the library or on the Internet, to take some time to visit an airport and talk with pilots to get some basic information about how to fly a plane. Even better, go through this book, write down any questions with which you had problems, and then ask the pilots for help. A hands-on demonstration will definitely help you remember the material.

This section covers the basics of flight for both fixed- and rotary-wing aircraft, including how aircraft are constructed; flight instruments and controls; flight theory and the flight envelope; basic aviation terminology; and basic flight maneuvers. We will go through this sequence with fixed-wing aircraft, then come back and revisit how rotary-wing aircraft are similar and how they are different.

While you're working your way through this section, make a note when you come to a concept that you don't fully understand based on the explanation in that particular section, but try to continue: Some ideas have to be explained one piece at a time, and the explanation will become clearer as you go along. For instance, it's impossible to explain aircraft controls without mentioning the control surfaces and what they do, but explaining what they do isn't very clear until you know what the three axes of movement are, which in turn don't make much sense unless explained in the context of cockpit controls and the airplane's control surfaces.

It's like listening to a class on a subject that's new to you, but having to wait until the end to ask any questions. Many of the questions you have will be answered as the information is explained, part by part. If you get to the end, however, and some ideas aren't clear yet, go back to that section and reread it; you will probably understand it better now that you have some of the other pieces of the puzzle in place. If that idea is still not clear to you, talk to a licensed pilot or do some more research on your own. You'll get it.

FIXED-WING AIRCRAFT

Although airplanes vary widely based on their design purposes and capacities, most have some version of the same basic components:

1. Fuselage
2. Wings
3. Landing gear
4. Powerplant
5. Tail assembly or empennage
6. Flight instruments/controls and control surfaces

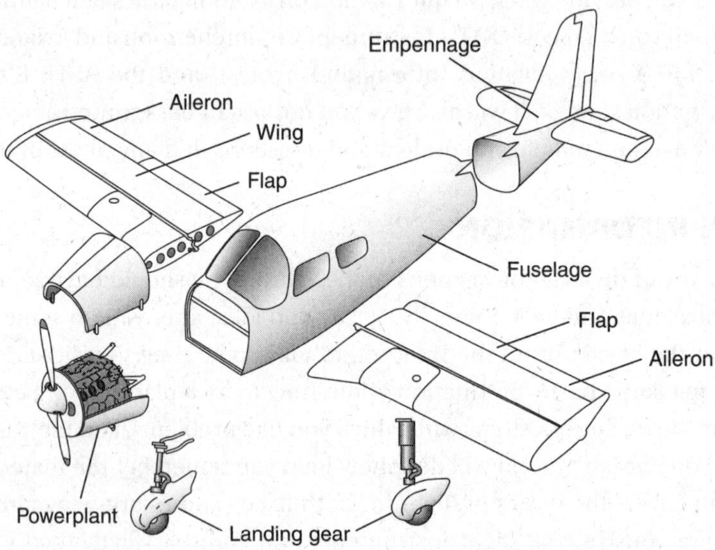

Figure 7.1 Basic fixed-wing aircraft construction

Fuselage

The *fuselage* or body of the airplane contains the cockpit, from which the pilots and flight crew control the aircraft's operations; the cabin, if the airplane carries any passengers; the cargo area if there is one; and attachment points for other major airplane components, such as the wings, tail section, and landing gear.

Single-engine propeller-driven airplanes usually have the engine in the front of the fuselage. There is a fireproof partition called a *firewall* between the engine compartment and the cockpit/cabin to protect the crew and passengers (if any) from a fire in the engine.

The two general design types of fuselage construction are *truss* and *monocoque.* Truss construction fuselages use steel or aluminum tubing in a series of triangular shapes (called trusses) to get the necessary strength and rigidity. Monocoque designs use bulkheads, stringers (running the length of the fuselage), and formers (perpendicular to the stringers) of various sizes and shapes to support a stretched or "stressed" skin.

Wings

The wings are airfoils attached to each side of the fuselage that serve as the main lifting surfaces supporting the airplane in flight. An *airfoil* is an aircraft part or surface (such as a wing, propeller blade, or rudder) that controls lift, direction, stability, thrust, or propulsion for the aircraft. Modern aircraft may have any one of a wide variety of wing designs, shapes, and sizes, based on the aircraft's purpose and design capabilities; the different types of wing shapes provide different capabilities, advantages, and disadvantages, but they all work basically the same way (we'll get into that shortly).

Wings may be attached to the fuselage at the top, middle, or bottom (hence the terms *high-wing, mid-wing,* and *low-wing*). How many wings an airplane has can also vary, but this is counted in pairs or sets (wouldn't want to have an airplane with only a left wing, for instance); airplanes with one set of wings are *monoplanes,* and those with two sets (usually stacked vertically) are called *biplanes.* There were a few triplanes early in the airplane's history, but you won't see them any more; there are still a few types of biplanes around (usually crop dusters and the like), but almost all planes today are monoplanes.

In terms of bracing and support, wings fall into one of two major categories, *cantilever* or *semi-cantilever.* A cantilever wing requires no external bracing, getting its support from internal wing spars, ribs, and stringers, as well as the construction of the wing's skin or covering. A semi-cantilever wing requires both internal bracing and external support from struts attached to the fuselage.

Attached to the rear (trailing) edges of the wings are two sets of control surfaces known as *ailerons* and *flaps* (see Figure 7.1). Ailerons extend from about the middle of the wing out toward the wingtip; they move in opposite directions to create aerodynamic forces that cause the airplane to roll. Flaps extend outward from near where the wing joins the fuselage (called the *wing root*) to about the middle of the wing's trailing edge. The flaps are usually flush with the rest of the wing surface during cruising (constant speed, neither climbing nor diving) flight; when they are extended, the flaps move downward together to increase the lift of the wing for takeoffs and landings.

In the flight theory section, we'll discuss in more detail how wings generate lift. For right now, though, let's hit the high points of how wings are shaped. First, we'll look at a cross section of a conventional wing shape or *airfoil.*

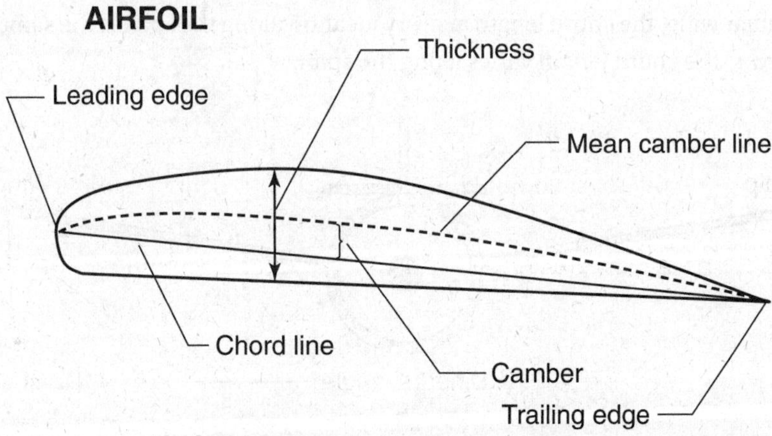

Figure 7.2 Airfoil cross section

Airfoil shapes are found on wings, fans, and propellers—any application where air needs to be moved. The airfoil shape provides lift when it splits the airstream through which it is moving. An airfoil usually has a somewhat thicker, rounded, front or leading edge, and a thinner trailing edge. In between the leading and trailing edge, an airfoil is curved; the top surface usually has a greater curve than the bottom surface. When a surface is curved, we say it has *camber.*

The popular explanation of how an airfoil or wing generates lift is based on Bernoulli's Principle. Because the top surface of the wing has more camber than the bottom surface, the air flows faster over the top of the wing than it does underneath. This means that there is less air pressure above the wing than there is underneath; the difference in air pressure above and below the wing causes lift. The primary advantages of the popular explanation of how lift occurs are (a) it's easy to understand, and (b) it has been taught for many years. Some of the questions you will see on your service's flight aptitude test may refer to this explanation, which is in fact more or less adequate at low speeds. However, we will see later in the flight theory section that the actual explanation for how lift occurs is based more on Newton's Laws than on Bernoulli's Principle.

Different airfoil shapes generate different amounts of lift and drag. If an airplane is designed to fly at low speeds (below 100 mph), it will have a different airfoil shape than an airplane designed to fly at supersonic speed (above about 761 mph). That's because the airflow behaves in slightly different ways at different speeds and at different altitudes. In general, low- to medium-speed airplanes have airfoils with more thickness and camber.

The distance from the leading edge of the wing to the trailing edge is called the *chord*; the line from the middle of the leading edge to the trailing edge (as depicted in Figure 7.2) is the *chord line,* which cuts the airfoil into an upper surface and a lower surface. If we plot the points that lie halfway between the upper and lower surfaces, we obtain a curve called the *mean camber line.* For a symmetric airfoil, where the upper surface has the same shape as the lower surface, the mean camber line is the same as the chord line—but in most cases, since the airfoil surface has less curvature on the bottom than the top, these are two separate lines. The maximum distance between the two lines is called the *camber,* which is a measure of the curvature of the airfoil (high camber means high curvature); the maximum distance between the upper and lower surfaces is called the *thickness.*

The ends of the wings are called the *wingtips,* and the distance from one wingtip to the other is called the *wingspan.* The shape of the wing viewed from above is called a *planform.* For a rectangular wing, the chord length at every location along the span is the same. For most other planforms, the chord length varies along the span.

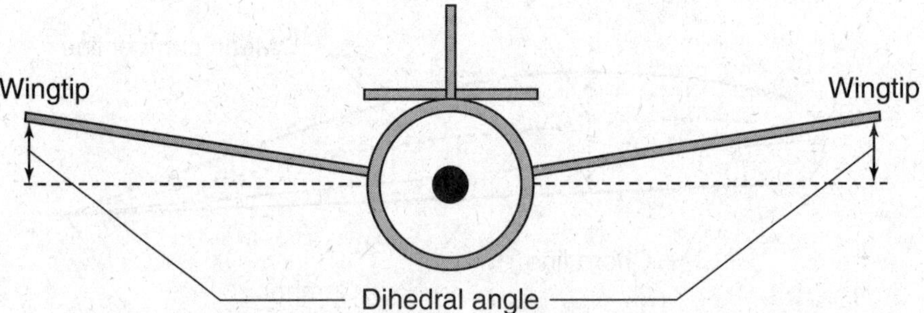

Figure 7.3 Front wing view showing dihedral

The front view of this wing shows that the left and right wings aren't truly horizontal (i.e., perpendicular to the fuselage), but instead meet at an angle called the *dihedral angle.* Dihedral is built into the design for roll stability; a wing with some dihedral will naturally return to its original position if it encounters a slight displacement. You may have noticed that most large airliner wings are designed with dihedral—you can tell by the fact that the wingtips are higher off the ground than the wing roots. Highly maneuverable fighter planes, on the other hand, don't have dihedral; in fact, some fighters have wingtips lower than the roots (called *anhedral*), giving the aircraft a higher roll rate.

Different wing planforms have different uses, characteristics, advantages, and disadvantages. An airplane's speed, maneuverability, and handling qualities are all very dependent on the shape of the wings. There are three basic wing types used on modern airplanes: straight, sweep, and delta.

Straight wings are mostly found on small, low-speed airplanes, as well as gliders and sailplanes. These wings give the most efficient lift at low speeds, but are not very good for high-speed flight, especially when approaching the speed of sound.

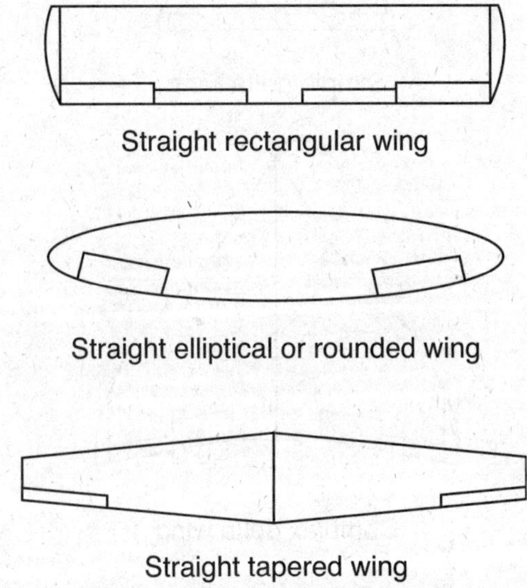

Figure 7.4 Straight-wing designs

The swept wing (either swept back or forward-swept) is the most common design for modern high-speed airplanes. The swept-wing design creates less drag than straight-wing designs, but is somewhat more unstable at low speeds. A sharply swept wing delays the formation of shock waves as the airplane nears the speed of sound. How much sweep a wing design is given depends on the design purpose for the airplane. A commercial jetliner has a moderate sweep, resulting in less drag while maintaining stability at lower speeds. High-speed aircraft like fighter planes have wings with a greater sweep, which do not generate much lift during low-speed flight and require relatively high-speed takeoffs and landings.

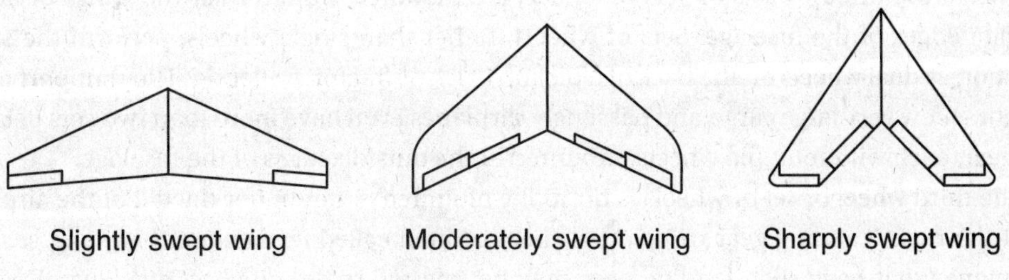

Figure 7.5 Swept-wing designs

A delta wing looks like a large triangle viewed from above. It has a high angle of sweep with a straight trailing edge. Airplanes with this type of wing design are designed to reach supersonic speeds, and also land at high speeds. This type of planform was found on the supersonic transport Concorde and the shuttle Orbiters, as well as some experimental aircraft and European fighters; the delta wing design was also used on the now-obsolete F-102 Delta Dart and F-106 Delta Dagger American fighters and the B-58 Hustler bomber.

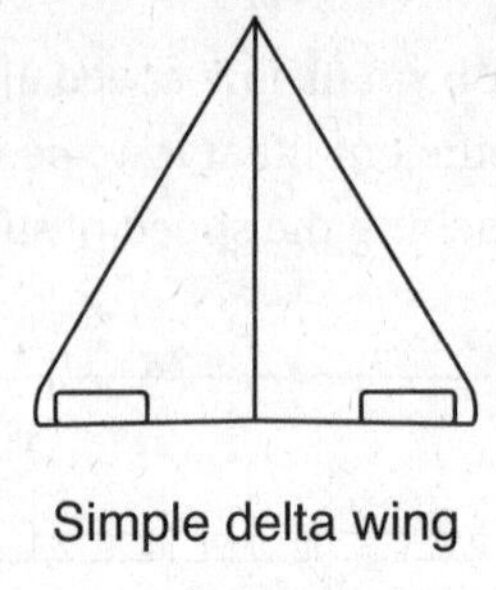

Simple delta wing

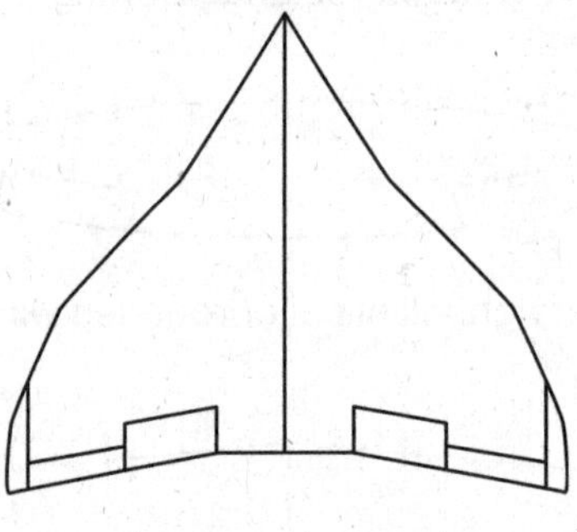

Complex delta wing

Figure 7.6 Delta wing designs

Landing Gear

The landing gear provides the main support for the airplane when it is on the ground. Landing gear usually consists of three wheels or sets of wheels—sometimes more for large or special-purpose aircraft—but airplanes can also be equipped with skis for landing on snow and ice, or floats to land on water.

Landing gear can be either retractable or nonretractable. Retractable gear can be mechanically pulled up into a cavity designed for them, with a door or doors closing over the opening to reduce drag and improve the airplane's performance. Nonretractable landing gear usually has fairings over the top half to reduce drag and improve the airplane's performance.

Two of the three wheels or sets of wheels are mounted either under the wings or at the outside edges of the fuselage. Sets of wheels, rather than single wheels, perform the same function as dual wheels on the back of a pickup truck or tractor-trailer rig: They support more weight. A few very large cargo and passenger airplanes even have more than two sets of landing gear, each with multiple wheels, mounted at the outside edges of the fuselage.

The third wheel or set of wheels is normally mounted either under the tail of the airplane or at the nose. Landing gear using a tailwheel is often called *conventional landing gear,* or the planes that have such landing gear may be referred to as *tailwheel airplanes.* Designs with the third wheel under the nose (a *nosewheel*) are commonly called *tricycle landing gear.*

In either case, a steerable tailwheel or nosewheel allows the airplane to be controlled during ground movement.

Powerplant

There are two main types of fixed-wing aircraft propulsion systems we will discuss here: propellers and jets. Propeller- or "prop"-driven planes get their *thrust* by the corkscrew action of one or more propellers with two or more blades each rotating very fast at the front of the engine, which pushes air backward with the result that the airplane is "pushed" forward in accordance with Newton's Third Law. The propeller blades are curved or slanted in a certain way to achieve this effect, and often the amount of the slant or *pitch* is variable—that is, the pilot can control just how much "pull" or *thrust* he wants the propeller to exert. Various designs, including the Wright brothers' original 1903 model, have placed the propeller at the back of the plane, resulting in the name *pusher prop*, but these are by far in the minority.

The powerplant of a propeller-driven plane is usually considered to include both the engine and the propeller. The primary function of the engine is to turn the propeller, but it also generates electrical power, provides a vacuum source for some flight instruments, and provides a heat source for the pilot and passengers in most small single-engine planes.

Propeller-driven airplanes may have either a *fixed-pitch* or *variable-pitch* propeller. A fixed-pitch propeller's pitch has a blade angle that can't be changed by the pilot. The propeller is connected directly to the engine's crankshaft; engine power rotates the crankshaft as well as the propeller, and the propeller converts the engine's rotary power into thrust. A variable-pitch propeller, also known as a *constant-speed* propeller, is more efficient than its fixed-pitch counterpart because the pilot can adjust the blade angle for the most efficient operation.

Single-engine propeller-driven airplanes usually have the engine attached to the front of the fuselage, covered by a cowling to streamline the airflow around the engine; it also helps cool the engine by ducting air around the cylinders. Multi-engine planes, whether propeller driven or jet, usually have the engines mounted under the wings in a nacelle, which surrounds the entire engine and performs the same functions as a cowling. Some jet engines are attached to the empennage, but these are in the minority.

Jet engines work by forcing incoming air into a tube or cylinder where the air is compressed, mixed with fuel, burned, and pushed exhausted at high speed to generate thrust. There are several variations of jet engines, including the turbojet, turbofan, and ramjet. These engines all operate by the same basic principles, but each has its own distinct advantages and disadvantages.

The critical part of a jet engine's operation is compressing the incoming air. Most jets employ a section of compressors, consisting of rotating blades that slow the incoming air to create high pressure. This compressed air is then forced into a combustion section, where it is mixed with fuel and burned. As the high-pressure gases are exhausted, they are passed through a turbine section with more rotating blades. In this region, the exhaust gases turn the turbine blades, which are connected by a shaft to the compressor blades at the front of the engine—which means that the exhaust turns the turbines that turn the compressors to bring in more air and keep the engine going. The combustion gases then continue to expand out through the nozzle, "pushing" backward to create a forward thrust.

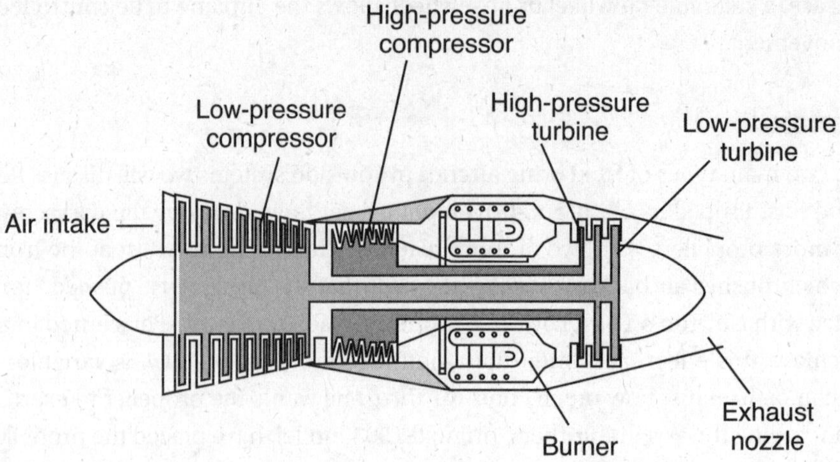

Figure 7.7 Turbojet engine cross section

Turbojets and turbofans can also be fitted with an *afterburner*. An afterburner is a tube placed between the turbine and the rear exhaust nozzle where additional fuel is added to the flow and ignited to provide increased thrust. However, afterburners greatly increase fuel consumption, so they can be used only for short periods.

Tail Assembly/Empennage

The technical name for the tail section of an airplane is the *empennage*; this includes the entire tail section, which consists of both fixed and movable control surfaces. The fixed surfaces are the vertical and horizontal stabilizers, and the movable surfaces include the elevators, the rudder, and any trim tabs.

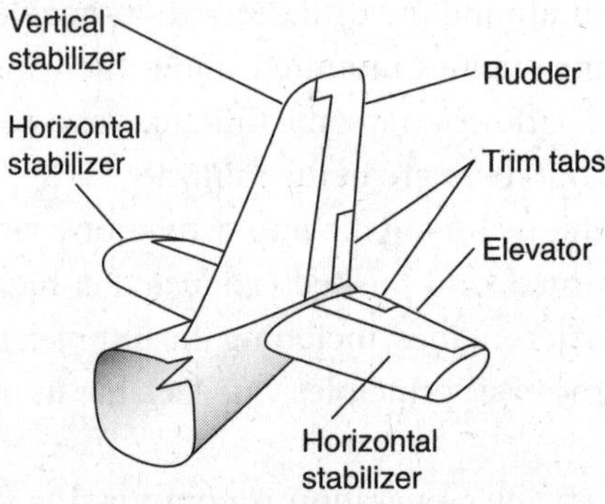

Figure 7.8 Conventional empennage

The elevators are movable control surfaces attached to the back or trailing edge of the horizontal stabilizers; they are used to move the nose of the airplane up or down during flight. Usually the two stabilizers are split, even at the back edge, by either the vertical stabilizer, the back end of the fuselage, or both; however, there are a few airplane designs where the trailing edge of the horizontal stabilizer is not split, and therefore there is only one elevator instead of two. For purposes of our discussion, however, we will consider the left and right horizontal stabilizers—and hence the attached elevators—to be split.

The rudder is a movable control surface attached to the back of the vertical stabilizer that is used to move the airplane's nose left and right during flight. The rudder is used in combination with the ailerons for turns while the airplane is flying. Some people incorrectly refer to the vertical stabilizer as the rudder, but now you know better.

Trim tabs are small movable segments of the trailing edge of the rudder, elevator(s), and ailerons. Controlled by the pilot in the cockpit, they reduce control pressures and decrease the pilot's workload.

NEWTON'S LAWS

British mathematician and philosopher Sir Isaac Newton put forth three basic laws of motion in the mid-1600s. Although we can be pretty confident that he wasn't thinking of aircraft flight characteristics when he proposed these laws, virtually everything that an aircraft does has something to do with one or more of his three laws of motion.

Newton's First Law of Motion (or Inertia), stated simply, maintains that a body at rest tends to remain at rest, and a body in motion tends to remain in motion (at the same speed and in the same direction) unless acted upon by an outside force. Stated differently, nothing in nature starts or stops moving until some outside force causes it to do so. This is connected with the concept of *inertia*, which is the property by which an object resists being accelerated in some different way from its current state.

Examples are the soccer ball that remains motionless (relative to Earth, anyway) on the ground until it is kicked, and the same soccer ball that keeps rolling until friction with the ground and the air around it slow it down and finally stop it. Likewise, an airplane parked on the ramp will stay there until enough force to move it is applied by its engines, a tow vehicle, a tornado, or something else.

Newton's Second Law of Motion is represented by the equation $F = ma$, where F is the *force* acting on an object, *m* stands for an object's *mass*, and *a* is the object's acceleration. According to this law, when an object is acted upon by a force, its resulting acceleration is directly proportional to the applied force and inversely proportional to the mass of the object. This means that force must be applied to overcome the inertia of an object: The greater the mass of the object, the greater the force needed to produce a particular acceleration.

Newton's Third Law of Motion is usually summarized like this: "For every action there is an equal and opposite reaction." Stated differently, when one object exerts a force on a second object, the second object exerts an equal and opposite force on the first object. This law is most clearly demonstrated in the aerospace world by the operation of jets and rockets: As hot gases are pushed out the back, they exert a forward push on the object from which they escape (such as the jet engine connected to the aircraft).

These laws need to be considered in the context of another of Newton's laws, that of *universal gravitation*. This law says that two objects attract each other with a force that is proportional to the product of their masses (i.e., their masses multiplied together), and inversely proportional to the square of the distance between them. This attraction is commonly known as *gravity*. Gravity accounts for the weight of an object on Earth (or some other planet, for that matter), and usually measures the pull of the large body (Earth, in this case) in pounds or kilograms.

It needs to be noted here that, although *mass* and *weight* are both commonly referred to in pounds or kilograms, *mass* is a constant that is unaffected by local gravitational conditions, whereas *weight* is a function of the planet's gravity at that point. In other words, regardless of the fact that an object can weigh six pounds on Earth, one pound on the moon (where gravity is one-sixth of that on Earth), or nothing at all in far outer space, its mass remains the same regardless—it will take the same amount of force in any of those places to accelerate it the same amount.

FLIGHT THEORY AND THE FLIGHT ENVELOPE

Four forces act upon an aircraft in flight: *lift*, *gravity* (or weight), *thrust*, and *drag*. Lift pushes the aircraft up (i.e., away from Earth's surface); weight pulls the aircraft down toward Earth (or, more precisely, toward Earth's center); thrust pushes the aircraft forward; and drag tends to slow the aircraft, pushing back on it as it moves forward.

The *flight envelope* consists of the different combinations of these factors and others that allow the aircraft to be flown safely. "Flying outside the envelope" is slang for some unsafe condition that caused problems in maintaining stability or even the ability to fly at all.

As mentioned earlier, the popular explanation of how an airfoil or wing generates lift is that the airfoil uses the aerodynamic forces identified by Bernoulli's Principle to provide *lift* to the wings and therefore the aircraft. Daniel Bernoulli, a Swiss mathematician, expanded on Newton's theories about the motion of fluids in his *Hydrodynamics*, published in 1783. Bernoulli's Principle says that as the velocity of a fluid increases, the pressure exerted by that fluid decreases. You can think of it that the faster a fluid (and air is a fluid) travels over a surface, the less time it has to exert pressure on any given part of that surface.

The popular explanation maintains that, because the top surface of the wing has more camber (curvature) than the bottom surface, the air flows faster over the top of the wing than it does underneath; this is because aerodynamic forces won't allow the air flowing over the upper surface to "lag behind," since that would create a vacuum at the trailing edge (and nature is very reluctant to allow vacuums to form). This faster airflow over the upper wing surface means that there is less air pressure above the wing than there is underneath; this difference in air pressure causes lift.

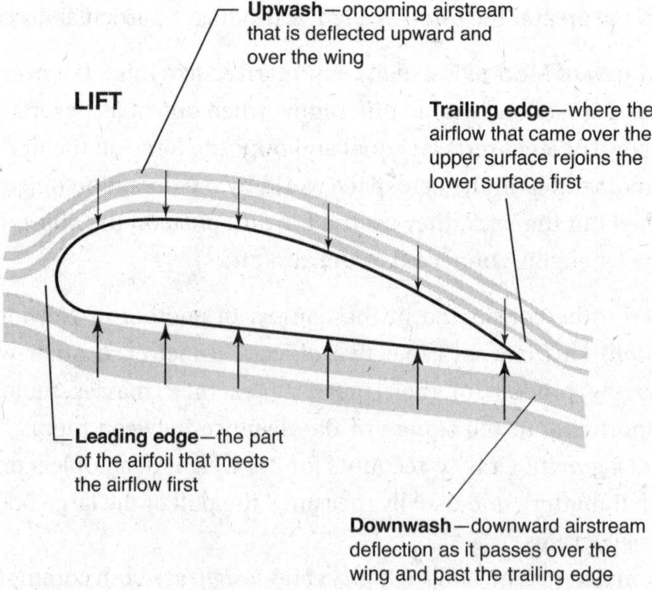

Figure 7.9 Popular explanation of lift produced by an airfoil

Some may wonder why the air goes faster over the top of the wing and what compels the same batch of air to join up with the air it was split from by the leading edge of the airfoil. This is where the popular explanation starts to wobble.

There is an alternative explanation for how a wing provides lift that relies on Newton's Laws of Motion instead of Bernoulli's Principle. The popular explanation assumes that the transit time for air split by the wing's leading edge is equal both under and over the wing, which is not borne out by wind tunnel testing. It also means that the popular explanation using Bernoulli's Principle has a hard time explaining inverted flight, symmetric wings, and changes in wing load in a steep turn or when pulling out of a dive.

Newton's Laws tell us that the wing must change something in the air around it (action) to get a reaction (lift). Figure 7.9 shows the airflow around a wing as it is often represented. Notice that as the air is approached by the wing, it splits and reforms behind the wing, going in whatever direction it was going in before (or standing still). *This wing has no lift.* There is no net *action* on the air, and therefore no *reaction* of lift on the wing. If the wing has no net effect on the air, the air can't have any net effect on the wing.

The alternative explanation proposes that, in order to generate lift, a wing must do something to the air. The wing splits the air (action), and lift is the reaction (see Newton's Third Law). By this explanation, lift is the result of upwash and downwash caused by the wing's movement through the air (see Figure 7.10). In this diagram, the air splits around the wing and leaves it at a slight downward angle. This downward-traveling air is the *downwash,* the action that creates lift as its reaction. In this figure, there has been a net change in the air after it passes over the wing—there is a force acting on the air and a reaction force acting on the wing. *This wing has lift.*

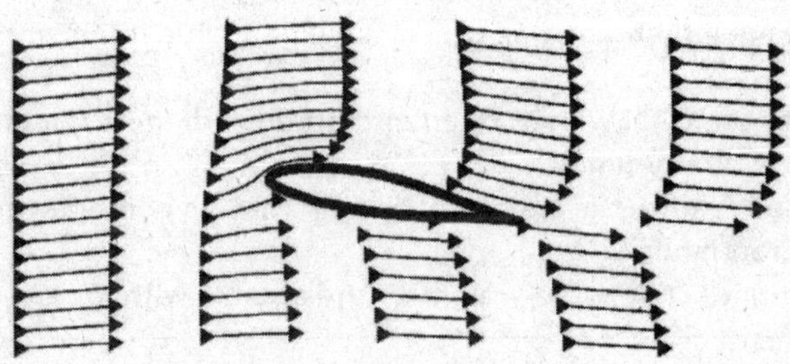

Figure 7.10 Newtonian airflow around a wing with lift

The summary here is that a wing produces lift by diverting air downward. This should be as easy to understand as saying that a propeller produces thrust by pushing air backward. Or, for another example: Who hasn't stuck their hand out of a moving car window and felt the force of the passing air push their hand upward (especially if you tilt the leading edge up a little bit, which diverts more air downward)? This is lift.

WARNING: The flight aptitude test you take may refer to Bernoulli's Principle as the cause of lift for an airfoil or wing. If this is the case, don't fight City Hall! Once you pass the test, make it through training, and get your wings, you can publicize the more accurate Newtonian explanation of what causes lift. Maybe you will be the one who gets this incorrect explanation updated after you get your wings. Regardless, now you are armed with both the popular explanation and what really happens.

A *stall* is caused by the separation of airflow from the wing's upper surface, resulting in a rapid decrease in lift—possibly to the extent of falling out of the sky. This separation happens from the trailing edge moving forward toward the leading edge, and allows a reverse airflow to creep in that presses down on the wing. A stall usually occurs gradually, and the first indications may be provided by a mushiness in the controls or a slight buffeting of the aircraft; stall warning devices that detect the airflow separation may also provide notice. To recover from a stall or imminent stall, the pilot must restore the smooth airflow by decreasing the angle of attack below the stalling angle, allowing normal lift dynamics to resume.

Weight is the force produced by the mass of the airplane interacting with Earth's gravitational field; it is the force that must be counteracted by lift to maintain flight.

Different kinds of weight are discussed in aviation circles:

- Basic Weight—the weight of the basic aircraft plus weapons, unusable fuel, oil, ballast, survival kits, oxygen, and any other internal or external equipment on board the aircraft that will not be disposed of during flight.
- Operating Weight—the sum of basic weight and items such as crew, crew baggage, steward equipment, pylons and racks, emergency equipment, special mission fixed equipment, and all other nonexpendable items not included in basic weight.
- Gross Weight—the total weight of an aircraft, including its contents and externally mounted items, at any time.
- Landing Gross Weight—the weight of the aircraft, its contents, and external items when the aircraft lands.
- Zero Fuel Weight (ZFW)—the weight of the aircraft without any usable fuel.

Profile drag or *parasitic drag* is experienced by all objects in an airflow, and is caused by resistance to the airplane pushing the air out of the way as it moves forward. This can be experienced by putting your hand out the window of a moving vehicle and then raising one finger out of alignment with the others.

The other type of drag is *induced drag*, which is the result of the production of lift. It is the part of the force produced by the wing that is parallel to the relative wind. Objects that create lift must also overcome this induced drag, also known as *drag-due-to-lift*.

Axes of Flight

Whenever an airplane changes its position in flight (*flight attitude*), we talk about movement around one or more of three *axes*—imaginary lines running through the airplane's center of gravity. The axes of an airplane can be thought of as imaginary axles around which the airplane turns, in the same way that a wheel rotates around an axle. At the point where all three axes intersect, each is at a 90-degree angle (a right angle) to the other two. The axis that runs lengthwise through the fuselage from the nose to the tail is the called the *longitudinal axis.* The axis that runs from wingtip to wingtip is called the *lateral axis.* The axis that passes vertically through the aircraft's center of gravity is called the *vertical axis* (see Figure 7.11).

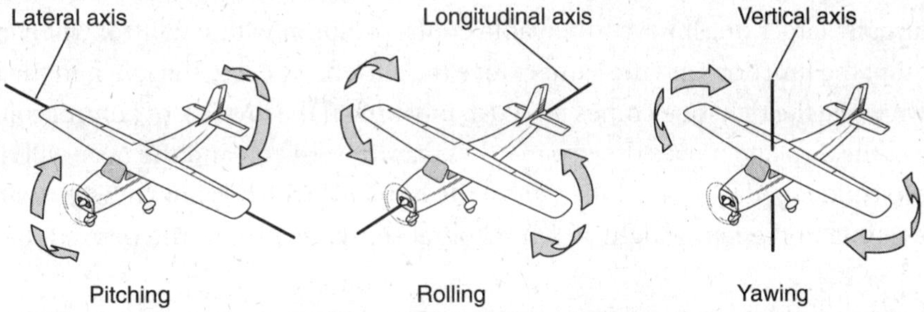

Figure 7.11 The three axes of flight

The airplane's motion around its longitudinal axis resembles the roll of a ship from side to side. In fact, the names used in describing movement around the airplane's three axes were originally nautical terms. Movement around the airplane's longitudinal axis is called *roll*; movement around its lateral axis is referred to as *pitch*; and movement around the vertical axis is known as *yaw*—a horizontal (left and right) movement of the airplane's nose. These three motions of the airplane are controlled by three control surfaces: roll is controlled by the ailerons; pitch is controlled by the elevators; and yaw is controlled by the rudder.

The Atmosphere

Our atmosphere is composed of 78 percent nitrogen, 21 percent oxygen, and one percent other gaseous elements, such as argon and helium. The heavier of these elements exhibit a natural tendency to remain closer to the surface of Earth, and the lighter elements are in the higher regions of the atmosphere. This explains why the vast majority of the atmosphere's oxygen, as one of the relatively heavier elements, is found less than 35,000 feet from the surface.

The atmosphere—the air surrounding Earth—has mass and weight. For instance, the weight of the atmosphere at sea level results in an average pressure of 14.7 pounds on each square inch of an object's surface. At 18,000 feet, however, the weight of the atmosphere is only about half of what it is at sea level.

Temperature, air pressure (depending in large part on altitude), and humidity play parts in an airplane's performance, largely by affecting the amount of lift produced by the airfoils. Warmer air, for instance, is less dense than cooler air and therefore produces less lift.

Flight Controls

A flight control system has two ends: the end where the pilot makes a change to a control in the cockpit, and the end where something on the outside of the aircraft changes and affects the airplane's performance (faster, slower, up, down, left, right, etc.). Implied in this are the mechanical, hydraulic, electronic, and other means of connecting these two ends—of having the expected result occur reliably from a certain movement of the cockpit controls.

There are two types of flight control systems, *primary* and *secondary.* The primary control systems are those needed to safely control an airplane during flight, including the ailerons, elevator/stabilator, and rudder. Secondary control systems, such as wing flaps and trim control systems, improve the airplane's performance or relieve the pilot from having to wrestle with excessive control forces.

In the cockpit, the pilot has three main ways to control the aircraft while in flight: the joystick or control wheel, the rudder pedals, and the throttle(s) for the engine(s).

The joystick controls *roll* (movement around the longitudinal axis, one wing up and one wing down) and *pitch* (movement around the lateral axis, nose up or nose down). Some airplanes (usually larger ones) have a movable control column with a control wheel mounted near the top; the functions are the same. Move the stick or wheel to the left, and the left wing goes down while the right one comes up. Push forward on the joystick or control column and the nose of the airplane moves downward; pull back toward you and the nose will rise.

The two rudder pedals control the *yaw* of the airplane, which is how much (or how little) the nose points to the left or right in a horizontal sense, relative to the desired direction of travel.

The engine throttles are considered flight controls because they are the main way for the pilot to regulate how much thrust the engine is producing. This is important because the pilot has to use all these controls in coordination to safely control the airplane; having the airplane at the proper attitude to climb higher, for example, does no good if the engine isn't producing enough thrust to accomplish the climb.

Primary Flight Controls

Airplane control systems are designed to provide the pilot a natural "feel"—one where the amount of force the pilot uses, as well as the resistance and other feedback felt by the pilot through the controls, are proportionate to the amount of actual movement by the control surfaces—but at the same time remain adequately responsive to the pilot's inputs on the controls. At low airspeeds, the controls usually feel soft and sluggish, and the airplane responds slowly to the controls. At higher speeds, the controls feel firmer and the response is quicker.

Moving one or more of the three primary flight control surfaces changes the airflow and pressure distribution over and around the airfoil (wings). These changes affect the lift and drag produced by the airfoil/control surface combination, which allows a pilot to control the airplane around its three axes of rotation.

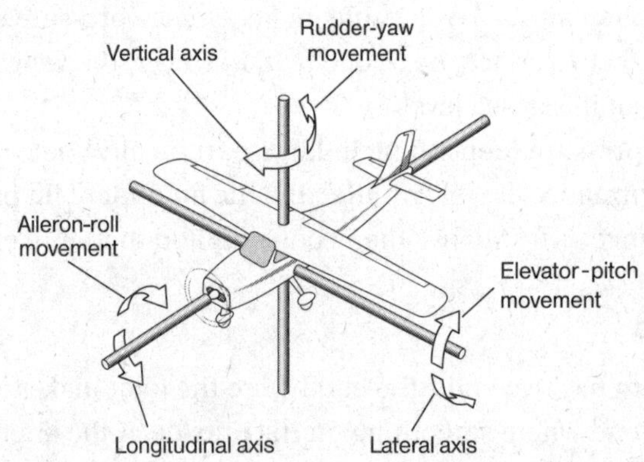

PRIMARY CONTROL SURFACE	AIRPLANE MOVEMENT	AXES OF ROTATION	TYPE OF STABILITY
Aileron	Roll	Longitudinal	Lateral
Elevator/stability	Pitch	Lateral	Longitudinal
Rudder	Yaw	Vertical	Directional

AILERONS

Ailerons control the airplane's movement around the longitudinal axis, also known as *roll.* They are attached to the outboard (the end farthest from the fuselage) trailing edge of each wing and move in opposite directions from each other.

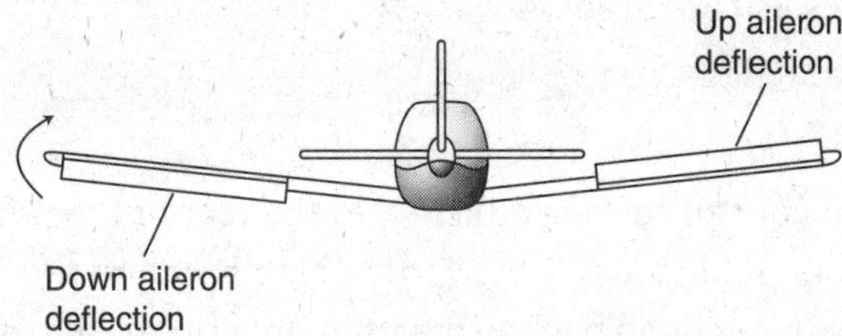

Figure 7.12 Ailerons

Moving the joystick or control wheel to the right causes the right aileron to move or *deflect* upward while the left aileron moves downward. The upward deflection of the right aileron decreases the camber of that wing, causing a decrease in lift that makes the right wing drop. The same aerodynamics in reverse on the left cause that wing to rise because of increased lift. The combined effects cause the airplane to roll to the right.

RUDDER

The rudder controls the airplane's movement around its vertical axis, called *yaw.* Like the other primary control surfaces, the rudder is a movable surface hinged to a fixed surface—in this case, to the vertical stabilizer. Moving the left or right rudder pedal causes the rudder to move in the same direction as the depressed pedal, and to the same relative extent. When the rudder is deflected into the airflow, the airflow exerts a horizontal force in the opposite direction.

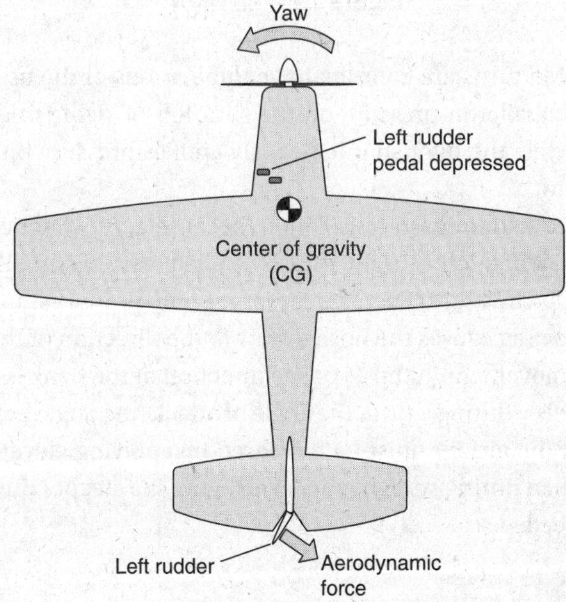

Figure 7.13 Rudder

By pushing the left pedal, the rudder moves left. This alters the airflow around the vertical stabilizer and rudder, creating a sideward force that moves the tail to the right and yaws the nose of the airplane to the left. Rudder effectiveness increases with speed, so large deflections at low speeds and small deflections at high speeds are usually what's required. In propeller-driven aircraft, any slipstream (rearward-flowing air pushed back by the propeller) flowing over the rudder increases its effectiveness.

ELEVATOR

The elevator is a hinged control surface attached to the rear of the horizontal stabilizer. On most planes, the elevators are divided by the vertical stabilizer and rudder; however, on some designs, the elevators are far enough back so that they are not two separated surfaces but one, called a *stabilator.*

The elevator controls the airplane's movement around its lateral axis, called *pitch.* Moving the joystick or control column to the rear (toward the pilot) causes the elevators to move or *deflect* air upward. The up-elevator position decreases the camber of the horizontal tail surface, creating a downward aerodynamic force greater than the slight tail-down force normal in most designs during straight and level flight. The overall effect causes the tail to move downward and the nose to pitch up, rotating around the plane's center of gravity (CG). Moving the joystick or control column forward, of course, has the opposite effect.

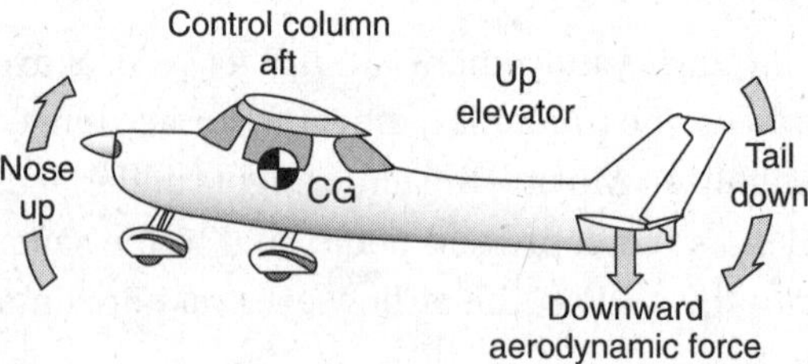

Figure 7.14 Elevator

All correctly executed turns are coordinated combinations of the use of ailerons, rudder, and elevators. Applying aileron pressure on the stick left or right is needed to achieve the desired bank angle, while the pilot simultaneously applies pressure on the rudder pedal to counteract adverse yaw.

Control surfaces are seldom used in isolation, because aerodynamic forces seldom work in only one direction. When left or right stick is applied, causing an aileron deflection that raises one wing, the downward-deflected aileron not only produces more lift, but also produces more drag. This drag causes the nose to yaw in the direction of the raised wing, called *adverse yaw.* Rudder movement in the opposite direction of the bank is used to compensate for adverse yaw. Likewise, during a turn, the angle of attack (the angle between the horizontal and the chord line of the airfoil) must be increased by applying elevator pressure because more lift is required than during straight and level flight. The steeper the turn, the more back elevator pressure is needed.

Secondary Flight Controls

Secondary flight control systems may consist of flaps, leading edge devices, spoilers, and trim systems.

FLAPS

Flaps are the most common high-lift devices. These surfaces, which are attached to the trailing edge of the wing, increase both lift and drag for any given angle of attack. Flaps allow a compromise between high cruising speed and low landing speed because they may be extended when needed and then retracted into the wing's structure when not needed.

LEADING EDGE DEVICES

High-lift devices also can be put on the leading edge of the airfoil. The most common types are fixed slats, movable slats, and leading edge flaps.

SPOILERS

On some airplanes, high-drag devices called spoilers are deployed from the wings to spoil the smooth airflow, reducing lift and increasing drag. Spoilers are used for roll control on some aircraft, one of the advantages being the elimination of adverse yaw. To turn right, for example, the spoiler on the right wing is raised, destroying some of the lift and creating more drag on the right. The right wing drops, and the airplane banks and yaws to the right. Deploying spoilers on both wings at the same time allows the aircraft to descend without gaining speed. Spoilers are also deployed to help shorten the ground roll after landing—by destroying lift, they transfer weight to the wheels, improving braking effectiveness.

TRIM SYSTEMS

Trim systems are used to relieve the pilot of the need to maintain constant pressure on the flight controls—just think how tired you would get if you had to hold the steering wheel a quarter turn to the right just to go *straight* down the highway. Trim systems usually consist of small hinged devices attached to the trailing edge of one or more of the primary flight control surfaces. They help minimize a pilot's workload by aerodynamically assisting movement and positioning of the flight control surface to which they are attached.

The most common trim system on small airplanes is a single trim tab attached to the trailing edge of the elevator, usually manually operated by a small control wheel or a crank. The cockpit control includes a tab position indicator; placing the trim control in nose-down position moves the tab to its full "up" position. With the tab up and into the airstream, the airflow over the horizontal tail surface forces the trailing edge of the elevator down. This causes the tail of the airplane to move up, and results in a nose-down pitch change.

In spite of the opposite direction movement of the trim tab and the elevator, trim control is natural to a pilot. If you have to exert constant back pressure on the control column, the need for nose-up trim is indicated. The normal trim procedure is to continue trimming until the airplane is balanced and the nose-heavy or tail-heavy condition is no longer apparent. Pilots normally establish the desired power, pitch, attitude, and configuration first, and then trim the airplane to relieve control pressures that may exist for that flight condition. Any time power, pitch, attitude, or configuration are changed, retrimming will normally be necessary to relieve the control pressures for the new flight condition.

Flight Instruments

Flight instruments enable a pilot to operate an airplane with optimal performance and increased safety, especially when flying long distances or in inclement weather conditions.

ALTIMETER

The altimeter measures height above a particular air pressure level, and therefore gives the pilot information about his altitude above the ground. Air is denser at sea level than at higher altitudes, so as altitude increases, atmospheric pressure decreases. The pressure altimeter is an anaeroid barometer that measures atmospheric pressure at the level where the altimeter is located, and presents an altitude in feet. Different altimeters can vary considerably, though, in how they show altitude; some have one pointer, whereas others have two or more. The dial of a typical altimeter is graduated, with numerals arranged clockwise from 0 to 9. The shortest hand indicates altitude in tens of thousands of feet, the intermediate hand in thousands of feet, and the longest hand in hundreds of feet.

Figure 7.15 Altimeter

This indicated altitude is precisely correct, though, only when the sea level barometric pressure is at what has been determined to be the "standard" (29.92 inches of mercury), the sea level free air temperature is "standard" (+15°C or 59°F), and the pressure and temperature decrease at a standard rate with an increase in altitude. Adjustments for nonstandard conditions are performed by setting the corrected pressure into a barometric scale on the face of the altimeter; only after this corrected setting is in place does the altimeter indicate the precise altitude.

TYPES OF ALTITUDE

Altitude is vertical distance above some point or level used as a reference. There are as many kinds of altitude as there are reference levels from which altitude is measured, and each may be used for specific reasons. Pilots are mainly concerned with five types of altitude:

- **INDICATED ALTITUDE**—The uncorrected altitude read directly from the altimeter when it is set to the current altimeter setting.
- **TRUE ALTITUDE**—The vertical distance of the airplane above sea level; the actual altitude. It is often expressed as feet above mean sea level (MSL); airport, terrain, and obstacle elevations on aeronautical charts are true altitudes.
- **ABSOLUTE ALTITUDE**—The vertical distance of an airplane above the terrain, or above ground level.
- **PRESSURE ALTITUDE**—The altitude indicated when the altimeter setting window (barometric scale) is adjusted to 29.92. This is the altitude above the standard datum plane, which is a theoretical level where air pressure (corrected to 15°C) equals 29.92 inches of mercury (Hg). Pressure altitude is used to compute density altitude, true altitude, true airspeed, and other performance data.
- **DENSITY ALTITUDE**—This altitude is pressure altitude corrected for variations from standard temperature. When conditions are standard, pressure altitude and density altitude are the same. If the temperature is above standard, the density altitude is higher than pressure altitude. If the temperature is below standard, the density altitude is lower than pressure altitude. This is an important altitude because it is directly related to the airplane's performance.

As an example, consider an airport with a field elevation of 5,048 feet MSL where the standard temperature is 5°C. Under these conditions, pressure altitude and density altitude are the same—5,048 feet. If the temperature changes to 30°C, the density altitude increases to 7,855 feet. This means an airplane would perform on takeoff as though the field elevation were 7,855 feet at standard temperature. Conversely, a temperature of –25°C would result in a density altitude of 1,232 feet. An airplane would have much better performance under these conditions because the denser air would produce more lift.

Hypoxia is a condition caused by insufficient oxygen in the bloodstream (in this context usually caused by unpressurized flight at too high an altitude). Symptoms are impaired reaction, confused thinking, poor judgment, fatigue, headaches, and sometimes euphoria; a prolonged condition can cause loss of consciousness and eventually death. A person with hypoxia may also show bluish lips and fingernail beds. This is generally not an issue below 10,000 feet altitude above mean sea level (MSL), although some people do not experience problems until higher elevations, and mountain climbers may be able to acclimatize themselves to much higher altitudes over time. Federal Aviation Administration (FAA) regulations only require oxygen for flights above 12,500 feet, but the rule of thumb for military flight operations above 10,000 feet is to use oxygen.

VERTICAL SPEED INDICATOR

The vertical speed indicator (VSI), sometimes called a vertical velocity indicator, indicates whether the airplane is climbing, descending, or in level flight. The rate of climb or descent is indicated in feet per minute. If properly calibrated, the VSI indicates zero in level flight. The vertical speed indicator is capable of displaying two different types of information:

- trend information that shows an immediate indication of an increase or decrease in the airplane's rate of climb or descent
- rate information that shows a stabilized rate of change in altitude

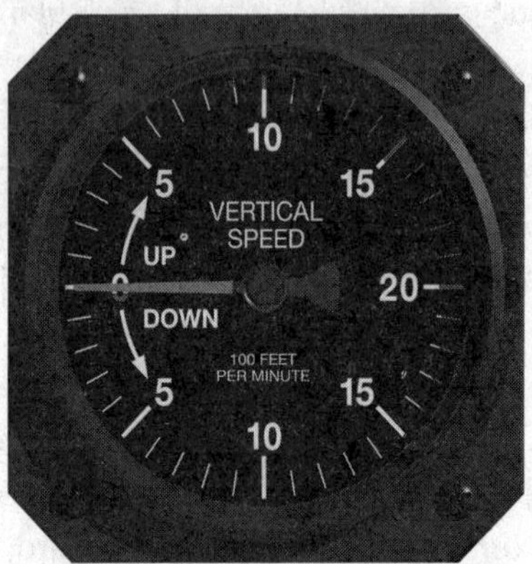

Figure 7.16 Vertical speed indicator

For example, if the airplane is maintaining a steady 500-foot-per-minute (fpm) climb and the nose is lowered slightly, the VSI immediately senses this change and indicates a decrease in the rate of climb. This first indication is called the *trend.* After a short time, the VSI needle stabilizes on the new rate of climb, which in this example is something less than 500 fpm. The time from the initial change in the rate of climb until the VSI displays an accurate indication of the new rate is called the *lag.* Some airplanes are equipped with an instantaneous vertical speed indicator (IVSI), which incorporates accelerometers to compensate for the lag in the typical VSI.

AIRSPEED INDICATOR

The airspeed indicator is a sensitive differential pressure gauge that measures and promptly shows the difference between *pitot* (impact) pressure and static pressure, the undisturbed atmospheric pressure at level flight. These two pressures will be equal when the airplane is parked on the ground in calm air. When the airplane moves through the air, the pressure on the pitot line becomes greater than the pressure in the static lines. This difference in pressure is registered by the airspeed pointer on the face of the instrument, which is calibrated in miles per hour, knots, or both.

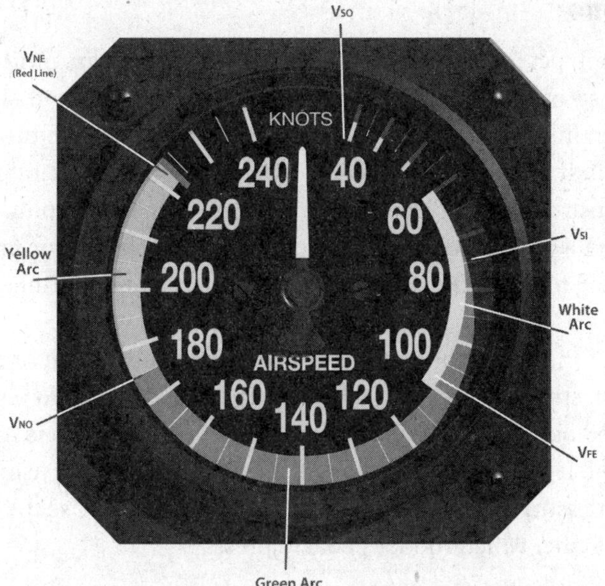

Figure 7.17 Airspeed indicator

There are four airspeed types, which you can remember by using the mnemonic **ICE-T**.

1. **INDICATED AIRSPEED**—measures air pressure reading from the pitot tube.
2. **CALIBRATED AIRSPEED**—airspeed calculated after accounting for aircraft mechanical and position errors (attitude).
3. **EQUIVALENT AIRSPEED**—airspeed calculated after compensating for compression effects; usually only needed at speeds over 200 mph.
4. **TRUE AIRSPEED**—airspeed calculated after accounting for temperature and atmospheric pressure changes.

- **WHITE ARC**—This arc is commonly referred to as the flap operating range, since its lower limit represents the full flap stall speed and its upper limit provides the maximum flap speed. Approaches and landings are usually flown at speeds within the white arc.
- **LOWER LIMIT OF WHITE ARC (V_{SO})**—The stall speed or the minimum steady flight speed in the landing configuration. In small airplanes, this is the power-off stall speed at the maximum landing weight in the landing configuration (gear and flaps down).
- **UPPER LIMIT OF WHITE ARC (V_{FE})**—The maximum speed with the flaps extended.
- **GREEN ARC**—Normal operating range of the airplane; most flying occurs within this range.
- **LOWER LIMIT OF GREEN ARC (V_{S1})**—The stall speed or minimum steady flight speed in a specified configuration; for most airplanes, this is the power-off stall speed at the maximum takeoff weight in the clean configuration (gear up if retractable, and flaps up).
- **UPPER LIMIT OF GREEN ARC (V_{NO})**—The maximum structural cruising speed; do not exceed this speed except in smooth air.
- **YELLOW ARC**—Caution range; fly within this range only in smooth air, and then only with caution.
- **RED LINE (V_{NE})**—Never-exceed speed; operating above this speed is prohibited, because it may result in damage or structural failure.

TURN INDICATORS

Airplanes use two types of turn indicators—the *turn-and-slip indicator* and the *turn coordinator.* Because of the way the gyro is mounted, the turn-and-slip indicator shows only the rate of turn in degrees per second. Because the gyro on the turn coordinator is set at an angle (canted), it initially also shows roll rate. Once the roll stabilizes, it indicates the rate of turn. Both instruments indicate turn direction and coordination, and also serve as a backup source of bank information in the event an attitude indicator fails. Coordination is achieved by referring to the *inclinometer,* which consists of a liquid-filled curved tube with a ball inside.

The inclinometer shows airplane yaw, the side-to-side movement of the airplane's nose. During coordinated, straight and level flight, gravity causes the ball to rest in the lowest part of the tube, centered between the reference lines. Coordinated flight is maintained by keeping the ball centered. If the ball is not centered, it can be centered by using the rudder. To do this, apply rudder pressure on the side where the ball is deflected. Use the simple rule of "step on the ball" to remember which rudder pedal to press.

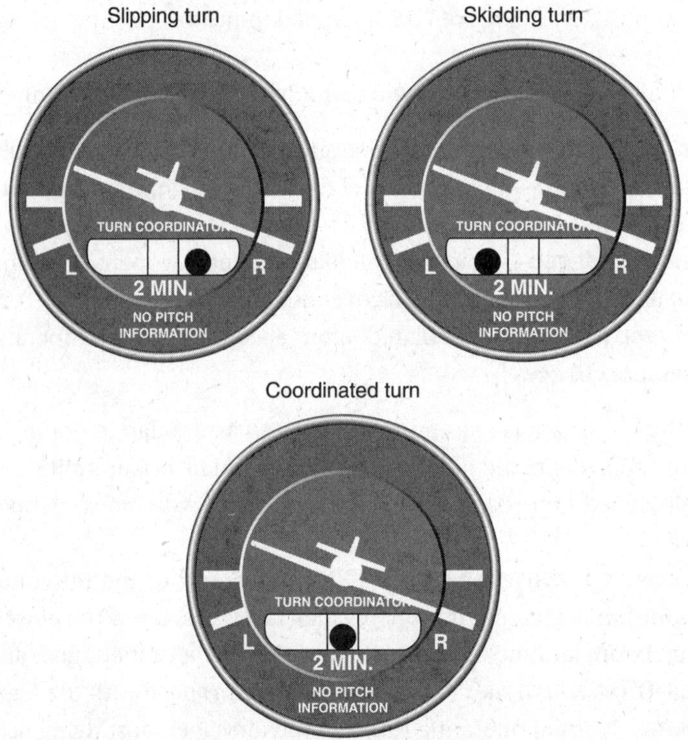

Figure 7.18 Turn coordinator

If aileron and rudder movements are coordinated during a turn, the ball remains centered in the tube. If aerodynamic forces are unbalanced, the ball moves away from the center of the tube.

ARTIFICIAL HORIZON

The *artificial horizon* (also called the *attitude indicator*), with its miniature airplane and horizon bar, displays a picture of the attitude of the airplane. The relationship of the miniature airplane to the horizon bar is the same as the relationship of the real airplane to the actual horizon. The instrument gives an instantaneous indication of even the smallest changes in attitude.

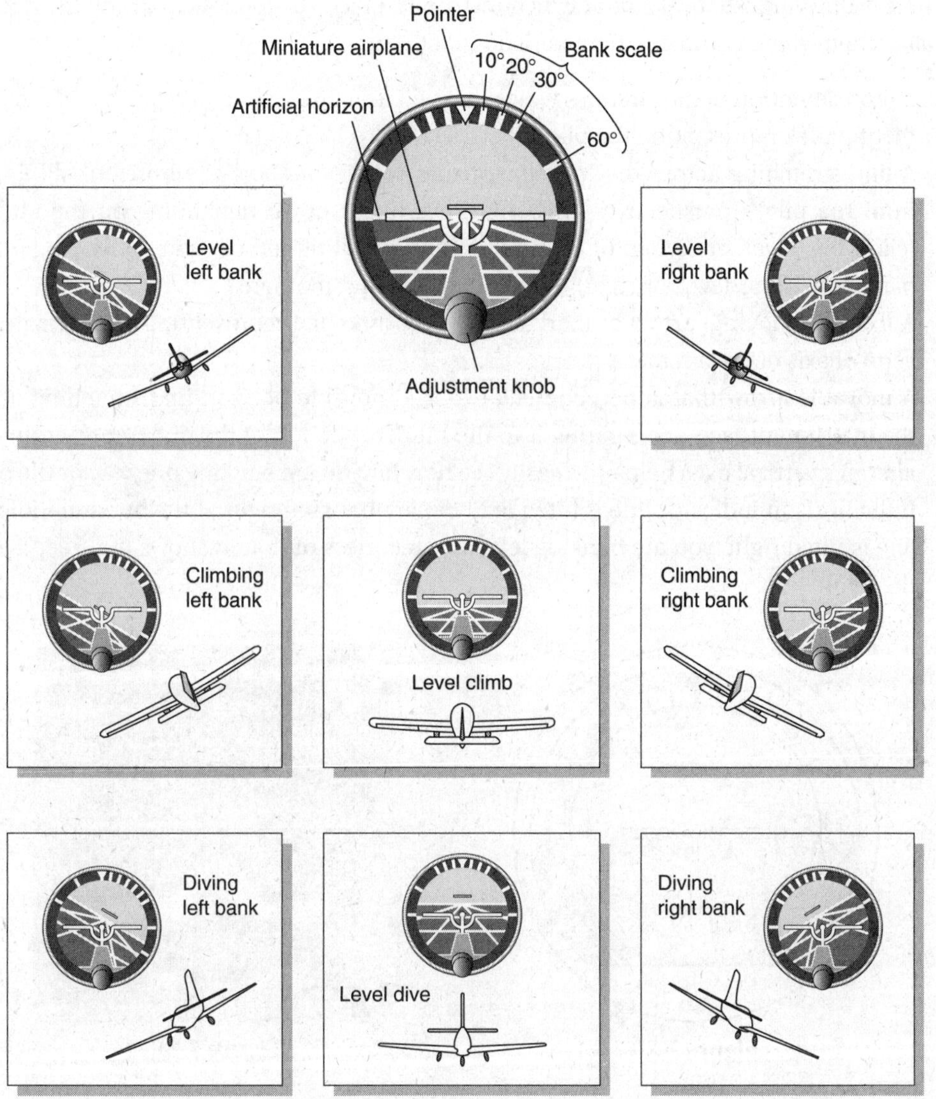

Figure 7.19 Artificial horizon

The gyro in the attitude indicator is mounted rigidly on a horizontal plane. The horizon bar represents the true horizon and is connected to the gyro, remaining in the horizontal plane as the airplane pitches or banks around its lateral or longitudinal axis, indicating the attitude of the airplane relative to the true horizon.

The pilot can use an adjustment knob to move the miniature airplane up or down to align it with the horizon bar as the pilot sees it from his position. Normally, the miniature airplane is adjusted so that the wings overlap the horizon bar when the airplane is in straight and level cruising flight.

The attitude indicator is reliable and the most realistic flight instrument on the instrument panel. What it shows is a very close approximation of the actual attitude of the airplane.

Different aircraft have different styles of artificial horizon instrument faces, but you don't need to be confused—the basics for all of them are the same. Although only the AFOQT actually has an Instrument Comprehension subtest using this instrument (and a magnetic compass), understanding what an artificial horizon shows you is a fundamental skill for all the military flight aptitude tests.

There is differing feedback about which instrument face version is actually on the AFOQT, but all of them share common characteristics, including:

- A representation of the aircraft's wings that will remain horizontal relative to the instrument panel, representing the pilot's perspective
- A line stretching across the instrument that represents how the horizon will appear from the pilot's perspective—this will move up or down depending on the attitude (climbing, level, or diving) of the aircraft, and it will tilt left or right depending on the bank (left, none/level, or right) of the aircraft at that moment
- A fixed (unmoving) arrow or mark at the top of the dial representing the "straight up" vertical axis of the aircraft
- A movable arrow that is perpendicular to the movable horizon line stretching across the instrument face—comparing it to the mark at the top of the dial (representing the aircraft's vertical axis) helps you easily see how far you are banking one way or the other
- If the horizon indicator line is tilted left, you are banking right; if the horizon indicator line is tilted right, you are banking left (the steepness of the tilt shows the steepness of the bank)

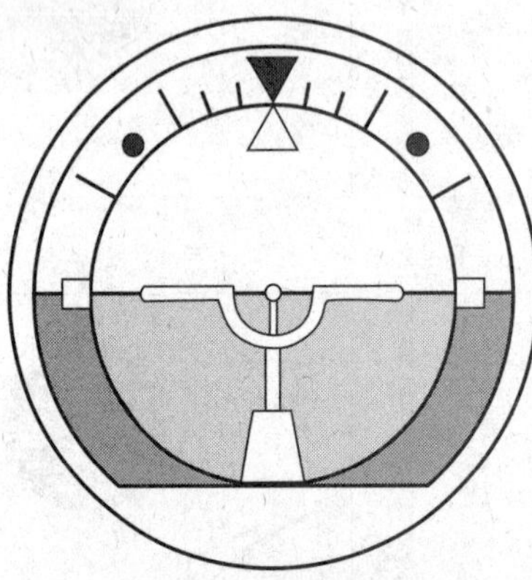

Figure 7.20

Figure 7.21

Figures 7.20 and 7.21 show other styles of artificial horizon instrument faces. One difference you will notice is that Figures 7.19 and 7.20 show instrument faces with hashmarks for 10, 20, 30, and 60 degrees of bank, while the type in Figure 7.21 shows just one hash mark at 45 degrees. Since it is the simplest, we will use the style in Figure 7.21 in the AFOQT practice test questions in this book.

> The AFOQT Instrument Comprehension questions will show you artificial horizon and compass heading instruments. Go to the compass heading *first*, and eliminate any answer choices that are not headed in the right direction. *Then* compare the remaining choices to the artificial horizon graphic to get the correct answer.

MAGNETIC COMPASS

The magnetic compass is usually the only direction-seeking instrument in the airplane. The compass card has letters for cardinal headings, and each 30-degree interval is represented by a number, the last zero of which is omitted. For example, 30° appears as a 3 and 300° appears as a 30. Between these numbers, the card is marked in 5-degree increments. The magnetic compass is required equipment in all airplanes.

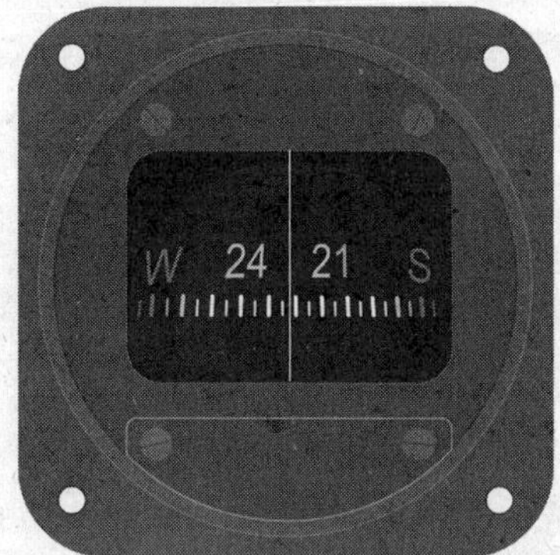

Figure 7.22 Magnetic compass

Although Earth's magnetic field lies *roughly* north and south, the magnetic poles don't exactly coincide with the geographic poles (which are used in the compilation of aeronautical charts). Therefore, at most places on Earth's surface, the direction-sensitive steel needles that seek Earth's magnetic field will not point to true north, but instead to magnetic north. Furthermore, local magnetic fields from mineral deposits and other conditions may distort Earth's magnetic field and cause additional errors.

VERTICAL CARD COMPASS

The vertical card compass is a newer design that significantly reduces the inherent error of the older compass models. It consists of an azimuth on a rotating vertical card, and resembles a heading indicator with a fixed miniature airplane to accurately represent the airplane's heading. The presentation is easy to read, and the pilot can see the complete 360° dial in relation to the airplane heading.

Figure 7.23 Vertical card compass

HEADING INDICATOR

The *heading indicator* or *directional gyro* is a mechanical (not magnetic) instrument that backs up and supplements the magnetic compass. Frequent magnetic compass errors make straight flight and precision turns to exact headings (directions) hard to accomplish, especially in turbulent air. A heading indicator, however, being mechanical, is not affected by the forces that make the magnetic compass difficult to interpret precisely.

Figure 7.24 Heading indicator

Some heading indicators receive a magnetic north reference from a magnetic slaving transmitter, and generally need no adjustment. Heading indicators that don't have this automatic north-seeking capability are called "free" gyros, and require periodic adjustment.

Basic Flight Maneuvers

There are four fundamental flight maneuvers on which all flying tasks are based: straight and level flight, turns, climbs, and descents. All controlled flight consists of one or more of these basic maneuvers.

Straight and level flight is flight where the pilot maintains a constant heading and altitude. It is accomplished by making immediate, measured corrections for deviations in direction and altitude from unintentional slight turns, descents, and climbs.

An aircraft turns by banking the wings in the direction of the desired turn. The pilot chooses a specific bank angle and applies control pressure on the stick or control wheel to achieve it. Once the bank angle is established, the pilot continues to exert the pressure to maintain the desired angle.

All four primary controls are used in close coordination when making turns:

- The ailerons bank the wings and so determine the rate of turn at any given airspeed.
- The elevator moves the nose of the airplane up or down in relation to the pilot, and perpendicular to the wings. In doing so, it both sets the pitch attitude in the turn and "pulls" the nose of the airplane around the turn.
- The throttle controls the engine, which provides thrust that may be used for airspeed to tighten the turn.

- The rudder offsets any yaw effects developed by the other controls. The rudder does not turn the airplane, as many people believe.

Turns are divided into three classes: shallow, medium, and steep.

- Shallow turns are those in which the bank is so shallow (less than about 20°) that the inherent lateral stability of the airplane acts to level the wings unless some aileron is applied to maintain the bank.
- Medium turns result from a degree of bank at which the airplane remains at a constant bank (approximately 20° to 45°).
- Steep turns result from a degree of bank (45° or more) at which the "over-banking tendency" of an airplane overcomes stability, and the bank increases unless aileron is applied to prevent it. Changing the direction of the wing's lift toward one side or the other causes the airplane to be pulled in that direction. The pilot does this by applying coordinated aileron and rudder to bank the airplane in the direction of the desired turn.

When an airplane is flying straight and level, the total lift force is acting perpendicular both to the wings and Earth. As the airplane is banked into a turn, lift then becomes a result of two components. The *vertical* lift component continues to act perpendicular to Earth and opposes gravity. The *horizontal* lift component (centripetal force) acts parallel to Earth's surface and opposes inertia (apparent centrifugal force). These two lift components act at right angles to each other, causing the resultant total lift force to act perpendicular to the banked wing of the airplane. It is the horizontal lift component that actually turns the airplane, not the rudder.

As the pilot applies aileron to bank the airplane, the lowered aileron on the rising wing produces a greater drag than the raised aileron on the lowered wing. This increased aileron yaws the airplane toward the rising wing, or opposite to the direction of turn. To counteract this adverse yawing moment, the pilot must apply rudder pressure simultaneously with aileron in the desired direction to produce a coordinated turn.

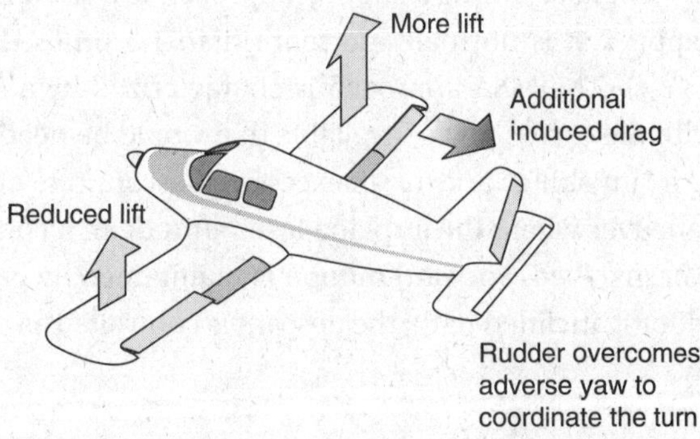

Figure 7.25 Coordinated turn to the left

CLIMBS AND CLIMBING TURNS

When an airplane enters a climb, it changes its flight path from level flight to an inclined plane or *climb attitude*. In a climb, weight no longer acts in a direction perpendicular to the flight path, but instead in a rearward direction. This causes an increase in total drag, requiring an increase in thrust (power) to balance the forces. An airplane can sustain a climb angle only when there is sufficient thrust to offset increased drag; therefore, a climb is limited by the thrust available.

A *normal climb* is performed at an airspeed recommended by the airplane manufacturer, and is generally somewhat higher than the airplane's *best rate of climb.* The additional airspeed provides better engine cooling, easier control, and better visibility over the nose. Normal climb is sometimes referred to as *cruise climb.* Complex or high-performance airplanes may have a specified cruise climb in addition to normal climb.

An airplane's *best rate of climb* (V_y) is performed at an airspeed where the most excess power is available over that required for level flight. This condition of climb will produce the most gain in altitude in the least amount of time (maximum rate of climb in feet per minute). The best rate of climb made at full allowable power is a maximum climb.

An airplane's *best angle of climb* (V_x) is performed at an airspeed that will produce the most altitude gain in a given distance. Best angle-of-climb airspeed (V_x) is considerably lower than best rate of climb (V_y), and is the airspeed where the most excess thrust is available over that required for level flight. The best angle of climb will result in a steeper climb, although the airplane will take longer to reach the same altitude than it would at its best rate of climb. The best angle of climb, therefore, is used in such situations as clearing obstacles after takeoff.

DESCENTS

When an airplane starts a descent, it changes its flight path from level to an inclined plane. There are three main categories of descents:

A *partial power descent* is the normal method of losing altitude, often called *cruise* or *enroute* descent. The airplane manufacturer normally recommends a setting of airspeed and power that will result in a target descent rate of 400–500 fpm. The airspeed may differ anywhere from cruise speed to that used on the downwind leg of the landing pattern. The pilot should keep the desired airspeed, pitch attitude, and power combination steady throughout the descent.

A descent at *minimum safe airspeed* (MSA) is a nose-high, power-assisted descent method mostly used for clearing obstacles during a landing approach to a short runway. The airspeed used for this type of approach is normally no more than 1.3 times the stall speed in the landing configuration (V_{S0}). The MSA approach is characterized by a steeper-than-normal descent angle, along with the excess power available that would be needed to produce acceleration at low airspeed if "mushing" and/or an excessive descent rate occur.

A *glide* is a basic maneuver where the airplane loses altitude in a controlled manner with little or no engine power involved. Forward motion is maintained by gravity pulling the airplane along its down-sloping inclined path; the descent is controlled as the pilot balances the forces of lift and gravity.

POWER AND PITCH

In addition to the dynamics already mentioned, the pilot must understand the effects of both power and elevator control as they work together during different flight conditions. Although there is a wide spectrum of combinations of conditions and settings, the overall rule of thumb for determining airspeed and altitude control runs something like this: *At any pitch attitude, the amount of power used will determine whether the airplane will climb, descend, or remain level at that altitude.*

In the majority of nose-down situations, a descent is the only possible flight condition. If you add power under these circumstances, it will only result in a descent at a faster airspeed. However, through a range of attitudes from only slightly nose-down to about 30° nose-up, a typical light aircraft can be made to climb, descend, or remain level based on the power used. In about the lower third of this range, the airplane will descend at idle power without stalling. As pitch attitude is increased, however, engine power is required to prevent a stall. Even more power will be required to maintain altitude, and yet more to climb. In a small plane, at a pitch attitude of about 30° nose-up, it will take all available power just to maintain altitude. A slight increase in the steepness of the climb, of a slight decrease in power, will result in a descent (whether the pilot intended it or not); again, this is known as "trying to fly outside the envelope." At that point, the slightest inducement will then further result in a stall.

ROTARY-WING AIRCRAFT

A helicopter creates lift in a unique way. It has a rotary "wing," compared to the fixed, stationary wing on an airplane. Where a fixed-wing aircraft has to be moving to produce lift from airflow over the airfoil or wing, a helicopter achieves it by manipulating its rapidly rotating main rotor blades, changing the angle at which they meet the air and diverting it downward. Like a wing, the lift provided by a rotor blade is proportional to its angle of attack. Unlike a wing, the speed of any given spot on the rotor blade increases with its distance from where it is connected to the *rotor hub*.

Helicopters in horizontal flight are subject to the same four forces as an airplane: lift, weight (or gravity), thrust, and drag. One difference, however, is that the thrust from a helicopter's rotors can be applied vertically, as when it's in a hover.

Just like a wing on an airplane, the lift on a wing or rotor blade is proportional to the amount of air diverted downward, multiplied by the vertical velocity of that air, so lift is proportional to the speed squared. That means that the lift of the rotor blade increases rapidly as the distance from the rotor hub increases.

The curved gray lines in Figure 7.26 show the lift produced by a rotor in hover with a constant angle of attack all along the length of the blade. You can see that most of the lift is produced near the blade tips. To improve this, many rotor blades are made with a twist so that the angle of attack decreases as the distance from the rotor hub increases, giving the more uniform lift distribution shown by the black line.

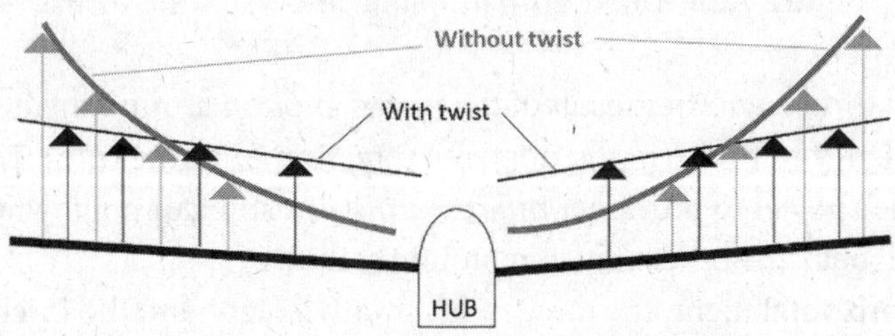

Figure 7.26 Lift distribution of rotor blades with and without a twist

Because the rotor blades are long and thin in cross section, they are fairly flexible. As a result of this and the higher lift loading as the distance from the hub increases, the rotors form a cone as they spin, something like a very shallow inverted ice cream cone.

Figure 7.27 Rotor tip-path plane

The rotor *tip-path plane* is a disk formed by the rotor tips as the rotors spin, often called the *rotor disk.* The force produced by the rotors is perpendicular to this plane. When the tip-path plane is tilted, as shown in Figure 7.28, the force is also tilted, and it can be separated into two components. The vertical component is the lift, which overcomes the weight of the helicopter and can, if large enough, cause the helicopter to increase its altitude. The horizontal component of the force is the thrust, used for forward motion, turns, or to slow the helicopter down.

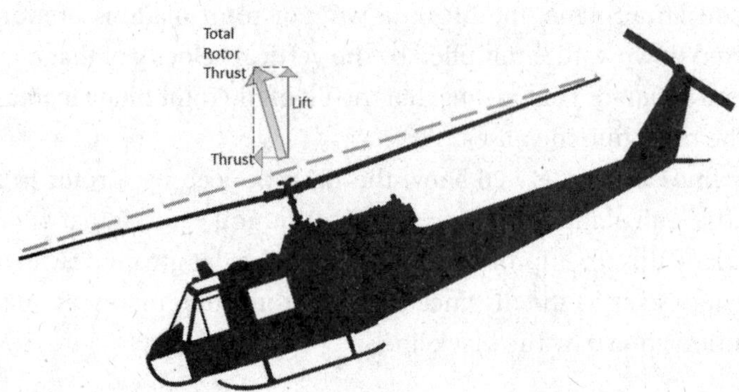

Figure 7.28 Tilted tip-path plane and resulting thrust

Besides lift and thrust, another result of the rotors' motion around the hub is the helicopter fuselage's tendency to rotate in the opposite direction from the rotor. The *tail rotor* uses some of the engine's power to provide *torque control* by pushing or pulling (depending on the helicopter) the tail back the other way to maintain stability.

In stabilized horizontal flight, the force of lift equals weight and the force of thrust equals drag. The difference between hovering and horizontal flight is that, in horizontal flight, the thrust force and drag force are acting horizontally while the lift and weight act vertically. If thrust exceeds drag, then the helicopter increases its horizontal speed. If drag is greater than thrust, then the helicopter decreases its horizontal speed. If lift is greater than weight, then the helicopter climbs. If weight is greater than lift, the helicopter descends. And, because of the helicopter's unique characteristics, horizontal flight is not limited to only the forward direction. This lift, weight, thrust, and drag relationship applies to any direction that the helicopter is moving (forward, sideways, or backward).

Controlling a helicopter's flight path and position is a little more complex than a fixed-wing aircraft. The pilot has three major flight controls: the *cyclic,* whereby the pilot controls longitudinal and lateral movement with a joystick to his front center; the *collective,* which controls pitch (by lifting or lowering the handle) as well as engine torque by means of a throttle that the pilot rotates around the collective handle; and the *directional control system,* where the pilot controls the tail rotor torque and how much or how little it is "pulling" or "pushing" the tail one way or the other. Let's examine these controls in a little more detail.

(Note: Unlike some airplanes, helicopters are very sensitive to pilot inputs and are therefore very responsive. Another difference is that the pilot in command of a helicopter normally sits on the right, as opposed to an airplane's pilot in command, who sits in the left-hand seat.)

The cyclic controls the direction of the tilt of the main rotor. While the helicopter rotors are spinning, if you move the stick forward, the main rotor will tilt forward. If you move the stick backward, the main rotor will tilt backward; move the cyclic to one side and it will tilt the main rotor disc to that side. This control changes the lift and thrust forces. The three axes of movement are still the same, and the terms used to describe movement around (or *about,* as it is sometimes called) any of these axes are the same as with fixed-wing craft.

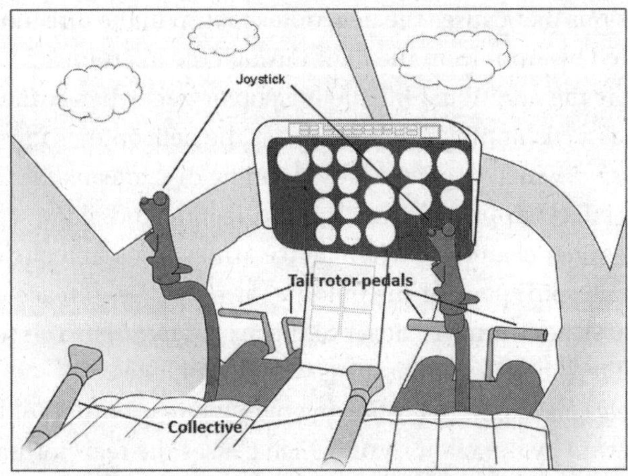

Figure 7.29 Primary helicopter cockpit controls

The collective is a long tube mounted at an angle to the cockpit floor to the left of the pilot; it controls the angle of the main rotor blades. If you pull the collective up, the angle of the main rotor blades increases (the leading edge of the rotor blades will move higher than the trailing edge of the rotor blade). This control affects the lift and thrust forces also. Wrapped around the collective is a throttle control the pilot operates by turning around the tube of the collective.

The tail rotor pedals at the pilot's feet control the pitch of the tail rotor blades and therefore how much the tail rotor pulls or pushes the tail of the aircraft.

To fly the helicopter, the pilot uses all of these controls in combination. By changing the lift and thrust of the main rotor with the cyclic and collective, the pilot can move the helicopter in any direction. Moving the cyclic forward moves the helicopter forward. Moving the cyclic to the left moves the helicopter to the left. Moving the cyclic to the left and forward moves the helicopter forward and to the left. Lifting the collective up causes the helicopter to climb. Lowering the collective causes the helicopter to descend. Moving the cyclic forward and lifting the collective causes the helicopter to increase its forward speed and may result in a climb, depending on how much the collective is raised. The pilot uses pressure from his feet on the tail rotor pedals to control whether the nose yaws left or right; left pedal moves the nose to the left, and right pedal moves the nose to the right.

If you increase the collective and the engine increases power (some helicopters have automatic engine controls that do this for you) to keep the same RPMs to the main rotor, the torque force that's trying to make the cabin spin around will also increase. This requires more left pedal (or pedal opposite to the direction that torque is trying to spin the helicopter) to keep the nose of the helicopter in the same place. So, an increase in collective needs to have an equal increase in pressure on the appropriate tail rotor pedal.

Autorotation is the action of turning a rotor system by airflow rather than engine power, which would be needed in, for instance, an engine failure situation. Airflow up through the rotor system during a power-off descent provides the energy to overcome blade drag and turn the rotor, slowing the descent of the helicopter to a manageable level.

The tail rotor is still important in an autorotation because the pilot needs to have some control over the yaw axis (left and right). During autorotation the tail rotor still turns because it is connected to the main rotor via a transmission; as long as the main rotor is turning (and the transmission is functioning properly), the tail rotor will be turning, too. Torque does not exist during an autorotation, but there is a little bit of drag/friction from the main rotors' and tail rotors' transmissions that causes the helicopter to turn in the direction of the main rotor spin. This is controlled by input from the pilot through the tail rotor.

Translational lift is the additional lift the helicopter gets when it flies out from its own downwash, which has a cushioning effect as long as the helicopter is low enough.

Gyroscopic precession, which applies to any spinning disc, means that a force applied to a spinning disc has its effect happen 90° later in the direction and plane of rotation.

Coriolis force (ice skater example): When an ice skater spins in a circle and her arms are out, they have a certain spin speed. If she pulls her arms in, the spin accelerates because the center of mass of the skater's arms is closer to the axis of rotation. The same thing happens in a helicopter if you replace the skater's arms with rotor blades.

The *transverse flow effect* is when air flowing over the rear portion of the main rotor disc is accelerated downward by the main rotor, which causes the rear portion to have a smaller angle of attack. This results in less lift to the rear portion of the rotor disc, but, because of gyroscopic precession, the result is felt 90° later.

AVIATION AND AEROSPACE HISTORICAL MILESTONES

1783: The French Montgolfier brothers fly in a hot-air balloon for 5.5 miles in 25 minutes.

1861–65: Observation balloons are used by both sides in the Civil War.

1896: American scientist Samuel Langley flies the first (unmanned) powered aircraft.

DEC. 17, 1903: American brothers Orville and Wilbur Wright achieve the first recognized powered, manned flight at Kitty Hawk, North Carolina.

NOV. 14, 1910: First airplane takeoff from a ship (USS *Birmingham*) by Eugene B. Ely.

JAN. 18, 1911: First successful shipboard landing (USS *Pennsylvania*) by Eugene B. Ely.

1913: Igor Sikorsky builds the first multi-engined aircraft in Russia.

1915: The United States establishes the National Advisory Committee for Aeronautics (NACA), the first government-sponsored support of aviation research and development.

1918: U.S. Air Mail service begins.

1919: The first transatlantic air crossing by the Navy and the first nonstop transatlantic air crossing.

1920: Launch of the first aircraft carrier, the USS *Langley*, CV-1.

1926: Robert H. Goddard, considered the father of American rocketry, launches the first liquid propellant rocket.

1927: Charles Lindbergh makes the first solo flight across the Atlantic in the *Spirit of St. Louis*.

1930: The first jet engine is designed and patented by Great Britain's Frank Whittle; however, it is not tested on an airplane until a decade later.

1930: The first practical helicopter design, developed by Russian Igor Sikorsky, has a large main rotor and a smaller vertical rotor on the tail boom, setting a standard for helicopter design still in use today.

1939–45: World War II ushers in mass production of U.S. aircraft, increasing from 500 a year to 50,000 a year by the war's end. The first jet aircraft, a German design, flies in 1939. Coordination of airpower with ground troops in Europe and amphibious landings in the Pacific proves to be a significant advantage for the Allies. The Battles of the Coral Sea and Midway in the Pacific are the first where enemy ships never see each other, and all attacks are by naval aircraft. The P-51 Mustang's laminar-flow wing reduces drag and improves aerodynamics, helping give it the range to escort Allied bombers into Germany. German Luftwaffe deploys the first operational jet, the Me-262 fighter-bomber, in 1944. The B-29 Superfortress is the first bomber with crew cabin pressurization and remote-controlled powered turrets; two B-29s drop atomic bombs on Hiroshima and Nagasaki that end the war in August 1945.

1946: The FH-1 Phantom is the first jet combat aircraft to operate from the deck of a U.S. aircraft carrier and the Navy's first airplane to fly 500 mph.

1947: Chuck Yeager, in the Bell X-1 rocket-powered research aircraft, is the first man to verifiably break the sound barrier. The first swept-wing jet fighter (F-86 Sabrejet) and the first swept-wing multi-engine bomber (B-47 Stratojet) are introduced. The U.S. Air Force is established.

1948: The Berlin Airlift supplies massive amounts of food, fuel, and other vital supplies to Allied West Berlin when East Germans and Soviets cut off ground access, keeping not only U.S. forces but West Berliners alive until tensions ease.

1950–53: The Korean War, launched by the North Korean invasion of South Korea, sees increasing use of jets and helicopters on a three-dimensional battlefield that, after seesaw defense and counterattack in 1950–51, settles down to a near-stalemate for the next two years.

1957: The Soviet Union launches the first satellite into space, beginning the space race between the United States and the U.S.S.R.

1958: The United States launches Explorer I, the first American satellite, into orbit.

1961: The Soviet Union's Yuri Gagarin becomes the first man in space, with a single orbit of Earth. U.S. Navy officer Alan Shepard becomes the first American in space on a suborbital flight in a one-man Mercury space capsule on May 5, 1961.

1962: U.S. Marine officer John Glenn is the first American to orbit Earth.

1963: The Mercury program ends and the Gemini program begins, using more sophisticated two-man capsules to develop space experience and skills leading to a lunar mission capability.

1965–74: Active phase of American involvement in the Vietnam War, characterized by increasing use of close air support, marginally effective strategic bombing, and the introduction of airmobile/air assault doctrine for the Army, which uses helicopters in coordination with ground forces. Near-total U.S. air superiority does not make up for political blunders at home, and public support dwindles until the withdrawal of troops is completed in 1974. North Vietnam takes over South Vietnam in 1975, uniting both under one Communist government.

1966: The Gemini program ends; the Apollo program begins, with the chief goal of putting a man on the moon.

1967: Three American astronauts are killed in a flash fire on the launch pad in *Apollo 1.*

1968: *Apollo 8* orbits the moon and returns.

1969: *Apollo 11* lands two men, civilian test pilot Neil Armstrong and Air Force officer Edwin "Buzz" Aldrin, on the moon on July 20, 1969. A British-French consortium conducts the first flight of the supersonic Concorde passenger jet.

1972: The first spacecraft to explore the outer solar system, *Pioneer 10,* is launched. After completing its study of Jupiter, its trajectory carried it outside the solar system into interstellar space—the first man-made craft to do so. *Pioneer 10* continued transmitting data until 2003, when its power source became too weak. By then, it was over 7.6 billion miles from Earth; in about two million years, it should reach the red giant Aldebaran, about 71 light-years away.

1973–74: *Skylab,* an American orbital space station, has three crews spend several months each in orbit, providing proof that man could tolerate weightlessness for extended periods.

1975: NASA collaborates with the Soviet space agency on the Apollo-Soyuz Test Project, where crews from each country rendezvoused and docked; the last flight of the Apollo-Saturn hardware.

1981: The first flight of the space shuttle *Columbia* on April 12, 1981.

1986: The space shuttle *Challenger* explodes during liftoff; all aboard are killed.

1986: The Russian space station *Mir* is launched.

1988: The F-117 Nighthawk stealth fighter enters operational service.

1991: The Persian Gulf War begins with a month-long aerial bombardment that drastically cuts Saddam Hussein's forces' communication, resupply, and antiaircraft capabilities.

1993: The B-2 Spirit stealth bomber enters operational service.

1998: The first components of the International Space Station are placed in orbit.

2000: The supersonic transatlantic passenger jet Concorde is retired from service; the first crew occupies the International Space Station.

2003: The space shuttle *Columbia* breaks up during reentry; all seven aboard are killed.

2004: Mars exploration rovers *Spirit* and *Opportunity* land on Mars; *Spirit* functions until 2010 and *Opportunity* is still functioning as of April 2018. *SpaceShipOne* becomes the first privately built craft to enter outer space.

2005: The F-22 Raptor, a stealth air superiority fighter, enters USAF service.

2010: The International Space Station marks 10 years of continuous human occupation.

2011: Space shuttle fleet retired.

2013: The U.S. Navy's unmanned X-47B executes successful carrier takeoffs and landings.

2015: The U.S. Marine Corps declares its first squadron of F-35B Lightning II STOVL stealth fighters ready for deployment.

2016: The U.S. Air Force declares its first squadron of conventional takeoff and landing F-35A Lightning II stealth fighters combat ready.

2018: The F-35C Lightning II—the Navy's carrier-capable variant of the stealth fighter family—completes fleet carrier qualifications.

AIRPORT AND RUNWAY INFORMATION

A *runway* is a strip of land on which aircraft can take off and land; it is part of the *maneuvering* or *movement area,* which also includes taxiways and other areas controlled by the air traffic control tower. Runway surfaces can be composed of a man-made material (usually asphalt, concrete, or a mixture) or natural ones, such as grass, dirt, or gravel.

Runways are named from 01–36 for a one-tenth value of their heading or direction, rounded to the nearest 10 degrees—so a runway pointing east (90°) would be "runway 09," a runway pointing west (270°) would be "runway 27," and so on.

Runways in North America use true or *geographic north* (also known as *grid north*) instead of *magnetic north* because magnetic compass needles point toward the magnetic north pole, which is in the Arctic Ocean about a thousand miles south of the geographic north pole. The magnetic north pole also actually moves from 5 to 25 miles (9 to 41 km) per year because of currents in the magma far below Earth's surface.

Since most runways can be used coming from or going to either direction, they can be considered to have two identities. "Runway 30" would be coming in from the southeast or taking off to the northwest with a heading of 300°, whereas the same runway would be referred to as "runway 12," coming in from the northwest or taking off to the southeast. The numbers always differ by 18, indicating a difference of 180° or half of the compass.

Runway numbers are also spoken one by one to avoid confusion. In the examples above, these would be spoken of as "runway three zero" and "runway one two" instead of "runway thirty" or "runway twelve."

If two or more runways are parallel, heading in the same direction (also known as *dual*), they are differentiated by adding "left," "center," or "right" to the number. For example, if two runways both run east/west, the northernmost runway when heading west (270°) would be runway 27R (spoken as "runway two seven right") and the other, runway 09L (spoken as "runway zero nine left"), when heading east (90°). These numbers are marked on the end of the runway, called the *threshold.* Runways will also usually have other markings besides the end number; they will probably have white stripes down the middle and solid white lines at the edges. Larger runways will also usually have a band of white stripes across the threshold and other markings to indicate an aiming point for aircraft touchdown and distance to the end of the runway.

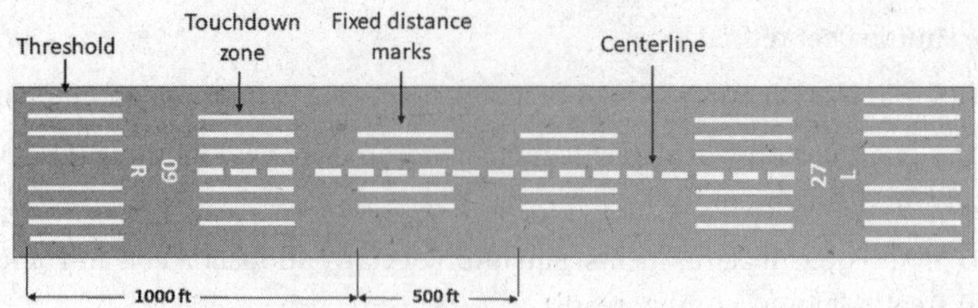

Figure 7.30 Typical runway oriented east/west

Fixed-wing aircraft usually try to take off and land into the wind to increase airflow over the wing and thereby increase lift, at the same time decreasing the ground speed needed.

Runways vary in size from general aviation airports as small as 800 ft. (244 m) long and 26 ft. (8 m) wide to international airports as large as 18,000 ft. (5,500 m) long and 260 ft. (80 m) wide. At sea level, a 10,000-ft. (3,000-m) runway can land virtually any aircraft. However, even an average size aircraft will need a longer runway at higher altitudes or in hotter, more humid conditions due to the decreased air density, which reduces lift and engine power.

A runway of at least 6,000 ft. (1,800 m) in length is usually adequate for aircraft weighing less than about 200,000 lbs. (90,000 kg). Larger aircraft usually require at least 8,000 ft. (2,400 m) at sea level and somewhat more at airports with higher altitudes. International "wide-body" flights, which carry substantial amounts of fuel and are therefore heavier, may also have landing requirements of up to 10,000 ft. (3,000 m) or more and takeoff requirements of up to 13,000 ft. (4,000 m) or more.

Runway markings are white, and may be outlined in black for greater visibility and contrast. Heliport landing area markings are also white, except for hospital heliports, which use a red "H" on a white cross. Markings for taxiways, areas not intended for use by aircraft, and holding positions—even if they are on a runway—are yellow.

There are three types of runways: *visual, nonprecision instrument,* and *precision instrument.* Visual runways such as those at small airstrips usually have no markings, but they may have threshold markings, designators, and centerlines. They do not provide an instrument-based landing procedure—pilots must be able to see the runway to use it. Also, radio communication may not be available, so pilots must be self-reliant.

Nonprecision instrument runways are most often seen at small- to medium-size airports. Depending on the surface, these runways may be marked with threshold markings, designators, centerlines, and sometimes a 1,000-ft. (304.80-km) or 1,500-ft. (457.20-km) mark known as an *aiming point.* They provide horizontal position guidance to planes on instrument approach.

Precision instrument runways, seen at medium- and large-size airports, usually consist of a blast pad/stopway, threshold, designator, centerline, aiming point, and touchdown zone marks at 500-ft. intervals from 500 ft. (152 m) to 3,000 ft. (914 m). Precision runways provide pilots with both horizontal and vertical guidance for instrument approaches.

Airports that allow night landings use runway lighting to mark their runways, including some or all of the following, among others:

- Approach Lighting System (ALS): a series of lightbars, strobe lights, or a combination of the two that extends outward from the approach end of the runway.

- Runway End Identification Lights (REIL): a pair of synchronized flashing lights installed at the runway threshold, one on each side. They can face the approach direction or be omnidirectional (visible from all directions). They enhance identification of a runway surrounded by other lighting or lacking contrast with the surrounding terrain, as well as during reduced visibility.
- Runway end lights: a pair of four lights on each side of precision instrument runways, extending the full width of the runway. These lights show green when viewed by approaching aircraft and red when seen from the runway to indicate the end of the runway to a departing aircraft.
- Runway edge lights: white elevated lights running the length of the runway on both sides. On precision instrument runways, the edge lighting becomes yellow in the last 2,000 ft. (610 m) or half the runway length, whichever is greater. Taxiways are differentiated by being bordered by omnidirectional blue lights, or by having green center lights, depending on the width of the taxiway and the complexity of the taxi pattern.
- Runway Centerline Lighting System (RCLS): white lights embedded in the surface of the runway along the centerline at 50-ft. (15-m) intervals, changing to alternating red and white 3,000 ft. (915 m) from the end of the runway, and then to red for the last 1,000 ft. (305 m).

Larger airports may also have a Visual Approach Slope Indicator (VASI), which is a system of lights that provides descent guidance information during an approach to a runway. The system uses red lights to indicate the upper glide path limits and white lights for lower limits. The VASI is visible for 3–5 miles during the day and up to 20 miles or more at night. The VASI's visual glide path provides safe obstruction clearance within about 10 degrees of the extended runway centerline and to up to four nautical miles from the runway threshold.

Runway lights are usually operated by the airport or airfield control tower. Smaller airports may not have lighted runways or runway markings; there may be nothing more than a wind sock beside a landing strip, particularly at small private airfields for light planes.

NAUTICAL INFORMATION

The U.S. Navy was founded on October 13, 1775, and the Department of the Navy was established on April 30, 1798. The Department of the Navy has three principal components: the Navy Department, consisting of executive offices mostly in Washington, D.C.; the operating forces, including the Marine Corps, the reserve components, and, in wartime, the U.S. Coast Guard (a component of the Department of Homeland Security in peacetime); and the shore establishment.

The U.S. Navy and the U.S. Marine Corps, two independent military services, comprise the Naval Services. The Navy has a traditional pyramidal structure; the management of money, personnel, and materiel in the Navy is no different than that of most large corporations.

The Navy's operating forces are subordinate to the six multiservice (joint) Geographic Combatant Commands: Northern Command, Southern Command, European Command, Pacific Command, Central Command, and Africa Command.

The independent carrier battle group or strike group is usually considered the primary building block of projecting power or responding to a crisis. Operating in international waters, the carrier battle group does not need the permission of a host country for landing or overflight rights, nor does it need to build or maintain bases in countries where a U.S. presence may cause political or other strains. Aircraft carriers are sovereign U.S. territory that can and do steam anywhere in international waters—and, it's useful to note, most of the surface of the globe is water.

By using the oceans both as a means of access and as a base, forward-deployed Navy and Marine forces are readily available to provide the United States with a flexible range of national response capabilities. These capabilities range from "simply showing the flag"—just a presence to let people in the region know that the United States is interested in what's going on—to insertion of forces ashore.

The typical air wing aboard a U.S. Navy aircraft carrier usually contains three to four FA-18 squadrons, one EA-6B squadron, and one E-2C squadron. They also include a logistic support squadron, an antisubmarine warfare helicopter squadron, and an antisurface warfare helicopter squadron. Flight operations resemble a well-choreographed ballet. Those involved in the "evolution" (one specific but multi-role task, such as launching aircraft, landing aircraft, or refueling at sea) have specific, clearly defined roles, and are easily recognizable by the color of their jerseys.

PURPLE: aviation fuels (nicknamed "grapes")

BLUE: plane handlers, aircraft elevator operators, airplane tractor drivers, messengers and phone talkers

GREEN: catapult and arresting gear crews, air wing maintenance personnel, cargo-handling personnel, ground support equipment troubleshooters, hook runners, photographer's mates, helicopter landing signal enlisted personnel

YELLOW: aircraft handling officers, catapult and arresting gear officers, plane directors

RED: ordnancemen, crash and salvage crews, explosive ordnance disposal

BROWN: air wing plane captains, air wing line leading petty officers

WHITE: air wing quality control personnel, squadron plane inspectors, the landing signal officer, air transfer officers, liquid oxygen crews, safety observers, medical personnel

The active duty Marine Corps is officially organized into three ground divisions and three aircraft wings, with a large combat support force formed into three service support groups. The Marine Corps Reserve consists of an additional ground division, aircraft wing, and support group. These divisions and wings can be considered the administrative structure for Marine units deployed in Marine Air-Ground Task Forces (MAGTFs). The MAGTF is the basic building block of Marine Corps operating forces, and is an integrated, combined-arms force made up of command, ground combat, aviation combat, and service support elements. Regardless of size—from relatively small, special purpose MAGTFs to multidivision-size Marine Expeditionary Forces (MEFs)—all MAGTFs are "expeditionary" forces, capable of carrying out specific missions. For example, MEFs comprising 40,000 or more troops are capable of amphibious assaults and sustained operations for up to 60 days without a resupply of ammunition, food, water, and other supplies.

Many nautical terms, phrases, and practices come from situations in the days when naval vessels were made of wood and propelled by the wind. By no means will all of these terms be tested on the Navy/Marine Corps/Coast Guard Aviation Selection Test Battery (ASTB-E); however, since test questions are closely guarded secrets and change from version to version and from time to time, it is wise for the examinee to be familiar with as much naval terminology as possible to gain the best possible understanding of a test question. Therefore, this section provides not only definitions but in some cases historical context.

Nautical Terms and Phrases

AHOY—ship-to-ship or ship-to-shore combination greeting and attention-getting term, usually when one party is unknown to the other.

AIRDALE—part of the aircraft-related crew.

ALL HANDS—a directive or reference applying to everyone hearing the message, usually directing them to perform their specific function as part of a collective task for the ship to accomplish, as in "All hands to quarters," "All hands up anchor," etc.

ANCHORS AWEIGH—the anchor has broken contact with the floor or surface at the bottom of the body of water.

ARRESTING CABLES—Each carrier-based aircraft has a tailhook, a hook bolted to an 8-foot bar extending from the after part of the aircraft. It is with the tailhook that the pilot catches one of the four steel cables stretched across the deck at 20-foot intervals, bringing the plane, traveling at 150 miles per hour, to a complete stop in about 320 feet. The cables are set to stop each aircraft at the same place on the deck, regardless of the size or weight of the plane.

AYE or **AYE AYE**—an acknowledgment of an order with the understanding that the receiver will execute it.

BARGE—small boat used to transport personnel or light cargo.

BEFORE THE MAST—generally refers to the enlisted part of the crew, especially when comparing them with officers. On sailing ships, this was a literal term referring to the physical location of the enlisted sailors' living quarters on the ship, which were in the forecastle (the part of the ship forward of or "before" the foremast).

BELAY—to make fast or secure to a pin or cleat, as in "belay that line."

"BELAY THAT"—disregard the order or information referred to, or cease work if the order has already been partially executed.

BILGE—water that has leaked into the ship and/or wastewater that can accumulate in a holding tank or empty space until it is pumped out.

BINNACLE LIST—a ship's sick list. On sailing ships, a binnacle was the stand on which the ship's compass was mounted; a list of men unable to report for duty was given to the officer or mate of the watch, who kept the list at the binnacle.

BLACK GANG or **BLACKGANG**—the engine room crew.

BLUEJACKET—enlisted sailor.

BOARDING A SMALL BOAT OR ENTERING A CAR—When boarding a small boat or entering a car, juniors enter first and take up the seats or the space beginning forward, leaving the most desirable seat for the senior. Seniors enter last and leave first.

BOATSWAIN or **BOSUN**—the sailor or petty officer in charge of the deck force or a specific section of the ship's crew.

BOOT CAMP—basic training given to new (recruit) sailors and Marines. During the Spanish-American War (1898–1902), sailors wore leggings called boots; this came to mean a Navy or Marine recruit.

BOOT ENSIGN—the most senior ensign of a Navy ship, squadron, or shore activity. In addition to his or her normal duties, the boot ensign teaches less-experienced ensigns about life at sea, planning and coordinating wardroom social activities, making sure that the officers' mess runs smoothly, and generally trying to make sure that the junior ensigns don't embarrass themselves or the Navy. Even though the position usually has little official authority, the boot ensign can also serve as the focus of the unit's expression of pride and spirit. Also called "bull ensign."

BOW—the front of the ship.

BRAVO ZULU—well done.

BRIDGE—This is every ship's primary control position when it is under way, and the place where all orders and commands affecting the ship, her movements, and routine originate.

"BRING SHIP TO ANCHOR"—bring the ship to a halt and drop the anchor.

BULKHEAD—a wall or other vertical surface, especially on a ship.

BUTTERBAR—someone with the lowest officer rank, pay grade O-1 ensign or second lieutenant, whose rank insignia is one gold-colored rectangular bar; usually carries a connotation of a lack of experience.

"CAST OFF ALL LINES"—disconnect or let go all lines connecting a ship with a dock or another ship.

CATAPULTS — The four steam-powered catapults on an aircraft carrier's deck thrust a 48,000-lb. aircraft 300 feet, from zero to 165 mph, in two seconds. On each plane's nose gear is a T-bar that locks into the catapult shuttle, which pulls the plane down the catapult's length. The flight deck crew can launch two aircraft and land one every 37 seconds in daylight, and one per minute at night.

"COME LEFT/RIGHT TO COURSE"—make a slight change in course or heading, usually less than 15 degrees.

COURSE—the ship's direction or compass heading, expressed in degrees or, less frequently, in cardinal directions.

COXSWAIN—the helmsman of a ship. Originally the coxswain (pronounced "coxun") was the swain (boy servant) in charge of the small cockboat kept aboard for the ship's captain, which was used to row him to and from the ship. With time this has come to mean the helmsman of any boat or ship, regardless of size.

DAVY JONES' LOCKER—the floor of the ocean.

DECK—floor or other horizontal surface, especially on a ship.

DOGWATCH—the period of time at sea between 4 and 6 P.M. (first dogwatch) or 6 and 8 P.M. (second dogwatch).

DRILL—a standardized sequence of actions designed to react to a possible situation; used to practice skills and improve proficiency.

DUFFLE or **DUFFEL**—a sailor's personal effects. Referring not only to the sailor's clothing but also the seabag in which he carries and stows it, the term comes from the Flemish town of Duffel near Antwerp, where a rough woolen cloth made there was often used to make the seabags.

EASE THE RUDDER—decrease the current rudder angle (with zero degrees being amidships). This command is normally given when the ship is turning too fast or is coming to the course required, e.g., "Ease your rudder to 5 degrees."

ELEVATORS—Each of a carrier's four deck-edge elevators can lift two aircraft from the cavernous hangar deck to the 4.5-acre flight deck in seconds.

FATHOM—a standardized nautical unit of measurement equaling six feet, usually referring to depth of water.

"GANGWAY"—get out of the way; make way for someone or something coming through an area.

GENERAL QUARTERS—all hands man their battle stations on the double (at a run).

HANDSOMELY—slowly and carefully.

HATCH—doorway.

HEAD—a ship's toilet, or, more generally, any toilet.

JONES, CAPTAIN JOHN PAUL (1747–1792)—acknowledged as the "Father of the American Navy," Revolutionary War naval hero. As a ship's captain, he made daring raids along the British coast, including the famous victory of the *Bonhomme Richard* over HMS *Serapis*, where Jones is reputed to have said, "I have not yet begun to fight!" when asked to surrender.

KEELHAUL—a naval punishment used by some European navies in the 15th and 16th centuries. A rope was rigged from yardarm to yardarm under the bottom of the ship, and the offender was secured to it, sometimes with weights on his legs. He was hoisted up to one yardarm and then dropped suddenly into the sea, hauled underneath the keel or bottom of the ship, and then hauled up to the other yardarm. Because many ships accumulated barnacles and other rough places on the underside of the ship's hull—and because it took a significant amount of time to haul the offender underneath a larger ship, all underwater—not all recipients survived the procedure.

KNOT—a unit of speed measuring one nautical mile (1.15 statute miles, 1.85 km) per hour.

"MAN OVERBOARD"—a command directing designated sailors to man their boat or boats and pick up the man as soon as possible; special conditions may apply for wartime.

"MAN YOUR BOAT"—a command for all hands or designated sailors to take their stations in the boats used for abandoning ship or moving outside the ship to another ship, dock, etc.

MARINE CORPS BIRTHDAY—One of the most famous Marine customs is the observance of the Marine Corps Birthday. Since 1921, the birthday of the Marine Corps has been officially celebrated each year on November 10, since it was on this date in 1775 that the Continental Congress resolved "that two Battalions of Marines be raised." Over the years, the event has been celebrated in a wide variety of ways, but the celebration generally involves the reading of an excerpt from the Marine Corps Manual and a birthday message from the Marine Corps Commandant; the cutting of a birthday cake by the commanding officer; and the presentation of the first and second pieces of cake to the oldest and youngest Marines present. In recent years, the ceremony for the Marine Corps Birthday observance by large posts and stations has been incorporated into written directives.

MAYDAY—internationally recognized distress call used on voice radio for vessels and people in serious trouble at sea or in the air. Derived from the French *m'aidez* ("help me") and officially recognized by an international telecommunications conference in 1948.

"MEATBALL"—a series of lights that aids carrier pilots when lining up for landing. In the center are amber and red lights with Fresnel lenses. Although the lights are always on, the Fresnel lens makes only one light at a time seem to glow, as the angle at which the pilot looks at the lights changes. If the lights appear above the green horizontal bar, the pilot is too high. If it is below, the pilot is too low, and if the lights are red, the pilot is very low. If the red lights on either side of the amber vertical bar are flashing, it is a wave-off, meaning "don't land."

NAUTICAL MILE—unit of measurement used in air and sea navigation equal to 1,852 meters or about 6,076 feet; derived from the length of one minute of arc of a great circle.

OFFICER OF THE DECK (OOD)—is always on the bridge when the ship is under way. Each OOD stands a four-hour watch and is the officer designated by the commanding officer to be in charge of the ship. The OOD is responsible for the safety and operation of the ship, including navigation, ship handling, communications, routine tests and inspections, reports, supervision of the watch team, and carrying out the Plan of the Day. Also on the bridge are the helmsman, who steers the ship, and the lee helmsman, who operates the engine order control, telling the engine room what speed to make. There are also lookouts, and the **boatswain's mate of the watch (BMOW)** who supervises the helmsman, lee helmsman, and lookouts. The **quartermaster of the watch** assists the OOD in navigation, reports all changes in weather, temperature, and barometer readings, and keeps the ship's log.

ON THE DOUBLE—quickly, on the run.

PORT—referring to the left side of a ship when facing the bow, or front.

"PRI-FLY"—Primary Flight Control ("Pri-Fly") is the control tower for the flight operations on the carrier. Here, the "air boss" controls takeoffs, landings, aircraft in the air near the ship, and the movement of planes on the flight deck, which resembles a well-choreographed ballet.

RUDDER AMIDSHIPS—orient the rudder along the long axis of the ship; straight ahead.

RUNNING LIGHTS—Required on all boats over 15 ft. (5 m) by international regulations, these lights are red on the left (port) side, green on the right (starboard) side, and white to the rear. Side running lights are visible from both the side and front of the craft.

SCUBA—an acronym for "self-contained underwater breathing apparatus."

SCUTTLEBUTT—gossip or rumors; because sailors stopped to talk and exchange gossip when they gathered at the cask of drinking water (called a "scuttlebutt") on board sailing ships, this became Navy slang referring to information or speculation, and eventually slang for any gossip or rumor. (A *butt* was a wooden cask for holding water or other liquids; to *scuttle* was to drill a hole, as when one taps a cask.)

SEMPER FIDELIS—Latin for "always faithful," the motto of the Marine Corps.

SEMPER PARATUS—Latin for "always ready," the motto of the Coast Guard.

SHIPSHAPE—in good order and function; squared away.

SMOKING LAMP—If it's "lit," you have permission to smoke; if it's not, you don't. Seldom used literally.

SONAR—underwater detection device using sound and echo detection.

STARBOARD—the right side as one is facing forward.

"STEADY AS YOU GO"—maintain the course the ship is on at the moment the command is given.

STERN—the rear of the ship.

STRIKING THE COLORS/ENSIGN/FLAG—Lowering or "striking" the ship's flag is the universally recognized sign of surrender.

"TOE THE LINE"—Once a literal command to gather on deck with one's toes on a line, now it means to give full obedience to orders or give extra attention to detail.

"TURN TO"—begin ship's work.

UNCOVER—to remove one's hat or headgear.

UP ANCHOR—raise the anchor and prepare to get under way.

"VERY WELL"—an officer's response indicating that a report is understood.

WARDROOM—the officer's dining room that is also used for meetings and other functions.

WATCHES—Watches at sea are divided into four-hour intervals:

Morning watch: 4 A.M. to 8 A.M. (0400–0800 hours)

Forenoon watch: 8 A.M. to noon (0800–1200 hours)

Afternoon watch: noon to 4 P.M. (1200–1600 hours)

Dogwatch: 4 P.M. to 8 P.M. (1600–2000 hours) (also divided into first and second dogwatches)

Nightwatch: 8 P.M. to midnight (2000–2400 hours)

Midwatch: midnight to 4 A.M. (2400–0400 hours)

"WHAT'S YOUR HEADING?"—a directive to report the course (compass heading) the ship is on.

Combatant Ship and Craft Categories

Category	Designation
Multi-Purpose Nuclear-Powered Aircraft Carrier	CVN
Surface Combatant	
Guided Missile Cruiser	CG
Guided Missile Destroyer	DDG
Guided Missile Frigate	FFG
Littoral Combat Ship	LCS
Submarine	
Nuclear-Powered Submarine	SSN
Nuclear-Powered Ballistic Missile Submarine	SSBN
Nuclear-Powered Guided Missile Submarine	SSGN
Amphibious Warfare	
General Purpose Amphibious Assault Ship	LHA
Multi-Purpose Amphibious Assault Ship	LHD
Amphibious Transport Dock	LPD
Dock Landing Ship	LSD
Mine Warfare	
Mine Countermeasures Ship	MCM
Combat Logistics (Underway Replenishment)	
Ammunition Ship	AE
Combat Store Ship	AFS
Oiler	AO
Fast Combat Support Ship	AOE
Dry Cargo and Ammunition Ship	AKE
Fleet Support	
Command Ship	LCC
Submarine Tender	AS
Joint High Speed Vessel	JHSV
Surveillance	AGOS
Salvage Ship	ARS

Amphibious Warfare Craft

Air Cushion Landing Craft	LCAC
Mechanized Landing Craft	LCM
Light Personnel Landing Craft	LCPL
Utility Landing Craft	LCU
Mark V Special Operations Craft	Mk V SOC
Naval Special Warfare Rigid-Hulled Inflatable Boat	NSW RHIB
SEAL Delivery Vehicle	SDV
Special Operations Craft-Riverine	SOC-R

Naval Aviation Unit Designations*

FRS	Fleet Readiness Squadron
HC	Helicopter Combat Support Squadron
HCS	Helicopter Combat Support Special Squadron
HM	Helicopter Mine Countermeasures Squadron
HMH	(Marine) Heavy Helicopter Squadron
HMLA	(Marine) Light Attack Helicopter Squadron
HMM	(Marine) Medium Helicopter Squadron
HMX	(Marine) Helicopter Squadron
HS	Helicopter Anti-Submarine Squadron
HSC	Helicopter Sea Combat Squadron
HSL	Light Helicopter Anti-Submarine Squadron
HSM	Helicopter Maritime Strike Squadron
HT	Helicopter Training Squadron
HUQ	Unmanned Helicopter Reconnaissance Squadron
MAG	Marine Aircraft Group
MAW	Marine Aircraft Wing
VAQ	Electronic Attack Squadron
VAW	Carrier Airborne Early Warning Squadron
VF	Fighter Squadron
VFA	Strike Fighter Squadron
VFC	Fighter Composite Squadron
VMAQ	(Marine) Electronic Warfare Squadron
VMFA	(Marine) Fighter-Attack Squadron
VMFA (AW)	(Marine) Fighter-Attack Squadron (All-Weather)
VMGR	(Marine) Refueler-Transport Squadron
VMM	(Marine) Medium-Lift Tilt-Rotor Squadron
VMR	(Marine) Transport Squadron
VMU	(Marine) Unmanned Aerial Vehicle Squadron
VP	Patrol Squadron
VQ	Fleet Air Reconnaissance Squadron
VR	Fleet Logistics Support Squadron
VS	Sea Control Squadron

*Note: This list is not all-inclusive; only the most common operational unit types are included.

8 Science Review

INTRODUCTION

Science can generally be divided into life, physical, and earth sciences, although there is a great deal of overlap between these categories. The science-related questions on the three military flight aptitude tests focus primarily on the physical sciences as they relate to aviation and aerospace concerns, so this review will focus on those areas, too, with special emphasis on mechanical comprehension.

THE SCIENTIFIC METHOD

The *scientific method* is an organized way of solving problems and explaining phenomena. It has evolved over many centuries with contributions from many cultures, with some early versions dating back to 1600 B.C. Today's versions differ in details and labels, but roughly follow the same thought process:

1. **OBSERVATION.** This step requires the accurate observation and recording of a specific occurrence. The accuracy of an initial sighting can be confirmed when a number of independent observers agree that they see the same set of circumstances occurring under the same conditions multiple times. This step includes collecting information, making observations, and asking questions, as appropriate.
2. **HYPOTHESIS.** A temporary or working conclusion based on a set of observations, or *hypothesis*, is usually a very general statement about why (based on the observations to that point) the scientist thinks something happens in the way that it does. It usually suggests the need for an experiment.
3. **EXPERIMENT.** Scientists perform *experiments* to test a specific hypothesis. Reliable experiments require controlled conditions and careful recording of data.
4. **THEORY.** A hypothesis becomes a *theory* when it is supported by one or more experiments; the original hypothesis is usually modified somewhat based on experimental data before it is acknowledged as a theory.
5. **LAW OR PRINCIPLE.** When a theory is repeatedly confirmed over a long period of time by multiple experiments, it is called a *law* or *principle*.

It's often helpful to identify a *mnemonic* (memory aid) for the steps in the scientific method.

- Observation
- Hypothesis
- Experiment
- Theory
- Law or principle

One way to help you remember these steps in order is to make up a sentence where each word starts with the same letter as the steps you want to remember (interestingly, most people remember odd or silly sentences better). A popular example is a sentence used to help remember the names and order of the planets in the solar system:

Mnemonic	Actual List
My	Mercury
Very	Venus
Eager	Earth
Mother	Mars
Just	Jupiter
Served	Saturn
Us	Uranus
Noodles	Neptune

When Pluto was still considered a planet, this sentence ended with "nine pizzas" instead of "noodles." There are lots of variations. For the steps in the scientific method, try, "**O**nly **H**eavy **E**ggs **T**aste **L**ousy." Even better, make up your own version—you will be more likely to remember it.

PHYSICAL SCIENCE

Meteorology

Meteorology is the study of *weather* (the condition of the atmosphere at a certain time and place) and *climate* (the average of weather conditions in a particular place over a span of time).

Further, weather describes the interaction of several atmospheric conditions—temperature, air pressure, wind, humidity, and so on—that are themselves influenced by other factors.

1. The local temperature is affected by the angle of the sun's rays, what season it is currently (and therefore the position of Earth relative to the sun), the length of the daylight period (also affected by the season), the altitude, the nearness of any large bodies of water, and so on.
2. The local air pressure depends mostly on temperature and humidity; warm air is lighter than cold air, and moist air is heavier than dry air. Changes in atmospheric pressure are measured on a *barometer*.
3. Wind is air moving from one place to another; it is caused by differences in air pressure. Winds move from areas of higher pressure to areas of lower pressure.

4. Humidity is the amount of moisture in the air; *relative humidity* is a percentage of how much water vapor the local air *could* hold at a given temperature. When the air is warm and dry, moisture on Earth's surface tends to *evaporate* (turn into vapor); when the air is *saturated* or completely filled with moisture, a decrease in temperature will cause the moisture in the air to *condense* (form droplets) and *precipitate* (fall) as rain, sleet, snow, or hail.

The Atmosphere

Earth's atmosphere has six layers that perform many functions, including keeping Earth's temperatures within an acceptable range, transmitting sound energy, and protecting us from most of the sun's harmful rays.

TROPOSPHERE

The troposphere is the densest part of the atmosphere; almost all weather is in this layer. It starts at Earth's surface and extends to an altitude of 5–9 miles (8–14.5 km) high.

STRATOSPHERE

The stratosphere starts just above the troposphere and extends to 31 miles (50 km) high. The ozone layer, which absorbs and scatters solar ultraviolet radiation, is in this layer.

MESOSPHERE

The mesosphere starts just above the stratosphere and extends up to 53 miles (85 km) above the surface. Meteors usually burn up in this layer of the atmosphere.

THERMOSPHERE

The thermosphere starts just above the mesosphere and extends out to about 370 miles (595 km). The northern lights (*aurora borealis*) phenomenon happens here, and most satellites orbit Earth in this layer.

EXOSPHERE

The upper limit of our atmosphere, the exosphere, extends from the top of the thermosphere out to about 6,200 miles (9,978 km).

IONOSPHERE

The ionosphere is an abundant layer of electrons and ionized atoms and molecules that stretches from about the top of the stratosphere (31 miles/50 km above Earth's surface) to the edge of space at about 600 miles (966 km), overlapping the mesosphere and the thermosphere. This dynamic region grows and shrinks based on solar conditions. The ionosphere is a critical link in the chain of sun–Earth interactions and is also what makes radio communications possible.

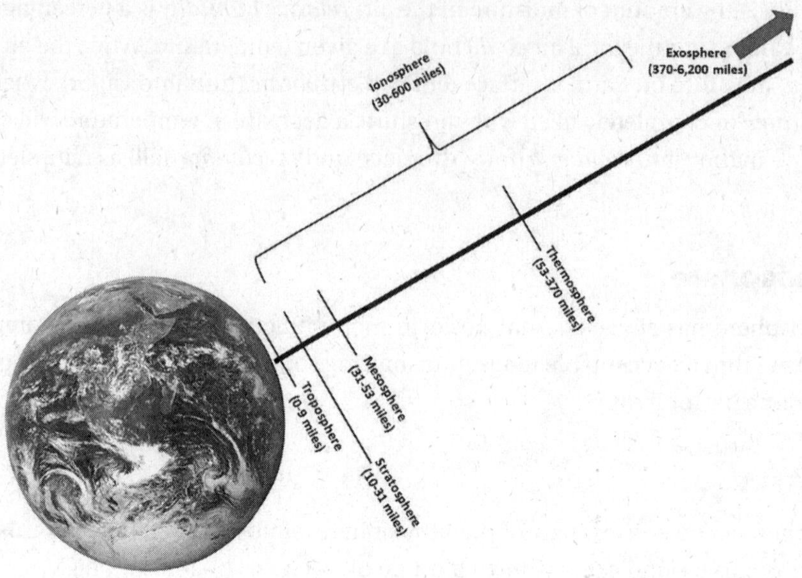

Figure 8.1 The layers of the atmosphere

CLOUDS

Clouds help regulate Earth's temperature and bring vital rain to different areas. Clouds develop out of the process of *convection,* which changes atmospheric moisture from a gas to a liquid.

As solar radiation heats the ground and the air immediately above it, the warmed air becomes lighter and rises upward. As the air rises, the temperature decreases, and so does the amount of water vapor the air can hold. This vapor rapidly condenses and forms clouds composed of many billions of tiny water droplets or ice crystals. These droplets are exceedingly small, averaging about 10 microns in diameter (a micron is one-millionth of a meter; ice crystals are much larger but less concentrated). Virtually all types of clouds and precipitation are due to rising air.

On the other hand, as air sinks, its temperature rises again, and its capacity for holding vapor increases. Then any cloud droplets tend to evaporate and the cloud itself disappears as evaporation changes moisture back from a liquid into a gas.

Clouds will also form where air masses collide—two different air masses can't mix unless they are very similar in temperature and moisture content. If a cold, dry air mass pushes into a warm, moist air mass, the warmer air is forced upward, rapidly producing clouds that bubble up, perhaps ultimately leading to lightning, thunder, and showers. If the cold air retreats, warm air pushing over it can bring a much slower process of lowering and thickening clouds and finally light precipitation in the form of light rain, mist, or drizzle.

Three major cloud classifications describe their appearance using Latin terms.

- Cirrus, from the Latin *cirro,* meaning "curly" or "fibrous"
- Stratus, from the Latin *strato,* suggesting sheets or layers
- Cumulus, from the Latin *cumulo,* indicating "heaped" or "piled"

By combining these with other terms, a number of different cloud combinations can be described. The Latin word for "shower" is *nimbus,* so the technical term for describing the cloud associated with thunderstorms is *cumulonimbus.*

Clouds are also categorized by how high above the ground they form.

- **HIGH CLOUDS:** *Cirrus, cirrostratus,* and *cirrocumulus* clouds are delicate wispy clouds at altitudes above 20,000 feet and are composed of ice crystals (at such altitudes, temperatures are perpetually below freezing).
- **MIDDLE CLOUDS:** *Altostratus, altocumulus,* and *nimbostratus* clouds are typically found between 6,000 and 20,000 feet in altitude.
- **LOW CLOUDS:** *Stratus, cumulus,* and *stratocumulus* clouds occur at altitudes of 6,000 feet or lower. Stratus clouds appear as smooth, even sheets, from which light rain and drizzle often fall (light snow or freezing drizzle during the winter). Fog is just a stratus cloud reaching to or sitting on the ground. Cumulus clouds can range in size from isolated balls of cotton to big heaps of mashed potatoes in the sky. They are often referred to as "fair weather clouds" because they usually aren't associated with precipitation, but occasionally they can grow into thunderstorms (*cumulonimbus*). They are convective clouds, caused by the sun heating the ground. Stratocumulus clouds, like altocumulus, can appear in a wide variety of different shapes and textures.
- **CLOUDS OF GREAT VERTICAL DEVELOPMENT:** These are the cumulonimbus clouds, often called *thunderheads* because they can bring torrential rain, vivid lightning, and thunder. The tops of such clouds may reach up to 60,000 feet or more; ice crystals get sheared off and are carried away by strong winds aloft, forming a flattened shield of cirrus that spreads out in the shape of an anvil. Sometimes hail—or, more rarely, a tornado—comes from a cumulonimbus cloud.

Astronomy

Astronomy is related to and interwoven with both physics and earth science. The *rotation* of Earth on its *axis* (an imaginary line running between the North and South Poles) causes day and night as one side or the other of the planet faces the sun. Earth's path, or *orbit,* around the sun is not perfectly circular, but it's Earth's *axial tilt* that causes the seasons. Earth's axis is tilted 23.5 degrees away from being exactly perpendicular (at right angles) to the plane of its orbit around the sun (you could say that Earth leans over somewhat instead of standing straight up). As Earth orbits the sun, its tilted axis stays pointing in the same direction in relation to its orbit, so throughout the year, different parts of Earth get more or less of the sun's direct rays, causing the seasons.

Earth is part of our *solar system,* which includes the sun and seven other planets (for a total of eight) with their various moons (see the table on page 174). Each *revolution* of Earth around the sun takes 365.25 days—which is why we have a leap year every four years, to balance out those accumulated extra quarter days.

The sun is the largest and most important body in our solar system, containing well over 99 percent of all the mass in the solar system (its diameter is more than a hundred times that of Earth). It provides the heat, light, and other energy that makes life on Earth possible. Electrically charged (and very hot) particles and plasma from the sun's outer layer—the *solar wind*—continually stream into space. These vary in density, temperature, and speed, bathing everything in the solar system, sometimes affecting normal magnetic and electromagnetic situations on the planets.

The four inner planets (Mercury, Venus, Earth, and Mars) consist mostly of iron and rock and are known as *terrestrial* (Earth-like) planets because they're somewhat similar to Earth in size and composition. The outer planets are huge and have thick, gaseous outer layers, mostly hydrogen and helium, giving them compositions more like the sun than Earth. Beneath their outer layers, the pressure of their thick atmospheres turns their insides into liquid, although they may have rocky cores. Rings of dust, rock, and ice chunks surround all the giant planets. Saturn's rings are the best known, but thin rings also encircle Jupiter, Uranus, and Neptune.

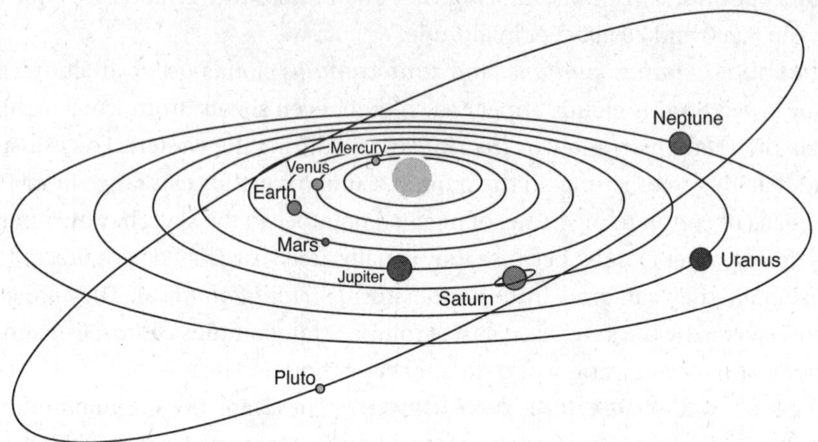

Figure 8.2 The solar system

There is also a band of *asteroids*—large, irregularly shaped chunks of rock, metals, and other materials—between the orbits of Mars and Jupiter, more than two and a half times as far away from the sun as Earth. Most of these asteroids are relatively small, from the size of boulders to a few thousand feet in diameter, but some are much larger (at least 16 are more than 150 miles in diameter). Although there are billions of them, scientists believe their total mass is still less than that of our moon.

Pluto was considered the ninth and most distant planet of our solar system from its discovery in 1930 until 2006, when the International Astronomical Union classified Pluto as a *dwarf planet*. However, not everyone in the scientific community agrees, and the discussion is still ongoing. You should keep Pluto's current status as a dwarf planet in mind because all three services' flight aptitude tests have been updated in the past few years. In fact, the AFOQT's Physical Science subtest is the most likely to include astronomy questions, and it is the most recently updated.

Solar System

Planet	Average distance from the sun (million miles)	Rank by size	Time for revolution	Number of moons
Mercury	36.0	8	88 days	0
Venus	67.2	6	225 days	0
Earth	93.0	5	365.25 days	1
Mars	141.6	7	687 days	2
Jupiter	483.8	1	12 years	67
Saturn	890.8	2	29 years	62
Uranus	1,784.8	3	84 years	27
Neptune	2,793.1	4	164 years	14

Occasionally, Earth's moon goes into *eclipse.* An eclipse happens when one astronomical body cuts off the light from another. A *lunar eclipse* happens when Earth comes directly between the sun and the moon, causing Earth's shadow (*umbra*) to fall directly on the moon. Since the moon shines only by way of light reflected from the sun, this position of Earth puts the moon into shadow.

In a *solar eclipse,* the moon is between Earth and the sun so that the umbra (moon's shadow) sweeps across Earth. Due to the relative size of the bodies involved, the moon's shadow is very narrow—only about 170 miles at its maximum. The *penumbra* is a much wider area of partial shadow where the sun's light is only partly cut off.

Two other types of astronomical bodies that you might be asked about are *comets* and *meteors.* Comets are mostly gaseous bodies that can be seen from Earth for periods ranging from a few days to months at a time. The *comet head* contains a small, brightly reflective nucleus made up of ice, frozen gases, and other particles. When a comet approaches the sun, these gases and particles stream off in the form of a *tail,* which can be as long as 100 million miles.

A meteor is a small piece of *extraterrestrial* (i.e., not from Earth) matter that becomes visible when it enters Earth's atmosphere. In the friction that goes along with its plunge toward Earth, a meteor heats up intensely, usually burning up before it reaches the ground. Those meteors large enough to reach Earth are called *meteorites.*

The glow of a meteor's appearance, as friction from the atmosphere heats it up, has led to it being (incorrectly) called a "shooting star" or a "falling star."

Electric Energy

Electrons are incredibly small, measuring only about 0.00000000000022 inch (that's twenty-two hundred-trillionths) in diameter. You may wonder how anything so small can be a source of energy. Much of the answer lies in the fact that electrons move at nearly the speed of light, or 186,282 miles per second. In metric terms that's about 300 million meters per second. Billions of them can move at once through a wire. The combination of speed and concentration together produces great energy. When a flow of electrons along a conductor occurs, this is commonly referred to as *current flow.*

Magnetism and Electricity

Magnetism and electricity are closely related. Magnetism is used to generate electricity, and electricity produces a magnetic field.

Magnetism is a force that acts between certain objects. The area around a magnet where the force is felt is called a *magnetic field.* Electricity flowing through a wire sets up a magnetic field around the wire. A coil of current-carrying wire becomes an *electromagnet* with the magnetic field strongest at the two ends of the coil, the north and south *poles.* The electromagnet remains magnetic only as long as the electricity flows through it. A magnetic field can also produce electricity. If you pass a wire across a magnetic field, electricity will be generated in the wire; electric generators are based on this principle. The relationship between electricity and magnetism is also used in transformers, relays, solenoids, and motors.

Electric Current

Electron current is defined as the directed flow of electrons, the direction of which is from a region of negative potential to a region of less negative potential or more positive potential.

Therefore, electric current can be said to flow from a negative potential to a positive potential. The direction is determined by the polarity of the voltage source.

Electric current is generally classified into two general types—direct current and alternating current. A *direct current* flows continuously in the same direction, whereas an *alternating current* periodically reverses direction.

A *circuit* is a pathway for the movement of electrons. An external force exerted on electrons to make them flow through a conductor is known as an *electromotive force,* or *emf,* and it's measured in volts. Electric pressure, potential difference, and emf mean the same thing. For electrons to move in a particular direction, it is necessary for a potential difference to exist between two points of the emf source. If 6,250,000,000,000,000,000 electrons pass a given point in one second, there is said to be one *ampere* (A) of current flowing. The same number of electrons stored on an object (a static charge) and not moving is called a *coulomb* (C).

The magnitude or "size" of a current is measured in *amperes.* A current of one ampere is said to flow when one coulomb of charge passes a point in one second. Expressed as an equation:

$$I = \frac{Q}{T}$$

Where: I = current in amperes
Q = charge in coulombs
T = time in seconds

Sometimes the ampere is too large a unit to be useful. Therefore the *milliampere* (mA), one-thousandth of an ampere, or the *microampere* (μA), one-millionth (0.000001) of an ampere, is used.

Current flow is assumed to be from negative (–) to positive (+) in the explanations here. Electron flow is negative (–) to positive (+), and we assume that current flow and electron flow are one and the same. This will make explanations simpler as we progress.

An *ammeter* is used to measure current flow in a circuit. A *milliammeter* is used to measure smaller amounts, and the *microammeter* is used to measure very small amounts of current. A *voltmeter* is used to measure voltage. In some instances it's possible to obtain a meter that will measure both voltage and current plus resistance. This is called a *multimeter,* or *volt-ohm-milliammeter.*

A material through which electricity passes easily is called a *conductor* because it has free electrons. In other words, a conductor offers very little resistance or opposition to the flow of electrons. All metals are conductors of electricity to some extent; some are much better than others. Silver, copper, and aluminum let electricity pass easily, and silver is a better conductor than copper. However, copper is used more frequently because it is cheaper. Aluminum is used as a conductor where light weight is important.

One of the most important reasons why some materials are good conductors—and some are not—is the presence of *free electrons.* If a material has many electrons that are free to move away from their atoms, that material will be a good conductor of electricity. Although free electrons usually move in a haphazard way, their movement can be controlled and results in the flow we call *electric current.*

Conductors may be in the form of bars, tubes, or sheets. The most familiar conductors are wire. Many sizes of wire are available; some are only the thickness of a hair, and other wires may be as thick as your arm.

To prevent conductors from touching at the wrong place, they are usually coated with plastic or cloth material called an *insulator*. An insulator is a material with very few, if any, free electrons. No known material is a perfect insulator; however, there are materials that are such poor conductors that they are classified as insulators, such as glass, dry wood, rubber, mica, and certain plastics.

In between the two extremes of conductors and resistors are *semiconductors*. Semiconductors in the form of transistors, diodes, and integrated circuits or chips are used every day in electronic devices. Materials used in the manufacture of transistors and diodes have a conductivity halfway between that of a good conductor and a good insulator. Therefore, the name *semi*conductor is given to them. Germanium and silicon are the two most commonly known semiconductor materials. Through the introduction of small amounts of other elements (called impurities), these nearly pure (99.999999 percent) elements become *limited* conductors.

The opposite of conductors are *resistors*. Resistors are devices used to give a measured amount of opposition or resistance to the flow of electrons. This opposition to current flow is measured in ohms (Ω) and indicates the amount of resistance a piece of material offers to the flow of electrons.

The unit of conductance is the *siemen* (formerly the mho, *ohm* spelled backward). Whereas the symbol used to represent the magnitude of resistance is the Greek letter omega (Ω), the symbol used to represent conductance is *S*. The relationship that exists between resistance and conductance is a reciprocal one; the reciprocal of a number is one divided by that number. If the resistance of a material is known, dividing its value into one will give its conductance. If the conductance is known, dividing its value into one will give its resistance.

Ohm's Law

German physicist Georg Ohm discovered the relationship between voltage, current, and resistance in 1827. He found that in any circuit where the only opposition to the flow of electrons is resistance, there is a relationship between voltage, current, and resistance. The strength of the current is directly proportional to the voltage and inversely proportional to the resistance.

Power

Power is defined as the *rate* at which work is done. It is expressed in metric measurement terms of watts (W) for power and joules (J) for energy work. A *watt* is the power that gives rise to the production of energy at the rate of 1 joule per second (W = J/s). A *joule* is the work done when the point of application of force of 1 newton is displaced a distance of 1 meter in the direction of the force (J = N × m).

It has long been the practice in this country to measure work in terms of horsepower (hp). Electric motors are still rated in horsepower and probably will be for some time, since the United States did not adopt metric standards for everything.

Power can be electric or mechanical. When a mechanical force is used to lift a weight, *work* is done. The rate at which the weight is moved is called *power*. *One horsepower* is defined as 33,000 lbs. being lifted 1 foot in one minute. Energy is consumed in moving a weight or when work is done. It takes 746 W of electric power to equal 1 hp.

The horsepower rating of electric motors is calculated by taking the voltage and multiplying it by the current drawn under full load. This power is measured in watts, so 1 volt times 1 ampere equals 1 watt. When put into a formula it reads as follows:

$$\text{Power} = \text{volts} \times \text{amperes or } P = E \times I$$

where E = voltage, or emf, and I = current, or intensity of electron flow

The kilowatt is commonly used to express the amount of electric energy used or available. Since the term *kilo* (k) means one thousand (1,000), a kilowatt (kW) is 1,000 watts. When the kilowatt is used in terms of power dissipated or consumed—by a home over a month, for instance—it is expressed in kilowatt hours. The unit kilowatt hour is abbreviated as kWh. It is the equivalent of one thousand watts used for a period of one hour. Electric bills are calculated or computed on an hourly basis and then read in the kWh units.

The *milliwatt* (mW) means one-thousandth (0.001) of a watt. The milliwatt is used in working with very small amplifiers and other electronic devices. For instance, a speaker used on a portable transistor radio could be rated as 100 milliwatts, or 0.1 W. Transistor circuits are designed in milliwatts, but powerline electric power is measured in kilowatts. Keep in mind that *kilo* means 1,000 and *milli* means 0.001 (one-thousandth).

Any time there is movement, there is resistance; this resistance is useful in electric and electronic circuits. Resistance makes it possible to generate heat, control electron flow, and supply the correct voltage to a device. Resistance in a conductor depends on four factors: material, length, cross-sectional area, and temperature. Resistance is measured by a unit called the *ohm*, symbolized by the Greek letter Ω (omega).

Some materials offer more resistance than others; it depends on the number of free electrons present in the material. The longer the wire or conductor, the more resistance it has, so resistance is said to vary *directly* with the length of the wire. However, resistance varies *inversely* with the size of the conductor in the cross section—in other words, the larger the wire, the smaller the resistance per foot of length.

For most materials, the higher the temperature, the higher the resistance. However, the exceptions to this are devices known as *thermistors*. Thermistors change resistance with temperature. They *decrease* in resistance with an increase in temperature. Thermistors are used in certain types of meters to measure temperature.

Resistance causes a voltage drop across a resistor when current flows through it. The voltage is dropped or dissipated as heat and must be eliminated into the air. Some variable resistors can be varied, but can also be adjusted for a particular setting. Resistors are available in various sizes, shapes, and wattage ratings.

Physics

Matter is defined as anything that occupies space and has mass. *Mass* is the quantity of matter that a substance possesses and, depending on the gravitational force acting on it, has a unit of weight assigned to it. Although its weight can vary, the mass of a body is constant and can be measured by its resistance to a change of position or motion.

For example, an astronaut who weighs 168 pounds here on Earth only weighs about 28 pounds on the moon, but the astronaut still has the same mass. This property of mass, to resist a change of position or motion, is called *inertia*. Since matter occupies space, we can compare the masses of various objects that occupy a particular unit of volume or amount of space. This relationship of mass to a unit of volume is called the *density* of a substance.

Energy

Energy is usually defined as the ability to do work. Energy may appear in a variety of forms—as light, heat, sound, mechanical energy, electrical energy, and chemical energy.

Two general classifications of energy are *potential energy* and *kinetic energy*. Potential energy is recognized as the result of the position of an object. Kinetic energy, on the other hand, is energy of motion. The difference between the two can be illustrated by a boulder on the slope of a mountain. While it remains on its high mountain ledge, the boulder has a great deal of potential energy due to its position above the valley floor. If the ledge crumbles, however, and the boulder falls, its potential energy is converted into kinetic energy.

MECHANICAL COMPREHENSION

This section reviews basic physics concepts and how simple machines make work easier.

Force

One of the basic concepts of physics is the concept of force. Force is something that can change the velocity of an object by making it start, stop, speed up, slow down, or change direction. When you take your foot off the gas pedal of a car, it doesn't suddenly come to a stop—it coasts on, only gradually losing its velocity. If you want the car to stop, you have to do something to it.

There are many types of force.

FRICTION

Your car has three controls whose function is to change its velocity: the gas pedal, the brake pedal, and the steering wheel. The brakes make use of the same force that stops your car if you just let it coast: friction.

Sliding friction is a force generated whenever two objects are in contact and there is relative motion between them. When something is moving, friction *always* acts in such a direction so as to retard (slow down) the relative motion. Thus, the direction of the force of friction on a moving object will always be directly opposite to the direction of the velocity. The brake shoes slow down the rotation of the wheels, and the tires slow the car until it comes to rest.

In the simplest case, friction can be measured by using a spring scale.

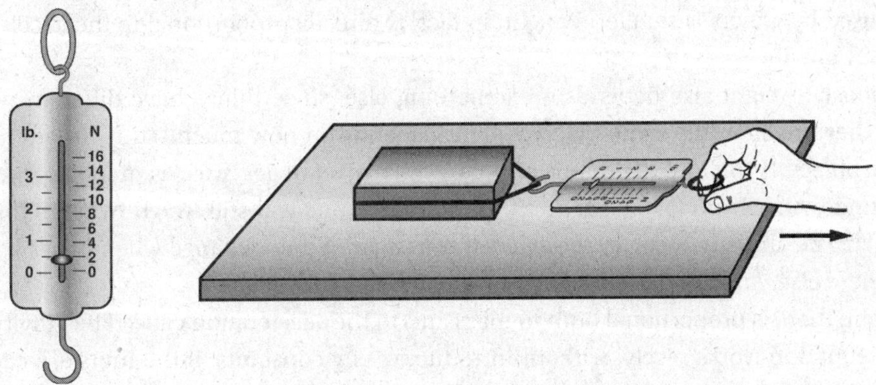

Figure 8.3 Sliding friction

A spring scale can be used to measure all kinds of forces. Basically, it measures the force pulling on its shackle. A spring scale is calibrated in force units—*pounds* or *newtons*. A newton (abbreviated N) is a fairly small unit of force; it takes 4.45 newtons to equal 1 pound.

The image in Figure 8.3 shows a spring scale being used to measure the force of sliding friction between a brick and the horizontal surface on which it is resting. The scale is pulling the brick along at constant speed. In this condition, the brick is said to be in *equilibrium*. Because its velocity is not changing, it follows that the net force acting on it is zero.

However, the spring scale is exerting a force, which is indicated on its face. This force is pulling the brick to the right. The brick can remain in equilibrium only if there is an equal force pulling it to the left, so that the net force acting on it is zero. In the situation shown, the only force pulling the brick to the left is the frictional force between the brick and the surface. Therefore the reading on the spring scale is equal to the force of friction.

Anyone who has ever moved furniture around or slid a box across the floor knows that the frictional force is greater when the furniture or the box is heavier. The force of friction does not change much as the object speeds up, but it depends very strongly on how hard the two surfaces are pressed together.

When a solid moves through a liquid, such as a boat moving through the water, there is a frictionlike force retarding the motion of the solid; this is called *viscous drag*. Like friction, it always acts opposite to velocity. Unlike friction, however, it increases greatly with speed, and it depends more on the shape of the object and on the nature of the liquid than on the object's weight. Gases also produce viscous drag, and you are probably most familiar with this as the air resistance that acts on a car at high speed.

GRAVITY

Probably the first law of physics that everyone learns is this: If you drop something, it falls. Since its velocity keeps on changing as it falls, there must be a force acting on it during the time that it's falling—this is *gravity*.

You can measure gravity by balancing it off with a spring scale. When you hang something on a spring scale and read the scale in pounds or newtons, you usually call the force of gravity acting on the object by a special name. You call it the *weight* of the object.

Weight is not a fixed property of an object; it varies with location. A person who weighs 160 pounds at the North Pole will check in at 159.2 pounds at the equator. If he should step on a scale on the moon, it would read only 27 pounds. Everything weighs less where the acceleration caused by gravity is smaller. Weight, in fact, is directly proportional to the acceleration caused by gravity.

Obviously, weight also depends on something else, since things have different weights even if they are all at the same place. Weight depends on how much "stuff" (matter) there is in the object. If you buy 10 pounds of sugar, you expect to get twice as much as if you buy five pounds. And if you take both sacks to the moon, one will still weigh twice as much as the other. The amount of sugar, the *mass* of the sugar, did not change when it was brought somewhere else. And the more sugar you have, the more it weighs.

Weight, then, is proportional both to mass and to the acceleration caused by gravity.

This equation works nicely, without introducing any constants, if the units are carefully defined. Mass is measured by pounds in the English system and in kilograms in the metric system. By definition, when you multiply the mass in kilograms by the acceleration in meters per second squared, the weight comes out in newtons.

To summarize: Weight—the force of gravity—is the product of mass and the acceleration caused by gravity.

ELASTIC RECOIL

The basic feature of a solid, as opposed to a liquid or a gas, is that it has a definite shape. It resists changes in its shape and, in so doing, exerts a force against whatever force is applied to it.

Look, for example, at the board supported at its ends, shown in Figure 8.4. If you push down on it, you bend it, and you can feel it pushing back on you. The harder you push, the more the board bends and the harder it pushes back. It bends just enough to push on you with the same force that you exert on it. The force it exerts is called *elastic recoil.*

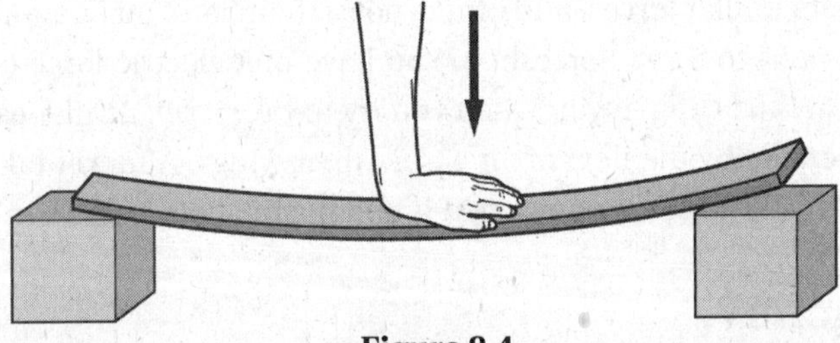

Figure 8.4

The same thing happens when you stand on the floor, or on the ground. You can't see the floor bend, but it bends just the same, just not very much. Even a feather resting on the floor bends it a little. The elastic recoil force needed to support the feather is very small, so the amount of bending is too small to detect.

A rope does not resist bending, but it certainly resists stretching. When a rope is stretched, it is said to be in a state of *tension.* The tension can be measured by cutting the rope and inserting a spring scale into it, as shown in Figure 8.5. The spring scale will read the tension in the rope, in pounds or newtons. If you pull with a force of 30 N, for example, the tension in the rope is 30 N, and that is what the scale will indicate. Something, such as the elastic recoil of the wall to which the scale is attached, must be pulling on the other end with a force of 30 N. The tension in the rope is the same throughout, and is equal to the elastic recoil force that the rope exerts at its ends.

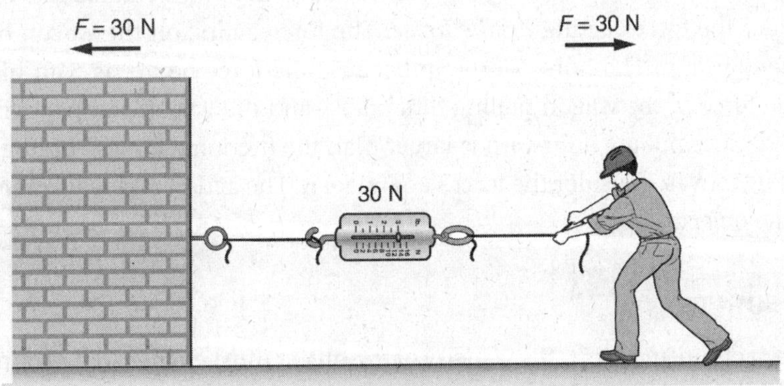

Figure 8.5

To summarize: A force applied to a solid distorts the shape of the solid, causing it to exert a force back on the force that distorted it.

BUOYANCY

If you take a deep breath and dive into a pool, you will have trouble keeping yourself submerged—something keeps pushing you up. That force is called *buoyancy.*

The force of buoyancy acts in an upward direction on anything submerged in a liquid or a gas. Buoyancy is the force that makes ships float and helium-filled balloons rise. A rock sinks because its weight is greater than the buoyancy of the water. A submerged cork rises because the buoyancy of the water exerts a force greater than its weight. When it reaches the surface, some of it emerges, but the rest is still under water. The amount under water is just enough to produce a buoyant force equal to its weight, so it stays put.

OTHER FORCES

There are some other familiar forces, and others not so familiar. You know about magnetism, which attracts iron nails to a red horseshoe. You have met electric force (static electricity), which makes a nylon shirt cling to you when you try to take it off. Airplanes stay up because of the lift force generated by the flow of air across their wings. A rocket takes off because of the force generated by the gases expanding in it and pushing out behind it.

ACTION AND REACTION

The batter steps up to the plate and takes a healthy swing, sending the ball into left field. The bat has exerted a large force on the ball, changing both the magnitude and the direction of its velocity. But the ball has also exerted a force on the bat, slowing it down. The batter feels this when the bat hits the ball.

Next time up, he strikes out. He has taken exactly the same swing, but exerts no force on anything (air doesn't count). The batter has discovered that it is impossible to exert a force unless there is something there to push back. Forces exist *only* in pairs. When object A exerts a force on object B, then B must exert a force on A. The two forces are sometimes called *action* and *reaction,* although which is which is often somewhat arbitrary. The two parts of the interaction are equal in magnitude, are opposite in direction, and act on different objects.

The law of action and reaction leads to an apparent paradox, if you are not careful how it is applied. The horse pulls on the wagon. If the force of the wagon pulling the horse the other way is the same, as the law insists, how can the horse and wagon get started?

The error in the reasoning is this: If you want to know whether the horse gets moving, you have to consider the forces acting *on the horse.* The force acting on the wagon has nothing to do with the question. The horse starts up because the force he exerts with his hooves is larger than the force of the wagon pulling him back—and the wagon starts moving because the force of the horse pulling it forward is larger than the frictional forces holding it back. To know something moves, consider the forces acting *on* it. The action and reaction forces *never* act on the same object.

BALANCED FORCES

If a single force acts on an object, the velocity of the object must change. If two or more forces act, however, their effects may eliminate each other. This is the condition of equilibrium, in which there is no net force and the velocity does not change. We saw such a condition in the case in which gravity is pulling an object down and the spring scale, used for weighing it, is pulling it upward.

An object in equilibrium may or may not be at rest. A parachutist, descending at constant speed, is in equilibrium. His weight is just balanced by the viscous drag on the parachute, which is why he put it on in the first place. A heavier parachutist falls a little faster; his speed increases until the viscous drag just balances his weight.

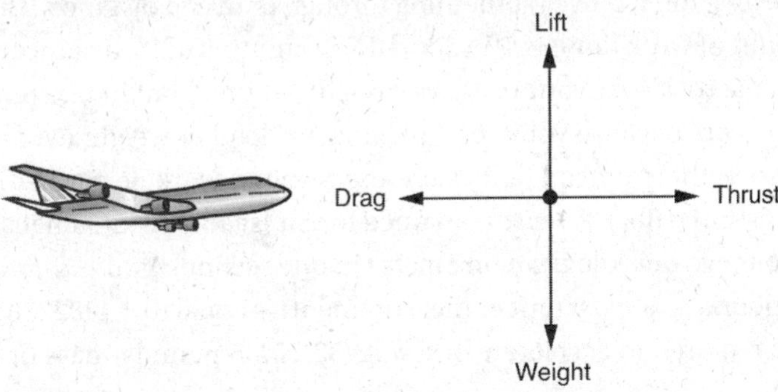

Balancing the vertical forces is not enough to produce equilibrium. An airplane traveling at constant speed is in equilibrium under the influence of four forces, two vertical and two horizontal. Vertical: Gravity (down) is just balanced by the lift (up) produced by the flow of air across the wing. Horizontal: Viscous drag (pulling back, slowing) is just balanced by the thrust of the engines (pushing forward). Both the vertical and the horizontal velocities are constant.

The brick in Figure 8.3, resting on a tabletop and being pulled along at constant speed, is another example. Vertical: The downward force of gravity is balanced by the upward force of the elastic recoil of the tabletop. Horizontal: The tension in the spring scale, pulling to the right, is balanced by the friction pulling it to the left, opposite to the direction of motion.

If an object is in equilibrium—at rest or moving at a constant speed in a straight line—the total force acting on it in any direction is exactly equal in magnitude to the force in the opposite direction.

Simple Machines

"Simple machines" are devices that make work easier by changing either the direction or magnitude of an applied force. Without thinking about it, we all use a multitude of simple machines every day—a light switch, a water faucet, a doorknob, a hammer, a car, or a knife, just to name a few.

There are six basic simple machines recognized in mechanical physics—the lever, the inclined plane, the wedge, the wheel and axle, the screw, and the pulley—and all of them have been in use for thousands of years. In theory, all complex machines are made up of parts derived from these six simple machines. The principles behind some of them were quantified by Archimedes, the Greek mathematician, engineer, and inventor.

And, even though not on the "official" list, we will discuss the hydraulic jack, as well as a few complex machines that are good examples of combinations of simple machines.

Simple machines are useful because of their ability to perform *work*, which is defined as applying force over a distance. The effort multiplied by the effort distance is called the *work input*, and the load multiplied by the load distance (distance the load travels) is the *work output*. Machines create a greater output force than the amount of force input to them; the ratio of these forces is the *mechanical advantage* of the machine. Simple machines can also be used in combinations to create even greater mechanical advantages, as in a bicycle.

The Work Principle

Work is done whenever a force moves something through or over a distance. The formula for measuring the amount of work done is $W = F \times d$ (force multiplied by distance). If you stand still holding a very large rock over your head, you might get tired, but in this physics context, you aren't doing any *work* because you aren't moving any load or weight over any distance.

The force to get something moved (and therefore result in work performed) is measured in newtons or pounds-force (lb_f). A *newton* (named for Sir Isaac Newton, English scientist) is the force required to move one kilogram one meter in one second. A *pound-force* (to prevent confusion with the pound as a *mass* unit of measurement) is equal to 4.44822162 newtons, or the amount of force required to accelerate one *slug* (32.17405 pounds-mass or lb_m) at a rate of 1 ft./sec.^{2}.

The purpose of a machine is to make it possible to exert a large force on the load with a smaller effort. You could say that a machine magnifies force or effort. The amount of this magnification—the ratio of load to effort—is called the *mechanical advantage* of the machine. It can be shown algebraically like this:

$$\text{MA} = \frac{F_L}{F_E}$$

Something else to consider in this area is the direction of a force applied to an object, and how that direction affects the amount of work that is done on the object. One way to look at it is that only the amount of force that's in the direction of movement counts. For example, look at Figure 8.6 below (the child pulling a smaller child on a sled).

Figure 8.6

The tension in the rope held by the larger child is pulling the sled forward, but, because it is applied at an angle, it is also lifting the sled somewhat. Since neither the angle of the rope nor the upward force applied to it are enough to overcome the force of gravity, only the component or part of the forward-directed force is doing the work of moving the sled.

The angle between the direction of actual movement and the direction in which the force is applied is known as *theta* (Greek symbol θ) and is measured in degrees. If we call the force that creates the tension in the rope to pull the sled *T*, the component of the force that actually pulls the sled forward is $T \cos \theta$, or *T* (tension) multiplied by the cosine of the angle theta.

You can probably understand just from the everyday intuitive application of these principles that the smaller the angle θ, the larger the effective force pulling the sled, and the smaller the amount of force that is spent trying to lift it. When θ = zero, the entire force contributes to moving the sled forward, and there is no effort spent lifting at all. On the other hand, when θ = 90°, the entire force is lifting the sled and nothing is pulling forward.

Most mechanical comprehension problems at this level are simplified—they do not, for instance, take into account the additional impact exerted by forces like friction with the ground, wind resistance (or the push from a tailwind), and so on. This leads us to the idea of a machine's *efficiency*: the ratio between the work output and the work input, expressed as a formula like this:

$$\text{efficiency} = \frac{W_{\text{out}}}{W_{\text{in}}}$$

Efficiency is usually expressed as a percentage that tells us what fraction of the work put into a machine comes out as useful work at the other end.

The next concept in this area that you need to know is the concept of *vectors.* A vector is any physical quantity that requires both a direction and an amount of force or *magnitude.* A vector is shown graphically as an arrow, where the length of the arrow represents the vector's magnitude, and the angle θ (sound familiar?) between the vector and a designated axis defines the vector's direction.

The Lever

Levers are a very common type of simple machine. A lever consists of a rigid bar that is supported at some point (the *fulcrum* or *pivot*), and has a load at some other point on the bar. The lever shown in Figure 8.7 is fairly typical. The load is the weight of the rock being lifted; the effort is the force exerted by the person trying to move the rock; and the fulcrum is the smaller rock supporting the lever.

Figure 8.7

Applying a force to one end of the bar causes it to pivot about the fulcrum, causing a magnification of the force applied to the load at another point along the bar. The torque or force around the pivot that is exerted by the worker is $F_E r_E$, where r_E (the *effort arm*) is the distance from the point where the effort is applied to the pivot. Similarly, the torque produced by the weight of the rock is $F_L r_L$, where r_L is the load arm. If the system is rotating in equilibrium, these two torques must have the same magnitude, so

$$F_E r_E = F_L r_L$$

from which we find that the mechanical advantage, F_L/F_E, is given by

$$MA_{lever} = \frac{r_E}{r_L}$$

Or, in other words, in a lever the mechanical advantage is equal to the ratio of effort arm to load arm.

For many kinds of levers, friction at the pivot is quite small, so efficiencies approach 100 percent, and the arm ratio is very near the force ratio. Usually, no correction is needed.

Levers are classified according to the relative positions of the pivot, load, and effort. The three classes of levers are represented by the tools shown in Figure 8.8. In the pliers (first-class lever), the pivot is between the effort and the load. In the nutcracker (second-class lever), it is the load that is between the other two. And in the sugar tongs (third-class lever), the effort is in the middle.

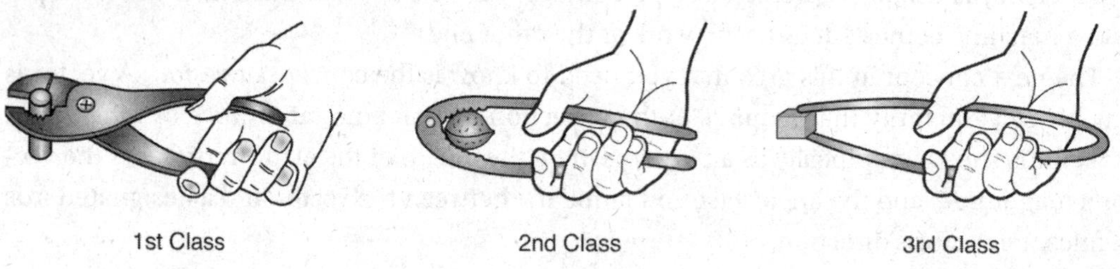

Figure 8.8

Note that in the third-class lever (the sugar tongs), the load arm is longer than the effort arm, so the mechanical advantage is less than 1. This lever magnifies distance at the expense of force.

Mechanical advantage is the ratio of load to effort; in a lever, it is equal to the ratio of effort arm to load arm.

THE INCLINED PLANE

An inclined plane is a plane (flat) surface set at an angle to another surface. This results in using less effort to achieve the same results by applying the required force over a longer distance. The most basic inclined plane is a ramp; it requires less force to move up or down a ramp to a different elevation than it does to climb or lower oneself to that height vertically.

For example, a wagon rolls downhill, propelled only by its own weight. But gravity pulls straight down, not at the angle of the road going down the hill. What makes the wagon go is a *component* of its weight, a part of its weight acting downhill, parallel to the surface the wagon rests on. A component of a force can act in any direction, not just vertically or horizontally. On the inclined plane, the weight of the wagon has two different effects: It acts *parallel* to the surface of the hill, pushing the wagon downhill; and it acts perpendicular (also called *normal*) to the surface, pushing the wagon into the surface. As the hill gets steeper, the parallel component becomes larger and the perpendicular (normal) component decreases.

When the wagon is resting on the surface, the elastic recoil of the surface is just enough to cancel the normal component of the wagon's weight. If the wagon is to stay in equilibrium, you have to pull on it, uphill, to prevent it from rolling away. If there is no friction, the uphill force needed is the same whether the wagon is standing still or going either uphill or downhill at a constant speed.

The situation is different if the wagon is moving and there is friction. If the wagon is going uphill, you have to pull harder, because the friction is working against you, holding it back. The total force you need to keep the wagon going is then equal to the parallel component of the weight plus the friction. On the other hand, if you are lowering the wagon down the hill, holding the rope to keep it from running away from you, friction is acting uphill, helping you hold the wagon back. Then the force you must exert is the parallel component of the weight *minus* the friction.

A ramp is a device commonly used to aid in lifting. To raise a heavy load a couple of feet onto a platform, it is common practice to place it on a dolly and wheel it up an inclined plane.

The work output of an inclined plane is the work that would have to be done to lift the load directly: the weight of the load times the vertical distance it goes. The work input is the actual force exerted in pushing the dolly up the ramp times the length of the ramp.

The ideal mechanical advantage of an inclined plane is equal to its length divided by its height.

THE WEDGE

A wedge—sometimes considered a specific type of inclined plane—is a double-inclined plane (i.e., both sides are inclined) that moves to exert a force along the lengths of its sides. The force is perpendicular to the inclined surfaces, so it pushes two objects (or portions of a single object) apart. Axes, knives, and chisels are all examples of wedges. The common door wedge used to keep an open door open uses the force on the surfaces of the door and floor to provide friction, rather than separate things, but it's still basically a wedge.

THE WHEEL AND AXLE

This simple machine involves a *wheel* attached to a rigid bar or *axle* in its center. A force applied to the wheel causes the axle to rotate, which can be used to magnify the output force (for example, by having a rope wind around the axle). Alternatively, a force applied to provide rotation to the axle translates into rotation of the wheel. The wheel and axle can be viewed as a type of lever that rotates around a center fulcrum. Ferris wheels, automobile wheels, and rolling pins are examples of wheel-and-axle machines.

THE SCREW

A screw is a shaft that has an inclined groove along its surface. It can also be thought of as an inclined plane wrapped around a cylinder. By rotating the screw (applying a *torque*), the force is applied perpendicular to the groove, thereby translating a rotational force into a linear one. Screws are frequently used to fasten objects together (as the hardware screw and bolt combination does), although the Babylonians developed a "screw" that could elevate water from a low-lying body to a higher one (which later came to be known as Archimedes' screw). Other examples of screws are propellers, fans, and most jar lids.

THE PULLEY

The pulley is a wheel with a groove along its edge where a rope or cable can be placed. It uses the principle of applying force over a longer distance—as well as the tension in the rope or cable—to reduce the magnitude of the force required to move the load. Complex systems of pulleys can be used to greatly reduce the force that must be applied to move an object.

For example, a piano mover, unable to fit the instrument into the staircase, decides to raise it outside the building to a window. He attaches it to a set of ropes and wheels that, somehow, make it possible for him to lift it with a force considerably smaller than the weight of the piano. How does this work?

Consider first the heavy block in Figure 8.9 suspended from two ropes. The upward force on the block is the tension (T) in the ropes, and the sum of the two tensions must equal the weight of the block. If the whole system is symmetrical, each rope is under tension equal to half the weight of the block.

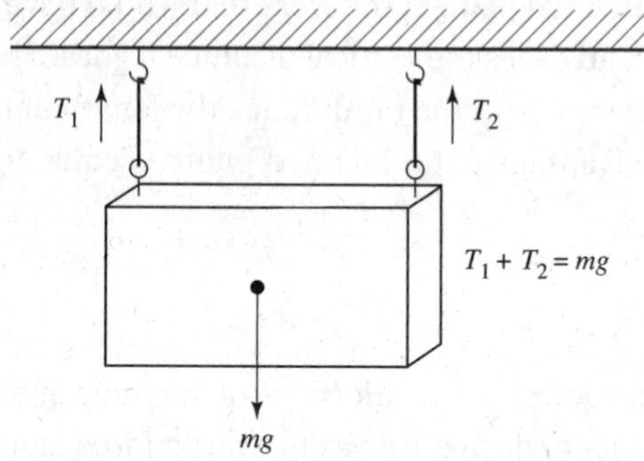

Figure 8.9

Now look at Figure 8.10, where the block has been attached to a wheel. There is now only one rope, which passes over the wheel. The tension in the rope is the same throughout; if it were different on one side than on the other, the wheel would turn until the tension on the two sides equalized. The tension in the rope is still only half the weight of the block, since it exerts *two* upward forces on the block. Now we have a system that helps in lifting things. Just fasten one end of the rope to a fixed support and pull on the other end (Figure 8.11). Now you can raise the block with a force equal to only half its weight.

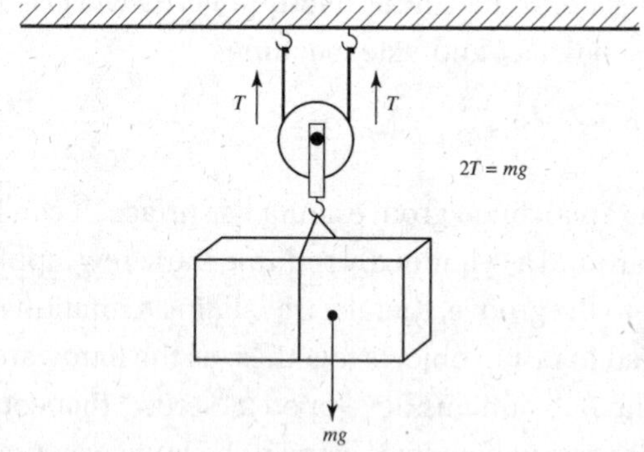

Figure 8.10

Are you getting something for nothing? Well, yes and no. True, you can now lift the weight with less force, but you have to pull the rope farther than you would if you lifted the block directly. Every time you pull 10 feet of rope through your hands, the block rises 5 feet. You might look at it this way: If the block rises 5 feet, *both* sides of the supporting rope have to shorten 5 feet, and the only way to accomplish this is to pull 10 feet of rope through. You raise the block with only half the force, but you have to exert the force through twice the distance.

You might prefer to pull in a downward direction rather than upward, and you can manage this by attaching a fixed wheel to the support and passing the rope around it as in Figure 8.12. The tension in the rope is still only half the weight of the block; the fixed pulley does nothing but change the direction of the force you exert.

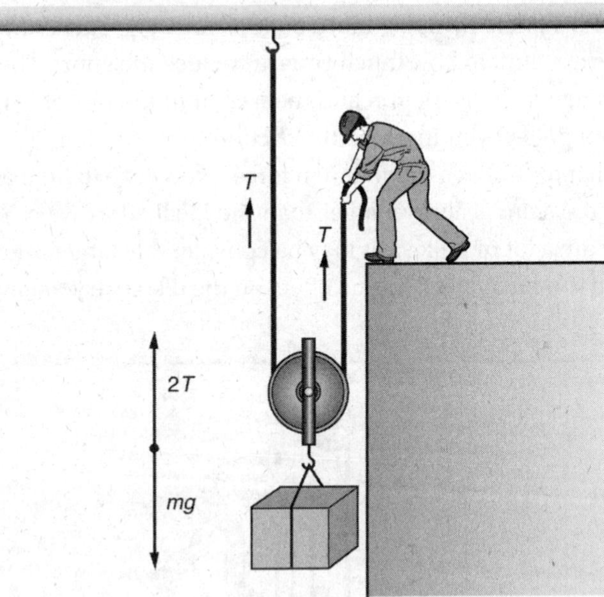

Figure 8.11

Let's learn some vocabulary. The weight of the object being lifted is called the *load*, and the distance it rises is the *load distance*. The force you exert on the rope is the *effort*, and the distance through which you exert that effort is the *effort distance*. With a single movable pulley in use, the effort is half the load and the effort distance is twice the load distance.

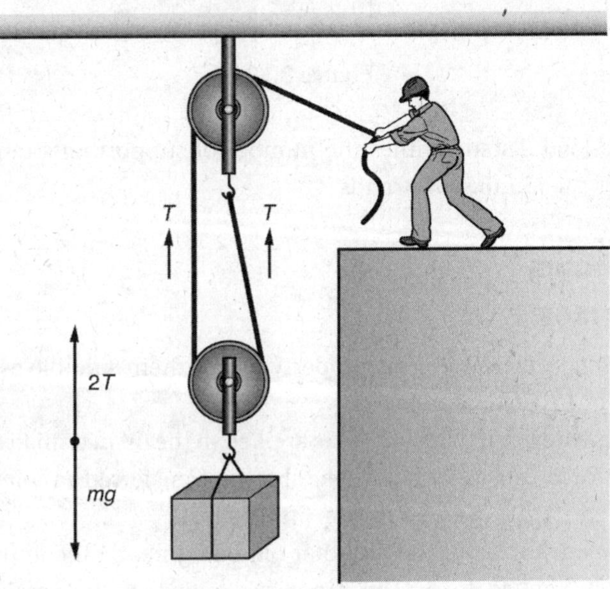

Figure 8.12

There are ways to string up a system of pulleys that will reduce the effort still further. Figure 8.13 shows how the same two pulleys can be connected to a rope in such a way as to divide the load among three strands of rope instead of two. This is done by fastening one end of the rope to the load instead of to the fixed support. Unfortunately, when you do this, you have to shorten all three strands when you raise the object, and the effort distance becomes three times the load distance. By using more pulleys you can reduce the effort still further. Unfortunately, there is a limit to how much you can reduce the effort. The analysis we did so far neglects a few things, such as friction and the weight of the movable pulleys themselves. Every time you add a pulley, you increase the friction in the system; if it is a movable pulley—the only kind that produces a reduction in force—you have to lift it along with the load. The effort in any real system is always larger than the ideal effort we calculated by dividing up the load. If there are a lot of pulleys, it may be considerably larger. And friction, although it increases the force you must exert, has no effect on the distance you have to pull that rope.

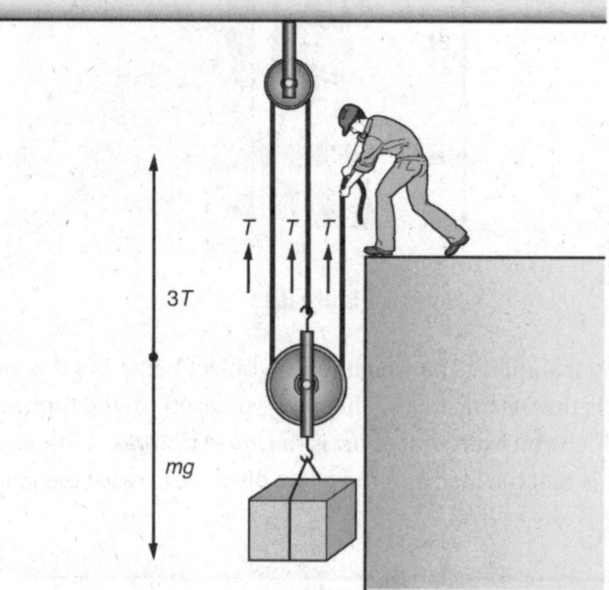

Figure 8.13

Effort distance is load distance times the number of supporting strands; effort is larger than load divided by the number of strands.

Complex Machines

THE HYDRAULIC JACK

Liquids are almost incompressible. This property makes them suitable as a means of transforming work from one type to another.

A hydraulic jack is a device in which force is applied to the oil in a small cylinder. As shown in Figure 8.14, this force causes some of the oil to be transferred to a larger cylinder. This forces the piston in the larger cylinder to rise, lifting a load.

This device takes advantage of the fact that oil, being nearly incompressible, transmits whatever pressure is applied to it. The pressure applied in the small cylinder appears unchanged in the big one, pushing up its piston.

The ideal mechanical advantage is the ratio between effort distance and load distance; for a hydraulic jack, it is equal to the ratio of the area of the load piston to that of the effort piston.

Figure 8.14

You may see a test problem that involves an application of these principles by showing you two cylinders of different sizes, connected by a hydraulic line or the equivalent, and each containing a piston that is either forcing the fluid in one cylinder down or being pushed up by actions in the other cylinder; alternatively, you may see a problem where there is a piston in only one cylinder. In either case, you will have to be able to understand the effects of mechanical advantage in these different-sized cylinders.

TIP

The volume of the oil being transferred from one piston to another does not change—only the size of the piston will change.

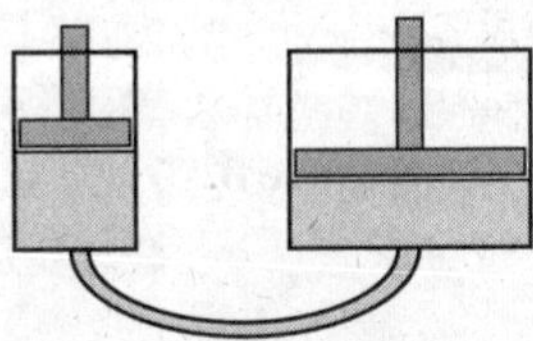

The question will give you some indication of the size of the cylinders, such as the diameter of the cylinder (or the piston within, which for purposes of the problem is assumed to be the same as the cylinder). It's good to remember that the volume of the oil being transferred from one piston to another does not change—only the dimensions of the piston change. Since the volume of a cylinder is $V = \pi r^2 d$ or ad (where a is the area of the circular part of the cylinder and d is the diameter of the cylinder), then $a_1 d_1 = a_2 d_2$, and the formula for mechanical advantage in this kind of problem is

$$\frac{a_2}{a_1} = \frac{d_1}{d_2}$$

where a_1 is the area of the smaller cylinder and a_2 is the area of the bigger cylinder, and d_1 is the vertical distance moved by the smaller cylinder and d_2 is the vertical distance moved by the larger cylinder. In a case where the smaller cylinder is two inches in diameter, for example, and the bigger one is eight inches, the mechanical advantage would be $\left(\frac{8}{2}\right) = 4$. Therefore, if the larger piston was pushed down one inch, the piston in the smaller cylinder would be correspondingly pushed upward four times that amount, or four inches. By the same token, if the piston in the smaller cylinder is pushed down four inches, for example, the piston in the larger cylinder would only be pushed upward one inch.

THE VISE

The vise of Figure 8.15 is a complex machine in which the handle acts as a lever operating a different kind of machine: a screw. How can we calculate the constants of this gadget? It would be very difficult to calculate the ratio of the force the jaws apply to the force on the handle. The best we can do is work with the distances.

A screw consists of a single continuous spiral wrapped around a cylinder. The distance between ridges is known as the *pitch* of the thread, as shown in Figure 8.16. Every time the screw makes one complete turn, the screw advances a distance equal to the pitch. In the vise, one complete turn is made when the end of the handle travels in a circle whose radius is the length of the handle (l). Therefore, when the effort moves a distance $2\pi l$, the load moves a distance equal to the pitch of the thread. Therefore, for a screw,

$$\text{ideal MA} = \frac{2\pi(\text{length of handle})}{\text{pitch of thread}}$$

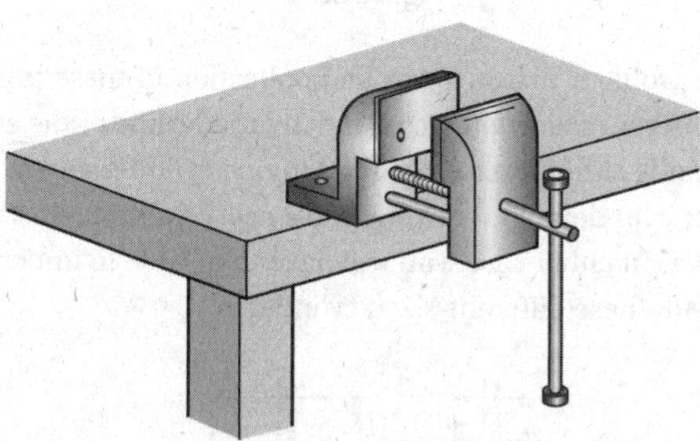

Figure 8.15

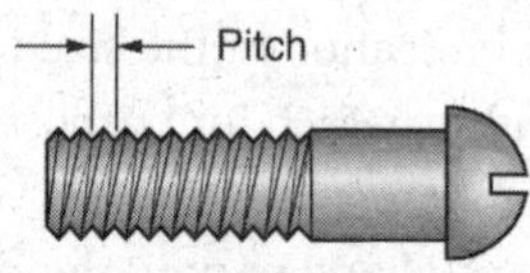

Figure 8.16

However, if you use this expression to calculate the forces, you will get it all wrong. The vise is a high-friction device. It has to be, for it is the friction that keeps it from opening when you tighten it. A vise is a self-locking machine because its efficiency is considerably under 50 percent.

Machines That Spin

What is the mechanical advantage of a winch, such as that shown in Figure 8.17? The principle is not much different from that of a lever. Because the crank and the shaft turn together, the torque exerted by the effort (the force on the handle) must be equal to the torque exerted by the load (the tension in the rope). The mechanical advantage, then, is the ratio of the radius of the crank to the radius of the shaft.

Figure 8.17

In mechanical devices, gears are commonly used to change torque. Consider the gears of Figure 8.18, for example. We assume that both gears are mounted on shafts of equal diameter, and that the small gear is driving the large one. What is the mechanical advantage of this combination?

Figure 8.18

First of all, the teeth must have the same size and spacing on both gears for them to mesh properly. With 12 teeth in the large gear and only four in the small one, the small gear has to make three complete revolutions to make the big one turn once. The large *load* or *driven* gear moves only one-third as far as the smaller *effort* or *driving* gear, and the ratio of the two distances is the same as the ratio of the number of teeth in the two gears. Then we can say that the ideal mechanical advantage of a gear is the ratio of the number of teeth in the load gear to the number of teeth in the effort gear, in this case 3:1.

Power

When a piano mover rigs his tackle to hoist a heavy piano up a vertical distance, he has to consider many factors. For one, the more pulleys he adds to the tackle setup, the longer it will take him to get the job done. If he has to pull more rope—using less force, to be sure—he will have to keep pulling for a longer time.

There is a definite limit to the amount of work the mover can do in a given time. The rate at which he does work is called his *power.* Power is work done per unit time.

The English unit of power is the foot-pound per second, and it takes 550 of them to make one horsepower. The SI unit is the joule per second, or *watt* (W). A horsepower is 746 watts. The watt is a very small unit, and the kilowatt (= 1,000 W) is commonly used.

In all the machines we have discussed so far, work comes out the load end as it goes in at the effort end. Thus, the power output of any machine is equal to the power input. Machines do not increase your power. A pulley or a windlass will spread the work out over a longer period of time, so that you can do it with the power available in your muscles and without straining for a force larger than convenient.

Mental Skills

9

Both the AFOQT and SIFT include subtests that measure your ability to visualize and understand the physical world around you. This chapter will help you review or develop the skills you need to score well on these tests:

- Block Counting (AFOQT)
- Situational Judgment (AFOQT)
- Table Reading (AFOQT)
- Simple Drawings (SIFT)
- Hidden Figures (SIFT)
- Spatial Apperception (SIFT)

In addition to preparing you for the Simple Drawings, Hidden Figures, and Spatial Apperception subtests of the SIFT and the Block Counting subtest of the AFOQT, this chapter will also discuss the skills you need to succeed on the Situational Judgment and Table Reading subtests of the AFOQT. While these two subtests don't require the same kind of visualization skills needed for the other subtests discussed above, they do require some mental skills of their own.

BLOCK COUNTING

The Block Counting subtest on the AFOQT has 30 questions that test your ability to analyze the spatial relationships of a three-dimensional collection of blocks to determine how many other blocks are touched by designated numbered blocks. For purposes of the test, you can consider that every block in the stack is the same size and shape as the other blocks. A block is considered to be touching the numbered block if any part touches it, even if it's only a corner or an edge. The key to doing well on this test section is being methodical. *Choose one side or edge of the numbered block in question and work your way (mentally) all the way around your numbered block to see how many other blocks are in contact with it.*

Let's look at an example:

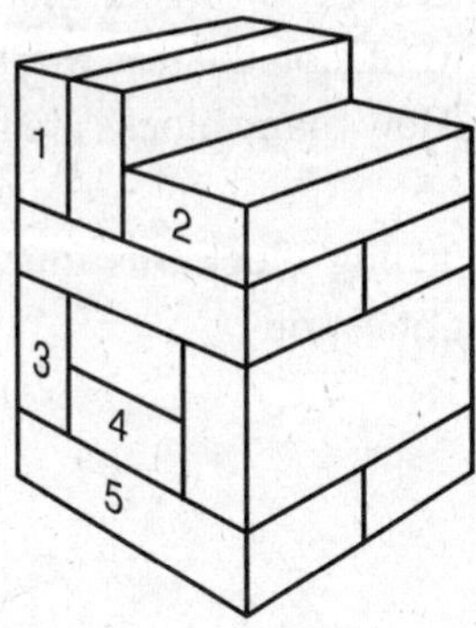

In this example, Block 1 is touching the block that is parallel to it (between Block 1 and Block 2), as well as the two blocks that are underneath and perpendicular (at right angles) to it, for a total of three blocks. Can you "see" that? Likewise, Block 2 is touching the block that is between it and Block 1, as well as the two blocks that are underneath and perpendicular, for a similar total of three blocks touched.

Block 3 is in a different circumstance, however; notice that Block 3 is edge-up at the back of this particular stack. Let's start at the top and work our way all the way around. First, notice the two blocks that are above and perpendicular to Block 3. Next, notice the two blocks (one of them numbered as Block 4) that are lying down where Block 3 is edge-up—both of them are in contact with Block 3's vertical face. Finally, there are the two blocks underneath and perpendicular to Block 3; one of them is numbered as Block 5. So, our total number of blocks in contact with Block 3 is six.

Before we look at the remaining numbered blocks, let's look at the way your possible answers are presented. This subtest is both like and unlike other multiple-choice tests. It is similar in that you will have several choices—in this case, five, designated as A through E—to pick from. Also, you will have to remain careful not to become confused between the several parallel lines of choices. However, there are no more or less attractive-sounding choices, nor are there clues you can deduce from the use of words such as *never* or *every*—there are only numbers in a table to pick from, with no difference between them except their value.

Now it's time to look at Block 4. Let's start at the back side of the stack, where we can readily see that Block 3 is touching Block 4. Then there is the block lying on top of Block 4, and then the one at the front of the stack that is perpendicular to Block 4 along its shorter axis, but parallel along the blocks' longer axis. Then, just as with Block 3, there are the two blocks at the bottom of the stack and perpendicular to Block 4's long axis. That's a total of five other blocks in the stack touching Block 4.

Key

Block	A	B	C	D	E
1	2	3	4	5	6
2	1	2	3	4	5
3	2	3	4	5	6
4	4	5	6	7	8
5	4	5	6	7	8

The stack of blocks will be presented to you with the table of possible answer choices alongside. Find the numbered block you are analyzing in the left-hand column and then read horizontally across the table until you find the number 5, which was the number of blocks touching Block 4. Reading up from the 5, you can see that the correct answer for Question 4 (which dealt with Block 4) is B. You would, on the test, mark choice B and move on to the next question, which deals with Block 5. How many blocks are touching Block 5? Go ahead—we'll wait.

Right, the number of blocks touching Block 5 is four, so we would mark choice A for Question 5 and move on to the next question.

SIMPLE DRAWINGS

In the Simple Drawings subtest of the Army's SIFT, each question will present five shapes; four are identical and one is different. Your task will be to identify the letter of the shape that's different. You will need to work quickly because there are 100 questions and you will only have two minutes—but don't guess! The score on this subtest comes from how many questions you get right, and wrong answers count against that score. It's unlikely that you will be able to get through all 100 questions in the time you're given, so focus on making the right choice for the ones you do answer. *Don't* start randomly guessing when you think time is about to run out—it can only decrease your score.

Here's an example:

P1.

(A) (B) (C) (D) (E)

As you can see, choice (D) is different from the others because it is not filled in, so that would be your choice.

"Slow is smooth, and smooth is fast."
—MG Lee Henry

This subtest is deceptively simple, but don't blow it off. Every point counts! If you get a passing score but it's only average or below average, you will *not* be able to retake the SIFT just to raise your score—you'll be stuck with it.

Everyone is different, but a technique that usually works is to pull your focus back and look at the whole question (all five shapes or figures) at one time. You will probably be able to identify the different shape faster this way versus looking at each choice sequentially. Only practice will tell you what technique works best for you.

HIDDEN FIGURES

The Hidden Figures subtest on the SIFT measures your ability to identify a simple figure hidden within a complex drawing. You will be given a series of five lettered figures—A, B, C, D, and E—followed by five numbered drawings. Your objective is to determine which lettered figure is contained within which numbered drawing. Each numbered drawing contains only one of the lettered figures, and the correct figure in each numbered drawing is always the same size and in the same rotational position as it appears in the preceding lettered figure. However, you may find the lettered shape in more than one drawing, or you may not find it at all—in other words, in each series of five, you may have one or more lettered figures that are not found, and others that are to be found more than once.

Sometimes you will be able to spot the figure in the drawing quickly, and sometimes it will take significant study. The drawing with the hidden figures often has overlapping shapes and lines that can create optical illusions, or at a minimum, mask the shape you are looking for. If you can spot the figure quickly, mark that answer on your answer sheet. However, it's not always easy to spot the hidden figures; it requires trial and error, and sometimes even the process of elimination.

The best technique to use here is to let your eye focus briefly on the figure you want to find, and then look at the numbered drawing. Think of it as letting a bloodhound sniff something belonging to the person you want him to search for or track. If you don't see the figure you're looking for in the first numbered drawing, refocus briefly on the shape to be found and go to the next numbered drawing, and so on until you find the shape. Then mark that answer on your answer sheet.

It can also be helpful, especially when you are searching for a complex shape, to focus your search on unique angles or other unusual facets of the figure. If you can find that particular angle, odd corner, or whatever, and then find it in the numbered drawing, chances are you have found the shape you're looking for—but be sure to confirm that the rest of the figure is there, too, and in the same size and rotational position as in the lettered example.

Let's look at an example series of five:

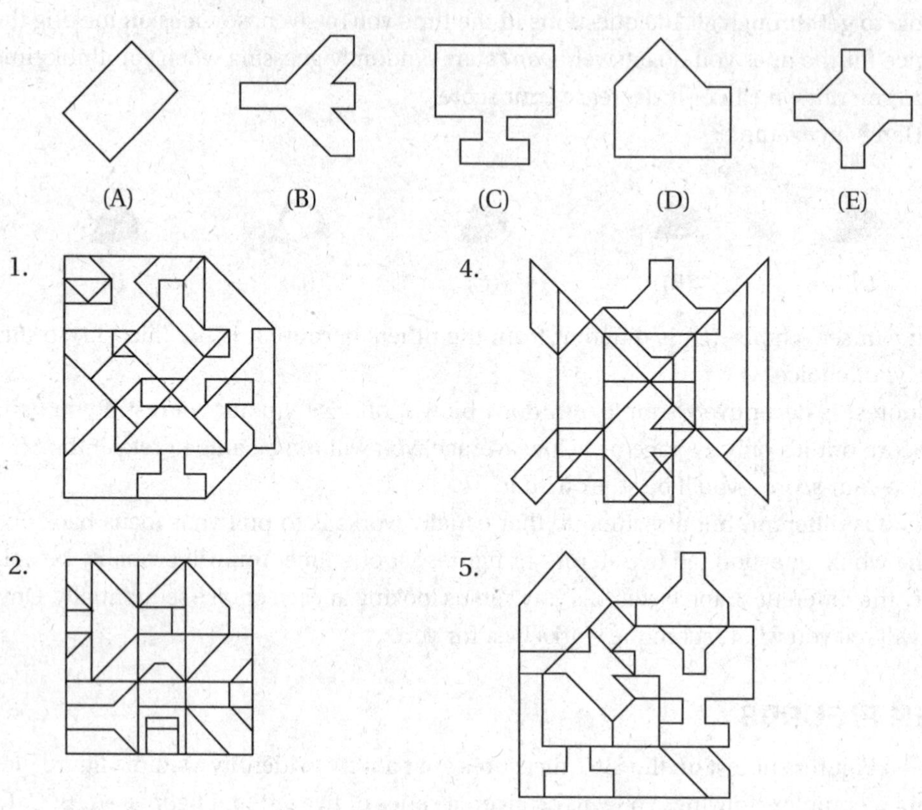

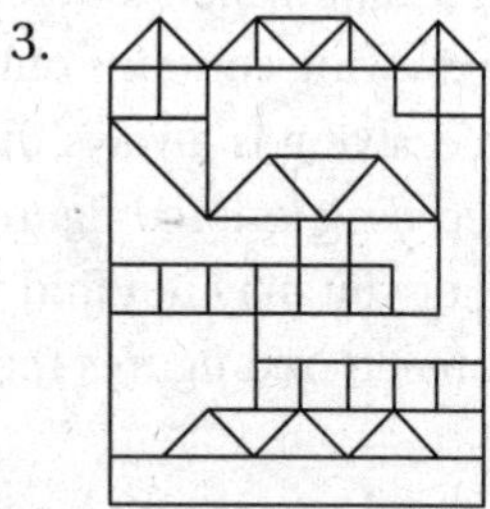

How did you do? The correct answers are as follows:

1. **A**
2. **B**
3. **C**
4. **B**
5. **D**

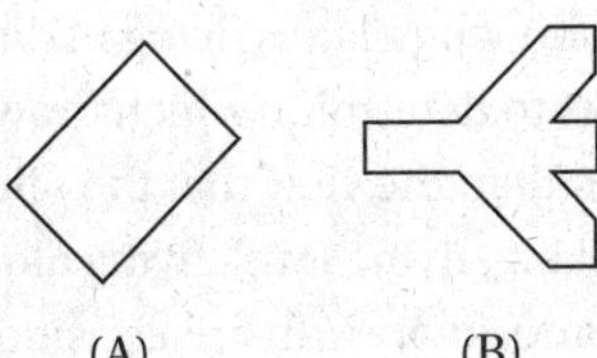
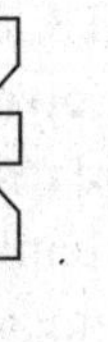
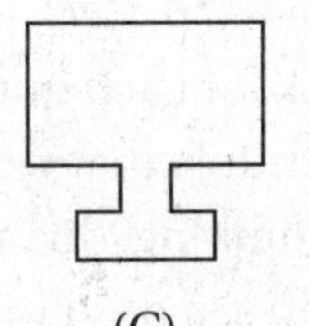
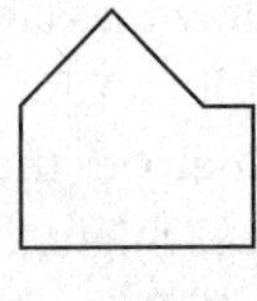
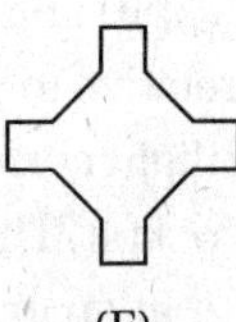

(A) (B) (C) (D) (E)

1. **(A)**

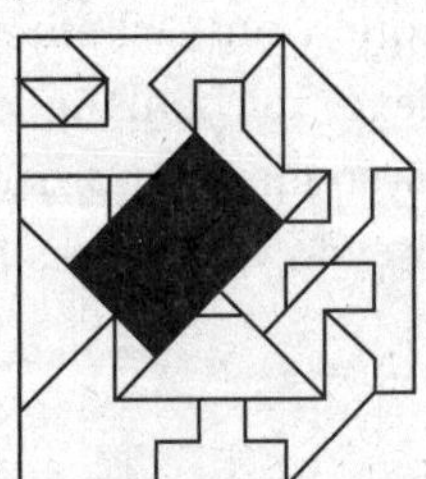

4. **(B)**

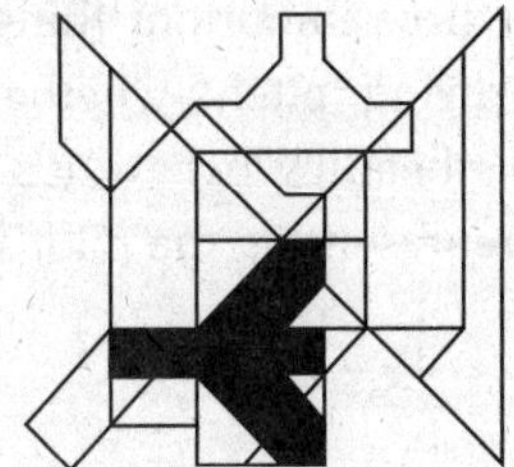

2. **(B)**

5. **(D)**

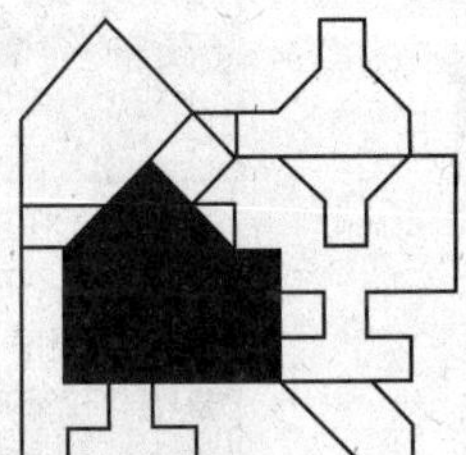

3. **(C)**

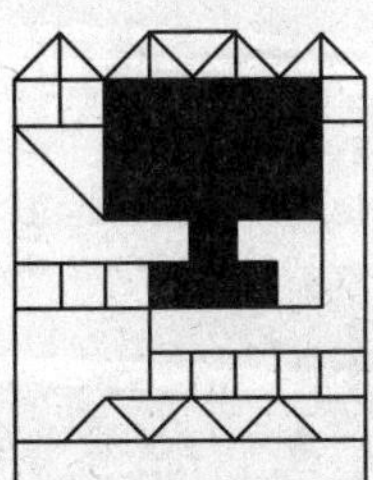

SPATIAL APPERCEPTION

The Spatial Apperception Test portion of the Army's SIFT measures your ability to perceive spatial relationships from differing orientations. Specifically, this test measures your ability to determine the attitude or position of an airplane in flight from a representation of the view through the cockpit windshield. Studies have indicated for decades that skill in determining spatial orientation has a significant role in predicting success in flight training.

On the test, you will be presented with an aerial view of the horizon (as if you were in an aircraft cockpit) and five drawings labeled A, B, C, D, and E, showing planes flying in different attitudes relative to a coastline. Your task for each question is to determine which drawing of a plane in flight correctly matches the attitude that would result in the view that the pilot sees from the cockpit. The planes might be climbing, diving, banking, flying level, flying along the coastline or at an angle to it, flying out to sea or in to land, and so on. You are considered to be looking out from the middle of your windscreen (the front part of the canopy, directly in front of the pilot).

You should look for three important things as you answer the questions: whether the airplane is climbing or diving (pitch); whether the plane is "wings level" or banking left or right; and the airplane's heading (where it's going). If you use a systematic approach of analyzing the drawing representing the pilot's view from the cockpit, you will be less likely to get confused.

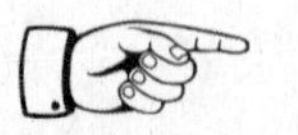

KEY

Dark Gray = Water
Light Gray = Land

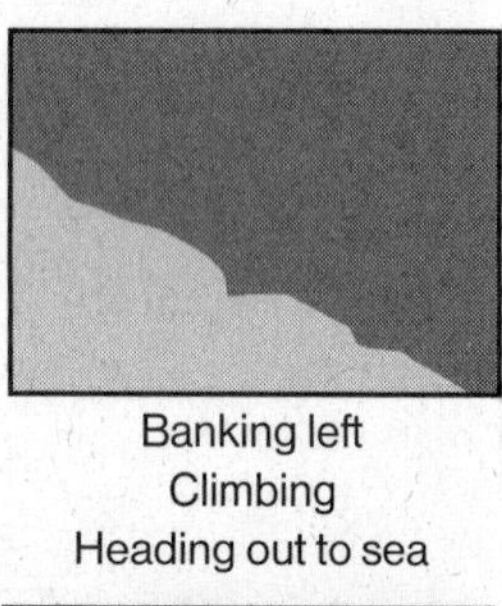

Banking left
Climbing
Heading out to sea

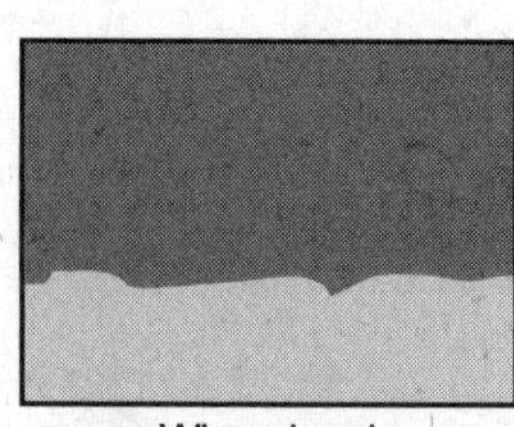

Wings level
Climbing
Heading out to sea

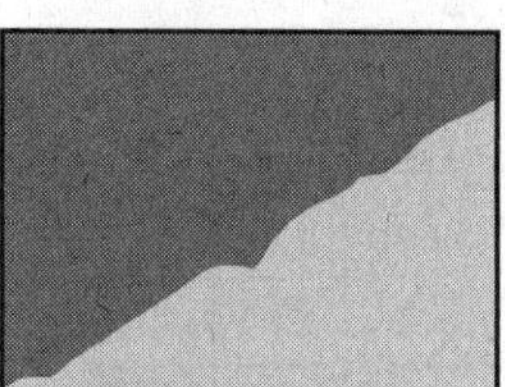

Banking right
Climbing
Heading out to sea

Banking left
Level flight
Heading out to sea

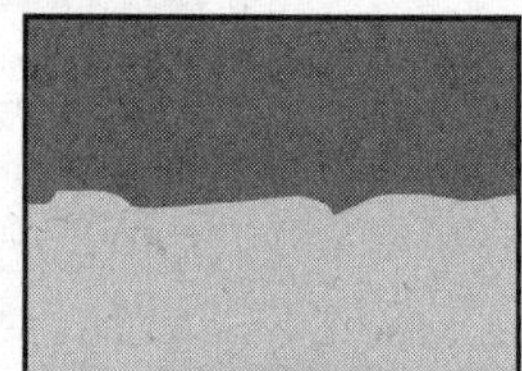

Wings level
Level flight
Heading out to sea

Banking right
Level flight
Heading out to sea

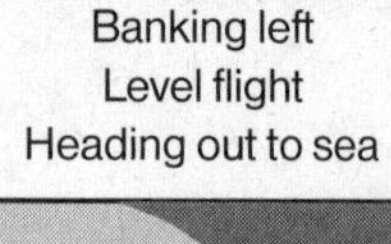

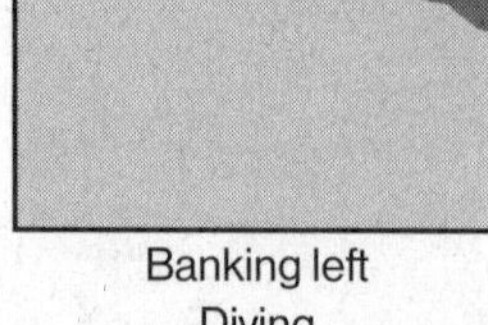

Banking left
Diving
Heading out to sea

Wings level
Diving
Heading out to sea

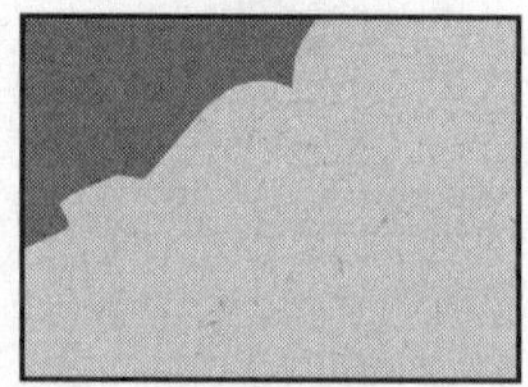

Banking right
Diving
Heading out to sea

The first thing you should look for to determine pitch is the *position* of the horizon, which indicates whether the plane is climbing, diving, or in level flight. If the horizon is above the middle of the picture, the plane is diving or descending. If it's below the middle, the plane is climbing. If the horizon is in the middle of the picture and level, the plane is in level flight.

Another way to think of this is to compare the area above and below the horizon line. If there is more area or space above the horizon than below, the plane is climbing. If there is more area underneath the horizon than above it, the plane is descending or diving. And, if the area above and below are about the same, the aircraft is in level flight. This technique is especially helpful when the airplane is in level flight but is banking one way or the other, causing the horizon to appear to tilt accordingly relative to the edges of the picture.

The next factor to consider is the *tilt* of the horizon. If it's tilted to the left, the airplane is banking to the right; if the horizon is tilted to the right, the airplane is banking to the left. If the horizon is level—tilted neither left nor right—then the plane is in level flight, not banking either left or right.

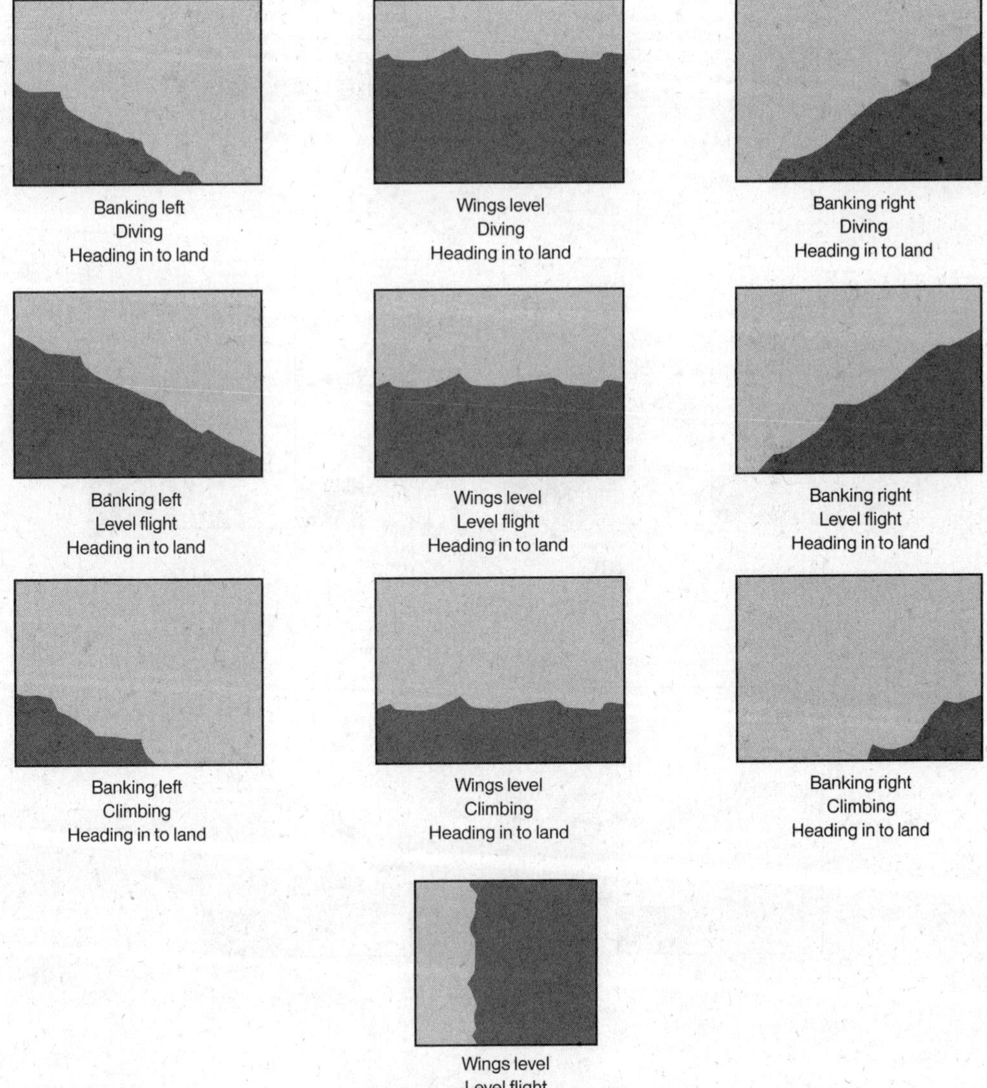

KEY

Dark Gray = Water
Light Gray = Land

The third thing to look for is the aircraft's *heading* (which direction it's going): out to sea, in from the sea, or along the coastline. This will be indicated by the representation of the land and water at the bottom of each of the five answer choices showing the airplane in flight. The lighter section is the land and the darker part represents the sea or ocean.

Now that we've discussed the view from the cockpit, let's talk about matching those views up to the external view of the airplane (looking at it from the outside).

Again, you have to approach this in a systematic way to maximize your chances for success. Determining whether the airplane is climbing, level, or diving is easy—if the nose is angled up relative to the page, it's climbing; if it's headed straight across the page, it's level; if it's angled downward, it's diving.

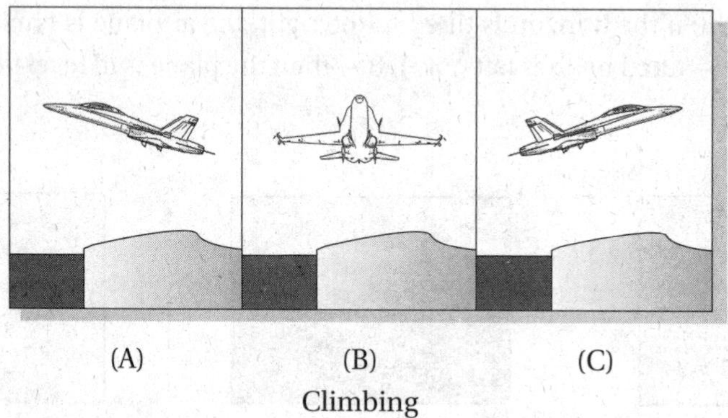

Climbing

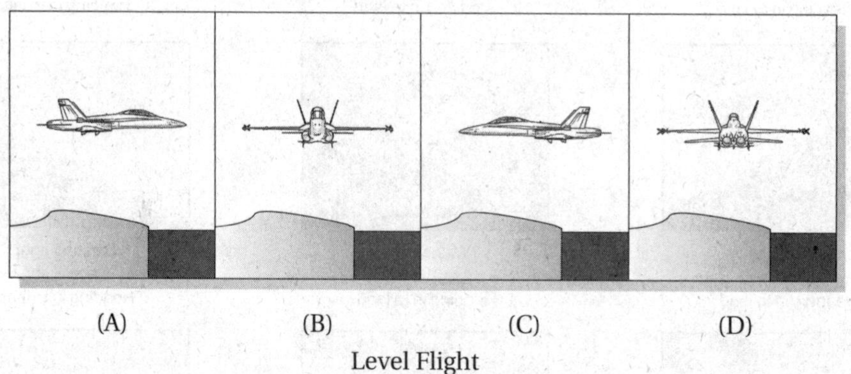

Level Flight

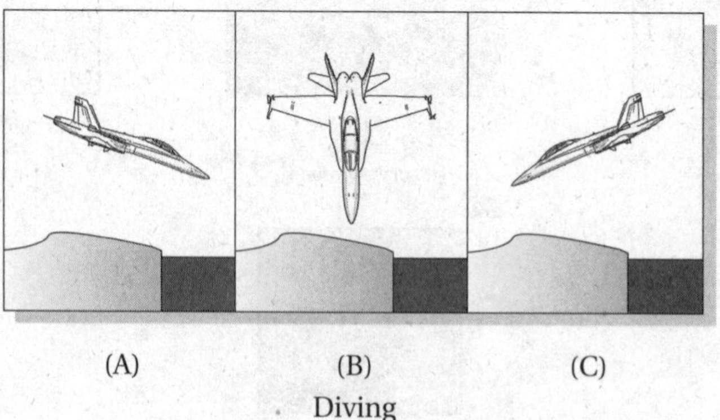

Diving

Determining the airplane's bank (or lack thereof) is as simple as seeing if the wings are level or not. If one wing is lower than the other, that's the direction of bank.

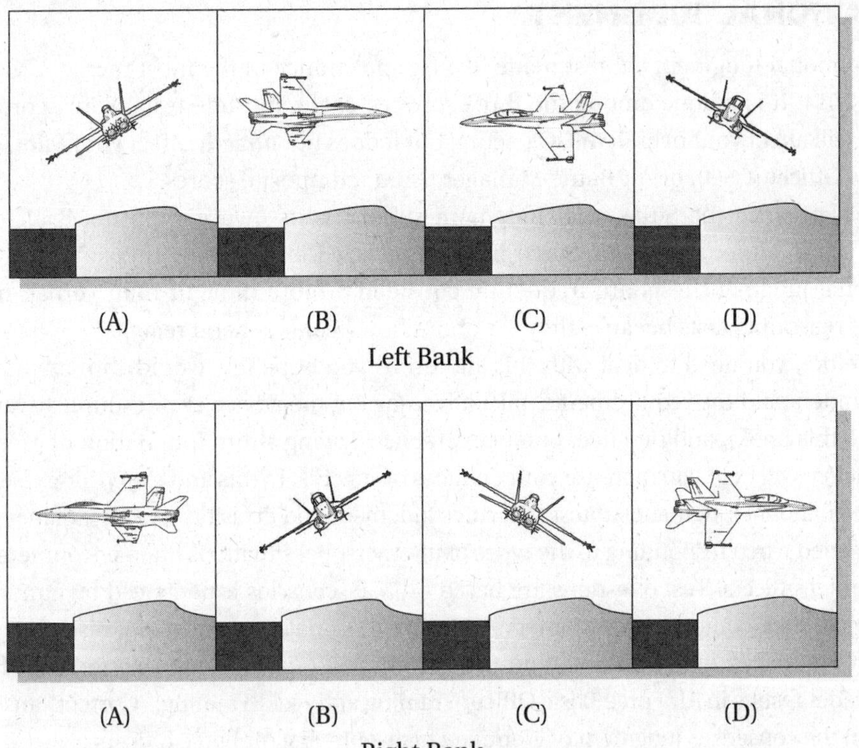

To determine whether the airplane is heading out to sea or in toward land, look at the land and water "bar" at the bottom of the illustration. If the lighter section underneath the airplane is on the right side of the picture and the nose of the airplane is pointed to the left, then the airplane is headed out to sea. Or, to look at it another way, if the pilot's viewpoint picture has sea above land with the horizon line and coastline parallel to each other, you are heading out to sea.

If the lighter segment underneath the airplane drawing is on the left side of the picture and the nose of the airplane is pointed to the left, then the airplane is headed toward land. Said differently, if the picture has land above sea, with the horizon line and coastline parallel to each other, you are heading in to land.

If the horizon line and coastline are perpendicular to each other you are heading down the coast. Here you just need to be aware of which way the coastline is—to your left or right—to make sure that you select the correct external view of the airplane.

And, if the horizon line and coastline are neither parallel nor perpendicular, then you are heading at a 45-degree angle relative to the coastline, either heading in toward land or out to sea.

SITUATIONAL JUDGMENT

The Situational Judgment subtest made its first appearance in the most recent AFOQT revision in 2014. It is unique among the three services' flight aptitude tests. Your score on this subtest will affect your overall AFOQT score, but it does not *directly* affect your Pilot, Combat Systems Officer (CSO), or Air Battle Manager (ABM) composite scores.

However, since the Situational Judgment subtest is its own composite, it affects your overall score, although the Air Force has not released exactly how this subtest affects it. Situational judgment tests are frequently considered more difficult than verbal, math, or abstract reasoning tests because they are about how *people* act and react.

Therefore, you need to deal with this subtest as you hopefully would with any new challenge: understand the requirements, take advantage of the advice and resources available to you (like this book), and practice, practice, practice! Laying a firm foundation of preparation and practice will help you increase your chances of success, in this and everything else you do.

"Good judgment comes from experience, and a lot of that comes from bad judgment." —Will Rogers, 1879–1935, American cowboy, actor, humorist, newspaper columnist, and social commentator

The Situational Judgment subtest measures judgment and decision-making abilities, such as those needed when responding to the types of interpersonal situations often encountered by Air Force junior officers. Test questions are based on real scenarios experienced by junior officers that require core competencies of integrity and professionalism, leadership, resource management, communication, innovation, and mentoring. Test questions are selected based on historical cadet results in Air Force Basic Officer Training and Field Training. "Correct" answers are based on the consensus judgment of identified high-potential Air Force officers.

In this subtest, you will be presented with a short scenario in which you will usually (but not always) be the leader of a small section, office, or the like. After presenting the situation, the question will give you five answer options and ask which would be the most effective and least effective ways to respond to the scenario.

You will have 35 minutes to answer 50 questions on 25 scenarios, meaning you will have a little more than a minute for each scenario. This is plenty of time if you stay focused—the scenarios usually run only about four to six sentences each. Although some actions may seem to be equally effective or ineffective, you only pick one of each—the best and the worst.

Here's an example right from the Air Force:

Situation I. You have recently been assigned to lead a section comprised of experienced subordinates, but you do not have a full understanding of the mission and tasks. Your subordinates are not helpful when you solicit ideas and information from them. You know it is necessary for you to understand your job and the other section members' jobs in order to effectively lead your section and accomplish the mission.

Possible actions:

(A) Contact the superior who assigned you to the section for further guidance.
(B) Contact the individual previously assigned to the section for guidance.
(C) Meet privately with the most senior subordinate to discuss the section's mission.
(D) Meet individually with each subordinate to get to know them personally.
(E) Call a section meeting, and emphasize that you need everyone's cooperation in order to help the section succeed.

1. Select the MOST EFFECTIVE action (A–E) in response to the situation.

2. Select the LEAST EFFECTIVE action (A–E) in response to the situation.

The Air Force AFOQT pamphlet containing this example says either choice (C) or choice (D) is considered most effective, and that choice (A) is considered the least effective. Thirty years of experience in the military tells me that choice (C) would be the most effective, *followed* by choice (D)—and that choice (A) would, in fact, be the least effective because it would show the superior who assigned you to that section that you are unable or unwilling to think on your own.

What this means to you as the test-taker is that you should read the scenario carefully and consider the choices thoroughly, but don't agonize over which one to pick—take your best shot and move on to the next scenario. Here are some useful tips for successfully working through these scenarios (as well as the ones in real life):

- Read the scenario carefully. Evaluate the relevance of each answer to solving the problem laid out in the scenario.
- Use only the information in the scenario. You will have to supplement this with your *general* knowledge of how the military works and how organizations and the people in them act and react—but don't make assumptions about *specific* resources or circumstances not mentioned in the scenario.
- Think about your response in light of the Air Force Core Values of *integrity first, service before self,* and *excellence in all we do* (discussed in more detail later in this section).
- Think about the effects of your response choices in light of the unit or organization's mission and purpose. Remember that the military can't afford to make excuses or arbitrarily miss deadlines.
- Take the initiative when you can to solve things at your level before you go to your supervisor or commander—but be willing to ask for help from your subordinates or colleagues when it seems appropriate.
- Don't jump over or skip levels in the chain of command or supervisory chain (military or civilian), either upward or downward. Put yourself in the shoes of your scenario superiors or subordinates and think about how each response choice would look from that perspective.
- Think about the effects of your scenario response choices on the situation, your team or unit, and the other people in your organization at both higher and lower levels.
- Prioritize which aspects of the scenario are most important to address first. Any answer option that does not move the situation forward will not be the "most effective" action to take. The "least effective" answer option will be one that makes the situation even worse.
- Don't look for the easy or short-term solution. Instead, seek to do what's right, even if it's tough—and balance your goals and agenda with those of your subordinates, colleagues, and the organization.
- Don't try to do everything yourself; keep your subordinates informed, ask their advice, and don't be afraid to delegate tasks to them while keeping everyone informed.
- Look for the most ethical solution. Any answer option that is even slightly unethical or dishonest to anyone involved will not be the correct one. Look for the most virtuous answer if there is one—demonstrating integrity, respect for others, and conscientiousness.
- Keep people in the scenario informed, both up and down the chain of command, in person if possible—especially when there is a disagreement, friction, or some other kind of contention.

- Look for a solution that emphasizes teamwork, listening to people, and helping people and teams get better. This may be a solution that puts your individual short-term desires at a lower priority.
- Look for a solution that builds and sustains positive, effective relationships within your team and across the broader organization.
- When an individual is the source of some problem or obstacle, don't be afraid to discuss it with him or her—but do so in private, and do it with an eye toward improving things in the scenario, not just telling him or her that he or she is wrong. A response option that involves criticizing someone in public is certainly not the "most effective," but it *will* almost certainly be a contender for "least effective."
- Look for a creative solution that goes beyond what look like the boundaries of the situation, without breaking the chain of command.
- Look for response choices that are distinct from each other. If two choices seem similar, one may be the most effective or least effective (or it may not)—but if two choices are similar to each other, one will not be the most effective and the other one the least effective.

To help you understand the values and qualities that apply to the scenarios and the actions considered most and least effective, here are some highlights of current Air Force doctrine and philosophy. This is not meant to be a recruiting section for the Air Force—but if you are going to take the AFOQT, this is to familiarize you with how the Air Force thinks about itself and its goals and what it considers important. This is not to say that the Army, the Navy, and the Marines don't have the same level of standards—they just don't have questions about them on their flight aptitude test.

Air Force Core Values

- **INTEGRITY FIRST**—An Airman is a person of integrity, courage, and conviction. He or she must be willing to control his or her impulses and exercise courage, honesty, and accountability in order to do what is right, even when no one is looking.
- **SERVICE BEFORE SELF**—An Airman's professional duties take precedence over personal desires. Every Airman is expected to have the discipline to follow rules, exhibit self-control, and possess respect for the beliefs, authority, and worth of others.
- **EXCELLENCE IN ALL WE DO**—An Airman strives for continual improvement in self and service in order to propel the Air Force further and to achieve greater accomplishment and performance for themselves and their community.

THE AIRMAN'S CREED

I AM AN AMERICAN AIRMAN.
I AM A WARRIOR.
I HAVE ANSWERED MY NATION'S CALL.

I AM AN AMERICAN AIRMAN.
MY MISSION IS TO FLY, FIGHT, AND WIN.
I AM FAITHFUL TO A PROUD HERITAGE,
A TRADITION OF HONOR,
AND A LEGACY OF VALOR.

I AM AN AMERICAN AIRMAN.
GUARDIAN OF FREEDOM AND JUSTICE,
MY NATION'S SWORD AND SHIELD,
ITS SENTRY AND AVENGER.
I DEFEND MY COUNTRY WITH MY LIFE.

I AM AN AMERICAN AIRMAN.
WINGMAN, LEADER, WARRIOR.
I WILL NEVER LEAVE AN AIRMAN BEHIND,
I WILL NEVER FALTER,
AND I WILL NOT FAIL.

The Air Force Vision

The U.S. Air Force is the world's preeminent force in air, space, and cyberspace. We maintain that distinction by maintaining our objective of global vigilance, reach, and power, and remaining true to our vision statement: The World's Greatest Air Force—Powered by Airmen, Fueled by Innovation. Through shared values, key capabilities, and upholding our Airman's Creed, we continue to achieve our mission and aim high in all we do.

The Air Force Mission

Fly, fight, and win in the air, space, and cyberspace.

Organization of the Air Force

MAJOR COMMANDS

The U.S. Air Force is subdivided into 10 major commands (MAJCOMs) which are directly subordinate to Headquarters, U.S. Air Force (HQ USAF), or the Air Staff. MAJCOM headquarters are *management* headquarters for a major segment of the Air Force, based on a functional or geographic perspective:

- **AIR COMBAT COMMAND**—provides Air Force component units for U.S. Northern Command, U.S. Southern Command, and U.S. Central Command
- **AIR EDUCATION AND TRAINING COMMAND**—recruits, trains, and educates Airmen of all ranks
- **AIR FORCE GLOBAL STRIKE COMMAND**—develops and provides combat-ready forces for global strike operations and nuclear deterrence
- **AIR FORCE MATERIEL COMMAND**—provides logistics support and research, development, and acquisition of Air Force weapons and equipment
- **AIR FORCE RESERVE COMMAND**—provides supervision of Air Force Reserve and Air National Guard forces and capabilities, helping to integrate them into active Air Force missions
- **AIR FORCE SPACE COMMAND**—develops and operates military space and cyberspace technologies and capabilities
- **AIR FORCE SPECIAL OPERATIONS COMMAND**—provides Air Force component units for U.S. Special Operations Command
- **AIR MOBILITY COMMAND**—provides airlift and aerial refueling for all U.S. Armed Forces
- **PACIFIC AIR FORCES**—provides Air Force component units for the U.S. Pacific Command
- **U.S. AIR FORCES IN EUROPE-AIR FORCES AFRICA**—provides Air Force component units for the U.S. European Command and the U.S. Africa Command

NUMBERED AIR FORCE

The numbered air force is a *tactical* echelon directly under an operational MAJCOM that supervises specific missions. Numbered air forces have operational units such as wings, groups, and squadrons assigned or attached to them.

WING

An Air Force wing has a distinct mission with a specific scope and reports to a numbered air force or HQ USAF. A wing is made up of one or more *groups* and is usually commanded by a colonel or a brigadier general.

GROUP

A group is made up of several *squadrons* and may have a single focus (i.e., operations, logistics, medical, etc.) or may be more independent, with several types of squadrons underneath it. It is commanded by a colonel.

SQUADRON

A squadron is considered the basic Air Force unit. A squadron is usually made up of *two flights* and (if it is a flying unit) has eight to 24 aircraft; it usually consists of a few hundred Airmen. It is usually commanded by a lieutenant colonel, but it can be commanded by a major or a captain, depending on its size and function.

FLIGHT

A flight is the smallest official Air Force unit. It is usually comprised of a dozen to over one hundred people and is commanded by a captain; if it is a flying unit, it typically has four aircraft.

ELEMENT

Although not officially recognized as a unit, a flight is usually broken up into three to four evenly distributed *elements,* usually led by a lieutenant, although in non-flying units it may be led by a senior NCO. In Air Force security forces, it may be called a *squad,* a term borrowed from the Army and Marines, whose land-based missions are similar.

For additional information about Air Force leadership, doctrine, and philosophy, go to: *http://www.doctrine.af.mil/Portals/61/documents/Volume_2/Volume-2-Leadership.pdf?ver=2017-09-17-123840-740*

TABLE READING

The Table Reading subtest of the AFOQT measures your ability to read a table quickly and accurately. It may seem like a mundane, overly simplistic task to accomplish accurately over and over again—but the Air Force considers it important enough that it feeds into your Pilot, CSO, and ABM composite scores.

For this subtest, you will be given a table similar to the one below (more about this shortly). Notice that the X values appear at the top of the table, and the Y values are shown on the left side of the table. The X values are the column values, and the Y values are the row values. For each test question, you are given an X value and a Y value. Your task is to find the block where the column and the row intersect, note the number that appears there, and then find this number among the five answer options.

		X VALUES						
		-3	-2	-1	0	+1	+2	+3
Y VALUES	+3	25	26	28	30	31	32	33
	+2	26	28	30	32	33	34	35
	+1	27	29	31	33	35	36	37
	0	29	30	32	34	36	37	38
	-1	30	32	33	35	37	38	40
	-2	31	33	34	36	38	39	41
	-3	32	34	35	37	39	40	42

	X	Y	(A)	(B)	(C)	(D)	(E)
1.	+1	+2	35	36	30	33	34

You can see that the column under the X value of +1 intersects with the row to the right of the Y value of +2 in a square that holds the number 33. Therefore, the correct answer is choice (D).

You will have 40 questions to answer in seven minutes, so you have only about 10 seconds per question—but that's plenty of time if you are methodical. Here's the trick: the actual test will have a much bigger table, and all 40 questions will be from that same table. You won't have a ruler to help you line up the rows and columns, so you will need to get your eyes and brain working together during this subtest.

PART III

Flight Aptitude Practice Tests

ANSWER SHEET
AFOQT #1

Subtest 1: Verbal Analogies

1. Ⓐ Ⓑ Ⓒ Ⓓ Ⓔ
2. Ⓐ Ⓑ Ⓒ Ⓓ Ⓔ
3. Ⓐ Ⓑ Ⓒ Ⓓ Ⓔ
4. Ⓐ Ⓑ Ⓒ Ⓓ Ⓔ
5. Ⓐ Ⓑ Ⓒ Ⓓ Ⓔ
6. Ⓐ Ⓑ Ⓒ Ⓓ Ⓔ
7. Ⓐ Ⓑ Ⓒ Ⓓ Ⓔ
8. Ⓐ Ⓑ Ⓒ Ⓓ Ⓔ
9. Ⓐ Ⓑ Ⓒ Ⓓ Ⓔ
10. Ⓐ Ⓑ Ⓒ Ⓓ Ⓔ
11. Ⓐ Ⓑ Ⓒ Ⓓ Ⓔ
12. Ⓐ Ⓑ Ⓒ Ⓓ Ⓔ
13. Ⓐ Ⓑ Ⓒ Ⓓ Ⓔ
14. Ⓐ Ⓑ Ⓒ Ⓓ Ⓔ
15. Ⓐ Ⓑ Ⓒ Ⓓ Ⓔ
16. Ⓐ Ⓑ Ⓒ Ⓓ Ⓔ
17. Ⓐ Ⓑ Ⓒ Ⓓ Ⓔ
18. Ⓐ Ⓑ Ⓒ Ⓓ Ⓔ
19. Ⓐ Ⓑ Ⓒ Ⓓ Ⓔ
20. Ⓐ Ⓑ Ⓒ Ⓓ Ⓔ
21. Ⓐ Ⓑ Ⓒ Ⓓ Ⓔ
22. Ⓐ Ⓑ Ⓒ Ⓓ Ⓔ
23. Ⓐ Ⓑ Ⓒ Ⓓ Ⓔ
24. Ⓐ Ⓑ Ⓒ Ⓓ Ⓔ
25. Ⓐ Ⓑ Ⓒ Ⓓ Ⓔ

Subtest 2: Arithmetic Reasoning

1. Ⓐ Ⓑ Ⓒ Ⓓ Ⓔ
2. Ⓐ Ⓑ Ⓒ Ⓓ Ⓔ
3. Ⓐ Ⓑ Ⓒ Ⓓ Ⓔ
4. Ⓐ Ⓑ Ⓒ Ⓓ Ⓔ
5. Ⓐ Ⓑ Ⓒ Ⓓ Ⓔ
6. Ⓐ Ⓑ Ⓒ Ⓓ Ⓔ
7. Ⓐ Ⓑ Ⓒ Ⓓ Ⓔ
8. Ⓐ Ⓑ Ⓒ Ⓓ Ⓔ
9. Ⓐ Ⓑ Ⓒ Ⓓ Ⓔ
10. Ⓐ Ⓑ Ⓒ Ⓓ Ⓔ
11. Ⓐ Ⓑ Ⓒ Ⓓ Ⓔ
12. Ⓐ Ⓑ Ⓒ Ⓓ Ⓔ
13. Ⓐ Ⓑ Ⓒ Ⓓ Ⓔ
14. Ⓐ Ⓑ Ⓒ Ⓓ Ⓔ
15. Ⓐ Ⓑ Ⓒ Ⓓ Ⓔ
16. Ⓐ Ⓑ Ⓒ Ⓓ Ⓔ
17. Ⓐ Ⓑ Ⓒ Ⓓ Ⓔ
18. Ⓐ Ⓑ Ⓒ Ⓓ Ⓔ
19. Ⓐ Ⓑ Ⓒ Ⓓ Ⓔ
20. Ⓐ Ⓑ Ⓒ Ⓓ Ⓔ
21. Ⓐ Ⓑ Ⓒ Ⓓ Ⓔ
22. Ⓐ Ⓑ Ⓒ Ⓓ Ⓔ
23. Ⓐ Ⓑ Ⓒ Ⓓ Ⓔ
24. Ⓐ Ⓑ Ⓒ Ⓓ Ⓔ
25. Ⓐ Ⓑ Ⓒ Ⓓ Ⓔ

Subtest 3: Word Knowledge

1. Ⓐ Ⓑ Ⓒ Ⓓ Ⓔ
2. Ⓐ Ⓑ Ⓒ Ⓓ Ⓔ
3. Ⓐ Ⓑ Ⓒ Ⓓ Ⓔ
4. Ⓐ Ⓑ Ⓒ Ⓓ Ⓔ
5. Ⓐ Ⓑ Ⓒ Ⓓ Ⓔ
6. Ⓐ Ⓑ Ⓒ Ⓓ Ⓔ
7. Ⓐ Ⓑ Ⓒ Ⓓ Ⓔ
8. Ⓐ Ⓑ Ⓒ Ⓓ Ⓔ
9. Ⓐ Ⓑ Ⓒ Ⓓ Ⓔ
10. Ⓐ Ⓑ Ⓒ Ⓓ Ⓔ
11. Ⓐ Ⓑ Ⓒ Ⓓ Ⓔ
12. Ⓐ Ⓑ Ⓒ Ⓓ Ⓔ
13. Ⓐ Ⓑ Ⓒ Ⓓ Ⓔ
14. Ⓐ Ⓑ Ⓒ Ⓓ Ⓔ
15. Ⓐ Ⓑ Ⓒ Ⓓ Ⓔ
16. Ⓐ Ⓑ Ⓒ Ⓓ Ⓔ
17. Ⓐ Ⓑ Ⓒ Ⓓ Ⓔ
18. Ⓐ Ⓑ Ⓒ Ⓓ Ⓔ
19. Ⓐ Ⓑ Ⓒ Ⓓ Ⓔ
20. Ⓐ Ⓑ Ⓒ Ⓓ Ⓔ
21. Ⓐ Ⓑ Ⓒ Ⓓ Ⓔ
22. Ⓐ Ⓑ Ⓒ Ⓓ Ⓔ
23. Ⓐ Ⓑ Ⓒ Ⓓ Ⓔ
24. Ⓐ Ⓑ Ⓒ Ⓓ Ⓔ
25. Ⓐ Ⓑ Ⓒ Ⓓ Ⓔ

Subtest 4: Math Knowledge

1. Ⓐ Ⓑ Ⓒ Ⓓ Ⓔ
2. Ⓐ Ⓑ Ⓒ Ⓓ Ⓔ
3. Ⓐ Ⓑ Ⓒ Ⓓ Ⓔ
4. Ⓐ Ⓑ Ⓒ Ⓓ Ⓔ
5. Ⓐ Ⓑ Ⓒ Ⓓ Ⓔ
6. Ⓐ Ⓑ Ⓒ Ⓓ Ⓔ
7. Ⓐ Ⓑ Ⓒ Ⓓ Ⓔ
8. Ⓐ Ⓑ Ⓒ Ⓓ Ⓔ
9. Ⓐ Ⓑ Ⓒ Ⓓ Ⓔ
10. Ⓐ Ⓑ Ⓒ Ⓓ Ⓔ
11. Ⓐ Ⓑ Ⓒ Ⓓ Ⓔ
12. Ⓐ Ⓑ Ⓒ Ⓓ Ⓔ
13. Ⓐ Ⓑ Ⓒ Ⓓ Ⓔ
14. Ⓐ Ⓑ Ⓒ Ⓓ Ⓔ
15. Ⓐ Ⓑ Ⓒ Ⓓ Ⓔ
16. Ⓐ Ⓑ Ⓒ Ⓓ Ⓔ
17. Ⓐ Ⓑ Ⓒ Ⓓ Ⓔ
18. Ⓐ Ⓑ Ⓒ Ⓓ Ⓔ
19. Ⓐ Ⓑ Ⓒ Ⓓ Ⓔ
20. Ⓐ Ⓑ Ⓒ Ⓓ Ⓔ
21. Ⓐ Ⓑ Ⓒ Ⓓ Ⓔ
22. Ⓐ Ⓑ Ⓒ Ⓓ Ⓔ
23. Ⓐ Ⓑ Ⓒ Ⓓ Ⓔ
24. Ⓐ Ⓑ Ⓒ Ⓓ Ⓔ
25. Ⓐ Ⓑ Ⓒ Ⓓ Ⓔ

ANSWER SHEET
AFOQT #1

Subtest 5: Reading Comprehension

1. Ⓐ Ⓑ Ⓒ Ⓓ Ⓔ
2. Ⓐ Ⓑ Ⓒ Ⓓ Ⓔ
3. Ⓐ Ⓑ Ⓒ Ⓓ Ⓔ
4. Ⓐ Ⓑ Ⓒ Ⓓ Ⓔ
5. Ⓐ Ⓑ Ⓒ Ⓓ Ⓔ
6. Ⓐ Ⓑ Ⓒ Ⓓ Ⓔ
7. Ⓐ Ⓑ Ⓒ Ⓓ Ⓔ
8. Ⓐ Ⓑ Ⓒ Ⓓ Ⓔ
9. Ⓐ Ⓑ Ⓒ Ⓓ Ⓔ
10. Ⓐ Ⓑ Ⓒ Ⓓ Ⓔ
11. Ⓐ Ⓑ Ⓒ Ⓓ Ⓔ
12. Ⓐ Ⓑ Ⓒ Ⓓ Ⓔ
13. Ⓐ Ⓑ Ⓒ Ⓓ Ⓔ
14. Ⓐ Ⓑ Ⓒ Ⓓ Ⓔ
15. Ⓐ Ⓑ Ⓒ Ⓓ Ⓔ
16. Ⓐ Ⓑ Ⓒ Ⓓ Ⓔ
17. Ⓐ Ⓑ Ⓒ Ⓓ Ⓔ
18. Ⓐ Ⓑ Ⓒ Ⓓ Ⓔ
19. Ⓐ Ⓑ Ⓒ Ⓓ Ⓔ
20. Ⓐ Ⓑ Ⓒ Ⓓ Ⓔ
21. Ⓐ Ⓑ Ⓒ Ⓓ Ⓔ
22. Ⓐ Ⓑ Ⓒ Ⓓ Ⓔ
23. Ⓐ Ⓑ Ⓒ Ⓓ Ⓔ
24. Ⓐ Ⓑ Ⓒ Ⓓ Ⓔ
25. Ⓐ Ⓑ Ⓒ Ⓓ Ⓔ

Subtest 6: Situational Judgment

1. Ⓐ Ⓑ Ⓒ Ⓓ Ⓔ
2. Ⓐ Ⓑ Ⓒ Ⓓ Ⓔ
3. Ⓐ Ⓑ Ⓒ Ⓓ Ⓔ
4. Ⓐ Ⓑ Ⓒ Ⓓ Ⓔ
5. Ⓐ Ⓑ Ⓒ Ⓓ Ⓔ
6. Ⓐ Ⓑ Ⓒ Ⓓ Ⓔ
7. Ⓐ Ⓑ Ⓒ Ⓓ Ⓔ
8. Ⓐ Ⓑ Ⓒ Ⓓ Ⓔ
9. Ⓐ Ⓑ Ⓒ Ⓓ Ⓔ
10. Ⓐ Ⓑ Ⓒ Ⓓ Ⓔ
11. Ⓐ Ⓑ Ⓒ Ⓓ Ⓔ
12. Ⓐ Ⓑ Ⓒ Ⓓ Ⓔ
13. Ⓐ Ⓑ Ⓒ Ⓓ Ⓔ
14. Ⓐ Ⓑ Ⓒ Ⓓ Ⓔ
15. Ⓐ Ⓑ Ⓒ Ⓓ Ⓔ
16. Ⓐ Ⓑ Ⓒ Ⓓ Ⓔ
17. Ⓐ Ⓑ Ⓒ Ⓓ Ⓔ
18. Ⓐ Ⓑ Ⓒ Ⓓ Ⓔ
19. Ⓐ Ⓑ Ⓒ Ⓓ Ⓔ
20. Ⓐ Ⓑ Ⓒ Ⓓ Ⓔ
21. Ⓐ Ⓑ Ⓒ Ⓓ Ⓔ
22. Ⓐ Ⓑ Ⓒ Ⓓ Ⓔ
23. Ⓐ Ⓑ Ⓒ Ⓓ Ⓔ
24. Ⓐ Ⓑ Ⓒ Ⓓ Ⓔ
25. Ⓐ Ⓑ Ⓒ Ⓓ Ⓔ
26. Ⓐ Ⓑ Ⓒ Ⓓ Ⓔ
27. Ⓐ Ⓑ Ⓒ Ⓓ Ⓔ
28. Ⓐ Ⓑ Ⓒ Ⓓ Ⓔ
29. Ⓐ Ⓑ Ⓒ Ⓓ Ⓔ
30. Ⓐ Ⓑ Ⓒ Ⓓ Ⓔ
31. Ⓐ Ⓑ Ⓒ Ⓓ Ⓔ
32. Ⓐ Ⓑ Ⓒ Ⓓ Ⓔ
33. Ⓐ Ⓑ Ⓒ Ⓓ Ⓔ
34. Ⓐ Ⓑ Ⓒ Ⓓ Ⓔ
35. Ⓐ Ⓑ Ⓒ Ⓓ Ⓔ
36. Ⓐ Ⓑ Ⓒ Ⓓ Ⓔ
37. Ⓐ Ⓑ Ⓒ Ⓓ Ⓔ
38. Ⓐ Ⓑ Ⓒ Ⓓ Ⓔ
39. Ⓐ Ⓑ Ⓒ Ⓓ Ⓔ
40. Ⓐ Ⓑ Ⓒ Ⓓ Ⓔ
41. Ⓐ Ⓑ Ⓒ Ⓓ Ⓔ
42. Ⓐ Ⓑ Ⓒ Ⓓ Ⓔ
43. Ⓐ Ⓑ Ⓒ Ⓓ Ⓔ
44. Ⓐ Ⓑ Ⓒ Ⓓ Ⓔ
45. Ⓐ Ⓑ Ⓒ Ⓓ Ⓔ
46. Ⓐ Ⓑ Ⓒ Ⓓ Ⓔ
47. Ⓐ Ⓑ Ⓒ Ⓓ Ⓔ
48. Ⓐ Ⓑ Ⓒ Ⓓ Ⓔ
49. Ⓐ Ⓑ Ⓒ Ⓓ Ⓔ
50. Ⓐ Ⓑ Ⓒ Ⓓ Ⓔ

Subtest 7: Self-Description Inventory (Omitted)

Subtest 8: Physical Science

1. Ⓐ Ⓑ Ⓒ Ⓓ Ⓔ
2. Ⓐ Ⓑ Ⓒ Ⓓ Ⓔ
3. Ⓐ Ⓑ Ⓒ Ⓓ Ⓔ
4. Ⓐ Ⓑ Ⓒ Ⓓ Ⓔ
5. Ⓐ Ⓑ Ⓒ Ⓓ Ⓔ
6. Ⓐ Ⓑ Ⓒ Ⓓ Ⓔ
7. Ⓐ Ⓑ Ⓒ Ⓓ Ⓔ
8. Ⓐ Ⓑ Ⓒ Ⓓ Ⓔ
9. Ⓐ Ⓑ Ⓒ Ⓓ Ⓔ
10. Ⓐ Ⓑ Ⓒ Ⓓ Ⓔ
11. Ⓐ Ⓑ Ⓒ Ⓓ Ⓔ
12. Ⓐ Ⓑ Ⓒ Ⓓ Ⓔ
13. Ⓐ Ⓑ Ⓒ Ⓓ Ⓔ
14. Ⓐ Ⓑ Ⓒ Ⓓ Ⓔ
15. Ⓐ Ⓑ Ⓒ Ⓓ Ⓔ
16. Ⓐ Ⓑ Ⓒ Ⓓ Ⓔ
17. Ⓐ Ⓑ Ⓒ Ⓓ Ⓔ
18. Ⓐ Ⓑ Ⓒ Ⓓ Ⓔ
19. Ⓐ Ⓑ Ⓒ Ⓓ Ⓔ
20. Ⓐ Ⓑ Ⓒ Ⓓ Ⓔ

ANSWER SHEET
AFOQT #1

Subtest 9: Table Reading

1. Ⓐ Ⓑ Ⓒ Ⓓ Ⓔ
2. Ⓐ Ⓑ Ⓒ Ⓓ Ⓔ
3. Ⓐ Ⓑ Ⓒ Ⓓ Ⓔ
4. Ⓐ Ⓑ Ⓒ Ⓓ Ⓔ
5. Ⓐ Ⓑ Ⓒ Ⓓ Ⓔ
6. Ⓐ Ⓑ Ⓒ Ⓓ Ⓔ
7. Ⓐ Ⓑ Ⓒ Ⓓ Ⓔ
8. Ⓐ Ⓑ Ⓒ Ⓓ Ⓔ
9. Ⓐ Ⓑ Ⓒ Ⓓ Ⓔ
10. Ⓐ Ⓑ Ⓒ Ⓓ Ⓔ
11. Ⓐ Ⓑ Ⓒ Ⓓ Ⓔ
12. Ⓐ Ⓑ Ⓒ Ⓓ Ⓔ
13. Ⓐ Ⓑ Ⓒ Ⓓ Ⓔ
14. Ⓐ Ⓑ Ⓒ Ⓓ Ⓔ
15. Ⓐ Ⓑ Ⓒ Ⓓ Ⓔ
16. Ⓐ Ⓑ Ⓒ Ⓓ Ⓔ
17. Ⓐ Ⓑ Ⓒ Ⓓ Ⓔ
18. Ⓐ Ⓑ Ⓒ Ⓓ Ⓔ
19. Ⓐ Ⓑ Ⓒ Ⓓ Ⓔ
20. Ⓐ Ⓑ Ⓒ Ⓓ Ⓔ
21. Ⓐ Ⓑ Ⓒ Ⓓ Ⓔ
22. Ⓐ Ⓑ Ⓒ Ⓓ Ⓔ
23. Ⓐ Ⓑ Ⓒ Ⓓ Ⓔ
24. Ⓐ Ⓑ Ⓒ Ⓓ Ⓔ
25. Ⓐ Ⓑ Ⓒ Ⓓ Ⓔ
26. Ⓐ Ⓑ Ⓒ Ⓓ Ⓔ
27. Ⓐ Ⓑ Ⓒ Ⓓ Ⓔ
28. Ⓐ Ⓑ Ⓒ Ⓓ Ⓔ
29. Ⓐ Ⓑ Ⓒ Ⓓ Ⓔ
30. Ⓐ Ⓑ Ⓒ Ⓓ Ⓔ
31. Ⓐ Ⓑ Ⓒ Ⓓ Ⓔ
32. Ⓐ Ⓑ Ⓒ Ⓓ Ⓔ
33. Ⓐ Ⓑ Ⓒ Ⓓ Ⓔ
34. Ⓐ Ⓑ Ⓒ Ⓓ Ⓔ
35. Ⓐ Ⓑ Ⓒ Ⓓ Ⓔ
36. Ⓐ Ⓑ Ⓒ Ⓓ Ⓔ
37. Ⓐ Ⓑ Ⓒ Ⓓ Ⓔ
38. Ⓐ Ⓑ Ⓒ Ⓓ Ⓔ
39. Ⓐ Ⓑ Ⓒ Ⓓ Ⓔ
40. Ⓐ Ⓑ Ⓒ Ⓓ Ⓔ

Subtest 10: Instrument Comprehension

1. Ⓐ Ⓑ Ⓒ Ⓓ
2. Ⓐ Ⓑ Ⓒ Ⓓ
3. Ⓐ Ⓑ Ⓒ Ⓓ
4. Ⓐ Ⓑ Ⓒ Ⓓ
5. Ⓐ Ⓑ Ⓒ Ⓓ
6. Ⓐ Ⓑ Ⓒ Ⓓ
7. Ⓐ Ⓑ Ⓒ Ⓓ
8. Ⓐ Ⓑ Ⓒ Ⓓ
9. Ⓐ Ⓑ Ⓒ Ⓓ
10. Ⓐ Ⓑ Ⓒ Ⓓ
11. Ⓐ Ⓑ Ⓒ Ⓓ
12. Ⓐ Ⓑ Ⓒ Ⓓ
13. Ⓐ Ⓑ Ⓒ Ⓓ
14. Ⓐ Ⓑ Ⓒ Ⓓ
15. Ⓐ Ⓑ Ⓒ Ⓓ
16. Ⓐ Ⓑ Ⓒ Ⓓ
17. Ⓐ Ⓑ Ⓒ Ⓓ
18. Ⓐ Ⓑ Ⓒ Ⓓ
19. Ⓐ Ⓑ Ⓒ Ⓓ
20. Ⓐ Ⓑ Ⓒ Ⓓ
21. Ⓐ Ⓑ Ⓒ Ⓓ
22. Ⓐ Ⓑ Ⓒ Ⓓ
23. Ⓐ Ⓑ Ⓒ Ⓓ
24. Ⓐ Ⓑ Ⓒ Ⓓ
25. Ⓐ Ⓑ Ⓒ Ⓓ

Subtest 11: Block Counting

1. Ⓐ Ⓑ Ⓒ Ⓓ Ⓔ
2. Ⓐ Ⓑ Ⓒ Ⓓ Ⓔ
3. Ⓐ Ⓑ Ⓒ Ⓓ Ⓔ
4. Ⓐ Ⓑ Ⓒ Ⓓ Ⓔ
5. Ⓐ Ⓑ Ⓒ Ⓓ Ⓔ
6. Ⓐ Ⓑ Ⓒ Ⓓ Ⓔ
7. Ⓐ Ⓑ Ⓒ Ⓓ Ⓔ
8. Ⓐ Ⓑ Ⓒ Ⓓ Ⓔ
9. Ⓐ Ⓑ Ⓒ Ⓓ Ⓔ
10. Ⓐ Ⓑ Ⓒ Ⓓ Ⓔ
11. Ⓐ Ⓑ Ⓒ Ⓓ Ⓔ
12. Ⓐ Ⓑ Ⓒ Ⓓ Ⓔ
13. Ⓐ Ⓑ Ⓒ Ⓓ Ⓔ
14. Ⓐ Ⓑ Ⓒ Ⓓ Ⓔ
15. Ⓐ Ⓑ Ⓒ Ⓓ Ⓔ
16. Ⓐ Ⓑ Ⓒ Ⓓ Ⓔ
17. Ⓐ Ⓑ Ⓒ Ⓓ Ⓔ
18. Ⓐ Ⓑ Ⓒ Ⓓ Ⓔ
19. Ⓐ Ⓑ Ⓒ Ⓓ Ⓔ
20. Ⓐ Ⓑ Ⓒ Ⓓ Ⓔ
21. Ⓐ Ⓑ Ⓒ Ⓓ Ⓔ
22. Ⓐ Ⓑ Ⓒ Ⓓ Ⓔ
23. Ⓐ Ⓑ Ⓒ Ⓓ Ⓔ
24. Ⓐ Ⓑ Ⓒ Ⓓ Ⓔ
25. Ⓐ Ⓑ Ⓒ Ⓓ Ⓔ
26. Ⓐ Ⓑ Ⓒ Ⓓ Ⓔ
27. Ⓐ Ⓑ Ⓒ Ⓓ Ⓔ
28. Ⓐ Ⓑ Ⓒ Ⓓ Ⓔ
29. Ⓐ Ⓑ Ⓒ Ⓓ Ⓔ
30. Ⓐ Ⓑ Ⓒ Ⓓ Ⓔ

Subtest 12: Aviation Information

1. Ⓐ Ⓑ Ⓒ Ⓓ Ⓔ
2. Ⓐ Ⓑ Ⓒ Ⓓ Ⓔ
3. Ⓐ Ⓑ Ⓒ Ⓓ Ⓔ
4. Ⓐ Ⓑ Ⓒ Ⓓ Ⓔ
5. Ⓐ Ⓑ Ⓒ Ⓓ Ⓔ
6. Ⓐ Ⓑ Ⓒ Ⓓ Ⓔ
7. Ⓐ Ⓑ Ⓒ Ⓓ Ⓔ
8. Ⓐ Ⓑ Ⓒ Ⓓ Ⓔ
9. Ⓐ Ⓑ Ⓒ Ⓓ Ⓔ
10. Ⓐ Ⓑ Ⓒ Ⓓ Ⓔ
11. Ⓐ Ⓑ Ⓒ Ⓓ Ⓔ
12. Ⓐ Ⓑ Ⓒ Ⓓ Ⓔ
13. Ⓐ Ⓑ Ⓒ Ⓓ Ⓔ
14. Ⓐ Ⓑ Ⓒ Ⓓ Ⓔ
15. Ⓐ Ⓑ Ⓒ Ⓓ Ⓔ
16. Ⓐ Ⓑ Ⓒ Ⓓ Ⓔ
17. Ⓐ Ⓑ Ⓒ Ⓓ Ⓔ
18. Ⓐ Ⓑ Ⓒ Ⓓ Ⓔ
19. Ⓐ Ⓑ Ⓒ Ⓓ Ⓔ
20. Ⓐ Ⓑ Ⓒ Ⓓ Ⓔ

Air Force Officer Qualifying Test (AFOQT) Practice Test #1

10

TEST FORMAT

The Air Force Officer Qualifying Test (AFOQT) measures aptitudes used by the U.S. Air Force to select candidates for officer commissioning programs and specific officer training programs, including pilot, combat systems officer, and air battle manager.

As discussed in Chapter 3, the AFOQT consists of 12 timed subtests. The scores from the individual subtests are combined in different ways to generate seven composite scores used to help predict success in selected USAF training programs.

			Rated Composites						
Subtest Name	**Number of Questions**	**Time Limit**	**Pilot**	**Combat Systems Officer (CSO)**	**Air Battle Manager (ABM)**	**Academic Aptitude**	**Verbal**	**Quantitative**	**Situational Judgment**
1. Verbal Analogies	25	8 mins			X	X	X		
2. Arithmetic Reasoning	25	29 mins				X		X	
3. Word Knowledge	25	5 mins		X		X	X		
4. Math Knowledge	25	22 mins	X	X	X	X		X	
5. Reading Comprehension	25	38 mins				X	X		X
6. Situational Judgment	50	35 mins							
7. Self-Description Inventory	240	45 mins							
8. Physical Science	20	10 mins							
9. Table Reading	40	7 mins	X	X	X				
10. Instrument Comprehension	25	5 mins	X		X				
11. Block Counting	30	4.5 mins		X	X				
12. Aviation Information	20	8 mins	X		X				

SUBTEST #1: VERBAL ANALOGIES

25 Questions

DIRECTIONS: This part of the test measures your ability to reason and see relationships between words. Choose the answer that best completes the analogy developed at the beginning of each question.

1. GLOVE is to HAND as SHOE is to
   (A) SOCK.
   (B) LEG.
   (C) FOOT.
   (D) TOE.
   (E) HORSE.

2. AIRCRAFT is to FLY as BOAT is to
   (A) STEER.
   (B) SINK.
   (C) SHIP.
   (D) LAND.
   (E) SAIL.

3. PLAN is to STRATEGY as FIGHT is to
   (A) STRUGGLE.
   (B) HIT.
   (C) BLOW.
   (D) BATTLE.
   (E) CONQUER.

4. TRAVEL is to DESTINATION as WORK is to
   (A) GOAL.
   (B) OFFICE.
   (C) LABOR.
   (D) LEISURE.
   (E) COMMUTE.

5. PLOW is to FIELD as RACQUET is to
   (A) BALL.
   (B) COURT.
   (C) GANGSTER.
   (D) HAND.
   (E) JUDGE.

6. SALUTE is to RESPECT as HUG is to
   (A) SQUEEZE.
   (B) GESTURE.
   (C) ARM.
   (D) EMBRACE.
   (E) AFFECTION.

7. GRAVITY is to PLANET as ODOR is to
   (A) SKUNK.
   (B) AROMA.
   (C) NOSE.
   (D) DEATH.
   (E) SIGHT.

8. FISHING ROD is to HOOK as KNIFE is to
   (A) BLADE.
   (B) BULLET.
   (C) CUT.
   (D) STEAK.
   (E) HANDLE.

9. BOOT is to HIKE as VISOR is to
   (A) FACE.
   (B) SUIT.
   (C) MOTORCYCLE.
   (D) HEAD.
   (E) WELD.

10. PUSH is to SHOVE as CLIMB is to
   (A) MOUNTAIN.
   (B) FALL.
   (C) WALK.
   (D) LINGER.
   (E) CLAMBER.

11. GROW is to MATURE as BLOOM is to

(A) ROSE.
(B) PETAL.
(C) FLOURISH.
(D) DECAY.
(E) BLOSSOM.

12. FUSELAGE is to BODY as

(A) TURRET is to TANK.
(B) LIFT is to DRAG.
(C) DIVING is to FALLING.
(D) WOOD is to OAK.
(E) COMPASS is to DIRECTION.

13. CLIMB is to RISE as DIVE is to

(A) SWIMMING POOL.
(B) ARC.
(C) FALL.
(D) DECREASE.
(E) SLIDE.

14. ROPE is to KNOT as THREAD is to

(A) SANDWICH.
(B) FABRIC.
(C) NEEDLE.
(D) SEWING.
(E) THIMBLE.

15. WATCH is to OBSERVE as SWITCH is to

(A) LIGHT FIXTURE.
(B) RAILROAD TRACK.
(C) HIDE.
(D) MOVE.
(E) REPLACE.

16. OBEY is to COMPLY as REPLY is to

(A) QUESTION.
(B) STATEMENT.
(C) ANSWER.
(D) REPOSE.
(E) REWIND.

17. HONOR is to HONESTY as TRUST is to

(A) DEPENDABILITY.
(B) TREASON.
(C) PROMPTNESS.
(D) INTELLIGENCE.
(E) EMPATHY.

18. SPEED is to DECELERATION as VELOCITY is to

(A) DISTANCE.
(B) THRUST.
(C) RAPIDITY.
(D) BRAKING.
(E) URGENCY.

19. COMPRESSION is to RAREFACTION as DENSE is to

(A) THIN.
(B) APOGEE.
(C) IGNORANT.
(D) COMPACTED.
(E) PROTECTION.

20. DELAY is to POSTPONE as PREVENT is to

(A) DETER.
(B) DISCOURAGE.
(C) OFFEND.
(D) DEFEND.
(E) SWITCH.

21. ADD is to SUBTRACT as GROW is to

(A) DECAY.
(B) MATURE.
(C) SHRINK.
(D) HEIGHT.
(E) DIVIDE.

22. LEFT is to PORT as RIGHT is to

(A) STARBOARD.
(B) DEPARTED.
(C) HARBOR.
(D) RED.
(E) GREEN.

23. ODOMETER is to DISTANCE as ALTIMETER is to

(A) ALTITUDE.
(B) DISTANCE.
(C) FUEL.
(D) INSTRUMENT.
(E) READOUT.

24. ELEVATOR is to HEIGHT as THRUST is to

(A) STAIRWAY.
(B) CLIMBING.
(C) ROCKET.
(D) ALTITUDE.
(E) FLIGHT.

25. LOOK is to INSPECT as ARRIVE is to

(A) DEPART.
(B) TRAVEL.
(C) LOCATE.
(D) ATTEND.
(E) NOTICE.

SUBTEST #2: ARITHMETIC REASONING

25 Questions

DIRECTIONS: This part of the test measures your ability to use arithmetic to solve problems. Each problem is followed by five possible answers. You are to decide which of the choices is most nearly correct.

1. A theater contains *x* rows, with *y* seats in each row. How many total seats are there in the theater?

(A) $x + y$
(B) $x - y$
(C) xy
(D) $y - x$
(E) $2x + y$

2. The sticker price of a new pickup truck was increased from $22,399 to $23,999 over last year's model. What was the approximate percentage of increase?

(A) 1.07%
(B) 7.1%
(C) 9.3%
(D) 71.4%
(E) 93.3%

3. During one season, a high school football quarterback attempted 82 passes and completed 57 of them. What is his completion percentage?

(A) 30.4%
(B) 69.5%
(C) 43.8%
(D) 81.7%
(E) 143.9%

4. Jaycie Marie has a 20-year term life insurance policy for $100,000. The annual premium is $12.00 per thousand. What is the total premium paid for this policy every six months?

(A) $600
(B) $1,200
(C) $100
(D) $2,400
(E) $24,000

5. If 2 pounds of smoked deli turkey breast cost $13.98, what is the cost of a 5-oz. portion?

(A) $0.44
(B) $0.87
(C) $1.40
(D) $2.20
(E) $4.36

6. If five shirts and four ties cost $173 and each tie costs $12, what is the cost of a shirt?

(A) $15.00
(B) $22.60
(C) $32.20
(D) $19.22
(E) $25.00

7. What is the volume of a container that is 23 feet long, 15 feet wide, and 11 feet high?

(A) 2,530 sq. ft.
(B) 3,450 cu. ft.
(C) 3,795 sq. ft.
(D) 3,795 cu. ft.
(E) 5,280 cu. ft.

8. The sister of a high school football player spent $119 on tickets for her family and friends to a playoff game. If tickets were $7 and $10, and she bought an equal number of both kinds of tickets, how many $7 tickets did she buy?

(A) 4
(B) 5
(C) 7
(D) 11
(E) 17

9. Amanda earns an average of $22 an hour in tips as a waitress at the best steak restaurant in town. If her hourly wage is $2.50 and she has to pay a 10% tip share to the hostesses and busboys, how much does she take home at the end of a day when she worked from 10:30 A.M. to 5:30 P.M.?

(A) $32.90
(B) $121.11
(C) $138.60
(D) $156.10
(E) $171.50

10. For a live performance of *The Nutcracker*, 76% of a 500-seat theater was occupied, and three-quarters of those attending were adults. How many children saw the performance?

(A) 95
(B) 100
(C) 76
(D) 285
(E) 350

11. Jonathan spent four hours studying, one hour raking leaves, 30 minutes doing laundry, and two hours watching TV. What percentage of his time was spent studying?

(A) 46.6%
(B) 50.0%
(C) 53.3%
(D) 57.1%
(E) 66.6%

12. June found a chandelier for the dining room for $1,400. However, since the model had been discontinued and the display had no factory packaging material, the store manager discounted the price to $1,150. What was the percentage of the reduction?

(A) 1.78%
(B) 13.0%
(C) 15.0%
(D) 17.9%
(E) 21.7%

13. Mackenzie bought a rectangular Persian rug with a perimeter measurement of 45 feet. If the long sides measure 15 feet each, how long is each short side of the rug?

(A) 7.5 ft.
(B) 10 ft.
(C) 12.5 ft.
(D) 15 ft.
(E) 20 ft.

14. In a flooring outlet, four customer service representatives each receive $320 a week, and two sales managers each earn $12 per hour plus an average $100 per day commission. What is the total weekly compensation paid to these six employees for a five-day, 40-hour work week?

(A) $2,420
(B) $3,240
(C) $2,260
(D) $4,520
(E) $7,080

15. A submarine sails x miles the first day, y miles the second day, and z miles the third day. What is the average number of miles sailed per day?

(A) $3xyz$
(B) $3 \cdot (x + y + z)$
(C) $(x + y + z) \div 3$
(D) $(x + y + z)$
(E) $xyz/3$

16. If a train can travel 500 miles in five hours, approximately how far can it travel in 15 minutes?

(A) 25 miles
(B) 30 miles
(C) 57 miles
(D) 125 miles
(E) 167 miles

17. Which of these is an example of similar figures?

(A) a pen and a pencil
(B) a motorcycle and a car
(C) a bicycle and a motorcycle
(D) an airplane and a scale model of that airplane
(E) an equilateral triangle and an isosceles triangle

18. Upon his death, a man's life insurance policies paid $750,000 to his wife and three children. The policies were set up to pay the wife and children in the ratio of 5:1:1:1. How much did the children receive altogether?

(A) $150,000
(B) $200,000
(C) $468,750
(D) $250,000
(E) $281,250

19. Although an air assault infantry company has 131 soldiers authorized, A Company has only 125 total soldiers assigned, of whom 4 percent are officers. How many enlisted soldiers are assigned to the company?

(A) 114
(B) 123
(C) 120
(D) 121
(E) 126

20. An electronics store owner buys 20 DVD players for the listed wholesale price of $80 apiece, but receives a 25% discount because he is a frequent customer of the wholesale dealer. He sells these DVD players at a 20% markup above the original wholesale price. What is his profit on each DVD player?

(A) $16
(B) $720
(C) $20
(D) $360
(E) $36

21. A mapmaker is told to prepare a map with a scale of 1 inch = 50 miles. If the actual ground distance between two points is 120 miles, how far apart should the mapmaker show them on the map?

(A) 0.4 in.
(B) 2.4 in.
(C) 1.2 in.
(D) 4.8 in.
(E) 8.4 in.

22. In the city of Woodway, houses are assessed at 80% of the purchase price. If Mr. Thomas buys a house in Woodway for $120,000 and real estate taxes are $4.75 per $100 of assessed valuation, how much property tax must he pay per year?

(A) $3,648
(B) $5,472
(C) $4,560
(D) $4,845
(E) $5,700

23. The fuel tank of a gasoline generator has enough capacity to operate the generator for one hour and 15 minutes. About how many times must the fuel tank be filled to run the generator from 6:15 P.M. to 7:00 A.M.?

(A) 9.4
(B) 10.2
(C) 10.8
(D) 11.5
(E) 12.0

24. When a highway was converted from nonpaid to a toll road, the traffic declined from 11,200 cars per day to 10,044. What was the percent of the decline in traffic?

(A) 10.3%
(B) 11.5%
(C) 10.1%
(D) 8.9%
(E) 79.3%

25. On Mr. Lee's trip, he first drives for two hours at 70 miles per hour. He then drives for another one and a half hours at 65 miles per hour. If his car gets 25 miles per gallon on the highway in this speed range, how many gallons of gas did he use for the trip?

(A) 5.4 gals.
(B) 8.2 gals.
(C) 8.4 gals.
(D) 9.5 gals.
(E) 11.2 gals.

SUBTEST #3: WORD KNOWLEDGE

25 Questions

DIRECTIONS: This part of the test measures verbal comprehension involving your ability to understand written language. For each question choose the answer that means the same as the capitalized word.

1. TACIT
   (A) silent
   (B) sour
   (C) ornament
   (D) talkative
   (E) pleasing

2. ALTITUDE
   (A) direction
   (B) old saying
   (C) demeanor
   (D) height
   (E) distance

3. PORTEND
   (A) feign
   (B) give warning beforehand
   (C) develop pores or holes
   (D) assume a pose
   (E) inhabit

4. ITINERARY
   (A) migrant
   (B) not permanent
   (C) cure-all
   (D) schedule
   (E) character

5. VEXATIOUS
   (A) annoying
   (B) contagious
   (C) at a high volume
   (D) insatiably hungry
   (E) having a moral fault

6. EQUIVALENT
   (A) complicated
   (B) inferior
   (C) superior
   (D) evident
   (E) equal

7. CRITERION
   (A) standard
   (B) disaster
   (C) environment
   (D) criticism
   (E) excerpt

8. MERCURIAL
   (A) having compassion
   (B) specious
   (C) unpredictably changeable
   (D) metallic
   (E) containing mercury

9. CRITICAL
   (A) conversational
   (B) influencing
   (C) dying
   (D) less worthy
   (E) most important

10. TELEMETRY
    - (A) mental communication
    - (B) marketing goods or services by telephone
    - (C) transmission of measurements made by automatic instruments
    - (D) study of climactic variations
    - (E) rashness, audacity

11. ANTAGONIST
    - (A) ally
    - (B) main character
    - (C) soothing to the stomach
    - (D) adversary
    - (E) one who causes pain

12. DIAGNOSE
    - (A) predict the outcome
    - (B) cut in two
    - (C) identify a situation
    - (D) antagonize
    - (E) speak about

13. KINETIC
    - (A) relating to the motion of material bodies
    - (B) referring to motion pictures
    - (C) moving at a high speed
    - (D) relating to sensory experience
    - (E) referring to a relative

14. RECTIFY
    - (A) dealing with the digestive system
    - (B) cause trouble or havoc
    - (C) get back
    - (D) correct
    - (E) give fresh life to

15. CAMOUFLAGE
    - (A) substitute
    - (B) conceal
    - (C) redeem
    - (D) divide
    - (E) twist

16. EQUIVOCAL
    - (A) equal
    - (B) poised
    - (C) overlapping
    - (D) removed
    - (E) evasive

17. CENTRIPETAL
    - (A) moving away from a center or axis
    - (B) relating to the feet
    - (C) having more than 100 petals
    - (D) moving toward a center or axis
    - (E) circular

18. DISCONSOLATE
    - (A) hopelessly sad
    - (B) cease using
    - (C) rearrange sloppily
    - (D) uncover
    - (E) recognize mentally

19. ANACHRONISTIC
    - (A) chronologically out of place
    - (B) cursed
    - (C) dealing with organism structure
    - (D) attribution of conscious thought to inanimate objects or animals
    - (E) existing before a war

20. MODULATE
    - (A) speak
    - (B) decay
    - (C) dry out
    - (D) adjust
    - (E) develop a mannerism

21. PICAYUNE

(A) unnoticed
(B) insignificant
(C) intense
(D) hot
(E) unfortunate

22. TENACIOUS

(A) annoying
(B) persistent
(C) religious
(D) hot-tempered
(E) cowardly

23. ENTENTE

(A) relaxation of tensions
(B) volition
(C) agreement providing for joint action
(D) freedom of entry or access
(E) concentrated

24. REDUNDANT

(A) brilliant
(B) held back
(C) repetitive
(D) unruly
(E) isolated

25. RECONNAISSANCE

(A) surveying expedition
(B) responsibility
(C) obligation
(D) resolution of differences
(E) rebirth

SUBTEST #4: MATH KNOWLEDGE

25 Questions

DIRECTIONS: This part of the test measures your ability to use learned mathematical relationships. Each problem is followed by five possible answers. Decide which one of the five answers is most nearly correct.

1. The expression "4 factorial" or 4! means

   (A) $\frac{1}{4}$
   (B) $\frac{1}{24}$
   (C) –2
   (D) 10
   (E) 24

2. An airplane is flying a circular or "racetrack" orbit around a 4,000-meter-high mountaintop. Assume the pilot flies a perfectly circular course. What is the distance in kilometers he travels each orbit if it is 40 kilometers from the mountaintop to the outer edge of his orbit? (Use pi = $\frac{22}{7}$.)

   (A) 13 km
   (B) 25 km
   (C) 126 km
   (D) 251 km
   (E) 503 km

3. The reciprocal of 7 to the nearest thousandth is

   (A) 0.143
   (B) 1.428
   (C) 14
   (D) 21
   (E) 49

4. The ten-thousandths digit of the square of 525 is

   (A) 2
   (B) 5
   (C) 6
   (D) 7
   (E) 0

5. The area of a square with a perimeter of 40 yards is

   (A) 100 sq. ft.
   (B) 180 sq. yds.
   (C) 300 sq. ft.
   (D) 300 sq. yds.
   (E) 900 sq. ft.

6. Solve the following equations for x.

   $$5x + 4y = 27$$
   $$x - 2y = 11$$

   (A) $x = \frac{5}{3}$
   (B) $x = 4.5$
   (C) $x = 9$
   (D) $x = 7$
   (E) $x = -3$

7. Find the square root of 85 correct to the nearest tenth.

   (A) 9.1
   (B) 9.2
   (C) 9.3
   (D) 9.4
   (E) 9.5

8. Solve for x: $8x - 2 - 5x = 8$

   (A) $x = 1.3$
   (B) $x = 3\frac{1}{3}$
   (C) $x = 2\frac{1}{2}$
   (D) $x = 7.0$
   (E) $x = -7.0$

9. $2(a-b)+4(a+3b)=$

(A) $6a-10b$
(B) $6a+2b$
(C) $8a^2+2b^2$
(D) $6a-2b$
(E) $6a+10b$

10. Which of the following is the smallest prime number greater than 200?

(A) 201
(B) 205
(C) 211
(D) 214
(E) 223

11. If a is a negative number, and ab is a positive number, then which of the following must be true?

(A) b is greater than a.
(B) a is greater than b.
(C) b is negative.
(D) b is positive.
(E) b is a whole integer.

12. What is the product of $(a+2)(a-5)(a+3)$?

(A) $a^3+2a^2+15a-30$
(B) a^3+6a^2-49
(C) $a^3-19a-30$
(D) $a^3+2a^2-15a+30$
(E) $a^3-19a+30$

13. Solve for z: $3z-5+2z=25-5z$

(A) $z=1$
(B) $z=3$
(C) $z=-3$
(D) $z=0$
(E) no solution

14. An architect has won a contract to place a memorial sculpture at each of the corners of the Pentagon in Washington, D.C. How many sculptures will there be?

(A) 4
(B) 5
(C) 6
(D) 7
(E) 8

15. If one of the angles of a right triangle is 30 degrees, what are the measurements of the other two angles?

(A) 30 degrees, 120 degrees
(B) 60 degrees, 45 degrees
(C) 60 degrees, 90 degrees
(D) 45 degrees, 90 degrees
(E) 45 degrees, 120 degrees

16. Factor $x^2-11x+30$

(A) $(x-6), (x-5)$
(B) $(x+6), (x-5)$
(C) $(x-10), (x-1)$
(D) $(x-3), (x+10)$
(E) $(x-6), (y+5)$

17. Solve $\frac{15a^3b^2c}{5abc}$

(A) $10abc$
(B) $3abc$
(C) $5a^2b^2$
(D) $3a^2b$
(E) $5a^2b^2c$

18. Two circles have the same center. If their radii are 7 in. and 10 in., find the area that is part of the larger circle but not part of the smaller one.

(A) 3 sq. in.
(B) 17 sq. in.
(C) 51π sq. in.
(D) 71π sq. in.
(E) 91π sq. in.

19. Amanda took five midterm tests for five different college classes; her average for all five tests was 88. That night at home, she could remember only her first four scores: 78, 86, 94, and 96. What was her score on the fifth test?

(A) 82
(B) 86
(C) 84
(D) 88
(E) 87

20. How many cubic yards of concrete are needed to make a concrete floor that measures 9′ × 12′ × 6″?

(A) 2
(B) 18
(C) 54
(D) 210
(E) 648

21. A new wildlife preserve is laid out in a perfect circle with a radius of 14 kilometers. The lion habitat is shaped like a wedge and has an 8-foot-high razor wire fence around it. Two inner sides of the fence meet at a 90-degree angle in the center of the base. How much ground space (area) does the lion habitat have?

(A) 140 sq. km
(B) 3.5 sq. km
(C) 210 sq. km
(D) 154 sq. km
(E) 35 sq. km

22. Factor $6x^2 + 3xy$.

(A) $2x(3x - y)$
(B) $x^2 + 3y$
(C) $x + 3y$
(D) $3x(2x + y)$
(E) $6x(x + y)$

23. A cylindrical container has a radius of 7″ and a height of 15″. How many gallons of hydraulic fluid can it hold? (There are 231 cubic inches in a gallon.)

(A) 15 gals.
(B) 14 gals.
(C) 140 gals.
(D) 10 gals.
(E) 23.1 gals.

24. A 10-foot-high ladder is resting against an 8-foot-high wall around a recreation area. If the top of the ladder is exactly even with the top of the wall, how far is the base of the ladder from the wall?

(A) 18 ft.
(B) 6 ft.
(C) 12 ft.
(D) 9 ft.
(E) 8 ft.

25. A cook is mixing fruit juice from concentrate for a catered event. Ten ounces of liquid contain 20% fruit juice and 80% water. He then further dilutes the mixture by adding 40 additional ounces of water. What is the percent of fruit juice in the new solution?

(A) 4%
(B) 10%
(C) 14%
(D) 18%
(E) 20%

SUBTEST #5: READING COMPREHENSION

25 Questions

DIRECTIONS: This subtest measures your ability to read and understand written material. Each passage is followed by a series of multiple-choice questions. You are to choose the option that best answers the question based on the passage. No additional information or specific knowledge is needed.

Reading Passage for Questions 1–5

In 1789, Congress established the Department of War, which bore responsibility for the United States Army, as well as the Navy and Marine Corps, until the Department of the Navy was established in 1798. The services functioned autonomously during this period, with the president, as commander in chief, their only common superior. Despite this outward independence, early American military history reflects the importance of what are now called joint (multi-service) and combined (multi-national) operations: the Revolutionary War was won when General George Washington successfully coordinated American and French naval and land forces to defeat British forces under Lord Cornwallis at Yorktown; naval operations by Commodore Thomas Macdonough, Jr. on Lake Champlain were a vital factor in successful ground campaigns against the British during the War of 1812; and the joint teamwork displayed by General Ulysses S. Grant and Admiral David Porter in the 1863 Vicksburg Campaign helped capture the last Confederate-controlled section of the Mississippi River.

However, instances of confusion, poor inter-service cooperation, and a lack of coordinated joint military action had an adverse impact on operations during the 1898 Cuban campaign of the Spanish-American War. As a result, the Secretary of War and the Secretary of the Navy created the Joint Army and Navy Board in 1903, charged with addressing "all matters calling for cooperation of the two services."

The Board was to be a continuing body that could plan for joint operations and resolve problems of common concern, but it accomplished little because it could not direct the implementation of concepts or enforce decisions. Instead, its main function wound up being commentary on problems submitted to it by the Secretaries of the Army and the Navy. Consequently, the Board had little or no impact on the conduct of joint operations during World War I, when similar joint command and control difficulties occurred as questions of seniority and command relationships between the Army Chief of Staff and the commander of the American Expeditionary Forces had to be resolved.

AFOQT #1

1. The primary purpose of this passage is to

   (A) describe the evolution of American joint military doctrine since the country's founding.
   (B) compare and contrast American and European employment of joint forces.
   (C) identify some of the results of both successful and unsuccessful American joint military operations.
   (D) provide a comprehensive historical account of coordination techniques between the Army and the Navy.
   (E) summarize lessons learned from American joint military operations.

2. In the first paragraph, the word "autonomously" most nearly means

   (A) without guidance.
   (B) independently.
   (C) secretly.
   (D) smoothly.
   (E) efficiently.

3. You can infer from the passage that

   (A) there was no standardized way of coordinating joint operations during the first century of American military operations.
   (B) conceiving and executing joint operations was very easy.
   (C) American military operations became continually more effective over the course of time.
   (D) joint operations became less necessary as warfare grew more complex during the 1700s and 1800s.
   (E) joint operations were primarily an Army responsibility during this time.

4. As used throughout the passage, the term "joint" means

   (A) involving more than one echelon of command.
   (B) involving more than one nation's forces on each side.
   (C) involving more than one service.
   (D) involving detailed planning.
   (E) involving specific intelligence and communications techniques.

5. With which statement would the author of this passage most likely agree?

   (A) "Joint military operations were uncommon before the advent of the airplane."
   (B) "The principles of joint operations have been well established and well known since ancient times."
   (C) "The part of the United States government involving the military was originally established with a clear view of the importance of joint operations."
   (D) "Joint military operations have been important throughout history."
   (E) "The American military had solved most of the challenges of joint operations by the time it entered World War I."

Reading Passage for Questions 6–10

Culture is both a "here and now" dynamic phenomenon and a coercive background structure that influences us in multiple ways. Culture is constantly reenacted and created by our interactions with others and shaped by our own behavior. When we are influential in shaping the behavior and values of others, we think of that as "leadership," which helps us create the conditions for new culture formation. At the same time, culture implies stability and sometimes rigidity in the sense that how we are supposed to perceive, feel, and act in a given society, organization, or occupation has been taught to us by our various socialization experiences and becomes prescribed as a way to maintain the "social order."

The "rules" of the social order make it possible to predict social behavior, get along with each other, and find meaning in what we do. Culture can be thought of as the foundation of the social order that we live in and of the rules we abide by. The culture of macrosystems, such as large societies, is more stable and ordered because of the length of time they have existed. Organizational cultures will vary in strength and stability as a function of the length and emotional intensity of their actual history from the time they were founded. Occupational cultures will vary from highly structured ones, such as medicine, to relatively fluid ones, such as management. Microcultures are the most variable and the most dynamic and, therefore, provide special opportunities to study culture formation and evolution.

The connection between culture and leadership is clearest in organizational cultures and microcultures. What we end up calling a culture in such systems is usually the result of the embedding of what a founder or a leader has imposed on a group that has worked out. In this sense, culture is ultimately created, embedded, evolved, and guided by leaders. At the same time, as the group matures and becomes more stable, culture comes to constrain, stabilize, and provide structure and meaning to the group members, even to the point of ultimately specifying what kind of leadership will be acceptable in the future. If elements of a given culture become dysfunctional, leaders have to surmount their own culture and speed up the normal evolution processes with forced, managed culture change programs. These dynamic processes of culture creation and management are the essence of leadership, and they make us realize that leadership and culture are two sides of the same coin.

6. The primary purpose of the passage is to
   - (A) compare and contrast functional and dysfunctional organizational cultures.
   - (B) define the types of structures of organizational cultures.
   - (C) provide a comprehensive historical overview of how cultures lead to social order.
   - (D) discuss the connections between organizational culture and leadership.
   - (E) identify what kind of organizational leaders are most effective.

7. Throughout the passage, the term "culture" is used to mean
   - (A) a refined understanding of the arts and other demonstrations of human intellectual achievement by a certain group.
   - (B) the attitudes and behaviors characteristic of a particular group or organization.
   - (C) defined written rules of operations codified in state or federal law.
   - (D) the set of tactics, techniques, and procedures required to accomplish the unit's mission.
   - (E) the perception of the best operating practices in the mind of the organization's most senior individual.

8. In the last paragraph, the word "dysfunctional" most nearly means
   - (A) an abnormality or impairment in the function of a bodily organ or system.
   - (B) a defining or contrasting difference between similar organizations.
   - (C) deviating from the norms of social behavior in a way that is regarded as bad or ineffective.
   - (D) preventing someone from giving his or her full attention to what he or she should be doing.
   - (E) extremely agitated or nearing hysteria.

9. You can infer from the passage that
   - (A) both leaders and members of an organization have an impact on its culture.
   - (B) only elected leaders have any lasting impact on the culture of a society.
   - (C) only the members of a group can really establish and define the culture of that group.
   - (D) the culture of highly structured organizations becomes less stable over time.
   - (E) the culture of societies becomes less structured over time due to innovation.

10. With which statement would the author of this passage most likely agree?
   - (A) "Leaders can be successful in any type of organization by following specific steps and processes."
   - (B) "Leadership that is attuned to its organization's culture is the most likely to be successful."
   - (C) "Occupational cultures are mostly the same, regardless of what area of expertise they address."
   - (D) "The connection between leadership and culture is seldom clear, especially in organizational cultures."
   - (E) "Cultural changes occur rapidly in large, established societies."

Reading Passage for Questions 11–15

Each nation practices intelligence collection and analysis in ways that are specific to that nation alone. This is true even among countries with a common heritage that share much of their intelligence, such as Australia, Canada, the United Kingdom, and the United States. The U.S. intelligence system is important to understand because it is the largest and most influential in the world—whether considered as an example, a competitor, or a target.

The *intelligence community* is made up of agencies and offices whose work is often related and sometimes combined, but who serve different needs and clients and work under different lines of control and authority. The intelligence community has grown to where and how it is without a master plan and as the result of evolving demands over time. It is often considered highly functional, but it is sometimes dysfunctional; it provides services that are multiple, varied, and supervised by different individuals and organizations, sometimes with different agendas.

Of the major national powers in the 20th and 21st centuries, the U.S. has the shortest history of significant intelligence operations outside of wartime emergencies. British intelligence operations date from the reign of Elizabeth I (1558–1603); French intelligence goes back to the time of Cardinal Richelieu (1624–1642); and Russian intelligence dates back to the reign of Ivan the Terrible (1533–1584). Even considering that the U.S. did not exist until 1776, American intelligence experience is still relatively brief: there was no hint of a serious U.S. national intelligence effort until 1940. Although some permanent and specific U.S. Army and Navy intelligence units were established in the 1800s, the U.S. did not have broader intelligence capabilities until just before World War II.

Much of the absence of U.S. intelligence efforts before WWII was driven by the fact that the U.S. had little interest in what went on outside its borders. The 1823 Monroe Doctrine—stating that the U.S. would resist any European efforts to colonize in the Western Hemisphere—addressed the United States' perceived basic security and foreign policy needs. The need for better intelligence became apparent only after the U.S. became a world power and became involved in international issues at the end of the 19th century.

Until the Cold War with the Soviet Union started in 1945, the U.S. severely limited spending on defense and related activities—including intelligence—during peacetime. Even in the 1940s, with WWII fully under way, intelligence was seen as a newcomer to the national security arena. Although Army and Navy intelligence efforts were well under way by then, they did not become robust until well into the 20th century. This meant that national level intelligence did not have any established supporters in government—but it did have rivals in the military services and the Federal Bureau of Investigation, neither of whom were keen to share their sources or information. With no firm roots of tradition or operational procedures, national intelligence was forced to create both under pressure, starting just before WWII, and throughout the Cold War that immediately followed.

Although the Monroe Doctrine may have contributed somewhat to the lack of a perceived need for U.S. national intelligence, it did assume a de facto U.S. vested interest in the international status quo, which became more pronounced after the 1898 Spanish-American War. With the acquisition of a small colonial empire, the U.S. achieved a satisfactory international position, largely self-sufficient and largely unthreatened. However, the 20th century saw the repeated rise of foreign powers whose policies directly threatened the status quo: Germany in WWI, the Axis Powers in WWII, and the Soviet Union during the Cold War. Responding to these threats became the mainstay of U.S. national security policy and gave focus to much of the operational side of U.S. intelligence efforts.

The terrorism threat in the late 20th and early 21st centuries fits much of the same pattern of an adversary who rejects the international status quo. However, the current crop of adversaries are not nation-states, although some have either overt or covert support of nation-states. This makes dealing with this threat much more challenging, since acceptance of the status quo by terrorists removes their stated reason for existence.

11. The primary idea of this passage is to
    - (A) analyze the current status of U.S. intelligence efforts versus the terrorist threat.
    - (B) compare and contrast U.S. and European intelligence successes throughout history.
    - (C) analyze the Monroe Doctrine's impact on U.S. foreign policy.
    - (D) provide an overview of U.S. national-level intelligence efforts since the nation's founding.
    - (E) discuss the structure of U.S. national-level intelligence efforts and agencies.

12. In the sixth paragraph, the word "vested" most nearly means
    - (A) entitled to a benefit as a legal right.
    - (B) fully or significantly involved or engaged.
    - (C) subject to forfeiture or dependent on some condition.
    - (D) supplied with a vest.
    - (E) having met the required threshold of contribution.

13. Which one of the following statements could you infer from the passage?
    - (A) The Axis Powers wanted to change the international status quo.
    - (B) The U.S. had a large colonial empire from its earliest days.
    - (C) The U.S. developed the Monroe Doctrine because it did not like the international status quo.
    - (D) U.S. national-level intelligence programs confirmed international intelligence that the FBI had developed.
    - (E) The American victory in the Spanish-American War began the United States' involvement with the Philippines.

14. The threat of terrorism in the 21st century is mentioned mainly to
    - (A) bring the narrative of U.S. national-level intelligence up to the present day.
    - (B) compare and contrast intelligence efforts against terrorism versus those against nation-states.
    - (C) both choice (A) and choice (B).
    - (D) neither choice (A) nor choice (B).
    - (E) examine terrorist groups' reasons for existence.

15. With which one of the following statements would the passage's author likely agree?
    - (A) "The U.S. national intelligence program has a long record of effectiveness."
    - (B) "The U.S. has always placed high importance on international involvement."
    - (C) "The U.S. has been considered a world power since the Civil War."
    - (D) "Although started relatively late in its national history, the U.S. national intelligence program is trying to make up for lost time."
    - (E) "The U.S. has a national intelligence program similar to those of its closest allies."

Reading Passage for Questions 16–20

A professional is a person of character and competence. As military professionals charged with the defense of the nation, joint leaders must be experts in the conduct of war. They must be moral individuals of both action and intellect, skilled at getting things done, while at the same time conversant in the military art.

Every joint leader is expected to be a student of the art and science of war. Officers especially are expected to have a solid foundation in military theory and philosophy, as well as a knowledge of military history and the timeless lessons to be gained from it. Leaders must have a strong sense of the great responsibility of their office; the resources they will expend in war include their fellow citizens.

Strong character and competence represent the essence of the U.S. joint military force and its leaders. Both are the products of lifelong learning and are embedded in joint professional military education.

Character is the aggregate of features and traits that form the individual nature of a person. In the context of the profession of arms, it entails moral and ethical adherence to our American values. Character is at the heart of the relationship of the profession with the American people and with each other.

Competence is central to the profession of arms. Competent performance includes both the technical competence to perform the relevant task to standard and the ability to demonstrate that skill when working with others. Those who will lead joint operations must develop skill in integrating forces into smoothly functioning joint teams.

U.S. military service is based on values that experience has proven to be vital for operational success. These values adhere to the most idealistic societal norms, are common to all the services, and represent the essence of military professionalism. Duty, honor, courage, integrity, and selfless service are the calling cards of the profession of arms. Integrity, competence, physical courage, moral courage, and teamwork all have a special impact on the conduct of joint operations.

Duty is our foremost value. It binds us together and conveys our moral commitment as defenders of the Constitution and servants of the nation. As members of the profession of arms, we fulfill our duty without consideration of self-interest, sacrificing our lives if needed. From duty comes responsibility.

Honor is the code of behavior that defines the ethical fulfillment of our duties. It is that quality that guides us to exemplify the ultimate in ethical and moral behavior; never to lie, cheat, or steal; to abide by an uncompromising code of integrity; to respect human dignity; and to have respect and concern for each other. Honor is the quality of maturity, dedication, trust, and dependability that commits members of the profession of arms to act responsibly, to be accountable for their actions, to fulfill obligations, and to hold others accountable for their actions.

The United States of America is blessed with Soldiers, Marines, Sailors, Airmen, and Coast Guardsmen whose courage knows no boundaries. Even in warfare characterized by advanced technology, individual fighting spirit and courage remain essential. Courage has both physical and moral aspects and encompasses both bravery and fortitude. Throughout history, physical courage has defined warriors. It is the ability to confront physical pain, hardship, death, or the threat of death. Physical courage in a leader is most often expressed in a willingness to act, even alone if necessary, in situations of danger and uncertainty. Moral courage is the ability to act rightly in the face of popular opposition or discouragement, including the willingness to stand up for what one believes to be right even if that stand is unpopular or contrary to conventional wisdom. This involves risk-taking, tenacity, and accountability.

Integrity is the quality of being honest and having strong moral principles. Integrity is the bedrock of our character and the cornerstone for building trust. Trust is an essential trait among service members—trust by seniors in the abilities of their subordinates and by juniors in the competence and support of their seniors. American service members must be able to rely on each other, regardless of the challenge at hand; they must individually and collectively say what they mean and do what they say.

Selfless service epitomizes the quality of putting our nation, our military missions, and others before ourselves. Members of the profession of arms do not serve to pursue fame, position, or money, but rather for the greater good. Selfless service is the enabler of teamwork, the cooperative effort by the members of a group to achieve common goals.

Members of the Armed Forces of the United States must internalize and embody these values. Their adherence to these values helps promulgate an attitude about joint warfighting, producing a synergy that multiplies the effects of their individual actions.

16. The primary purpose of this passage is to
    (A) compare and contrast the U.S. military with other nations' militaries.
    (B) identify the essential professional qualities of U.S. joint military leaders and service members.
    (C) discuss how members of the profession of arms apply their values in their daily lives.
    (D) praise the courage of U.S. service members.
    (E) encourage joint leaders to be students of the art and science of war.

17. In the passage's next to last paragraph, the word "epitomizes" most nearly means
    (A) to be a perfect example of something.
    (B) to suddenly perceive the essential nature of something.
    (C) to only last for a short time.
    (D) to make equal or equivalent.
    (E) to emphasize or encourage.

18. Which one of the following statements could you infer based solely on the information in the passage?
    (A) Military leaders who do not embody the values mentioned in the passage would have difficulty being effective in the American military.
    (B) It is understood that military personnel must look out for themselves first.
    (C) Physical courage is easier to demonstrate than moral courage.
    (D) Character cannot be learned in the same way that technical competence can.
    (E) Trust is not essential if everyone follows orders properly.

19. Fellow citizens being referred to as resources to be expended is meant to

(A) emphasize the dehumanizing aspect of war.
(B) illustrate the costs associated with the responsibility of military leadership.
(C) demonstrate the capacity for unemotional calculation needed in military leaders.
(D) be symbolic only, since people are not resources.
(E) prevent military leaders from becoming too cautious.

20. With which one of the following statements would the passage's author likely agree?

(A) "Courage consists of not being afraid in the face of hazardous situations."
(B) "Character cannot be learned, but instead must be inside an individual from birth."
(C) "Values cannot be learned, but instead must be inside an individual from birth."
(D) "Only leaders are required to have and maintain strong character and values."
(E) "All service members, but especially officers, are expected to have and maintain strong character and values."

Reading Passage for Questions 21–25

Leadership is the art and science of influencing and directing people to accomplish the assigned mission. This highlights two fundamental elements of leadership: the mission to be accomplished and the people who accomplish it. All facets of Air Force leadership should support these two basic elements. Effective leadership transforms human potential into effective performance in the present and prepares capable leaders for the future. The Air Force needs these leaders to accomplish the national objectives set for national security, to defend the safety of our people and our nation, when those objectives require the use of armed force.

Leadership does not equal command, but all commanders should be leaders. Any Air Force member can be a leader and can positively influence those around him or her to accomplish the mission. This is the Air Force concept of leadership, and all aspects of Air Force leadership should support it. The vast majority of Air Force leaders are not commanders. These individuals, who have stepped forward to lead others in accomplishing the mission, simultaneously serve as both leaders and followers at every level of the Air Force, from young Airmen working in the life support shop, to captains at wing staffs, to civilians in supply agencies, to generals at the Pentagon. Desirable behavioral patterns of these leaders and followers are identified in Air Force doctrine and should be emulated in ways that improve the performance of individuals and units. Leaders positively influence their entire organization without necessarily being the commander.

The primary task of a military organization is to perform its mission. The leader's primary responsibility is to motivate and direct people to carry out the unit's mission successfully. A leader must never forget the importance of the personnel themselves to that mission.

People perform the mission. They are the heart of the organization. Without their actions, a unit will fail to achieve its objectives. A leader's responsibilities include the care, support, and development of the unit's personnel. Successful leaders have continually ensured that the needs of the people in their unit are met promptly and properly.

All Air Force leaders share the same goal: to accomplish their organization's mission. Upon entering the Air Force, members take an oath, signifying their personal commitment to support and defend the Constitution of the United States and a commitment and willingness to serve their country for the duration of their Air Force careers. The oath is a solemn promise to do one's duty and meet one's responsibilities. The oath espouses the responsibility to lead others in the exercise of one's duty.

Regardless of duty location, occupational specialty, or job position, all Airmen must embody the warrior ethos, tough-mindedness, tireless motivation, an unceasing vigilance, and a willingness to sacrifice their own lives for their country, if necessary. Air Force Airmen, military and civilian, are committed to being the world's premier air and space force. This is the warrior ethos.

The abilities of a leader, which are derived from innate capabilities and built through experience, education, and training, can be improved upon through deliberate development. Using the Air Force leadership components is the means by which Airmen can achieve excellence—by living the Air Force core values, developing enduring leadership competencies, acquiring professional and technical competence, and then acting on such abilities to accomplish the unit's mission while taking care of the unit's personnel. Core values permeate leadership at all levels at all times. Leaders at the more junior levels must demonstrate the personal leadership competencies needed to create a cohesive unit fully supportive of its mission. Mid-level leaders will use the people and team leadership competencies to advance the organization's responsibilities within the framework of the operational mission. The more senior the leader, the more crucial his or her influence is on the institutional excellence of the organization. The abilities to influence people, improve performance, and accomplish a mission—the leadership actions—are part of all levels of leadership.

21. The primary purpose of the passage is to
    - (A) compare the different mission sets of U.S. Air Force organizations.
    - (B) describe the legal obligations of commanders.
    - (C) define U.S. Air Force leadership.
    - (D) prescribe acceptable levels of risk during mission accomplishment.
    - (E) focus on the contribution of Airmen at all levels.

22. Which one of the following statements could you infer based solely on the information in the passage?
    - (A) All leaders must be proficient in the full spectrum of leadership techniques.
    - (B) Leaders are mostly born, not made.
    - (C) Some lower-level missions could be handled by automated equipment.
    - (D) Commanders can delegate their leadership responsibility.
    - (E) Different organizational levels require different leadership styles.

23. According to the passage, successful leaders must
    - (A) continually ensure that the needs of their unit's people are met promptly and properly.
    - (B) hold subordinate leaders accountable for failure to accomplish the mission.
    - (C) decide which Air Force core values apply to a situation and then apply the appropriate leadership techniques.
    - (D) take into account individual unit members' professional development needs when assigning tasks.
    - (E) avoid any appearance of not accepting the individual values of unit members.

24. In the passage's sixth paragraph, the word "ethos" most nearly means

(A) the characteristic emotional atmosphere of the group or organization.
(B) the distinguishing character or guiding beliefs of a group.
(C) the primary mission of the organization, as assigned by higher headquarters.
(D) the prevailing level of correct technical decisions made during operations.
(E) the logical outcome of the organization's mission statement.

25. With which one of the following quotes would the passage's author likely agree?

(A) "Life is like a dogsled team. If you ain't the lead dog, the scenery never changes."
(B) "Never forget that only dead fish swim with the stream."
(C) "Leadership involves finding a parade and getting in front of it."
(D) "Don't bring me a problem without a solution."
(E) "Ultimately, leadership is not about glorious crowning acts. It's about keeping your team focused on a goal and motivated to do their best to achieve it."

SUBTEST #6: SITUATIONAL JUDGMENT

50 Questions

DIRECTIONS: This subtest measures your judgment in responding to interpersonal situations similar to those you may encounter as an officer. Your responses will be scored relative to the consensus judgment of a wide sample of experienced U.S. Air Force officers. For each situation, you must respond to two questions. First, select which one of the five actions listed you judge as the MOST EFFECTIVE action in response to the situation. Second, select which one of the five actions listed you judge as the LEAST EFFECTIVE action in response to the situation.
NOTE: Select only one action (A–E) for each question.

Situation 1. You have recently been assigned to lead a section made up of experienced and technically proficient Airmen, but you don't have a solid understanding of the section's mission, nor of its day-to-day routine. The senior NCO is on extended leave due to a family emergency out of state. The section members present on your first day are not immediately helpful when you ask them for information. You know you need to understand your job and the other section members' jobs in order to effectively lead the section and accomplish the mission.

Possible actions:
(A) Contact the previous section leader and ask for suggestions.
(B) Call the senior NCO on his emergency leave contact number.
(C) Contact the superior who assigned you to the section for further guidance.
(D) Meet one-on-one with the most senior section member present to learn about the section's mission and its daily routine.
(E) Call a section meeting and let them know your priorities and what changes you would like to see.

1. Select the MOST EFFECTIVE action (A–E) in response to the situation.

2. Select the LEAST EFFECTIVE action (A–E) in response to the situation.

Situation 2. You are in charge of a project supported by people who do not fall directly under your supervision, including a civilian engineer. The engineer always provides update briefings in your meetings with the commander, who is superior in authority to the engineer and your immediate supervisors. When answering technical questions about the project, the engineer often leaves out relevant facts. You recognize the engineer is filtering his responses, sometimes to the point of being untruthful.

Possible actions:
(A) Speak up during the meeting to present the full, unfiltered information yourself.
(B) Immediately after the meeting, discuss your concerns privately with the engineer.
(C) Immediately after the meeting, notify the engineer's supervisor of your concerns.
(D) Immediately after the meeting, notify your supervisor of your concerns to seek advice.
(E) Immediately after the meeting, meet privately with the commander to present the full, unfiltered information.

3. Select the MOST EFFECTIVE action (A–E) in response to the situation.

4. Select the LEAST EFFECTIVE action (A–E) in response to the situation.

Situation 3. You are a section leader on a field exercise, and, after a late conclusion of the day's training activities, your section is ready to bed down for the night. However, the section's tent, which is large enough to hold all 10 section members but takes four people to set up, has not been put up yet. No one in the section wants to put up the tent, even though they know it may rain; they all say they just want to go to sleep. What should you do?

Possible actions:
(A) Let the section sleep in the open and put up the tent tomorrow.
(B) Tell the section that everyone will work together to set up the tent.
(C) Tell the section that the first four Airmen to volunteer to put up the tent will have light duty tomorrow.
(D) Explain that you understand that everyone is tired, but the tent needs to be put up and they need to get it done while you check in with the command post to get some answers about tomorrow's events.
(E) Firmly tell the senior NCO that the tent *will* be set up in the next 30 minutes or that tomorrow will be a very hard day for everyone.

5. Select the MOST EFFECTIVE action (A–E) in response to the situation.

6. Select the LEAST EFFECTIVE action (A–E) in response to the situation.

Situation 4. You are the assistant operations officer for a refueling wing participating in an international exercise. During a video teleconference, you are finding it difficult to understand the briefing officer for another wing in the exercise for whom English is obviously a second language. You have met her several times before at conferences and also in a technical school you both attended. Your previous experience is that she is smart and capable, but you noticed before that she has a tendency to speak very quickly when nervous, making her already noticeable accent very strong. You can see that the other people in the same room are having the same problem you are. What should you do?

Possible actions:
(A) After the call is over, mention your concerns to the others in the room and suggest that everyone compare notes to ensure they had the same understanding of what she was saying.
(B) After the other wing's briefing officer has finished her portion, send her a text message suggesting that she might benefit from slowing her speaking rate, since there were some participants in the room with you who found it challenging to understand her.
(C) Mention your concerns to the wing operations officer (who was present in the room) after the call, offering to speak to the other wing's briefing officer if the operations officer wants you to, explaining that you have an existing working relationship with her.
(D) Call your colleague afterward to ask what she thinks about the state of exercise planning and mention that at times you found it difficult to understand what she was saying, adding that she obviously knew what she was talking about but suggesting that slowing down her delivery a little would help everyone better understand her information.
(E) Interrupt the briefer's presentation when she pauses and ask politely if she could please slow down her delivery because the audio reception is not 100%.

7. Select the MOST EFFECTIVE action (A–E) in response to the situation.

8. Select the LEAST EFFECTIVE action (A–E) in response to the situation.

Situation 5. You are the officer in charge of A Flight in a newly activated security service squadron, which has just spent the past three weeks concentrating on weapons qualification. Your squadron commander calls you in to discuss your flight's results, which report that your machine gunners are not fully qualified since they only fired on the 10-meter range; the transition range has not been built yet. However, the qualification manual specifies that gunners must fire on the transition range to be certified as fully qualified. The squadron commander can't understand why B and C Flights reported all machine gunners as fully qualified, while your report did not: "You all fired on the only range we have. And besides, that's how we did it in the same situation back at Michaelson Airbase." You know that some of your senior NCOs served under this commander before at Michaelson Airbase overseas. What do you do?

Possible actions:

(A) Tell him you will correct your report to match B and C Flights so that the squadron doesn't look incompetent—after all, you did the best you could with the assets available.

(B) Respectfully decline to change your report, but ask about any other bases nearby that have a transition range.

(C) Tell him you would like to research the matter and confer with your NCOs.

(D) Decline to change your report and suggest it could be leverage to get higher headquarters to get the transition range built more quickly.

(E) Ask permission for your flight to build a field expedient transition range over the weekend with materials at hand.

9. Select the MOST EFFECTIVE action (A–E) in response to the situation.

10. Select the LEAST EFFECTIVE action (A–E) in response to the situation.

Situation 6. You are the senior NCO in an operations flight. When you first arrived, you directed the section leaders to counsel their Airmen on their performance—good and bad—every month, and to keep written records. Three months later, you find the section leaders' counseling records are sloppy, incomplete, or nonexistent. What do you do?

Possible actions:

(A) Write up an official counseling on the section leaders to show them how to keep counseling records and to prepare the way for disciplinary actions if your orders continue to be executed poorly.

(B) Chew the section leaders out for ignoring your instructions, but keep no written record.

(C) Draft a counseling annex to the flight Standing Operating Procedure (SOP) so you can point to it the next time your directions are carried out poorly.

(D) Talk to the section leaders as a group to find out if they know how to properly conduct formal counseling as well as why it's important.

(E) Talk to the section leaders individually to find out if they know how to properly conduct formal counseling as well as why it's important.

11. Select the MOST EFFECTIVE action (A–E) in response to the situation.

12. Select the LEAST EFFECTIVE action (A–E) in response to the situation.

Situation 7. You are the leader of a dismounted "presence patrol" through an Iraqi village that was until recently occupied by hard-core terrorist fighters. Intelligence has told you that the terrorists told the villagers that the American forces' primary objective was to defile their mosques and make their children work for U.S. forces. As you walk down both sides of the dusty main road through the village (which will take you past the mosque), an angry crowd starts to gather, yelling and shaking their fists at your patrol. The sun is bright, your patrol's body armor is hot and uncomfortable, and you can tell your patrol members' tempers are fraying, too. What do you do?

Possible actions:

(A) Tell the patrol to use their weapons to warn away the mob; they have to understand that they will lose any confrontation.

(B) Turn around, exit the village, and find a route around the village to get to your destination; there's no benefit to touching off this powder keg.

(C) Tell the patrol to take a knee, point their weapons at the ground, take off their sunglasses, and smile; the villagers need to understand that your patrol is not a threat.

(D) Tell your interpreter to use a bullhorn to tell the crowd that you are just passing through; the villagers need to know your peaceful intentions.

(E) Tell the patrol to get closer together and speed up their progress through the village; the sooner you get out of here, the better.

13. Select the MOST EFFECTIVE action (A–E) in response to the situation.

14. Select the LEAST EFFECTIVE action (A–E) in response to the situation.

Situation 8. You are the third-highest ranking person in an Air Force coordination cell that is part of a newly established joint (multi-service) Coalition (multi-national) peacekeeping headquarters. You have never been on a peacekeeping mission before, but the group of senior NCOs in your cell have experience in both peacekeeping and multiple wartime deployments. The cell's senior officer (officer in charge, or OIC) is at a week-long conference on another continent, and the executive officer (second senior person) just got medically evacuated due to a heart attack, leaving you in charge. You are glad that an Army lieutenant in the land operations cell is a friend from college; it's nice to see a friendly face among all the strangers. You have just returned from a mission briefing at Coalition headquarters for an operation where Air Force assets have a major role. What do you do?

Possible actions:

(A) Go to the cell's senior NCO, confess that you don't have any idea what to do next, and ask him to take over until the OIC returns.

(B) Make an emergency call to the OIC and ask him if he can return immediately.

(C) Get the cell together, explain the mission brief you just received, and ask the group what they think needs to be done and whose roles fit into each task.

(D) Make an emergency call to the OIC and ask him what you should do.

(E) Ask your college friend in the land operations cell what he thinks you should do.

15. Select the MOST EFFECTIVE action (A–E) in response to the situation.

16. Select the LEAST EFFECTIVE action (A–E) in response to the situation.

Situation 9. You are the unmarried commander of a maintenance flight when you meet Lieutenant Davidson, a recently divorced pilot in a flying wing on the same base. You discover you have many of the same interests, including waterskiing. You also discover that you are a distant cousin of the commander of Lieutenant Davidson's unit and even attended the same large high school, although separated by a couple of years. You begin dating Lieutenant Davidson from time to time, and you reserve rooms for a particular weekend at a beach area where waterskiing is popular. However, the flying wing is short of pilots (there have even been complaints about the high operations tempo), and on the Friday before your beach trip, Lieutenant Davidson gets notified of a short-notice weekend mission. Lieutenant Davidson calls you to say, "I'd really rather go to the beach like we planned, but I've been assigned to a mission this weekend. Unless you can talk my commander out of it, the trip is off." What do you do?

Possible actions:

(A) Call Lieutenant Davidson's first-line supervisor and inquire if there is another pilot who could perform the weekend mission.

(B) Tell Lieutenant Davidson to find a replacement for the mission or you will find a replacement for the beach trip.

(C) Tell Lieutenant Davidson that that suggestion is completely unprofessional, and not to call you until after the weekend.

(D) Decline to call your cousin, the flying unit's commander, and suggest rescheduling the trip.

(E) Call your cousin, Lieutenant Davidson's commander, and ask as a personal and family favor if there is another pilot who could perform the weekend mission.

17. Select the MOST EFFECTIVE action (A–E) in response to the situation.

18. Select the LEAST EFFECTIVE action (A–E) in response to the situation.

Situation 10. You have been working in your security service unit for more than a year, and you are acting as a mentor to a new member of the unit, helping him understand his role and tasks. You are currently very busy, working to meet a tight deadline on some essential work that is vital for a legal case; in fact, your report needs to be completed within the next three hours. The person you are mentoring is having difficulty understanding how to use one of the automated reporting applications, and he has come to you for help with his own report that is due in two hours. If the new unit member does not submit his report on time, it will not only break the unit's two-year streak of on-time submissions, but it will also make you look like a poor leader and mentor. What do you do?

Possible actions:

(A) Help the new unit member, and then hurry up and finish your own report.

(B) Suggest that the new unit member look at the SOP and online FAQs for help with his issue.

(C) Ask for an extension to the deadlines for both reports.

(D) Tell the new unit member you will help him, but you are very busy so it will have to be later—no sense in both of you missing your deadlines.

(E) Ask a colleague to help the new unit member.

19. Select the MOST EFFECTIVE action (A–E) in response to the situation.

20. Select the LEAST EFFECTIVE action (A–E) in response to the situation.

Situation 11. You are a junior staff officer in the Current Operations Flight of an operations support squadron. The Plans flight leader (a different office within the squadron) asks you if you can do some work for her during a period when your flight is not only extraordinarily busy but also shorthanded. The correct procedure for one flight requesting help from another is for one flight leader to coordinate with the other flight leader, rather than approaching individual staff officers directly. Based on the Plans flight leader's initial request, you estimate the work will take two to three focused hours to complete. How do you respond to the Plans flight leader's request?

Possible actions:

(A) Tell the Plans flight leader that you will have to ask your flight leader for permission to help her.

(B) Tell the Plans flight leader that you would like to help her, but that your flight is not only shorthanded but also unusually busy, and it's just not possible.

(C) Tell the Plans flight leader that you would like to help her, but that your flight is not only shorthanded but also unusually busy, and ask her to coordinate through your flight leader.

(D) Tell the Plans flight leader that you will work it into your schedule, and then complete your own work as quickly as possible to get to the extra work from the Plans flight leader.

(E) Tell the Plans flight leader that you will do your best to help, and then ask your Current Operations coworkers if they can share some of your existing workload.

21. Select the MOST EFFECTIVE action (A–E) in response to the situation.

22. Select the LEAST EFFECTIVE action (A–E) in response to the situation.

Situation 12. You work in the International Operations area of an upper-level headquarters, and part of your set of responsibilities is to obtain visas for staff members who need to travel to other countries outside U.S. military installations. You get a phone call from a senior NCO in the intelligence section requesting a visa for a specific country that you know usually takes several weeks to be granted. The person requesting the visa needs to have it by the end of the week as he must begin his travel (which was directed by his two-star general) Monday morning.

Possible actions:

(A) Call your contact in the embassy for the country concerned to set up an appointment to bring in the American traveler's documents for expedited handling.

(B) Tell the traveler that he needs to take extra care to avoid errors or gaps when filling out his visa request.

(C) Tell the traveler that the time available will make the request challenging, but you will do what you can to arrange the visa for him.

(D) Explain to the traveler that his requested timeline is too short and that you will not be able to help him get a visa.

(E) Call your supervisor and ask for instructions.

23. Select the MOST EFFECTIVE action (A–E) in response to the situation.

24. Select the LEAST EFFECTIVE action (A–E) in response to the situation.

Situation 13. Your convoy of two armored wheeled vehicles and two lighter, unarmored High Mobility Multipurpose Wheeled Vehicles (HMMWVs) has a mission to replace three malfunctioning communications relays near the Afghanistan–Pakistan border. These relays are essential for both ground and air operations in this area, which has a shifting mix of friendly and unfriendly tribes. The spring thaws have made the ground extremely muddy in places and, between the second and third relays, one of your HMMWVs gets badly mired in the deep mud between rocks at a fast-flowing stream crossing. While your convoy attempts to pull it out, one of the armored vehicles breaks an axle. When this happens, two Airmen are injured, one seriously (you think his leg is broken), but neither's injury is life-threatening anytime soon. What do you do?

Possible actions:

(A) Abandon the vehicle with the broken axle, cross load all personnel and equipment on the remaining vehicles, and return to base.

(B) Call your commander and ask for instructions.

(C) Call for an aerial medical evacuation for the injured personnel, set up security around the accident site, wait for the medevac and vehicle recovery team to show up, and then continue the mission.

(D) Send out the remaining HMMWV to find a local friendly tribe to help you.

(E) Leave two Airmen with the injured personnel and disabled vehicle, call in a recovery team for both, and continue the mission.

25. Select the MOST EFFECTIVE action (A–E) in response to the situation.

26. Select the LEAST EFFECTIVE action (A–E) in response to the situation.

Situation 14. Airman Belton is new to the unit—fresh out of his basic and technical training—and hesitantly approaches you as his team leader in the maintenance bay, saying, "I have a problem I'd like to talk to you about." You stop what you're doing and ask him to continue. He says, "I have this new checking account, and it's the first one I've ever had. I have lots of checks left, but for some reason the base exchange is saying they're no good." You realize that Airman Belton probably does not understand that there must be money in his bank account to cover checks written against the account. What do you do?

Possible actions:

(A) Since you have to finish a report for the commander before you can leave for the day, tell Airman Belton to come see you at 0900 tomorrow morning so you can discuss it some more and see what you can do to help.

(B) Since you don't want to seem like you are talking down to him, tell him to check with Airman Curley, who has been in the unit for almost a year.

(C) Ask a few more questions to confirm your initial assessment, and then tell Airman Belton to bring his checkbook to your office in an hour. Before this meeting, look up the Internet addresses for online Air Force and civilian personal financial readiness information.

(D) Tell Airman Belton that he needs to make friends with Google to handle his personal problems; you have a report for the commander to finish.

(E) Call over the next most senior team member, explain Airman Belton's situation and your assessment of it, and ask him to help the new kid.

27. Select the MOST EFFECTIVE action (A–E) in response to the situation.

28. Select the LEAST EFFECTIVE action (A–E) in response to the situation.

Situation 15. You are the section leader for the installation-wide inventory management office. Staff Sergeant (SSgt) Nelson is your most competent section member. She has the lowest error rate, she always beats her deadlines, and she is very knowledgeable about the inventory management software, as well as obscure regulations about the base's specialized property and equipment. She is well aware of her value to the section and is not ashamed to use it in arguments with other team members, even when it's irrelevant. Other section members say she is a know-it-all and avoid any interaction with her, both on and off duty, even though the base is in a somewhat isolated area. What should you do?

Possible actions:

(A) Tell SSgt Nelson that you appreciate her professional contribution, but you need her to use her expertise to help the section and its members, not just to win arguments.
(B) Don't get involved. As long as SSgt Nelson doesn't mind being left out, her social status is none of your business.
(C) Encourage the team not to take her comments personally.
(D) Ask SSgt Nelson why she behaves the way she does. Tell her that if she doesn't make an effort to get along with the rest of the section, you'll have to transfer her to a more individual, less responsible position.
(E) Move SSgt Nelson to a separate office to reduce her interactions with other section members.

29. Select the MOST EFFECTIVE action (A–E) in response to the situation.

30. Select the LEAST EFFECTIVE action (A–E) in response to the situation.

Situation 16. Your unit is working furiously on a project that will likely be incorporated into the next Air Force Instruction (regulation) on this subject. Your deadline is next week, and you are a little behind schedule, although you hope to make up the time as you wrap things up. Your unit is subdivided into smaller work teams for this project, and you meet regularly with each team to review their progress and help solve problems. In one of your meetings, you discover that one team did not document their work, despite such documentation being part of their specified task's requirements. Asking them to document their work now will inevitably cause further delays. What do you do?

Possible actions:

(A) Tell the team to start documentation from this point forward.
(B) Tell the entire unit that everyone will work with this team over the weekend to catch up.
(C) Move someone from another team in your unit to help this team complete their documentation.
(D) Tell the team to complete the documentation, regardless of the significant overtime hours needed to correct their omission.
(E) Work with the team leader in question to establish some weekend documentation catch-up sessions where you will also attend and help.

31. Select the MOST EFFECTIVE action (A–E) in response to the situation.

32. Select the LEAST EFFECTIVE action (A–E) in response to the situation.

Situation 17. Senior Airman (SA) Mitchell just reported to the unit this week. He is still learning unit SOPs and procedures, and today you gave him some material to study. An hour before the normal end of the day, SA Mitchell steps into your office and says he has finished studying the material and has even completed some practice exercises. He asks you if it's OK for him to leave now since he is going to a wedding this evening and doesn't want to be late. There isn't anything else in particular you need him to do today, but work hours are important to you.

Possible actions:

(A) Refuse his request and explain that if he has special needs, he should ask in advance.
(B) Give him permission to leave since he has finished his tasks and has an unusual reason.
(C) Give him permission to leave, but on the next day talk to him about working hours.
(D) Allow him to leave 15 minutes early. You want to help but you also want him to get used to regular work hours.
(E) Allow him to leave now, but tell him to come in an hour early tomorrow.

33. Select the MOST EFFECTIVE action (A–E) in response to the situation.

34. Select the LEAST EFFECTIVE action (A–E) in response to the situation.

Situation 18. Your section has a heavy workload of specified tasks that are needed to enable a large unit to deploy overseas; this is the first of four such units that will need the same level of work from your understaffed section. You schedule a two-hour workshop for the entire section to improve the speed of operations and to synchronize tasks. One of your team leaders tells you he does not want his team to attend the training, citing their heavy workload. What do you do?

Possible actions:

(A) Move some of that team leader's tasks to another team so that all teams can attend the workshop.
(B) Tell the team leader that the workshop is mandatory and that he and his team must attend since there are three more deploying units that will need this level of attention from the entire section.
(C) Explain the importance of the workshop to the team leader but empower him to decide whether his team will attend.
(D) Go over the team leader's task list and prioritize them for him to identify time for his section to attend the training.
(E) Tell the team leader that his team can either be at the workshop or he can get a reprimand in writing.

35. Select the MOST EFFECTIVE action (A–E) in response to the situation.

36. Select the LEAST EFFECTIVE action (A–E) in response to the situation.

Situation 19. Everyone in your office has been issued replacements for their previous worn-out computer systems—except for you. What do you do?

Possible actions:

(A) Assume that this is a mistake and speak to your first-line supervisor.
(B) Confront your first-line supervisor about why you are being treated unfairly.
(C) Take the new computer system from one of your coworkers who is on temporary duty elsewhere.
(D) Ask for a transfer.
(E) File a complaint with the base Inspector General.

37. Select the MOST EFFECTIVE action (A–E) in response to the situation.

38. Select the LEAST EFFECTIVE action (A–E) in response to the situation.

Situation 20. Over the past few weeks, your directorate keeps running out of paper, printer ink, and other office supplies, even though you have seen boxes of new supplies arrive on three different occasions. For the last three days, you notice a coworker leaving the office with a large backpack that looks like it is filled and heavy. What do you do?

Possible actions:

(A) Inform your first-line supervisor that you suspect your coworker is stealing.
(B) Use your smartphone to record a video of your coworker leaving with a full backpack.
(C) Don't do anything. Office supplies are not your responsibility, and if someone is stealing, they will be caught.
(D) Ask some of your other coworkers if they have noticed anything suspicious lately.
(E) Ask your coworker about what you have seen.

39. Select the MOST EFFECTIVE action (A–E) in response to the situation.

40. Select the LEAST EFFECTIVE action (A–E) in response to the situation.

Situation 21. After completing your first substantive project in a new assignment, you are happy with the results and believe your performance is up to, if not above, the standard. Your supervisor sends you an email that gives you some brief feedback, explaining that most areas of the assignment were in fact not up to standard. You did not expect such negative feedback. Your supervisor asks to meet with you in a few days. What do you do?

Possible actions:

(A) Review the project requirements before the meeting and evaluate what you could have done better. During the meeting, ask your supervisor to elaborate on the feedback so that you understand what to do better.
(B) Ask to see your supervisor as soon as possible. Ask respectfully how you failed to meet expectations and what you should have done differently.
(C) Don't let the feedback have a negative effect on you. When you meet with your supervisor, listen to what he has to say but don't dwell on it—you know that you did your best, and that's all anyone can do.
(D) Tell a coworker about the negative feedback and ask him or her to review your work and give you their opinion.
(E) Draft a reply email to your supervisor explaining why your project work was in fact up to standard.

41. Select the MOST EFFECTIVE action (A–E) in response to the situation.

42. Select the LEAST EFFECTIVE action (A–E) in response to the situation.

Situation 22. Due to a reorganization, your supervisor is now responsible for an additional section, and he has transferred you there to be the section leader. You are shocked at how inefficient and outdated some of the processes and systems are in that section. In fact, an Air Force policy memo that came out six months ago specified changes in these exact areas. Suddenly, your supervisor needs to go on emergency leave for the next three to four weeks, and you are now not only in charge of the new section, but you are also the acting supervisor for the entire department. How do you proceed?

Possible actions:

(A) Await your supervisor's return to discuss your concerns and work out a plan together.
(B) Wait for at least two weeks to see what the impact of the current processes are before taking action.
(C) Implement steps directly to bring the new section's processes up-to-date.
(D) Identify an acting section leader for the new section, tell him or her about the updated policies, and ask him or her to come up with a plan to bring things up to date.
(E) Email your supervisor, asking for guidance at your supervisor's convenience based on the emergency leave situation.

43. Select the MOST EFFECTIVE action (A–E) in response to the situation.

44. Select the LEAST EFFECTIVE action (A–E) in response to the situation.

Situation 23. You have two very important deadlines to meet by the end of your working day. However, it is becoming clear, two hours before close of business, that you are in danger of missing both deadlines. What do you do?

Possible actions:

(A) Identify what's left to do and prioritize the critical tasks for the time remaining; work late to get both done before you leave today.
(B) Focus on still doing a quality job even if you miss one or both deadlines.
(C) Speed up your remaining tasks so that you will still be able to meet both deadlines.
(D) Identify the less important project, and make a call to see if you can renegotiate its delivery date. Then focus on finishing the more important project.
(E) Identify the project furthest from completion, and make a call to see if you can renegotiate its delivery date. Then work late to finish the more nearly completed project.

45. Select the MOST EFFECTIVE action (A–E) in response to the situation.

46. Select the LEAST EFFECTIVE action (A–E) in response to the situation.

Situation 24. Your flight leader has assigned your team a new, innovative project that he believes could increase productivity and decrease time spent tremendously. He is very excited about it, and he seems to expect you to feel the same way. However, when he describes the project's details, you begin to have doubts—the costs seem high, the time estimates seem low, and you are not sure that the units you support would benefit as much from the increased productivity as your flight leader expects. What do you do?

Possible actions:

(A) Thank your flight leader for the assignment, but discuss your concerns with the flight leader's supervisor to get guidance.

(B) Take the project, and thank your flight leader. Later, on your own, make adjustments to his plan that you think might help.

(C) Show appreciation for his choice to assign the project to your team, but mention that you have some additional thoughts on the matter and voice your concerns.

(D) Tell your flight leader that you're concerned that not everything will work out as expected, and point out the issues that concern you.

(E) Go along with the project. Your flight leader has more information than you do and has probably thought everything through. There's no reason to drop a project he believes in so much before it even begins.

47. Select the MOST EFFECTIVE action (A–E) in response to the situation.

48. Select the LEAST EFFECTIVE action (A–E) in response to the situation.

Situation 25. At the end of a particularly hectic day, under the pressure of multiple overlapping deadlines and briefings, you accidentally send an e-mail with attachments that contain internal decision-making documents to the wrong person (same first and last name, same rank, but different middle initial). What do you do?

Possible actions:

(A) Find your supervisor, explain what happened, and let him or her deal with any problems.

(B) Decide to ignore your error, send the e-mail to the correct person, and leave things like that.

(C) Send the e-mail to the right person, and delete the message to the wrong recipient from your "Sent Items" folder.

(D) Immediately send a follow-up e-mail to the "wrong" e-mail recipient, or if possible telephone him or her, apologizing and explaining your mistake. Then send the e-mail to the correct person.

(E) Leave the office, and deal with any problems tomorrow.

49. Select the MOST EFFECTIVE action (A–E) in response to the situation.

50. Select the LEAST EFFECTIVE action (A–E) in response to the situation.

SUBTEST #7: SELF-DESCRIPTION INVENTORY

The Self-Description Inventory measures personal characteristics and traits. The inventory consists of a list of 240 statements; your task is to read each statement carefully and decide how much that statement applies to you. You will then indicate how much you agree that a particular statement applies to you or describes you by using the following scale:

(A) Strongly disagree
(B) Moderately disagree
(C) Neither agree nor disagree
(D) Moderately agree
(E) Strongly agree

Since you have 240 statements and only 45 minutes for this test, you should work quickly—but you should answer all the questions. Choose your answer from your first impression by comparing yourself with other people in your same age group and of the same sex. Don't spend a long time thinking about what the "right" answer is—there is no right or wrong answer to any question. Mark a choice for all the statements, even if you're not completely sure of the answer. Again, your first impression will be the best indicator.

Following are some statements that are representative of the type you will see on the AFOQT Self-Description Inventory.

1. I generally get along well with most people.
2. I always try to finish what I start.
3. People often get upset with me for not showing up on time.
4. I usually place my work goals ahead of personal interests or hobbies.
5. I get nervous when I have to speak in public.
6. I try to avoid large gatherings or crowds of people if I can.
7. I am not comfortable supervising others.
8. I like to listen to different types of music.
9. I usually wind up being the leader in whatever group I am in.
10. I have higher work standards than most people I know.
11. I like being involved in group activities.
12. I like being on time or even ahead of time.
13. I like meeting new people.
14. I like being where the action is.
15. I am pleased when friends stop by to see me.
16. I am reluctant to turn in an assignment unless it is perfect.
17. I am neater than most people I know.
18. I am usually afraid to voice my opinion because others may disagree.
19. I prefer an evening at home alone to a night on the town with friends.
20. I like new challenges.

SUBTEST #8: PHYSICAL SCIENCE

20 Questions

DIRECTIONS: This subtest measures your knowledge in the area of science. Each of the questions or incomplete statements is followed by five choices. Your task is to decide which one of the choices best answers the question or completes the statement.

1. What is energy called that is derived from the sun?
   (A) hydroelectric
   (B) solar
   (C) geothermal
   (D) volcanic
   (E) kinetic

2. The rotation of Earth on its axis causes
   (A) tides.
   (B) day and night.
   (C) the seasons.
   (D) axial tilt.
   (E) magnetic anomalies.

3. Matter exists in one of three states or conditions: __________, __________, or __________.
   (A) element, compound, mixture
   (B) solid, liquid, gas
   (C) physical, chemical, molecular
   (D) physical, inertial, chemical
   (E) reactive, nonreactive, inert

4. The reaction between sodium, metal, and water can be classified as
   (A) single replacement.
   (B) double replacement.
   (C) decomposition.
   (D) synthesis.
   (E) aggregation.

5. Potential energy is due to __________, and kinetic energy is __________.
   (A) the position of an object, energy of motion
   (B) an object's acceleration, steady movement
   (C) the reaction between certain elements, velocity in a straight line
   (D) how much faster an object could theoretically go, speed plus rate of acceleration
   (E) potential inertia, actual inertia

6. Which substance can be used to treat drinking water of questionable purity?
   (A) ammonia
   (B) iodine
   (C) chlorine
   (D) hydrogen chloride
   (E) ethylene glycol

7. In the International System of Units, the way to measure mass is known as the
   (A) kilogram.
   (B) kilometer.
   (C) ampere.
   (D) ohm.
   (E) henry.

8. An atom has
   (A) a greater number of electrons than protons.
   (B) a smaller number of electrons than protons.
   (C) the same number of protons as electrons.
   (D) the same number of protons as neutrons.
   (E) always one more electron than neutrons.

9. The total number of atoms in a molecule of $CuSO_4 \cdot 5H_2O$ is
   (A) 15.
   (B) 18.
   (C) 21.
   (D) 29.
   (E) 33.

10. A magnetic compass points in the direction of
    (A) true north.
    (B) the geographic north pole.
    (C) the magnetic north pole.
    (D) the local magnetic field.
    (E) grid north.

11. The four types of chemical reactions are
    (A) combination, sublimation, single replacement, and double replacement.
    (B) combination, decomposition, single replacement, and double replacement.
    (C) catalyzation, decomposition, single replacement, and equilibrium.
    (D) catalyzation, sublimation, double replacement, and saturation.
    (E) catalysis, morpholysis, single replacement, and double replacement.

12. The kinetic energy of a 1-kilogram mass, dropped from a height of 1 meter, just before it hits the ground is approximately
    (A) 1 joule.
    (B) 10 joules.
    (C) 100 joules.
    (D) 1,000 joules.
    (E) 10,000 joules.

13. A 120-V electrical power supply produces $\frac{1}{2}$ A to the load. The power delivered is
    (A) 60 watts.
    (B) 60 ohms.
    (C) 120 watts.
    (D) 240 watts.
    (E) 240 ohms.

14. Resistance—the tendency for a material to oppose the flow of electrons—is measured in
    (A) volts.
    (B) watts.
    (C) ohms.
    (D) amperes.
    (E) current.

15. When a lever is balanced on its fulcrum, the force on one arm
    (A) is greater than the force on the other.
    (B) matches the force on the other.
    (C) is less than the force on the other.
    (D) depends on the placement of the fulcrum.
    (E) is directly inverse to the length of the moment arm.

16. A magnifying glass is what kind of lens used on objects how far away?
    (A) convex lens used for objects beyond one focal length
    (B) convex lens used for objects closer than one focal length
    (C) concave lens used for objects beyond one focal length
    (D) concave lens used for objects closer than one focal length
    (E) none of the above

17. The three methods of heat transfer are
    (A) mechanical energy, heat energy, and steam power.
    (B) combustion, convection, and radiation.
    (C) insulation, convection, and wave motion.
    (D) radiation, conduction, and convection.
    (E) invection, convection, and conduction.

18. Frictional forces usually do NOT
    (A) oppose motion.
    (B) decrease kinetic energy.
    (C) increase kinetic energy.
    (D) increase potential energy.
    (E) produce wear.

19. For a solar eclipse to take place, the
    (A) moon must be between the sun and Earth.
    (B) Earth's axis of rotation must point toward the sun.
    (C) moon must be in its last crescent phase.
    (D) Earth must be between the sun and the moon.
    (E) Earth and the moon must be on opposite sides of the sun.

20. The speed of a wave is
    (A) equal to or less than the frequency of the wave multiplied by the wavelength.
    (B) equal to the frequency of the wave divided by the wavelength.
    (C) equal to the frequency of the wave multiplied by the wavelength.
    (D) equal to or greater than the wavelength multiplied by the frequency of the wave.
    (E) equal to or less than the wavelength divided by its frequency.

SUBTEST #9: TABLE READING

40 Questions

DIRECTIONS: This subtest measures your ability to read a table quickly and accurately. All the questions on this subtest are based on the following table. Notice that the X values appear at the top of the table and the Y values are shown on the left side of the table. The X values are the column values and the Y values are the row values. For each test question, you are given an X value and a Y value; your task will be to find the box where the selected column and row meet, note the number that appears there, and then find that same number among the answer options for each question.

Y \ X	–20	–19	–18	–17	–16	–15	–14	–13	–12	–11	–10	–9	–8	–7	–6	–5	–4	–3	–2	–1
20	50	51	52	53	54	55	56	57	58	59	60	61	62	63	64	65	66	67	68	69
19	51	52	53	54	55	56	57	58	59	60	61	62	63	64	65	66	67	68	69	70
18	52	53	54	55	56	57	58	59	60	61	62	63	64	65	66	67	68	69	70	71
17	53	54	55	56	57	58	59	60	61	62	63	64	65	66	67	68	69	70	71	72
16	54	55	56	57	58	59	60	61	62	63	64	65	66	67	68	69	70	71	72	73
15	55	56	57	58	59	60	61	62	63	64	65	66	67	68	69	70	71	72	73	74
14	56	57	58	59	60	61	62	63	64	65	66	67	68	69	70	71	72	73	74	75
13	57	58	59	60	61	62	63	64	65	66	67	68	69	70	71	72	73	74	75	76
12	58	59	60	61	62	63	64	65	66	67	68	69	70	71	72	73	74	75	76	77
11	59	60	61	62	63	64	65	66	67	68	69	70	71	72	73	74	75	76	77	78
10	60	61	62	63	64	65	66	67	68	69	70	71	72	73	74	75	76	77	78	79
9	61	62	63	64	65	66	67	68	69	70	71	72	73	74	75	76	77	78	79	80
8	62	63	64	65	66	67	68	69	70	71	72	73	74	75	76	77	78	79	80	81
7	63	64	65	66	67	68	69	70	71	72	73	74	75	76	77	78	79	80	81	82
6	64	65	66	67	68	69	70	71	72	73	74	75	76	77	78	79	80	81	82	83
5	65	66	67	68	69	70	71	72	73	74	75	76	77	78	79	80	81	82	83	84
4	66	67	68	69	70	71	72	73	74	75	76	77	78	79	80	81	82	83	84	85
3	67	68	69	70	71	72	73	74	75	76	77	78	79	80	81	82	83	84	85	86
2	68	69	70	71	72	73	74	75	76	77	78	79	80	81	82	83	84	85	86	87
1	69	70	71	72	73	74	75	76	77	78	79	80	81	82	83	84	85	86	87	88
0	70	71	72	73	74	75	76	77	78	79	80	81	82	83	84	85	86	87	88	89
–1	71	72	73	74	75	76	77	78	79	80	81	82	83	84	85	86	87	88	89	90
–2	72	73	74	75	76	77	78	79	80	81	82	83	84	85	86	87	88	89	90	91
–3	73	74	75	76	77	78	79	80	81	82	83	84	85	86	87	88	89	90	91	92
–4	74	75	76	77	78	79	80	81	82	83	84	85	86	87	88	89	90	91	92	93
–5	75	76	77	78	79	80	81	82	83	84	85	86	87	88	89	90	91	92	93	94
–6	76	77	78	79	80	81	82	83	84	85	86	87	88	89	90	91	92	93	94	95
–7	77	78	79	80	81	82	83	84	85	86	87	88	89	90	91	92	93	94	95	96
–8	78	79	80	81	82	83	84	85	86	87	88	89	90	91	92	93	94	95	96	97
–9	79	80	81	82	83	84	85	86	87	88	89	90	91	92	93	94	95	96	97	98
–10	80	81	82	83	84	85	86	87	88	89	90	91	92	93	94	95	96	97	98	99
–11	81	82	83	84	85	86	87	88	89	90	91	92	93	94	95	96	97	98	99	100
–12	82	83	84	85	86	87	88	89	90	91	92	93	94	95	96	97	98	99	100	101
–13	83	84	85	86	87	88	89	90	91	92	93	94	95	96	97	98	99	100	101	102
–14	84	85	86	87	88	89	90	91	92	93	94	95	96	97	98	99	100	101	102	103
–15	85	86	87	88	89	90	91	92	93	94	95	96	97	98	99	100	101	102	103	104
–16	86	87	88	89	90	91	92	93	94	95	96	97	98	99	100	101	102	103	104	105
–17	87	88	89	90	91	92	93	94	95	96	97	98	99	100	101	102	103	104	105	106
–18	88	89	90	91	92	93	94	95	96	97	98	99	100	101	102	103	104	105	106	107
–19	89	90	91	92	93	94	95	96	97	98	99	100	101	102	103	104	105	106	107	108
–20	90	91	92	93	94	95	96	97	98	99	100	101	102	103	104	105	106	107	108	109

0	1	2	3	4	5	6	7	8	9	10	11	12	13	14	15	16	17	18	19	20
70	71	72	73	74	75	76	77	78	79	80	81	82	83	84	85	86	87	88	89	90
71	72	73	74	75	76	77	78	79	80	81	82	83	84	85	86	87	88	89	90	91
72	73	74	75	76	77	78	79	80	81	82	83	84	85	86	87	88	89	90	91	92
73	74	75	76	77	78	79	80	81	82	83	84	85	86	87	88	89	90	91	92	93
74	75	76	77	78	79	80	81	82	83	84	85	86	87	88	89	90	91	92	93	94
75	76	77	78	79	80	81	82	83	84	85	86	87	88	89	90	91	92	93	94	95
76	77	78	79	80	81	82	83	84	85	86	87	88	89	90	91	92	93	94	95	96
77	78	79	80	81	82	83	84	85	86	87	88	89	90	91	92	93	94	95	96	97
78	79	80	81	82	83	84	85	86	87	88	89	90	91	92	93	94	95	96	97	98
79	80	81	82	83	84	85	86	87	88	89	90	91	92	93	94	95	96	97	98	99
80	81	82	83	84	85	86	87	88	89	90	91	92	93	94	95	96	97	98	99	100
81	82	83	84	85	86	87	88	89	90	91	92	93	94	95	96	97	98	99	100	101
82	83	84	85	86	87	88	89	90	91	92	93	94	95	96	97	98	99	100	101	102
83	84	85	86	87	88	89	90	91	92	93	94	95	96	97	98	99	100	101	102	103
84	85	86	87	88	89	90	91	92	93	94	95	96	97	98	99	100	101	102	103	104
85	86	87	88	89	90	91	92	93	94	95	96	97	98	99	100	101	102	103	104	105
86	87	88	89	90	91	92	93	94	95	96	97	98	99	100	101	102	103	104	105	106
87	88	89	90	91	92	93	94	95	96	97	98	99	100	101	102	103	104	105	106	107
88	89	90	91	92	93	94	95	96	97	98	99	100	101	102	103	104	105	106	107	108
89	90	91	92	93	94	95	96	97	98	99	100	101	102	103	104	105	106	107	108	109
90	91	92	93	94	95	96	97	98	99	100	101	102	103	104	105	106	107	108	109	110
91	92	93	94	95	96	97	98	99	100	101	102	103	104	105	106	107	108	109	110	111
92	93	94	95	96	97	98	99	100	101	102	103	104	105	106	107	108	109	110	111	112
93	94	95	96	97	98	99	100	101	102	103	104	105	106	107	108	109	110	111	112	113
94	95	96	97	98	99	100	101	102	103	104	105	106	107	108	109	110	111	112	113	114
95	96	97	98	99	100	101	102	103	104	105	106	107	108	109	110	111	112	113	114	115
96	97	98	99	100	101	102	103	104	105	106	107	108	109	110	111	112	113	114	115	116
97	98	99	100	101	102	103	104	105	106	107	108	109	110	111	112	113	114	115	116	117
98	99	100	101	102	103	104	105	106	107	108	109	110	111	112	113	114	115	116	117	118
99	100	101	102	103	104	105	106	107	108	109	110	111	112	113	114	115	116	117	118	119
100	101	102	103	104	105	106	107	108	109	110	111	112	113	114	115	116	117	118	119	120
101	102	103	104	105	106	107	108	109	110	111	112	113	114	115	116	117	118	119	120	121
102	103	104	105	106	107	108	109	110	111	112	113	114	115	116	117	118	119	120	121	122
103	104	105	106	107	108	109	110	111	112	113	114	115	116	117	118	119	120	121	122	123
104	105	106	107	108	109	110	111	112	113	114	115	116	117	118	119	120	121	122	123	124
105	106	107	108	109	110	111	112	113	114	115	116	117	118	119	120	121	122	123	124	125
106	107	108	109	110	111	112	113	114	115	116	117	118	119	120	121	122	123	124	125	126
107	108	109	110	111	112	113	114	115	116	117	118	119	120	121	122	123	124	125	126	127
108	109	110	111	112	113	114	115	116	117	118	119	120	121	122	123	124	125	126	127	128
109	110	111	112	113	114	115	116	117	118	119	120	121	122	123	124	125	126	127	128	129
110	111	112	113	114	115	116	117	118	119	120	121	122	123	124	125	126	127	128	129	130

	X	Y	(A)	(B)	(C)	(D)	(E)
1.	+4	+19	74	75	76	86	57
2.	+2	–8	99	101	100	28	98
3.	–9	–1	82	83	84	28	81
4.	+9	+5	90	91	92	93	94
5.	0	–6	69	106	95	96	97
6.	+9	–7	116	106	107	105	117
7.	+2	+2	109	99	90	91	92
8.	+8	+5	93	94	95	96	97
9.	+4	–4	98	89	90	97	96
10.	–3	+3	103	83	93	84	73
11.	0	–7	94	95	96	98	97
12.	+6	+8	87	88	89	98	107
13.	–9	–8	86	87	89	108	90
14.	+1	0	91	89	88	90	92
15.	+3	–1	84	95	92	93	94
16.	+1	+6	86	87	84	85	88
17.	+3	–5	96	97	98	99	100
18.	–10	+18	61	62	63	64	65
19.	+20	–12	123	124	122	120	121
20.	+17	+13	93	94	95	96	97

	X	Y	(A)	(B)	(C)	(D)	(E)
21.	–9	+14	68	66	67	65	69
22.	+15	+3	112	113	103	102	101
23.	–12	–16	94	95	93	96	92
24.	+7	+11	86	87	84	88	85
25.	–13	–13	89	90	91	92	93
26.	–16	+6	68	67	66	69	65
27.	–16	+19	52	54	56	58	55
28.	–4	+1	82	86	83	85	84
29.	–9	–6	84	85	87	86	88
30.	+19	0	111	108	109	107	110
31.	–4	+7	78	79	80	82	85
32.	+6	–18	114	115	117	112	113
33.	–18	+11	61	59	60	63	62
34.	+14	–17	118	119	120	121	122
35.	+2	+12	79	82	81	80	83
36.	+13	–7	108	109	110	112	111
37.	–9	0	81	82	83	85	79
38.	+8	–6	103	104	105	102	106
39.	+16	–6	111	110	113	109	112
40.	+19	+8	98	102	103	101	99

SUBTEST #10: INSTRUMENT COMPREHENSION

25 Questions

DIRECTIONS: This subtest measures your ability to determine the position of an airplane in flight from reading instruments showing its compass heading (direction), amount of climb or dive, and degree of bank to the right or left. In each problem, the left-hand dial is labeled ARTIFICIAL HORIZON. On the face of the dial, the small aircraft fuselage silhouette remains stationary, whereas the positions of the white line and the white pointer vary with changes in the position of the aircraft in which the instrument is located.

The white line represents the HORIZON LINE. The white pointer shows the degree of BANK to the right or left.

If the airplane is neither climbing nor diving, the horizon line is directly on the fuselage silhouette, as in dial 1 below.

If the airplane is climbing, the fuselage silhouette is seen between the horizon line and the pointer, as shown in dial 2 below. The greater the amount of climb, the greater the distance between the horizon line and the fuselage silhouette.

If the airplane is diving, the horizon line is seen between the fuselage silhouette and the pointer, as shown in dial 3 below. The greater the amount of dive, the greater the distance between the horizon line and the fuselage silhouette.

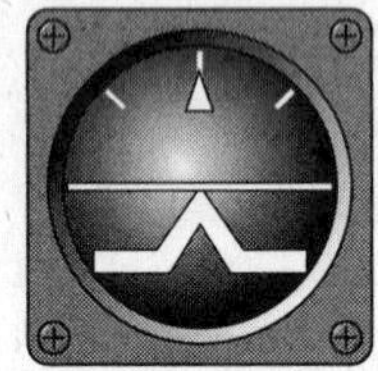

ARTIFICIAL HORIZON

Dial 1

ARTIFICIAL HORIZON

Dial 2

ARTIFICIAL HORIZON

Dial 3

If the airplane has no bank, the white pointer is seen to point to zero, as in dial 1 above.

If the airplane is banked to the pilot's left, the pointer is seen to the right of zero, as in dial 2 above.

If the airplane is banked to the pilot's right, the pointer is seen to the left of zero, as in dial 3 above.

The HORIZON LINE tilts as the aircraft is banked and is always at right angles to the pointer.

Dial 1 shows an airplane neither climbing nor diving, with no bank.
Dial 2 shows an airplane climbing and banked 45° to the pilot's right.
Dial 3 shows an airplane diving and banked 45° to the pilot's left.

In each problem, the right-hand dial is labeled COMPASS. On this dial, the nose of the plane shows the compass direction in which the airplane is headed. Dial 4 shows the airplane headed north, dial 5 shows it headed west, and dial 6 shows it headed northwest.

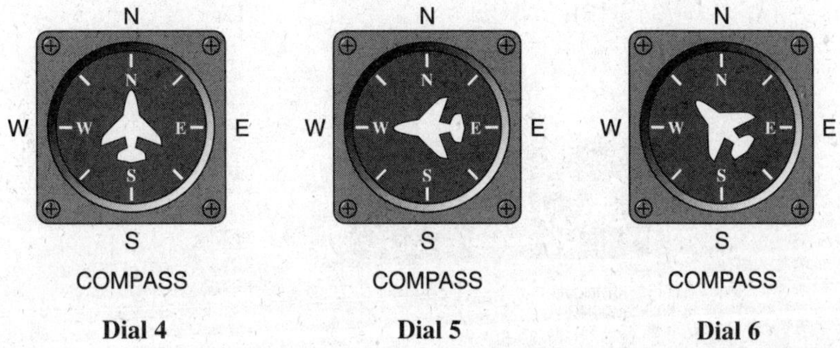

Each problem consists of two dials and four silhouettes of airplanes in flight. Your task is to determine which one of the four airplanes is MOST NEARLY in the position indicated by the two dials. You are always looking north at the same altitude in each of the four airplanes' silhouettes. East is always to your right as you look at the page. In the sample question below, the dial labeled ARTIFICIAL HORIZON shows that the airplane is NOT banked, and is neither climbing nor diving. The COMPASS shows that it is headed south. The only one of the four airplane silhouettes that meets these specifications is in the box lettered (A), so the answer to the sample question is (A).

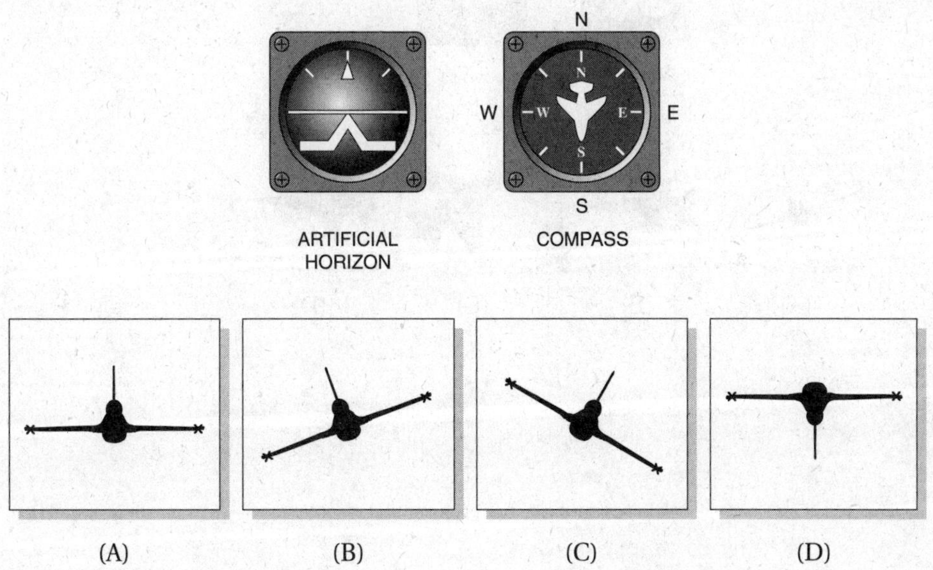

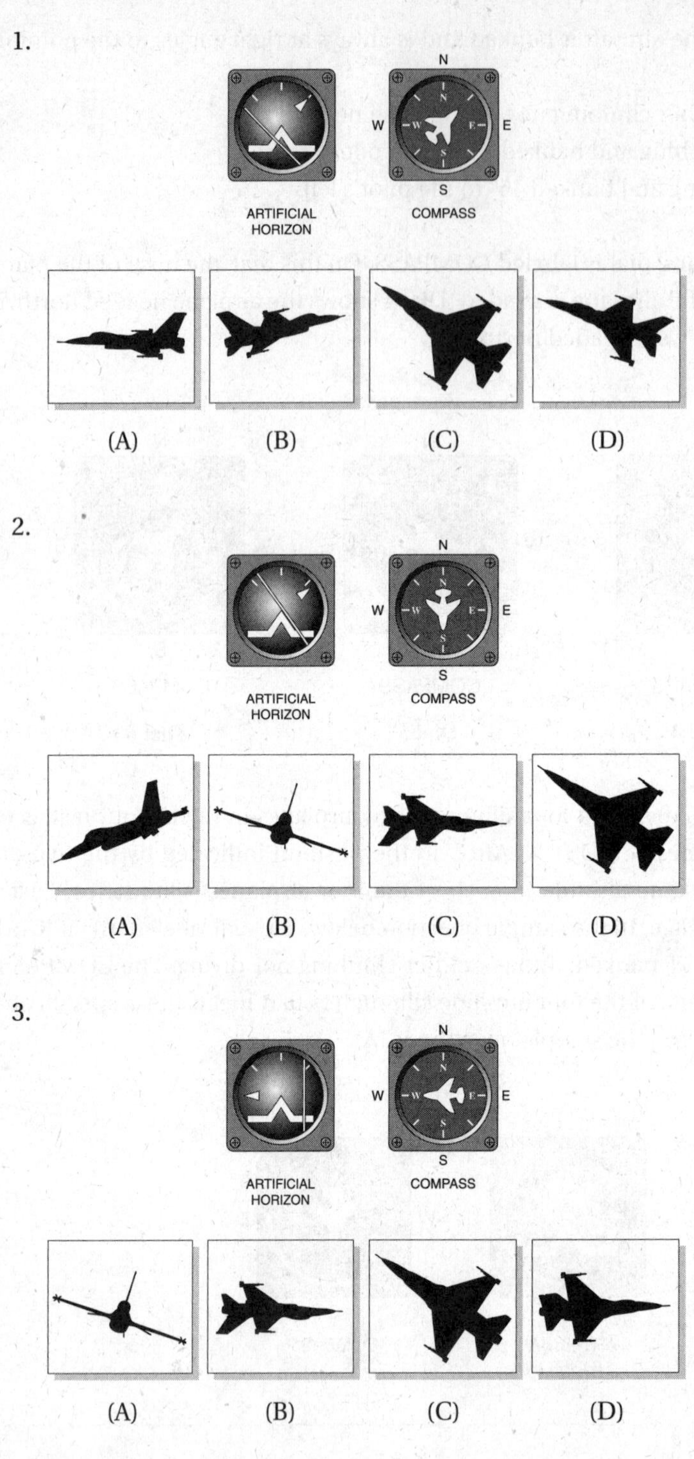
1.
ARTIFICIAL HORIZON
COMPASS
N
S
W
E
(A)
(B)
(C)
(D)
2.
ARTIFICIAL HORIZON
COMPASS
N
S
W
E
(A)
(B)
(C)
(D)
3.
ARTIFICIAL HORIZON
COMPASS
N
S
W
E
(A)
(B)
(C)
(D)

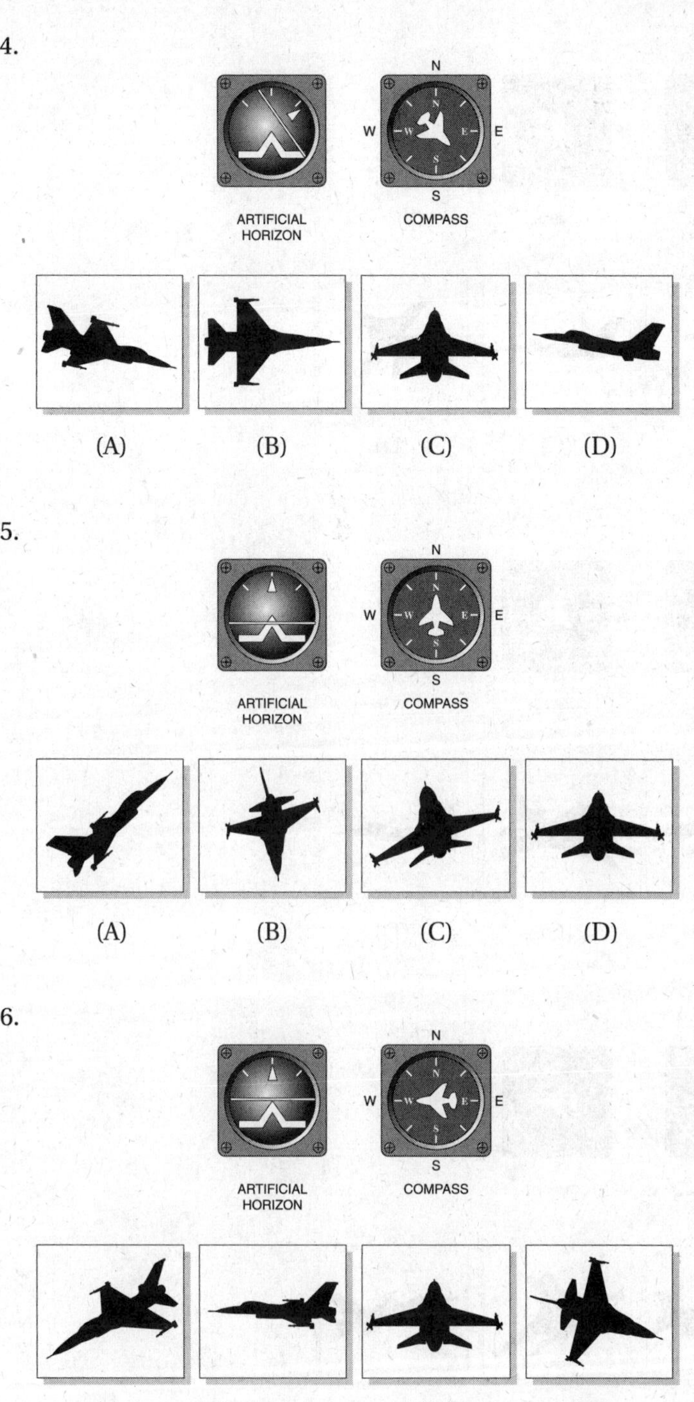
4.
N
W
E
S
ARTIFICIAL HORIZON
COMPASS
(A)
(B)
(C)
(D)
5.
N
W
E
S
ARTIFICIAL HORIZON
COMPASS
(A)
(B)
(C)
(D)
6.
N
W
E
S
ARTIFICIAL HORIZON
COMPASS
(A)
(B)
(C)
(D)

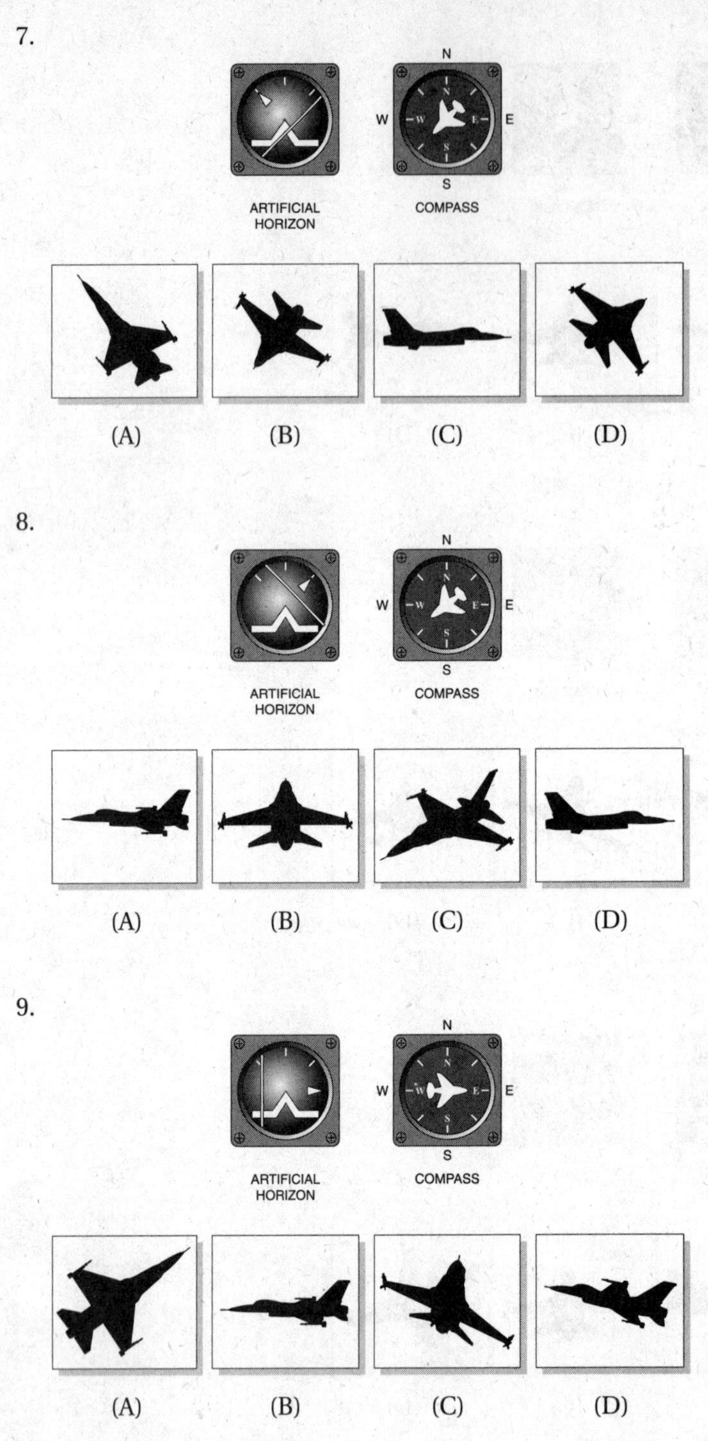
7.
N
W
E
S
ARTIFICIAL HORIZON
COMPASS
(A)
(B)
(C)
(D)
8.
N
W
E
S
ARTIFICIAL HORIZON
COMPASS
(A)
(B)
(C)
(D)
9.
N
W
E
S
ARTIFICIAL HORIZON
COMPASS
(A)
(B)
(C)
(D)

10.

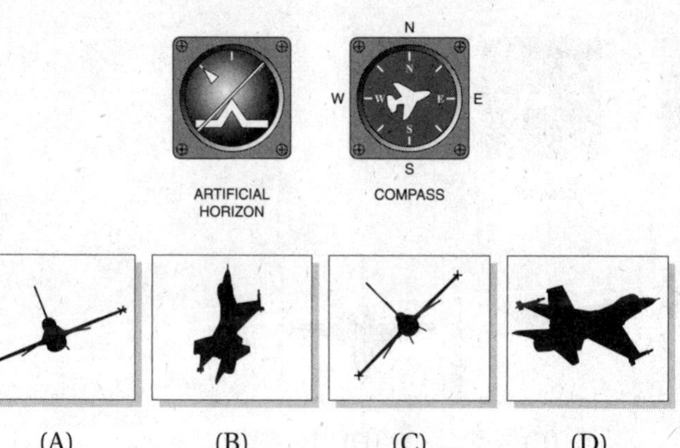

(A) (B) (C) (D)

11.

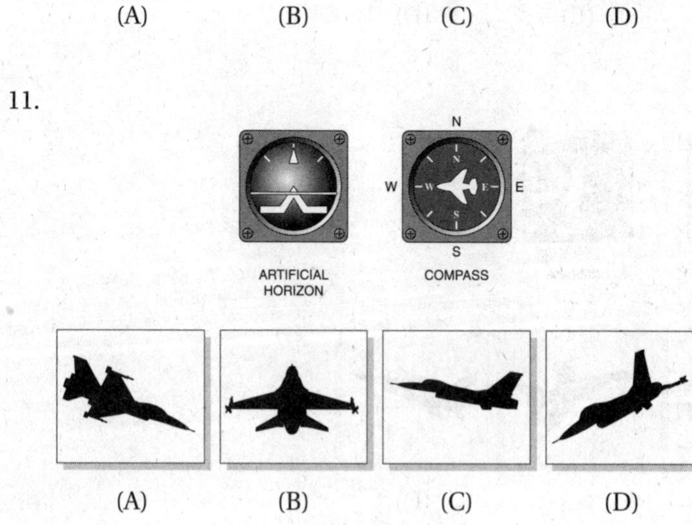

(A) (B) (C) (D)

12.

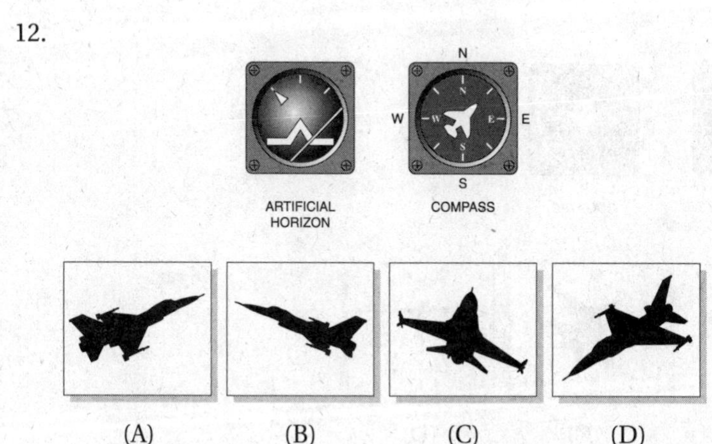

(A) (B) (C) (D)

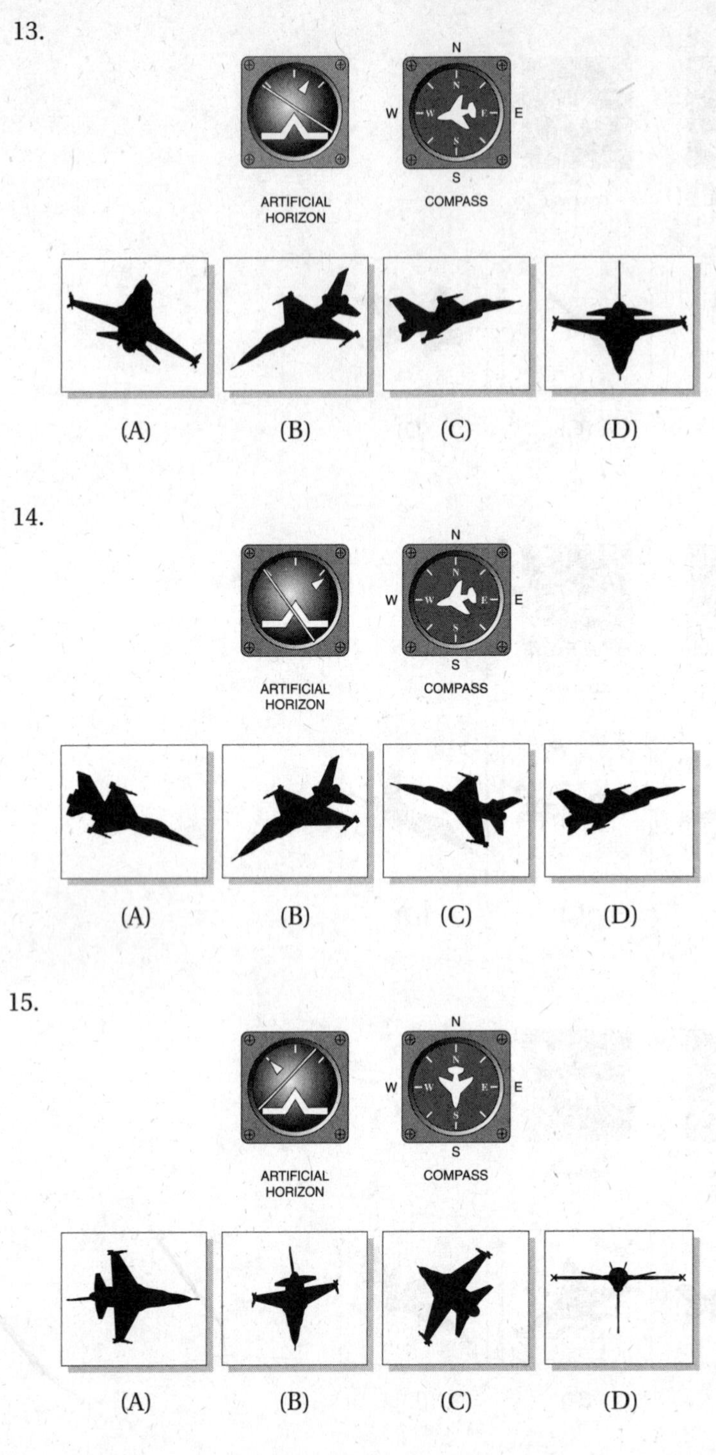
13.
N
W
E
S
ARTIFICIAL HORIZON
COMPASS
(A)
(B)
(C)
(D)
14.
N
W
E
S
ARTIFICIAL HORIZON
COMPASS
(A)
(B)
(C)
(D)
15.
N
W
E
S
ARTIFICIAL HORIZON
COMPASS
(A)
(B)
(C)
(D)

16.

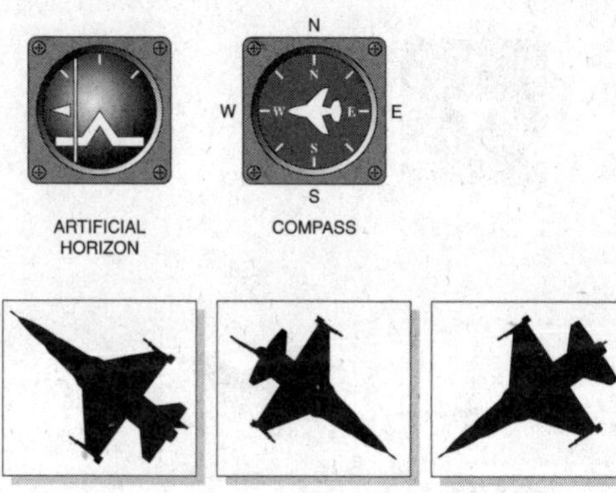

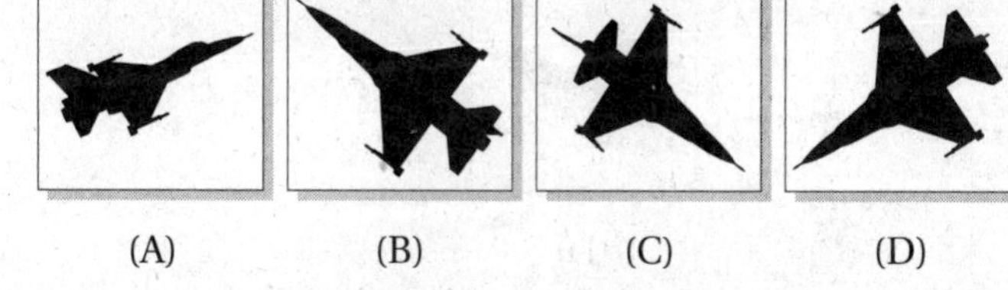

(A) (B) (C) (D)

17.

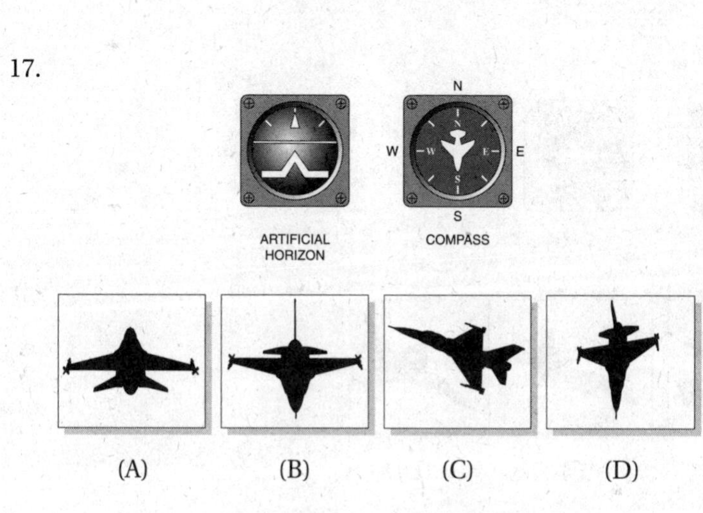

(A) (B) (C) (D)

18.

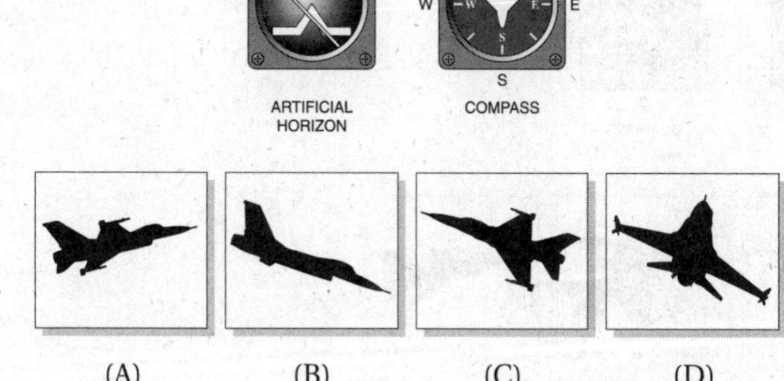

(A) (B) (C) (D)

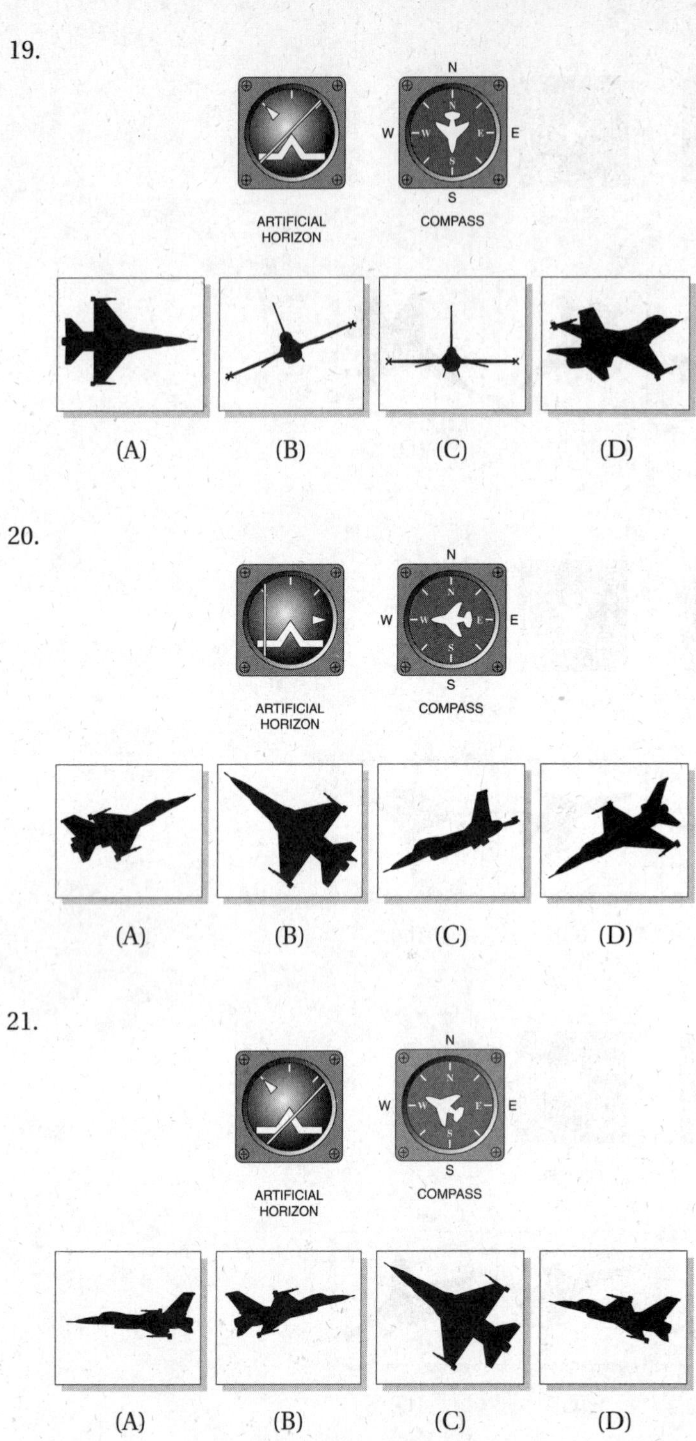
19.
N
W
E
S
ARTIFICIAL HORIZON
COMPASS
(A)
(B)
(C)
(D)
20.
N
W
E
S
ARTIFICIAL HORIZON
COMPASS
(A)
(B)
(C)
(D)
21.
N
W
E
S
ARTIFICIAL HORIZON
COMPASS
(A)
(B)
(C)
(D)

22.

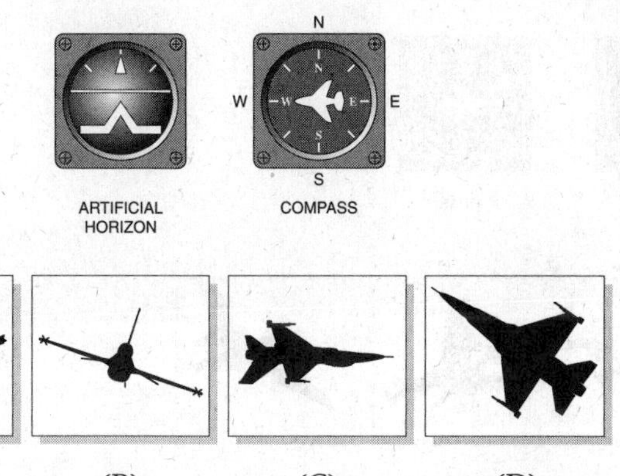

(A) (B) (C) (D)

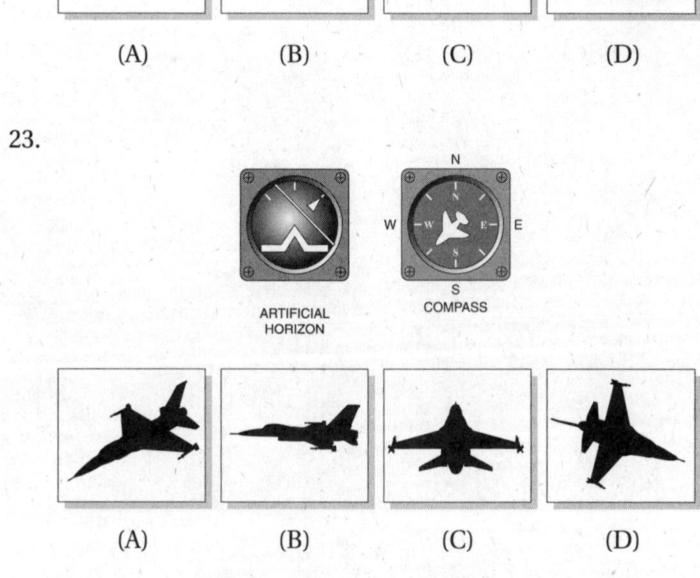

23.

(A) (B) (C) (D)

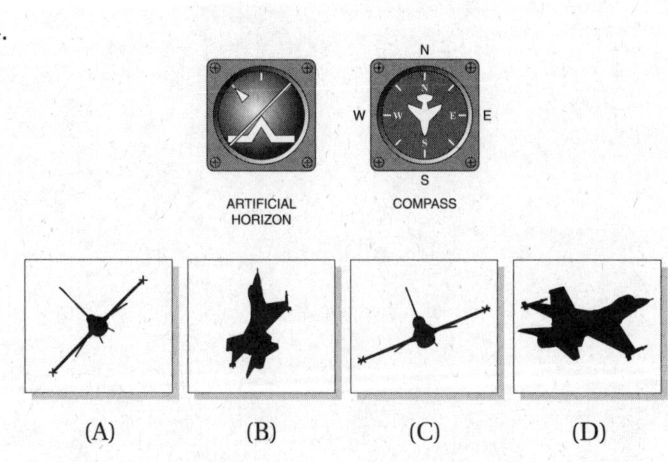

24.

(A) (B) (C) (D)

25.

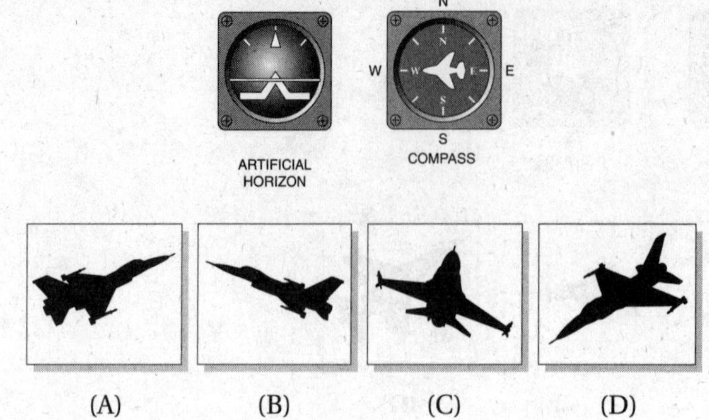

SUBTEST #11: BLOCK COUNTING

30 Questions

DIRECTIONS: This part of the test measures your ability to "see into" a three-dimensional pile of blocks. Given a certain numbered block, your task is to determine how many other blocks it touches. *All of the blocks in each pile are the same size and shape.*

Questions 1–5

	KEY				
Block	**A**	**B**	**C**	**D**	**E**
1	2	3	4	5	6
2	1	2	3	4	5
3	2	3	4	5	6
4	4	5	6	7	8
5	4	5	6	7	8

Questions 6–10

	KEY				
Block	**A**	**B**	**C**	**D**	**E**
6	4	5	6	7	8
7	3	4	5	6	7
8	4	5	6	7	8
9	4	5	6	7	8
10	2	3	4	5	6

Questions 11–15

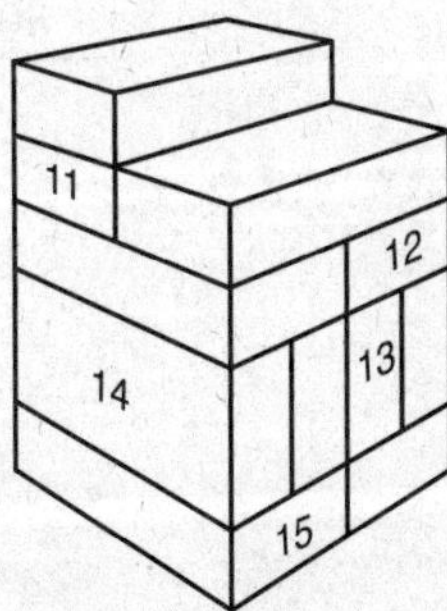

	KEY				
Block	**A**	**B**	**C**	**D**	**E**
11	3	4	5	6	7
12	3	4	5	6	7
13	3	4	5	6	7
14	3	4	5	6	7
15	2	3	4	5	6

Questions 16–20

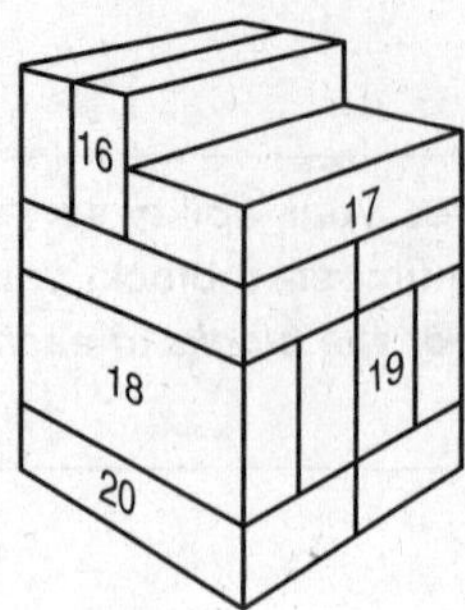

Block	KEY A	B	C	D	E
16	3	4	5	6	7
17	2	3	4	5	6
18	3	4	5	6	7
19	3	4	5	6	7
20	1	2	3	4	5

Questions 21–25

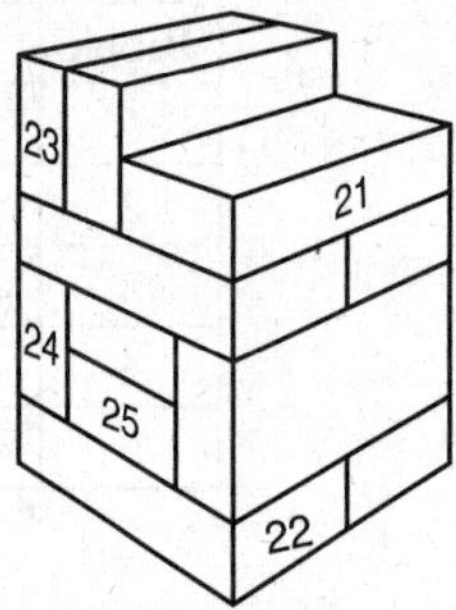

Block	KEY A	B	C	D	E
21	2	3	4	5	6
22	3	4	5	6	7
23	6	5	4	3	2
24	3	4	5	6	7
25	6	5	4	3	2

Questions 26–30

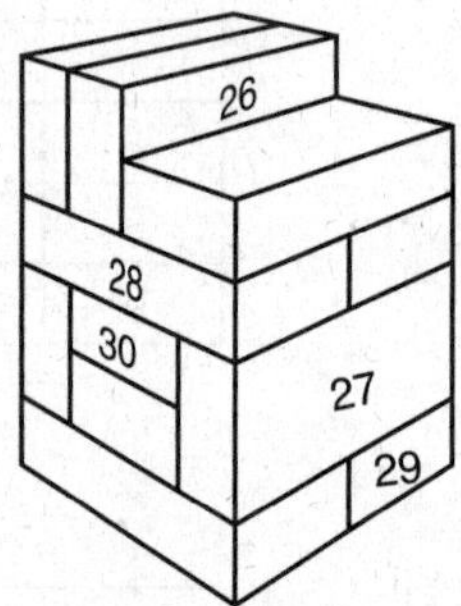

Block	KEY A	B	C	D	E
26	2	3	4	5	6
27	3	4	5	6	7
28	7	6	5	4	3
29	3	4	5	6	7
30	4	5	6	7	8

SUBTEST #12: AVIATION INFORMATION

20 Questions

1. When in the down (extended) position, wing flaps provide
   (A) increased lift and decreased drag.
   (B) decreased lift and increased drag.
   (C) increased lift and increased drag.
   (D) increased lift only.
   (E) decreased wing camber (curvature).

2. Municipal airports often provide at least one extended or unusually long runway to facilitate the takeoff of
   (A) heavily loaded aircraft in calm conditions.
   (B) lightly loaded aircraft taking off in a crosswind.
   (C) small aircraft in rainy weather.
   (D) aircraft with higher than average climbing speeds.
   (E) rotary-wing aircraft in trail formation.

3. The small hinged section on the elevator of most airplanes is known as the
   (A) aileron.
   (B) flap.
   (C) stabilator.
   (D) elevon.
   (E) trim tab.

4. The rearward retarding force on the airplane known as drag is opposed by
   (A) lift.
   (B) thrust.
   (C) weight.
   (D) laminar air flow.
   (E) compression.

5. At night, airport taxiways are identified by omnidirectional edge lights that are ________ in color.
   (A) red
   (B) white
   (C) alternating red and white
   (D) blue
   (E) green

A F O Q T # 1

6. A runway with the Approach Lighting System (ALS) would show an incoming pilot

    (A) a pair of synchronized flashing lights at the runway threshold.
    (B) a series of lightbars and/or strobe lights extending outward from the runway approach end.
    (C) white elevated lights running the length of the runway on both sides.
    (D) white lights embedded in the runway centerline at 50-foot intervals.
    (E) unidirectional blue lights.

7. The thrust of a turbojet is developed by compressing air in the inlet and compressor, mixing the air with fuel and burning it in the combustor, and

    (A) venting the combusted air through side nozzles.
    (B) rerouting the airflow through the compressor for extra power.
    (C) expanding the gas stream through the turbine and nozzle.
    (D) using the resulting accelerated airflow to turn the propeller shaft.
    (E) diffusing the gas stream through the designated relief valves.

8. A ramjet engine consists of

    (A) an intake, a compressor, a combustion chamber, and an outlet.
    (B) an inlet, a turbine, a compressor, and a nozzle.
    (C) an intake, a compression chamber, and a nozzle.
    (D) an inlet, a combustion zone, and a nozzle.
    (E) an inlet, a compression chamber, a turbine, and a nozzle.

9. The four forces that act on an aircraft in flight are

    (A) lift, gravity, thrust, and drag.
    (B) lift, mass, propulsion, and resistance.
    (C) aerodynamics, mass, propulsion, and drag.
    (D) lift magnitude, mass, thrust, and drag.
    (E) roll, pitch, yaw, and magnitude.

10. For a fixed-wing aircraft, lift is generated ______________ to the direction of flight.

    (A) parallel
    (B) reciprocal
    (C) proportionate
    (D) vectored
    (E) perpendicular

11. The angle formed by the chord of an airfoil or wing and the direction of the relative wind is known as the

    (A) critical angle.
    (B) stall angle.
    (C) angle of pitch.
    (D) delta angle.
    (E) angle of attack.

12. Pitot tubes furnish data to an instrument that is used by aircraft pilots in about the same way that a(n) ___________ is used by an automobile driver.

(A) pressure transducer
(B) odometer
(C) speedometer
(D) tachometer
(E) ohmmeter

13. The part of an airplane that holds the cargo and/or passengers—and provides a base for the other aircraft parts—is known as the

(A) fuselage.
(B) empennage.
(C) cargo compartment.
(D) cockpit array.
(E) static line.

14. On a conventional fixed-wing aircraft, the ___________ maintain(s) pitch and the ___________ maintain(s) yaw.

(A) elevators, rudder
(B) horizontal stabilizers, vertical stabilizer
(C) elevons, stabilator
(D) rudder, elevators
(E) trim tabs, wing flaps

15. ___________ are additional hinged rear sections mounted to the wing near the body that are deployed downward on takeoff and landing to increase the amount of force produced by the wing.

(A) Ailerons
(B) Elevators
(C) Flaps
(D) Trim tabs
(E) Elevons

16. Which one of the following does not affect density altitude?

(A) temperature
(B) atmospheric pressure
(C) humidity
(D) wind velocity
(E) altitude

AFOQT #1

17. The degree of movement of an aircraft around its longitudinal axis is known as

    (A) pitch.
    (B) sideslip.
    (C) yaw.
    (D) angle of attack.
    (E) bank.

18. The Venturi theory of lift says that faster airflow over the curved upper portion of a wing surface causes

    (A) decreased pressure according to Bernoulli's equation.
    (B) increased pressure according to Avogadro's constant.
    (C) increased drag proportionate to crosswinds.
    (D) decreased drag proportionate to the thrust vector.
    (E) decreased drag perpendicular to the thrust vector.

19. The maneuver in which a rotary-wing aircraft (helicopter) is maintained in nearly motionless flight over a ground reference point at a constant altitude and heading (direction) is known as

    (A) feathering.
    (B) autorotation.
    (C) hovering.
    (D) torque balance.
    (E) freewheeling.

20. The ratio of the speed of an aircraft to the speed of sound in the air around it is the aircraft's

    (A) compressibility factor.
    (B) Mach angle.
    (C) Mach number.
    (D) aerodynamic heating ratio.
    (E) isentropic threshold.

ANSWERS AND EXPLANATIONS

Subtest #1: Verbal Analogies

Check your answers below and refer to the explanation for each question you missed. Use the table to record right and wrong answers.

	✔	✘		✔	✘		✔	✘		✔	✘		✔	✘
1. C			**6. E**			**11. E**			**16. C**			**21. C**		
2. E			**7. A**			**12. A**			**17. A**			**22. A**		
3. D			**8. A**			**13. C**			**18. D**			**23. A**		
4. A			**9. E**			**14. B**			**19. A**			**24. D**		
5. B			**10. E**			**15. E**			**20. A**			**25. D**		

1. **(C)** GLOVE is to HAND as SHOE is to **FOOT**. This is a "tool to user" analogy; a shoe is a protective, warming cover for the foot in the same way that a glove performs the same functions for the hand.

2. **(E)** AIRCRAFT is to FLY as BOAT is to **SAIL**. This is an "object to function" analogy; an aircraft is a means of conveyance or transportation used to fly, just as a boat is a means of transportation used to sail.

3. **(D)** PLAN is to STRATEGY as FIGHT is to **BATTLE**. This is an "action to result" analogy; one does the first to make the second happen or come into being.

4. **(A)** TRAVEL is to DESTINATION as WORK is to **GOAL**. This is another "action to result" analogy—you travel to reach your destination, and you work to get to or achieve your goal.

5. **(B)** PLOW is to FIELD as RACQUET is to **COURT**. A plow is a tool or implement to be used on a field, just as a racquet is an implement used on a court.

6. **(E)** SALUTE is to RESPECT as HUG is to **AFFECTION**. This is a form of a "result to cause" analogy; a salute is a physical gesture resulting from respect held for another, and a hug is a physical symbol of affection (the cause of the result or physical action).

7. **(A)** GRAVITY is to PLANET as ODOR is to **SKUNK**. Another "result to cause" analogy; gravity is caused by the presence of a planet in roughly the same way that odor is caused by or comes from a skunk.

8. **(A)** FISHING ROD is to HOOK as KNIFE is to **BLADE**. This is a "whole to part" analogy. A hook is the part of a fishing rod that actually enables the rod's function to be fulfilled (to catch fish), in the same way that the blade is the part of a knife that fulfills the function of a knife (to cut). Choice (E) is not correct because, even though a handle *is* part of a knife, it is not the part that performs the primary function of the tool in the way that the blade is.

9. **(E)** BOOT is to HIKE as VISOR is to **WELD**. In the same way that a boot protects and helps the hiker, a visor protects and helps the welder—an "object to function" analogy.

10. **(E)** PUSH is to SHOVE as CLIMB is to **CLAMBER**. This is an analogy of language; *push* and *shove* mean nearly the same thing, as do *climb* and *clamber.*

11. **(E)** GROW is to MATURE as BLOOM is to **BLOSSOM**. *Grow* and *mature* mean very nearly the same thing, as do *bloom* and *blossom*—another language-based analogy.

12. **(A)** FUSELAGE is to BODY as **TURRET is to TANK**. This is a "part to whole" analogy. *Fuselage* is a specific term for the main part of the body of an airplane; *turret* is a term for the main part of a tank.

13. **(C)** CLIMB is to RISE as DIVE is to **FALL**. Although it may at first appear to be a language analogy—these word pairs almost seem like synonyms—this is actually an "action to result" analogy. A pilot causes his airplane to climb in order to rise, whereas he causes the plane to dive in order to fall or lose altitude.

14. **(B)** ROPE is to KNOT as THREAD is to **FABRIC**. This is a "part to whole" analogy; a rope is used to make a knot, just as a thread is manipulated to make fabric.

15. **(E)** WATCH is to OBSERVE as SWITCH is to **REPLACE**. Here we have an analogy of language—both these pairs of words are synonyms.

16. **(C)** OBEY is to COMPLY as REPLY is to **ANSWER**. Both these pairs of words are synonyms—another language analogy.

17. **(A)** HONOR is to HONESTY as TRUST is to **DEPENDABILITY**. This is an "action to result" analogy; honor is a result of consistent honesty, just as trust is a by-product of consistent dependability.

18. **(D)** SPEED is to DECELERATION as VELOCITY is to **BRAKING**. This is an "action to result" analogy. When an automobile driver, for instance, decreases his speed in a car (usually by stepping on the brake pedal), it is called *deceleration*; decreased velocity, similarly, is usually caused by braking.

19. **(A)** COMPRESSION is to RAREFACTION as DENSE is to **THIN**. Sound is made up of successive compression and rarefaction waves in the air—respectively, thickened and thinned areas resulting from the source of the sound. This is an analogy of language—these are opposites, or antonyms.

20. **(A)** DELAY is to POSTPONE as PREVENT is to **DETER**. *Delay* and *postpone* mean the same thing, to put something off or do it later; *prevent* and *deter* both mean to stop something from happening. This is another analogy of language, since these are basically synonyms.

21. **(C)** ADD is to SUBTRACT as GROW is to **SHRINK**. *Add* and *subtract* are opposite concepts, as are *grow* and *shrink*. This is an analogy of language, since they are antonyms.

22. **(A)** LEFT is to PORT as RIGHT is to **STARBOARD**. This is an analogy of language; *port* is an aviation and nautical term for *left,* and *starboard* refers to the right side or direction.

23. **(A)** ODOMETER is to DISTANCE as ALTIMETER is to **ALTITUDE**. In the same way that an odometer measures road distance traveled, an altimeter measures an aircraft's altitude above Earth. Although a compass needle points to the north because of magnetic attraction, it does not *measure* where the user is. This is an "object to function" analogy.

24. **(D)** ELEVATOR is to HEIGHT as THRUST is to **ALTITUDE.** This is a somewhat tricky "cause to effect" analogy; in the same way that an elevator on an airplane (or an elevator in a building) causes you to gain or lose height above the ground, thrust from a rocket or jet engine determines your altitude. "STAIRWAY is to BUILDING" is not the right answer—even though it could be thought of as close—because a stairway is static and does not move; the user must furnish the moving power (his or her legs), rather than being moved by an external source of power. Test-takers need to be aware of possible multiple meanings for certain words.

25. **(D)** LOOK is to INSPECT as ARRIVE is to **ATTEND.** This is an "action to result" analogy; one must first look in order to inspect, in the same way that one has to arrive before one can attend (a meeting, for example).

Subtest #2: Arithmetic Reasoning

Check your answers below and refer to the explanation for each question you missed. Use the table to record right and wrong answers.

	✔	✘		✔	✘		✔	✘		✔	✘		✔	✘
1. C			6. E			11. C			16. A			21. B		
2. B			7. D			12. D			17. D			22. C		
3. B			8. C			13. A			18. E			23. B		
4. A			9. D			14. B			19. C			24. A		
5. D			10. A			15. C			20. E			25. D		

1. **(C)** To calculate the number of total seats in the theater, multiply the number of rows (x) by the number of seats in each row (y). This expression is written as $\boldsymbol{xy}$.

2. **(B)** First, find the amount of the price increase.

$$\$23,999 - \$22,399 = \$1,600$$

Multiply the amount of the increase by 100, then divide by the original price.

3. **(B)** Multiply the number of completed passes by 100, and then divide it by the number of attempted passes. The result will be the percentage.

$$57 \times 100 = 5,700$$

$$\frac{5,700}{82} = 69.5 = \mathbf{69.5\%}$$

4. **(A)** There are 100 units of \$1,000 in \$100,000. Thus, Jaycie Marie pays 100 × \$12 (or \$1,200) every year in premiums, or \$100 every month. Therefore, every six months, Jaycie Marie pays $\frac{1}{2}$ of \$1,200 (or six times \$100), which equals **\$600.**

5. **(D)** There are 16 ounces in 1 pound. Therefore, if 2 pounds of smoked deli turkey breast cost \$13.98, then 1 pound costs \$6.99.

$$1 \text{ oz. costs } \$6.99 \div 16 = \$0.44$$
$$5 \text{ oz. cost } \$0.44 \times 5 = \mathbf{\$2.20}$$

6. **(E)** Find the cost of four ties:

$$4 \times \$12 = \$48$$

Find the cost of the shirts alone:

$$\$173 - \$48 = \$125$$

Find the cost of one shirt:

$$\$125 \div 5 = \mathbf{\$25.00}$$

7. **(D)** The formula for the volume of an object with parallel sides and right-angle corners is:

$$\text{Length } l \times \text{width } w \times \text{height } h \text{ or}$$

$$l \times w \times h$$

$$23 \text{ ft.} \times 15 \text{ ft.} \times 11 \text{ ft.} = \mathbf{3{,}795 \text{ cu. ft.}} \text{ ("cubic feet")}$$

8. **(C)** Let x be the number of tickets bought at each price (remember, the sister bought the same number of both kinds of tickets). So,

$$7x + 10x = 119$$

Now combine the terms and continue solving the equation for x.

$$17x = 119$$

$$\frac{17x}{17} = \frac{119}{17}$$

$$x = \frac{119}{17}$$

$$x = \mathbf{7}$$

9. **(D)** First, calculate the amount of Amanda's hourly wages for a shift of 10:30 A.M. to 5:30 P.M., which is seven hours.

$$7 \times \$2.50 = \$17.50$$

Next, calculate the amount of Amanda's tips for her seven-hour shift.

$$7 \times \$22 = \$154$$

Now, calculate the amount of her tips she has to share with the busboys and hostesses.

$$\$154 \times .10 = \$15.40$$

Now add everything up.

Wages	$17.50
Tips	+ $154.00
Tip share	– $15.40
Net pay	**$156.10**

10. **(A)** First, calculate the number of total attendees by multiplying the total seats available by the percentage.

$$500 \times .76 = 380$$

Since "three quarters" (75%) of those attending were adults, that means that one quarter or 25% were children (which is the final result we are trying to find). Therefore, multiply

AFOQT #1

the number of total attendees by the percentage of children to find out how many children saw the performance.

$$380 \times .25 = \mathbf{95} \textbf{ children}$$

11. **(C)** Add all the blocks of time together.

$$4 + 1 + .5 + 2 = 7.5 \text{ hours total}$$

Now multiply the time spent studying (four hours) by 100 and divide it by the total time.

$$4 \times 100 = 400$$
$$400 \div 7.5 = \mathbf{53.3\%}$$

12. **(D)** Subtract the discounted price from the original price.

$$\$1{,}400 - \$1{,}150 = \$250$$

Now multiply the amount of the discount by 100 and divide it by the original price.

$$\$250 \times 100 = 25{,}000$$
$$25{,}000 \div 1{,}400 = 17.857142 = \mathbf{17.9\%}$$

13. **(A)** The formula for the perimeter of a rectangle is

$$P = 2l \times 2w$$

If the long sides of the rug measure 15 feet each, then both long sides together equal 30 feet. Subtract the length of both long sides from the total perimeter measurement.

$$45 - (2 \times 15) = 45 - 30 = 15 \text{ ft.}$$

Now we have the part of the perimeter made up by the short sides, but we need to divide it by two to get the length of each short side.

$$15 \text{ ft.} \div 2 = \mathbf{7.5 \text{ ft.}}$$

14. **(B)** First add up the wages made by the four customer service reps.

$$\$320 \times 4 = \$1{,}280$$

Now calculate how much the two sales reps make each week.

$$2 \text{ sales reps} \times [(\$12 \text{ per hr.} \times 40 \text{ hrs.}) + (5 \text{ days per week} \times \$100)] =$$
$$2 \text{ sales reps} \times (\$480 + \$500) =$$
$$2 \text{ sales reps} \times \$980 = \$1{,}960 \text{ per week}$$

Now add the pay for the four customer service reps to the pay for the two sales managers.

$$\$1{,}280 + \$1{,}960 = \mathbf{\$3{,}240}$$

15. **(C)** To find an average, add the values for each day together and then divide by the total number of days: $\boldsymbol{(x + y + z) \div 3}$

16. **(A)** First find the number of miles per hour the train travels.

$$500 \text{ miles} \div 5 \text{ hours} = 100 \text{ miles per hour (mph)}$$

Now calculate how many miles the train travels in one minute.

$$100 \text{ mph} \div 60 \text{ minutes} = 1.67 \text{ miles per minute}$$

AFOQT #1

AFOQT #1

Now multiply the train's speed in miles per minute by the number of minutes in question.

$$1.67 \text{ miles per minute} \times 15 \text{ minutes} \approx \mathbf{25\ miles}$$

17. **(D)** Two figures are "similar" in the mathematical sense if they have the same shape; they may or may not have the same size. **An airplane and a scale model of that airplane** have the same shape and are therefore similar.

18. **(E)** Start by letting x equal one share of the insurance money. According to the ratio, the wife received five shares ($5x$) and the children received one share (x) apiece for a total of eight shares. Divide the total amount by the total number of shares.

$$\$750,000 \div 8 = \$93,750 \text{ per share}$$

Now multiply the amount of each share by the total number of shares received by the children.

$$\$93,750 \times 3 = \mathbf{\$281,250}$$

19. **(C)** If 4% of the unit are officers, then the percent of enlisted men is:

$$100\% - 4\% = 96\%$$

To find the number of enlisted men, multiply the total number by 96% or .96.

$$125 \text{ total soldiers} \times 0.96 = \mathbf{120} \text{ enlisted soldiers}$$

20. **(E)** First find the discount received from the wholesale dealer for each DVD player by multiplying the listed price by the discount percentage.

$$\$80 \times .25 = \$20$$

Now find the final price per DVD player paid to the wholesale dealer.

$$\$80 - \$20 = \$60$$

Now find the retail markup by multiplying the markup percentage by the original wholesale price.

$$\$80 \times .20 = \$16$$

Now find the retail price for which the electronics store owner sells the DVD players to his customers by adding the markup amount to the listed wholesale amount.

$$\$80 + \$16 = \$96$$

To find the profit, subtract the retail price from the actual price paid to the wholesale dealer.

$$\$96 - \$60 = \mathbf{\$36} \text{ profit per DVD player}$$

21. **(B)** Since 1 inch represents 50 miles, divide the ground distance (120 miles) by the scale (50 miles to the inch) to find the number of inches required to represent 120 miles.

$$120 \div 50 = \mathbf{2.4}$$

22. **(C)** Multiply the purchase price of the home by the assessment rate to find the assessed value.

$$120,000 \times .80 = \$96,000 \text{ (assessed value)}$$

Find the number of hundreds in the assessed value.

$$\$96,000 \div 100 = 960 \text{ (hundreds)}$$

Multiply the number of hundreds by the tax rate.

$$960 \times \$4.75 = \mathbf{\$4,560} \text{ (property tax)}$$

23. **(B)** First find the total time needed to run the generator = 12 hours and 45 minutes or 12.75 minutes. Now divide the total time needed to run the generator by the amount of time each tank of fuel will last.

$$12.75 \div 1.25 = \mathbf{10.2} \text{ tanks of fuel}$$

24. **(A)** First find the amount of the decline in traffic.

$$11,200 \text{ cars} - 10,044 = 1,156 \text{ fewer cars per day}$$

Now multiply the amount of traffic decrease by 100 and then divide it by the amount of original traffic. This will yield the percentage decrease without further calculation.

$$1,156 \times 100 = 115,600$$

$$115,600 \div 11,200 = \mathbf{10.3\%} \text{ decrease}$$

25. **(D)** First calculate the distances driven during the two legs of the trip.

$$\text{Leg 1: } 2 \text{ hours} \times 70 \text{ mph} = 140 \text{ miles}$$

$$\text{Leg 2: } 1.5 \text{ hours} \times 65 \text{ mph} = 97.5 \text{ miles}$$

$$140 \text{ miles} + 97.5 \text{ miles} = 237.5 \text{ miles}$$

Now divide the total distance traveled by the car's gas mileage rate.

$$237.5 \text{ miles} \div 25 \text{ mpg} = \mathbf{9.5 \text{ gals.}}$$

Subtest #3: Word Knowledge

Check your answers below and refer to the explanation for each question you missed. Use the table to record right and wrong answers.

	✔	✘		✔	✘		✔	✘		✔	✘		✔	✘
1. A			6. E			11. D			16. E			21. B		
2. D			7. A			12. C			17. D			22. B		
3. B			8. C			13. A			18. A			23. C		
4. D			9. E			14. D			19. A			24. C		
5. A			10. C			15. B			20. D			25. A		

1. **(A)** TACIT means **silent** or unspoken.

2. **(D)** ALTITUDE means **height**, which *is* a measure of distance, but height is more specific and therefore the most accurate answer.

3. **(B)** To PORTEND is to **give warning beforehand**, as when building storm clouds portend a storm. To *feign* is to *pretend*; to assume a pose is to *portray.*

4. **(D)** ITINERARY means **schedule.**

5. **(A)** VEXATIOUS means to be **annoying**. A contagious disease is said to be *virulent*; someone who is insatiably hungry is *voracious.*

6. **(E)** EQUIVALENT means **equal**.

7. **(A)** CRITERION means a **standard** of judgment.

8. **(C)** MERCURIAL means **unpredictably changeable**, referring both to the speed of the mythical Roman god Mercury and the unpredictable physical nature of the element itself—mercury on a supposedly flat surface will flow in unexpected directions with the smallest provocation. Someone who is *merciful* is said to be compassionate; *specious* means tawdrily attractive or *meretricious.*

9. **(E)** CRITICAL means **most important**. A seriously ill or injured patient may be classified as "critical," but that does not necessarily mean the patient is dying. It just means that they are at risk of dying; therefore this is the **most important** classification, and the hospital staff pays extra attention to their status and needs.

10. **(C)** TELEMETRY means the **transmission of measurements made by automatic instruments**. Mental communication is *telepathy*; marketing goods or services by telephone is *telemarketing*; the study of climactic variations (i.e., weather) is *meteorology*; and *temerity* means "acting with rashness or audacity."

11. **(D)** ANTAGONIST means **adversary**. A main character is a *protagonist.*

12. **(C)** DIAGNOSE means to **identify a situation**. A prognosis is a prediction of the outcome.

13. **(A)** KINETIC means **relating to the motion of material bodies**. Something relating to the movies may be referred to as *cinematic*; someone moving at a high speed may be called *frenetic*; and things relating to a sensory experience are *kinesthetic.*

14. **(D)** RECTIFY means to **correct**.

15. **(B)** CAMOUFLAGE means to **conceal**.

16. **(E)** EQUIVOCAL means **evasive**. Another word for *equal* is *equivalent.*

17. **(D)** CENTRIPETAL means **moving toward a center or axis.** Moving away from an axis is *centrifugal*; having two feet is *bipedal.*

18. **(A)** DISCONSOLATE means **hopelessly sad**. To cease using is to *discontinue*; to rearrange sloppily is to *disarrange*; to uncover is to *discover*; and to recognize mentally is to *discern.*

19. **(A)** ANACHRONISTIC means **chronologically out of place**. To be cursed is to be *anathematized*; *anatomy* deals with an organism's physical structure; the attribution of conscious thought to inanimate objects or animals is *animism*; and things or situations existing before a war are described as *antebellum.*

20. **(D)** MODULATE means to **adjust**. To speak is to *enunciate*; to dry out is to *desiccate.*

21. **(B)** PICAYUNE means exceedingly small or **insignificant**. When something is intense—such as an emotion or a jalapeño pepper—we may say that it is "piquant."

22. **(B)** TENACIOUS means **persistent**. A hot-tempered person may be called "pugnacious."

23. **(C)** ENTENTE means **an agreement providing for** (or leading to) **joint action**. The relaxation of tensions or disagreements, especially between nations, is known as *détente*; *volition* means the same as *intent*, which is the state of mind with which an act is done; *freedom of entry or access* is often known as *entrée*.

24. **(C)** REDUNDANT means **repetitive** or having more than needed of something.

25. **(A)** RECONNAISSANCE means a **surveying expedition** or scouting trip to see how an area is set up, or the like. A rebirth or revival (especially cultural) is a *renaissance*.

Subtest #4: Math Knowledge

Check your answers below and refer to the explanation for each question you missed. Use the table to record right and wrong answers.

	✔	✘		✔	✘		✔	✘		✔	✘		✔	✘
1. E			6. D			11. C			16. A			21. D		
2. D			7. B			12. C			17. D			22. D		
3. A			8. B			13. B			18. C			23. D		
4. D			9. E			14. B			19. B			24. B		
5. E			10. C			15. C			20. A			25. A		

1. **(E)** A factorial is the product of all the positive integers from 1 to a given number. The expression "4 factorial" or 4! means $1 \times 2 \times 3 \times 4 = \mathbf{24}$.

2. **(D)** The formula for the circumference of a circle is

$$d \text{ (diameter)} \times \pi = \text{circumference}$$

The pilot flies in a circle with a radius of 40 km and therefore a diameter of 80 km.

$$80 \text{ km} \times \frac{22}{7} = \text{circumference}$$

$$\frac{80 \times 22}{7} = \text{circumference}$$

$$\frac{1{,}760}{7} = \text{circumference}$$

$$\mathbf{251 \text{ km}} = \text{circumference}$$

3. **(A)** The reciprocal of any number is 1 over that number. The reciprocal of 7 to the nearest thousandth is $\frac{1}{7} = \mathbf{0.143}$.

4. **(D)** The square of any number is that number times itself. The square of 525 is:

$$\begin{array}{r} 525 \\ \times \;\; 525 \\ \hline 275{,}625 \end{array}$$

Therefore the ten-thousandths digit of the square of 525 is **7**.

AFOQT #1

5. **(E)** The area of a square with four sides of length s is $s \times s$ or s^2. A square with a perimeter of 40 yards has four sides where length = 10 yards. This means that the area of this square is 10 yds. × 10 yds. = 100 sq. yds. Since this is not one of the choices, let's convert it to square feet:

$$\frac{100 \text{ yds.}^2}{1} \times \frac{9 \text{ ft.}^2}{1 \text{ yd.}^2} = \mathbf{900\ ft.^2}$$

The tricky part to remember here is that there are 9 square feet in a square yard (3 ft. times 3 ft.), not just the 3 feet to 1 yard we are used to thinking about in linear terms.

6. **(D)** To solve these equations for x, start by finding a way to get rid of y: Multiply both sides of the second equation by 2.

$$2(x - 2y) = 2 \times 11$$
$$2x - 4y = 22$$

Then add the new form of the second equation to the first equation and solve for x.

$$\begin{array}{r} 5x + 4y = 27 \\ +\ 2x - 4y = 22 \\ \hline 7x = 49 \\ \mathbf{x = 7} \end{array}$$

7. **(B)** One way to solve this is to square each of the possible answers to see which one is closest to 85.

$$\begin{array}{r} 9.1 \\ \times 9.1 \\ \hline 91 \\ +\ 819 \\ \hline 82.81 \end{array} \quad \begin{array}{r} 9.2 \\ \times 9.2 \\ \hline 184 \\ +\ 828 \\ \hline 84.64 \end{array} \quad \begin{array}{r} 9.3 \\ \times 9.3 \\ \hline 279 \\ +\ 837 \\ \hline 86.49 \end{array} \quad \begin{array}{r} 9.4 \\ \times 9.4 \\ \hline 376 \\ +\ 846 \\ \hline 88.36 \end{array} \quad \begin{array}{r} 9.5 \\ \times 9.5 \\ \hline 475 \\ +\ 855 \\ \hline 90.25 \end{array}$$

The squares of 9.2 and 9.3 are closer to 85 than the squares of 9.1, 9.4, or 9.5. Now find the difference between the square of each of the closest numbers and 85.

$$(9.2) \quad \begin{array}{r} 85.00 \\ -\ 84.64 \\ \hline 0.36 \end{array} \qquad (9.3) \quad \begin{array}{r} 86.49 \\ -\ 85.00 \\ \hline 1.49 \end{array}$$

The square of 9.2 is closer to 85 than the square of 9.3. Therefore, the square root of 85 to the nearest tenth is **9.2**.

8. **(B)** To solve for x, combine all similar terms and set the equation equal to 0.

$$(8x - 5x) + (-2 - 8) = 0$$

Do the operations inside the parentheses first.

$$(3x) + (-10) = 0 \quad \text{or}$$
$$3x - 10 = 0$$

Next, add 10 to each side to undo the subtraction.

$$3x - 10 + 10 = 0 + 10$$
$$3x = 10$$

Finally, divide each side by 3 to find the value of x. You are undoing the multiplication to find the value of a single x.

$$\frac{3x}{3} = \frac{10}{3}$$

$$\mathbf{x = 3\frac{1}{3}}$$

9. **(E)** Clear the parentheses by multiplying $(a - b)$ by 2 and $(a + 3b)$ by 4. Line up similar terms and add.

$$2(a - b) + 4(a + 3b) =$$

$$\begin{array}{r} 2a - 2b \\ +\ 4a + 12b \\ \hline \mathbf{6a + 10b} \end{array}$$

10. **(C)** A prime number is a number larger than 1 that has only itself and 1 as factors—i.e., it can be evenly divided only by itself and 1. The number 201 is divisible by 3. The number 205 is divisible by 5. The number **211**, however, is a prime number.

11. **(C)** The product of a negative number and a positive number is always negative. The result of multiplying (product) two negative numbers is always a positive number. Since ab is positive, and a is negative, ***b* must be negative**, too.

12. **(C)** Set this up as a two-stage multiplication problem. Remember that when you multiply terms with opposite signs, the product is negative (i.e., it has a minus sign).

$$\begin{array}{r} a + 2 \\ \times\ a - 5 \\ \hline -5a - 10 \\ +\ a^2 + 2a \\ \hline a^2 - 3a - 10 \end{array}$$

$$\begin{array}{r} a^2 - 3a - 10 \\ \times\ \quad a + 3 \\ \hline 3a^2 - 9a - 30 \\ +\ a^3 - 3a^2 - 10a \\ \hline \mathbf{a^3 - 19a - 30} \end{array}$$

13. **(B)** Begin by combining like terms.

$$3z - 5 + 2z = 25 - 5z$$
$$5z - 5 = 25 - 5z$$

Next, add $5z$ to each side to eliminate the $-5z$ from the right side.

$$5z - 5 + 5z = 25 - 5z + 5z$$
$$10z - 5 = 25$$

Now, add 5 to each side to cancel out the remaining subtraction.

$$10z - 5 + 5 = 25 + 5$$
$$10z = 30$$
$$\mathbf{z = 3}$$

14. **(B)** A pentagon is a five-sided figure, which therefore has five corners. If the architect places a sculpture at each corner, there will be **five** sculptures.

15. **(C)** Every right triangle contains an angle of 90 degrees. This particular right triangle also has an angle of 30 degrees. To find the third angle, subtract the sum of these two angles from 180 degrees.

$$180 - (30 + 90) =$$
$$180 - 120 =$$
$$60 = \text{degrees in third angle}$$

The other two angles are **60 and 90 degrees.**

16. **(A)** Find the factors of the first term in the trinomial—the factors of x^2 are x and x.

$$(x\quad)(x\quad)$$

Then, look at the last factor in the trinomial—in this case, it has a plus sign. This means that both factors of the trinomial are either positive or negative. Which one, though? Since we see that the middle term ($-11x$) has a minus sign, both factors must have minus signs.

$$(x -\quad)(x -\quad)$$

The next step is to find the factors of 30. There are several numbers you can multiply to get 30—30 × 1, 10 × 3, 15 × 2, etc. However, the two multipliers that you use have to also combine somehow to give you the middle term, which is 11. When 5 and 6 are multiplied, they give you 30; when they're added, they give you 11. We know the factors have minus signs, so the factors of 30 are actually –6 and –5.

$$\mathbf{(x - 6)(x - 5)}$$

17. **(D)** Divide only similar terms. First divide numbers and then letters. When dividing powers of a letter (variable), just subtract the exponents.

$$\frac{15a^3b^2c}{5abc} = \frac{15}{5} \times \frac{a^3}{a} \times \frac{b^2}{b} \times \frac{c}{c} = \mathbf{3a^2b}$$

18. **(C)** The formula for the area of a circle is $\pi \times r^2$. Find the area of the larger circle first.

$$\pi \times 10^2 = 100\pi \text{ sq. in.}$$

Then find the area of the smaller circle.

$$\pi \times 7^2 = 49\pi \text{ sq. in.}$$

To find the part of the larger circle that the smaller one doesn't touch, subtract the smaller area from the larger one.

$$100 - 49 = \mathbf{51\pi\ sq.\ in.}$$

19. **(B)** The simplest way to solve this is to form an equation with x as the unknown grade.

$$\frac{78+86+96+94+x}{5} = 88$$

$$\frac{354+x}{5} = 88$$

Multiply both sides by 5. This will cancel out the division so you will no longer have a fraction to deal with, but instead whole numbers.

$$5 \times \frac{354 + x}{5} = 88 \times 5$$

Simplify both sides of the equation.

$$354 + x = 440$$
$$x = 440 - 354$$
$$x = \mathbf{86} \text{ (missing grade)}$$

20. **(A)** First, change all measurements to yards.

$$9' = 3 \text{ yds.} \quad 12' = 4 \text{ yds.} \quad 6'' = \frac{1}{6} \text{ yd.}$$

To find the volume of the concrete (the volume of a rectangle), multiply the length times the width times the height.

$$3 \times 4 \times \frac{1}{6} =$$

$$12 \times \frac{1}{6} = \mathbf{2} \text{ cu. yds.}$$

21. **(D)** First, find the area of the entire new wildlife preserve. Since the preserve is in the shape of a circle, use the formula for the area of a circle (area = π times the square of the radius or $A = \pi \times r^2$).

$$A = \pi \times r^2$$
$$A = \frac{22}{7} \times (14)^2 = \frac{22}{7} \times 196 = 616 \text{ sq. km}$$

The lion habitat area is a wedge formed by a 90-degree angle at the center of the circle.

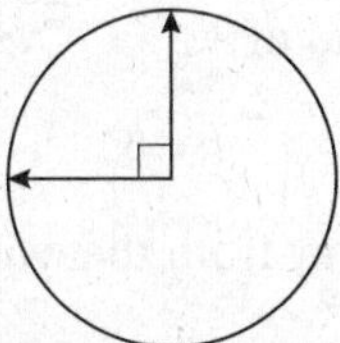

Since a circle has 360 degrees, we can find the part of the preserve that belongs to the lion habitat, and then reduce that fraction to its simplest term.

$$\frac{90}{360} = \frac{1}{4}$$

Next find what this fraction of the whole equals in square kilometers.

$$\frac{1}{4} \times \frac{616}{1} = \mathbf{154 \text{ sq. km}}$$

AFOQT #1

22. **(D)** Find the highest common factor that will divide into the numerical coefficients, 6 and 3, which is 3. Then find the highest literal factor that will divide into x^2 and xy, which is x (note that y is not contained in the first term at all). The next step is to divide the highest common factor, $3x$, into $6x^2 + 3xy$ to find the remaining factor. Thereby we see that the factors are $\mathbf{3x\,(2x + y)}$.

23. **(D)** To find the volume (V) of a cylinder, multiply π times the square of the radius (r) times the height (h).

$$V = \pi \times r^2 \times h$$

$$V = \frac{22}{7} \times \left(\frac{7}{1} \times \frac{7}{1}\right) \times \frac{15}{1}$$

$$V = 154 \times 15$$

$$V = 2{,}310 \text{ cu. in. (volume)}$$

To find the number of gallons this cylinder will hold, divide its volume by 231.

$$2{,}310 \div 231 = \mathbf{10\ gals.}$$

24. **(B)** The wall, the ladder, and the ground in the recreation area form a right triangle. The ladder is on a slant and is opposite the right angle formed by the wall and the ground. In this position, the ladder is the "hypotenuse" of the right triangle. In geometry, the Pythagorean theorem states that the square of the hypotenuse (c^2) of a right triangle equals the sum of the squares of the other two sides ($a^2 + b^2$).

$$a^2 + b^2 = c^2$$

$$8^2 + b^2 = 10^2$$

Solve by doing the arithmetic operations and by clearing one side of the equation for b^2.

$$64 + b^2 = 100$$

$$b^2 = 100 - 64$$

$$b^2 = 36$$

Then find the square root of b^2 and of 36.

$$b = 6$$

The base of the ladder is **6 feet** away from the wall.

25. **(A)** First find how many ounces of the original mixture were fruit juice.

$$10 \times 20\% = 10 \times .2 = 2 \text{ oz.}$$

Next, find the total number of ounces in the new mixture.

$$10 + 40 = 50 \text{ oz.}$$

Then find what part of the new mixture is fruit juice and convert that to a percentage.

$$\frac{2}{50} = \frac{4}{100} = \mathbf{4\%}$$

Subtest #5: Reading Comprehension

Check your answers below and refer to the explanation for each question you missed. Use the table to record right and wrong answers.

	✔	✘		✔	✘		✔	✘		✔	✘		✔	✘
1. C			6. D			11. D			16. B			21. C		
2. B			7. B			12. B			17. A			22. E		
3. A			8. C			13. A			18. A			23. A		
4. C			9. A			14. C			19. B			24. B		
5. D			10. B			15. D			20. E			25. E		

1. **(C)** The primary purpose of this passage is to **identify some of the results of both successful and unsuccessful American joint military operations.** Although the passage does mention historical examples of American joint military operations from the Revolutionary War through World War I, it does not discuss the evolution of doctrine (how operations are conducted) (choice (A)), nor does it compare American and European joint operations (choice (B)). The passage is also too short to provide a comprehensive historical account (choice (D)) or summarize lessons learned from American joint military operations (choice (E)).

2. **(B)** In the first paragraph, the word "autonomously" most nearly means **independently.** The context gives strong clues, since the end of that sentence says that the president was the Army and the Navy's "only common superior"—i.e., the only higher authority they shared was the very top of the pyramid—and the very next sentence mentions the "outward independence" of the Army and the Navy. Additionally, the root *auto* means "self," as in the *automobile* that doesn't need horses or oxen to pull it.

3. **(A)** You can infer from the passage that **there was no standardized way of coordinating joint operations during the first century of American military operations.** You can deduce this from the fact that it took until 1903 to form any kind of organization or office responsible for coordinating Army and Navy operations. The numerous failures cited show that joint operations were not easy (choice (B)), and those same failures demonstrated that American military operations did not in fact become continually more effective over time (choice (C)). The increasing complexity of warfare during the 1700s and 1800s is not mentioned in the passage, although it is true—and that increasing complexity made joint operations more necessary, not less necessary (choice (D)). Since joint operations means "operations involving more than one service," the idea of joint operations being primarily an Army responsibility is a contradiction in terms (choice (E)).

4. **(C)** As used throughout the passage, the term "joint" means **involving more than one service.** The third sentence of the first paragraph parenthetically defines "joint" as "multi-service."

5. **(D)** This passage's author would most likely agree with the statement that **"Joint military operations have been important throughout history."** The passage cites multiple instances of joint operations before the airplane was invented (choice (A)), and the unsuccessful examples illustrate that joint operational principles were neither well

established nor well known throughout history, much less since ancient times (choice (B)). The joint fumbles involving American forces, as listed in the passage, demonstrate that there was no such thing as a clear view of the importance of joint operations (choice (C)), and the last paragraph specifically refutes the statement in choice (E).

6. **(D)** The primary purpose of the passage is to **discuss the connections between organizational culture and leadership**. This is summed up neatly in the last sentence of the passage that calls leadership and culture "two sides of the same coin."

7. **(B)** Throughout the passage, the term "culture" is used to mean **the attitudes and behaviors characteristic of a particular group or organization**. This is demonstrated by the discussion of culture's role in the first paragraph, which notes that culture largely determines "how we are supposed to perceive, feel, and act in a given society."

8. **(C)** In the last paragraph, the word "dysfunctional" most nearly means **deviating from the norms of social behavior in a way that is regarded as bad or ineffective**. You can infer the word's meaning from the rest of the sentence, where "dysfunctional" cultural elements are cited as the impetus that causes the need for leaders to make changes.

9. **(A)** You can infer from the passage that **both leaders and members of an organization have an impact on its culture**. The passage repeatedly mentions the impact that both leaders and group or organizational members have on the organization's culture—how members of the group are supposed to perceive, feel, and act.

10. **(B)** The statement with which the passage's author would most likely agree is **"Leadership that is attuned to its organization's culture is the most likely to be successful."** While this is implied in several places throughout the passage, the last paragraph's discussion of leadership and culture being two sides of the same coin is the most obvious.

11. **(D)** The primary idea of this passage is to **provide an overview of U.S. national-level intelligence efforts since the nation's founding**. Although the other answer choices are touched on in the passage, they are not examined in detail.

12. **(B)** In the sixth paragraph, the word "vested" most nearly means **fully or significantly involved or engaged**. This term originated in the financial world, frequently relating to matching retirement fund contributions from an employer. However, as is done in this passage, its usage has expanded to show acknowledged and demonstrated interest in a subject by an individual or an organization.

13. **(A)** From the information in the passage, you could infer that **the Axis Powers wanted to change the international status quo**. The Axis Powers are mentioned in the sixth paragraph among the list of foreign powers "whose policies directly threatened the status quo."

14. **(C)** The threat of terrorism in the 21st century is mentioned mainly to bring the narrative of U.S. national-level intelligence up to the present day and to compare and contrast intelligence efforts against terrorism versus those against nation-states (**both choice (A) and choice (B)**). The passage does not discuss terrorist groups' reasons for existence.

15. **(D)** The passage's author would likely agree with the following statement: **"Although started relatively late in its national history, the U.S. national intelligence program is trying to make up for lost time."** All the other statements are directly contradicted by information in the passage.

16. **(B)** The primary purpose of this passage is to **identify the essential professional qualities of U.S. joint military leaders and service members**. The militaries of other nations are not mentioned (choice (A)). The passage only directly discusses professional conduct, not personal conduct (choice (C)). The passage neither praises the courage of U.S. service members (choice (D)) nor encourages joint leaders to be students of the art and science of war (choice (E))—it states these conditions as requirements, not just as something to be encouraged.

17. **(A)** In the passage's next to last paragraph, the word "epitomizes" most nearly means **to be a perfect example of something**; in this case, selfless service perfectly embodies "putting our nation, our military missions, and others before ourselves."

18. **(A)** Based solely on the information in the passage, it would be reasonable to infer that **military leaders who do not embody the values mentioned in the passage would have difficulty being effective in the American military**. Since the passage makes it clear that these values are the standards and requirements of the American military, someone who does not embody these values would be judged as not meeting the appropriate standards. Not only would that individual have a hard time being effective, but he or she would likely be asked to leave.

19. **(B)** Fellow citizens being referred to as resources to be expended is meant to **illustrate the costs associated with the responsibility of military leadership**. This statement is meant to emphasize the potentially high cost of the loss of human life. People are the most important resources in any organization, especially in the military—and part of leadership is balancing risk (including the potential loss of life) with the potential for mission accomplishment.

20. **(E)** The passage's author would likely agree with the following statement: **"All service members, but especially officers, are expected to have and maintain strong character and values."** Courage is not the absence of fear, but its mastery (choice (A)), and the passage specifically makes the points that character and values can and must be learned (choices (B) and (C)). The passage also makes the point that all service members—not just leaders—are required to have and maintain strong character and values (choice (D)).

21. **(C)** The primary purpose of the passage is to **define U.S. Air Force leadership**. The first sentence of the passage lays out the framework, and then goes into more detail about the elements of U.S. Air Force leadership and how they are or should be applied. The other answer choices are touched on in the passage, but only in support of the passage's primary purpose, defining U.S. Air Force leadership.

22. **(E)** Based on the information in the passage, you could infer that **different organizational levels require different leadership styles**. The last paragraph discusses the differences and similarities of junior, mid-level, and senior leaders.

23. **(A)** According to the passage, successful leaders must **continually ensure that the needs of their unit's people are met promptly and properly**. This is laid out in the last sentence of the fourth paragraph.

24. **(B)** In the passage's sixth paragraph, the word "ethos" most nearly means **the distinguishing character or guiding beliefs of a group**. The distinguishing characteristics and attitudes of the warrior ethos are laid out directly in the sixth paragraph, and indirectly

throughout the passage. While these attitudes and characteristics are backed up by both emotions and logic, and require correct technical decisions in support of mission accomplishment, the warrior ethos encompasses all of these and more.

25. **(E)** The quote that the passage's author would likely agree with is: **"Ultimately, leadership is not about glorious crowning acts. It's about keeping your team focused on a goal and motivated to do their best to achieve it."** While the other quotes may be interesting for their metaphors or hard-nosed pithiness, they run counter to all the ideas expressed in the passage, while choice (E) encapsulates those ideas.

Subtest #6: Situational Judgment

Check your answers below and refer to the explanation for each question you missed. Use the table to record right and wrong answers.

			✔	✘
Situation 1	1. Most Effective	**D**		
	2. Least Effective	**B**		
Situation 2	3. Most Effective	**B**		
	4. Least Effective	**E**		
Situation 3	5. Most Effective	**B**		
	6. Least Effective	**A**		
Situation 4	7. Most Effective	**D**		
	8. Least Effective	**E**		
Situation 5	9. Most Effective	**B**		
	10. Least Effective	**A**		
Situation 6	11. Most Effective	**E**		
	12. Least Effective	**B**		
Situation 7	13. Most Effective	**C**		
	14. Least Effective	**A**		
Situation 8	15. Most Effective	**C**		
	16. Least Effective	**A**		
Situation 9	17. Most Effective	**D**		
	18. Least Effective	**E**		
Situation 10	19. Most Effective	**E**		
	20. Least Effective	**D**		
Situation 11	21. Most Effective	**C**		
	22. Least Effective	**E**		
Situation 12	23. Most Effective	**A**		
	24. Least Effective	**D**		
Situation 13	25. Most Effective	**C**		
	26. Least Effective	**E**		
Situation 14	27. Most Effective	**C**		
	28. Least Effective	**E**		

			✔	✘
Situation 15	29. Most Effective	**A**		
	30. Least Effective	**B**		
Situation 16	31. Most Effective	**E**		
	32. Least Effective	**B**		
Situation 17	33. Most Effective	**C**		
	34. Least Effective	**A**		
Situation 18	35. Most Effective	**B**		
	36. Least Effective	**E**		
Situation 19	37. Most Effective	**A**		
	38. Least Effective	**E**		
Situation 20	39. Most Effective	**E**		
	40. Least Effective	**C**		
Situation 21	41. Most Effective	**B**		
	42. Least Effective	**E**		
Situation 22	43. Most Effective	**D**		
	44. Least Effective	**A**		
Situation 23	45. Most Effective	**A**		
	46. Least Effective	**B**		
Situation 24	47. Most Effective	**C**		
	48. Least Effective	**A**		
Situation 25	49. Most Effective	**D**		
	50. Least Effective	**E**		

Situation 1

Choice (D) is the most effective choice. When members of the chain of command are elsewhere, a subordinate (usually the most senior person) steps up to fill in. Also, people sometimes act differently one-on-one than when they are in a group; showing the senior NCO's acting replacement that you trust him or her will likely help you get an informative response. Ideally, the superior who assigned you to lead the section would already have given you an idea of its mission and daily routine (choice (C)); since he or she didn't (and since you didn't ask when you got the job), it makes sense to find out what you can before going back to that superior. The section's situation may have changed since the previous section leader departed (choice (A)), but whether it has or not, it makes more sense to save this option for later when you have specific questions. Likewise, calling a section meeting to let the section know what changes you want (choice (E)) should happen *after* you find out what the section's mission and routine are—and probably long after even that, when you have had time to gather enough information to make a solid assessment. **Calling the senior section NCO while he is on emergency leave (choice (B)) is the last thing you want to do if you can avoid it**—his mind will be focused on the reason he is on emergency leave (not the job), and you have plenty of other options to try first.

Situation 2

The most effective action is choice (B). You are in charge of the project, so go directly to the source of the problem, the engineer. You want to do this privately so that you can both be frank but professional, without the obstacles to communication caused by addressing the issue in an open meeting. Choices (C), (D), and (E) are all in a race to be the least effective action, but the "winner" **(i.e., least effective) is choice (E)**, which violates two tenets of leadership. Problems should be handled at the lowest level possible, but in this action, not only did you not try to deal with it yourself, but you bypassed both the engineer and your own supervisors when you went directly to the commander. One of the major parts of a subordinate leader's role is to handle problems at his or her level so that the next level up does not have to. When those subordinate leaders don't even get the chance to do their job and solve problems at their level, nothing good happens—after you present the full, unfiltered information to the commander, he is going to go back to the engineer's supervisor to set him straight and to your supervisor to teach you about the chain of command—or maybe find a replacement.

Situation 3

Choice (B) is the most effective action, as it will get the tent put up the quickest with the fairest distribution of work. **Choice (A) is the least effective action** since it does not take care of the section's personnel, exposing them unnecessarily to the risk of sleeping in the rain and abdicating your responsibility as a leader—regardless of the section members' lack of willingness to do what is not only the right thing, but also an easy right thing.

Situation 4

Choice (D) is the most effective action. It is tactful and professional, but does not sweep the problem under the rug. The briefer would probably appreciate honest feedback from someone she knows at least a little, directly and sooner, instead of second-hand criticism later. Adapting one's briefing/communication style is very important in the increasingly common circumstance of a video or audio teleconference. In this case (as in most cases), it's important to be honest but tactful at the same time. Choice (A) would likely be perceived as talking badly about someone behind his or her back; while your intentions might be honorable, it undermines a colleague and will likely be seen by others as unprofessional. It's also likely that a distorted version of your comments will make it back to the briefer. In choice (B), it may seem like you are doing the briefer a favor by immediately but discreetly bringing the issue to her attention, but doing it during the call is more likely to throw her off balance than help her. Additionally, using text messaging instead of speaking to her directly can lead to misinterpretation; she may not take your comments in the constructive manner you intend them to be. Choice (C) does not use your own communication skills to their best advantage and may be seen as just complaining. **Choice (E) is the least effective action.** Although it provides timely, direct feedback, it is also unnecessarily embarrassing to the briefing officer involved and is therefore unprofessional. It may get the briefing officer to slow down, but you (and your unit) will reap far more negative consequences than that action is worth.

Situation 5

Choice (B) is the most effective action because it maintains your integrity but creatively seeks a solution that will improve the situation. **Choice (A) is the least effective action**, as it gives away your integrity, shows your Airmen that you are more interested in doing the easy thing than doing the right thing, and does not seek to improve the situation. The qualification manual's standards were put in place for a reason; it is unwise to disregard them and cover it up as your Airmen will not be operationally trained and ready at the level you are reporting them to be.

Situation 6

Choice (E) is the most effective action; many times noncompliance with a leader's directions results from not knowing how, or not knowing why, compliance is important. **Choice (B) is the least effective action**, as it ignores the possible training/knowledge shortfall in the section leaders, and it also demonstrates a "do as I say, not as I do" attitude on your part. There's also an old saying: "If it's not written down, it didn't happen."

Situation 7

The seemingly unconventional **choice (C) is actually the most effective action**, while **choice (A) is the most strikingly ineffective action** of the other bad choices listed. This situation is based on an actual occurrence in Najaf, Iraq, in 2003. Army Lieutenant Colonel (LTC) Christopher P. Hughes was leading soldiers from his battalion toward Najaf, one of Iraq's holy cities, to secure the town and protect both the mosque and a Muslim cleric who had been put under house arrest by deposed dictator Saddam Hussein. However, Ba'athist agitators started to spread the rumor that the Americans were coming not to protect the mosque and its associated Shrine of Ali, but to invade it. The previously friendly Iraqis around the patrol turned angry and started shouting and throwing rocks. The American troops were hot in their chemical protective suits and hadn't slept in two to three days; tempers began to fray. However, LTC Hughes held his rifle upside down—showing that he had no intention of using it—and moved among his troops, ordering them to take a knee, lower their weapons, and smile. He also told them to take off their sunglasses, which made them more human to the surrounding Iraqis. Once the crowd quieted, he told his men to back up, turn around, and walk away, rather than backing away—which in Arab culture shows fear. The next day, after the agitators were removed and confusion cleared up, the same unit entered Najaf peacefully.

Situation 8

Choice (C) is the most effective action here—when the leader does not have experience in an area but has experienced subordinate leaders, it's almost always a good idea to get their input; it also reinforces an attitude of professional respect in the unit that will pay big dividends. **Choice (A) is the least effective action**, as it abdicates your duty as a leader. Even if a leader doesn't have any idea what to do, the leader's job is to *figure out* what to do.

Situation 9

This situation illustrates some of the potential difficulties romantic relationships between service members with different ranks or levels of influence can cause. **Choice (D) is the most effective action** because it gives the appropriate level of importance to professional and personal concerns: you did not try to use undue influence to get Lieutenant Davidson out of a mission (choices (A) and (E)), and you did not allow an unforeseen change to damage your relationship (choices (B) and (C)). Of these unethical and ill-advised options, **choice (E) is the least effective action.**

Situation 10

Choice (E) is likely the most effective action here. Since you have not been initially successful in helping the new unit member, a colleague may be more successful in reaching him—and you do have your own report to do on your own deadline. One note here: it's a good idea to explain to the new unit member what you are doing and why, so that he can see he is not being pushed aside as unimportant, while at the same time freeing yourself up to fulfill your individual responsibility. **Choice (D) is the least effective action**, as it tells the new unit member that he is not important in your eyes when you make no effort to balance competing needs or bring in new resources to help everyone accomplish their missions.

Situation 11

Choice (C) is the most effective action. Willingness to help other sections of the unit is important, but this should be coordinated with your flight leader since your flight is not only shorthanded but also unusually busy; your flight leader also might have other work scheduled that you don't know about yet, so it's important to give the leader a chance to do his or her job. Coordination between the two flight leaders also makes possible rearranging more than one person's workload in case that is the best solution. Choices (B) and (E) are both ineffective choices, but **choice (E) is the least effective** because it denies your flight leader the chance to do his or her job and manage your flight's overall workload.

Situation 12

Choice (A) is the most effective action; using your initiative to work around problems is beneficial (the opposite of choice (E)). It's important to make others involved fully aware of any potential challenges or problems (choices (B) and (C)), while making sure you are actually taking the most appropriate practical steps to prevent the problem from occurring. Telling the traveler that his request is impossible without even trying to arrange it **(choice (D)) is the least effective action.**

Situation 13

Choice (C) is the most effective action, and **choice (E) is the least effective action**, although choices (A), (D), and (B) are not far behind for the title of "worst idea." Choice (C) maintains the security of the people and equipment while still finishing this important mission as soon as possible. Choice (E) puts the injured Airmen and the other two team members in unnecessary, possibly severe, danger by leaving this small element by itself with no guarantee of when help is going to arrive; it also unnecessarily increases the danger to the rest of the convoy by leaving it with two fewer Airmen. Likewise, just abandoning the damaged vehicle (choice (A)) is the same as donating it to the enemy, while calling the commander to ask for instructions (choice (B)) requires him to do his job and yours also—he will be informed of your status, and if he wants you to do something different, he will tell you.

Situation 14

Choice (C) is the most effective action, while **choice (E) is the least effective action** you can choose here, although choice (D) is a close second for the least effective option. When a junior service member says, "I have a problem," it is vital, if there is any way possible, to stop and give that individual your full attention as his leader—solving problems is the leader's job. This tells Airman Belton that he matters, that he is part of the team, and that team members help each other. What may seem like an obvious problem to an experienced person isn't necessarily so obvious to an inexperienced individual. Although Airman Belton's problem may seem funny or even ridiculous, you don't laugh, and you make sure—nonverbal cues are important—that your tone of voice and facial expressions don't convey contempt or disregard for Airman Belton. It's acceptable to delay the full conversation for a short time to allow you to gather resources that will help him, but waiting till tomorrow (choice (A)) tells him that he is not important and that you are not interested in helping him solve his problem—plus, he could go somewhere else tonight, write some hot checks, and get into trouble. It's also not a good idea to send him to someone else or call someone else over (choice (B)) to tell him or her about Airman Belton's situation. Not only is it your job to help, but you are opening Airman Belton up to unnecessary embarrassment and even humiliation—not a good way to inspire loyalty, and it still doesn't guarantee that the problem will be solved.

Situation 15

Your goal must be to improve overall section performance, not just avoid friction; therefore, **the most effective action is choice (A)**, and **the least effective action is choice (B)**. Any organization is made up of people, and arguments due to individual instead of section focus mean time lost and performance reduced. Not getting involved ignores the problem, and isolating SSgt Nelson (choices (D) and (E)) may reduce day-to-day sparks, but it will probably make the problem worse in the long run. Asking the rest of the section to go along with her behavior (choice (C)) will only pour gas on the fire.

Situation 16

Choice (E) is the most effective action, and **choice (B) is the least effective action**. Putting your weekend time in to help this team with their documentation sends a powerful message about maintaining standards and that you are more interested in results than recrimination. Making the rest of the unit help this team catch up will not help them get their own tasks done on time, and it will make them resent the team with the missing documentation.

Situation 17

The most effective action here is choice (C), and **the least effective action is choice (A)**. SA Mitchell has in fact completed the tasks given to him for today, and, being brand new, is not aware of your extra emphasis on maintaining work hours. Choice (C) balances mission accomplishment (studying the material you gave him) with personal needs (the wedding) but informs him about unit standards in a timely manner. Choice (A) (and choice (D), for that matter) emphasize your power to keep him in the workplace, but without any particular reason. Choice (E) might be effective, but it would require your instructions to him about what to do in that early hour, and it would require someone else to come in early, too—again, without a particular associated benefit or need.

AFOQT #1

Situation 18

Choice (B) is the most effective action, and **choice (E) is the least effective action.** Enforcing the section-wide requirement maintains standards and prevents degrading the workshop's effectiveness, since it's hard to synchronize tasks with a team who isn't there. Explaining the importance of the workshop and its benefit to the entire section enables the team leader to present the requirement to his team as if it was his own. Choice (E) is an arbitrary enforcement of your authority and presents a penalty for noncompliance that may be excessive—and, what's more, could be prevented by a little reasoning with the team leader.

Situation 19

Choice (A) is the most effective action—if you don't have the appropriate equipment to do your job, speaking to your first-line supervisor (who is responsible for seeing that you get your job done) is the right thing to do. **Choice (E) is the least effective action**, although the other remaining choices aren't too far behind. Filing a complaint might be appropriate if your supervisor told you to shut up and deal with the situation, but it's more appropriate (and usually more effective) to ask your question to successive levels of your chain of command rather than jumping all the way up to the base Inspector General. Asking for a transfer (choice (D)) is a permanent solution to a short-term problem that may not even exist, since it assumes (like choice (B)) that you are being treated unfairly without even asking. You may be next on the list to get a new system.

Situation 20

The most effective action is choice (E), and **the least effective action is choice (C).** Asking your coworker gives you a direct but non-confrontational option—for example, you might learn that the coworker you suspect may have actually started going to the gym after work—that goes directly to the issue at hand. Ignoring the problem does not resolve it, and it may continue indefinitely. Spying on your coworker (choice (B)) does not qualify as taking solution-oriented action, but it does qualify as wasting your own time—and if your suspicions are unfounded, maybe even a little creepy. Relaying your suspicions to your supervisor (choice (A)) leverages the chain of command, but you haven't given your coworker the opportunity to even answer a question, much less explain. Asking your other coworkers if they have noticed anything suspicious lately (choice (D)) might uncover something, but it could start destructive rumors just as easily.

Situation 21

Choice (B) is the most effective action, and **choice (E) is the least effective action** in this scenario. Since you have a different idea of the standard than your supervisor does, waiting a few days means you are in unknown territory until then, which puts you at risk of making the situation worse. Asking how you can do better is a good idea—remember, it is your supervisor who understands and must maintain performance standards, not you or your coworker. Arguing that your performance was acceptable without more information is unproductive at best, and doing it over email is even worse, since email is not a conversation and also denies you the nonverbal cues (as opposed to the face-to-face meeting) that can help you better understand your situation.

Situation 22

Choice (D) is the most effective action, while **choice (A) is the least effective action.** Since it's clear, based on an approved policy memo, that the new section's processes need to be updated, immediate action—not waiting—is needed. However, since you are also the acting department head for now, you need to delegate getting those changes started in the new section while you run the department. When the department head gets back and you can focus on your new section, you will be able to give the situation more detailed and direct attention.

Situation 23

This one is tricky and in the real world would partially depend on details not given in the scenario and the personalities and priorities involved. However, given the information in this scenario, **choice (A) is the most effective action**, and **choice (B) is the least effective action.** The best outcome is to meet both deadlines with a quality product, and the worst outcome is to miss one or both deadlines, especially if the project owner doesn't know your part will be late. Quality is important, but so is timeliness. Communicating with whomever you will turn the projects in to is also important, but if you call for an extension, the very reasonable question will be: "Why didn't you identify this need earlier?"

Situation 24

The most effective action is choice (C), and **the least effective action is choice (A)**. It's always good to acknowledge someone's effort to make things better, especially if it's your leadership. By the same token, you should respectfully express your concerns, and hopefully you and your flight leader can work out solutions together—two heads are indeed frequently better than one. Choice (A) is the least effective action because, if you take this action, then you don't communicate openly with your flight leader, but you do make him look bad and demonstrate your own unprofessional behavior (and possibly lack of understanding of the project) by going to his boss without consulting him.

Situation 25

Choice (D) is the most effective action, and **choice (E) is the least effective action.** If you follow choice (D), you admit and take responsibility for your error, taking immediate steps to fix the mistake. The other choices all represent some level of "responsibility avoidance"—choice (A) will call into question in your supervisor's mind why he or she should keep you around—with choice (E) being the most extreme.

Subtest #7: Self-Description Inventory

There are no right or wrong answers to the questions on this subtest.

Subtest #8: Physical Science

Check your answers below and refer to the explanation for each question you missed. Use the table to record right and wrong answers.

	✔	✘		✔	✘		✔	✘		✔	✘
1. B			**6. B**			**11. B**			**16. D**		
2. B			**7. A**			**12. B**			**17. D**		
3. B			**8. C**			**13. A**			**18. D**		
4. A			**9. C**			**14. C**			**19. A**		
5. A			**10. D**			**15. B**			**20. C**		

1. **(B)** Energy that is derived from the sun is called **solar** energy. *Hydroelectric power* is derived from the movement of water—for example, water pouring over the top of a dam, turning one or more turbines, and thereby generating electricity. *Geothermal* energy is energy produced by harnessing heat from Earth, usually from deep below the surface.
2. **(B)** The rotation of Earth on its axis causes **day and night**. *Tides* are caused by the gravitational pull of the sun and Earth's moon. *The seasons* are caused by the tilt of Earth's axis, which brings parts of Earth closer to the sun at different times of the year. The fact that *Earth's axis is tilted* is not caused by Earth's rotation on its axis.
3. **(B)** Matter exists in one of three states or conditions: **solid**, **liquid**, or **gas**. Frequently, a substance's state may be affected by adding or removing heat, such as when heat melts ice into liquid water and then turns that ice into steam. Recent higher-level science texts add a fourth state, *plasma*, which is different from a gas because it is electrically conductive.
4. **(A)** Chemical reactions may be classified into four main types. In composition (direct combination), two or more elements or compounds combine to form a more complex substance. *Decomposition* (the reverse of composition) occurs when a complex compound breaks down to simpler compounds of basic elements. Replacement takes place when one substance in a compound is freed and another takes its place. *Double* (or ionic) *replacement* occurs when ions in a solution combine to form a new product that then leaves the solution. $2Na + 2HOH \rightarrow 2NaOH + H_2$ is a **single replacement** reaction where one sodium atom replaces just one of the hydrogen atoms in each water molecule.
5. **(A)** Potential energy is due to **the position of an object**, and kinetic energy is **energy of motion**. A boulder perched at the top edge of a long, steep mountainside downslope is said to have *potential energy.* If whatever is propping up the boulder gives way and it rolls down the slope, the boulder at that point will have *kinetic energy.*
6. **(B)** **Iodine** crystals in a small bottle of water make a saturated aqueous solution; a few milliliters of this solution added to a quart of water will destroy most organisms in an hour.
7. **(A)** The **kilogram** is the unit of mass used by the International System of Units, or SI (for Systéme International d'Unités). The *kilometer* is a unit of length (1,000 meters); the *ampere* is a unit of electric current; the *ohm* measures electrical resistance; and the *henry*

is a unit of electrical inductance, which is the ability of a coil to oppose any change in circuit current.

8. **(C)** An atom has **the same number of protons as electrons**.

9. **(C)** The hydrate $CuSO_4 \cdot 5H_2O$ contains 6 atoms in the salt $CuSO_4$ (1Cu + 1S + 4O). The 5 loosely bonded water molecules contain 15 atoms (10H + 5O). The total number of atoms is 6 + 15 = **21**.

10. **(D)** A magnetic compass is influenced by all magnetic sources in its vicinity and aligns itself according to the net **local magnetic field**; normally, this means pointing to the *magnetic north pole,* but not when there is a stronger magnetic influence nearby.

11. **(B)** The four types of chemical reactions are **combination, decomposition, single replacement, and double replacement**.

12. **(B)** In this example, gravitational potential energy is converted into kinetic energy. The kinetic energy is equal to the mass of the object, *m,* multiplied by the acceleration caused by the force of gravity, *g,* multiplied by the distance or height involved, *h.* Thus,

$$m \times g \times h = 1 \text{ kilogram} \times 9.8 \text{ m/sec} \times 1 \text{ meter} = 9.8 \text{ J (approximately } \mathbf{10\ J}\text{)}.$$

13. **(A)** The power delivered when a 120-volt electrical power supply produces $\frac{1}{2}$ amp to the load is **60 watts**. This is calculated by the formula:

Power (measured in watts) = volts (measuring electricity) × amperes (measuring intensity)

or

$$P = E \times I$$
$$P = 120 \text{ V} \times 0.5 \text{ A}$$
$$P = 60 \text{ W}$$

14. **(C)** Resistance, which is the tendency for a material to oppose the flow of electrons, is measured in **ohms**, named after German physicist Georg Ohm, who discovered the relationship between voltage, current, and resistance in 1827.

15. **(B)** When a lever is balanced on its fulcrum, the force on one arm **matches the force on the other**; this system is in equilibrium. If a load is placed on one end of such a lever but not the other, the balance is upset, and the lever will tilt to the side with the load on it (think of one person on a seesaw). If we lift the load (the person gets off the seesaw) or apply a similar load to the other end of the lever (think of the second person getting onto the seesaw), the system becomes balanced again.

16. **(D)** A magnifying glass is a **concave lens used for objects closer than one focal length.** The object held closer than one focal length from a convex lens will produce a virtual magnified image.

17. **(D)** The three methods of heat transfer are **radiation, conduction, and convection.** *Conduction,* as the transfer of heat between atoms as they collide within a substance, is usually the most efficient method for solids. *Convection* involves a fluid (such as a liquid or air) being heated and then expanding and traveling away from the heat source, typically displacing other parts of the fluid, which then get heated, etc. Thermal (not nuclear) *radiation* comes from the emission of electromagnetic waves, which carry the energy away from the emitting object.

18. **(D)** Frictional forces usually do NOT **increase potential energy**. The friction force *does* tend to *oppose motion*, slow the object down, and *produce wear* between contacting surfaces.

19. **(A)** For a solar eclipse to take place, the **moon must be between the sun and Earth.** Because the moon is directly between Earth and the sun—and because Earth and the moon are still moving and line up only relatively briefly—the moon only seems to block out the sun from a certain perspective; the moon's shadow (umbra) is very narrow, only about 170 miles in width.

20. **(C)** The speed of a wave is **equal to the frequency of the wave multiplied by the wavelength**. This equation, known as the *wave equation*, shows the mathematical relationship between the speed of a wave (v) and its wavelength (λ) and frequency (f). Using the symbols v, λ, and f, the equation can be rewritten as:

$$v = f \cdot \lambda$$

Subtest #9: Table Reading

Check your answers below. Use the table to record right and wrong answers.

	✔	✘		✔	✘		✔	✘		✔	✘		✔	✘
1. B			**9. A**			**17. C**			**25. B**			**33. A**		
2. C			**10. D**			**18. B**			**26. A**			**34. D**		
3. A			**11. E**			**19. C**			**27. E**			**35. D**		
4. E			**12. B**			**20. B**			**28. D**			**36. C**		
5. D			**13. C**			**21. C**			**29. C**			**37. A**		
6. B			**14. A**			**22. D**			**30. C**			**38. B**		
7. C			**15. E**			**23. A**			**31. B**			**39. E**		
8. A			**16. D**			**24. A**			**32. A**			**40. D**		

Subtest #10: Instrument Comprehension

Check your answers below. Use the table to record right and wrong answers.

	✔	✘		✔	✘		✔	✘		✔	✘		✔	✘
1. B			**6. B**			**11. C**			**16. D**			**21. D**		
2. B			**7. A**			**12. A**			**17. B**			**22. A**		
3. C			**8. C**			**13. B**			**18. D**			**23. A**		
4. A			**9. A**			**14. C**			**19. B**			**24. C**		
5. D			**10. D**			**15. B**			**20. B**			**25. B**		

Answer	Nose	Bank	Heading
1. **(B)**	UP	LEFT	NE
2. **(B)**	LEVEL	LEFT	S
3. **(C)**	UP	RIGHT	W
4. **(A)**	DOWN	LEFT	SE
5. **(D)**	UP	ZERO	N
6. **(B)**	LEVEL	LEFT	W
7. **(A)**	UP	RIGHT	SW
8. **(C)**	DOWN	LEFT	SW
9. **(A)**	UP	LEFT	E
10. **(D)**	LEVEL	RIGHT	ENE
11. **(C)**	UP	ZERO	W
12. **(A)**	UP	RIGHT	NE
13. **(B)**	DOWN	LEFT	WSW
14. **(C)**	UP	LEFT	WSW
15. **(B)**	DOWN	RIGHT	S
16. **(D)**	DOWN	RIGHT	W
17. **(B)**	DOWN	ZERO	S
18. **(D)**	UP	LEFT	S
19. **(B)**	LEVEL	RIGHT	S
20. **(B)**	UP	LEFT	W
21. **(D)**	UP	RIGHT	NW
22. **(A)**	DOWN	ZERO	W
23. **(A)**	DOWN	LEFT	SW
24. **(C)**	LEVEL	RIGHT	S
25. **(B)**	UP	ZERO	W

Subtest #11: Block Counting

Check your answers below. Use the table to record right and wrong answers.

	✔	✘		✔	✘		✔	✘		✔	✘		✔	✘
1. B			**7. E**			**13. B**			**19. D**			**25. B**		
2. C			**8. B**			**14. A**			**20. D**			**26. C**		
3. E			**9. C**			**15. C**			**21. B**			**27. D**		
4. B			**10. D**			**16. B**			**22. B**			**28. A**		
5. A			**11. B**			**17. B**			**23. D**			**29. B**		
6. D			**12. C**			**18. A**			**24. D**			**30. B**		

Subtest #12: Aviation Information

Check your answers below and refer to the explanation for each question you missed. Use the table to record right and wrong answers.

	✔	✘		✔	✘		✔	✘		✔	✘
1. C			6. B			11. E			16. D		
2. A			7. C			12. C			17. E		
3. E			8. D			13. A			18. A		
4. B			9. A			14. B			19. C		
5. D			10. E			15. C			20. C		

1. **(C)** Being in the down or extended position means that the wing flaps are pivoted downward from hinged points on the trailing edge of the wing. This effectively increases the wing camber or curvature, resulting in **increased lift and increased drag**; this allows the airplane to climb or descend at a steeper angle or a slower airspeed.

2. **(A)** **Heavily loaded aircraft** are slower and therefore take longer to achieve flying speed, so a longer runway is needed to develop the lift required for takeoff. Also, a take-off in **calm** or **nearly calm** air takes away the increased wind speed advantage derived from taking off into the wind. Therefore, many municipal or regional airports have a longer runway to accommodate airplanes needing a longer takeoff roll because of one or both of these conditions.

3. **(E)** The small hinged section on the elevator of most airplanes is called the **trim tab.** The trim tab helps prevent or minimize pilot fatigue by relieving control pressure at the desired flight angle—in other words, the pilot does not have to spend physical and mental energy keeping the elevator at a certain angle to maintain a certain attitude (climbing, level flight, or diving).

4. **(B)** The rearward retarding force on the airplane known as drag is opposed by **thrust,** which propels the aircraft through the air.

5. **(D)** At night, airport taxiways are identified by omnidirectional edge lights that are **blue** in color.

6. **(B)** A runway with the Approach Lighting System (ALS) would show an incoming pilot **a series of lightbars and/or strobe lights extending outward from the runway approach end.**

7. **(C)** The thrust of a turbojet is developed by compressing air in the inlet and compressor, mixing the air with fuel and burning it in the combustor, and **expanding the gas stream through the turbine and nozzle.**

8. **(D)** The ramjet engine consists of **an inlet, a combustion zone, and a nozzle.** The ramjet does not have a compressor and turbine as the turbojet does. Air enters the inlet, where it is compressed; it then enters the combustion zone, where it is mixed with fuel and burned. The hot gases are then expelled through the nozzle, developing thrust. Ramjet operation depends on the inlet to decelerate the incoming air to increase the pressure in the combustion zone. The pressure increase makes it possible for the ramjet

to operate: The higher the velocity of the incoming air, the more the pressure increase. It is for this reason that the ramjet operates best at high supersonic velocities. At subsonic velocities, the ramjet is inefficient, and, to start the ramjet, air must first enter the inlet at a relatively high velocity.

9. **(A)** The four forces that act on an aircraft in flight are **lift, gravity, thrust, and drag**.

10. **(E)** For a fixed-wing aircraft, lift is generated **perpendicular** to the direction of flight.

11. **(E)** The angle formed by the chord of an airfoil or wing and the direction of the relative wind is known as the **angle of attack**.

12. **(C)** Pitot tubes furnish data to an instrument that is used by aircraft pilots in about the same way that a **speedometer** is used by an automobile driver.

13. **(A)** The part of an airplane that holds the cargo and/or passengers—and provides a base for the other aircraft parts—is known as the **fuselage**.

14. **(B)** On a conventional fixed-wing aircraft, the **horizontal stabilizers** maintain pitch and the **vertical stabilizer** maintains yaw. If the pilot wishes to *change* pitch or yaw, he uses the elevators and rudder, respectively.

15. **(C)** **Flaps** are additional hinged rear sections mounted to the wing near the body that are deployed downward on takeoff and landing to increase the amount of upward force produced by the wing. *Ailerons* are mounted farther out on the wing, away from the body, and can change or control the roll of the aircraft. *Elevators* are the hinged rear part of the horizontal stabilizer and can change the aircraft's pitch (up and down orientation). *Trim tabs* are small hinged surfaces on the rear of the elevators that help prevent or minimize pilot fatigue by relieving control pressure at the desired flight angle. *Elevons* are movable flight surfaces on delta wing aircraft that help control roll and pitch.

16. **(D)** Density altitude is a theoretical air density that exists under standard conditions at a certain altitude—a "rule of thumb" guideline. The four factors that affect density altitude are altitude, atmospheric pressure, humidity, and temperature.

17. **(E)** The degree of movement of an aircraft around its longitudinal axis is known as **bank**; the movement itself is known as "roll."

18. **(A)** The Venturi theory of lift says that faster airflow over the curved upper portion of a wing surface causes **decreased pressure according to Bernoulli's equation**. Although this has been the widely accepted explanation for many years, emerging research is beginning to account for inconsistencies between theoretical and actual airfoil pressures and other performance results. However, the still widely recognized Venturi theory is correct in many major aspects and does accurately describe some airfoil performance characteristics.

19. **(C)** The maneuver in which a rotary-wing aircraft (helicopter) is maintained in nearly motionless flight over a ground reference point at a constant altitude and heading (direction) is known as **hovering**. It is usually done at a relatively low altitude.

20. **(C)** The ratio of the speed of an aircraft to the speed of sound in the air around it is the aircraft's **Mach number**, named in honor of Ernst Mach, a late-nineteenth-century physicist who studied gas dynamics.

ANSWER SHEET
AFOQT #2

Subtest 1: Verbal Analogies

1. Ⓐ Ⓑ Ⓒ Ⓓ Ⓔ	8. Ⓐ Ⓑ Ⓒ Ⓓ Ⓔ	15. Ⓐ Ⓑ Ⓒ Ⓓ Ⓔ	22. Ⓐ Ⓑ Ⓒ Ⓓ Ⓔ
2. Ⓐ Ⓑ Ⓒ Ⓓ Ⓔ	9. Ⓐ Ⓑ Ⓒ Ⓓ Ⓔ	16. Ⓐ Ⓑ Ⓒ Ⓓ Ⓔ	23. Ⓐ Ⓑ Ⓒ Ⓓ Ⓔ
3. Ⓐ Ⓑ Ⓒ Ⓓ Ⓔ	10. Ⓐ Ⓑ Ⓒ Ⓓ Ⓔ	17. Ⓐ Ⓑ Ⓒ Ⓓ Ⓔ	24. Ⓐ Ⓑ Ⓒ Ⓓ Ⓔ
4. Ⓐ Ⓑ Ⓒ Ⓓ Ⓔ	11. Ⓐ Ⓑ Ⓒ Ⓓ Ⓔ	18. Ⓐ Ⓑ Ⓒ Ⓓ Ⓔ	25. Ⓐ Ⓑ Ⓒ Ⓓ Ⓔ
5. Ⓐ Ⓑ Ⓒ Ⓓ Ⓔ	12. Ⓐ Ⓑ Ⓒ Ⓓ Ⓔ	19. Ⓐ Ⓑ Ⓒ Ⓓ Ⓔ	
6. Ⓐ Ⓑ Ⓒ Ⓓ Ⓔ	13. Ⓐ Ⓑ Ⓒ Ⓓ Ⓔ	20. Ⓐ Ⓑ Ⓒ Ⓓ Ⓔ	
7. Ⓐ Ⓑ Ⓒ Ⓓ Ⓔ	14. Ⓐ Ⓑ Ⓒ Ⓓ Ⓔ	21. Ⓐ Ⓑ Ⓒ Ⓓ Ⓔ	

Subtest 2: Arithmetic Reasoning

1. Ⓐ Ⓑ Ⓒ Ⓓ Ⓔ	8. Ⓐ Ⓑ Ⓒ Ⓓ Ⓔ	15. Ⓐ Ⓑ Ⓒ Ⓓ Ⓔ	22. Ⓐ Ⓑ Ⓒ Ⓓ Ⓔ
2. Ⓐ Ⓑ Ⓒ Ⓓ Ⓔ	9. Ⓐ Ⓑ Ⓒ Ⓓ Ⓔ	16. Ⓐ Ⓑ Ⓒ Ⓓ Ⓔ	23. Ⓐ Ⓑ Ⓒ Ⓓ Ⓔ
3. Ⓐ Ⓑ Ⓒ Ⓓ Ⓔ	10. Ⓐ Ⓑ Ⓒ Ⓓ Ⓔ	17. Ⓐ Ⓑ Ⓒ Ⓓ Ⓔ	24. Ⓐ Ⓑ Ⓒ Ⓓ Ⓔ
4. Ⓐ Ⓑ Ⓒ Ⓓ Ⓔ	11. Ⓐ Ⓑ Ⓒ Ⓓ Ⓔ	18. Ⓐ Ⓑ Ⓒ Ⓓ Ⓔ	25. Ⓐ Ⓑ Ⓒ Ⓓ Ⓔ
5. Ⓐ Ⓑ Ⓒ Ⓓ Ⓔ	12. Ⓐ Ⓑ Ⓒ Ⓓ Ⓔ	19. Ⓐ Ⓑ Ⓒ Ⓓ Ⓔ	
6. Ⓐ Ⓑ Ⓒ Ⓓ Ⓔ	13. Ⓐ Ⓑ Ⓒ Ⓓ Ⓔ	20. Ⓐ Ⓑ Ⓒ Ⓓ Ⓔ	
7. Ⓐ Ⓑ Ⓒ Ⓓ Ⓔ	14. Ⓐ Ⓑ Ⓒ Ⓓ Ⓔ	21. Ⓐ Ⓑ Ⓒ Ⓓ Ⓔ	

Subtest 3: Word Knowledge

1. Ⓐ Ⓑ Ⓒ Ⓓ Ⓔ	8. Ⓐ Ⓑ Ⓒ Ⓓ Ⓔ	15. Ⓐ Ⓑ Ⓒ Ⓓ Ⓔ	22. Ⓐ Ⓑ Ⓒ Ⓓ Ⓔ
2. Ⓐ Ⓑ Ⓒ Ⓓ Ⓔ	9. Ⓐ Ⓑ Ⓒ Ⓓ Ⓔ	16. Ⓐ Ⓑ Ⓒ Ⓓ Ⓔ	23. Ⓐ Ⓑ Ⓒ Ⓓ Ⓔ
3. Ⓐ Ⓑ Ⓒ Ⓓ Ⓔ	10. Ⓐ Ⓑ Ⓒ Ⓓ Ⓔ	17. Ⓐ Ⓑ Ⓒ Ⓓ Ⓔ	24. Ⓐ Ⓑ Ⓒ Ⓓ Ⓔ
4. Ⓐ Ⓑ Ⓒ Ⓓ Ⓔ	11. Ⓐ Ⓑ Ⓒ Ⓓ Ⓔ	18. Ⓐ Ⓑ Ⓒ Ⓓ Ⓔ	25. Ⓐ Ⓑ Ⓒ Ⓓ Ⓔ
5. Ⓐ Ⓑ Ⓒ Ⓓ Ⓔ	12. Ⓐ Ⓑ Ⓒ Ⓓ Ⓔ	19. Ⓐ Ⓑ Ⓒ Ⓓ Ⓔ	
6. Ⓐ Ⓑ Ⓒ Ⓓ Ⓔ	13. Ⓐ Ⓑ Ⓒ Ⓓ Ⓔ	20. Ⓐ Ⓑ Ⓒ Ⓓ Ⓔ	
7. Ⓐ Ⓑ Ⓒ Ⓓ Ⓔ	14. Ⓐ Ⓑ Ⓒ Ⓓ Ⓔ	21. Ⓐ Ⓑ Ⓒ Ⓓ Ⓔ	

Subtest 4: Math Knowledge

1. Ⓐ Ⓑ Ⓒ Ⓓ Ⓔ	8. Ⓐ Ⓑ Ⓒ Ⓓ Ⓔ	15. Ⓐ Ⓑ Ⓒ Ⓓ Ⓔ	22. Ⓐ Ⓑ Ⓒ Ⓓ Ⓔ
2. Ⓐ Ⓑ Ⓒ Ⓓ Ⓔ	9. Ⓐ Ⓑ Ⓒ Ⓓ Ⓔ	16. Ⓐ Ⓑ Ⓒ Ⓓ Ⓔ	23. Ⓐ Ⓑ Ⓒ Ⓓ Ⓔ
3. Ⓐ Ⓑ Ⓒ Ⓓ Ⓔ	10. Ⓐ Ⓑ Ⓒ Ⓓ Ⓔ	17. Ⓐ Ⓑ Ⓒ Ⓓ Ⓔ	24. Ⓐ Ⓑ Ⓒ Ⓓ Ⓔ
4. Ⓐ Ⓑ Ⓒ Ⓓ Ⓔ	11. Ⓐ Ⓑ Ⓒ Ⓓ Ⓔ	18. Ⓐ Ⓑ Ⓒ Ⓓ Ⓔ	25. Ⓐ Ⓑ Ⓒ Ⓓ Ⓔ
5. Ⓐ Ⓑ Ⓒ Ⓓ Ⓔ	12. Ⓐ Ⓑ Ⓒ Ⓓ Ⓔ	19. Ⓐ Ⓑ Ⓒ Ⓓ Ⓔ	
6. Ⓐ Ⓑ Ⓒ Ⓓ Ⓔ	13. Ⓐ Ⓑ Ⓒ Ⓓ Ⓔ	20. Ⓐ Ⓑ Ⓒ Ⓓ Ⓔ	
7. Ⓐ Ⓑ Ⓒ Ⓓ Ⓔ	14. Ⓐ Ⓑ Ⓒ Ⓓ Ⓔ	21. Ⓐ Ⓑ Ⓒ Ⓓ Ⓔ	

ANSWER SHEET
AFOQT #2

Subtest 5: Reading Comprehension

1. Ⓐ Ⓑ Ⓒ Ⓓ Ⓔ
2. Ⓐ Ⓑ Ⓒ Ⓓ Ⓔ
3. Ⓐ Ⓑ Ⓒ Ⓓ Ⓔ
4. Ⓐ Ⓑ Ⓒ Ⓓ Ⓔ
5. Ⓐ Ⓑ Ⓒ Ⓓ Ⓔ
6. Ⓐ Ⓑ Ⓒ Ⓓ Ⓔ
7. Ⓐ Ⓑ Ⓒ Ⓓ Ⓔ
8. Ⓐ Ⓑ Ⓒ Ⓓ Ⓔ
9. Ⓐ Ⓑ Ⓒ Ⓓ Ⓔ
10. Ⓐ Ⓑ Ⓒ Ⓓ Ⓔ
11. Ⓐ Ⓑ Ⓒ Ⓓ Ⓔ
12. Ⓐ Ⓑ Ⓒ Ⓓ Ⓔ
13. Ⓐ Ⓑ Ⓒ Ⓓ Ⓔ
14. Ⓐ Ⓑ Ⓒ Ⓓ Ⓔ
15. Ⓐ Ⓑ Ⓒ Ⓓ Ⓔ
16. Ⓐ Ⓑ Ⓒ Ⓓ Ⓔ
17. Ⓐ Ⓑ Ⓒ Ⓓ Ⓔ
18. Ⓐ Ⓑ Ⓒ Ⓓ Ⓔ
19. Ⓐ Ⓑ Ⓒ Ⓓ Ⓔ
20. Ⓐ Ⓑ Ⓒ Ⓓ Ⓔ
21. Ⓐ Ⓑ Ⓒ Ⓓ Ⓔ
22. Ⓐ Ⓑ Ⓒ Ⓓ Ⓔ
23. Ⓐ Ⓑ Ⓒ Ⓓ Ⓔ
24. Ⓐ Ⓑ Ⓒ Ⓓ Ⓔ
25. Ⓐ Ⓑ Ⓒ Ⓓ Ⓔ

Subtest 6: Situational Judgment

1. Ⓐ Ⓑ Ⓒ Ⓓ Ⓔ
2. Ⓐ Ⓑ Ⓒ Ⓓ Ⓔ
3. Ⓐ Ⓑ Ⓒ Ⓓ Ⓔ
4. Ⓐ Ⓑ Ⓒ Ⓓ Ⓔ
5. Ⓐ Ⓑ Ⓒ Ⓓ Ⓔ
6. Ⓐ Ⓑ Ⓒ Ⓓ Ⓔ
7. Ⓐ Ⓑ Ⓒ Ⓓ Ⓔ
8. Ⓐ Ⓑ Ⓒ Ⓓ Ⓔ
9. Ⓐ Ⓑ Ⓒ Ⓓ Ⓔ
10. Ⓐ Ⓑ Ⓒ Ⓓ Ⓔ
11. Ⓐ Ⓑ Ⓒ Ⓓ Ⓔ
12. Ⓐ Ⓑ Ⓒ Ⓓ Ⓔ
13. Ⓐ Ⓑ Ⓒ Ⓓ Ⓔ
14. Ⓐ Ⓑ Ⓒ Ⓓ Ⓔ
15. Ⓐ Ⓑ Ⓒ Ⓓ Ⓔ
16. Ⓐ Ⓑ Ⓒ Ⓓ Ⓔ
17. Ⓐ Ⓑ Ⓒ Ⓓ Ⓔ
18. Ⓐ Ⓑ Ⓒ Ⓓ Ⓔ
19. Ⓐ Ⓑ Ⓒ Ⓓ Ⓔ
20. Ⓐ Ⓑ Ⓒ Ⓓ Ⓔ
21. Ⓐ Ⓑ Ⓒ Ⓓ Ⓔ
22. Ⓐ Ⓑ Ⓒ Ⓓ Ⓔ
23. Ⓐ Ⓑ Ⓒ Ⓓ Ⓔ
24. Ⓐ Ⓑ Ⓒ Ⓓ Ⓔ
25. Ⓐ Ⓑ Ⓒ Ⓓ Ⓔ
26. Ⓐ Ⓑ Ⓒ Ⓓ Ⓔ
27. Ⓐ Ⓑ Ⓒ Ⓓ Ⓔ
28. Ⓐ Ⓑ Ⓒ Ⓓ Ⓔ
29. Ⓐ Ⓑ Ⓒ Ⓓ Ⓔ
30. Ⓐ Ⓑ Ⓒ Ⓓ Ⓔ
31. Ⓐ Ⓑ Ⓒ Ⓓ Ⓔ
32. Ⓐ Ⓑ Ⓒ Ⓓ Ⓔ
33. Ⓐ Ⓑ Ⓒ Ⓓ Ⓔ
34. Ⓐ Ⓑ Ⓒ Ⓓ Ⓔ
35. Ⓐ Ⓑ Ⓒ Ⓓ Ⓔ
36. Ⓐ Ⓑ Ⓒ Ⓓ Ⓔ
37. Ⓐ Ⓑ Ⓒ Ⓓ Ⓔ
38. Ⓐ Ⓑ Ⓒ Ⓓ Ⓔ
39. Ⓐ Ⓑ Ⓒ Ⓓ Ⓔ
40. Ⓐ Ⓑ Ⓒ Ⓓ Ⓔ
41. Ⓐ Ⓑ Ⓒ Ⓓ Ⓔ
42. Ⓐ Ⓑ Ⓒ Ⓓ Ⓔ
43. Ⓐ Ⓑ Ⓒ Ⓓ Ⓔ
44. Ⓐ Ⓑ Ⓒ Ⓓ Ⓔ
45. Ⓐ Ⓑ Ⓒ Ⓓ Ⓔ
46. Ⓐ Ⓑ Ⓒ Ⓓ Ⓔ
47. Ⓐ Ⓑ Ⓒ Ⓓ Ⓔ
48. Ⓐ Ⓑ Ⓒ Ⓓ Ⓔ
49. Ⓐ Ⓑ Ⓒ Ⓓ Ⓔ
50. Ⓐ Ⓑ Ⓒ Ⓓ Ⓔ

Subtest 7: Self-Description Inventory (Omitted)

Subtest 8: Physical Science

1. Ⓐ Ⓑ Ⓒ Ⓓ Ⓔ
2. Ⓐ Ⓑ Ⓒ Ⓓ Ⓔ
3. Ⓐ Ⓑ Ⓒ Ⓓ Ⓔ
4. Ⓐ Ⓑ Ⓒ Ⓓ Ⓔ
5. Ⓐ Ⓑ Ⓒ Ⓓ Ⓔ
6. Ⓐ Ⓑ Ⓒ Ⓓ Ⓔ
7. Ⓐ Ⓑ Ⓒ Ⓓ Ⓔ
8. Ⓐ Ⓑ Ⓒ Ⓓ Ⓔ
9. Ⓐ Ⓑ Ⓒ Ⓓ Ⓔ
10. Ⓐ Ⓑ Ⓒ Ⓓ Ⓔ
11. Ⓐ Ⓑ Ⓒ Ⓓ Ⓔ
12. Ⓐ Ⓑ Ⓒ Ⓓ Ⓔ
13. Ⓐ Ⓑ Ⓒ Ⓓ Ⓔ
14. Ⓐ Ⓑ Ⓒ Ⓓ Ⓔ
15. Ⓐ Ⓑ Ⓒ Ⓓ Ⓔ
16. Ⓐ Ⓑ Ⓒ Ⓓ Ⓔ
17. Ⓐ Ⓑ Ⓒ Ⓓ Ⓔ
18. Ⓐ Ⓑ Ⓒ Ⓓ Ⓔ
19. Ⓐ Ⓑ Ⓒ Ⓓ Ⓔ
20. Ⓐ Ⓑ Ⓒ Ⓓ Ⓔ

ANSWER SHEET
AFOQT #2

Subtest 9: Table Reading

1. Ⓐ Ⓑ Ⓒ Ⓓ Ⓔ	11. Ⓐ Ⓑ Ⓒ Ⓓ Ⓔ	21. Ⓐ Ⓑ Ⓒ Ⓓ Ⓔ	31. Ⓐ Ⓑ Ⓒ Ⓓ Ⓔ
2. Ⓐ Ⓑ Ⓒ Ⓓ Ⓔ	12. Ⓐ Ⓑ Ⓒ Ⓓ Ⓔ	22. Ⓐ Ⓑ Ⓒ Ⓓ Ⓔ	32. Ⓐ Ⓑ Ⓒ Ⓓ Ⓔ
3. Ⓐ Ⓑ Ⓒ Ⓓ Ⓔ	13. Ⓐ Ⓑ Ⓒ Ⓓ Ⓔ	23. Ⓐ Ⓑ Ⓒ Ⓓ Ⓔ	33. Ⓐ Ⓑ Ⓒ Ⓓ Ⓔ
4. Ⓐ Ⓑ Ⓒ Ⓓ Ⓔ	14. Ⓐ Ⓑ Ⓒ Ⓓ Ⓔ	24. Ⓐ Ⓑ Ⓒ Ⓓ Ⓔ	34. Ⓐ Ⓑ Ⓒ Ⓓ Ⓔ
5. Ⓐ Ⓑ Ⓒ Ⓓ Ⓔ	15. Ⓐ Ⓑ Ⓒ Ⓓ Ⓔ	25. Ⓐ Ⓑ Ⓒ Ⓓ Ⓔ	35. Ⓐ Ⓑ Ⓒ Ⓓ Ⓔ
6. Ⓐ Ⓑ Ⓒ Ⓓ Ⓔ	16. Ⓐ Ⓑ Ⓒ Ⓓ Ⓔ	26. Ⓐ Ⓑ Ⓒ Ⓓ Ⓔ	36. Ⓐ Ⓑ Ⓒ Ⓓ Ⓔ
7. Ⓐ Ⓑ Ⓒ Ⓓ Ⓔ	17. Ⓐ Ⓑ Ⓒ Ⓓ Ⓔ	27. Ⓐ Ⓑ Ⓒ Ⓓ Ⓔ	37. Ⓐ Ⓑ Ⓒ Ⓓ Ⓔ
8. Ⓐ Ⓑ Ⓒ Ⓓ Ⓔ	18. Ⓐ Ⓑ Ⓒ Ⓓ Ⓔ	28. Ⓐ Ⓑ Ⓒ Ⓓ Ⓔ	38. Ⓐ Ⓑ Ⓒ Ⓓ Ⓔ
9. Ⓐ Ⓑ Ⓒ Ⓓ Ⓔ	19. Ⓐ Ⓑ Ⓒ Ⓓ Ⓔ	29. Ⓐ Ⓑ Ⓒ Ⓓ Ⓔ	39. Ⓐ Ⓑ Ⓒ Ⓓ Ⓔ
10. Ⓐ Ⓑ Ⓒ Ⓓ Ⓔ	20. Ⓐ Ⓑ Ⓒ Ⓓ Ⓔ	30. Ⓐ Ⓑ Ⓒ Ⓓ Ⓔ	40. Ⓐ Ⓑ Ⓒ Ⓓ Ⓔ

Subtest 10: Instrument Comprehension

1. Ⓐ Ⓑ Ⓒ Ⓓ	8. Ⓐ Ⓑ Ⓒ Ⓓ	15. Ⓐ Ⓑ Ⓒ Ⓓ	22. Ⓐ Ⓑ Ⓒ Ⓓ
2. Ⓐ Ⓑ Ⓒ Ⓓ	9. Ⓐ Ⓑ Ⓒ Ⓓ	16. Ⓐ Ⓑ Ⓒ Ⓓ	23. Ⓐ Ⓑ Ⓒ Ⓓ
3. Ⓐ Ⓑ Ⓒ Ⓓ	10. Ⓐ Ⓑ Ⓒ Ⓓ	17. Ⓐ Ⓑ Ⓒ Ⓓ	24. Ⓐ Ⓑ Ⓒ Ⓓ
4. Ⓐ Ⓑ Ⓒ Ⓓ	11. Ⓐ Ⓑ Ⓒ Ⓓ	18. Ⓐ Ⓑ Ⓒ Ⓓ	25. Ⓐ Ⓑ Ⓒ Ⓓ
5. Ⓐ Ⓑ Ⓒ Ⓓ	12. Ⓐ Ⓑ Ⓒ Ⓓ	19. Ⓐ Ⓑ Ⓒ Ⓓ	
6. Ⓐ Ⓑ Ⓒ Ⓓ	13. Ⓐ Ⓑ Ⓒ Ⓓ	20. Ⓐ Ⓑ Ⓒ Ⓓ	
7. Ⓐ Ⓑ Ⓒ Ⓓ	14. Ⓐ Ⓑ Ⓒ Ⓓ	21. Ⓐ Ⓑ Ⓒ Ⓓ	

Subtest 11: Block Counting

1. Ⓐ Ⓑ Ⓒ Ⓓ Ⓔ	9. Ⓐ Ⓑ Ⓒ Ⓓ Ⓔ	17. Ⓐ Ⓑ Ⓒ Ⓓ Ⓔ	25. Ⓐ Ⓑ Ⓒ Ⓓ Ⓔ
2. Ⓐ Ⓑ Ⓒ Ⓓ Ⓔ	10. Ⓐ Ⓑ Ⓒ Ⓓ Ⓔ	18. Ⓐ Ⓑ Ⓒ Ⓓ Ⓔ	26. Ⓐ Ⓑ Ⓒ Ⓓ Ⓔ
3. Ⓐ Ⓑ Ⓒ Ⓓ Ⓔ	11. Ⓐ Ⓑ Ⓒ Ⓓ Ⓔ	19. Ⓐ Ⓑ Ⓒ Ⓓ Ⓔ	27. Ⓐ Ⓑ Ⓒ Ⓓ Ⓔ
4. Ⓐ Ⓑ Ⓒ Ⓓ Ⓔ	12. Ⓐ Ⓑ Ⓒ Ⓓ Ⓔ	20. Ⓐ Ⓑ Ⓒ Ⓓ Ⓔ	28. Ⓐ Ⓑ Ⓒ Ⓓ Ⓔ
5. Ⓐ Ⓑ Ⓒ Ⓓ Ⓔ	13. Ⓐ Ⓑ Ⓒ Ⓓ Ⓔ	21. Ⓐ Ⓑ Ⓒ Ⓓ Ⓔ	29. Ⓐ Ⓑ Ⓒ Ⓓ Ⓔ
6. Ⓐ Ⓑ Ⓒ Ⓓ Ⓔ	14. Ⓐ Ⓑ Ⓒ Ⓓ Ⓔ	22. Ⓐ Ⓑ Ⓒ Ⓓ Ⓔ	30. Ⓐ Ⓑ Ⓒ Ⓓ Ⓔ
7. Ⓐ Ⓑ Ⓒ Ⓓ Ⓔ	15. Ⓐ Ⓑ Ⓒ Ⓓ Ⓔ	23. Ⓐ Ⓑ Ⓒ Ⓓ Ⓔ	
8. Ⓐ Ⓑ Ⓒ Ⓓ Ⓔ	16. Ⓐ Ⓑ Ⓒ Ⓓ Ⓔ	24. Ⓐ Ⓑ Ⓒ Ⓓ Ⓔ	

Subtest 12: Aviation Information

1. Ⓐ Ⓑ Ⓒ Ⓓ Ⓔ	6. Ⓐ Ⓑ Ⓒ Ⓓ Ⓔ	11. Ⓐ Ⓑ Ⓒ Ⓓ Ⓔ	16. Ⓐ Ⓑ Ⓒ Ⓓ Ⓔ
2. Ⓐ Ⓑ Ⓒ Ⓓ Ⓔ	7. Ⓐ Ⓑ Ⓒ Ⓓ Ⓔ	12. Ⓐ Ⓑ Ⓒ Ⓓ Ⓔ	17. Ⓐ Ⓑ Ⓒ Ⓓ Ⓔ
3. Ⓐ Ⓑ Ⓒ Ⓓ Ⓔ	8. Ⓐ Ⓑ Ⓒ Ⓓ Ⓔ	13. Ⓐ Ⓑ Ⓒ Ⓓ Ⓔ	18. Ⓐ Ⓑ Ⓒ Ⓓ Ⓔ
4. Ⓐ Ⓑ Ⓒ Ⓓ Ⓔ	9. Ⓐ Ⓑ Ⓒ Ⓓ Ⓔ	14. Ⓐ Ⓑ Ⓒ Ⓓ Ⓔ	19. Ⓐ Ⓑ Ⓒ Ⓓ Ⓔ
5. Ⓐ Ⓑ Ⓒ Ⓓ Ⓔ	10. Ⓐ Ⓑ Ⓒ Ⓓ Ⓔ	15. Ⓐ Ⓑ Ⓒ Ⓓ Ⓔ	20. Ⓐ Ⓑ Ⓒ Ⓓ Ⓔ

Air Force Officer Qualifying Test (AFOQT) Practice Test #2

11

Please turn to the beginning of Chapter 10, page 217, for more information about the breakdown and scoring attributes of the Air Force Officer Qualifying Test (AFOQT).

SUBTEST #1: VERBAL ANALOGIES

25 Questions

DIRECTIONS: This part of the test measures your ability to reason and see relationships between words. Choose the answer that best completes the analogy developed at the beginning of each question.

1. CROWDED is to URBAN as SPARSE is to
   (A) SLOWER.
   (B) RURAL.
   (C) SUBURBAN.
   (D) INDUSTRIAL.
   (E) CALM.

2. WATCH is to WATCHED as THROW is to
   (A) THROWED.
   (B) THROWN.
   (C) THROWER.
   (D) THREW.
   (E) TOSSED.

3. WRENCH is to PLUMBER as HAMMER is to
   (A) NAIL.
   (B) CARPENTER.
   (C) CONSTRUCTION.
   (D) BUILDING.
   (E) FOREMAN.

4. NATURAL is to ARTIFICIAL as
   (A) COOK is to WAITER.
   (B) BIRTH is to MATURITY.
   (C) CREATE is to DESTROY.
   (D) CUT is to DISSECT.
   (E) TEAR is to WATER.

5. BACON is to PIGS as HAMBURGER is to
   (A) VEAL.
   (B) BEEF.
   (C) FOWL.
   (D) HORSES.
   (E) CATTLE.

6. KANGAROO is to POUCH as
   (A) BEAR is to CAVE.
   (B) GLOVE is to BALL.
   (C) WEB is to SPIDER.
   (D) BUTTERFLY is to COCOON.
   (E) FISH is to SCHOOL.

7. BEHAVE is to CANDY as DISOBEY is to
   (A) RELINQUISH.
   (B) REPRIMAND.
   (C) ARGUMENT.
   (D) DISHONESTY.
   (E) DISRUPTION.

8. XXII is to IXXX as 22 is to
   (A) 29.
   (B) 31.
   (C) 32.
   (D) 51.
   (E) 13.

9. AMUSING is to FUNNY as ODD is to
   (A) EVEN.
   (B) EXTRA.
   (C) FELLOW.
   (D) DISTINCT.
   (E) UNUSUAL.

10. HONOR is to COURAGE as
    (A) LIGHT is to DARKNESS.
    (B) KNOWLEDGE is to WISDOM.
    (C) SELFISHNESS is to GREED.
    (D) DUTY is to COUNTRY.
    (E) KEY is to IGNITION.

11. ATLANTA is to GEORGIA as DALLAS is to

(A) FORT WORTH.
(B) BIRMINGHAM.
(C) COWBOYS.
(D) TEXAS.
(E) LOUISIANA.

12. CLOCK is to WATCH as

(A) LAKE is to STREAM.
(B) OCEAN is to RIVER.
(C) WATER is to FISH.
(D) BOAT is to SAIL.
(E) LAKE is to POND.

13. STABLE is to HORSE as

(A) HOUSE is to HUMAN.
(B) MOTHER is to DAUGHTER.
(C) BOOK is to LIBRARY.
(D) SEAMSTRESS is to CLOTH.
(E) WATER is to DUCK.

14. SQUIRREL is to TREE as GOPHER is to

(A) FOREST.
(B) BUSH.
(C) LAKE.
(D) GROUND.
(E) HOLLOW.

15. INFANCY is to CHILDHOOD as ENGAGEMENT is to

(A) DRIVE TRAIN.
(B) LOVE.
(C) MARRIAGE.
(D) RING.
(E) BRIDE.

16. TRAVEL is to AUTO as

(A) TRAIN is to WHISTLE.
(B) WATER is to DRINK.
(C) SOLDIER is to SAILOR.
(D) EAT is to SPOON.
(E) MEAT is to POTATOES.

17. ABU DHABI is to MUSCAT as

(A) CAIRO is to INCIRLIK.
(B) BEIRUT is to DAMASCUS.
(C) AUSTIN is to BATON ROUGE.
(D) OMAN is to YEMEN.
(E) LONDON is to HAMBURG.

18. SURGEON is to SCALPEL as FIREMAN is to

(A) SIREN.
(B) DALMATIAN.
(C) HELMET.
(D) WATER HOSE.
(E) POLICEMAN.

19. FRAME is to PAINTING as

(A) FENCE is to YARD.
(B) CLOUD is to SKY.
(C) BOOK is to COVER.
(D) PARK is to RANGER.
(E) JACK is to TIRE.

20. CASCADE is to WATERFALL as

(A) FISH is to RIVER.
(B) WARN is to HURRICANE.
(C) LAKE is to SAIL.
(D) CROSS is to OCEAN.
(E) MEANDER is to STREAM.

21. INFORM is to ENLIGHTEN as SING is to

(A) MELODY.
(B) ENTERTAIN.
(C) REFRAIN.
(D) CONFESS.
(E) WHISTLE.

22. PECAN is to PIE as CHOCOLATE is to

(A) BROWN.
(B) FROSTING.
(C) CHIPS.
(D) CAKE.
(E) DESSERT.

23. WALK is to MARCH as

(A) READ is to STUDY.
(B) FOOT is to TREAD.
(C) RUN is to STOP.
(D) WALTZ is to RUMBA.
(E) RAP is to JAZZ.

24. KABUL is to AFGHANISTAN as

(A) PENSACOLA is to FLORIDA.
(B) CALCUTTA is to INDIA.
(C) JAPAN is to KOREA.
(D) CAIRO is to EGYPT.
(E) CANCUN is to HONDURAS.

25. PERPLEX is to ENLIGHTEN as MIXTURE is to

(A) INDIVIDUAL.
(B) ADDITIVE.
(C) SETTLE.
(D) SOLIDIFY.
(E) SOCIAL.

SUBTEST #2: ARITHMETIC REASONING

25 Questions

DIRECTIONS: This part of the test measures your ability to use arithmetic to solve problems. Each problem is followed by five possible answers. You are to decide which of the choices is most nearly correct.

1. A particular flight is composed of 11 enlisted men and one noncommissioned officer. A squadron of 132 enlisted men is to be divided into flights. How many noncommissioned officers will be needed?

   (A) 11
   (B) 12
   (C) 13
   (D) 10
   (E) 14

2. An employee earns $350 per week. A total of $27.75 is withheld for federal income taxes, $5.65 for FICA (Social Security taxes), $9.29 for state income taxes, and $3.58 for the employee's retirement fund. How much will her net pay for the week be?

   (A) $314.73
   (B) $304.73
   (C) $303.73
   (D) $313.73
   (E) $305.73

3. Temperature readings on a certain day ranged from a low of –4°F to a high of 16°F. What was the average temperature for the day?

   (A) 10°
   (B) 6°
   (C) 12°
   (D) 8°
   (E) 20°

4. On a scale drawing, $\frac{1}{4}$ inch represents 1 foot. How long would a line on the drawing have to be to represent a length of $3\frac{1}{2}$ feet?

   (A) $\frac{3}{4}$ in.
   (B) $\frac{7}{8}$ in.
   (C) $1\frac{7}{8}$ in.
   (D) $1\frac{1}{4}$ in.
   (E) $1\frac{3}{4}$ in.

5. During a sale, an auto dealership offers a 15% discount on the list price of a used car. What would be the discount on a car that lists for $13,620?

   (A) $900.00
   (B) $11,577.00
   (C) $204.30
   (D) $2,043.00
   (E) $20.43

6. The price of gasoline rose from $2.90 to $3.08 per gallon. What was the percent of increase?

   (A) 3.2%
   (B) 6.2%
   (C) 6.4%
   (D) 10.6%
   (E) 1.6%

7. A team won 70% of the 40 games it played. How many games did it lose?

(A) 28
(B) 30
(C) 22
(D) 12
(E) 7

8. A flight is scheduled for departure at 3:50 P.M. If the flight takes 2 hours and 55 minutes, at what time is it scheduled to arrive at its destination?

(A) 5:05 P.M.
(B) 6:05 P.M.
(C) 6:15 P.M.
(D) 6:45 P.M.
(E) 6:50 P.M.

9. How many 4-oz. candy bars are there in a 3-lb. package of candy?

(A) 12
(B) 16
(C) 48
(D) 9
(E) 24

10. What is the fifth term of the series $2\frac{5}{6}$, $3\frac{1}{2}$, $4\frac{1}{6}$, $4\frac{5}{6}$, . . . ?

(A) $5\frac{1}{6}$
(B) $5\frac{1}{2}$
(C) $5\frac{5}{6}$
(D) $6\frac{1}{6}$
(E) $5\frac{1}{4}$

11. In a restaurant, Max orders an entree with vegetables for $12.50, dessert for $3.50, and coffee for $1.25. If the tax on meals is 8%, what tax should be added to his check?

(A) $.68
(B) $.80
(C) $1.00
(D) $1.28
(E) $1.38

12. A 55-gallon drum of oil is to be used to fill cans that hold 2 quarts each. How many cans can be filled from the drum?

(A) 55
(B) $27\frac{1}{2}$
(C) 110
(D) 220
(E) 165

13. In a factory that makes wooden spindles, a lathe operator takes 45 minutes to do the finish work on nine spindles. How many hours will it take him to finish 96 spindles at the same rate?

(A) 8
(B) 72
(C) 9
(D) 10
(E) 45

14. A triangle has two equal sides. The third side has a length of 13 feet, 2 inches. If the perimeter of the triangle is 40 feet, what is the length of one of the equal sides?

(A) 13 ft., 4 in.
(B) 26 ft., 10 in.
(C) 13 ft., 11 in.
(D) 13 ft., 5 in.
(E) 10 ft., 3 in.

15. A lawn is 21 feet wide and 39 feet long. How much will it cost to weed and feed it if a gardening service charges $.40 per square yard for this treatment?

(A) $109.20
(B) $36.40
(C) $327.60
(D) $24.00
(E) $218.40

16. Amanda drove for 7 hours at a speed of 48 miles per hour. Her car gets 21 miles per gallon of gas. How many gallons of gas did she use?

(A) 24
(B) 14
(C) 18
(D) 16
(E) 21

17. Two partners operate a business that shows a profit for the year of $63,000. Their partnership agreement calls for them to share the profits in the ratio 5:4. How much of the profit should go to the partner who gets the larger share?

(A) $35,000
(B) $28,000
(C) $32,000
(D) $36,000
(E) $24,000

18. A purchaser paid $17.16 for an article that had recently been increased in price by 4%. What was the price of the article before the increase?

(A) $17.00
(B) $17.12
(C) $16.50
(D) $16.47
(E) $17.20

19. In a clothing factory, 5 workers finish production of 6 garments each per day, 3 others turn out 4 garments each per day, and one worker turns out 12 per day. What is the average number of garments produced per worker per day?

(A) $2\frac{2}{9}$
(B) 6
(C) 4
(D) $7\frac{1}{3}$
(E) $5\frac{1}{9}$

20. A man makes a 255-mile trip by car. He drives the first two hours at 45 miles per hour. At what speed must he travel for the remainder of the trip in order to arrive at his destination five hours after he started the trip?

(A) 31 mph
(B) 50 mph
(C) 51 mph
(D) 55 mph
(E) 49 mph

21. A contractor bids $300,000 as his price for erecting a building. He estimates that $\frac{1}{10}$ of this amount will be spent for masonry materials and labor, $\frac{1}{3}$ for lumber and carpentry, $\frac{1}{5}$ for plumbing and heating, and $\frac{1}{6}$ for electrical and lighting work. The remainder will be his profit. How much profit does he expect to make?

(A) $24,000
(B) $80,000
(C) $60,000
(D) $50,000
(E) $48,000

22. The list price of a TV set is $325, but the retailer offers successive discounts of 20% and 30%. What price would a customer actually pay?

(A) $182.00
(B) $270.00
(C) $162.50
(D) $176.67
(E) $235.50

23. A certain brand of motor oil is regularly sold at a price of two quart cans for $1.99. On a special sale, a carton containing six of the quart cans is sold for $5.43. What is the saving per quart if the oil is bought at the special sale?

(A) $.27
(B) $.09
(C) $.54
(D) $.5425
(E) $.18

24. A worker earns $7.20 an hour. She is paid time and a half for overtime beyond a 40-hour week. How much will she earn in a week in which she works 43 hours?

(A) $295.20
(B) $320.40
(C) $432.00
(D) $464.40
(E) $465.12

25. A tree 36 feet high casts a shadow 8 feet long. At the same time, another tree casts a shadow 6 feet long. How tall is the second tree?

(A) 30 ft.
(B) 27 ft.
(C) 24 ft.
(D) 32 ft.
(E) 28 ft.

SUBTEST #3: WORD KNOWLEDGE

25 Questions

DIRECTIONS: This part of the test measures verbal comprehension involving your ability to understand written language. For each question choose the answer that means the same as the capitalized word.

1. SIMULTANEOUS
   (A) versatile
   (B) imitation
   (C) false appearance
   (D) concurrent
   (E) indefinite

2. PARAGON
   (A) triangular structure
   (B) prototype
   (C) wax figure
   (D) partially departed
   (E) peacemaker

3. DEMONSTRABLE
   (A) evident
   (B) able to be refuted
   (C) able to be torn down
   (D) possessed by demons
   (E) countable

4. CONTROVERSY
   (A) vehicles moving together
   (B) a school of music
   (C) armed police force
   (D) disagreement
   (E) agreement to commit wrong

5. TEMERITY
   (A) automatic readings
   (B) presumptuous daring
   (C) mental communication
   (D) tiresome
   (E) story prepared for television

6. SCRUTINY
   (A) point of conscience or ethics
   (B) obligation
   (C) revolt of a ship's crew
   (D) careful inspection
   (E) a room adjoining the kitchen

7. JETTISON
   (A) discard
   (B) long pier
   (C) uninteresting or empty
   (D) build shoddily
   (E) compete for advantage

8. CONCILIATE
   (A) speak briefly
   (B) form in the mind
   (C) placate
   (D) set apart as sacred
   (E) confuse

9. ARBITRARY
   (A) orderly
   (B) fervent
   (C) lacking consistency
   (D) disputed
   (E) selected at random

10. ENVISAGE
    (A) conceive
    (B) wrap around
    (C) articulate
    (D) designate
    (E) paint one's face

AFOQT #2

11. SCLEROTIC

(A) mentally disturbed
(B) having hardened arteries
(C) remote
(D) despicable
(E) educational

12. PARTISAN

(A) adherent
(B) divided
(C) not complete
(D) over-hasty
(E) part of speech

13. INCEPTION

(A) careful examination
(B) divine guidance
(C) ever-present feature
(D) beginning
(E) revolt against authority

14. DERIVATIVE

(A) having a bad reputation
(B) disconnected
(C) serving to prove
(D) deprived of vitality
(E) following from

15. PERVASIVE

(A) influential
(B) focused on wrong
(C) lasting indefinitely
(D) on the outer part
(E) permeating

16. INANITY

(A) mental unbalance
(B) exemption from penalty
(C) statement lacking sense
(D) dishonesty
(E) official approval

17. PLAUSIBLE

(A) unemotional
(B) deniable
(C) believable
(D) great quantity
(E) flexible

18. CONDUCIVE

(A) able to transmit electricity
(B) contributive
(C) compressed
(D) simultaneous
(E) ignitable

19. ENSEMBLE

(A) coordinated group or outfit
(B) bring together
(C) naval officer rank
(D) rake with gunfire
(E) tail section

20. DELETERIOUS

(A) with careful thought
(B) behind schedule
(C) very tasty
(D) harmful
(E) removed from the total

21. LITIGATION

(A) marking or outlining
(B) coastland waters
(C) governmental ruling
(D) legal case
(E) chemical test for acid or base

22. IMPRIMATUR

(A) not having to do with monkeys
(B) improper
(C) signature
(D) official policy
(E) controversial decision

23. DECELERATE

(A) belittle
(B) remove approval
(C) speed up
(D) slow down
(E) deny

24. UNILATERAL

(A) obligating one side only
(B) the same throughout
(C) sideways motion
(D) wavelike motion
(E) having one compartment

25. INTRANSIGENT

(A) doing things in a new way
(B) knowing without being told
(C) in between boundaries
(D) courageous
(E) uncompromising

SUBTEST #4: MATH KNOWLEDGE

25 Questions

DIRECTIONS: This part of the test measures your ability to use learned mathematical relationships. Each problem is followed by five possible answers. Decide which one of the five answers is most nearly correct.

1. What is 4% of 0.0375?

   (A) 0.0015
   (B) 0.9375
   (C) 0.0775
   (D) 0.15
   (E) 0.015

2. What number multiplied by $\frac{2}{3}$ will give a product of 1?

   (A) $-\frac{2}{3}$
   (B) $-\frac{3}{2}$
   (C) $\frac{3}{2}$
   (D) $\frac{4}{6}$
   (E) $\frac{2}{3}$

3. What is the value of the expression $x^2 - 5xy + 2y$ if $x = 3$ and $y = -2$?

   (A) –25
   (B) –27
   (C) 32
   (D) 35
   (E) –32

4. Solve the following inequality: $x - 3 < 14$

   (A) $x < 11$
   (B) $x < 17$
   (C) $x = 11$
   (D) $x > 17$
   (E) $x > 11$

5. Multiply $7a^3b^2c$ by $3a^2b^4c^2$.

   (A) $10a^5b^6c^3$
   (B) $21a^5b^6c^2$
   (C) $21a^6b^8c^2$
   (D) $21a^5b^6c^3$
   (E) $10a^6b^8c^2$

6. A floor is made up of hexagonal tiles, some of which are black and some of which are white. Every black tile is completely surrounded by white tiles. How many white tiles are there around each black tile?

   (A) 4
   (B) 5
   (C) 6
   (D) 8
   (E) 7

7. The value of 8^0 is

   (A) 8
   (B) 0
   (C) 1
   (D) $\frac{1}{8}$
   (E) 80

8. If $2x - 3 = 37$, what is the value of x?

   (A) 17
   (B) 38
   (C) 20
   (D) 80
   (E) 34

AFOQT #2

9. An audience consists of M people. $\frac{2}{3}$ of the audience are adults. Of the adults, $\frac{1}{2}$ are males. How many adult males are in the audience?

(A) $\frac{1}{6}M$

(B) $M - \frac{2}{3} - \frac{1}{2}$

(C) $\frac{1}{3}M$

(D) $M - \frac{1}{3}$

(E) $\frac{2}{3}M$

10. What is the value of $(0.2)^3$?

(A) 0.008
(B) 0.8
(C) 0.006
(D) 0.6
(E) 0.06

11. If $x^2 + x = 6$, what is the value of x?

(A) 6 or −1
(B) 1 or −6
(C) 2 or −3
(D) 3 or −2
(E) 0 or −3

12. What is the number of square inches in the area of a circle whose diameter is 28 inches? $\left(\text{Use } \frac{22}{7} \text{ for the value of } \pi.\right)$

(A) 616
(B) 88
(C) 44
(D) 1,232
(E) 22

13. The expression $\frac{x^2+2x-3}{x+3}$ cannot be evaluated if x has a value of

(A) 0
(B) −1
(C) 3
(D) −3
(E) 1

14. If $\sqrt{x+11} = 9$, what is the value of x?

(A) −2
(B) −8
(C) 70
(D) 7
(E) 10

15. The points A (2, 7) and B (5, 11) are plotted on coordinate graph paper. What is the distance from A to B?

(A) 7
(B) 5
(C) 25
(D) 14
(E) 5

16. Solve the following equation for y:
$ay - bx = 2$

(A) $\frac{2+bx}{a}$

(B) $2 + bx - a$

(C) $\frac{2}{a-bx}$

(D) $\frac{2}{a} - bx$

(E) $bx - 2a$

17. For a special mission, one soldier is to be chosen at random from among three infantrymen, two artillerymen, and five tank crewmen. What is the probability that an infantryman will be chosen?

(A) $\frac{3}{10}$

(B) $\frac{1}{10}$

(C) $\frac{1}{3}$

(D) $\frac{3}{7}$

(E) $\frac{1}{7}$

18. A cylindrical post has a cross section that is a circle with a radius of 3 inches. A piece of cord can be wound around it exactly seven times. How long is the piece of cord? $\left(\text{Use } \frac{22}{7} \text{ as the value of } \pi.\right)$

(A) 66 in.
(B) 42 in.
(C) 198 in.
(D) 132 in.
(E) 84 in.

19. A naval task force is to be made up of a destroyer, a supply ship, and a submarine. If four destroyers, two supply ships, and three submarines are available from which to choose, how many different combinations are possible for the task force?

(A) 9
(B) 24
(C) 8
(D) 12
(E) 16

20. The basis of a cylindrical can is a circle whose diameter is 2 inches. Its height is 7 inches. How many cubic inches are there in the volume of the can? $\left(\text{Use } \frac{22}{7} \text{ for the value of } \pi.\right)$

(A) $12\frac{4}{7}$ cu. in.
(B) 22 cu. in.
(C) 44 cu. in.
(D) 88 cu. in.
(E) 66 cu. in.

21. A rectangular vegetable garden 16 yards long and 4 yards wide is completely enclosed by a fence. To reduce the amount of fencing used, the owner replaced the garden with a square one having the same area. How many yards of fencing did he save?

(A) 4
(B) 6
(C) 8
(D) 16
(E) 12

22. The value of $\sqrt{164}$ to the nearest integer is

(A) 18
(B) 108
(C) 42
(D) 13
(E) 26

AFOQT #2

23. What is the maximum number of boxes, each measuring 3 inches by 4 inches by 5 inches, that can be packed into a storage space measuring 1 foot by 2 feet by 2 feet, 1 inch?

(A) 120
(B) 60
(C) 15
(D) 48
(E) 24

24. A circle passes through the four vertices of a rectangle that is 8 feet long and 6 feet wide. How many feet are there in the radius of the circle?

(A) 14
(B) $2\frac{1}{2}$
(C) 10
(D) 5
(E) $7\frac{1}{2}$

25. There are 12 liters of a mixture of acetone in alcohol that is $33\frac{1}{3}$% acetone. How many liters of alcohol must be added to the mixture to reduce it to a mixture containing 25% acetone?

(A) 1
(B) 2
(C) 4
(D) 6
(E) 8

AFOQT #2

SUBTEST #5: READING COMPREHENSION

25 Questions

DIRECTIONS: This subtest measures your ability to read and understand written material. Each passage is followed by a series of multiple-choice questions. You are to choose the option that best answers the question based on the passage. No additional information or specific knowledge is needed.

Reading Passage for Questions 1–5

The State Partnership Program (SPP) is a joint Department of Defense (DoD) security cooperation program, managed and administered by the National Guard Bureau, executed and coordinated by the geographic combatant commands, with personnel provided by the Air and Army National Guard. It is an innovative, small-footprint tool that supports the security cooperation goals of the geographic combatant commanders and the U.S. Chief of Mission for the respective partner nation involved.

The SPP has built enduring relationships for more than 23 years that, as of the end of Fiscal Year (FY) 2016, included 70 partnerships with 76 countries spread across all six geographic combatant commands. By the end of FY 2016, three new partnerships had received initial approval from the Office of the Under Secretary of Defense for Policy, as well as Department of State concurrence, but designation of partner states by the Chief of the National Guard Bureau and final approval by the DoD had not yet been completed.

All 54 U.S. states and territories with National Guard elements have at least one SPP partnership. Over the course of more than two decades, the SPP has evolved to meet the changing requirements of the DoD's security cooperation efforts. From helping to reform Eastern Europe's military establishments after the Cold War to helping partner nations participate in coalition operations and improve their disaster response capabilities, the SPP's enduring relationships have provided uniquely valuable support in the accomplishment of geographic combatant commanders' security cooperation goals. The National Guard remains committed to maintaining the enduring relationships that the SPP provides to help ensure U.S. strategic access, sustain and increase U.S. presence and influence, and enhance partner nation defense, security force, and disaster response capabilities in support of regional U.S. goals.

The SPP builds cumulative benefits for both the United States and the partner nation over time through recurring individual, professional, and institutional contacts and relationships. These benefits go beyond just enhanced influence and access for the United States—they generate trust, the essential ingredient for successful operations when times are tough or when changes need to be made.

The invaluable trust engendered by enduring SPP relationships has, over the 23-year course of the program so far, resulted in a total of 38 partner nations who have deployed personnel in support of Operations Iraqi Freedom, Inherent Resolve, and Enduring Freedom, or the North Atlantic Treaty Organization (NATO)-led International Security Assistance Force (ISAF) in Afghanistan. Of those, 16 partner nations made co-deployment with personnel from their partner state a condition of their deployment in support of coalition operations, and 17 partner nations deployed forces to both Iraq and Afghanistan. Further, a total of 52 SPP partner nations—approximately three-quarters of the total—are contributing to or have contributed to United Nations peacekeeping missions around the world. These additional faces and forces not only demonstrate international support for multinational action in areas affected by international tensions and natural disasters, but they also reduce the amount of U.S. forces needed in those same areas.

1. The primary purpose of this passage is to provide

   (A) justification for funding the SPP in FY 2016.
   (B) an overview of how the SPP got started.
   (C) an overview of the SPP as a program at the end of FY 2016.
   (D) a history of SPP partner nations and coalition operations.
   (E) an accounting of SPP expenses during FY 2016.

2. In the last paragraph, the word "engendered" most nearly means

   (A) guided.
   (B) recognized.
   (C) degraded.
   (D) started and supported.
   (E) enabled.

3. You can infer from the passage that

   (A) the SPP has lost many of its original members.
   (B) the benefits that the U.S. receives due to the SPP go beyond just monetary measurements.
   (C) the SPP is primarily a program to benefit warfighting efforts.
   (D) the relationships between SPP participants are strictly professional.
   (E) the SPP requires a great deal of attention from both the DoD and the geographic combatant commanders.

4. As used throughout the passage, the term "partner nation" means

   (A) a foreign country partnered with the National Guard of a U.S. state or territory.
   (B) a foreign country with treaty obligations to the U.S.
   (C) the nation where a major U.S. exercise is held.
   (D) opponents to coalition activities.
   (E) a country that shares identical goals with the U.S.

5. With which statement would the author of this passage most likely agree?

   (A) "The SPP is a very expensive program that is difficult to fund."
   (B) "Security cooperation with friendly foreign nations strengthens the defense of both the U.S. and the friendly foreign nations."
   (C) "The U.S. has very few SPP partner nations, compared to the total number of nations in the world."
   (D) "The U.S. needs to mind its own business around the world unless another country asks for our help."
   (E) "Allies and partners do not need to practice or train together until attacked by an opponent."

Reading Passage for Questions 6–10

The United States relies on the Internet and the systems and data of cyberspace for a wide range of critical services. The Internet connects billions of people, helps deliver goods and services globally, and brings ideas and knowledge to those who would otherwise lack access. The United States' reliance on cyberspace leaves us vulnerable in the face of a real and dangerous cyber threat, as state and non-state actors plan to conduct disruptive and destructive cyberattacks on the networks of our critical infrastructure and steal U.S. intellectual property to undercut our technological and military advantage.

The DoD cyber strategy guides the development of its cyber forces to strengthen its cyber defense and cyber deterrence posture. The DoD's policy focuses on building cyber capabilities and organizations for its three cyber missions: defending DoD networks, systems, and information; defending the United States and its interests against cyberattacks of significant consequence; and providing integrated cyber capabilities to support military operations and contingency plans. The strategy sets five strategic goals and establishes specific objectives for the DoD to achieve over the next five years and beyond.

Today's cyberspace environment, including the increasing severity and sophistication of the cyber threat to U.S. interests, requires the DoD to maintain an updated strategy. The DoD has the largest network in the world, and it must take aggressive steps to defend its networks, secure its data, and mitigate risks to DoD missions. In 2012, the president directed the DoD to organize and plan to defend the nation against cyberattacks of significant consequence in concert with other U.S. government agencies, and the DoD soon began to build a Cyber Mission Force (CMF) to carry out its cyber missions.

To build the force of the future, the DoD must attract the best talent, the best ideas, and the best technology to public service. To do so, the DoD is building strong bridges to the private sector as well as to the research institutions that make the United States such an innovative nation. The private sector and America's research institutions design and build the networks of cyberspace, provide cybersecurity services, and research and develop advanced capabilities. The DoD continues its strong historic partnerships with the private sector and these research institutions, and it will strengthen those ties to discover and validate new ideas for cybersecurity for the DoD and for the country as a whole.

Deterrence is a key part of the DoD's cyber strategy. Deterrence of cyberattacks on U.S. interests will be achieved through the totality of U.S. actions, including stated policy, substantial indications and warning capabilities, defensive posture, effective response procedures, and the overall resiliency of U.S. networks and systems. The DoD is building and maintaining ready forces and capabilities to conduct cyberspace operations to defend the DoD Information Network (DoDIN), secure DoD data, and mitigate risks to DoD missions. The DoD will defend the U.S. homeland and our vital interests from significant disruptive or destructive cyberattacks. The DoD is building and maintaining viable cyber options and planning the use of those options to control conflict escalation and shape the conflict environment at all stages. It is also building and maintaining robust international alliances and partnerships to deter shared threats and increase international security and stability.

6. The primary purpose of this passage is to provide
   (A) justification for funding DoD cyber operations.
   (B) an overview of how DoD cyber defense efforts got started.
   (C) an overview of the DoD's cyberspace defense strategy.
   (D) a history of DoD cyber defensive and offensive operations after 2012.
   (E) a status report of the operational capability of the Cyber Mission Force.

7. In the second paragraph, the word "strategic" most nearly means
   (A) over-arching, high-level.
   (B) dramatic, distinctive.
   (C) well-defined.
   (D) interconnected with international partners.
   (E) speculative.

8. You can infer from the passage that
   (A) the DoD understands that a certain number of cyberattacks by adversarial nation-states will succeed.
   (B) the DoD understands that it must stand alone among all U.S. government agencies to defend the homeland against cyberattacks.
   (C) the DoD will focus the greatest amount of its energy on developing cyberattack capabilities to deter potential adversaries.
   (D) there are cyber components to many DoD operations around the world.
   (E) the DoD will assume responsibility for comprehensive cyber defense of U.S. small businesses to maintain our economic edge.

9. As used throughout the passage, the term "deterrence" means
   (A) discouraging potential attackers.
   (B) an incidental part of U.S. cyber strategy.
   (C) conducting preventive cyberattacks on enemies who are likely to attack us.
   (D) defining risks to our shared significant cyber capabilities.
   (E) providing detailed open information about DoD systems to show potential attackers our resilience.

10. With which statement would the author of this passage most likely agree?
   (A) "Cyber system redundancy is the most effective way to defend against cyberattacks on key systems."
   (B) "National cyber security is a key element of national survival in the 21st century."
   (C) "The United States is strong enough and advanced enough that it doesn't have to put much effort into cyber defense."
   (D) "Cyber defense is the primary responsibility of the Department of Defense."
   (E) "Fortunately, the DoD has a sufficient number of cyber experts now employed so it does not have to actively recruit any new ones in the near future."

Reading Passage for Questions 11–15

The Air Force core values are a statement of the institutional values and principles of conduct that provide the moral framework for military activities. The professional Air Force ethic consists of three fundamental and enduring values: *integrity first, service before self,* and *excellence in all we do.* This ethic is the set of values that guide the way Airmen live and perform. Success hinges on the incorporation of these values into the character of every Airman. In today's time-compressed, dynamic, and dangerous operational environment, an Airman does not have the luxury of examining each issue at leisure. He or she must fully internalize these values in order to be better prepared in all situations—to maintain integrity, to serve others before self, to perform with excellence, and to encourage others to do the same. The Air Force core values are a commitment that each Airman makes when joining the Air Force. These values provide a foundation for leadership, decision-making, and success, no matter the level of an Airman's assignment, the difficulty of the task at hand, or the dangers presented by the mission.

There are four reasons why the Air Force recognizes these core values as fundamental to its people:

- The core values identify the attributes all Airmen should have. All Air Force personnel must possess integrity first. A person's "self" must take a back seat to Air Force service: rules must be acknowledged and followed faithfully; other personnel must be respected as persons of fundamental worth; discipline and self-control must be demonstrated always; and there must be faith in the system. The Air Force demands that each of us place service before self. It is imperative that we seek excellence in all we do—whether the form is product or service excellence, resources excellence, community excellence, or operations excellence.
- The core values point to what is universal and unchanging in the profession of arms. The values are road signs that invite us to consider key features of the requirements of professional service, but they cannot hope to point to or pick out everything. By examining integrity, service, and excellence, we also eventually discover the importance of duty, honor, country, dedication, fidelity, competence, and a host of other professional requirements and attributes.
- They help us get a fix on the ethical climate of an organization. Big-ticket scandals grow out of a climate of ethical erosion. Because some believe our operating procedures or the requirements levied upon them from above are absurd, they tend to "cut corners" or "skate by." As time goes by, these actions become easier, and they become habitual until the person can no longer distinguish between the "important" tasking or rules and the "stupid" ones. Lying on official forms becomes second nature. Placing personal interests ahead of the mission becomes a natural response. These individuals then develop a "good enough for government work" mentality. In such a climate of corrosion, the core values can bring a person back to recognition of what is important: integrity, service, and excellence.
- They serve as beacons vectoring us back to the path of professional conduct. Adherence to the core values ensures that the Air Force will not degrade from a climate of ethical commitment into a climate of corrosion.

The Air Force recognizes these core values as universal and unchanging in the profession of arms. They provide the standards with which to evaluate the ethical climate of all Air Force organizations. Finally, when needed in the cauldron of war, they are the beacons vectoring the individual back to the path of professional conduct and the highest ideals of integrity, service, and excellence.

11. From the specific examples mentioned, you can infer from the passage that

    (A) these core values have not always been universally applied.
    (B) these core values have historically been consistently applied.
    (C) other, more detailed, standards and requirements are not needed if these values are observed and applied.
    (D) standards and requirements for ethical conduct change over time, even if slowly.
    (E) these core values only apply to peacetime service, not to the stresses of combat operations.

12. The primary purpose of this passage is to

    (A) fully explore the importance of Air Force core values in everyday life.
    (B) focus on the most important Air Force core values and why they predominate.
    (C) articulate how the values and standards that derive from these core values support specific standards and requirements.
    (D) provide an overview of Air Force core values and explain why they are important.
    (E) explain why balancing the core values is important as situations change over time.

13. In the fourth bullet point and in the last paragraph, the word "vectoring" most nearly means

    (A) consistently pushing.
    (B) guiding and directing.
    (C) holding up as a standard.
    (D) including in ongoing movements.
    (E) stopping or obstructing.

14. With which statement would the author of this passage most likely disagree?

    (A) "Core values identify the principles by which all people, military or civilian, should live by."
    (B) "Core values should reflect the changing nature of the profession of arms."
    (C) "Core values identify organizational principles of conduct that provide the moral framework for military activities around the world."
    (D) "By examining integrity, service, and excellence, we also eventually discover the importance of many other professional requirements and attributes."
    (E) "Placing personal interests ahead of the mission becomes a natural response when the core value of selfless service is ignored."

15. According to the passage, Air Force success

    (A) is a function of balancing these core values against operational requirements as situations change and evolve.
    (B) is the product of enlightened leadership, superior technology, and correct application of doctrine.
    (C) depends on every Airman's personal values that he or she learned as he or she grew up and matured professionally.
    (D) hinges on the incorporation of these values into the character of every Airman.
    (E) comes from taking the time to think about how to apply these core principles to every situation.

Reading Passage for Questions 16–20

In the 23 months of its World War II existence, the 15th Air Force—operating mostly from a complex of airfields in southern Italy previously used by Axis forces—destroyed all gasoline production within range in southern Europe; knocked out all the major aircraft factories in its area of operations; and destroyed 6,282 enemy aircraft in the air or on the ground.

The 15th Air Force crippled the Axis transportation system throughout half of occupied Europe with repeated fighter and bomber attacks, sometimes also helping to disperse enemy counterattacks or paving the way for advancing Allied land forces. The 15th Air Force dropped 303,842 tons of bombs on enemy targets in nine countries across Europe, including military installations in eight capital cities. Its combat personnel made 148,955 heavy bomber sorties and 87,732 fighter sorties against the enemy. It lost 3,364 aircraft and 21,617 personnel killed, wounded, missing, or taken prisoner—20,430 bomber crewmen and 1,187 fighter pilots.

The 15th Air Force's overall mission was to attack enemy oil facilities, air forces, communications, and ground forces. Most vital of the 15th Air Force's oil-related targets was the complex of refineries in Ploesti, Romania, which contributed almost a third of the entire Axis oil and gasoline supply. Ploesti was protected by three German and Romanian fighter groups, as well as by hundreds of well-concealed and well-integrated heavy and medium caliber antiaircraft guns, when the 15th Air Force, along with the night bombers of the Royal Air Force (RAF) 205th Group, conducted a series of attacks from April 5 to August 19, 1944. The 15th Air Force and RAF bombers flew 5,287 sorties, dropping 12,870 tons of bombs. The cost was 237 Allied heavy bombers (15 of them RAF), 10 dive bombers, and 39 escort fighters. More than 2,200 American Airmen were lost, but the campaign reduced the Axis refineries' production to only 10 percent of previous levels. The 15th Air Force followed up the Ploesti attacks by dropping 10,000 tons of bombs on three synthetic oil plants in Silesia and one in Poland. By February 1945, the 15th Air Force's attacks reduced these plants' combined production to 20 percent of what it had been eight months before.

The 15th Air Force also contributed significantly to Allied air supremacy in Europe by conducting devastating attacks on German fighter manufacturing complexes in Wiener Neustadt and Regensburg. By May 1944, these facilities were only producing about 250 aircraft a month instead of the Axis' planned production of 650 aircraft a month. Even during the campaigns against enemy oil facilities and air forces, the 15th Air Force was also attacking enemy communications and transportation systems far behind the front lines, disrupting supply movement from Axis industrial centers within an 800-mile radius of the 15th Air Force's Italian airfields.

The 15th Air Force also supported ground operations in Italy, bombing Axis targets at Salerno, Anzio, and Cassino during the Rome campaign. On April 15, 1945, the 15th Air Force put up a record-breaking 93 percent of its available aircraft to soften up the approaches to Bologna in one of the final missions of the Italian campaign.

A unique aspect of the 15th Air Force's operations was the rescue and repatriation of aircrews shot down in enemy territory. No other air force conducted escape operations in so many countries. The 15th Air Force returned 5,650 personnel by air, surface vessel, or on foot through enemy lines. In more than 300 "reunion" operations, the 15th Air Force brought Airmen safely back from Tunisia, Italy, France, Switzerland, Greece, Albania, Bulgaria, Romania, Hungary, Yugoslavia, Austria, and Germany.

16. The primary purpose of this passage is to
   (A) provide a record of the individual heroism and grit of the 15th Air Force's WWII leadership.
   (B) summarize the 15th Air Force's operations in Italy during WWII.
   (C) recount the 15th Air Force's unique contribution to rescuing downed aircrews.
   (D) applaud the 15th Air Force's outstanding aircraft maintenance and repair capabilities and achievements.
   (E) detail the 15th Air Force's contributions to the Ploesti oil facility bombing efforts.

17. In the fourth paragraph, the word "devastating" is used to mean
   (A) representing the moral superiority of the Allied cause versus the Axis cause.
   (B) resulting from careful planning by American and British air staffs.
   (C) causing great emotional distress because of the loss of life.
   (D) causing heavy damage to German aircraft manufacturing facilities.
   (E) causing severe casualties among the Allied bomber crews.

18. What was the primary way that the 15th Air Force's attacks on Axis oil facilities and aircraft manufacturing complexes contributed to Allied air supremacy?
   (A) They demoralized enemy workers and military strategists.
   (B) They reduced the amount of oil and gasoline available for aircraft manufacturing facilities.
   (C) They reduced the number of cargo aircraft available to resupply Axis troops.
   (D) They demoralized the civilian population, which started opposing the Nazi regime.
   (E) They reduced the number of enemy aircraft available to oppose Allied operations.

19. Which of the following statements could you infer based on information in the passage?
   (A) The ground operations at Salerno and Anzio led to heavy casualties due to stiff German resistance and poor Allied planning.
   (B) The 15th Air Force was deactivated after almost two years of operations in Italy.
   (C) The Wiener Neustadt and Regensburg aircraft facilities were two of the three largest Axis aircraft manufacturing complexes.
   (D) The 15th Air Force commenced operations on November 1, 1943, with six heavy bomber groups and three fighter groups transferred from the previously existing 12th Air Force.
   (E) The low-level raids on Ploesti by Eighth and Ninth Air Force bombers on August 1, 1944, were costly and not very effective.

20. With which one of the following statements would the passage's author likely agree?
   (A) "The 15th Air Force played a major role in the successful Allied landings at Normandy."
   (B) "The 15th Air Force greatly decreased Axis oil production in southern Italy."
   (C) "The 15th Air Force played a major role in the Allied victory over the Axis powers in WWII."
   (D) "The 15th Air Force played a major role in the Allied reconquest of Italy."
   (E) "The 15th Air Force made a major contribution in the Allied liberation of Italy."

Reading Passage for Questions 21–25

More than 1,100 U.S. institutions of higher learning offer military precommissioning training in Reserve Officer Training Corps (ROTC) programs under Title 10, U.S. Code. Six of those schools are designated in law as Senior Military Colleges (SMCs):

- Norwich University, Northfield, VT (1813)
- The Virginia Military Institute, Lexington, VA (1839)
- The Citadel, Charleston, SC (1842)
- The University of North Georgia (formerly North Georgia College), Dahlonega, GA (1873)
- The Virginia Polytechnic Institute and State University (commonly known as Virginia Tech), Blacksburg, VA (1872)
- Texas A&M University, College Station, TX (1876)

SMCs differ from other colleges and universities in that they have a "full-time" uniformed Corps of Cadets with its own identity outside the ROTC programs. This provides a daily military environment in which the cadets are subject to military discipline. SMC cadets do not incur a military obligation by membership in their school's Corps of Cadets, but SMC ROTC graduates are guaranteed an active duty commission if desired upon graduation. Additionally, the Defense Department can, without notice, close, reduce, or suspend regular ROTC programs during a total mobilization to make the cadre available for assignment elsewhere—but not so for the SMCs.

All six SMCs started as military colleges or academies, but now all but one (VMI) allow civilian students, too. Five of the six SMCs (all but the University of North Georgia) offer Army, Air Force, and Navy/Marine ROTC—and average Corps of Cadets membership at both Texas A&M and The Citadel usually exceeds 2,000, making them the nation's largest cadet organizations outside the federal service academies. One SMC is a private school (Norwich), while the other five are state-supported.

However, despite their differences, all six SMCs share a dedication to academic excellence—perhaps because of their military-driven focus on mission accomplishment, adherence to standards, and the highest levels of professional and personal conduct. The five public SMCs are all ranked in the 25 "Top Public Schools" nationwide, and all are ranked in the top 100 schools nationally or in their region. Four are ranked in the top 30 nationally for their undergraduate engineering programs, and three are ranked in the top 25 for best value by two major publications.

The SMCs' traditions of excellence and dedication to service are well demonstrated by the accomplishments of their alumni, many of whom did not graduate because military service got in the way—sometimes permanently. Especially at the outbreak of World War I and World War II, many SMC students resigned to enlist immediately; some did not return.

The Citadel lists 289 general or flag officers among its former students, including five four-star and 32 three-star officers. Eleven Medal of Honor recipients were Citadel alumni.

There are 138 Norwich University graduates who have served as U.S. general or flag officers, plus another 26 graduates who served as generals in foreign armies. Eight Norwich alumni have received the Medal of Honor.

During World War II, more than 14,000 Texas A&M alumni ("Aggies") served as officers—more than the U.S. Military and Naval academies combined, and more than three times the contribution of any other SMC. Since its founding, some 269 Texas A&M alumni have achieved flag rank, including nine four-stars and 31 three-stars. Eight Aggies have been awarded the Medal of Honor.

The University of North Georgia lists 54 general or flag officers (admirals) among their alumni, including two four-stars, seven three-stars, and one Medal of Honor recipient.

Seven VMI alumni have received the Medal of Honor, and 266 have served as U.S. generals or admirals—in fact, VMI is the only U.S. military college whose graduates include the top four-star generals of three services: two Marine Corps Commandants, a Chief of Staff of the Army, and a Chief of Staff of the Air Force. Another 16 alumni have gone on to flag rank in foreign militaries.

Virginia Tech alumni rolls include seven Medal of Honor recipients and 97 general officers and admirals, including three four-star and 11 three-star officers. The class with the greatest number of flag officers was the Class of 1941.

21. The primary purpose of this passage is to
    (A) compare the number of generals and admirals between the SMCs.
    (B) compare and contrast the size of the SMCs.
    (C) validate the SMCs' ROTC suspension exclusion in times of full mobilization.
    (D) provide an overview of Senior Military College enrollment.
    (E) explain what Senior Military Colleges are and why they are important.

22. In the first paragraph, the word "precommissioning" most nearly means
    (A) in preparation for being commissioned as an officer.
    (B) in preparation for entering into naval service.
    (C) before receiving a security clearance.
    (D) in preparation for being a noncommissioned officer.
    (E) in preparation for being a general officer.

23. From the information in the passage, you can infer that
    (A) some of the Medal of Honor winners from Virginia Tech may have fought in the Civil War.
    (B) some of the graduates from The Citadel may have fought in the Civil War.
    (C) some of the general officers from Texas A&M may have fought during the War of 1812.
    (D) the University of North Georgia is preparing future admirals.
    (E) all the SMCs' alumni are also graduates of their respective schools.

24. According to the passage, which of these statements is not true?
    (A) Some Norwich and VMI graduates have gone on to high rank in foreign military establishments.
    (B) The SMCs focus more on military excellence and precommissioning training than on academic programs.
    (C) Five of the six SMCs offer all three types of ROTC.
    (D) SMC cadets do not incur a military obligation just by being members of their school's Corps of Cadets.
    (E) More Texas A&M alumni served as officers in WWII than the combined total of officers from the U.S. Naval Academy and Military Academy.

25. With which statement would the author of this passage most likely agree?
    (A) "The law should be changed to treat SMCs the same as other schools that offer ROTC."
    (B) "The benefits of the SMCs are not enough to continue the extra investment they require."
    (C) "The benefits of the SMCs more than compensate for the extra investment they require."
    (D) "SMC graduates on the whole don't perform any better than graduates from regular colleges with ROTC."
    (E) "SMC programs focus too much on military preparation and not enough on academics."

SUBTEST #6: SITUATIONAL JUDGMENT

50 Questions

DIRECTIONS: This subtest measures your judgment in responding to interpersonal situations similar to those you may encounter as an officer. Your responses will be scored relative to the consensus judgment of a wide sample of experienced U.S. Air Force officers. For each situation, you must respond to two questions. First, select which one of the five actions listed you judge as the MOST EFFECTIVE action in response to the situation. Second, select which one of the five actions listed you judge as the LEAST EFFECTIVE action in response to the situation.

NOTE: Select only one action (A–E) for each question.

Situation 1. You have been assigned to a high-level staff in a new organization that deals with technical subject matter that you are experienced with. During the first few months, your supervisor took extra time and effort to familiarize you with local procedures and contacts, coaching you through your first several major projects. Now you believe that you can handle more autonomy and independence in the course of fulfilling your duties and that you don't need as much of your supervisor looking over your shoulder, even though it was helpful in the beginning. What do you do?

Possible actions:

(A) Pay extra attention to the quality of your work—both content and form—to show your supervisor that you can handle things on your own now.

(B) Ask for a meeting with your supervisor to discuss your working relationship.

(C) Ask for advice from a more experienced coworker after your first annual performance evaluation.

(D) Decrease your level of contact with your supervisor, ask fewer questions, and make more decisions without consultation; he will get the hint.

(E) Send your supervisor an e-mail, respectfully requesting less close supervision so that you can get more experience doing your own work.

1. Select the MOST EFFECTIVE action (A–E) in response to the situation.

2. Select the LEAST EFFECTIVE action (A–E) in response to the situation.

Situation 2. You are being promoted to replace your previous supervisor and supervise the section in which you already work. The section consists of two teams, with a dozen people total, whom you appreciate—they are hard-working, collaborative, and focused on mission accomplishment. Your personal relationships with them are solid, you believe that they support you, and you believe that you can lead and motivate them. You feel concerned, however, about the tight deadlines that your section has to meet on a regular basis due to its mission. Which of the following would be the most and least helpful in meeting the section's deadlines?

Possible actions:

(A) Use your good relationship with all of the section members to motivate them.

(B) Visit with all of the section members individually to get an update on their progress.

(C) Schedule work assignments transparently and regularly have team leaders update you on their progress and challenges.

(D) Delegate tasks to the two team leaders, and minimize contact with the other section members.

(E) Send regular e-mail reminders about deadlines to all of the section members.

3. Select the MOST EFFECTIVE action (A–E) in response to the situation.

4. Select the LEAST EFFECTIVE action (A–E) in response to the situation.

Situation 3. You are assigned to take over a 20-Airman security forces squad. An initial walk through the arms room shows that many weapons are not only dirty, but some are even rusty. You call your four fire team leaders together and tell them that weapons will be cleaned to standard today before anyone is released to go home. You instruct the team leaders to inspect every weapon in their team by 1600 and that you will inspect a sampling across the teams by 1700. At 1630, your sampling shows that most weapons are still unacceptable. What do you do?

Possible actions:

(A) Re-emphasize the importance of clean and serviceable weapons to the fire team leaders, and then release everyone for the day.

(B) Tell the fire team leaders that you will re-inspect a sampling of the weapons at 1800 tonight; no one goes home until they are clean.

(C) Tell the fire team leaders you will re-inspect all weapons at noon tomorrow and that no one will go home tomorrow until all weapons are satisfactory.

(D) Tell the fire team leaders that you are going to write them up for failing to supervise their Airmen adequately.

(E) Conduct an in-ranks inspection of the entire squad at 1700.

5. Select the MOST EFFECTIVE action (A–E) in response to the situation.

6. Select the LEAST EFFECTIVE action (A–E) in response to the situation.

Situation 4. You are working on a research and analysis project with a peer coworker who just went on sick leave, but who is scheduled to return tomorrow. The project is ultimately to support the operations of another squadron. You are glad that your coworker is returning soon because the deadline assigned by your mutual supervisor is now only a week away. Suddenly, you learn that your coworker's sick leave is being extended for four weeks. Your work on the project is at a standstill because it depends on the work your colleague was supposed to do. What do you do?

Possible actions:

(A) Await the return of your colleague since your work has gone as far as it can without your coworker's input.

(B) Inform your supervisor of the project's status, and ask for someone else to work with you on it.

(C) Call your working-level contact in the squadron who will ultimately receive the project, and ask him or her to extend the deadline.

(D) Inform your supervisor of the project's status, and ask if you should finish it on your own.

(E) Inform your supervisor of the project's status, and ask for an extension so that your coworker can do his part of the work.

7. Select the MOST EFFECTIVE action (A–E) in response to the situation.

8. Select the LEAST EFFECTIVE action (A–E) in response to the situation.

Situation 5. Your section is assigned to work on a project that will potentially revolutionize flightline maintenance operations throughout the Air Force. Your flight leader meets with you to go over the details together and establish specific tasks and milestones. He tells you that completing this project to a high standard would not only increase aircraft availability by up to 20 percent, but it would also put the whole squadron in the lead for an Air Force or even Department of Defense maintenance unit award. What do you do?

Possible actions:

(A) Gather the entire section, ask for their ideas on the project, and then assign tasks for each individual based on their skills. Schedule weekly full-section meetings where everyone can share their progress and exchange ideas.

(B) Send an e-mail to the two team leaders in the section, introducing the project and delegating tasks to each section. Emphasize the project's importance, and ask them to stay focused on it, putting it as a high priority and contacting you about any difficulties.

(C) Take an active part in the project by assigning the most crucial tasks to yourself; use the most experienced team members for other assignments.

(D) Meet with the team leaders to brainstorm ways to approach the project, and then meet with the entire section to give everyone the full scope of the project, laying out tasks for each section and emphasizing the project's importance.

(E) To get the section to feel involved and take responsibility, have a section meeting to introduce the project and its required tasks. Then let everyone choose what they want to work on individually.

9. Select the MOST EFFECTIVE action (A–E) in response to the situation.

10. Select the LEAST EFFECTIVE action (A–E) in response to the situation.

Situation 6. After completing a tour as an instructor for field medics, you have been assigned as a grader for the base-wide medical recertification field training exercise. MSgt. McCann—who is now your section leader—goes through your station and fails the task because he exceeded the time standard by four seconds. Just before you record the score, MSgt. McCann pulls you aside. "I need this certification, or I will be reassigned out of my specialty," he says, "and you know I can't get promoted if I am not assigned to a job in my specialty. You can really help me out here. It's only four seconds, no big deal, right? How about showing a little loyalty?" What do you do?

Possible actions:

(A) It's obvious that MSgt. McCann knows his stuff but is just a little rusty. Mark him as passing.

(B) As your section leader, MSgt. McCann can make your life from here on out easy or hard. Mark him as passing.

(C) Tell MSgt. McCann that you can't mark him as passing when he didn't pass and that you are going to report the fact that he even asked for you to mark him as passing. When the exercise is over, though, ask for a transfer.

(D) Tell MSgt. McCann that as much as you want to help him out, your highest loyalty is to the Airmen to whom your section will have to provide medical treatment and that you will help him out after hours with his skills so he can pass a retest.

(E) In the spirit of cooperation, tell MSgt. McCann that you will pass him if you can take your upcoming vacation with your family without being charged for the leave days.

11. Select the MOST EFFECTIVE action (A–E) in response to the situation.

12. Select the LEAST EFFECTIVE action (A–E) in response to the situation.

Situation 7. You are a project leader, responsible for coordinating the activities of four team members. You find out that two team members won't be able to meet the agreed-upon internal deadlines for their share of the tasks. Even after all four team members finish their work, you will still need time to consolidate their input and put the project into its final form. In a recent meeting, your squadron commander had reminded everyone of the importance of meeting deadlines. What do you do?

Possible actions:

(A) Give some of the workload from the two team members who are having difficulties to the two who aren't having difficulties; do not cut into the time you have for final project consolidation.
(B) Discuss the cause of the delays with the two team members who are having difficulties, evaluate the remaining workload and time available, and determine an action plan to finish the project on time.
(C) Shorten the time you have allowed for project consolidation, and require daily updates from the two team members who are having difficulties.
(D) Ask the two team members who are behind to work additional hours in order to meet their deadlines.
(E) Ask for an extension of the project deadline, mentioning the two team members who are having difficulties.

13. Select the MOST EFFECTIVE action (A–E) in response to the situation.

14. Select the LEAST EFFECTIVE action (A–E) in response to the situation.

Situation 8. You are in a meeting with several peers where one of the members is acting in a very disruptive manner, making negative and sarcastic remarks and not respecting anyone else's input, and in general is making it very difficult for the meeting to accomplish its purpose. What do you do?

Possible actions:

(A) Speak to the individual directly but professionally during the meeting.
(B) Speak to the individual privately after the meeting.
(C) Leave the individual alone, and continue the meeting as well as possible.
(D) Speak to your supervisor after the meeting.
(E) Speak to his supervisor after the meeting.

15. Select the MOST EFFECTIVE action (A–E) in response to the situation.

16. Select the LEAST EFFECTIVE action (A–E) in response to the situation.

Situation 9. You just completed a course at your supervisor's request. While at the course, you learned that some of your unit's procedures are not in line with broader Air Force and Department of Defense policies on protecting personal and confidential information. Everyone in your unit at your level and up has already completed the same course, including your supervisor and her boss, but to your knowledge no one has identified this inconsistency. You will be the first to draw attention to your unit's incorrect procedures. What do you do?

Possible actions:

(A) Send an e-mail to everyone in your unit, with copies of higher policies attached, and tell them that they need to start observing the correct procedures.
(B) Copy the relevant pages from the course materials, and put them on your supervisor's desk.
(C) Send the course materials and the higher policies to your supervisor, and cc her supervisor to get the quickest leadership emphasis on correcting your unit's procedures.
(D) Speak with your supervisor immediately, give her copies of the relevant policies, and ask if you can help implement the correct procedures.
(E) Ask the course instructor to contact your supervisor to discuss correct procedures in this area.

17. Select the MOST EFFECTIVE action (A–E) in response to the situation.

18. Select the LEAST EFFECTIVE action (A–E) in response to the situation.

Situation 10. You are in charge of security for U.S. forces at a joint overseas base occupied by both U.S. forces and a partner nation. Military personnel from the partner nation are responsible for manning a number of entry checkpoints and guarding several secure areas. However, there have been four incidents in three days where local civilian contractors from the partner nation have either entered the base without being checked or have wandered into what are supposed to be secure areas. What do you do?

Possible actions:

(A) Assign U.S. troops to periodically monitor the partner nation's guards.
(B) Discuss the recent lapses with the partner nation guard force commander, and ask him to encourage his guards to do a better job.
(C) Ask your commander to tell his partner nation counterpart that he is assigning all guard duties to U.S. troops.
(D) Tell the partner nation guard force commander forcefully that his guards are doing a poor job, and do it in front of witnesses so that he can't cover it up.
(E) After clearing it with your own commander, suggest to the partner nation guard force commander that checkpoints and area patrols be jointly manned by partner nation and U.S. troops to provide additional intercultural training for both guard forces.

19. Select the MOST EFFECTIVE action (A–E) in response to the situation.

20. Select the LEAST EFFECTIVE action (A–E) in response to the situation.

Situation 11. You are part of a working group for a project involving landing rights for an international security cooperation exercise. You have to work with a member of another staff section in your headquarters. Your staff section's principal (i.e., senior officer) has determined a well-defined, specific plan of action for each step in the project. After a week has passed, you realize that your colleague from the other staff section is not following the plan and that he is not meeting his intermediate milestone objectives, which is having a negative effect on the overall progress of the project. What do you do?

Possible actions:

(A) Discuss the situation with your colleague and together formulate a plan to make up for lost time to achieve the project's deadline.

(B) Update the head of the working group so that he can discuss the situation with your colleague in the other staff section.

(C) Send your colleague an e-mail, asking him if there is something wrong and cc his supervisor and your supervisor.

(D) Wait for the work done by the other staff section's representative to catch up to the plan. In the meantime, focus on your own intermediate objectives.

(E) Update your first-line supervisor so that she can talk to your colleague's supervisor.

21. Select the MOST EFFECTIVE action (A–E) in response to the situation.

22. Select the LEAST EFFECTIVE action (A–E) in response to the situation.

Situation 12. In order to get to where you can guide ammunition and medical resupply back to your unit, which is in contact with the enemy, you find that you must cross a stream that is about 40 feet wide. Time is critical. A blizzard has been blowing all day, and the stream is frozen over—but because of the snow, you can't tell how thick the ice is. You see two planks about 10 feet long near the point where you want to cross. You also see on your map that there is a bridge about two miles downstream. What do you do?

Possible actions:

(A) Walk very slowly and carefully across the ice.

(B) Run rapidly across the ice.

(C) Walk the two miles downstream to the bridge, and use it to cross over.

(D) Cross with the aid of the planks, pushing one ahead of the other and walking on them.

(E) Break a hole in the ice near the edge of the stream to see how deep the stream is.

23. Select the MOST EFFECTIVE action (A–E) in response to the situation.

24. Select the LEAST EFFECTIVE action (A–E) in response to the situation.

Situation 13. You just attended a two-day internal training class presented by your section leader. While talking with other members of your section privately after the class, several of them were critical of how your section leader presented the large amount of material. You believe that your section leader is unaware of this feedback—and besides, you thought the presentation of the material in the class was adequate, and even good in spots. What do you do?

Possible actions:

(A) Don't mention any feedback about the class to your section leader.

(B) Thank your section leader for the class, and tell him that you think it went well; don't mention the reactions of the other section members.

(C) Tell the other section members that they ought to give their feedback to the section leader if they feel strongly about it.

(D) Tell your section leader about the negative feedback from the other section members without bringing up any names.

(E) Suggest to the section leader that he conduct an after-action review, where everyone is encouraged to voice their feedback, even if it is negative.

25. Select the MOST EFFECTIVE action (A–E) in response to the situation.

26. Select the LEAST EFFECTIVE action (A–E) in response to the situation.

Situation 14. The base where you are stationed is on the edge of a large city. A fellow section member and friend has told you he is under constant financial stress due to loans he obtained before joining the Air Force as well as due to current expenses. He is married with two children, and he has recently gotten a second job on the weekends to pay his bills; you believe this is a little risky because your unit sometimes has weekend exercises. You have noticed that since he has had this second job, the quality of his work has gone down. What do you do as a first step?

Possible actions:

(A) Lend your coworker some money to get him over the hump.

(B) Discuss your concerns with your coworker.

(C) Discuss your concerns with the section leader.

(D) Suggest to your coworker that he speak with a financial consultant.

(E) Discuss your concerns with your coworker's spouse.

27. Select the MOST EFFECTIVE action (A–E) in response to the situation.

28. Select the LEAST EFFECTIVE action (A–E) in response to the situation.

Situation 15. Among other duties, you provide administrative support to a large team of government civilian engineers. Due to the many projects your office handles, all engineers are required to enter the time they spend on specific projects into a database so that costs can be allocated appropriately. Last month, as a favor to one engineer who was having personal problems, you entered the data for his time spent per project. Now, the rest of the engineers are expecting you to do the same for them. It's not part of your job requirement and would prevent you from accomplishing most, if not all, of your assigned responsibilities. What do you do?

Possible actions:

(A) Enter the engineers' time-per-project data as they now expect.
(B) Offer to enter all the engineers' time-per-project data, but only if they take you to lunch once a week.
(C) Remind all the engineers that it is their responsibility to enter in their own data, and decline any future requests.
(D) Intentionally enter incorrect data for all the engineers into the database to guarantee that they don't ask you again.
(E) Ask your supervisor to convince the engineers to take responsibility for entering their own time-per-project data.

29. Select the MOST EFFECTIVE action (A–E) in response to the situation.

30. Select the LEAST EFFECTIVE action (A–E) in response to the situation.

Situation 16. You work in a large resource management office, part of a four-person team (all with different portfolios) under the same section leader and the flight leader above her. Another team member has asked you to review a report that he will present at this week's team meeting, to be led by the section leader, with the flight leader also probably attending. Although the part of the report that your colleague shows you seems fine, you notice that the analysis in another section seems to be missing some important conclusions, which is not up to established standards. Your colleague seems satisfied about that part of the report and doesn't seem to be interested in your assessment of it. What do you do?

Possible actions:

(A) Stay out of it. If your colleague isn't interested in your opinion, that's up to him—and there's always the chance that you are mistaken.
(B) Let it go right now, but ask questions during the presentation that make the missing conclusions noticeable.
(C) Discuss it with your mutual section leader, and try to get her to persuade your colleague of those conclusions' importance.
(D) Discuss your concerns with your colleague, and explain the logic of your recommendation to add the missing conclusions.
(E) Try to get the other team members to persuade your colleague that he needs to add the missing conclusions.

31. Select the MOST EFFECTIVE action (A–E) in response to the situation.

32. Select the LEAST EFFECTIVE action (A–E) in response to the situation.

Situation 17. After 18 months as section leader, your flight leader appointed an individual previously unknown to you as your assistant section leader. This individual immediately came across to you and the rest of the section as self-serving, arrogant, and disloyal, and the last three weeks have been very stressful. Your section's morale, which was previously superb, is now passing mediocre on the way to terrible. Now, the flight leader is asking for your recommendation about sending your assistant section leader to a month-long military school that will probably result in her transfer to a different squadron for a position of greater responsibility. It would also accelerate her chances for promotion to the same rank that you hold. What do you do?

Possible actions:
(A) Since this school will almost certainly result in her transfer, you tell your flight leader that you support her attending that school.
(B) You tell your flight leader that you support sending her to that school since the idea came from him, but you express your concerns about her performance and potential.
(C) You tell your flight leader that she is not ready for greater responsibility and that you do not support her attending that school, and request her transfer to another squadron for a fresh start.
(D) You do not recommend her attending that school, and you discuss your expectations for improved performance with her, documenting the meeting in writing.
(E) You send your flight leader an e-mail saying that you do not support her attending that school, and you cc your assistant section leader.

33. Select the MOST EFFECTIVE action (A–E) in response to the situation.

34. Select the LEAST EFFECTIVE action (A–E) in response to the situation.

Situation 18. You are a flight leader in a support squadron, and you have recently come up with a new procedure that you believe would improve the tracking and timeliness of work orders. Some of your senior NCO section leaders agree with making the change, and some don't—you haven't changed anything yet, and you are still weighing the pros and cons. One of your section leaders expresses his strong disagreement to your supervisor, the squadron commander, without consulting you at all. What do you do?

Possible actions:
(A) Don't respond to your critics in order to prevent unnecessary conflict.
(B) Ask that section leader at the next weekly meeting why he felt it was necessary to unprofessionally violate the chain of command by going over your head.
(C) Meet with that section leader one-on-one to let him know that going around the chain of command is unacceptable, but also to get a better understanding of his objections.
(D) Relieve that section leader from his position, and request his immediate transfer—he can't be trusted.
(E) Since you want to maintain your section leaders' loyalty and trust, only implement some of the changes to lessen their objections.

35. Select the MOST EFFECTIVE action (A–E) in response to the situation.

36. Select the LEAST EFFECTIVE action (A–E) in response to the situation.

Situation 19. You are a moderately experienced planner in a joint (multi-service) operational headquarters. A peer on the operations staff brings you a draft operations order for an upcoming major exercise, asking you to look it over and give her your input tomorrow, since you are known for the quality of your work and this needs to be perfect. You know this biannual exercise is a make-or-break event for the senior staff and the whole headquarters, and this is the first time you have been asked for your input. What do you do?

Possible actions:

(A) Thank her, and let her know that you will be happy to review the order. Ask her when she could go over any questions you might have.

(B) Thank her, and make time for it very soon; go over your thoughts on the order with your supervisor before reviewing it with your colleague in the operations section.

(C) Leave the task until the end of the day; you already have more tasks than you can practically accomplish on your "to do" list.

(D) Ask her if there is someone else who could do it. You are grateful that she trusts you, but you don't want to cause a shortfall if you miss something.

(E) Respectfully ask her to check with your supervisor first.

37. Select the MOST EFFECTIVE action (A–E) in response to the situation.

38. Select the LEAST EFFECTIVE action (A–E) in response to the situation.

Situation 20. You are the NCOIC of a maintenance section that consists of eight Airmen divided into two teams. The shop safety policy requires members of the section to take off all their jewelry while repairing electrical equipment. There are even two large signs that state this policy on opposite walls of the shop. Despite this, you notice that one of your Airmen who is repairing a generator still has her watch on. What do you do?

Possible actions:

(A) Since the generator is not turned on at the moment, the risk of injury is low, so you decide you'll talk to her later about the policy.

(B) Tell the Airman to step away from the generator, remind her of the policy, and have her take her watch off before returning to her work.

(C) Find the Airman's team leader, and have him make the correction immediately.

(D) Make a note to send an e-mail to the entire section about safety practices.

(E) Yell across the shop for everyone to stop what they are doing and look around to see if they see any safety hazards.

39. Select the MOST EFFECTIVE action (A–E) in response to the situation.

40. Select the LEAST EFFECTIVE action (A–E) in response to the situation.

Situation 21. The squadron-level pre-inspection before next week's base-level Operational Readiness Inspection categorized your section's deficiencies into two categories, minor and major, although they are in multiple functional areas. The squadron commander's primary emphasis seems to be on safety, while the base leadership constantly emphasizes readiness to deploy. There are dozens of minor deficiencies but only five major deficiencies. What do you do?

Possible actions:

(A) Assign each section member a specific set of minor deficiencies to correct so that the inspectors will see that your section is making progress.
(B) Prioritize all the deficiencies from largest to smallest, and tackle the biggest ones first, regardless of functional area.
(C) Focus on correcting all the safety-related deficiencies to make your squadron commander happy.
(D) Prioritize the functional areas, and assign teams for each, directing them to immediately start correcting the minor deficiencies and give you a plan for correcting the major deficiencies first thing in the morning.
(E) Focus on correcting all the readiness-related deficiencies first to make the base inspectors happy.

41. Select the MOST EFFECTIVE action (A–E) in response to the situation.

42. Select the LEAST EFFECTIVE action (A–E) in response to the situation.

Situation 22. Your section has been tasked to represent your squadron in the annual base-wide fitness test competition two weeks from Friday. Three section members have asked to be excused from the competition since they barely pass their fitness tests anyway and don't want to hurt the section's chances of winning. What do you do?

Possible actions:

(A) Assign them other duties on the day of the competition; since they will not be competing, there's no sense in making them do the train-up.
(B) Tell them that they are part of the section and that they will participate in the train-up and the competition itself.
(C) Require them to participate in the train-up, but give them a three-day pass starting the Friday of the competition.
(D) Tell them that they will participate in the train-up, and you will decide later.
(E) Request their transfer to another section for their disloyalty.

43. Select the MOST EFFECTIVE action (A–E) in response to the situation.

44. Select the LEAST EFFECTIVE action (A–E) in response to the situation.

Situation 23. You are assigned to work on a project along with a coworker who has been in the unit longer than you have. Since he has never demonstrated any significant ambitions or aspirations to develop professionally, he does not put much effort into your mutual project. What is your first step?

Possible actions:

(A) Accept the situation, and do your part of the project to the best of your ability, but no more; the rest is up to your coworker.
(B) Ask your supervisor to speak to your coworker to get him to do his part of the project to an acceptable standard.
(C) Discuss the situation with your supervisor, and ask for your coworker to be replaced on the project.
(D) If the project is not completed successfully and on time, you are concerned that it will reflect badly not only on you, but also on your unit, so you put in the extra time to complete the project on your own.
(E) Discuss the situation with your coworker, and try to negotiate a fair distribution of effort as well as his agreement to do his part.

45. Select the MOST EFFECTIVE action (A–E) in response to the situation.

46. Select the LEAST EFFECTIVE action (A–E) in response to the situation.

Situation 24. You have been placed in charge of a small team that trains new recruiters. Your most effective trainer tells you that he has a medical procedure scheduled for next Monday that will require at least two weeks of recovery. He scheduled the procedure and recovery time months ago, before you took charge of the team; back then, his absence would not have interfered with a class. However, since then the training schedule has changed because there are so many new recruiters to train before the end of the fiscal (budget) year. There are strict limits on class size for each trainer, and trainers have to be school-trained and certified to teach these classes. What is the first thing you do?

Possible actions:

(A) Ask your supervisor for another trainer to fill in for the one with a medical procedure.
(B) Inform your supervisor of the issue, and then research the availability of certified instructors in your area—maybe you can borrow one from another unit or base.
(C) Tell the trainer with the scheduled procedure that he will have to find a certified replacement before he can have his procedure.
(D) Tell the trainer with the scheduled procedure that he will have to reschedule it.
(E) Tell your supervisor that you will not be able to train the full load of new recruiters before the end of the fiscal year.

47. Select the MOST EFFECTIVE action (A–E) in response to the situation.

48. Select the LEAST EFFECTIVE action (A–E) in response to the situation.

Situation 25. At a planning meeting that includes your supervisor and the logistics officer, a disagreement springs up between them about what is necessary for an upcoming exercise. You know the two do not get along personally or professionally and that they are in constant disagreement. They surprise you by asking for your opinion—basically asking you to choose a side. Even though this is not very professional conduct, you have to respond somehow, and you do have some experience from three similar exercises. What do you do?

Possible actions:

(A) You agree with the position of your supervisor; since he is directly above you, he has more influence on your duties and can make your life easy or hard.

(B) You go along with the position of the logistics officer, who has experience gained from supporting several different types of exercises.

(C) You compare the advantages and disadvantages of each position, and recommend a middle course without getting involved in their conflict.

(D) Respectfully decline to make a recommendation, saying that either method would be equally successful.

(E) Respectfully decline to make a recommendation immediately, saying that the question needs more study.

49. Select the MOST EFFECTIVE action (A–E) in response to the situation.

50. Select the LEAST EFFECTIVE action (A–E) in response to the situation.

SUBTEST #7: SELF-DESCRIPTION INVENTORY

The Self-Description Inventory measures personal characteristics and traits. The inventory consists of a list of 240 statements; your task is to read each statement carefully and decide how much that statement applies to you. You will then indicate how much you agree that a particular statement applies to you or describes you by using the following scale:

(A) Strongly disagree
(B) Moderately disagree
(C) Neither agree nor disagree
(D) Moderately agree
(E) Strongly agree

Since you have 240 statements and only 45 minutes for this test, you should work quickly—but you should answer all the questions. Choose your answer from your first impression by comparing yourself with other people in your same age group and of the same sex. Don't spend a long time thinking about what the "right" answer is—there is no right or wrong answer to any question. Mark a choice for all the statements, even if you're not completely sure of the answer. Again, your first impression will be the best indicator.

Following are some statements that are representative of the type you will see on the AFOQT Self-Description Inventory.

1. I often get distracted from my original goals.
2. I am comfortable being the leader of a group.
3. I am usually on time and prepared for the day's activities.
4. I usually place my work goals ahead of personal interests or hobbies.
5. I enjoy speaking to a large group of people.
6. People often refer to me as a natural leader.
7. I am more comfortable being a member of a group than the leader.
8. I like to visit art museums by myself.
9. I believe that finishing a job on time is more important than how well it's done.
10. Many people put in too much effort on little things.
11. I do not like being involved in group activities.
12. I expect other people to show up on time.
13. I dislike having to meet new people.
14. I like being the center of attention.
15. I am annoyed when people drop in without advance notice.
16. I have a hard time getting along with people unless I know them well.
17. My personal interests and hobbies are very important to me.
18. I am seldom reluctant to voice my opinion in a group setting.
19. It is easy and enjoyable for me to learn new things.
20. I like going to new places.

SUBTEST #8: PHYSICAL SCIENCE

20 Questions

DIRECTIONS: This subtest measures your knowledge in the area of science. Each of the questions or incomplete statements is followed by five choices. Your task is to decide which one of the choices best answers the question or completes the statement.

1. The most accurate description of Earth's atmosphere is that it is made up of

   (A) 78% oxygen, 19% nitrogen, and 2% carbon dioxide, with trace amounts of nitrogen, water vapor, and dust particles.
   (B) 3% water vapor, 78% ozone, and 20% nitrogen.
   (C) 20% oxygen, 77% hydrogen, 3% carbon dioxide, and some water vapor.
   (D) 21% oxygen, 78% nitrogen, .03% carbon dioxide, trace amounts of rare gases, water vapor, and some dust particles.
   (E) 77% oxygen, 21% hydrogen, and 2% carbon dioxide, with trace amounts of nitrogen, water vapor, and dust particles.

2. A vibrating tuning fork, placed in a vacuum under a bell jar, will

   (A) have the pitch of its sound raised.
   (B) have the pitch of its sound lowered.
   (C) be inaudible.
   (D) crack the thick glass of the bell jar.
   (E) experience no change in its audible tone or pitch.

3. The three ingredients found most often in commercial fertilizers are

   (A) iron, calcium, and magnesium.
   (B) nitrogen, phosphorus, and potassium.
   (C) sulfur, phosphorus, and iron.
   (D) magnesium, iron, and calcium.
   (E) iron, sulfur, and magnesium.

4. The barometric pressure at a particular location directly depends on ____________.

   (A) its temperature and humidity
   (B) its solar wind flares and its local wind speed
   (C) its local wind speed and temperature
   (D) its humidity and the local prevailing wind speed
   (E) its atmospheric salinity and saturation

5. What is the correct formula for "dry ice"?

   (A) HO_2
   (B) CO_2
   (C) H_2O_2
   (D) C_2O
   (E) $H_6O_6C_6$

AFOQT #2

6. When an airplane is in flight, the air pressure on the bottom surface of the wing is

(A) less than on the top surface.
(B) more than on the top surface.
(C) either more or less than on the top surface, depending on the speed of the airplane.
(D) either more or less than on the top surface, depending on the shape of the wing.
(E) the same, regardless of airspeed or attitude.

7. In a vacuum, radio waves and visible light waves have the same

(A) frequency.
(B) speed.
(C) intensity.
(D) wavelength.
(E) appearance.

8. Inertia is the property of matter to

(A) resist a change of position or motion.
(B) resist a change of volume or shape.
(C) resist a change of composition.
(D) interact or not interact with other substances.
(E) accelerate going downhill.

9. The density of a substance is determined by

(A) dividing its mass by its volume.
(B) the relationship of its volume to its chemical state.
(C) the inverse of its weight compared to its volume.
(D) how much it resists acceleration.
(E) dividing its weight at one atmosphere by its volume.

10. Parallel rays of light, after reflection from a plane (flat) mirror, will be

(A) converged.
(B) parallel.
(C) diffused.
(D) absorbed.
(E) invisible.

11. Object 1, with a mass of 4 kilograms, and Object 2, with a mass of 10 kilograms, are dropped simultaneously from a resting position 500 meters high. Neglecting air resistance, what is the ratio of the speed of Object 1 to the speed of Object 2 at the end of four seconds?

(A) 2:5
(B) 1:1
(C) 1:4
(D) 1:8
(E) 2:1

12. On the basis of their atomic structure, atoms are considered __________ if they can lend electrons and __________ if they borrow electrons.

(A) inert, nonmetals
(B) metals, inert
(C) nonmetals, metals
(D) metals, nonmetals
(E) reactive, nonreactive

13. Isotopes of the same element have the same number of

(A) electrons.
(B) protons.
(C) electrons and protons.
(D) neutrons and protons.
(E) electrons and neutrons.

14. Erosion and depletion are problems associated with

(A) blood circulation.
(B) baldness.
(C) soil conservation.
(D) cardiovascular exercise.
(E) ozone hole maintenance.

15. An insulator is a material with

(A) many free electrons.
(B) few free electrons.
(C) few free protons.
(D) many free ions.
(E) a variable number of neutrons.

16. Which of the following is a chemical change?

(A) vaporizing 1 gram of water
(B) melting ice
(C) magnetizing an iron rod
(D) mixing graphite flakes with oil
(E) burning 1 kilogram of wood

17. A seesaw is an example of

(A) an inclined plane.
(B) the pulley principle.
(C) a wedge.
(D) a lever.
(E) a combined machine.

18. In atomic structure, what is the negative particle that orbits the atom's nucleus?

(A) neutron
(B) proton
(C) meson
(D) isotope
(E) electron

19. Light from the sun takes approximately how long to reach Earth?

(A) eight days
(B) four hours
(C) eight minutes
(D) two years
(E) nine seconds

20. A liquid has ______________, and ______________.

(A) definite volume, takes the shape of its container
(B) no definite volume, expands to fill its container
(C) no definite shape, exerts pressure on its container based on the container's shape
(D) a definite shape, exerts constant pressure on its container
(E) indefinite volume, contracts to fit in the space available

AFOQT #2

SUBTEST #9: TABLE READING

40 Questions

DIRECTIONS: This subtest measures your ability to read a table quickly and accurately. All the questions on this subtest are based on the following table. Notice that the X values appear at the top of the table and the Y values are shown on the left side of the table. The X values are the column values and the Y values are the row values. For each test question, you are given an X value and a Y value; your task will be to find the box where the selected column and row meet, note the number that appears there, and then find that same number among the answer options for each question.

Y \ X	–20	–19	–18	–17	–16	–15	–14	–13	–12	–11	–10	–9	–8	–7	–6	–5	–4	–3	–2	–1
20	50	51	52	53	54	55	56	57	58	59	60	61	62	63	64	65	66	67	68	69
19	51	52	53	54	55	56	57	58	59	60	61	62	63	64	65	66	67	68	69	70
18	52	53	54	55	56	57	58	59	60	61	62	63	64	65	66	67	68	69	70	71
17	53	54	55	56	57	58	59	60	61	62	63	64	65	66	67	68	69	70	71	72
16	54	55	56	57	58	59	60	61	62	63	64	65	66	67	68	69	70	71	72	73
15	55	56	57	58	59	60	61	62	63	64	65	66	67	68	69	70	71	72	73	74
14	56	57	58	59	60	61	62	63	64	65	66	67	68	69	70	71	72	73	74	75
13	57	58	59	60	61	62	63	64	65	66	67	68	69	70	71	72	73	74	75	76
12	58	59	60	61	62	63	64	65	66	67	68	69	70	71	72	73	74	75	76	77
11	59	60	61	62	63	64	65	66	67	68	69	70	71	72	73	74	75	76	77	78
10	60	61	62	63	64	65	66	67	68	69	70	71	72	73	74	75	76	77	78	79
9	61	62	63	64	65	66	67	68	69	70	71	72	73	74	75	76	77	78	79	80
8	62	63	64	65	66	67	68	69	70	71	72	73	74	75	76	77	78	79	80	81
7	63	64	65	66	67	68	69	70	71	72	73	74	75	76	77	78	79	80	81	82
6	64	65	66	67	68	69	70	71	72	73	74	75	76	77	78	79	80	81	82	83
5	65	66	67	68	69	70	71	72	73	74	75	76	77	78	79	80	81	82	83	84
4	66	67	68	69	70	71	72	73	74	75	76	77	78	79	80	81	82	83	84	85
3	67	68	69	70	71	72	73	74	75	76	77	78	79	80	81	82	83	84	85	86
2	68	69	70	71	72	73	74	75	76	77	78	79	80	81	82	83	84	85	86	87
1	69	70	71	72	73	74	75	76	77	78	79	80	81	82	83	84	85	86	87	88
0	70	71	72	73	74	75	76	77	78	79	80	81	82	83	84	85	86	87	88	89
–1	71	72	73	74	75	76	77	78	79	80	81	82	83	84	85	86	87	88	89	90
–2	72	73	74	75	76	77	78	79	80	81	82	83	84	85	86	87	88	89	90	91
–3	73	74	75	76	77	78	79	80	81	82	83	84	85	86	87	88	89	90	91	92
–4	74	75	76	77	78	79	80	81	82	83	84	85	86	87	88	89	90	91	92	93
–5	75	76	77	78	79	80	81	82	83	84	85	86	87	88	89	90	91	92	93	94
–6	76	77	78	79	80	81	82	83	84	85	86	87	88	89	90	91	92	93	94	95
–7	77	78	79	80	81	82	83	84	85	86	87	88	89	90	91	92	93	94	95	96
–8	78	79	80	81	82	83	84	85	86	87	88	89	90	91	92	93	94	95	96	97
–9	79	80	81	82	83	84	85	86	87	88	89	90	91	92	93	94	95	96	97	98
–10	80	81	82	83	84	85	86	87	88	89	90	91	92	93	94	95	96	97	98	99
–11	81	82	83	84	85	86	87	88	89	90	91	92	93	94	95	96	97	98	99	100
–12	82	83	84	85	86	87	88	89	90	91	92	93	94	95	96	97	98	99	100	101
–13	83	84	85	86	87	88	89	90	91	92	93	94	95	96	97	98	99	100	101	102
–14	84	85	86	87	88	89	90	91	92	93	94	95	96	97	98	99	100	101	102	103
–15	85	86	87	88	89	90	91	92	93	94	95	96	97	98	99	100	101	102	103	104
–16	86	87	88	89	90	91	92	93	94	95	96	97	98	99	100	101	102	103	104	105
–17	87	88	89	90	91	92	93	94	95	96	97	98	99	100	101	102	103	104	105	106
–18	88	89	90	91	92	93	94	95	96	97	98	99	100	101	102	103	104	105	106	107
–19	89	90	91	92	93	94	95	96	97	98	99	100	101	102	103	104	105	106	107	108
–20	90	91	92	93	94	95	96	97	98	99	100	101	102	103	104	105	106	107	108	109

0	1	2	3	4	5	6	7	8	9	10	11	12	13	14	15	16	17	18	19	20
70	71	72	73	74	75	76	77	78	79	80	81	82	83	84	85	86	87	88	89	90
71	72	73	74	75	76	77	78	79	80	81	82	83	84	85	86	87	88	89	90	91
72	73	74	75	76	77	78	79	80	81	82	83	84	85	86	87	88	89	90	91	92
73	74	75	76	77	78	79	80	81	82	83	84	85	86	87	88	89	90	91	92	93
74	75	76	77	78	79	80	81	82	83	84	85	86	87	88	89	90	91	92	93	94
75	76	77	78	79	80	81	82	83	84	85	86	87	88	89	90	91	92	93	94	95
76	77	78	79	80	81	82	83	84	85	86	87	88	89	90	91	92	93	94	95	96
77	78	79	80	81	82	83	84	85	86	87	88	89	90	91	92	93	94	95	96	97
78	79	80	81	82	83	84	85	86	87	88	89	90	91	92	93	94	95	96	97	98
79	80	81	82	83	84	85	86	87	88	89	90	91	92	93	94	95	96	97	98	99
80	81	82	83	84	85	86	87	88	89	90	91	92	93	94	95	96	97	98	99	100
81	82	83	84	85	86	87	88	89	90	91	92	93	94	95	96	97	98	99	100	101
82	83	84	85	86	87	88	89	90	91	92	93	94	95	96	97	98	99	100	101	102
83	84	85	86	87	88	89	90	91	92	93	94	95	96	97	98	99	100	101	102	103
84	85	86	87	88	89	90	91	92	93	94	95	96	97	98	99	100	101	102	103	104
85	86	87	88	89	90	91	92	93	94	95	96	97	98	99	100	101	102	103	104	105
86	87	88	89	90	91	92	93	94	95	96	97	98	99	100	101	102	103	104	105	106
87	88	89	90	91	92	93	94	95	96	97	98	99	100	101	102	103	104	105	106	107
88	89	90	91	92	93	94	95	96	97	98	99	100	101	102	103	104	105	106	107	108
89	90	91	92	93	94	95	96	97	98	99	100	101	102	103	104	105	106	107	108	109
90	91	92	93	94	95	96	97	98	99	100	101	102	103	104	105	106	107	108	109	110
91	92	93	94	95	96	97	98	99	100	101	102	103	104	105	106	107	108	109	110	111
92	93	94	95	96	97	98	99	100	101	102	103	104	105	106	107	108	109	110	111	112
93	94	95	96	97	98	99	100	101	102	103	104	105	106	107	108	109	110	111	112	113
94	95	96	97	98	99	100	101	102	103	104	105	106	107	108	109	110	111	112	113	114
95	96	97	98	99	100	101	102	103	104	105	106	107	108	109	110	111	112	113	114	115
96	97	98	99	100	101	102	103	104	105	106	107	108	109	110	111	112	113	114	115	116
97	98	99	100	101	102	103	104	105	106	107	108	109	110	111	112	113	114	115	116	117
98	99	100	101	102	103	104	105	106	107	108	109	110	111	112	113	114	115	116	117	118
99	100	101	102	103	104	105	106	107	108	109	110	111	112	113	114	115	116	117	118	119
100	101	102	103	104	105	106	107	108	109	110	111	112	113	114	115	116	117	118	119	120
101	102	103	104	105	106	107	108	109	110	111	112	113	114	115	116	117	118	119	120	121
102	103	104	105	106	107	108	109	110	111	112	113	114	115	116	117	118	119	120	121	122
103	104	105	106	107	108	109	110	111	112	113	114	115	116	117	118	119	120	121	122	123
104	105	106	107	108	109	110	111	112	113	114	115	116	117	118	119	120	121	122	123	124
105	106	107	108	109	110	111	112	113	114	115	116	117	118	119	120	121	122	123	124	125
106	107	108	109	110	111	112	113	114	115	116	117	118	119	120	121	122	123	124	125	126
107	108	109	110	111	112	113	114	115	116	117	118	119	120	121	122	123	124	125	126	127
108	109	110	111	112	113	114	115	116	117	118	119	120	121	122	123	124	125	126	127	128
109	110	111	112	113	114	115	116	117	118	119	120	121	122	123	124	125	126	127	128	129
110	111	112	113	114	115	116	117	118	119	120	121	122	123	124	125	126	127	128	129	130

	X	Y	(A)	(B)	(C)	(D)	(E)
1.	–4	–19	104	105	106	103	107
2.	+18	+9	100	101	98	102	99
3.	–12	+11	67	76	68	66	69
4.	–2	–8	96	94	97	95	98
5.	–10	+16	62	63	64	65	66
6.	–10	–15	91	93	96	94	95
7.	+2	+8	83	84	85	86	87
8.	+7	–3	97	98	99	100	101
9.	–11	+17	63	61	64	65	62
10.	+12	–6	107	108	106	109	110
11.	0	0	87	91	88	89	90
12.	+17	–8	113	115	114	112	116
13.	–9	–10	91	88	92	90	88
14.	+2	+10	80	83	82	81	79
15.	–5	–1	84	85	87	86	88
16.	–14	+10	67	66	65	68	63
17.	+12	+17	87	85	86	84	83
18.	–2	–5	95	92	91	93	94
19.	+10	–1	101	102	99	103	98
20.	–5	+9	67	75	57	77	76

	X	Y	(A)	(B)	(C)	(D)	(E)
21.	−2	−7	97	98	94	93	95
22.	+5	−3	100	98	99	97	96
23.	+11	−16	119	118	117	116	115
24.	+8	+14	84	82	85	86	83
25.	+16	−1	107	106	105	104	103
26.	+9	−4	99	100	101	102	103
27.	−11	−18	99	98	97	96	95
28.	+17	+19	89	86	87	88	90
29.	−9	+7	77	76	74	75	73
30.	+6	+7	90	91	89	93	88
31.	+11	−6	107	106	105	104	103
32.	−14	−8	88	82	86	84	83
33.	+2	−15	109	108	107	106	105
34.	+15	+8	100	95	99	98	97
35.	+11	+7	94	95	96	97	98
36.	+7	−7	102	106	104	108	110
37.	−1	−5	94	95	96	97	98
38.	+16	+4	101	104	103	102	100
39.	−12	−12	86	87	88	89	90
40.	−1	−1	94	93	92	91	90

SUBTEST #10: INSTRUMENT COMPREHENSION

25 Questions

DIRECTIONS: This subtest measures your ability to determine the position of an airplane in flight from reading instruments showing its compass heading (direction), amount of climb or dive, and degree of bank to the right or left. In each problem, the left-hand dial is labeled ARTIFICIAL HORIZON. On the face of the dial, the small aircraft fuselage silhouette remains stationary, whereas the positions of the white line and the white pointer vary with changes in the position of the aircraft in which the instrument is located.

The white line represents the HORIZON LINE. The white pointer shows the degree of BANK to the right or left.

If the airplane is neither climbing nor diving, the horizon line is directly on the fuselage silhouette, as in dial 1 below.

If the airplane is climbing, the fuselage silhouette is seen between the horizon line and the pointer, as shown in dial 2 below. The greater the amount of climb, the greater the distance between the horizon line and the fuselage silhouette.

If the airplane is diving, the horizon line is seen between the fuselage silhouette and the pointer, as shown in dial 3 below. The greater the amount of dive, the greater the distance between the horizon line and the fuselage silhouette.

ARTIFICIAL HORIZON

Dial 1

ARTIFICIAL HORIZON

Dial 2

ARTIFICIAL HORIZON

Dial 3

If the airplane has no bank, the white pointer is seen to point to zero, as in dial 1 above.

If the airplane is banked to the pilot's left, the pointer is seen to the right of zero, as in dial 2 above.

If the airplane is banked to the pilot's right, the pointer is seen to the left of zero, as in dial 3 above.

The HORIZON LINE tilts as the aircraft is banked and is always at right angles to the pointer.

Dial 1 shows an airplane neither climbing nor diving, with no bank.
Dial 2 shows an airplane climbing and banked 45° to the pilot's right.
Dial 3 shows an airplane diving and banked 45° to the pilot's left.

In each problem, the right-hand dial is labeled COMPASS. On this dial, the nose of the plane shows the compass direction in which the airplane is headed. Dial 4 shows the airplane headed north, dial 5 shows it headed west, and dial 6 shows it headed northwest.

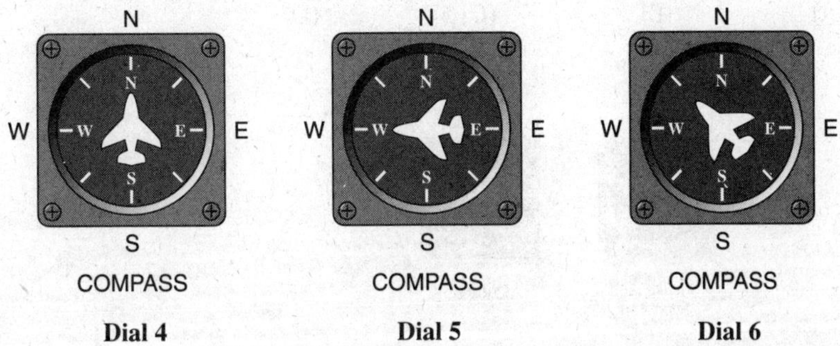

Dial 4 **Dial 5** **Dial 6**

Each problem consists of two dials and four silhouettes of airplanes in flight. Your task is to determine which one of the four airplanes is MOST NEARLY in the position indicated by the two dials. You are always looking north at the same altitude in each of the four airplanes' silhouettes. East is always to your right as you look at the page. In the sample question below, the dial labeled ARTIFICIAL HORIZON shows that the airplane is NOT banked, and is neither climbing nor diving. The COMPASS shows that it is headed south. The only one of the four airplane silhouettes that meets these specifications is in the box lettered (A), so the answer to the sample question is (A).

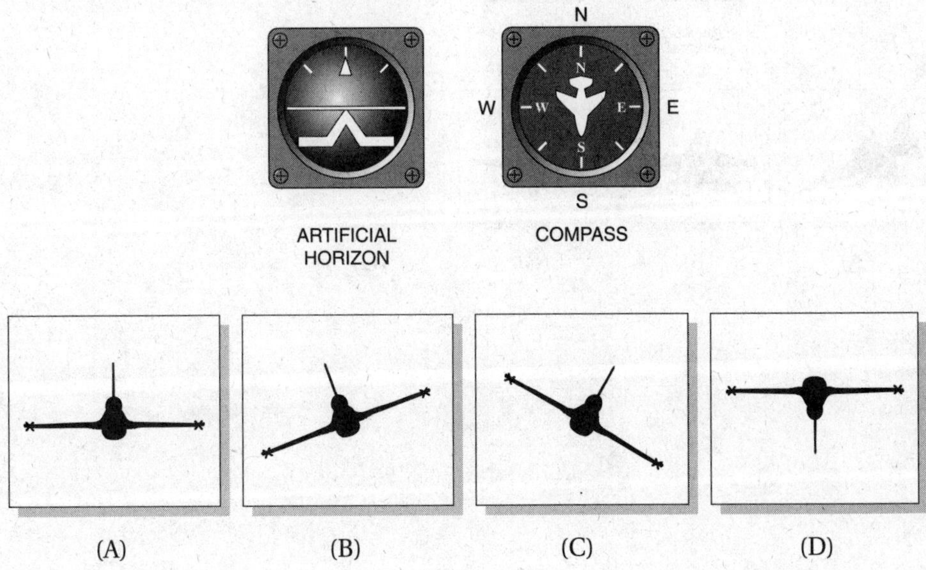

(A) (B) (C) (D)

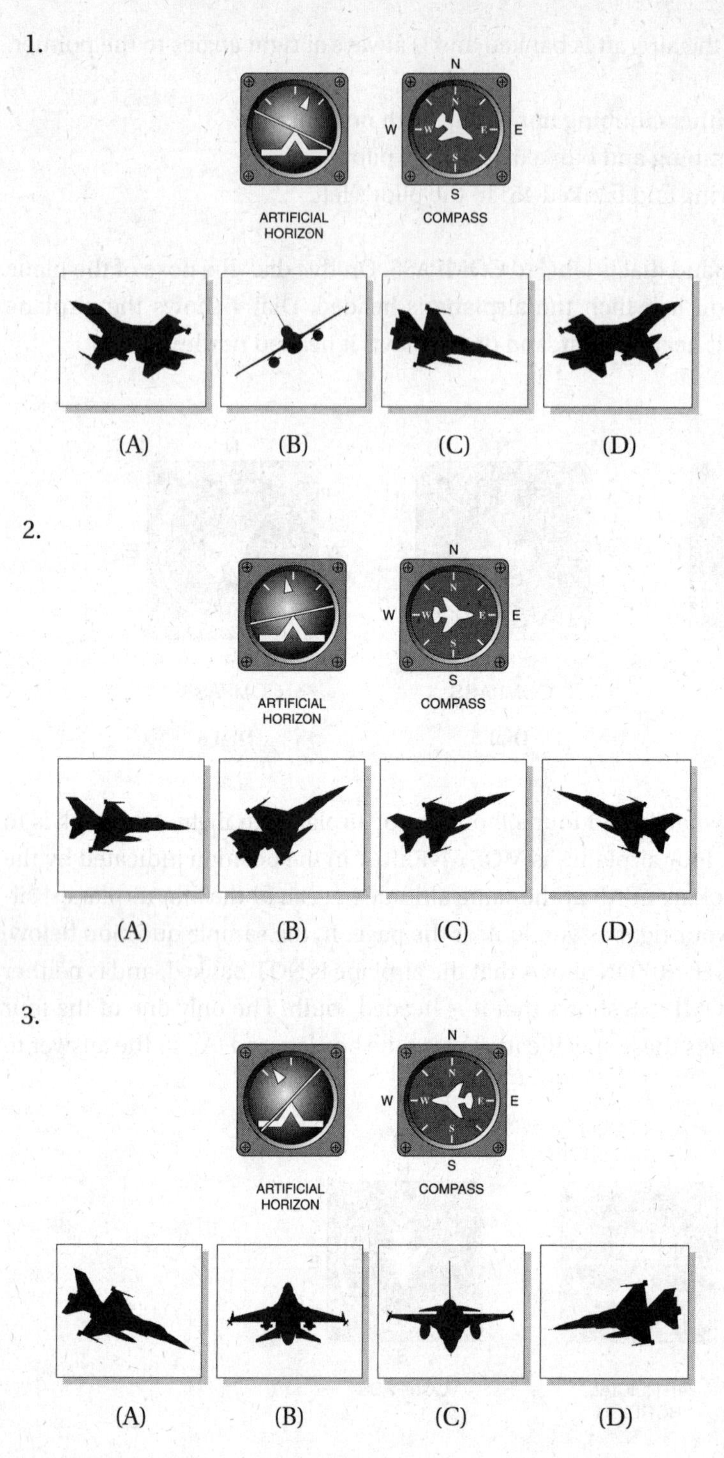
1.
N
W
E
S
ARTIFICIAL HORIZON
COMPASS
(A)
(B)
(C)
(D)
2.
N
W
E
S
ARTIFICIAL HORIZON
COMPASS
(A)
(B)
(C)
(D)
3.
N
W
E
S
ARTIFICIAL HORIZON
COMPASS
(A)
(B)
(C)
(D)

AFOQT #2

4.

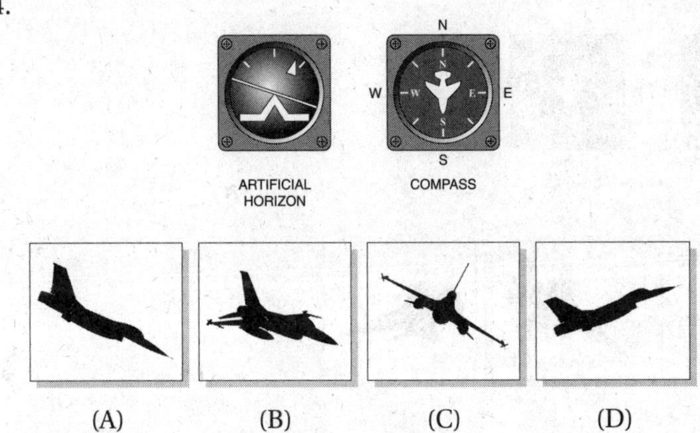
N
W
E
S
ARTIFICIAL HORIZON
COMPASS
(A)
(B)
(C)
(D)

5.

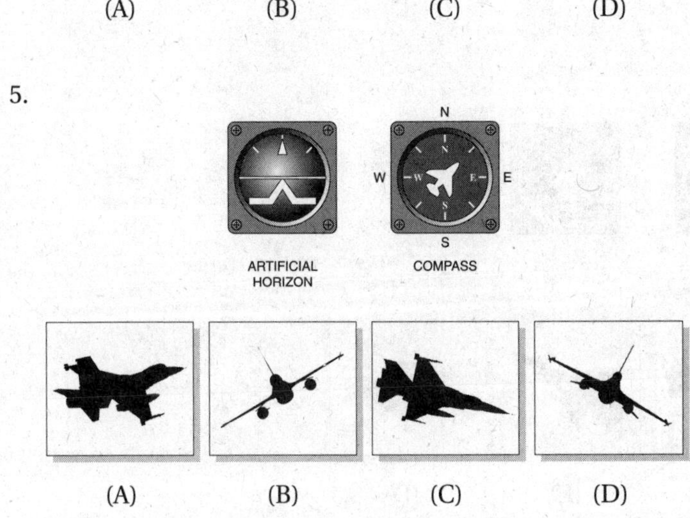
N
W
E
S
ARTIFICIAL HORIZON
COMPASS
(A)
(B)
(C)
(D)

6.

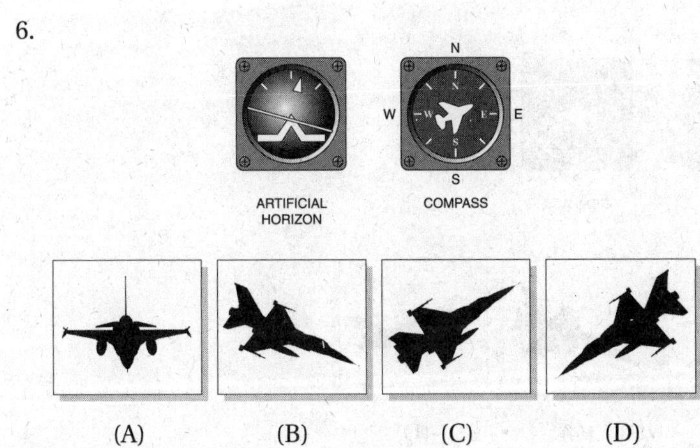
N
W
E
S
ARTIFICIAL HORIZON
COMPASS
(A)
(B)
(C)
(D)

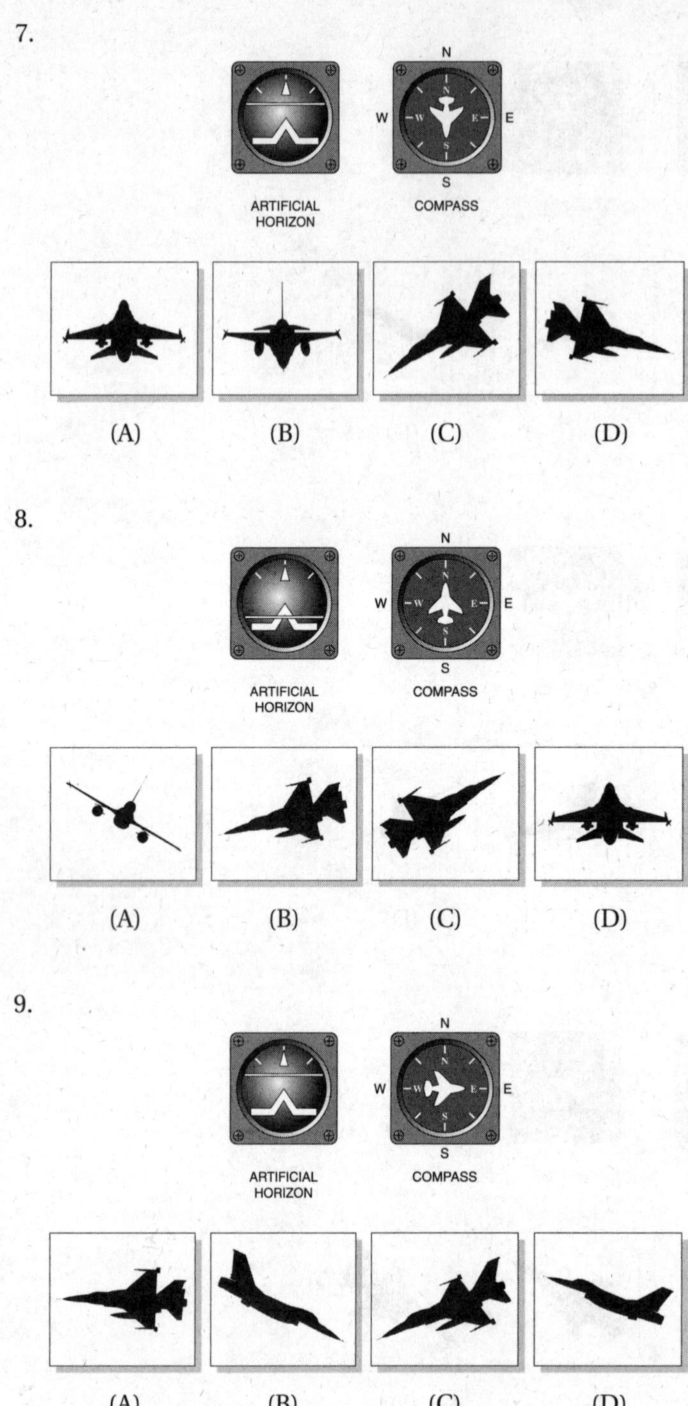
7.
N
W
E
S
ARTIFICIAL HORIZON
COMPASS
(A)
(B)
(C)
(D)
8.
N
W
E
S
ARTIFICIAL HORIZON
COMPASS
(A)
(B)
(C)
(D)
9.
N
W
E
S
ARTIFICIAL HORIZON
COMPASS
(A)
(B)
(C)
(D)

10.

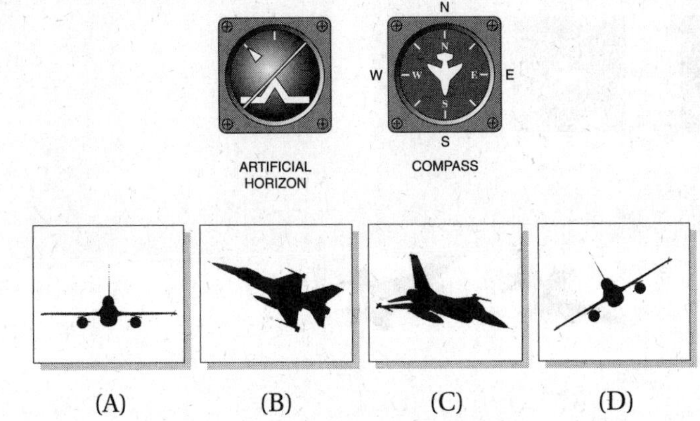
N
W
E
S
ARTIFICIAL HORIZON
COMPASS
(A)
(B)
(C)
(D)

11.

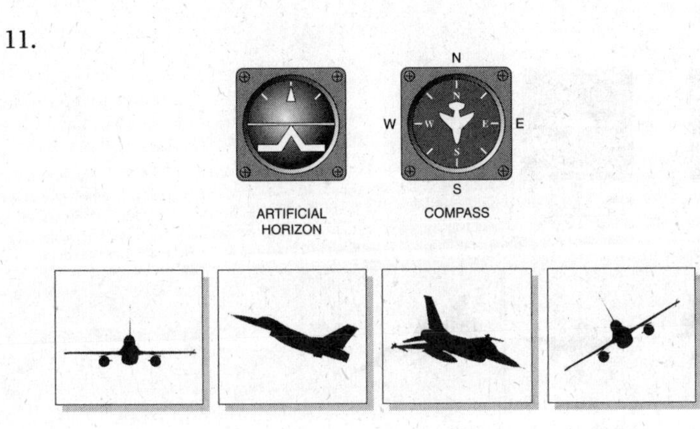
N
W
E
S
ARTIFICIAL HORIZON
COMPASS
(A)
(B)
(C)
(D)

12.

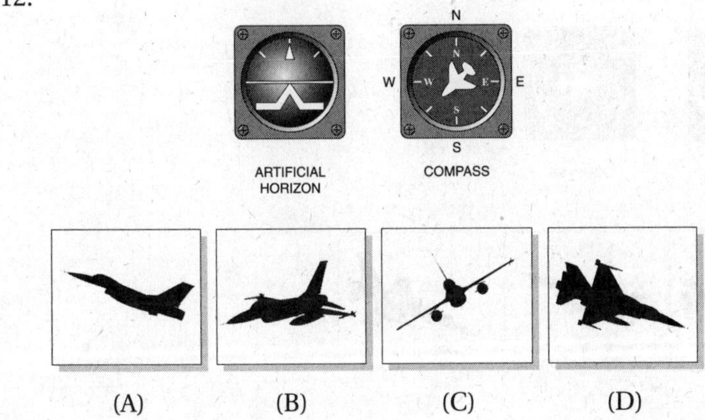
N
W
E
S
ARTIFICIAL HORIZON
COMPASS
(A)
(B)
(C)
(D)

13.

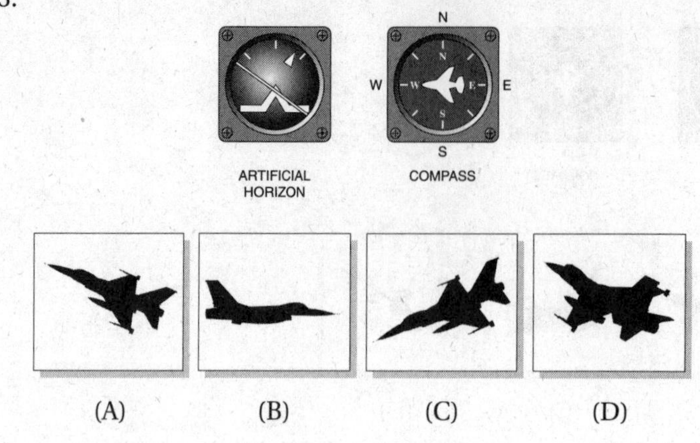
N
W
E
S
ARTIFICIAL HORIZON
COMPASS
(A)
(B)
(C)
(D)

14.

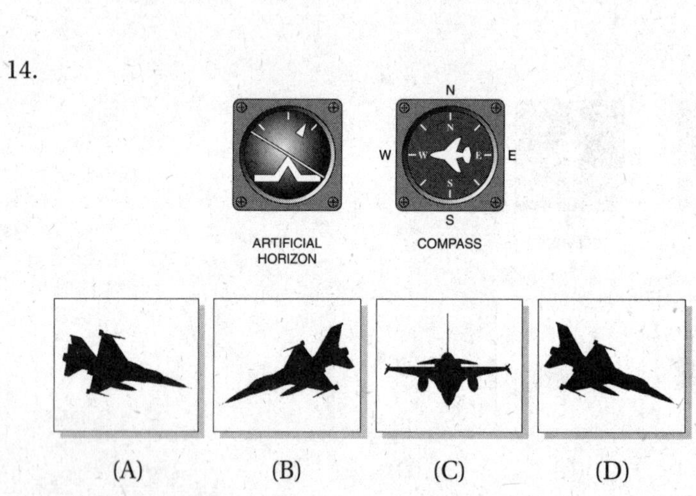
N
W
E
S
ARTIFICIAL HORIZON
COMPASS
(A)
(B)
(C)
(D)

15.

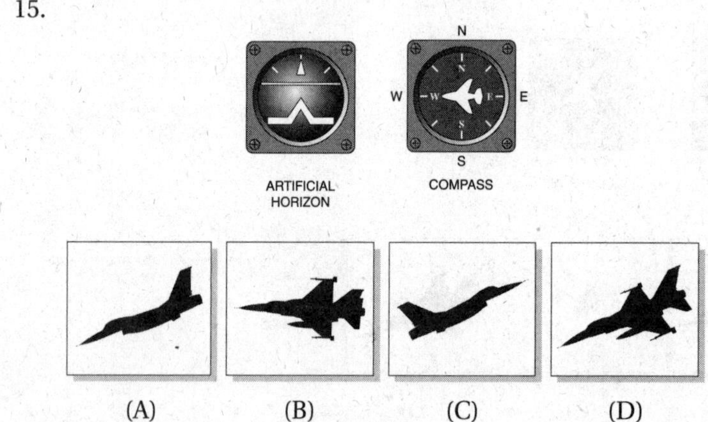
N
W
E
S
ARTIFICIAL HORIZON
COMPASS
(A)
(B)
(C)
(D)

16.

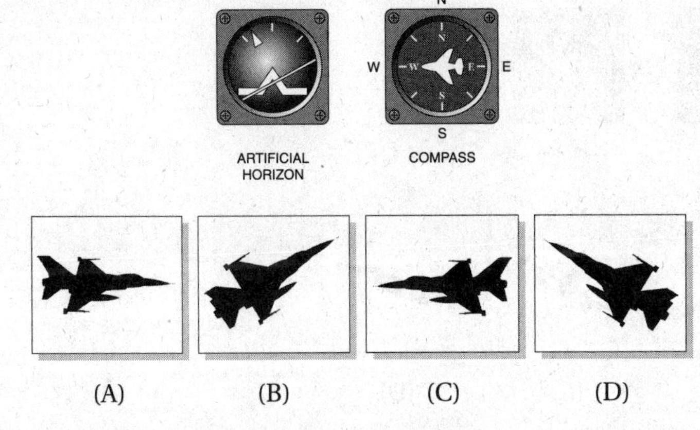

(A) (B) (C) (D)

17.

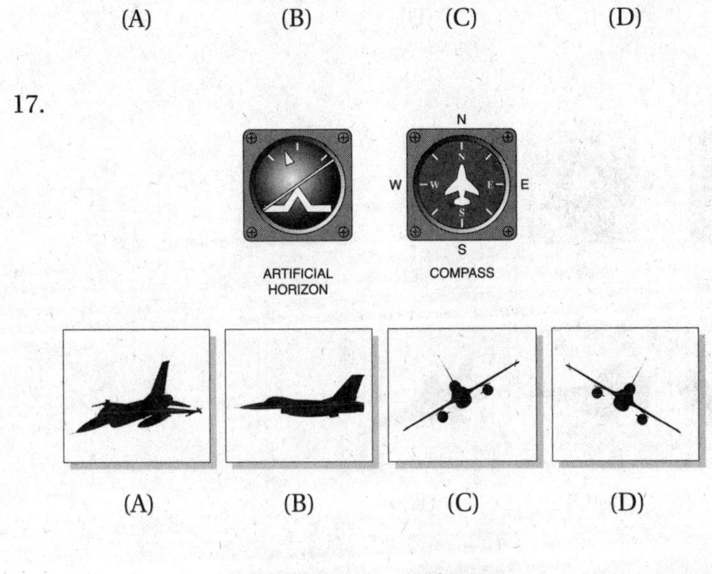

(A) (B) (C) (D)

18.

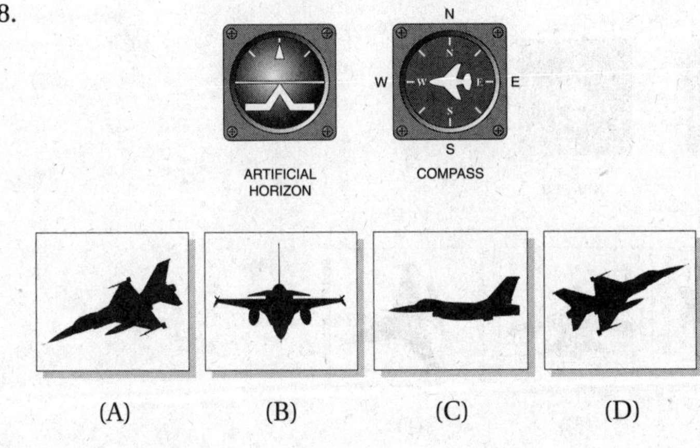

(A) (B) (C) (D)

19.

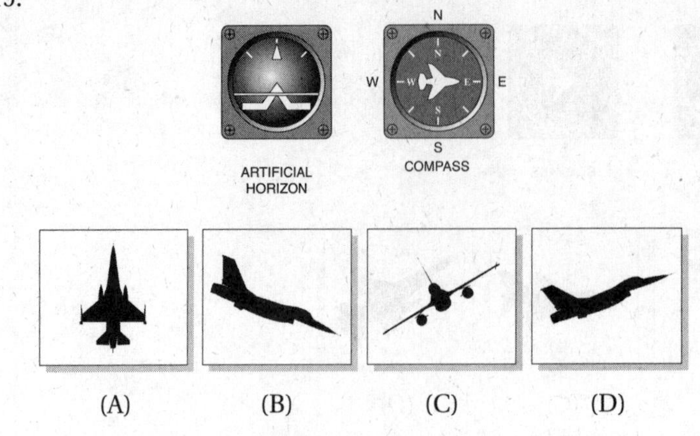

20.

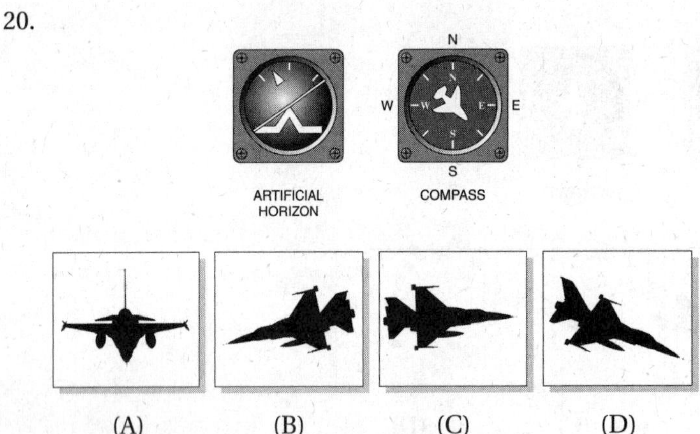

21.

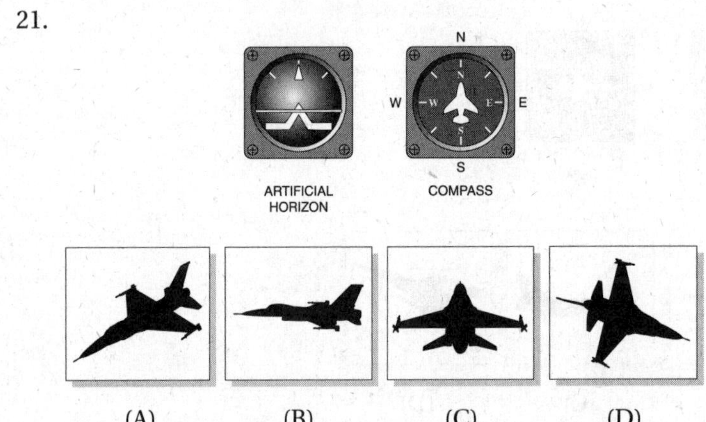

AFOQT #2

22.

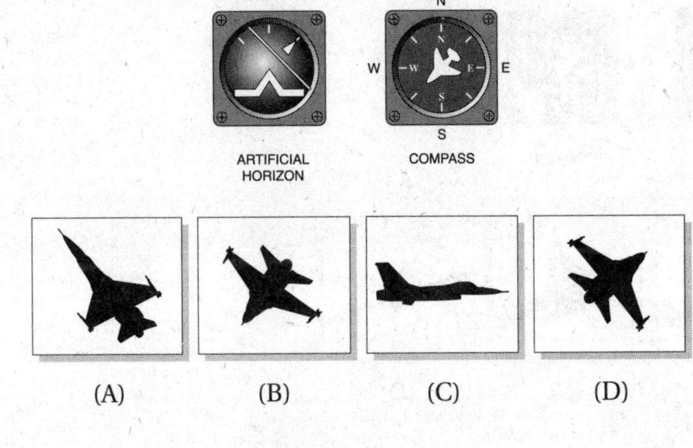
ARTIFICIAL HORIZON
N
W
E
S
COMPASS
(A)
(B)
(C)
(D)

23.

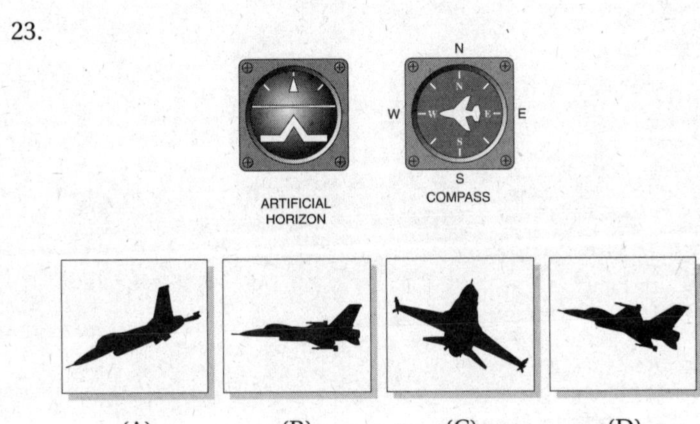
ARTIFICIAL HORIZON
N
W
E
S
COMPASS
(A)
(B)
(C)
(D)

24.

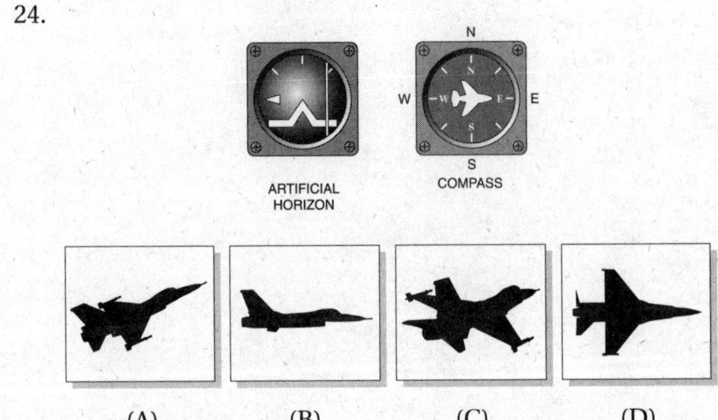
ARTIFICIAL HORIZON
N
W
E
S
COMPASS
(A)
(B)
(C)
(D)

25.

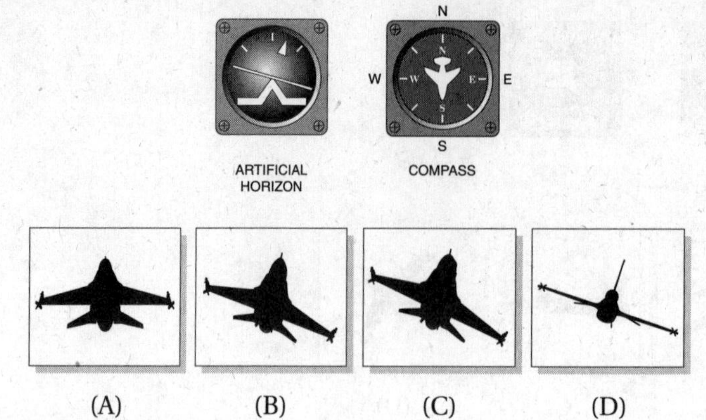

(A) (B) (C) (D)

AFOQT #2

SUBTEST #11: BLOCK COUNTING

30 Questions

DIRECTIONS: This part of the test measures your ability to "see into" a three-dimensional pile of blocks. Given a certain numbered block, your task is to determine how many other blocks it touches. *All of the blocks in each pile are the same size and shape.*

Questions 1–5

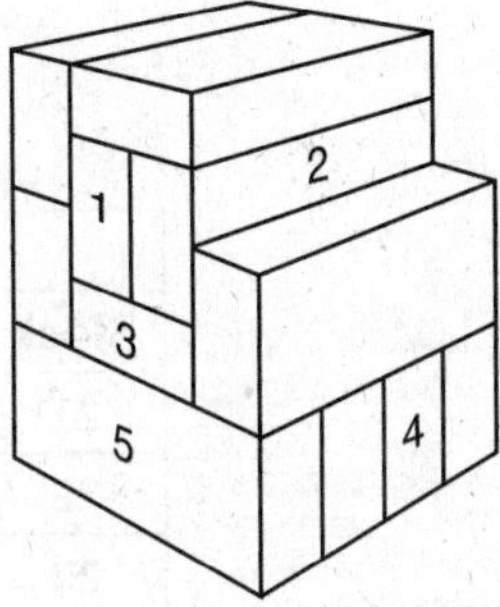

	KEY				
Block	**A**	**B**	**C**	**D**	**E**
1	2	3	4	5	6
2	3	4	5	6	7
3	4	5	6	7	8
4	3	4	5	6	7
5	3	4	5	6	7

Questions 6–10

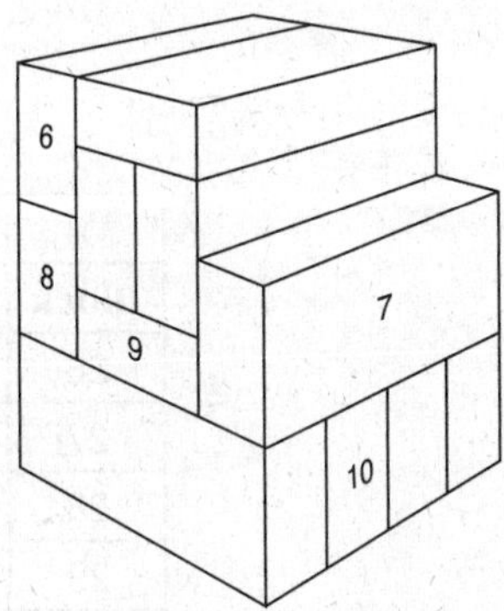

	KEY				
Block	**A**	**B**	**C**	**D**	**E**
6	2	3	4	5	6
7	4	5	6	7	8
8	4	5	6	7	8
9	4	5	6	7	8
10	4	5	6	7	8

Questions 11–15

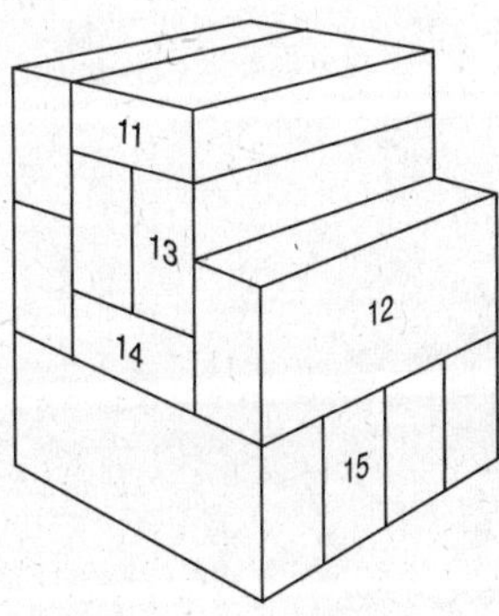

	KEY				
Block	**A**	**B**	**C**	**D**	**E**
11	3	4	5	6	7
12	4	5	6	7	8
13	3	4	5	6	7
14	4	5	6	7	8
15	3	4	5	6	7

Questions 16–20

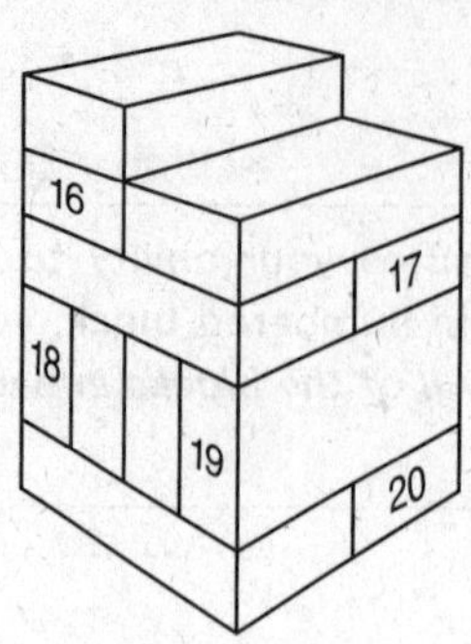

	KEY				
Block	**A**	**B**	**C**	**D**	**E**
16	3	4	5	6	7
17	3	4	5	6	7
18	4	5	6	7	8
19	3	4	5	6	7
20	2	3	4	5	6

Questions 21–25

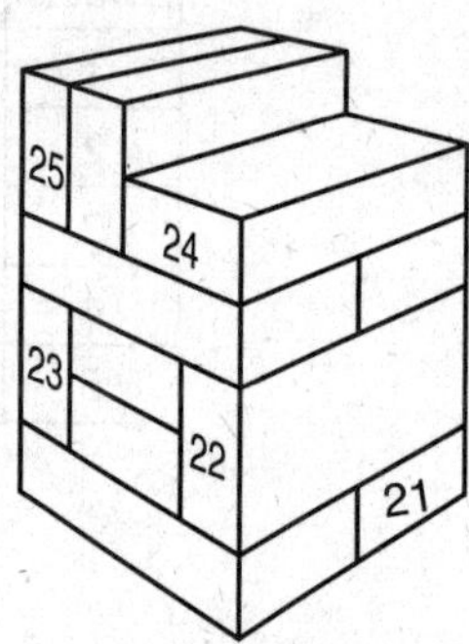

	KEY				
Block	**A**	**B**	**C**	**D**	**E**
21	2	3	4	5	6
22	3	4	5	6	7
23	6	5	4	3	2
24	3	4	5	6	7
25	6	5	4	3	2

Questions 26–30

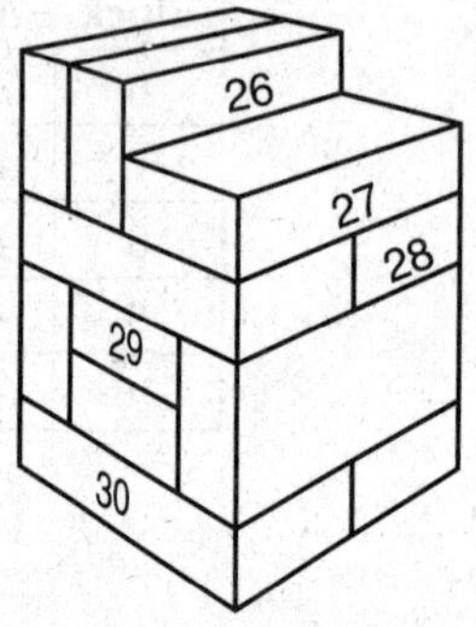

	KEY				
Block	**A**	**B**	**C**	**D**	**E**
26	2	3	4	5	6
27	3	4	5	6	7
28	7	6	5	4	3
29	3	4	5	6	7
30	1	2	3	4	5

SUBTEST #12: AVIATION INFORMATION

20 Questions

1. In a level turn, the acceleration experienced by the aircraft and its pilot in the direction perpendicular to the wing is solely determined by the

   (A) relative airspeed.
   (B) angle of attack.
   (C) bank angle.
   (D) altitude.
   (E) local air density and temperature.

2. The flight envelope of an aircraft is

   (A) the airspeed at which it achieves takeoff.
   (B) the region of altitude and airspeed in which it can be operated.
   (C) the volume of air it displaces in flight.
   (D) the envelope containing the aircraft registration documents.
   (E) the geographical area covered by the officially filed flight plan.

3. The locus of points equidistant from the upper and lower surfaces of an airfoil is called the

   (A) angle of attack.
   (B) leading airfoil edge.
   (C) upper camber measurement.
   (D) mean camber line.
   (E) wing chord.

4. The straight line joining the ends of the mean camber line is called the

   (A) lower camber curve.
   (B) mean airfoil throughpoint.
   (C) wing chord.
   (D) angle of attack.
   (E) relative lift threshold line.

5. A(n) ___________ is the point at which the airflow over the wings ceases to be a smooth (laminar) flow and the wing starts to lose lift.

   (A) Mach threshold
   (B) tactile feedback
   (C) relative wind camber
   (D) maximum bank limit
   (E) aerodynamic stall

6. The two basic types of drag are
   - (A) parasitic and induced.
   - (B) simple and complex.
   - (C) high pressure and low pressure.
   - (D) induced and incidental.
   - (E) parasitic and peripheral.

7. An airfoil's efficiency, either a wing or a rotor blade, is __________ at high altitudes by the __________ air density.
   - (A) increased, lesser
   - (B) increased, greater
   - (C) decreased, lesser
   - (D) decreased, greater
   - (E) increased, stable

8. The degree of movement of an aircraft around its lateral axis is known as
   - (A) yaw.
   - (B) roll.
   - (C) bank.
   - (D) pitch.
   - (E) sideslip.

9. When the flaps are extended, the camber of the wing is
   - (A) enlarged proportionate to the airspeed.
   - (B) decreased proportionate to the angle of attack.
   - (C) unchanged.
   - (D) decreased.
   - (E) increased.

10. A helicopter's cyclic control is a mechanical linkage used to change the pitch of the main rotor blades
    - (A) all at the same time.
    - (B) at a selected point in its circular pathway.
    - (C) proportionate to the engine RPMs.
    - (D) in conjunction with the desired speed.
    - (E) for vertical flight only.

11. When the rotor blades of a helicopter are spinning fast enough in a clockwise direction to generate lift, a phenomenon known as ___________ causes the body of the helicopter to have a tendency to turn in a counterclockwise direction.

(A) centrifugal force
(B) centripedal force
(C) lateral roll
(D) torque
(E) autorotation

12. Pulling back (toward the pilot) on the control column or joystick of a fixed-wing aircraft will cause the aircraft to

(A) increase its RPMs.
(B) decrease its RPMs.
(C) maintain its angle of attack.
(D) pitch down.
(E) pitch up.

13. Contra-rotating propellers, a complex way of applying the maximum power of a single piston or turboprop aircraft engine, uses two propellers

(A) rotating in the same direction arranged one behind the other.
(B) rotating in opposite directions arranged one behind the other.
(C) rotating in opposite directions on opposite sides of the engine nacelle.
(D) rotating in the same direction on opposite sides of the engine nacelle.
(E) rotating asynchronously in the same direction.

14. The abbreviation VTOL, applied to aircraft other than helicopters, means

(A) Vertical Transmission Of Lift.
(B) Very Turbulent Opposite Launching.
(C) Vertical Take-Off and Landing.
(D) Velocity Transmitted to Onboard Lines.
(E) Virtual Transmission Operation Line.

15. Delta wing aircraft have a wing in the form of a triangle, named after the Greek uppercase letter delta (Δ), and no

(A) vertical stabilizer.
(B) flaps.
(C) horizontal stabilizer.
(D) stabilizing canard.
(E) ogival structure.

16. The Visual Approach Slope Indicator (VASI) is a system of lights designed to provide visual descent guidance information to the pilot during a runway approach. The system uses ______ lights to indicate the upper limits of the glide path and ______ lights for the lower limits.

    (A) red, white
    (B) white, red
    (C) blue, white
    (D) red, green
    (E) green, red

17. A biplane has

    (A) two wings arranged one behind the other.
    (B) two wings arranged one above the other.
    (C) two horizontal stabilizers, one above the other.
    (D) two horizontal stabilizers, one in front of the other.
    (E) two engines, one on each wing.

18. A coordinated turn (change of heading direction) includes both ______ of the airplane.

    (A) pitch and yaw
    (B) roll and bank
    (C) roll and pitch
    (D) pitch and roll
    (E) roll and yaw

19. ______ is induced by use of a movable rudder controlled by ______ in the cockpit.

    (A) Roll, ailerons
    (B) Bank, control column
    (C) Change of pitch, collective
    (D) Yaw, rudder pedals
    (E) Power dive, trim tabs

20. Moving the control column or joystick to the left or right affects the ______ rather than indicating the ______

    (A) angle of pitch, angle of attack.
    (B) angle of bank, rate of roll.
    (C) rate of roll, angle to which the aircraft will roll.
    (D) degree of bank, relative airspeed.
    (E) degree of roll, angle of yaw.

ANSWERS AND EXPLANATIONS

Subtest #1: Verbal Analogies

Check your answers below and refer to the explanation for each question you missed. Use the table to record right and wrong answers.

	✔	✘		✔	✘		✔	✘		✔	✘		✔	✘
1. B			6. D			11. D			16. D			21. B		
2. D			7. B			12. E			17. B			22. D		
3. B			8. A			13. A			18. D			23. A		
4. C			9. E			14. D			19. A			24. D		
5. E			10. C			15. C			20. E			25. A		

1. **(B)** CROWDED is to URBAN as SPARSE is to **RURAL**. This can be viewed as an analogy of description or an analogy of association; an urban area can be described as crowded with people in the same way that a rural area has only a sparse amount of people. Stated another way, an urban area is commonly associated with being crowded, whereas a rural area is usually associated with being sparsely populated. Both descriptive words (adjectives) refer to the amount of people in a given area, but the other adjective choices (slower, industrial, calm) describe other possible conditions of an urban or rural area. A suburban area is another category altogether, in between urban and rural.
2. **(D)** WATCH is to WATCHED as THROW is to **THREW**. This is an association of language; *watched* is the past tense of *watch*, so the correct choice to complete the analogy with *throw* is its past tense, *threw*. THROWED is not a standard conjugation of the verb *throw* (or *to throw*)—otherwise known as "improper English," and therefore not a correct choice. *Thrown* is the past participle form of *throw*—it needs the auxiliary or helping verb *has* to be used properly. A *thrower* is the person who throws—not a form of the verb itself—and *tossed* is not a form of *throw* at all, just a word that is close in meaning.
3. **(B)** WRENCH is to PLUMBER as HAMMER is to **CARPENTER**. This is a "tool to user" analogy. Pliers are the plumber's primary tool in the same way that a hammer is one of the carpenter's primary tools. A nail is used by a carpenter, but it becomes part of the structure the carpenter builds, as opposed to being a tool used on many different jobs. None of the other choices is a tool used by anyone.
4. **(C)** NATURAL is to ARTIFICIAL as **CREATE is to DESTROY**. This is an analogy of language—in this case, we have opposites or antonyms. *Cook* to *waiter* is a relationship, but not one of opposites. *Birth* and *maturity* are at different places on the spectrum of age, but not completely opposite ends of that spectrum. *Cut* and *dissect* are basically synonyms, and a *tear* is partially made out of *water*, so they can't be anything approaching opposites.
5. **(E)** BACON is to PIGS as HAMBURGER is to **CATTLE**. This is a "part to whole" analogy. Bacon comes from pigs and hamburger comes from cows or cattle; both are a certain way to prepare meat from the source animal. *Veal* is a special kind of beef, coming as it does from young cows (i.e., calves). *Beef* is a general term for the meat that comes from

AFOQT #2

cattle; *fowl* is another word for birds (the implication is edible ones in this case); horses are animals, but are not normally used as a meat source.

6. **(D)** KANGAROO is to POUCH as **BUTTERFLY is to COCOON**. This is an analogy of association, although it may seem to be a "part to whole"—the pouch and the cocoon are protective coverings that help the kangaroo and butterfly, respectively, to develop physically and mature. A *bear* can enter a *cave*, but the cave is a shelter or hiding place, not a covering. A *ball* can go into a *glove*, but this analogy is not equivalent because neither the ball nor the glove is living, and therefore the glove can't be a developmental aid. The *web* is something made by the *spider* to catch its prey, and a *fish* can be a member of a *school*—but that's a group, not a covering.

7. **(B)** BEHAVE is to CANDY as DISOBEY is to **REPRIMAND**. This is an "action to result" analogy: if a child, for instance, behaves well, he or she may be rewarded with candy—whereas a child who disobeys will likely receive a reprimand. *Relinquish* means to let go of something, which doesn't make sense as a result of disobedience. An *argument* may ensue if directions are disobeyed, but the weak correlation (i.e., relationship) between cause and effect (it may or may not happen, very uncertain) makes this answer not nearly as strong as reprimand; besides, the implication is strong in the first analogy of a parent- or adult-to-young-child relationship, which doesn't really fit with the *argument* answer. *Dishonesty* and *disruption* may in fact be associated with disobedience, but there is again not nearly as clear a path of relationship as between disobey and reprimand.

8. **(A)** XXII is to IXXX as 22 is to **29**. This is a very easy numerical or mathematical analogy; all we are really asked to do is reproduce the relationship of XXII (22) to IXXX (29) in Arabic numerals rather than Roman.

9. **(E)** AMUSING is to FUNNY as ODD is to **UNUSUAL**. This is an association of language, since amusing and funny are basically synonyms. *Even* is an antonym (opposite) of odd, even though it is an opposite of a different meaning of odd. *Extra* is almost a synonym for yet another meaning of odd—as used in, "He picked up the odd scrap of bread here and there"; in this context, odd means *occasional* or *scattered. Fellow* has no relevant relationship to odd except as a distraction, because of the common phrase or cliché of *odd fellow. Distinct*, like *fellow*, is only a distracting filler choice—so don't fall for it.

10. **(C)** HONOR is to COURAGE as **SELFISHNESS is to GREED**. You can look at this analogy either as one of association or as "action to result"—when one has honor in one's character, one is likely to exhibit courage; in the same way, when a person has selfishness as part of their internal makeup, they will probably show some degree of greed. *Light* and *darkness* are opposites, rather than such associated qualities as honor and courage. *Knowledge* and *wisdom* are without doubt associated qualities, but *knowledge* is not a character trait—it is something one either has or doesn't. By the same token, *duty* is usually viewed as an externally imposed obligation; even if one feels *duty* to one's *country*, that is the object of the obligation, not the external manifestation of the inner quality. And, of course, a *key* does go into an *ignition* to start a car, but these are inanimate objects, not qualities of living beings.

11. **(D)** ATLANTA is to GEORGIA as DALLAS is to **TEXAS**. This is a geographical analogy (city-state/city-state); Atlanta is a very large metropolitan city in Georgia, just as Dallas is a very large metropolitan city in Texas. *Fort Worth* is another city in Texas, but this

doesn't fit the city-state/city-state pattern; *Birmingham* is a large city in Alabama; *cowboys* (either the real kind or the football team) are associated with Dallas but don't fit the pattern; and *Louisiana*, although adjacent to Texas, does not fit the pattern, either.

12. **(E)** CLOCK is to WATCH as **LAKE is to POND**. This is an analogy of association; a clock is a larger version of a watch in much the same way that a lake is a larger version of a pond. *Stream* does not properly complete the analogy pattern, since it has a current and can be said to move "from" one place to another, whereas a *lake* does not have an appreciable current and stays in one place, so to speak. Viewed another way, a stream is a linear feature, whereas a lake is not; either way, *stream* is an incorrect choice. For much the same reasons, *ocean* and *river* are incorrect choices. *Water* and *fish* fit the pattern even less, since *fish* is either a verb or denotes a living thing—and *boat* and *sail* fit the pattern even more poorly (a *sail* is either part of a boat or it is a verb), even though they are associated terms.
13. **(A)** STABLE is to HORSE as **HOUSE is to HUMAN**. This is an analogy of association; for the second pair, we are looking for something that is a dwelling place or shelter for a living thing. The only choice here that is even close is house and human. *Water* and *duck* are the closest contenders, but, although water is certainly associated with ducks, it is not a shelter or dwelling for them.
14. **(D)** SQUIRREL is to TREE as GOPHER is to **GROUND**. Here we have yet another analogy of association; a squirrel lives in a tree, so we are looking for where in the wild a gopher lives. Since gophers live in holes in the ground—and not in the *forest* (too broad of a general area), nor in a *bush* or *lake* or *hollow* (either in a particular tree or in a forest)—(D) is the correct choice here.
15. **(C)** INFANCY is to CHILDHOOD as ENGAGEMENT is to **MARRIAGE**. This may best be viewed as an analogy of association; both of the first terms are immediate preparatory stages for the conditions mentioned as second terms. *Drive train* is a nonsense distracter choice; *love* usually comes before engagement, not after; a *ring* traditionally comes as a symbol of engagement rather than a stage; and a *bride* is what results from a marriage, but is a person and not a stage of development.
16. **(D)** TRAVEL is to AUTO as **EAT is to SPOON**. This is a "function to object" analogy, since travel can be done in an auto, just as eating can be done with a spoon. A *train* does *whistle*, but that's not its primary function; in addition, the order is reversed ("object to function" instead of "function to object"), so it doesn't fit the pattern, either. *Water* is something that is consumed in the act of its use as a *drink*, so that doesn't fit the pattern, either; *soldiers* and *sailors* are different categories of military personnel—just as *meat* and *potatoes* are different food items, so those choices don't fit, either.
17. **(B)** ABU DHABI is to MUSCAT as **BEIRUT is to DAMASCUS**. This is a geographical analogy; Abu Dhabi and Muscat are capitals of adjacent countries (United Arab Emirates and Oman, respectively), and Beirut and Damascus are likewise capitals of adjacent countries (Lebanon and Syria, respectively). *Cairo* is the capital of Egypt and *Incirlik* is the capital of Turkey, but those countries are not adjacent; *London* is the capital of England, but the German city of *Hamburg* is not that country's capital and England

and Germany aren't adjacent. *Austin* and *Baton Rouge* are state capitals but not national capitals; and *Oman* and *Yemen* are countries, not cities.

18. **(D)** SURGEON is to SCALPEL as FIREMAN is to **WATER HOSE**. This is a "user to tool" analogy; a surgeon uses a scalpel to do his job (perform surgery), just as a fireman uses a water hose to put out fires. A *siren* is also a tool used by a fireman, but it is used to get to the scene of a fire, not to do the fireman's job of putting out the fire; likewise, a fireman may use a *helmet* for protection, but, again, he does not use it to perform his primary function. The *dalmatian* is a dog traditionally associated with firehouses, but it is not used to put out fires, either—and a *policeman* is a different type of emergency responder, by no means a tool used by the fireman.

19. **(A)** FRAME is to PAINTING as **FENCE is to YARD**. This is an analogy of association—specifically, the first object outlines and contains the second object. A *cover* does contain the pages of a *book*, but it does not outline the book in the same way as the correct choices. A *cloud* is an object in the *sky* ("part to whole"); a *park* is watched over by a *ranger* (an analogy of association but not the right kind); and a *jack* is used to change a *tire*—again, an analogy of association, but not the right kind.

20. **(E)** CASCADE is to WATERFALL as **MEANDER is to STREAM**. This is a "function to object" analogy—what the waterfall does is cascade, and what the stream does is meander; these are transitive, movement-oriented functions of inanimate things. *Fish* are living things that live in the water of a *river* in this case, but that water is the only connection to the analogy to which we are supposed to relate. *Warn* is something that the authorities do before a *hurricane*—there is no direct connection between the verb *warn* and the noun *hurricane*, because the hurricane neither warns nor gets warned; there must exist the help of people to complete the connection, such as it is. *Lake* is to *sail* also has a water-based connection, but this is an object that moves on top of the water, rather than the way the body of water itself moves. And, finally, *cross* is to *ocean* requires the presence of an implied direct object (whatever is crossing the ocean), which means again that there is not a direct connection, and that the analogy is not the correct choice.

21. **(B)** INFORM is to ENLIGHTEN as SING is to **ENTERTAIN**. This is an "action to result" analogy; when you *inform* someone of new information, you *enlighten* them. In the same way, when you *sing* for or to someone, you can *entertain* them (depending on the quality of the singing!). A *melody* and a *refrain* are things that you can sing—"whats" and not "results." *Confess* is a distracter choice, and *whistle*, although still musical, is in a "next-door-neighbor" category to singing—it's not a result.

22. **(D)** PECAN is to PIE as CHOCOLATE is to **CAKE**. This is an analogy of association where the first term of the base analogy is a main ingredient of the dessert named as the second term. *Brown* describes chocolate but nothing more—it is not an ingredient. *Frosting* denotes an optional outer part of a dessert, but, again, it is not an ingredient of that dessert. Chocolate *chips* can be an ingredient of a dessert, but are unlikely to be the primary ingredient. And *dessert*, of course, rather than being an appropriate second half of the analogy, is a general term for a sweet eaten after the main meal.

23. **(A)** WALK is to MARCH as **READ is to STUDY**. This is a "general to specific" analogy pattern—a certain type of walking is marching, just as a certain type of reading is

studying. A *tread* is either one impact on the ground of a *foot*, or it's the sound that *foot* makes; *run* and *stop* are opposites; *waltz* and *rumba* are two different types of dance, just as *rap* and *jazz* are different types of music—in this context, you could call these two "specific to specific" analogies, if there were such a category.

24. **(D)** KABUL is to AFGHANISTAN as **CAIRO is to EGYPT**. This is a geographical analogy; Kabul is the capital of Afghanistan, just as Cairo is the capital of the country of Egypt. *Pensacola* is a city (not even the capital) of the state of *Florida*, which is not, of course, a country unto itself. *Calcutta* is a large city—but, again, not the capital—of *India*; *Japan* and *Korea* are two different countries; and *Cancun* is a resort city in Mexico, which is a different Central American country than its neighboring country *Honduras*.

25. **(A)** PERPLEX is to ENLIGHTEN as MIXTURE is to **INDIVIDUAL**. This is an analogy of language. Perplex means to confuse or otherwise fail to gain understanding, whereas to enlighten is to grant or help achieve that understanding; these are opposites (antonyms). Likewise, mixture and individual are opposite terms. An *additive* is something that might result in a mixture; a poorly combined mixture might have some of its components *settle* to the bottom of its container. Those same components that settled might eventually *solidify*, but in any case we can't tell whether the new solid was a mixture or a pure, individual material; and *social* is a distracter choice, meant to cause the test-taker to think of a mixture of different people instead of mixture's opposite, individual.

Subtest #2: Arithmetic Reasoning

Check your answers below and refer to the explanation for each question you missed. Use the table to record right and wrong answers.

	✔	✘		✔	✘		✔	✘		✔	✘		✔	✘
1. A			**6. B**			**11. E**			**16. D**			**21. C**		
2. C			**7. D**			**12. C**			**17. A**			**22. A**		
3. B			**8. D**			**13. A**			**18. C**			**23. B**		
4. B			**9. A**			**14. D**			**19. B**			**24. B**		
5. D			**10. B**			**15. B**			**20. D**			**25. B**		

1. **(A)** The total number of Airmen in the squadron (132) divided by the total number in each flight (11 Airmen plus one NCO equals 12 total) gives the number of flights in the squadrons.

$$132 \div 12 = \mathbf{11}$$

Eleven noncommissioned officers are needed, one for each flight.

2. **(C)** Find the total of all the amounts withheld.

$$\$27.75 + \$5.65 + \$9.29 + \$3.58 = \$46.27$$

Net pay is the salary for the week minus the total of all withholdings.

$$\begin{aligned}\text{Net pay} &= \$350.00 - \$46.27 \\ &= \mathbf{\$303.73}\end{aligned}$$

AFOQT #2

3. **(B)** The average is the sum of the high and low temperatures divided by two. However, we have to be careful not to get tangled up in the fact that the high and low temperatures cross the "zero" line, giving us positive and negative numbers. There are 20 degrees between –4° and 16°F,

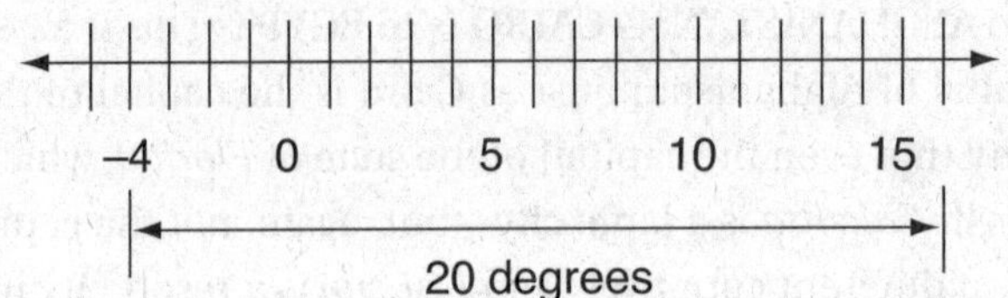

so when we divide 20 by 2, we get 10 degrees, which we have to add to –4° to give us the final answer of **6°F**.

4. **(B)** If $\frac{1}{4}$ inch represents 1 foot, then $\frac{3}{4}$ inch will represent 3 feet. $\frac{1}{2}$ foot will be represented by one-half of $\frac{1}{4}$ inch, or $\frac{1}{8}$ inch. Thus, $3\frac{1}{2}$ feet will be represented by $\frac{3}{4}$ inch plus $\frac{1}{8}$ inch, or $\mathbf{\frac{7}{8}}$ **inch**.

5. **(D)** The discount will be 15% (or 0.15) of the list price, $13,620.

$$\$13{,}620 \times 0.15 = \mathbf{\$2{,}043.00}$$

6. **(B)** Find the increase in price by subtracting the original price from the new price per gallon.

$$\text{Increase in price} = \$3.08 - \$2.90 = \$0.18$$

The percent of increase is the rise in price, multiplied by 100, divided by the original price.

$$(\$0.18 \times 100) \div \$2.90 = \mathbf{6.2\%}$$

7. **(D)** The number of games won is 70% (or 0.70) of the number of games played, 40.

$$\text{Number of games won} = 0.70(40) = 28$$

The number of games lost is the total number played minus the number won.

$$\text{Number of games lost} = 40 - 28 = \mathbf{12}$$

8. **(D)** The time of arrival is 2 hours and 55 minutes after the departure time of 3:50 P.M. By 4:00 P.M., the flight has taken 10 minutes of the total flight time of 2 hours and 55 minutes. 2 hours and 45 minutes remain, and 2 hours and 45 minutes after 4:00 P.M. is **6:45 P.M.**

9. **(A)** There are 16 oz. in 1 lb. Therefore, 4 of the 4-oz. candy bars will make 1 lb. A 3-lb. package will hold 3 times 4 or **12** bars.

10. **(B)** Find the relationship between each pair of successive numbers in the series. It is helpful to change $3\frac{1}{2}$ to $3\frac{3}{6}$ to see the relationships. Each term of the series is obtained by adding $\frac{4}{6}$ to the preceding term. The fifth term is $5\frac{3}{6}$ or $\mathbf{5\frac{1}{2}}$.

11. **(E)** First add the prices of the three items ordered to get the cost of the meal before the tax.

$$\$12.50 + \$3.50 + \$1.25 = \$17.25$$

The tax is 8% (or 0.08) of the cost of the meal.

$$0.08 \times \$17.25 = \mathbf{\$1.38}$$

12. **(C)** There are 4 quarts in 1 gallon; therefore, a 55-gallon drum holds 4×55 quarts.

$$4 \times 55 \text{ qts.} = 220 \text{ qts.}$$

If each can holds 2 quarts, the number of cans filled is 220 divided by 2.

$$220 \div 2 = \mathbf{110} \text{ cans}$$

13. **(A)** Since it takes 45 minutes to finish nine spindles, it takes five minutes to finish each spindle ($45 \div 9 = 5$). So, the number of minutes it takes to finish 96 spindles is:

$$5 \times 96 = 480$$

$$480 \text{ minutes} \div 60 \text{ minutes} = \mathbf{8} \text{ hours}$$

14. **(D)** The perimeter, 40 feet, is the sum of the lengths of all three sides. The sum of the lengths of the two equal sides is the difference between the perimeter and the length of the third side. The sum of the lengths of two equal sides

$$= 40 \text{ ft.} - 13 \text{ ft., } 2 \text{ in.}$$
$$= 39 \text{ ft., } 12 \text{ in.} - 13 \text{ ft., } 2 \text{ in.}$$
$$= 26 \text{ ft., } 10 \text{ in.}$$

The length of one side is obtained by dividing the sum by 2.
The length of one equal side equals **13 ft., 5 in.**

15. **(B)** Since 3 feet = 1 yard, convert the length and width to yards by dividing their dimensions in feet by 3. The area of a rectangle is the product of its length and width.

$$\text{Area} = 7 \times 13 = 91 \text{ sq. yds.}$$

The cost for the entire lawn is obtained by multiplying the area in square yards by the cost per square yard.

$$91 \times \$.40 = \mathbf{\$36.40}$$

16. **(D)** Find the number of miles traveled by multiplying the rate, 48 mph, by the time, seven hours.

$$48 \times 7 = 336 \text{ miles}$$

The number of gallons of gas used is the number of miles driven divided by the number of miles per gallon.

$$336 \div 21 = \mathbf{16}$$

17. **(A)** If the profits are shared in the ratio 5:4, one partner gets $\frac{5}{9}$ of the profits and the other gets $\frac{4}{9}$. Note that $\frac{5}{9} + \frac{4}{9} = 1$, the whole profit. The larger share is $\frac{5}{9}$ of the profit, $63,000, or **$35,000.**

18. **(C)** Consider the original price as 100%. Then the price after an increase of 4% is 104%. To find the original price, divide the price after the increase, $17.16, by 104% (or 1.04).

    $17.16 ÷ 1.04 = $16.50
    $16.50 = original price

19. **(B)** 5 workers making 6 garments each = 30 garments per day plus 3 workers making 4 garments each = 12 garments per day plus 1 worker making 12 garments each = 12 garments per day = 54 garments per day.

    Divide the total number of workers (5 + 3 + 1 = 9) into the total number of garments produced per day:

    54 garments per day ÷ 9 workers = **6** garments per worker per day

20. **(D)** The distance traveled by driving at 45 mph for 2 hours is 2 × 45 = 90 miles. The remainder of the 255-mile trip is 255 – 90, or 165 miles.

    To finish the trip in 5 hours, the driver has 5 – 2 = 3 hours still to drive. To find the rate of travel for a distance of 165 miles driven in 3 hours, divide the distance by the time.

    165 miles ÷ 3 hours = **55 mph**

21. **(C)** Calculate and add up the contractor's expenses:

Masonry materials and labor	$300,000 ÷ 10 = $ 30,000
Lumber and carpentry	$300,000 ÷ 3 = $100,000
Plumbing and heating	$300,000 ÷ 5 = $ 60,000
Electrical and lighting work	$300,000 ÷ 6 = $ 50,000
Total	$240,000

    Subtract his expenses from the total bid:

    $300,000 – $240,000 = **$60,000** profit

22. **(A)** The first discount of 20% means that a customer actually pays 80% $\left(\text{or } \frac{4}{5}\right)$ of the list price. The second successive discount of 30% means that a customer actually pays 70% $\left(\text{or } \frac{7}{10}\right)$ of the price determined after the first discount. The price the customer actually pays is the list price multiplied by the portions determined from each discount or ($325)(0.80)(0.70) = **$182.00.**

23. **(B)** At 2 quarts for $1.99, each quart costs

    $1.99 ÷ 2 = $.995 per qt.

    At 6 quarts for $5.43, each quart costs

    $5.43 ÷ 6 = $.905 per qt.

    The savings per quart is

    $.995 – $.905 = **$.09** per qt. savings

24. **(B)** For the regular 40 hours, the worker earns $\$7.20 \times 40 = \$288.00$. If the regular wage is $7.20 per hour, then overtime paid at time and a half is $\$7.20 \times 1.5 = \$10.80$. The three hours of overtime earn the worker a total of $32.40. Add the regular time wages to the overtime wages:

$$\$288.00 + \$32.40 = \mathbf{\$320.40} \text{ total pay}$$

25. **(B)** The ratio of the heights of the two trees will be the same as the ratio of the lengths of their shadows. The ratio of the length of the shadow of the second tree to the length of the shadow of the first tree is $\frac{6}{8}$ or $\frac{3}{4}$.

Thus, the height of the second tree is $\frac{3}{4}$ of the height of the 36-foot tree.

$$36 \text{ ft.} \times \frac{3}{4} = \mathbf{27 \text{ ft.}}$$

Subtest #3: Word Knowledge

Check your answers below and refer to the explanation for each question you missed. Use the table to record right and wrong answers.

	✔	✘		✔	✘		✔	✘		✔	✘		✔	✘
1. D			6. D			11. B			16. C			21. D		
2. B			7. A			12. A			17. C			22. C		
3. A			8. C			13. D			18. B			23. D		
4. D			9. E			14. E			19. A			24. A		
5. B			10. A			15. E			20. D			25. E		

1. **(D)** SIMULTANEOUS means **concurrent** or happening at the same time. *Versatile* means having the ability to change from one task to another, or to be used in more than one way; an *imitation* or *false appearance* could be thought of as a *simulation*, which has the same root as *simultaneous* but a different final meaning; *indefinite* means "having no precise limits" or "vague."

2. **(B)** PARAGON means a **prototype** or original example. A *triangular structure* is a pyramid; a *wax figure* is made from paraffin.

3. **(A)** DEMONSTRABLE means **evident** or provable. *Able to be refuted* is deniable; something that is *able to be torn down* is something that can be demolished; and another word for *countable* is denumerable.

4. **(D)** CONTROVERSY means **disagreement** or argument. *Vehicles moving together* are a convoy; a *school of music* is a conservatory; an *armed police force* is a constabulary; and an *agreement* by people *to commit* a crime or *wrong* act is a conspiracy.

5. **(B)** TEMERITY means **presumptuous daring** or rash boldness. *Automatically* transmitted *readings* are telemetry; *mental communication* is telepathy; and a *story prepared for television* is a teleplay.

6. **(D)** SCRUTINY means a **careful inspection**, often at close range or with a critical attitude. A *point of conscience or ethics* is a scruple; an *obligation* is a duty; a *revolt of a ship's crew* is a mutiny; and the *room adjoining the kitchen*—especially in a large, older-style house or mansion—is a scullery.

7. **(A)** To JETTISON an object is to **discard** it. A *long pier* is known as a jetty; something that is *uninteresting or empty* is jejune; to *build shoddily* is to jerry-build; to *compete for advantage* or position, especially in a crowd, is to jostle.

8. **(C)** CONCILIATE means to **placate**. To *speak briefly* is to speak in a concise way; to *form in the mind* is to conceive; to *set apart as sacred* is to consecrate; and to *confuse* is to confound.

9. **(E)** ARBITRARY means **selected at random**, as opposed to an orderly or arranged manner. *Fervent* means ardent or intense; one who is *lacking consistency* could be thought of as erratic; and *disputed* could be thought of as arguing or controversial.

10. **(A)** ENVISAGE means **conceive**. To *articulate* is to enunciate or explain; to *designate* is to set apart or mark. To *paint one's face* is a distracter choice because it has an indirect reference to a common root, *visage* (meaning "face"), which still, however, does not apply to this question.

11. **(B)** SCLEROTIC means **having hardened arteries**. *Mentally disturbed* is neurotic.

12. **(A)** PARTISAN means an **adherent** or "one who takes the part of another"; by World War II, this had grown to include resistance members or guerillas in an occupied country, such as France when it was occupied by Nazi Germany. *Divided* means to be partitioned; *not complete* means partial; *over-hasty* could be thought of as precipitant; and a participle is one type of a *part of speech*.

13. **(D)** INCEPTION means **beginning**. A *careful examination* is an inspection; *divine guidance* is often thought of as inspiration; an *ever-present feature* is often referred to as an institution; and a *revolt against authority* is an insurrection.

14. **(E)** DERIVATIVE means **following** (or deriving) **from** something that has gone or occurred before. A synonym for *serving to prove* is demonstrative; and something that is *deprived of vitality* is said to be deanimated.

15. **(E)** PERVASIVE means **permeating**—as when an odor goes all through a room, to every corner, it is said to be pervasive. Being *influential*, on the other hand, is much the same as being persuasive; something that is *on the outer part* can be said to be peripheral.

16. **(C)** An INANITY is a **statement lacking sense**, as when someone wakes from a dream and says, "The sinks can't fly back to the kitchen because their lacquer has expired." This word (inanity) is often confused with insanity, which is *mental unbalance*.

17. **(C)** PLAUSIBLE means **believable**. Someone who is *unemotional* could be said to be phlegmatic, and something that is *flexible* is considered pliable.

18. **(B)** CONDUCIVE means **contributive**—it sets up the conditions for something that follows, as when you have a comfortable, quiet setting that is conducive to studying this book. This is often confused with being *able to transmit electricity*, which is conductive, and *ignitable*, which is another word for combustible. A synonym for *simultaneous* is also concurrent.

19. **(A)** ENSEMBLE means a **coordinated group or outfit**. To *bring together* is to assemble; the lowest *naval officer rank* is an ensign; to *rake with gunfire* along its length is to enfilade the enemy position; and an airplane's *tail section* is also known as the empennage.

20. **(D)** DELETERIOUS means **harmful**. This is another word that sounds a little like several other words, so some people get them confused. To do something *with careful thought* is to deliberate; someone who is *behind schedule* is delinquent; a dish that is *very tasty* is said to be delectable; and, when a part is *removed from the total*, it has been deleted.

21. **(D)** LITIGATION is nothing more than a **legal case**. *Marking or outlining* is called lineation; *coastland waters* are referred to as a littoral area or littorals; a *governmental ruling* by an elected body is known as legislation; and a *chemical test for acid or base* is known as a litmus test.

22. **(C)** IMPRIMATUR means a **signature**, usually one meaning approval by an authority. It has nothing to do with primates.

23. **(D)** DECELERATE means to **slow down**. To *belittle* someone is to denigrate them; to *remove* or withdraw *approval* in an official capacity is to decertify; to *speed up* is to accelerate; and to *deny* is to denegate.

24. **(A)** UNILATERAL means **obligating one side only**. Being *the same throughout* is to be uniform; a *sideways motion* can involve a common root, lateral; making a *wavelike motion* is to undulate; and an object or thing that *has one compartment* can be correctly called unilocular or unicameral.

25. **(E)** INTRANSIGENT means **uncompromising**. *Doing things in a new way* can be thought of as innovative; *knowing without being told* is intuitive; something that is *in between boundaries* is interstitial; and a *courageous* act can also be called intrepid.

Subtest #4: Math Knowledge

Check your answers below and refer to the explanation for each question you missed. Use the table to record right and wrong answers.

	✔	✘		✔	✘		✔	✘		✔	✘		✔	✘
1. A			**6. C**			**11. C**			**16. A**			**21. C**		
2. C			**7. C**			**12. A**			**17. A**			**22. D**		
3. D			**8. C**			**13. D**			**18. D**			**23. A**		
4. B			**9. C**			**14. C**			**19. B**			**24. D**		
5. D			**10. A**			**15. B**			**20. B**			**25. C**		

1. **(A)** Multiply 0.0375 by 4% (or 0.04).

$$0.0375 \times 0.04 = 0.001500 = \mathbf{0.0015}$$

Note that the product has as many decimal places as there are in the multiplicand and multiplier combined, but the two final zeros may be dropped, since they are to the right of the decimal point and at the end.

2. **(C)** If a number is multiplied by its reciprocal (also called its multiplicative inverse), the product is 1. The reciprocal of a fraction is found by inverting the fraction. The reciprocal of $\frac{2}{3}$ is $\frac{3}{2}$, that is, $\frac{2}{3} \times \frac{3}{2} = 1$.

3. **(D)** Substitute 3 for x and –2 for y in the expression $x^2 - 5xy + 2y$.

$$(3)^2 - 5(3)(-2) + 2(-2)$$
$$9 - 15(-2) - 4$$
$$9 + 30 - 4$$
$$\mathbf{35}$$

4. **(B)** $x - 3 < 14$ is an inequality that states that x minus 3 is less than 14. To solve the inequality, add 3 to both sides of it.

$$x - 3 + 3 < 14 + 3$$
$$\mathbf{x < 17}$$

The result says that the inequality is true for any value of x less than 17. Try it for some value of x less than 17—for example, $x = 10$.

$$10 - 3 < 14$$
$$7 < 14 \text{ is a true statement}$$

5. **(D)** To multiply $7a^3b^2c$ by $3a^2b^4c^2$, first multiply the numerical coefficients, 7 and 3.

$$7 \times 3 = 21$$

Powers of the same base, such as a^3 and a^2, are multiplied by adding their exponents; thus, $a^3 \times a^2 = a^5$.

$$(a^3b^2c) \times (a^2b^4c^2) = a^5b^6c^3$$

Note that c should be regarded as c^1 when adding exponents. The combined result for $(7a^3b^2c) \times (3a^2b^4c^2) = \mathbf{21a^5b^6c^3}$.

6. **(C)** A hexagon has six sides. Each of the six sides of the black tile must touch a side of a white tile, so there are **6** white tiles surrounding each black tile.

7. **(C)** x^0 is defined as always equal to 1, provided that x does not equal 0; therefore, $8^0 = \mathbf{1}$.

8. **(C)** The equation $2x - 3 = 37$ means that "twice a number minus 3 is equal to 37." To arrive at a value for x, we first eliminate –3 on the left side. This can be done by adding 3 to both sides of the equation, thus undoing the subtraction.

$$2x - 3 + 3 = 37 + 3$$
$$2x = 40$$

To eliminate the 2, we undo the multiplication by dividing both sides of the equation by 2.

$$\frac{2x}{2} = \frac{40}{2}$$
$$x = \mathbf{20}$$

AFOQT #2

9. **(C)** If $\frac{2}{3}$ of M people are adults, then $\frac{2}{3}M$ represents the number of adults. If $\frac{1}{2}$ of $\frac{2}{3}M$ are males, then $\frac{1}{2} \times \frac{2}{3}M = \mathbf{\frac{1}{3}M}$, represents the number of adult males.

10. **(A)** $(0.2)^3$ means $0.2 \times 0.2 \times 0.2$.
Multiply the first two numbers:

$$0.2 \times 0.2 = 0.04$$

Now multiply by the remaining number:

$$0.04 \times 0.2 = \mathbf{0.008}$$

11. **(C)** Rewrite the equation as $x^2 + x - 6 = 0$. The left side of the equation can now be factored:

$$(x + 3)(x - 2) = 0$$

This result says that the product of two factors, $(x + 3)$ and $(x - 2)$, equals 0. But if the product of two factors equals 0, then either or both must equal 0:

$$x + 3 = 0 \text{ or } x - 2 = 0$$

Subtract 3 from both sides of the left equation to isolate x on one side, and add 2 to both sides of the right equation to accomplish the same result:

$$x + 3 - 3 = 0 - 3 \qquad x - 2 + 2 = 0 + 2$$
$$x = \mathbf{-3} \qquad x = \mathbf{2}$$

12. **(A)** The area of a circle is πr^2 where $\pi = \frac{22}{7}$ and r represents the length of the radius. A radius is one-half the length of a diameter. Therefore, if the diameter is 28 inches, the radius of the circle is 14 inches.

$$\begin{aligned}\text{Area of circle} &= \frac{22}{7} \times \frac{14}{1} \times \frac{14}{1}\\ &= \frac{44}{1} \times \frac{14}{1}\\ &= \frac{616}{1}\\ &= \mathbf{616}\text{ sq. in.}\end{aligned}$$

13. **(D)** If $x = -3$, the denominator of

$$\frac{x^2 + 2x - 3}{x + 3}$$

will equal 0. Division of 0 is undefined, so x cannot equal **–3**.

14. **(C)** The given equation means that a number is added to 11, the square root of the result is taken, and the result equals 9. The square root sign (or radical sign) can be removed by squaring both sides of the equation.

$$(\sqrt{x + 11})^2 = 9^2$$
$$x + 11 = 81$$

AFOQT #2

Isolate x on one side of the equation by subtracting 11 from both sides.

$$x + 11 - 11 = 81 - 11$$
$$x = \mathbf{70}$$

15. **(B)**

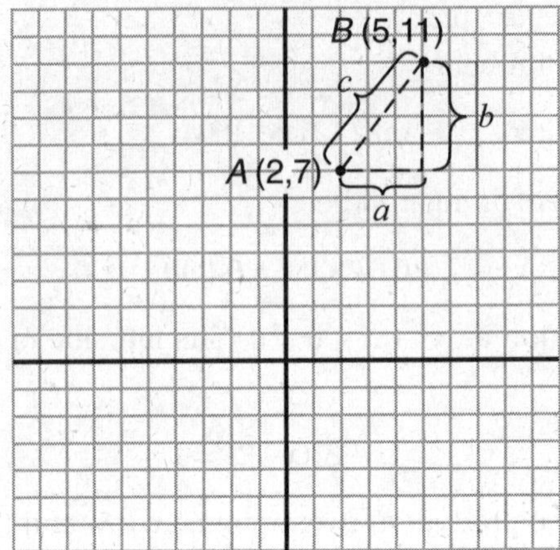

Plot the points. When a pair of numbers is given as the coordinates of a point, the first number is the x-value (the distance right or left from the origin or (0, 0) point). The second number is the y-value (or distance up or down). Form the right triangle as shown in the diagram. The horizontal leg has a length of 5 – 2, or 3; the vertical leg has a length of 11 – 7, or 4. The distance A to B is the hypotenuse of the right triangle. Let $x = \overline{AB}$. By the Pythagorean theorem, the square of the length of the hypotenuse equals the sum of the squares of the lengths of the legs.

$$x^2 = 3^2 + 4^2$$
$$x^2 = 9 + 16$$
$$x^2 = 25$$

The equation $x^2 = 25$ means that x times x equals 25. Therefore, $x = \mathbf{5}$.

16. **(A)** The given equation, $ay - bx = 2$, is to be solved for y. Isolate the y term on one side of the equation by adding bx to both sides.

$$ay - bx + bx = 2 + bx$$
$$ay = 2 + bx$$

This gives us y multiplied by a. To obtain y alone, undo the multiplication by dividing both sides of the equation by a.

$$\frac{ay}{a} = \frac{(2+bx)}{a}$$
$$y = \boldsymbol{\frac{(2+bx)}{a}}$$

17. **(A)** The probability of a particular event occurring is the number of favorable outcomes divided by the total possible number of outcomes. Because there are three possible infantrymen to choose, there are three possible favorable outcomes for choosing an infantryman. A choice may be made from among three infantrymen, two artillerymen, and five tank crewmen, so there are 3 + 2 + 5, or 10, possible outcomes in total. The probability of choosing an infantryman is, therefore, $\boldsymbol{\frac{3}{10}}$.

18. **(D)** A length of cord that will wind around once is equal to the circumference of the circle whose radius is 3 inches. The circumference of a circle equals $2\pi r$ where $\pi = \frac{22}{7}$ and r is the radius.

$$\text{Circumference} = \frac{2}{1} \times \frac{22}{7} \times \frac{3}{1} = \frac{132}{7} \text{ inches}$$

If the cord can be wound around the post seven times, its length is seven times the length of one circumference.

Length of cord = **132 inches**

19. **(B)** There are four possible choices for the destroyer. Each of these choices may be coupled with any of the two choices for the supply ship. Each such destroyer–supply ship combination may in turn be coupled with any of the three possible choices for the submarine. Thus, there are $4 \times 2 \times 3$, or **24**, different combinations possible.

20. **(B)** The volume of a cylinder is equal to the product of its height and the area of its base. The base is a circle. The area of a circle is πr^2, where $\pi = \frac{22}{7}$ and r is the radius. Since the diameter is 2 inches, the radius (which is one-half the diameter) is 1 inch.

A = Area of the base

$A = \pi(r^2)$

$A = \frac{22}{7}(1^2)$

$A = \frac{22}{7}$

V = Volume of the cylinder

h = height of the cylinder

$V = A \times h$

$V = \frac{22}{7}$ sq. in. $\times$ 7 in.

V = **22 cu. in.**

21. **(C)**

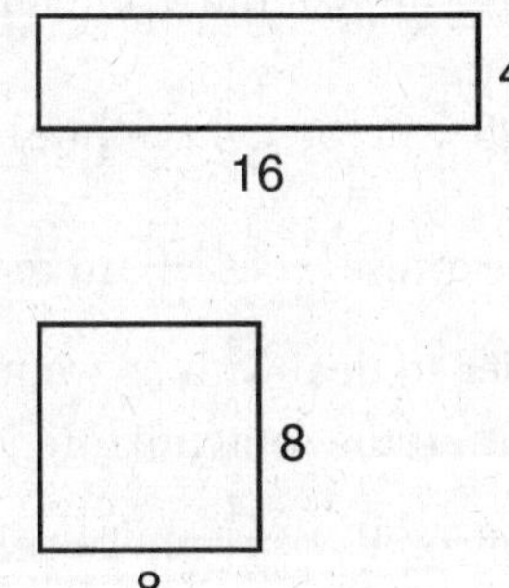

The area of the rectangular garden is equal to the product of its length and width.

Area of rectangle = $16 \times 4 = 64$ square yards

For the square to have the same area, 64 square yards, its sides must each be 8 yards long, since $8 \times 8 = 64$ square yards. The fence around the rectangular garden has a length of $16 + 4 + 16 + 4$, or 40, yards. The fence around the square garden has a length of 4×8, or 32, yards. Thus, the saving in fencing material is $40 - 32$, or **8**, yards.

22. **(D)** $\sqrt{164}$ stands for the square root of 164, or the number that when multiplied by itself equals 164. We know that $12 \times 12 = 144$ and that $13 \times 13 = 169$. Therefore, $\sqrt{164}$ lies between 12 and 13. It is nearer to **13** since 164 is nearer to 169 than it is to 144.

23. **(A)** The storage space measurements of 1 foot × 2 feet × 2 feet, 1 inch can be converted to inches as 12 inches × 24 inches × 25 inches. Boxes measuring 3 inches × 4 inches × 5 inches can be stacked so that four of the 3-inch sides make up the 12-inch storage dimension, six of the 4-inch sides fill the 24-inch storage dimension, and five of the 5-inch sides fill the 25-inch storage dimension. There will therefore be $4 \times 6 \times 5$, or **120**, boxes packed into the storage space.

24. **(D)**

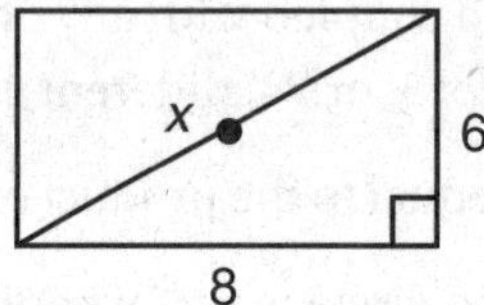

If the circle passes through all four vertices of the rectangle, its diameter will be a diagonal of the rectangle. Since a rectangle's angles are right angles, the diagonal forms a right triangle with two sides of the rectangle. Let x = the length of the diagonal. By the Pythagorean theorem, in a right triangle the square of the length of the hypotenuse is equal to the sum of the squares of the legs.

$$x^2 = 8^2 + 6^2$$
$$x^2 = 64 + 36$$
$$x^2 = 100$$

$x^2 = 100$ means that x times $x = 100$; therefore, $x = 10$ feet. But 10 is a diameter of the circle, and a radius of a circle is one-half the diameter. Hence, the radius is **5** feet.

25. **(C)** If the original mixture is $33\frac{1}{3}\%$ $\left(\text{or } \frac{1}{3}\right)$ acetone, then $\frac{1}{3}$ of the mixture of 12 liters, or 4 liters, is acetone. We can express $\frac{1}{3}$ as $\frac{4}{12}$ to represent the ratio of acetone to the total mixture; this will be easier to deal with as we make our calculations, since there are 12 liters in the total mixture. If the total mixture is increased by x liters, the ratio of acetone to the total mixture becomes $\frac{4}{(12+x)}$. To solve this problem, we then have to set this as equal to 25%, which we will still express here as $\frac{1}{4}$ to make our calculations easier.

$$\frac{4}{(12+x)} = \frac{1}{4}$$

Our next objective is to solve for x by getting it by itself on one side of the equation. To undo the division on both sides of the equation, first multiply both sides by 4 and then by $(12 + x)$.

AFOQT #2

$$4 \times \left(\frac{4}{(12+x)}\right) = 4 \times \left(\frac{1}{4}\right)$$

$$\frac{16}{12+x} = 1$$

$$\frac{(12+x)\times 16}{12+x} = (12 + x) \times 1$$

$$16 = 12 + x$$
$$16 - 12 = 12 + x - 12$$
$$4 = x$$

Subtest #5: Reading Comprehension

Check your answers below and refer to the explanation for each question you missed. Use the table to record right and wrong answers.

	✔	✘		✔	✘		✔	✘		✔	✘		✔	✘
1. C			6. C			11. A			16. B			21. E		
2. D			7. A			12. D			17. D			22. A		
3. B			8. D			13. B			18. E			23. B		
4. A			9. A			14. B			19. B			24. B		
5. B			10. B			15. D			20. E			25. C		

1. **(C)** The primary purpose of this passage is to provide **an overview of the SPP as a program at the end of FY 2016.** The passage starts by defining the program, what it does, and who is involved in it. Then, it gives the program's overall status as of the end of FY 2016. It does not discuss, in any detail, the program's funding (choice (A)), beginnings (choice (B)), history (choice (D)), or expenses (choice (E)).

2. **(D)** In the last paragraph, the word "engendered" most nearly means **started and supported**. Although "enabled" (choice (E)) is closer than the other choices to the dictionary definitions of *caused or gave rise to* and *generated,* the best answer is "started and supported" (choice (D)). You can also tell from how it is used in the sentence that it has something to do with starting, which is more than just enabling.

3. **(B)** You can infer from the passage that **the benefits that the U.S. receives due to the SPP go beyond just monetary measurements.** This is indicated by such words and phrases as "innovative," "uniquely valuable support," and "invaluable trust," and most clearly by the fourth paragraph, which states that "these benefits go beyond just enhanced influence and access for the United States."

4. **(A)** As used throughout the passage, the term "partner nation" means **a foreign country partnered with the National Guard of a U.S. state or territory**. Treaties (choice (B)), exercises (choice (C)), and identical goals (choice (E)) are neither mentioned nor implied in the passage, and it is very clear that *partner nation* does not mean an opponent (choice (D)).

5. **(B)** The statement with which the passage's author would most likely agree is: **"Security cooperation with friendly foreign nations strengthens the defense of both the U.S. and the friendly foreign nations."** The last paragraph discusses SPP partner nation support of operations that support the U.S.-led coalition in Iraq and Afghanistan. It also discusses how having this support helps reduce the level of U.S. forces needed in areas affected by international tensions and natural disasters.

6. **(C)** The primary purpose of this passage is to provide **an overview of the DoD's cyberspace defense strategy**. The DoD's cyber funding (choice (A)), beginnings (choice (B)), history (choice (D)), and capabilities (choice (E)) are not mentioned, and the passage discusses DoD cyber operations in only very broad terms.

7. **(A)** In the second paragraph, the word "strategic" most nearly means **over-arching** or **high-level**. In addition to the fact that this sentence discusses DoD (and therefore high-level) planning over the next five years, the word *strategic* usually means something at a high level, or with great impact, or both.

8. **(D)** It is possible to infer from the passage that **there are cyber components to many DoD operations around the world**. Every paragraph in the passage mentions the DoD either defending itself or U.S. national interests against a variety of enemies and potential enemies. Since the U.S. has DoD members around the world, it is a short step to infer that many DoD operations around the world have some sort of cyber-related component to them.

9. **(A)** As used throughout the passage, the term "deterrence" means **discouraging potential attackers**. The word "deter" in any context means to stop, prevent, or discourage someone else from taking an action, and the same holds true in this passage.

10. **(B)** The statement with which the passage's author would most likely agree is: **"National cyber security is a key element of national survival in the 21st century."** The first paragraph talks about the United States' vulnerability due to its reliance on cyberspace in many areas, and cyber security's importance to U.S. survival is also strongly implied by the emphasis the passage puts on deterring, defending against, and defeating cyberattacks.

11. **(A)** From the specific examples mentioned, you can infer from the passage that **these** (Air Force current) **core values have not always been universally applied**. One specific reference is in the fourth bullet point, which states that these Air Force core values "serve as beacons vectoring us *back* to the path of professional conduct" [emphasis added]. The use of the word *back* clearly implies that people at least sometimes deviate from the path laid out by these values—you can't go back to something if you haven't left it. Choice (B) is the opposite of choice (A), and the other choices contradict specific statements in the passage.

12. **(D)** The primary purpose of this passage is to **provide an overview of Air Force core values and explain why they are important.** Although the points made in the passage imply that these core values should be adhered to in both professional and personal situations, the passage's sole emphasis is on professional conduct, thus eliminating choice (A). The passage does not prioritize or say that one should strike a balance between the three core values mentioned, eliminating choices (B) and (E). The second bullet paragraph states

that the core values "point to what is *universal* and *unchanging* in the profession of arms" [emphasis added], citing the values as road signs illuminating key features, but noting that they cannot "point to or pick out everything." This eliminates the "specific standards and requirements" mentioned in choice (C).

13. **(B)** In the fourth bullet point and in the last paragraph, the word "vectoring" most nearly means **guiding and directing**. In physics, a vector has both a direction and a magnitude; in Air Force parlance, a vector is a direction of travel to reach a desired destination. It does not push—eliminating choice (A)—nor is it stationary like a standard, eliminating choice (C). The word's usage implies a change of direction from the current one, ruling out choice (D), and choice (E) is the opposite of this word's meaning in any context.

14. **(B)** The statement with which the passage's author would most likely disagree is: **"Core values should reflect the changing nature of the profession of arms."** The passage specifically states that "the core values point to what is universal and unchanging in the profession of arms." The other choices are all quotes that the passage's author would most likely agree with.

15. **(D)** According to the passage, Air Force success **hinges on the incorporation of these values into the character of every Airman**. This sentence is taken directly from the fourth sentence of the passage's first paragraph.

16. **(B)** The primary purpose of this passage is to **summarize the 15th Air Force's operations in Italy during WWII**. The passage does not mention individual heroics, thus ruling out choice (A), and choices (C), (D), and (E) only mention specific items within the passage rather than its purpose as a whole.

17. **(D)** In the fourth paragraph, the word "devastating" is used to mean **causing heavy damage to German aircraft manufacturing facilities**. The passage uses "devastating" in the context of "attacks on German fighter manufacturing complexes in Wiener Neustadt and Regensburg."

18. **(E)** The primary way that the 15th Air Force's attacks on Axis oil facilities and aircraft manufacturing complexes contributed to Allied air supremacy was that **they reduced the number of enemy aircraft available to oppose Allied operations**. Choices (A), (B), and (C) may have been true to some extent, but the ultimate result of the drop in oil and gasoline availability, combined with the reduction in new aircraft production, was that fewer Axis aircraft were available to oppose Allied air and ground operations.

19. **(B)** The first sentence of the passage mentions the 15th Air Force's 23 months of existence during WWII, implying that it was no longer active after those 23 months, and hence was deactivated after almost two years (i.e., 24 months). The facts listed in the other choices are in fact correct, but they are not mentioned in the passage.

20. **(E)** The passage's author would likely agree with the following statement: **"The 15th Air Force made a major contribution in the Allied liberation of Italy."** The passage does not discuss the Allied landings at Normandy in France (choice (A)). The decrease in Axis oil production due to 15th Air Force bombing was in facilities in Romania, Silesia, and Poland, not southern Italy, thus eliminating choice (B). While the 15th Air Force's role was important, its 23 months of regional operations in the 45 months of global war probably don't qualify it as a "major" contributor to the overall Allied victory, ruling out choice (C).

Finally, there was no Allied "reconquest" of Italy, as the Allies had not conquered it before and were only interested in defeating the expansionist Italian dictatorial government that was one of the Axis powers.

21. **(E)** The primary purpose of this passage is to **explain what Senior Military Colleges are and why they are important**. The passage discusses SMCs as a category of colleges and universities that go beyond just having ROTC programs, and it gives some specific information about each school. The other choices are too specific to address the overall purpose of the passage.

22. **(A)** In the first paragraph, the word "precommissioning" most nearly means **in preparation for being commissioned as an officer**. "Commissioning" is what happens when a student or cadet first becomes an officer, regardless of service. Choice (B) is both too narrow and too broad: it mentions only service in the Navy, not in the Army, and the naval service it mentions does not specify service as an officer. Receiving a security clearance is not a matter of training, but instead involves an outside agency evaluating an individual's risk and reliability factors, ruling out choice (C). Neither choice (D) nor choice (E) addresses training that happens before a cadet becomes an officer.

23. **(B)** From the information in the passage, you can infer that **some of the graduates from The Citadel may have fought in the Civil War**. Since The Citadel was established in 1842—19 years before the outbreak of the Civil War—its graduates would indeed have been likely to have been involved in Civil War campaigns. In fact, after it seceded, South Carolina even called The Citadel's cadets into wartime service multiple times. Both Virginia Tech and Texas A&M were established after the Civil War, eliminating choices (A) and (C). The University of North Georgia only has Army ROTC, thereby making it unlikely that any future admirals are there right now, so you can rule out choice (D). The passage specifically mentions that many SMC alumni did not graduate because service in wartime interrupted their enrollment, and that some did not return, so choice (E) is incorrect.

24. **(B)** According to the passage, the following statement is not true: **"The SMCs focus more on military excellence and precommissioning training than on academic programs."** The passage specifically states that the SMCs share a dedication to academic excellence and supports that statement with information about high academic rankings for some SMCs. The other choices are statements that are all specifically mentioned in the passage.

25. **(C)** The author would most likely agree with the following statement: **"The benefits of the SMCs more than compensate for the extra investment they require."** The writer of the passage offers many examples of high standards and high academic rankings for the SMCs as well as high accomplishments by their alumni—the apparently disproportionate number of generals, admirals, and Medal of Honor winners, for example. The overall tone of the passage does not support the statements in choices (A), (B), and (D). The passage specifically mentions the high academic rankings for several SMCs, refuting choice (E).

Subtest #6: Situational Judgment

Check your answers below and refer to the explanation for each question you missed. Use the table to record right and wrong answers.

			✔	✘
Situation 1	1. Most Effective	**B**		
	2. Least Effective	**E**		
Situation 2	3. Most Effective	**C**		
	4. Least Effective	**E**		
Situation 3	5. Most Effective	**C**		
	6. Least Effective	**A**		
Situation 4	7. Most Effective	**D**		
	8. Least Effective	**A**		
Situation 5	9. Most Effective	**D**		
	10. Least Effective	**C**		
Situation 6	11. Most Effective	**D**		
	12. Least Effective	**E**		
Situation 7	13. Most Effective	**B**		
	14. Least Effective	**E**		
Situation 8	15. Most Effective	**A**		
	16. Least Effective	**C**		
Situation 9	17. Most Effective	**D**		
	18. Least Effective	**C**		
Situation 10	19. Most Effective	**E**		
	20. Least Effective	**D**		
Situation 11	21. Most Effective	**A**		
	22. Least Effective	**D**		
Situation 12	23. Most Effective	**D**		
	24. Least Effective	**C**		
Situation 13	25. Most Effective	**E**		
	26. Least Effective	**A**		
Situation 14	27. Most Effective	**B**		
	28. Least Effective	**C**		
Situation 15	29. Most Effective	**C**		
	30. Least Effective	**B**		
Situation 16	31. Most Effective	**D**		
	32. Least Effective	**B**		
Situation 17	33. Most Effective	**D**		
	34. Least Effective	**A**		
Situation 18	35. Most Effective	**C**		
	36. Least Effective	**D**		

			✔	✘
Situation 19	37. Most Effective	**B**		
	38. Least Effective	**D**		
Situation 20	39. Most Effective	**B**		
	40. Least Effective	**D**		
Situation 21	41. Most Effective	**D**		
	42. Least Effective	**A**		
Situation 22	43. Most Effective	**B**		
	44. Least Effective	**C**		
Situation 23	45. Most Effective	**E**		
	46. Least Effective	**A**		
Situation 24	47. Most Effective	**B**		
	48. Least Effective	**E**		
Situation 25	49. Most Effective	**C**		
	50. Least Effective	**D**		

Situation 1

The most effective action here is choice (B), while **the least effective action is choice (E)**. Respectfully asking your supervisor in person how he thinks you are doing, while expressing gratitude for his extra coaching during the first few months, will give you useful feedback, regardless of how he answers. It also has the advantages of being clear and direct. If he expresses an increasing level of satisfaction, it will open the door for you to ask for more elbow room, and it doesn't present you as a know-it-all. Sending an e-mail is acceptable for short, factual messages or things that have to be communicated to many people at once. However, since this is a *relationship* question, it deserves a face-to-face meeting that directly addresses your desire for looser supervision—and gets you feedback, which is always beneficial whether you like it or not.

Situation 2

Choice (C) is the most helpful way to meet section deadlines, and **choice (E) is the least helpful or effective way**. Scheduling work assignments transparently—where everyone has visibility not only of tasks, but also of progress and deadlines—and having the team leaders keep you regularly updated would be the best way to handle things, even if everyone was new to each other; it will be even more effective in this environment. Sending e-mail deadline reminders as your primary method of leadership and management would waste the advantage of the good personal relationships you already have, and it would also undercut the subordinate team leaders (also a problem with choice (B)).

Situation 3

Choice (C) is the most effective action in this scenario, and **choice (A) is the least effective action**. Although it's clear that firm enforcement will be necessary to meet the standard, weapons this bad will take some time to clean properly, so another inspection at 1700 or even 1800 will likely not be productive. By the same token, just talking about the importance of clean weapons with no follow-through will not likely be productive, either.

Situation 4

Choice (D) is the most effective action here, and **the least effective action is choice (A).** Choice (D) shows your supervisor that you are paying attention to the situation as it changes and that you can see how it will affect your unit's scheduled tasks, and it demonstrates initiative on your part by offering to finish the project on your own. It also allows your supervisor to do his or her job, which is to manage your unit's projects and make decisions about how to allocate resources—which choice (C) does not allow since you would inappropriately bypass your supervisor to work directly with the "customer" unit. Choice (B) is the next most effective action, but it does not show any willingness on your part to do more than the minimum requirements. Choices (E) and (A) are successively less positive choices, as they demonstrate a bigger deficit in initiative and willingness to work hard on your part.

Situation 5

Choice (D) is the most effective action, while **choice (C) is the least effective action.** You have two major managerial tasks here: use the experience and supervisory skills of your team leaders, and get the whole section enthusiastic about the project. You do this by first meeting with the team leaders to rough out the plan, and then meeting with the entire section to ensure that everyone understands the project's full scope, importance, and impact. Only then can you turn it back over to the team leaders to keep track of their team's tasks, making sure that the appropriate type and amount of progress is being made. Taking it all on yourself and leaving the "less important" routine tasks to your subordinates cuts your team leaders out of the loop and tells them that you don't trust them—and it will probably overload what you can reliably accomplish. While choice (C) is in fact the worst option, any option that bypasses the team leaders or doesn't help the section understand the importance of the project is not destined for success either.

Situation 6

The most effective—and the most ethical—action here is choice (D), and **the least effective—and least ethical—action is choice (E)**, although choices (A) and (B) are not far behind for the least effective and least ethical action. By upholding the standard but offering to help MSgt. McCann brush up on his skills, you have balanced two strong but competing forces pulling you in different directions.

Situation 7

In this situation, **choice (B) is the most effective action**, although parts of choices (C) and (D) may have merit. **Choice (E) is the least effective action**, although choice (A) is not far behind in lack of wisdom. In any problem or challenge, you should first seek to understand not only what the problem is, but what is causing it—hence your discussion with the two team members who are having difficulties. Only then can you realistically hope to come up with an effective action plan; the actions in choices (C) and (D) may be part of that action plan, but they are not solutions by themselves. Likewise, asking for an extension of the project deadline when you haven't found out what's causing the delay—much less taken any actions to solve the problem at your level, with your resources, and still on time—does not address your obligation to solve things at your level when possible.

Situation 8

The most effective action is choice (A), and **the least effective action is choice (C)**. If the disruption was less than what is described here, it might be best to talk to the individual privately. However, if the disruption is keeping the meeting from accomplishing its purpose, direct action—although still professional—is justified. Leaving the disruptor alone would not solve the problem and would probably encourage continuation. Telling your supervisor implies not taking action during the meeting, and, unless you and the disruptor work for the same supervisor, wastes your supervisor's time. Telling the disruptive individual's supervisor again implies action after the fact and could very well be perceived as grade school tattling.

Situation 9

The most effective action in this situation is choice (D), and **the least effective action is choice (C)** (although choices (A), (B), and (E) are also very bad choices). Using your chain of command, with documentation of the necessary changes in hand, is the right way to address this issue and possibly become part of the solution. Bypassing your supervisor and announcing the problem outside your unit is neither wise nor your responsibility, and it will reflect poorly on you, your supervisor, and your unit. However, if addressed correctly, and if your supervisor is a good leader, she may even put a positive spotlight on you when she tells her supervisor and the rest of your unit that procedures have to change.

Situation 10

Dealing with other cultures in joint (multi-national) situations is often tricky, especially for U.S. personnel without much experience in doing so. Here, **the best action is likely choice (E)**, and **the least effective action is certainly choice (D)**, although choices (A), (B), and (C) are also pretty bad options. Many cultures place very high importance on maintaining their dignity and not being embarrassed, and sensitivities to criticism can be further aggravated by U.S. forces having visibly more resources or the like. "Just feedback" or "constructive criticism" can be perceived as a serious insult with long-lasting international implications. Chances are that the partner nation guard force commander knows about the lapses and is frustrated by them. Offering a face-saving way to provide U.S. help, without creating a "know-it-all U.S. big brother helping out the poor incompetent partner nation little brother" impression, can be a workable solution for all concerned.

Situation 11

Choice (A) is the most effective action in this situation, since problems should be solved as directly as possible and at the lowest level possible. **Choice (D) is the least effective action** of the actions listed because it does nothing and assumes that the problem will go away on its own—never a good idea. However, choice (C) is almost as bad since you don't approach your colleague directly to discuss the situation before bringing it up to a supervisory level—there's almost always some part of the situation you don't know about, and you are likely to both build ill will and pick up a reputation as a backstabber.

Situation 12

Choice (D) is the most effective action, and **choice (C) is the least effective action**. Using the planks to distribute your weight balances speed (remember, you have to guide ammunition and resupply back to your unit as soon as possible) with mitigating the risk of the ice breaking. Walking slowly and running rapidly are both great ways to break through the ice, and seeing how deep the stream is doesn't really matter—it's how thick the ice is that matters. Likewise, walking two miles downstream to the bridge is the worst option because it reduces your risk but almost certainly means that other members of your unit will die because you took so long to get the ammunition and medical resupply back to them.

Situation 13

Choice (E) is the most effective action, while **choice (A)—doing nothing—is the least effective action**. An after-action review (AAR) is a forum where even the most junior person can respectfully express his or her opinion about the conduct of an exercise or event. No one gets better without feedback—if the class was substandard, the section leader needs to know it. If the criticism was unfounded, misdirected, or otherwise not completely valid, the people offering those opinions should have the opportunity to come to that understanding themselves.

Situation 14

The most effective action is choice (B), and **the least effective action is choice (C)**. Discussing your concerns with your coworker as a first step is a good idea because you have knowledge of your friend/coworker's situation, and you may be able to offer a more objective perspective. Choice (D) is not a bad choice, but it shouldn't be the first step—your friend/coworker may have already talked with a financial consultant or with one of the various military financial counseling resources. Lending him money (choice (A)) is certainly not the first step—he hasn't asked, and it won't solve his problem. Choice (E) is not a good idea because it is meddling too far into a private situation, but it is not as bad as choice (C), which makes what is, after all, your coworker's issue visible to the chain of command before your coworker has a chance to solve it himself.

Situation 15

Choice (C) is the most effective action in this situation, and **choice (B) is the least effective action**. Direct, respectful communication is almost always the answer if it is not bypassing levels of the chain of command. Choice (A) is not really an option unless you want to neglect your own duties, and choices (B) and (D) involve damaging your own integrity, which you should always avoid.

Situation 16

Choice (D) is the most effective action, and it's a race between choices (B), (C), and (E) for the least effective action, although **choice (B) is likely the least effective action** of the bunch. Again, direct but respectful conversation at the lowest level possible to address the issue is the preferred course of action. Choices (C) and (E) are not only unlikely to succeed, but both will make you look like a know-it-all or worse to either your supervisor or to the rest of the team. Choice (B), however, makes you appear to be the opposite of a team player as well as a know-it-all to both your teammates and the next two levels up at the same time.

Situation 17

The most effective action—although probably the most painful for you—is choice (D), and **the least effective action is choice (A)**. You should have had a face-to-face meeting, laying out your expectations, soon after her assignment, but it's never too late to start doing the right thing. If she straightens up and performs better—even if it takes a while and much effort—your section will gain a valuable member; if she doesn't perform better, you will have a written basis to request her transfer or recommend other action. Supporting her school attendance may get her out of your hair, but she will then be inflicted on another unit at a higher level than she is now—and you will have failed by intentionally avoiding your responsibilities as a leader. Although it's not the absolute worst possible choice of those presented, copying a subordinate on a negative e-mail message to your leadership, especially without an explanation or a prior discussion, is highly unprofessional. This kind of discussion must be face-to-face, both with your flight leader and with your assistant section leader.

Situation 18

The most effective action is choice (C), and **the least effective action is choice (D)**. While it's important to maintain standards and the flow of the chain of command, if that section leader went around you to the squadron commander, he apparently feels pretty strongly about his objections. You need to understand why this experienced NCO went around you (he knows better), and you also need to consider whether your leadership or communication style or other attributes are contributing to the objections. It's very seldom necessary (and often counterproductive) to hammer down objections or point out procedural fouls in a group setting, and firing an NCO is something that should only be done after a series of documented, unresolved issues, and only after consultation with your boss.

Situation 19

Choice (B) is the most effective action, and **choice (D) is the least effective action.** By prioritizing something that greatly affects the entire headquarters ahead of your other tasks, you are being a team player. By going over your thoughts on it with your supervisor, you are not only multiplying the quality that your section adds to the order, but you are also demonstrating your trust in and support of your chain of command, which will be reciprocated. Pushing the task off until the end of the day—when you are no longer at your best and when you may not get to it at all—puts your individual tasks above something that greatly affects the whole headquarters, which is inappropriate at best. Being afraid to take a swing at it because you might miss something misses the opportunity for both you and the order to be improved.

Situation 20

Choice (B) is the most effective action, and **choice (D) is the least effective action**. Ideally, you would want to reinforce the chain of command—as well as training your team leaders—by finding the team leader and having him make the correction. However, since this is a safety situation, and the Airman might be hurt while you are looking for the team leader, you need to make an on-the-spot correction. Sending an e-mail to the whole section does not solve the immediate problem, does not reinforce the chain of command, and will possibly be ignored.

Situation 21

Choice (D) is the most effective action, and **choice (A) is the least effective action**. Inspections are not about making anyone in particular "happy"—they are about meeting standards. As section leader, you are responsible for both accomplishing the mission and taking care of your people—this includes prioritizing their work, setting deadlines, and checking results. Major deficiencies, by definition, are more important than minor deficiencies—but the fact of the matter is that you will have to address both at the same time to some extent. You may want to prioritize working on deficiencies related to safety and readiness above other areas, or you may not, depending on the details—but you are responsible for the results. Don't confuse results with "making progress" or "making an effort."

Situation 22

Choice (B) is the most effective action, and **choice (C) is the least effective action** (although it has stiff competition for worst idea from choices (A), (D), and (E)). Unit cohesion and loyalty are important and can be reinforced by overcoming obstacles together. Avoidance of hardship or challenges should not be rewarded with easier duties or a three-day pass just to hide these three below-average physical specimens for the purposes of the competition. The leader is responsible for communicating his or her vision of where the unit needs to go to its members and for getting their buy-in when possible. The leader is also responsible for setting and enforcing standards—and once you make one exception, especially to "game" a competitive result, you are sliding off that mountain at high speed.

Situation 23

The most effective course of action is choice (E), and **the least effective action is choice (A)**. You should always try to solve problems at the lowest level possible with direct, respectful communication of goals, standards, and who's going to do what. Doing only what you have to do is not very different from the low-effort attitude of your underachieving coworker.

Situation 24

The most effective action here is choice (B), and **the least effective action is choice (E)**. Being a leader means taking responsibility for solving problems at your level whenever possible, including finding innovative approaches, while still keeping your chain of command informed about challenges you may be facing. Putting the burden on the trainer with the scheduled procedure is an abdication of your responsibility as a leader, as is asking your supervisor to find you another trainer without making any effort to do so yourself. Worst of all is just giving up on being able to accomplish the mission—i.e., surrendering without a fight.

Situation 25

The most effective action here is choice (C), and **the least effective action is choice (D)**. They did ask you for your opinion, so if you can in fact use the experience you have to make a logical recommendation that combines considerations from both perspectives, good for you—the next best contender would be choice (E). Making a recommendation based on what is easiest for you is never the way to go—it should be about what is best for the mission and for the unit. Saying that the issue needs more research or analysis may work, but just saying that both ways are equally successful will virtually guarantee that your opinion will not be asked for again.

Subtest #7: Self-Description Inventory

There are no right or wrong answers to the questions on this subtest.

Subtest #8: Physical Science

Check your answers below and refer to the explanation for each question you missed. Use the table to record right and wrong answers.

	✔	✘		✔	✘		✔	✘		✔	✘
1. D			**6. B**			**11. B**			**16. E**		
2. C			**7. B**			**12. D**			**17. D**		
3. B			**8. A**			**13. C**			**18. E**		
4. A			**9. A**			**14. C**			**19. C**		
5. B			**10. B**			**15. B**			**20. A**		

1. **(D)** The most accurate description of Earth's atmosphere is that it is made up of **21% oxygen, 78% nitrogen, .03% carbon dioxide, trace amounts of rare gases, water vapor, and some dust particles**.
2. **(C)** Since sound consists of vibrations passed through a medium such as air, in an environment where there is nothing to transmit the sound there will be no sound—so the tuning fork will **be inaudible**.
3. **(B)** Most plants need **nitrogen**; they also need **phosphorus and potassium**. Plants need only traces of other elements, so they are not a priority for companies that produce fertilizers.
4. **(A)** The barometric pressure at a particular location directly depends on **its temperature and humidity**. Solar flares and wind speed have nothing to do with barometric pressure.
5. **(B)** "Dry ice" is solid carbon dioxide (**CO_2**), made by cooling this gas to –80 degrees Celsius. In this case, CO_2 goes directly from a gaseous state to a solid—and then, when it warms above the temperature needed to keep it a solid, it goes directly back to a gas.

6. **(B)** An airplane wing is curved on the top and relatively flat on the bottom (this shape is called an airfoil). Because nature avoids having a vacuum whenever possible (the cliché is that "nature abhors a vacuum"), air flowing over the top surface is forced to flow faster over the top of the wing than under the bottom surface to avoid having a partial vacuum at the trailing (back) edge of the wing. This faster-flowing air results in less air pressure on the top surface of the wing than underneath. The scientific principle behind this was first described by Swiss mathematician Daniel Bernoulli (1700–1782): in any flowing fluid, as the speed of the fluid becomes greater, the pressure becomes less.

7. **(B)** Radio waves and visible light waves are two forms of electromagnetic radiation. Therefore, they have the same **speed** as all electromagnetic waves in a vacuum—that is, the speed of light.

8. **(A)** Inertia is the property of matter to **resist a change of position or motion**. This is addressed by Newton's First Law of Motion, which states that an object at rest stays at rest and an object in motion stays in motion (at the same speed and in the same direction) unless acted on by an unbalanced force.

9. **(A)** The density of a substance is determined by **dividing its mass by its volume**. For any particular substance, there's a linear relationship between its mass and its volume: when one increases, so does the other, and vice versa.

10. **(B)** Parallel light rays each strike the mirror at a different point. Because the mirror has a plane (flat) surface, the rays are still **parallel** after reflection.

11. **(B)** All freely falling objects, regardless of their mass, fall toward Earth with equal acceleration. Any two objects that begin to fall at the same instant will have equal velocities at the end of four seconds, or at any other time interval. Therefore, the ratio of their speeds will be **1:1**.

12. **(D)** On the basis of their atomic structure, atoms are considered **metals** if they can lend electrons and **nonmetals** if they borrow electrons. The periodic table is organized so that elements with similar chemical and physical properties are aligned in columns or groups. Metals that form the left-hand two-thirds of the periodic table tend to form compounds by losing or "lending" electrons.

13. **(C)** All atoms of the same element have the same number of protons. Neutral atoms have the same number of **electrons and protons** (protons are inside the atom's nucleus, and electrons are outside of it). Atoms of the same element may differ in the number of neutrons.

14. **(C)** **Soil** is eroded by the action of wind, water, and ice; it can also be depleted by the removal of organic matter or minerals.

15. **(B)** An insulator is a material that has tightly held electrons and very **few** (if any) **free electrons**. This means that it can be used to protect the conductor, since the insulator will not allow free electrons from the conductor to knock loose any tightly held electrons of the insulator material.

16. **(E)** Combustion (**burning**) is a chemical process; the others listed are not.

17. **(D)** A seesaw is an example of **a lever**. Specifically, a seesaw is an example of a first-class lever, where the fulcrum is placed between the applied force and the load. Which

end has the load and which end has the applied force changes as each person alternates using their legs to push off from the ground.

18. **(E)** The **electron** is the negatively charged particle that circles the nucleus of an atom. A *neutron* is neutral (has no charge), and a *proton* is positively charged; a *meson* has both positive and negative charges. An *isotope* is an atom of the same element that has a different number of neutrons.

19. **(C)** Light travels in a vacuum at 186,282 miles per second, and Earth is 92,955,807 miles from the sun. This means that light from the sun reaches Earth in about **eight minutes** and 19 seconds. (Even if you rounded off the speed of light to 186,000 mps and the Earth–sun distance to 93,000,000 miles, the result would be only one second different—eight minutes and 20 seconds.)

20. **(A)** A liquid has **definite volume**, and **takes the shape of its container**.

Subtest #9: Table Reading

Check your answers below. Use the table to record right and wrong answers.

	✔	✘		✔	✘		✔	✘		✔	✘		✔	✘
1. B			9. E			17. B			25. A			33. C		
2. E			10. B			18. D			26. E			34. E		
3. A			11. E			19. A			27. C			35. A		
4. A			12. B			20. E			28. D			36. C		
5. C			13. A			21. E			29. C			37. A		
6. E			14. C			22. B			30. C			38. D		
7. B			15. D			23. C			31. A			39. E		
8. D			16. B			24. A			32. D			40. E		

Subtest #10: Instrument Comprehension

Check your answers below. Use the table to record right and wrong answers.

	✔	✘		✔	✘		✔	✘		✔	✘		✔	✘
1. C			6. C			11. A			16. D			21. C		
2. A			7. B			12. B			17. D			22. B		
3. D			8. D			13. A			18. C			23. A		
4. C			9. B			14. B			19. D			24. D		
5. A			10. D			15. A			20. D			25. D		

Answer	Nose	Bank	Heading
1. **(C)**	DOWN	LEFT	SE
2. **(A)**	LEVEL	RIGHT	E
3. **(D)**	DOWN	LEFT	W
4. **(C)**	UP	LEFT	S
5. **(A)**	LEVEL	ZERO	NE
6. **(C)**	UP	RIGHT	NE
7. **(B)**	DOWN	ZERO	S
8. **(D)**	UP	ZERO	N
9. **(B)**	DOWN	ZERO	E
10. **(D)**	LEVEL	RIGHT	S
11. **(A)**	LEVEL	ZERO	S
12. **(B)**	LEVEL	ZERO	SW
13. **(A)**	UP	LEFT	W
14. **(B)**	DOWN	LEFT	W
15. **(A)**	DOWN	ZERO	W
16. **(D)**	UP	RIGHT	W
17. **(D)**	LEVEL	RIGHT	N
18. **(C)**	LEVEL	ZERO	W
19. **(D)**	UP	ZERO	E
20. **(D)**	DOWN	RIGHT	SE
21. **(C)**	UP	ZERO	N
22. **(B)**	DOWN	LEFT	SW
23. **(A)**	DOWN	ZERO	W
24. **(D)**	LEVEL	LEFT	E
25. **(D)**	LEVEL	LEFT	S

Subtest #11: Block Counting

Check your answers below. Use the table to record right and wrong answers.

	✔	✘		✔	✘		✔	✘		✔	✘		✔	✘
1. D			**7. C**			**13. B**			**19. C**			**25. D**		
2. B			**8. D**			**14. E**			**20. D**			**26. C**		
3. E			**9. E**			**15. C**			**21. C**			**27. A**		
4. C			**10. B**			**16. B**			**22. D**			**28. A**		
5. B			**11. A**			**17. E**			**23. A**			**29. C**		
6. B			**12. C**			**18. B**			**24. A**			**30. D**		

Subtest #12: Aviation Information

Check your answers below and refer to the explanation for each question you missed. Use the table to record right and wrong answers.

	✔	✘		✔	✘		✔	✘		✔	✘
1. C			6. A			11. D			16. A		
2. B			7. C			12. E			17. B		
3. D			8. D			13. B			18. E		
4. C			9. E			14. C			19. D		
5. E			10. B			15. C			20. C		

1. **(C)** In a level turn, the acceleration experienced by the aircraft and its pilot in the direction perpendicular to the wing is solely determined by the **bank angle**. Regardless of the aircraft type, its altitude, the density of the air, the temperature, or any other factor, the G-load (or load factor) experienced by the aircraft and pilot is related only to the bank angle. A Cessna 150 at 100 knots in a 60° bank will experience two Gs (twice the force of normal Earth gravity), just as an F-16 will at 500 knots at the same bank angle.

2. **(B)** The flight envelope of an aircraft is **the region of altitude and airspeed in which it can be operated.**

3. **(D)** The locus of points equidistant from the upper and lower surfaces of an airfoil is called the **mean camber line**.

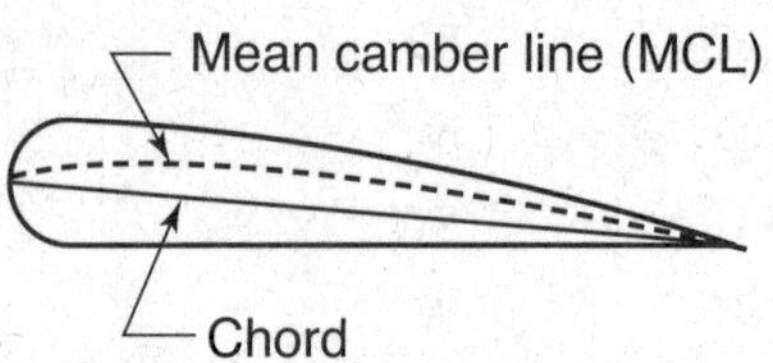

4. **(C)** The straight line joining the ends of the mean camber line is called the **wing chord.**

5. **(E)** An **aerodynamic stall** is the point at which the airflow over the wings ceases to be a smooth (laminar) flow and the wing starts to lose lift.

6. **(A)** The two basic types of drag are **parasitic drag and induced drag**. Parasitic drag is the resistance of the aircraft to the air through which it moves; it increases with the square of the object's speed through the air. The second basic type of drag is called induced drag; it's related to the wing's production of lift. At low airspeed and high angles of attack, induced drag increases and becomes a large factor.

7. **(C)** An airfoil's efficiency, either a wing or a rotor blade, is **decreased** at high altitudes by the **lesser** air density.

8. **(D)** The degree of movement of an aircraft around its lateral axis is known as **pitch.**

9. **(E)** When the flaps are extended, the camber of the wing is **increased**. Effectively, the wing becomes larger and more curved. The flaps, mounted inboard of the ailerons, are probably the most commonly used lift device. They increase the lift capability of the

airfoil (wing) to its maximum potential, which means an aircraft can become or remain airborne at lower speeds. They also permit a shorter ground roll on landing when used as airbrakes.

10. **(B)** A helicopter's cyclic control is a mechanical linkage used to change the pitch of the main rotor blades **at a selected point in its circular pathway**. For instance, if the pilot adjusts the cyclic pitch so that the rotor blades have more "bite" into the air (i.e., more lift) when they pass over the tail than when they pass over the nose of the helicopter, the aircraft travels forward.

11. **(D)** When the rotor blades of a helicopter are spinning fast enough in a clockwise direction to generate lift, a phenomenon known as **torque** causes the body of the helicopter to have a tendency to turn in a counterclockwise direction.

12. **(E)** Pulling back (toward the pilot) on the control column or joystick of a fixed-wing aircraft will cause the aircraft to **pitch up**, that is, for the nose to rise.

13. **(B)** Contra-rotating propellers, a complex way of applying the maximum power of a single piston or turboprop aircraft engine, uses two propellers **rotating in opposite directions arranged one behind the other**. Power is transferred from the engine via a planetary gear transmission. When airspeed is low, the air mass going back through the propeller disk (thrust) causes a significant amount of tangential or rotational airflow to be created by the spinning blades; the energy of this tangential airflow is wasted in a single-propeller design. To use this wasted resource, the placement of a second propeller behind the first takes advantage of the already-disturbed airflow.

14. **(C)** The abbreviation VTOL, applied to aircraft other than helicopters, means **Vertical Take-Off and Landing**.

15. **(C)** Delta wing aircraft have a wing in the form of a triangle, named after the Greek uppercase letter delta (Δ) and no **horizontal stabilizer**. The primary advantage of this design is that the wing's leading edge remains behind the shock wave generated by the aircraft's nose when flying at supersonic speeds, which is an improvement on traditional wing designs.

16. **(A)** The Visual Approach Slope Indicator (VASI) is a system of lights designed to provide visual descent guidance information during a runway approach. The system uses **red** lights to indicate the upper limits of the glide path and **white** lights for the lower limits. It is visible from 3–5 miles during the day and up to 20 miles or more at night. The visual glide path of the VASI provides safe obstruction clearance within ±10 degrees of the extended runway centerline and to 4 nautical miles from the runway threshold.

17. **(B)** A biplane has **two wings arranged one above the other**.

18. **(E)** A coordinated turn (change of heading direction) includes both **roll and yaw** of the airplane.

19. **(D)** **Yaw** is induced by use of a movable rudder controlled by **rudder pedals** in the cockpit.

20. **(C)** Moving the control column or joystick to the left or right affects the **rate of roll** rather than indicating the **angle to which the aircraft will roll**.

ANSWER SHEET
SIFT #1

Subtest 1: Simple Drawings (SD)

1. Ⓐ Ⓑ Ⓒ Ⓓ Ⓔ
2. Ⓐ Ⓑ Ⓒ Ⓓ Ⓔ
3. Ⓐ Ⓑ Ⓒ Ⓓ Ⓔ
4. Ⓐ Ⓑ Ⓒ Ⓓ Ⓔ
5. Ⓐ Ⓑ Ⓒ Ⓓ Ⓔ
6. Ⓐ Ⓑ Ⓒ Ⓓ Ⓔ
7. Ⓐ Ⓑ Ⓒ Ⓓ Ⓔ
8. Ⓐ Ⓑ Ⓒ Ⓓ Ⓔ
9. Ⓐ Ⓑ Ⓒ Ⓓ Ⓔ
10. Ⓐ Ⓑ Ⓒ Ⓓ Ⓔ
11. Ⓐ Ⓑ Ⓒ Ⓓ Ⓔ
12. Ⓐ Ⓑ Ⓒ Ⓓ Ⓔ
13. Ⓐ Ⓑ Ⓒ Ⓓ Ⓔ
14. Ⓐ Ⓑ Ⓒ Ⓓ Ⓔ
15. Ⓐ Ⓑ Ⓒ Ⓓ Ⓔ
16. Ⓐ Ⓑ Ⓒ Ⓓ Ⓔ
17. Ⓐ Ⓑ Ⓒ Ⓓ Ⓔ
18. Ⓐ Ⓑ Ⓒ Ⓓ Ⓔ
19. Ⓐ Ⓑ Ⓒ Ⓓ Ⓔ
20. Ⓐ Ⓑ Ⓒ Ⓓ Ⓔ
21. Ⓐ Ⓑ Ⓒ Ⓓ Ⓔ
22. Ⓐ Ⓑ Ⓒ Ⓓ Ⓔ
23. Ⓐ Ⓑ Ⓒ Ⓓ Ⓔ
24. Ⓐ Ⓑ Ⓒ Ⓓ Ⓔ
25. Ⓐ Ⓑ Ⓒ Ⓓ Ⓔ
26. Ⓐ Ⓑ Ⓒ Ⓓ Ⓔ
27. Ⓐ Ⓑ Ⓒ Ⓓ Ⓔ
28. Ⓐ Ⓑ Ⓒ Ⓓ Ⓔ
29. Ⓐ Ⓑ Ⓒ Ⓓ Ⓔ
30. Ⓐ Ⓑ Ⓒ Ⓓ Ⓔ
31. Ⓐ Ⓑ Ⓒ Ⓓ Ⓔ
32. Ⓐ Ⓑ Ⓒ Ⓓ Ⓔ
33. Ⓐ Ⓑ Ⓒ Ⓓ Ⓔ
34. Ⓐ Ⓑ Ⓒ Ⓓ Ⓔ
35. Ⓐ Ⓑ Ⓒ Ⓓ Ⓔ
36. Ⓐ Ⓑ Ⓒ Ⓓ Ⓔ
37. Ⓐ Ⓑ Ⓒ Ⓓ Ⓔ
38. Ⓐ Ⓑ Ⓒ Ⓓ Ⓔ
39. Ⓐ Ⓑ Ⓒ Ⓓ Ⓔ
40. Ⓐ Ⓑ Ⓒ Ⓓ Ⓔ
41. Ⓐ Ⓑ Ⓒ Ⓓ Ⓔ
42. Ⓐ Ⓑ Ⓒ Ⓓ Ⓔ
43. Ⓐ Ⓑ Ⓒ Ⓓ Ⓔ
44. Ⓐ Ⓑ Ⓒ Ⓓ Ⓔ
45. Ⓐ Ⓑ Ⓒ Ⓓ Ⓔ
46. Ⓐ Ⓑ Ⓒ Ⓓ Ⓔ
47. Ⓐ Ⓑ Ⓒ Ⓓ Ⓔ
48. Ⓐ Ⓑ Ⓒ Ⓓ Ⓔ
49. Ⓐ Ⓑ Ⓒ Ⓓ Ⓔ
50. Ⓐ Ⓑ Ⓒ Ⓓ Ⓔ
51. Ⓐ Ⓑ Ⓒ Ⓓ Ⓔ
52. Ⓐ Ⓑ Ⓒ Ⓓ Ⓔ
53. Ⓐ Ⓑ Ⓒ Ⓓ Ⓔ
54. Ⓐ Ⓑ Ⓒ Ⓓ Ⓔ
55. Ⓐ Ⓑ Ⓒ Ⓓ Ⓔ
56. Ⓐ Ⓑ Ⓒ Ⓓ Ⓔ
57. Ⓐ Ⓑ Ⓒ Ⓓ Ⓔ
58. Ⓐ Ⓑ Ⓒ Ⓓ Ⓔ
59. Ⓐ Ⓑ Ⓒ Ⓓ Ⓔ
60. Ⓐ Ⓑ Ⓒ Ⓓ Ⓔ
61. Ⓐ Ⓑ Ⓒ Ⓓ Ⓔ
62. Ⓐ Ⓑ Ⓒ Ⓓ Ⓔ
63. Ⓐ Ⓑ Ⓒ Ⓓ Ⓔ
64. Ⓐ Ⓑ Ⓒ Ⓓ Ⓔ
65. Ⓐ Ⓑ Ⓒ Ⓓ Ⓔ
66. Ⓐ Ⓑ Ⓒ Ⓓ Ⓔ
67. Ⓐ Ⓑ Ⓒ Ⓓ Ⓔ
68. Ⓐ Ⓑ Ⓒ Ⓓ Ⓔ
69. Ⓐ Ⓑ Ⓒ Ⓓ Ⓔ
70. Ⓐ Ⓑ Ⓒ Ⓓ Ⓔ
71. Ⓐ Ⓑ Ⓒ Ⓓ Ⓔ
72. Ⓐ Ⓑ Ⓒ Ⓓ Ⓔ
73. Ⓐ Ⓑ Ⓒ Ⓓ Ⓔ
74. Ⓐ Ⓑ Ⓒ Ⓓ Ⓔ
75. Ⓐ Ⓑ Ⓒ Ⓓ Ⓔ
76. Ⓐ Ⓑ Ⓒ Ⓓ Ⓔ
77. Ⓐ Ⓑ Ⓒ Ⓓ Ⓔ
78. Ⓐ Ⓑ Ⓒ Ⓓ Ⓔ
79. Ⓐ Ⓑ Ⓒ Ⓓ Ⓔ
80. Ⓐ Ⓑ Ⓒ Ⓓ Ⓔ
81. Ⓐ Ⓑ Ⓒ Ⓓ Ⓔ
82. Ⓐ Ⓑ Ⓒ Ⓓ Ⓔ
83. Ⓐ Ⓑ Ⓒ Ⓓ Ⓔ
84. Ⓐ Ⓑ Ⓒ Ⓓ Ⓔ
85. Ⓐ Ⓑ Ⓒ Ⓓ Ⓔ
86. Ⓐ Ⓑ Ⓒ Ⓓ Ⓔ
87. Ⓐ Ⓑ Ⓒ Ⓓ Ⓔ
88. Ⓐ Ⓑ Ⓒ Ⓓ Ⓔ
89. Ⓐ Ⓑ Ⓒ Ⓓ Ⓔ
90. Ⓐ Ⓑ Ⓒ Ⓓ Ⓔ
91. Ⓐ Ⓑ Ⓒ Ⓓ Ⓔ
92. Ⓐ Ⓑ Ⓒ Ⓓ Ⓔ
93. Ⓐ Ⓑ Ⓒ Ⓓ Ⓔ
94. Ⓐ Ⓑ Ⓒ Ⓓ Ⓔ
95. Ⓐ Ⓑ Ⓒ Ⓓ Ⓔ
96. Ⓐ Ⓑ Ⓒ Ⓓ Ⓔ
97. Ⓐ Ⓑ Ⓒ Ⓓ Ⓔ
98. Ⓐ Ⓑ Ⓒ Ⓓ Ⓔ
99. Ⓐ Ⓑ Ⓒ Ⓓ Ⓔ
100. Ⓐ Ⓑ Ⓒ Ⓓ Ⓔ

Subtest 2: Hidden Figures (HF)

1. Ⓐ Ⓑ Ⓒ Ⓓ Ⓔ
2. Ⓐ Ⓑ Ⓒ Ⓓ Ⓔ
3. Ⓐ Ⓑ Ⓒ Ⓓ Ⓔ
4. Ⓐ Ⓑ Ⓒ Ⓓ Ⓔ
5. Ⓐ Ⓑ Ⓒ Ⓓ Ⓔ
6. Ⓐ Ⓑ Ⓒ Ⓓ Ⓔ
7. Ⓐ Ⓑ Ⓒ Ⓓ Ⓔ
8. Ⓐ Ⓑ Ⓒ Ⓓ Ⓔ
9. Ⓐ Ⓑ Ⓒ Ⓓ Ⓔ
10. Ⓐ Ⓑ Ⓒ Ⓓ Ⓔ
11. Ⓐ Ⓑ Ⓒ Ⓓ Ⓔ
12. Ⓐ Ⓑ Ⓒ Ⓓ Ⓔ
13. Ⓐ Ⓑ Ⓒ Ⓓ Ⓔ
14. Ⓐ Ⓑ Ⓒ Ⓓ Ⓔ
15. Ⓐ Ⓑ Ⓒ Ⓓ Ⓔ
16. Ⓐ Ⓑ Ⓒ Ⓓ Ⓔ
17. Ⓐ Ⓑ Ⓒ Ⓓ Ⓔ
18. Ⓐ Ⓑ Ⓒ Ⓓ Ⓔ
19. Ⓐ Ⓑ Ⓒ Ⓓ Ⓔ
20. Ⓐ Ⓑ Ⓒ Ⓓ Ⓔ
21. Ⓐ Ⓑ Ⓒ Ⓓ Ⓔ
22. Ⓐ Ⓑ Ⓒ Ⓓ Ⓔ
23. Ⓐ Ⓑ Ⓒ Ⓓ Ⓔ
24. Ⓐ Ⓑ Ⓒ Ⓓ Ⓔ
25. Ⓐ Ⓑ Ⓒ Ⓓ Ⓔ
26. Ⓐ Ⓑ Ⓒ Ⓓ Ⓔ
27. Ⓐ Ⓑ Ⓒ Ⓓ Ⓔ
28. Ⓐ Ⓑ Ⓒ Ⓓ Ⓔ
29. Ⓐ Ⓑ Ⓒ Ⓓ Ⓔ
30. Ⓐ Ⓑ Ⓒ Ⓓ Ⓔ
31. Ⓐ Ⓑ Ⓒ Ⓓ Ⓔ
32. Ⓐ Ⓑ Ⓒ Ⓓ Ⓔ
33. Ⓐ Ⓑ Ⓒ Ⓓ Ⓔ
34. Ⓐ Ⓑ Ⓒ Ⓓ Ⓔ
35. Ⓐ Ⓑ Ⓒ Ⓓ Ⓔ
36. Ⓐ Ⓑ Ⓒ Ⓓ Ⓔ
37. Ⓐ Ⓑ Ⓒ Ⓓ Ⓔ
38. Ⓐ Ⓑ Ⓒ Ⓓ Ⓔ
39. Ⓐ Ⓑ Ⓒ Ⓓ Ⓔ
40. Ⓐ Ⓑ Ⓒ Ⓓ Ⓔ
41. Ⓐ Ⓑ Ⓒ Ⓓ Ⓔ
42. Ⓐ Ⓑ Ⓒ Ⓓ Ⓔ
43. Ⓐ Ⓑ Ⓒ Ⓓ Ⓔ
44. Ⓐ Ⓑ Ⓒ Ⓓ Ⓔ
45. Ⓐ Ⓑ Ⓒ Ⓓ Ⓔ
46. Ⓐ Ⓑ Ⓒ Ⓓ Ⓔ
47. Ⓐ Ⓑ Ⓒ Ⓓ Ⓔ
48. Ⓐ Ⓑ Ⓒ Ⓓ Ⓔ
49. Ⓐ Ⓑ Ⓒ Ⓓ Ⓔ
50. Ⓐ Ⓑ Ⓒ Ⓓ Ⓔ

ANSWER SHEET
SIFT #1

Subtest 3: Army Aviation Information Test (AAIT)

1. Ⓐ Ⓑ Ⓒ Ⓓ Ⓔ	11. Ⓐ Ⓑ Ⓒ Ⓓ Ⓔ	21. Ⓐ Ⓑ Ⓒ Ⓓ Ⓔ	31. Ⓐ Ⓑ Ⓒ Ⓓ Ⓔ
2. Ⓐ Ⓑ Ⓒ Ⓓ Ⓔ	12. Ⓐ Ⓑ Ⓒ Ⓓ Ⓔ	22. Ⓐ Ⓑ Ⓒ Ⓓ Ⓔ	32. Ⓐ Ⓑ Ⓒ Ⓓ Ⓔ
3. Ⓐ Ⓑ Ⓒ Ⓓ Ⓔ	13. Ⓐ Ⓑ Ⓒ Ⓓ Ⓔ	23. Ⓐ Ⓑ Ⓒ Ⓓ Ⓔ	33. Ⓐ Ⓑ Ⓒ Ⓓ Ⓔ
4. Ⓐ Ⓑ Ⓒ Ⓓ Ⓔ	14. Ⓐ Ⓑ Ⓒ Ⓓ Ⓔ	24. Ⓐ Ⓑ Ⓒ Ⓓ Ⓔ	34. Ⓐ Ⓑ Ⓒ Ⓓ Ⓔ
5. Ⓐ Ⓑ Ⓒ Ⓓ Ⓔ	15. Ⓐ Ⓑ Ⓒ Ⓓ Ⓔ	25. Ⓐ Ⓑ Ⓒ Ⓓ Ⓔ	35. Ⓐ Ⓑ Ⓒ Ⓓ Ⓔ
6. Ⓐ Ⓑ Ⓒ Ⓓ Ⓔ	16. Ⓐ Ⓑ Ⓒ Ⓓ Ⓔ	26. Ⓐ Ⓑ Ⓒ Ⓓ Ⓔ	36. Ⓐ Ⓑ Ⓒ Ⓓ Ⓔ
7. Ⓐ Ⓑ Ⓒ Ⓓ Ⓔ	17. Ⓐ Ⓑ Ⓒ Ⓓ Ⓔ	27. Ⓐ Ⓑ Ⓒ Ⓓ Ⓔ	37. Ⓐ Ⓑ Ⓒ Ⓓ Ⓔ
8. Ⓐ Ⓑ Ⓒ Ⓓ Ⓔ	18. Ⓐ Ⓑ Ⓒ Ⓓ Ⓔ	28. Ⓐ Ⓑ Ⓒ Ⓓ Ⓔ	38. Ⓐ Ⓑ Ⓒ Ⓓ Ⓔ
9. Ⓐ Ⓑ Ⓒ Ⓓ Ⓔ	19. Ⓐ Ⓑ Ⓒ Ⓓ Ⓔ	29. Ⓐ Ⓑ Ⓒ Ⓓ Ⓔ	39. Ⓐ Ⓑ Ⓒ Ⓓ Ⓔ
10. Ⓐ Ⓑ Ⓒ Ⓓ Ⓔ	20. Ⓐ Ⓑ Ⓒ Ⓓ Ⓔ	30. Ⓐ Ⓑ Ⓒ Ⓓ Ⓔ	40. Ⓐ Ⓑ Ⓒ Ⓓ Ⓔ

Subtest 4: Spatial Apperception Test (SAT)

1. Ⓐ Ⓑ Ⓒ Ⓓ Ⓔ	8. Ⓐ Ⓑ Ⓒ Ⓓ Ⓔ	15. Ⓐ Ⓑ Ⓒ Ⓓ Ⓔ	22. Ⓐ Ⓑ Ⓒ Ⓓ Ⓔ
2. Ⓐ Ⓑ Ⓒ Ⓓ Ⓔ	9. Ⓐ Ⓑ Ⓒ Ⓓ Ⓔ	16. Ⓐ Ⓑ Ⓒ Ⓓ Ⓔ	23. Ⓐ Ⓑ Ⓒ Ⓓ Ⓔ
3. Ⓐ Ⓑ Ⓒ Ⓓ Ⓔ	10. Ⓐ Ⓑ Ⓒ Ⓓ Ⓔ	17. Ⓐ Ⓑ Ⓒ Ⓓ Ⓔ	24. Ⓐ Ⓑ Ⓒ Ⓓ Ⓔ
4. Ⓐ Ⓑ Ⓒ Ⓓ Ⓔ	11. Ⓐ Ⓑ Ⓒ Ⓓ Ⓔ	18. Ⓐ Ⓑ Ⓒ Ⓓ Ⓔ	25. Ⓐ Ⓑ Ⓒ Ⓓ Ⓔ
5. Ⓐ Ⓑ Ⓒ Ⓓ Ⓔ	12. Ⓐ Ⓑ Ⓒ Ⓓ Ⓔ	19. Ⓐ Ⓑ Ⓒ Ⓓ Ⓔ	
6. Ⓐ Ⓑ Ⓒ Ⓓ Ⓔ	13. Ⓐ Ⓑ Ⓒ Ⓓ Ⓔ	20. Ⓐ Ⓑ Ⓒ Ⓓ Ⓔ	
7. Ⓐ Ⓑ Ⓒ Ⓓ Ⓔ	14. Ⓐ Ⓑ Ⓒ Ⓓ Ⓔ	21. Ⓐ Ⓑ Ⓒ Ⓓ Ⓔ	

Subtest 5: Reading Comprehension Test (RCT)

1. Ⓐ Ⓑ Ⓒ Ⓓ Ⓔ	6. Ⓐ Ⓑ Ⓒ Ⓓ Ⓔ	11. Ⓐ Ⓑ Ⓒ Ⓓ Ⓔ	16. Ⓐ Ⓑ Ⓒ Ⓓ Ⓔ
2. Ⓐ Ⓑ Ⓒ Ⓓ Ⓔ	7. Ⓐ Ⓑ Ⓒ Ⓓ Ⓔ	12. Ⓐ Ⓑ Ⓒ Ⓓ Ⓔ	17. Ⓐ Ⓑ Ⓒ Ⓓ Ⓔ
3. Ⓐ Ⓑ Ⓒ Ⓓ Ⓔ	8. Ⓐ Ⓑ Ⓒ Ⓓ Ⓔ	13. Ⓐ Ⓑ Ⓒ Ⓓ Ⓔ	18. Ⓐ Ⓑ Ⓒ Ⓓ Ⓔ
4. Ⓐ Ⓑ Ⓒ Ⓓ Ⓔ	9. Ⓐ Ⓑ Ⓒ Ⓓ Ⓔ	14. Ⓐ Ⓑ Ⓒ Ⓓ Ⓔ	19. Ⓐ Ⓑ Ⓒ Ⓓ Ⓔ
5. Ⓐ Ⓑ Ⓒ Ⓓ Ⓔ	10. Ⓐ Ⓑ Ⓒ Ⓓ Ⓔ	15. Ⓐ Ⓑ Ⓒ Ⓓ Ⓔ	20. Ⓐ Ⓑ Ⓒ Ⓓ Ⓔ

Subtest 6: Math Skills Test (MST)

1. Ⓐ Ⓑ Ⓒ Ⓓ Ⓔ	6. Ⓐ Ⓑ Ⓒ Ⓓ Ⓔ	11. Ⓐ Ⓑ Ⓒ Ⓓ Ⓔ	16. Ⓐ Ⓑ Ⓒ Ⓓ Ⓔ
2. Ⓐ Ⓑ Ⓒ Ⓓ Ⓔ	7. Ⓐ Ⓑ Ⓒ Ⓓ Ⓔ	12. Ⓐ Ⓑ Ⓒ Ⓓ Ⓔ	17. Ⓐ Ⓑ Ⓒ Ⓓ Ⓔ
3. Ⓐ Ⓑ Ⓒ Ⓓ Ⓔ	8. Ⓐ Ⓑ Ⓒ Ⓓ Ⓔ	13. Ⓐ Ⓑ Ⓒ Ⓓ Ⓔ	18. Ⓐ Ⓑ Ⓒ Ⓓ Ⓔ
4. Ⓐ Ⓑ Ⓒ Ⓓ Ⓔ	9. Ⓐ Ⓑ Ⓒ Ⓓ Ⓔ	14. Ⓐ Ⓑ Ⓒ Ⓓ Ⓔ	19. Ⓐ Ⓑ Ⓒ Ⓓ Ⓔ
5. Ⓐ Ⓑ Ⓒ Ⓓ Ⓔ	10. Ⓐ Ⓑ Ⓒ Ⓓ Ⓔ	15. Ⓐ Ⓑ Ⓒ Ⓓ Ⓔ	20. Ⓐ Ⓑ Ⓒ Ⓓ Ⓔ

Subtest 7: Mechanical Comprehension Test (MCT)

1. Ⓐ Ⓑ Ⓒ Ⓓ Ⓔ	6. Ⓐ Ⓑ Ⓒ Ⓓ Ⓔ	11. Ⓐ Ⓑ Ⓒ Ⓓ Ⓔ	16. Ⓐ Ⓑ Ⓒ Ⓓ Ⓔ
2. Ⓐ Ⓑ Ⓒ Ⓓ Ⓔ	7. Ⓐ Ⓑ Ⓒ Ⓓ Ⓔ	12. Ⓐ Ⓑ Ⓒ Ⓓ Ⓔ	17. Ⓐ Ⓑ Ⓒ Ⓓ Ⓔ
3. Ⓐ Ⓑ Ⓒ Ⓓ Ⓔ	8. Ⓐ Ⓑ Ⓒ Ⓓ Ⓔ	13. Ⓐ Ⓑ Ⓒ Ⓓ Ⓔ	18. Ⓐ Ⓑ Ⓒ Ⓓ Ⓔ
4. Ⓐ Ⓑ Ⓒ Ⓓ Ⓔ	9. Ⓐ Ⓑ Ⓒ Ⓓ Ⓔ	14. Ⓐ Ⓑ Ⓒ Ⓓ Ⓔ	19. Ⓐ Ⓑ Ⓒ Ⓓ Ⓔ
5. Ⓐ Ⓑ Ⓒ Ⓓ Ⓔ	10. Ⓐ Ⓑ Ⓒ Ⓓ Ⓔ	15. Ⓐ Ⓑ Ⓒ Ⓓ Ⓔ	20. Ⓐ Ⓑ Ⓒ Ⓓ Ⓔ

Army Selection Instrument for Flight Training (SIFT) Practice Test #1

12

TEST FORMAT

The Army's SIFT is completely automated; there is no paper version, so you don't have to worry about whether you filled in the little bubble on the answer sheet correctly to get credit for your answer.

As a reminder, this is how the SIFT is organized:

Subtest	Abbrev.	Number of Questions	Time Limit
Simple Drawings	SD	100	2 mins
Hidden Figures	HF	50	5 mins
Army Aviation Information Test	AAIT	40	30 mins
Spatial Apperception Test	SAT	25	10 mins
Reading Comprehension Test	RCT	20	30 mins
Math Skills Test	MST	Varies	40 mins
Mechanical Comprehension Test	MCT	Varies	15 mins

Again, the subtests are different, so there are different strategies and techniques needed to do your best.

Subtest 1: Simple Drawings (SD)

In the Simple Drawings subtest, you will be given five shapes, four of which are identical and one of which is different. Your task is to identify the letter of the shape that's different and move on quickly—there are 100 questions and only two minutes—but don't guess! The SD score is a result of how many questions you get right, and wrong answers are deducted from your score. It's unlikely that you'll be able to get through all the questions in the time allotted, so concentrate on choosing the right answer for the ones you do answer—and don't start randomly guessing as time is about to expire.

Here's an example question:

P1.

As you can see, choice (D) is different because it's not filled in, so that would be your choice.

Subtest 2: Hidden Figures (HF)

The Hidden Figures subtest measures your ability to "see" and identify a simple figure hidden within a complex drawing. You will be given a series of five lettered figures, followed by five numbered drawings. Your objective is to determine which lettered figure is contained within each numbered drawing.

Again, like the Simple Drawings subtest, work quickly and don't guess—you have 50 questions and only five minutes allotted, but once you get rolling they will come easier. Remember, though, that you get your HF score from how many problems you get right; wrong answers are deducted from your score—so concentrate on making the right choice, and don't start randomly guessing as time is about to expire.

Here's an example:

P2.

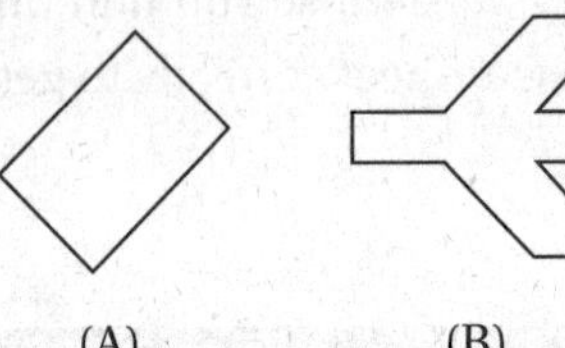
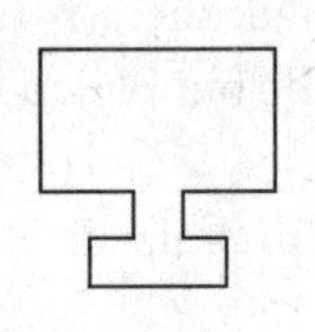
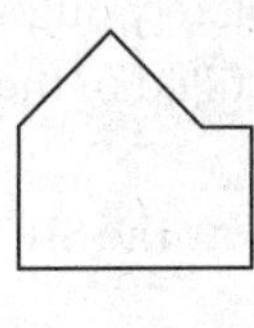
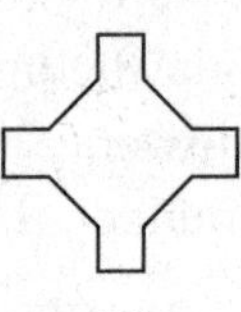

(A) (B) (C) (D) (E)

1.

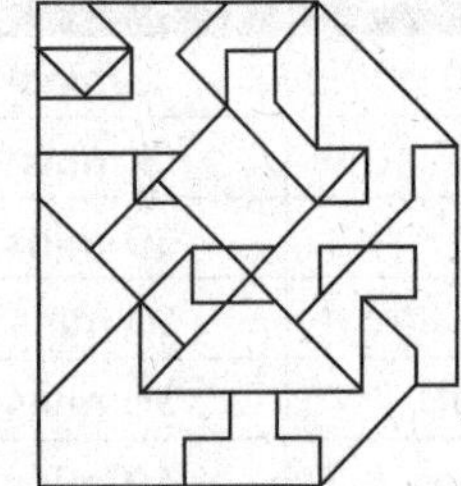

4.

2.

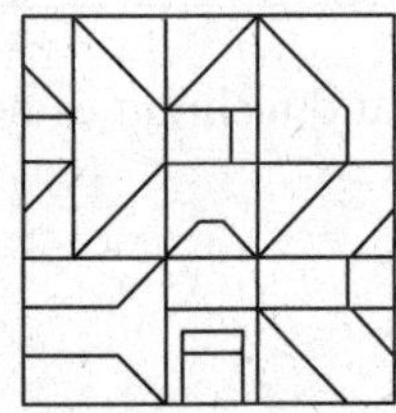

5.

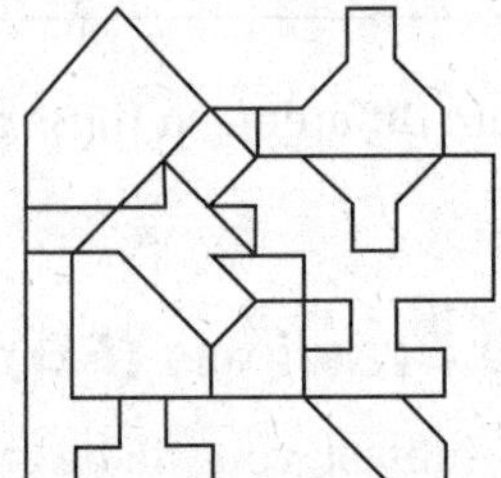

3.

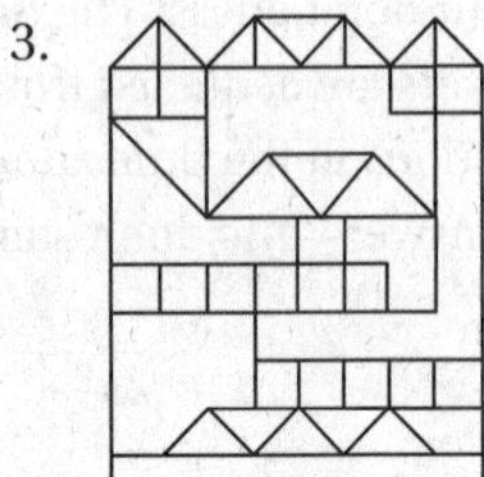

How did you do? The correct answers are as follows:

1. **A**
2. **B**
3. **C**
4. **B**
5. **D**

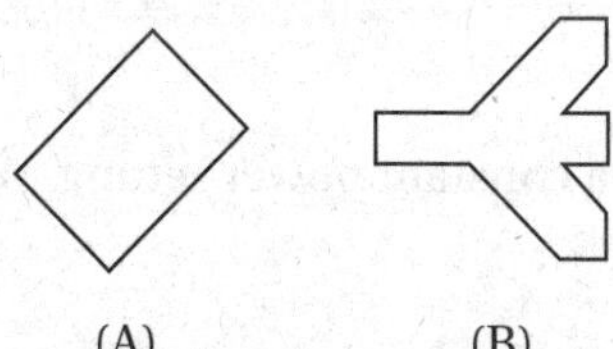

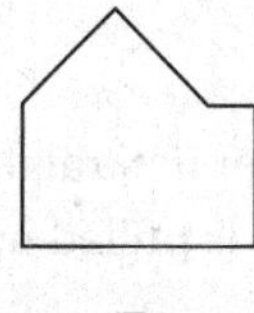
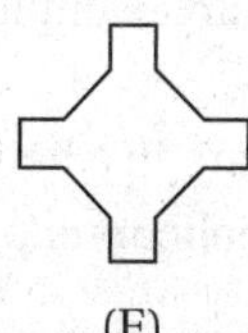

(A) (B) (C) (D) (E)

1. **(A)**

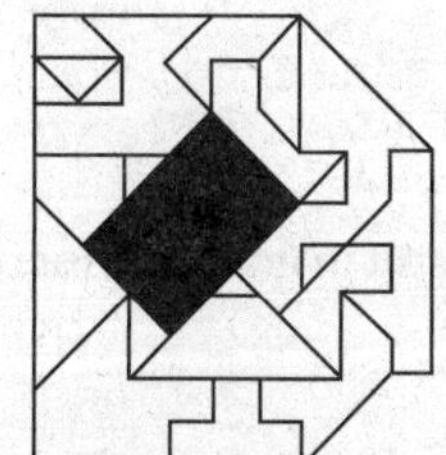

2. **(B)**

3. **(C)**

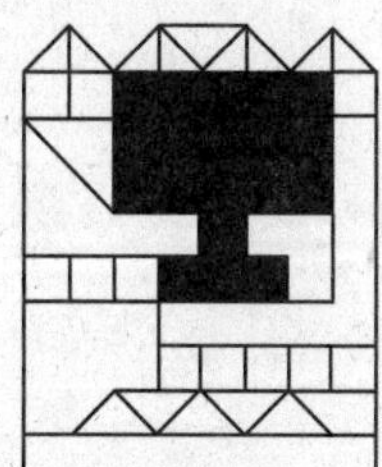

4. **(B)**

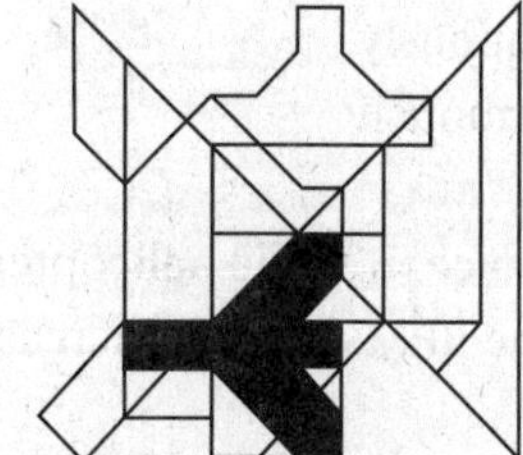

5. **(D)**

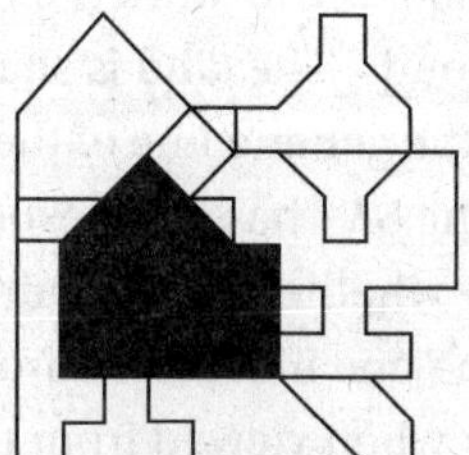

Subtest 3: Army Aviation Information Test (AAIT)

This subtest assesses your level of knowledge of the basics of rotary-wing flight, as well as terminology and concepts relevant to Army aviation. You will have 40 multiple-choice questions to answer in 30 minutes. This subtest has a fixed number of questions and is not adaptive. Unlike the first two subtests, any unanswered questions will be graded as incorrect. Therefore, if time is about to expire, you will benefit by taking just enough time on the remaining questions to bypass obviously wrong answer choices and make educated guesses.

Here's an example:

P3. You are in a helicopter in straight and level flight with a constant power setting. When the helicopter's nose is pulled up, the altitude will

(A) remain the same.
(B) initially increase.
(C) initially decrease.
(D) increase continuously.
(E) decrease continuously.

The correct answer is choice (B)—the helicopter's momentum will result in an initial increase in altitude, even if engine RPMs are not increased.

Subtest 4: Spatial Apperception Test (SAT)

The SAT measures your ability to determine the position of an aircraft in flight relative to the view the pilot would see looking forward out of the cockpit. In this view, you will usually have some land, water, and clouds. The land is shaded lightly, and the water is darker. The clouds will help you determine the general line of the horizon, since the bottom of the clouds will be parallel to the horizon.The SAT has 25 questions, which you will have 10 minutes to answer. Your task is to determine whether the aircraft is banking, diving, climbing, or in level flight—then you must choose the one illustration from a series of five that best represents how that same aircraft would look when viewed from the outside.

Here's an example:

P4:

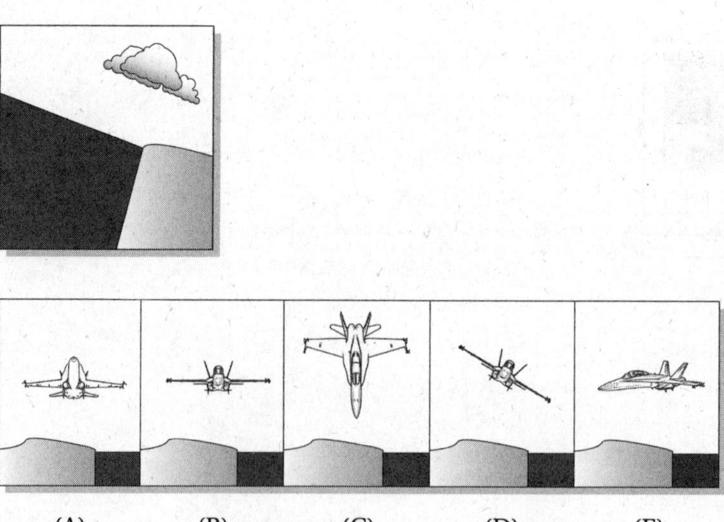

The correct answer is choice (D). Since the horizon is tilted to the right, you (as the pilot) are banking to the left; since the horizon is roughly in the middle of the view, you are in level flight; the water is on your left and the land on the right, with your path of forward progress leading generally along the coast. The only answer choice that matches all these conditions is choice (D).

Subtest 5: Reading Comprehension Test (RCT)

The RCT measures your vocabulary and reading skills. It consists of 20 multiple-choice questions, which you will have 30 minutes to answer. Again, it is not adaptive, so if time is getting short, try to blaze through the last few questions, since unanswered questions will be counted as incorrect.

Read the passage associated with each question carefully, then choose the response that best answers the question based on the passage.

> A noted communications researcher found that only 7 percent of our feelings and attitudes are communicated with words, 38 percent through tone of voice, and a whopping 55 percent through nonverbal expressions and body language. These numbers are astonishing, but that's only part of the picture. The communications channels that we best control and best understand have the least impact—and the channels over which we have the least control, and that we understand the least, are by far the most important.

P5. According to the above passage,

(A) 55 percent of what we say is understood through tone of voice.
(B) verbal communication is what gets the message across.
(C) we have the most control over the most important aspects of how we communicate.
(D) written communication is more precise than verbal communication.
(E) more than half of our communication is through nonverbal expressions and body language.

The correct answer is choice (E); even though choice (D) may be true, too, the passage does not address whether written communication is more precise than verbal communication.

Subtest 6: Math Skills Test (MST)

The MST is one of two adaptive subtests on the SIFT; it evaluates your knowledge of basic arithmetic and your problem-solving ability using math. Although you can expect to see 20–30 questions on this subtest, you may see more or less depending on how you do, as the program tailors its questions to your demonstrated level of proficiency.

Here's an example:

P6. Mrs. H.B. drove her Volvo S70 four-door sedan from Waco to Corpus Christi at an average speed of 68 miles per hour, including two rest stops of 10 minutes each. Her car, on average, gets highway mileage of 30 miles per gallon. If her car used 9.5 gallons of gas, how many hours did she travel?

(A) 4 hrs., 45 min.
(B) 3 hrs., 30 min.
(C) 4 hrs., 12 min.
(D) 4 hrs., 2 min.
(E) none of the above

The answer is choice (C), 4.2 hours (4 hours, 12 minutes). Although we are given lots of numbers and information in the problem (car model, city names, how long her rest stops were), some of it is not relevant. To solve this problem:

$$9.5 \text{ gallons of gas} \times 30 \text{ miles per gallon} = 285 \text{ miles traveled}$$
$$285 \text{ miles} \div 68 \text{ mph} = 4.2 \text{ hrs. (4 hrs., 12 min.)}$$

Again, since this subtest is adaptive, it is not wise to guess, even if time is about to run out.

Subtest 7: Mechanical Comprehension Test (MCT)

This subtest—one of two adaptive subtests on the SIFT—measures your understanding of general mechanical principles by (in most cases) showing you a diagram and asking you a question about the mechanical principle(s) illustrated there.

You can expect to see about 20 questions in the 15 minutes you have allotted, although since the MCT is adaptive, you may see more or less depending on your demonstrated knowledge in this area.

P7. At which point should one pull down to raise the weight more easily: at point A or at point B?

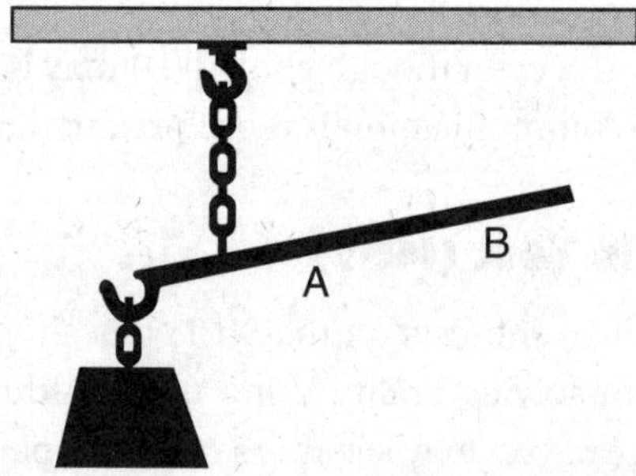

The correct answer is point B. Pulling down at point B makes more leverage available because of the longer length of the lever. (The distance from the fulcrum—the point of attachment to the hanging chain—is farther to point B than to point A, resulting in a longer effective lever length, and hence requiring less force to raise the weight at B than at A.)

SUBTEST 1: SIMPLE DRAWINGS (SD)

100 Questions

1. (A) (B) (C) (D) (E)

2. (A) (B) (C) (D) (E)

3.  (A) (B) (C) (D) (E)

4.  (A) (B) (C) (D) (E)

5.  (A) (B) (C) (D) (E)

6.  (A) (B) (C) (D) (E)

7. (A) (B) (C) (D) (E)

8.  (A) (B) (C) (D) (E)

9. (A) (B) (C) (D) (E)

10. (A) (B) (C) (D) (E)

11. (A) (B) (C) (D) (E)

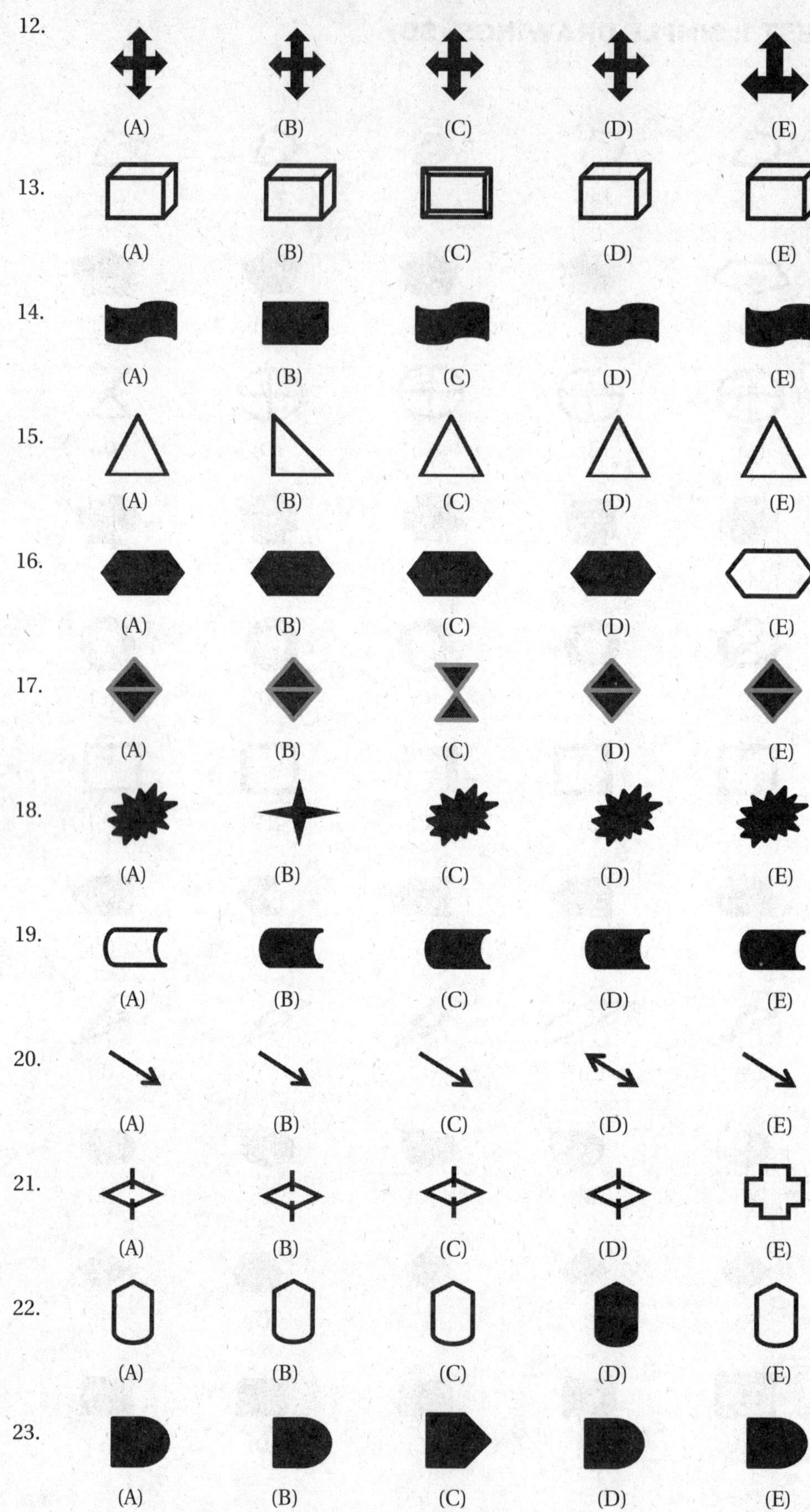
12.
(A) (B) (C) (D) (E)
13.
(A) (B) (C) (D) (E)
14.
(A) (B) (C) (D) (E)
15.
(A) (B) (C) (D) (E)
16.
(A) (B) (C) (D) (E)
17.
(A) (B) (C) (D) (E)
18.
(A) (B) (C) (D) (E)
19.
(A) (B) (C) (D) (E)
20.
(A) (B) (C) (D) (E)
21.
(A) (B) (C) (D) (E)
22.
(A) (B) (C) (D) (E)
23.
(A) (B) (C) (D) (E)

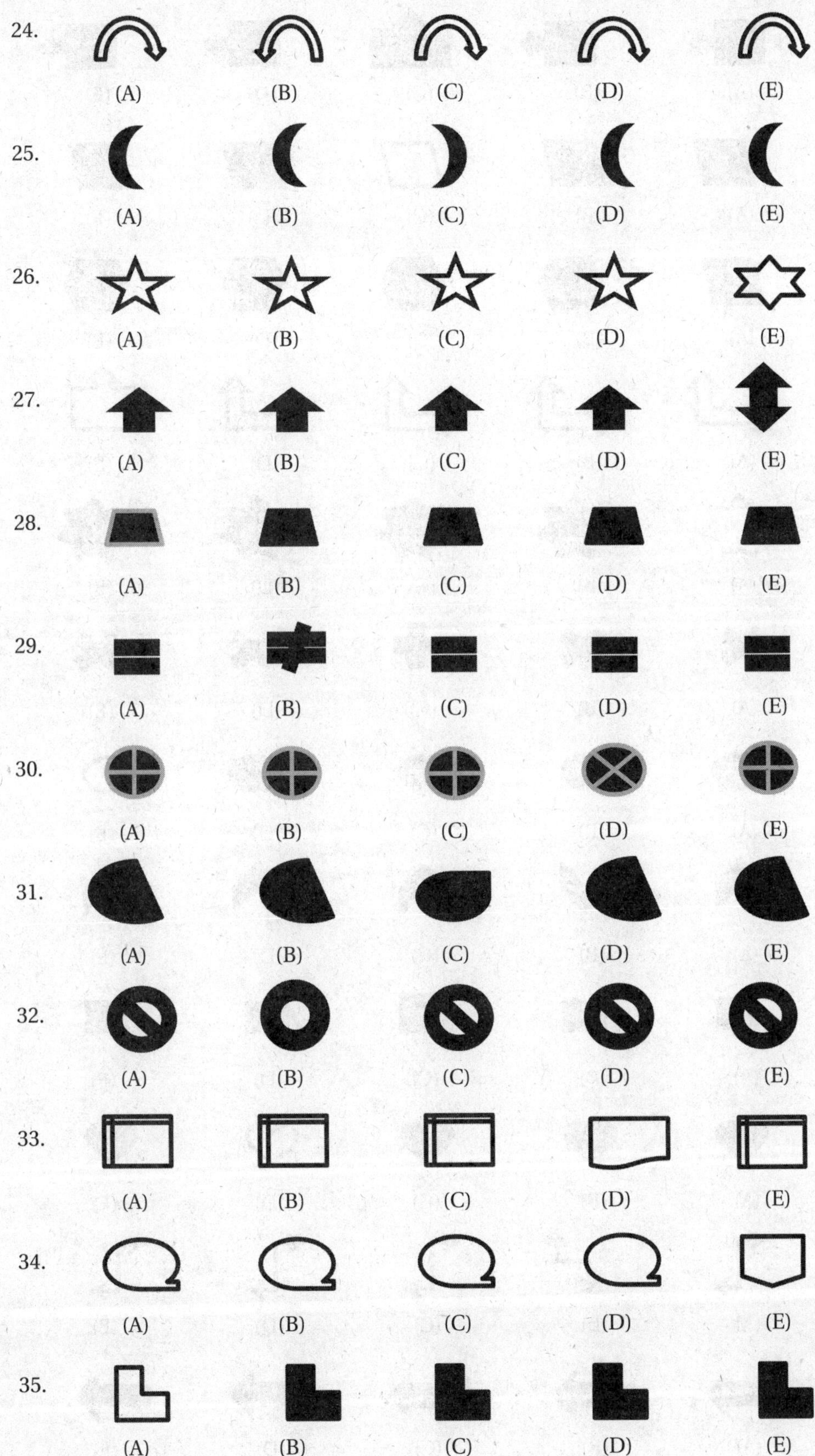
24.
(A)
(B)
(C)
(D)
(E)
25.
(A)
(B)
(C)
(D)
(E)
26.
(A)
(B)
(C)
(D)
(E)
27.
(A)
(B)
(C)
(D)
(E)
28.
(A)
(B)
(C)
(D)
(E)
29.
(A)
(B)
(C)
(D)
(E)
30.
(A)
(B)
(C)
(D)
(E)
31.
(A)
(B)
(C)
(D)
(E)
32.
(A)
(B)
(C)
(D)
(E)
33.
(A)
(B)
(C)
(D)
(E)
34.
(A)
(B)
(C)
(D)
(E)
35.
(A)
(B)
(C)
(D)
(E)

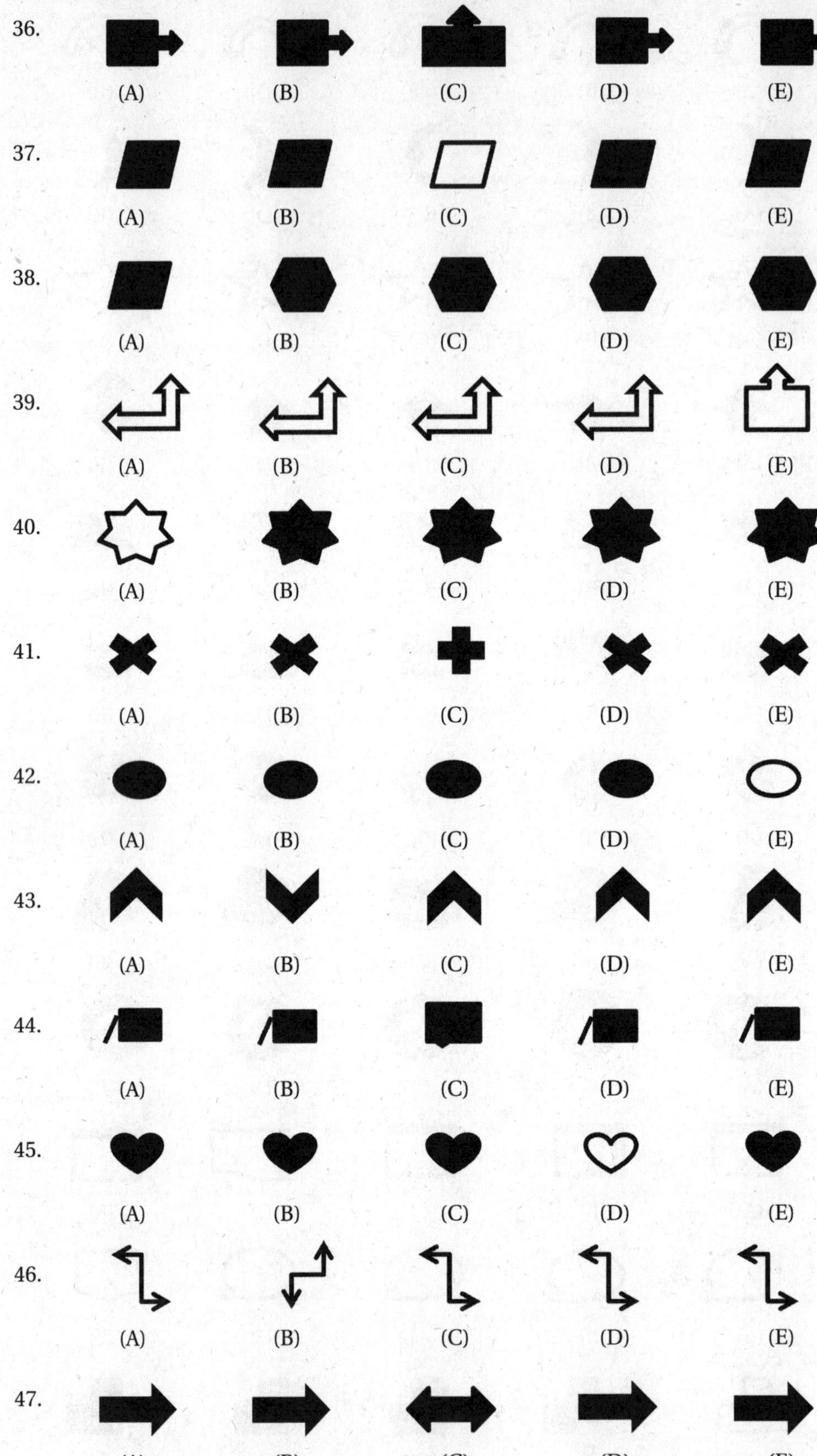
36.
(A) (B) (C) (D) (E)
37.
(A) (B) (C) (D) (E)
38.
(A) (B) (C) (D) (E)
39.
(A) (B) (C) (D) (E)
40.
(A) (B) (C) (D) (E)
41.
(A) (B) (C) (D) (E)
42.
(A) (B) (C) (D) (E)
43.
(A) (B) (C) (D) (E)
44.
(A) (B) (C) (D) (E)
45.
(A) (B) (C) (D) (E)
46.
(A) (B) (C) (D) (E)
47.
(A) (B) (C) (D) (E)

48. (A) (B) (C) (D) (E)

49. (A) (B) (C) (D) (E)

50. (A) (B) (C) (D) (E)

51. (A) (B) (C) (D) (E)

52. (A) (B) (C) (D) (E)

53. (A) (B) (C) (D) (E)

54. (A) (B) (C) (D) (E)

55. (A) (B) (C) (D) (E)

56. (A) (B) (C) (D) (E)

57. (A) (B) (C) (D) (E)

58. (A) (B) (C) (D) (E)

59. (A) (B) (C) (D) (E)

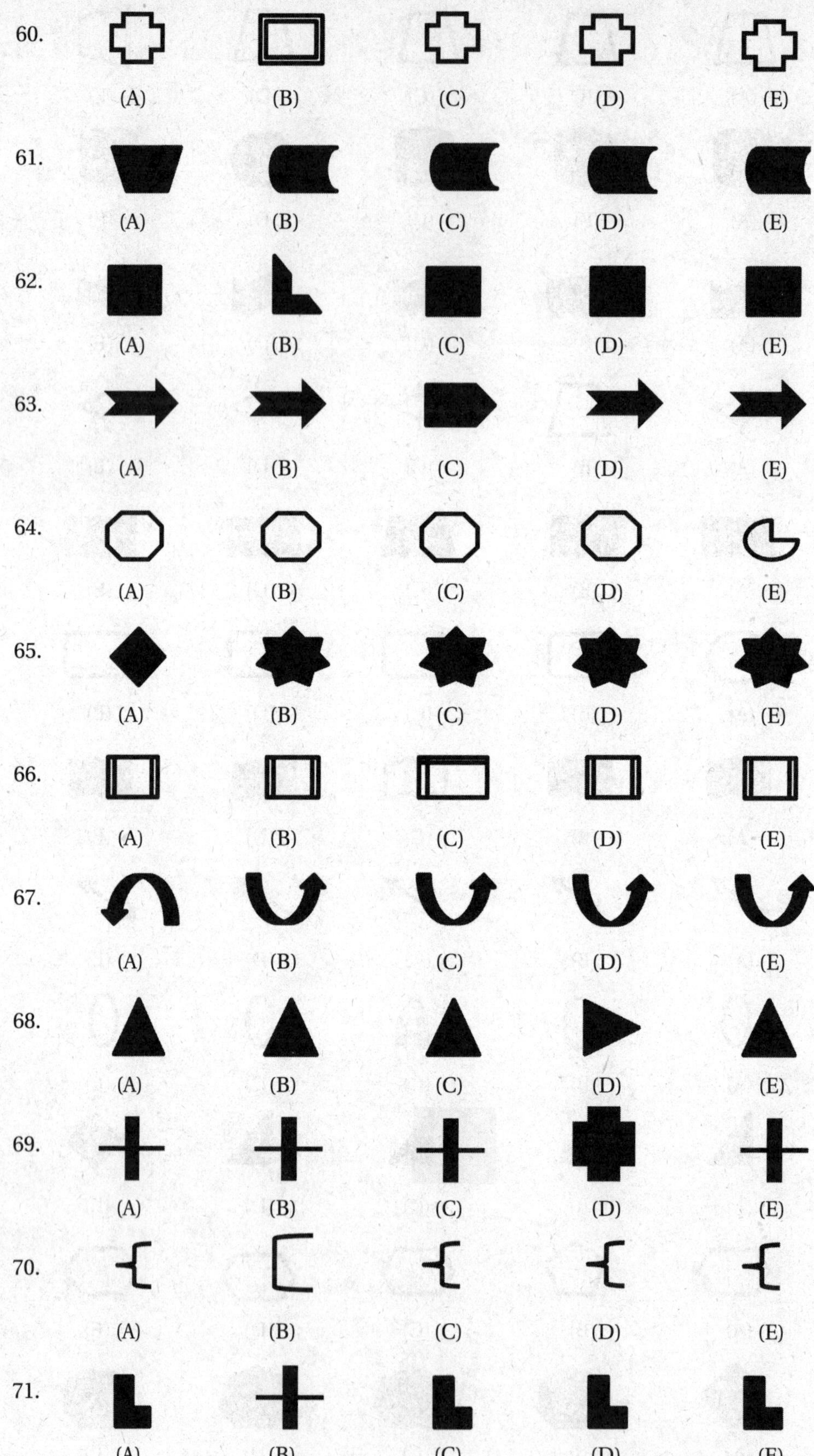
60.
(A)
(B)
(C)
(D)
(E)
61.
(A)
(B)
(C)
(D)
(E)
62.
(A)
(B)
(C)
(D)
(E)
63.
(A)
(B)
(C)
(D)
(E)
64.
(A)
(B)
(C)
(D)
(E)
65.
(A)
(B)
(C)
(D)
(E)
66.
(A)
(B)
(C)
(D)
(E)
67.
(A)
(B)
(C)
(D)
(E)
68.
(A)
(B)
(C)
(D)
(E)
69.
(A)
(B)
(C)
(D)
(E)
70.
(A)
(B)
(C)
(D)
(E)
71.
(A)
(B)
(C)
(D)
(E)

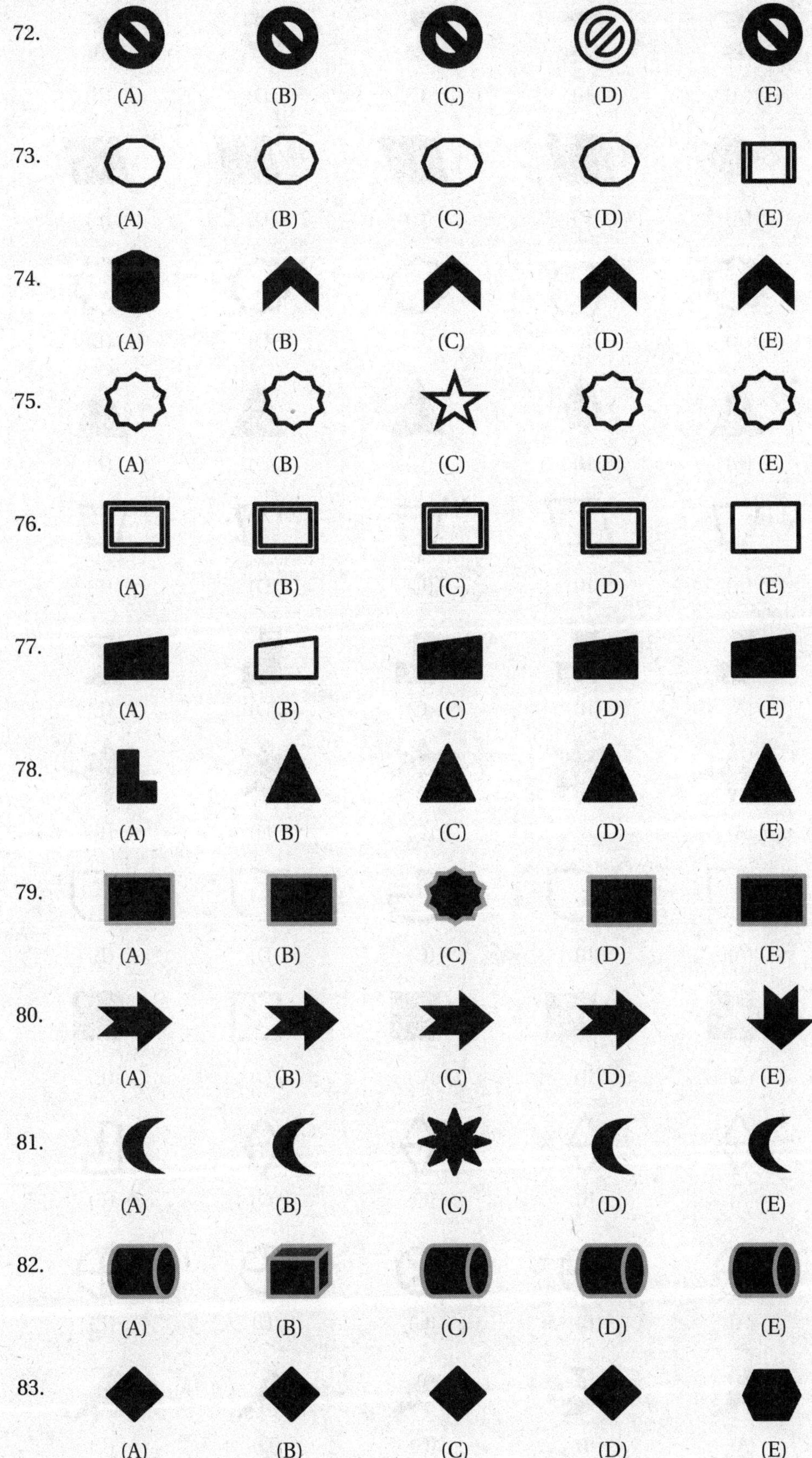
72.
(A) (B) (C) (D) (E)
73.
(A) (B) (C) (D) (E)
74.
(A) (B) (C) (D) (E)
75.
(A) (B) (C) (D) (E)
76.
(A) (B) (C) (D) (E)
77.
(A) (B) (C) (D) (E)
78.
(A) (B) (C) (D) (E)
79.
(A) (B) (C) (D) (E)
80.
(A) (B) (C) (D) (E)
81.
(A) (B) (C) (D) (E)
82.
(A) (B) (C) (D) (E)
83.
(A) (B) (C) (D) (E)

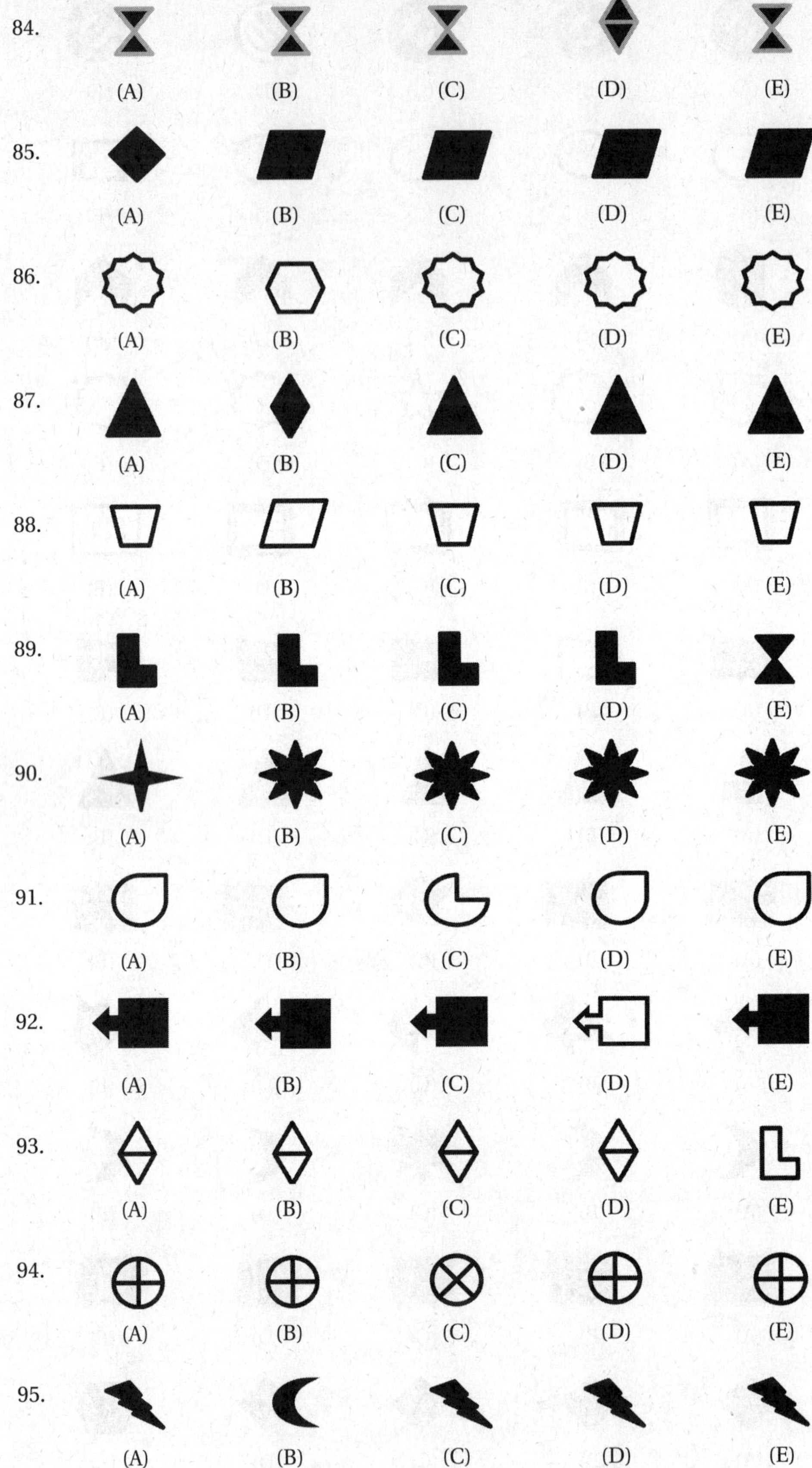
84.
(A) (B) (C) (D) (E)
85.
(A) (B) (C) (D) (E)
86.
(A) (B) (C) (D) (E)
87.
(A) (B) (C) (D) (E)
88.
(A) (B) (C) (D) (E)
89.
(A) (B) (C) (D) (E)
90.
(A) (B) (C) (D) (E)
91.
(A) (B) (C) (D) (E)
92.
(A) (B) (C) (D) (E)
93.
(A) (B) (C) (D) (E)
94.
(A) (B) (C) (D) (E)
95.
(A) (B) (C) (D) (E)

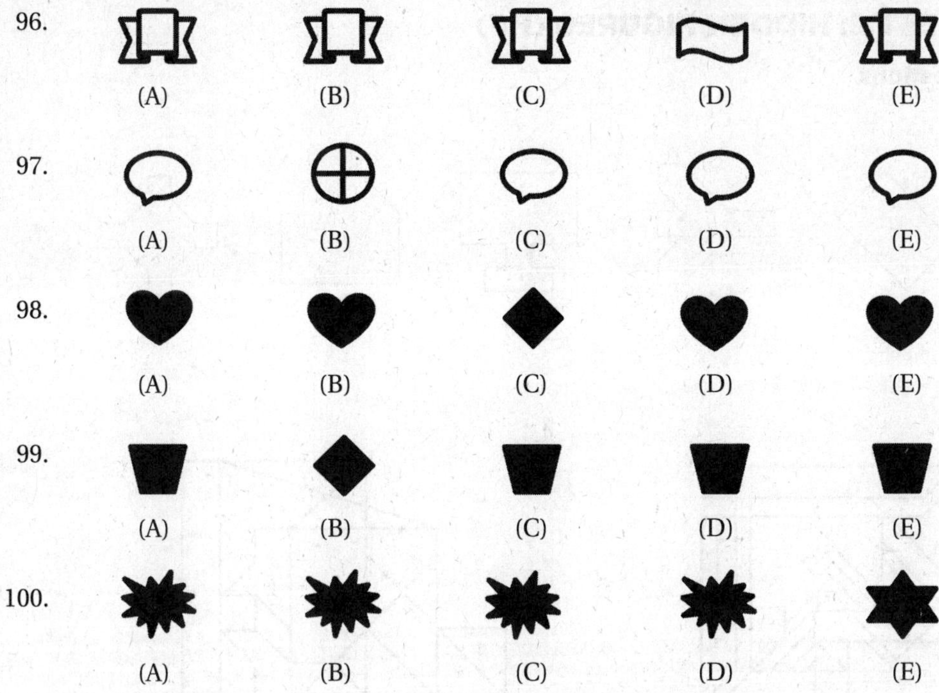
96.
(A) (B) (C) (D) (E)
97.
(A) (B) (C) (D) (E)
98.
(A) (B) (C) (D) (E)
99.
(A) (B) (C) (D) (E)
100.
(A) (B) (C) (D) (E)

SUBTEST 2: HIDDEN FIGURES (HF)

50 Questions

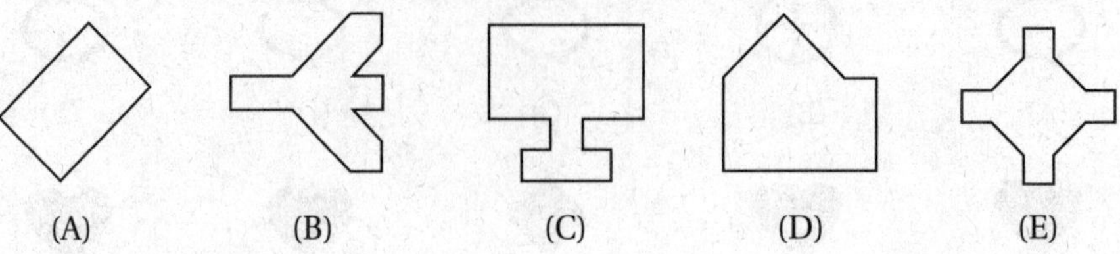

1.

4.

2.

5.

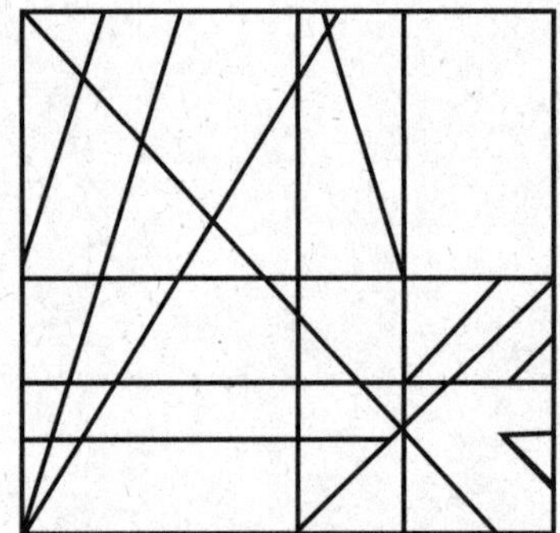

3.

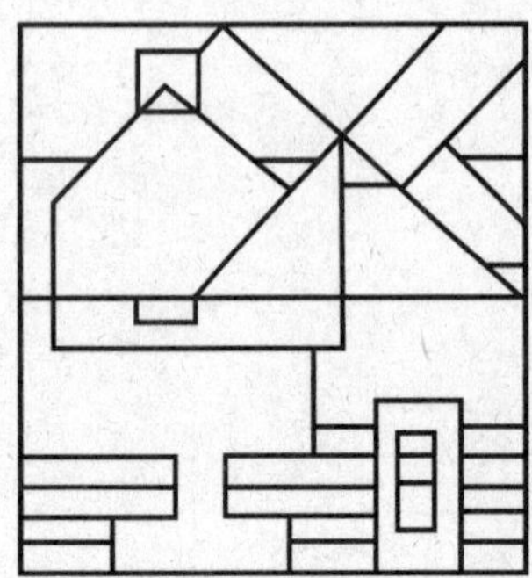

(A)

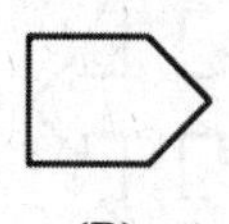

(B)

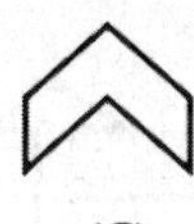

(C)

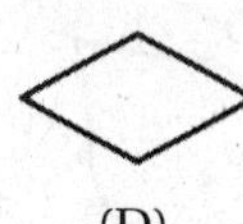

(D)

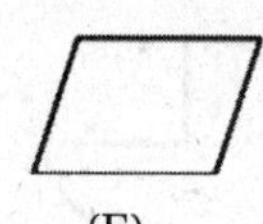

(E)

6.

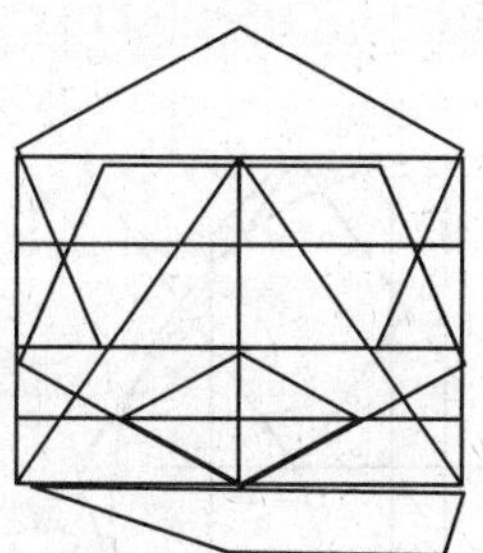

9.

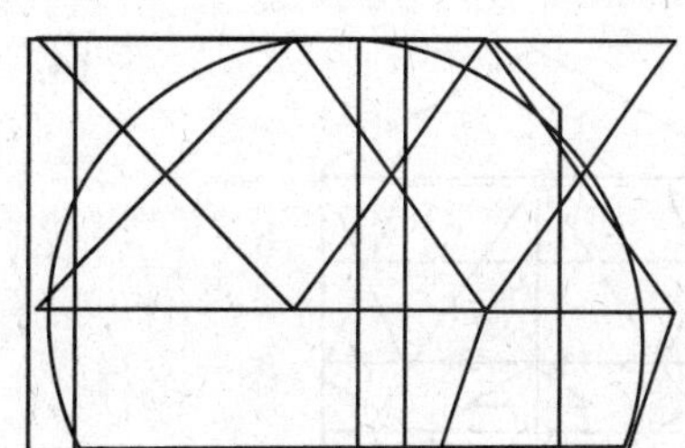

7.

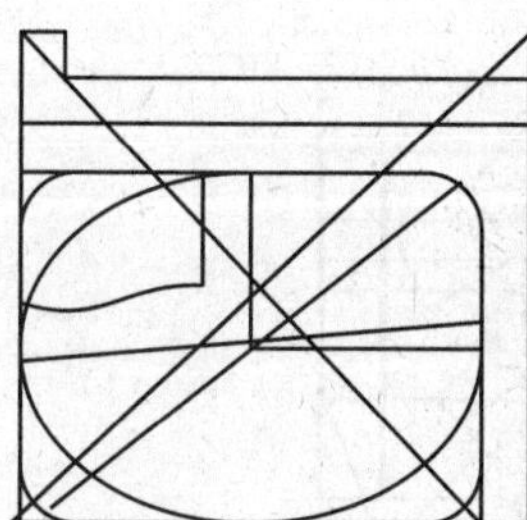

10.

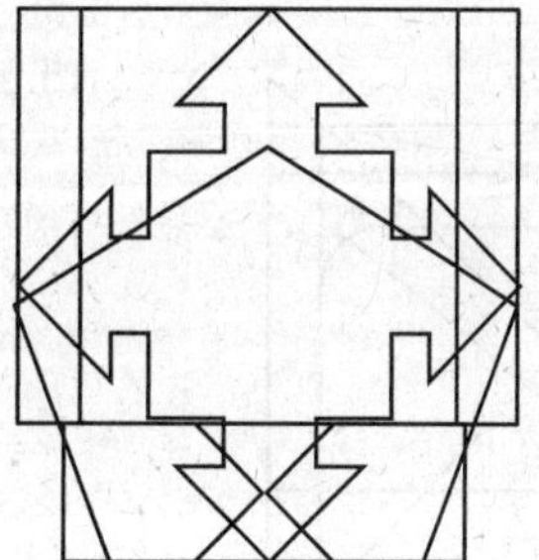

8.

SIFT #1

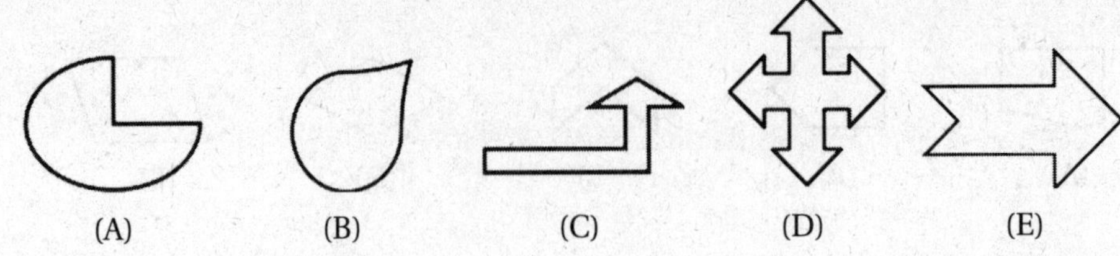

11.

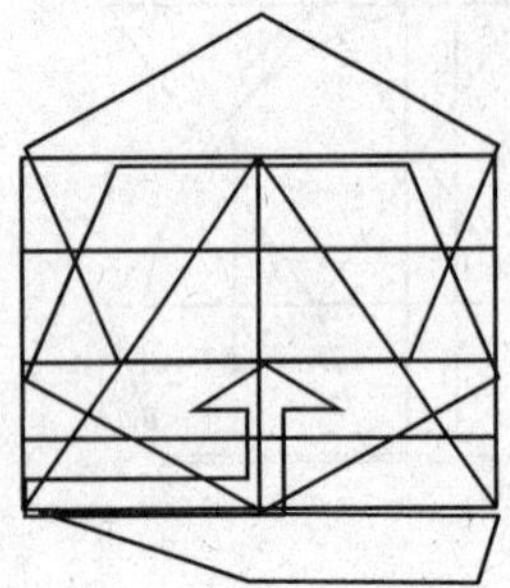

12.

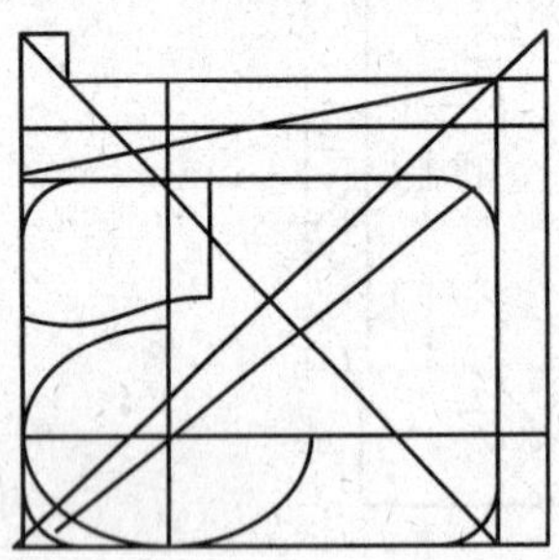

13.

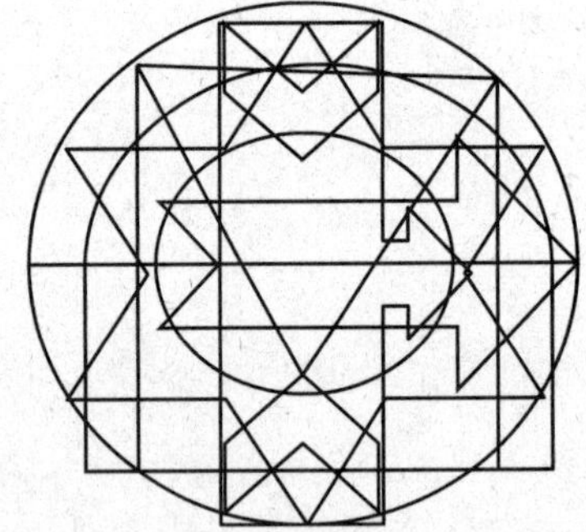

14.

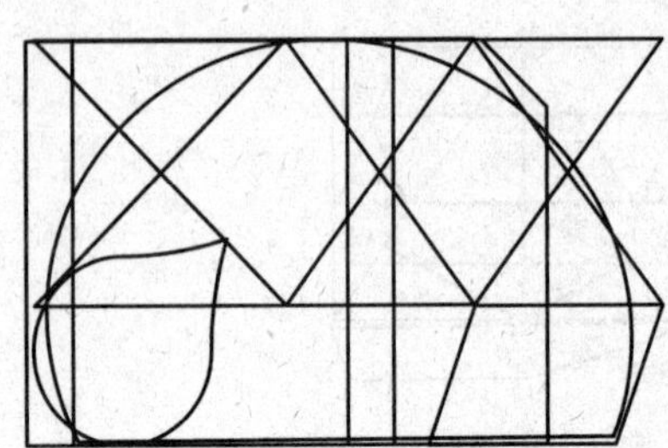

15.

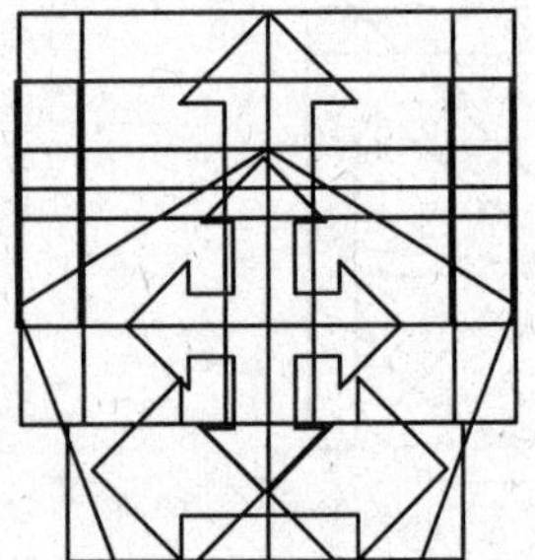

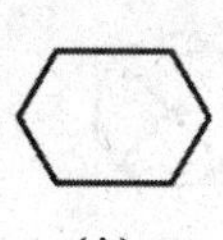
(A)

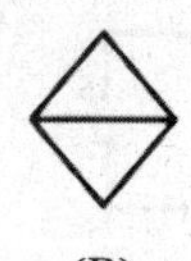
(B)

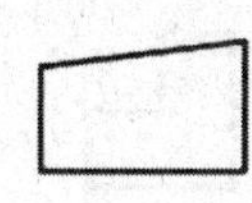
(C)

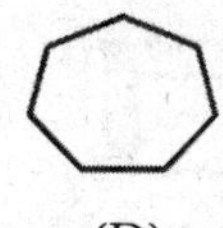
(D)

(E)

16.

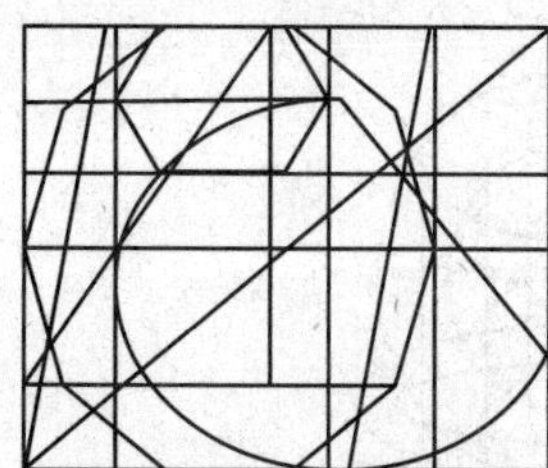

19.

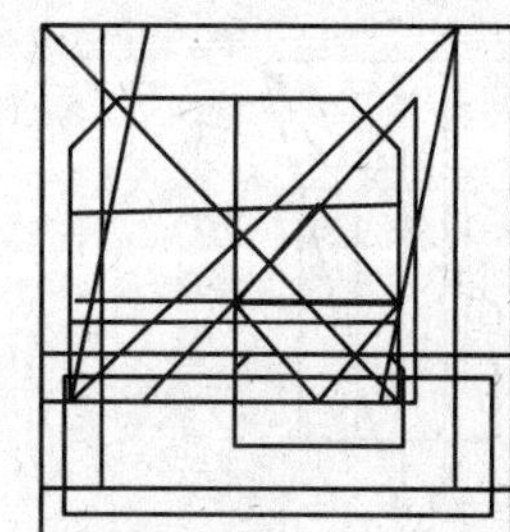

17.

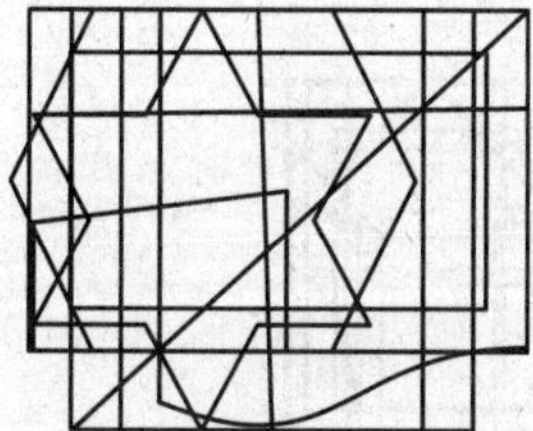

20.

18.

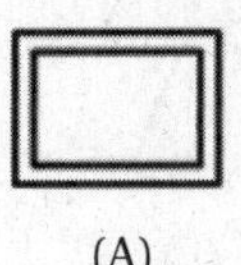
(A)

(B)

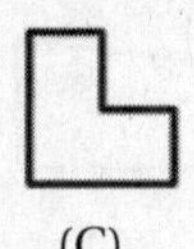
(C)

(D)

(E)

21.

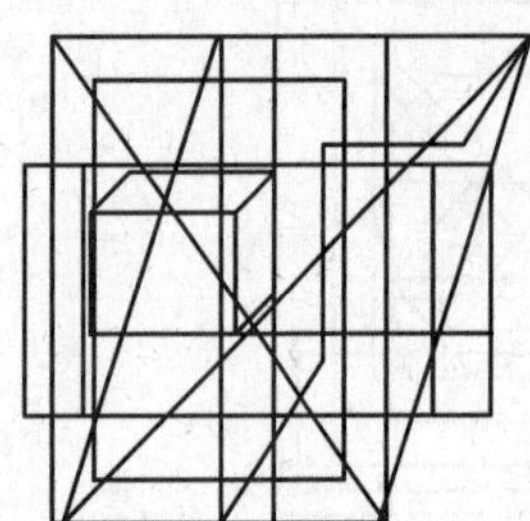

24.

22.

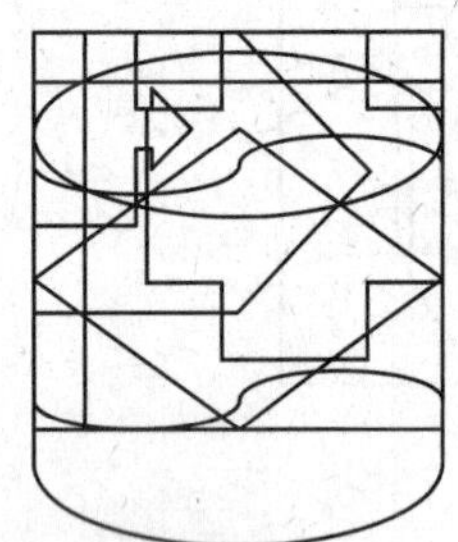

25.

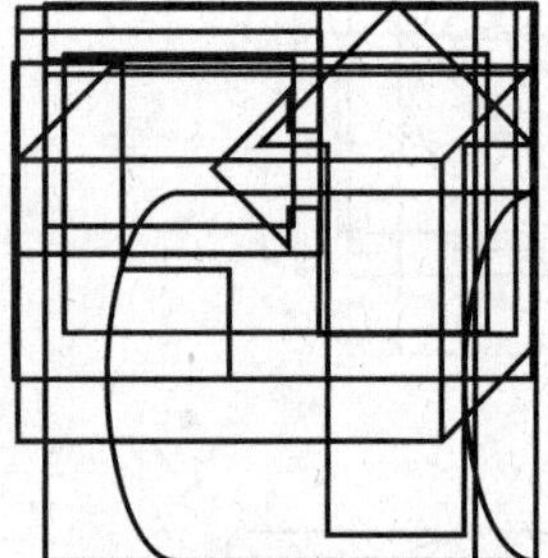

23.

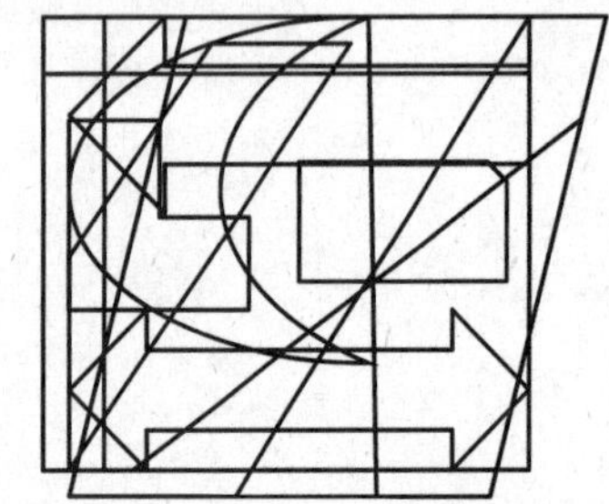

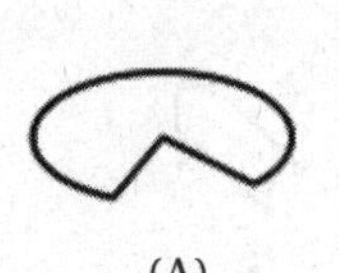
(A)

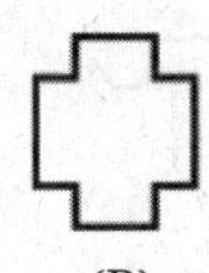
(B)

(C)

(D)

(E)

26.

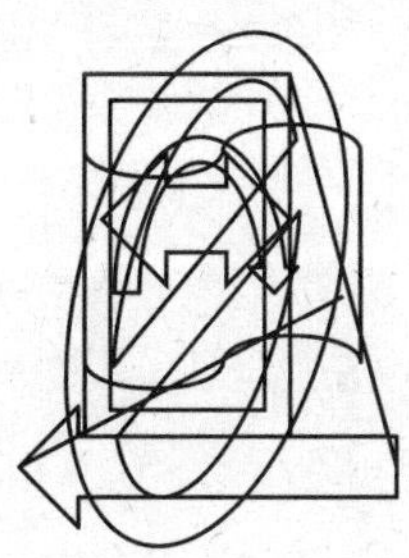

27.

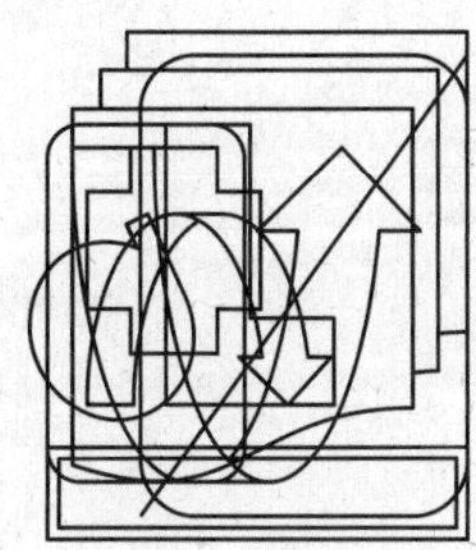

28.

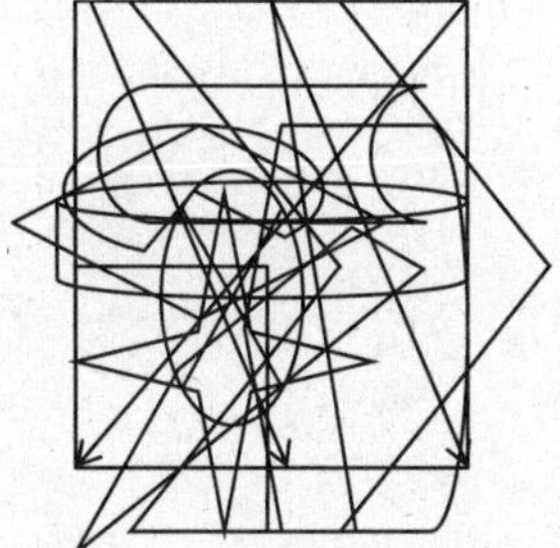

29.

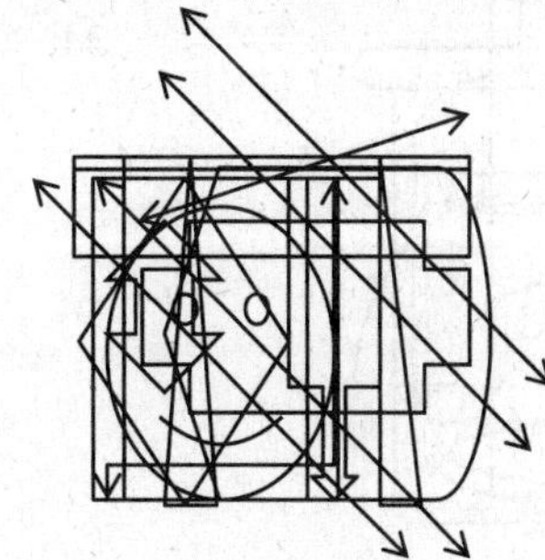

30.

SIFT #1

SIFT #1

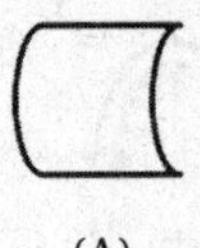
(A)

(B)

(C)

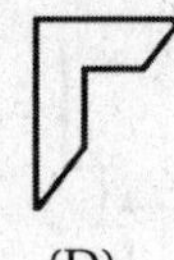
(D)

(E)

31.

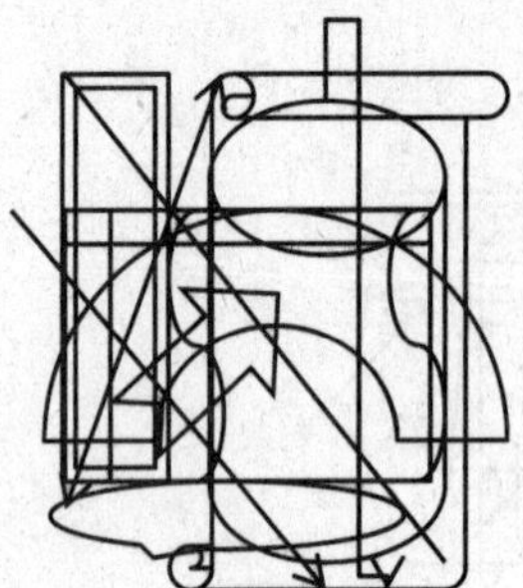

34.

32.

35.

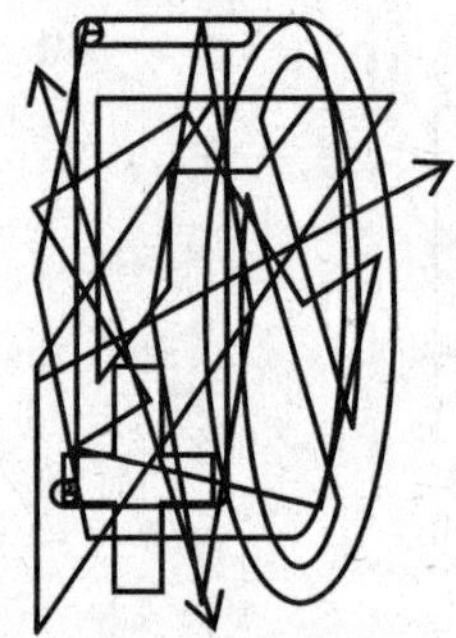

33.

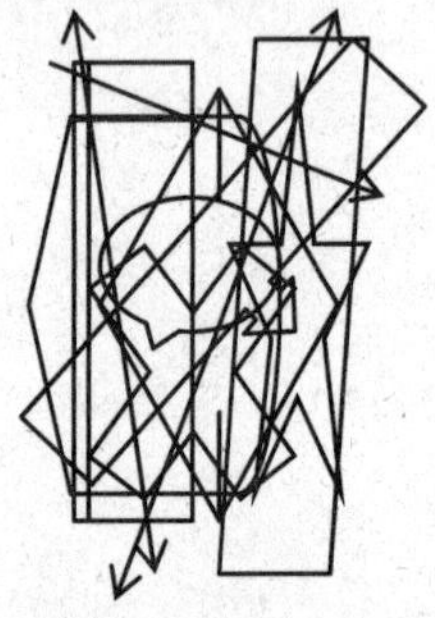

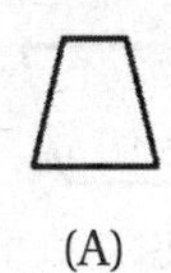

(A)

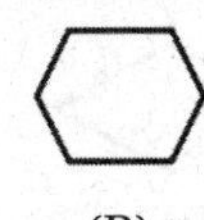

(B)

(C)

(D)

(E)

36.

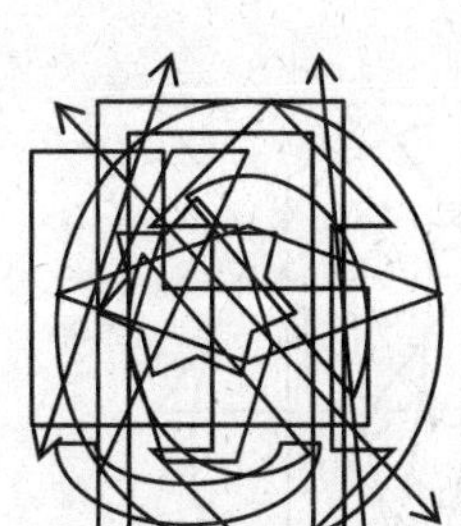

39.

37.

40.

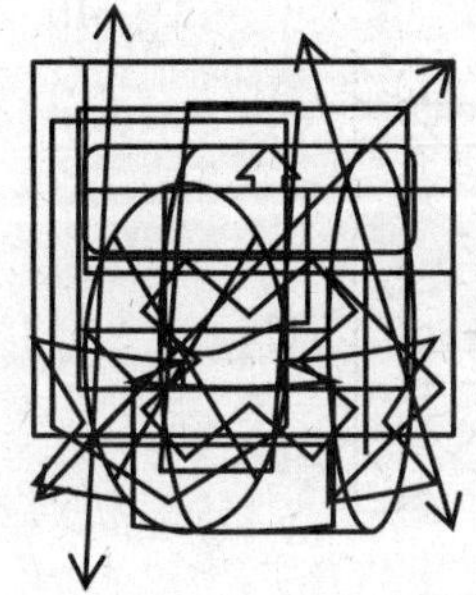

38.

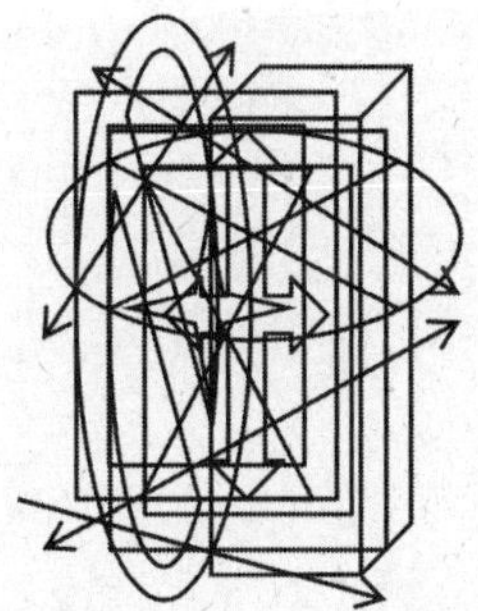

SIFT #1

(A)

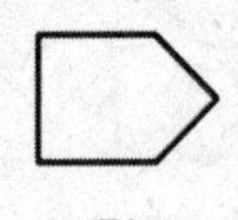
(B)

(C)

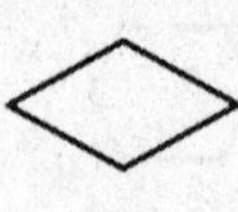
(D)

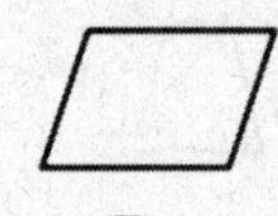
(E)

41.

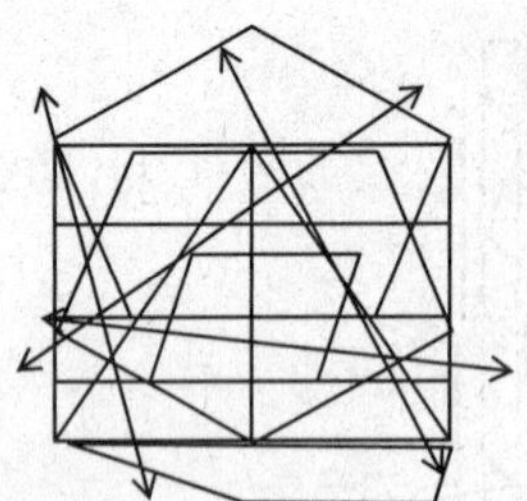

44.

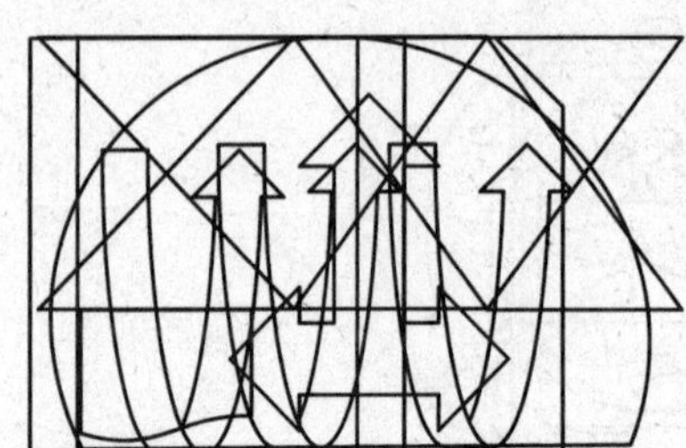

42.

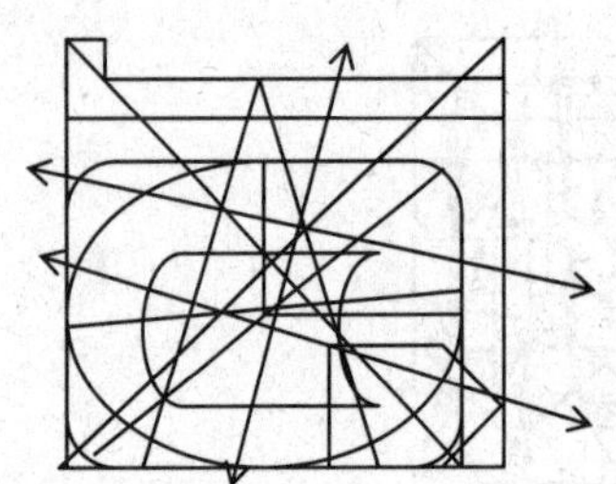

45.

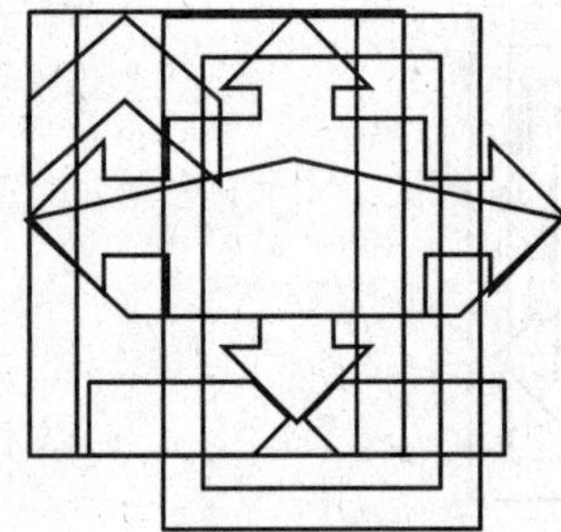

43.

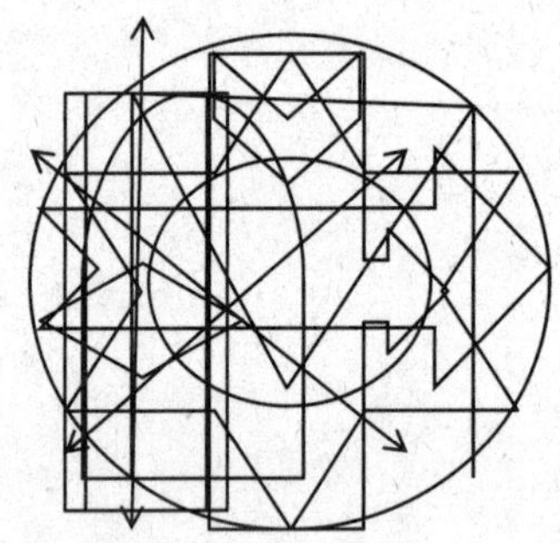

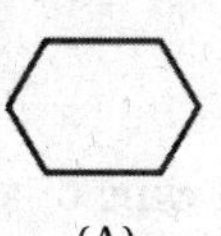
(A)

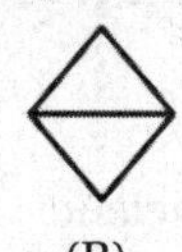
(B)

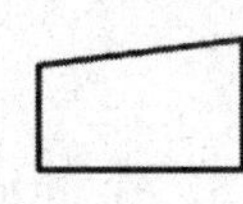
(C)

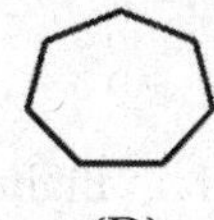
(D)

(E)

46.

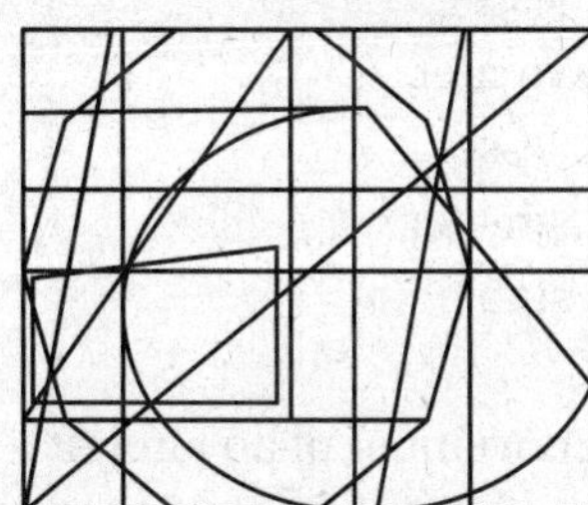

47.

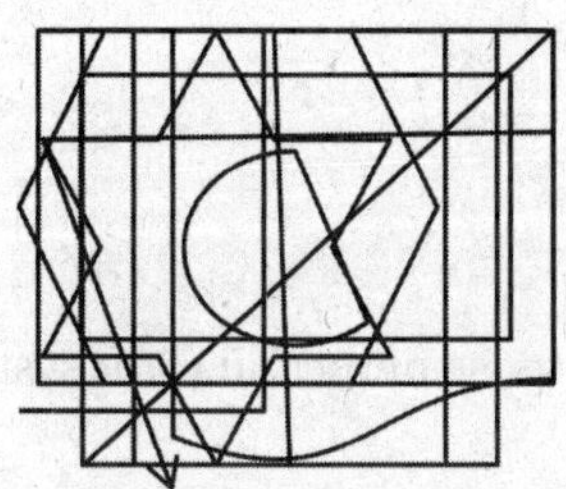

48.

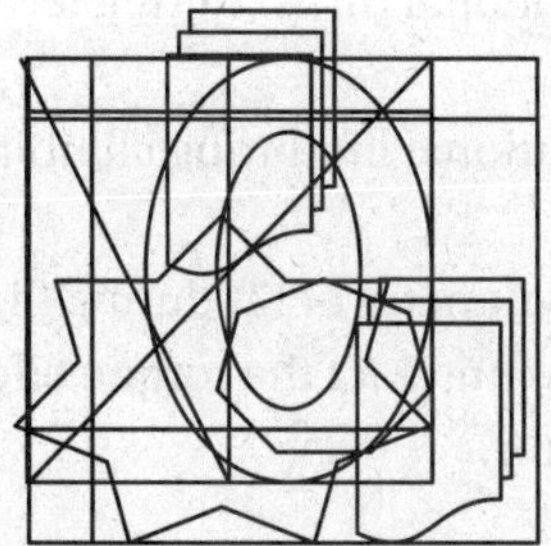

49.

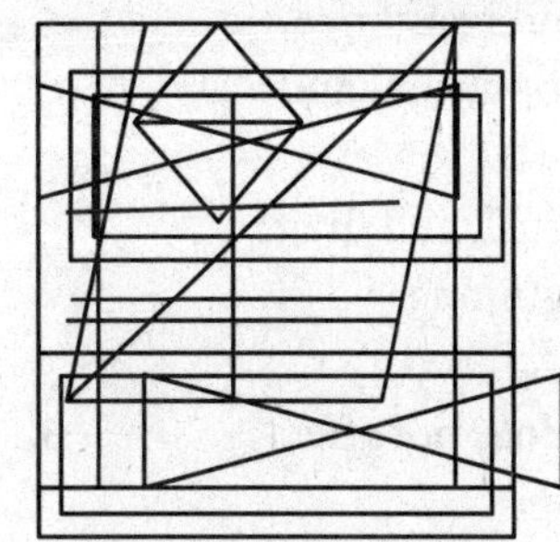

50.

SIFT #1

SIFT #1

SUBTEST 3: ARMY AVIATION INFORMATION TEST (AAIT)

40 Questions

1. The four forces that act on an aircraft in flight are

   (A) lift, gravity, thrust, and drag.
   (B) lift, mass, propulsion, and resistance.
   (C) aerodynamics, mass, propulsion, and drag.
   (D) lift magnitude, mass, thrust, and drag.
   (E) roll, pitch, yaw, and magnitude.

2. Which one of the following does not affect density altitude?

   (A) temperature
   (B) atmospheric pressure
   (C) humidity
   (D) wind velocity
   (E) altitude

3. The maneuver in which a rotary-wing aircraft (helicopter) is maintained in nearly motionless flight over a ground reference point at a constant altitude and heading (direction) is known as

   (A) feathering.
   (B) autorotation.
   (C) hovering.
   (D) torque balance.
   (E) freewheeling.

4. The flight envelope of an aircraft is

   (A) the airspeed at which it achieves takeoff.
   (B) the region of altitude and airspeed in which it can be operated.
   (C) the volume of air it displaces in flight.
   (D) the envelope containing the aircraft registration documents.
   (E) the geographical area covered by the officially filed flight plan.

5. An airfoil's efficiency, either a wing or a rotor blade, is ________ at high altitudes by the __________ air density.

   (A) increased, lesser
   (B) increased, greater
   (C) decreased, lesser
   (D) decreased, greater
   (E) increased, stable

6. The degree of movement of an aircraft around its lateral axis is known as

   (A) yaw.
   (B) roll.
   (C) bank.
   (D) pitch.
   (E) sideslip.

7. The primary purpose of the tail rotor system is to

   (A) maintain the aircraft's stability during pitch up and down maneuvers.
   (B) provide additional thrust during level flight.
   (C) provide additional lift during climbing and diving.
   (D) correct dissymmetry of lift during flight.
   (E) balance or counteract the torque effect of the main rotor.

8. Takeoff from a slope in a helicopter with skid-type landing gear is normally done by

   (A) turning the tail upslope to reduce the danger of the tail rotor striking the ground.
   (B) making a smooth running takeoff if the ground surface is smooth.
   (C) simultaneously applying downslope cyclic control and collective pitch.
   (D) bringing the aircraft to a level attitude before completely leaving the ground.
   (E) rapidly increasing collective pitch and upslope cyclic controls to avoid sliding downslope.

9. "True altitude" is defined as

(A) the horizontal distance of the aircraft above the coastline.
(B) the vertical distance of the aircraft above mean sea level.
(C) the vertical distance of the aircraft above the terrain.
(D) the uncorrected distance of the aircraft above the pressure gradient.
(E) the adjusted vertical distance measured by density altitude.

10. A helicopter's cyclic control is a mechanical linkage used to change the pitch of the main rotor blades

(A) all at the same time.
(B) at a selected point in its circular pathway.
(C) proportionate to the engine RPMs.
(D) in conjunction with the desired speed.
(E) for vertical flight only.

11. When the rotor blades of a helicopter are spinning fast enough in a clockwise direction to generate lift, a phenomenon known as __________ causes the body of the helicopter to have a tendency to turn in a counterclockwise direction.

(A) centrifugal force
(B) centripedal force
(C) lateral roll
(D) torque
(E) autorotation

12. "Absolute altitude" is defined as

(A) the vertical adjustment corrected for variations from standard conditions.
(B) the vertical distance of the aircraft above the density pressure gradient.
(C) the vertical distance of the aircraft above sea level.
(D) the vertical distance of the aircraft above the terrain or ground level.
(E) the horizontal distance of the aircraft above mean sea level.

13. The differential in lift between that of the advancing rotor blade and that of the retreating rotor blade is called

(A) translational lift.
(B) transitional torque.
(C) dissymmetry of lift.
(D) centripedal differential.
(E) translating tendency.

14. Foot pedals in the helicopter cockpit give the pilot the ability to

(A) smoothly enter transitional lift.
(B) stabilize rotor RPMs.
(C) be prepared to autorotate at any time.
(D) control engine RPMs.
(E) control the torque effect.

15. "Density altitude" is defined as

(A) the pressure altitude reading corrected for variations from standard temperature.
(B) the true altitude reading corrected for variations in inches of mercury.
(C) the uncorrected standard reading listed on the standard datum plane.
(D) the vertical distance of the aircraft above the highest obstacle.
(E) the vertical distance of the aircraft above the nearest sea level reading.

16. The cyclic controls the

(A) pitch of the helicopter.
(B) engine RPMs.
(C) torque effect.
(D) direction of the tilt of the main rotor.
(E) gyroscopic precession of the rotor blades.

17. Moving the cyclic forward and significantly raising the collective will cause the helicopter to

(A) increase its forward speed.
(B) increase its forward speed and begin to climb.
(C) immediately increase its altitude without increasing forward velocity.
(D) nose over.
(E) stall.

SIFT #1

18. Conventional American helicopters have a main rotor that
   (A) turns in a counterclockwise direction.
   (B) turns in a clockwise direction.
   (C) defeats translational torque.
   (D) experiences two stages of gyroscopic precession.
   (E) has two rotor blades of fixed pitch only.

19. Translational lift is
   (A) the lift needed to initially leave the ground.
   (B) the cushioning effect encountered in a low hover.
   (C) another name for Coriolis force.
   (D) the additional lift gained when the helicopter leaves its downwash.
   (E) the decreased lift suffered when the helicopter leaves its downwash.

20. Gyroscopic precession happens when
   (A) a force applied to a spinning disc has its effect 90 degrees later in the opposite direction of rotation.
   (B) a force applied to a spinning disc has its effect 180 degrees later in the opposite direction of rotation.
   (C) a force applied to a spinning disc has its effect 90 degrees later in the direction and plane of rotation.
   (D) a force applied to a spinning disc has its effect 180 degrees later in the direction and plane of rotation.
   (E) none of the above

21. One useful tool for the illustration of aerodynamic forces at work is a *vector,* which is a
   (A) direction expressed in degrees.
   (B) quantity described by size alone.
   (C) quantity with a magnitude and a direction.
   (D) position described by latitude and longitude.
   (E) location described by universal transverse Mercator coordinates.

22. As a rotor system begins to turn, the blades start to rise from their drooping position due to
   (A) centripetal force.
   (B) centrifugal force.
   (C) Coriolis force.
   (D) relative resultant wind.
   (E) rotor flapping.

23. Significant "coning" of the rotor disk can cause
   (A) a decrease in lift due to a decrease in effective disk area.
   (B) a decrease in lift due to increased torque that must be counteracted.
   (C) an increase in lift due to increased angle of attack.
   (D) an increase in drag due to increased resultant relative wind.
   (E) excessive rotor flapping.

24. In tandem rotor and coaxial helicopters,
   (A) the two rotor systems turn in the same direction to increase lift capability.
   (B) the two rotor systems alternate to conserve power.
   (C) the two rotor systems' blades do not flap to avoid hitting each other.
   (D) the two rotor systems turn in opposite directions, canceling the torque effect.
   (E) an antitorque rotor is still required.

25. Most American-built single-rotor helicopters turn the main rotor
   (A) in a clockwise direction.
   (B) in a counterclockwise direction.
   (C) in either direction as dictated by atmospheric conditions.
   (D) against the wind.
   (E) slower than tandem or European helicopters to achieve the same lift.

26. An increase in blade pitch through application of collective

(A) generates the additional lift needed to hover.
(B) decreases lift, allowing the helicopter to descend.
(C) allows the helicopter to turn laterally.
(D) allows the helicopter to slow its forward acceleration.
(E) allows the helicopter to fly backward.

27. "Ground effect" is ___________ rotor system efficiency due to interference of the airflow ___________ .

(A) unpredictable, when hovering too close to the ground for power settings
(B) decreased, when blade pitch is increased near the ground
(C) decreased, when blade pitch is decreased near the ground
(D) increased, when blade pitch is decreased
(E) increased, when near the ground

28. A helicopter has four flight control inputs: the ___________, ___________, ___________, and ___________ .

(A) throttle, cyclic, collective, rudder pedals
(B) cyclic, collective, antitorque pedals, throttle
(C) collective, swashplate, throttle, cyclic
(D) control bar, collective, trim control, throttle
(E) throttle, joystick, cyclic, collective

29. The collective pitch control is used to

(A) make simultaneous changes to the pitch angle of the main rotor blades.
(B) make sequential changes to the pitch angle of the main rotor blades.
(C) make simultaneous changes to the pitch angle of the tail rotor blades.
(D) prevent inadvertent collective pitch movement.
(E) keep rotor RPMs constant when pitch is changed.

30. A twist grip throttle is usually mounted

(A) next to the correlator or governor.
(B) on the cyclic pitch control.
(C) on the end of the collective lever.
(D) between the pilot and copilot seats.
(E) next to the manifold pressure control.

31. With the antitorque pedals in the neutral position, the tail rotor has a medium positive pitch angle, thereby

(A) yawing the nose of the helicopter slightly to the right.
(B) yawing the nose of the helicopter slightly to the left.
(C) approximately equaling the torque of the main rotor.
(D) raising the tail and lowering the nose.
(E) lowering the tail and causing the nose to pitch up.

32. Main rotor systems are classified as rigid, semirigid, or fully articulated according to

(A) how the main rotor blades are attached and move relative to the main rotor hub.
(B) how many degrees the individual blades flex from the horizontal.
(C) the amount of gyroscopic precession allowed by the hub.
(D) the material they are made of.
(E) the amount of engine power used to get the blades turning from a cold start.

33. The lift generated by an airfoil directly depends on all of the following factors *except*

(A) airflow speed.
(B) air density.
(C) actual altitude.
(D) total area of the segment or airfoil.
(E) angle of attack between the air and the airfoil.

SIFT #1

34. The angle between the chord line of a wing or airfoil and the direction of relative wind or airflow is called the

(A) degree of yaw.
(B) angle of deflection.
(C) angle of attack.
(D) degree of roll.
(E) angle of pitch.

35. When the pilot of a fixed-wing aircraft pushes forward on the control stick, the elevators will

(A) retract.
(B) extend.
(C) move downward.
(D) move upward.
(E) assume a neutral position.

36. Another form of antitorque system is the "fan-in-tail" system or *fenestron*, which

(A) uses the Coanda effect to maintain directional control.
(B) uses a series of rotating blades shrouded within a vertical tail.
(C) produces a low pressure, high volume of ambient air to pressurize the composite tailboom.
(D) uses a rotating direct jet thruster to maintain directional control.
(E) places the tail rotor on the opposite side of the tail from the usual arrangement.

37. Most ______________ helicopters use ______________ engines because they are relatively simple and inexpensive to operate.

(A) experimental, reciprocating (piston)
(B) training, turbine
(C) larger, turbine
(D) training, reciprocating (piston)
(E) larger, reciprocating (piston)

38. For both helicopters and fixed-wing aircraft, VFR stands for

(A) Vector Following Requirement.
(B) Volume Fluctuation Regulator.
(C) Velocity Falloff Restriction.
(D) Vertical Flight Regulator.
(E) Visual Flight Rules.

39. If a helicopter's center of gravity (CG) is too far forward of the rotor mast,

(A) the helicopter has a nose-low attitude during a hover.
(B) the pilot may not be able to decelerate sufficiently to bring the helicopter to a stop.
(C) excessive rearward cyclic displacement may be needed to maintain a hover when there is no wind.
(D) all of the above
(E) none of the above

40. Image intensifier (I2) systems

(A) amplify light in both the visible and ultraviolet (UV) spectrum segments.
(B) amplify absorbed and reflected infrared (IR) energy only.
(C) amplify light in both visible and near infrared (IR) spectrum segments.
(D) amplify ambient low-level visible light only.
(E) amplify both reflected and emitted infrared (IR) light only.

SUBTEST 4: SPATIAL APPERCEPTION TEST (SAT)

25 Questions

This subtest measures your ability to determine the position of an aircraft in flight in relation to the view a pilot would see when looking out the front of the cockpit.

This subtest consists of 25 questions, which you will have 10 minutes to answer.

For each question, you will see a series of six pictures. The first picture will depict a view of the landscape that a pilot would see when looking out the front of the cockpit. You are to determine whether the aircraft is climbing, diving, banking, or in level flight, and choose the picture that best represents the same aircraft when viewed from the outside.

1. 

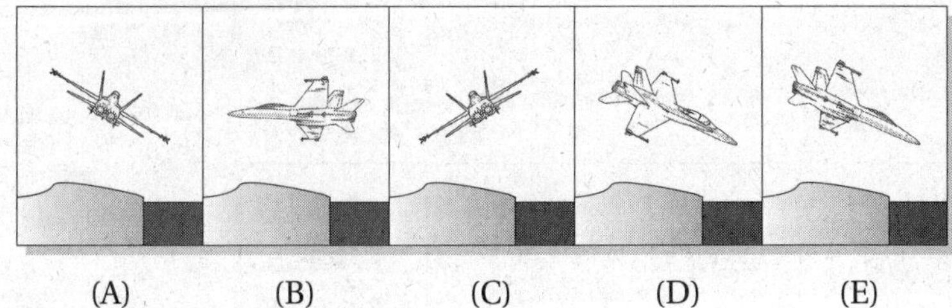

(A) (B) (C) (D) (E)

2. 

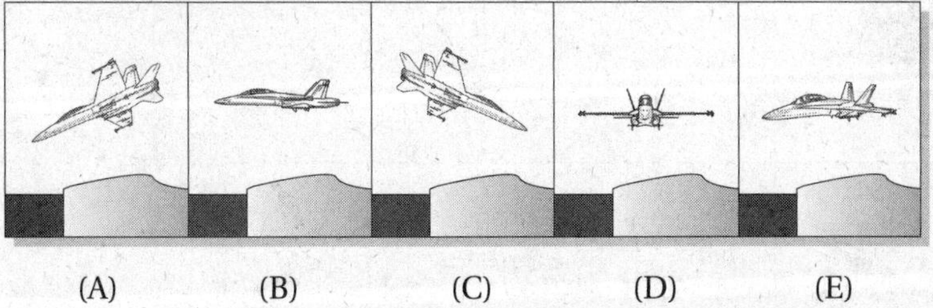

(A) (B) (C) (D) (E)

SIFT #1

3.

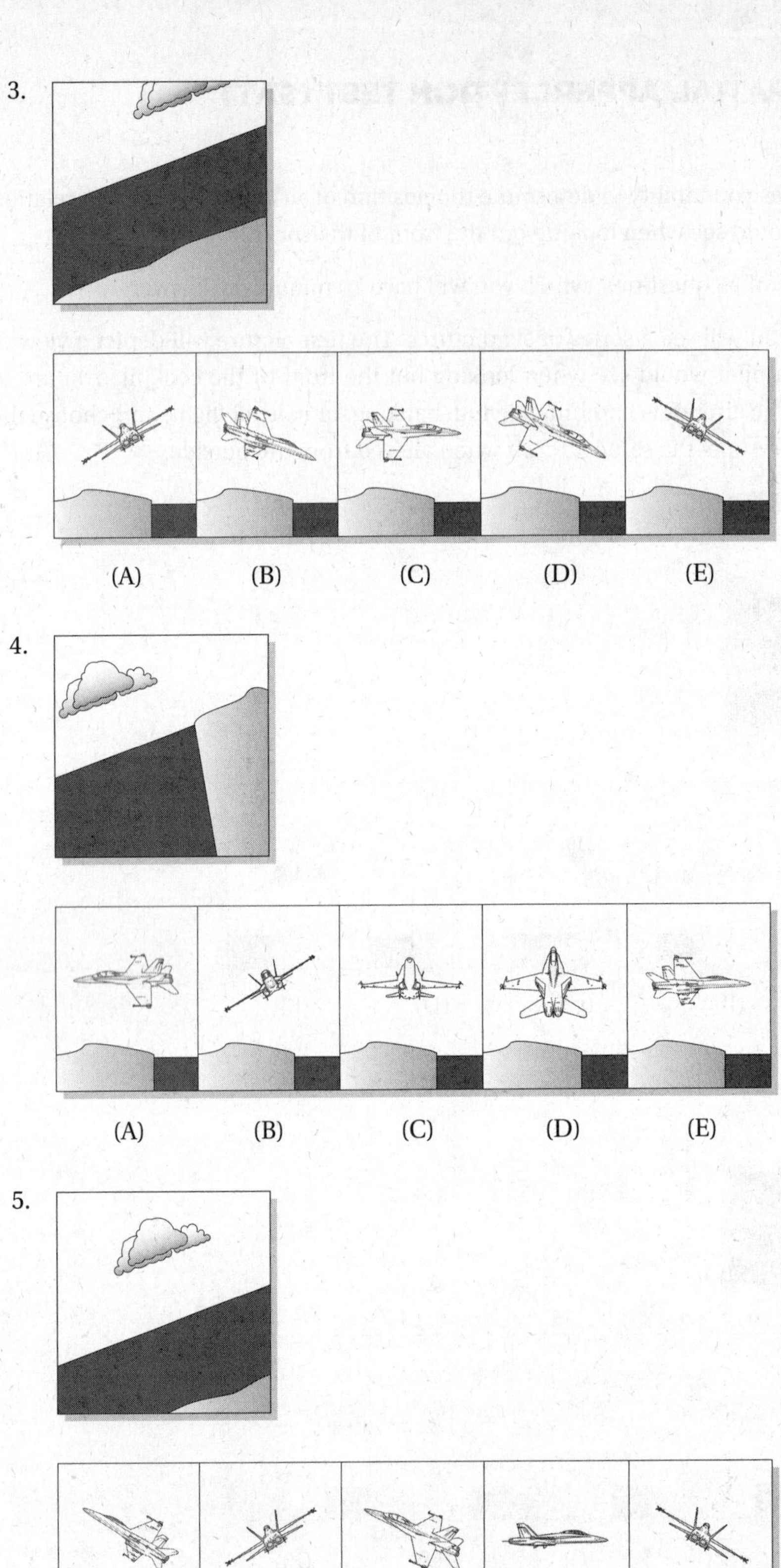

(A) (B) (C) (D) (E)

4.

(A) (B) (C) (D) (E)

5.

(A) (B) (C) (D) (E)

6.

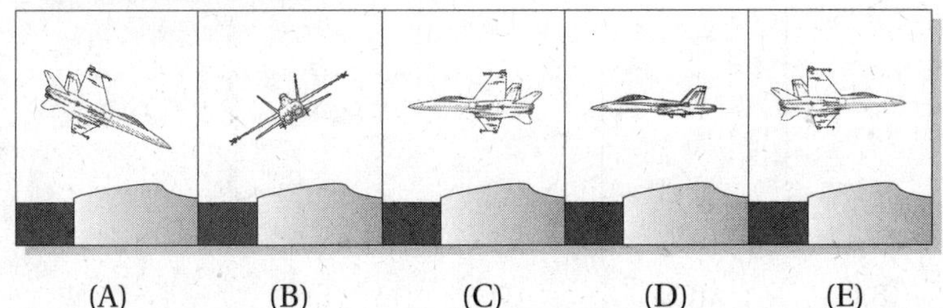

(A) (B) (C) (D) (E)

7.

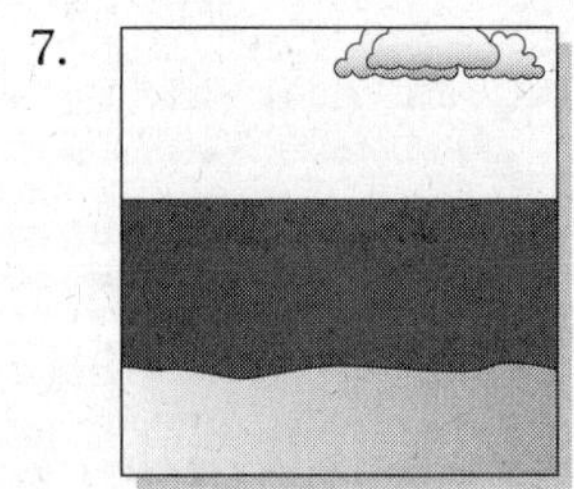

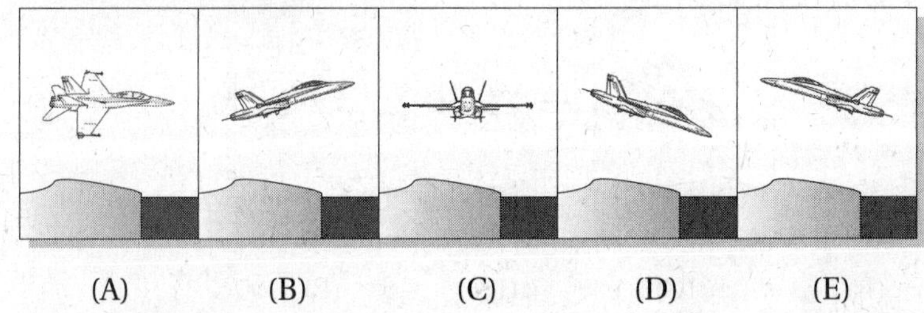

(A) (B) (C) (D) (E)

8.

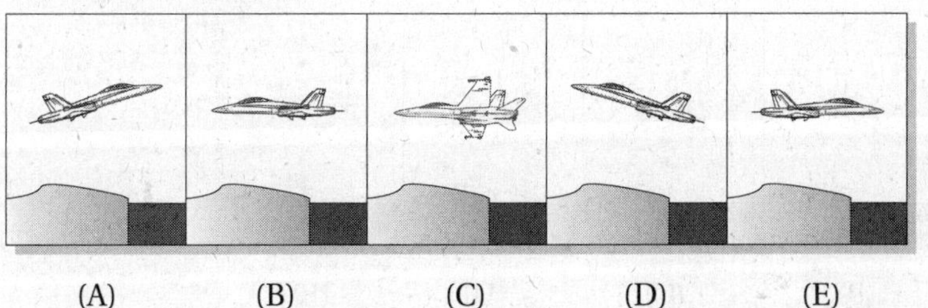

(A) (B) (C) (D) (E)

9.

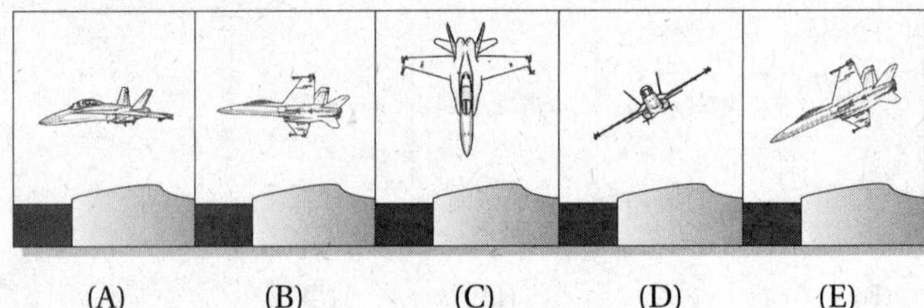

(A) (B) (C) (D) (E)

10.

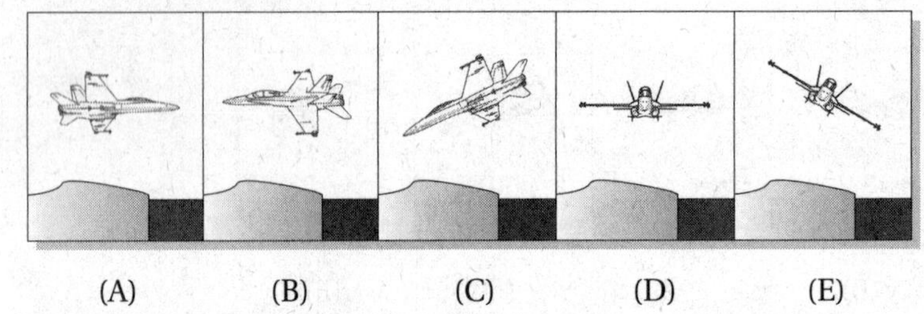

(A) (B) (C) (D) (E)

11.

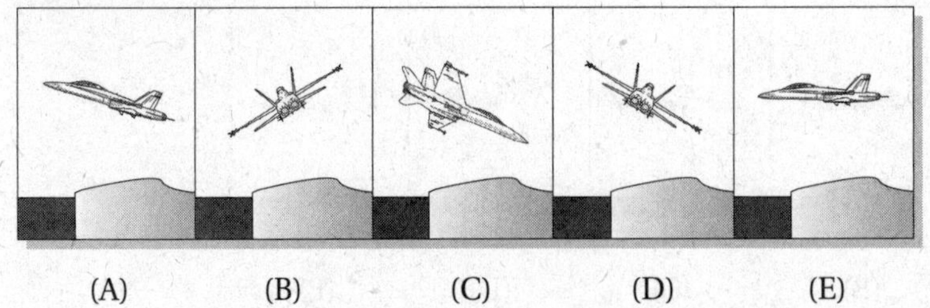

(A) (B) (C) (D) (E)

12. 

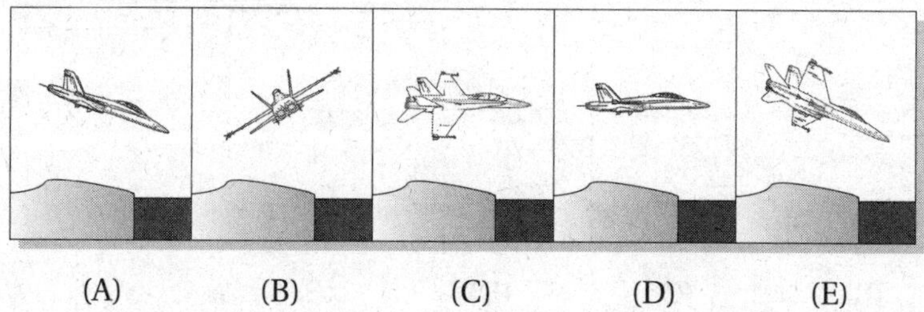

(A) (B) (C) (D) (E)

13. 

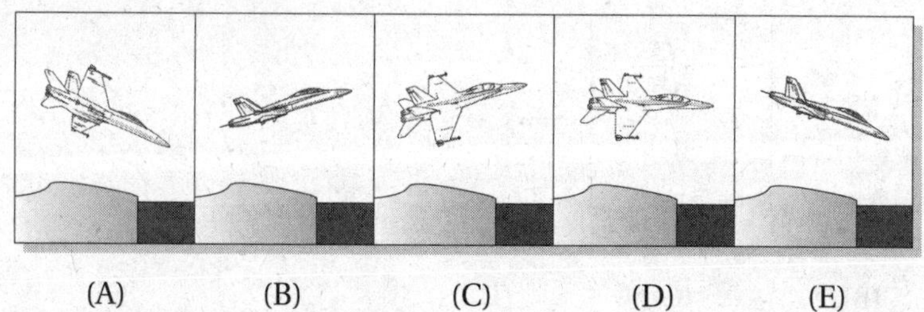

(A) (B) (C) (D) (E)

14. 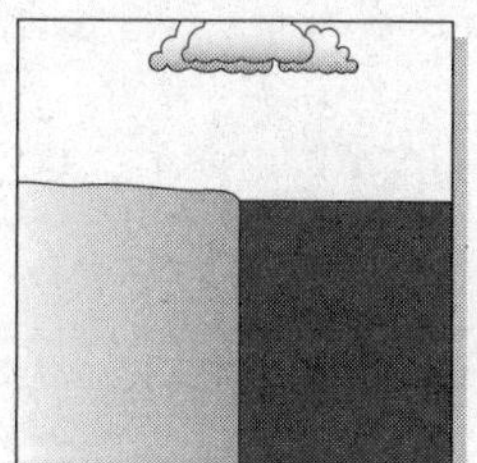

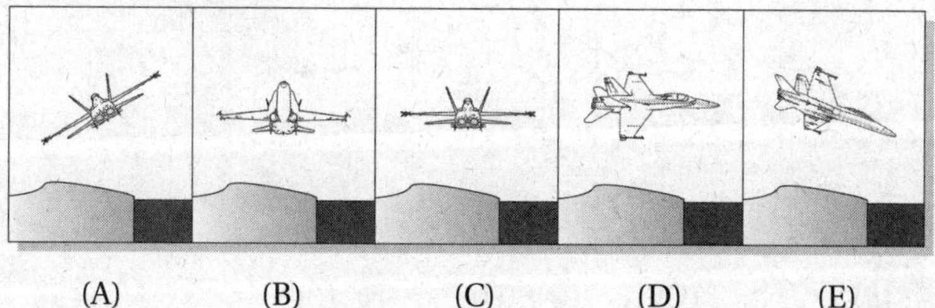

(A) (B) (C) (D) (E)

15.

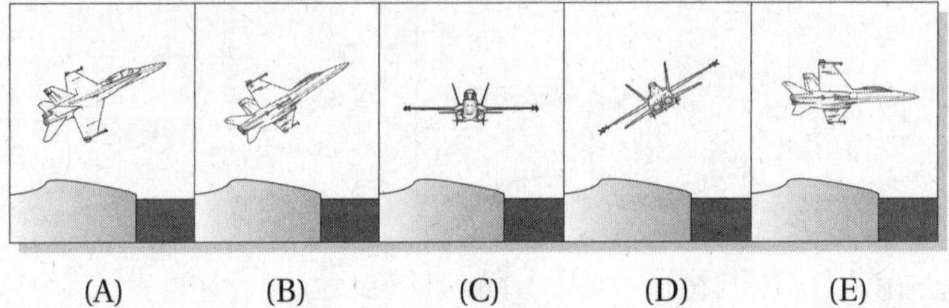

(A) (B) (C) (D) (E)

16.

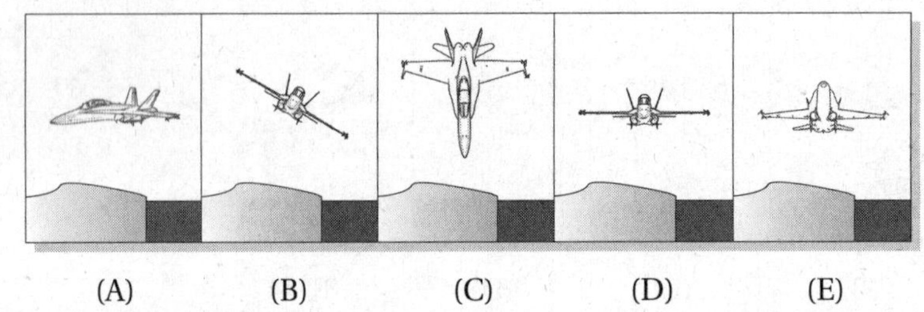

(A) (B) (C) (D) (E)

17.

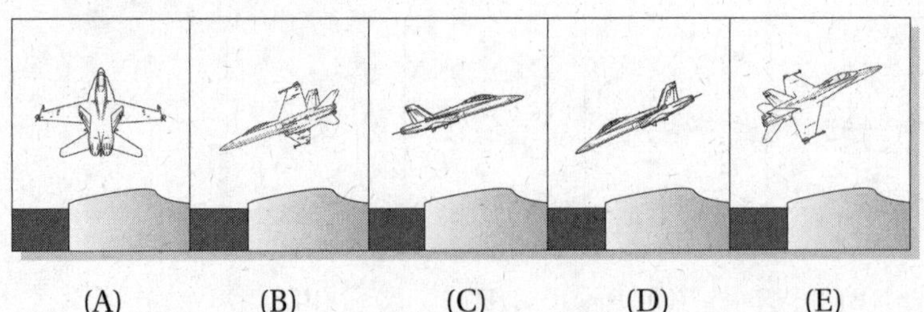

(A) (B) (C) (D) (E)

18. 

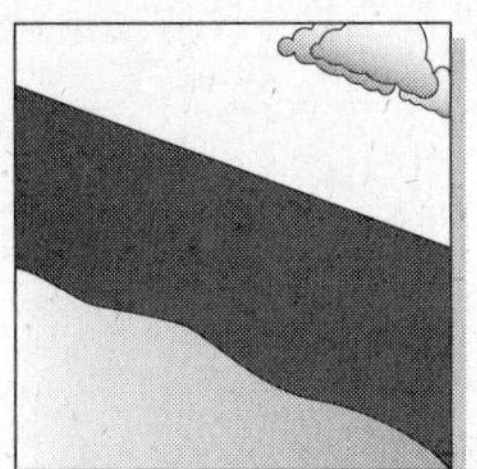

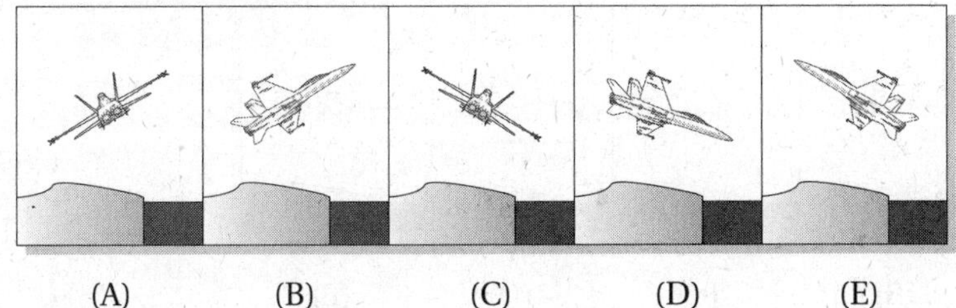

(A) (B) (C) (D) (E)

19.

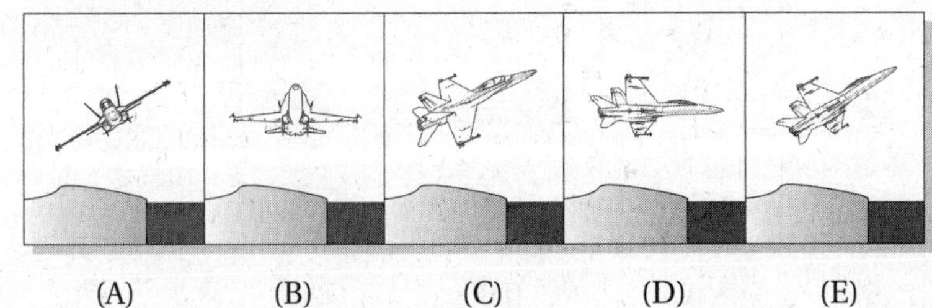

(A) (B) (C) (D) (E)

20.

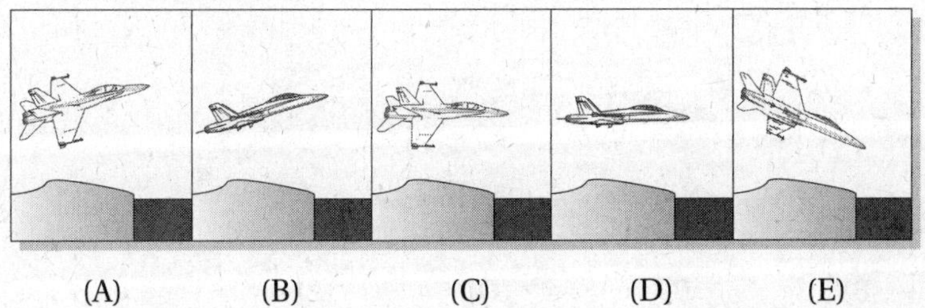

(A) (B) (C) (D) (E)

21.

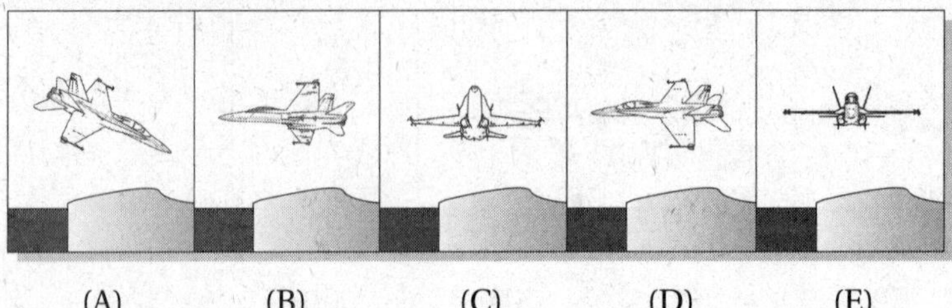

(A) (B) (C) (D) (E)

22.

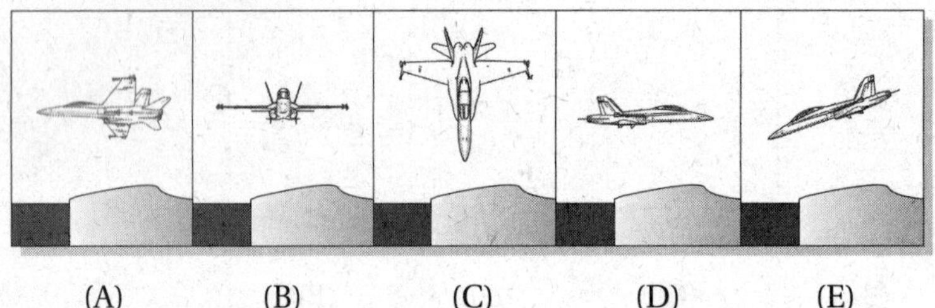

(A) (B) (C) (D) (E)

23.

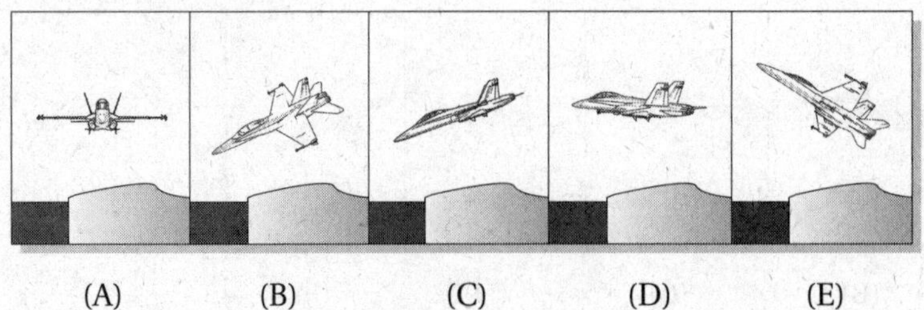

(A) (B) (C) (D) (E)

24.

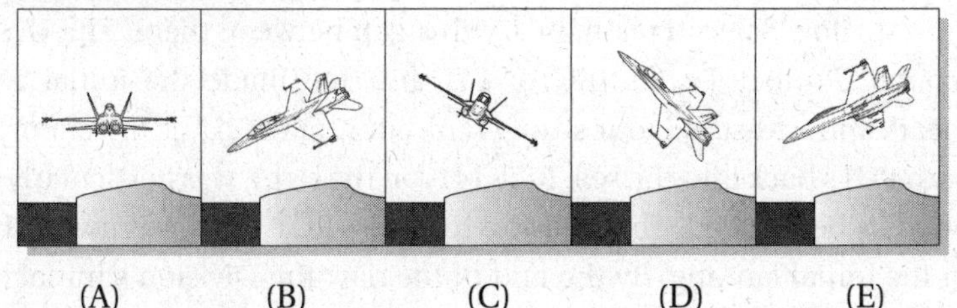

(A) (B) (C) (D) (E)

25.

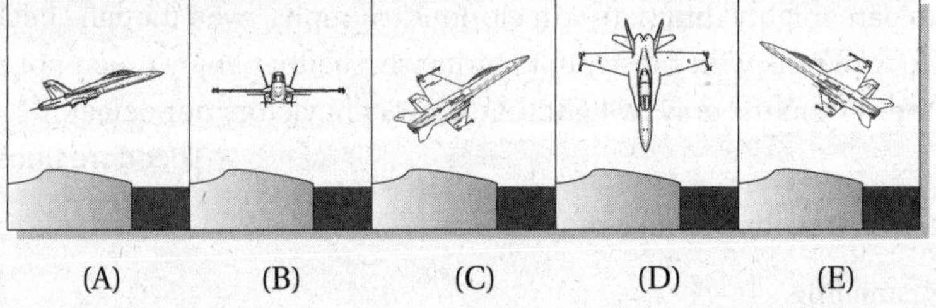

(A) (B) (C) (D) (E)

SIFT #1

SUBTEST 5: READING COMPREHENSION TEST (RCT)

20 Questions

1. The U.S. Fifth Army, commanded by Gen. Mark Clark, landed south of Salerno at 0330 hours on September 9, 1943. Within Fifth Army, the U.S. VI Corps landed south of the Sele River and the British 10th Corps landed north of the river; both landings were closely supported by aircraft and naval gunfire. By the end of the day, both corps held a beachhead on the shallow Salerno plain, but with a gap between them. The U.S. 36th Division's Regimental Combat Teams (RCTs) 141 and 142 made the initial assault, secured a beachhead, and withstood four strong tank counterattacks as the enemy tried futilely to push both RCTs back into the sea. RCT 141, on the right, was particularly hard-pressed but retained its beachhead. The Division reserve—RCT 143—was committed in the center during the initial landing. By the end of the day, the Division's initial objectives on the left flank and in the center had been secured.

   According to this passage, Regimental Combat Team 143 was

   (A) pushed back into the sea.
   (B) held in reserve throughout the operation.
   (C) committed on the left flank.
   (D) committed between RCT 141 and 142.
   (E) landed at the mouth of the Sele River.

2. "Far better it is to dare mighty things, to win glorious triumphs, even though checkered by failure, than to take rank with those poor spirits who neither enjoy much nor suffer much, because they live in the gray twilight that knows not victory nor defeat."

   —Theodore Roosevelt

   In the passage above, the phrase "take rank" means

   (A) become bad-smelling.
   (B) to win triumphs.
   (C) to join a group.
   (D) to get promoted.
   (E) to not be checkered.

3. Leaders must create an organizational culture driven by actual, shared values that are calls to action, not just high-sounding platitudes. Leaders must challenge assumptions, take courageous risks, and inspire others by example and integrity. They must also, however, still be humble, give credit to others, and follow through. In this way they create the legacy that shows the organization's members what "right" looks like.

   The author of this passage believes that a leadership position

   (A) is a reward for previous hard work and service.
   (B) is based on maintaining current policies.
   (C) is a time to finally let others do the work.
   (D) is an obligation to challenge the status quo and take calculated risks.
   (E) shows organizational members what leadership privileges look like.

4. Discipline is the most important element for successful multiaircraft formations. On an individual basis, discipline consists of self-control, maturity, and sound judgment in a high-stress, emotionally charged environment. Teamwork is an integral part of discipline; each individual must evaluate his or her own actions and how these actions will affect both the flight and mission accomplishment. Discipline within a flight has a synergistic effect. If the flight lead and wingmen know their respective duties, they will work together as a team. Experience and realistic training leads to solid and professional air discipline.

   The author of the above passage believes that, if the flight lead and wingmen know their duties, they will

   (A) better be able to accomplish the mission.
   (B) work together as a team.
   (C) receive realistic training.
   (D) be showing self-control in a low-stress environment.
   (E) be an integral part of the team.

5. LLC stands for "Limited Liability Corporation," meaning that the business owners' personal liability for business debts is limited. Without the protection of LLC laws, the owner or owners of a business can be held personally liable for their business's debts and obligations. The idea of limited liability got its start in Germany in the late 1800s. By the 1940s, the idea had gained acceptance in 17 countries, but the United States was not one of them. In 1977, Wyoming became the first state to pass an LLC law modeled on the German statute. Many other states eventually passed their own versions, although most of them are at least slightly different from one another.

   Why is the idea of limited liability helpful to business owners?

   (A) because it is a tradition dating back to the 19th century
   (B) because it is now legal in all 50 states
   (C) because it can limit their personal risk
   (D) because it lets them take care of their business obligations with personal funds
   (E) because it lets people avoid business liabilities

6. We have focused so much on mandating diversity that we have lost sight of why diversity is a good thing. The benefit of having different kinds of people working together is that they bring their various experiences and insights to help the organization accomplish shared goals. These different parts of the whole are important because, when they are joined together, they make a stronger, more capable totality. It is the strengthened unity and capability resulting from diversity that is important, not just diversity for its own sake.

   What does the writer say about different kinds of people working together?

   (A) It's important because it strengthens the entire organization or group.
   (B) It is important for its own sake.
   (C) It takes their minds off their personal problems.
   (D) Working together is too difficult to be important.
   (E) It only happens when diversity is mandated by government.

7. U.S. Army rotary-wing aviation has a proud heritage of providing support to units on the battlefield. Army aviation relies on highly skilled aviators to fly the different types of rotary-wing aircraft needed to conduct demanding and often hazardous combat and support functions throughout the battlespace and around the world. The Army relies on an extensive selection process to sort through the many volunteers applying for flight training and subsequent service as aviators. The process includes an interview with a current Army aviator and passing a physical examination, as well as successful completion of an aptitude test measuring different dimensions considered necessary for effectiveness as an Army aviator.

   How are potential Army aviators chosen for flight training?

   (A) by ordering those with qualities needed for success to flight school to be aviators
   (B) by examining applicants for characteristics needed for success as aviators
   (C) by interviewing current Army aviators who pass a physical examination
   (D) by conducting demanding and often hazardous combat and support missions
   (E) by relying on highly skilled aviators to fly different types of rotary-wing aircraft

8. Piloting a helicopter requires a great deal of training and skill, as well as continuous attention to the aircraft. The pilot must think in three dimensions and must use both arms and both legs constantly to keep the helicopter in the air. Coordination, control touch, and timing are all used simultaneously when flying a helicopter.

   What is the most important overall characteristic of a pilot discussed in this passage?

   (A) having a great deal of training and skill
   (B) the ability to pay attention to the aircraft after a great deal of training
   (C) the ability to use both arms and both legs simultaneously
   (D) coordinating, control touch, and timing
   (E) the ability to constantly coordinate multiple mental and physical actions

9. The saying goes that the A-10 Thunderbolt II ground attack jet isn't a plane with a gun—it's a gun with a plane built around it. The signature belching of its 30 mm Avenger cannon has been one of the most welcome sounds to U.S. and Coalition ground troops in Iraq and Afghanistan over the last decade. When a convoy in Afghanistan was attacked while patrolling a highway, its 60 soldiers were pinned behind their vehicles facing heavy Taliban fire from a nearby treeline. One A-10 flew over as a show of force—often enough to make the enemy break contact due to the Thunderbolt II's reputation for heavy firepower—but enemy fire on the ground increased. One A-10 marked the area with two rockets, then his wingman came in and strafed the enemy positions—but the Taliban just moved closer to the friendly forces. The A-10s came in for a low-angle strafe, 75 ft. above the enemy's positions and 50 m away from friendly troops. Over the next two hours, the Warthogs flew 15 gun passes, fired nearly all 2,300 of their 30 mm rounds, and dropped three 500-lb. bombs on the enemy fighters. The enemy eventually gave up their attack and the convoy was able to return to its base.

What was the most hazardous moment mentioned in this passage?

(A) when the convoy was pinned down by enemy fire from a nearby treeline
(B) when one A-10 flew over the Taliban as a show of force
(C) when the A-10s fired on enemy forces just 50 m away from friendly troops
(D) when the A-10s had fired almost all of their 30 mm cannon rounds
(E) when the Air Force suggested retiring the entire A-10 fleet to save money

10. "It may seem to you conceited to suppose that you can do anything important toward improving the lot of mankind. But this is a fallacy. You must believe that you can help bring about a better world. A good society is produced only by good individuals, just as truly as a majority in a presidential election is produced by the votes of single electors. Everybody can do something toward creating in his own environment kindly feelings rather than anger, reasonableness rather than hysteria, happiness rather than misery."

—Bertrand Russell

If this passage had to be summed up on a bumper sticker, what would it say?

(A) Everybody can come together to fight hysteria.
(B) A good society will win a majority in presidential elections.
(C) It is better to be happy than miserable.
(D) When you make your local area better, you contribute to a better world.
(E) Protecting the environment keeps people from getting angry.

11. "No state has an inherent right to survive through conscript troops, and in the long run no state ever has. Roman matrons used to say to their sons: 'Come back with your shield, or on it.' Later on, this custom declined. So did Rome."

—Robert A. Heinlein

According to this passage, what did Roman matrons (mothers of grown sons) believe?

(A) that their sons should either perform honorably in battle or die trying
(B) that losing one's shield was a crime punishable by death
(C) that conscript [drafted] troops used their shields as stretchers
(D) that Rome would fall if their sons lost their shields
(E) that their sons must above all else hang on to their equipment

SIFT #1

12. The U.S. Army's experience in China started in the early 1900s, when the 15th Infantry Regiment took up its station in Tientsin after the Boxer Rebellion. Army officers also served as intelligence and language officers with the military attaché's office for almost as far back. During this period, American officers were mostly uninvolved observers of Chinese affairs but the Army's interest in China's military potential increased after Japan's invasion of China in 1937. The Chinese resisted with only minimal outside aid for four years, but the United States enlarged its military role in China soon after Japan's attack on Pearl Harbor in December 1941.

    According to the passage, when did the U.S. Army begin advising Chinese Nationalist combat forces?

    (A) in the early 1900s, after the Boxer Rebellion
    (B) when the 15th Infantry Regiment was stationed in Tientsin
    (C) when American Army officers served as intelligence and language officers
    (D) officers began their advisory assignments after a tour with the military attaché
    (E) the passage does not address American Army advisers to Nationalist Chinese forces

13. Malalai was born about 1861 in the small village of Khig, about three miles southwest of the town of Maiwand in the southern Afghan province of Kandahar. In 1880, Afghanistan was occupied for the second time by British-Indian forces trying to colonize and annex the area. Malalai's father, a shepherd, and her fiancé joined with Afghan forces in a large attack on British-Indian forces in Maiwand in July 1880. Like many Afghan women, Malalai was there to help tend to the wounded and provide water and spare weapons. Local sources maintain this was also supposed to be her wedding day. When the Afghan army was losing morale despite superior numbers, Malalai took the Afghan flag and shouted to her fiancé: "Young love! If you don't fall in the battle of Maiwand, by God, someone is saving you as a symbol of shame!" This inspired the Afghan fighters to redouble their efforts. When a leading flag bearer was killed, Malalai went forward and held up his flag, singing an inspirational poem—but then Malalai was herself struck down and killed. However, her encouragement spurred her countrymen on to victory. After the battle, Malalai was honored for her efforts and buried in her native village of Khig, where her grave remains today, viewed by those in the region as a shrine.

    What was Malalai's major contribution to the Afghan victory?

    (A) She helped tend the wounded and provided water and spare weapons.
    (B) She inspired her fiancé and his fellow Afghans that they should die or be shamed.
    (C) She sang to comfort a wounded flag bearer.
    (D) She was buried with honor in her native village, where her grave is today a shrine.
    (E) She married an Afghan fighter and inspired him to lead Afghan forces.

14. Until the establishment of the Aviation School at Fort Rucker, Alabama, in 1955, Army aviation had a not entirely undeserved reputation for being sort of a military Siberia. One applied for aviation duty the morning following the party at which one had insulted the colonel's lady, for instance. Once in aviation, it was difficult—verging on the impossible—to return to the ground Army. There was a certain resentment toward, for example, artillery captains who had never fired a cannon and yet, because of flight pay, were being paid more than artillery majors who had spent their careers in fire direction centers and on the gun lines. But the Korean War, and the establishment of the Aviation School and Center, changed this. Professionals in the ground Army saw the prospect in a flying Army not only of a new way of waging war but an even greater chance of advancement based on smarts and skills.

    What factors changed the reputation of Army aviation?

    (A) resentment toward captains on flight pay who made more than nonflying majors
    (B) the Korean War and the opportunity for earning flight pay
    (C) the establishment of the Aviation School and the Korean War
    (D) professionals in the flying army who saw new chances for advancement
    (E) the establishment of the Aviation Center and the opportunity for earning flight pay

15. The Sabalauski Air Assault School—a fast-paced, two-week course that is challenging both physically and mentally—is located at Fort Campbell, Kentucky. Its primary mission is training soldiers and leaders to conduct airmobile and air assault helicopter operations; it also trains a limited number of personnel from other services. Instruction includes aircraft identification and orientation, helicopter insertion and extraction, slingload operations, pathfinder operations, and rappelling and fast-roping techniques. Although the Sabalauski Air Assault School at Fort Campbell is considered to be the "original" air assault school, other Army-approved air assault schools either exist or have existed under its oversight at Fort Rucker, Alabama; Fort Hood, Texas; Camp Gruber, Oklahoma; Schofield Barracks, Hawaii; Fort Benning, Georgia; and elsewhere.

    What is the primary mission of the Sabalauski Air Assault School?

    (A) to challenge soldiers and leaders physically and mentally
    (B) overseeing air assault schools set up at other military installations worldwide
    (C) helicopter identification, orientation, and maintenance, as well as slingload operations
    (D) training soldiers and leaders to conduct airmobile and air assault helicopter operations
    (E) training personnel from all U.S. services to conduct airmobile and air assault helicopter operations

SIFT #1

16. Light dragoons (mounted infantry) were not considered a permanent part of the Army after the Revolutionary War because horses were expensive to procure and maintain. Dragoons were raised on an "as needed" basis for service on the Northwest Territory frontier (present-day Ohio, Indiana, and Illinois) in the 1790s and again for the War of 1812. During the War of 1812, only sabers and pistols were issued to the dragoons, but this was not just to save money—the saber was considered the primary mounted weapon, with the pistol next in importance. Westward expansion revived the importance of dragoons, and on March 2, 1833, Congress added a regiment of dragoons to the Army establishment. This unit was renamed the First Regiment of Dragoons when a second regiment was formed in 1836. The .52 caliber Hall-North Carbine, first issued to dragoons in 1833, was the first percussion weapon and the first breech-loading weapon adopted by any government in the world. Starting in 1851, new uniform regulations introduced the frock coat for everyone, but by 1858 cavalry and dragoons had a coat that was only waist length; the primary dividing line between uniform types was whether a soldier was mounted or not—an indication of the growing role of cavalry and dragoons in nineteenth century warfare.

    What is the primary subject of this passage?

    (A) efforts to save money after the Revolutionary War
    (B) the increasing acceptance and importance of dragoons in the Army
    (C) the weapons used by dragoons during the Civil War
    (D) early American infantry uniforms and accessories
    (E) the impact of organizational changes on Army uniforms in the 1800s

17. The Air Force and ground forces—Army and Marines—carried their longstanding and fundamental disagreement over air mission priorities into the Persian Gulf War. The Air Force's priorities were—as they had been—strategic attack and interdiction. The Army's and Marines' priorities—as they had been—were close air support of troops on the ground. This dispute had its roots in attitudes developed during and after World War I, demonstrated in World War II, and further exacerbated in Korea. It had been arm-wrestled all the way up the chain to the Secretary of Defense in Vietnam, and it remains a friction point (and sometimes worse) today. The Air Force continued to press its strategic air campaign even as the Army and Marines were preparing for the ground war—not necessarily a bad thing, but not necessarily a balanced situation, either: strategic targets got two-thirds of daily sorties while battlefield shaping (preparation for the ground offensive) got the leftovers. It took the theater commander and the chairman of the Joint Chiefs (both Army four-stars) to reverse the priorities and mission balances.

    From this passage, one can infer that

    (A) all the services agreed on battlefield objectives and strategies.
    (B) the disagreement over priorities between air and ground forces affects how wars are fought.
    (C) the Secretary of Defense was an arm-wrestling aficionado.
    (D) close air support has always been given first priority in wartime.
    (E) the Air Force's strategic air campaign got first priority throughout the Gulf War.

18. The Big Bang is the moment, almost 14 billion years ago, when matter appeared in an incredible energy explosion; all the matter that currently exists in our universe originated here. The appearance of particles from what is understood to be a previous condition of nothingness cannot be explained by modern science, so many cosmologists have decided to accept (for now) that understanding this event is impossible with today's technology. Quantum physicists believe they may have a clue in their study of particles that appear and disappear without obvious cause, but they are not agreed about just what that means. Some scientists, however, believe that the Big Bang was caused by the will and idea of a divine being—a supreme architect of the universe.

    From this passage, one can infer that

    (A) scientists are generally not religious.
    (B) scientists have no idea why the Big Bang occurred.
    (C) scientists are divided about what caused the Big Bang to happen.
    (D) scientists believe that today's technology is not getting any better.
    (E) scientists believe that, since "Nature abhors a vacuum," the vacuum of nothingness caused the Big Bang to occur.

19. Since a sense of responsibility—not just for oneself, but for others—is the mark of an adult, the dividing line between being a child and being a grown-up is the willingness to accept that responsibility. This is true of every individual and organization, regardless of age or honor, culture or country. Those who avoid accepting responsibility for their actions and inactions may seem either charming or contemptible, but they are similarly juvenile in their denial of their proper role, no matter what the calendar says. In a small child this is, of course, not only excusable but expectable—children truly don't understand yet, although most start picking up on it a little by the time they are six or eight. It's those who are old enough to understand but make the decision, consciously or unconsciously, not to accept responsibility for themselves and their actions—they cause most of the trouble and unhappiness and tragedy in the world. The rules don't apply to them, not really; it wasn't their fault; everyone else was doing it; it wasn't their responsibility; it was just too hard; they didn't want to get involved. Those who take up the mantle of adulthood and responsibility may bear it like a gloomy burden they are condemned to carry or drag against their wishes, but the happiest among us bear it easily, like the honor that it is—knowing that they themselves are not and cannot be perfect, but who are grateful for the opportunity to try.

    From this passage, one can infer that the writer believes that

    (A) a refusal to accept responsibility for one's actions comes from fear of consequences.
    (B) accepting responsibility can be either charming or contemptible.
    (C) there is a dividing line between the childlike and the juvenile.
    (D) the burden of responsibility for saving lives is a mark of adulthood.
    (E) people who don't accept responsibility are not as happy as those who do.

20. During the 1942 siege of Bataan, the American commander Lt. Gen. Jonathan Wainwright decided to visit the front lines. When Japanese artillery started exploding at treetop level, the Navy lieutenant driving the jeep and everyone else nearby dove into foxholes—except for Wainwright, who had noticed a captain he knew from earlier days in Virginia. Wainwright took the captain by the arm, asked him how he was, and sat with him on sandbags with his back to the enemy, continuing to talk with him during the length of the bombardment, exposed to enemy shellfire. When the shelling finally stopped, Wainwright got back into his jeep. On the way back to headquarters, the Navy lieutenant asked Wainwright why he had exposed himself to enemy fire the way he had. Wainwright told him: "A general in the United States Army does his best to give his men arms and ammunition, food, medicine, and recreation. We have none of these things. The men are starving. We are running out of ammunition. . . .What can I give them? What can I do for my men? The only thing I can give them now is morale. My life is not worth as much as you think it is. I can give them morale and my presence on the front line is not the waste you think it is. When I sat on the sandbags, I did it deliberately. They want their general and they want to know he is here. I do that, and I do it for a good reason."

    From this passage, one can infer that Lt. Gen. Wainwright

    (A) believed in sharing the dangers his men faced every day.
    (B) overestimated his own importance to the war effort.
    (C) underestimated the danger of artillery fire.
    (D) did not care about resupplying his men or about their safety.
    (E) believed that the Navy lieutenant acted in a cowardly manner.

SUBTEST 6: MATH SKILLS TEST (MST)

20 Questions

1. If 2 lbs. of Greek-style yogurt with fruit cost \$3.00, what is the pro rata cost of a 2-oz. portion, rounded off to the nearest cent?

   (A) \$0.18
   (B) \$0.19
   (C) \$0.37
   (D) \$0.10
   (E) \$0.21

2. What is the product of $(3a - 2)$ and $(a + 3)$?

   (A) $4a + 2$
   (B) $3a^2 - 6$
   (C) $3a^2 - 2a + 6$
   (D) $3a^2 + 7a - 6$
   (E) $3a^2 - 4a + 2$

3. Amanda drove through various traffic and weather conditions for 3 hours to meet with a client. Her average speed was 50 mph for the first hour, 72 mph for the second hour, and 46 mph for the third hour. If her red 2012 Ford Mustang gets an average of 23 miles per gallon of gas, how many gallons of gas did she use on her trip?

   (A) 2.4 gals.
   (B) 4.8 gals.
   (C) 7.3 gals.
   (D) 5.3 gals.
   (E) 9.7 gals.

4. A road-building contractor needs eight barrels of water to wet down a half-mile of gravel base roadway to keep the dust down. How many barrels of water does he need to wet down 3.5 miles of the same kind of roadway?

   (A) 24
   (B) 32
   (C) 64
   (D) 56
   (E) 40

5. A portable fence installed around a small temporary rectangular parking lot 40 ft. long and 36 ft. wide is disassembled and moved to completely enclose a square garden, with no gaps and nothing left over. What is the length in feet of one side of the square garden?

   (A) 38 ft.
   (B) 18 ft.
   (C) 42 ft.
   (D) 76 ft.
   (E) 32 ft.

6. A Navy F/A-18E Super Hornet and an Air Force F-35A Lightning II leave Carswell Joint Reserve Base at the same time. The F/A-18E is flying due east at 260 mph, and the F-35A is flying due west at 340 mph. How long will it be (in hours and minutes) until the planes are 1,800 miles apart?

   (A) 2:30
   (B) 2:40
   (C) 3:00
   (D) 4:30
   (E) 6:00

7. In an organizational day formation of 1st Battalion, 327th Infantry Regiment, 574 soldiers were present, about 92% of whom were enlisted personnel. How many officers were in the formation?

   (A) 45
   (B) 46
   (C) 47
   (D) 528
   (E) 529

SIFT #1

8. A ground surveillance radar (GSR) set can detect moving individuals out to a radius of 10 km. If the radar is used to cover a 36-degree segment of the circle around the radar, how many square km of area will it cover? (Use 3.14 as the value of π.)

   (A) 6.28 sq. km
   (B) 12.56 sq. km
   (C) 31.4 sq. km
   (D) 62.8 sq. km
   (E) 360 sq. km

9. Mrs. Queenby drove her Ford Focus sedan from Nashville to Cincinnati at an average speed of 68 miles per hour, not including two rest stops of 10 minutes each. Her car gets average highway mileage of 30 miles per gallon. If her car used 9.5 gallons of gas, about how much time did she actually spend driving?

   (A) 4 hours, 48 minutes
   (B) 3 hours, 30 minutes
   (C) 4 hours, 12 minutes
   (D) 4 hours, 2 minutes
   (E) 3 hours, 58 minutes

10. An aviation task force is to be composed of one company of AH-64 Apache attack helicopters, one company of UH-60 Black Hawk helicopters, and one company of CH-47 Chinook helicopters. There are four Apache companies available for the mission, two companies of Black Hawks, and three companies of Chinooks. How many different combinations of helicopter companies are possible for the task force?

    (A) 9
    (B) 24
    (C) 8
    (D) 12
    (E) 16

11. A CH-47D Chinook is flying a circular orbit around the landing zone (LZ), where it is going to pick up a long-range reconnaissance unit when it calls in. Assuming the pilot flies a perfectly circular course, what is the distance in kilometers he travels each orbit if it is 40 km from the LZ to the outer edge of his orbit? (Use $22/7 = \pi$.)

    (A) 126 km
    (B) 80 km
    (C) 340 km
    (D) 502 km
    (E) 251 km

12. A floor is made up of hexagonal tiles, some of which are brown and some of which are tan. Every brown tile is completely surrounded by tan tiles. How many tan tiles are there around each brown tile?

    (A) 4
    (B) 5
    (C) 6
    (D) 7
    (E) 8

13. Describe the following sequence in mathematical terms: 5, 10, 20, 40, 80, and 160.

    (A) ascending geometric sequence
    (B) descending geometric sequence
    (C) ascending arithmetic sequence
    (D) descending arithmetic sequence
    (E) ascending rounded sequence

14. Travis is going to sell his Dodge Ram 2500 Laramie pickup truck because he is being deployed and wants to buy a new truck when he gets back. A co-worker in another section has agreed to buy it for Blue Book retail valuation. Travis originally bought the truck for $43,999, but the Blue Book retail value has decreased 12% since then. What will the co-worker pay for the truck?

(A) $38,719
(B) $31,999
(C) $38,971
(D) $39,179
(E) $33,999

15. What is $x^3y^4z^{-5} / x^{-2}y^{-3}z^2$?

(A) xyz^{-3}
(B) $x^5y^7z^{-7}$
(C) $x^6y^{-12}z^{-10}$
(D) xy^6z^{-3}
(E) $x^{-5}y^{-6}z^7$

16. If x is positive, and $x^2/4$ and $x/4$ both yield the same result, what is the value of x?

(A) 1
(B) –1
(C) 0
(D) 4
(E) –4

17. Find the average of the sum of the numbers 1 through 1,000.

(A) 500
(B) 500.5
(C) 501
(D) 625
(E) 499.5

18. If $16^r = 4^{-1/t}$, what is rt?

(A) 2
(B) –2
(C) 1
(D) –1
(E) –.5

19. The first of three consecutive odd integers, multiplied by four, is six more than the result of multiplying two by the third integer. Find the integers.

(A) 7, 9, 11
(B) 5, 7, 9
(C) 3, 5, 7
(D) 9, 11, 13
(E) 1, 3, 5

20. A die is rolled 81 times and the number 3 came up 33 times. Based on this data, for the 82nd roll of the die, what is the probability that the 3 will land facing up?

(A) 3/81
(B) 3/82
(C) 33/81
(D) 33/82
(E) 3/33

SIFT #1

SUBTEST 7: MECHANICAL COMPREHENSION TEST (MCT)

20 Questions

This subtest evaluates your understanding of general mechanical principles by showing you drawings or pictures, and then asking questions about the mechanical principles indicated. There are 20 questions on this subtest, which you will have 15 minutes to answer. For each question, choose the best answer; there is only *one* right answer to every question.

1. Gear B is intended to mesh with

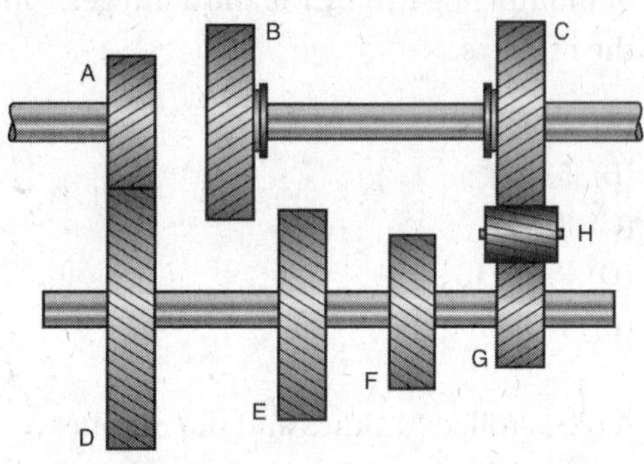

(A) gear A only.
(B) gear D only.
(C) gear E only.
(D) gear F only.
(E) all of the above gears.

2. As cam A makes one complete turn, the setscrew hits the contact point how many times?

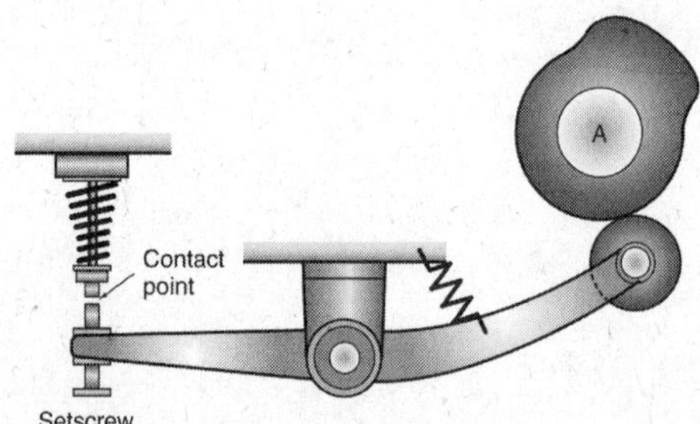

(A) once
(B) twice
(C) three times
(D) four times
(E) not at all

3. If gear A makes 14 revolutions, gear B will make

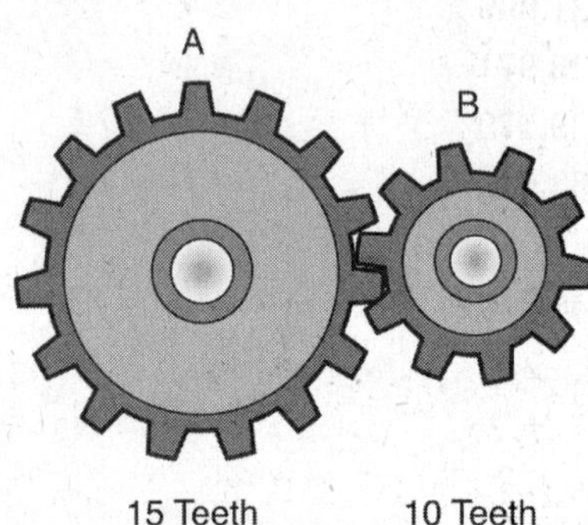

(A) 21 revolutions.
(B) 28 revolutions.
(C) 14 revolutions.
(D) 17 revolutions.
(E) 9 revolutions.

4. Which of the other gears is moving in the same direction as Gear 2?

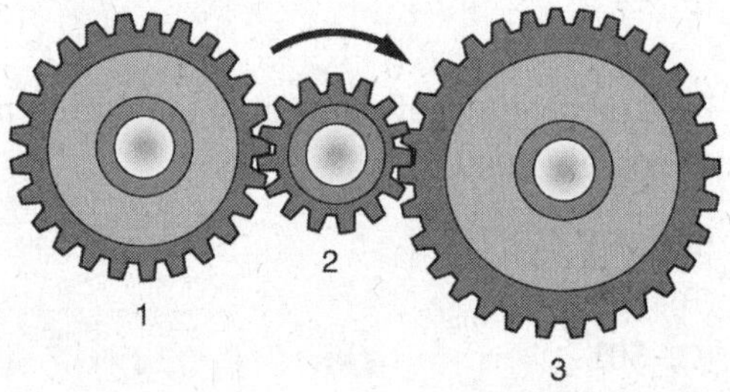

(A) gear 1
(B) gear 3
(C) neither of the other gears
(D) gears 1 and 3
(E) both of the other gears

5. Floats X and Y are measuring the specific gravity of two different liquids. Which float indicates the liquid with the highest specific gravity?

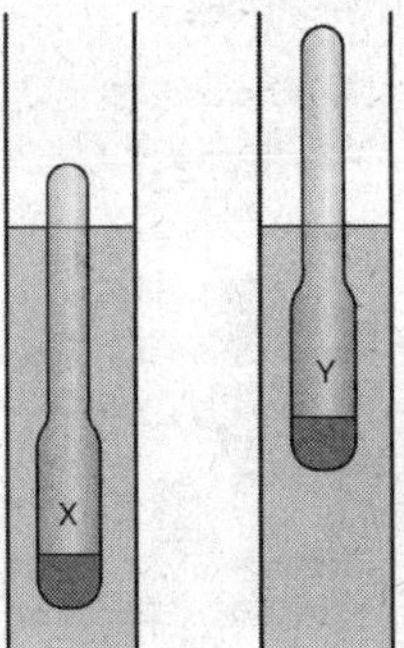

(A) Y
(B) X
(C) neither X nor Y
(D) both X and Y are the same
(E) cannot be determined from the information given

6. The wheelbarrow is an example of a

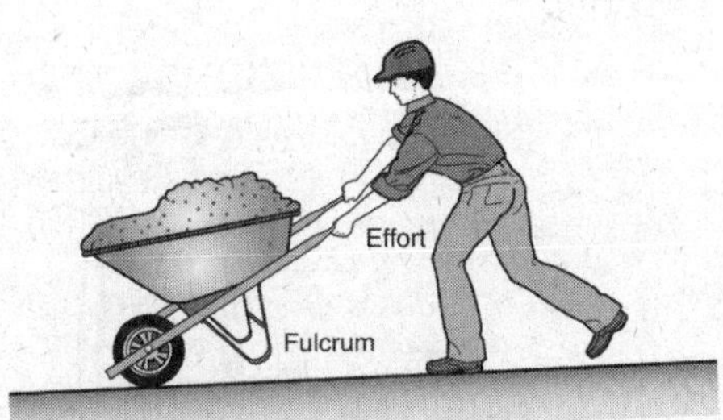

(A) first-class lever.
(B) second-class lever.
(C) third-class lever.
(D) load-bearing mechanism.
(E) first- and third-class lever.

7. In the figure, the angle θ is important, because when it is

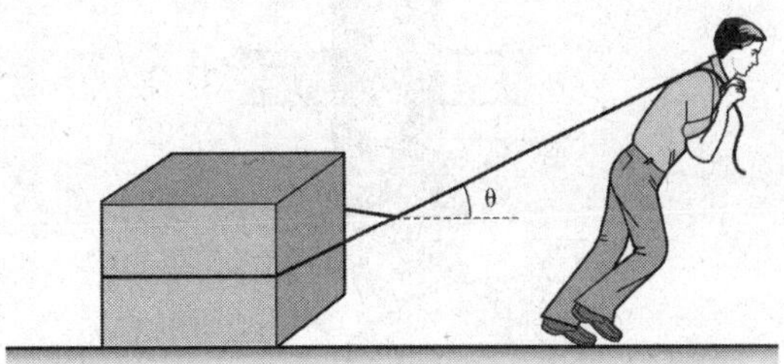

(A) 0 (zero) degrees, the entire force is dragging the box.
(B) 90 degrees, the entire force is lifting the box.
(C) 45 degrees, it is equally lifting and dragging the box.
(D) both lifting and dragging to some extent between 0 and 90 degrees.
(E) all of the above

8. Pliers are an example of a

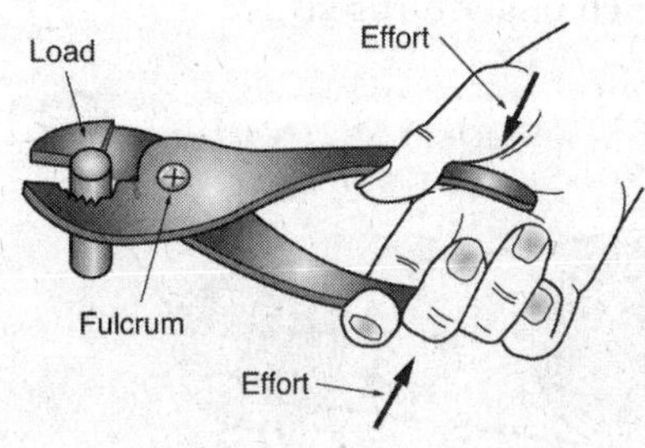

(A) first-class lever.
(B) second-class lever.
(C) third-class lever.
(D) first- and second-class lever.
(E) second- and third-class lever.

SIFT #1

9. The follower is at its highest position between points

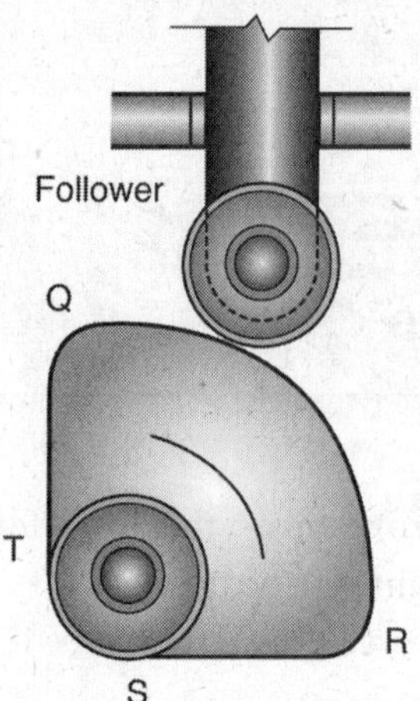

(A) Q and R.
(B) R and S.
(C) S and T.
(D) T and Q.
(E) T and R.

10. If pulley A is the driver and turns in direction 1, which pulley turns faster?

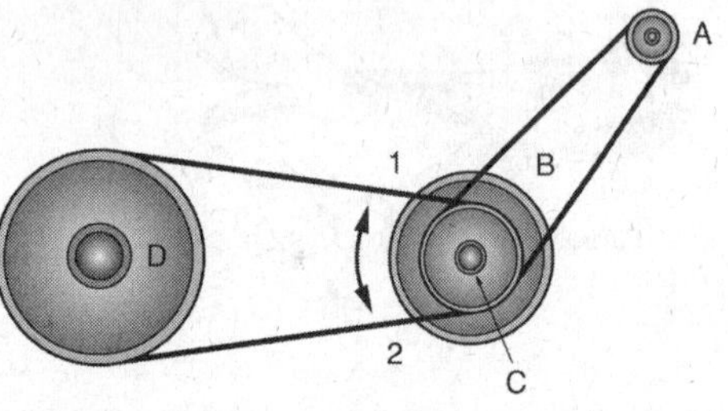

(A) A
(B) B
(C) C
(D) D
(E) A and D are equal.

11. Which shaft or shafts are turning in the same direction as shaft X?

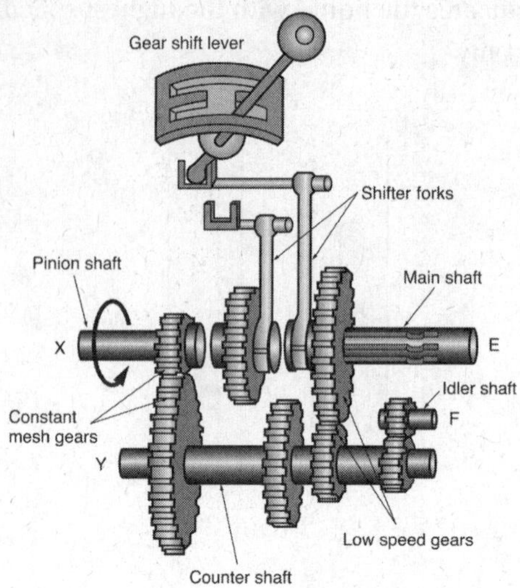

(A) Y
(B) Y and E
(C) F
(D) E and F
(E) E, F, and Y

12. The human arm as depicted below is an example of a

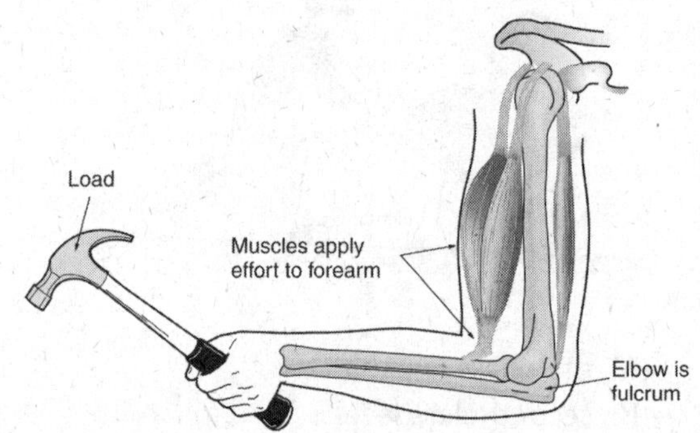

(A) first-class lever.
(B) second-class lever.
(C) third-class lever.
(D) second- and third-class lever.
(E) first- and second-class lever.

13. If arm H is held fixed as gear B turns in direction 2, gear

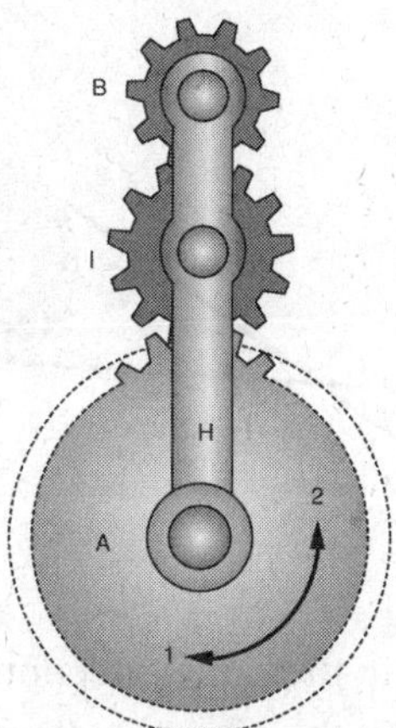

(A) A will turn in direction 1.
(B) A will turn in direction 2.
(C) I must turn in direction 2.
(D) A must be held fixed.
(E) B will spin freely.

14. Two 30-pound blocks are attached to the ceiling using ropes, as shown below. Which of the following statements is true?

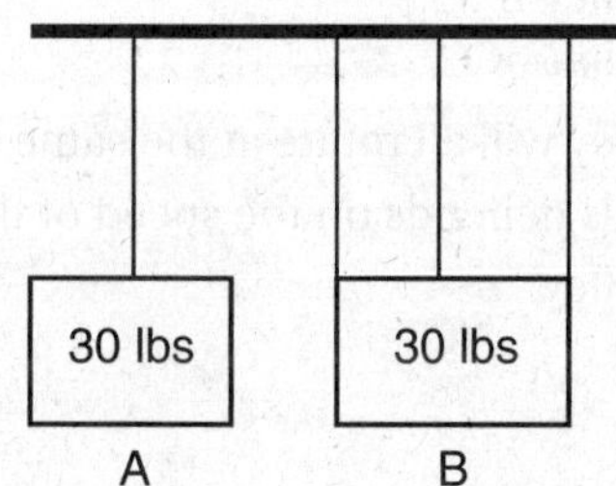

(A) All the ropes are under the same amount of tension.
(B) The rope holding block A is under $\frac{1}{3}$ of the tension of the ropes holding block B.
(C) The ropes supporting block B are under $\frac{1}{3}$ of the tension of the rope holding block A.
(D) The rope supporting block A is under twice the tension of the ropes holding block B.
(E) The ropes supporting block B are under $\frac{1}{6}$ of the tension of the rope holding block A.

15. As the shaft in the illustration below spins faster in a clockwise direction, balls A and B will

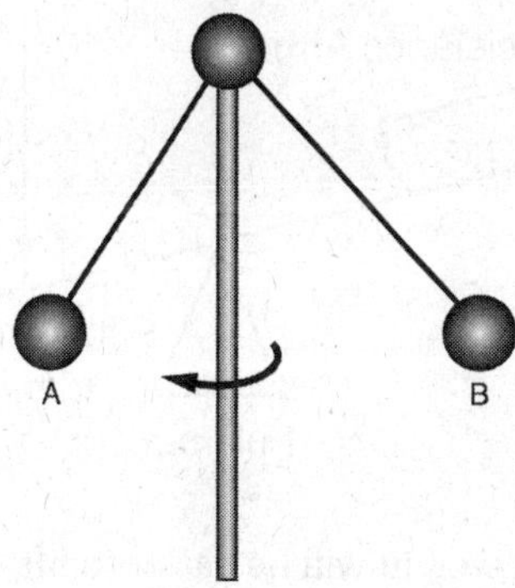

(A) move outward and downward.
(B) move outward and upward.
(C) move up.
(D) move down.
(E) stay at the same level.

16. Water flows into a water tower at a rate of 120 gallons per hour and flows out at the rate of 2 gallons per minute. The level of water in the tower will

(A) remain the same.
(B) lower.
(C) rise.
(D) rise initially, then lower.
(E) lower initially, then rise.

SIFT #1

17. In the illustration below, if the fulcrum is moved farther away from the weight on the resistance arm, the result will be that

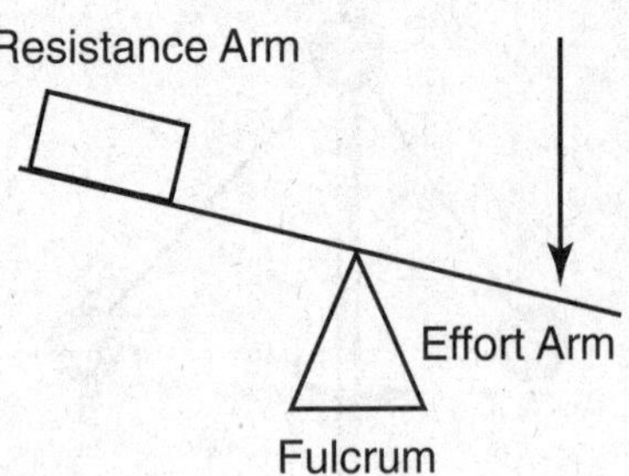

(A) the weight will be easier to lift, and will travel higher.
(B) the weight will be easier to lift, and will not travel as high.
(C) the weight will take more effort to lift, and will travel higher.
(D) the weight will take more effort to lift, and will not travel as high.
(E) the weight will take the same amount of effort to lift, and will travel the same height.

18. What is the difference between weight and mass?

(A) Weight can be changed by buoyancy, but mass is relative to gravity.
(B) Mass remains constant, but weight depends on altitude.
(C) Weight remains constant, but mass depends on altitude.
(D) Mass can be changed by buoyancy, but weight is relative to gravity.
(E) There is no difference between mass and weight.

19. In the illustration below, if pulley A is rotating in the direction indicated, then pulley C will

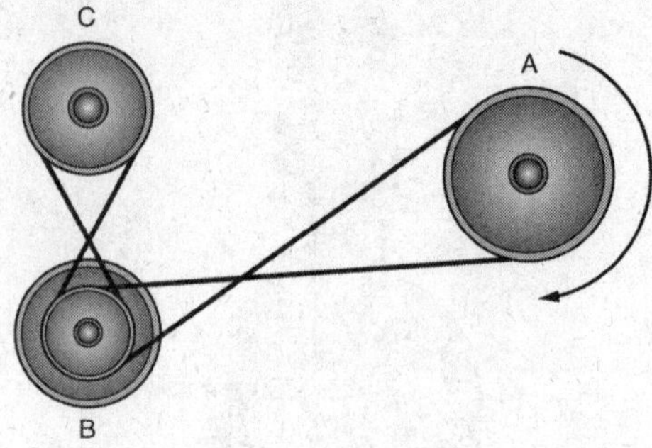

(A) rotate in the same direction as pulley B.
(B) rotate in the same direction as pulleys A and B.
(C) rotate in the opposite direction of pulleys A and B.
(D) rotate in the same direction as pulley A.
(E) none of the above

20. In the pulley system shown in problem 19, which pulley will rotate the fastest?

(A) pulley A
(B) pulley B
(C) pulley C
(D) They will all rotate at the same speed.
(E) This depends on the speed of the drive pulley.

ANSWERS AND EXPLANATIONS

Subtest 1: Simple Drawings (SD)

	✔	✘		✔	✘		✔	✘		✔	✘
1. C			26. E			51. B			76. E		
2. A			27. E			52. C			77. B		
3. E			28. A			53. A			78. A		
4. B			29. B			54. C			79. C		
5. A			30. D			55. D			80. E		
6. C			31. C			56. C			81. C		
7. D			32. B			57. E			82. B		
8. B			33. D			58. B			83. E		
9. A			34. E			59. A			84. D		
10. D			35. A			60. B			85. A		
11. A			36. C			61. A			86. B		
12. E			37. C			62. B			87. B		
13. C			38. A			63. C			88. B		
14. B			39. E			64. E			89. E		
15. B			40. A			65. A			90. A		
16. E			41. C			66. C			91. C		
17. C			42. E			67. A			92. D		
18. B			43. B			68. D			93. E		
19. A			44. C			69. D			94. C		
20. D			45. D			70. B			95. B		
21. E			46. B			71. B			96. D		
22. D			47. C			72. D			97. B		
23. C			48. E			73. E			98. C		
24. B			49. D			74. A			99. B		
25. C			50. B			75. C			100. E		

Subtest 2: Hidden Figures (HF)

	✔	✘		✔	✘		✔	✘		✔	✘		✔	✘
1. C			11. C			21. B			31. E			41. E		
2. E			12. A			22. D			32. C			42. B		
3. D			13. E			23. C			33. B			43. D		
4. A			14. B			24. E			34. A			44. A		
5. B			15. D			25. A			35. D			45. C		
6. D			16. A			26. E			36. D			46. C		
7. A			17. C			27. B			37. A			47. E		
8. C			18. E			28. A			38. C			48. D		
9. E			19. B			29. C			39. B			49. B		
10. B			20. D			30. D			40. E			50. A		

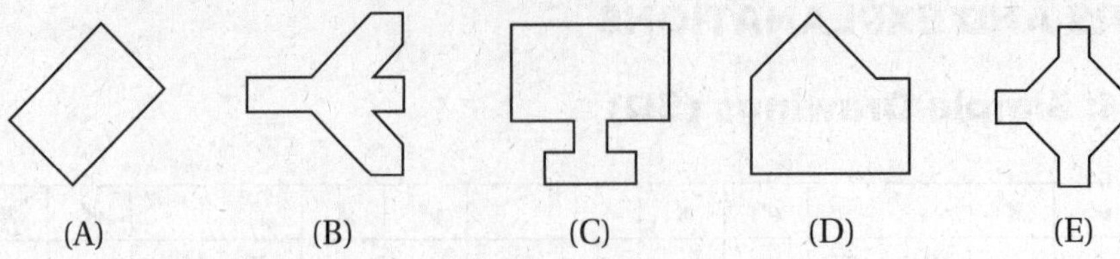

1. **(C)**

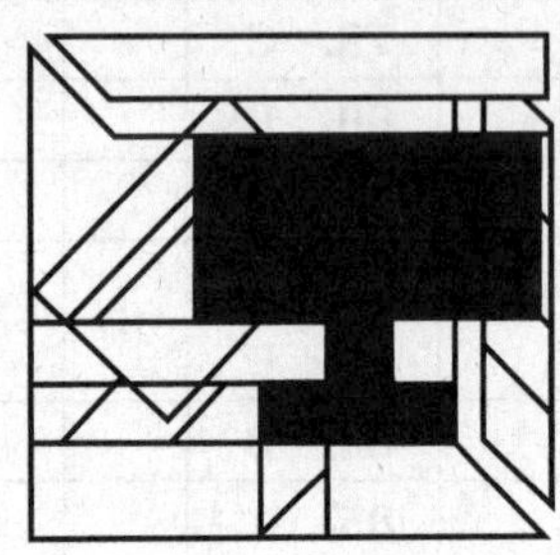

4. **(A)**

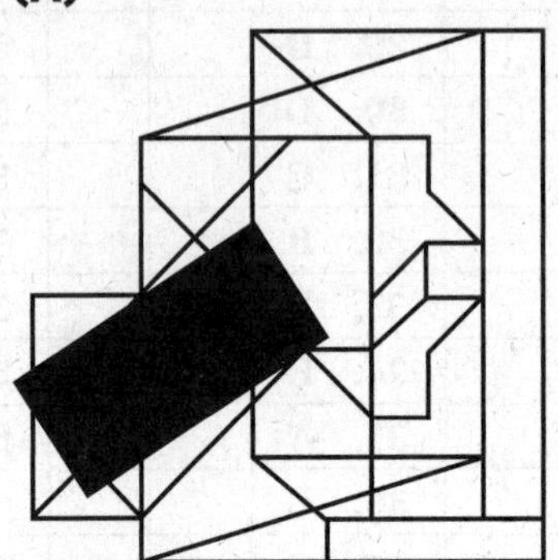

2. **(E)**

5. **(B)**

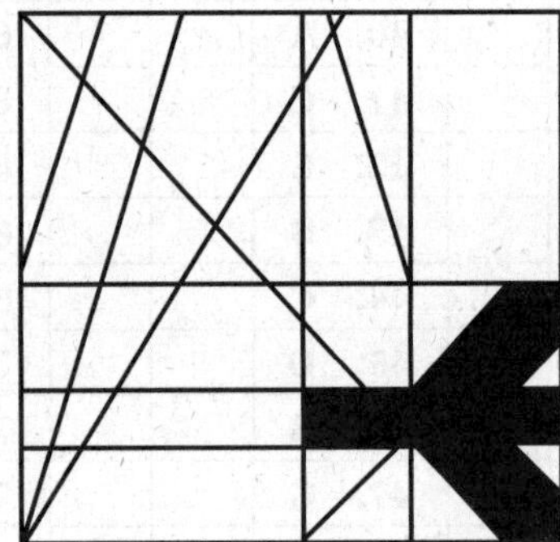

3. **(D)**

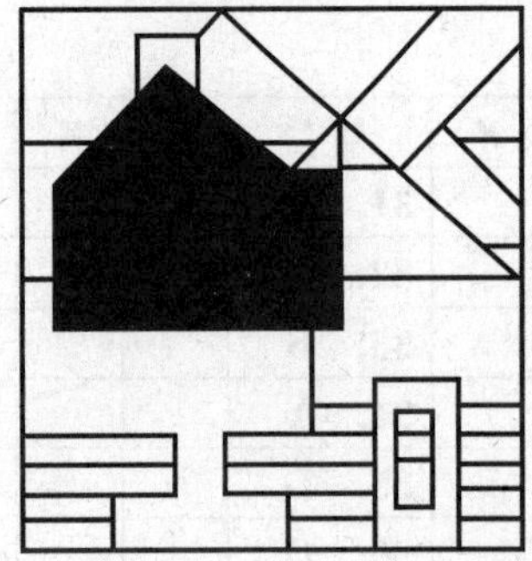

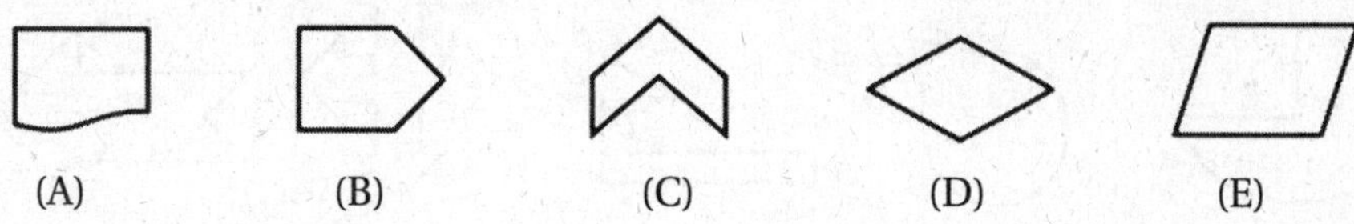

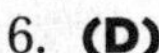
6. **(D)**

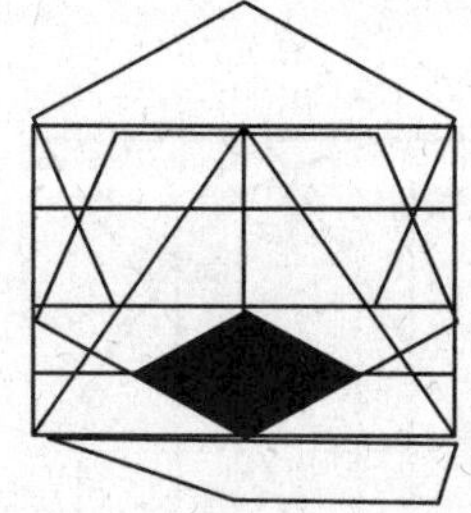

9. **(E)**

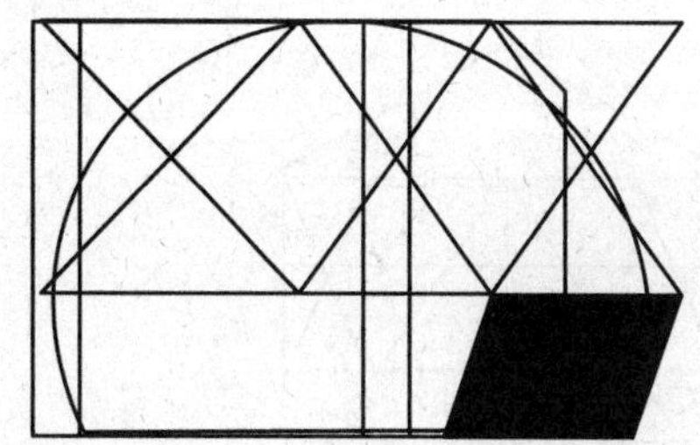

7. **(A)**

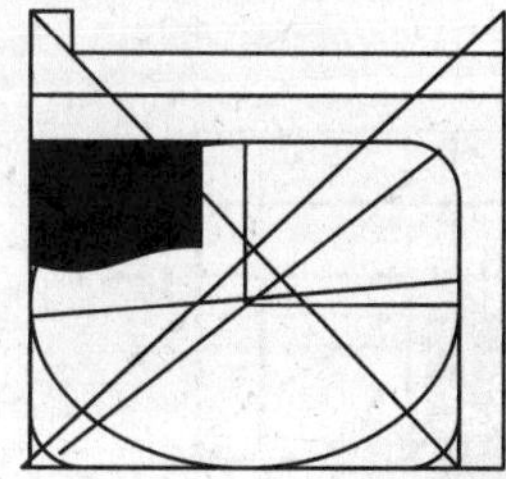

10. **(B)**

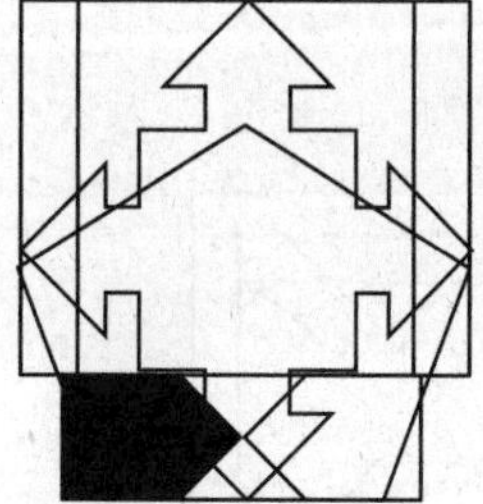

8. **(C)**

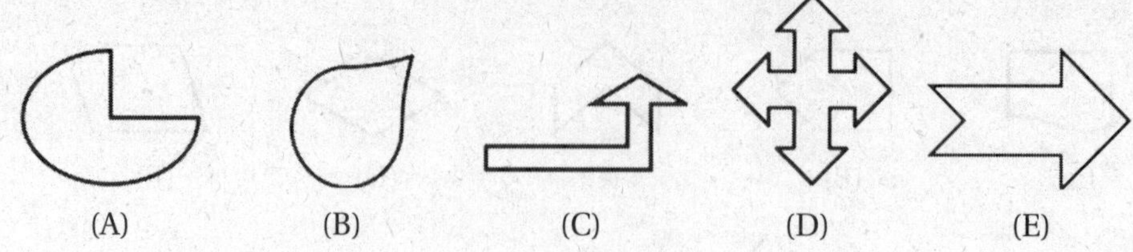

11. **(C)**

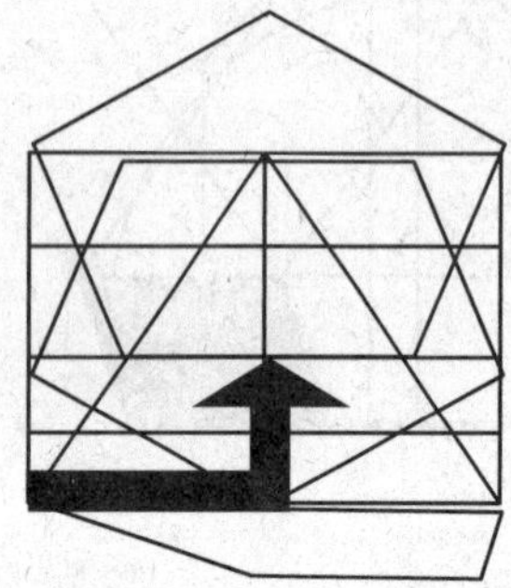

12. **(A)**

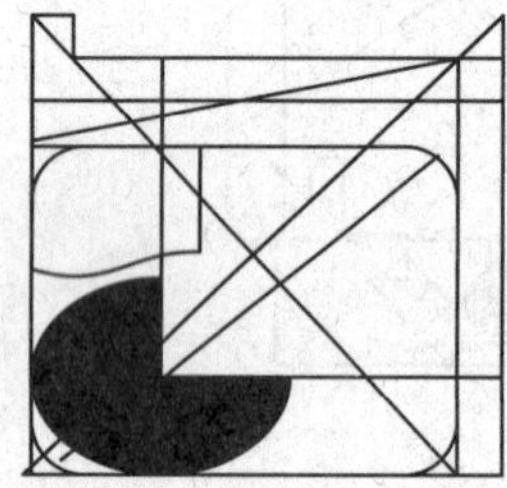

13. **(E)**

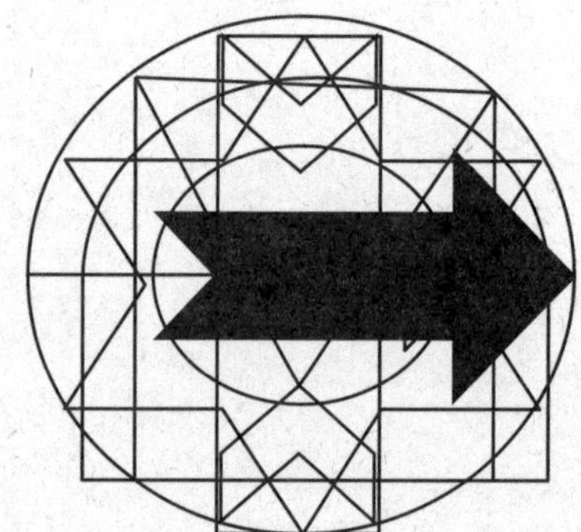

14. **(B)**

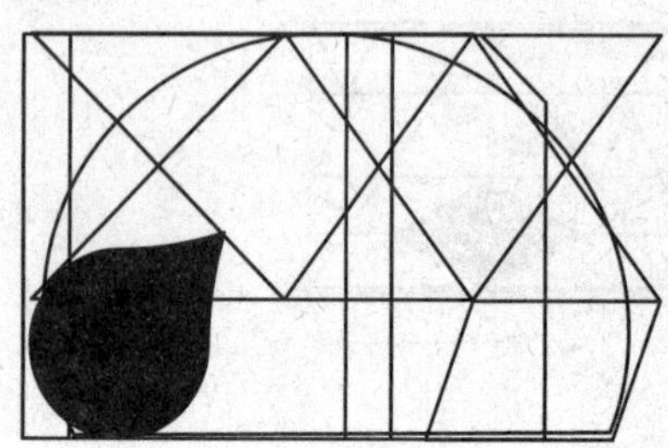

15. **(D)**

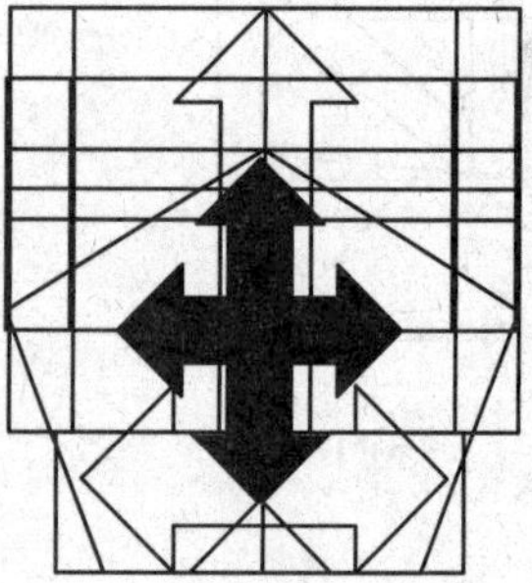

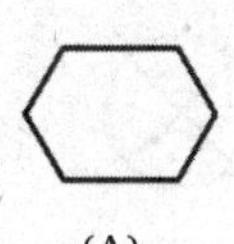

(A)

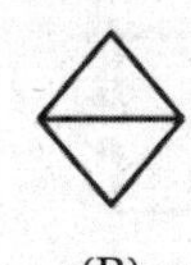

(B)

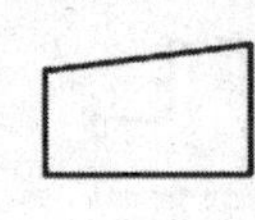

(C)

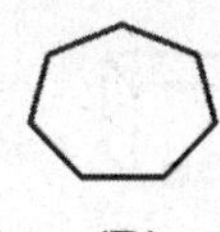

(D)

(E)

16. **(A)**

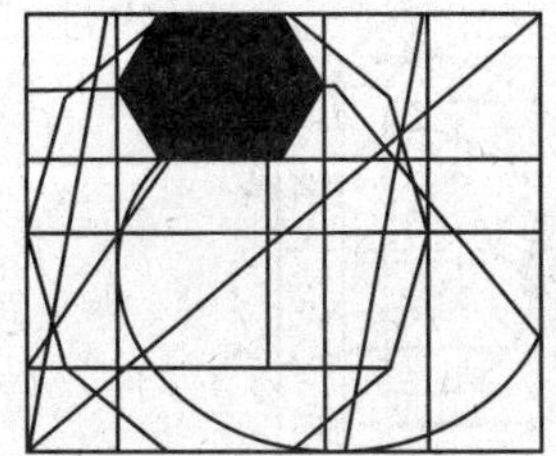

17. **(C)**

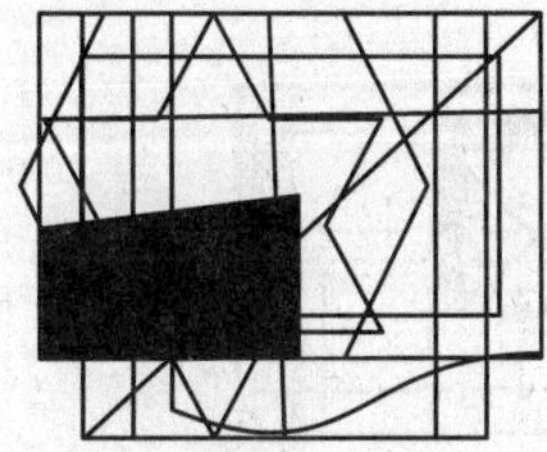

18. **(E)**

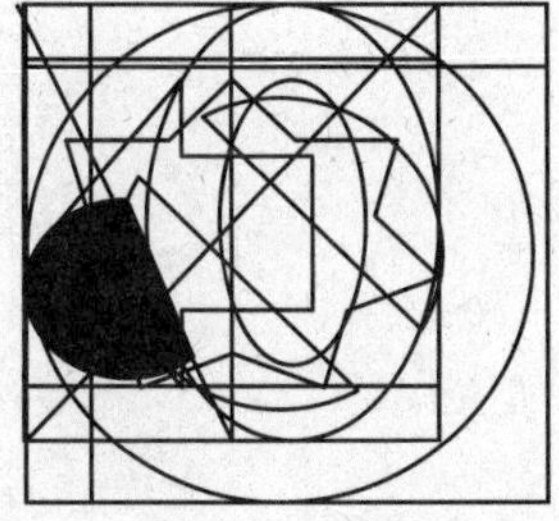

19. **(B)**

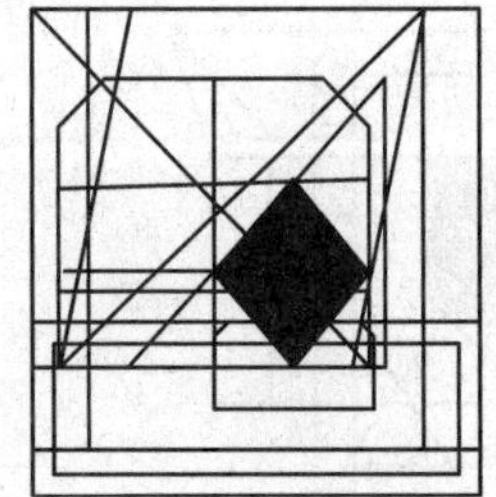

20. **(D)**

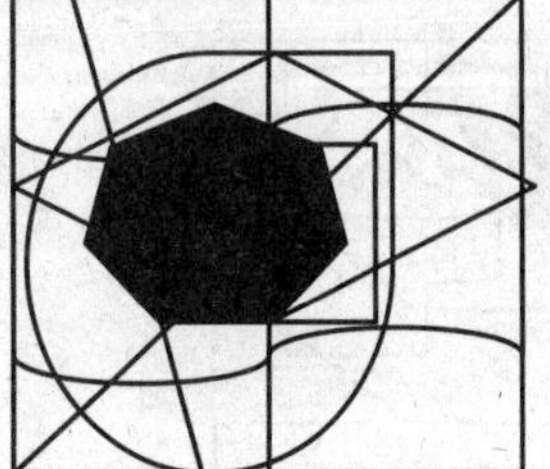

SIFT #1

(A)

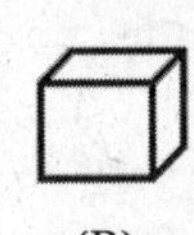
(B)

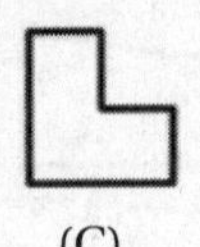
(C)

(D)

(E)

21. **(B)**

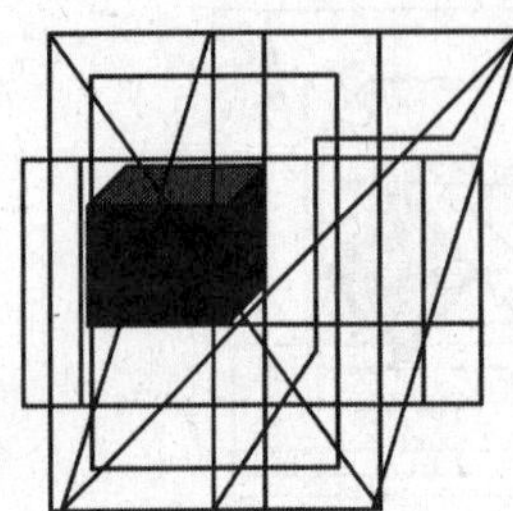

22. **(D)**

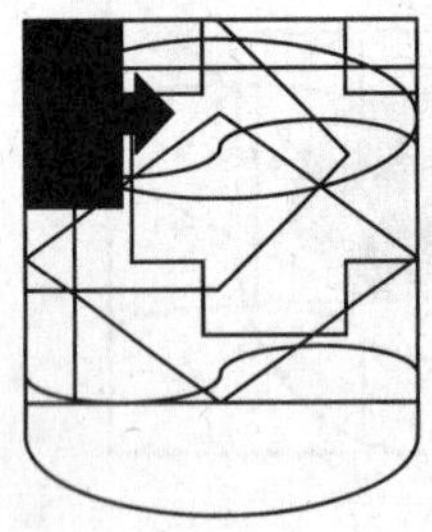

23. **(C)**

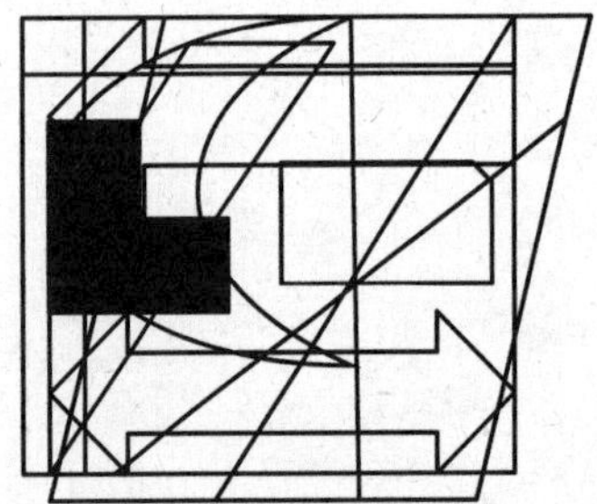

24. **(E)**

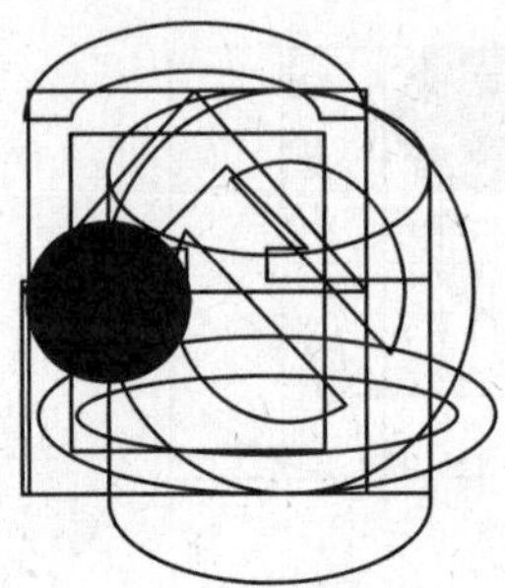

25. **(A)**

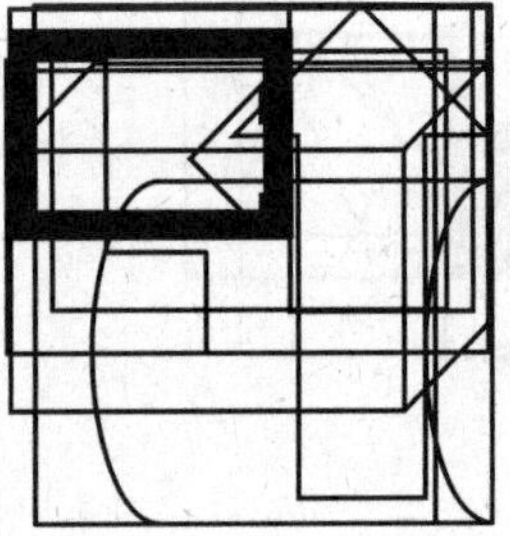

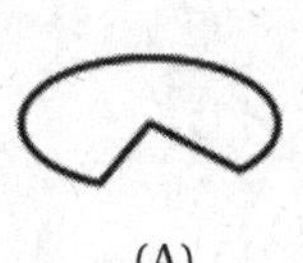
(A)

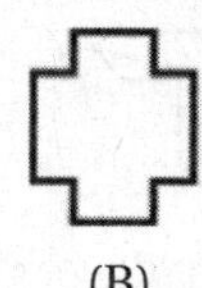
(B)

(C)

(D)

(E)

26. **(E)**

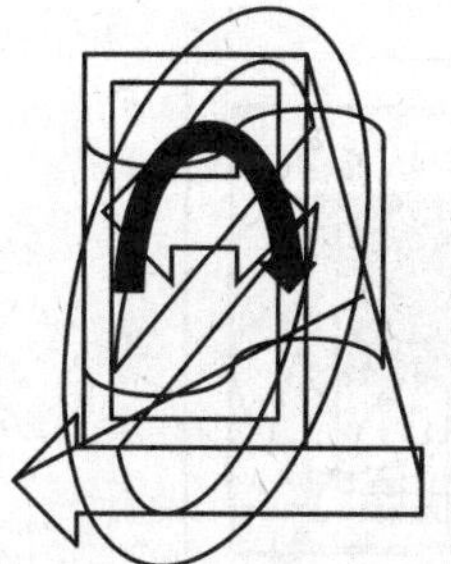

29. **(C)**

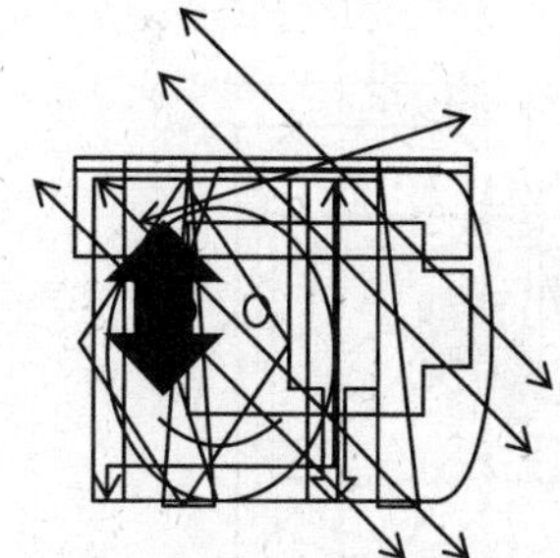

27. **(B)**

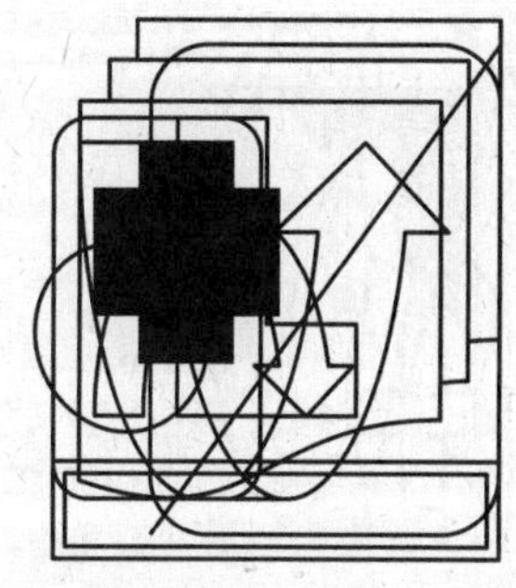

30. **(D)**

28. **(A)**

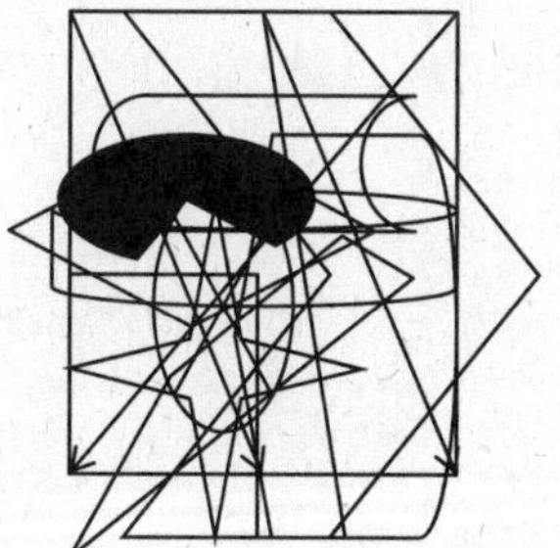

SIFT #1

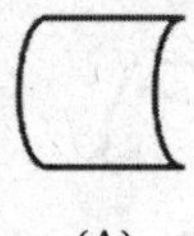
(A)

(B)

(C)

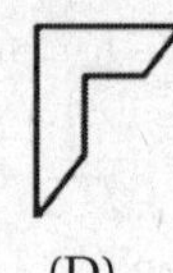
(D)

(E)

31. **(E)**

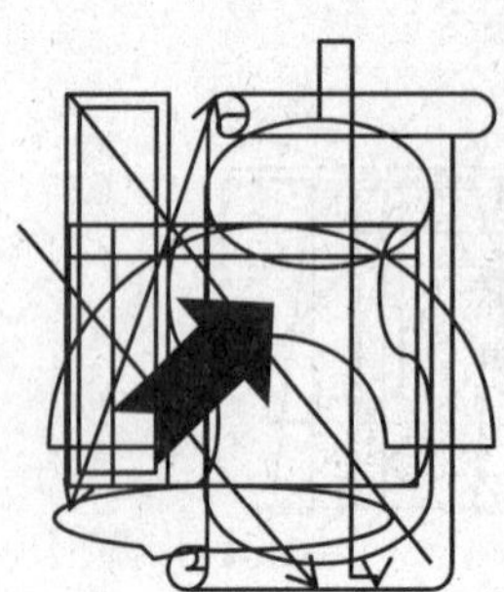

32. **(C)**

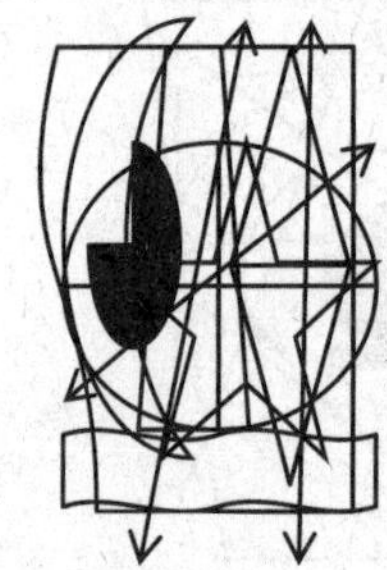

33. **(B)**

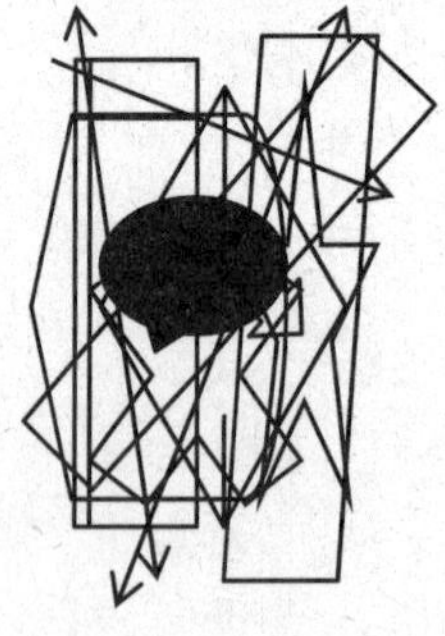

34. **(A)**

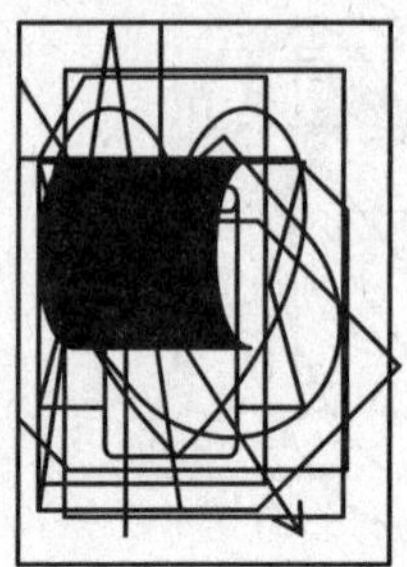

35. **(D)**

SIFT #1

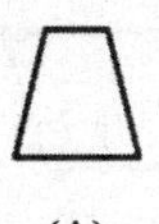
(A)

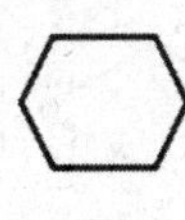
(B)

(C)

(D)

(E)

36. **(D)**

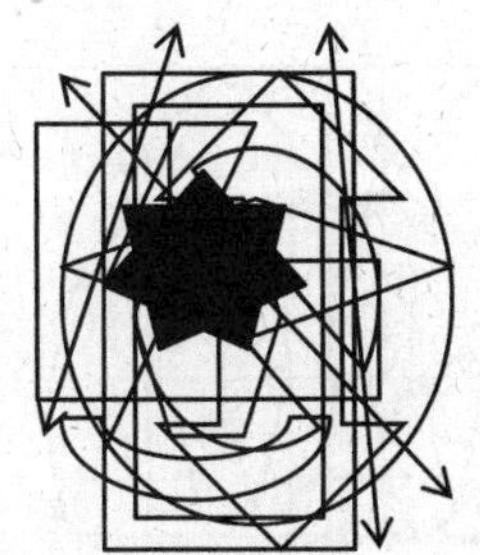

37. **(A)**

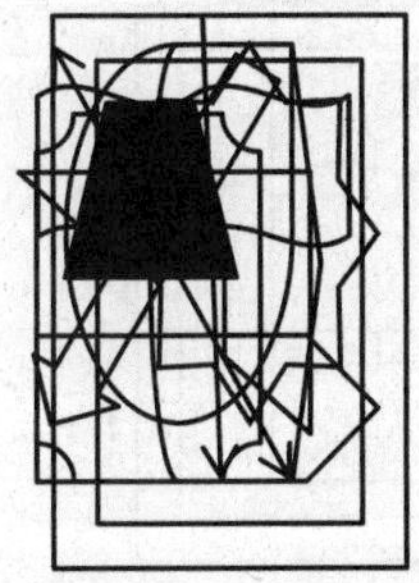

38. **(C)**

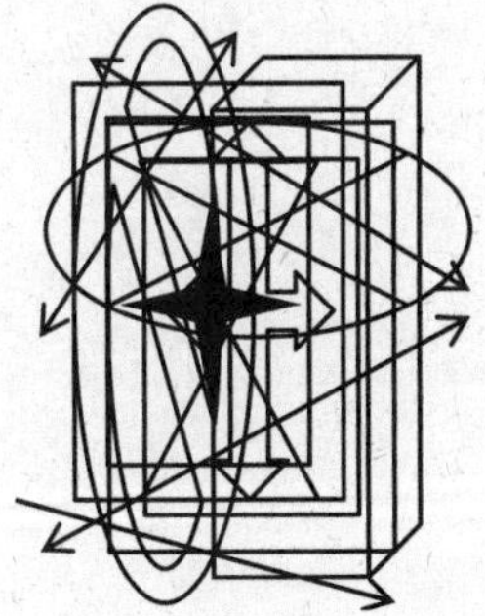

39. **(B)**

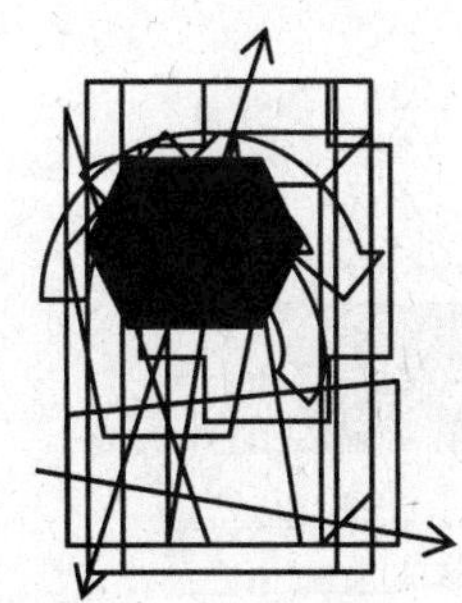

40. **(E)**

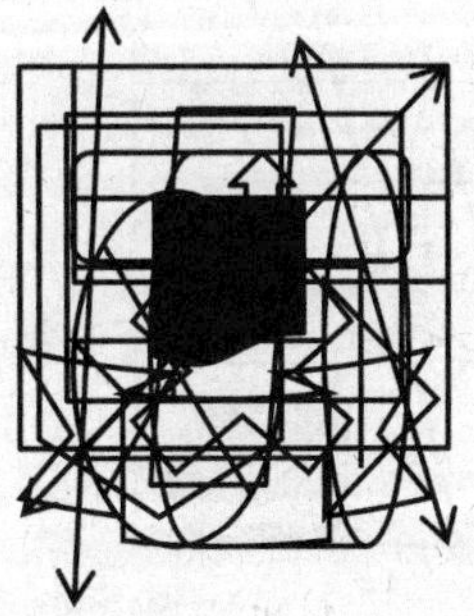

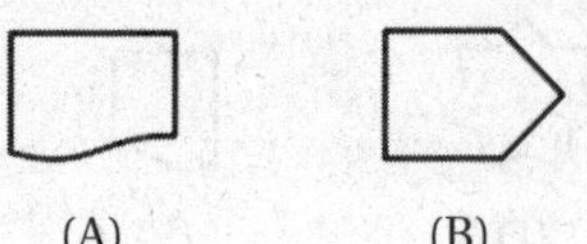
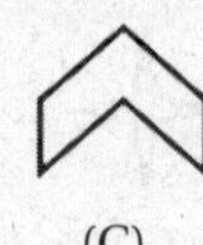
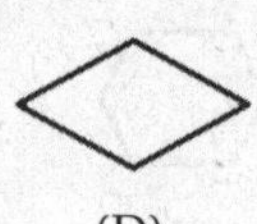

(A) (B) (C) (D) (E)

41. **(E)**

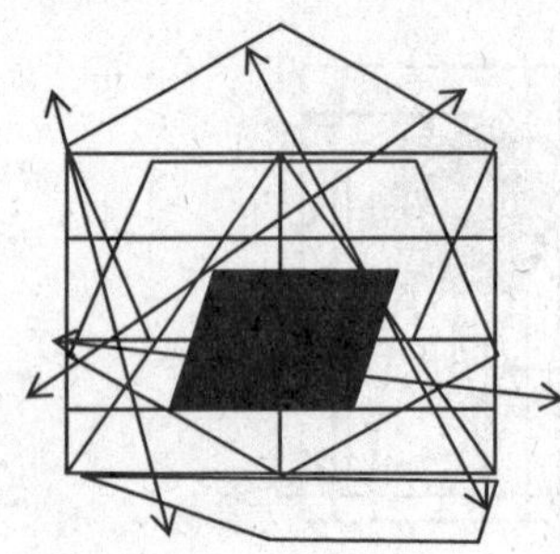

42. **(B)**

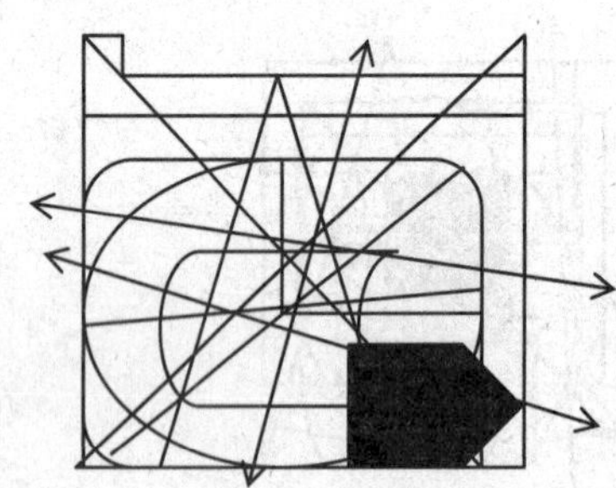

43. **(D)**

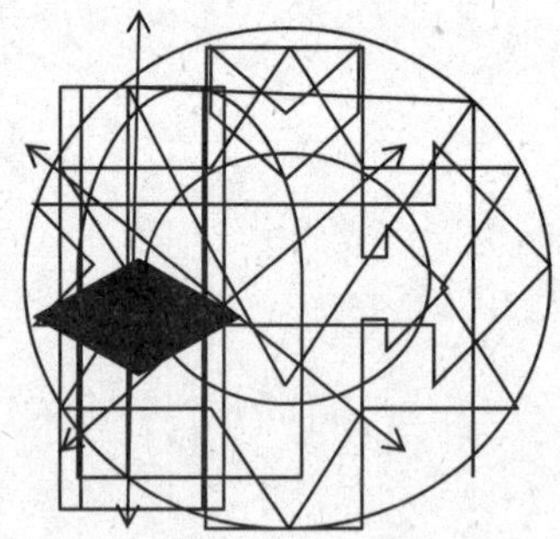

44. **(A)**

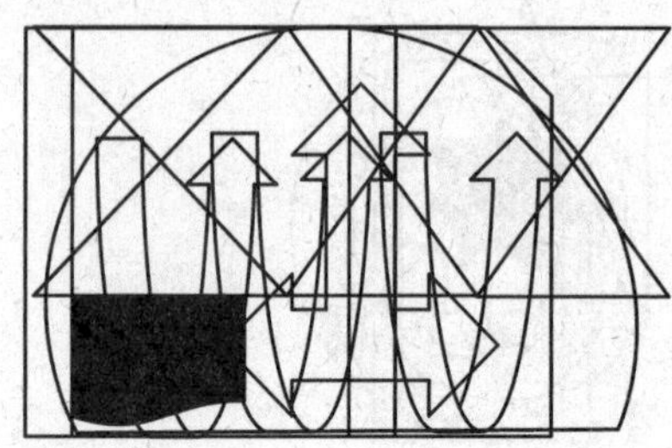

45. **(C)**

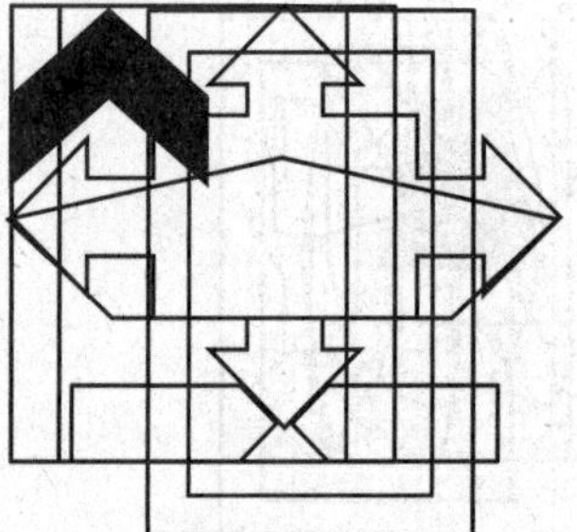

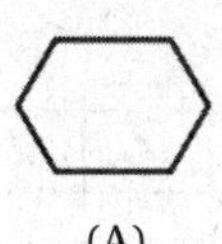

(A)

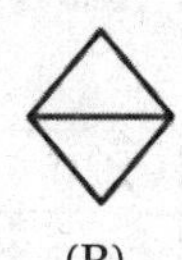

(B)

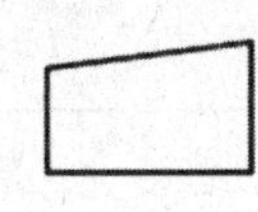

(C)

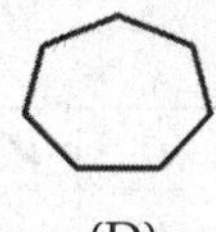

(D)

(E)

46. **(C)**

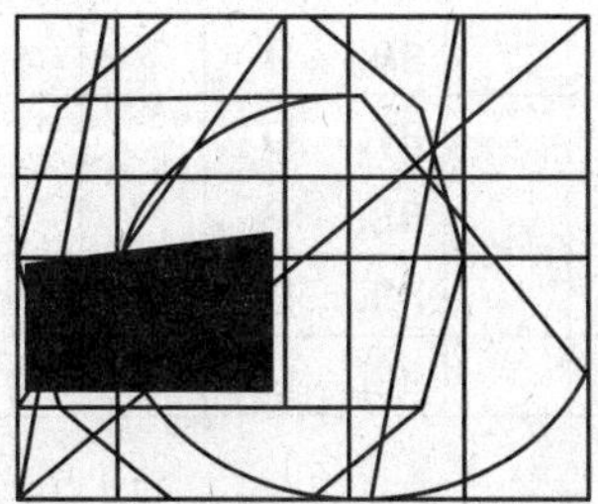

47. **(E)**

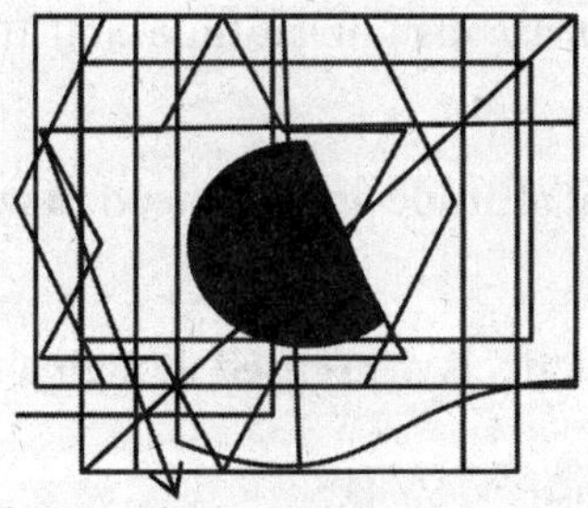

48. **(D)**

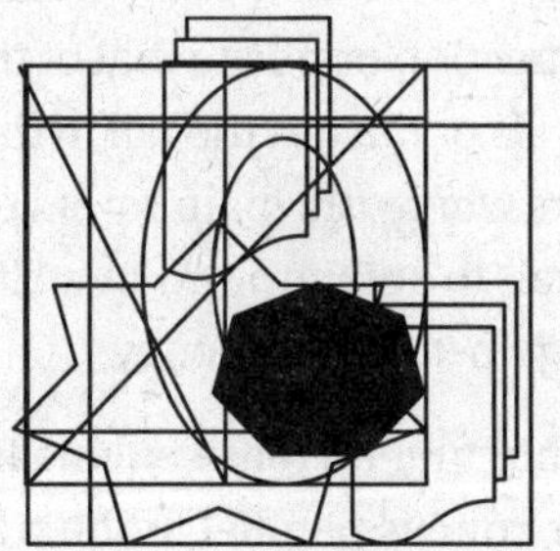

49. **(B)**

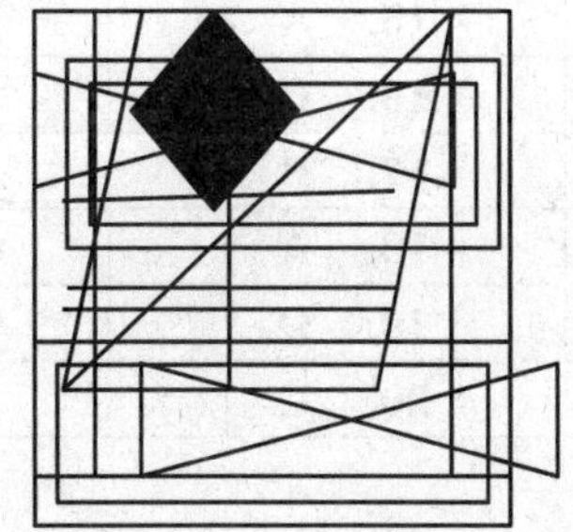

50. **(A)**

SIFT #1

Subtest 3: Army Aviation Information Test (AAIT)

	✔	✘		✔	✘		✔	✘		✔	✘
1. A			11. D			21. C			31. C		
2. D			12. D			22. B			32. A		
3. C			13. C			23. A			33. C		
4. B			14. E			24. D			34. C		
5. C			15. A			25. B			35. C		
6. D			16. D			26. A			36. B		
7. E			17. B			27. E			37. D		
8. D			18. A			28. B			38. E		
9. B			19. D			29. A			39. D		
10. B			20. C			30. C			40. C		

1. **(A)** The four forces that act on an aircraft in flight are **lift, gravity, thrust, and drag**.
2. **(D)** Of the five factors listed, **wind velocity** does not affect density altitude.
3. **(C)** The maneuver in which a rotary-wing aircraft (helicopter) is maintained in nearly motionless flight over a ground reference point at a constant altitude and heading (direction) is known as **hovering**.
4. **(B)** The flight envelope of an aircraft is **the region of altitude and airspeed in which it can be operated**.
5. **(C)** An airfoil's efficiency, either a wing or a rotor blade, is **decreased** at high altitudes by the **lesser** air density.
6. **(D)** The degree of movement of an aircraft around its lateral axis is known as **pitch**.
7. **(E)** The primary purpose of the tail rotor system is to **balance or counteract the torque effect of the main rotor**. The "torque effect" is caused by the rotation of the main rotors, which gives the fuselage the tendency to rotate in the direction opposite that of the main rotor. The tail rotor counteracts the torque effect and pulls or pushes the tail in the direction opposite that of the rotors. In American helicopters where the main rotors rotate in a counterclockwise direction, the tendency is for the tail to spin around in a clockwise direction; the tail rotor either pulls or pushes the tail against that tendency.
8. **(D)** For a takeoff from a sloping surface, the pilot should first increase engine RPMs to takeoff level and move the cyclic stick so that the rotor cone is parallel to the true horizon instead of the slope. Apply up-collective pitch and apply pedal to maintain heading. As the downslope skid rises and the helicopter approaches a level attitude, move the cyclic stick back to the neutral position and take the helicopter straight up to a hover before moving away from the slope. The tail should not be turned upslope because of the danger of the tail rotor striking the surface.
9. **(B)** "True altitude" is defined as **the vertical distance of the aircraft above mean sea level**.
10. **(B)** A helicopter's cyclic control is a mechanical linkage used to change the pitch of the main rotor blades **at a selected point in its circular pathway**.

11. **(D)** When the rotor blades of a helicopter are spinning fast enough in a clockwise direction to generate lift, a phenomenon known as **torque** causes the body of the helicopter to have a tendency to turn in a counterclockwise direction.

12. **(D)** "Absolute altitude" is defined as **the vertical distance of the aircraft above the terrain or ground level.**

13. **(C)** The differential in lift between that of the advancing rotor blade and that of the retreating rotor blade is called **dissymmetry of lift.**

14. **(E)** Foot pedals in the helicopter cockpit give the pilot the ability to **control the torque effect.**

15. **(A)** "Density altitude" is defined as **the pressure altitude reading corrected for variations from standard temperature.**

16. **(D)** The cyclic controls the **direction of the tilt of the main rotor.**

17. **(B)** Moving the cyclic forward and significantly raising the collective will cause the helicopter to **increase its forward speed and begin to climb.**

18. **(A)** Conventional American helicopters have a main rotor that **turns in a counterclockwise direction.**

19. **(D)** Translational lift is **the additional lift gained when the helicopter leaves its downwash.**

20. **(C)** Gyroscopic precession happens when **a force applied to a spinning disc has its effect 90 degrees later in the direction and plane of rotation.**

21. **(C)** One useful tool for the illustration of aerodynamic forces at work is a *vector*, which is **a quantity with a magnitude and a direction**. A direction expressed in degrees is an *azimuth*; a quantity described by size alone is a *scalar*; a position described by latitude and longitude can be called a *coordinate*; and a location described by universal transverse Mercator coordinates is a *grid coordinate.*

22. **(B)** As a rotor system begins to turn, the blades start to rise from their drooping position due to **centrifugal force**, which tends to make rotating bodies move away from the center of rotation.

23. **(A)** Significant "coning" of the rotor disk on a helicopter can cause **a decrease in lift due to a decrease in effective disk area.**

24. **(D)** In tandem rotor and coaxial helicopters, **the two rotor systems turn in opposite directions, canceling the torque effect.**

25. **(B)** Most American-built single-rotor helicopters turn the main rotor **in a counterclockwise direction.**

26. **(A)** An increase in blade pitch through application of collective **generates the additional lift needed to hover,** so long as the lift produced by the rotor system is equal to the total weight of the helicopter.

27. **(E)** "Ground effect" is **increased** rotor system efficiency due to interference of the airflow **when near the ground.**

SIFT #1

28. **(B)** A helicopter has four flight control inputs: the **cyclic, collective, antitorque pedals,** and **throttle**.

29. **(A)** The collective pitch control is used to **make simultaneous changes to the pitch angle of the main rotor blades.** The collective pitch control is normally just called the "collective" for short.

30. **(C)** A twist grip throttle is usually mounted **on the end of the collective lever.**

31. **(C)** With the antitorque pedals in the neutral position, the tail rotor has a medium positive pitch angle, thereby **approximately equaling the torque of the main rotor.**

32. **(A)** Main rotor systems are classified as rigid, semirigid, or fully articulated according to **how the main rotor blades are attached and move relative to the main rotor hub.**

33. **(C)** The lift generated by an airfoil directly depends on all of the following factors except **actual altitude.** While the altitude may affect such factors as air density, the altitude of the aircraft or airfoil does not *directly* affect the lift generated by the airfoil.

34. **(C)** The angle between the chord line of a wing or airfoil and the direction of relative wind or airflow is called the **angle of attack.**

35. **(C)** When the pilot of a fixed-wing aircraft pushes forward on the control stick, the elevators will **move downward.** This pushes the tail of the aircraft upward and the nose downward.

36. **(B)** Another form of antitorque system is the "fan-in-tail" system or *fenestron,* which **uses a series of rotating blades shrouded within a vertical tail.** This design provides an improved margin of safety during ground operations, since the blades are located in a circular duct and are therefore less likely to come into contact with people or objects.

37. **(D)** Most **training** helicopters use **reciprocating (piston)** engines because they are relatively simple and inexpensive to operate.

38. **(E)** For both helicopters and fixed-wing aircraft, VFR stands for **Visual Flight Rules.**

39. **(D)** If a helicopter's center of gravity (CG) is too far forward of the rotor mast, the helicopter has a nose-low attitude during a hover; the pilot may not be able to decelerate sufficiently to bring the helicopter to a stop; and excessive rearward cyclic displacement may be needed to maintain a hover when there is no wind **(all of the above).**

40. **(C)** Image intensifier (I2) systems **amplify light in both visible and near infrared (IR) spectrum segments.**

Subtest 4: Spatial Apperception Test (SAT)

	✔	✘		✔	✘		✔	✘		✔	✘		✔	✘
1. A			6. C			11. B			16. B			21. D		
2. E			7. D			12. A			17. D			22. C		
3. D			8. E			13. C			18. D			23. B		
4. B			9. E			14. C			19. E			24. C		
5. A			10. A			15. D			20. B			25. A		

Answer	Pitch	Bank	Heading
1. **(A)**	level flight	right	coastline left
2. **(E)**	level flight	wings level	45° right of the coastline
3. **(D)**	diving	right	out to sea
4. **(B)**	level flight	right	coastline right
5. **(A)**	climbing	right	out to sea
6. **(C)**	level flight	right	out to sea
7. **(D)**	diving	wings level	out to sea
8. **(E)**	level flight	wings level	out to sea
9. **(E)**	diving	right	out to sea
10. **(A)**	level flight	left	out to sea
11. **(B)**	level flight	left	coastline left
12. **(A)**	diving	wings level	out to sea
13. **(C)**	climbing	right	out to sea
14. **(C)**	level flight	wings level	coastline left
15. **(D)**	level flight	left	coastline left
16. **(B)**	level flight	left	coastline right
17. **(D)**	diving	wings level	out to sea
18. **(D)**	diving	left	out to sea
19. **(E)**	climbing	left	out to sea
20. **(B)**	climbing	wings level	out to sea
21. **(D)**	level flight	left	out to sea
22. **(C)**	diving	wings level	coastline right
23. **(B)**	diving	left	out to sea
24. **(C)**	climbing	left	out to sea
25. **(A)**	climbing	wings level	out to sea

Subtest 5: Reading Comprehension Test (RCT)

	✔	✘		✔	✘		✔	✘		✔	✘
1. D			6. A			11. A			16. B		
2. C			7. B			12. E			17. B		
3. D			8. E			13. B			18. C		
4. B			9. C			14. C			19. E		
5. C			10. D			15. D			20. A		

1. **(D)** According to this passage, Regimental Combat Team 143 was **committed between RCT 141 and 142.**

2. **(C)** In the passage above, the phrase "take rank" means **to join a group**, as in when one becomes part of a military formation standing in ranks (lines).

3. **(D)** The author of this passage believes that a leadership position **is an obligation to challenge the status quo and take calculated risks.**
4. **(B)** The author of the above passage believes that, if the flight lead and wingmen know their duties, they will **work together as a team.**
5. **(C)** Why is the idea of limited liability helpful to business owners? **Because it can limit their personal risk.**
6. **(A)** What does the writer say about different kinds of people working together? **It's important because it strengthens the entire organization or group.**
7. **(B)** How are potential Army aviators chosen for flight training? **By examining applicants for characteristics needed for success as aviators.**
8. **(E)** What is the most important overall characteristic of a pilot discussed in this passage? **The ability to constantly coordinate multiple mental and physical actions.**
9. **(C)** What was the most hazardous moment mentioned in the above passage? **When the A-10s fired on enemy forces just 50 m away from friendly troops.**
10. **(D)** If this passage had to be summed up on a bumper sticker, what would it say? **When you make your local area better, you contribute to a better world.**
11. **(A)** According to this passage, what did Roman matrons (mothers of grown sons) believe? **That their sons should either perform honorably in battle or die trying.**
12. **(E)** According to the passage, when did the U.S. Army begin advising Chinese Nationalist combat forces? **The passage does not address American Army advisers to Nationalist Chinese forces.**
13. **(B)** What was Malalai's major contribution to the Afghan victory? **She inspired her fiancé and his fellow Afghans that they should die or be shamed.**
14. **(C)** What factors changed the reputation of Army aviation? **The establishment of the Aviation School and the Korean War.**
15. **(D)** What is the primary mission of the Sabalauski Air Assault School? **Training soldiers and leaders to conduct airmobile and air assault helicopter operations.**
16. **(B)** What is the primary subject of this passage? **The increasing acceptance and importance of dragoons in the Army.**
17. **(B)** From this passage, one can infer that **the disagreement over priorities between air and ground forces affects how wars are fought.**
18. **(C)** From this passage, one can infer that **scientists are divided about what caused the Big Bang to happen.**
19. **(E)** From this passage, one can infer that the writer believes that **people who don't accept responsibility are not as happy as those who do.** While the conclusions in choices (A) and (D) could logically proceed from some of the principles stated in the passage, they are not addressed as such and therefore cannot be accurately inferred from this passage alone.
20. **(A)** From this passage, one can infer that Lt. Gen. Wainwright **believed in sharing the dangers his men faced every day.**

Subtest 6: Math Skills Test (MST)

	✔	✘		✔	✘		✔	✘		✔	✘
1. B			6. C			11. E			16. A		
2. D			7. B			12. C			17. B		
3. C			8. C			13. A			18. E		
4. D			9. C			14. A			19. A		
5. A			10. B			15. B			20. C		

1. **(B)** There are 16 ounces in a pound. Therefore, if 2 lbs. of yogurt cost \$3.00, 1 lb. costs \$1.50. One ounce would be 1/16 of that:

$$\$1.50 \div 16 = \$0.09375$$

so 2 ounces would cost twice that:

$$\$0.09375 \times 2 = \$0.1875 = \mathbf{\$0.19}$$

2. **(D)** Set this up like a basic multiplication problem (because that's what it is). Multiply each term of $(3a - 2)$ by a and write the results as the first line of partial products (remember that the product of multiplying a positive number by a negative number is always negative). Next, multiply each term of $(3a-2)$ by (positive) 3 and write the results as the second line of partial products. Add the partial products as you would for any multiplication problem to get the final answer:

$$\begin{array}{r} 3a-2 \\ \times \ a+3 \\ \hline 3a^2-2a \quad \\ + \qquad 9a-6 \\ \hline \mathbf{3a^2+7a-6} \end{array}$$

3. **(C)** First we have to calculate how far Amanda traveled. To do that, we add the average speed for each of the 3 hours Amanda was on the road (since she drove for only an hour at each average speed, we don't have to calculate the average speed for her entire trip):

$$50 + 72 + 46 = 168$$

Then we divide the total miles driven, 168, by the average mileage (miles per gallon) Amanda's vehicle gets:

$$168 \div 23 = \mathbf{7.3\ gals.}$$

4. **(D)** Here's the simple way to do this: if the contractor needs 8 barrels to wet down a half mile, he will need 16 barrels of water to wet down a mile. That means he needs $16 \times 3 = 48$ barrels to sprinkle 3 miles; add in the 8 barrels for the last half mile, and you get $48 + 8 =$ **56** barrels to wet down 3.5 miles.

5. **(A)** If the same fence fits around the rectangular parking lot and the square garden, then their perimeters are equal. The perimeter of a rectangle is the sum of the lengths of its four sides:

$$P_{rect} = 40 + 36 + 40 + 36 = 152 \text{ ft.}$$

SIFT #1

The perimeter of a square is the sum of its four equal sides, so the length of one side is the perimeter divided by 4:

$$152 \div 4 = \mathbf{38\ ft.}$$

6. **(C)** In the first hour, the two planes will be a combined distance of 340 + 260 = 600 miles apart. Find out how long it will take for the two to be 1,800 miles apart by dividing:

$$1{,}800 \text{ miles} \div 600 \text{ mph} = \mathbf{3} \text{ hours}$$

7. **(B)** If 92% of the formation consisted of enlisted personnel, then the percentage of officers was 8%. To find the number of officers:

$$574 \text{ (total personnel)} \times .08 \text{ (percentage of officers)} = 45.92 \text{ officers}$$

Since we can't have .92% of a person (also, notice that the problem said "about 92%" were enlisted), we round that up to **46** officers for the correct answer.

8. **(C)** The GSR can cover a complete circle with a radius of 10 km. Because the 36-degree wedge (think of a slice of pie) is not a triangle (the base, part of the radius, is curved), we should first find the area of the circle that makes up the entire range of the GSR. To do this, we use the formula $A = \pi r^2$, where r is the radius:

$$A = 3.14 \times 10^2 = 3.14 \times 100 = 314 \text{ sq. km}$$

We know that there are 360 degrees in a circle; if the radar is used to cover a 36-degree portion of that circle, then that amount of area will be represented by the fraction

$$\frac{\text{number of degrees covered}}{\text{number of degrees in a circle}}$$

$$\frac{36 \text{ degrees}}{360 \text{ degrees}} = \frac{1}{10}$$

$$\frac{1}{10} \times 314 \text{ sq. km} = \mathbf{31.4\ sq.\ km}$$

9. **(C)** We are given a lot of information here that does not actually affect the problem, so the first thing we need to do is identify what information we need and what we don't. We don't need to know the model of her car; it doesn't matter what cities; and the length of her rest stops doesn't matter, because we are only asked how much time she actually spent driving. So the way to attack this problem is:

$$9.5 \text{ gallons of gas} \times 30 \text{ miles per gallon} = 285 \text{ miles traveled}$$

$$285 \text{ miles} \div 68 \text{ miles per hour} = 4.2 \text{ hours} = \mathbf{4\ hours,\ 12\ minutes}$$

(A tenth of an hour = .1 × 60 minutes = 6 minutes, so .2 hour = 12 minutes)

10. **(B)** There are four possible choices of the Apache company for the task force. Each of these choices could be paired with either of the two available Black Hawk companies. Each of these Apache–Black Hawk pairings could in turn be paired up with any of the three available Chinook companies. Therefore, there are $4 \times 2 \times 3 =$ **24** different combinations possible.

11. **(E)** The formula for the circumference of a circle is:

$$C \text{ (circumference)} = d \text{ (diameter)} \times \pi$$

The Chinook pilot flies in a circle with a radius of 40 km and, therefore, a diameter of 80 km:

$$C = 80 \text{ km} \times 22/7$$
$$C = (80 \times 22)/7$$
$$C = (1{,}760)/7$$
$$C = \mathbf{251 \text{ km}}$$

12. **(C)** A hexagon has six sides. Each of the six sides of a brown tile must touch the side of a tan tile, so there are six (**6**) tan tiles surrounding each brown tile.

13. **(A)** We can see that the sequence of numbers we are given starts with a low number and increases, so we know this is an ascending sequence. We can also see that every number is double the number before it, so this is an **ascending geometric sequence**. An arithmetic sequence proceeds by adding or subtracting the same number over and over again, for example: 20, 18, 16, 14, 12.

14. **(A)** The price of Travis' truck when he bought it was $43,999 but the current Blue Book valuation is 12% less. This means that the price his co-worker will pay is 88% (that is, 100% minus 12%) of $43,999. To get that number, multiply $43,999 × 0.88 = **$38,719**.

15. **(B)** To simplify this expression, we need to remember that dividing different exponents of the same variable is the same as multiplying by the opposite sign of the second term. The next thing to do is to add exponents of the same variables for the final result—watch your signs!

$$x^3y^4z^{-5}/x^{-2}y^{-3}z^2 =$$
$$x^3y^4z^{-5} \times x^2y^3z^{-2} =$$
$$x^{(3+2)}y^{(4+3)}z^{(-5-2)} = \mathbf{x^5y^7z^{-7}}$$

16. **(A)** We are told that $x^2/4$ and $x/4$ both yield the same result, so we can deduce that the two expressions are equal, and can be simplified:

$$x^2/4 = x/4$$

$$x^2 = x$$

The only possible values for this situation are 1 and 0. Since we are told that x is positive and 0 is neither positive nor negative, the answer is **1**.

17. **(B)** What we are looking for is to add up all the numbers from 1 to 1,000, so that's 1 + 2 + 3 . . . + 998 + 999 + 1,000! One way to do this, obviously, is to just add up all the numbers, divide by 1,000, and there you go. Surely there's an easier way—and there is. What we find is that if you add the first and last numbers together, starting with 1 and 1,000, you get 1,001. Okay, but thinking of all those numbers along a number line, if we move inward and add the next pair of "first and last," 2 and 999, we still get 1,001. So, do this 500 times, since we are looking at pairs of integers, and proceed from there:

$$1{,}001 \times 500 = 500{,}500$$

Divide that by 1,000 to get the average, and we get our final answer:

$$500{,}500 \div 1{,}000 = \mathbf{500.5}$$

18. **(E)** Looking at the equation, we see that 16^r is the same as 4^{2r}. So . . .

$$4^{2r} = 4^{-1/t}$$

Dividing both sides by 4 gives us just the exponents to work with:

$$2r = -1/t$$

Divide by 2 to get *r* by itself:

$$r = -.5/t$$

Now multiply by *t*:

$$rt = -.5$$

19. **(A)** If the first integer = *x*, then, since we are looking for the next consecutive odd integer, the second integer = *x* + 2 and the third integer = *x* + 4. Since four times the first integer equals six more than the product of two and the third integer:

$$4x = 6 + 2(x + 4)$$
$$4x = 6 + 2x + 8$$
$$2x = 14$$
$$x = 7$$

Therefore, the first integer is 7, the second integer is *x* + 2 = 7 + 2 = 9, and the third integer is *x* + 4 = 7 + 4 = 11.

20. **(C)** The probability of an event occurring is the number of trials in which the event occurred over (divided by) the total number of trials. In this case, that's **33/81** (or, simplified, 11/27). If no trials had occurred, we would say that there was a statistically even chance of any of the six sides showing up, or 1 chance out of 6 (1/6).

Subtest 7: Mechanical Comprehension Test (MCT)

	✔	✘		✔	✘		✔	✘		✔	✘
1. C			**6. B**			**11. D**			**16. A**		
2. A			**7. E**			**12. C**			**17. C**		
3. A			**8. A**			**13. B**			**18. B**		
4. C			**9. A**			**14. C**			**19. D**		
5. A			**10. A**			**15. B**			**20. B**		

1. **(C)** Gears A and D are in constant mesh, and F is too small.
2. **(A)** When the lobe (high spot) on cam A makes contact with the follower (roller) on the contact arm, the contact will close. Because cam A has only one lobe, the contacts will close **one** time per revolution.
3. **(A)** To calculate the revolutions of gear B, use this formula: $r = \frac{(D \times R)}{d}$ where

   D = number of teeth on gear A;
   R = revolutions of gear A;
   d = number of teeth on gear B;
   r = revolutions of gear B;

$$r = \frac{(D \times R)}{d}$$

$$r = \frac{(15 \times 14)}{10}$$

$$r = \frac{210}{10}$$

$$r = \mathbf{21}$$

4. **(C)** Gears that are meshed turn in opposite directions. Gear 2 is turning clockwise; gears 1 and 3 are turning counterclockwise.
5. **(A)** Hydrometers use floats to measure specific gravity. Specific gravity is the weight of a liquid compared with the weight of the water. The liquid with the highest specific gravity will cause the float to rise higher in the glass tube.
6. **(B)** On a **second-class lever**, the fulcrum is at one end, the effort is at the other end, and the load is in between.
7. **(E)** The angle of the rope, θ, determines if the box is being pulled or dragged along the floor or being lifted from the floor. That means it can be both lifted and pulled along any angle that is more than 0 degrees and less than 90 degrees.
8. **(A)** The fulcrum is positioned between the effort and the load on a **first-class lever**.
9. **(A)** The shaft of the pivot is at T and S. The high spot (lobe) of the cam is between **Q and R**.
10. **(A)** When a series of pulleys is connected by drive belts, the pulley with the smallest diameter rotates at the highest speed; the smallest pulley will turn the fastest.
11. **(D)** When gears are meshed, they turn in opposite directions. X and Y are therefore turning in opposite directions. However, because both **E and F** are meshed with Y, they are both turning in the same direction as X.
12. **(C)** On a **third-class lever**, the fulcrum is at one end, the load is at the other, and the effect is between the fulcrum and the load.
13. **(B)** Two meshed gears turn in opposite directions. When an idler gear (gear I is the idler in this example) is placed between the two, both turn in the same direction. The idler gear turns in direction 1.
14. **(C)** Because there are three ropes supporting block B, they are under $\frac{1}{3}$ of the tension as the rope supporting block A.
15. **(B)** Centrifugal force from the spin (it doesn't matter which direction) will cause the balls to move **outward**, and the tension on the strings holding them will result in the balls moving **upward**.
16. **(A)** Water is flowing into the water tower at 120 gallons per hour. To convert that to gallons per minute, we divide 120 gallons by the 60 minutes in an hour, resulting in a rate of 2 gallons per minute coming into the water tower. Therefore, the level of water in the tower will **remain the same**.

SIFT #1

17. **(C)** The farther away the fulcrum is from the resistance arm, the greater the amount of force that is required to lift the weight and the higher the resistance arm will travel.

18. **(B)** **Mass remains constant, but the weight of an object depends on its altitude**—or, said differently, its distance from the gravitational pull of Earth.

19. **(D)** Pulley C will **rotate in the same direction as pulley A**. Pulley A causes pulley B to rotate in the opposite direction from pulley A, and pulley B causes pulley C to rotate in the opposite direction from pulley B—which (there being only two directions of rotation available) is the same direction as pulley A.

20. **(B)** **Pulley B** will rotate the fastest. In the same way as meshing gears, the smaller the pulley in a system, the faster it rotates.

ANSWER SHEET
SIFT #2

Subtest 1: Simple Drawings (SD)

1. Ⓐ Ⓑ Ⓒ Ⓓ Ⓔ
2. Ⓐ Ⓑ Ⓒ Ⓓ Ⓔ
3. Ⓐ Ⓑ Ⓒ Ⓓ Ⓔ
4. Ⓐ Ⓑ Ⓒ Ⓓ Ⓔ
5. Ⓐ Ⓑ Ⓒ Ⓓ Ⓔ
6. Ⓐ Ⓑ Ⓒ Ⓓ Ⓔ
7. Ⓐ Ⓑ Ⓒ Ⓓ Ⓔ
8. Ⓐ Ⓑ Ⓒ Ⓓ Ⓔ
9. Ⓐ Ⓑ Ⓒ Ⓓ Ⓔ
10. Ⓐ Ⓑ Ⓒ Ⓓ Ⓔ
11. Ⓐ Ⓑ Ⓒ Ⓓ Ⓔ
12. Ⓐ Ⓑ Ⓒ Ⓓ Ⓔ
13. Ⓐ Ⓑ Ⓒ Ⓓ Ⓔ
14. Ⓐ Ⓑ Ⓒ Ⓓ Ⓔ
15. Ⓐ Ⓑ Ⓒ Ⓓ Ⓔ
16. Ⓐ Ⓑ Ⓒ Ⓓ Ⓔ
17. Ⓐ Ⓑ Ⓒ Ⓓ Ⓔ
18. Ⓐ Ⓑ Ⓒ Ⓓ Ⓔ
19. Ⓐ Ⓑ Ⓒ Ⓓ Ⓔ
20. Ⓐ Ⓑ Ⓒ Ⓓ Ⓔ
21. Ⓐ Ⓑ Ⓒ Ⓓ Ⓔ
22. Ⓐ Ⓑ Ⓒ Ⓓ Ⓔ
23. Ⓐ Ⓑ Ⓒ Ⓓ Ⓔ
24. Ⓐ Ⓑ Ⓒ Ⓓ Ⓔ
25. Ⓐ Ⓑ Ⓒ Ⓓ Ⓔ
26. Ⓐ Ⓑ Ⓒ Ⓓ Ⓔ
27. Ⓐ Ⓑ Ⓒ Ⓓ Ⓔ
28. Ⓐ Ⓑ Ⓒ Ⓓ Ⓔ
29. Ⓐ Ⓑ Ⓒ Ⓓ Ⓔ
30. Ⓐ Ⓑ Ⓒ Ⓓ Ⓔ
31. Ⓐ Ⓑ Ⓒ Ⓓ Ⓔ
32. Ⓐ Ⓑ Ⓒ Ⓓ Ⓔ
33. Ⓐ Ⓑ Ⓒ Ⓓ Ⓔ
34. Ⓐ Ⓑ Ⓒ Ⓓ Ⓔ
35. Ⓐ Ⓑ Ⓒ Ⓓ Ⓔ
36. Ⓐ Ⓑ Ⓒ Ⓓ Ⓔ
37. Ⓐ Ⓑ Ⓒ Ⓓ Ⓔ
38. Ⓐ Ⓑ Ⓒ Ⓓ Ⓔ
39. Ⓐ Ⓑ Ⓒ Ⓓ Ⓔ
40. Ⓐ Ⓑ Ⓒ Ⓓ Ⓔ
41. Ⓐ Ⓑ Ⓒ Ⓓ Ⓔ
42. Ⓐ Ⓑ Ⓒ Ⓓ Ⓔ
43. Ⓐ Ⓑ Ⓒ Ⓓ Ⓔ
44. Ⓐ Ⓑ Ⓒ Ⓓ Ⓔ
45. Ⓐ Ⓑ Ⓒ Ⓓ Ⓔ
46. Ⓐ Ⓑ Ⓒ Ⓓ Ⓔ
47. Ⓐ Ⓑ Ⓒ Ⓓ Ⓔ
48. Ⓐ Ⓑ Ⓒ Ⓓ Ⓔ
49. Ⓐ Ⓑ Ⓒ Ⓓ Ⓔ
50. Ⓐ Ⓑ Ⓒ Ⓓ Ⓔ
51. Ⓐ Ⓑ Ⓒ Ⓓ Ⓔ
52. Ⓐ Ⓑ Ⓒ Ⓓ Ⓔ
53. Ⓐ Ⓑ Ⓒ Ⓓ Ⓔ
54. Ⓐ Ⓑ Ⓒ Ⓓ Ⓔ
55. Ⓐ Ⓑ Ⓒ Ⓓ Ⓔ
56. Ⓐ Ⓑ Ⓒ Ⓓ Ⓔ
57. Ⓐ Ⓑ Ⓒ Ⓓ Ⓔ
58. Ⓐ Ⓑ Ⓒ Ⓓ Ⓔ
59. Ⓐ Ⓑ Ⓒ Ⓓ Ⓔ
60. Ⓐ Ⓑ Ⓒ Ⓓ Ⓔ
61. Ⓐ Ⓑ Ⓒ Ⓓ Ⓔ
62. Ⓐ Ⓑ Ⓒ Ⓓ Ⓔ
63. Ⓐ Ⓑ Ⓒ Ⓓ Ⓔ
64. Ⓐ Ⓑ Ⓒ Ⓓ Ⓔ
65. Ⓐ Ⓑ Ⓒ Ⓓ Ⓔ
66. Ⓐ Ⓑ Ⓒ Ⓓ Ⓔ
67. Ⓐ Ⓑ Ⓒ Ⓓ Ⓔ
68. Ⓐ Ⓑ Ⓒ Ⓓ Ⓔ
69. Ⓐ Ⓑ Ⓒ Ⓓ Ⓔ
70. Ⓐ Ⓑ Ⓒ Ⓓ Ⓔ
71. Ⓐ Ⓑ Ⓒ Ⓓ Ⓔ
72. Ⓐ Ⓑ Ⓒ Ⓓ Ⓔ
73. Ⓐ Ⓑ Ⓒ Ⓓ Ⓔ
74. Ⓐ Ⓑ Ⓒ Ⓓ Ⓔ
75. Ⓐ Ⓑ Ⓒ Ⓓ Ⓔ
76. Ⓐ Ⓑ Ⓒ Ⓓ Ⓔ
77. Ⓐ Ⓑ Ⓒ Ⓓ Ⓔ
78. Ⓐ Ⓑ Ⓒ Ⓓ Ⓔ
79. Ⓐ Ⓑ Ⓒ Ⓓ Ⓔ
80. Ⓐ Ⓑ Ⓒ Ⓓ Ⓔ
81. Ⓐ Ⓑ Ⓒ Ⓓ Ⓔ
82. Ⓐ Ⓑ Ⓒ Ⓓ Ⓔ
83. Ⓐ Ⓑ Ⓒ Ⓓ Ⓔ
84. Ⓐ Ⓑ Ⓒ Ⓓ Ⓔ
85. Ⓐ Ⓑ Ⓒ Ⓓ Ⓔ
86. Ⓐ Ⓑ Ⓒ Ⓓ Ⓔ
87. Ⓐ Ⓑ Ⓒ Ⓓ Ⓔ
88. Ⓐ Ⓑ Ⓒ Ⓓ Ⓔ
89. Ⓐ Ⓑ Ⓒ Ⓓ Ⓔ
90. Ⓐ Ⓑ Ⓒ Ⓓ Ⓔ
91. Ⓐ Ⓑ Ⓒ Ⓓ Ⓔ
92. Ⓐ Ⓑ Ⓒ Ⓓ Ⓔ
93. Ⓐ Ⓑ Ⓒ Ⓓ Ⓔ
94. Ⓐ Ⓑ Ⓒ Ⓓ Ⓔ
95. Ⓐ Ⓑ Ⓒ Ⓓ Ⓔ
96. Ⓐ Ⓑ Ⓒ Ⓓ Ⓔ
97. Ⓐ Ⓑ Ⓒ Ⓓ Ⓔ
98. Ⓐ Ⓑ Ⓒ Ⓓ Ⓔ
99. Ⓐ Ⓑ Ⓒ Ⓓ Ⓔ
100. Ⓐ Ⓑ Ⓒ Ⓓ Ⓔ

Subtest 2: Hidden Figures (HF)

1. Ⓐ Ⓑ Ⓒ Ⓓ Ⓔ
2. Ⓐ Ⓑ Ⓒ Ⓓ Ⓔ
3. Ⓐ Ⓑ Ⓒ Ⓓ Ⓔ
4. Ⓐ Ⓑ Ⓒ Ⓓ Ⓔ
5. Ⓐ Ⓑ Ⓒ Ⓓ Ⓔ
6. Ⓐ Ⓑ Ⓒ Ⓓ Ⓔ
7. Ⓐ Ⓑ Ⓒ Ⓓ Ⓔ
8. Ⓐ Ⓑ Ⓒ Ⓓ Ⓔ
9. Ⓐ Ⓑ Ⓒ Ⓓ Ⓔ
10. Ⓐ Ⓑ Ⓒ Ⓓ Ⓔ
11. Ⓐ Ⓑ Ⓒ Ⓓ Ⓔ
12. Ⓐ Ⓑ Ⓒ Ⓓ Ⓔ
13. Ⓐ Ⓑ Ⓒ Ⓓ Ⓔ
14. Ⓐ Ⓑ Ⓒ Ⓓ Ⓔ
15. Ⓐ Ⓑ Ⓒ Ⓓ Ⓔ
16. Ⓐ Ⓑ Ⓒ Ⓓ Ⓔ
17. Ⓐ Ⓑ Ⓒ Ⓓ Ⓔ
18. Ⓐ Ⓑ Ⓒ Ⓓ Ⓔ
19. Ⓐ Ⓑ Ⓒ Ⓓ Ⓔ
20. Ⓐ Ⓑ Ⓒ Ⓓ Ⓔ
21. Ⓐ Ⓑ Ⓒ Ⓓ Ⓔ
22. Ⓐ Ⓑ Ⓒ Ⓓ Ⓔ
23. Ⓐ Ⓑ Ⓒ Ⓓ Ⓔ
24. Ⓐ Ⓑ Ⓒ Ⓓ Ⓔ
25. Ⓐ Ⓑ Ⓒ Ⓓ Ⓔ
26. Ⓐ Ⓑ Ⓒ Ⓓ Ⓔ
27. Ⓐ Ⓑ Ⓒ Ⓓ Ⓔ
28. Ⓐ Ⓑ Ⓒ Ⓓ Ⓔ
29. Ⓐ Ⓑ Ⓒ Ⓓ Ⓔ
30. Ⓐ Ⓑ Ⓒ Ⓓ Ⓔ
31. Ⓐ Ⓑ Ⓒ Ⓓ Ⓔ
32. Ⓐ Ⓑ Ⓒ Ⓓ Ⓔ
33. Ⓐ Ⓑ Ⓒ Ⓓ Ⓔ
34. Ⓐ Ⓑ Ⓒ Ⓓ Ⓔ
35. Ⓐ Ⓑ Ⓒ Ⓓ Ⓔ
36. Ⓐ Ⓑ Ⓒ Ⓓ Ⓔ
37. Ⓐ Ⓑ Ⓒ Ⓓ Ⓔ
38. Ⓐ Ⓑ Ⓒ Ⓓ Ⓔ
39. Ⓐ Ⓑ Ⓒ Ⓓ Ⓔ
40. Ⓐ Ⓑ Ⓒ Ⓓ Ⓔ
41. Ⓐ Ⓑ Ⓒ Ⓓ Ⓔ
42. Ⓐ Ⓑ Ⓒ Ⓓ Ⓔ
43. Ⓐ Ⓑ Ⓒ Ⓓ Ⓔ
44. Ⓐ Ⓑ Ⓒ Ⓓ Ⓔ
45. Ⓐ Ⓑ Ⓒ Ⓓ Ⓔ
46. Ⓐ Ⓑ Ⓒ Ⓓ Ⓔ
47. Ⓐ Ⓑ Ⓒ Ⓓ Ⓔ
48. Ⓐ Ⓑ Ⓒ Ⓓ Ⓔ
49. Ⓐ Ⓑ Ⓒ Ⓓ Ⓔ
50. Ⓐ Ⓑ Ⓒ Ⓓ Ⓔ

ANSWER SHEET
SIFT #2

Subtest 3: Army Aviation Information Test (AAIT)

1. Ⓐ Ⓑ Ⓒ Ⓓ Ⓔ
2. Ⓐ Ⓑ Ⓒ Ⓓ Ⓔ
3. Ⓐ Ⓑ Ⓒ Ⓓ Ⓔ
4. Ⓐ Ⓑ Ⓒ Ⓓ Ⓔ
5. Ⓐ Ⓑ Ⓒ Ⓓ Ⓔ
6. Ⓐ Ⓑ Ⓒ Ⓓ Ⓔ
7. Ⓐ Ⓑ Ⓒ Ⓓ Ⓔ
8. Ⓐ Ⓑ Ⓒ Ⓓ Ⓔ
9. Ⓐ Ⓑ Ⓒ Ⓓ Ⓔ
10. Ⓐ Ⓑ Ⓒ Ⓓ Ⓔ
11. Ⓐ Ⓑ Ⓒ Ⓓ Ⓔ
12. Ⓐ Ⓑ Ⓒ Ⓓ Ⓔ
13. Ⓐ Ⓑ Ⓒ Ⓓ Ⓔ
14. Ⓐ Ⓑ Ⓒ Ⓓ Ⓔ
15. Ⓐ Ⓑ Ⓒ Ⓓ Ⓔ
16. Ⓐ Ⓑ Ⓒ Ⓓ Ⓔ
17. Ⓐ Ⓑ Ⓒ Ⓓ Ⓔ
18. Ⓐ Ⓑ Ⓒ Ⓓ Ⓔ
19. Ⓐ Ⓑ Ⓒ Ⓓ Ⓔ
20. Ⓐ Ⓑ Ⓒ Ⓓ Ⓔ
21. Ⓐ Ⓑ Ⓒ Ⓓ Ⓔ
22. Ⓐ Ⓑ Ⓒ Ⓓ Ⓔ
23. Ⓐ Ⓑ Ⓒ Ⓓ Ⓔ
24. Ⓐ Ⓑ Ⓒ Ⓓ Ⓔ
25. Ⓐ Ⓑ Ⓒ Ⓓ Ⓔ
26. Ⓐ Ⓑ Ⓒ Ⓓ Ⓔ
27. Ⓐ Ⓑ Ⓒ Ⓓ Ⓔ
28. Ⓐ Ⓑ Ⓒ Ⓓ Ⓔ
29. Ⓐ Ⓑ Ⓒ Ⓓ Ⓔ
30. Ⓐ Ⓑ Ⓒ Ⓓ Ⓔ
31. Ⓐ Ⓑ Ⓒ Ⓓ Ⓔ
32. Ⓐ Ⓑ Ⓒ Ⓓ Ⓔ
33. Ⓐ Ⓑ Ⓒ Ⓓ Ⓔ
34. Ⓐ Ⓑ Ⓒ Ⓓ Ⓔ
35. Ⓐ Ⓑ Ⓒ Ⓓ Ⓔ
36. Ⓐ Ⓑ Ⓒ Ⓓ Ⓔ
37. Ⓐ Ⓑ Ⓒ Ⓓ Ⓔ
38. Ⓐ Ⓑ Ⓒ Ⓓ Ⓔ
39. Ⓐ Ⓑ Ⓒ Ⓓ Ⓔ
40. Ⓐ Ⓑ Ⓒ Ⓓ Ⓔ

Subtest 4: Spatial Apperception Test (SAT)

1. Ⓐ Ⓑ Ⓒ Ⓓ Ⓔ
2. Ⓐ Ⓑ Ⓒ Ⓓ Ⓔ
3. Ⓐ Ⓑ Ⓒ Ⓓ Ⓔ
4. Ⓐ Ⓑ Ⓒ Ⓓ Ⓔ
5. Ⓐ Ⓑ Ⓒ Ⓓ Ⓔ
6. Ⓐ Ⓑ Ⓒ Ⓓ Ⓔ
7. Ⓐ Ⓑ Ⓒ Ⓓ Ⓔ
8. Ⓐ Ⓑ Ⓒ Ⓓ Ⓔ
9. Ⓐ Ⓑ Ⓒ Ⓓ Ⓔ
10. Ⓐ Ⓑ Ⓒ Ⓓ Ⓔ
11. Ⓐ Ⓑ Ⓒ Ⓓ Ⓔ
12. Ⓐ Ⓑ Ⓒ Ⓓ Ⓔ
13. Ⓐ Ⓑ Ⓒ Ⓓ Ⓔ
14. Ⓐ Ⓑ Ⓒ Ⓓ Ⓔ
15. Ⓐ Ⓑ Ⓒ Ⓓ Ⓔ
16. Ⓐ Ⓑ Ⓒ Ⓓ Ⓔ
17. Ⓐ Ⓑ Ⓒ Ⓓ Ⓔ
18. Ⓐ Ⓑ Ⓒ Ⓓ Ⓔ
19. Ⓐ Ⓑ Ⓒ Ⓓ Ⓔ
20. Ⓐ Ⓑ Ⓒ Ⓓ Ⓔ
21. Ⓐ Ⓑ Ⓒ Ⓓ Ⓔ
22. Ⓐ Ⓑ Ⓒ Ⓓ Ⓔ
23. Ⓐ Ⓑ Ⓒ Ⓓ Ⓔ
24. Ⓐ Ⓑ Ⓒ Ⓓ Ⓔ
25. Ⓐ Ⓑ Ⓒ Ⓓ Ⓔ

Subtest 5: Reading Comprehension Test (RCT)

1. Ⓐ Ⓑ Ⓒ Ⓓ Ⓔ
2. Ⓐ Ⓑ Ⓒ Ⓓ Ⓔ
3. Ⓐ Ⓑ Ⓒ Ⓓ Ⓔ
4. Ⓐ Ⓑ Ⓒ Ⓓ Ⓔ
5. Ⓐ Ⓑ Ⓒ Ⓓ Ⓔ
6. Ⓐ Ⓑ Ⓒ Ⓓ Ⓔ
7. Ⓐ Ⓑ Ⓒ Ⓓ Ⓔ
8. Ⓐ Ⓑ Ⓒ Ⓓ Ⓔ
9. Ⓐ Ⓑ Ⓒ Ⓓ Ⓔ
10. Ⓐ Ⓑ Ⓒ Ⓓ Ⓔ
11. Ⓐ Ⓑ Ⓒ Ⓓ Ⓔ
12. Ⓐ Ⓑ Ⓒ Ⓓ Ⓔ
13. Ⓐ Ⓑ Ⓒ Ⓓ Ⓔ
14. Ⓐ Ⓑ Ⓒ Ⓓ Ⓔ
15. Ⓐ Ⓑ Ⓒ Ⓓ Ⓔ
16. Ⓐ Ⓑ Ⓒ Ⓓ Ⓔ
17. Ⓐ Ⓑ Ⓒ Ⓓ Ⓔ
18. Ⓐ Ⓑ Ⓒ Ⓓ Ⓔ
19. Ⓐ Ⓑ Ⓒ Ⓓ Ⓔ
20. Ⓐ Ⓑ Ⓒ Ⓓ Ⓔ

Subtest 6: Math Skills Test (MST)

1. Ⓐ Ⓑ Ⓒ Ⓓ Ⓔ
2. Ⓐ Ⓑ Ⓒ Ⓓ Ⓔ
3. Ⓐ Ⓑ Ⓒ Ⓓ Ⓔ
4. Ⓐ Ⓑ Ⓒ Ⓓ Ⓔ
5. Ⓐ Ⓑ Ⓒ Ⓓ Ⓔ
6. Ⓐ Ⓑ Ⓒ Ⓓ Ⓔ
7. Ⓐ Ⓑ Ⓒ Ⓓ Ⓔ
8. Ⓐ Ⓑ Ⓒ Ⓓ Ⓔ
9. Ⓐ Ⓑ Ⓒ Ⓓ Ⓔ
10. Ⓐ Ⓑ Ⓒ Ⓓ Ⓔ
11. Ⓐ Ⓑ Ⓒ Ⓓ Ⓔ
12. Ⓐ Ⓑ Ⓒ Ⓓ Ⓔ
13. Ⓐ Ⓑ Ⓒ Ⓓ Ⓔ
14. Ⓐ Ⓑ Ⓒ Ⓓ Ⓔ
15. Ⓐ Ⓑ Ⓒ Ⓓ Ⓔ
16. Ⓐ Ⓑ Ⓒ Ⓓ Ⓔ
17. Ⓐ Ⓑ Ⓒ Ⓓ Ⓔ
18. Ⓐ Ⓑ Ⓒ Ⓓ Ⓔ
19. Ⓐ Ⓑ Ⓒ Ⓓ Ⓔ
20. Ⓐ Ⓑ Ⓒ Ⓓ Ⓔ

Subtest 7: Mechanical Comprehension Test (MCT)

1. Ⓐ Ⓑ Ⓒ Ⓓ Ⓔ
2. Ⓐ Ⓑ Ⓒ Ⓓ Ⓔ
3. Ⓐ Ⓑ Ⓒ Ⓓ Ⓔ
4. Ⓐ Ⓑ Ⓒ Ⓓ Ⓔ
5. Ⓐ Ⓑ Ⓒ Ⓓ Ⓔ
6. Ⓐ Ⓑ Ⓒ Ⓓ Ⓔ
7. Ⓐ Ⓑ Ⓒ Ⓓ Ⓔ
8. Ⓐ Ⓑ Ⓒ Ⓓ Ⓔ
9. Ⓐ Ⓑ Ⓒ Ⓓ Ⓔ
10. Ⓐ Ⓑ Ⓒ Ⓓ Ⓔ
11. Ⓐ Ⓑ Ⓒ Ⓓ Ⓔ
12. Ⓐ Ⓑ Ⓒ Ⓓ Ⓔ
13. Ⓐ Ⓑ Ⓒ Ⓓ Ⓔ
14. Ⓐ Ⓑ Ⓒ Ⓓ Ⓔ
15. Ⓐ Ⓑ Ⓒ Ⓓ Ⓔ
16. Ⓐ Ⓑ Ⓒ Ⓓ Ⓔ
17. Ⓐ Ⓑ Ⓒ Ⓓ Ⓔ
18. Ⓐ Ⓑ Ⓒ Ⓓ Ⓔ
19. Ⓐ Ⓑ Ⓒ Ⓓ Ⓔ
20. Ⓐ Ⓑ Ⓒ Ⓓ Ⓔ

13 Army Selection Instrument for Flight Training (SIFT) Practice Test #2

Please turn to the beginning of Chapter 12, page 415, for more information about the breakdown and scoring attributes of the Army's Selection Instrument for Flight Training (SIFT).

SUBTEST 1: SIMPLE DRAWINGS (SD)

100 Questions

1. (A) (B) (C) (D) (E)

2. (A) (B) (C) (D) (E)

3. (A) (B) (C) (D) (E)

4. (A) (B) (C) (D) (E)

5. (A) (B) (C) (D) (E)

6. (A) (B) (C) (D) (E)

7. (A) (B) (C) (D) (E)

8. (A) (B) (C) (D) (E)

9. (A) (B) (C) (D) (E)

10. (A) (B) (C) (D) (E)

11. (A) (B) (C) (D) (E)

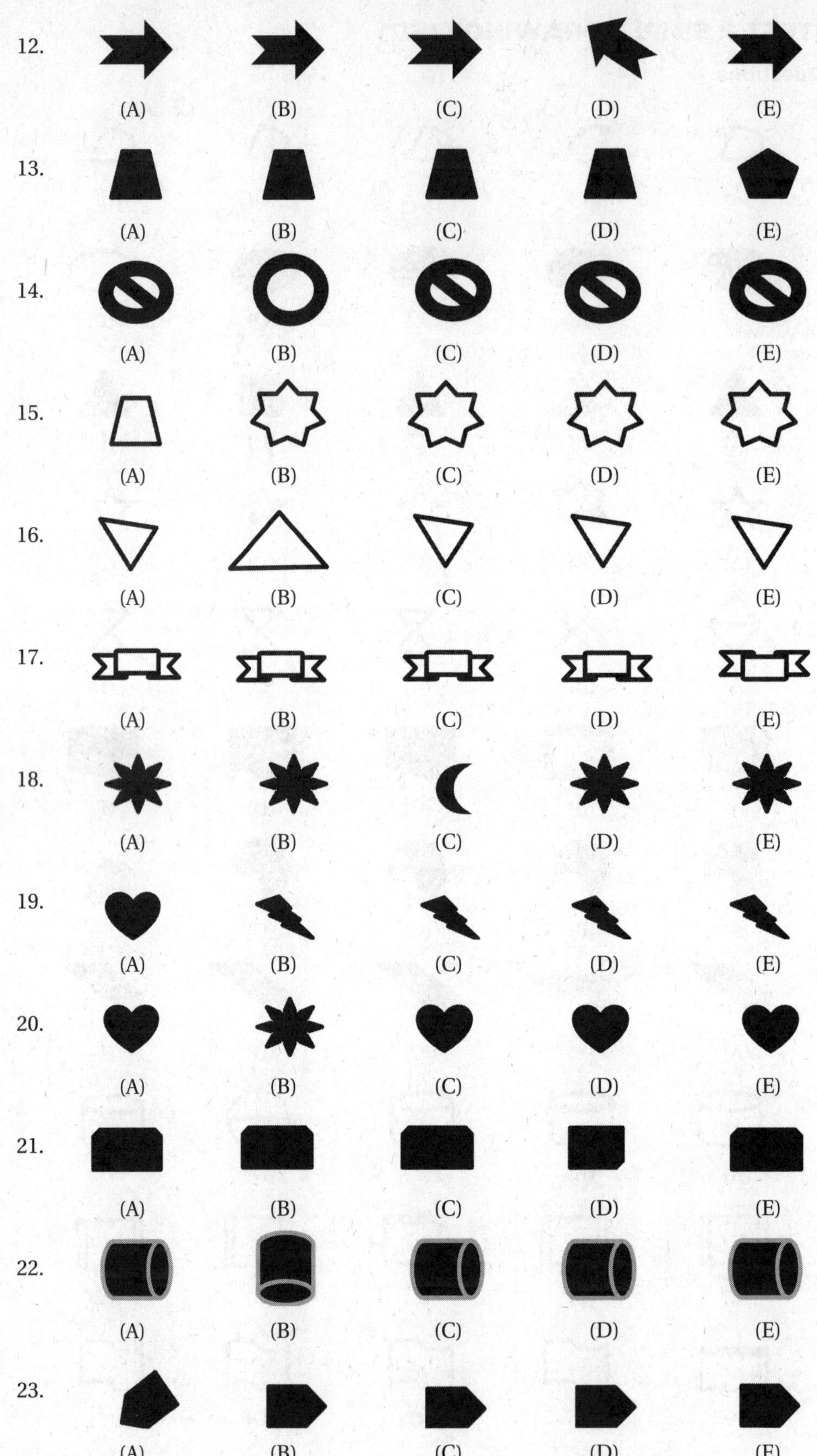
12.
(A)
(B)
(C)
(D)
(E)
13.
(A)
(B)
(C)
(D)
(E)
14.
(A)
(B)
(C)
(D)
(E)
15.
(A)
(B)
(C)
(D)
(E)
16.
(A)
(B)
(C)
(D)
(E)
17.
(A)
(B)
(C)
(D)
(E)
18.
(A)
(B)
(C)
(D)
(E)
19.
(A)
(B)
(C)
(D)
(E)
20.
(A)
(B)
(C)
(D)
(E)
21.
(A)
(B)
(C)
(D)
(E)
22.
(A)
(B)
(C)
(D)
(E)
23.
(A)
(B)
(C)
(D)
(E)

SIFT #2

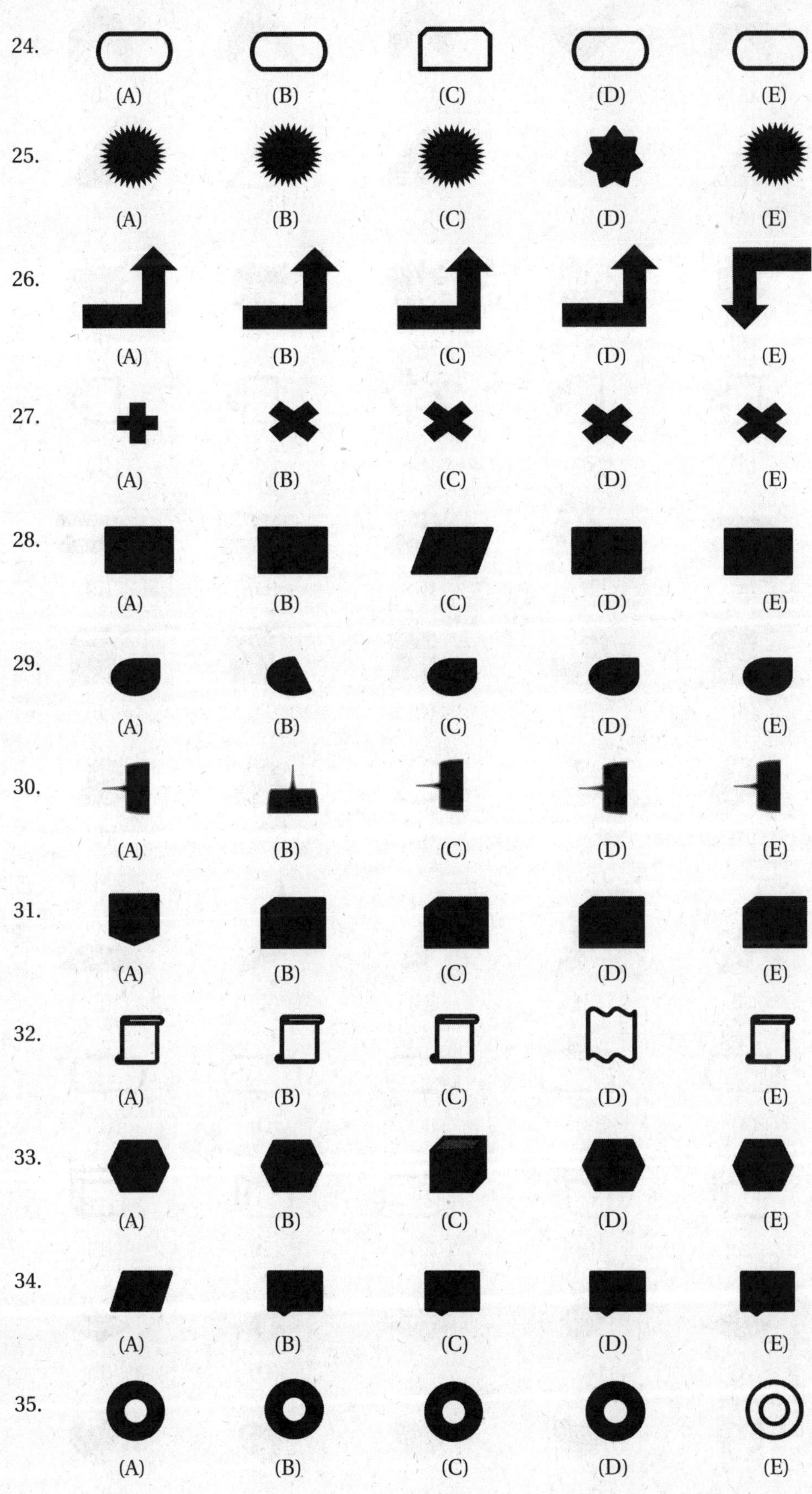
24. (A) (B) (C) (D) (E)
25. (A) (B) (C) (D) (E)
26. (A) (B) (C) (D) (E)
27. (A) (B) (C) (D) (E)
28. (A) (B) (C) (D) (E)
29. (A) (B) (C) (D) (E)
30. (A) (B) (C) (D) (E)
31. (A) (B) (C) (D) (E)
32. (A) (B) (C) (D) (E)
33. (A) (B) (C) (D) (E)
34. (A) (B) (C) (D) (E)
35. (A) (B) (C) (D) (E)

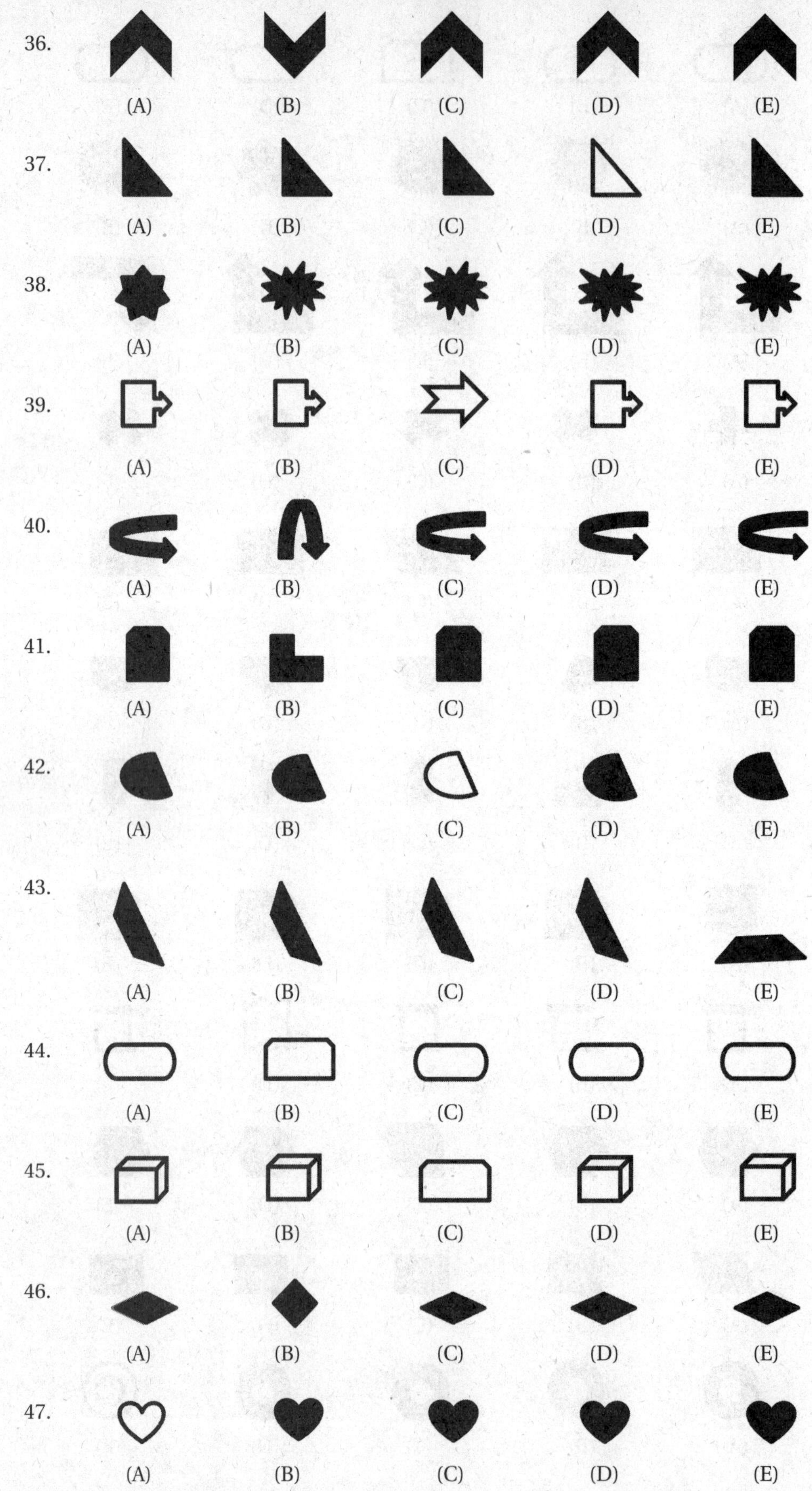
36.
(A)
(B)
(C)
(D)
(E)
37.
(A)
(B)
(C)
(D)
(E)
38.
(A)
(B)
(C)
(D)
(E)
39.
(A)
(B)
(C)
(D)
(E)
40.
(A)
(B)
(C)
(D)
(E)
41.
(A)
(B)
(C)
(D)
(E)
42.
(A)
(B)
(C)
(D)
(E)
43.
(A)
(B)
(C)
(D)
(E)
44.
(A)
(B)
(C)
(D)
(E)
45.
(A)
(B)
(C)
(D)
(E)
46.
(A)
(B)
(C)
(D)
(E)
47.
(A)
(B)
(C)
(D)
(E)

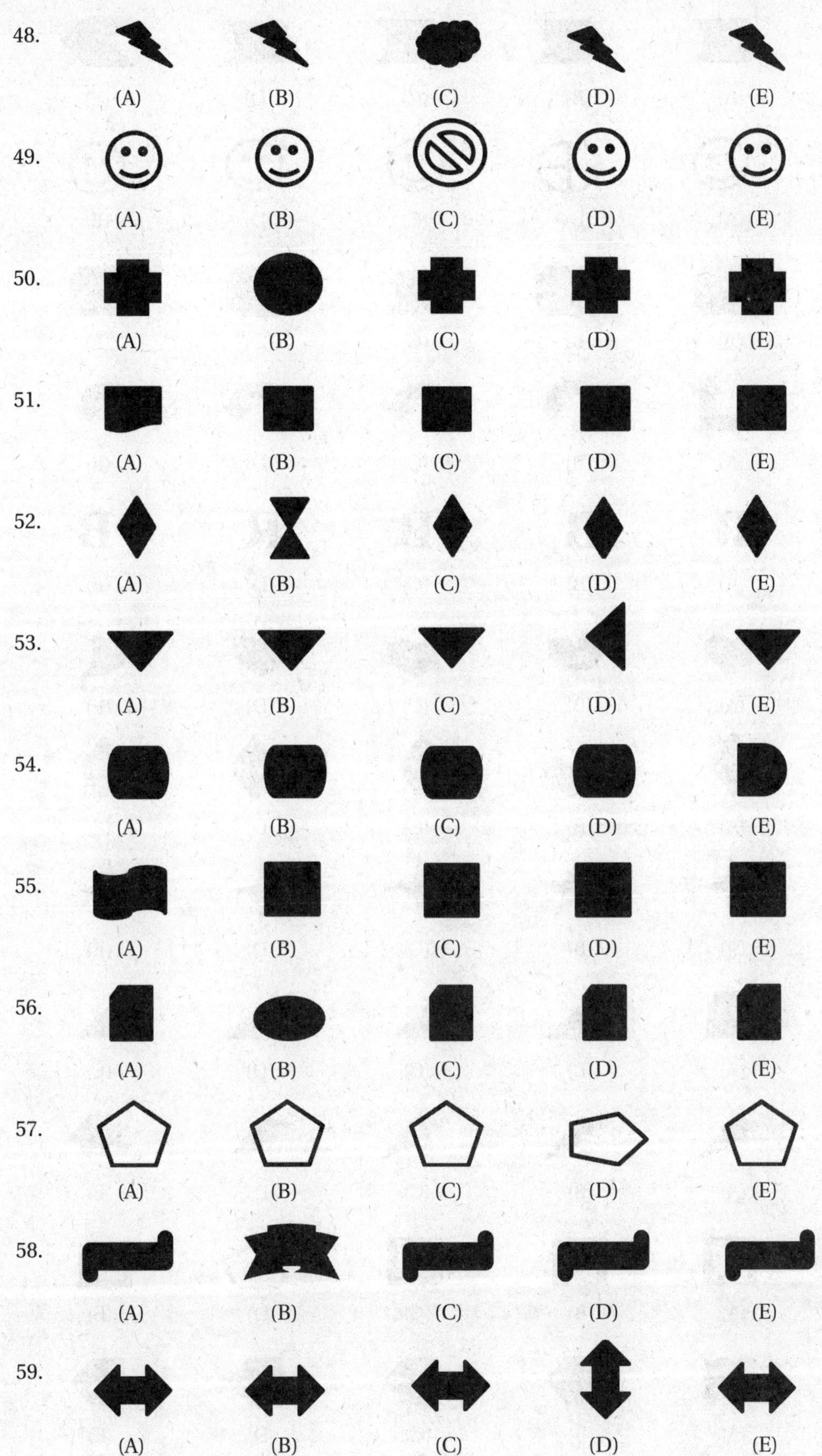
48.
(A)
(B)
(C)
(D)
(E)
49.
(A)
(B)
(C)
(D)
(E)
50.
(A)
(B)
(C)
(D)
(E)
51.
(A)
(B)
(C)
(D)
(E)
52.
(A)
(B)
(C)
(D)
(E)
53.
(A)
(B)
(C)
(D)
(E)
54.
(A)
(B)
(C)
(D)
(E)
55.
(A)
(B)
(C)
(D)
(E)
56.
(A)
(B)
(C)
(D)
(E)
57.
(A)
(B)
(C)
(D)
(E)
58.
(A)
(B)
(C)
(D)
(E)
59.
(A)
(B)
(C)
(D)
(E)

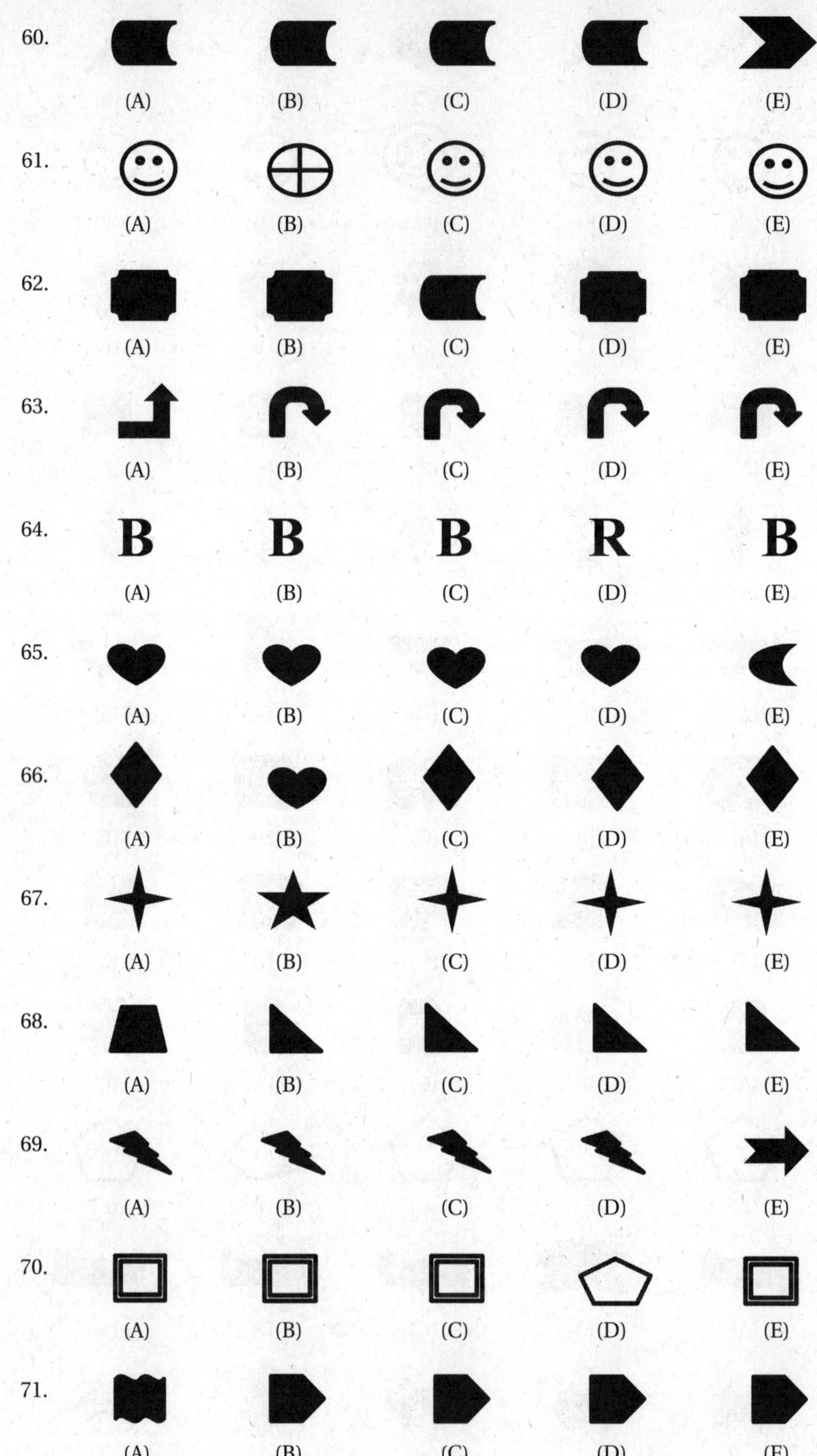
60.
(A)
(B)
(C)
(D)
(E)
61.
(A)
(B)
(C)
(D)
(E)
62.
(A)
(B)
(C)
(D)
(E)
63.
(A)
(B)
(C)
(D)
(E)
64.
B
B
B
R
B
(A)
(B)
(C)
(D)
(E)
65.
(A)
(B)
(C)
(D)
(E)
66.
(A)
(B)
(C)
(D)
(E)
67.
(A)
(B)
(C)
(D)
(E)
68.
(A)
(B)
(C)
(D)
(E)
69.
(A)
(B)
(C)
(D)
(E)
70.
(A)
(B)
(C)
(D)
(E)
71.
(A)
(B)
(C)
(D)
(E)

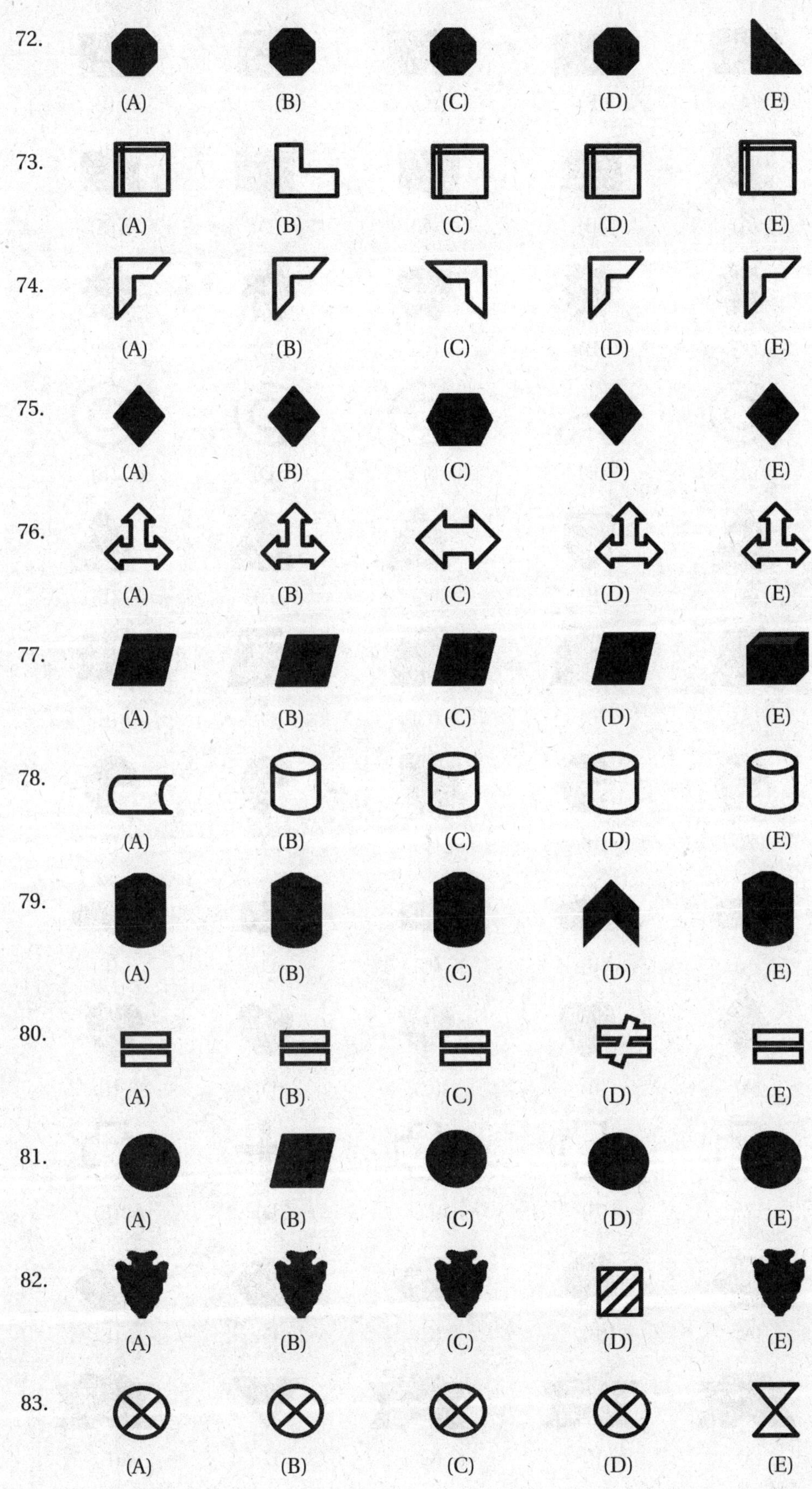
72.
(A)
(B)
(C)
(D)
(E)
73.
(A)
(B)
(C)
(D)
(E)
74.
(A)
(B)
(C)
(D)
(E)
75.
(A)
(B)
(C)
(D)
(E)
76.
(A)
(B)
(C)
(D)
(E)
77.
(A)
(B)
(C)
(D)
(E)
78.
(A)
(B)
(C)
(D)
(E)
79.
(A)
(B)
(C)
(D)
(E)
80.
(A)
(B)
(C)
(D)
(E)
81.
(A)
(B)
(C)
(D)
(E)
82.
(A)
(B)
(C)
(D)
(E)
83.
(A)
(B)
(C)
(D)
(E)

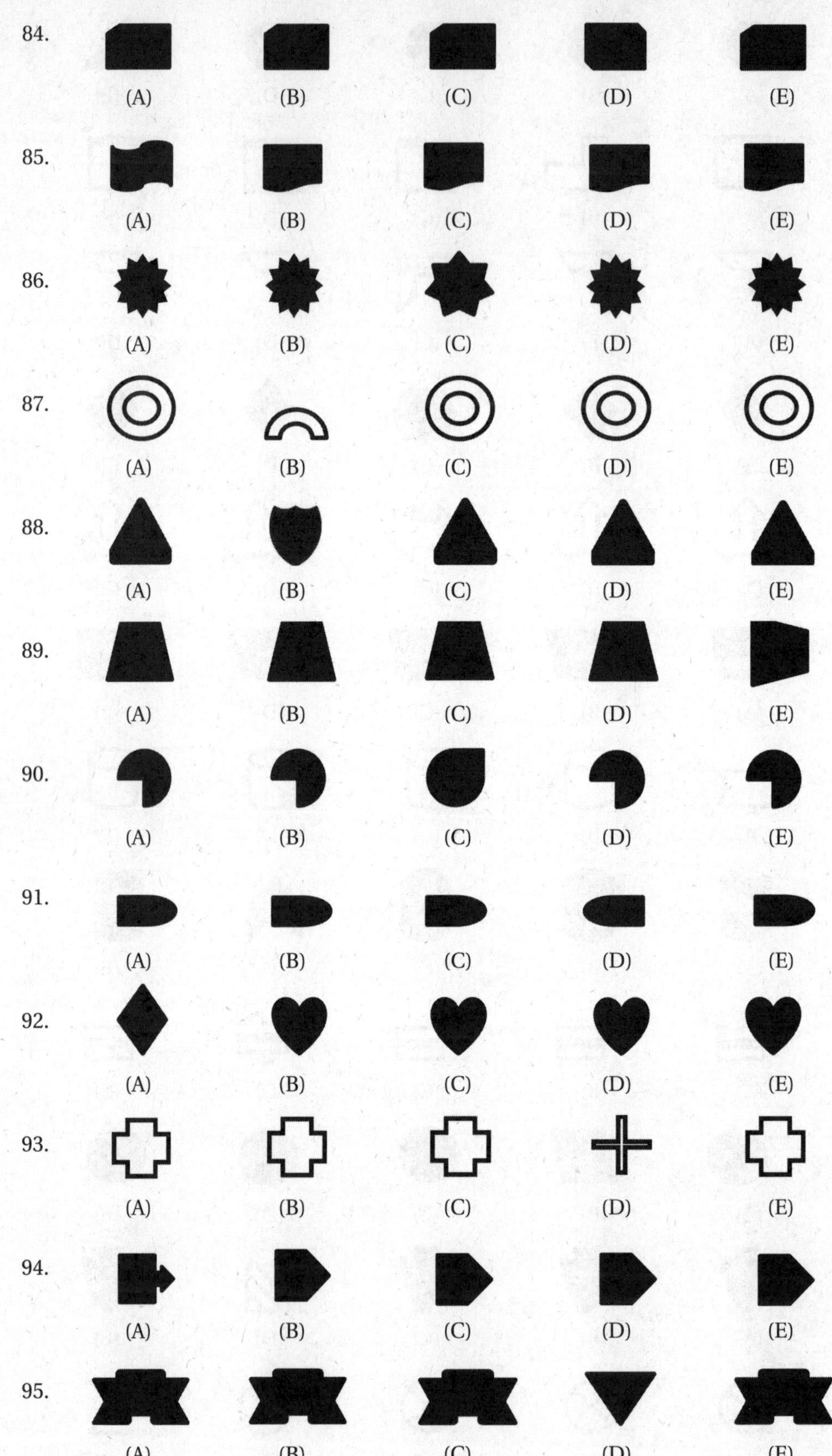
84.
(A) (B) (C) (D) (E)
85.
(A) (B) (C) (D) (E)
86.
(A) (B) (C) (D) (E)
87.
(A) (B) (C) (D) (E)
88.
(A) (B) (C) (D) (E)
89.
(A) (B) (C) (D) (E)
90.
(A) (B) (C) (D) (E)
91.
(A) (B) (C) (D) (E)
92.
(A) (B) (C) (D) (E)
93.
(A) (B) (C) (D) (E)
94.
(A) (B) (C) (D) (E)
95.
(A) (B) (C) (D) (E)

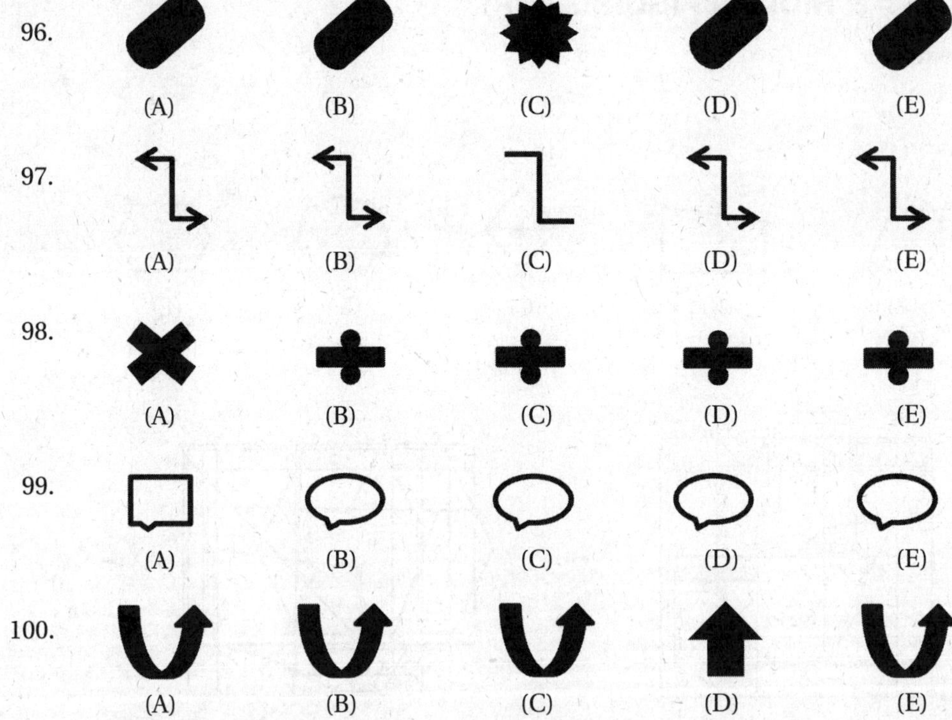

SIFT #2

SUBTEST 2: HIDDEN FIGURES (HF)

50 Questions

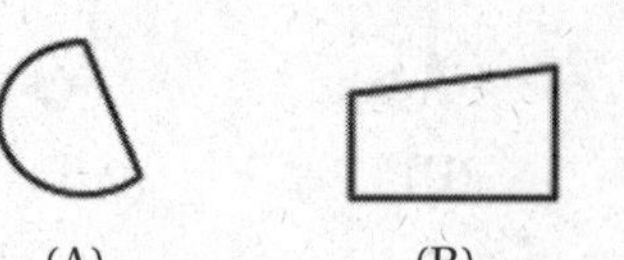
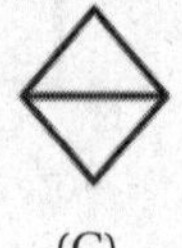
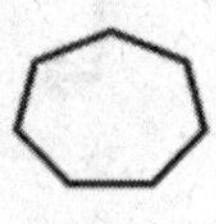
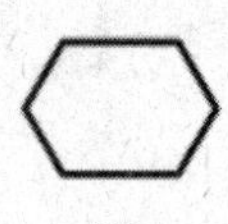

(A) (B) (C) (D) (E)

1.

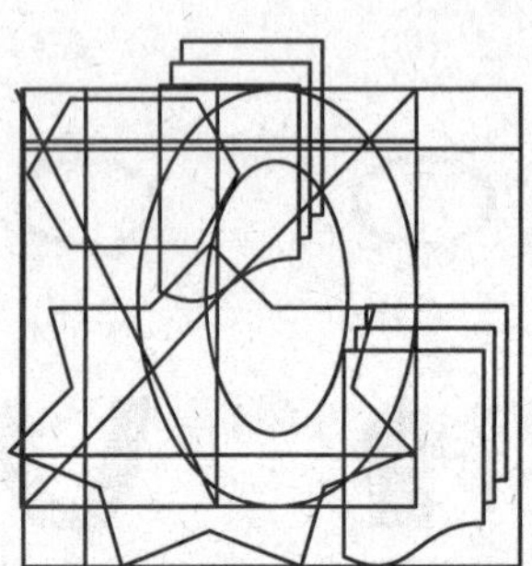

2.

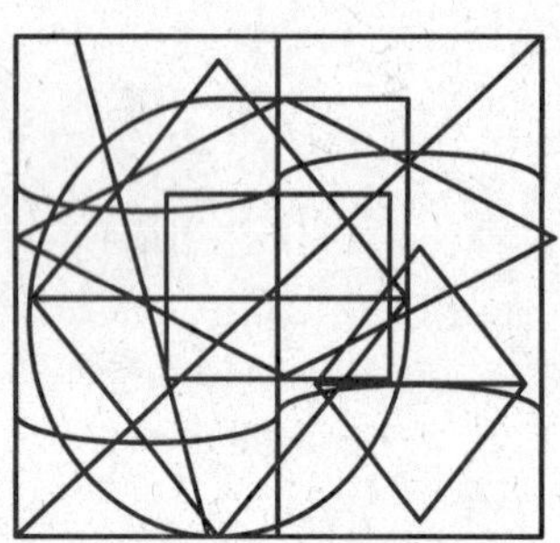

3.

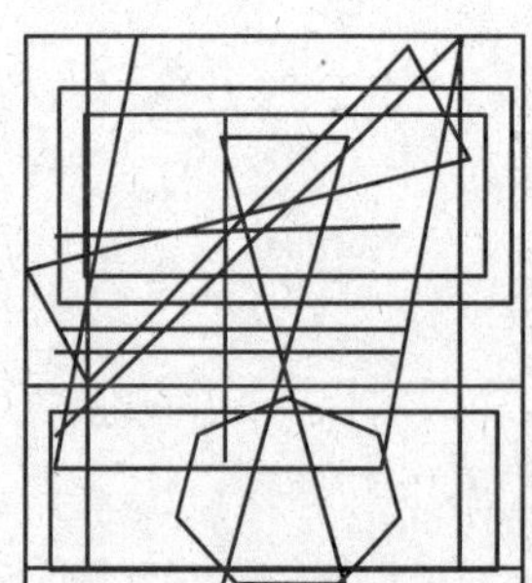

4.

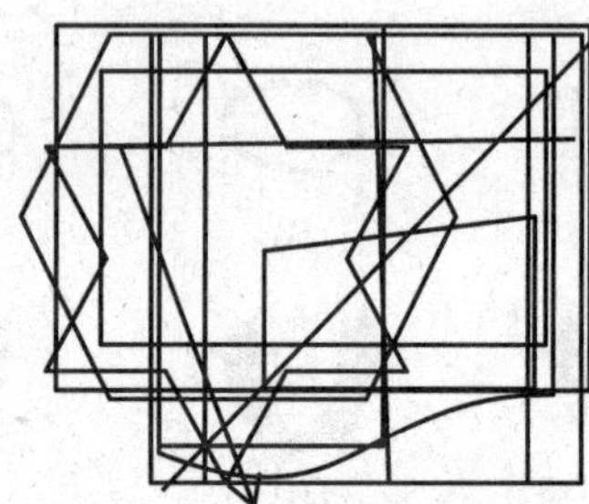

5.

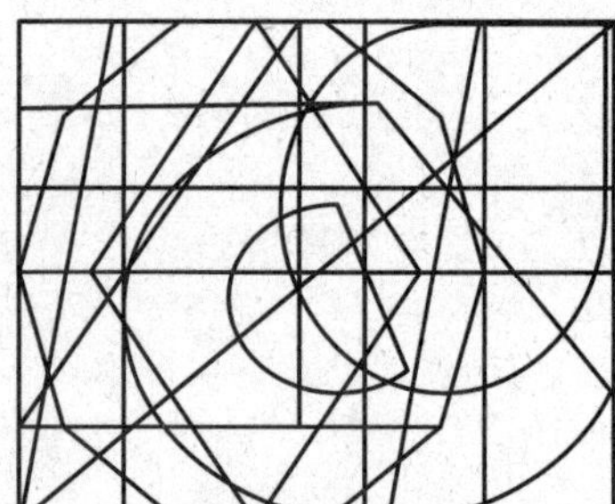

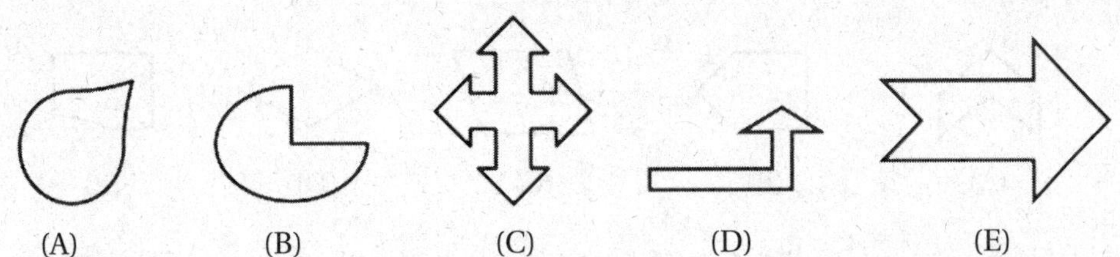

(A) (B) (C) (D) (E)

6.

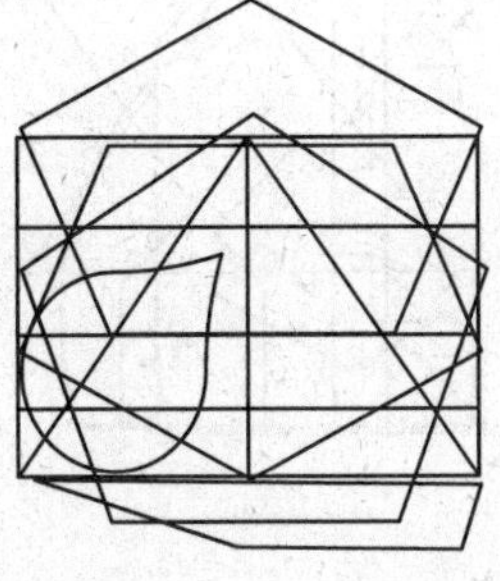

7.

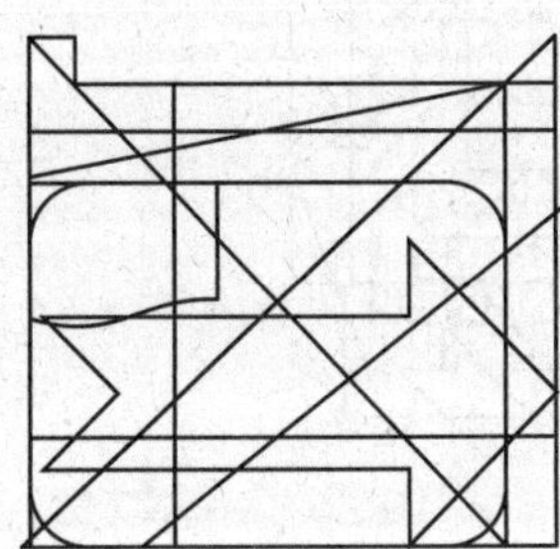

8.

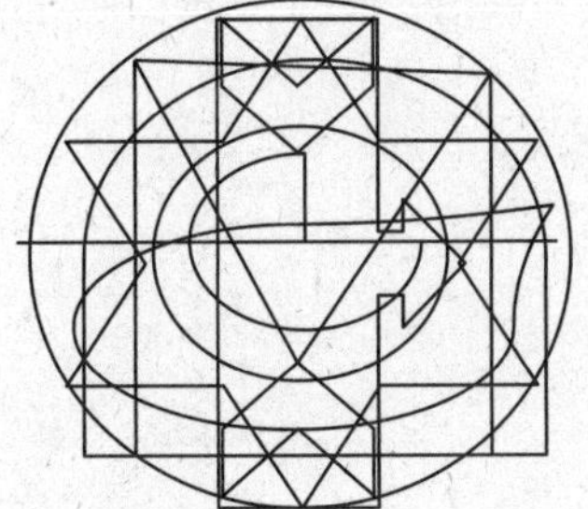

9.

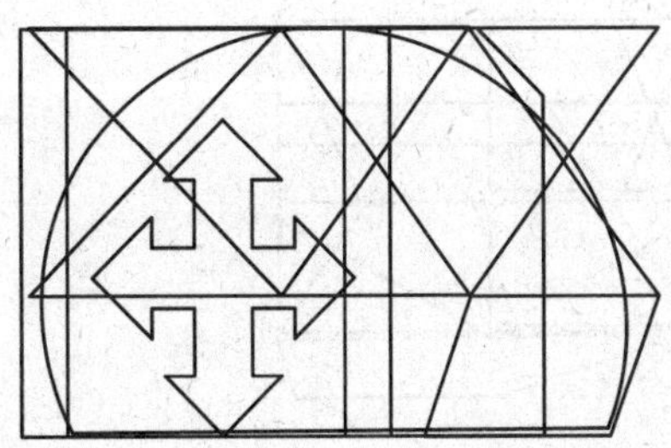

10.

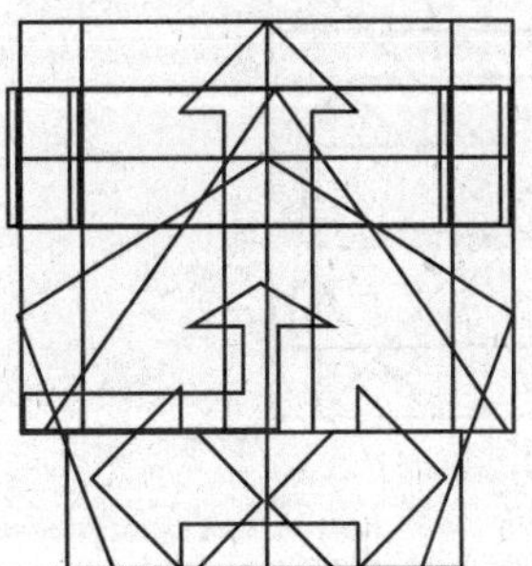

SIFT #2

(A)

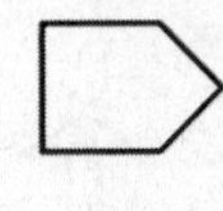
(B)

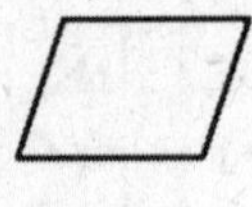
(C)

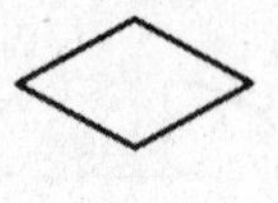
(D)

(E)

11.

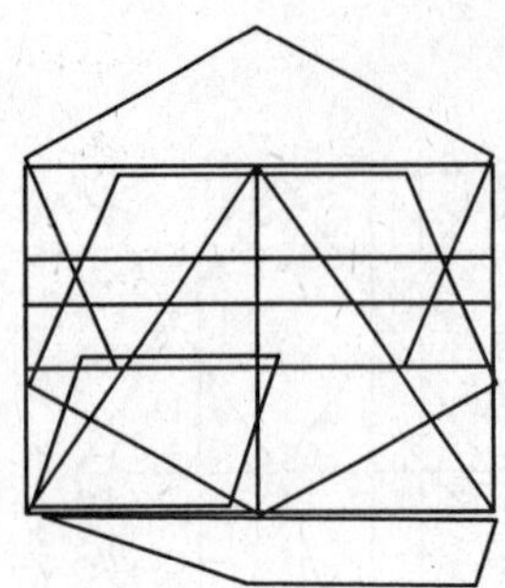

14.

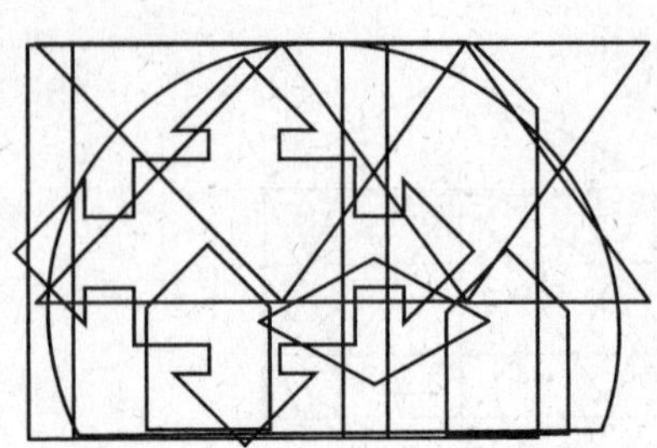

12.

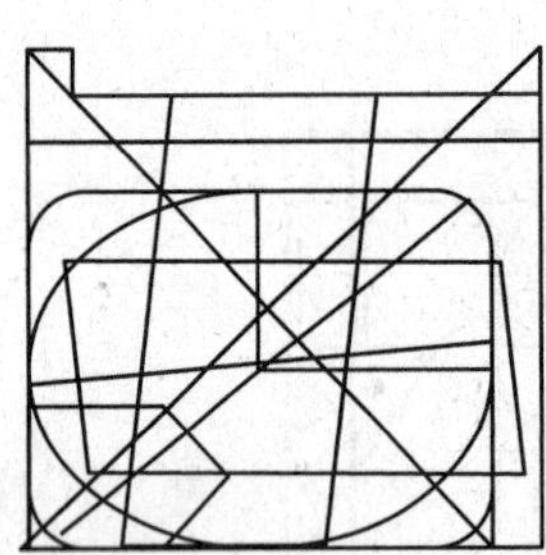

15.

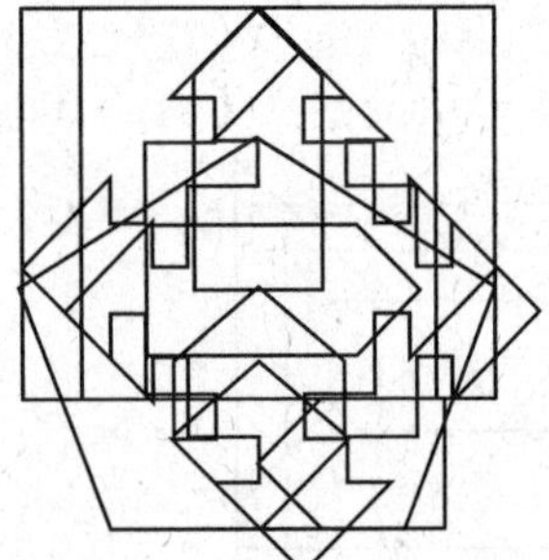

13.

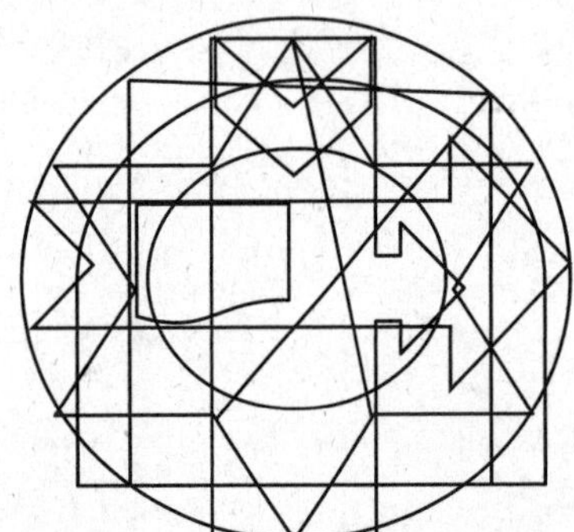

SIFT #2

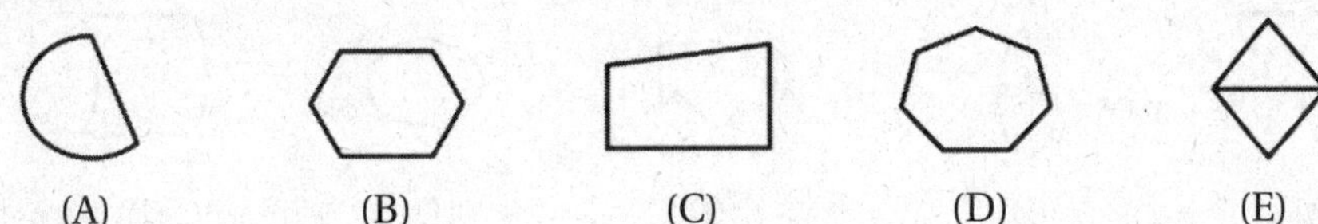

16.

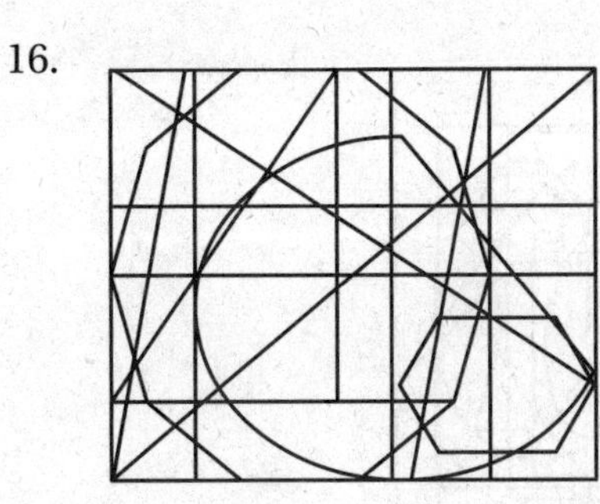

17.

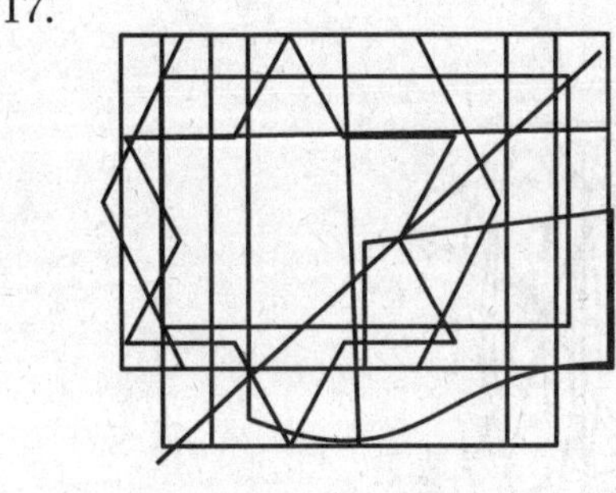

18.

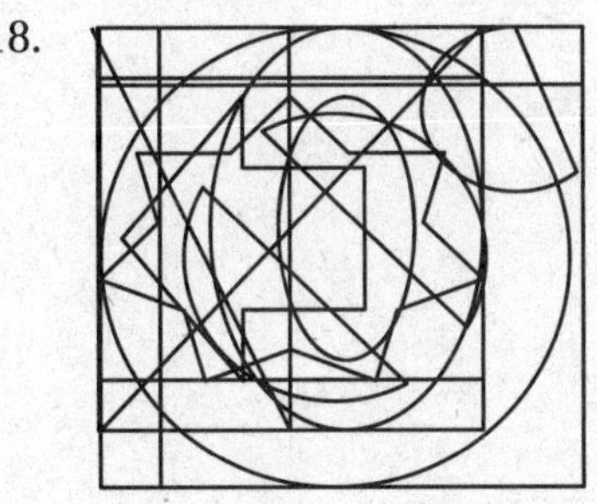

19.

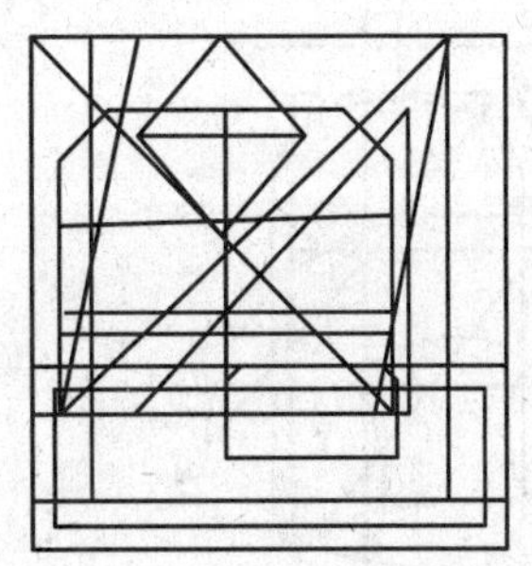

20.

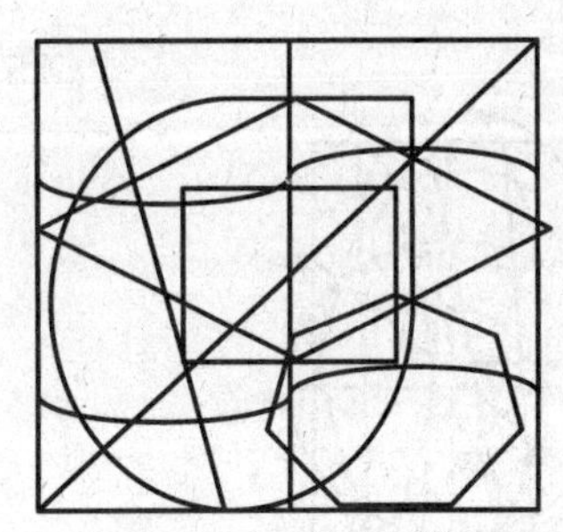

(A)

(B)

(C)

(D)

(E)

21.

22.

23.

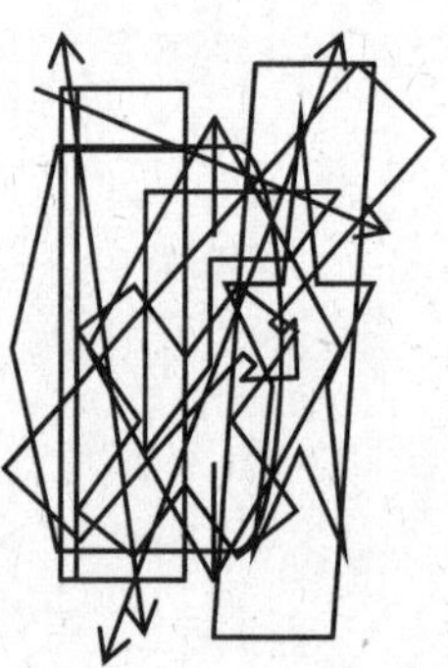

24.

25.

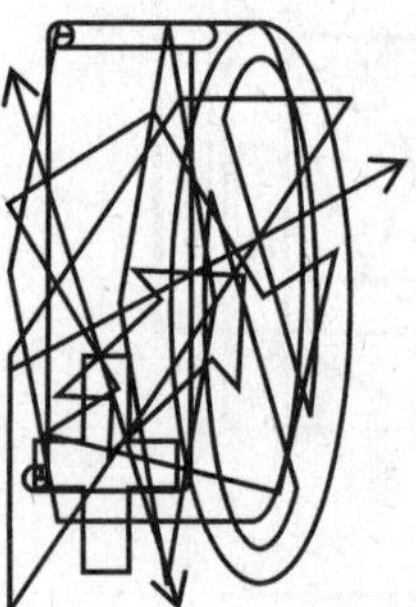

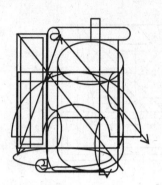

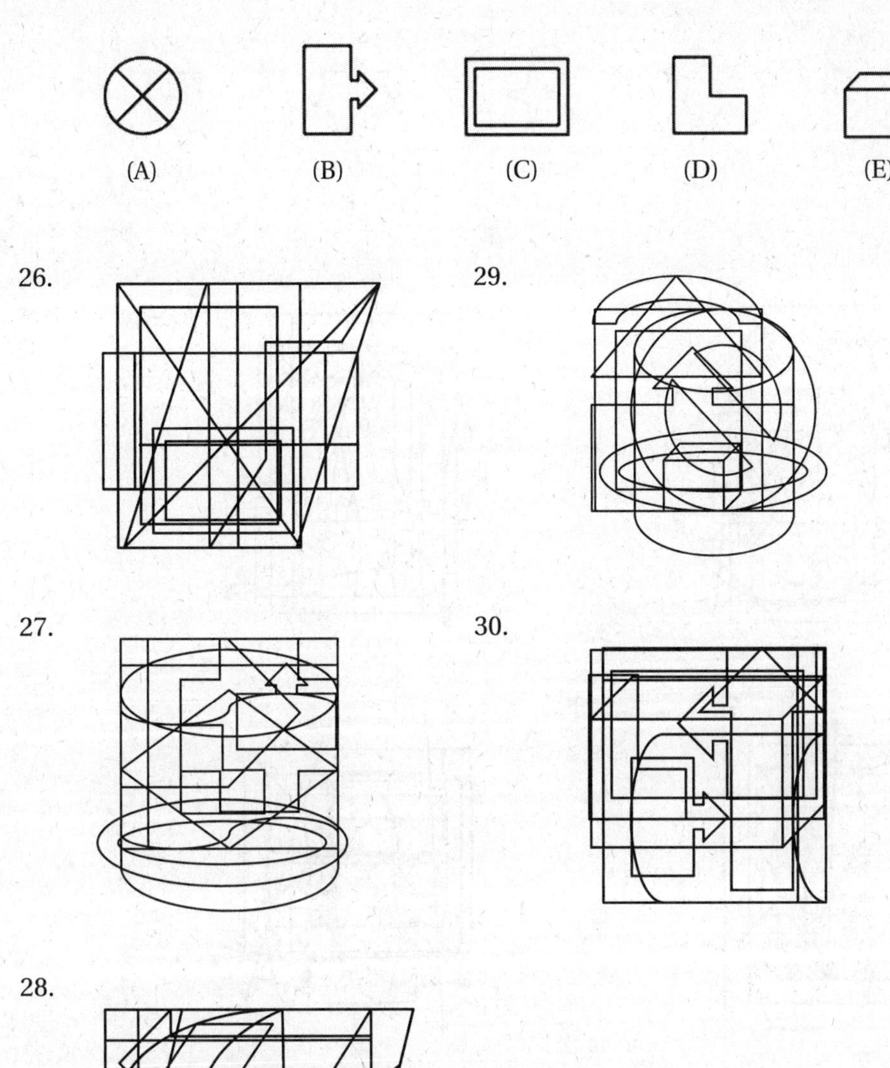
(A)
(B)
(C)
(D)
(E)
26.
27.
28.
29.
30.

(A)

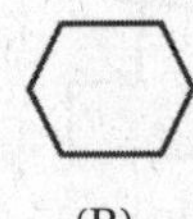
(B)

(C)

(D)

(E)

31.

32.

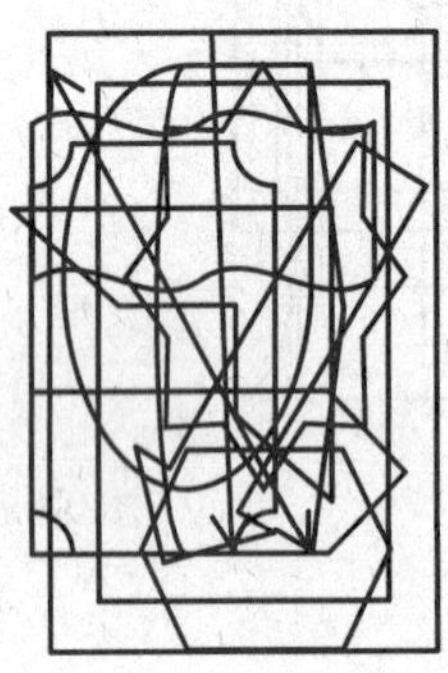

33.

34.

35.

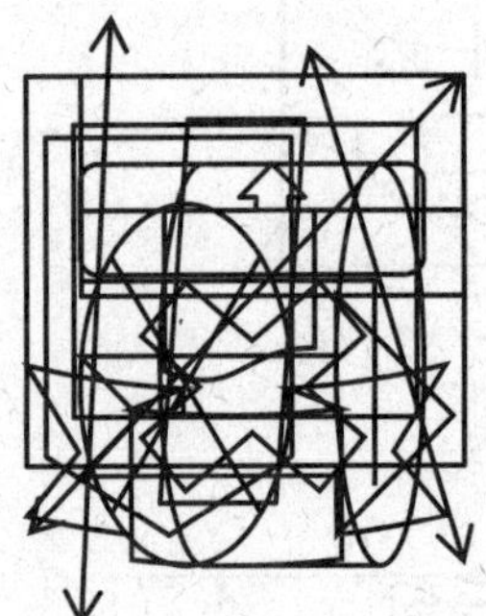

SIFT #2

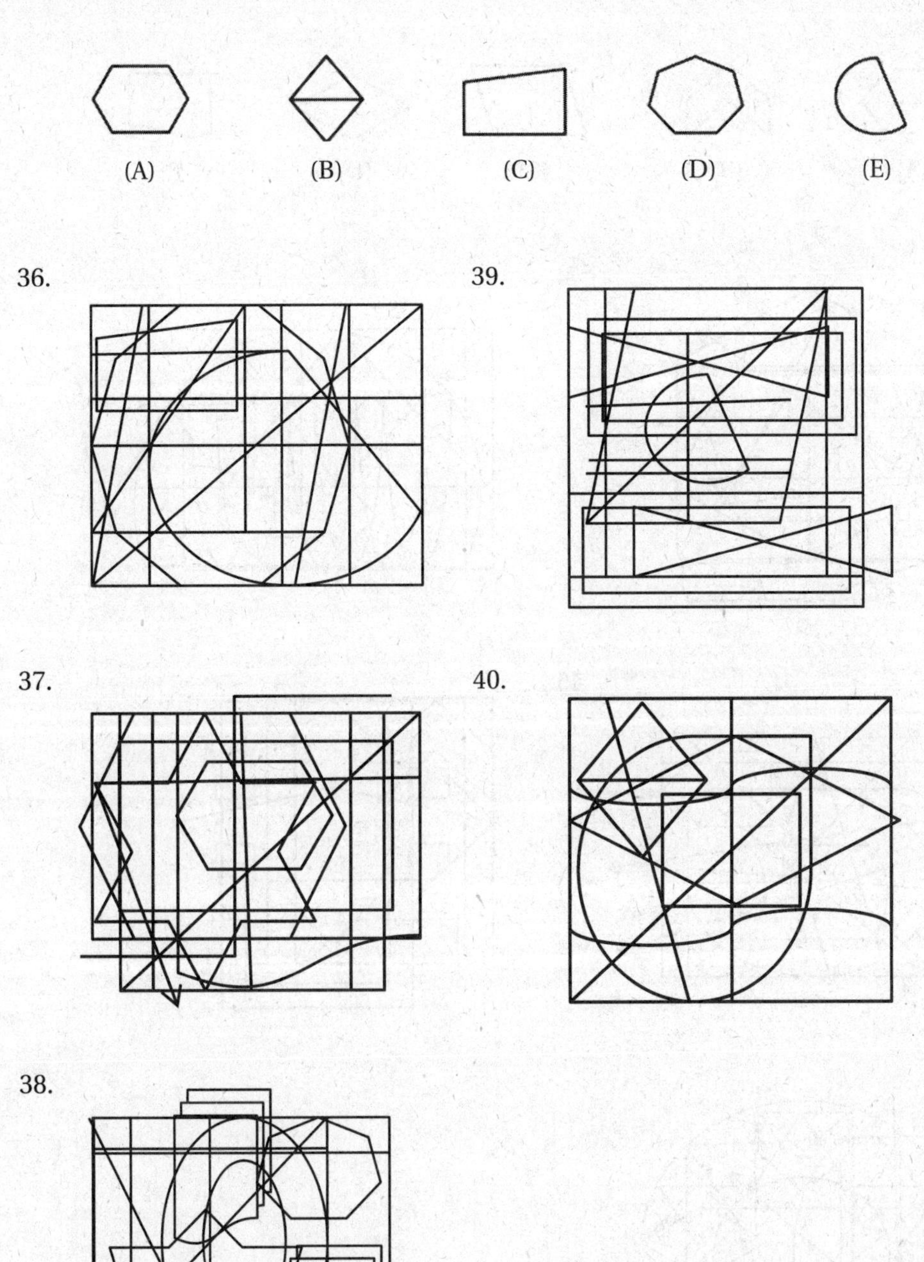
(A)
(B)
(C)
(D)
(E)
36.
39.
37.
40.
38.

SIFT #2

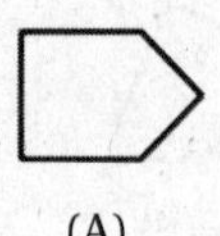

(A)

(B)

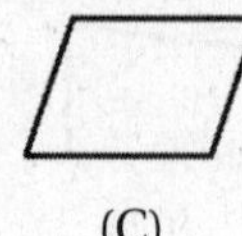

(C)

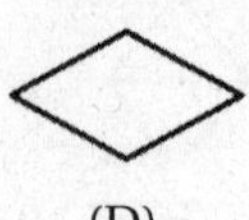

(D)

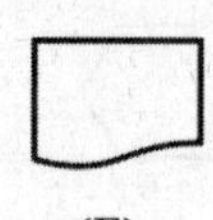

(E)

41.

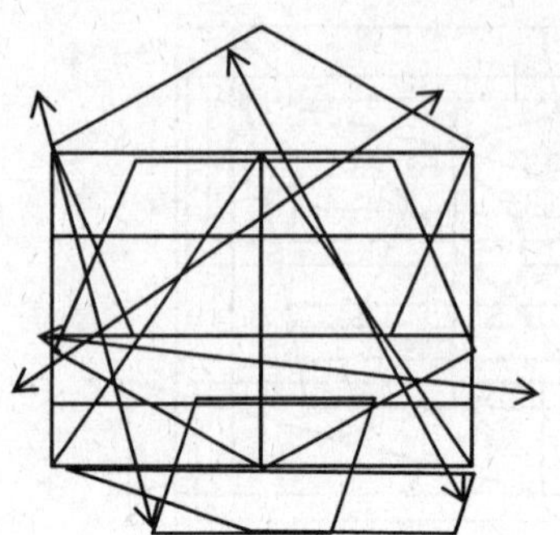

42.

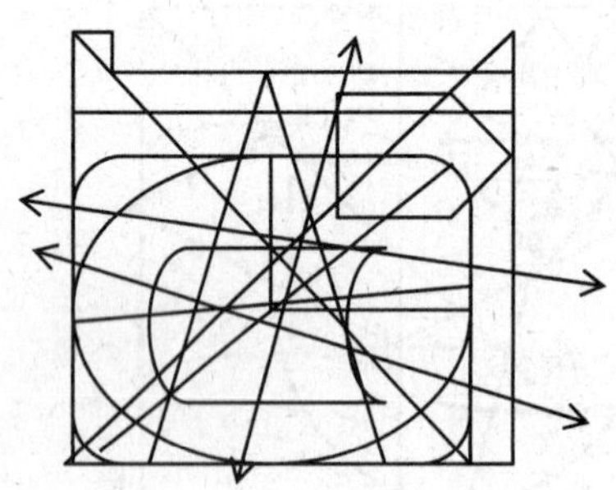

43.

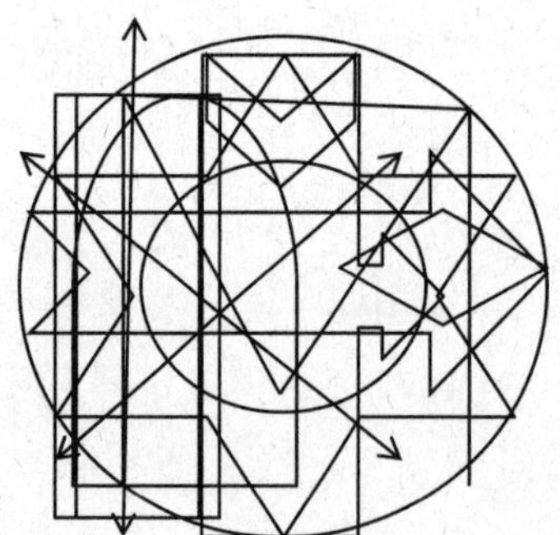

44.

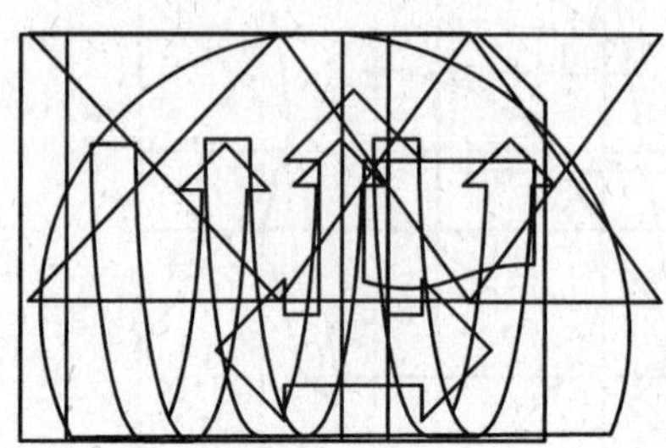

45.

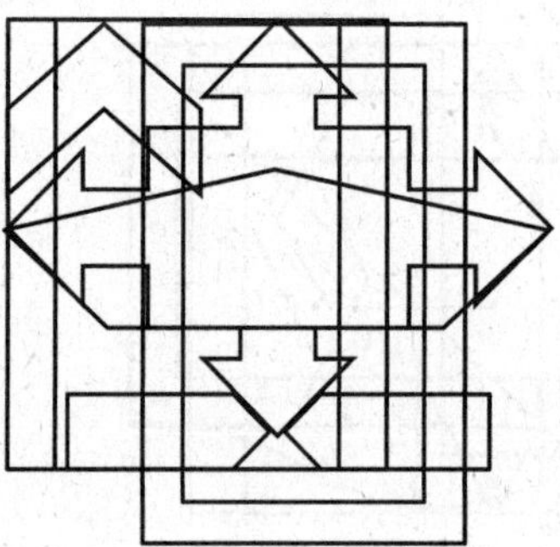

SIFT #2

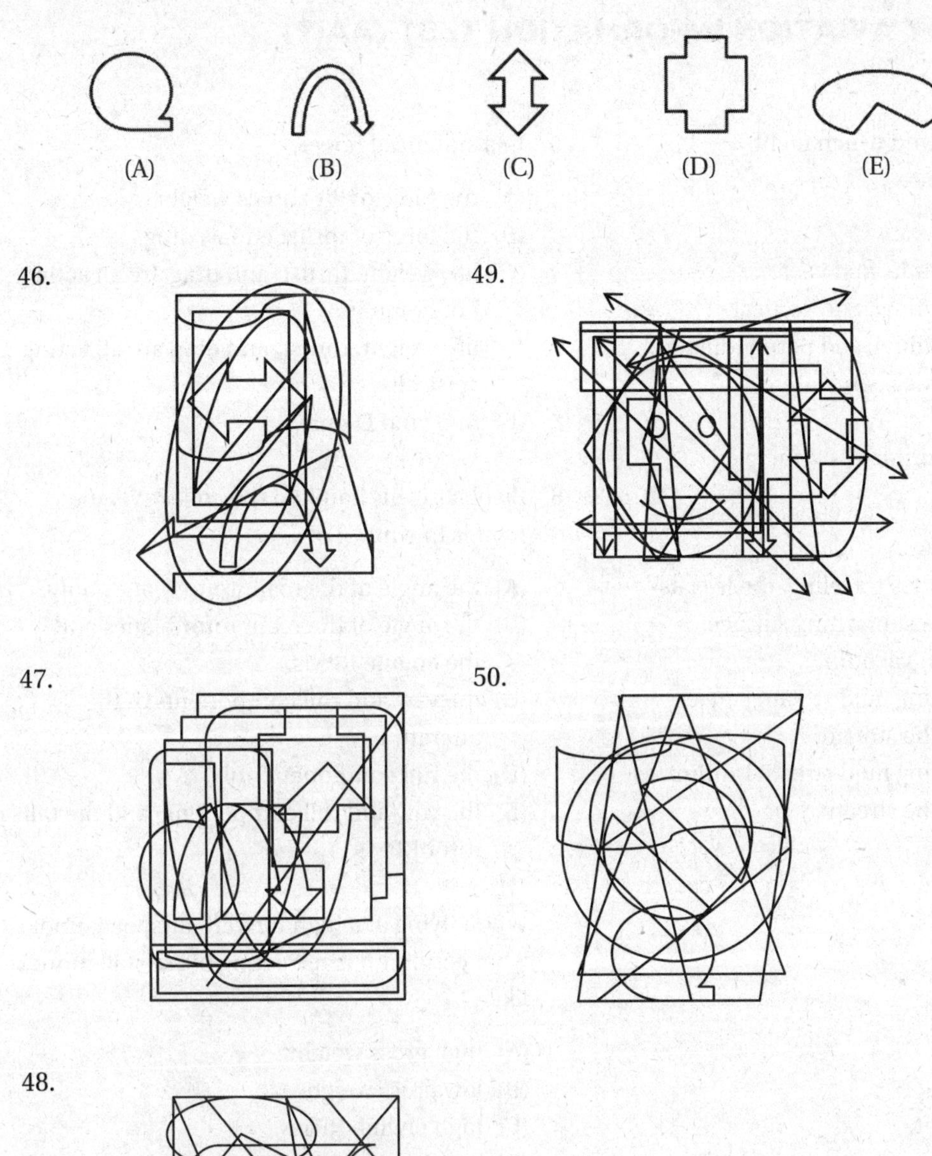

SIFT #2

SUBTEST 3: ARMY AVIATION INFORMATION TEST (AAIT)

40 Questions

1. The three axes around which flight movement occurs are

   (A) roll, pitch, and yaw.
   (B) latitude, longitude, and vector.
   (C) lateral, longitudinal, and vertical.
   (D) lateral, longitudinal, and perpendicular.
   (E) horizontal, vertical, and lateral.

2. One way to state Bernoulli's Principle is

   (A) the faster a fluid is traveling, the more smoothly it flows.
   (B) the faster a fluid is traveling, the less its pressure on the supporting surface.
   (C) nature abhors a vacuum.
   (D) a slower-traveling fluid stream causes turbulence in the stream.
   (E) a slower-traveling fluid stream minimizes turbulence in the stream.

3. The amount of an airfoil's curvature is called its

   (A) angle of attack.
   (B) chord.
   (C) camber.
   (D) lift ratio.
   (E) Langley number.

4. Earth's atmosphere is composed of

   (A) 78% nitrogen, 21% oxygen, and 1% other gases.
   (B) 87% nitrogen, 12% oxygen, and 1% other gases.
   (C) 67% nitrogen, 31% oxygen, and 2% other gases.
   (D) 77% nitrogen, 22% oxygen, and 1% other gases.
   (E) 76% helium, 22% oxygen, and 2% other gases.

5. In a stabilized hover,

   (A) the force of lift equals weight.
   (B) the force of thrust equals drag.
   (C) lift, weight, thrust, and drag are all acting horizontally.
   (D) lift, weight, thrust, and drag are all acting vertically.
   (E) A, B, and D only.

6. By placing his hand on the collective, the pilot is in control of

   (A) the angle of the main rotor blades only.
   (B) the angle of the main rotor blades and the engine RPMs.
   (C) the yaw and roll components of the aircraft.
   (D) the roll component only.
   (E) the yaw and roll components and the tail rotor RPMs.

7. When flying at a high forward airspeed, under what condition is retreating blade stall more likely?

   (A) high gross weight
   (B) low gross weight
   (C) high engine RPMs
   (D) low density altitude
   (E) wide, sweeping turns

8. Transient torque occurs in

   (A) single-rotor helicopters when longitudinal cyclic is applied.
   (B) single-rotor helicopters when lateral cyclic is applied.
   (C) single-rotor helicopters when excess power is applied.
   (D) single-rotor helicopters when cyclic back pressure is applied.
   (E) double-rotor helicopters when making a sharp turn.

9. Autorotation is
   (A) engaging the autopilot when the helicopter is in forward flight.
   (B) engaging the autopilot when the helicopter is in a hover.
   (C) turning a rotor system by airflow rather than engine power.
   (D) part of the engine shutoff and spool-down procedure.
   (E) changing the pitch of the rotor blades to achieve maximum efficiency.

10. During autorotation, the tail rotor
   (A) is not a factor.
   (B) does not rotate.
   (C) is still needed to control yaw.
   (D) spins freely on its own.
   (E) is regulated automatically.

11. The transverse flow effect
   (A) results in less lift to the rear portion of the rotor disc.
   (B) results in more lift to the rear portion of the rotor disc.
   (C) results in more lift to the front portion of the rotor disc.
   (D) results in less lift to the front portion of the rotor disc.
   (E) none of the above

12. A lighted heliport can be identified by
   (A) a white, yellow, and green rotating beacon.
   (B) a white, yellow, and red rotating beacon.
   (C) blue lights around a square landing area.
   (D) red and green alternating flashing lights.
   (E) red and blue alternating flashing lights.

13. When a helicopter in a hover has a tendency to drift in the direction of tail rotor thrust, this is called
   (A) gyroscopic regression.
   (B) gyroscopic progression.
   (C) gyroscopic precession.
   (D) translating tendency.
   (E) transverse flow effect.

14. The best way to perform a quick stop is to
   (A) raise the collective and push forward on the cyclic.
   (B) lower the collective and pull back on the cyclic.
   (C) pull back on the cyclic and decrease engine RPMs.
   (D) push forward on the cyclic and decrease engine RPMs.
   (E) return all controls to the neutral position.

15. The collection of factors that facilitates maximum helicopter performance is
   (A) low altitude, low temperature, and high humidity.
   (B) low altitude, low temperature, and low humidity.
   (C) low altitude, high temperature, and high humidity.
   (D) high altitude, low temperature, and high humidity.
   (E) high altitude, high temperature, and high humidity.

16. The cyclic controls the
   (A) pitch of the helicopter.
   (B) engine RPMs.
   (C) torque effect.
   (D) direction of the tilt of the main rotor.
   (E) gyroscopic precession of the rotor blades.

17. Moving the cyclic forward and significantly raising the collective will cause the helicopter to

(A) increase its forward speed.
(B) increase its forward speed and begin to climb.
(C) immediately increase its altitude without increasing forward velocity.
(D) nose over.
(E) stall.

18. Conventional American helicopters have a main rotor that

(A) turns in a counterclockwise direction.
(B) turns in a clockwise direction.
(C) defeats translational torque.
(D) experiences two stages of gyroscopic precession.
(E) has two rotor blades of fixed pitch only.

19. Translational lift is

(A) the lift needed to initially leave the ground.
(B) the cushioning effect encountered in a low hover.
(C) another name for Coriolis force.
(D) the additional lift gained when the helicopter leaves its downwash.
(E) the decreased lift suffered when the helicopter leaves its downwash.

20. Gyroscopic precession happens when

(A) a force applied to a spinning disc has its effect 90 degrees later in the opposite direction of rotation.
(B) a force applied to a spinning disc has its effect 180 degrees later in the opposite direction of rotation.
(C) a force applied to a spinning disc has its effect 90 degrees later in the direction and plane of rotation.
(D) a force applied to a spinning disc has its effect 180 degrees later in the direction and plane of rotation.
(E) none of the above

21. Increasing collective (power) while maintaining constant airspeed will cause the helicopter to

(A) climb.
(B) descend.
(C) pitch nose-up sharply.
(D) pitch nose-down sharply.
(E) autorotate.

22. Profile drag, developing from the frictional resistance of the blades passing through the air, does not change significantly with the airfoil's angle of attack, but

(A) increases proportionately when airspeed increases.
(B) increases significantly when airspeed increases.
(C) increases moderately when airspeed increases.
(D) decreases moderately when airspeed increases.
(E) decreases significantly when airspeed increases.

23. Induced drag is generated by

(A) profile drag and skin friction.
(B) the high-pressure area above the blade.
(C) the low-pressure area below the blade.
(D) vortices at the rotor's trailing edge and tips.
(E) airflow circulation around the rotor blade as it creates lift.

24. A rotor blade's angle of attack (AOA) is

(A) usually lower at higher airspeeds and higher at lower airspeeds.
(B) usually higher at higher airspeeds and lower at lower airspeeds.
(C) a function of the power applied to the antitorque rotor.
(D) always the same relative to the rotor mast.
(E) a function of induced drag vortices.

25. Airfoils are used to produce lift, as well as

(A) thrust or propulsion.
(B) control, blade twist, and counteracting dissymmetry of lift.
(C) stability, control, and thrust or propulsion.
(D) stability, thrust, and facilitating torque.
(E) stability, control, and radial engine cooling.

26. In a vertical autorotative descent in still air, the forces that cause the blades to turn are

(A) similar for all blades regardless of their position in the plane of rotation, making dissymmetry of lift from airspeed not a factor.
(B) similar for all blades regardless of their position in the plane of rotation, making dissymmetry of lift from airspeed a factor.
(C) dissimilar for all blades regardless of their position in the plane of rotation, making dissymmetry of lift from airspeed not a factor.
(D) dissimilar for all blades regardless of their position in the plane of rotation, making dissymmetry of lift from airspeed a factor.
(E) a result of the downward flow of relative wind.

27. On a helicopter, a governor is a device that

(A) is found only on piston-engine helicopters.
(B) senses main and tail rotor RPMs and makes adjustments to keep torque balanced.
(C) senses rotor and engine RPMs and makes adjustments to keep rotor RPMs constant.
(D) senses rotor and engine RPMs and adjusts to keep engine RPMs constant.
(E) governs the pitch angle on the main rotor blades.

28. A correlator is a mechanical connection between the collective lever and the engine throttle. When the collective lever is raised,

(A) the flap angle of the main rotor blades is increased.
(B) the flap angle of the main rotor blades is decreased.
(C) the angle of incidence of the tail rotor is decreased.
(D) power is automatically increased.
(E) power is automatically decreased.

29. The antitorque pedals, located on the cabin floor by the pilot's feet, control the _____ and therefore the _____ of the tail rotor blades or other antitorque system.

(A) pitch, RPMs
(B) RPMs, pitch
(C) RPMs, thrust
(D) thrust, pitch
(E) pitch, thrust

30. Main rotor systems are classified according to how the main rotor blades are attached and move relative to the main rotor hub. There are three primary types:

(A) rigid, semirigid, and fully articulated
(B) rigid, semirigid, and bearingless
(C) underslung, overslung, and fully articulated
(D) teetering, feathering, and bearingless
(E) rigid, teetering, and feathering

31. A fully articulated rotor system allows each blade to

(A) lead/lag (move back and forth in the plane of rotation).
(B) flap independent of the other blades (move up and down about an inboard mounted hinge).
(C) feather (rotate around the pitch axis to change lift).
(D) all of the above
(E) none of the above

32. On a typical helicopter airspeed indicator a green arc indicates the aircraft's

    (A) airspeed limit beyond which structural damage could occur.
    (B) normal operating speed range.
    (C) maximum safe autorotation speed.
    (D) maximum continuous power setting.
    (E) normal altitude operating range.

33. More power is required during ____________ than any other helicopter flight regime.

    (A) takeoff
    (B) landing
    (C) transitional flight
    (D) hovering
    (E) autorotation

34. The three major factors that affect helicopter performance are

    (A) pressure altitude, center of gravity, and wind.
    (B) density altitude, weight, and wind.
    (C) density altitude, weight, and relative airspeed.
    (D) altitude above ground, center of gravity, and airspeed.
    (E) humidity, weight, and relative airspeed.

35. The four fundamentals of flight—on which all maneuvers are based—are

    (A) hovers, turns, climbs, and descents.
    (B) hovers, climbs, descents, and autorotation.
    (C) straight and level flight, turns, climbs, and descents.
    (D) straight and level flight, climbs, descents, and autorotation.
    (E) horizontal flight, vertical flight, yaws, and pitches.

36. The helicopter pilot can use the pedals to control

    (A) heading, direction of turn, and rate of turn at hover.
    (B) heading, rate of ascent, and rate of descent.
    (C) direction of travel, helicopter position, and rate of turn.
    (D) direction of travel, heading, and hover height.
    (E) hover height, rate of ascent, and rate of turn.

37. Airspeed in straight and level flight is determined by the

    (A) RPMs of the main rotor.
    (B) forward-tilting attitude of the rotor disk relative to the horizon.
    (C) rear-tilting attitude of the rotor disk relative to the horizon.
    (D) use of the collective.
    (E) thickness of the horizontal stabilizers.

38. A slip occurs when the helicopter slides sideways toward the center of the turn, and is caused by

    (A) insufficient main rotor RPMs during the conduct of the turn.
    (B) too much collective applied during the conduct of the turn.
    (C) too little collective pressure applied during the conduct of the turn.
    (D) not enough antitorque pedal pressure in the direction of the turn.
    (E) too much antitorque pedal pressure in the direction of the turn.

39. A normal approach to a hover before landing uses a descent profile of

   (A) between 7 and 12 degrees starting about 100–300 feet above ground level.
   (B) between 7 and 12 degrees starting about 300–500 feet above ground level.
   (C) between 12 and 15 degrees starting about 100–300 feet above ground level.
   (D) between 12 and 15 degrees starting about 300–500 feet above ground level.
   (E) between 15 and 20 degrees starting about 500 feet above ground level.

40. Nap-of-the-Earth (NOE) flight is conducted

   (A) at constant altitude and airspeed as dictated by threat avoidance.
   (B) at relatively constant airspeeds and low altitudes conforming to Earth's contours.
   (C) at varying airspeeds as close to Earth's surface as vegetation and obstacles permit.
   (D) following 500 ft. above the highest elevation features available at low speeds.
   (E) offset from and 200 ft. above the highest terrain features at moderate to high speeds.

SUBTEST 4: SPATIAL APPERCEPTION TEST (SAT)

25 Questions

This subtest measures your ability to determine the position of an aircraft in flight in relation to the view a pilot would see when looking out the front of the cockpit.

This subtest consists of 25 questions, which you will have 10 minutes to answer.

For each question, you will see a series of six pictures. The first picture will depict a view of the landscape that a pilot would see when looking out the front of the cockpit. You are to determine whether the aircraft is climbing, diving, banking, or in level flight, and choose the picture that best represents the same aircraft when viewed from the outside.

1.

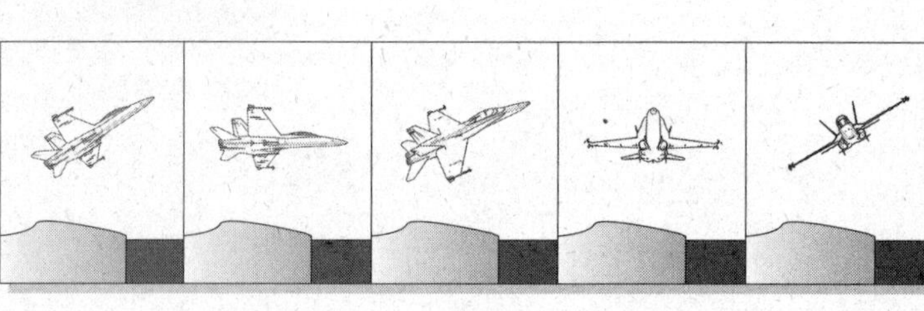

(A) (B) (C) (D) (E)

2.

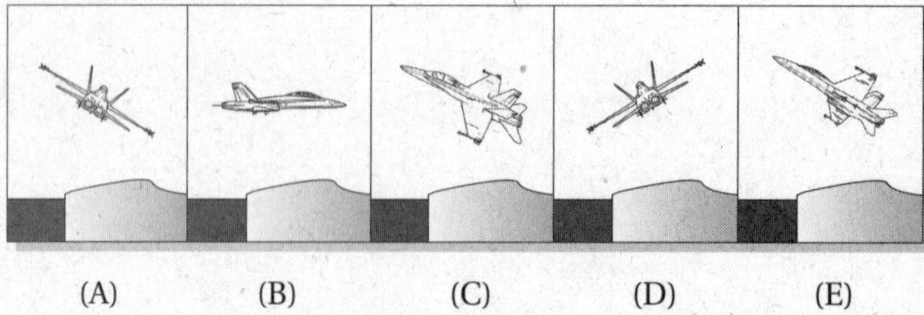

(A) (B) (C) (D) (E)

3.

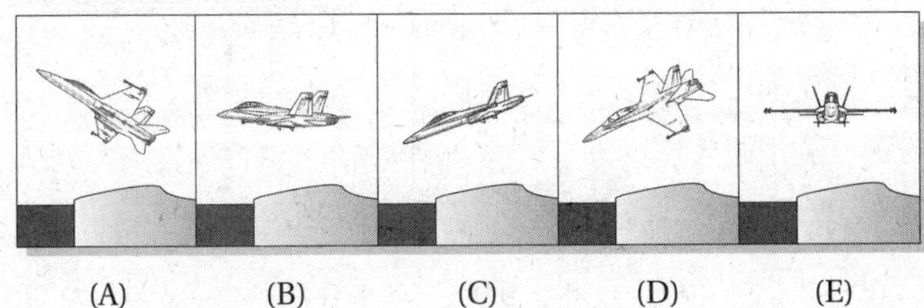

(A) (B) (C) (D) (E)

4.

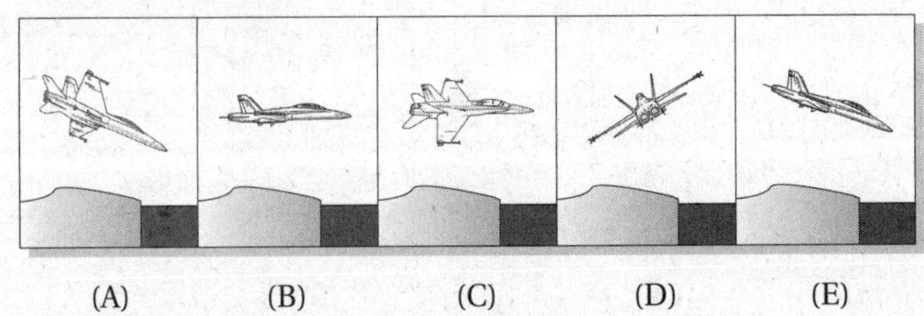

(A) (B) (C) (D) (E)

5.

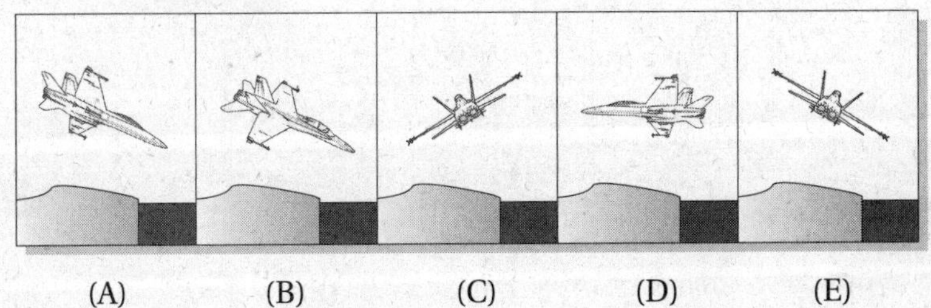

(A) (B) (C) (D) (E)

6.

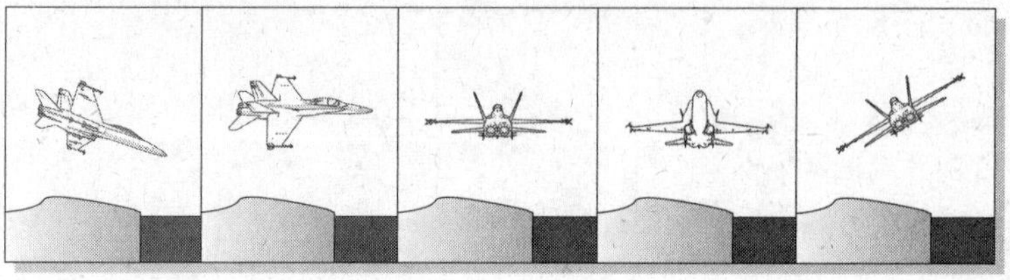

(A) (B) (C) (D) (E)

7.

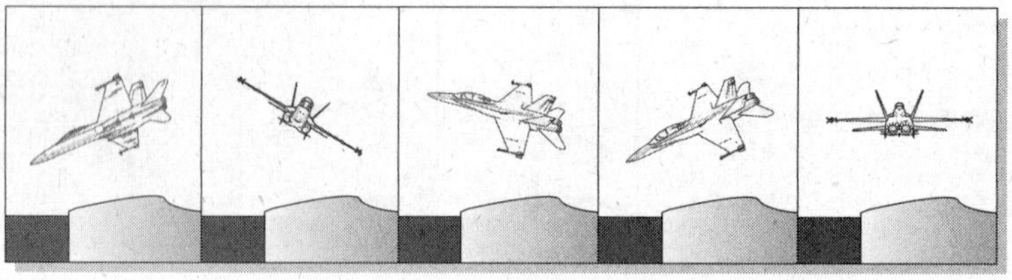

(A) (B) (C) (D) (E)

8.

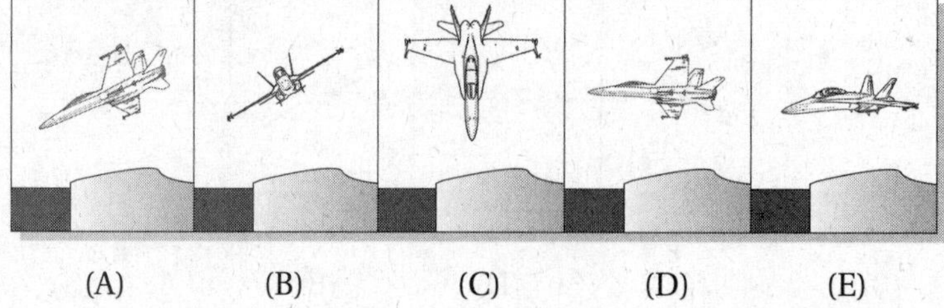

(A) (B) (C) (D) (E)

9.

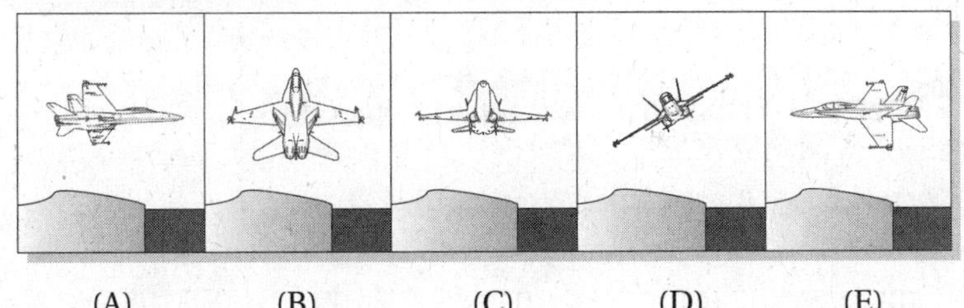

(A) (B) (C) (D) (E)

10. 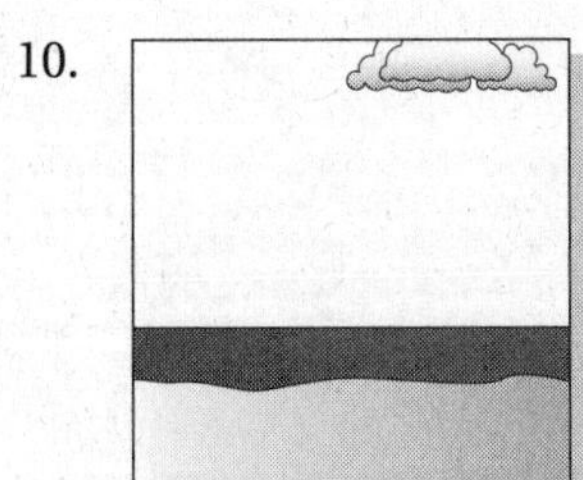

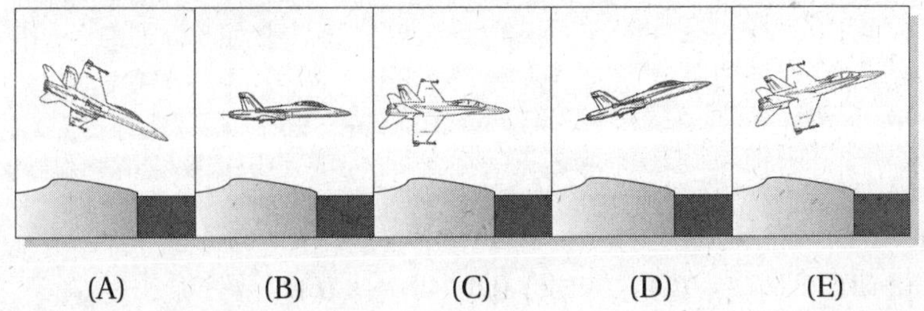

(A) (B) (C) (D) (E)

11. 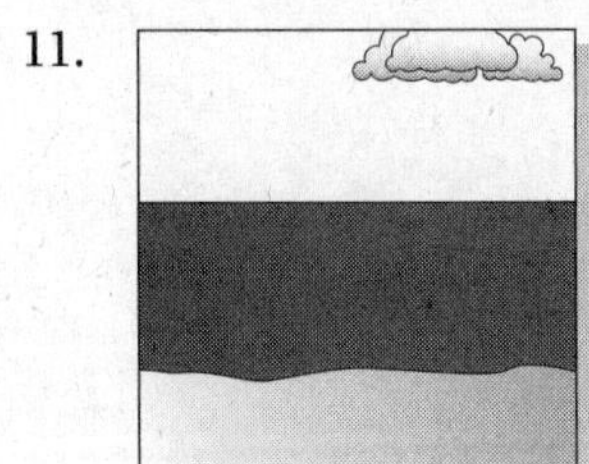

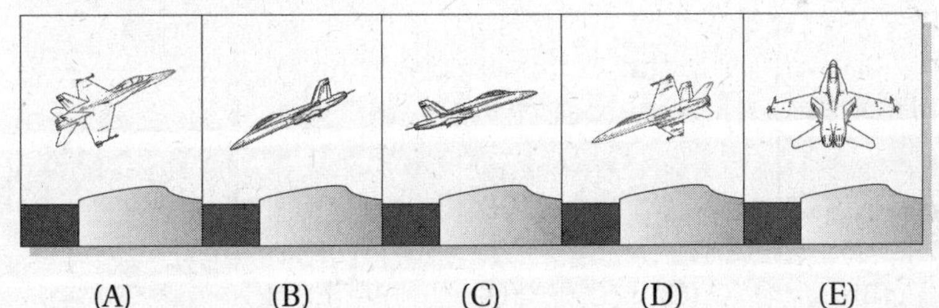

(A) (B) (C) (D) (E)

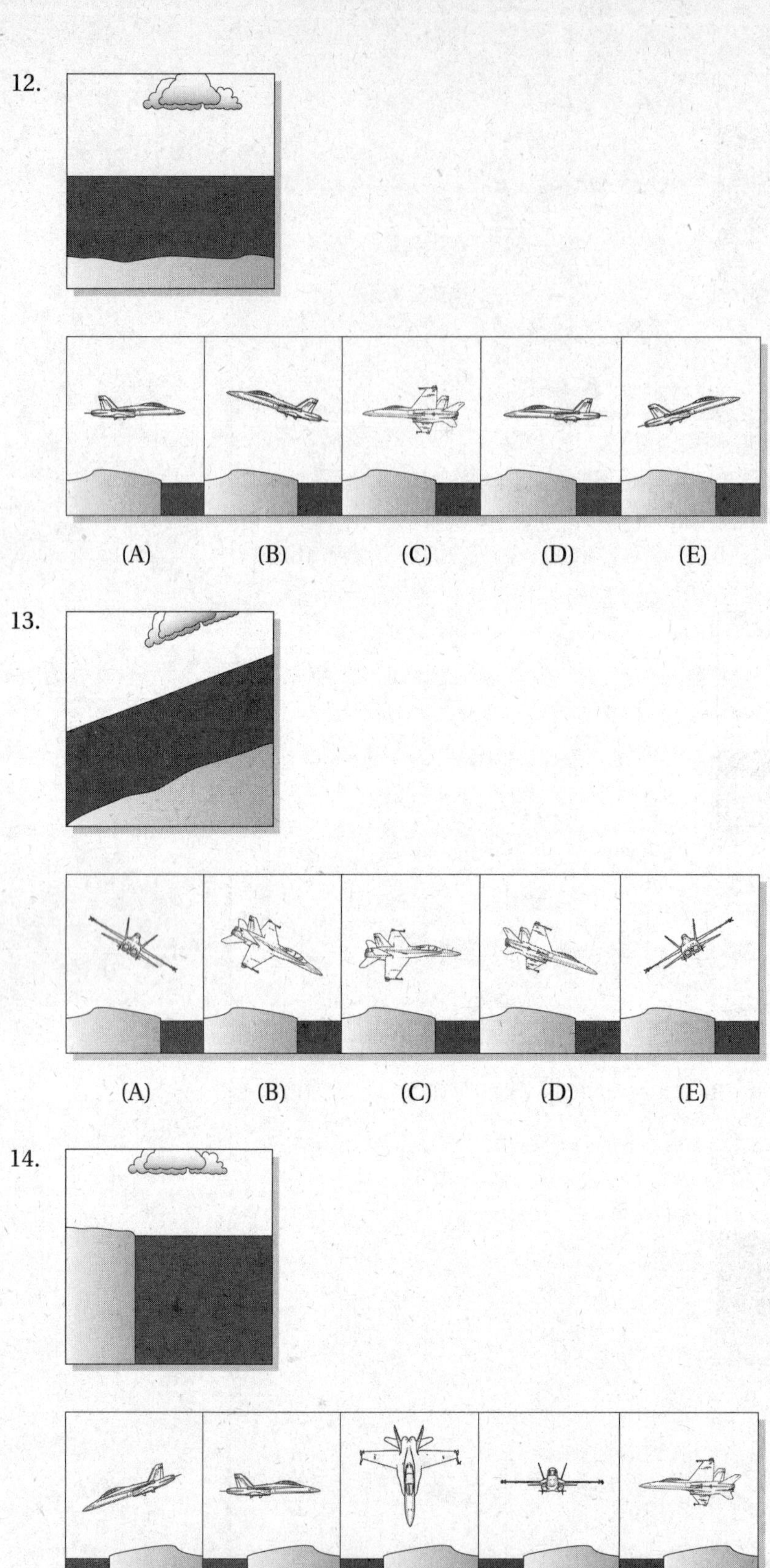

SIFT #2

15.

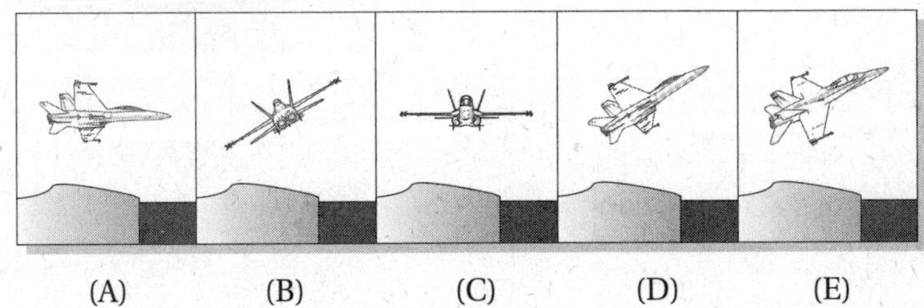

(A) (B) (C) (D) (E)

16.

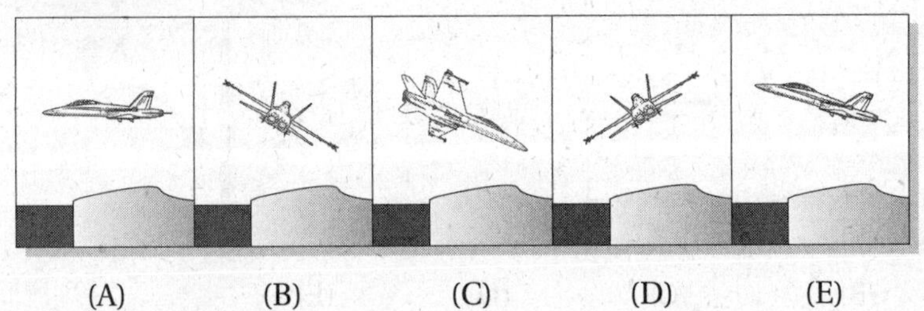

(A) (B) (C) (D) (E)

17.

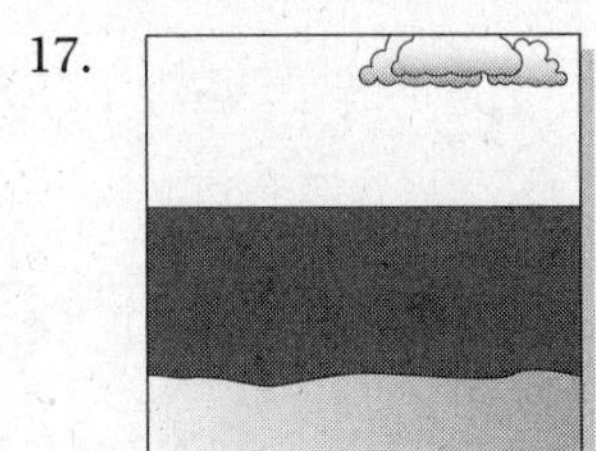

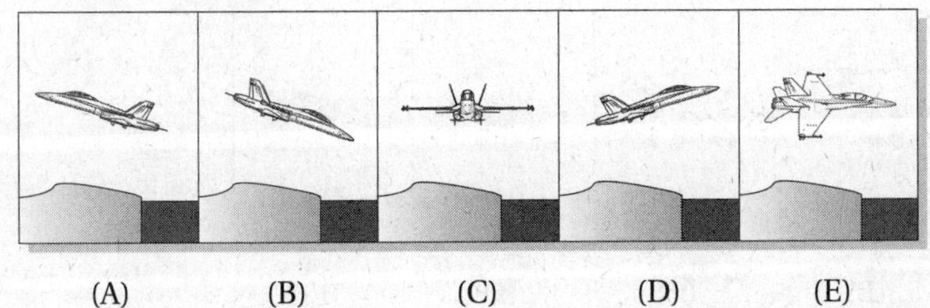

(A) (B) (C) (D) (E)

SIFT #2

18.

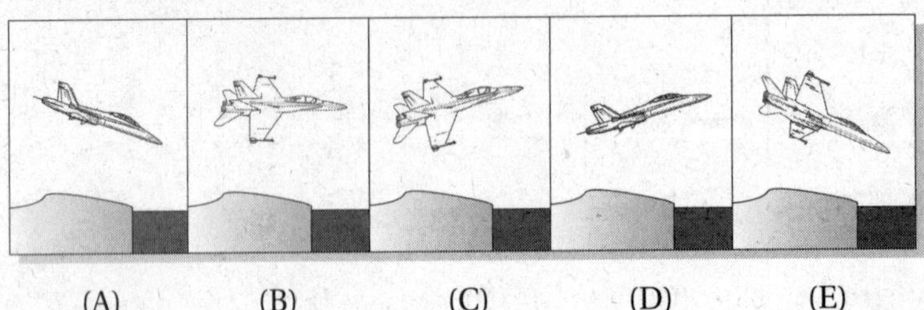

(A) (B) (C) (D) (E)

19.

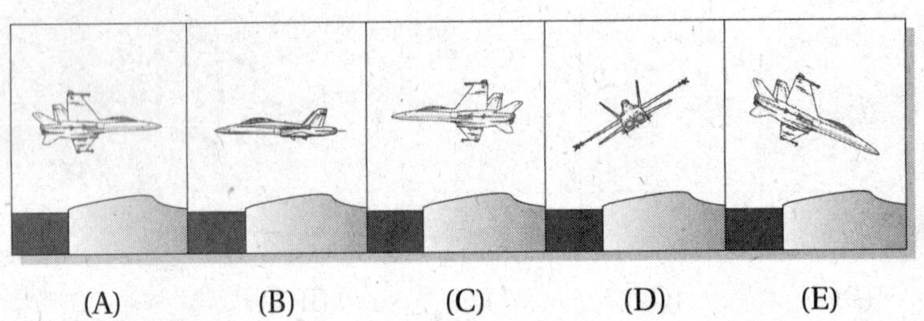

(A) (B) (C) (D) (E)

20.

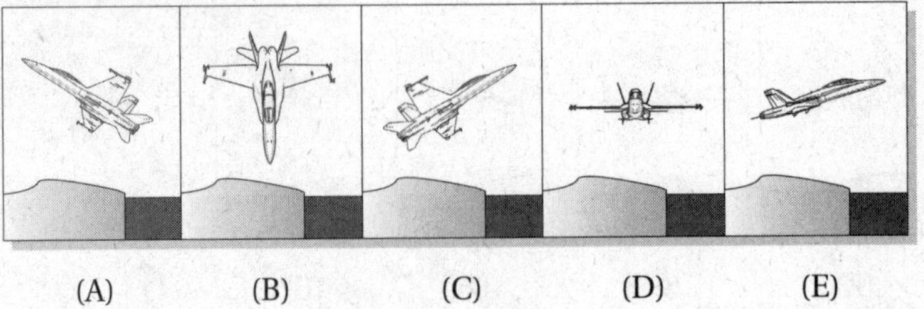

(A) (B) (C) (D) (E)

21.

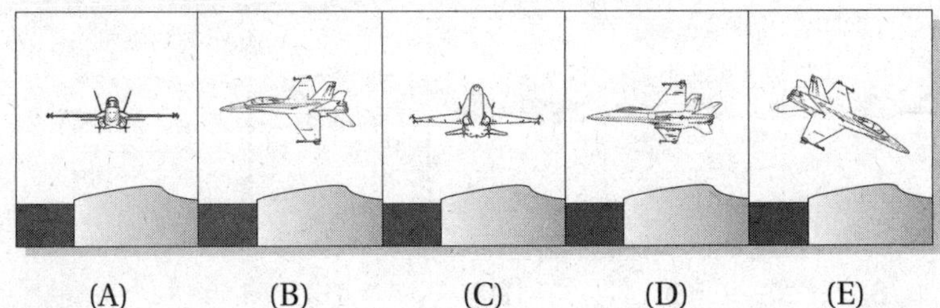

(A) (B) (C) (D) (E)

22.

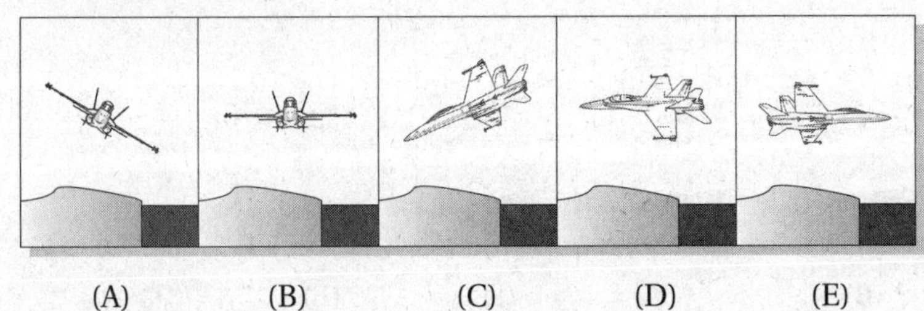

(A) (B) (C) (D) (E)

23.

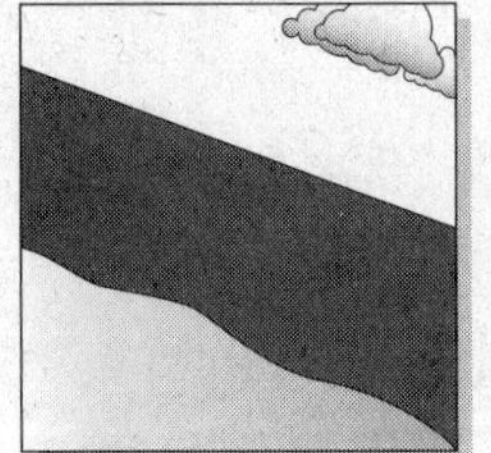

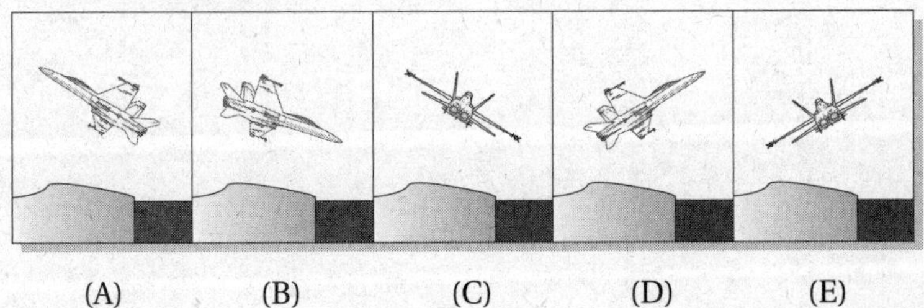

(A) (B) (C) (D) (E)

24.

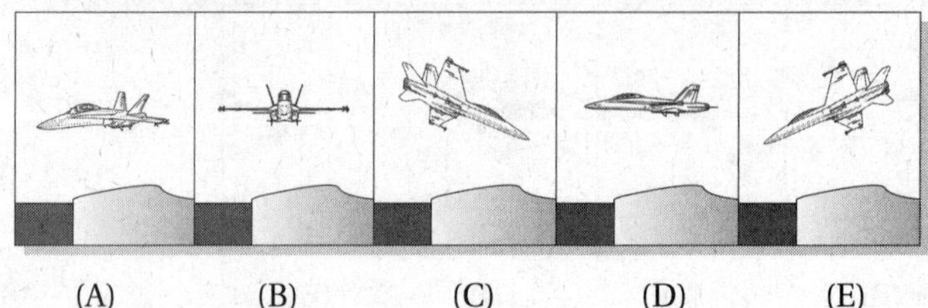

(A) (B) (C) (D) (E)

25.

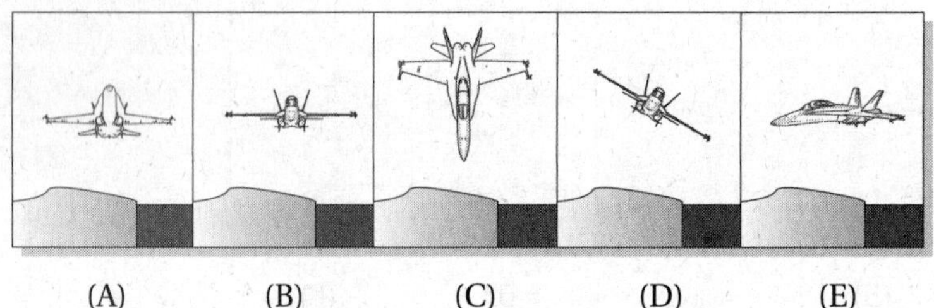

(A) (B) (C) (D) (E)

SUBTEST 5: READING COMPREHENSION TEST (RCT)

20 Questions

1. American military members who willingly defend the free world in the fringe areas are no longer the responsible citizen-soldiers who won World War II and then went back home, glad to have helped but done with that duty. The warrior who will fight a phantom foe in jungle and desert and mountain range and city; who will patiently (if sometimes clumsily) advise and mentor the armies of allies and waverers and recent foes alike, in the hopes of working him- or herself out of a job in that region; this warrior both is and is not the stuff of which legions have been made. They defend the far frontier not as unquestioning, conscripted masses but as creative, committed individuals with multiple competencies who volunteer to answer their calling. These days, he or she is not always a full-time soldier or sailor or airman or Marine; the Reserve and National Guard components of the various services are full of these warriors, not just the active duty "regular" component as it once was. Their devotion is often measured not only in hardships endured but in family sacrifices, missed civilian paychecks and promotions, and children's birthdays and weddings witnessed via Skype if at all.

   The writer of this passage implies that

   (A) National Guard and Reserve warriors are better than the active duty military.
   (B) both the American military and culture have changed significantly since World War II.
   (C) American military recruiting methods have changed significantly since World War II.
   (D) the American military traces its roots to the Roman legions.
   (E) American military members are not as responsible as those who won World War II.

2. "An armed society is a polite society. Manners are good when one may have to back up his acts with his life."

   —Robert A. Heinlein

   From this quote, we can infer that Heinlein

   (A) valued courtesy.
   (B) was willing to voice a possibly unpopular or controversial opinion.
   (C) supported the Second Amendment to the U.S. Constitution.
   (D) all of the above
   (E) none of the above

3. Raoul Wallenberg arrived in Budapest, Hungary, in July 1944 as a Swedish diplomat with a mission: save as many Hungarian Jews as possible from death at Nazi hands. Using a combination of guile, persuasion, falsified documents, and his own diplomatic immunity, his nearly single-handed efforts saved some 25,000 Jews from execution—some literally snatched from death chamber lines. As the Soviet Army neared Budapest in December 1944, Wallenberg persuaded the German general commanding the shrinking Nazi garrison to spare 70,000 more Jews marked for extermination. On January 17, 1945, Wallenberg met with Soviet Army officials to negotiate for food, medicine, and blankets—and was never heard from again. Soviet authorities initially told the Swedish government that Wallenberg had been taken into "protective custody," and said nothing else until 1947, when they disavowed any knowledge of his arrest or whereabouts. In 1957, the Soviet story became that Wallenberg had died of a heart attack in 1947—but between then and 1981, former Gulag prisoners have reported encounters with Wallenberg.

   From this passage, it is reasonable to infer that

   (A) Wallenberg may have died in 1981.
   (B) Wallenberg was an American citizen.
   (C) Soviet Army prisoner records were classified.
   (D) Wallenberg was Jewish.
   (E) Wallenberg had Hungarian family members.

4. Before the airplane provided a means of transporting people—and of killing them—it was used mainly to give them pleasure and thrills. A great flying meeting in the years before the First World War afforded not only spectacle, education, and (for the venturesome few) aerial initiation, but also employment to professional exhibition pilots of several countries. These aerial showmen were the heroes of their time, and nowhere were their evolutions better presented to better effect and warmer appreciation than at the London Aerodrome. Steep banks, glides, and dives were what the crowd loved, and flying in a wind of any strength filled them with astonishment. And there was, of course, always the risk of an accident.

   From this passage, it is reasonable to conclude that

   (A) pilots were looked down upon until the First World War.
   (B) airplane rides at county fairs were not very expensive.
   (C) the writer is a NASCAR fan.
   (D) the writer is from London.
   (E) the writer is unhappy that airplanes started being used in warfare rather than just as entertainment.

5. Young Rudyard Kipling's earliest years in Bombay were blissfully happy, in an India full of exotic sights and sounds. However, at the tender age of just 5 he was sent back to England to stay with a foster family in Southsea, where he was very unhappy. When he was 12 he moved to a boarding school, the United Services College at Westward Ho!, where the headmaster encouraged his literary ability. Despite poor eyesight that handicapped him on the athletic field, he began to blossom. At age 16, he successfully sought to return to Lahore in 1882, where his parents now lived, to work on the *Civil and Military Gazette*, and later on its sister paper the *Pioneer* in Allahabad.

   From this passage about Rudyard Kipling we can infer that

   (A) India was an important British ally.
   (B) Kipling's father worked for the British government.
   (C) Kipling's parents worked for the Indian government.
   (D) Kipling's father worked for a British multinational company.
   (E) Kipling had a good relationship with his parents.

6. An entirely new form of long-range weapon was born with the V2 rocket, which the Germans began to fire on London in the fall of 1944. The "V" was for *Vergeltungswaffen*, or "revenge weapon." The V2 was the first large rocket missile and, unlike the pulse-jet-propelled V1, could not be intercepted once it had been launched because of its high speed and its trajectory, which actually took it out of Earth's atmosphere before coming back to dive into its target. First test-fired successfully in October 1942, a properly functioning V2 reached a height of about 60 miles at the top of its arc, and could hit areas nearly 200 miles away. The V2 reached a speed of 3,500 mph before its rocket burned out, and people near its impact point heard both a sonic boom and an explosion. Even without an explosive warhead, test model V2s left an impact crater 45 feet deep and 120 feet across. Fired from tractor-drawn trailers, lots of effort went into concealing V2 launch sites; some rockets aimed at London were launched from between avenues of trees in the Dutch town of Wassenaar near the Hague, which provided excellent natural concealment.

   The V2 was

   (A) a short-range, high-speed weapon without an explosive warhead.
   (B) an evolution of the V1 rocket design, which could be intercepted.
   (C) tested for two years before it was used on London.
   (D) the first manned rocket used in warfare.
   (E) a high-speed Dutch rocket used on London during World War II.

7. The difference between performance and effectiveness boils down to the quality of the result. Performance in this context is just showing up—"I did what I was supposed to"—which, while essential, is no guarantee of success. Excellence does not happen by chance; it is the result of intention, effort, and adherence to a standard. "Just showing up" is sometimes claimed to be the majority of success—and it's true that those who don't show up fail 100 percent of the time. However, without the determination to do more than just show up, failure is likely—now accompanied by the waste of time and other resources. We know where the road paved with good intentions leads, but without those intentions nothing good happens. Good intentions without serious effort die stillborn. Effort is important, too—but we must not confuse effort with results. Only effort focused by dedication to a high standard, backed up by the determination to reach that standard, results in excellence. Our monument to accomplishment is built in stages, one atop the other and needing all those below, with a flag flying at the pinnacle that says, "Nothing worthwhile is ever easy."

   From this passage, we can infer that the writer

   (A) believes that just showing up is the majority of success.
   (B) does not have much patience with people who don't try very hard.
   (C) has had a lifetime of easy successes.
   (D) is probably an architect or builder.
   (E) likes people who achieve things easily.

8. A Shoulder Sleeve Insignia—abbreviated as "SSI"—is a distinctive cloth patch worn on the left sleeve of a uniform just below the shoulder seam indicating assignment to a particular Army organization. Its design must be approved by The Institute of Heraldry (TIOH). SSI of a design approved by TIOH are authorized and prescribed for wear on the green service uniform and utility (Class C) uniforms of the following echelons: armies, corps, regional support commands, divisions, corps support commands, separate brigades and brigade combat teams not assigned to division, and separate regiments not organic to a group, brigade, or division. Personnel assigned to units not authorized an SSI will wear the SSI of the lowest level command to which the unit is assigned. As an exception, personnel assigned to training support regiments and battalions will wear the SSI of the training support division to which assigned or aligned. Soldiers assigned to a Warrior Transition Unit will continue to wear their organizational headgear and SSI authorized from their last unit of assignment. Cadre assigned to U.S. Army Medical Command will wear the U.S. Army Medical Command SSI. Personnel attached to Headquarters Company, U.S. Army, who are assigned to or performing duty with HQDA staff agencies and offices of the DoD, will wear the Army logo SSI on the Class C uniform.

   From this passage, we learn that soldiers belonging to a unit not authorized an SSI wear the

   (A) SSI of the lowest level command to which the unit is assigned.
   (B) SSI of the highest level command to which the unit is assigned.
   (C) SSI of the lowest level command to which the unit is assigned, unless they are assigned to a training support regiment or battalion.
   (D) SSI of the next level command to which the unit is assigned, unless they are assigned to a training support regiment or battalion.
   (E) SSI authorized from their last unit of assignment.

9. After the 3rd Battalion, 187th Regimental Combat Team returned from Korea to its base in Japan in 1952, the infantry companies all adopted animal nicknames or mascots starting with the same letter as the company designation. K Company had a king cobra, L Company had a lion, and so on. The men of I Company, though, had trouble finding an appropriate figurehead—until they came up with the IBU (which stood for "I is the Best Unit"). The IBU had the antlers of a moose, the head of a lion, the body of a gorilla, and the tail of an alligator; it wore jump boots, had main and reserve parachutes strapped on, and carried a pistol in one hand and a knife in the other. The fierce, mythical mascot caught on, and many members of the company had its image tattooed on their left calf. When the unit was redesignated as A Company, 327th Airborne Battle Group in 1956, morale dropped as the IBU Warriors thought they would have to abandon their mascot. When the mascot was kept and renamed Abu, however, morale once again picked up and today's soldiers of A Company, 1st Battalion, 327th Infantry Regiment still proudly call themselves "Abu Warriors."

   The mythical Abu mascot traces its heritage to

   (A) A Company, 327th Airborne Battle Group.
   (B) I Company, 3rd Battalion, 327th Regimental Combat Team.
   (C) A Company, 1st Battalion, 327th Infantry Regiment.
   (D) I Company, 187th Brigade Combat Team.
   (E) I Company, 187th Regimental Combat Team.

10. The history of the propeller reaches as far back as the twelfth century, when windmills began to dot the landscape of Western Europe. The blades of these windmills—essentially large wood-and-cloth paddles—took energy from the wind to power mechanical grinding mills. It was only a small intellectual leap to think of this process in reverse: to power the blades mechanically to add energy to the air and produce thrust. Leonardo da Vinci developed a helical screw for a sixteenth-century helicopter toy; later, after the first successful manned balloon flights in 1783, J. P. Blanchard mounted a hand-driven propeller to a balloon, but it was not a practical propulsion device. Numerous other efforts to power hot-air balloons with hand-cranked propellers followed, but none were successful. It was not until 1852 that a propeller connected to a steam engine allowed Henri Giffard to guide his airship over Paris at a top speed of five miles per hour.

    Propellers as a practical means of propulsion

    (A) date back to the twelfth century.
    (B) were first designed by Leonardo da Vinci.
    (C) were invented by J. P. Blanchard in the 1780s.
    (D) started with windmills.
    (E) were first used by Henri Giffard in 1852.

11. By the late 1920s, the reciprocating engine-propeller combination was so completely accepted as the means of airplane propulsion that other concepts were mostly discounted. In particular, jet propulsion was viewed as technically infeasible. For example, the National Advisory Committee for Aeronautics (NACA) reported in 1923 that jet propulsion was "impractical," but their studies had been aimed at airspeeds of 250 mph or less, where jet propulsion really is impractical. In 1934, the British government still held a similar opinion. Although an Englishman, Frank Whittle, was the first to operate a jet engine successfully in 1937, it was only on a test stand, and it was a private venture not yet supported by the British government. The first jet to fly was an independently conceived gas-turbine German experimental aircraft that first took off in 1939 and, reaching a top speed of 435 mph, eventually reversed the German government's initial disinterest.

    The first jet airplane

    (A) had a British-made engine and a German design.
    (B) flew in 1937, designed by Englishman Frank Whittle.
    (C) was studied by NACA and deemed "impractical."
    (D) was a German design first flown in 1939.
    (E) was supported by both the British and German governments.

12. If science is right, human beings only use about 10 percent of their brain's capacity. That those who suffer from stroke and brain injuries can often relearn tasks associated with the specific area of brain atrophy or damage confirms this belief. The mind is capable of much more than we have discovered. There are a number of ways to increase personal and organizational creativity. It takes effort, but the benefits are well beyond bottom-line considerations, because creativity influences every aspect of life—even its quality and length. A 1991 *Life* magazine article examined nuns in their eighties and nineties, none of whom showed any evidence of Alzheimer's disease. Their one common thread was that they worked on jigsaw puzzles every day, and in doing so, apparently held off the ravaging effects of brain deterioration.

    The bumper sticker summary of this passage would be

    (A) If You've Got It, Flaunt It.
    (B) Use It or Lose It.
    (C) If You Think Education Is Expensive, Try Ignorance.
    (D) Getting Older Ain't for Sissies.
    (E) Old Age and Treachery Beats Youth and Enthusiasm.

13. It is a pilot's inherent responsibility to be alert at all times for and in anticipation of all circumstances, situations, and conditions affecting the safe operation of the aircraft. For example, a pilot should expect to find air traffic at any time or place. At or near both civil and military airports and in the vicinity of known training areas, a pilot should expect concentrated air traffic and realize concentrations of air traffic are not limited to these places.

    According to this passage, it is a pilot's responsibility to

    (A) be relaxed at all times in order to react quickly to other aircraft in the area.
    (B) always be on the lookout for other aircraft, even when not near an airport.
    (C) stay out of concentrated traffic areas unless necessary to be in them.
    (D) anticipate areas with low concentrations of air traffic.
    (E) ensure each airport's published glide slope is safe for his aircraft.

14. When Korea held its first democratic election in May 1948 under United Nations supervision, about 95 percent of registered voters in the south cast ballots for members of a national assembly. Soviet authorities, however, banned the election in the north and refused to allow UN officials to enter North Korea. The newly elected National Assembly went to work forming a government. In July 1948 the first constitution in four millennia of Korean history was promulgated by the National Assembly, and three days later the deputies elected Dr. Syngman Rhee to a four-year presidential term. The Republic of Korea was acknowledged by the UN General Assembly as the only valid government in Korea; thirty-two nations formally recognized the republic, but UN membership was denied by a Soviet veto in April 1949. The North Korean regime accused Dr. Rhee of a variety of crimes, and caricatured members of his government as responsible for problems actually caused by North Korean provocations. For example, although 80 percent of the Republic of Korea's electric power came from the north, the communists periodically cut off the flow of electricity and then criticized the Seoul government for failing to bring prosperity to the south.

    From this passage, it can be inferred that

    (A) South Korea's initial constitution was not effective.
    (B) South Koreans did not like their constitution.
    (C) South Korea was initially a barren country.
    (D) South Korea never got a chance to join the United Nations.
    (E) there were more North Korean provocations than just cutting off power.

15. Promotion selection boards for Army officers will use the "fully qualified" method of selection when the maximum number of officers to be selected, as established by the SA, equals or exceeds the number of officers above, in, and below the promotion zone. Under this method, a fully qualified officer is one of demonstrated integrity, who has shown that he or she is qualified professionally and morally to perform the duties expected of an officer in the next higher grade. The term *qualified professionally* means meeting the requirements in a specific branch, functional area, or skill. Promotion selection boards will use the "best qualified" method when the board must recommend fewer than the total number of officers to be considered for promotion. However, no officer will be recommended under this method unless a majority of the board determines that he or she is fully qualified for promotion. As specified in the MOI for the applicable board, officers will be recommended for promotion to meet specific branch, functional area, or skill requirements if fully qualified for promotion.

    Promotion selection boards use the "best qualified" method when the

    (A) maximum number of officers to be selected equals or exceeds the number of officers above, in, and below the promotion zone.
    (B) maximum number of officers to be selected is less than the number of officers above, in, and below the promotion zone.
    (C) board can recommend more officers than the total number considered.
    (D) board can recommend the same number of officers as the total considered.
    (E) board is limited to recommending fewer officers than the total considered.

16. In the passage for Question 15 above, what can you conclude from the context that the abbreviations "SA" and "MOI" mean?

    (A) Situational Awareness, Methods of Instruction
    (B) Situational Analysis, Methods of Instruction
    (C) Secretary of the Army, Memorandum of Instruction
    (D) Secretary of the Air Force, Meaning Oriented Interface
    (E) System Administrator, Memorandum of Instruction

17. Inertial Reference Units (IRUs) are self-contained systems comprising gyros and accelerometers that provide aircraft attitude (pitch, roll, and heading), position, and velocity information in response to signals resulting from inertial effects on system components. Once aligned with an initial known position, IRUs continuously calculate position and velocity. IRU position accuracy decays with time; this degradation is known as "drift." Inertial Navigation Systems (INSs) combine the components of an IRU with an internal navigation computer. By programming a series of waypoints, these systems will navigate along a predetermined track.

    Which of the following factors would probably make the most contribution to the accuracy of IRU and INS navigation?

    (A) establishing alignment with an accurate initial starting point
    (B) maintaining a solid four-satellite Global Positioning Satellite system fix
    (C) maintaining radio contact with airfields along the planned route
    (D) maintaining homing beacon reverse bearings to airfields along the planned route
    (E) minimizing drift through programming accurate waypoints

18. The Army generates operationally ready units through a structured progression of training and mission preparation called Army force generation (ARFORGEN). The ARFORGEN ensures that every deploying unit is the best led, trained, and equipped force possible. It is a continuous and structured process of generating Active Component (AC) and Reserve Component (RC) forces that provide increasing unit readiness over time with units moving through the force pools in the operational readiness cycle. This process results in trained, ready, and cohesive forces prepared for operational deployment. At the same time, it establishes a basis to predictively schedule potential deployments on an Army-wide scale while reducing uncertainty for soldiers, families, employers, and communities that support installations. The ARFORGEN allows AC forces to plan on one potential deployment in three years and RC forces to plan for one potential deployment in five years. If deployment to a combat theater is not necessary for a particular unit, it may be scheduled for a major OCONUS exercise or rotational positioning overseas for a period of less than nine months.

    What is the primary purpose of ARFORGEN?

    (A) to guarantee the timing of AC and RC deployments five years ahead of time
    (B) to predict which AC unit will deploy where three years ahead of time
    (C) to predictively schedule potential deployments for AC and RC units
    (D) to provide increasing readiness over time for soldiers, families, and employers
    (E) to define operational readiness cycles for AC and RC units

19. The Global Positioning System (GPS) is a satellite-based radio navigation system that broadcasts a signal used by receivers to determine precise position anywhere in the world. The receiver tracks multiple satellites and determines a pseudorange measurement that is then used to determine the user's location. A minimum of four satellites is necessary to establish an accurate three-dimensional position. The Department of Defense (DoD) is responsible for operating the GPS satellite constellation and monitors the GPS satellites to ensure proper operation. Every satellite's orbital parameters (ephemeris data) are sent to each satellite for broadcast as part of the data message embedded in the GPS signal. The GPS coordinate system is the Cartesian Earth-centered Earth-fixed coordinates as specified in the World Geodetic System 1984 (WGS-84).

    How many satellites receive ephemeris data?

    (A) 3
    (B) 4
    (C) 24
    (D) 26
    (E) all of them

20. There is strong evidence that many military victories once thought amazing or unexplainable are the result of creative leadership. It has always been so, whether recognized or not. Regardless of its mechanisms, war remains an equation of human beings and their minds and hearts. No stockpiling of mere things can offset a superiority of minds. When Hannibal burned his boats in A.D 219 and crossed the uncrossable Alps; when Cortes burned his boats thirteen centuries later and conquered an empire; when Col. Joshua Chamberlain told the men of the 20th Maine to "swing like a gate" and drove his opponents from the field; and when then-Lt. Col. Chris Hughes told his battalion to take a knee, and then to smile at crowding Iraqis, thereby defusing a brewing conflict over a mosque—none of these measures was in any manual. None had been taught in any school (although they are now, as examples of creativity). Today's leaders have to know the doctrinal solutions to common challenges—but they must also know when and how to "color outside the lines" to accomplish the mission.

    The author of this passage believes that leaders

    (A) have to know when to burn their boats.
    (B) must be able to apply uncommon solutions to uncommon challenges.
    (C) should smile after burning their boats.
    (D) must apply creative solutions to common problems.
    (E) must stockpile a superiority of creative minds.

SIFT #2

SUBTEST 6: MATH SKILLS TEST (MST)

20 Questions

1. If $x + 9 = 10$, then x equals

(A) –1
(B) 1
(C) 2
(D) 0
(E) 9/10

2. If $a - 5 = 7$, then a equals

(A) 2
(B) –2
(C) 12
(D) –12
(E) 5/7

3. What is the product of $(4y - 3)(y + 2)$?

(A) $4y^2 + 11y + 6$
(B) $4y^2 + 11y - 6$
(C) $4y^2 + 3y + 6$
(D) $4y^2 + 5y - 6$
(E) $4y^2 + 4y - 6$

4. At Norwich University, 41 percent of the 1,400 cadets participate in intramural athletics, and about 27 percent of those are rooks (freshmen). If this number is one-third of the total rook class, how many total rooks are there?

(A) 64
(B) 155
(C) 465
(D) 52
(E) 378

5. Fort Shackleford has a large pool in the shape of a pentagon. If the Morale, Welfare, and Recreation office wants to hire a lifeguard for each side of the pool, what is the minimum number they will need to hire? Lifeguards are limited to one 4-hour shift per day with a 30-minute meal break and, during the peak summer season, the pool stays open from 1000 to 1800.

(A) 4
(B) 5
(C) 10
(D) 15
(E) 16

6. If a carpenter cuts the largest possible circular tabletop from a piece of wood that is two feet square, how much wood will be left over? Use 3.14 for π.

(A) 0.86 sq. ft.
(B) 1.0 sq. ft.
(C) 1.72 sq. ft.
(D) 1.86 sq. ft.
(E) 2.0 sq. ft.

7. The measure of one of the equal angles of an isosceles triangle is 50 degrees. What is the measure of the angle opposite the unequal side?

(A) 120
(B) 180
(C) 100
(D) 130
(E) 80

8. A room in Mackenzie's new house measures 19 ft. × 10 ft., with an 8-ft. ceiling. If she wants to paint the walls and ceiling, how many square feet will she have to cover?

(A) 232 sq. ft.
(B) 422 sq. ft.
(C) 464 sq. ft.
(D) 654 sq. ft.
(E) 1,308 sq. ft.

9. Operating by itself, Pump 1 can empty the Schmutzig-Merder Waste Treatment Facility initial holding tank in six hours, but Pump 2 can empty the same holding tank in four hours. How many minutes will it take the two pumps to empty the holding tank if they are both operating at the same time?

(A) 120
(B) 144
(C) 272
(D) 444
(E) 600

10. A metal cube weighs 5 lbs. How many pounds will another cube made of the same metal weigh if its sides are twice as long?

(A) 10
(B) 25
(C) 40
(D) 50
(E) 60

11. Out of the sophomore class of 373 students at Stony Rock High School, 101 are taking Spanish and 82 are taking German. Of those taking a language, 14 are taking both. How many sophomores are not taking a language at all?

(A) 162
(B) 176
(C) 183
(D) 197
(E) 204

12. $(\sqrt{3} - \sqrt{2})^2 =$

(A) $6 + 2(\sqrt{6})$
(B) $-1 + 2(\sqrt{6})$
(C) $1 - 2(\sqrt{6})$
(D) $5 - 2(\sqrt{3} + \sqrt{2})$
(E) $5 - 2(\sqrt{6})$

13. The distance from point A to point B is 5 km; the distance from point B to point C is 2 km. Which of the following is the best choice for the distance from point A to point C?

(A) 3 km
(B) 7 km
(C) 5 km
(D) choice (A) or (B)
(E) choice (A), (B), or (C)

14. *JKLM* is a parallelogram. If the length of *JL* = 3, and triangle *JLM* is an equilateral triangle, what is the perimeter of the parallelogram?

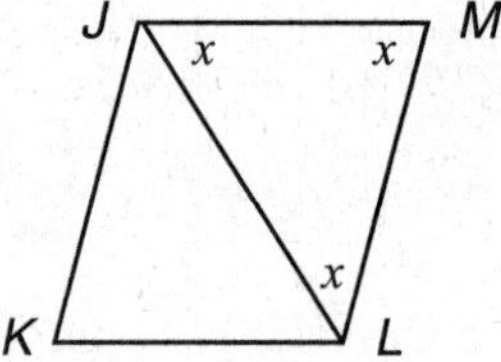

(A) $3\sqrt{9}$
(B) 9
(C) 12
(D) $\frac{5}{3}$
(E) 15

SIFT #2

15. Lieutenant Highspeed saved $1,047 while he was in his Basic Officer Leader Course. If he deposits 90% of this amount in the local credit union at his first duty station, in an account with a 3.2% simple annual interest rate, how much will he have in the credit union at the end of 32 months, presuming he can leave the account alone? The formula to calculate simple interest is interest = principal × rate × time.

(A) $1,035.68
(B) $1,136.46
(C) $1,003.57
(D) $1,024.98
(E) $1,022.81

16. Which of these angle measure sets would fit a right triangle?

(A) 40°, 40°, 100°
(B) 60°, 60°, 60°
(C) 40°, 50°, 90°
(D) 40°, 40°, 90°
(E) 30°, 45°, 90°

17. The maximum airspeed for a UH-60L Black Hawk is 156 knots; cruise speed is 120–145 knots. What percentage increase is maximum speed over minimum cruise speed?

(A) 7.6%
(B) 30.0%
(C) 33.3%
(D) 43.2%
(E) 24.8%

18. The internal Allowable Cargo Load (ACL) of a CH-47D Chinook is 31 combat-equipped troops estimated at 250 lbs. each. If a 100-round ammo can of linked .50 caliber ammunition weighs 35 lbs., about how many rounds of .50 cal ammo can safely accompany a 4-man fire team? Assume all ammo stays packed in cans for transport, and round to the nearest hundred rounds.

(A) 775,000
(B) 675,000
(C) 154,000
(D) 19,300
(E) 22,140

19. An increase in temperature decreases the hovering ceiling for all helicopters, and decreases in temperature have the opposite effect; this occurs in an evenly graduated manner for Helicopter X. The hovering ceiling (in ground effect) chart for Helicopter X in humid air at 60° F shows 3,900 ft. and 1,300 ft. at 100° F. Based on the data above, what hovering ceiling would you expect when similarly loaded in humid air at 20° F?

(A) 2,600 ft.
(B) 3,200 ft.
(C) 3,900 ft.
(D) 5,200 ft.
(E) 6,500 ft.

20. In 1950, the U.S. Army had 715 pilots and 1,242 aircraft; in 1970, the Army had 22,250 aviators and 11,446 aircraft. What is the difference, expressed as a percentage, in the ratio of aviators to aircraft between the two years? In other words, for every aviator, how many aircraft were there in each of the two specified years? Round your final answer to the nearest tenth of a percentage point.

(A) increase of 70.4%
(B) decrease of 70.4%
(C) decrease of 70.6%
(D) decrease of 31.1%
(E) increase of 82.2%

SUBTEST 7: MECHANICAL COMPREHENSION TEST (MCT)

20 Questions

This subtest evaluates your understanding of general mechanical principles by showing you drawings or pictures, and then asking questions about the mechanical principles indicated. There are 20 questions on this subtest, which you will have 15 minutes to answer. For each question, choose the best answer; there is only *one* right answer to every question.

1. If gear B is the driving gear and it makes 6 revolutions, how many revolutions will gear A make?

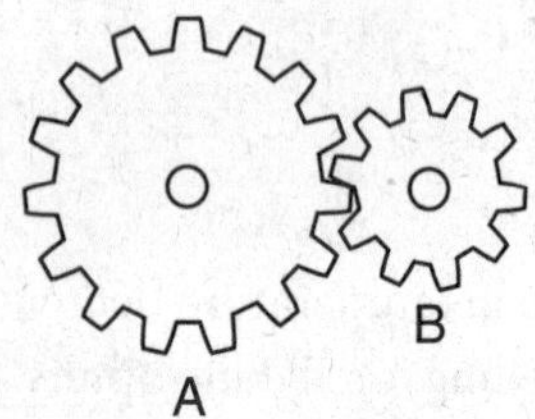

(A) 2
(B) 4
(C) 6
(D) 8
(E) 9

2. If block A, on which the lever is resting, is moved closer to block B,

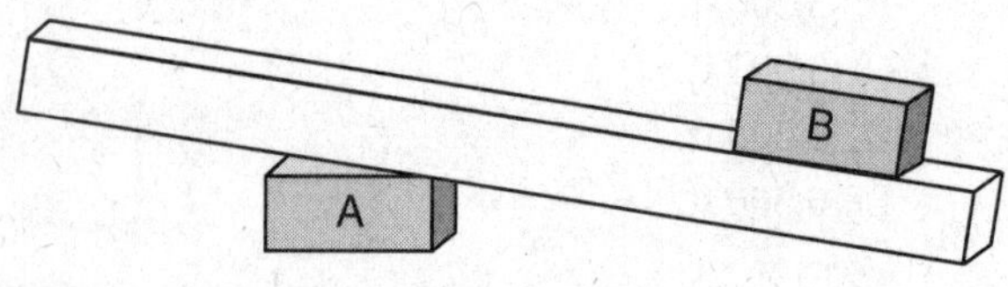

(A) there will be no change in the effort required to lift block B to the same height.
(B) it will be harder to lift block B but it will go higher.
(C) it will be easier to lift block B and it will go higher.
(D) it will be harder to lift block B and it will not be lifted to the same height.
(E) it will be easier to lift block B but it will not be lifted as high.

3. If pulley C is rotating clockwise, what direction will pulley A rotate?

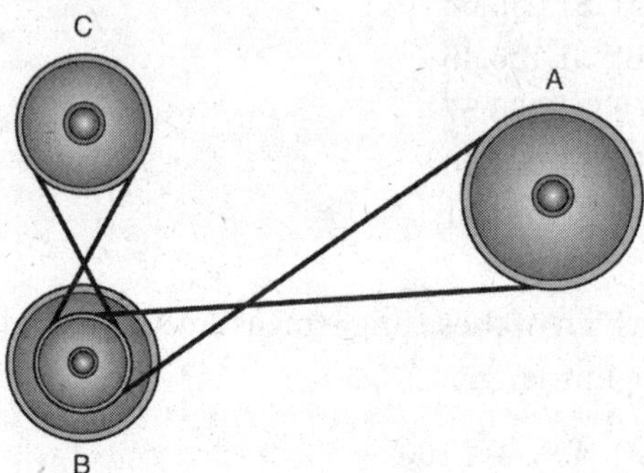

(A) clockwise
(B) counterclockwise
(C) insufficient information to answer
(D) pulley A will not rotate
(E) the same direction as pulley B

4. In the pulley system above, which pulley will rotate the fastest?

(A) pulley A
(B) pulley B
(C) pulley C
(D) all will rotate at the same speed
(E) insufficient information to answer

5. If the cisterns of both water towers A and B are the same size and the same height above the ground, and both begin with a full water level, which water tower will be able to provide more water to the thirsty troops below?

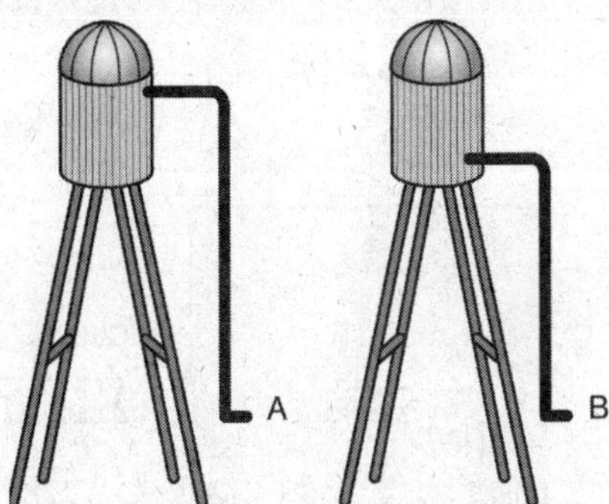

(A) water tower A
(B) water tower B
(C) both will provide the same amount
(D) unable to tell from the information provided
(E) depends on local wind shear

6. Which weight exerts more pull on the horizontal bar from which both weights hang by strings as shown?

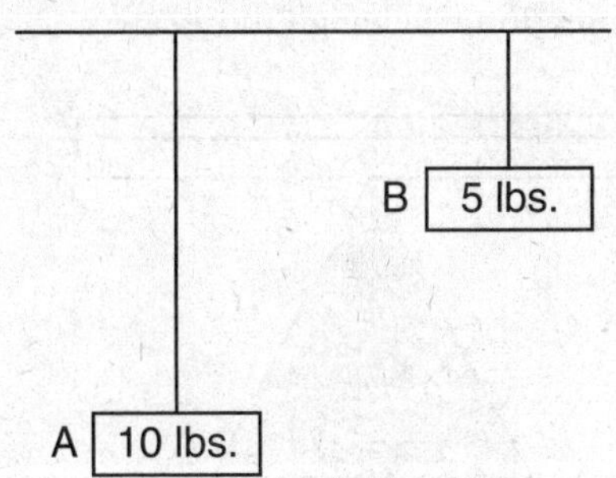

(A) A
(B) B
(C) both exert the same pull
(D) cannot tell from the information given
(E) none of the above

7. The wheels below are connected by a belt as shown. If the larger wheel makes 2 revolutions, how many revolutions will the smaller wheel make?

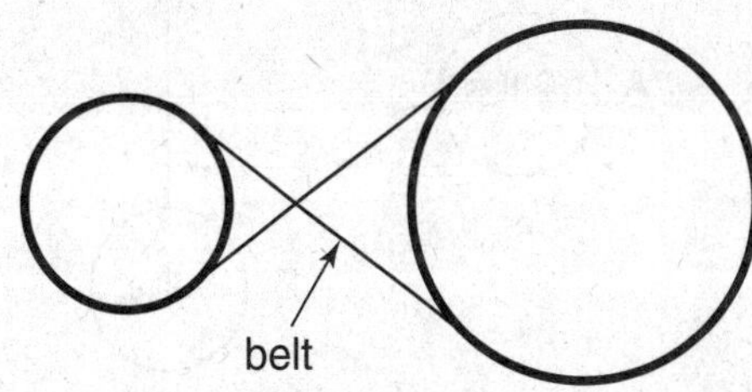

(A) less than one
(B) one
(C) two
(D) more than two
(E) none of the above

8. The force required to balance the lever shown below would be

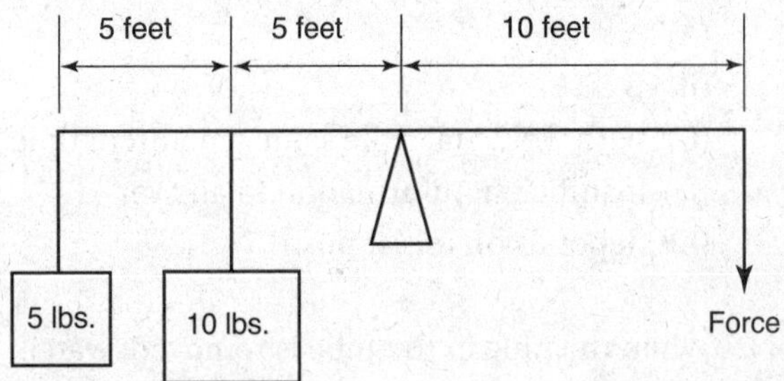

(A) 10 pounds
(B) 15 pounds
(C) 20 pounds
(D) 25 pounds
(E) 30 pounds

SIFT #2

9. Which pendulum takes more time to make one complete swing?

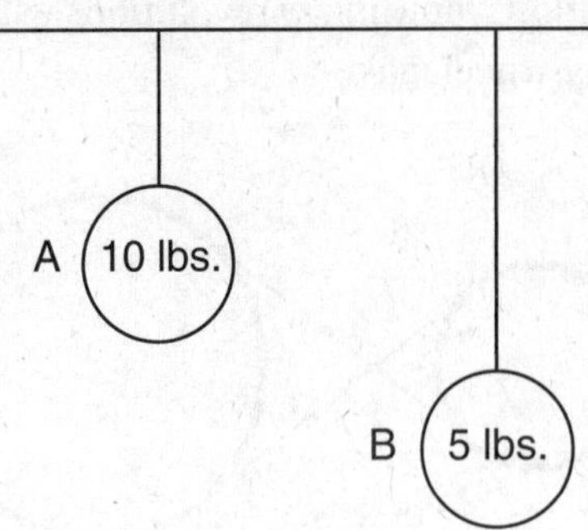

(A) A
(B) B
(C) both take the same amount of time
(D) insufficient information to answer
(E) depends on initial push

10. In the diagram above, if pendulum A was the same length as pendulum B, which pendulum would take less time to make one swing?

(A) A
(B) B
(C) both would take the same amount of time
(D) insufficient information to answer
(E) depends on initial push

11. When the plug in the tube is removed, water will flow

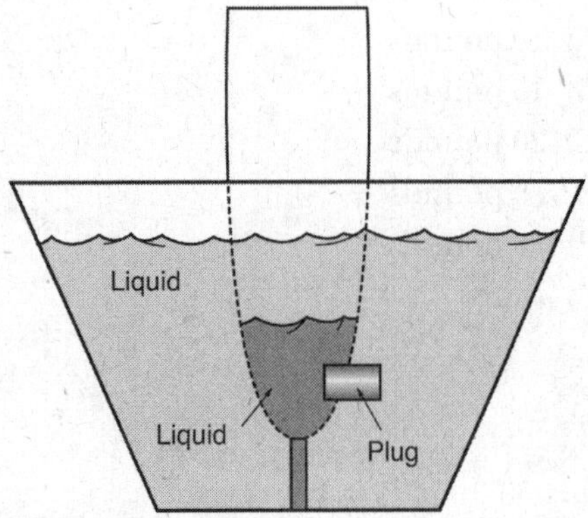

(A) into the tube.
(B) out of the tube.
(C) in neither direction.
(D) impossible to tell
(E) depends on atmospheric pressure

12. In the water system below, assume that the main tank begins in an empty state and that all the valves are closed. In order for the tank to fill approximately halfway and maintain that level, which valves would have to be open?

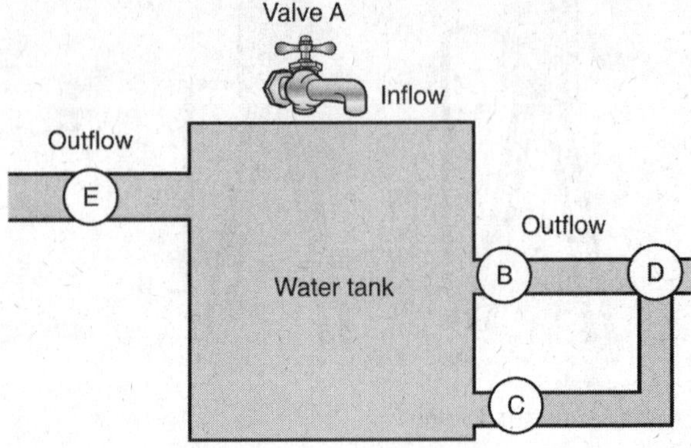

(A) A, B, and C
(B) A, B, and D
(C) A, E, and B
(D) A, E, and C
(E) B, C, and D

13. You balance a wooden beam on a fulcrum at its center of gravity (CG). If you then mark the CG and cut the beam in two at that point, which section will weigh more?

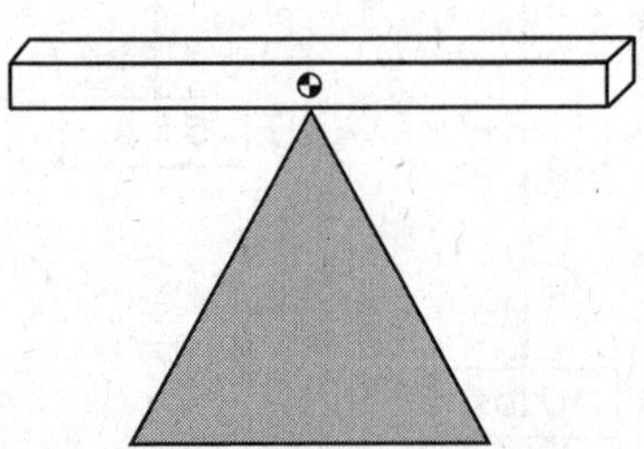

(A) the lefthand portion
(B) the righthand portion
(C) the bigger segment
(D) the smaller segment
(E) both segments will weigh the same

SIFT #2

14. In the depicted arrangement of pulleys and belts, which pulley will have the highest number of revolutions per minute (RPMs)?

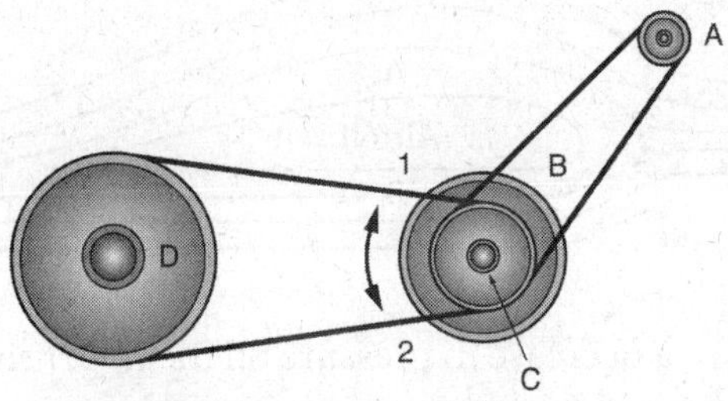

(A) pulley A
(B) pulley B
(C) pulley C
(D) pulley D
(E) cannot tell from the information given

15. Two cylinders, A and B, contain hydraulic fluid to the same level and are connected by a hydraulic line as shown. If the surface area of the piston in cylinder A is 3 square inches, the surface area of the piston in cylinder B is 6 square inches, and the piston in cylinder B is pressed down 1 inch, what will happen to the piston in cylinder A?

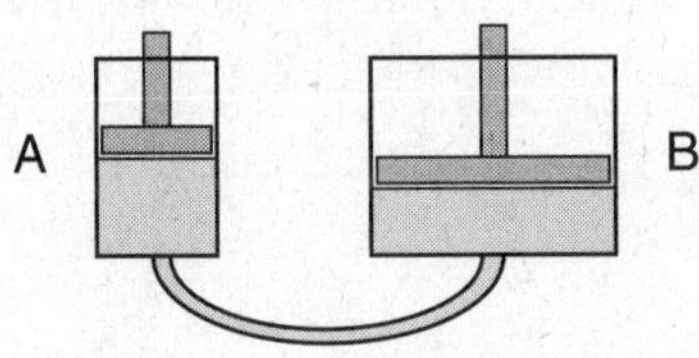

(A) It will rise 1/4 inch.
(B) It will rise 2 inches.
(C) It will rise 3 inches.
(D) It will rise 4 inches.
(E) cannot tell from the information given

16. In the diagram below, if gear A is the driving gear turning clockwise, what directions will gears B, C, and D turn?

(A) B counterclockwise, C counterclockwise, and D counterclockwise
(B) B clockwise, C clockwise, and D clockwise
(C) B clockwise, C counterclockwise, and D clockwise
(D) B counterclockwise, C clockwise, and D counterclockwise
(E) B counterclockwise, C counterclockwise, and D clockwise

17. In the diagram above, what is the mechanical advantage of gear A to gear D?

(A) 1:1
(B) 1:2
(C) 1:4
(D) 1:8
(E) 1:24

18. When two or more forces act in such a way that their combination has a net effect of zero, what is this condition called?

(A) similarity
(B) equilibrium
(C) equilateral
(D) notionality
(E) equestrianism

19. The descent of an airborne paratrooper is primarily affected by what physical forces?

(A) gravity and thrust
(B) gravity and temperature
(C) thrust and temperature
(D) drag and gravity
(E) lift and drag

20. Most of the lift on an aircraft's wings is because of

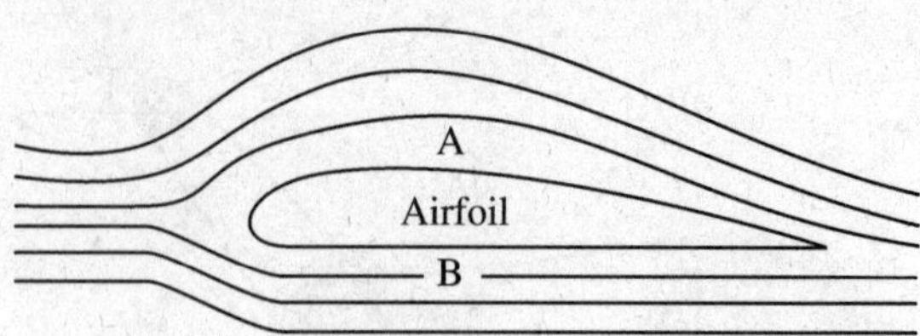

(A) a decrease in pressure on the upper side of the wing (A).
(B) a decrease in pressure on the bottom side of the wing (B).
(C) a vacuum created under the wing at (B).
(D) an increase in pressure on the upper side of the wing (A).
(E) none of the above

SIFT #2

ANSWERS AND EXPLANATIONS

Subtest 1: Simple Drawings (SD)

	✔	✘		✔	✘		✔	✘		✔	✘
1. B			26. E			51. A			76. C		
2. E			27. A			52. B			77. E		
3. D			28. C			53. D			78. A		
4. B			29. B			54. E			79. D		
5. A			30. B			55. A			80. D		
6. B			31. A			56. B			81. B		
7. E			32. D			57. D			82. D		
8. B			33. C			58. B			83. E		
9. D			34. A			59. D			84. D		
10. C			35. E			60. E			85. A		
11. A			36. B			61. B			86. C		
12. D			37. D			62. C			87. B		
13. E			38. A			63. A			88. B		
14. B			39. C			64. D			89. E		
15. A			40. B			65. E			90. C		
16. B			41. B			66. B			91. D		
17. E			42. C			67. B			92. A		
18. C			43. E			68. A			93. D		
19. A			44. B			69. E			94. A		
20. B			45. C			70. D			95. D		
21. D			46. B			71. A			96. C		
22. B			47. A			72. E			97. C		
23. A			48. C			73. B			98. A		
24. C			49. C			74. C			99. A		
25. D			50. B			75. C			100. D		

Subtest 2: Hidden Figures (HF)

	✔	✘		✔	✘		✔	✘		✔	✘		✔	✘
1. E			11. C			21. E			31. A			41. C		
2. C			12. B			22. D			32. B			42. A		
3. D			13. E			23. A			33. D			43. D		
4. B			14. D			24. B			34. C			44. E		
5. A			15. A			25. C			35. E			45. B		
6. A			16. B			26. C			36. C			46. B		
7. E			17. C			27. D			37. A			47. D		
8. B			18. A			28. A			38. D			48. E		
9. C			19. E			29. E			39. E			49. C		
10. D			20. D			30. B			40. B			50. A		

(A)

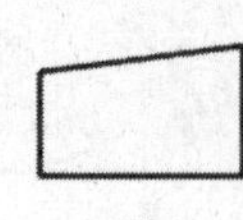

(B)

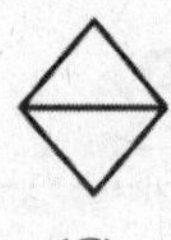

(C)

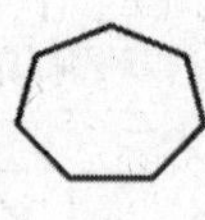

(D)

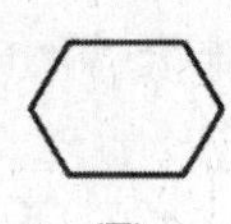

(E)

1. **(E)**

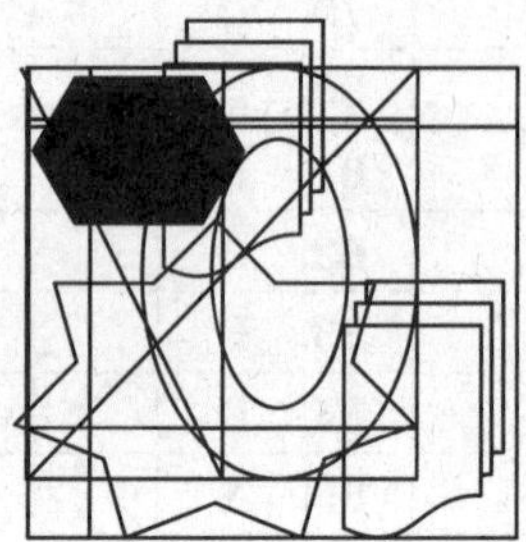

2. **(C)**

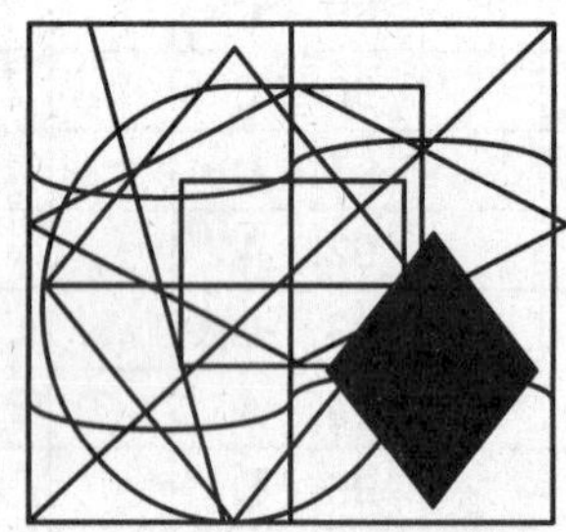

3. **(D)**

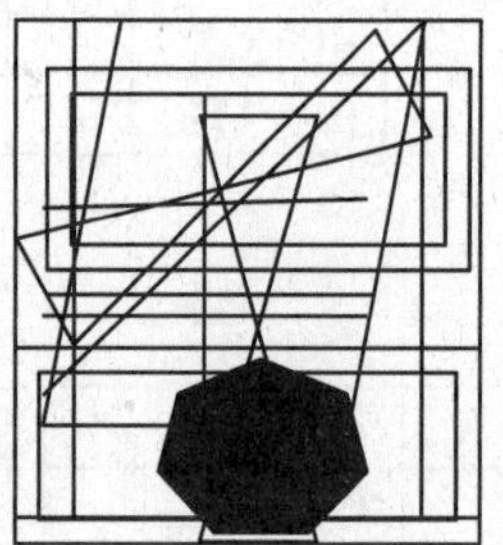

4. **(B)**

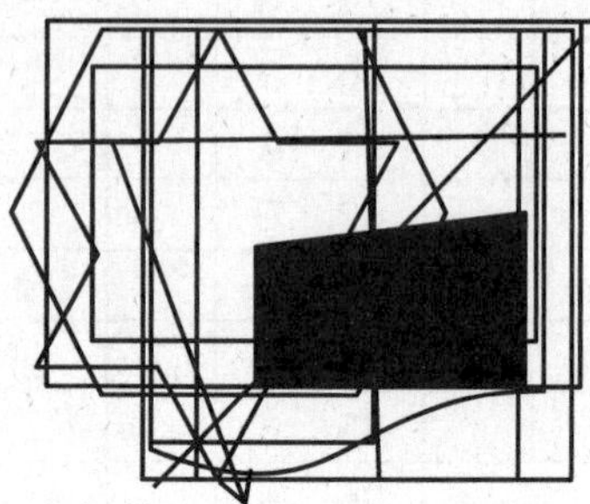

5. **(A)**

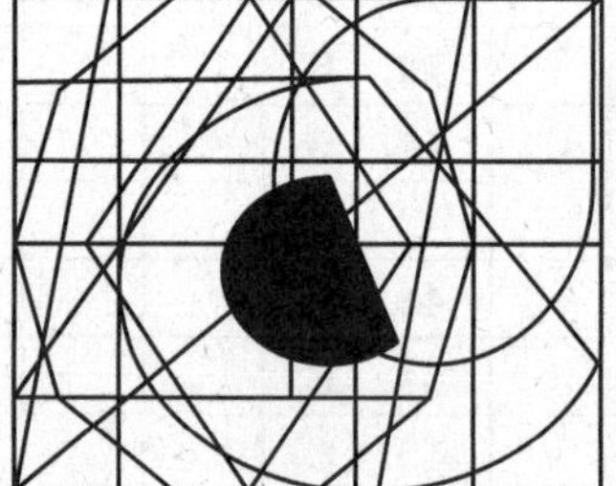

SIFT #2

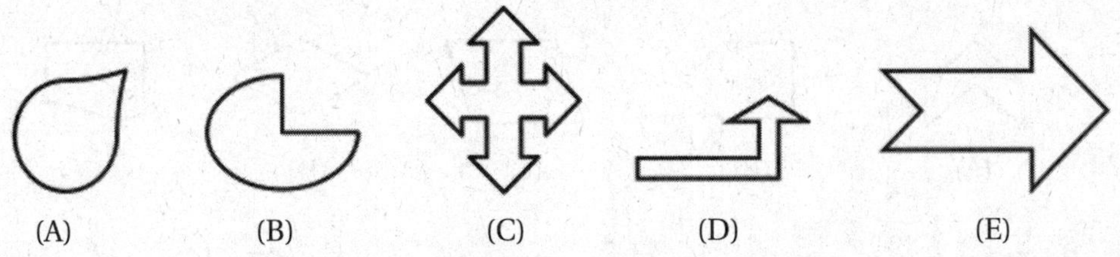

6. **(A)**

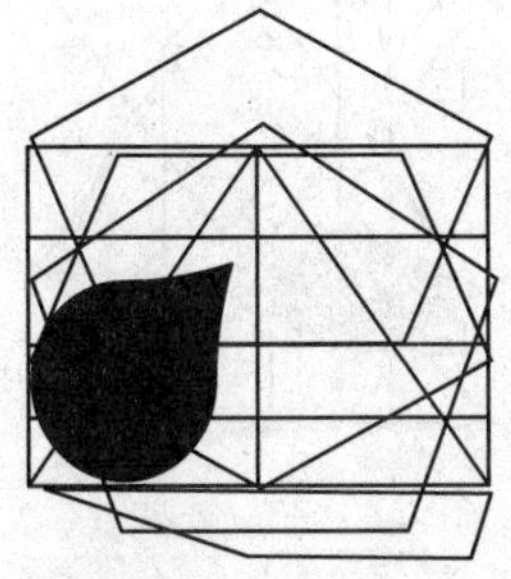

7. **(E)**

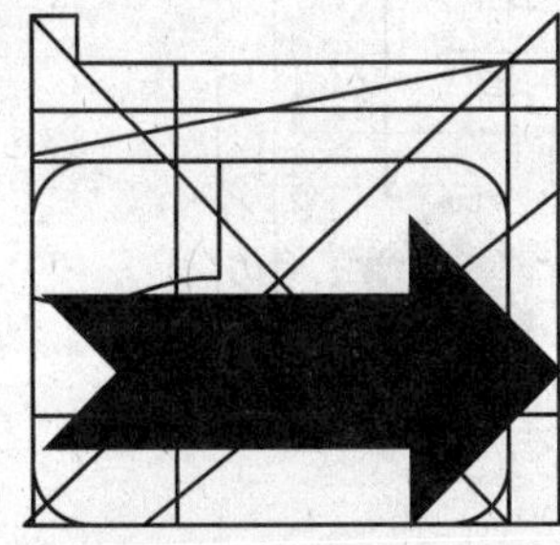

8. **(B)**

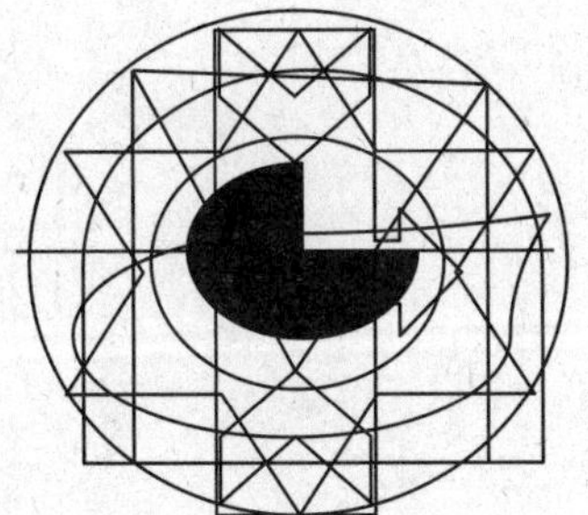

9. **(C)**

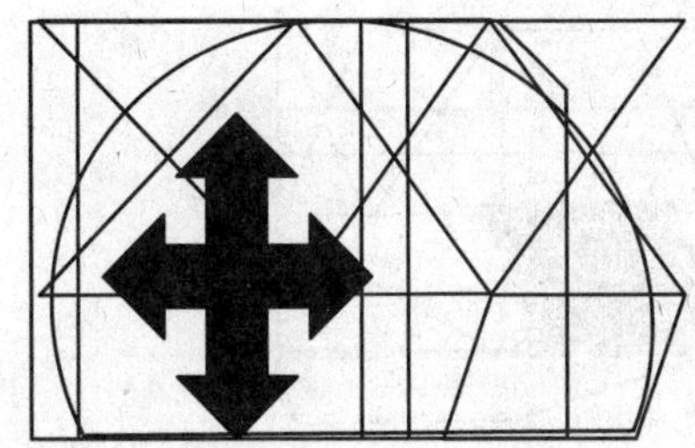

10. **(D)**

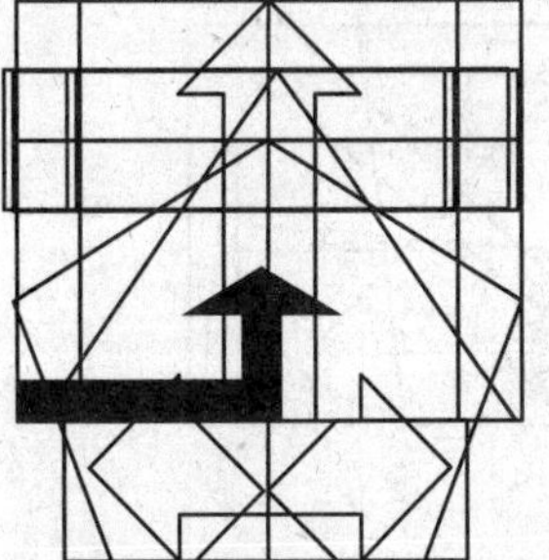

SIFT #2

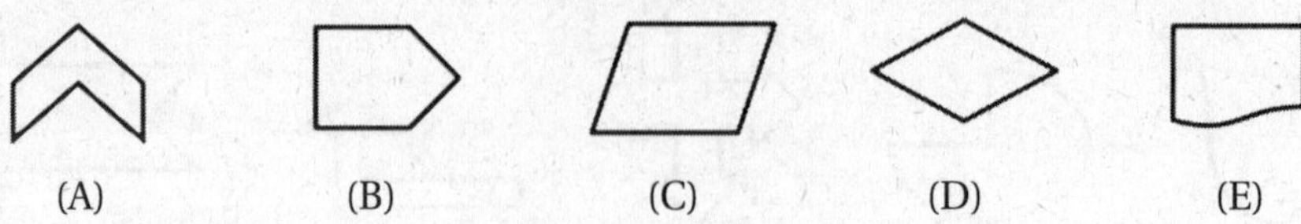

11. **(C)**

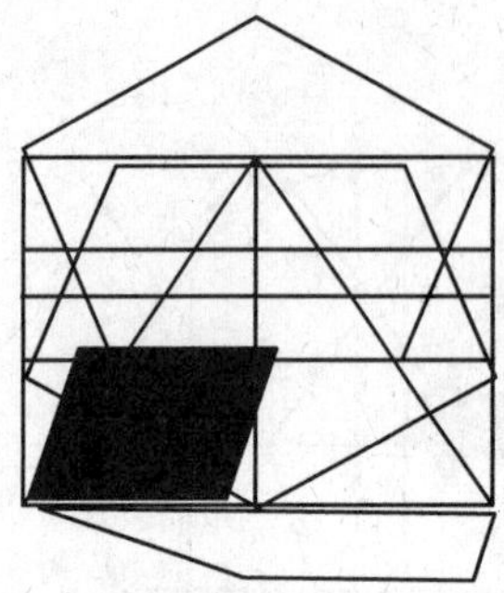

14. **(D)**

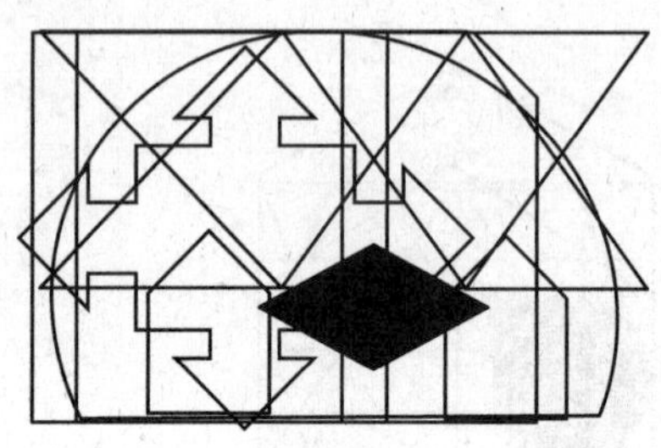

12. **(B)**

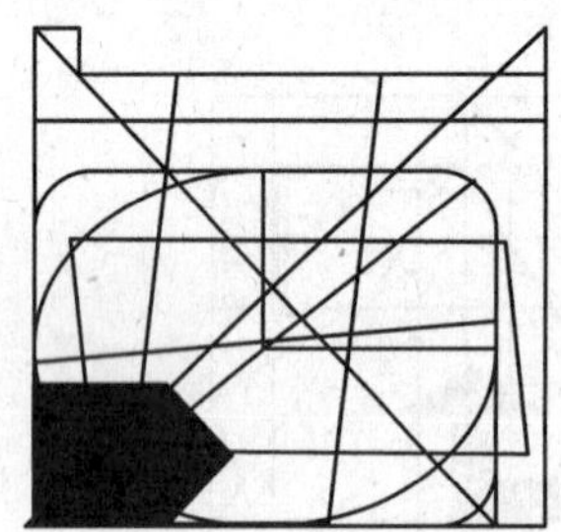

15. **(A)**

13. **(E)**

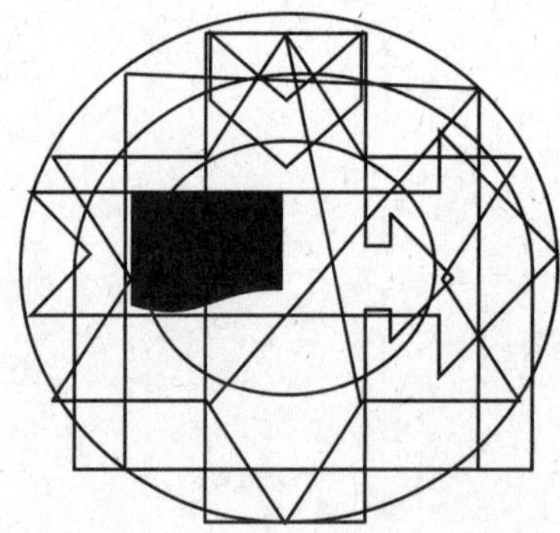

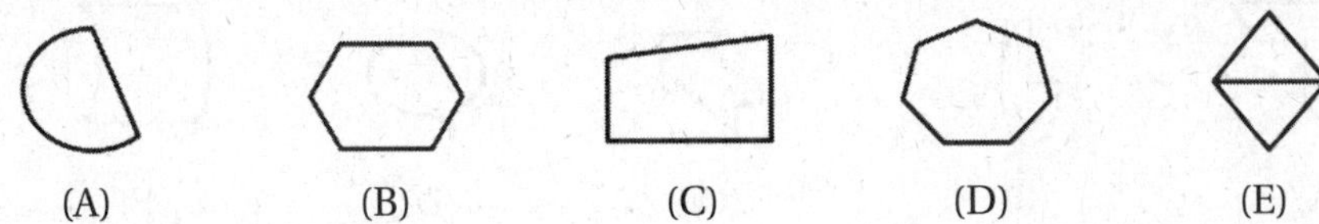

16. **(B)**

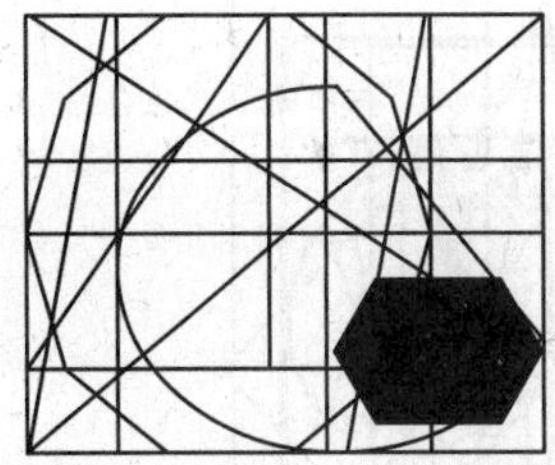

17. **(C)**

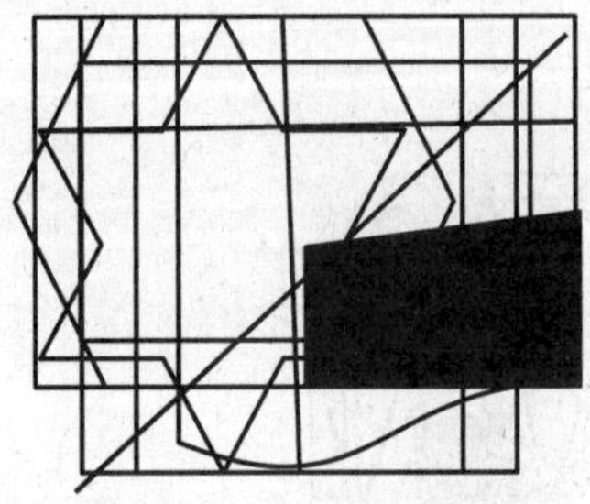

18. **(A)**

19. **(E)**

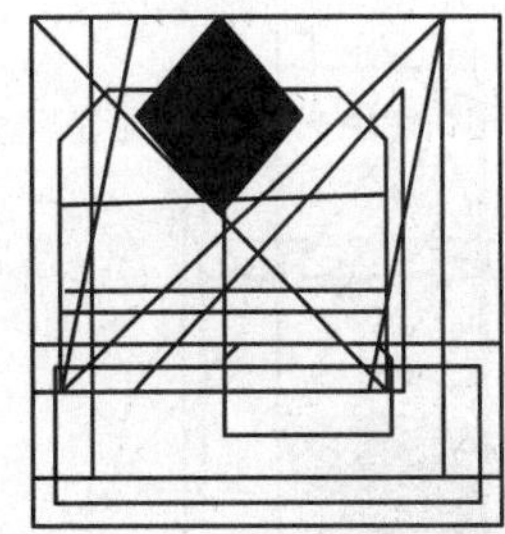

20. **(D)**

(A)

(B)

(C)

(D)

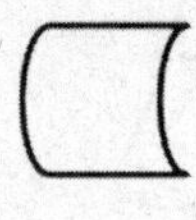
(E)

21. **(E)**

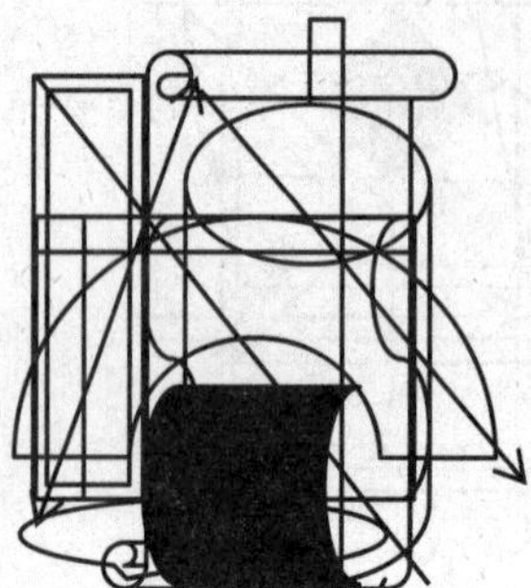

24. **(B)**

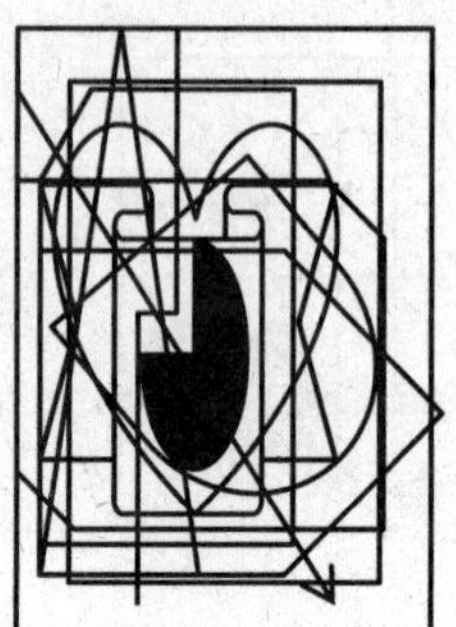

22. **(D)**

25. **(C)**

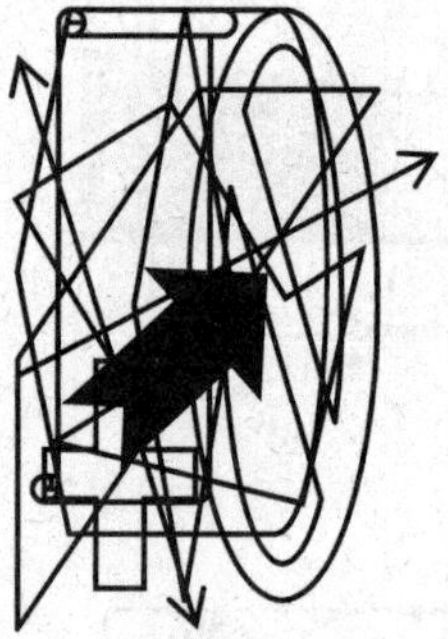

23. **(A)**

(A)

(B)

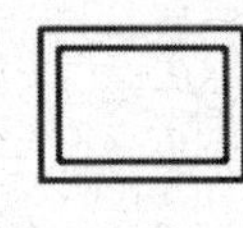

(C)

(D)

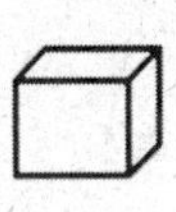

(E)

26. **(C)**

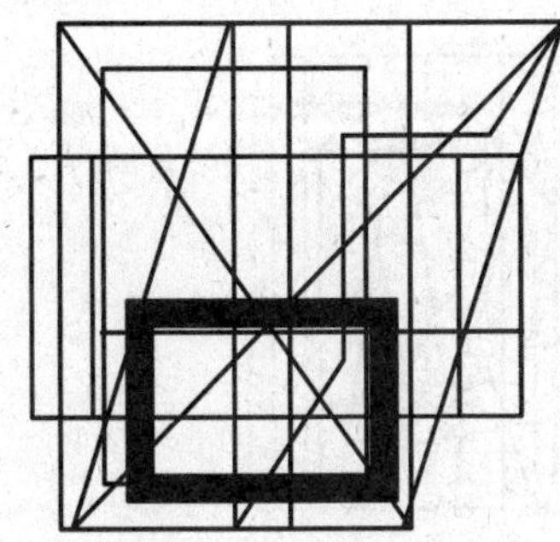

29. **(E)**

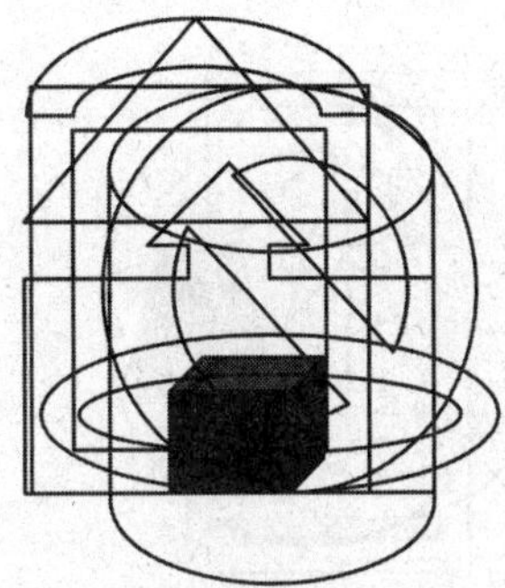

27. **(D)**

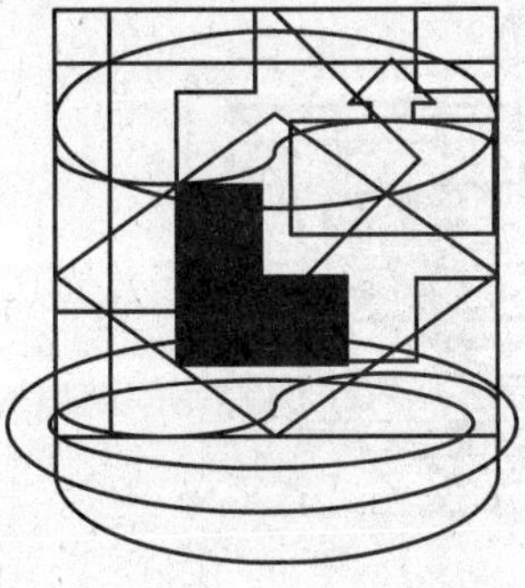

30. **(B)**

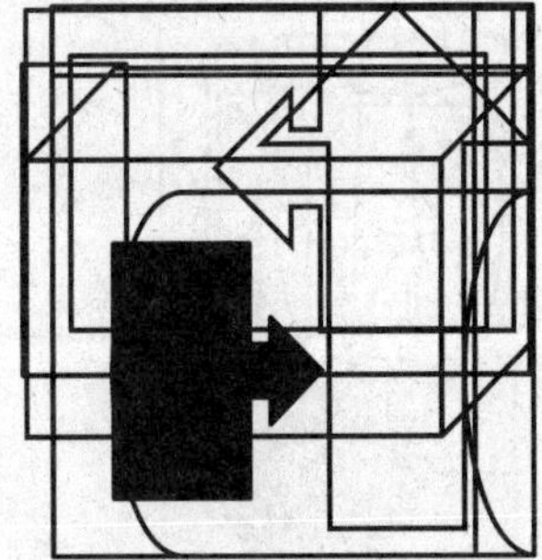

28. **(A)**

SIFT #2

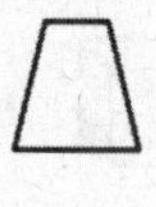
(A)

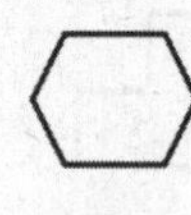
(B)

(C)

(D)

(E)

31. **(A)**

32. **(B)**

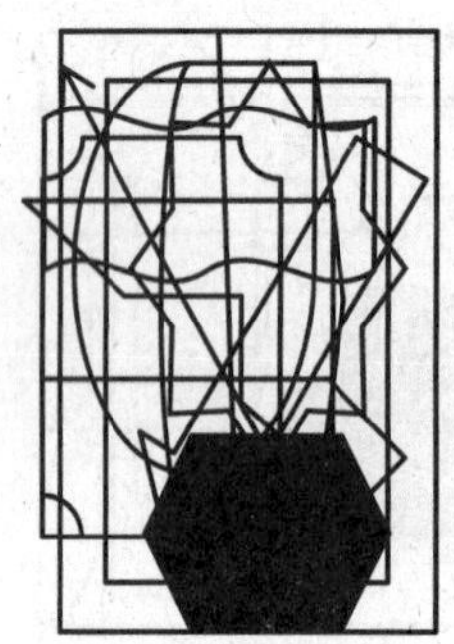

33. **(D)**

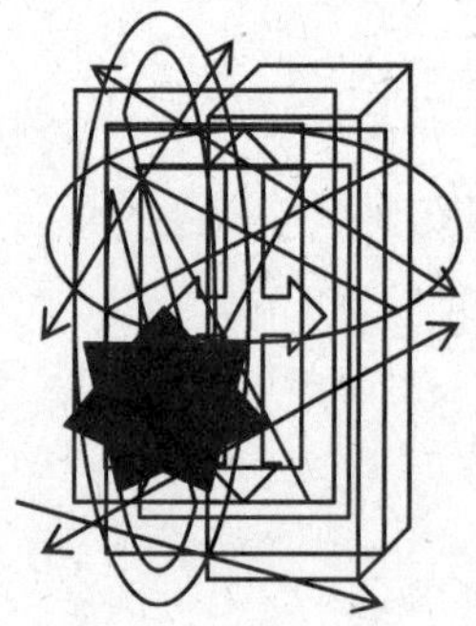

34. **(C)**

35. **(E)**

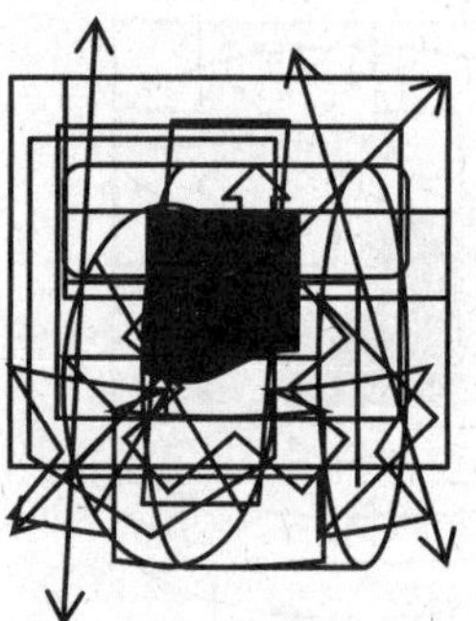

SIFT #2

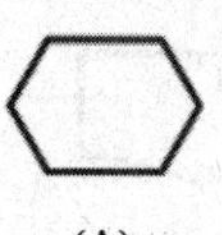
(A)

(B)

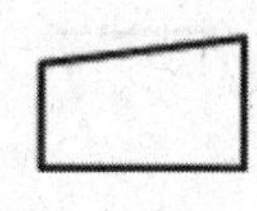
(C)

(D)

(E)

36. **(C)**

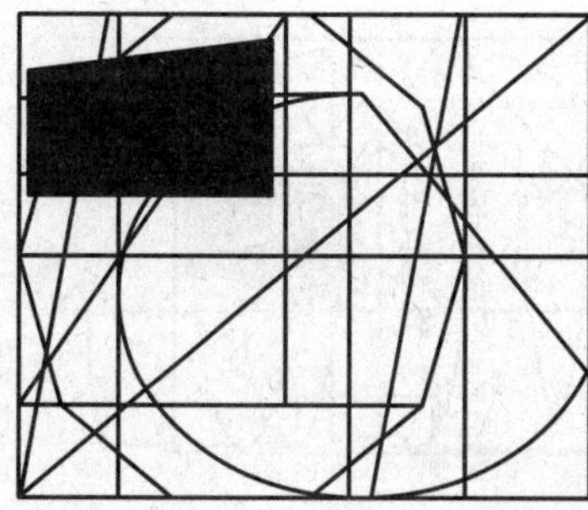

37. **(A)**

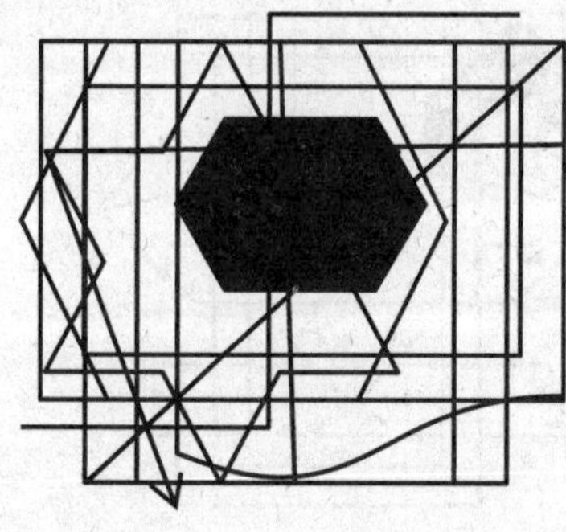

38. **(D)**

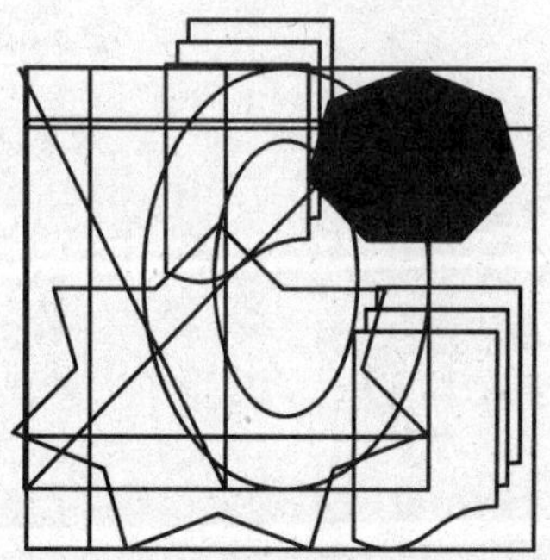

39. **(E)**

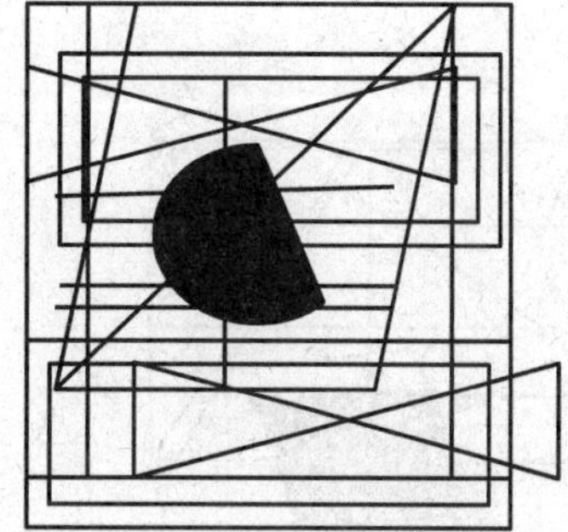

40. **(B)**

SIFT #2

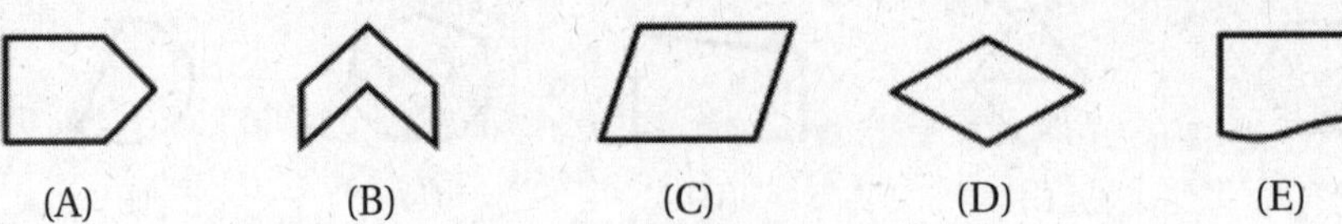

41. **(C)**

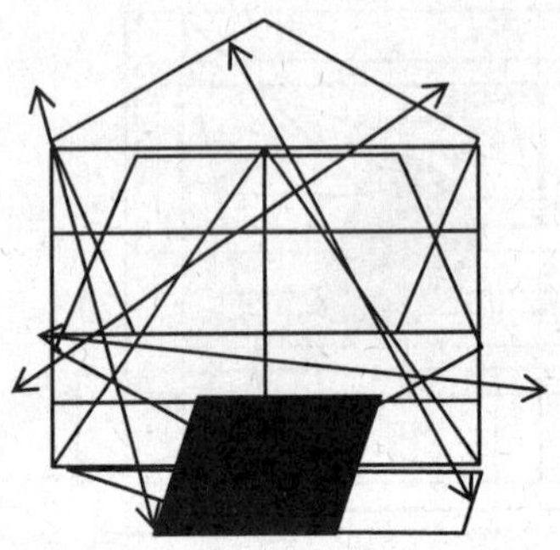

44. **(E)**

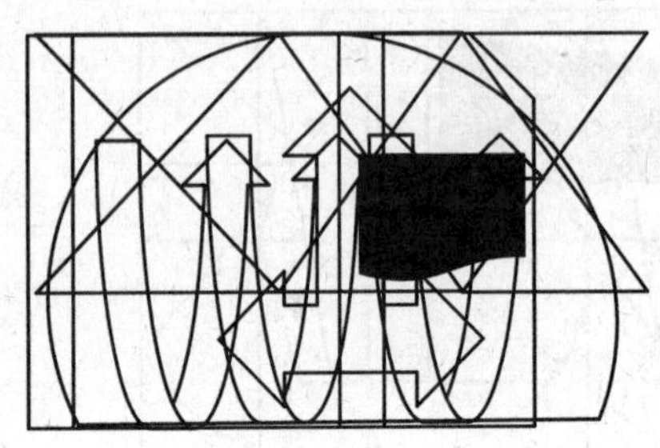

42. **(A)**

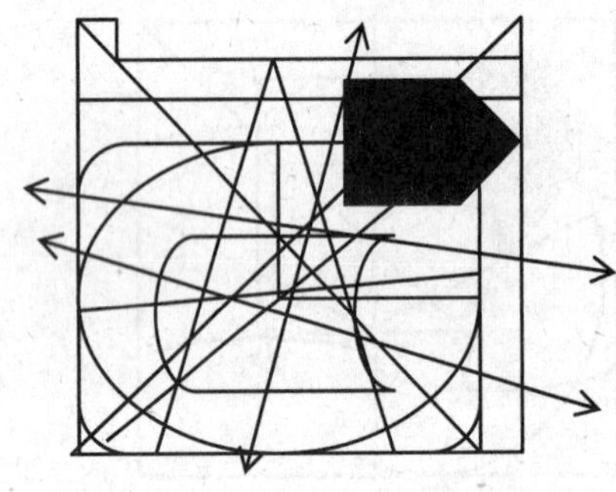

45. **(B)**

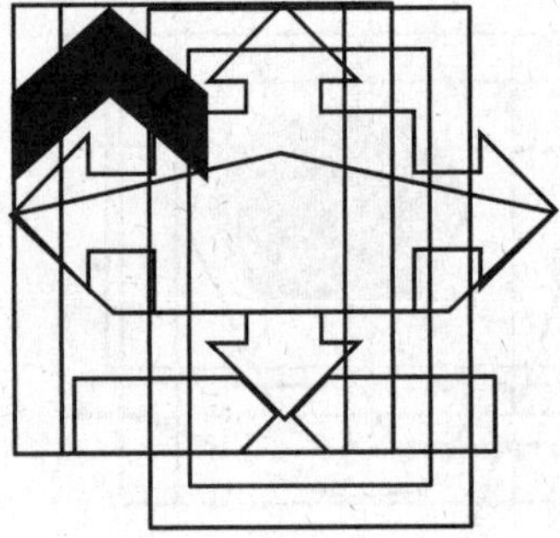

43. **(D)**

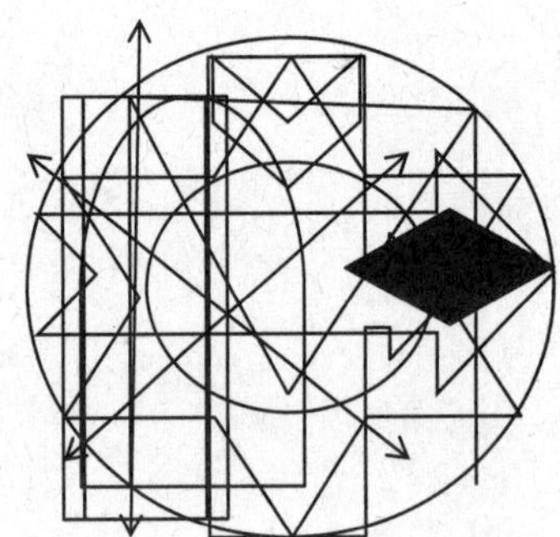

(A)

(B)

(C)
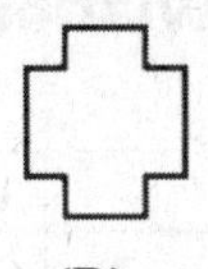
(D)

(E)

46. **(B)**

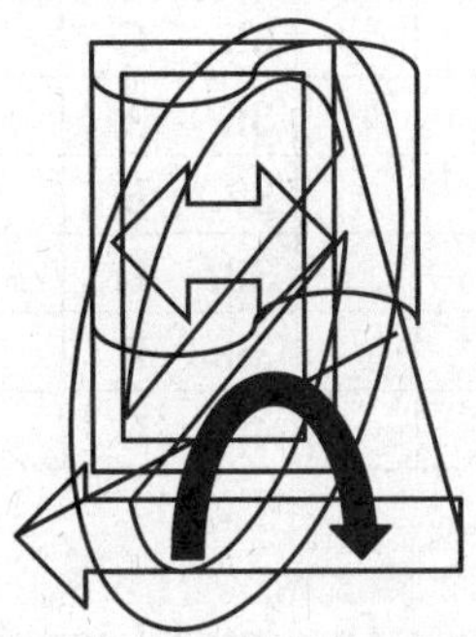

49. **(C)**

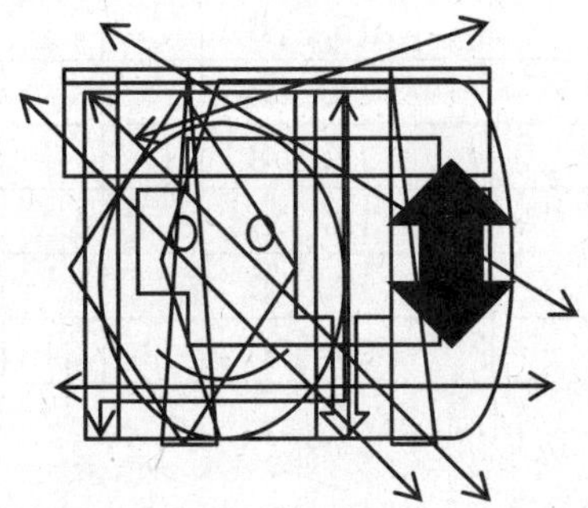

47. **(D)**

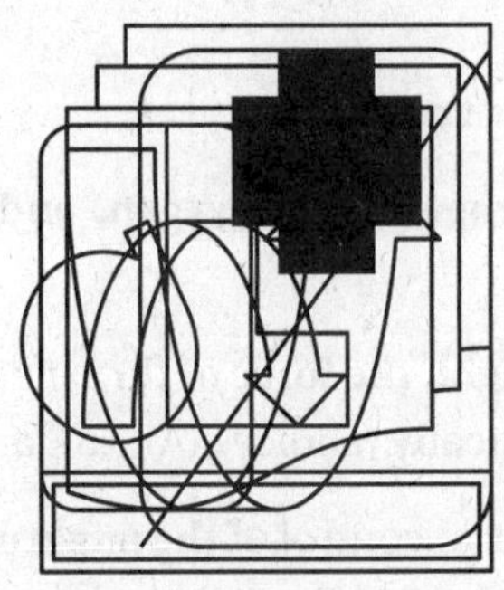

50. **(A)**

48. **(E)**

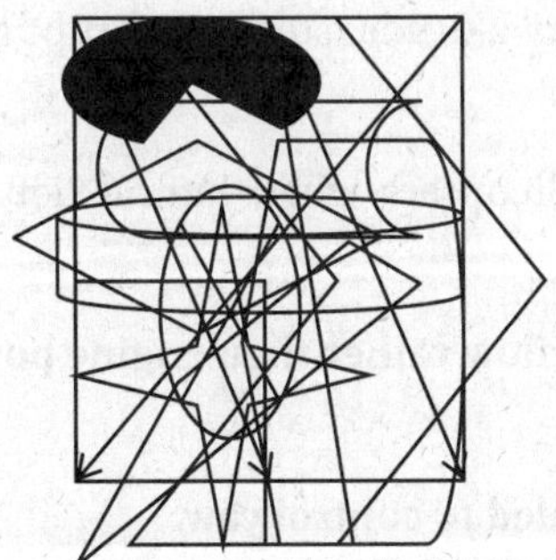

Subtest 3: Army Aviation Information Test (AAIT)

	✔	✘		✔	✘		✔	✘		✔	✘
1. C			11. A			21. A			31. D		
2. B			12. A			22. C			32. B		
3. C			13. D			23. E			33. D		
4. A			14. B			24. A			34. B		
5. E			15. B			25. C			35. C		
6. B			16. D			26. A			36. A		
7. A			17. B			27. C			37. B		
8. B			18. A			28. D			38. D		
9. C			19. D			29. E			39. B		
10. C			20. C			30. A			40. C		

1. **(C)** The three axes around which flight movement occurs are **lateral, longitudinal, and vertical**.
2. **(B)** One way to state Bernoulli's Principle is **the faster a fluid is traveling, the less its pressure on the supporting surface**.
3. **(C)** The amount of an airfoil's curvature is called its **camber**.
4. **(A)** Earth's atmosphere is composed of **78% nitrogen, 21% oxygen, and 1% other gases**.
5. **(E)** In a stabilized hover, **the force of lift equals weight, the force of thrust equals drag,** and **lift, weight, thrust, and drag are all acting vertically** (choices (A), (B), and (D)).
6. **(B)** By placing his hand on the collective, the pilot is in control of **the angle of the main rotor blades and the engine RPMs**. Lifting the collective affects the angle of the main rotor blades, and the throttle can be twisted with the same hand holding the collective.
7. **(A)** When flying at a high forward airspeed, retreating blade stall is likely under conditions of **high gross weight**, low RPMs, high density altitude, steep or abrupt turns, and turbulent air.
8. **(B)** Transient torque occurs in **single-rotor helicopters when lateral** (left or right) **cyclic is applied**.
9. **(C)** Autorotation is **turning a rotor system by airflow rather than engine power**, such as during an engine failure.
10. **(C)** During autorotation, the tail rotor **is still needed to control yaw**.
11. **(A)** The transverse flow effect occurs when air flowing over the rear portion of the main rotor disc is accelerated downward by the main rotor, which causes the rear portion to have a smaller angle of attack. This **results in less lift to the rear portion of the rotor disc**, but, because of gyroscopic precession, the result is felt 90 degrees later.
12. **(A)** A lighted heliport can be identified by **a white, yellow, and green rotating beacon**.

13. **(D)** When a helicopter in a hover has a tendency to drift in the direction of tail rotor thrust, this is called **translating tendency**.

14. **(B)** The best way to perform a quick stop is to **lower the collective and pull back on the cyclic**.

15. **(B)** The collection of factors that facilitates maximum helicopter performance is **low altitude, low temperature, and low humidity**.

16. **(D)** The cyclic controls the **direction of the tilt of the main rotor**.

17. **(B)** Moving the cyclic forward and significantly raising the collective will cause the helicopter to **increase its forward speed and begin to climb**.

18. **(A)** Conventional American helicopters have a main rotor that **turns in a counterclockwise direction**.

19. **(D)** Translational lift is **the additional lift gained when the helicopter leaves its downwash**.

20. **(C)** Gyroscopic precession happens when **a force applied to a spinning disc has its effect 90 degrees later in the direction and plane of rotation**.

21. **(A)** Increasing collective (power) while maintaining constant airspeed will cause the helicopter to **climb**. When a helicopter is stable in a flight mode, it has very little pitch deflection up or down.

22. **(C)** Profile drag, developing from the frictional resistance of the blades passing through the air, does not change significantly with the airfoil's angle of attack, but **increases moderately when airspeed increases**.

23. **(E)** Induced drag is generated by **airflow circulation around the rotor blade as it creates lift**. The high-pressure area beneath the blade joins the low-pressure area above the blade at the trailing edge and rotor tips. This causes a spiral or vortex that trails behind each blade whenever lift is being produced. These vortices deflect the air downward in the vicinity of the blade, creating an increase in downwash.

24. **(A)** A rotor blade's angle of attack (AOA) is **usually lower at higher airspeeds and higher at lower airspeeds**. The main rotor's AOA has nothing directly to do with the power applied to the antitorque rotor (if that helicopter even has one). The collective pitch control (or just "collective") changes the pitch angle of all the main rotor blades collectively (i.e., all at the same time) and independently of their position; this changes the blades' AOA relative to the mast.

25. **(C)** Airfoils are used to produce lift, as well as **stability, control, and thrust or propulsion**. An example of an airfoil being used for stability is a fin, for control an elevator, and for thrust or propulsion a propeller or rotor. Certain airfoils, such as rotor blades, combine some of these functions. The main and tail rotor blades of the helicopter are airfoils, and air is forced to pass around the blades by mechanically powered rotation. In some conditions, parts of the fuselage, such as the vertical and horizontal stabilizers, can become airfoils.

26. **(A)** In a vertical autorotative descent in still air, the forces that cause the blades to turn are **similar for all blades regardless of their position in the plane of rotation, making**

dissymmetry of lift from airspeed not a factor. During an autorotation, the *upward* flow of relative wind permits the main rotor blades to rotate at their normal speed; in effect, the blades are "gliding" in their rotational plane.

27. **(C)** On a helicopter, a governor is a device that **senses rotor and engine RPMs and makes adjustments to keep rotor RPMs constant**. In normal operations, once rotor RPMs are set, the governor keeps them constant, and there is no need to make any throttle adjustments. Governors are common on all turbine helicopters (since it's a function of the turbine engine's fuel control system), and used on some piston-powered helicopters.
28. **(D)** A *correlator* is a mechanical connection between the collective lever and the engine throttle. When the collective lever is raised, **power is automatically increased**. When the collective is lowered, power is decreased. This system maintains RPMs close to the desired value, but still requires adjustment of the throttle for fine-tuning.
29. **(E)** The antitorque pedals, located on the cabin floor by the pilot's feet, control the **pitch** and therefore the **thrust** of the tail rotor blades or other antitorque system. RPMs of the tail rotor blades, along with the main rotor blades, are controlled by the throttle. Note: The antitorque pedals are sometimes (incorrectly) called "rudder pedals" because that is what the same kind of pedals are called in an airplane, and because they control the motion of the helicopter in the same plane (no pun intended) around the vertical or *z* axis.
30. **(A)** Main rotor systems are classified according to how the main rotor blades are attached and move relative to the main rotor hub. There are three primary types: **rigid, semirigid, and fully articulated.** An *underslung* rotor system is a type of semirigid system that mitigates the lead/lag forces by mounting the blades slightly lower than the usual plane of rotation, so the lead and lag forces are minimized. As the blades cone upward, the center of pressures of the blades are almost in the same plane as the hub. Whatever stresses are remaining bend the blades for compliance. The *teetering* hinge in a semirigid rotor system allows the main rotor hub to tilt, while the *feathering* hinge enables the pitch angle of the blades to change.
31. **(D)** A fully articulated rotor system allows each blade to **lead/lag (move back and forth in the plane of rotation)**, **flap independent of the other blades (move up and down about an inboard mounted hinge)**, and **feather (rotate around the pitch axis to change lift)** so **all of the above**.
32. **(B)** On a typical helicopter airspeed indicator a green arc indicates the aircraft's **normal operating speed range**. The airspeed limit beyond which structural damage could occur, or "never exceed" speed (V_{NE}), is indicated by a red arc. Maximum safe autorotation speed is sometimes marked by a blue line.
33. **(D)** More power is required during **hovering** than any other helicopter flight regime. Obstructions aside, if a hover can be maintained, a takeoff can be made, especially with the additional benefit of translational lift.
34. **(B)** The three major factors that affect helicopter performance are **density altitude, weight, and wind**. Airspeed is the speed at which a helicopter moves through the atmosphere and is unaffected by wind. Atmospheric wind affects only the groundspeed, or

speed at which the helicopter is moving over Earth's surface. Humidity alone is usually not considered an important factor in calculating density altitude and helicopter performance, but it does contribute. There are no rules of thumb used to compute the effects of humidity on density altitude, but some manufacturers include charts with 80 percent relative humidity columns as additional information. There appears to be an approximately 3–4 percent reduction in performance compared with dry air at the same altitude and temperature; it's reasonable to expect a decrease in hovering and takeoff performance in high-humidity conditions. Although 3–4 percent may seem insignificant, it can cause an accident when the helicopter is operating at the edge of its performance envelope. Additionally, at higher gross weights, the increased power required to hover produces more torque, which means more antitorque thrust is required. In some helicopters during high-altitude operations, the maximum antitorque produced by the tail rotor during a hover may not be sufficient to overcome torque even if the gross weight is within limits.

35. **(C)** The four fundamentals of flight—on which all maneuvers are based—are **straight and level flight, turns, climbs, and descents**. All controlled flight maneuvers consist of one or more of these.

36. **(A)** The helicopter pilot can use the pedals to control **heading, direction of turn, and rate of turn at hover**. Hover height, rate of ascent, and rate of descent are controlled with the collective. Helicopter position and the direction of travel are controlled by the cyclic. Don't confuse *heading*—which way the longitudinal axis of the helicopter is "pointing," or which way the pilot is facing when looking forward through the canopy—with *direction of travel*, which is relative to the whole airframe: forward, backward, left, or right.

37. **(B)** Airspeed in straight and level flight is determined by the **forward-tilting attitude of the rotor disk relative to the horizon**. However, the collective must be adjusted as necessary to control airspeed and altitude, even if it's constant.

38. **(D)** A slip occurs when the helicopter slides sideways toward the center of the turn, and is caused by **not enough antitorque pedal pressure in the direction of the turn**.

39. **(B)** A normal approach to a hover before landing uses a descent profile of **between 7 and 12 degrees starting about 300–500 feet above ground level**.

40. **(C)** Nap-of-the-Earth (NOE) flight is conducted **at varying airspeeds as close to Earth's surface as vegetation and obstacles permit**. It is a military flight mode designed to minimize detection by enemy forces or systems.

Subtest 4: Spatial Apperception Test (SAT)

	✔	✘		✔	✘		✔	✘		✔	✘		✔	✘
1. A			6. C			11. B			16. D			21. B		
2. E			7. C			12. A			17. B			22. E		
3. D			8. A			13. B			18. C			23. B		
4. E			9. D			14. C			19. C			24. A		
5. E			10. D			15. B			20. E			25. D		

Answer	Pitch	Bank	Heading
1. **(A)**	climbing	left	out to sea
2. **(E)**	climbing	right	out to sea
3. **(D)**	diving	left	out to sea
4. **(E)**	diving	wings level	out to sea
5. **(E)**	level flight	right	coastline left
6. **(C)**	level flight	wings level	coastline left
7. **(C)**	climbing	left	out to sea
8. **(A)**	diving	right	out to sea
9. **(D)**	level flight	right	coastline right
10. **(D)**	climbing	wings level	out to sea
11. **(B)**	diving	wings level	out to sea
12. **(A)**	level flight	wings level	out to sea
13. **(B)**	diving	right	out to sea
14. **(C)**	diving	wings level	coastline right
15. **(B)**	level flight	left	coastline left
16. **(D)**	level flight	left	coastline left
17. **(B)**	diving	wings level	out to sea
18. **(C)**	climbing	right	out to sea
19. **(C)**	level flight	right	out to sea
20. **(E)**	climbing	wings level	out to sea
21. **(B)**	level flight	left	out to sea
22. **(E)**	level flight	left	out to sea
23. **(B)**	diving	left	out to sea
24. **(A)**	level flight	wings level	out to sea at an angle
25. **(D)**	level flight	left	coastline right

Subtest 5: Reading Comprehension Test (RCT)

	✔	✘		✔	✘		✔	✘		✔	✘
1. C			6. C			11. D			16. C		
2. D			7. B			12. B			17. A		
3. A			8. C			13. B			18. C		
4. E			9. E			14. E			19. E		
5. E			10. E			15. E			20. B		

1. **(C)** The writer of this passage implies that **American military recruiting methods have changed significantly since World War II**. This is *implied* because the writer dwells on how the individuals who make up both active and reserve forces are different; therefore, if the people recruited are significantly different—if they "both are and are not the stuff of which legions were once made," we may reasonably infer or deduce that recruiting methods are different. Although both the American military and American culture have, in fact, changed a great deal since WWII, the writer does not address American culture, and no inference is therefore possible.

2. **(D)** From this quote, we can infer that Heinlein valued courtesy; was willing to voice a possibly unpopular or controversial opinion; and supported the Second Amendment to the U.S. Constitution (which guarantees the right to keep and bear arms), so the answer is **all of the above**.

3. **(A)** From this passage, it is reasonable to infer that **Wallenberg may have died in 1981**, the year of his last reported sighting in the Soviet prison system. Wallenberg was in fact made an honorary American citizen in 1981 in an effort to resolve his status—but this was not mentioned in the passage. Soviet Army prisoner records may or may not have been classified, but the passage does not address this even by implication—and he would have been handed over to other, non-Army, Soviet authorities if he had in fact been sent to the Gulag archipelago and its infamous camps. Wallenberg was not in fact Jewish, nor did he have Hungarian relatives. He had, however, been an apprentice to a Hungarian Jewish import/export business owner in Sweden in 1936; when his boss found it too difficult to travel to Hungary, Wallenberg was given the reins of the firm's foreign division.

4. **(E)** From this passage, it is reasonable to conclude that **the writer is unhappy that airplanes started being used in warfare rather than just as entertainment**.

5. **(E)** From this passage about Rudyard Kipling we can infer that **Kipling had a good relationship with his parents**; his first five years with his parents are described as "blissfully happy," and he apparently moved back with them voluntarily at age sixteen ("he successfully sought to return to Lahore . . ."). India was a British colony—not ally—at the time. Nowhere in the passage does it mention who Kipling's father (most married women did not work at this time) worked for; in fact, he was an art teacher, illustrator, and museum curator.

6. **(C)** The V2 was **tested for two years before it was used on London**. The passage states that it was first fired on London in the fall of 1944, and later mentions that it was first successfully test-fired in October 1942, about two years previously. The phrase "First

SIFT #2

test-fired successfully in October 1942" implies that it had tests before then that were not successful, but this is not definitive.

7. **(B)** From this passage, we can infer that the writer **does not have much patience with people who don't try very hard**. The writer says that "'just showing up' is *sometimes claimed* to be the majority of success"—which doesn't sound like the writer agrees. Since the passage emphasizes the amount of effort needed to achieve excellent results—especially by quoting the maxim that "Nothing worthwhile is ever easy"—it does not follow that success has come easily to him or that he likes people who achieve things easily; probably just the opposite. The fact that the writer uses a metaphor of building a "monument to accomplishment" does not necessarily point to him being an architect or builder; he did not use specialized or technical terms indicating a high level of professional knowledge, and the building metaphor was only used toward the end of the passage.

8. **(C)** From this passage, we learn that soldiers belonging to a unit not authorized an SSI wear **the SSI of the lowest level command to which the unit is assigned, unless they are assigned to a training support regiment or battalion.**

9. **(E)** The mythical Abu mascot traces its heritage to **I Company, 187th Regimental Combat Team**. Although the Abu itself only goes back to A Company, 327th Airborne Battle Group in 1956, the question asks about the mascot's *heritage* or ancestors—providing the link back to the IBU of I Company, 187th Regimental Combat Team.

10. **(E)** Propellers as a practical means of propulsion **were first used by Henri Giffard in 1852**. Although rotating slanted blades do trace their heritage to windmills in the twelfth century, propellers *as a practical means of propulsion* date back only to Henri Giffard's use of one connected to a steam engine in 1852.

11. **(D)** The first jet airplane **was a German design first flown in 1939**. The passage states that the first jet airplane to fly "was an independently conceived gas-turbine German experimental aircraft that first took off in 1939."

12. **(B)** The bumper sticker summary of this passage would be **Use It or Lose It**. The passage discusses how people's minds can overcome brain injuries by using new areas, and how senior citizens can stay mentally alert by keeping their brains agile.

13. **(B)** According to this passage, it is a pilot's responsibility to **always be on the lookout for other aircraft, even when not near an airport**.

14. **(E)** From this passage, it can be inferred that **there were more North Korean provocations than just cutting off power**.

15. **(E)** Promotion selection boards use the "best qualified" method when the **board is limited to recommending fewer officers than the total considered.**

16. **(C)** In the passage for Question 15 above, what can you conclude from the context that the abbreviations "SA" and "MOI" mean? **Secretary of the Army, Memorandum of Instruction.**

17. **(A)** Which of the following factors would probably make the most contribution to the accuracy of IRU and INS navigation? **Establishing alignment with an accurate initial starting point**. Since IRUs and INSs are "self-contained" (stated in the first sentence), they do not communicate with GPS satellites or airfields along the planned route. Waypoints are not programmed into IRUs, only INSs, and the question asks about both systems.

18. **(C)** What is the primary purpose of ARFORGEN? **To predictively schedule potential deployments for AC and RC units.** It does not *guarantee* when a unit will deploy, certainly not three or five years ahead of time. It does not provide readiness for soldiers, families, and employers; it helps provide readiness for units over time and reduces uncertainty for soldiers, families, and employers. Operational readiness cycles are defined as part of the ARFORGEN framework; that is not its primary purpose.

19. **(E)** How many satellites receive ephemeris data? **All of them.** The passage does not specify how many GPS satellites there are, but it does state that every satellite's ephemeris data are sent to each satellite for broadcast as part of the data message embedded in the GPS signal.

20. **(B)** The author of this passage believes that leaders **must be able to apply uncommon solutions to uncommon challenges.**

Subtest 6: Math Skills Test (MST)

	✔	✘		✔	✘		✔	✘		✔	✘
1. B			6. A			11. E			16. C		
2. C			7. E			12. E			17. B		
3. D			8. D			13. E			18. D		
4. C			9. B			14. C			19. E		
5. C			10. C			15. E			20. B		

1. **(B)** If $x + 9 = 10$, then x equals 1. The first thing to do here is to get the variable x by itself on one side of the equation. So, if we subtract 9 from each side, that will leave the variable x by itself and we will quickly see what it is equal to:

$$x + 9 = 10$$
$$x + 9 - 9 = 10 - 9$$
$$x = \mathbf{1}$$

2. **(C)** If $a - 5 = 7$, then a equals 12. As is often the case, the first thing to do is to get the variable a alone on one side of the equation. So, if we add 5 to each side, it's still an "equation" (equal on both sides), but it lets us get the variable a by itself:

$$a - 5 = 7$$
$$a - 5 + 5 = 7 + 5$$
$$a = \mathbf{12}$$

3. **(D)** This is an order of operations drill. Multiply the first term by each of the terms in the second group, then do the same for the second:

$$(4y - 3)(y + 2)$$
$$(4y \times y) + (4y \times 2) + (-3 \times y) + (-3 \times 2)$$
$$4y^2 + 8y - 3y - 6$$
$$\mathbf{4y^2 + 5y - 6}$$

4. **(C)** First, calculate how many cadets participate in intramural athletics:

$$1{,}400 \times .41 = 574$$

SIFT #2

So, if 27 percent of these 574 cadets are rooks, we find the number of rooks in intramural athletics:

$$574 \times .27 = 154.98$$

The problem did say "about 27 percent," so we can round this up to 155. If this is then one-third of the total number of cadets in the rook class, we just multiply by 3 to get **465** total rooks.

5. **(C)** A pentagon is a five-sided figure, so one lifeguard per side means five lifeguards at any one time. However, due to the restriction of only four hours a day, with the pool being open for eight hours, that will need to be doubled to **ten** lifeguards. This is the minimum number, and assumes that lifeguards will not take their meal break until after their shift.
6. **(A)** First, find the area of the square before the circle is cut from it:

$$A = s^2$$
$$A = 2\text{ ft.}^2 = 4\text{ sq. ft.}$$

Next, find the area of the circle, using the formula $A = \pi r^2$. The largest possible circle will be 2 feet across—the same size as the sides of the square—so the radius will be half that (1 foot).

$$A = \pi r^2$$
$$A = 3.14 \times 1^2 = 3.14\text{ sq. ft.}$$

Last, subtract the area of the circle from the area of the square it came from:

$$4\text{ sq. ft.} - 3.14\text{ sq. ft.} = \mathbf{0.86\text{ sq. ft.}}$$

7. **(E)** In an isosceles triangle, two of the sides are equal. This means that the angles opposite them are equal, too; if one is 50 degrees, so is the other. To find the measure of the angle opposite the unequal side, start by adding the measure of the two equal angles:

$$50 + 50 = 100\text{ degrees}$$

To find the measure of the third angle, subtract 100 from 180, which is the total of the measures of the angles of any triangle:

$$180 - 100 = \mathbf{80}\text{ degrees}$$

8. **(D)** First, find the surface area of the ceiling. Since it is opposite the floor, it has the same length and width:

$$A = lw = 19 \times 10 = 190\text{ sq. ft.}$$

Next, find the square footage of two of the facing or opposite walls—let's start with the walls formed by the room's length and height:

$$19\text{ ft.} \times 8\text{ ft.} = 152\text{ sq. ft.}$$
$$152\text{ sq. ft.} \times 2\text{ walls} = 304\text{ sq. ft.}$$

Next, find the area of the two walls formed by the width and height of the room:

$$10\text{ ft.} \times 8\text{ ft.} = 80\text{ sq. ft.}$$
$$80\text{ sq. ft.} \times 2\text{ walls} = 160\text{ sq. ft.}$$

Finally, combine the areas of all the walls and the ceiling:

$$304 + 160 + 190 = \mathbf{654\ sq.\ ft.} \text{ to be painted}$$

9. **(B)** If a task can be completed in x units of time, after one unit of time $1/x$ of the task will be completed. So here we see that after one hour, Pump 1 by itself would have emptied 1/6 of the holding tank, and Pump 2 would have emptied 1/4 of it. However, since we are asked to find out how long it will take both pumps working together, let's see how much of the tank the two pumps working together will have emptied after an hour:

Pump 1 = 1/6
Pump 2 = 1/4
(lowest common denominator = 12)

Pump 1 = 2/12
Pump 2 = + 3/12
After 1 hour = 5/12

Now for the second principle needed to solve this problem: If x/y of a task can be completed in one unit of time, then the completion of the entire task will take the reciprocal of the original fraction. That means that it will take 12/5 hours for both pumps to empty the tank—but we are asked for the answer in minutes, so we multiply by the 60 minutes in an hour:

$$12/5 \times 60 = 720/5 = \mathbf{144} \text{ minutes}$$

10. **(C)** Since the problem does not give us a specific length of the sides of the cube, we have to think of ratios—how the size of the first cube relates to the second cube. The good part about this is that we can pick a size, work things out, and in doing so come to understand the principles involved. So, if the sides of our first cube are 2 units long, the length of the second cube's sides will be 4 units. Since the formula for the volume of a cube is simply the cube (x^3) of the length of the sides, the volume of the first cube will be 8 ($2 \times 2 \times 2$) cubic units, and the volume of the second cube will be 64 ($4 \times 4 \times 4$) cubic units—a ratio of 8 : 64 or 1 : 8 (if you want to have even more confidence that you are on the right track, pick another value for the length of the sides of the original cube and work things through again to confirm). This means that, since weight is proportional to volume, the weight of the second cube will be $5 \times 8 =$ **40** lbs.

11. **(E)** The number of students who are taking only Spanish is 101 – 14 = 87. The number of students who are taking only German is 82 – 14 = 68. The number of students taking only Spanish, only German, or both is 87 + 68 + 14 = 169. Thus, the number of students not taking any language at all is the total number of students minus the number of students taking only Spanish, only German, or both: 373 – 169 = **204**.

12. **(E)** Expand and resolve this as you would any other $(a + b)^2$ expression:

$$(\sqrt{3} - \sqrt{2})^2 =$$
$$(\sqrt{3} - \sqrt{2})(\sqrt{3} - \sqrt{2}) =$$
$$3 - (\sqrt{3} \times \sqrt{2}) - (\sqrt{2} \times \sqrt{3}) + 2 =$$
$$3 - (\sqrt{6}) - (\sqrt{6}) + 2 = \mathbf{5 - 2(\sqrt{6})}$$

SIFT #2

13. **(E)** Don't assume that points A, B, and C are on a straight line. Draw a diagram with 5 km between A and B; then draw a circle around point B with a radius of 2 km. Point C is somewhere on the perimeter of that circle, with a minimum distance of 3 km from point A and a maximum distance of 7 km. Any distance between those two can be correct.

14. **(C)** Since triangle *JLM* is an equilateral triangle, not only are all its angles equal (as shown in the diagram), but all its sides are equal, too. Since $JL = 3$, *JM* and *ML* also equal 3. Further, since the overall figure is a parallelogram and triangle *JLM* is an equilateral triangle, then triangle *JKL* is an equilateral triangle, too, with the same dimensions as triangle *JLM*. Therefore, each side of the parallelogram = 3 and the perimeter is $3 \times 4 =$ **12.**

15. **(E)** Lieutenant Highspeed deposits 90% of \$1,047 = .9 × \$1,047 = \$942.30 (remember to move the decimal two places to the left to convert a percentage to a decimal); this is his principal. We know the rate of 3.2% converts to a decimal of .032, and 32 months is $2\frac{2}{3}$ or 2.67 years:

$$I = prt$$
$$I = \$942.30 \times .032 \times 2.67 = \$80.51$$

Adding back in the original principal (\$80.51 + \$942.30) gives us a total of **\$1,022.81**.

16. **(C)** The measures of the angles of any triangle have to add up to 180°, or it's not a triangle. Further, a right triangle, by definition, has one angle that is 90°. Only choice (C) fits these criteria.

17. **(B)** First find the difference between max airspeed (156 knots) and minimum cruise speed (120 knots):

$$156 - 120 = 36 \text{ knots}$$

Now determine what percentage 36 knots is of 120 knots—we can most easily do this by setting up a proportion and then cross-multiplying:

$$\frac{36}{120} = \frac{x}{100}$$
$$(36 \cdot 100) = 120x$$
$$\frac{3{,}600}{120} = x$$
$$\mathbf{30} = x$$

18. **(D)** 31 combat-equipped troops at 250 lbs. each would weigh 7,750 lbs. Subtract the weight of the 4-man fire team (4 × 250 = 1,000 lbs.) and that leaves 6,750 lbs. of internal lift capacity for ammunition. 6,750 lbs. divided by 35 lbs. per ammo can gives us 192.8 (round off to 193) cans or **19,300** rounds at 100 rounds per can.

19. **(E)** For Helicopter X, the problem specifies that increases and decreases in hovering ceiling due to temperature are evenly graduated. Therefore, since a 40-degree increase in temperature decreases the hovering ceiling by 2,600 ft., it's reasonable for this problem to expect that a 40-degree decrease in temperature would result in a 2,600-foot increase in hovering ceiling.

20. **(B)** First determine the aviator-to-aircraft ratio (i.e., how many aircraft per pilot) for both years. The 1950 ratio was 715:1242 or 1:1.737 (divide the second number of aircraft by the number of aviators for a 1:x ratio). For 1970, the ratio was 22,250:11,446 or 1:0.514. Next, determine the amount of change in the aircraft part of the ratio:

$$1.737 - 0.514 = 1.223$$

Next, compare the difference to the 1950 number of aircraft and calculate it as a percentage; do this by using a proportion and cross-multiplying:

$$\frac{1.223}{1.737} = \frac{x}{100}$$

$$1.737x = 122.3$$

$$x = \frac{122.3}{1.737}$$

$$x = 70.409\% = 70.4\%$$

So, we see that even though there were nine times as many aircraft, it was still a *decrease* in the *ratio* of aviators to aircraft, because the number of aviators increased by more than 31 times. In other words, in 1950 there were almost two aircraft for every aviator, while in 1970 there were roughly two aviators for every aircraft. The answer is a **decrease in the ratio of pilots to aircraft of 70.4%.**

Subtest 7: Mechanical Comprehension Test (MCT)

	✔	✘		✔	✘		✔	✘		✔	✘
1. B			6. A			11. A			16. D		
2. E			7. D			12. B			17. A		
3. A			8. A			13. E			18. B		
4. B			9. B			14. A			19. D		
5. B			10. C			15. D			20. A		

1. **(B)** Gear A will turn **4** times. Counting the number of teeth in the two gears tells us that the mechanical advantage of the larger gear A is 3:2, since gear A has 15 teeth and gear B has 10 teeth. Divide the number of gear B revolutions (6) by the advantage of the larger gear A (3). Then multiply by the ratio for the smaller gear (2): $\frac{6}{3} = 2$. $2 \times 2 = 4$.

2. **(E) It will be easier to lift block B but it will not be lifted as high.** If block A under the lever beam is moved toward block B on top of the lever beam, the moment for a particular force exerted will increase, since the fulcrum is now further from the force; this will make block B easier to lift. However, the height to which block B on the end of the lever beam can be raised decreases the closer block A is moved toward block B.

3. **(A)** By rotating clockwise, pulley C will cause pulley B to rotate counterclockwise, which will in turn cause pulley A to rotate **clockwise.**

4. **(B) Pulley B** will rotate the fastest because it is the smallest.

5. **(B) Water tower B** will be able to provide the most water, because its outlet pipe is near the bottom and can let almost all of its contents out, while the outlet pipe on tower A is

SIFT #2

near the top and will stop providing water as soon as A's water level drops below where the pipe leaves the cistern.

6. **(A)** The string holding the 10-lb. weight exerts more pull; the fact that that string is longer makes no difference.

7. **(D)** We are not told the sizes of the two wheels, but we can see that one is larger than the other. If the two wheels are connected by a belt, the small wheel will be forced to turn faster and complete more turns than the larger wheel.

8. **(A)** The force required to balance the lever shown would be **10 lbs.** because the sum of the moments on each side of the fulcrum must be zero. To calculate this, we would set it up like this:

$$F \times d = F \times d$$

where F is the force or weight involved and d is the distance from the fulcrum. Therefore,

$$\begin{aligned}(5 \text{ lbs.} \times 10 \text{ ft.}) + (10 \text{ lbs.} \times 5 \text{ ft.}) &= F \times 10 \text{ ft.}\\ 50 \text{ ft.-lbs.} + 50 \text{ ft.-lbs.} &= F \times 10 \text{ ft.}\\ 100 \text{ ft.-lbs.}/10 \text{ ft.} &= F\\ 10 \text{ lbs.} &= F\end{aligned}$$

9. **(B)** The length of time taken for one swing depends on the length of the string, not the weight.

10. **(C) Both would take the same amount of time** to make one swing; the length of time taken for one swing depends on the length of the string, not the weight at the end of it.

11. **(A)** When the plug is removed, water will flow **into the tube** to equalize the water level both inside and outside the tube.

12. **(B) Valves A, B, and D** must be open for the tank to fill halfway and maintain that level. Water flows in through valve A (so any choice not including valve A is a nonstarter), and flows out when the tank is half full through valve B—but, for that water to leave the system, valve D must also be open.

13. **(E) Both segments will weigh the same.** If this were not the case, then you would not have been able to balance the beam at its CG because gravity would have been acting unequally on the two (still-joined) segments of the beam; the center of gravity wouldn't have been the center of gravity at all if you couldn't balance the beam there. Also, if the beam was regularly proportioned, both segments will be very close to the same size, allowing only for density variations in the wood itself.

14. **(A) Pulley A** will have the highest number of RPMs (i.e., will turn the fastest). In any arrangement of connected pulleys, the smaller pulley will turn faster than the larger pulley—it has to "keep up" and therefore turns faster. Pulleys B and D appear to be of the same size, while pulley A is the smaller of the connected pulleys and therefore turns fastest.

15. **(D) The piston in cylinder A will rise 4 inches.** The formula for mechanical advantage in this kind of problem is

$$\frac{a_2}{a_1} = \frac{d_1}{d_2}$$

where a_1 is the area of the smaller cylinder and a_2 is the area of the bigger cylinder, and d_1 is the vertical distance moved by the smaller cylinder and d_2 is the vertical distance moved by the larger cylinder. In this case the smaller cylinder has a surface area of 3 square inches and the larger cylinder has a surface area of 6 square inches. Therefore, using the formula on page 572:

$$\frac{6^2}{3^2} = \frac{d_1}{1}$$

$$\frac{36}{9} = d_1$$

$$4 = d_1$$

The piston in cylinder A will move up 4 inches.

16. **(D) B counterclockwise, C clockwise, and D counterclockwise.** Each driven gear in succession turns in the opposite direction from the gear that is driving it.

17. **(A)** The mechanical ratio of gear A to gear D is **1:1** because all four gears have the same number of teeth and will therefore turn at the same rate.

18. **(B)** When two or more act in such a way that their combination has a net effect of zero (i.e., they cancel each other out), the condition is called **equilibrium**.

19. **(D)** The descent of a paratrooper under his parachute is primarily affected by **drag** (air resistance) **and gravity**.

20. **(A)** When oncoming air meets the leading edge of the airfoil (wing), part goes over the top and part flows underneath. The air flowing over the top of the wing has to go farther than the air underneath, because it must meet again at the far side of the wing—physical laws act together to prevent or minimize vacuums in most cases. Because the air flowing over the top must go faster than that underneath, the pressure on the top of the wing is decreased, whereas the pressure underneath the wing remains relatively unchanged. Therefore, most of the lift on an aircraft's wing is because of a decrease in pressure on the wing's upper side.

ANSWER SHEET
ASTB-E #1

Subtest 1: Math Skills Test (MST)

1. Ⓐ Ⓑ Ⓒ Ⓓ
2. Ⓐ Ⓑ Ⓒ Ⓓ
3. Ⓐ Ⓑ Ⓒ Ⓓ
4. Ⓐ Ⓑ Ⓒ Ⓓ
5. Ⓐ Ⓑ Ⓒ Ⓓ
6. Ⓐ Ⓑ Ⓒ Ⓓ
7. Ⓐ Ⓑ Ⓒ Ⓓ
8. Ⓐ Ⓑ Ⓒ Ⓓ
9. Ⓐ Ⓑ Ⓒ Ⓓ
10. Ⓐ Ⓑ Ⓒ Ⓓ
11. Ⓐ Ⓑ Ⓒ Ⓓ
12. Ⓐ Ⓑ Ⓒ Ⓓ
13. Ⓐ Ⓑ Ⓒ Ⓓ
14. Ⓐ Ⓑ Ⓒ Ⓓ
15. Ⓐ Ⓑ Ⓒ Ⓓ
16. Ⓐ Ⓑ Ⓒ Ⓓ
17. Ⓐ Ⓑ Ⓒ Ⓓ
18. Ⓐ Ⓑ Ⓒ Ⓓ
19. Ⓐ Ⓑ Ⓒ Ⓓ
20. Ⓐ Ⓑ Ⓒ Ⓓ
21. Ⓐ Ⓑ Ⓒ Ⓓ
22. Ⓐ Ⓑ Ⓒ Ⓓ
23. Ⓐ Ⓑ Ⓒ Ⓓ
24. Ⓐ Ⓑ Ⓒ Ⓓ
25. Ⓐ Ⓑ Ⓒ Ⓓ
26. Ⓐ Ⓑ Ⓒ Ⓓ
27. Ⓐ Ⓑ Ⓒ Ⓓ
28. Ⓐ Ⓑ Ⓒ Ⓓ
29. Ⓐ Ⓑ Ⓒ Ⓓ
30. Ⓐ Ⓑ Ⓒ Ⓓ

Subtest 2: Reading Comprehension Test (RCT)

1. Ⓐ Ⓑ Ⓒ Ⓓ
2. Ⓐ Ⓑ Ⓒ Ⓓ
3. Ⓐ Ⓑ Ⓒ Ⓓ
4. Ⓐ Ⓑ Ⓒ Ⓓ
5. Ⓐ Ⓑ Ⓒ Ⓓ
6. Ⓐ Ⓑ Ⓒ Ⓓ
7. Ⓐ Ⓑ Ⓒ Ⓓ
8. Ⓐ Ⓑ Ⓒ Ⓓ
9. Ⓐ Ⓑ Ⓒ Ⓓ
10. Ⓐ Ⓑ Ⓒ Ⓓ
11. Ⓐ Ⓑ Ⓒ Ⓓ
12. Ⓐ Ⓑ Ⓒ Ⓓ
13. Ⓐ Ⓑ Ⓒ Ⓓ
14. Ⓐ Ⓑ Ⓒ Ⓓ
15. Ⓐ Ⓑ Ⓒ Ⓓ
16. Ⓐ Ⓑ Ⓒ Ⓓ
17. Ⓐ Ⓑ Ⓒ Ⓓ
18. Ⓐ Ⓑ Ⓒ Ⓓ
19. Ⓐ Ⓑ Ⓒ Ⓓ
20. Ⓐ Ⓑ Ⓒ Ⓓ
21. Ⓐ Ⓑ Ⓒ Ⓓ
22. Ⓐ Ⓑ Ⓒ Ⓓ
23. Ⓐ Ⓑ Ⓒ Ⓓ
24. Ⓐ Ⓑ Ⓒ Ⓓ
25. Ⓐ Ⓑ Ⓒ Ⓓ
26. Ⓐ Ⓑ Ⓒ Ⓓ
27. Ⓐ Ⓑ Ⓒ Ⓓ

Subtest 3: Mechanical Comprehension Test (MCT)

1. Ⓐ Ⓑ Ⓒ
2. Ⓐ Ⓑ Ⓒ
3. Ⓐ Ⓑ Ⓒ
4. Ⓐ Ⓑ Ⓒ
5. Ⓐ Ⓑ Ⓒ
6. Ⓐ Ⓑ Ⓒ
7. Ⓐ Ⓑ Ⓒ
8. Ⓐ Ⓑ Ⓒ
9. Ⓐ Ⓑ Ⓒ
10. Ⓐ Ⓑ Ⓒ
11. Ⓐ Ⓑ Ⓒ
12. Ⓐ Ⓑ Ⓒ
13. Ⓐ Ⓑ Ⓒ
14. Ⓐ Ⓑ Ⓒ
15. Ⓐ Ⓑ Ⓒ
16. Ⓐ Ⓑ Ⓒ
17. Ⓐ Ⓑ Ⓒ
18. Ⓐ Ⓑ Ⓒ
19. Ⓐ Ⓑ Ⓒ
20. Ⓐ Ⓑ Ⓒ
21. Ⓐ Ⓑ Ⓒ
22. Ⓐ Ⓑ Ⓒ
23. Ⓐ Ⓑ Ⓒ
24. Ⓐ Ⓑ Ⓒ
25. Ⓐ Ⓑ Ⓒ
26. Ⓐ Ⓑ Ⓒ
27. Ⓐ Ⓑ Ⓒ
28. Ⓐ Ⓑ Ⓒ
29. Ⓐ Ⓑ Ⓒ
30. Ⓐ Ⓑ Ⓒ

Subtest 4: Aviation and Nautical Information Test (ANIT)

1. Ⓐ Ⓑ Ⓒ Ⓓ
2. Ⓐ Ⓑ Ⓒ Ⓓ
3. Ⓐ Ⓑ Ⓒ Ⓓ
4. Ⓐ Ⓑ Ⓒ Ⓓ
5. Ⓐ Ⓑ Ⓒ Ⓓ
6. Ⓐ Ⓑ Ⓒ Ⓓ
7. Ⓐ Ⓑ Ⓒ Ⓓ
8. Ⓐ Ⓑ Ⓒ Ⓓ
9. Ⓐ Ⓑ Ⓒ Ⓓ
10. Ⓐ Ⓑ Ⓒ Ⓓ
11. Ⓐ Ⓑ Ⓒ Ⓓ
12. Ⓐ Ⓑ Ⓒ Ⓓ
13. Ⓐ Ⓑ Ⓒ Ⓓ
14. Ⓐ Ⓑ Ⓒ Ⓓ
15. Ⓐ Ⓑ Ⓒ Ⓓ
16. Ⓐ Ⓑ Ⓒ Ⓓ
17. Ⓐ Ⓑ Ⓒ Ⓓ
18. Ⓐ Ⓑ Ⓒ Ⓓ
19. Ⓐ Ⓑ Ⓒ Ⓓ
20. Ⓐ Ⓑ Ⓒ Ⓓ
21. Ⓐ Ⓑ Ⓒ Ⓓ
22. Ⓐ Ⓑ Ⓒ Ⓓ
23. Ⓐ Ⓑ Ⓒ Ⓓ
24. Ⓐ Ⓑ Ⓒ Ⓓ
25. Ⓐ Ⓑ Ⓒ Ⓓ
26. Ⓐ Ⓑ Ⓒ Ⓓ
27. Ⓐ Ⓑ Ⓒ Ⓓ
28. Ⓐ Ⓑ Ⓒ Ⓓ
29. Ⓐ Ⓑ Ⓒ Ⓓ
30. Ⓐ Ⓑ Ⓒ Ⓓ

Navy/Marine Corps/ Coast Guard Aviation Selection Test Battery (ASTB-E) Practice Test #1

14

TEST FORMAT

The Aviation Selection Test Battery (ASTB-E) is used by the U.S. Navy, the Marine Corps, and the Coast Guard to select flight training candidates from those officers and officer applicants who wish to become aviators. It is also used for all U.S. Navy Officer Candidate School applicants, not just potential aviators.

Subtest	Abbrev.	Number of Questions	Time Limit
Math Skills Test	MST	20–30	Up to 40 mins
Reading Comprehension Test	RCT	20–30	Up to 30 mins
Mechanical Comprehension Test	MCT	20–30	Up to 15 mins
Aviation and Nautical Information Test	ANIT	Up to 30	Up to 15 mins
Naval Aviation Trait Facet Inventory	NATFI	88	N/A
Performance-Based Measures	PBM	Six sections	N/A
Biographical Inventory with Response Verification	BI-RV	Varies based on individual	Not timed or proctored

Unless you are deployed aboard a ship, the ASTB-E is administered on the secure web-based testing platform known as Automated Pilot Examination (APEX); APEX platforms are also equipped with headphones and a video-game-like joystick. If you are deployed aboard a ship at sea, there are paper testing options, but you will need to contact your ship's testing or education officer to get details on what is available in your situation.

The first four ASTB-E subtests are all adaptive. The PBM is an interactive multimedia test that assesses motor skills, spatial ability, reaction time, and multitasking abilities. The BI-RV may be taken on any web-enabled computer by an examinee with a user name and password provided by an examiner. This may be (but is not required to be) an APEX-equipped workstation.

The Math Skills Test (MST) has 20–30 questions. You have up to 40 minutes to complete this subtest, which assesses your knowledge of arithmetic, algebra, and geometry skills and knowledge, as well as statistics, probability, and exponents (including negative and fractional). Some questions will be word problems, and some will involve equations. There will also be questions that require solving for variables, time/rate/distance calculations, fractions, square roots, and the calculation of geometric shapes' areas, angles, and perimeters.

You will not be allowed to use a calculator for either the paper or computerized version of the MST.

The RCT has 20–30 questions, and you will have up to 30 minutes to answer them. The questions will present you with a short passage to read, and then you will have to select the answer choice that can be deduced or inferred from the information given to you in the passage.

The MCT has 20–30 questions, which you will have up to 15 minutes to solve. It tests your ability to comprehend and reason with mechanical applications and simple physics rules.

The ANIT has up to 30 questions, and you will have up to 15 minutes to answer those questions. This subtest measures your knowledge of aviation history, nautical terminology and procedures, and aviation-related concepts such as aircraft components, aerodynamic principles, and flight rules and regulations.

The NATFI is a "forced-choice" computer-adaptive personality inventory consisting of 88 questions. "Forced choice" means that you have to pick one of the pairs of alternatives offered as being more applicable to you—what you like, what you would do, how you are. The actual questions are not released by the Navy, and, as a result of this, no practice questions are included here.

The PBM is a set of interactive, multimedia, performance-based tests that are similar to some video games. It tests your motor skills, spatial abilities (how well you think in three dimensions), reaction time, ability to concentrate despite distractions, multitasking abilities, physical dexterity, and hand-eye coordination. When taking the PBM, you will use a joystick and throttle combination (sometimes known as a "hands-on throttle and stick" setup) and headphones. All of these will be provided to you by the test site. Due to its hands-on nature, this subtest cannot be tested here in this book.

The Biographical Inventory with Response Verification (BI-RV) is an unproctored (unsupervised) subtest taken outside of the APEX environment as a separate testing session. It takes anywhere from 45 minutes to two hours to complete, and it does not have to be completed in a single session. The Navy actually recommends that you get it done before you take the rest of the ASTB-E if you can; your recruiter can help you with this. Again, due to its nature—it's not a test, it's a listing of what you've done in certain areas up to this point in your life—practice questions are not included here.

SUBTEST 1: MATH SKILLS TEST (MST)

30 Questions

1. You need eight barrels of water to sprinkle $\frac{1}{2}$ mile of roadway. How many barrels of water do you need to sprinkle $3\frac{1}{2}$ miles of roadway?

   (A) 7
   (B) 15
   (C) 50
   (D) 56

2. A snapshot 8 inches long and 6 inches wide is to be enlarged so that its length will be 12 inches. How many inches wide will the enlarged snapshot be?

   (A) 8
   (B) 6
   (C) 9
   (D) 10

3. Maddalyn has an ordinary life insurance policy with a face value of $10,000. At her age, the annual premium is $24.00 per thousand. What is the total premium paid for this policy every six months?

   (A) $100
   (B) $120
   (C) $240
   (D) $400

4. If 2 pounds of cottage cheese cost $3.20, what is the cost of a 3-ounce portion of cottage cheese?

   (A) $0.30
   (B) $0.20
   (C) $0.25
   (D) $0.15

5. Jonathan drove for 12 hours at an average speed of 55 miles per hour. If his car covered 22 miles for each gallon of gas consumed, how many gallons of gas did he use?

   (A) 32 gals.
   (B) 34 gals.
   (C) 36 gals.
   (D) 30 gals.

6. Max earns $7.50 per hour. If he works from 8:45 A.M. until 5:15 P.M., with one hour off for lunch, how much does he earn in one day?

   (A) $58.50
   (B) $56.25
   (C) $55.00
   (D) $53.75

7. If five shirts and three ties cost $52 and each tie costs $4, what is the cost of a shirt?

   (A) $6.00
   (B) $8.00
   (C) $10.00
   (D) $7.50

8. What is the fifth term in this series: 5; 2; 9; 6; ____?

   (A) 16
   (B) 15
   (C) 14
   (D) 13

9. In a theater audience of 500 people, 80% were adults. How many children were in the audience?

(A) 20
(B) 50
(C) 100
(D) 125

10. A brand-name dining room table usually sells for $240, but because it has been the display model and is a little shopworn, the store manager lets it go for $210. What is the percent of reduction?

(A) $12\frac{1}{2}\%$
(B) $14\frac{2}{7}\%$
(C) $16\frac{2}{3}\%$
(D) $18\frac{3}{4}\%$

11. Mr. and Mrs. Asher bought a repossessed house for an investment for $55,000. It was assessed at 80% of the purchase price. If the real estate tax was $4.74 per $100, how much tax did the Ashers pay?

(A) $2,085.60
(B) $1,985.60
(C) $2,607.00
(D) $285.60

12. The scale on a particular map is 1 inch = 50 miles. On this map, two cities are $2\frac{1}{2}$ inches apart. What is the actual distance between the two cities?

(A) 75 miles
(B) 100 miles
(C) 225 miles
(D) 125 miles

13. A shipment of 2,200 lbs. of fertilizer is packed in 40-oz. bags. How many bags are needed for the shipment?

(A) 800
(B) 880
(C) 780
(D) 640

14. A TV set priced at $400 was reduced 25% during a weekend sale. In addition, there was a 10% discount for cash. What was the cash price of the TV set during the sale?

(A) $130
(B) $260
(C) $270
(D) $320

15. In a store, four clerks each get paid $255 per week, and two part-timers each earn $120. What is the average weekly salary paid to these six workers?

(A) $200.00
(B) $210.00
(C) $187.50
(D) $190.00

16. The perimeter of a rectangle is 40 feet. If the length is 15 feet, 6 inches, what is the width of the rectangle?

(A) 4 ft., 6 in.
(B) 9 ft., 6 in.
(C) 5 ft., 6 in.
(D) 5 ft.

17. What is the result of dividing 0.675 by 0.9?

(A) 7.5
(B) 0.075
(C) 75
(D) 0.75

18. Two planes leave the same airport, traveling in opposite directions. One is flying at a speed of 340 miles per hour, the other at 260 miles per hour. In how many hours will the two planes be 3,000 miles apart?

(A) 5
(B) 3.75
(C) 6
(D) 10

19. What is the cost of 5 feet, 3 inches of plastic slipcover material that sells for \$8 per foot?

(A) \$14.00
(B) \$42.00
(C) \$23.00
(D) \$21.12

20. If 1 gallon of milk costs \$3.84, what is the cost of 3 pints?

(A) \$1.44
(B) \$2.82
(C) \$2.04
(D) \$1.96

21. A man left \$72,000 in his will to his wife and son. The ratio of the wife's share to the son's share was 5:3. How much did his wife receive?

(A) \$27,000
(B) \$14,000
(C) \$45,000
(D) \$54,000

22. A recipe calls for $2\frac{1}{2}$ ounces of chocolate and $\frac{1}{2}$ cup of corn syrup. If only 2 ounces of chocolate are available, how much corn syrup should be used?

(A) $\frac{1}{2}$ cup
(B) $\frac{1}{3}$ cup
(C) $\frac{2}{5}$ cup
(D) $\frac{3}{10}$ cup

23. A ship sails x miles the first day, y miles the second day, and z miles the third day. What was the average distance covered per day?

(A) $3(x + y + z)$
(B) $(x + y + z) \div 3$
(C) $3xyz$
(D) $(xyz) \div 3$

24. A man invests \$6,000 at 5% annual interest. How much more must he invest at 6% annual interest so that his annual income from both investments is \$900?

(A) \$3,000
(B) \$5,000
(C) \$8,000
(D) \$10,000

ASTB-E #1

25. Which of these is an example of similar figures?

(A) a plane and a scale model of that plane
(B) a pen and a pencil
(C) a motorcycle and a car
(D) an equilateral triangle and a right triangle

26. Find the numerical value of $5a^2b - 3ab^2$ if $a = 7$ and $b = 4$.

(A) 846
(B) 644
(C) 488
(D) 224

27. If the circumference of a circle is divided by the length of its diameter, what is the result?

(A) 2
(B) 27
(C) π
(D) 7

28. A businesswoman spends $\frac{1}{5}$ of her small company's gross income for office rent, and $\frac{3}{8}$ of the remainder of the company's income for salaries. What part of her income does she spend for salaries?

(A) $\frac{23}{40}$
(B) $\frac{3}{10}$
(C) $\frac{1}{2}$
(D) $\frac{3}{4}$

29. Using the following formula, find the value of C when $F = 50$.

$$C = \frac{5}{9}(F - 32)$$

(A) 10
(B) 18
(C) 90
(D) 40

30. What is the average of these temperature readings, taken on a cold day last winter?

6:00 A.M.	–12 degrees
7:00 A.M.	–7 degrees
8:00 A.M.	–2 degrees
9:00 A.M.	0 degrees
10:00 A.M.	+6 degrees

(A) 0 degrees
(B) 2 degrees
(C) –1 degree
(D) –3 degrees

SUBTEST 2: READING COMPREHENSION TEST (RCT)

27 Questions

Specialized warships, even ships suitable for war, are relatively recent in origin. They have always been expensive to build and they require handling by specialist crews. Their construction and operation therefore demand considerable disposable wealth, probably the surplus of a ruler's revenue; and if the earliest form of fighting at sea was piratical rather than political in motive, we must remember that even the pirate needs capital to start in business. The first navies may or may not have been anti-piratical in purpose—the advantages conferred by the ability to move forces or supplies along rivers or coasts may have first prompted rulers to maintain warships—but navies are, by definition, more costly than individual ships. Whichever way it is looked at, fighting on water has cost more than fighting on land from the start.

1. According to this passage, navies

   (A) are necessary to project power.
   (B) are more expensive to have and maintain than individual ships.
   (C) were always piratical in nature.
   (D) are an ancient invention that brought revenue to rulers.

Dr. Albert Mehrabian, a noted researcher in the field of nonverbal communication (UCLA), found that only 7 percent of our feelings and attitudes are communicated with words, 38 percent via tone of voice, and a whopping 55 percent through nonverbal expressions. These numbers are astonishing, but that's only part of the picture . . . the communications channels over which we have the most control, and understand the best, have the least amount of impact. And the channels over which we have the least control, and understand the least, have the most impact.

2. According to the above passage,

   (A) 55 percent of what we say is understood through tone of voice.
   (B) verbal communication is what gets the message understood.
   (C) we have the most control over the most important aspects of how we communicate.
   (D) more than half of our communication is through nonverbal expressions.

3. <u>Conflagration</u> most nearly means

   (A) a secret or conspiratorial message.
   (B) a seizure by a higher authority.
   (C) a large and destructive fire.
   (D) the act of letting the air out of an inflatable object.

4. Inurbane most nearly means

   (A) rude or uncouth.
   (B) nonsensical.
   (C) smooth and polished.
   (D) having great value.

5. Alluvial most nearly means

   (A) dating to ancient times.
   (B) covered with sediment deposited by flowing water.
   (C) small, insignificant.
   (D) referring to land held in absolute ownership.

Genghis Khan; original name Temujin, c. 1162–1227. Mongol conqueror. Became leader of a destitute clan; defeated other clan leaders; proclaimed Universal Ruler (Genghis Khan) of all the Mongols (1206); consolidated his authority among Mongols (1206–12); made his capital at Karakorum. Invaded northern China (1211), capturing Peking (1215); made conquests in the west (c. 1216–23), overcoming Khwārezm while his generals subdued what is now Iran, Iraq, and part of Russia; died on campaign (1226–27) against Tangut kingdom of Hsi Hsia. A conciliatory leader and military genius. Father of Ögödei (his successor) and Chagatai.

6. In the passage above, what word is used incorrectly?

   (A) destitute
   (B) subdued
   (C) capital
   (D) conciliatory

The way the Roman legions came to serve so far from the Roman army's birthplace and to embrace so wide a range of recruits began during the Punic Wars with Carthage. That city, a Phoenician colony, first fell into conflict with the Romans when the latter's success in subduing their Italian neighbors drew them south to Sicily, which Carthage regarded as within its sphere of influence; Rome's confrontation with Pyrrhus, also an enemy of Carthage, weakened its position on the island. In 265 B.C. the two powers found themselves at war over Sicily, and the war rapidly expanded, by both land and sea, until the Carthaginians had to concede defeat and the Romans established control over Sicily. While Rome added Corsica and Sardinia to these beginnings of its overseas empire, and made its first inroads into the land of the Gauls, Carthage responded by campaigning along the Mediterranean coast of Spain against cities that were Rome's allies. The siege of Saguntum in 219 B.C. brought war on afresh; it lasted 17 years, ended in Carthaginian defeat only after Rome barely avoided catastrophe, and established the Romans as the dominant Mediterranean power.

7. What area were the Romans and Carthaginians fighting over in 265 B.C.?

   (A) Gaul
   (B) Sicily
   (C) Carthage
   (D) Saguntum

8. Rhetoric most nearly means

   (A) the persuasive use of language to influence listeners or readers.
   (B) a painful pathological condition of the joints.
   (C) a regulated pattern of long and short notes or beats.
   (D) referring to a continuously variable electrical resistor.

9. Exemplify most nearly means

   (A) to test or measure for quality.
   (B) worthy of being imitated.
   (C) to illustrate by example.
   (D) to breathe out.

In any planning, especially strategic planning, it is vitally important to select the "right" objectives. In fact, some would suggest that this is the primary role of strategic planning. In addition to setting the "right" objectives, part of the job of planning is to determine the best means of achieving the objectives and, further, to facilitate effective communication and review of the means as the plan is executed. In order to select the "right" objectives, the planners must, among other things, do their work in the context of the higher-order purposes of the organization.

10. According to the passage above, how must strategic planners choose appropriate goals?

    (A) by selecting the "right" objectives
    (B) by facilitating effective communication
    (C) in the context of the higher-order purposes of the organization
    (D) by reviewing the means as the plan is executed

ASTB-E #1

The traditions of Freemasonry have evolved over many centuries and from many sources. They are a powerful source of the cement that gels a Lodge and Freemasons into one sacred band. Often, the traditions are never codified into law but are taught from mouth to ear. They can be modified (slowly) to fit the needs of the organization. Most Lodges adhere to the same traditions, but some may have adopted some of their own. As members become aware of the traditions, they soon learn that they are part of something larger than themselves.

11. According to the passage above, the traditions of Freemasonry teach new members that

    (A) they are part of something larger than themselves.
    (B) new members can quickly change traditions to meet the organization's needs.
    (C) traditions are never written in concrete.
    (D) there is only one source for traditional laws of Freemasonry.

12. Captain Agnew had located the Italian convoy—and brought his "Force K" into the most favorable attacking position—by means of radar; for the Italians, who possessed no such weapon, the darkness remained <u>impenetrable</u>, and their surprise was consequently complete.

    <u>Impenetrable</u> most nearly means

    (A) not perceptible to the touch.
    (B) unprejudiced.
    (C) free from blemish.
    (D) not capable of being pierced or entered.

Texas A&M University, with its main campus in College Station, Texas, is one of only a few select academic institutions to hold triple federal designation as a Land Grant, Sea Grant, and Space Grant university. Offering almost 400 undergraduate and graduate degrees, it has awarded more than 480,000 degrees since its establishment as a military college in 1876. The first public institution of higher learning established in Texas, its main campus is the third-largest nationwide, with more than 62,500 students for the 2017–2018 school year and a well-established campus of 5,200 acres. It was ranked fourth among national public universities in the "Best Value Schools" category of the 2018 *U.S. News and World Report* "Best Colleges" issue. Home to the George Bush Presidential Library and Museum, it conducts research valued at almost $900 million annually and has an endowment valued at more than $9.8 billion, ranking it second among all U.S. public universities and seventh overall.

13. According to the passage above, what is Texas A&M University's enrollment ranking nationally?

    (A) $9.8 billion
    (B) second
    (C) third
    (D) fourth

14. Drogue most nearly means

(A) a one-humped domesticated camel widely used in northern Africa.
(B) to slobber or drool.
(C) a male bee who performs no work and produces no honey.
(D) a funnel-shaped device at the end of a hose of a tanker aircraft.

Babe Ruth was much more than simply the quintessential slugger who reigned over the great revolution in hitting. No modern athletic hero has exceeded Ruth's capacity to project multiple images of brute power, the natural, uninhibited man, and the fulfillment of the legendary American success formula. Ruth was living proof that the lone individual could still rise from mean, vulgar beginnings to fame and fortune, to a position of public recognition equaled by few men in American history. His mighty home runs represented a dramatic finality, a total clearing of the bases with one mighty swat.

15. According to this passage, the reader can infer that Babe Ruth's childhood was

(A) privileged, upper economic class.
(B) focused on teamwork.
(C) uninhibited.
(D) poor, lower economic class.

16. Aircraft carriers provide a credible, sustainable, independent forward presence and conventional ______________ in peacetime.

(A) appearance
(B) assimilation
(C) obscuration
(D) deterrence

Most drivers try to drive safely. A major part of safe driving is driving at the right speed. But what is the "right" speed? Is it 20 miles per hour, or 35, or 60? That question may be hard to answer. On some city streets and in heavy traffic, 20 miles per hour could be too fast, even if it's within the posted speed limit. On a superhighway, 35 miles per hour could be too slow. Of course, a good driver must follow the speed limit, but he must also use good judgment. The "right" speed will vary depending on the number of cars, the road surface and its condition, and the driver's visibility.

17. The general theme of this passage is that a good driver

(A) drives at 35 miles an hour.
(B) adjusts to different driving conditions.
(C) always drives at the same speed.
(D) always follows the speed limit.

18. "Negotiation in the classic _______________ sense assumes parties more anxious to agree than to disagree." [Dean Acheson]

    (A) diplomatic
    (B) aggressive
    (C) automatic
    (D) attacking

About three-fourths of the surface of Earth is water. Of the 336 million cubic miles of water, most (97.2%) is found in the oceans and is salty. Glaciers at both poles hold to themselves another 2 percent of the total. Less than 1 percent (0.8%) is available as freshwater for people to use—and much of that is not near people who need it.

19. The amount of freshwater available for people to use is

    (A) 97.2%.
    (B) 0.8%.
    (C) two-tenths.
    (D) 2%.

20. Transmogrify most nearly means

    (A) to change into a different or bizarre shape or form.
    (B) to displace an object from one position to another.
    (C) to reverse or interchange the order of two or more objects.
    (D) to pass beyond a human limit.

There are a number of different varieties of quarks: there are thought to be at least six "flavors," which we call up, down, strange, charmed, bottom, and top. Each flavor comes in three "colors": red, green, and blue. (It should be emphasized that these terms are just labels: quarks are much smaller than the wavelength of visible light and so do not have any color in the normal sense. It is just that modern physicists seem to have more imaginative ways of naming new particles and phenomena—they no longer restrict themselves to Greek!) A proton or neutron is made up of three quarks, one of each color. A proton contains two up quarks and one down quark; a neutron contains two down and one up. We can create particles made up of the other quarks (strange, charmed, bottom, and top), but these all have a much greater mass and decay very rapidly into protons and neutrons.

21. According to the passage above, how many different types of "flavors" of quarks are there?

    (A) 2
    (B) 3
    (C) 6
    (D) 12

Nucleic acids are found in all living organisms, from viruses to man. They received their name because of their discovery in the nuclei of white blood cells and fish sperm by Swiss physiologist Johann Miescher (who founded the first physiological institute in Switzerland) in 1869. However, it is now well established that nucleic acids occur outside the cell nucleus as well.

22. Nucleic acids are found

    (A) only in human cells.
    (B) only in viruses.
    (C) in all living organisms.
    (D) only in the cell nucleus.

23. Galley navies, with their oared ships and limited carrying capacities, were never autonomous instruments of strategy but extensions—or, more accurately, partners—of armies on land.

    Autonomous most nearly means

    (A) catalytic.
    (B) independent.
    (C) native to a particular place.
    (D) operating without human involvement.

The War of 1812 was in many ways one of the most unfortunate events in American history. For one reason, it was needless; the British Orders in Council that had caused the worst irritation were being unconditionally repealed just as Congress declared war. For another, the United States suffered from internal divisions of the gravest kind. While the South and West favored war, New York and New England in general opposed it, and toward its end important New England groups went to the very edge of disloyalty. For a third reason, the war was far from glorious in a military sense: the American army was in wretched shape to fight.

24. The above passage characterizes the War of 1812 as

    (A) a war for which the military was unprepared.
    (B) an unnecessary conflict.
    (C) an unfortunate event.
    (D) all of the above

ASTB-E #1

25. Abusive excise taxes burdened agriculture and mining, while the tariff gave Spanish manufacturers and traders an exclusive ____________, which they exploited by charging ruinous prices for goods.

    (A) advertisement
    (B) insouciance
    (C) diversification
    (D) monopoly

The Tao-te-ching (The Way and Its Power) is the basic text of the Chinese philosophy and religion known as Taoism. It is made up of 81 short chapters or poems that describe a way of life marked by quiet effortlessness and freedom from desire. This is thought to be achieved by following the creative, spontaneous life force of the universe, called the Tao. The book is attributed to Lao-tzu, but it was probably written in the third century B.C.

26. The Tao-te-ching

    (A) is the basic text of the Chinese universe.
    (B) describes a way of life marked by effortless desire.
    (C) is made up of 81 chapters and a short poem.
    (D) was probably not written by Lao-tzu, even though it is attributed to him.

27. In the first land skirmish of the Cuban campaign, the Marines quickly overcame enemy resistance and established the base at Guantanamo Bay.

    Skirmish most nearly means

    (A) long siege.
    (B) negotiation.
    (C) small battle.
    (D) reconnaissance.

SUBTEST 3: MECHANICAL COMPREHENSION TEST (MCT)

30 Questions

1. Gear B is intended to mesh with

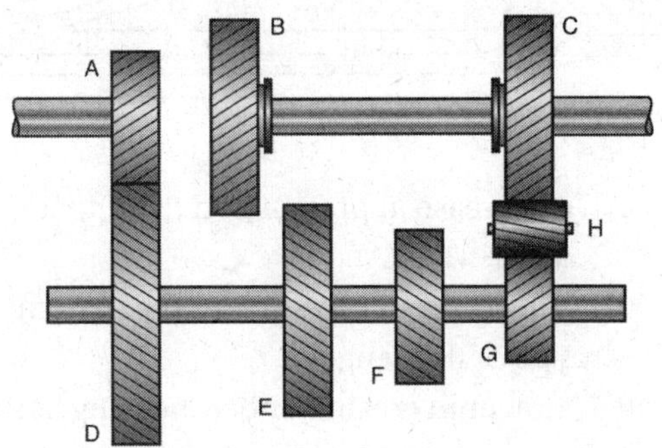

(A) gear A only.
(B) gear D only.
(C) gear E only.

2. As cam A makes one complete turn, the setscrew hits the contact point how many times?

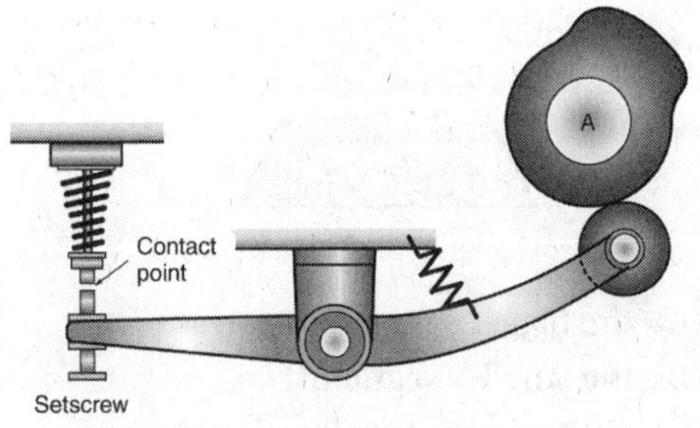

(A) once
(B) twice
(C) three times

3. If gear A makes 14 revolutions, gear B will make

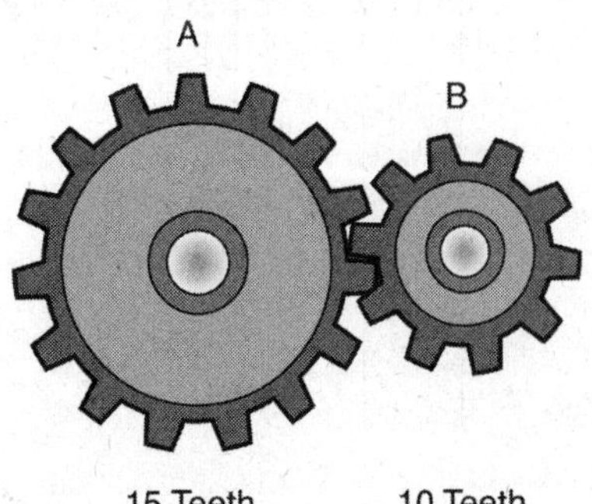

(A) 21 revolutions.
(B) 28 revolutions.
(C) 14 revolutions.

4. Which of the other gears is moving in the same direction as gear 2?

(A) gear 1
(B) gear 3
(C) neither of the other gears

5. Floats X and Y are measuring the specific gravity of two different liquids. Which float indicates the liquid with the highest specific gravity?

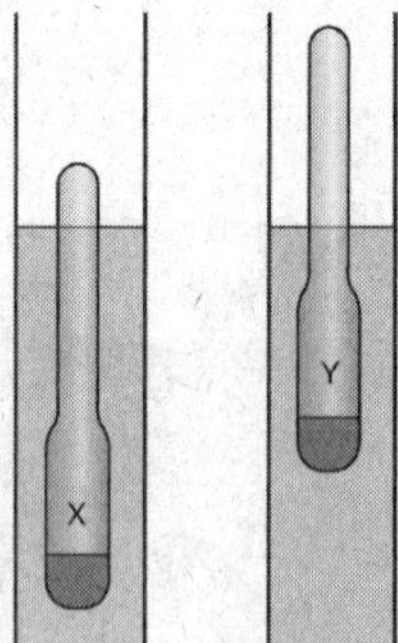

(A) Y
(B) X
(C) neither X nor Y

6. The wheelbarrow is an example of a

(A) first-class lever.
(B) second-class lever.
(C) third-class lever.

7. Most of the lift on an aircraft's wings is because of

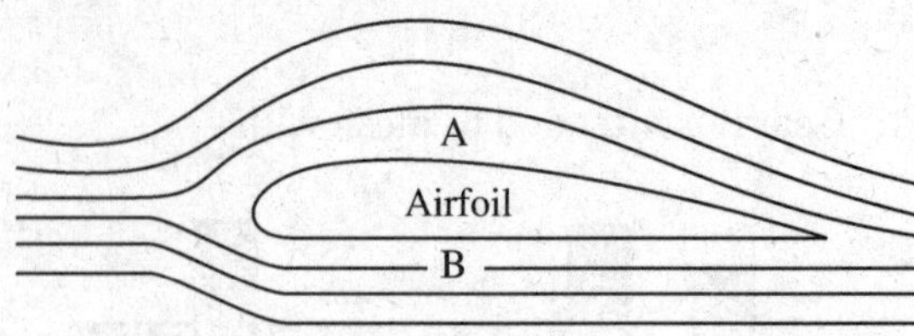

(A) a decrease in pressure on the upper side of the wing (A).
(B) a decrease in pressure on the bottom side of the wing (B).
(C) a vacuum created under the wing at (B).

8. You balance a wooden beam on a fulcrum at its center of gravity (CG). If you then mark the CG and cut the beam in two at that point, which section will weigh more?

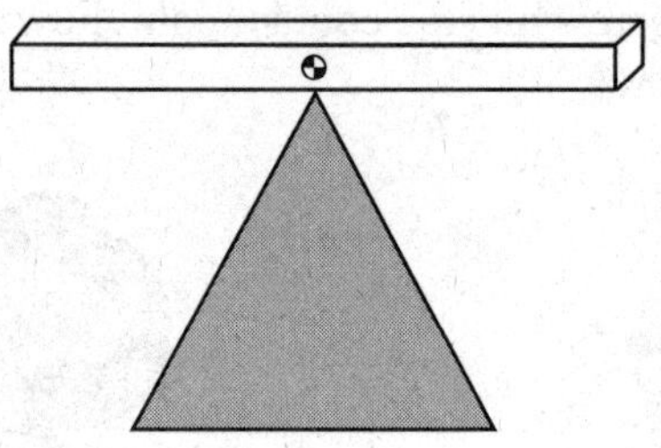

(A) the bigger segment
(B) the smaller segment
(C) both segments will weigh the same

9. In the depicted arrangement of pulleys and belts, which pulley will have the highest number of revolutions per minute (RPMs)?

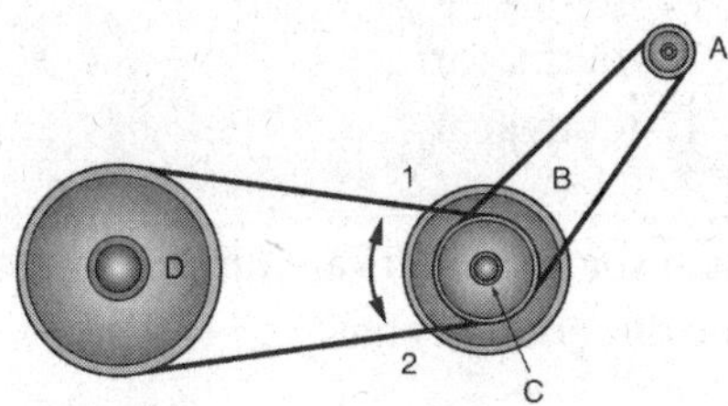

(A) pulley A
(B) pulley B
(C) pulley C

10. If gear B is the drive gear and makes 12 revolutions, how many revolutions will gear A make?

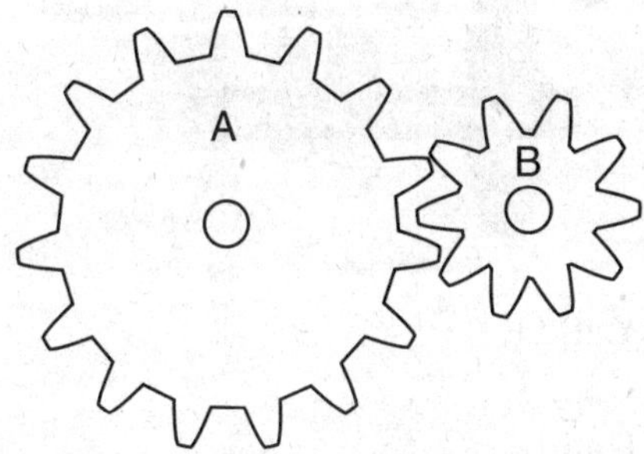

(A) 4
(B) 8
(C) 18

11. In the diagram above, if gear B is the drive gear and it is turning clockwise, what direction will gear A turn?

(A) clockwise
(B) counterclockwise
(C) gear A is free spinning

12. Two cylinders containing hydraulic fluid, A and B, are connected by a hydraulic line as shown. If the diameter of cylinder A is 3 inches and the diameter of cylinder B is 6 inches, and the piston in cylinder B presses down 1 inch, what will happen to the piston in cylinder A?

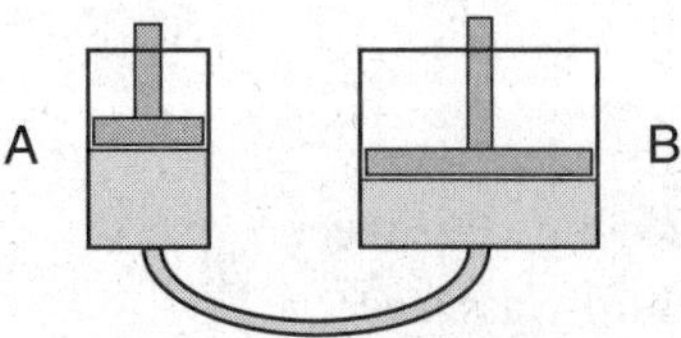

(A) It will rise one-half inch.
(B) It will rise one inch.
(C) It will rise two inches.

13. In the figure, the angle θ is important, because when it is

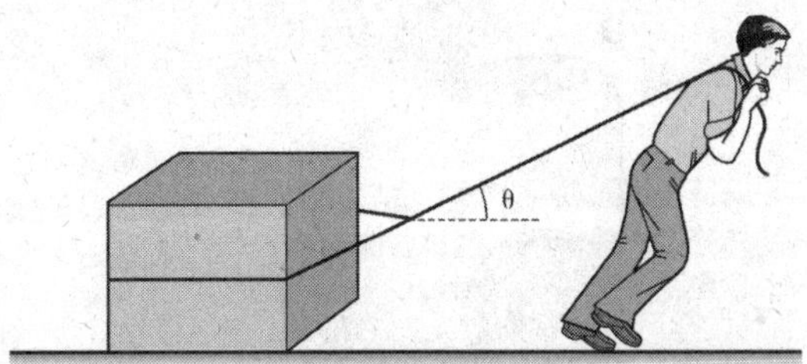

(A) 0 (zero) degrees, the entire force is dragging the box.
(B) 90 degrees, the entire force is lifting the box.
(C) both of the above

14. Pliers are an example of a

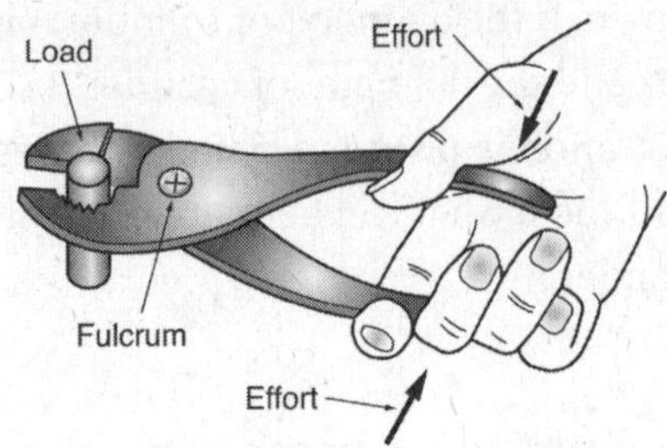

(A) first-class lever.
(B) second-class lever.
(C) third-class lever.

15. The follower is at its highest position between points

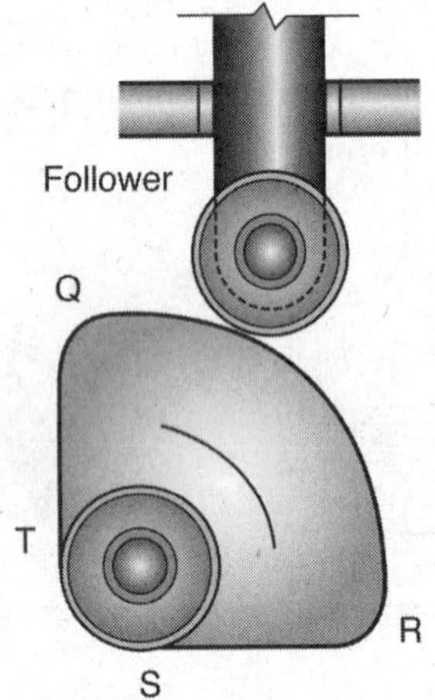

(A) Q and R.
(B) R and S.
(C) S and T.

16. If pulley A is the driver and turns in direction 1, which pulley turns faster?

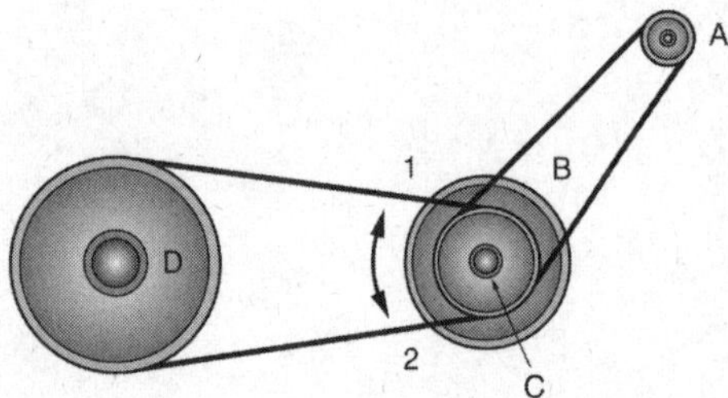

(A) A
(B) B
(C) C

17. The greatest amount of mechanical advantage of power is attained when an 11-tooth gear drives a(n)

(A) 29-tooth gear.
(B) 11-tooth gear.
(C) 47-tooth gear.

18. Which shaft or shafts are turning in the same direction as shaft X?

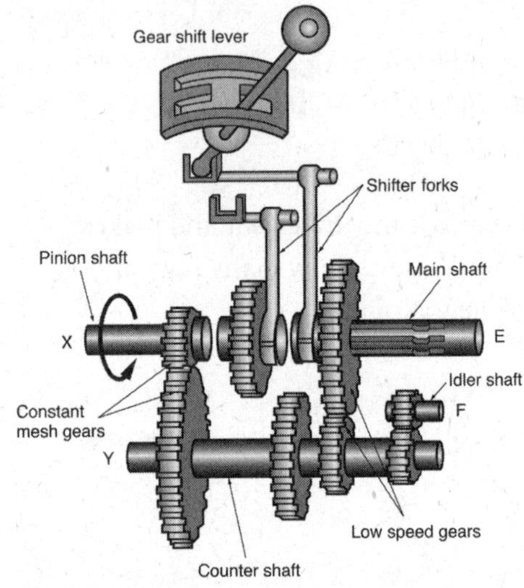

(A) Y and E
(B) F
(C) E and F

19. The human arm as depicted below is an example of a

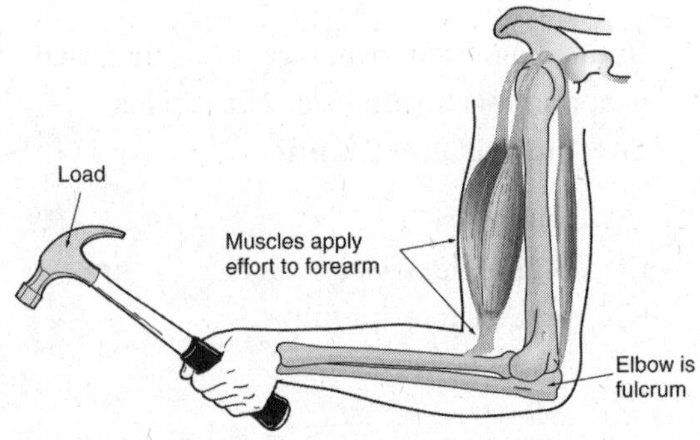

(A) first-class lever.
(B) second-class lever.
(C) third-class lever.

20. If arm H is held fixed as gear B turns in direction 2, gear

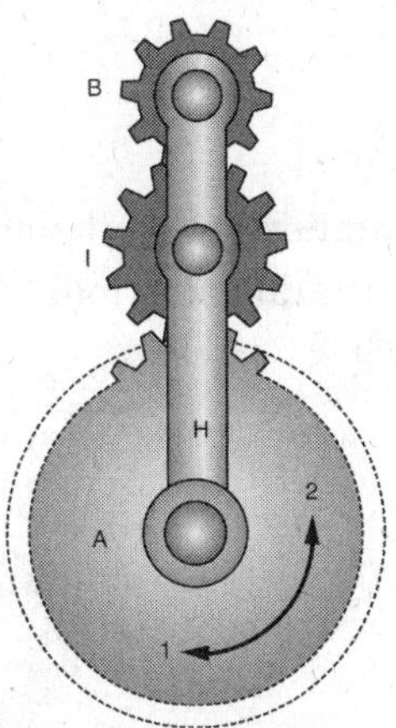

(A) A will turn in direction 1.
(B) A will turn in direction 2.
(C) I must turn in direction 2.

21. Two 30-pound blocks are attached to the ceiling using ropes, as shown below. Which of the following statements is true?

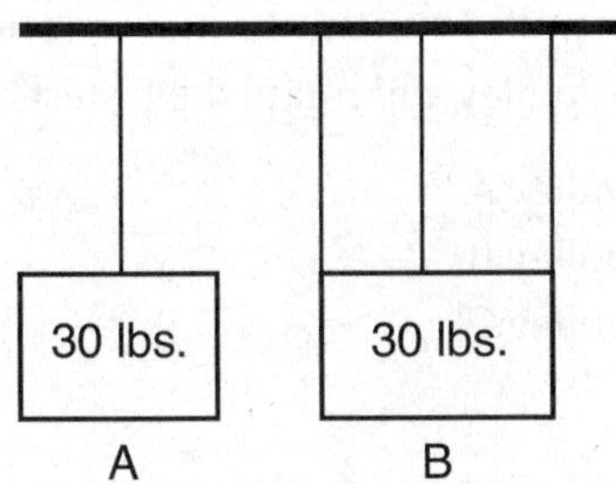

(A) All the ropes are under the same amount of tension.
(B) The rope holding block A is under $\frac{1}{3}$ of the tension of the ropes holding block B.
(C) The ropes supporting block B are under $\frac{1}{3}$ of the tension of the rope holding block A.

22. An ax is what type of mechanical device?

(A) cutting
(B) inclined plane
(C) chopping

23. A 400-lb. pallet needs to be moved into a trailer whose floor is 3 feet off the ground. In order to reduce to $\frac{1}{3}$ the amount of effort needed to move the pallet by lifting it straight up, we need an inclined plane ________ feet long.

(A) 4
(B) 9
(C) 12

24. As the shaft in the illustration below spins faster in a clockwise direction, balls A and B will

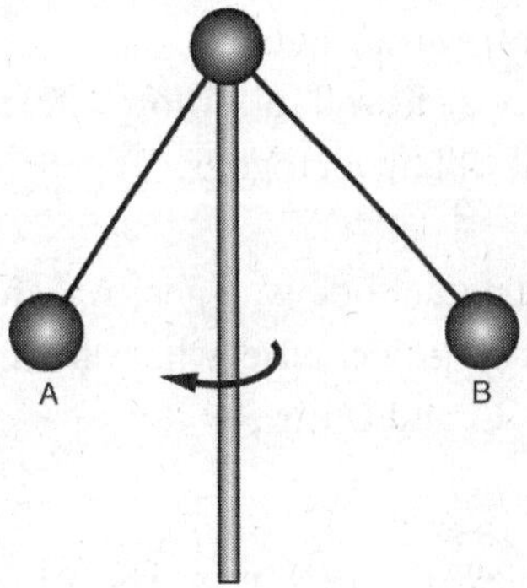

(A) move outward and downward.
(B) move outward and upward.
(C) move up.

25. Water flows into a water tower at a rate of 120 gallons per hour and flows out at the rate of 2 gallons per minute. The level of water in the tower will

(A) remain the same.
(B) lower.
(C) rise.

26. In the illustration below, if the fulcrum is moved farther away from the weight on the resistance arm, the result will be that

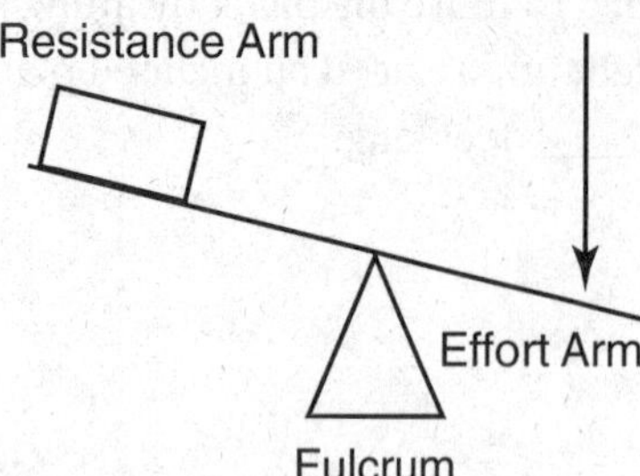

(A) the weight will be easier to lift, and will travel higher.
(B) the weight will be easier to lift, and will not travel as high.
(C) the weight will take more effort to lift, and will travel higher.

27. In the diagram below, if gear A is the driving gear turning clockwise, what directions will gears B, C, and D turn?

(A) B counterclockwise, C counterclockwise, and D counterclockwise
(B) B clockwise, C clockwise, and D clockwise
(C) B counterclockwise, C clockwise, and D counterclockwise

28. In the diagram for problem 27, what is the mechanical advantage of gear A to gear D?

(A) 1:1
(B) 1:2
(C) 1:4

29. In the illustration below, if pulley A is rotating in the direction indicated, then pulley C will

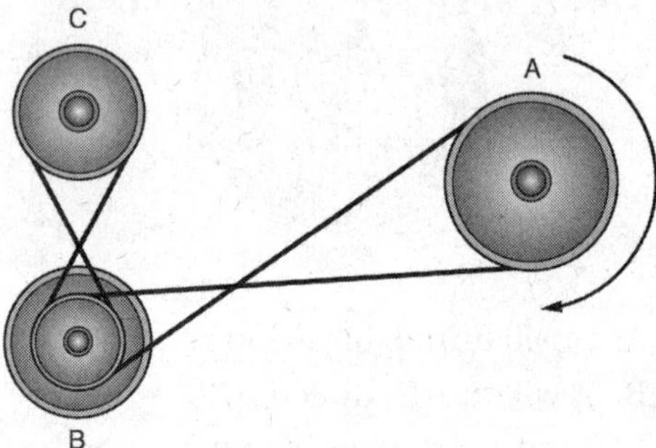

(A) rotate in the same direction as pulley B.
(B) rotate in the same direction as pulleys A and B.
(C) rotate in the same direction as pulley A.

30. In the pulley system shown in problem 29, which pulley will rotate the fastest?

(A) pulley A
(B) pulley B
(C) pulley C

SUBTEST 4: AVIATION AND NAUTICAL INFORMATION TEST (ANIT)

30 Questions

1. What do the terms *port, starboard, fore,* and *aft* mean?

   (A) left, right, up, and down
   (B) right, left, above, and below
   (C) left, right, in front, and behind
   (D) right, left, behind, and in front

2. On an aircraft carrier deck, what color shirt would a plane handler or tractor driver wear?

   (A) green
   (B) blue
   (C) purple
   (D) yellow

3. The angle between the chord line of a wing or airfoil and the direction of the relative wind or airflow is called the

   (A) angle of pitch.
   (B) degree of roll.
   (C) angle of deflection.
   (D) angle of attack.

4. A wall or vertical surface within a ship is called a

   (A) bulkhead.
   (B) bilgeway.
   (C) gangway.
   (D) keel.

5. A conventional fixed-wing aircraft is controlled around its longitudinal axis by means of the

   (A) ailerons.
   (B) elevators.
   (C) rudder.
   (D) trim tab.

6. Two statute miles are equal to

   (A) 2.0 nautical miles.
   (B) 1.74 nautical miles.
   (C) 2.3 nautical miles.
   (D) 2.3 knots.

7. The altimeter typically shows the height of the aircraft above a particular pressure level in

   (A) feet.
   (B) hundreds of feet.
   (C) thousands of feet.
   (D) hundreds of meters.

8. The time of 7 P.M. would be expressed using the 24-hour clock as

   (A) 0700.
   (B) 1400.
   (C) 1700.
   (D) 1900.

9. When a pilot pulls back on the control stick, the elevators will

   (A) extend.
   (B) retract.
   (C) move upward.
   (D) move downward.

10. The order given to the helmsman to align the rudder with the keel of the ship is

    (A) "Ease the rudder."
    (B) "Rudder amidships."
    (C) "Steady as you go."
    (D) "Align your rudder."

11. If one end of a runway was numbered 09, what number would designate the other end of the same runway?

(A) 90
(B) 27
(C) 18
(D) 10

12. The coordinates of latitude and longitude are used to express ___________ in ___________.

(A) direction, degrees
(B) position, degrees
(C) distance, time
(D) location, meridians

13. Which of the following engines could operate outside Earth's atmosphere?

(A) jet engine
(B) turbofan engine
(C) rocket engine
(D) four-stroke diesel engine

14. The bridge of a ship is where

(A) all orders and commands affecting the ship originate.
(B) the lookout is stationed.
(C) the captain has his quarters.
(D) the ship's officers meet and consume their meals.

15. Which of the following is a flight instrument?

(A) tachometer
(B) fuel flow indicator
(C) control column
(D) altimeter

16. The tailhook of a carrier-borne aircraft is used to

(A) catch one of four arresting cables stretched across the deck.
(B) position the aircraft on the deck for launch.
(C) engage with the catapult T-bar before launch.
(D) stabilize the aircraft on the deck elevator.

17. *VFR* stands for

(A) Velocity Flight Resistance.
(B) Venturi Flight Resonance.
(C) Vertical Flight Rules.
(D) Visual Flight Rules.

18. A nautical mile is approximately

(A) 1,760 yds.
(B) 5,280 ft.
(C) 6,076 ft.
(D) 7,676 ft.

19. The four aerodynamic forces acting on an aircraft in flight are

(A) gravity, lift, thrust, and friction.
(B) lift, gravity, thrust, and drag.
(C) velocity, drag, lift, and thrust.
(D) lift, gravity, velocity, and drag.

20. A flashing green air traffic control directed to an aircraft on the ground is a signal that the pilot

(A) should radio the tower.
(B) should stop taxiing.
(C) has clearance to take off.
(D) has clearance to taxi.

21. The Latin phrase *Semper Paratus* is the motto of the

(A) U.S. Navy Submarine Service.
(B) U.S. Marine Corps.
(C) U.S. Marine Air Wing.
(D) U.S. Coast Guard.

22. The *empennage* of an airplane is usually referred to as the

(A) vertical stabilizer.
(B) horizontal stabilizer.
(C) main body.
(D) tail section.

23. On an aircraft carrier, the standard watch length for the Officer of the Deck is

(A) two hours.
(B) four hours.
(C) six hours.
(D) eight hours.

24. ________________ are designed to help minimize a pilot's workload by aerodynamically assisting movement and position of the flight control surfaces to which they are attached.

(A) Labor-saving devices
(B) Secondary flight controls
(C) Trim systems
(D) Spoilers

25. The Carrier Strike Group could be employed in a variety of roles, such as

(A) protection of commercial and/or military shipping.
(B) protection of a Marine amphibious force.
(C) establishing a naval presence in support of national interests.
(D) all of the above

26. Ailerons

(A) extend from the midpoint of the wing outward toward the tip.
(B) create aerodynamic forces that cause the airplane to roll.
(C) move in opposite directions.
(D) all of the above

27. "Pri-Fly" is

(A) the facility where U.S. military aircraft are designed.
(B) the control tower for flight operations on an aircraft carrier.
(C) the two-aircraft section that has priority for launch from a carrier.
(D) where carrier aircraft get refueled and serviced.

28. The two types of turn indicators used in an aircraft are

(A) turn-and-slip indicator and attitude indicator.
(B) attitude indicator and automatic gyroscope.
(C) turn-and-slip indicator and turn coordinator.
(D) left and right indicators.

29. In the Navy, the term *Bravo Zulu* has come to traditionally mean

(A) well done.
(B) two hours later than Greenwich Mean (Zulu) time.
(C) two hours earlier than Greenwich Mean (Zulu) time.
(D) beyond the zone.

30. When an airplane banks into a turn,

(A) the horizontal lift component acts parallel to Earth's surface and opposes inertia.
(B) the horizontal lift component acts parallel to Earth's surface and opposes gravity.
(C) the horizontal lift component acts perpendicular to Earth's surface and opposes inertia.
(D) the horizontal lift component acts perpendicular to Earth's surface and opposes gravity.

ANSWERS AND EXPLANATIONS

Subtest 1: Math Skills Test (MST)

	✔	✘		✔	✘		✔	✘		✔	✘		✔	✘
1. D			7. B			13. B			19. B			25. A		
2. C			8. D			14. C			20. A			26. B		
3. B			9. C			15. B			21. C			27. C		
4. A			10. A			16. A			22. C			28. B		
5. D			11. A			17. D			23. B			29. A		
6. B			12. D			18. A			24. D			30. D		

1. **(D)** You need eight barrels of water to sprinkle $\frac{1}{2}$ mile. You need 16 barrels of water to sprinkle 1 mile. You need 3×16 (or 48) barrels to sprinkle 3 miles. Therefore, you need 48 + 8 (or **56**) barrels to sprinkle $3\frac{1}{2}$ miles.

2. **(C)** Because the picture and its enlargement are similar figures, the lengths have the same ratio as the widths.

$$\frac{\text{length of picture}}{\text{length of enlargement}} = \frac{\text{width of picture}}{\text{width of enlargement}}$$

$$\frac{8}{12} = \frac{6}{\text{width of enlargement } (x)}$$

To solve this, cross-multiply the measurements, using x for the one you don't know.

$$8 \times x = 12 \times 6 = 72$$

$$x = \frac{72}{8} = \mathbf{9} \text{ (width)}$$

3. **(B)** There are ten units of $1,000 in $10,000. Thus, Maddalyn pays $10 \times \$24$ (or $240) each year in premiums. That means that every six months, she pays $\frac{1}{2}$ of $240, or **$120**.

4. **(A)** There are 16 ounces in a pound. Therefore, if 2 pounds of cottage cheese cost $3.20, then 1 pound of cottage cheese costs $1.60. One ounce costs ($1.60 ÷ 16) = $0.10, so 3 ounces cost 3 × $0.10 = **$0.30.**

5. **(D)** To find the distance Jonathan drove, multiply the hours by the miles per hour. Thus,

$$12 \times 55 = 660 \text{ (distance covered)}$$

To find the number of gallons he used, divide the distance by the miles for each gallon. Thus,

$$660 \div 22 = \mathbf{30 \text{ (gallons used)}}$$

6. **(B)** From 8:45 A.M. to 4:45 P.M. is 8 hours; from 4:45 P.M. to 5:15 P.M. is $\frac{1}{2}$ hour.

Subtract Max's lunch hour:

$$8\frac{1}{2} - 1 = 7\frac{1}{2} \text{ (or 7.5 hours)}$$

Multiply his work hours by his hourly rate.

$$7.5 \times \$7.50 = \mathbf{\$56.25} \text{ (day's salary)}$$

7. **(B)** Find the cost of three ties: $3 \times \$4 = \$12$
Subtract $12 (cost of three ties) from the total cost, $52:

$$\$52 - \$12 = \$40$$

Divide $40 (cost of all five shirts) by the number of shirts to find the cost of one shirt:

$$\$40 \div 5 = \mathbf{\$8}$$

8. **(D)** Find the relationship between each pair of numbers in the series. Thus,

$$(5; 2)\ 5 - 3 = 2$$
$$(2; 9)\ 2 + 7 = 9$$
$$(9; 6)\ 9 - 3 = 6$$

The pattern so far is – 3, + 7, – 3. To continue the series, add 7 to the fourth number in the series: 6 + 7 = **13**

9. **(C)** If 80% of the audience was adults, then the percentage of children was

$$100\% - 80\% = 20\% \ (0.2)$$

To find the number of children, multiply

$$500 \times 0.2 = 100.0 = \mathbf{100} \text{ children}$$

10. **(A)** Find the amount of reduction by subtracting.

$$\$240 - \$210 = \$30$$

To find the percentage of reduction, divide the amount of the reduction by the original price.

$$\frac{\$30}{\$240} = \frac{1}{8}$$

Multiply the numerator, 1, by 100 and then divide by the denominator, 8, to get the percentage.

$$\frac{100}{8} = \mathbf{12\frac{1}{2}\%}$$

11. **(A)** Multiply the cost of the home by the assessment rate.

$$\$55{,}000 \times 80\% = \$55{,}000 \times 0.8 = \$44{,}000$$

The property tax is $4.74 for each $100 in $44,000.

$$\$44{,}000 \div 100 = 440 \text{ (hundreds)}$$
$$\$4.74 \times 440 = \mathbf{\$2{,}085.60} \text{ (tax)}$$

12. **(D)** If 1 inch equals 50 miles, then $2\frac{1}{2}$ inches (or 2.5 inches) equal $2.5 \times 50 =$ **125 miles.**

13. **(B)** One pound equals 16 ounces. Find the number of ounces in 2,200 lbs. by multiplying.

$$2{,}200 \times 16 = 35{,}200 \text{ ounces}$$

Find the number of 40-oz. bags needed to pack 35,200 ounces by dividing.

$$35{,}200 \div 40 = \mathbf{880} \text{ bags}$$

14. **(C)** Find the first reduction and the weekend sale price. (25% is the same as .25).

$$\$400 \times .25 = \$100 \text{ (first reduction)}$$
$$\$400 - \$100 = \$300 \text{ (weekend sale price)}$$

Use the weekend sale price to find the reduction for paying cash and the final price (10% = 0.1).

$$\$300 \times 0.1 = \$30 \text{ (second reduction)}$$
$$\$300 - \$30 = \mathbf{\$270} \text{ (cash price)}$$

15. **(B)** Find the combined salaries of the four clerks.

$$\$255 \times 4 = \$1{,}020$$

Find the combined salaries of the part-timers.

$$\$120 \times 2 = \$240$$

Add both totals and divide by 6 for the average.

$$\$1{,}020 + \$240 = \$1{,}260$$
$$\$1{,}260 \div 6 = \mathbf{\$210} \text{ (average salary)}$$

16. **(A)** The perimeter of a rectangle is equal to the sum of the two lengths and two widths. If 15 feet, 6 inches $\left(15\frac{1}{2} \text{ feet}\right)$ equal 1 length, then

$$2 \times 15\frac{1}{2} = 31 \text{ ft. (2 lengths)}$$
$$40 - 31 = 9 \text{ ft. (both widths)}$$
$$9 \div 2 = \mathbf{4\frac{1}{2} \text{ ft.}} \text{ (1 width)}$$

17. **(D)** Before dividing by a decimal, do what is needed to clear the decimal point in the divisor—and then, of course, you have to perform the same operation to the dividend to have the same number. In this case, to make 0.9 a whole number, we multiply it by 10, and then multiply the top number by the same amount.

$$\frac{0.675}{0.9} = \frac{6.75}{9} = \mathbf{0.75}$$

18. **(A)** In the first hour, the two planes will be a combined distance of 340 + 260 miles apart. Thus,

$$340 + 260 = 600 \text{ miles apart in 1 hour}$$

Find how many hours it will take them to be 3,000 miles apart by dividing.

$$3{,}000 \div 600 = \mathbf{5} \text{ (hours)}$$

19. **(B)** Multiply the cost per foot by the length of the material. 12 inches equal 1 foot and 3 inches equal $\frac{1}{4}$ foot; therefore 5 feet, 3 inches equal $5\frac{1}{4}$ feet (or 5.25 feet).

$$\$8 \times 5.25 = \mathbf{\$42}$$

20. **(A)** Find the cost of one pint. (There are 8 pints in 1 gallon.)

$$\$3.84 \div 8 = \$0.48$$

Find the cost of 3 pints.

$$\$0.48 \times 3 = \mathbf{\$1.44}$$

21. **(C)** Begin by letting x equal one share of the inheritance. According to the ratio, the widow received 5 shares ($5x$), and the son received 3 shares ($3x$). Together, they inherited \$72,000. This can be written as an equation.

$$5x + 3x = \$72,000$$

Solve for x by combining similar terms.

$$8x = \$72,000$$
$$x = \$9,000 \text{ (one share)}$$

Multiply the value of one share by the number of shares the mother received.

$$5x = \mathbf{\$45,000} \text{ (mother's share)}$$

22. **(C)** Begin by setting up a statement of proportion.

$$\frac{\text{chocolate}}{\text{chocolate}} = \frac{\text{corn syrup (recipe)}}{\text{corn syrup (amount available)}}$$

$$\frac{2\frac{1}{2}}{2} = \frac{\frac{1}{2}}{x} \text{ (or) } \frac{\frac{5}{2}}{2} = \frac{\frac{1}{2}}{x}$$

Simplify each side of the proportion.

(a) $\frac{5}{2} \div \frac{2}{1} = \frac{5}{2} \times \frac{1}{2} = \frac{5}{4}$

(b) $\frac{1}{2} \div \frac{x}{1} = \frac{1}{2} \times \frac{1}{x} = \frac{1}{2x}$

Then solve the proportion by cross-multiplying.

$$\frac{5}{4} = \frac{1}{2x} \text{ (or) } 10x = 4$$

Divide each side of the equation by 10 to find the value of x.

$$10x = 4$$
$$x = \frac{4}{10}$$
$$= \mathbf{\frac{2}{5}} \textbf{ cup} \text{ of corn syrup}$$

ASTB-E #1

ASTB-E #1

23. **(B)** To find the average of three numbers, divide their sum by 3.

$$x + y + z \text{ (sum of three numbers)}$$

$$\frac{x + y + z}{3} \text{ (sum of numbers, divided by 3)}$$

24. **(D)** First find the income he gets on the \$6,000 at 5% annual interest.

$$\$6{,}000 \times 0.05 = \$300.00 \text{ (income)}$$

Next, find how much more interest he wants to earn in a year.

$$\$900 - \$300 = \$600 \text{ (additional interest)}$$

This \$600 will equal 6% of the amount (x) he has to invest. Write this as an equation.

$$\$600 = 0.06x$$

To solve for x, divide each side of the equation by 0.06 (clear the decimal in the divisor).

$$\frac{\$600.00}{0.06} = \left(\frac{0.06}{0.06}\right)x$$

$$\$10{,}000 = x$$

$$\text{(new amount needed) } x = \mathbf{\$10{,}000}$$

25. **(A)** Two figures are similar if they have the same shape. They may or may not have the same size. **A plane and a scale model of that plane** have the same shape and are therefore similar.

26. **(B)** Solve by substituting the given number values for the algebraic letters and then working out the arithmetic operations.

$$a = 7,\ b = 4$$

$$5a^2b - 3ab^2 =$$

$$5(7^2)(4) - 3(7)(4^2) =$$

$$5(49)(4) - 3(7)(16) =$$

$$245(4) - 21(16) =$$

$$980 - 336 = \mathbf{644}$$

27. **(C)** The formula for the circumference (C) of a circle can be written in terms of its radius (R) or its diameter (D).

$$C = 2 \times R \times \pi \quad \text{or} \quad C = D \times \pi$$

Therefore, if you divide the circumference of a circle by its diameter, you are left with $\boldsymbol{\pi}$.

28. **(B)** If the businesswoman spends $\frac{1}{5}$ of her income for rent, she has $\frac{4}{5}$ of her income left. She then spends $\frac{3}{8}$ of the remainder on salaries. To calculate what that amount is, cross-multiply the remaining income $\left(\frac{4}{5}\right)$ by the fraction spent on salaries:

$$\frac{4}{5} \times \frac{3}{8} = \frac{12}{40} = \mathbf{\frac{3}{10}} \text{ (salaries)}$$

29. **(A)** Solve by substituting the number value for F, and then doing the arithmetic operations.

$$C=\frac{5}{9}(F-32)$$
$$C=\frac{5}{9}(50-32)$$
$$C=\frac{5}{9}\times(18)$$
$$C=\mathbf{10}$$

30. **(D)** To obtain the average, add the five temperatures and divide the total by 5.

Add:

$$-12+(-7)+(-2)+0+6=-21+6=-15$$

Divide:

$$-15\div 5=\mathbf{-3}$$

Subtest 2: Reading Comprehension Test (RCT)

	✔	✘		✔	✘		✔	✘		✔	✘		✔	✘
1. B			7. B			13. C			19. B			25. D		
2. D			8. A			14. D			20. A			26. D		
3. C			9. C			15. D			21. C			27. C		
4. A			10. C			16. D			22. C					
5. B			11. A			17. B			23. B					
6. D			12. D			18. A			24. D					

1. **(B)** According to this passage, navies **are more expensive to have and maintain than individual ships.** The passage says that "navies are, by definition, more costly than individual ships."
2. **(D)** According to the passage, **more than half of our communication is through nonverbal expressions.** The passage says that 55 percent of our feelings and attitudes are communicated with nonverbal expressions.
3. **(C)** Conflagration, a noun, most nearly means **a large and destructive fire**. A "secret or conspiratorial message" might be a *confidential communication*; a "seizure by a higher authority" would be a *confiscation*; and "the act of letting the air out of an inflatable object" is *deflation.*
4. **(A)** Inurbane, an adjective, most nearly means **rude or uncouth**. Another word for "nonsensical" is *inane*; an *urbane* person is smooth and polished (the opposite of inurbane); and another word for "covered with water" is *inundated.*
5. **(B)** Alluvial, an adjective, most nearly means **covered with sediment deposited by flowing water**. Something that dates to ancient times could be called *antediluvian* ("before the flood"); something small or insignificant is *trivial*; land that is held in

ASTB-E #1

absolute ownership, without any obligation to a feudal lord, is known as *allodium* (a noun); and an *alloy* (a noun) is one metal mixed with others.

6. **(D)** In the passage, the word **conciliatory** is used incorrectly to describe the leadership of a "conqueror" who, by military conquest and force of arms, subdued much of the Asian continent. The word conciliatory applies to someone who makes peace through friendly, calming negotiations, rather than someone who uses warfare to conquer new territory.

7. **(B)** The passage says that "Carthage . . . first fell into conflict with the Romans when the [Romans'] success . . . drew them south to **Sicily** . . . In 265 B.C., the two powers found themselves at war over Sicily."

8. **(A)** Rhetoric, a noun, most nearly means **the persuasive use of language to influence listeners or readers**. A pathological condition of the joints is *rheumatism*; a regulated pattern of long and short notes or beats is a *rhythm*; a continuously variable electrical resistor is a *rheostat*; and a parallelogram with unequal adjacent sides is a *rhombus*.

9. **(C)** Exemplify, a verb, most nearly means **to illustrate by example**. To test or measure for quality is to *examine*; something worthy of being imitated may be called *exemplary* (an adjective); to breathe out is to *exhale*; and to tear or wear the skin off of something is to *excoriate* it.

10. **(C)** The passage says that "in order to select the 'right' objectives, the planners must, among other things, do their work **in the context of the higher-order purposes of the organization**."

11. **(A)** The passage says, "As members become aware of the traditions, they soon learn that **they are part of something larger than themselves**."

12. **(D)** Impenetrable means **not capable of being pierced or entered**, so the correct choice here is choice (D); the Italians, with no radar, had no way to pierce or see through the darkness of night, and so were surprised by Captain Agnew's British fleet. If something is not perceptible to the touch, it is *impalpable*; something or someone who is unprejudiced is said to be *impartial*; something free from blemish is *immaculate*; and something that is incapable of being moved is (you've guessed it by now) *immovable*.

13. **(C)** The passage says that Texas A&M's main campus is the "third-largest nationwide," and then lists the number of students enrolled there. This shows that "**third**-largest" refers to enrollment, not the geographic size of the campus: the "well-established campus" implies that its size has been the same for some time. Choice (A) refers to the size of the school's *endowment*, which means donated money or other financial assets meant to be invested to grow the principal and provide additional income for future expenditures and investments.

14. **(D)** Drogue, a noun, most nearly means **a funnel-shaped device at the end of a hose of a tanker aircraft**. A one-humped domesticated camel widely used in northern Africa is a *dromedary*; to slobber or drool is to *drivel* (a verb); a male bee who performs no work and produces no honey is a *drone*; and the verb that means to make a continuous, low, humming sound is also to *drone*.

15. **(D)** The passage says that "Ruth was living proof that the lone individual could still rise from mean, vulgar beginnings to fame and fortune." *Rising* from *mean, vulgar beginnings* shows that Ruth started his life in lower-level economic circumstances and rose higher as an adult.

16. **(D)** Aircraft carriers provide a credible, sustainable, independent forward presence and conventional **deterrence** in peacetime. *Deterrence* means to prevent or discourage someone (in this case, other nations) from doing something—in this example, to discourage them from attacking us by showing strength and thereby persuading other countries that they will not be able to attack us successfully. *Appearance* does not make sense as an answer in this context; *assimilation* means absorbing and incorporating something; *obscuration* is making something hidden, unclear, or indistinct; and *insipience* is foolishness or a lack of wisdom.

17. **(B)** The general theme of this passage is that a good driver **adjusts to different driving conditions.**

18. **(A)** Negotiation in the classic **diplomatic** sense assumes parties more anxious to agree than to disagree [Dean Acheson]. None of the other choices presented make sense in the context given.

19. **(B)** The amount of freshwater available for people to use is, as stated in the passage, **0.8%.**

20. **(A)** Transmogrify most nearly means **to change into a different or bizarre shape or form**. To displace an object from one position to another is to *transport* it; to reverse or interchange the order of two or more objects is to *transpose* them; to pass beyond a human limit is to *transcend* that limit; and someone or something that passes away or decreases with time is a *transient.*

21. **(C)** According to the passage, there are **six** different types of "flavors" of quarks: up, down, strange, charmed, bottom, and top.

22. **(C)** Nucleic acids are found **in all living organisms**, as stated in the first sentence of the passage.

23. **(B)** Autonomous means **independent** or self-sustaining.

24. **(D)** The passage calls the War of 1812 "unfortunate," says that one of the chief causes of the war was being repealed even as Congress was declaring war (making it unnecessary), and further says that the army was in "wretched shape," clearly implying unpreparedness.

25. **(D)** The critical clue here is the word *exclusive* before the blank to be filled in; none of the other choices presented make sense in the context given.

26. **(D)** The passage says that the Tao-te-ching "is attributed to Lao-tzu, but it was probably written in the third century B.C." This clearly implies that Lao-tzu (who lived during the sixth century B.C.) did not write the book.

27. **(C)** A skirmish is a **small battle**, so the correct answer is choice (C).

Subtest 3: Mechanical Comprehension Test (MCT)

	✔	✘		✔	✘		✔	✘		✔	✘		✔	✘
1. C			7. A			13. C			19. C			25. A		
2. A			8. C			14. A			20. B			26. C		
3. A			9. A			15. A			21. C			27. C		
4. C			10. B			16. A			22. B			28. A		
5. A			11. B			17. C			23. B			29. C		
6. B			12. C			18. C			24. B			30. B		

1. **(C)** Gears A and D are in constant mesh, and F is too small.
2. **(A)** When the lobe (high spot) on cam A makes contact with the follower (roller) on the contact arm, the contact will close. Because cam A has only one lobe, the contacts will close **one** time per revolution.
3. **(A)** To calculate the revolutions of gear B, use this formula: $r = \frac{(D \times R)}{d}$ where

   D = number of teeth on gear A
   R = revolutions of gear A
   d = number of teeth on gear B
   r = revolutions of gear B

   $$r = \frac{(D \times R)}{d}$$

   $$r = \frac{(15 \times 14)}{10}$$

   $$r = \frac{210}{10}$$

   $$r = \mathbf{21}$$

4. **(C)** Gears that are meshed turn in opposite directions. Gear 2 is turning clockwise; gears 1 and 3 are turning counterclockwise.
5. **(A)** Hydrometers use floats to measure specific gravity. Specific gravity is the weight of a liquid compared with the weight of the water. The liquid with the highest specific gravity will cause the float to rise higher in the glass tube.
6. **(B)** On a **second-class lever**, the fulcrum is at one end, the effort is at the other end, and the load is in between.
7. **(A)** When oncoming air meets the leading edge of the airfoil (wing), part goes over the top and part flows underneath. The air flowing over the top of the wing has to go farther than the air underneath because it must meet again at the far side of the wing—physical laws act together to prevent or minimize vacuums in most cases. Because the air flowing over the top must go faster than that underneath, the pressure on the top of the wing is decreased, whereas the pressure underneath the wing remains relatively unchanged. Therefore, most of the lift on an aircraft's wing is because of a decrease in pressure on the wing's upper side.

8. **(C) Both segments will weigh the same.** If this were not the case, then you would not have been able to balance the beam at its CG because gravity would have been acting unequally on the two (still-joined) segments of the beam; the center of gravity wouldn't have been the center of gravity at all if you couldn't balance the beam there. Also, if the beam was regularly proportioned, both segments will be very close to the same size, allowing only for density variations in the wood itself.

9. **(A) Pulley A will have the highest number of RPMs (i.e., it will turn the fastest).** In any arrangement of connected pulleys, the smaller pulley will turn faster than the larger pulley—it has to "keep up" and therefore turns faster. Pulleys B and D appear to be of the same size, while pulley A is the smaller of the connected pulleys and therefore turns fastest.

10. **(B)** Gear A has 15 teeth and gear B has 10 teeth, so the gear ratio is 3:2. This means that for every three turns that the smaller drive gear B makes, the larger drive gear A only makes two. So, if gear B makes 12 revolutions (the "3" part of the gear ratio), divide that by one-third to find out what "1" is, then multiply by the "2" part of the gear ratio to get the number of revolutions that gear A will make. $12 \div 3 = 4$; $4 \times 2 =$ **8.**

11. **(B)** Regardless of gear ratio, when two meshing gears turn and the drive wheel turns one way (in this example, clockwise), the driven gear turns the other way (**counterclockwise**).

12. **(C) The piston in cylinder A will rise two inches.** The formula for mechanical advantage in this kind of problem is

$$\frac{a_2}{a_1} = \frac{d_1}{d_2}$$

where a_1 is the area of the smaller cylinder and a_2 is the area of the bigger cylinder, and d_1 is the vertical distance moved by the smaller cylinder and d_2 is the vertical distance moved by the larger cylinder. In this case the smaller cylinder is 3 inches in diameter and the bigger one is 6 inches. Therefore, the mechanical advantage is $\left(\frac{6}{3}\right) = 2$. Therefore we take the one inch moved by the larger cylinder and multiply it by the mechanical advantage to see that the piston in the smaller cylinder A will be forced upward by two inches.

13. **(C)** The angle of the rope, θ, determines if the box is being pulled or dragged along the floor or being lifted from the floor. That means it can be both lifted and pulled along any angle that is more than 0 degrees and less than 90 degrees.

14. **(A)** The fulcrum is positioned between the effort and the load on a **first-class lever.**

15. **(A)** The shaft of the pivot is at T and S. The high spot (lobe) of the cam is between **Q and R.**

16. **(A)** When a series of pulleys is connected by drive belts, the pulley with the smallest diameter rotates at the highest speed; the smallest pulley will turn the fastest.

17. **(C)** The greater the difference between the number of teeth of the two meshed gears, the greater the torque.

18. **(C)** When gears are meshed, they turn in opposite directions. X and Y are therefore turning in opposite directions. However, because both **E and F** are meshed with Y, they are both turning in the same direction as X.

ASTB-E #1

19. **(C)** On a **third-class lever**, the fulcrum is at one end, the load is at the other, and the effect is between the fulcrum and the load.

20. **(B)** Two meshed gears turn in opposite directions. When an idler gear (gear I is the idler in this example) is placed between the two, both turn in the same direction. The idler gear turns in direction 1.

21. **(C)** Because there are three ropes supporting block B, they are under $\frac{1}{3}$ of the tension as the rope supporting block A.

22. **(B)** An ax is classified as a wedge, which is a type of **inclined plane.**

23. **(B)** To reduce to $\frac{1}{3}$ the effort of moving an object to a height of 3 feet, we need an inclined plane or ramp that is three times the amount of the height: $3 \times 3 = \mathbf{9}$

24. **(B)** Centrifugal force from the spin (it doesn't matter which direction) will cause the balls to move **outward**, and the tension on the strings holding them will result in the balls moving **upward.**

25. **(A)** Water is flowing into the water tower at 120 gallons per hour. To convert that to gallons per minute, we divide 120 gallons by the 60 minutes in an hour, resulting in a rate of 2 gallons per minute coming into the water tower. Therefore, the level of water in the tower will **remain the same.**

26. **(C)** The farther away the fulcrum is from the resistance arm, the greater the amount of force that is required to lift the weight and the higher the resistance arm will travel.

27. **(C) B counterclockwise, C clockwise, and D counterclockwise.** Each driven gear in succession turns in the opposite direction from the gear that is driving it.

28. **(A)** The mechanical ratio of gear A to gear D is **1:1** because all four gears have the same number of teeth and will therefore turn at the same rate.

29. **(C) Pulley C will rotate in the same direction as pulley A.** Pulley A causes pulley B to rotate in the opposite direction from pulley A, and pulley B causes pulley C to rotate in the opposite direction from pulley B—which (there being only two directions of rotation available) is the same direction as pulley A.

30. **(B) Pulley B** will rotate the fastest. In the same way as meshing gears, the smaller the pulley in a system, the faster it rotates.

Subtest 4: Aviation and Nautical Information Test (ANIT)

	✔	✘		✔	✘		✔	✘		✔	✘		✔	✘
1. C			7. C			13. C			19. B			25. D		
2. B			8. D			14. A			20. D			26. D		
3. D			9. C			15. D			21. D			27. B		
4. A			10. B			16. A			22. D			28. C		
5. A			11. B			17. D			23. B			29. A		
6. B			12. B			18. C			24. C			30. A		

1. **(C)** *Port* is nautical terminology for "**left**," *starboard* means "**right**," *fore* means "**in front** (of)," and *aft* means "**behind**."
2. **(B)** On an aircraft carrier deck, **blue** shirts are worn by plane handlers, tractor drivers, aircraft elevator operators, messengers, and phone talkers.
3. **(D)** The angle between the chord line of a wing or airfoil and the direction of the relative wind or airflow is called the **angle of attack**.
4. **(A)** A wall or vertical surface within a ship is called a **bulkhead**.
5. **(A)** A conventional fixed-wing aircraft is controlled around its longitudinal axis (roll) by means of the **ailerons**. Elevators control movement around the lateral axis (pitch); the rudder controls movement around the vertical axis (yaw). Flaps increase both lift and drag, and are normally used during takeoffs and landings.
6. **(B)** Two statute miles are equal to **1.74 nautical miles**. A nautical mile is equal to 1.15 statute miles—so, to convert from statute miles to nautical miles, you must divide by 1.15. A knot is a measure of speed of one nautical mile per hour.
7. **(C)** The altimeter typically shows the height of the aircraft above a particular pressure level in **thousands of feet**.
8. **(D)** The time of 7 P.M. would be expressed using the 24-hour clock as **1900**.
9. **(C)** When a pilot pulls back on the control stick, the elevators will **move upward**. This pushes the tail of the aircraft downward and the nose upward.
10. **(B)** The order given to the helmsman to align the rudder with the keel of the ship is **"Rudder amidships."**
11. **(B)** If one end of a runway was numbered 09, what number would designate the other end of the same runway? The correct answer is **27**. Runways are given two-digit numbers based on the magnetic compass heading or azimuth of the runway in tens of degrees. Runway 09 would therefore be the runway facing 90 degrees or due east; the opposite direction, due west, would have a designation of 27, for 270 degrees.
12. **(B)** The coordinates of latitude and longitude are used to express **position** in **degrees**.
13. **(C)** Which of the following engines could operate outside Earth's atmosphere? A **rocket engine** is the only choice that could operate outside the atmosphere because all the other engines require oxygen to operate.
14. **(A)** The bridge of a ship is where **all orders and commands affecting the ship originate**.

ASTB-E #1

15. **(D)** Which of the following is a flight instrument? An **altimeter** is a flight instrument. The tachometer and fuel flow indicator are engine instruments; the control column isn't an instrument; and the trim tab is a secondary flight control.

16. **(A)** The tailhook of a carrier-borne aircraft is used to **catch one of four arresting cables stretched across the deck.**

17. **(D)** *VFR* stands for **Visual Flight Rules**, which means visually establishing the aircraft's attitude with reference to the natural horizon.

18. **(C)** A nautical mile is approximately **6,076 feet**, or about 1.15 statute miles.

19. **(B)** The four aerodynamic forces acting on an aircraft in flight are **lift, gravity, thrust, and drag**.

20. **(D)** A flashing green air traffic control directed to an aircraft on the ground is a signal that the pilot **has clearance to taxi**.

21. **(D)** The Latin phrase *Semper Paratus* is the motto of the **U.S. Coast Guard**. The meaning of the phrase is "Always Ready." The Marine Corps motto is *Semper Fidelis* ("Always Faithful").

22. **(D)** The *empennage* of an airplane is usually referred to as the **tail section**.

23. **(B)** On an aircraft carrier, the standard watch length for the Officer of the Deck is **four hours**.

24. **(C)** **Trim systems** are designed to help minimize a pilot's workload by aerodynamically assisting movement and position of the flight control surfaces to which they are attached.

25. **(D)** The Carrier Strike Group could be employed in a variety of roles, such as **all of the above**. The CSG's mission can be protection of commercial and/or military shipping, protection of a Marine amphibious force, or establishing a naval presence in support of national interests.

26. **(D)** Ailerons extend from the midpoint of the wing outward toward the tip (choice (A)), create aerodynamic forces that cause the airplane to roll (choice (B)), and move in opposite directions (choice (C)), so the answer is **all of the above**.

27. **(B)** "Pri-Fly" is **the control tower for flight operations on an aircraft carrier**.

28. **(C)** The two types of turn indicators used in an aircraft are the **turn-and-slip indicator and turn coordinator**. The turn-and-slip indicator shows the rate of turn in degrees per second; the turn coordinator can initially show the roll rate (because the gyroscope is canted), and then shows rate of turn. Both instruments indicate turn direction and coordination of the turn, and also serve as a backup source of bank information in the circumstance where an attitude indicator fails.

29. **(A)** In the Navy, the term *Bravo Zulu* has come to traditionally mean **well done**. Although the phrase's origin is uncertain, the most common explanation is that it was a signal sent by Admiral William F. Halsey to members of his naval task force after defeating the Japanese in the Battle of the Solomon Islands during World War II.

30. **(A)** When an airplane banks into a turn, **the horizontal lift component acts parallel to Earth's surface and opposes inertia**. The vertical lift component continues to act perpendicular to Earth's surface and opposes gravity.

ANSWER SHEET
ASTB-E #2

Subtest 1: Math Skills Test (MST)

1. Ⓐ Ⓑ Ⓒ Ⓓ	9. Ⓐ Ⓑ Ⓒ Ⓓ	17. Ⓐ Ⓑ Ⓒ Ⓓ	25. Ⓐ Ⓑ Ⓒ Ⓓ
2. Ⓐ Ⓑ Ⓒ Ⓓ	10. Ⓐ Ⓑ Ⓒ Ⓓ	18. Ⓐ Ⓑ Ⓒ Ⓓ	26. Ⓐ Ⓑ Ⓒ Ⓓ
3. Ⓐ Ⓑ Ⓒ Ⓓ	11. Ⓐ Ⓑ Ⓒ Ⓓ	19. Ⓐ Ⓑ Ⓒ Ⓓ	27. Ⓐ Ⓑ Ⓒ Ⓓ
4. Ⓐ Ⓑ Ⓒ Ⓓ	12. Ⓐ Ⓑ Ⓒ Ⓓ	20. Ⓐ Ⓑ Ⓒ Ⓓ	28. Ⓐ Ⓑ Ⓒ Ⓓ
5. Ⓐ Ⓑ Ⓒ Ⓓ	13. Ⓐ Ⓑ Ⓒ Ⓓ	21. Ⓐ Ⓑ Ⓒ Ⓓ	29. Ⓐ Ⓑ Ⓒ Ⓓ
6. Ⓐ Ⓑ Ⓒ Ⓓ	14. Ⓐ Ⓑ Ⓒ Ⓓ	22. Ⓐ Ⓑ Ⓒ Ⓓ	30. Ⓐ Ⓑ Ⓒ Ⓓ
7. Ⓐ Ⓑ Ⓒ Ⓓ	15. Ⓐ Ⓑ Ⓒ Ⓓ	23. Ⓐ Ⓑ Ⓒ Ⓓ	
8. Ⓐ Ⓑ Ⓒ Ⓓ	16. Ⓐ Ⓑ Ⓒ Ⓓ	24. Ⓐ Ⓑ Ⓒ Ⓓ	

Subtest 2: Reading Comprehension Test (RCT)

1. Ⓐ Ⓑ Ⓒ Ⓓ	8. Ⓐ Ⓑ Ⓒ Ⓓ	15. Ⓐ Ⓑ Ⓒ Ⓓ	22. Ⓐ Ⓑ Ⓒ Ⓓ
2. Ⓐ Ⓑ Ⓒ Ⓓ	9. Ⓐ Ⓑ Ⓒ Ⓓ	16. Ⓐ Ⓑ Ⓒ Ⓓ	23. Ⓐ Ⓑ Ⓒ Ⓓ
3. Ⓐ Ⓑ Ⓒ Ⓓ	10. Ⓐ Ⓑ Ⓒ Ⓓ	17. Ⓐ Ⓑ Ⓒ Ⓓ	24. Ⓐ Ⓑ Ⓒ Ⓓ
4. Ⓐ Ⓑ Ⓒ Ⓓ	11. Ⓐ Ⓑ Ⓒ Ⓓ	18. Ⓐ Ⓑ Ⓒ Ⓓ	25. Ⓐ Ⓑ Ⓒ Ⓓ
5. Ⓐ Ⓑ Ⓒ Ⓓ	12. Ⓐ Ⓑ Ⓒ Ⓓ	19. Ⓐ Ⓑ Ⓒ Ⓓ	26. Ⓐ Ⓑ Ⓒ Ⓓ
6. Ⓐ Ⓑ Ⓒ Ⓓ	13. Ⓐ Ⓑ Ⓒ Ⓓ	20. Ⓐ Ⓑ Ⓒ Ⓓ	27. Ⓐ Ⓑ Ⓒ Ⓓ
7. Ⓐ Ⓑ Ⓒ Ⓓ	14. Ⓐ Ⓑ Ⓒ Ⓓ	21. Ⓐ Ⓑ Ⓒ Ⓓ	

Subtest 3: Mechanical Comprehension Test (MCT)

1. Ⓐ Ⓑ Ⓒ	9. Ⓐ Ⓑ Ⓒ	17. Ⓐ Ⓑ Ⓒ	25. Ⓐ Ⓑ Ⓒ
2. Ⓐ Ⓑ Ⓒ	10. Ⓐ Ⓑ Ⓒ	18. Ⓐ Ⓑ Ⓒ	26. Ⓐ Ⓑ Ⓒ
3. Ⓐ Ⓑ Ⓒ	11. Ⓐ Ⓑ Ⓒ	19. Ⓐ Ⓑ Ⓒ	27. Ⓐ Ⓑ Ⓒ
4. Ⓐ Ⓑ Ⓒ	12. Ⓐ Ⓑ Ⓒ	20. Ⓐ Ⓑ Ⓒ	28. Ⓐ Ⓑ Ⓒ
5. Ⓐ Ⓑ Ⓒ	13. Ⓐ Ⓑ Ⓒ	21. Ⓐ Ⓑ Ⓒ	29. Ⓐ Ⓑ Ⓒ
6. Ⓐ Ⓑ Ⓒ	14. Ⓐ Ⓑ Ⓒ	22. Ⓐ Ⓑ Ⓒ	30. Ⓐ Ⓑ Ⓒ
7. Ⓐ Ⓑ Ⓒ	15. Ⓐ Ⓑ Ⓒ	23. Ⓐ Ⓑ Ⓒ	
8. Ⓐ Ⓑ Ⓒ	16. Ⓐ Ⓑ Ⓒ	24. Ⓐ Ⓑ Ⓒ	

Subtest 4: Aviation and Nautical Information Test (ANIT)

1. Ⓐ Ⓑ Ⓒ Ⓓ	9. Ⓐ Ⓑ Ⓒ Ⓓ	17. Ⓐ Ⓑ Ⓒ Ⓓ	25. Ⓐ Ⓑ Ⓒ Ⓓ
2. Ⓐ Ⓑ Ⓒ Ⓓ	10. Ⓐ Ⓑ Ⓒ Ⓓ	18. Ⓐ Ⓑ Ⓒ Ⓓ	26. Ⓐ Ⓑ Ⓒ Ⓓ
3. Ⓐ Ⓑ Ⓒ Ⓓ	11. Ⓐ Ⓑ Ⓒ Ⓓ	19. Ⓐ Ⓑ Ⓒ Ⓓ	27. Ⓐ Ⓑ Ⓒ Ⓓ
4. Ⓐ Ⓑ Ⓒ Ⓓ	12. Ⓐ Ⓑ Ⓒ Ⓓ	20. Ⓐ Ⓑ Ⓒ Ⓓ	28. Ⓐ Ⓑ Ⓒ Ⓓ
5. Ⓐ Ⓑ Ⓒ Ⓓ	13. Ⓐ Ⓑ Ⓒ Ⓓ	21. Ⓐ Ⓑ Ⓒ Ⓓ	29. Ⓐ Ⓑ Ⓒ Ⓓ
6. Ⓐ Ⓑ Ⓒ Ⓓ	14. Ⓐ Ⓑ Ⓒ Ⓓ	22. Ⓐ Ⓑ Ⓒ Ⓓ	30. Ⓐ Ⓑ Ⓒ Ⓓ
7. Ⓐ Ⓑ Ⓒ Ⓓ	15. Ⓐ Ⓑ Ⓒ Ⓓ	23. Ⓐ Ⓑ Ⓒ Ⓓ	
8. Ⓐ Ⓑ Ⓒ Ⓓ	16. Ⓐ Ⓑ Ⓒ Ⓓ	24. Ⓐ Ⓑ Ⓒ Ⓓ	

Navy/Marine Corps/ Coast Guard Aviation Selection Test Battery (ASTB-E) Practice Test #2

15

Please turn to the beginning of Chapter 14, page 577, for more information about the breakdown and scoring attributes of the Aviation Selection Test Battery (ASTB-E).

SUBTEST 1: MATH SKILLS TEST (MST)

30 Questions

1. Jonathan earns $350 (before taxes) every two weeks at his part-time job. His withholdings are $27.75 for federal income taxes, $5.65 for Social Security (FICA), and $12.87 for Medicare tax. How much will his net paycheck be?

   (A) $314.73
   (B) $304.73
   (C) $303.73
   (D) $313.73

2. A computer-generated award certificate 9 inches long and 6 inches wide has to be enlarged so that its length will be 12 inches. How many inches wide will the enlarged certificate be?

   (A) 8
   (B) 6
   (C) 9
   (D) 10

3. June C. has a certificate of deposit for $10,000 at a compound annual interest percentage rate of six percent. How much interest will she gain if she does not touch the CD for two years?

   (A) $11,236
   (B) $10,636
   (C) $1,200
   (D) $1,236

4. If 2 lbs. of jelly beans cost $3.20, what is the cost of 3 oz.?

   (A) $0.30
   (B) $0.20
   (C) $0.25
   (D) $0.15

5. Mrs. H.B. drove her Volvo S80 four-door sedan from Waco to San Antonio at an average speed of 60 miles per hour, including two rest stops of 10 minutes each. Her car gets average highway mileage of 30 miles per gallon. If her car used 7 gallons of gas, how many hours did she travel?

   (A) 3 hrs.
   (B) 3.5 hrs.
   (C) 2.1 hrs.
   (D) 7.0 hrs.

6. James earns $17.50 per hour. If he works from 7:45 A.M. until 5:30 P.M., with 1 hour off for lunch, about how much does he earn in one day?

   (A) $170.63
   (B) $163.37
   (C) $147.88
   (D) $153.13

7. A basketball team won 70% of the 40 games it played. How many games did it lose?

   (A) 28
   (B) 30
   (C) 22
   (D) 12

8. EconoAir Flight 1776 is scheduled for departure at 3:50 P.M. If the flight takes 2 hours and 55 minutes, at what time is it scheduled to arrive at its destination?

   (A) 5:05 P.M.
   (B) 6:05 P.M.
   (C) 6:15 P.M.
   (D) 6:45 P.M.

9. How many 4-oz. candy bars are there in a 3-lb. package of candy?

(A) 12
(B) 16
(C) 48
(D) 9

10. What is the fifth term of the series $2\frac{5}{6}$, $3\frac{1}{2}$, $4\frac{1}{6}$, $4\frac{5}{6}$, . . . ?

(A) $5\frac{1}{6}$

(B) $5\frac{1}{2}$

(C) $5\frac{5}{6}$

(D) $6\frac{1}{6}$

11. In a steakhouse, a guest orders a small steak entree with vegetables for $12.50, dessert for $3.50, and coffee for $1.25. If the tax on meals is 8%, what tax should be added to his check?

(A) $0.68
(B) $0.80
(C) $1.28
(D) $1.38

12. A mechanic's warehouse is going to use a 55-gallon drum of oil to fill cans that hold 2 quarts each. How many cans can be filled from the drum?

(A) 55
(B) $27\frac{1}{2}$
(C) 110
(D) 220

13. On production line 2A in the Lee County wooden product factory, a lathe operator takes 45 minutes to do the finish work on 9 spindles. How many hours will it take him to finish 96 spindles at the same rate?

(A) 8
(B) 12
(C) 10
(D) 9

14. A triangle has two equal sides. The third side has a length of 13 feet, 2 inches. If the perimeter of the triangle is 40 feet, what is the length of one of the equal sides?

(A) 13 ft., 4 in.
(B) 26 ft., 10 in.
(C) 13 ft., 11 in.
(D) 13 ft., 5 in.

15. A lawn is 21 feet wide and 39 feet long. How much will it cost Jan to weed and feed it if a gardening service charges $0.40 per square yard for this treatment?

(A) $109.20
(B) $36.40
(C) $327.60
(D) $24.00

16. The perimeter of a rectangle is 40 feet. If the length is 15 feet, 6 inches, what is the width of the rectangle?

(A) 4 ft., 6 in.
(B) 9 ft., 6 in.
(C) 5 ft., 6 in.
(D) 5 ft.

17. Two partners operate a business that shows a profit for the year equal to $63,000. Their partnership agreement calls for them to share the profits in the ratio 5:4. How much of the profit should go to the partner who gets the larger share?

(A) $35,000
(B) $28,000
(C) $32,000
(D) $36,000

18. A purchaser paid $17.16 for an article that had recently been increased in price by 4%. What was the price of the article before the increase?

(A) $17.00
(B) $17.12
(C) $16.50
(D) $16.47

19. In a clothing factory, 5 workers finish production of 6 garments each per day, 3 others turn out 4 garments each per day, and one worker turns out 12 per day. What is the average number of garments produced per worker per day?

(A) $2\frac{2}{9}$
(B) 6
(C) 4
(D) $7\frac{1}{3}$

20. Travis makes a 255-mile trip by car. He drives the first 2 hours at 45 miles per hour. At what speed must he travel for the remainder of the trip in order to arrive at his destination 5 hours after he started the trip?

(A) 31 mph
(B) 50 mph
(C) 51 mph
(D) 55 mph

21. A contractor bids $300,000 as his price for erecting a building. He estimates that $\frac{1}{10}$ of this amount will be spent for masonry materials and labor, $\frac{1}{3}$ for lumber and carpentry, $\frac{1}{5}$ for plumbing and heating, and $\frac{1}{6}$ for electrical and lighting work. The remainder will be his profit. How much profit does he expect to make?

(A) $24,000
(B) $80,000
(C) $60,000
(D) $50,000

22. The list price of a TV set is $325, but the retailer offers successive discounts of 20% and 30%. What price does a customer actually pay?

(A) $182.00
(B) $270.00
(C) $162.50
(D) $176.67

23. A certain brand of motor oil is regularly sold at a price of 2 quart cans for $1.99. On a special sale, a carton containing 6 of the quart cans is sold for $5.43. What is the saving per quart if the oil is bought at the special sale?

(A) $0.27
(B) $0.09
(C) $0.54
(D) $0.5425

24. A worker earns $7.20 an hour. She is paid time and a half for overtime beyond a 40-hour week. How much will she earn in a week in which she works 43 hours?

(A) $295.20
(B) $320.40
(C) $432.00
(D) $464.40

25. A tree 36 feet high casts a shadow 8 feet long. At the same time, another tree casts a shadow 6 feet long. How tall is the second tree?

(A) 30 ft.
(B) 27 ft.
(C) 24 ft.
(D) 32 ft.

26. Find the numerical value of $(5)(a)(2)(b) - (3)(a)(b)(2)$ if $a = 7$ and $b = 4$.

(A) 244
(B) 124
(C) 112
(D) 224

27. If the circumference of a circle is divided by the length of its diameter, what is the result?

(A) 2
(B) 27
(C) π
(D) 7

28. For a special mission, 1 soldier is to be chosen at random from among 3 infantrymen, 2 artillerymen, and 5 tank crewmen. What is the probability that an infantryman will be chosen?

(A) $\frac{3}{10}$
(B) $\frac{1}{10}$
(C) $\frac{1}{3}$
(D) $\frac{3}{7}$

29. A naval task force is to be made up of a destroyer, a supply ship, and a submarine. If 4 destroyers, 2 supply ships, and 3 submarines are available from which to choose, how many different combinations are possible for the task force?

(A) 9
(B) 24
(C) 8
(D) 12

30. The base of a cylindrical can is a circle whose diameter is 2 inches. Its height is 7 inches. How many cubic inches are there in the volume of the can?
$\left(\text{Use } \frac{22}{7} \text{ for the value of } \pi.\right)$

(A) $12\frac{4}{7}$ cu. in.
(B) 22 cu. in.
(C) 44 cu. in.
(D) 88 cu. in.

SUBTEST 2: READING COMPREHENSION TEST (RCT)

27 Questions

The tactical effect of speech is not only that it improves cohesion—from which comes unified action—but that it is the vital spark in all maneuver. Speech galvanizes the desire to work together. It is the beginning of the urge to get something done. Until there is speech, each soldier is likely to think of his situation in purely negative terms; with the coming of speech, he starts to face up to it. If you doubt this, put yourself in the middle of a group of men who have just been pinned down by close-range sniper fire. What happens? These men will hug the dirt or snuggle up to the nearest log or boulder or building remnant, but they won't do anything constructive about their situation until one of them makes a specific suggestion: "It's too hot; let's get out of here," or "You cover me while I work my way up to that treeline."

1. According to this passage, soldiers

    (A) like to take cover from snipers.
    (B) have to communicate first before they get anything done.
    (C) are more likely to get pinned down if they don't communicate.
    (D) think only in negative terms.

By September 23, the Communists were in obvious retreat. The 1st Cavalry Division received the mission of pushing up the central corridor toward the X Corps beachhead at Inchon. The division commander organized Task Force 777 (built mostly around elements of Custer's onetime unit, the 7th Cavalry), which was to drive north—disregarding flanks and lateral contact—avoid decisive engagement with the retreating enemy, and move night and day to effect a linkup. The 3rd Battalion, 7th Cavalry, under Lt. Col. James H. Lynch, was reinforced and designated "Task Force Lynch"—this was the pointy end of the 1st Cavalry Division's spearhead. By midmorning of September 26, with little more than a hundred miles to go, Lynch's troopers were bypassing gaggles of disorganized, leaderless North Korean People's Army soldiers, and were cheered by villagers whose homes were still on fire in the wake of the retreating invaders. Lynch's lead group of three Pershing tanks plowed ahead so far and so fast that they outran even radio contact. By ten that night, they had made contact with the 31st Infantry Regiment north of Osan—but only after a blaze of hair-trigger American antitank fire at the unexpected visitors took off the head of a tank crewman in one of the Pershings.

2. According to the above passage,

    (A) the 7th Cavalry was commanded by Custer during the Civil War.
    (B) Task Force 777 reached Inchon on September 26.
    (C) the 31st Infantry Regiment reached Inchon on September 26.
    (D) Task Force Lynch linked up with the 31st Infantry but suffered a friendly fire casualty.

ASTB-E #2

3. Anomaly most nearly means

   (A) bitter hostility or open hatred.
   (B) an abnormality or irregularity.
   (C) a collection of songs or stories.
   (D) boldness.

4. Cacophony most nearly means

   (A) a sound made by a chicken or other domesticated bird.
   (B) bad handwriting.
   (C) a winged staff symbolizing the medical profession.
   (D) a jarring, discordant sound or noise.

5. Xenophobe most nearly means

   (A) a person who is afraid of foreigners or strangers.
   (B) a person who does not like foreigners or strangers.
   (C) a person who has a deep hatred of women.
   (D) a light that flashes at rapid, predetermined intervals.

A credibility check has its roots in a leader's history as it is known by other people; it has to do with reputation. Reputation is human collateral—the security we pledge to guarantee the performance of our obligations as leaders, friends, colleagues, and citizens. It is what supports the (usually natural) human instinct to *want* to trust. Reputation is to be derided and cared for—a damaged one lowers people's perceptions of a leader's worth and hence their motivation to follow.

6. In the passage above, what word is used incorrectly?

   (A) collateral
   (B) security
   (C) derided
   (D) obligations

During the Battle of the Bulge, the town of Bastogne was occupied by the American 101st Airborne Division to control the vital crossroads there, but surrounded by the German Army as it tried to unexpectedly slice through a lightly held sector to the port of Antwerp. On December 22, 1944, four Germans under a flag of truce, carrying a surrender demand, approached the lines of the 327th Infantry Regiment on the outskirts of Bastogne. The message cited the progress of attacking German forces farther west as evidence of the futility of holding out at Bastogne, and demanded the surrender of the encircled town within two hours. The surrender demand was delivered to acting division commander Brig. Gen. Anthony C. McAuliffe as he was about to leave his headquarters to congratulate the defenders of a roadblock who had driven off a heavy attack. He dropped the message on the floor, said "Nuts," and left. When he returned, his staff reminded him of the message, which he at first had not taken seriously; McAuliffe asked his staff what they thought should be the reply. The division operations officer said, "That first remark of yours would be hard to beat." So the message delivered to the Germans read, "To the German Commander: Nuts! The American Commander." The confused German major asked if this was affirmative or negative; he was told by the 327th's regimental commander that it was "decidedly not affirmative."

7. Why was the 101st Airborne Division holding out at Bastogne?

   (A) to protect the vital nut and berry agricultural center at Bastogne
   (B) to set up a roadblock
   (C) to deny the Germans an important crossroads
   (D) to serve as an affirmative symbol of Allied resistance

8. What news did the German major have to take back to his commander?

   (A) The Americans would surrender within two hours.
   (B) The Americans would surrender, but not within two hours.
   (C) The Americans would not surrender.
   (D) The Americans would not surrender the nut plantations west of Bastogne.

9. Incentive most nearly means

   (A) a motivation or benefit for doing something.
   (B) capable of producing new ideas.
   (C) copied or adapted from something else.
   (D) moderate or cautious.

Our current understanding of the motion of objects dates back to Newton and Galileo. Before then, people held to Aristotle's ideas that the "natural state" of an object was to be at rest, and that it moved only if it was caused to move by some force. Aristotle also thought one could figure out all the principles governing the universe by reason alone; there was no need to physically verify those conclusions by experimentation or observation—so no one until Galileo checked to see if bodies of differing weights *actually* fell at different velocities. The story goes that Galileo dropped weights from the leaning tower of Pisa, but whether or not this is actually true, we know that he did roll balls of differing weights down a smooth slope (an easier experiment because the speeds are less). Galileo's experiment showed that each body increased its speed at the same rate, no matter what its weight. His work was then used by Newton to deduce his three laws of motion.

10. According to the passage above,

    (A) Aristotle's experiments formed the basis of Galileo's and Newton's work.
    (B) different weights fall at different speeds from the Leaning Tower of Pisa.
    (C) different weights fall at the same speed from the Leaning Tower of Pisa.
    (D) balls of differing weights roll downhill at the same rate.

The least considerable man among us has an interest equal to the proudest nobleman in the laws and constitution of his country, and is equally called upon to make a generous contribution in support of them—whether it be the heart to conceive, the understanding to direct, or the hand to execute.

11. According to the passage above,

    (A) all citizens have an obligation to do what they can to make their country better.
    (B) all citizens should make an equal contribution to running their country.
    (C) rich people should contribute more to their nation since they have more.
    (D) poor people should contribute more to their country since there are more of them.

As a citizen, you are to be a quiet and peaceable subject, true to your government, and just to your country; you are not to <u>countenance</u> disloyalty or rebellion, but patiently submit to legal authority, and conform with cheerfulness to the government of the country in which you live.

12. <u>Countenance</u> most nearly means

    (A) face.
    (B) start.
    (C) enumerate.
    (D) consider.

ASTB-E #2

The "zero tolerance on fighting" policy many of our schools have instituted sounds great at first, but it's actually a smokescreen that lets school leaders avoid tough decisions while teaching kids the wrong lessons. The biggest problem happens when the student who is attacked gets swept up in the punishment net along with the one who started the fight—unless he doesn't fight back and lets himself get pummeled. It is morally wrong to teach our kids that the attacked person is invariably as much in the wrong as the attacker. The correct solution, instead, is a balanced application of reasonable judgment by administrators, backed up by a determination to tell the truth to parents. Parents, too, have an obligation—to recognize that their little angel may not be perfect, and not to sue the school because a teacher or principal told them an unpleasant truth.

13. The author of this passage believes that

    (A) "zero tolerance on fighting" policies sound great.
    (B) administrators should sue parents whose children get into fights.
    (C) parents should sue school personnel who tell them something they don't want to hear.
    (D) the student who defends himself should be viewed differently than the attacker.

14. Posterity most nearly means

    (A) the back side of an object or person.
    (B) a series of small signs or posters.
    (C) great honor or recognition.
    (D) future descendants or generations.

It is either exceptionally naïve or depressingly cynical to equate an analysis of incomplete facts that turns out to be wrong with knowing untruths (otherwise known as "lies"). Military, political, and economic intelligence—information about a known or potential adversary or competitor—is especially open to gaps, misinterpretation, and other confusion. Perfect information seldom if ever exists even in non-adversarial situations, much less when the adversary is actively trying to deny you the facts—or sell you the wrong ones. The quest for perfectly complete and accurate information results in analysis paralysis: the inability to make a decision until you have *all* the information, which is never going to happen.

15. According to this passage, the reader can infer that the author

    (A) likes to make decisions based on 100% accurate information.
    (B) knows that complete information will eventually be available.
    (C) believes that acting on incomplete information is often necessary.
    (D) wants to give accurate information to potential adversaries or competitors.

16. Quandary most nearly means

    (A) a swampy area that impedes the movement of people or vehicles.
    (B) a stanza of four lines in poetry.
    (C) divided into four sections.
    (D) deep uncertainty about a choice; a dilemma.

After Texas broke away from Mexico and became a republic, the new nation's government made halting but significant steps toward a public education system. In 1839, the Texas House passed a law calling for three leagues (13,285 acres) to be set aside in each county for a "primary school or academy," and 50 leagues to be set aside for two colleges. However, the official system of public schools did not even begin to become a reality until after Texas was admitted to the Union as a state in 1845.

17. The passage primarily discusses

    (A) the relationship of leagues to acres.
    (B) early steps toward public education in Texas.
    (C) steps taken by private organizations to improve public education.
    (D) how Texas became a republic and then a state in the Union.

18. There is no room in this ________ for hyphenated Americanism. The one absolutely certain way of bringing this nation to ruin, of preventing all possibility of its continuing to be a nation at all, would be to permit it to become a tangle of squabbling nationalities. [Theodore Roosevelt]

    (A) improbability
    (B) country
    (C) diversity
    (D) science

Perhaps the most valuable result of all education is the ability to make yourself do the thing you have to do, when it ought to be done, whether you like it or not; it is the first lesson that ought to be learned; and however early a man's training begins, it is probably the last lesson that he learns thoroughly. [Thomas Henry Huxley]

19. If the passage above had to be summarized, it would be

    (A) Don't Procrastinate.
    (B) Support Early Childhood Education.
    (C) If You Think Education Is Expensive, Try Ignorance.
    (D) A Smart Man Does What He's Supposed to Do.

20. Discernment most nearly means

(A) to treat differently due to race or color.
(B) a preference for always being at the center of events.
(C) insight; the ability to see things clearly.
(D) scientific knowledge of natural phenomena.

An ultimate British victory was certain for three main reasons. First, the 1.5 million inhabitants of the British colonies in 1754 were tenacious, resourceful, and growing quickly—while New France had fewer than 100,000 people, brave but scattered and deficient in initiative. Second, the British held a better strategic geographical position. While operating on interior lines of communication and transportation, they could effectively strike westward at what is now Pittsburgh, northwestward toward Niagara, and northward toward Quebec and Montreal. They also had a better navy, could more quickly reinforce and supply their troops, and could lay siege to Quebec by water. Finally, they proved able to produce better leaders in both the civilian and military realms.

21. What does the author of the passage state were the three main reasons why the British victory in North America was "certain"?

(A) more people, more land, more ships
(B) more people, better commerce, better military
(C) fewer people, better geographical position, more leaders
(D) more people, better geographical position, better leaders

Chlorophyll can be any one of almost a dozen kinds of green pigments present in most plant cells. Chlorophyll is able to convert the energy from sunlight into carbohydrates, which plants form from carbon dioxide and water from the environment. The carbohydrates in turn become a source of energy for animals and humans when the plant material is eaten.

22. Chlorophyll uses ________________ to make carbohydrates.

(A) water and carbon dioxide
(B) pigments, water, and carbon dioxide
(C) animal waste, water, and carbon dioxide
(D) sunlight, carbon dioxide, and water

The most common cold weather injury is frostbite. Severe cold, especially for a prolonged period, can severely constrict the blood vessels, reducing the normal flow of warm blood to exposed body parts. The symptoms usually include a very cold feeling in the exposed skin area, followed by full or partial loss of feeling. The skin may appear flushed or reddish at first, but later it becomes white or grayish yellow. Because of the loss of feeling, the victim is often unaware of the injury.

23. The best remedy for frostbite is

    (A) vigorous rubbing of the affected area to create friction and therefore heat.
    (B) removal of tight clothing and gradual warming of the area.
    (C) immediate heating of the affected area, followed by vigorous exercise.
    (D) not addressed in this passage.

Far better it is to dare mighty things, to win glorious triumphs, even though checkered by failure, than to take rank with those poor spirits who neither enjoy much nor suffer much, because they live in the gray twilight that knows not victory nor defeat. [Theodore Roosevelt]

24. The above passage encourages the reader to

    (A) make the effort to accomplish challenging goals.
    (B) live in the gray twilight so as not to suffer much.
    (C) dare to outrank the poor.
    (D) devote one's life to public service.

25. Leaders demonstrate that they value other people when they listen to them, trust them, and are ___________ and willing to listen to reports of unproductive or unpleasant information—even when it involves the leader himself.

    (A) spontaneous
    (B) receptive
    (C) disarming
    (D) characteristic

In 1949, the Federal Communications Commission (FCC) instituted its Fairness Doctrine, which required broadcasters to "afford reasonable opportunity for the discussion of conflicting views of public importance." The Personal Attack rule in that Doctrine required broadcasters to provide rebuttal time to anyone of whom a less-than-complimentary opinion had been spoken on the air. This resulted in self-imposed inhibitions on political speech to avoid federal prosecution, as well as loss of income by trying to comply. By 1987, however, it was recognized that the Doctrine was "antagonistic to the freedom of expression guaranteed by the First Amendment," and the speech-stifling regulation was itself stifled—or rather, gleefully strangled by those who were willing to engage in the give-and-take of a fair public debate.

26. The Fairness Doctrine was

    (A) instituted in 1987 and is still in effect today.
    (B) recognized as antagonistic to freedom of expression.
    (C) a reasonable opportunity to respond to broadcast attacks.
    (D) a vast right-wing conspiracy.

27. If a nation expects to be ignorant and free, in a state of __________, it expects what never was and never will be. [Thomas Jefferson]

    (A) siege
    (B) negotiation
    (C) civilization
    (D) nature

SUBTEST 3: MECHANICAL COMPREHENSION TEST (MCT)

30 Questions

1. If gear B is the driving gear and it makes 6 revolutions, how many revolutions will gear A make?

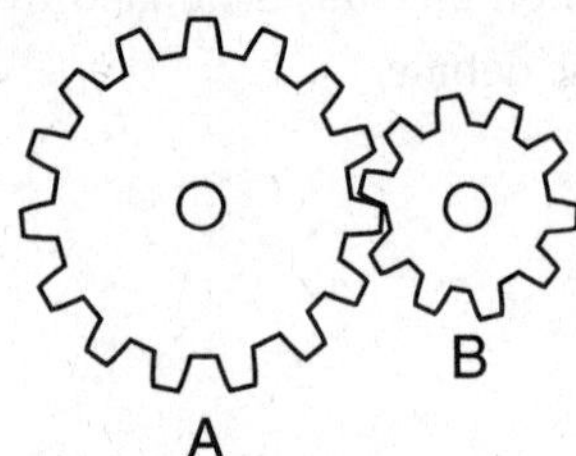

(A) 2
(B) 4
(C) 6

2. The wheels below are connected by a belt as shown. If the larger wheel makes 2 revolutions, how many revolutions will the smaller wheel make?

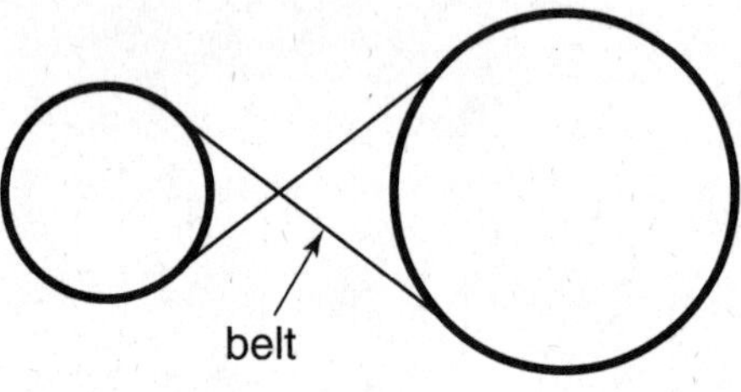

(A) one
(B) two
(C) more than two

3. In the diagram in problem 2, if the wheel on the left turns counterclockwise, which way will the wheel on the right turn?

(A) clockwise
(B) counterclockwise
(C) unable to tell from the information given

4. If block A, on which the lever is resting, is moved closer to block B,

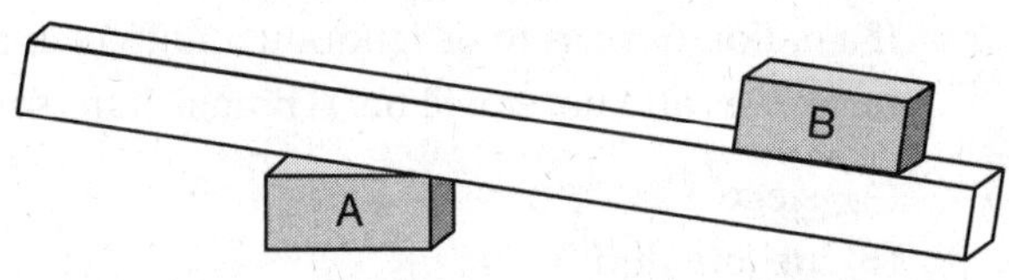

(A) there will be no change in the effort required to lift block B to the same height.
(B) it will be harder to lift block B but it will go higher.
(C) it will be easier to lift block B but it will not be lifted as high.

5. A gear system derives the greatest amount of mechanical advantage if a 7-tooth gear drives a

(A) 27-tooth gear.
(B) 7-tooth gear.
(C) 28-tooth gear.

6. Recruit Highspeed is assigned to cross a fast-moving stream by swimming it while facing at a right angle to the banks. If he maintains his perpendicular orientation correctly during his swim, where will he arrive on the far bank?

   (A) upstream of his departure point
   (B) downstream of his departure point
   (C) directly across from his departure point

7. If pulley C is rotating clockwise, what direction will pulley A rotate?

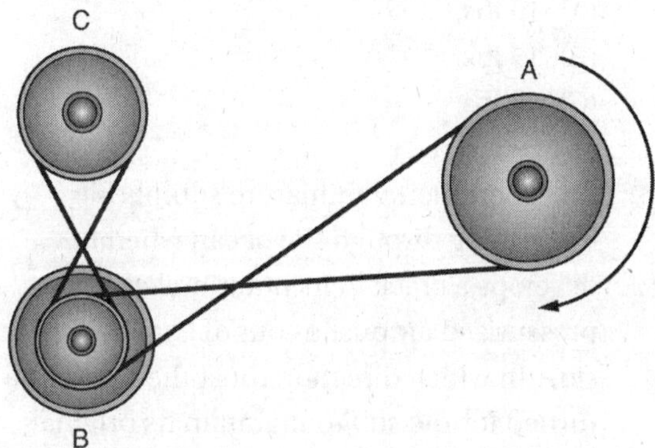

   (A) clockwise
   (B) counterclockwise
   (C) insufficient information to answer

8. In the pulley system above, which pulley will rotate the fastest?

   (A) pulley A
   (B) pulley B
   (C) pulley C

9. If the cisterns of both water towers A and B are the same size and the same height above the ground, and both begin with a full water level, which water tower will be able to provide more water to the thirsty troops below?

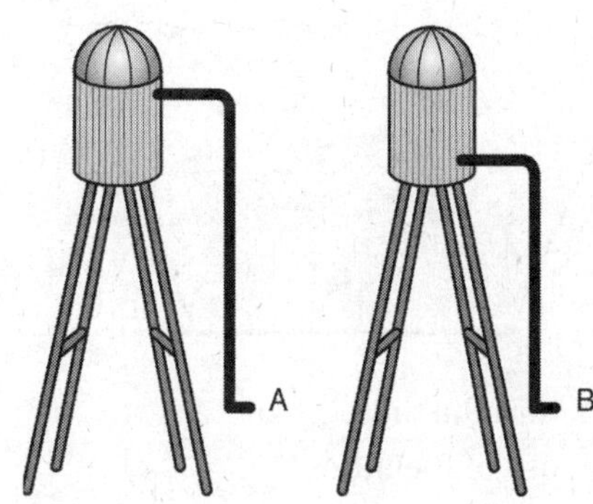

   (A) water tower A
   (B) water tower B
   (C) both will provide the same amount

10. If a bullet from a rifle is fired at a 1 degree angle above the horizontal, at what point will it have the highest velocity?

   (A) when it leaves the muzzle
   (B) midway between the muzzle and the top of its arc
   (C) at the top of its arc

11. When the plug in the tube is removed, water will flow

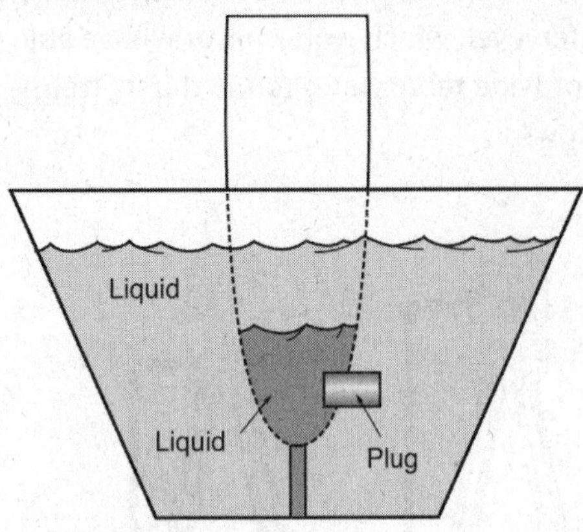

(A) into the tube.
(B) out of the tube.
(C) in neither direction.

12. Which weight exerts more pull on the horizontal bar from which both weights hang by strings as shown?

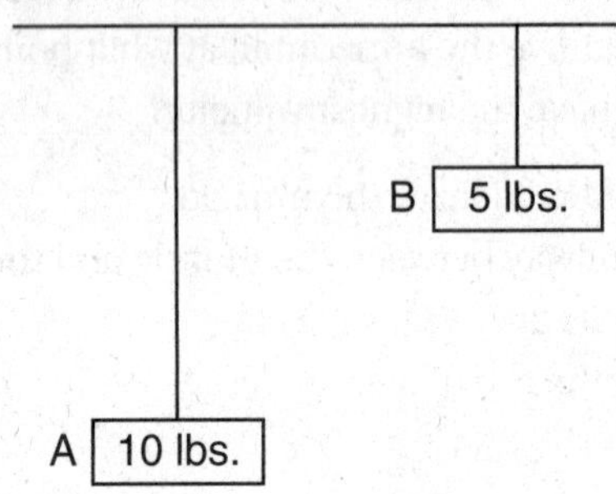

(A) A
(B) B
(C) both exert the same pull

13. The force required to balance the lever shown below would be

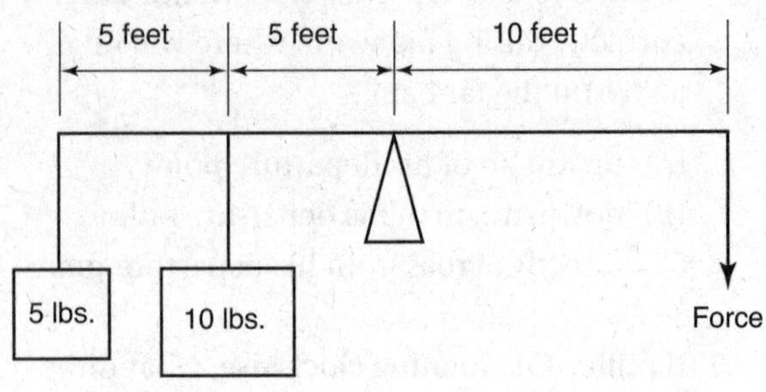

(A) 10 lbs.
(B) 15 lbs.
(C) 20 lbs.

14. An experimental miniature submarine is traveling through the ocean when it develops a crack in its outer hull and pressurized air pushes out of its lower right side. In which direction must the rudder be turned for the sub to maintain its original heading?

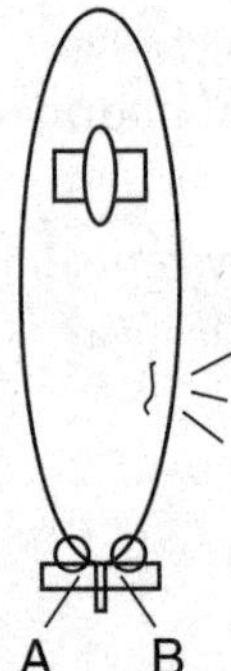

(A) A
(B) B
(C) no rudder correction is necessary

ASTB-E #2

15. In the water system below, assume that the main tank begins in an empty state and that all the valves are closed. In order for the tank to fill approximately halfway and maintain that level, which valves would have to be open?

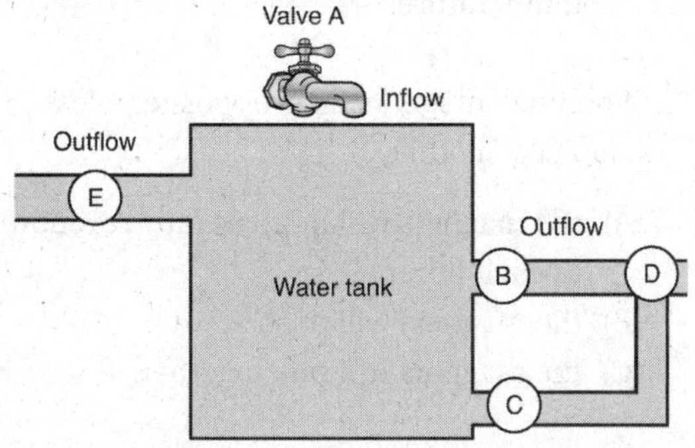

(A) A, B, and C
(B) A, B, and D
(C) A, E, and B

16. Which pendulum takes more time to make one complete swing?

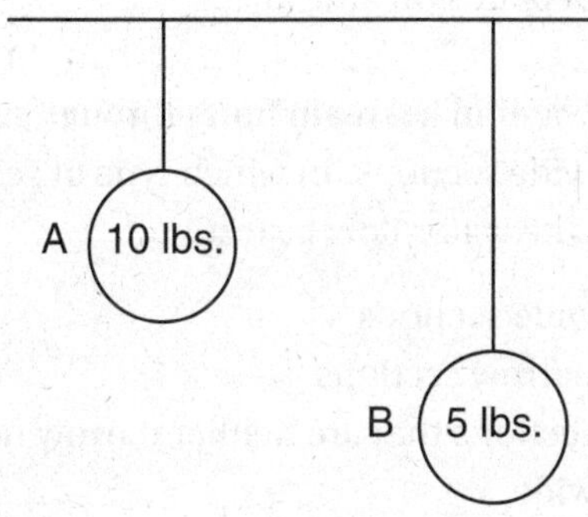

(A) A
(B) B
(C) both take the same amount of time

17. In the diagram for problem 16, if pendulum A was the same length as pendulum B, which pendulum would take less time to make one swing?

(A) A
(B) B
(C) both would take the same amount of time

18. If two resistors and a battery are arranged as shown in each circuit, which circuit arrangement has a greater resistance?

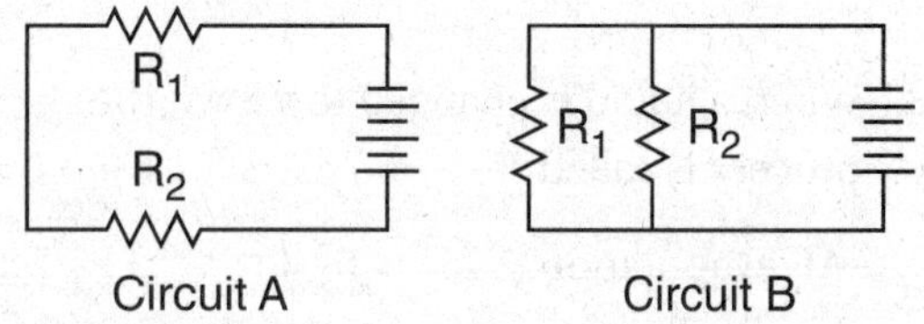

(A) circuit A
(B) circuit B
(C) both circuits have the same resistance

19. When two or more forces act in such a way that their combination has a net effect of zero, what is this condition called?

(A) similarity
(B) equilibrium
(C) equilateral

20. The descent of an airborne paratrooper by parachute is primarily affected by what physical forces?

(A) gravity and thrust
(B) gravity and temperature
(C) drag and gravity

21. Heat is transferred from one location to another by conduction, convection, and

(A) condensation.
(B) evaporation.
(C) radiation.

22. When a salt is dissolved in water, it causes

(A) an increase in the freezing point of the solution.
(B) a decrease in the freezing point of the solution.
(C) no significant difference in the freezing point of the solution.

23. When a liquid is changed to vapor, the process is called

(A) evaporation.
(B) distillation.
(C) dehydration.

24. When water that is being heated is confined to a closed container so that the steam cannot escape, the pressure inside the container increases and the temperature of the boiling water

(A) decreases.
(B) increases.
(C) stays the same.

25. If pulley A is the driver and turns counterclockwise, which pulley will turn the slowest?

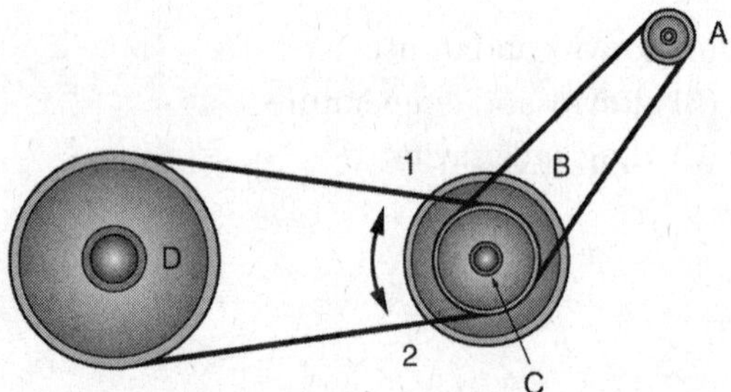

(A) pulley A
(B) pulley C
(C) pulley D

26. Compressing the air in a closed space will

(A) increase the volume and raise the temperature.
(B) increase the volume and lower the temperature.
(C) decrease the volume and raise the temperature.

27. When two magnets have opposite poles facing each other,

(A) the magnets will not have any reaction to each other.
(B) the magnets will push apart.
(C) the magnets will pull together.

28. What is the difference between weight and mass?

(A) Weight can be changed by buoyancy, but mass is relative to gravity.
(B) Mass remains constant, but weight depends on altitude.
(C) Weight remains constant, but mass depends on altitude.

29. The water in a stream flows through narrow and wide sections. In which type of section does the water flow fastest?

(A) wide sections
(B) narrow sections
(C) sections that are neither narrow nor wide

30. Static electricity is

(A) direct currect (DC).
(B) alternating current (AC).
(C) none of the above

SUBTEST 4: AVIATION AND NAUTICAL INFORMATION TEST (ANIT)

30 Questions

1. If a fixed-wing aircraft has tricycle landing gear, it

   (A) has landing gear supporting the nose of the aircraft.
   (B) has three sets of landing gear evenly spaced under the aircraft.
   (C) has three sets of landing gear mounted closely together.
   (D) has three sets of landing gear spaced longitudinally along the fuselage.

2. A floor or horizontal surface on a ship is called a

   (A) divider.
   (B) gangway.
   (C) deck.
   (D) spewcatcher.

3. What is the nickname for the EA-6B?

   (A) Growler
   (B) Prowler
   (C) Tomcat
   (D) Hornet

4. Who was Yuri Gagarin?

   (A) inventor of the helicopter
   (B) Father of the Navy
   (C) first man into space
   (D) first woman into space

5. The wings of an airplane design are angled upward. This is called

   (A) armature.
   (B) angulation.
   (C) attitude of attack.
   (D) dihedral.

6. Who is considered to be the Father of the Navy?

   (A) John Paul Jones
   (B) John Paul Sartre
   (C) John Paul
   (D) Albert Thayer Mahan

7. Where is the bow of a ship?

   (A) in the back
   (B) below decks
   (C) underneath
   (D) in the front

8. The time of 5 A.M. would be expressed using the 24-hour clock as

   (A) 0500.
   (B) 0700.
   (C) 1500.
   (D) 1700.

9. When a pilot pushes forward on the control stick, the elevators will

   (A) extend.
   (B) retract.
   (C) move upward.
   (D) move downward.

10. From where is longitude measured?

    (A) the prime meridian
    (B) the equator
    (C) the international date line
    (D) Greenwich Village

11. If one end of a runway was numbered 10, what number would designate the other end of the same runway?

(A) 11
(B) 28
(C) 12
(D) 20

12. From where is latitude measured?

(A) the prime meridian
(B) the equator
(C) the international date line
(D) Greenwich, England

13. Who was the first American to complete an orbital space mission?

(A) Alan Shepard
(B) John Glenn, Jr.
(C) Neil Armstrong
(D) Deke Slayton

14. What were the names, in chronological order, of the three primary American manned space programs?

(A) Gemini, Apollo, Challenger
(B) Dynasoar, Redstone, Saturn
(C) Redstone, Gemini, Mercury
(D) Mercury, Gemini, Apollo

15. For the F/A-18 aircraft, what does "F/A" stand for?

(A) fighter, advanced
(B) fighter/attack
(C) fueler, airborne
(D) fighter/assault

16. What is hypoxia?

(A) too much oxygen in the bloodstream, resulting in euphoria
(B) too little oxygen in the bloodstream, resulting in blackout
(C) too much smallpox vaccine, resulting in mild smallpox symptoms
(D) an early stage of rust below the waterline of a ship

17. A ship's gunwales are

(A) the upper edges of the vessel's sides.
(B) the mounts where machine guns are mounted.
(C) the areas where fire can be observed.
(D) the fire control direction center.

18. Above what altitude would you normally need oxygen?

(A) 5,500 ft.
(B) 10,000 ft.
(C) 12,000 ft.
(D) 14,200 ft.

19. Who first broke the sound barrier, and in what year?

(A) Billy Mitchell, 1942
(B) Charles Lindbergh, 1952
(C) Robert Goddard, 1949
(D) Chuck Yeager, 1947

20. Who was the first man to walk on the moon?

(A) Neil Young
(B) Tip O'Neal
(C) Neil Armstrong
(D) Lance Armstrong

21. The Latin phrase *Semper Fidelis* is the motto of the

(A) U.S. Navy.
(B) U.S. Central Command.
(C) U.S. Air Force.
(D) U.S. Marine Corps.

22. Who was the first American woman in space and in what year?
    (A) Sally Wright, 1981
    (B) Sally Forth, 1985
    (C) Sally Ride, 1983
    (D) June Cleaver, 1982

23. A ship designated with a hull number starting with "CG" is what kind of ship?
    (A) fleet command ship
    (B) battleship, cruise missile
    (C) nuclear-propelled aircraft carrier
    (D) guided missile cruiser

24. The first conflict to see widespread use of the helicopter was the
    (A) Korean War.
    (B) Vietnam War.
    (C) Cuban Missile Crisis.
    (D) Persian Gulf War.

25. Aircraft position lights
    (A) should be on from dusk till dawn.
    (B) show red on the left wing.
    (C) show green on the right wing.
    (D) all of the above

26. The first American spacecraft to explore the outer solar system was the
    (A) *Pioneer 1.*
    (B) *Pioneer 10.*
    (C) *Freedom 7.*
    (D) *Voyager 2.*

27. The four types of airspeed are
    (A) instrument, calibrated, equilibrium, and true.
    (B) indicated, calculated, equivalent, and temperature-dependent.
    (C) indicated, calibrated, equivalent, and true.
    (D) instrument, calibrated, equivalent, and true.

28. The airspeed indicator measures and shows the difference between
    (A) equivalent and indicated airspeed.
    (B) true airspeed and equivalent groundspeed.
    (C) above-ground altitude and altitude above mean sea level (MSL).
    (D) impact and static pressure.

29. The typical air wing aboard a U.S. Navy aircraft carrier usually includes
    (A) 2–3 fighter/attack squadrons, an electronic defense squadron, a command and control squadron, a logistic support squadron, and two anti-surface warfare helicopter squadrons.
    (B) a fighter/attack squadron, an electronic attack squadron, a command and control squadron, a logistic support squadron, an antisubmarine warfare helicopter squadron, and an anti-surface warfare helicopter squadron.
    (C) 3–4 fighter/attack squadrons, an electronic attack squadron, a reconnaissance squadron, a logistic support squadron, an antisubmarine warfare helicopter squadron, and an anti-surface warfare helicopter squadron.
    (D) 3–4 fighter/attack squadrons, an electronic attack squadron, a command and control squadron, a logistic support squadron, an antisubmarine warfare helicopter squadron, and an anti-surface warfare helicopter squadron.

30. A nuclear-powered aircraft carrier has what designation?
    (A) CV
    (B) CVN
    (C) CGN
    (D) CVA

ANSWERS AND EXPLANATIONS

Subtest 1: Math Skills Test (MST)

	✔	✘		✔	✘		✔	✘		✔	✘		✔	✘
1. C			7. D			13. A			19. B			25. B		
2. A			8. D			14. D			20. D			26. C		
3. D			9. A			15. B			21. C			27. C		
4. A			10. B			16. A			22. A			28. A		
5. B			11. D			17. A			23. B			29. B		
6. D			12. C			18. C			24. B			30. B		

1. **(C)** First, total up all the withholding amounts.

$$\$27.75 + \$5.65 + \$12.87 = \$46.27$$

Jonathan's net pay is his salary for the pay period minus the total of all the withholdings.

$$\text{Net pay} = \$350.00 - \$46.27 = \mathbf{\$303.73}$$

2. **(A)** Because the certificate and its enlargement are similar (i.e., proportional) figures, the lengths will have the same ratio as the widths; if the length is increased by a given proportion, then the width will be increased by the same proportion or percentage of its original size.

$$\frac{\text{length of original}}{\text{length of enlargement}} = \frac{\text{width of original}}{\text{width of enlargement}}$$

$$\frac{9}{12} = \frac{6}{\text{width of enlargement}}$$

To solve this, cross-multiply the measurements, using x for the one you don't know.

$$9 \times x = 12 \times 6$$
$$9x = 72$$
$$\frac{9x}{9} = \frac{72}{9}$$
$$x = \mathbf{8}$$

The width of the enlarged certificate is 8 inches.

3. **(D)** There is a standard equation to calculate compound interest, but you don't need to remember it to work this problem. You can work it as a simple multiplication problem (interest rate times the amount in the CD at that time) and repeat it for each time period in the problem (in this case only two years).

$$\$10{,}000 \times .06 = 600 \text{ (first year's interest)}$$
$$(10{,}000 + 600) \times .06 = \text{(second year's interest)}$$
$$10{,}600 \times .06 = 636 \text{ (second year's interest)}$$

So, the total interest—make sure you pay attention to what the question asks for—for the two years is $600 + $636 = **$1,236.**

4. **(A)** There are 16 oz. in a lb. Therefore, if two lbs. of jelly beans cost \$3.20, then one lb. costs \$1.60. The cost of one oz. is (\$1.60 ÷ 16) = \$0.10, so three oz. cost 3 × \$0.10 = **\$0.30.**

5. **(B)** We are given a lot of numbers and information here, so the first thing to do is identify what we need and what we don't. It doesn't matter what model of car Mrs. H.B. drove, and it doesn't matter that she stopped twice for 10 minutes each, since we are given her average speed for the trip. So, the way to attack this problem is:

   7 gallons of gas × 30 miles per gallon = 210 miles traveled
   210 miles ÷ 60 miles per hour = **3.5 hours**

6. **(D)** From 7:45 A.M. to 5:30 P.M. with an hour off for lunch is 8 hours and 45 minutes, or 8.75 hours. Multiply James' work hours by his hourly rate.

   8.75 × \$17.50 = **\$153.13** (one day's wages)

7. **(D)** The number of games won is 70% (or 0.70) of the number of games played, 40.

   Number of games won = 0.70(40) = 28

   The number of games lost is the total number played minus the number won.

   Number of games lost = 40 – 28 = **12**

8. **(D)** The time of arrival is 2 hours and 55 minutes after the departure time of 3:50 P.M. By 4:00 P.M., the flight has taken 10 minutes of the total flight time of 2 hours and 55 minutes. 2 hours and 45 minutes remain, and 2 hours and 45 minutes after 4:00 P.M. is **6:45 P.M.**

9. **(A)** There are 16 oz. in 1 lb. Therefore, 4 of the 4-oz. candy bars will make 1 pound. A 3-lb. package will hold 3 times 4 or **12** bars.

10. **(B)** Find the relationship between each pair of successive numbers in the series. It is helpful to change $3\frac{1}{2}$ to $3\frac{3}{6}$ in order to see the relationships. Each term of the series is obtained by adding $\frac{4}{6}$ to the preceding term. The fifth term is $5\frac{3}{6}$ or $\mathbf{5\frac{1}{2}}$.

11. **(D)** First add the prices of the three items ordered to get the cost of the meal before the tax.

    \$12.50 + \$3.50 + \$1.25 = \$17.25

    The tax is 8% (or 0.08) of the cost of the meal.

    0.08 × \$17.25 = **\$1.38**

12. **(C)** There are four quarts in one gallon; therefore, a 55-gallon drum holds 4 × 55 quarts.

    4 × 55 quarts = 220 quarts

    If each can holds two quarts, the number of cans filled is 220 divided by 2.

    220 ÷ 2 = **110** cans

ASTB-E #2

13. **(A)** Since it takes 45 minutes to finish nine spindles, it takes five minutes to finish each spindle ($45 \div 9 = 5$). So, the number of minutes it takes to finish 96 spindles is:

$$5 \times 96 = 480$$

$$480 \text{ minutes} \div 60 \text{ minutes} = \mathbf{8} \textbf{ hours}$$

14. **(D)** The perimeter, 40 feet, is the sum of the lengths of all three sides. The sum of the lengths of the two equal sides is the difference between the perimeter and the length of the third side. The sum of the lengths of two equal sides

$$\begin{aligned} &= 40 \text{ ft.} - 13 \text{ ft., } 2 \text{ in.} \\ &= 39 \text{ ft., } 12 \text{ in.} - 13 \text{ ft., } 2 \text{ in.} \\ &= 26 \text{ ft., } 10 \text{ in.} \end{aligned}$$

The length of one side is obtained by dividing the sum by 2. The length of one equal side = **13 ft., 5 in.**

15. **(B)** Since 3 feet = 1 yard, convert the length and width to yards by dividing their dimensions in feet by 3. The area of a rectangle is the product of its length and width.

$$\text{Area} = 7 \times 13 = 91 \text{ sq. yds.}$$

The cost for the entire lawn is obtained by multiplying the area in square yards by the cost per square yard.

$$91 \times \$.40 = \mathbf{\$36.40}$$

16. **(A)** The perimeter of a rectangle is equal to the sum of the two lengths and two widths. If 15 feet, 6 inches $\left(15\frac{1}{2} \text{ feet}\right)$ equal 1 length, then

$$2 \times 15\frac{1}{2} = 31 \text{ ft. (2 lengths)}$$

$$40 - 31 = 9 \text{ ft. (both widths)}$$

$$9 \div 2 = \mathbf{4\frac{1}{2}} \textbf{ ft.} \text{ (1 width)}$$

17. **(A)** First add both partners' shares together to find the value of one share ($5 + 4 = 9$), and then divide the total profit by nine: $63,000 ÷ 9 = $7,000. Then multiply the value of one share by the number of shares held by the partner who holds the most shares to find out how much he gets: $7,000 × 5 = **$35,000.**

18. **(C)** The current (recently increased) price is 4% more than the previous price, so it is 104% of that amount; we want to find out what 100% (the old price) was. Set up a proportion with x representing the unknown original price over 100 (for its percentage) and the new price over 104, then cross-multiply and solve for x:

$$\frac{x}{100} = \frac{17.16}{104}$$

$$104x = 17.16 \times 100$$

$$104x = 1{,}716$$

$$\frac{104x}{104} = \frac{1{,}716}{104}$$

$$x = 16.50$$

The original price was **$16.50.**

ASTB-E #2

19. **(B)** First find the total number of garments produced in a day by all nine workers:

$$(5 \times 6) + (3 \times 4) + 12 = 30 + 12 + 12 = 54$$

Now divide the total garments produced per day (54) by the total number of workers (9) to find out that the average number of garments produced per day per worker is **6**.

20. **(D)** After driving the first two hours at 45 mph, Travis has covered 90 miles (45 mph × 2 hours = 90 miles). Subtract this from the total distance of 255 and we see that he has 165 miles remaining to go in three hours (five hours total trip time minus the two hours he already drove). Divide 165 miles by those three hours and we see that Travis must travel at **55 mph** to make it to his destination on time.

21. **(C)** Break down the contractor's costs by applying the fractional costs to the total:

Masonry materials: $\$300{,}000 \times \frac{1}{10} =$	\$30,000
Lumber and carpentry: $\$300{,}000 \times \frac{1}{3} =$	\$100,000
Plumbing and heating: $\$300{,}000 \times \frac{1}{5} =$	\$60,000
Electrical and lighting: $\$300{,}000 \times \frac{1}{6} =$	+ \$50,000
Total costs =	\$240,000

Subtract the contractor's costs (\$240,000) from his bid (\$300,000) and we see that his profit will be **\$60,000.**

22. **(A)** The key to getting the right answer here is careful reading: the discounts are *successive*—they follow one after the other. We apply the first discount of 20% by multiplying \$325 by 20% or 0.2, reaching the intermediate step answer of \$65, and then subtracting that \$65 from the \$325 original price to get a price of \$260 after the first discount. Now do the same thing for the second discount of 30%:

$$\$260 \times 0.3 = \$78$$
$$\$260 - \$78 = \$182$$

So we see that the final price paid by the customer after two successive discounts is **\$182.**

23. **(B)** First find the price *per quart* at the regular price (notice that the regular price is \$1.99 for *two* cans, not just one). \$1.99 divided by two is \$0.995; hold onto that and don't round it off yet. Now, for the sale price *per quart*, divide \$5.43 by the six quart cans to get \$0.905 per quart. Subtract the sale price *per quart* from the regular price *per quart* and we see that the savings on the sale is **\$0.09** per quart.

24. **(B)** First find how much she makes for her regular 40-hour work week: 40 × \$7.20 = \$288. Now, for the three hours beyond 40 that she worked, her pay per hour is 1.5 × \$7.20 = \$10.80. Add the overtime pay for three hours (3 × \$10.80 = \$32.40) to her regular pay of \$288 and we see that \$288 + \$32.40 = **\$320.40.**

25. **(B)** Since light rays are parallel to each other and the angle from the light source (the sun) would be the same, the shadows will be proportionate to the height of the tree. Set up a proportion where x is the height of the second tree:

$$\frac{8}{36} = \frac{6}{x}$$
$$8x = 36 \times 6$$
$$8x = 216$$
$$x = 27$$

The height of the second tree is **27 ft.**

26. **(C)** All you have to do here is substitute the values for a and b listed and follow the order of operations:

$$(5)(a)(2)(b) - (3)(a)(b)(2)$$
$$(5 \times 7 \times 2 \times 4) - (3 \times 7 \times 4 \times 2)$$
$$(280) - (168) = \mathbf{112}$$

27. **(C)** The definition of π is the circumference of a circle divided by the length of its diameter.

28. **(A)** The probability of a particular event occurring is the number of favorable outcomes divided by the total possible number of outcomes. Since there are three possible infantrymen to choose, there are three possible favorable outcomes for choosing an infantryman. Since a choice may be made from among three infantrymen, two artillerymen, and five tank crewmen, there are 3 + 2 + 5, or 10, possible outcomes in total. The probability of choosing an infantryman is, therefore, $\mathbf{\frac{3}{10}}$.

29. **(B)** There are four possible choices for the destroyer. Each of these choices may be coupled with any of the two choices for the supply ship. Each such destroyer–supply ship combination may in turn be coupled with any of the three possible choices for the submarine. Thus, there are $4 \times 2 \times 3$, or **24**, different combinations possible.

30. **(B)** The volume of a cylinder is equal to the product of its height and the area of its base. The base is a circle.

The area of a circle is πr^2, where $\pi = \frac{22}{7}$ and r is the radius. Since the diameter is 2 inches, the radius (which is one-half the diameter) is 1 inch.

A = Area of the base

$A = \pi(r^2)$

$A = \frac{22}{7}(1^2)$

$A = \frac{22}{7}$

V = Volume of the cylinder

h = height of the cylinder

$V = A \times h$

$V = \frac{22}{7}$ sq. in. $\times$ 7 in.

$V =$ **22 cu. in.**

Subtest 2: Reading Comprehension Test (RCT)

	✔	✘		✔	✘		✔	✘		✔	✘		✔	✘
1. B			7. C			13. D			19. D			25. B		
2. D			8. C			14. D			20. C			26. B		
3. B			9. A			15. C			21. D			27. C		
4. D			10. D			16. D			22. D					
5. A			11. A			17. B			23. D					
6. C			12. D			18. B			24. A					

1. **(B)** According to this passage, soldiers **have to communicate first before they get anything done**. The passage states that "speech [communication] is the vital spark in all maneuver" and speech "is the beginning of the urge to get something done."

2. **(D)** According to this passage, **Task Force Lynch linked up with the 31st Infantry but suffered a friendly fire casualty.**

3. **(B)** Anomaly most nearly means **an abnormality or irregularity**. "Bitter hostility or open hatred" is *animosity*; "a collection of songs or stories" is an *anthology*; another word for "boldness" is *audacity*.

4. **(D)** Cacophony most nearly means **a jarring, discordant sound or noise**. "Bad handwriting" is *cacography*; and a "winged staff symbolizing the medical profession" is a *caduceus* (it also usually has two serpents twined around the staff).

5. **(A)** Xenophobe most nearly means **a person who is afraid of foreigners or strangers**. A person who has a deep hatred of women is a *misogynist*; and a light that flashes at rapid, predetermined intervals is a *strobe* light.

6. **(C)** In the passage, the word **derided** is used incorrectly. Derided refers to treating something with ridicule or contemptuous humor. The passage makes the point strongly that a good reputation is something that is worth a lot, especially to a leader.

7. **(C)** The 101st Airborne Division was holding out at Bastogne **to deny the Germans an important crossroads.**

8. **(C)** The German major who approached the American lines with a German surrender demand had to tell his commander that **the Americans would not surrender**. The passage states that the American slang reply was clarified for the German officer as "decidedly not affirmative."

9. **(A)** Incentive most nearly means **a motivation or benefit for doing something**. Someone who is "capable of producing new ideas" could be said to be *inventive* or *innovative*; something that is "copied or adapted from something else" is *derivative*; someone who is "moderate or cautious" could be said to be *conservative*; and someone who is "unaware of the thoughts or feelings of others" would be *insensitive*.

10. **(D)** The passage explains that Galileo's experiment showed that **balls of differing weights roll downhill at the same rate**. The passage casts doubt on whether Galileo

actually dropped different weights from the Leaning Tower of Pisa, which rules out choice (C).

11. **(A)** The gist of the passage is that **all citizens have an obligation to do what they can to make their country better**. It states that "the least considerable man . . . has an interest equal to the proudest nobleman . . . and is equally called upon . . . ."

12. **(D)** Countenance in this context most nearly means **consider** or agree with. In a different context, *countenance* does in fact refer to one's face or expression, but not here.

13. **(D)** The author of this passage believes that **the student who defends himself should be viewed differently than the attacker**. The passage states that "the biggest problem happens when the student who is attacked gets swept up in the punishment net along with the one who started the fight," and "it is morally wrong to teach our kids that the attacked person is invariably as much in the wrong as the attacker."

14. **(D)** Posterity most nearly means **future descendants or generations**. The "back side of an object or person" would be the *posterior.*

15. **(C)** According to this passage, the reader can infer that the author **believes that acting on incomplete information is often necessary**. The passage states that "the quest for perfectly complete . . . information results in . . . the inability to make a decision until you have *all* the information, *which is never going to happen* [emphasis added]." Therefore, we can conclude that the author believes the opposite, giving us our answer.

16. **(D)** Quandary most nearly means **deep uncertainty about a choice; a dilemma**. A swampy area that impedes the movement of people or vehicles can be called a *quagmire*; a stanza of four lines is a *quatrain*; and something consisting of four parts can be called *quarternary.*

17. **(B)** The passage *primarily* discusses **early steps toward public education in Texas**. The passage touches on how many acres are in a league, as well as the fact that Texas was a republic and then became a state—but those are not the *primary* points made in the passage. Although it would be relevant, the passage does not even mention steps taken by private organizations to improve public education, nor opposition to public education in the Republic of Texas.

18. **(B)** It is clear in this quote—both from the context and the other references to the "nation"—that President Roosevelt was speaking of the entire country or nation. Of the choices given, **country** is the only one that makes sense in the context given.

19. **(D)** The author's *main* point in this passage is that education (resulting in a "smart man") enables us to do what we have to do at the appropriate time, whether we want to or not. The other choices make valid points, but they are not the main point of this passage.

20. **(C)** Discernment most nearly means **insight** or **the ability to see things clearly**.

21. **(D)** The author of the passage maintains that the three main reasons why the British victory in North America was "certain" were **more people, better geographical position,** and **better leaders**.

22. **(D)** Chlorophyll uses **sunlight, carbon dioxide, and water** to make carbohydrates.

23. **(D)** The best remedy for frostbite is **not addressed in this passage.**

24. **(A)** The passage encourages the reader to **make the effort to accomplish challenging goals.**

25. **(B)** Leaders demonstrate that they value other people when they listen to them, trust them, and are **receptive** and willing to listen to reports of unproductive or unpleasant information—even when it involves the leader himself. **Receptive** is the only choice that makes sense in the context given.

26. **(B)** The Fairness Doctrine was **recognized as antagonistic to freedom of expression** in 1987 and is no longer public policy.

27. **(C)** "If a nation expects to be ignorant and free, in a state of **civilization**, it expects what never was and never will be." [Thomas Jefferson] This is the only choice that makes sense in the given context.

Subtest 3: Mechanical Comprehension Test (MCT)

	✔	✘		✔	✘		✔	✘		✔	✘		✔	✘
1. B			7. A			13. A			19. B			25. C		
2. C			8. B			14. A			20. C			26. C		
3. A			9. B			15. B			21. C			27. C		
4. C			10. A			16. B			22. B			28. B		
5. C			11. A			17. C			23. A			29. B		
6. B			12. A			18. A			24. B			30. C		

1. **(B)** Gear A will turn **4** times. Counting the number of teeth in the two gears tells us that the mechanical advantage of the larger gear A is 3:2, since gear A has 15 teeth and gear B has 10 teeth. Divide the number of gear B revolutions (6) by the advantage of the larger gear A (3). Then multiply by the ratio for the smaller gear (2): $\frac{6}{3} = 2$. $2 \times 2 = 4$.

2. **(C)** We are not told the sizes of the two wheels, but we can see that one is larger than the other. If the two wheels are connected by a belt, the small wheel will be forced to turn faster and complete more turns than the larger wheel.

3. **(A)** If the wheel on the left turns counterclockwise, the wheel on the right will turn **clockwise.**

4. **(C) It will be easier to lift block B but it will not be lifted as high.** If block A under the lever beam is moved toward block B on top of the lever beam, the moment for a particular force exerted will increase, since the fulcrum is now further from the force; this will make block B easier to lift. However, the height to which block B on the end of the lever beam can be raised decreases the closer block A is moved toward block B.

5. **(C)** The greater the difference between the number of teeth of the two meshed gears, the greater the torque or mechanical advantage.

6. **(B)** Recruit Highspeed will arrive on the far bank **downstream of his departure point**, because he will be pushed downstream while he swims at right angles to the banks. If he wanted to arrive directly across the stream from his departure point, he would have to swim upstream at a sufficient angle to compensate for the force of the water pushing him downstream.

7. **(A)** By rotating clockwise, pulley C will cause pulley B to rotate counterclockwise, which will in turn cause pulley A to rotate **clockwise.**

8. **(B)** **Pulley B** will rotate the fastest because it is the smallest.

9. **(B)** **Water tower B** will be able to provide the most water, because its outlet pipe is near the bottom and can let almost all of its contents out, while the outlet pipe on tower A is near the top and will stop providing water as soon as A's water level drops below where the pipe leaves the cistern.

10. **(A)** The bullet will have its highest velocity at the point where it **leaves the muzzle** of the rifle. After that, gravity and friction will combine to continually slow it down until it hits its target.

11. **(A)** When the plug is removed, water will flow **into the tube** to equalize the water level both inside and outside the tube.

12. **(A)** The string holding the 10-pound weight exerts more pull; the fact that that string is longer makes no difference.

13. **(A)** The force required to balance the lever shown would be **10 pounds** because the sum of the moments on each side of the fulcrum must be zero. To calculate this, we would set it up like this:

$$F \times d = F \times d$$

where F is the force or weight involved and d is the distance from the fulcrum. Therefore,

$$(5 \text{ lbs.} \times 10 \text{ ft.}) + (10 \text{ lbs.} \times 5 \text{ ft.}) = F \times 10 \text{ ft.}$$
$$50 \text{ ft.-lbs.} + 50 \text{ ft.-lbs.} = F \times 10 \text{ ft.}$$
$$100 \text{ ft.-lbs.}/10 \text{ ft.} = F$$
$$10 \text{ lbs.} = F$$

14. **(A)** The air pushing out of the crack in the hull will tend to push the rear of the sub to the left and hence the nose of the sub will veer to the right. To compensate for this, a left rudder correction must be used.

15. **(B)** **Valves A, B, and D** must be open for the tank to fill halfway and maintain that level. Water flows in through valve A (so any choice not including valve A is a nonstarter), and flows out when the tank is half full through valve B—but, for that water to leave the system, valve D must also be open.

16. **(B)** The length of time taken for one swing depends on the length of the string, not the weight.

17. **(C)** **Both would take the same amount of time** to make one swing; the length of time taken for one swing depends on the length of the string, not the weight at the end of it.

18. **(A) Circuit A** would have the greater resistance. As the electrical current makes its trip from one polarity of the battery to the other on circuit A, it has no choice but to pass through two resistors. However, on circuit B, the current will follow the path of least resistance and take a "shortcut" that only passes through one resistor.

19. **(B)** When two or more act in such a way that their combination has a net effect of zero (i.e., they cancel each other out), the condition is called **equilibrium**.

20. **(C)** The descent of an airborne paratrooper by parachute is *primarily* affected by **drag** (air resistance) **and gravity**.

21. **(C)** There are three ways of transferring heat from one place to another: conduction, convection, and **radiation**.

22. **(B)** Putting salt into the water increases the specific gravity of the solution and **lowers its freezing point**.

23. **(A)** Changing a liquid to a gas or vapor is called **evaporation**. Boiling is one method of accomplishing this process.

24. **(B)** Heating a closed container of boiling water increases the pressure of the water vapor (steam) inside the container and **increases** the temperature of the water.

25. **(C)** The largest pulley will turn the slowest.

26. **(C)** Compressing the air in a closed space will **decrease the volume and raise the temperature**. The diesel engine—which does not use a spark plug—is an example of this principle. As a piston moves up on its compression stroke, air in the cylinder is compressed, and then ignition takes place when fuel is injected into the cylinder. The increased temperature of the compressed air provides the heat needed for combustion, so no spark plug is needed.

27. **(C)** When two magnetic objects have opposite poles facing each other, they will attract each other.

28. **(B) Mass remains constant, but the weight of an object depends on its altitude**—or, said differently, its distance from the gravitational pull of Earth.

29. **(B)** The water will flow fastest through the **narrowest sections**.

30. **(C)** Static electricity is definitely not theoretical, and is also neither AC nor DC—hence its accurately descriptive name, static electricity.

Subtest 4: Aviation and Nautical Information Test (ANIT)

	✔	✘		✔	✘		✔	✘		✔	✘		✔	✘
1. A			7. D			13. B			19. D			25. D		
2. C			8. A			14. D			20. C			26. B		
3. B			9. D			15. B			21. D			27. C		
4. C			10. A			16. B			22. C			28. D		
5. D			11. B			17. A			23. D			29. D		
6. A			12. B			18. B			24. A			30. B		

1. **(A)** If a fixed-wing aircraft has tricycle landing gear, it **has landing gear supporting the nose of the aircraft**.
2. **(C)** A floor or horizontal surface on a ship is called a **deck**.
3. **(B)** The official nickname for the EA-6B is the **Prowler**.
4. **(C)** Yuri Gagarin, a Soviet cosmonaut, was the **first man into space** in 1961.
5. **(D)** When the wings of an airplane design are angled upward, it is called **dihedral**.
6. **(A)** **John Paul Jones** is considered to be the Father of the U.S. Navy.
7. **(D)** The bow of a ship is the most forward part, i.e., **the front**.
8. **(A)** The time of 5 A.M. would be expressed using the 24-hour clock as **0500**.
9. **(D)** When a pilot pushes forward on the control stick, the elevators will **move downward**, causing the nose to pitch down, following which the aircraft usually descends.
10. **(A)** Longitude is measured from **the prime meridian** in Greenwich, England.
11. **(B)** If one end of a runway was numbered 10 (meaning its orientation was 100 degrees by the compass), the other end of the same runway would be numbered **28** for 280 degrees.
12. **(B)** Latitude is measured from **the equator**.
13. **(B)** The first American to complete an orbital space mission was **John Glenn, Jr.** Alan Shepard was the first American into space, but his mission was suborbital (i.e., his capsule did not travel a complete orbit around Earth).
14. **(D)** The three primary American manned space programs, in chronological order, were **Mercury**, **Gemini**, and **Apollo**.
15. **(B)** The dual-role F/A-18 Hornet and SuperHornet are designated as **fighter/attack** aircraft.
16. **(B)** Hypoxia is **too little oxygen in the bloodstream, resulting in blackout**.
17. **(A)** A ship's gunwales are **the upper edges of the vessel's sides**.
18. **(B)** You would normally need oxygen if you were going to fly above **10,000 feet**.
19. **(D)** The first man to verifiably break the sound barrier was **Chuck Yeager** in the Bell X-1 rocketplane, in **1947**.

20. **(C)** **Neil Armstrong** was the first man to walk on the moon on July 21, 1969.

21. **(D)** The Latin phrase *Semper Fidelis* ("Always Faithful") is the motto of the **U.S. Marine Corps.**

22. **(C)** The first American woman in space was **Sally Ride** in **1983**.

23. **(D)** A ship designated with a hull number starting with "CG" is a **guided missile cruiser**.

24. **(A)** The first conflict to see widespread use of the helicopter was the **Korean War**, where the helicopter first began to be used for medical evacuation and command and control.

25. **(D)** Aircraft position lights should be on from dusk till dawn and show red on the left wing, green on the right, and white on the tail (**all of the above**).

26. **(B)** The first American spacecraft to explore the outer solar system was the ***Pioneer 10***.

27. **(C)** The four types of airspeed are **indicated, calibrated, equivalent, and true**.

28. **(D)** The airspeed indicator is a sensitive differential pressure gauge that measures and promptly shows the difference between *pitot* (**impact**) pressure, and **static pressure**, the undisturbed atmospheric pressure at level flight.

29. **(D)** The typical air wing aboard a U.S. Navy aircraft carrier usually includes **3–4 fighter/attack squadrons, an electronic attack squadron, a command and control squadron, a logistic support squadron, an antisubmarine warfare helicopter squadron, and an anti-surface warfare helicopter squadron.**

30. **(B)** A nuclear-powered aircraft carrier has a **CVN** designation starting its hull number.

Abbreviations and Acronyms

AAA	Anti-aircraft artillery
ABM	Air Battle Manager
ACIP	Aviation Career Incentive Pay
ACL	Allowable Cargo Load
ACP	Aviation Continuation Pay
ACT	A major college entrance exam, formerly known as the American College Test
ADA	Air Defense Artillery (an Army officer branch)
AETC	Air Education and Training Command (USAF)
AFAST	Army Flight Aptitude Selection Test (obsolete)
AFB	Air Force Base
AFI	Air Force Instruction (service regulation)
AFOQT	Air Force Officer Qualifying Test
AFROTC	Air Force Reserve Officer Training Corps
AGL	Above ground level
AGM	Air-to-ground missile
AIM	Air intercept missile; also aeronautical information manual
AIRMET	Airman's meteorological information
ALS	Approach Lighting System
AMRAAM	Advanced Medium-Range Air-to-Air Missile
ANG	Air National Guard
APEX	Automated Pilot Examination (Navy)
API	Aviation Preflight Indoctrination
APU	Auxiliary power unit
AR	Army Regulation
ARNG	Army National Guard
ASCP	Airman Scholarship and Commissioning Program
ASTB-E	Aviation Selection Test Battery (Navy/Marine Corps/Coast Guard flight aptitude test battery) (series E)
ASVAB	Armed Services Vocational Aptitude Battery
ASW	Anti-submarine warfare
ATC	Air traffic control
AW	Aviation Warfare specialist (Navy rating)

AWACS	Airborne Warning and Control System
C2 or C^2	Command and Control
CAC	Combat Aircrew (USMC specialty)
CAS	Close air support
CASEVAC	Casualty Evacuation
CCMD	Combatant Command
CG	Center of gravity; also commanding general
CIA	Central Intelligence Agency
CINC	Commander in Chief
CJCS	Chairman, Joint Chiefs of Staff
CNGB	Chief, National Guard Bureau
CNO	Chief of Naval Operations
CO	Commanding Officer
CONUS	Continental United States
CPG	Copilot/gunner
CRRC	Combat Rubber Raiding Craft
CSA	Chief of Staff of the Army
CSAF	Chief of Staff of the Air Force
CSAR	Combat search and rescue
CSO	Combat Systems Officer
CSPI	College Student Pre-commissioning Initiative
DA	Department of the Army
DC	Direct current; also District of Columbia
DHS	Department of Homeland Security
DoD	Department of Defense
DoD FLIP	Department of Defense Flight Information Publication
ENJJPT	Euro-NATO Joint Jet Pilot Training
ETA	Estimated time of arrival
ETL	Effective translational lift
EW	Electronic warfare
FAA	Federal Aviation Administration
FAR	Federal Aviation Regulation
FLIP	Flight Information Publication
FOD	Foreign object damage
FPM	Feet per minute
GPA	Grade point average
GPS	Global Positioning System
GRE	Graduate Record Exam
GWOT	Global War on Terror/Terrorism
HARM	High-speed anti-radiation missile; an air-to-air missile that guides itself to its target by homing in on the target's radar or other electronic emissions
Hg	Symbol for the element mercury
HMMWV	High-Mobility, Multi-purpose, Wheeled Vehicle

HQMC	Headquarters, Marine Corps
HUD	Head-up display
IATA	International Air Transport Association
IFF	Identification Friend or Foe
IFR	Instrument flight rules
IGE	In-ground effect
IP	Instructor pilot
IR	Infrared
ISR	Intelligence, Surveillance, and Reconnaissance
JATO	Jet-assisted takeoff
JCS	Joint Chiefs of Staff
JPATS	Joint Primary Aircraft Training System
JSOC	Joint Special Operations Command
JSUPT	Joint Specialized Undergraduate Pilot Training
kg	Kilograms
lbs.	Pounds
LZ	Landing zone
MAGTF	Marine Air-Ground Task Force
MEDEVAC	Medical Evacuation
MEF	Marine Expeditionary Force
MEPS	Military Entrance Processing Station
MEU	Marine Expeditionary Unit
MPH or mph	Miles per hour
MSA	Minimum safe airspeed
MSL	Mean sea level
NAC	Naval Air Crewman (Navy rating)
NAS	National Airspace System; also Naval Air Station
NASA	National Aeronautics and Space Administration
NATO	North Atlantic Treaty Organization
NAVAID	Navigational aid
NCO	Noncommissioned officer; enlisted subordinate leaders from corporal through sergeant major in the Army and Marine Corps; staff sergeant through chief master sergeant in the Air Force; and from petty officer third class through master chief petty officer in the Navy and Coast Guard
NFO	Naval Flight Officer
NGB	National Guard Bureau; a four-star general organization with policy and regulatory oversight of the Army and Air National Guard; the Chief, National Guard Bureau is a member of the Joint Chiefs of Staff and reports directly to the Secretary of Defense
NM or nm	Nautical miles
NOE	Nap-of-the-Earth
NROTC	Navy Reserve Officer Training Corps
NTSB	National Transportation Safety Board

NVD	Night vision device
NVG	Night vision goggles
NWS	National Weather Service
OAR	Officer Aptitude Rating (Navy/Marine Corps ASTB-E)
OCC	Officer Candidate Course (USMC)
OCONUS	Outside [the] Continental United States
OCS	Officer Candidate School (Army, Navy, Coast Guard)
OEF	Operation Enduring Freedom (Afghanistan)
OGE	Out-of-ground effect
OIF	Operation Iraqi Freedom (Iraq)
OND	Operation New Dawn (Iraq)
ONE	Operation Noble Eagle (post-9/11 homeland defense)
OOD	Officer of the deck
OTS	Officer Training School (USAF)
PCSM	Pilot Candidate Selection Method
PLC	Platoon Leaders Course (USMC)
PSI or psi	Pounds (of pressure) per square inch
PZ	Pickup zone
RATO	Rocket-assisted takeoff
RCLS	Runway Centerline Lighting System
REIL	Runway End Identification Lights
RIO	Radar Intercept Officer
ROTC	Reserve Officer Training Corps (usually Army ROTC when not otherwise specified)
RPM or rpm	Revolutions per minute
SA	Situational awareness
SAM	Surface-to-air missile
SAR	Search and rescue
SAT	A major college entrance exam, formerly known as the Scholastic Aptitude Test
SEAD	Suppression of enemy air defenses
SF	Special Forces (Army)
SIFT	Selection Instrument for Flight Training (U.S. Army flight aptitude test)
SLAM	Standoff Land Attack Missile (U.S. Navy)
SNA	Student Naval Aviator
SOCOM	Special Operations Command, a joint (all-service) headquarters
SOP	Standard operating procedure; also standing operating procedures
SSN	Social Security number; also nuclear-powered attack submarine designation
STOVL	Short Take-Off and Vertical Landing
TAS	True airspeed
TBAS	Test of Basic Aviation Skills
TBS	The Basic School (USMC)

TTP	Tactics, techniques, and procedures
UAE	United Arab Emirates
UAV	Unmanned aerial vehicle
UK	United Kingdom
USA	United States of America; also United States Army
USAF	United States Air Force
USAFA	United States Air Force Academy
USAFR	United States Air Force Reserve
USAR	United States Army Reserve
USASOC	United States Army Special Operations Command
USCG	United States Coast Guard
USMA	United States Military Academy
USMC	United States Marine Corps
USMCR	United States Marine Corps Reserve
USNA	United States Naval Academy
USNR	United States Navy Reserve
USS	United States Ship
UTM	Universal Transverse Mercator
VASI	Visual Approach Slope Indicator
VFR	Visual flight rules
V/STOL	Vertical/Short Takeoff and Landing
VTOL	Vertical Takeoff and Landing
WOCS	Warrant Officer Candidate School (Army)
WOFT	Warrant Officer Flight Training (Army program)
XO	Executive Officer; usually the second in command

Bibliography

15thaf.org. "15th Air Force Summary," *http://www.15thaf.org/index.htm*, accessed December 26, 2017.

Aerospaceweb.org. "C-17 Cargo Capabilities," *http://www.aerospaceweb.org/question/planes/q0115a.shtml*, posted March 16, 2003, accessed November 11, 2017.

Airbus Helicopters. "UH-72A Lakota Specifications," *http://airbushelicoptersinc.com/products/UH-72A-specifications.asp*, accessed December 3, 2017.

Aleshire, Peter. *Eye of the Viper: The Making of an F-16 Pilot.* Guilford, CT: Lyons Press, 2004.

Anderson, David F., and Scott Eberhardt. *Understanding Flight, 2nd Edition.* New York: The McGraw-Hill Companies, 2010.

Anderson, John D., Jr. *Introduction to Flight.* New York: McGraw-Hill, Inc., 1978.

Army-technology.com. "UH-72A Lakota Light Utility Helicopter," *www.army-technology.com/projects/uh-72a-lakota/*, accessed December 3, 2017.

Asimov, Isaac. *Asimov's Chronology of the World: The History of the World From the Big Bang to Modern Times.* New York: HarperCollins Publishers, 1991.

Association of Former Students of Texas A&M University, The. "Roll Call for the Absent," *www.aggienetwork.com/muster/song_rollcall.aspx*, accessed December 3, 2017.

Ballard, Michael B. *Vicksburg: The Campaign That Opened the Mississippi.* Chapel Hill, NC: University of North Carolina Press, 2004.

Baum, Dan. "Battle Lines," *The New Yorker Magazine*, January 17, 2005, *https://www.newyorker.com/magazine/2005/01/17/battle-lessons*, accessed December 24, 2017.

Becker, Cajus. *Hitler's Naval War.* New York: Kensington Publishing Corp., 1974.

Benitez, Mike. "Air Force in Crisis, Part I: Why Pilot Retention Matters Right Now," *War on the Rocks Media, LLC*, February 28, 2018, *https://warontherocks.com/2018/02/air-force-crisis-part-pilot-retention-matters-right-now/*, accessed April 1, 2018.

Boeing Company. "V-22 Osprey," *http://www.boeing.com/defense/v-22-osprey/*, accessed December 3, 2017.

Boeing Company. "V-22 Osprey Guidebook," *www.boeing.com/ospreynews/2011/issue_02/final_2011_2012_guidebook.pdf,* posted 2011, accessed December 3, 2017.

Burton, James G. *The Pentagon Wars: Reformers Challenge the Old Guard.* Annapolis, MD: Naval Institute Press, 1993.

Butterworth, William E. *Flying Army: The Modern Air Arm of the U.S. Army.* Garden City, NY: Doubleday & Co., 1971.

Charlton, James (editor). *The Military Quotation Book.* New York: St. Martin's Press, 1990.

Chiles, James R. *The God Machine: From Boomerangs to Black Hawks, a Social History of the Helicopter.* New York: Random House Publishing Group, 2008.

Chiles, James R. "The Stealth Bomber Elite." *Air & Space Magazine,* September 2013.

Clancy, Tom. *Carrier: A Guided Tour of an Aircraft Carrier.* New York: Berkley Publishing Group, 1999.

Cole, David. *Survey of U.S. Army Uniforms, Weapons, and Accoutrements.* Washington, DC: U.S. Army Center of Military History, 2007.

Correll, John T. "The Reformers." *Air Force Magazine,* February 2008.

Cowley, Michael, and Ellen Domb. *Beyond Strategic Vision.* Newton, MA: Butterworth-Heinemann, 1997.

Cox, Matthew. "Welsh: F-22 Flew to Drone's Rescue Off Iran Coast." *Military.com News* (online), September 17, 2013.

Currie, Col. (Ret.) (Dr.) Karen, Col. (Ret.) John Conway, Col. (Ret.) Scott Johnson, Lt. Col. (Dr.) Brian Landry, and Dr. Adam Lowther. "Air Force Leadership Study: The Need for Deliberate Development," *Air University Press,* 2012.

Davies, Steve, and Doug Dildy. *F-15 Eagle Engaged: The World's Most Successful Jet Fighter.* Oxford, UK: Osprey Publishing, 2007.

Defense Industry Daily. "Last of the Globemasters: The Final C-17 Orders," *https://www.defenseindustrydaily.com/last-of-the-globemasters-the-usafs-final-orders-05283/,* June 28, 2017, accessed November 11, 2017.

Department of the Air Force. "Officer Qualifying Test (AFOQT) Information Pamphlet." August 1, 2015.

Department of the Air Force. "Officer Training School: Find the Leader in You," *https://www.airforce.com/education/military-training/ots/,* accessed November 5, 2017.

Department of the Air Force. "Pilot Candidate Selection Method: Test of Basic Aviation Skills (PCSM/TBAS)," *http://access.afpc.af.mil/pcsmdmz/faq2_0.html,* accessed November 5, 2017.

Department of the Air Force. "U.S. Air Force ROTC," *https://www.afrotc.com/,* accessed November 5, 2017.

Departments of the Air Force, Army, and Navy. *Air Force Joint Instruction 16-401/Army Regulation 70-50/NAVAIRINST 8800.3B,* "Designating and Naming Military Aerospace Vehicles," March 14, 2005.

Department of the Navy. "SECNAV Instruction 1532.1: U.S. Navy and Marine Corps Aviation Selection Test Battery," *Office of the Secretary of the Navy,* October 31, 2013.

Dickstein, Corey. "Navy SEAL, to Receive Medal of Honor Monday, Tells His Story," *Stars and Stripes,* February 26, 2016 edition, *https://www.stripes.com/news/navy/navy-seal-to-receive-medal-of-honor-monday-tells-his-story-1.396290,* accessed December 30, 2017.

Duran, Terry L. *Barron's ASVAB: Armed Services Vocational Aptitude Battery, 12th Edition,* Hauppauge, New York: Barron's Educational Series, 2018.

Eckstein, Megan. "Marines Would Save $1B if F-35 Entered Service Faster; F-18 Hornets Struggling to Stay Mission-Ready," USNI News, *https://news.usni.org/2017/03/28/davis-marines-would-save-1billion-in-o-f-18s-struggling-to-stay-mission-ready,* posted March 28, 2017, accessed December 3, 2017.

Fehrenbach, Theodore R. *This Kind of War: A Study in Unpreparedness.* New York: McMillan Company, 1963.

FlightGlobal.com. "Directory: World Air Forces," *https://www.flightglobal.com/assets/getasset.aspx?ItemID=26061,* posted June 11, 2008, accessed November 11, 2017.

Foss, Joe, and Matthew Brennan. *Top Guns.* New York: Simon & Schuster, 1991.

Fredriksen, John C. *Warbirds: An Illustrated Guide to U.S. Military Aircraft 1915–2000.* Santa Barbara, CA: ABC-Clio, 1999.

Gallicchio, Marc. "Army Advisers and Liaison Officers and the 'Lessons' of America's Wartime Experience in China." *The U.S. Army and World War II: Selected Papers from the Army's Commemorative Conferences,* Washington, DC: United States Army Center of Military History, 1998.

Glines Jr., Carroll V. *The Compact History of the United States Air Force.* New York: Hawthorn Books, 1973.

GlobalSecurity.org. "F-35 Joint Strike Fighter (JSF) Lightning II," *https://www.globalsecurity.org/military/systems/aircraft/f-35-specs.htm,* accessed December 3, 2017.

GlobalSecurity.org. "F-35C Carrier Variant Joint Strike Fighter (JSF)," *https://www.globalsecurity.org/military/systems/aircraft/f-35c.htm,* accessed December 3, 2017.

Groom, Winston. *1942: The Year That Tried Men's Souls.* New York: Atlantic Monthly Press, 2005.

Gross, John (editor). *Rudyard Kipling: The Man, His Work and His World.* London: Weidenfeld & Nicolson, 1972.

Grossnik, Roy A. *A Dictionary of American Naval Aviation Squadrons.* Washington, DC: Naval Historical Center, Department of the Navy, 1995.

Gschwandtner, Gerhard, with Pat Garnett. *Nonverbal Selling Power.* Upper Saddle River, NJ: Prentice Hall, Inc., 1995.

Guest, Tom. "Tradition: A Pillar in Freemasonry." *Texas Mason Magazine,* Fall 2006.

Gunston, Bill (editor-in-chief). *Chronicle of Aviation.* London: Chronicle Communications, Ltd., 1992.

Hastings, Max (editor). *The Oxford Book of Military Anecdotes.* New York: Oxford University Press, 1985.

Hawking, Stephen W. *A Brief History of Time (New Edition).* New York: Bantam Books, 2017.

Headquarters, Department of the Air Force. Air Force Instruction (AFI) 11-202, Volume 3, Flying Operations: General Flight Rules, November 28, 2012.

Headquarters, Department of the Army. *Army Regulation 135-155: Promotion of Commissioned Officers and Warrant Officers Other Than General Officers.* Washington, DC: HQ, Department of the Army, July 13, 2004.

Headquarters, Department of the Army. *Army Regulation 350-1: Army Training and Leader Development.* Washington, DC: HQ, Department of the Army, August 19, 2014.

Headquarters, Department of the Army. *Army Regulation 670-1: Wear and Appearance of Army Uniforms and Insignia.* Washington, DC: HQ, Department of the Army, March 31, 2014.

Headquarters, Department of the Army. *Department of the Army Pamphlet 670-1: Guide to the Wear and Appearance of Army Uniforms and Insignia.* Washington, DC, May 25, 2017.

Headquarters, Department of the Army. *Field Manual (FM) 3-04.203, Fundamentals of Flight.* Washington, DC: Department of the Army, 2007.

Headquarters, Department of the Navy. Department of the Navy Flight Training Instruction, *Contact,* Helicopter Advanced Phase, TH-57C, CNATRA P-457 (Rev. 01-15). Corpus Christi, TX: Chief of Naval Air Training, 2015.

Headquarters, U.S. Marine Corps. "2017 Marine Aviation Plan," *www.aviation.marines.mil/Portals/11/2017%20MARINE%20AVIATIOIN%20PLAN.pdf,* accessed December 1, 2017.

Heinl, Robert D., Jr. *Victory at High Tide: The Inchon-Seoul Campaign.* New York: J.B. Lippincott Co., 1968.

Helis.com. "Elicotteri Meridionali CH-47C Chinook in Al Quwwat al-Jawwiya al-Libyya," *http://www.helis.com/database/modelorg/1367/,* accessed November 19, 2017.

Hibbeler, R.C. *Statics and Dynamics, 12th Edition.* Upper Saddle River, NJ: Pearson Prentice Hall, 2010.

Historic Naval Ships Association. "HNSA Ships: United States of America," *www.hnsa.org/ship-location/united-states-of-america/,* accessed December 4, 2017.

Hoyle, Craig. "France Receives First C-130J Transport," *FlightGlobal.com, https://www.flightglobal.com/news/articles/france-receives-first-c-130j-transport-444553/,* posted January 2, 2018; accessed January 4, 2018.

Hughes, Christopher P. *War on Two Fronts: An Infantry Commander's War in Iraq and the Pentagon.* Philadelphia, PA: Casemate Publishers, 2007.

Jackson, Robert. *The Encyclopedia of Military Aircraft.* Bath, UK: Parragon Books, Ltd., 2009.

Jane's 360. "Paris Air Show 2017: Boeing Officials Reveal Production Plans for Qatari Eagles," *http://www.janes.com/article/71508/paris-air-show-2017-boeing-officials-reveal-production-plans-for-qatari-eagles*, posted June 19, 2017; accessed November 19, 2017.

Jenkins, Dennis R. *F/A-18 Hornet: A Navy Success Story*. New York: McGraw-Hill, 2000.

Joint Chiefs of Staff. *Joint Publication (JP) 1, Doctrine for Armed Forces of the United States*, March 25, 2013.

Keegan, John. *A History of Warfare*. New York: Alfred A. Knopf, 1993.

Keller, John. "Next Year's DoD Budget Makes Substantial Cuts In Military Procurement; Aircraft Buying Hit Hard," *Military & Aerospace Electronics Online Magazine*, *http://www.militaryaerospace.com/articles/2017/06/aircraft-procurement-dod-budget.html*, posted June 9, 2017; accessed November 10, 2017.

Kern, Florence, and Barbara Voulgaris. *Traditions of the United States Coast Guard*. Washington, DC: Office of the Historian, U.S. Coast Guard, 1990.

Kotter, John P. *Leading Change*. Boston, MA: Harvard Business School Press, 1996.

Kouzes, James M., and Barry Z. Posner. *Credibility*. San Francisco, CA: Jossey-Bass, Inc., 1993.

Laird, Robbin F. "A 21st-Century Concept of Air and Military Operations," *Defense Horizons*, *https://web.archive.org/web/20090920031810/http://www.ndu.edu/ctnsp/defense_horizons/DH_66.pdf*, March 2009; accessed December 1, 2017.

Legal Information Institute. "10 U.S. Code § 2111a—Support for Senior Military Colleges," *https://www.law.cornell.edu/uscode/text/10/2111a*, accessed December 29, 2017.

Longyard, William H. *Who's Who in Aviation History*. Novato, CA: Presidio Press, 1994.

Lowenthal, Mark M. *Intelligence: From Secrets to Policy, 5th Edition*. Washington, DC: CQ Press College, 2012.

Mabus, Ray. "U.S. Navy and Marine Corps Aviation Selection Test Battery." Official memorandum (SECNAVINST 1532.1). Office of the Secretary of the Navy, Washington, DC, October 31, 2013.

Macdonough, Rodney. *The Life of Commodore Thomas Macdonough*. South Usher: Fort Hill Press, 1909.

Marshall, S.L.A. *Men Against Fire: The Problem of Battle Command in Future War*. Gloucester, MA: Peter Smith, 1947.

Matloff, Maurice (editor). *American Military History, Vol. I: 1775–1902*. Conshohocken, PA: Combined Books, 1996.

McDermott, Tricia. "A Calm Colonel's Strategic Victory," *CBS News online*, *https://www.cbsnews.com/news/a-calm-colonels-strategic-victory/*, posted March 15, 2006; accessed December 24, 2017.

Military.com. "First Marine Corps F-35B Squadron Readies for Pacific Deployment," *https://www.military.com/daily-news/2017/05/31/first-marine-corps-f-35b-squadron-readies-for-pacific-deployment.html*, posted April 18, 2017; accessed December 1, 2017.

Mrazek, Col. James E. "Rembrandts of the Military Art." *Army Magazine*, July 1965.

Murray, Williamson, and Allan R. Millett. *Military Innovation in the Interwar Period.* New York: Cambridge University Press, 1996.

National Aeronautics and Space Administration (NASA). "Beginner's Guide to Aerodynamics Activities," *https://www.grc.nasa.gov/WWW/K-12/BGA/BGAindex.html,* accessed December 3, 2017.

National Defense University. *Joint Forces Staff College Student Text 1, Academic Year 2017,* January 2017.

NATO Support and Procurement Agency. "Strategic Airlift Capability: Boeing C-17 Globemaster III," *https://www.sacprogram.org/en/Pages/Boeing-C-17-Globemaster-III.aspx,* accessed November 11, 2017.

Naval Air Systems Command. "EA-6B Prowler," *www.navair.navy.mil/index.cfm?fuseaction=home.display&key=C8B54023-C006-4699-BD20-9A45FBA02B9A,* accessed December 3, 2017.

Naval Air Systems Command. "F/A-18 A-D Hornet," *www.navair.navy.mil/index.cfm?fuseaction=home.displayPlatform&key=32F08227-0DE1-437F-93AB-C7241517AA8D,* accessed December 2, 2017.

Naval Air Systems Command. "P-8A Poseidon," *www.navair.navy.mil/index.cfm?fuseaction=home.display&key=cfd01141-cd4e-4db8-a6b2-7e8fbfb31b86,* posted September 2017; accessed December 3, 2017.

Naval Service Training Command Officer Development Office. "NROTC: Naval Reserve Officer Training Corps," *http://www.nrotc.navy.mil/about.html,* accessed November 10, 2017.

Nevins, Allan, and Harry Steele Commager, with Jeffrey Morris. *A Pocket History of the United States, 9th Revised Edition.* New York: Simon & Schuster, 1992.

New Century Foundation. "American Renaissance: College Student Pre-Commissioning Initiative (Scholarship Program)," *https://www.amren.com/news/2013/07/college-student-pre-commissioning-initiative-scholarship-program/,* posted July 15, 2013; accessed November 10, 2017.

New York Public Library Desk Reference. New York: Simon & Schuster, 1989.

Norwich University. "Corps of Cadets," *http://cadets.norwich.edu/,* accessed December 31, 2017.

O'Leary, Colonel (Retired) Jeffrey. *The Centurion Principles.* Nashville, TN: Thomas Nelson, Inc., 2004.

Pawlyk, Oriana. "START Lanced the B-1's Nukes, but the Bomber Will Still Get New Bombs," *http://www.military.com/daily-news/2017/07/12/start-lanced-the-b-1s-nukes-but-bomber-will-still-get-new-bombs.html,* posted July 12, 2017; accessed November 10, 2017.

Polmar, Norman, with Richard R. Burgess. *The Naval Institute Guide to the Ships and Aircraft of the U.S. Fleet.* Annapolis, MD: Naval Institute Press, 2013.

Prophet, Wallace W. "Performance Measurement in Helicopter Training and Operations." Alexandria, VA: Human Resources Research Organization, April 1972.

Rader, Benjamin G. *Baseball: A History of America's Game.* Chicago: University of Illinois Press, 1992.

"Raptors Perform First Intercept of Russian Bombers." *Air Force Magazine* (online), December 14, 2007.

Reed, Allen. "Aggie Honored for Military Service, Joins Medal of Honor Hall of Honor," Bryan-College Station Eagle, *http://www.theeagle.com/news/local/aggie-honored-for-military-service-joins-medal-of-honor-hall/article_3049be3d-796d-56ee-8d47-79bc3de3c7fc.html,* posted November 8, 2013; accessed December 30, 2017.

Russell, Edward T., and Robert M. Johnson. *Africa to the Alps: The Army Air Forces in the Mediterranean Theater.* Air Force History and Museums Program, 1999.

Schein, Edgar H. *Organizational Culture and Leadership, 4th Edition.* New York: John Wiley & Sons, 2010.

Smith, James M. "Service Cultures, Joint Cultures, and the US Military." *Airman-Scholar,* Winter 1998.

Snow, Shawn. "Aviation Pay Nearly Doubles as Corps Suits its Qualified Pilots," *Marine Corps Times,* February 27, 2018, *https://www.marinecorpstimes.com/news/your-marine-corps/2018/02/27/marines-nearly-double-aviation-incentive-pay/,* accessed April 1, 2018.

Taylor, John W.R., and Kenneth Munson. *History of Aviation.* New York: Crown Publishers, 1972.

Texas Aggie Corps of Cadets Association. "Flag Officers," *http://corpsofcadets.org/flag-officers/,* accessed December 31, 2017.

Texas A&M University. "Texas A&M University at a Glance," *http://www.tamu.edu/about/at-a-glance.html,* accessed January 15, 2018.

United States Air Force. "Leadership and Force Development: Air Force Doctrine Document 1-1," February 18, 2006.

United States Air Force Air Combat Command Public Affairs Office. "Fact Sheet: A-10 Thunderbolt II," *http://www.af.mil/About-Us/Fact-Sheets/Display/Article/104490/a-10-thunderbolt-ii/,* posted September 22, 2015; accessed November 10, 2017.

United States Air Force Air Combat Command Public Affairs Office. "Fact Sheet: EC-130H Compass Call," *http://www.af.mil/About-Us/Fact-Sheets/Display/Article/104550/ec-130h-compass-call/,* posted September 23, 2015; accessed November 19, 2017.

United States Air Force Air Combat Command Public Affairs Office. "Fact Sheet: F-15 Eagle," *https://archive.is/20120730162301/http://www.af.mil/information/factsheets/factsheet.asp?fsID=101,* posted May 21, 2012; accessed November 19, 2017.

United States Air Force Air Combat Command Public Affairs Office. "Fact Sheet: F-16 Fighting Falcon," *http://www.af.mil/About-Us/Fact-Sheets/Display/Article/104505/f-16-fighting-falcon/,* posted September 23, 2015; accessed November 20, 2017.

United States Air Force Air Combat Command Public Affairs Office. "Fact Sheet: F-22 Raptor," *http://www.af.mil/About-Us/Fact-Sheets/Display/Article/104506/f-22-raptor/*, posted September 23, 2015; accessed December 3, 2017.

United States Air Force Air Combat Command Public Affairs Office. "Fact Sheet: HC-130J Combat King II," *http://www.af.mil/About-Us/Fact-Sheets/Display/Article/104468/hc-130j-combat-king-ii/*, posted September 19, 2011; accessed November 19, 2017.

United States Air Force Air Mobility Command Public Affairs Office, "Fact Sheet: C-17 Globemaster III," *http://www.af.mil/About-Us/Fact-Sheets/Display/Article/104523/c-17-globemaster-iii/*, posted October 1, 2015; accessed November 11, 2017.

United States Air Force Air Mobility Command Public Affairs Office, "Fact Sheet: C-130 Hercules," *http://www.af.mil/About-Us/Fact-Sheets/Display/Article/104517/c-130-hercules/*, posted May 2014; accessed November 19, 2017.

United States Air Force Curtis E. LeMay Center for Doctrine Development and Education. "Volume 2, Leadership: The Air Force Core Values," *http://www.doctrine.af.mil/Portals/61/documents/Volume_2/V2-D05-Core-Values.pdf?ver=2017-09-17-123835-303*, posted August 8, 2015; accessed December 26, 2017.

United States Air Force Global Strike Command Public Affairs Office. "Fact Sheet: B-1B Lancer," *http://www.af.mil/About-Us/Fact-Sheets/Display/Article/104500/b-1b-lancer/*, posted December 16, 2015; accessed November 10, 2017.

United States Air Force Global Strike Command Public Affairs Office. "Fact Sheet: B-2 Spirit," *http://www.af.mil/About-Us/Fact-Sheets/Display/Article/104482/b-2-spirit/*, posted December 16, 2015; accessed November 11, 2017.

United States Air Force Global Strike Command Public Affairs Office. "Fact Sheet: B-52 Stratofortress," *http://www.af.mil/About-Us/Fact-Sheets/Display/Article/104465/b-52-stratofortress/*, posted December 16, 2015; accessed November 11, 2017.

United States Air Force Special Operations Command (AFSOC) Public Affairs Office. "Fact Sheet: AC-130U," *http://www.af.mil/About-Us/Fact-Sheets/Display/Article/104486/ac-130u/*, posted January 20, 2016; accessed November 10, 2017.

United States Army Aviation Center of Excellence. "Policy Memorandum for the Selection Instrument for Flight Training (SIFT)," Fort Rucker, AL, November 27, 2012.

United States Army Recruiting Command. "Frequently Asked Questions about the SIFT," *http://www.usarec.army.mil/hq/warrant/*, accessed December 3, 2017.

United States Department of Defense. "Fact Sheet: The Department of Defense (DoD) Cyber Strategy, April 2015," *https://www.defense.gov/Portals/1/features/2015/0415_cyber-strategy/Department_of_Defense_Cyber_Strategy_Fact_Sheet.pdf*, accessed December 25, 2017.

United States Department of Defense. "State Partnership Program: Fiscal Year 2016 Report to Congress," approved December 2017.

United States Department of Defense. "The United States Military Rank Insignia," *https://www.defense.gov/About/Insignias/*, accessed December 3, 2017.

United States Department of Transportation, Federal Aviation Administration. *Aeronautical Information Manual: Official Guide to Basic Flight Information and ATC Procedures* (with Change 3). St. Louis, MO: U.S. Government Printing Office, 2013.

United States Department of Transportation, Federal Aviation Administration, Airmen Testing Standards Branch. *Aircraft Weight and Balance Handbook (FAA-H-8083-1A).* Oklahoma City, OK: U.S. Government Printing Office, 2007.

United States Department of Transportation, Federal Aviation Administration, Airmen Testing Standards Branch. *Helicopter Flying Handbook 2012 (FAA-H-8083-21A).* Oklahoma City, OK: U.S. Government Printing Office, 2012.

United States Department of Transportation, Federal Aviation Administration, Airmen Testing Standards Branch. *Pilot's Handbook of Aeronautical Knowledge (FAA-H-8083-25).* Oklahoma City, OK: U.S. Government Printing Office, 2008.

United States Marine Corps Recruiting Command. "Officer Programs," *http://www.mcrc.marines.mil/Marine-Officer/Officer-Programs/*, accessed November 10, 2017.

United States Naval Academy. "Class of 2015 Statistics," *https://www.usna.edu/NewsCenter/2015/05/usna-graduates-class-of-2015.php*, posted May 26, 2015; accessed November 10, 2017.

United States Naval Academy. "Class of 2016 Statistics," *https://www.usna.edu/NewsCenter/2016/05/027-16-graduation-class-of-2016.php*, posted May 27, 2016; accessed November 10, 2017.

United States Naval Academy. "Class of 2017 Statistics," *https://www.usna.edu/NewsCenter/2017/05/class-of-2017-statistics.php*, posted May 24, 2017; accessed November 10, 2017.

United States Naval Institute News. "Navy Wants to Buy 80 More Super Hornets for $7.1B Over the Next Five Years," *https://news.usni.org/2017/06/13/navy-intends-to-buy-80-more-super-hornets-in-fydp-to-ease-fighter-shortfall*, posted June 13, 2017; accessed November 20, 2017.

United States Navy Medicine Operational Training Center. "ASTB-E Frequently Asked Questions," *http://www.med.navy.mil/sites/nmotc/nami/pages/astbfrequentlyaskedquestions.aspx*, accessed December 2, 2017.

United States Navy Medicine Operational Training Center. "ASTB-E Overview," *www.med.navy.mil/sites/nmotc/nami/pages/astboverview.aspx*, accessed December 2, 2017.

United States Navy Medicine Operational Training Center. "ASTB-E Sample Questions," *www.med.navy.mil/sites/nmotc/nami/documents/astb_samplequestions_14nov2013.pdf*, accessed December 2, 2017.

U.S. News and World Report. "10 Universities with the Biggest Endowments," *https://www.usnews.com/education/best-colleges/the-short-list-college/articles/2017-09-28/10-universities-with-the-biggest-endowments,* posted September 28, 2017; accessed January 15, 2018.

U.S. News and World Report. "Norwich University," *https://www.usnews.com/best-colleges/norwich-university-3692,* accessed December 30, 2017.

U.S. News and World Report. "Texas A&M University—College Station," *https://www.usnews.com/best-colleges/texas-am-college-station-10366,* accessed December 30, 2017.

U.S. News and World Report. "The Citadel," *https://www.usnews.com/best-colleges/citadel-3423/overall-rankings,* accessed December 30, 2017.

U.S. News and World Report. "University of North Georgia," *https://www.usnews.com/best-colleges/north-georgia-state-1585,* accessed December 30, 2017.

U.S. News and World Report. "Virginia Military Institute," *https://www.usnews.com/best-colleges/vmi-3753,* accessed December 30, 2017.

U.S. News and World Report. "Virginia Tech," *https://www.usnews.com/best-colleges/virginia-tech-3754,* accessed December 30, 2017.

University Archives of Virginia Tech. "General & Flag Officers of Virginia Tech," *https://spec.lib.vt.edu/archives/125th/cadets/generals.htm,* accessed December 30, 2017.

Virginia Military Institute. "VMI General and Flag Ranks Officers," *http://www.vmi.edu/archives/genealogy-biography-alumni/vmi-alumni-in-the-military/general-and-flag-rank-officers/,* accessed December 31, 2017.

Virginia Military Institute. "VMI Medal of Honor Recipients," *http://www.vmi.edu/archives/genealogy-biography-alumni/vmi-alumni-in-the-military/vmi-medal-of-honor-recipients/,* accessed December 31, 2017.

Webster's New Biographical Dictionary. Springfield, MA: Merriam-Webster, Inc., 1988.

Weinraub, Bernard. "U.S. Jets Hit 'Terrorist Centers' in Libya; Reagan Warns of New Attacks if Needed." *The New York Times,* April 15, 1986.

Williams, Mary H. *The U.S. Army in World War II: Chronology 1941–1945.* Washington, DC: Center for Military History, 1958.

Withington, Thomas. *B-1B Lancer Units in Combat.* Botley, Oxford, UK: Osprey Publishing, 2006.

Woodall, James R. *Texas Aggie Medals of Honor.* College Station, TX: Texas A&M University Press, 2010.

Young, Hugh D., Roger A. Freedman, and A. Lewis Ford. *University Physics, 12th Edition.* San Francisco, CA: Pearson Addison-Wesley, 2008.

Glossary

ABSOLUTE ALTITUDE—The actual distance an object is above the ground.

ABSOLUTE PRESSURE—Pressure measured from the reference point of zero pressure, or a vacuum.

ACCELERATION—Force involved in overcoming inertia; may be defined as a change in velocity per unit of time.

ACCELEROMETER—A part of an inertial navigation system (INS) that accurately measures the force of acceleration in one direction.

ADJUSTABLE-PITCH PROPELLER—A propeller with blades whose pitch can be adjusted on the ground with the engine not running, but which cannot be adjusted in flight; also referred to as a ground-adjustable propeller. Sometimes also used to refer to constant-speed propellers that are adjustable in flight.

ADVANCING BLADE—The rotor blade moving in the same direction as the body of the helicopter. In helicopters with counterclockwise main rotor blade rotation (viewed from above), the advancing blade is in the right half of the rotor disk area during forward movement.

ADVERSE YAW—A condition of flight in which the nose of an airplane tends to yaw toward the outside of the turn. This is caused by the higher induced drag on the outside wing, which is also producing more lift. Induced drag is a byproduct of the lift associated with the outside wing.

AILERONS—Primary flight control surfaces mounted on the trailing edge of an airplane wing, near the tip. Ailerons control roll about the longitudinal axis.

AIR DENSITY—The density of the air in terms of mass per unit volume. Dense air has more molecules per unit volume than thinner air. The density of air decreases with altitude above the surface of Earth and with increasing temperature. Cooler air is denser than warmer air.

AIRFOIL—Any surface designed to obtain a useful reaction of lift or negative lift as it moves through the air.

AIRSPEED—Rate of an aircraft's progress through the air.

AIRSPEED INDICATOR—A differential pressure gauge that measures the dynamic pressure of the air through which the aircraft is flying. Displays the craft's airspeed, typically in knots.

ALTIMETER—An instrument that indicates flight altitude by sensing pressure changes and displaying altitude in feet or meters.

AMBIENT PRESSURE—The air pressure in the area immediately surrounding the aircraft.

AMBIENT TEMPERATURE—The temperature of the air immediately surrounding the aircraft.

ANGLE OF ATTACK—The angle between an airfoil's chord line and the relative wind.

ANGLE OF INCIDENCE—For an airplane, the angle formed by the chord line of the wing and a line parallel to the longitudinal axis of the airplane. For a helicopter, angle of incidence is the angle between the blade chord line and the plane of rotation of the rotor system—a mechanical angle rather than an aerodynamic angle. In the absence of induced flow and/or aircraft airspeed, angle of attack and angle of incidence are the same. Whenever relative wind is modified by induced flow or aircraft airspeed, a helicopter's angle of attack is different from angle of incidence.

ANTITORQUE PEDAL—The pedal used to control the pitch of the tail rotor or air diffuser in a NOTAR® system.

APPROACH LIGHTING SYSTEM (ALS)—Provides lights that penetrate the atmosphere far enough from touchdown to give directional, distance, and glidepath information for safe transition from instrument to visual flight.

ARTICULATED ROTOR—A rotor system in which each of the main rotor blades is connected to the rotor hub in such a way that it is free to change its pitch angle (move up and down and fore and aft) in its plane of rotation.

ASYMMETRIC THRUST (also known as P-factor)—The tendency for an aircraft to yaw to the left due to the descending propeller blade on the right producing more thrust than the ascending blade on the left. This occurs when the aircraft's longitudinal axis is in a climbing attitude in relation to the relative wind. The P-factor would be to the right if the aircraft had a counter-clockwise rotating propeller.

ATTITUDE INDICATOR—An instrument that reflects the airplane's attitude in relation to the horizon.

AUTOPILOT—An automatic flight control system that keeps an aircraft in level flight or on a set course. Automatic pilots can be directed by the pilot, or they may be coupled to a radio navigation signal.

AUTOROTATION—The condition of helicopter flight during which the main rotor is driven only by aerodynamic forces, with no power from the engine.

AXES OF AN AIRCRAFT—Three imaginary lines that pass through an aircraft's center of gravity. The axes can be considered as imaginary axles around which the aircraft rotates. The three axes pass through the center of gravity at 90-degree angles to one another. The axis from nose to tail is the longitudinal axis (pitch), the axis that passes from wingtip to wingtip is the lateral axis (roll), and the axis that passes vertically through the center of gravity is the vertical axis (yaw).

AXIS OF ROTATION—The imaginary line about which the rotor rotates. It is represented by a line drawn through the center of, and perpendicular to, the tip-path plane.

BASIC EMPTY WEIGHT—The weight of the standard aircraft, operational equipment, unusable fuel, and full operating fluids, including full engine oil.

BERNOULLI'S PRINCIPLE—A principle that explains how the pressure of a moving fluid varies with its speed of motion. An increase in the speed of movement causes a decrease in the fluid's pressure.

BLADE CONING—An upward sweep of rotor blades as a result of lift and centrifugal force.

BLADE FEATHER OR FEATHERING (also **CYCLIC FEATHERING**)—The mechanical change of pitch or angle of incidence of individual rotor blades, independent of other blades in the system.

BLADE FLAP—The ability of a rotor blade to move in a vertical direction; blades may flap independently or in unison.

BLADE GRIP—The part of the hub assembly to which the rotor blades are attached; sometimes also called "blade forks."

BLADE LEAD OR LAG—The fore and aft movement of the rotor blade in its plane of rotation. It is sometimes called "hunting" or "dragging."

BLADE LOADING—The load imposed on rotor blades, determined by dividing the total weight of the helicopter by the combined area of all the rotor blades.

BLADE ROOT—The part of the blade that attaches to the blade grip.

BLADE SPAN—The length of a blade from its tip to its root.

BLADE STALL—The condition of the rotor blade when it is operating at an angle of attack greater than the maximum angle of lift.

BLADE TIP—The part of the blade that is farthest from the rotor hub.

BLADE TRACK—The relationship of the blade tips in the plane of rotation. Blades that are "in track" will move in the same plane of rotation.

BLADE TRACKING—The mechanical procedure used to bring the rotor blades into an acceptable relationship with one another under dynamic conditions so that all blades rotate on a common plane.

BLADE TWIST—The variation in the angle of incidence of a blade between the root and the tip.

BLOWBACK—The tendency of the rotor disk to tilt toward the rear during transition to forward flight, resulting from unequal airflow.

CALIBRATED AIRSPEED (CAS)—The indicated airspeed of an aircraft, corrected for installation and instrumentation errors.

CAMBER—The camber of an airfoil is the characteristic curve of its upper and lower surfaces. The upper camber or curve is normally more pronounced, while the lower camber is usually comparatively flat. This causes the velocity of the airflow immediately above the wing to be much higher than that below the wing.

CANARD—A horizontal surface mounted ahead of the main wing to provide longitudinal stability and control. It may be a fixed, movable, or variable geometry surface, with or without control surfaces.

CEILING—The height above Earth's surface of the lowest layer of clouds, which is reported as broken or overcast, or the vertical visibility into an obscuration.

CENTER OF GRAVITY (CG or **CoG)**—The point at which an aircraft would balance if it were possible to suspend it at that point. It is the theoretical point at which the entire weight of the aircraft is assumed to be concentrated for purposes of balance calculations. The location depends on the distribution of weight in the aircraft.

CENTER OF PRESSURE—The point where the resultant of all the aerodynamic forces acting on an airfoil intersects the chord.

CENTRIFUGAL FORCE—An outward force opposing centripetal force, resulting from the effect of inertia during a turn.

CENTRIPETAL FORCE—A center-seeking force directed inward toward the center of rotation created by the horizontal component of lift in turning flight.

CHIP DETECTOR—A warning device that alerts the pilot to abnormal wear in a transmission or engine, consisting of a magnetic plug inside the transmission. The magnet attracts any metal particles that have come loose from the bearings or other transmission parts. Most chip detectors have warning lights on the instrument panel that illuminate when metal particles are picked up.

CHORD—An imaginary straight line between the leading and trailing edges of an airfoil section.

CHORDWISE AXIS—For semirigid rotors, a term used to describe the flapping or teetering axis of the rotor.

COAXIAL ROTOR—A rotor system utilizing two rotors turning in opposite directions on the same centerline. This system is used to eliminate the need for a tail rotor.

COLLECTIVE PITCH CONTROL ("COLLECTIVE")—The control for changing the pitch of all the rotor blades in the main rotor system equally and simultaneously and, consequently, the amount of lift or thrust that is generated.

COMPASS ROSE—A small circle graduated in 360-degree increments, to show direction expressed in degrees.

CORIOLIS EFFECT—The tendency of a rotor blade to increase or decrease its velocity in its plane of rotation when the center of mass moves closer to or farther from the axis of rotation.

COURSE—The intended direction of flight in the horizontal plane measured in degrees from north.

CRITICAL ANGLE OF ATTACK—The angle of attack at which a wing stalls regardless of airspeed, flight attitude, or weight.

CYCLIC FEATHERING—The mechanical change of the angle of incidence (pitch) of individual rotor blades, independent of other blades in the system.

CYCLIC PITCH CONTROL—The control for changing the pitch of each rotor blade individually as it rotates through one cycle to govern the tilt of the rotor disk and, consequently, the direction and velocity of horizontal movement.

DEAD RECKONING—Navigation of an aircraft solely by means of computations based on airspeed, course, heading, wind direction and speed, groundspeed, and elapsed time.

DENSITY ALTITUDE—Pressure altitude corrected for nonstandard temperature variations.

DEVIATION—Compass error caused by magnetic disturbances from the electrical and metal components in the aircraft. The correction for this error is displayed on a compass correction card placed near the magnetic compass of the aircraft.

DIHEDRAL—The positive acute angle between the lateral axis of an airplane and a line through the center of a wing or horizontal stabilizer. Dihedral contributes to the lateral stability of an airplane.

DIRECT CONTROL—The ability to maneuver a helicopter by tilting the rotor disk and changing the pitch of the rotor blades.

DIRECT SHAFT TURBINE—A single-shaft helicopter turbine engine in which the compressor and power section are mounted on a common driveshaft.

DISK AREA—The area swept by the blades of the rotor. It is a circle with its center at the hub and has a radius of one blade length.

DISK LOADING—The total helicopter weight divided by the rotor disk area.

DISSYMMETRY OF LIFT—The unequal lift across the rotor disk resulting from the difference in the velocity of air over the advancing blade half and the velocity of air over the retreating blade half of the rotor disk area.

DRAG—An aerodynamic force on a body acting parallel and opposite to relative wind.

ELEVATOR—The horizontal, movable primary control surface in the tail section or empennage of an airplane. The elevator is hinged to the trailing edge of the fixed horizontal stabilizer.

EMPENNAGE—The section of the airplane that consists of the vertical stabilizer, the horizontal stabilizer, and the associated control surfaces.

FEATHERING—The action that changes the pitch angle of the rotor blades by rotating them around their feathering (spanwise) axis.

FEATHERING AXIS—The axis about which the pitch angle of a rotor blade is varied. Sometimes referred to as "spanwise axis."

FEEDBACK—The transmittal of forces initiated by aerodynamic action on rotor blades to the cockpit controls.

FLAPPING—The vertical movement of a blade about a flapping hinge.

FLAPPING HINGE—The hinge that permits the rotor blade to flap and thus balance the lift generated by the advancing and retreating blades.

FLAPS—Hinged portion of the trailing edge between the ailerons and fuselage. In some aircraft, ailerons and flaps are interconnected to produce full-span "flaperons." In either case, flaps change the lift and drag on the wing.

FLARE—A maneuver expending vertical momentum accomplished prior to landing, designed to slow an aircraft.

FLIGHT LEVEL (FL)—A measure of altitude (in hundreds of feet) used by aircraft flying above 18,000 feet with the altimeter set at 29.92" Hg (inches of mercury).

FLIGHT PATH—The line, course, or track along which an aircraft is flying or is intended to be flown.

FORCE (F)—The energy applied to an object that attempts to cause the object to change its direction, speed, or motion. In aerodynamics, it is expressed as F, T (thrust), L (lift), W (weight), or D (drag), usually in pounds.

FOREIGN OBJECT DAMAGE (FOD)—Damage to a gas turbine engine caused by an object being sucked into the engine while it is running. Debris from runways or taxiways can cause foreign object damage during ground operations, and the ingestion of ice and birds can cause FOD in flight.

GOUGE—Slang for study material, or, more generally, information of any kind.

GRAVITY (WEIGHT)—One of the four main forces acting on an aircraft. Equivalent to the actual weight of the helicopter. It acts downward toward the center of Earth.

GROSS WEIGHT—The sum of the basic empty weight and useful load.

GROUND EFFECT—The condition of slightly increased air pressure below an airplane wing or helicopter rotor system that increases the amount of lift produced. It exists within a height of approximately one wingspan or one rotor diameter above the ground. It results from a reduction in upwash, downwash, and wingtip vortices, and provides a corresponding decrease in induced drag.

GROUND RESONANCE—Self-excited vibration occurring whenever the frequency of oscillation of the blades about the lead-lag axis of an articulated rotor becomes the same as the natural frequency of the fuselage.

GROUNDSPEED—Speed over the ground in the direction the aircraft is going at that moment.

GYROSCOPIC PRECESSION—An inherent quality of rotating bodies, which causes an applied force to be manifested 90 degrees in the direction of rotation from the point where the force is applied.

HEAD-UP DISPLAY (HUD)—A special type of flight-viewing screen that allows the pilot to watch flight instruments and other data while looking through the windshield of the aircraft for other traffic, the approach lights, or the runway.

HOLDING PATTERN—A racetrack pattern, involving two turns and two legs, used to keep an aircraft within a prescribed airspace with respect to a geographic point or "fix." A standard pattern uses right turns, while a "nonstandard" pattern uses left turns.

HUNTING—Movement of a rotor blade with respect to the other blades in the plane of rotation, sometimes also called "leading" or "lagging."

IN-GROUND EFFECT (IGE) HOVER—Hovering close to the surface (usually less than one rotor diameter distance above the surface) under the influence of ground effect.

INDICATED AIRSPEED (IAS)—Shown on the aircraft instrument airspeed indicator, this is the airspeed indicator reading uncorrected for instrument, position, and other errors. Indicated airspeed means the speed of an aircraft as shown by its pitot static airspeed indicator calibrated to reflect standard atmosphere adiabatic compressible flow at sea level, uncorrected for airspeed system errors. Calibrated airspeed (CAS) is IAS corrected for instrument errors, position error (due to incorrect pressure at the static port), and installation errors.

INDICATED ALTITUDE—The altitude read directly from the altimeter (uncorrected) when it is set to the current altimeter setting.

INDUCED DRAG—That part of the total drag that is created by the production of lift.

INDUCED FLOW—The component of air flowing vertically through the rotor system resulting from the production of lift.

INERTIA—The property of matter by which it will remain at rest or in a state of uniform motion in the same direction unless acted upon by an external force.

INERTIAL NAVIGATION SYSTEM (INS)—A computer-based navigation system that tracks the movement of an aircraft via signals produced by onboard accelerometers. The initial location of the aircraft is entered into the computer, and all subsequent movement of the aircraft is sensed and used to keep the position updated. An INS does not require any inputs from outside signals.

INSTRUMENT FLIGHT RULES (IFR)—Rules and regulations established by the FAA to govern flight under conditions in which flight by outside visual reference is not safe. IFR flight depends on flying by reference to instruments in the flight deck, and navigation is accomplished by reference to electronic signals.

INSTRUMENT LANDING SYSTEM (ILS)—An electronic system that provides both horizontal and vertical guidance to a specific runway, used to execute a precision instrument approach procedure.

KNOT—A unit of speed equal to one nautical mile per hour.

LEAD AND LAG—The fore (lead) and aft (lag) movement of the rotor blade in the plane of rotation.

LEADING EDGE—The part of an airfoil that meets the airflow first.

LICENSED EMPTY WEIGHT—Basic empty weight not including full engine oil, just undrainable oil.

LIFT—One of the four main forces acting on an aircraft, it acts perpendicular to the relative wind.

LOAD FACTOR—The ratio of a specified load weight to the total weight of the aircraft.

MARRIED NEEDLES—A term used when two hands on an instrument dial are superimposed one over the other, as on the engine/rotor tachometer.

MAST—The component that supports the main rotor.

MAST BUMPING—Action of the rotor head striking the mast, occurring on underslung rotors only.

NACELLE—A streamlined enclosure on an aircraft in which an engine is mounted. On multiengine propeller-driven airplanes, the nacelle is normally mounted on the leading edge of the wing.

NAVIGATIONAL AID (NAVAID)—Any visual or electronic device, airborne or on the surface, that provides point-to-point guidance information or position data to aircraft in flight.

NIGHT—The time between the end of evening civil twilight and the beginning of morning civil twilight, as published in the American Air Almanac.

NORMALLY ASPIRATED ENGINE—An engine that does not compensate for decreases in atmospheric pressure through turbocharging or other means.

NOTICE TO AIRMEN (NOTAM)—A notice filed with an aviation authority to alert aircraft pilots of any hazards en route or at a specific location. The authority in turn provides means of disseminating relevant NOTAMs to pilots.

OUT-OF-GROUND EFFECT (OGE) HOVER—In a helicopter, hovering a distance greater than one disk diameter above the surface. Because induced drag is greater while hovering out-of-ground effect, this takes more power than a hover in ground effect.

OUTER MARKER—A marker beacon at or near the glideslope intercept altitude of an ILS approach. It is normally located four to seven miles from the runway threshold, on the extended centerline of the runway.

PARASITE (PARASITIC) DRAG—The part of total drag created by the form or shape of the aircraft's parts.

PAYLOAD—The combined weight of passengers and cargo.

PENDULAR ACTION—The lateral (left or right) or longitudinal (forward or backward) oscillation of the helicopter fuselage as it is suspended from the rotor system.

PITCH—The movement of the aircraft about its lateral, or *pitch*, axis. For a helicopter, movement of the cyclic forward or aft causes the nose of the helicopter to pitch up or down.

PITCH ANGLE—The angle between the chord line of the rotor blade and the reference plane of the rotor plane of rotation.

PRESSURE ALTITUDE—The height above the standard sea-level pressure level of 29.92" Hg (inches of mercury). It is obtained by setting 29.92 in the barometric pressure window and reading the altimeter.

PROFILE DRAG—Drag incurred from frictional or parasitic resistance of the blades passing through the air. It does not change significantly with the angle of attack of the airfoil section, but it increases moderately as airspeed increases.

RESULTANT RELATIVE WIND—Airflow from rotation that is modified by induced flow.

RETREATING BLADE—Any blade, located in a semicircular part of the rotor disk, in which the blade direction of movement is opposite to the direction of flight.

RETREATING BLADE STALL—A stall that begins at or near the tip of a blade in a helicopter because of the high angles of attack required to compensate for dissymmetry of lift.

RIGID ROTOR—A rotor system permitting blades to feather, but not flap or hunt.

ROLL—The movement of the aircraft about its longitudinal axis. For a helicopter, movement of the cyclic right or left causes the helicopter to tilt in that direction.

ROTATIONAL VELOCITY—The component of relative wind produced by the rotation of the rotor blades.

ROTOR—A complete system of rotating airfoils creating lift for a helicopter.

ROTOR BRAKE—A device used to slow down and stop the rotor blades during shutdown.

ROTOR FORCE—The force produced by the rotor, comprising rotor lift and rotor drag.

RUDDER—The movable primary control surface mounted on the trailing edge of the vertical fin (vertical stabilizer) of an airplane. Movement of the rudder rotates the airplane about its vertical axis.

SEMIRIGID ROTOR—A rotor system in which the blades are fixed to the hub, but are free to flap and feather.

SERVICE CEILING—The maximum density altitude where the best rate-of-climb airspeed will produce a 100-foot-per-minute climb at maximum weight while in a clean configuration with maximum continuous power.

SHAFT TURBINE—A turbine engine used to drive an output shaft, commonly used in helicopters.

SKID—A flight condition in which the rate of turn is too great for the angle of bank.

SLIP—A flight condition in which the rate of turn is too slow for the angle of bank.

SPAN—The dimension of a rotor blade or airfoil from root to tip.

SPLIT NEEDLES—A term used to describe the position of the two needles on the engine/rotor tachometer when the two needles are not superimposed.

STANDARD ATMOSPHERE—A hypothetical atmosphere based on averages in which the surface temperature is 59°F (15°C), the surface pressure is 29.92" (1013.2 millibars) of mercury at sea level, and the temperature lapse rate is approximately 3.5°F (2°C) per 1,000 feet.

STEADY-STATE FLIGHT—The type of flight experienced when a helicopter is in unaccelerated, straight and level flight, and all forces are in balance.

SYMMETRICAL AIRFOIL—An airfoil having the same shape on the top and bottom.

TAIL ROTOR (ANTITORQUE ROTOR)—A rotor turning in a plane perpendicular to that of the main rotor and parallel to the longitudinal axis of the fuselage. It is used to control or counteract the torque of the main rotor and to provide movement about the yaw axis of the helicopter.

TEETERING HINGE—A hinge that permits the rotor blades of a semirigid rotor system to flap as a unit.

THRUST—The force developed by the rotor blades acting parallel to the relative wind and opposing the forces of drag and weight.

TIP-PATH PLANE—The imaginary circular plane outlined by the rotor blade tips as they make a cycle of rotation.

TORQUE—(1) A resistance to turning or twisting. (2) Forces that produce a twisting or rotating motion. (3) In an airplane, the tendency of the aircraft to turn (roll) in the opposite direction of the rotation of the engine and propeller. (4) In helicopters with a single, main rotor system, the tendency of the helicopter to turn in the opposite direction of the main rotor rotation.

TRAILING EDGE—The rearmost edge of an airfoil.

TRANSLATING TENDENCY—The tendency of the single-rotor helicopter to move laterally during hovering flight. Also called tail rotor drift.

TRANSLATIONAL LIFT—The additional lift obtained when entering forward flight, due to the increased efficiency of the rotor system.

TRANSVERSE-FLOW EFFECT—The condition of increased drag and decreased lift in the aft portion of the rotor disk caused by the air having a greater induced velocity and angle in the aft portion of the disk.

TRUE AIRSPEED—Actual airspeed, determined by applying a correction for pressure altitude and temperature to the CAS.

TRUE ALTITUDE—The vertical distance of the airplane above sea level—the actual altitude. It is often expressed as feet above mean sea level (MSL). Airport, terrain, and obstacle elevations on aeronautical charts are true altitudes.

TURBOSHAFT ENGINE—A turbine engine transmitting power through a shaft as would be found in a turbine helicopter.

TWIST GRIP—The power control on the end of the collective control.

UNDERSLUNG—A rotor hub that rotates below the top of the mast, as on semirigid rotor systems.

UNLOADED ROTOR—The state of a rotor when rotor force has been removed, or when the rotor is operating under a low or negative G condition.

USEFUL LOAD—The difference between the *gross weight* and the *basic empty weight.* It includes the flight crew, useable fuel, drainable oil (if applicable), and payload.

VARIATION—The angular difference between true north and magnetic north; indicated on charts by isogonic lines. Also known as *declination.*

VECTORING—Navigational guidance by assigning headings.

VISUAL APPROACH SLOPE INDICATOR (VASI)—A visual aid using lights arranged to provide descent guidance information during the approach to the runway. A pilot on the correct glideslope will see red lights over white lights.

VISUAL FLIGHT RULES (VFR)—Flight rules adopted by the FAA governing aircraft flight using visual references. VFR operations specify the amount of ceiling and the visibility the pilot must have to operate according to these rules. When the weather conditions are such that the pilot cannot operate according to VFR, he or she must use instrument flight rules (IFR).

VORTEX RING STATE ("SETTLING WITH POWER")—A transient condition of downward flight (descending through air after just previously being accelerated downward by the rotor) during which an appreciable portion of the main rotor system is being forced to operate at angles of attack above maximum. Blade stall starts near the hub and progresses outward as the rate of descent increases.

YAW—The movement of an aircraft around its vertical axis.

Index

T

U

V

W

Y

place at the Maison Aury That Stéphanie had taken up her position—it had been necessary to hire domestics like everyone else—after the departure of the three young women with the names of jewels…their familiarity too disturbed, the hussies…their atmosphere, as they put it…not astonishing, in view of Madame's behavior…who spent the night away four nights out of seven...

"And in fact, saving your respects, the worst of prostitutes couldn't hold a candle to her."

"But in that case," Cahoche had said, with a cold laugh, "perhaps she's no longer interesting."

Frignot, turning very red, had stopped eating, the fork that he was holding aloft trembling slightly.

"What are you saying?" he had stammered. Then, pulling himself together, with a coarse laugh: "On the contrary..."

Denis, returning one day earlier than the date announced in the telegram from the hospital, had not found Lène at the château. She had not returned until the next day. She confessed that she had emerged from Méran's arms. She blamed Denis. After he had accepted the liaison with Brionne, he had allowed her to be carried away several times. Not without stupor, Lène had seen him complacent regarding the actress' artificial milieu. She accused Denis of having, under cover of the business affairs vaguely mentioned in the telegram, satisfied some unacknowledged passion. Denis talked about a dizzy spell, a short stay in Lugnault's establishment. He had not wanted to alarm his friends...

One point remained extremely obscure. Why had he not had the auto with him?" The chauffeur had reported that, having taken Monsieur to Bellevue railway station, he had seen him get into a third-class carriage.

Rather than admit his visits to the poor, Denis preferred to let Lène suspect the worst turpitudes.

Incoherences. Sometimes, he went with her to discreet parties in which opium and cocaine concurred with sensualities in which the mediocre intellectuality of the habitués was

me…the great unfortunate, the great incurable, whom neither money, nor words, nor art, nor science…nothing in the world…can bandage... Me, who has lost the earth..."

The invalid trembles; again the blood flows to his face.

"But that's very old, all that I told you there, Lugnault. It's over. I've rediscovered the earth. Better, even. I've…I don't know exactly what I found, just now…before the faint. It will come back. It's something admirable…the elixir of life. With which to go forth…in spite of your blessed marvelous apparatus…like a young eagle-hunter in the mountains… with which never to buckle, to give in to the suffering...

"A verity. It will come back…the salvation, the joy, henceforth ineradicable. A verity…all suns... Lugnault…!"

4

I

The Maire had given his administratees the pretext for his departure of the necessity of a cure for his wife. Madame Cahoche was not so very ill that a sojourn in Paris was necessary to put it right. In reality, Cahoche preferred to leave the Séneçois to shift for themselves. Frignot had kept him punctually up to date of with the crumbling of Denis' work. The two men met in fixed dates in a small restaurant near the Gare de Lyon. Frignot gave him the latest news. Everything was collapsing.

"They're beginning to cut down the sculpted trees in Telluire wood."

"Why? To carry the trees home as souvenirs?"

"For heating."

The factory had suffered an accident to the current; no one had demanded that it be restored. The price of the current had reached too high a level. And people got far less help from the factory when it was a matter of repairing machines. A large number, following the example of Lauvin and Chaleix, had gone back to tools, and apparatus drawn by horses and oxen. The trouble was greater, the profits less, but the results were more reliable. Electroculture was suffering serious breakdowns, and the château was no longer interested.

The great profiteer of Denis' revolutions, in the final analysis, was Lampreux, the notary in Crennes, charged with selling the farms, the fields and the commercial capital of those who, having become rich enough to live at their ease anywhere, had left Sénecé, where their habits of pleasure and the facile life found less and less satisfaction. There were many new faces in the village. The paint on the houses in the main street, discolored by the sun and the rain, was not renewed, or even scraped off, by the newcomers. The

Séneçoises were gradually abandoning their extra
accoutrements in the face of the disapproval of the n
ers, who could not understand the causes of such a pro
esthetic. Some young women had gone to Paris to
artists that had once lodged with them. Some young m
going blindly about the world, in search of employn
their imprecise talents.

At the château, half of the beautiful electrical
that did everything were no longer working. Leveil, w
more often in Paris than in Sénecé, had started tea
course near the Gare Montparnasse. Draguin made v
cessantly, trying to sell his inventions. Frignot did no
whether it was because lack of money was affectin
messieurs too...

"Good God!" Cahoche had cut in. "Money! And
extraordinary people who surrounded Denis? There w
entists among them, inventions capable of making mill
it were only Draguin's famous rain at will..."

"Oh, many avatars on that side too," said Frignot
business of rain, even in the best of weather, was neve
pletely perfected..."

And, all things considered, the diminution of curre
supply rendered by the business, had hindered the re
And then again, Monsieur Denis no longer being the
man, everyone around him sensed that... In brief, he co
say exactly whether it was lack of money or because
messieurs no longer found pleasure at Sénecé. There v
sum, still enough money to pay for Madame's fantasie
was more beautiful than ever…although, with the life sl
she would age quickly!

The intimacy of the château was displayed base
tween the two collaborators. Frignot had attached a cha
maid to Lène's service who was avid for tips, from wh
had not hidden the Maire's passion; she made excelle
ports. Combining the words and attitudes of Denis ar
friends with the treasons of young Stéphanie, he br
Cahoche a faithful account if the ravages that were t

impotent to invent refinements of its own accord; sometimes, careless of Lène's absences, he cloistered himself in his room. For entire days he read, meditated, wrote feverishly, tore up what he had written and began again.

He delved into the hermetic sciences that had disorientated and dazzled him at twenty, seeking to confront his organic idea of joy with the original truths distorted in kabbalas and theosophies, to shore up with them a proof of the eternal reality of the force of Joy. But he lost himself in the gibberish of the great initiates, their frantic grandiloquence around a few unformulatable data. The objective attempts of the metaphysical schools disappointed him. He made contact with the last and most notorious representatives of High Magic. One of them, the last confidant of Éliphas Lévi, and who had doubtless received from him the secret of voyaging through the superior worlds and commanding the indigenes of the invisible, was an old man paralyzed in both legs; another, in the exoteric employment of the Bureau of Indirect Taxation, who did not fail to let it be known that Christ had appeared to him personally, solemnly pronounced verities of the communal school.

Several beings cohabited in Denis, and the one who accepted the most bizarre perversions, as well as the one whose searched stubbornly, however disappointing the results of his investigations were, the supreme testimony of the Occult were united in a general being who was admiring bliss.

"He's going senile," Frignot translated it to Cahoche. "He only has one word in his mouth: *admirable*; everything is *admirable*. Even the most utter idiot…even the most disgusting of satyrs..."

One morning, Denis had told Lène about a strange dream. He had seen himself in a miserable café in an eccentric quarter, sitting at a table with a whore. She had combined with her caresses a singular and troubling performance of her legs, with feet shod in slippers...

Lène had laughed. It seemed in consequence that the dream had engendered an obsession.

"If they're not satirical inventions...," said Frignot. "Madame talked about it one evening to women who often come to the château, with whom she spends nights drinking and amusing herself…if one can call them women…and you ought to see their faces the next day! And the odors of the pharmacy! Madame, to give pleasure to Monsieur, goes, dressed like a tramp, into little cafés in dirty quarters; Monsieur arrives there after her; they pretend not to know one another, and Madame has to have mischievously, tucking up her dress…I don't know what. She boasts about it! And all the other sluts laugh. One of them asked to go with them one of these evenings..."

Lubricious games were designed behind Cahoche's forehead; his eyelids fluttered. As Frignot went on, the condescending smile on the Maire's face failed to hide the rise of erotic surges of blood to his face.

"It's certain that thinking of a woman like Madame spending her time in all that can be known and imagined in matters of swinish pleasure…one would soon go mad...a satyr oneself...fit to be locked up one day, or die a little sooner..."

One day, Frignot said:

"Men who are worth less than you have had her. That little brigand Stéphanie isn't stealing her money. When Madame comes back from her adventures she's there, with her little cares, and without having the appearance of doing anything, gets her to talk, flattering her, sometimes playing the wide-eyed novice, sometimes the sly one who knows what's what...

"There are means for you to arrive at what you want so much. One, for example, would be to introduce yourself into the societies into which Madame goes. There are times, it seems, when it's as if everyone there is mad. No one knows any longer what they're doing, they fall on one another, men, women. Supposing that you were there…you could jump on the beauty…bang bang, it's done. One explains later..."

Cahoche replied, haughtily: "My dear Frignot, you don't have the slightest idea of the sentiments that incline me toward Madame Aury..."

"Permit me, M'sieur Cahioche," Frignot interjected, "but I'm beginning to understand, a little..."

"You show it very poorly. It's not a matter for me of one of those brief possessions of a tramp surprising a milkmaid. Whatever the degree might be to which Madame Aury has fallen, she remains in my eyes the creature who was surrounded by more luxury, homage and passion than a queen. If, at the moment when I sense myself to be the elect, the master, the sovereign of that sovereign, I think, at the same time, that in that suave church of all the carnal perfections and all terrestrial refinements, burns the very fire of hell, and the science of all lusts, I don't deny that that thought...I won't hide it from you that that thought warms my blood a little in advance."

"Fair enough, M'sieu Cahoche. You talk very finely."

"It's to tell you how far away from your suggestion are the results that I expect from Stéphanie's shrewd efforts. What I want is for the woman desired since the time of her full splendor, facing me, fully lucid and consenting... All the more so because possession by surprise would only be for a moment, and God knows what an epilogue, at the recovery of the senses...! And what I want…also…is, once the step is taken, to be considered as a lover, one of whose embraces has not completed all that might be expected of him. I want to be involved, but alongside my beautiful demon, guided by her, in these fêtes…where lubricity becomes an art…equal to the other arts, and which, like them, demands all the ingenuity and all the science of its servitors..."

"I can almost see what you mean," Frignot interjected, again. "That's not easy to arrange. I'll have a chat with Stéphanie..."

"She's been told that you're in the process of dying of love for her," Frignot reported, piteously, "that it's consuming you. She asked that we shouldn't forget to notify her of the date of your interment. She would try to go, in between the milliner and taking tea. Stéphanie insinuated that you had been the terror of all the girls in Sénecé, that the prettiest had passed through your hands…"

"I like that better."

"Madame said...I'll put it bluntly; what you want is to succeed. She said: 'With his beard? Impossible! Let no one ever talk to me about a bearded man. What horror!'"

"If that's all it is, I'll gladly sacrifice my beard," said Cahoche. "But what story shall I tell my wife?"

He brought a photograph of himself, clean-shaven, to Frignot. "Here. And find out exactly what she's says."

At the next meeting, Frignot was again very vague.

"Stéphanie has done everything she could. You understand that it would require an absolutely exceptional occasion. In the time when you were running after Madame, if that had reached a conclusion..."

"What a joke! Then, there was Aury. I was running…a long way behind. After the accident, everything became possible again...and now..."

"In sum, this is it, Madame said that you have the most frightful of faults, in her eyes..."

"Great God! What?"

"She finds you banal, M'sieur Cahoche."

"Damn!" said the other, flabbergasted. "I didn't expect that. So?"

"Well, I don't know. Perhaps it's necessary for you to do something extraordinary..."

"Perhaps I could murder my wife?" suggested Cahoche, sarcastically.

"Of course," said Frignot, in the same tone.

They ate in silence. As Cahoche accompanied Frignot to the station, he let his anger out.

"Damned bitch!" he growled. "You let her know that if I do her a bad turn one day, she'll know what it has cost her to have played me for a fool!"

Left alone, he reflected, furiously.

"Logically, it can't be so. It's because she's so terribly not banal that I desire her…like a wild beast! If I were so banal... Get away! My desire would be frightened…turned toward others, more facile, average... But if I'm not so banal...if I'm the man of my desire...why aren't I capable? She's right, in sum, to demand in a lover something…something…of her measure. It's that she's been so spoiled... Love, fortune, happiness, artists, women, the handsomest of men. What's left? A murderer? Perhaps she hasn't yet had one of those. Oho! Look out, Cahoche..." The Maire stopped on the edge of the sidewalk, and mopped his brow mechanically. "Dangerous ideas to let linger in the brain...when one has a wild beast in the heart..."

II

Everything has been arranged. To celebrate his return to Sénecé, the owner of the Château d'Hercors will throw a party. The village will dance on the lawns. Games for the boys and girls in the illuminated park. Galettes, brioches, wine in profusion. The domesticity of the Aury household will come when its service is concluded. That is arranged. No one will remain at the château but Frignot and Stéphanie. Lène is ready. Denis is of no account: in his room, scribbling page after page, which he tears up into little pieces and throws into the basket, or making tables turn, or following with staring eyes, his body leaden, one of the ideas that makes him walk through the rooms by day, going past people, blind and deaf to everything that surrounds him.

Frignot is on watch behind the gate. An almost silent rolling of the auto, headlights extinct. A muffled peep of the horn. He opens the gate. The auto, driven by Cahoche, on his own, goes in, and stoops. The Maire jumps down in the driveway. Frignot clicks his teeth. Cahoche has a face the color of his false collar, whose glazed edges collapse under the chin into a soft cushion. The two men go through the door with the high windows framed in bronze and climb the dark stairway, Frignot slips away, and disappears. Lène is sitting in the hall. A single blue-tinted lamp is illuminated above the divan on which she is sitting. Outside that corner of uncertain light, shadow. The vague whiteness, that the extremity of the fall, of the Bacchus. Cahoche advances at a firm and decided pace. He keeps his hands in the pocket of his overcoat. The lamp brightens abruptly. The lips, in the shaven face, are violently tensed, half retracted and tremulous. The dilated eyes are ablaze.

"Here I am," he says, his voice hoarse.

"Bonjour, my dear," says Lène. "She extends her hand to him. She is dressed in a sheath of red silk held up blue-steel epaulettes. Arms bare. Feet bare, in blue brocade mules. "Sit down. Delighted to see you."

A scent of ether emanates from her. Cahoche remains standing.

"I'm delighted too…but impossible to..." The voice chokes. The body is shaken by a shudder. The hands must have clenched in the pockets and trapped the will.

The neck swells, the voice become firm. "…To make small talk. Not the time. I'm the man. One can talk. Give me your hands..."

"To do what, my dear Cahoche?" asked Lène, who seems perfectly self-controlled—and yet her gaze vacillates slightly when it settles on the haggard and grim face.

"So that I can be sure of holding you a little, already…to emphasize what I have to say to you..."

She gives her hands. A viscous sensation in one of her wrists. She snatches the hand away and looks.

"It's blood. It's the proof. One minute, my beauty. Give back your wrist. Ah!

He squeezed the two wrists, sinks down, and sticks his palms, with massive voluptuousness, in silky contact with Lène's hand.

"Good work. At dinner, she drank something in her coffee that was to make her ill her an hour or two later. The fête's in full swing. You can hear the music from here. I said to the servants: it's nothing; a minor malaise. I accompanied her to her room. I laid her down on the bed. The hands leave traces around the neck. I preferred the old system of the pillow... Perhaps you'd be more seduced if I arrived covered in blood like a butcher... I regret. Necessary to be content with this...."

He threw something that he had taken from his pocket on to the dress. Lène started with fright.

"It's her finger. The one she always had in the air when she said to me: 'Cahoche, you're the most cynical...' There, that's what I have to tell you. First of all, I'm going to have you, right away, still warm from the crime…famous, eh? And then I'll go back. Neither seen nor known. It'll be easy. I mingle with the fête, I clink glasses, I think I might even dance. I apologize for my poor wife. I kept her company for a while to help her sleep. I left her sound asleep. What a good husband, that Cahoche. Once the guests have gone, I go up to my bedroom. I go to see how the invalid is. I discover the crime. I howl. I telephone. I beg the prosecutor to come. They can telephone Sherlock Holmes. I'm distraught. The story of the severed finger will make a fine subject for a feuilleton. Let them run around. The knife for the finger is in the well. As for suspecting me…I'm at the party, until the end. Now, I'm up to it. I'll answer all the questions. When I feel myself weakening. I'll come to drink you..."

He approaches his myopic eyes to Lène's, until their foreheads collide. His fingers put two iron bracelets around her wrists. His nostrils breathe in the odor of ether and the odor of flesh. His mouth continues talking and moving, almost colliding with Lène's.

"I'll drink you, the alcohol that was running through my brain when I killed her, which is, at this moment, my very blood. We're going to have a good time. The investigation will be closed and some unknown sentenced to death in his absence. What's left? Remorse? I'll give that to you to chew on. If I experience a need for punishment I name you my executioner. You can beat me, tear me apart, tear out my blood with your lips. Murderer's blood…that ought to worth as much as cocaine..."

One of the hands releases one of the wrists and the arm goes to Lène's waist, causes the woman to fold up. She falls on the divan.

Something swoops down upon Cahoche's back; two enormous hands envelop his throat; he is drawn irresistibly backwards, loses his balance. A body is spread over his own, crushing it.

"If it's blood of which you have too much, my Maire, I can aid you to bleed it… Don't move, Madame!" cries Frignot to Lène, standing up stupidly. "I have marvelous things to tell you. A moment's patience. A little account to settle with my friend Cahoche."

A hand abandons the neck. Cahoche struggles; his arms are maintained by Frignot's knees; the grip on his throat is choking him.

"Look, my Maire," says Frignot, taking a stout wallet from his pocket, "here are all your sous. It's all there. With that of the restaurant bills. I don't owe you anything. You thought that it was for your money that I was operating? Bloody fool that you are!"

He relaxes the strangulation slightly.

"Breathe a little, in order to listen to this. You too, Madame—this concerns you. It was seeing this gross fellow talk about you as a woman one might perhaps have one day that started to work on me... I tell you this, Madame…Oh, in God's name, don't move, friend Cahoche, or I'll squeeze hard. Perhaps you'll catch the train that's taking your lady to the Eternal Father. I can say, Madame, before God and men, that I would never have dared lift my eyes... You weren't a woman…you were like a divinity on the earth Eh! In God's name, you too, don't try to call out—there's no one here! This is it. If I've accepted to listen to this bandit, it was because I found that M'sieur Denis had demolished all the good habits…including mine. In brief, nothing to see with you. And then, very softly, to understand it, I said to myself: the day when she's on the point of making merry with the Maire, there's no longer any reason why it wouldn't be with anyone... that's how far you've fallen...and I've fallen! That's what decided me. And the most culpable in all of this—to each is due—is the Monsieur! With all his nonsense that had turned the heads of everyone around. I took my time...but I've understood in the end. Joy, he said...on seeing the way your conducted yourself, I said to myself: Is that what it is, Joy? Well, I understand! And why shouldn't I have my share too?"

He shook Cahoche's head.

"You're going to make yourself scarce, friend Cahoche, like a coward. You have just enough time to go save your head. Tomorrow, it will be light. If that still sings to you, and the gendarmes haven't taken you away, we'll see how things can be arranged. Perhaps it will be your turn for Joy. Me, I'm going to have mine!"

Light inundates the hall, fully illuminating the tragic and burlesque scene. Denis is on the threshold of the gallery, his hand still on the commutator.

Frignot, with a start, has released Cahoche. The Maire, crimson and staggering, has fled, grunting fragments of phrases...

The sound of the auto engine starting, its glide over the sand of the park.

Lène has bounded toward Denis, is clinging to him. "It's horrible. Protect me."

Frignot, after a moment of bewilderment, has steadied himself on his legs and marches toward the invalid. Denis raises his cane. Lène takes refuge behind him behind the Bacchus, against which Denis, having taken a step back, is leaning.

Frignot hurls himself upon Denis, grabs him, shakes him, but is nonplussed by the metal carcass and its weight. Meanwhile, the heavy cane lashes him repeatedly.

"I'll have her!" Frignot cries. In the bodily struggle, one of Denis' steel arms has gripped his shoulder; he tries to disengage it, to knock the invalid down, to leap on Lène.

Denis has dropped his cane. Desperately, he tries to immobilize the man. And he cries, his eyes wild, bulging, with a little drool on his lips: "The man who will surpass me...Lène. There…there he is!"

Lène tries to move closer, to help Denis, to strike the brute, but Frignot frees himself. Terrified, she flees into the gallery; the fluid sheath of silk constructed for gesture of nonchalant grace hinders her run; it gives way, splits, over the flamboyant flesh.

Frignot has seen. With an enormous oath, he pushes Denis away with a merciless thrust. Denis collapses. He launches himself after Lène.

Aha! The slut is naked!

Denis' head is spinning; as he falls into oblivion, he has time to hear the sound of a door slamming, a key turning…blows of feet and fists against the door, frantic oaths...

His eyes blink, open. In the empty hall the same bright light. An armchair overturned by Cahoche as he fled, a little blue slipper, over there in the gallery...

The misty gaze encounters, as it wanders, the dazzling statue, stops, rises along the pulpy body, reaches the empty eyes, embraces the blissful and mocking face, fixes upon the immutable laugh.

A similar laugh is designed on Denis' stupid face; his lips stir and stammer words, flakes of frozen thought...

"Are you content? You've seen them. Look what they've made of me... Look what I've made of myself... Look what the verity that you made me speak, perfect image…has become in passing through the verity of the worlds, still too heavy…and over which you go all the same, continuing to dance and laugh, your foot striking its earth full of seed, your hand raising the cup full of juice... Ha ha! You'll endure…veridical image, more cruelly insulting to our snail-like verity than all the lying images of distress!"

The body drags itself toward the pedestal; the groping hands encounter the cane.

"Ha ha! That at least, no one…after me…is led astray by your ferocious counsel…statue too soon erected...on the edge of a world to come…and behind which the man who hears your laughing tone...staggers and breaks…among the larvae of impossible verity..."

He lifts himself up, with immense effort, his hands reaching the feet of the god, hanging on, hoisting up the body, which rasps the pedestal, the cane blindly striking the marble, fragments leaping from the face, the fingers that hold the chalice, the vine-branches that circle the forehead. The blows resonate in the silence and the sound echoes and makes the glass in the gallery and the cupola vibrate, like the bursts of laughter of the god.

Lène appears at the end of the gallery, advances prudently, stops, sees from a distance Denis lying, unmoving, at the foot of the mutilated marble.

Reaching him, she bends over, listens for his breathing…passes on, goes to stand up the armchair knocked over by Cahoche, and comes back toward. But she stops again. Some distance from the divan where she was sitting, a small, yellowing cylindrical mass lies on the carpet. She looks around, picks up a newspaper lying on the big table, wraps the small debris in it, and sticks the package as best she can in the waistband of her peignoir. Then she goes to turn a commutator.

The lamps go out. The light of the nascent dawn tints the hall with gray. Lène goes back to Denis.

"My poor king…," she says.

She kneels down, lifts his head, tries to stand up, lifting the body, pauses for breath and tries again. Unable to succeed, she passes her bare arms under Denis' armpits, and slowly, walking backwards, bent over the burden, her hair falling down and partly covering his face, she drags the body along the gallery, toward the bedrooms.

III

The sun strikes Lène in the face, waking her up. Stéphanie has drawn the large curtains.

"It's noon, Madame. I came in several times, but Madame was sleeping so soundly…I have things to tell Madame."

"Me too. Go telephone Doctor Lugnault and ask him to come as soon as possible. Monsieur had a bout of fever last night. I succeeded in putting him to bed. I hope that with a few days of tranquility... Also telephone Mademoiselle Brionne and tell her that if she's free at the moment, it would give me the greatest pleasure to have her at the château for a few days, with a few of her friends. That will help me support a little better life with Monsieur while he's ill... Your turn."

"Oh!" says Stéphanie, turning toward the fireplace. "Madame lit a fire?"

"Yes. It was very late, after having cared for Monsieur. I was frozen. The radiators are extinct..."

"If Madame had called me…"

"To strike a match under a faggot ready prepared? Anyway, you were doubtless dancing at the Cahoches..."

"A fine evening, Madame…there's been a frightful crime. Madame Cahoche has been murdered..."

"How?" exclaims Lène, sitting on her bed.

"The murderer stifled her with a pillow and cut off one of her fingers. As I tell Madame. Otherwise, nothing was stolen. Monsieur Cahoche is in a frightful state. The château's full of policemen. And what's very serious is that Monsieur Frignot has disappeared."

"Frignot. I don't see the connection…"

"At any rate' they're searching for him, and it's on him that suspicions are weighing."

A silence between the two women. Lène moves hair away from her forehead, gently.

"And your idea?"

"My idea?" Stéphanie places a peignoir on an armchair near the bed. "My idea will be Madame's."

Lène yawns lightly. "I'm not sufficiently awake yet to have an opinion."

"It's in case they find that poor Monsieur Frignot and he tells stories."

"What stories, my dear Stéphanie? If he has stories to tell, how can they concern me?"

"Or me?" says Stéphanie, hesitantly.

Lène makes her fingernails glisten in the sunlight.

"Monsieur Cahoche was in love with me, and sometimes asked Frignot and you to serve his cause with me. You're too devoted to me and know my sentiments too well to have accepted. On the other hand, you earn a good enough living here not to have been tempted by the bribes you were offered. As for Frignot, I don't know anything about his dealings with Monsieur Cahoche, I never have known anything, and don't want to know anything. All that has no connection with the horrible drama you've told me about..."

"Very well, Madame."

Stéphanie goes to push a few ashes that have overflowed from the hearth back into the fireplace, among which are charred pieces of a newspaper.

"A good enough living here? To tell the truth, Madame..."

Lène looks at the girl, and then stretches herself.

"We can always reach an understanding about questions of money, my dear Stéphanie. Will you go and telephone the doctor and Mademoiselle Brionne. And then, bring me some chocolate and something to nibble. I'm as hungry as a wolf."

"I can't leave you depressed, my rose," says Brionne. Unfortunately, I can only stay for a few hours. I'm starting rehearsals tomorrow for a play that will run for a thousand...it's as if one held them. In any case, I've brought little Loulia here. Sixteen years in the raspberries. She's a sister of

Hetchine's. Her, it's the piano. A child prodigy. For the rest, her sister's example has attracted her, and prepared her, for a heap of little things. A pretty garden to bring into flower. I confide her to you. She'll distract you. When you're tired, she'll play you anything you like, from Bach and Debussy to the most piquant moderns."

"Hmm…the piano...at this time! We need as little noise as possible around the invalid."

"It's going badly?"

"The doctor came yesterday. If Denis has escaped physically, the fall has almost capsized his reason. It wasn't going very well on that side, you know..."

"Why, the beautiful statue is damaged!"" says Brionne stopping in front of the Bacchus.

"Yes. It was in the course of his fit that he lashed out at it. I'll tell you about it. Let's get some refreshments."

Stéphanie comes into the hall.

"Madame…while I was dressing Madame a young man has arrived from Paris, who asked to see Madame."

"Who?"

"He told the gardener that he was an artist in Paris, that he was from Sénecé, and that a long time ago, when he was a child, Madame had a dress made after a picture he had drawn in his schoolbook."

"What's that story? I don't remember that at all. What's his name?"

"Something like Avy…Annevy. He asked permission to wait, to see whether Madame would like to see him. That he has something important to say to her... He's been in the park for nearly two hours."

"Zut!" said Lène. "I don't have time for this. Have you see him, this boy. What's he like?"

"Good looking, Madame.

"Good. Have him wait here. I'll come back."

A young man of about twenty has been contemplating the Bacchus. He turns round, advances toward Lène and immediately blushes with embarrassment

"I beg your pardon, Madame…you've probably forgotten me…so many things have happened. This is what it's about… After Monsieur Aury's accident…many people left…including my parents…the miller Mannevy. We went to live in Paris. I couldn't do anything else than be an artist. Perhaps because of you…in the time…the dress…"

"I remember," says Lène, politely.

"My parents did their best to make me take up a trade…but the art was stronger. I started trying my hand at sculpture… Masters encouraged me. And then, I reflected a great deal…"

He interrupts himself, searches for words, his face becoming very serious.

"Monsieur Aury's ideas had opened a world of thoughts to me. I've formed a great vision of life…and I'd like to express everything that's within me…in a work…for which you might consent to pose, Madame...

"I'd like to make…a statue of Joy..."

Intermediary Note by the Translator

In his introduction to the unfortunately-curtailed new edition of *L'Arche* that he issued in 1961, Pierre Versins claimed that Albin Michel told the author that *Le Bacchus mutilé* would never be reprinted, because it was "unreadable"—information he presumably obtained from Henriette Sauret, from whom he sought permission for the reprint. One presumes that the book was accepted for publication by an employee and that Michel did not read it prior to publication. It is not immediately obvious what Michel meant by "unreadable," although three possibilities spring to mind.

Michel might have thought the novel difficult because of its narrative method, which continually introduces new characters and then abandons them again once they have played their part in the unfolding tragedy, which switches repeatedly between past and present tenses, and sometimes deploys a kind of stream-of-consciousness that might have seemed rather avantgardish, especially in the elaborate account of Denis' delirium following his encounter with Cécelle. This is, however, highly unlikely, in that none of these devices actually makes the book any less readable—arguably quite the reverse—and none of them is really all that unusual for 1922.

Michel might also have thought that Denis Aury's theory of transcendental Joy would be incomprehensible to the average reader—which, of course, it is, that being, in a sense, the whole point of it. It is also highly unlikely that the suspicion in question occasioned the remark, because Michel was far too experienced a publisher not to know that many readers have a very high tolerance level for the incomprehensible, even when it is not—as it is in this case—being deployed in the seemingly-good cause of offering glimpses of something new, far-reaching and highly desirable.

By far the likeliest hypothesis, it seems to me, is that Albin Michel thought the novel "unreadable" because the final section is so utterly, relentlessly and savagely despairing, offering not the slightest crumb of comfort to any reader previously seduced into sympathy for Denis and Lène. In his treatment of his main characters—and thus of any readers who had identified with them—the author is brutally, abominably cruel, to an extent very rarely seen even in the many other agonized expressions of disenchantment written in the aftermath of the Great War. As its translator, inevitably involved more intimately than most readers, I can testify that I have never encountered anything else remotely as distressing in the other 180+ volumes I have translated to date, or any of the thousands of books that I have read, and would never have imagined beforehand that any book could horrify me so profoundly.

Every editor and publisher knows that readers love "happy endings," and can only routinely excuse tragic and *conte cruel* endings because of the curious sense of bittersweet moral uplift definitive of the sense of tragedy and the element of black comedy in the latter. Every editor knows, too, that many readers feel literally betrayed if a text does not deliver, if not a happy ending, at least some other potential psychological compensation. Perhaps, however, even though *Le Bacchus mutilé* is certainly extreme in aggressively denying readers what most of them routinely want, it is a trifle over the top to call the book "unreadable." The story-line goes beyond tragedy, and its ironic last line is far more saddening than black comic, with the result that the book is, indeed a difficult and painful read—but that is, in a sense, what makes it such a unique and valuable literary work, and constitutes its true brilliance. There is no starker challenge to conventional reader expectations, no sterner test of imaginative moral fiber. It is precisely because it is so nearly "unreadable" that every serious reader should want to read it, and should be glad of having read it.

The extent to which the final chapters of the book devastate the characters of Denis and Lène, inflicting far worse degradations on both of them than mere death, is all the more astonishing because of the extent to which the author and his protagonist share ideas and a biography. There is a sense in which, in trashing Denis so viciously, Arnyvelde is trashing his own youthful hopes and ambitions. Doubtless the assault is exaggerated; having finished the novel, the author did, after all, get on with his life and job, and soon started writing another book in which those hopes and ambitions surfaced again, albeit still somewhat mutilated. Perhaps, in fact, "venting" his feelings of disillusionment and distress in the final chapters of the novel helped him get past them, or even get rid of them. In any case, for a writer to attack himself through characters based on himself, for whatever reason, is fair game. What is more suspect, in terms of fairness, is seeming to do it to other people.

What might Henriette Sauret have thought of the appalling portrait of Lène painted in the final pages of *Le Bacchus mutilé*, if she saw the slightest hint of herself in the character? What might she have thought, in the certain knowledge that, even if she did not see any of herself in Lène, other people would be likely to imagine some connection?

Because she was a highly intelligent woman, a writer and a theoretically-aware feminist, Henriette Sauret would have known, in fact, that Lène is not in any sense a representation of her, but is merely a sophisticated version of a commonplace fantasy figure of a kind with which male writers love to supply their fictional alter egos: a supremely beautiful, supremely docile sexual possession and social trophy; mutilating her character is, in a sense, merely an extension of the mutilation of the author's own dreams and obsessions via the character of Denis. By the same token, however, Henriette Sauret would also have known that there is a marked tendency among males in general to attempt to impose aspects of that fantasy projection on their actual wives, however ill-fitting it might be and whatever trouble the expectations generated by the illusion might cause; and she would also have known, in consequence, that there was certainly a possibility of some connection between Lène and herself in Arnyvelde's mind.

Then again, the fact that Lène is a mere fantasy figure does not mean that Henriette Sauret had nothing to do with the black mood that caused Arnyvelde to vent his feelings so cruelly in the final chapters of the novel, if only because she was presumably unable, for a while, to help him get over it. As to whether the details of the final section of *La Bacchus mutilé* offer any clues to further causes of the author's evident distress, that is a matter of pure conjecture. Lène states forthrightly in the text that her own inability to render any assistance to Denis is entirely his fault, for refusing to accept that assistance, and she is right—as Denis agrees himself—but even if Henriette bore no more responsibility for Arnyvelde's distress than a temporary inability to help, and even if Arnyvelde accepted that it was his fault and not hers, the fact remains that he must have known, whether he did it in a spirit of malevolence or not, that his demolition of the character of Lène would rebound and reflect to some degree on his actual wife.

In fact, that repercussion and reflection does not seem to have had any dire effect on their marriage. Their only child, Jérôme, was born in March 1921, possibly after the writing of the text had been completed, although Henriette was probably pregnant while he was writing it. At any rate, that birth must have marked a new point of departure for their life together. We know, in any case, that Arnyvelde went on to write another book, which, while certainly retaining a strong measure of disenchantment, and featuring therein an alter ego with a "dead heart," goes some way providing the note of partial redemption that the text of *Le Bacchus mutilé* so brutally refuses. Furthermore, it deliberately employs a redeemed Lène as a key character, albeit one who remains mostly in the wings, while her offspring take center stage, replacing her as a version of the ultimate male fantasy—and, indeed, the text goes to considerable length to provide an elaborate argument and analysis regarding her status in that regard. Most indicative of all, however, as a measure of repentance of the possibility that the demolition of Lène in the earlier book might have had repercussions for his wife, is the fact that the author added the following dedication to *On demande un homme…*:

> *To my wife*
> *Henriette Sauret-Arnyvelde*
> *I dedicate this novel*
> *of the Palais Gioia*
> *in order that her name might be at the threshold of this book*
> *as it is at all the thresholds*
> *of my effort and my happiness*

MAN WANTED
or, THE STRANGE TOURNAMENT OF LOVE

I

1. Interview at the Palais Gioia[32]

"My five daughters are to be taken—say rather, to be conquered, if you have no fear of emphasis. No distinction of class or race before those who attempt the adventure. One single law at stake: to please. Each of my children has a dowry of twenty-five million. We're transposing into the most modern conditions in the world the old appeal for suitors, that of mythology and folklore. It's for you to report it and spread your announcement in such a way that it attracts the rarest of men here."

"I shall immediately venture a question which everyone is bound to ask themselves. Why, with the regal dowries that Mesdemoiselles d'Aldezza will receive, do you feel the need to make this appeal? Are not the demoiselles, quite naturally, the object of a host of solicitations?"

"Admit that their pretentions seek individuals of such singular quality..."

"Madame, an advertisement of a few lines would not do justice to such a picturesque item of information. There is a system that we call editorial publicity. It consists of obtaining, for a fee proportional to the circulation of the paper, an article in the news section, which, thanks to the skill of its writer,

[32] I have retained the French spelling of Palais used in the text, as the edifice concerned is in France, in spite of its Italian name (which means, of course, Joy).

takes away the reader's impression that what they are being told serves particular interests."

"I leave that up to you," said the Contessa.

The representative of the Radia agency looks at the marble walls of the hall, and the furniture in precious woods, each item of which gives evidence of having been conceived for the palace.

"Excuse me for introducing the question of money at this point. If I've understood your intention correctly, it's in the principal newspapers of each country..."

"In all the newspapers of every country. We want to reach even the most obscure and distant individuals. Among those for whom that we're searching, one might perhaps be a solitary dreamer who has exiled himself to some lost region and only riffles negligently through a small local paper."

"Those little papers, Madame, compare to the great as gadflies to cattle."

"I would worry about a single omission."

"This publicity, absolutely universal, will correspond to a disbursement so…formidable… Permit me, Madame, to submit to you a procedure that is both simpler and infinitely richer in consequences. What if we envisage the news that you want to give us as sufficiently attractive to obtain, in its own right, a reverberation equal to that which you desire? It's us, Radia, that would be obliged to you, and will be glad, privileged with a new item of the first order, to deliver it to the world in such a form that it will excite the most legitimate emotion throughout the world."

"What do you mean?"

"Instead of considering us uniquely as your intermediary, you consent to grant me what is vulgarly known as an interview. The rest is our affair. Can you imagine, Madame, that we, who are proud to be, in the eyes of the press, the best-informed and the most expert distributor of the sensational, have been seeking a means of entering into relations with you since you were installed here two months ago. A thousand details put our attention on the alert for a decorous reason to ringing at your gate. You have taken the trouble to invite us. We are obliged to you, Madame."

"Very nicely said. Let's try the interview. I fear that you might be exaggerating the interest of it."

"Certainly not. The singularity of the announcement you propose has only served to heighten our curiosity. You're Italian?"

"French. My first marriage was to an industrialist...who was at the same time a kind of apostle. After a long widowhood I encountered the Comte d'Aldezza. I lost the Comte a few years ago."[33]

"Is the choice of this Savoyard residence an effect of hazard or a particular dilection?"

"Both. A sojourn in Evian, an excursion in the surroundings, this lake and its wild surroundings enchanted my daughters and myself. Is it very captivating?"

"No, but that will follow your enchantment."

"To have negotiated with the commune the property of the lake, had the honest wooden chalet to which a few families came on holiday demolished, and had this villa constructed in its stead..."

"This Palais, Madame. Everyone who talks about it calls it a Palais. They say the *Palais Gioia*. Why?"

"I don't know. From the name of one of my daughters, presumably."

"The entire region is occupied with your magnificence. Their description will be a factor marvelously propitious to the atmosphere we want to create."

---

[33] In order to make this account consonant with the chronology of *Le Bacchus mutilé*, which undoubtedly extends into the mid-1930s, it would be necessary to suppose that the present story is set in the 1950s, but the backcloth of the story explicitly denies such a distant futuristic setting in its references to the moderately recent Great War, so it is necessary to assume that the events of the previously novel have ben tacitly shifted back in time.

"I confide myself to your experience. If you would like to make a tour of the property..."

Above the hall the muffled sound of an organ is audible.

"Beautiful music, Madame."

"By Handel."

"One of Mesdemoiselles your daughters? Shall I have the honor of being introduced to Mesdemoiselles d'Aldezza?"

"That's Vénerise. She's the only one here at present. I'll gladly show her to you. Her sisters left this morning on an excursion."

"Italian, that pretty name?"

"Entirely whimsical. Inspired, like the other four—Marden, Mercerelle, Gioia and Samion, by the symbolism of one of the seven days and corresponding to the dominant nature of the child who bears it..."[34]

The organ falls silent. At that moment a light tread descends in leaps a nearby staircase. Through the door of the hall open to the park the Radia representative sees, passing along the broad amber pathway that separates the perron from the lake, a tall semi-naked young woman in a crimson woolen tunic, shod in red sandals. She is running. Her hair, cut short at

---

[34] This scheme links the name Vénerise to Vendredi (Friday), Marden to Mardi (Tuesday), Mercerelle to Mercredi (Wednesday), Gioia to Jeudi (Thursday) and Samion to Samedi (Saturday). The reference to dominant nature has no connection with the English nursery rhyme associating different characters with children born on the different days of the week, and the apparent modes of derivation are somewhat inconsistent, Gioia relating to *joie* [joy], not to Jupiter, and Vénerise relating to *vénération* [reverence], not to Venus, while Mercerelle apparently relates to *mercerie* [mercery] in the sense of trading as well as *Mercure* [Mercury, the messenger], although Marden does seem to relate to Mars in the martial sense. Samion presumably relates, like Samedi, to the vulgar Latin *sambati* [Sabbath].

the nape, dances in the heavy bounds of a single tawny mass; a squirrel flees in front of her.

The interviewer has advanced as far as the perron. The squirrel grips the trunk of one of the old trees that border the lake, reaching the branches in a flash. With an imperious and lithe gesture, the young woman catches one of the nearest branches, hoists herself up, reaches the foliage and continues her pursuit. "Illi! Illi!" she cried to the animal as she scales the branches, agile and confident.

Illi has leapt from that tree to another, and she launches herself into the void in her turn.

"The fool!" exclaims the Contessa.

The branch that receives the impact of the red huntress bends. The latter equilibrates herself as it curves, lodges herself astride it, and swings, renouncing her pursuit and laughing at the squirrel perched in the fragile topmost branches.

A great flame released from the impetuously-oscillated branch; the plunge of a body fallen with the violence of a dive into the russet water of the lake, where black and white swans are gliding—and the laughing naiad, her hair steaming, swims toward the terrified swans, catches up with one of them, seizes it, imprisons it in the crook of her bare arm, and soothes it, the red beak confounded with the shine of the tunic.

"Marvelous!" exclaims the Radia man. "Mademoiselle Vénerise...."

"I thought Vénerise was alone," says the Contessa. "I was mistaken. Marden was there too."

2. 1280. Rap.

Abbeville railway station, 20:20. Delvêque only comes out of the waiting room at the moment when the Calais-Paris express is moving off, leaps into a first-class carriage and advances along the corridor, looking nonchalantly at the passengers. Anglo-Saxon face with snub nose, looks like a music-hall impresario or a racehorse trainer. In the last compartment, one man, alone, is sleeping.

Delvêque puts a hand in his jacket and goes in. At the slight sound he makes as he sits down the passenger wakes up. Delvêque looks at his neighbor with a smile that broadens. A thin fellow of about thirty, short black beard, slender moustache, gold-rimmed spectacles, pensive forehead under a traveling cap, the other, slightly astonished at first by that smile, looks away and takes out his cigarette case. Delvêque extracts a cigar from his jacket, bites it and leans forward, raising his hat, toward the passenger's lighter.

"Thanks, Dal Morre."

"You're welcome, Monsieur…?"

"Delvêque. The little turn in London went well? The necklace? At Old Sam's?"

The passenger smiles benevolently "I don't understand. You must be confusing..."

"Don't think so."

"At any rate, I'd be grateful if you didn't interrupt me."

"Pooh!"

"I'm the Marquis de…"

"Beria-Berians. I know. The examining magistrate knows too. That's where we're going when we get off the train. Beria-Berians for the hunters at the Ritz, Dal Morre for the girls at the Carlton. Your mother's name is Berana and she's a herbalist in Barcelona. The last job, at the Ritz, was less skillful than usual. Your cane with the ivory handle was found. It was a girl who gave you away without meaning to.

"The cashier said: 'This is the Marquis' cane.'

"The girl, who was settling her bill, said: 'It looks like Henri's...'

"I happened to be there—let's say by chance. 'Henri…?' I asked. 'Dal Morre, a friend of mine. Let me see…'

"Why do you carry the same cane as the Marquis and as Dal Morre?

"Looking at the girl, I said: "Is it definitely his?' 'There's a mechanical device that makes it easy to recognize,' she said. She pressed on one of the little moldings and, with all due respect, the robe of one of the sculpted Chinamen opened up. The cashier blushed."

"Your story is quite amusing and passes the time in a carriage. It's true that I stayed one night at the Ritz and left a cane there of rare workmanship."

"It's true, too, that the necklace disappeared the night you had a bed there—I won't say slept. You booked your room in the afternoon. Then you asked the floor attendant to show you the lavatories. When the attendant had gone, as you went back downstairs, you went past the door of the American lady with the necklace. Knock knock! I little squirt of the oil syringe into the lock. No one saw a thing. The facility of working by night. You have an *ouistiti* to pick the lock.[35] Nothing grates because of the oil."

"My dear Monsieur..."

"Delvêque."

"One weak point in your anecdote. I went back to bed last night at five in the morning. The night porter will testify to that. What time I would I have been…burgling?"

"We know your system. An accomplice books a room on the same night as you. You come back early, and in all the coming and going no one pays any attention to you. You don't budge from your room. In the middle of the night you pull your job and go back to bed. Your accomplice arrives at five o'clock in the morning and gives your name to the night-porter, half asleep. You make your exit under the eyes of the day porter at eight. By the time the theft is discovered and the two porters are questioned, you're already in Old Sam's shop on the other side of the Channel."

"Well imagined. If I ever want to be a hotel rat, I'll take advantage of your information."

---

[35] This argot usage of the term *ouistiti*—literally, a kind of monkey—does not seem to have reached dictionaries, but subsequent details of the plot suggest that it is a device by means of which a key left in a lock can be turned within it from the other side of the door.

The train slows down and stops at Amiens station. A woman passes alongside the train, selling the Paris papers. The Marquis stands up.

"No tricks, fellow!"

"My intention is to buy the evening newspapers, with your permission."

"Get one for me, then."

The Marquis comes to sit down again, holds *Paris-Soir* out to Delvêque and calmly unfolds the *Intransigeant*."

"Calling yourself a hotel rat—that's good!" jokes Delvêque. "They call you the Great Workman in the bars where the petty four-sou burglars hang out. We know your pedigree from A to Z."

"Let's hear it. I don't mind telling you that I have a certain talent as a writer. If the pedigree is piquant, I'll write an article about it for the *Heraldo*."

"Keep talking. I know that you're a writer. We have the book that you published. 'A pity,' the boss said, 'that the brain that did that serves a burglar.' *Toward the Light!* Full of Latin, historical portraits, declamations on justice. Your Light is anarchy, isn't it?"

"I'm sorry, but with regard to me, I haven't the slightest idea what you're talking about."

"An anarchist and a believer. At church three times a week. If you confess, what must the curés hear!"

"The pedigree?"

"There was once a lady who called herself the Comtesse de Hourtheil. Beautiful appearance, stays in palaces. She's the one who perfected the hotel rat genre. Oil syringe, *ouistiti*, etc. One day, you meet. You already had a few thefts to your credit. But above all…take off your spectacles."

"Why?"

"Don't quibble, Marquis. Take off the specs."

"I'll lend myself to all your whims. I don't dislike having a laugh."

Delvêque moves his face closer. The Marquis submits to the examination serenely.

"I'm not an oculist. The physicians at the Prefecture will recognize it better than me. In brief, it appears that you're a nyctalope. What an accomplice for La Hourtheil! A good-looking fellow, liberated, who can see in the dark! The association doesn't last long. She confides all her little secrets to you. She's been nicknamed the queen of hotel rats. No such thing. There's soon a king. As for the worthy lady, soon discarded. Ingrate!"

"And then?"

"That's all?"

"Nice—but for an article, a little thin."

"The examining magistrate won't be as demanding as the *Heraldo*."

"Would you like to leave it there for now? I'd like to look through the papers."

"Scan away, There'll be time to resume the conversation when we arrive."

The Marquis settles down comfortably and reads. Delvêque runs his eyes over his own paper. "Pooh! There's no mention of the necklace." He folds up *Paris-Soir*, puts it in the inside pocket of his coat, and says, mockingly: "They'll be talking about it tomorrow."

The Marquis' attention is suddenly caught. He says: "Are you determined that we're going to see the magistrate?"

"Yes indeed."

"It's just that we'd be wasting precious time—mine, the magistrate's and yours."

"Not sure. Without indiscretion, what's so urgent, Marquis? Something in the paper? The arrival of another necklace to collect?"

"No. Dowries of twenty-five million put up for competition."

"Another American hoax."

"Not so far away." The Marquis holds out the paper to the policeman. "Look."

"No thanks," says Delvêque. "Read it to me if you want. I prefer to keep my hands free."

"Your mistrust is an unparalleled rudeness. As is addressing me as *tu*. If you were to find that you were mistaken on my account, you'd be in trouble."

"That true," says Delvêque, placidly. "Risks of the profession." After a moment's silence, slightly annoyed, he added: "And the article?"

"There it is. Third column. From Thonon, by a correspondent of the Radia agency.

"D'Alezza," says Delvêque. "I know that name. It was an Italian multimillionaire. He married a widow who's been an actress in her youth. He threw parties in his house in the Avenue Friedland. I went there several times, sometimes dressed as a guest, sometimes as a flunkey. Because of the collections. It's not only necklaces that attract thieves."

"You've seen the daughters?"

"I don't remember. They must have been in bed. It was seven or eight years ago. Kids."

The train slows down in order to go through Creil. Delvêque hands the paper back to the Marquis.

"Funny business. Searching for husbands when one has a twenty-five million dowry…"

"Would you care to lend me your paper?" asks the Marquis. "It might have a different version from the *Intran...*"

Delvêque opens his jacket. In a flash, the Marquis has bounded on the lapels of Delvêque's garment and dragged them down over the upper arms, paralyzing them. Before the policeman, standing up violently, can get free, a solid punch on the chin stuns him and knocked him down on to the banquette.

The Marquis snatches his valise from the luggage-rack, opened the door and leaps down on to the trackside, shouting: "Add that to your pedigree, old chap!"

3. We were ten girls in a meadow[36]
All ten of us to marry
There was Chine
There was Dine...

"That's lucky," said the pilot. We're arriving just in time to see Mont Blanc at sunrise. We'll be over Ontriond before all the Alps are lit up."[37]

"We've made good time."

"Isn't that what you wanted? You know, I thank you for the opportunity that you're giving me. I've never spent such hours here. It's chic, eh?"

Five thousand meters beneath the airplane, Lake Geneva is shining, a kind of great brown puddle, like a drinking-trough surrounded by white-tinted monsters. The sky over the chains, black in the west, passes in the east from amethyst to green, and large expanses of saffron soon unfurl for the aviators a yellow daylight that the mountains are not yet receiving. Suddenly, between the fleecy white masses beneath the plane, one of them turns pink. The summit of Mont Blanc welcomes the sun just as the top of the star appears to the aviators, an enormous red arc that transmutes all of space for them, while the Alps and the lake, scarcely emerged from their torpor, remain in gray shadow."

"Greetings, Phoebus!" cries the pilot. "Isn't it grandiose, Monsieur?"

---

[36] These words are from a popular children's song, which might have played some part in inspiring the central motif of the story; the reader will remember that the amareur dramatists of Sénecé were putting on a pageant based in it in the previous novel.

[37] "Ontriond" is a substitute for Montriond, as "Lurzine" is for Morzine, although Thonon and Evian, being slightly more distant from the presumed seting the the story, retain the names they have in our world.

“Beautiful,” his companion replies. “But I think we’re going a little too fast now. When we arrive at Ontriond, everybody will still be asleep.”

“Well, tell me what time you want to land. We’ll take a little tour beforehand.”

“I’m hesitant. Someone else might have had the same idea as me...”

“Do you want us to circle above the region? We’d see them coming.”

“That’s true. It’s necessary to reach the palace at about eight o’clock.”

“The moment when the demoiselles are probably having their chocolate.”

“Indeed...”

“I understand. You want to have your effect. You’re right. It’s very smart. It’s a matter of managing the fall, putting down delicately on one of the lawns in front, avoiding the lake.”

“If you make me take a bath, it’ll all be spoiled.”

The day is born. In the gilded air, clouds glide like flakes of nacre beneath the plane.

“Now we’re over Thonon,” says the pilot. Look down there—Lurzine…Ontriond…that hundred-sou piece ablaze to the right of Outriond is the lake.”

The early risers at the palace have seen the apparatus pass back and forth over Ontriond, describe circles in a regular fashion over the surrounding mountains, the Grandforts, the Volze, Ansaux, the Gognon. Suddenly, plunging vertically toward the lake, the airplane falls. A fearful cry from a domestic has brought on to the terrace of the façade the Contessa, in a violet silk gandourah, and a tall young woman with vaporous blonde hair coifing her like a helmet of golden foam. She is dressed in a white dalmatic, her bare feet shod in silver mules.

The two women follow the fall of the frail vessel with anguish. A thousand meters from the ground, the latter rights itself with a broad turn, and, stabilized, its wings sparkling in the sunlight, resumes its descent in graceful spirals.

The Contessa burst out laughing "In our honor, those acrobatics?"

"Perhaps it's a new suitor."

"A little early, but it's possible. Let's go prepare ourselves to receive him worthily."

"Go, Maman. I'd like to catch him as he exits his bird. He won't wait there, and I'd be amused."

Having flown over the palace, the airplane is landing softly on one of the lawns. One of the aviators emerges from the cabin. He takes off his helmet and furry combination. A beardless and robust young man appears in sporting costume, and comes straight toward the motionless young woman.

"Bonjour, Mademoiselle. Am I in the home of Madame d'Aldezza?"

"Yes, Monsieur."

"Is it too early for me to introduce myself to Madame d'Aldezza or one of her daughters?"

"I'm Gioia d'Aldezza."

"I salute you, Mademoiselle. My name is Herbert Lesielt. Yesterday evening, in Paris, I was reading in a café at about six o'clock, the article concerning you and your sisters. A few moments later, the speaker of the wireless in the establishment repeated the news, but in a more ostentatious fashion. 'Challenge!' cried a voice, which must at that moment have been colliding with millions of ears. 'Challenge of amour, thrown down by the Palais Gioia to all those who hold the true scepter of amour...' The listeners, a trifle nonplussed at first, mostly laughed. One fat drinker said: 'It must be a trap set by the Salvation Army…old girls…and the love that of Jesus.' Others began making jokes, of which I didn't hear the end. I immediately telephoned Le Bourget and asked for an apparatus to be prepared. At one o'clock in the morning we took off. Here I am. I imagine that I'm the first to respond to the challenge."

"No."

A slight chagrin in Herbert Lesielt's gaze—but that earnest gaze immediately becomes calm again.

"At the moment when you were telephoning, another presented himself here, whom my sister Mercerelle received. That was Monsieur Vernail."

"The manufacturer?"

"Yes."

"He knows you? He had been alerted personally?"

"No."

"It wasn't possible to arrive more rapidly than I have."

"It's necessary to admit that it was."

"I'm glad. Vernail's a man of the highest caliber. If I'm acceptable, I'll stay."

"It's the presence of Monsieur Vernail that decided you?"

"It's connected to one of the sentiments that brought me here."

"A sentiment other than our conquest?"

"Yes."

"You're very frank."

"Indeed."

"What sentiment?"

"The desire to compete with the men most representative of what a man is, in the most elevated sense of the world. I supposed that many of them would take up your challenge."

"We supposed so too. But your frankness is odd…dangerous, perhaps, given that we might believe ourselves to be a sufficient goal."

"Why dangerous? I imagine that if I succeed in showing myself to be superior to men of the caliber of Vernail, I might perhaps please whichever of you I might love."

"Perhaps." She laughs.

"I'll stay. I assume that I'll find a hotel or lodgings in the neighborhood. I'd be glad to know when I shall have the honor of paying my respects to your mother. Will you permit me to send my bird away?"

Herbert returns to the airplane, exchanges a few words with the pilot, goes to the propeller and starts it spinning. Then, after shaking the aviator's hand, he returns to Gioia. The plane starts moving, and takes off before reaching the end of the lawn. As it rises up, Herbert says: "Adieu, my beloved swan."

"Oh, Monsieur!" says the young woman. "None of us is Elsa von Brabant."[38]

"Are you sure of that?"

"I believe so."

"There are subtle jails. Your appeal allowed the supposition of a dream...in sum, an ideal doubtless singularly difficult to attain."

"Yes."

"You are, therefore—you and your sisters—prisoners of that ideal. It complicates you, forbids you the union, even the love, to which daughters of your condition, but less demanding, could claim more simply."

"Indeed. And you, Monsieur…Lohengrin…I've forgotten your name…"

"Herbert Lesielt."

"Will you keep the secret, like the ancestor of Montsalvat, of your estate and origin?"

"I'm more modern. If I have secrets, they're much more complex than those on an elector's card. My father is the general paymaster in the Nord. I am, or rather have been, a poet. Now, I'm a man who has lost his heart..."

"Oh!"

"To begin with, I was a young idler rhyming vaguely in his province, and who, subsequent to having a poem appear in the *Mercure*, came to Paris to make contact with arts and letters. Verses here and there, in minor periodicals...then I was

[38] Elsa von Brabant is the heroine of Richard Wagner's opera *Lohengrin* (1850), whose hero makes his spectacular arrival in a vessel drawn by a swan.

ambitious to produce a great work…which became impossible at the moment when I thought I was ready to realize it.

"In brief…I dreamed a song that had to decree nothing less than a new face of human being and the world. I wanted, before writing it, to know what human being really was, beyond the ethics through which the war had just strewn is ten million deaths. What better field of experiment than myself? I offered myself to a host of trials: spiritual, sentimental, physical... There I discovered the power of the will... It would be too complicated to tell you how I arrived at very curious results…at a strange force over instincts, desires and a certain number of ill-defined energies...

"One day, I judged myself to be ready to describe my results, my vision of humankind armed with will, and rich with the prodigious powers over the world that modern science confers upon it. I was about to display an entirely new human being...and found myself before a blank sheet. Blank…like cotton wool, like the Pole, like a shroud. Nothing. No faculty of exteriorization.

"Have you read a tale by Alexandre Arnoux, which features a certain Val-Braquin, whose sensibility has been stolen? I surpassed that Val-Braquin.[39] I had stolen my own sensibility. My mastery over my desires, my impulses, had frozen the desire and the passion within me, closed the door to spontaneous and quivering reception. I wandered with my aimless will in a desert…until yesterday, at six o'clock. At six o'clock, I took up the challenge of the Palais Gioia."

"You've come here to love, and you left without your heart!"

"The adventure offered here is the only one that appears to me to be of a magnitude to enable me to recover it."

---

[39] *Écoute s'il pleut* [See if it's Raining] (1923) by Alexandre Arnoux (1884-1973), a prolific writer of fantastic fictions in the symbolist tradition; the work in question reflects the disenchantment following the end of the Great War in quasi-allegorical terms.

"It will be necessary," said Gioia, "to recommence your story with a little more detail for my sister Samion. She's a metaphysician. You'll be able to talk to her about will. She's even studied magic a little."

Herbert smiles disdainfully.

An auto draws up silently outside the gate. A corpulent man of about forty, with a face simultaneously debonair and shrewd, gets out.

"That must be Vernail," says Gioia.

"You haven't seen him yet?"

"No. He only met Mercerelle and Maman yesterday."

The gravel squeaks under the solid tread of the newcomer.

"Bonjour, Mademoiselle Mercerelle," says Vernail.

"Monsieur," says Gioia. "I assume that you are Monsieur Vernail."

"I had the honor yesterday..."

"Of seeing my sister Mercerelle. She told me about your visit. That's why I guessed... I'm Gioia."

"Ah! Of course! In fact, your sister was brunette… Forgive me, Mademoiselle. But you resemble her in an unusual fashion..."

"All five of us resemble one another," says Gioia. "May I introduce to you Monsieur Lesielt."

The two men bow to one another.

"Monsieur," says Herbert, "I arrived just now in an airplane, having set out a short time after the appearance of the news with which you're familiar. I thought I would be the first one here. I'm told that you were far ahead of me..."

"I have no merit in that," says Vernail. "The news editor of a large evening paper owed me a few favors, and we had a little agreement. I have the same agreement with the editor in chief of a morning paper. Those excellent comrades telephone me as soon as information from the agencies reach them that they deem susceptible of interesting me. That renders me precious services. I knew at ten o'clock yesterday morning what you read at six in the evening. At midday, my Vernail 60 sports car passed through the Porte de Bercy." He turns to Gioia. "Shall I have the pleasure of seeing Mademoiselle Mercerelle?" he asks.

"Please excuse her; she's not feeling very well. As for my other sisters, Vénerise and Samion have gone to Geneva with Marden, who's driving the car."

II

1. Rajah-I-Rajan Amarjit Singh

The grating of pliers and levers in wooden crates from which nails are being extracted, the trumpeting of elephants, the furious sounds of horses' hooves on the cinders, the clink of metal vases colliding as they emerges from the crates...

The guests of the Splendid whose windows overlook the courtyard have been snatched from their sleep at dawn. Harassed by the persistence of the racket they have got up to take a look, and have not gone back to bed.

In the courtyard of the palatial hotel there is a swarm of Hindus dressed in kaftans and coiffed in multicolored turbans. Some are hauling crates of heavy jewelry and piles of gaudy fabrics; others, under the surveillance of officers clad in scarlet and gold are putting brocade blankets and saddles on fine black horses with white hooves. Three kneeling camels, with their eyes closed, are allowing themselves to be laden with bales and vividly-colored tents. Beyond them, two immobile elephants are similarly being laden, by means of ladders leaning against either side of their ribs. To one side, served by Hindus in violet damask, is a third elephant, this one white, each foot circled by a precious bracelet, its breast armored with a gold plate ocellated with emeralds, its tusks ornamented with massive emerald-studded gold rings. An immense brocade carpet rattling with gems caparisons it, all the way to the ground. On top of it is a tall ivory carina, the doors of which are open on two pink silk seats decorated with silver lamé.

His Highness Amarjit, Rajah of Ezrapur, whom the press never name without automatically adding "the most Parisian of Maharajahs," had been taking a rest, in a sports jacket, from generals, Russian ballets and charity balls at the Splendid in Thonon, only accompanied by his secretary and a few servants, when Monsieur Vernail arrived at the hotel. Soon, the latter, having summoned two secretaries and put himself in permanent contact by wireless with his factories in Suresnes, made no secret of the fact that he was taking part in the same tournament whose stake was a Contessina d'Aldezza.

In the meantime, Doctor Athanase Kariakopoulos, the tutor of the young hereditary prince of Ornania, was inscribing his name and that of his lord in the Splendid's register. Prince Costantino—Stani for short—was rarely seen; he spent his days at the Palais Gioia.

The local papers reported the arrival at the Majestic in Saint-Jean d'Aulph of the European middleweight boxing champion Béron. Even Béron in the lists, a candidate for the Gioia Cup, a famous Golden Bowl!

A room had been taken at the Hotel Froetzer in Lurzine by a young Japanese engineer, Inukai Ozaki, about whom it was known that he had installed workshops at the foot of the Grandforts and was working there on the construction of aviation materials capable of supporting altitudes superior to twenty thousand meters. He too was frequenting the Contessa's home.

Amarjit Singh, who had not taken the Ontriond challenge seriously, and had judged at first that the premium would only attract a few adventurers, suddenly found himself amused and piqued. An effusion of nationalism warmed him up, which caused him to see the triumph of the old Orient as a fine stake to risk in the cosmopolitan contest. One radio message after another to Jasgraun, the capital of Ezrapur, ordered the sending, without delay, via Marseilles, of his elephants, dromedaries, cavalry officers and all the elements—fabrics, perfumes, jewels—of his indigenous pomp.

Then he went in person to pay a visit to the Prefect, soliciting authorization to establish a camp site, with his Thousand-and-One Nights, in the Bois d'Arlans, which was adjacent to Lac d'Ontriond. The functionary acquiesced. The government, which prohibits religious processions, had not foreseen the cortege of a Maharajah going to play the gallant with his white elephant, his dignitaries and the baggage of a royal camp.

Throughout the hotel, bells ring, which are heard outside by the incessantly-growing crowd. Strokes of a gong and curt orders in the courtyard. The gate opens. The horses go out first, led by hand by Hindus in black silk kaftans, belted and coifed in white. While the cavalry assembles, facing the terrace of the hotel, the Rajah's elephant advances, preceded by two guides in brocade tunics, and mounted by a mahout with a naked black torso ornamented by an ivory necklace. The royal beast comes to a halt before the perron. One of the Maharajah's officers, who is standing on the terrace, makes a sign. The officers appear in their turn, head toward the horses, mount up and draw their curved swords. The clicks of kodaks crepitate in the crowd. Rumors of admiration and pleasure run around, along with sarcastic remarks, protestations of modesty and wonderment. Rajah-I-Rajan Amarjit Singh is on the threshold

The most Parisian of the princes of Asia is clad in a long silk robe embroidered with gold, his pink silk trousers secured at the ankles by two heavy bracelets of gemstones. A necklace of emeralds wound ten times around the neck terminates on his breast with a giant emerald. His pink brocade turban is surmounted by a diamond plume. He is a young man with dark eyes, his visage bisected by a small brown moustache and framed by a think necklace of undulating and curly black beard.

Next to him stands his secretary, Balbir Kanwar Narasa, a strangely svelte, beardless young man with green eyes. He is dressed in a blue brocade robe, also covered with jewels and coifed in a golden turban with a plume of sapphires.

An ebony and ivory stepladder is stood up against the elephant. The Rajah's companion climbs up, unrolls a golden scarf that he takes from the cushions, and covers the ivory back of the seats, Amarjit Singh climbs up in his turn, sits down, and then extends his finger majestically. The gesture is repeated by one of the guides to the mahout, and the elephant sets off. The other two follow, along with the camels with their mountains of luggage, surrounded by servants. Then the officers on the black horses launch forward and gallop along the cortege.

A man in the crowd shrugs his shoulders nervously. “Barnum!” he says, when Amarjit appears. He spoils the pleasure of his neighbors.

Some kind of electrician in blue overalls, looks on, hesitant and angry. “All that for one man,” he mutters. “Misery of the world!” Between his clenched teeth he adds: “A nice bomb under all that…!”

“Calm down, eh!” said a neighbor with a child astride his shoulders.

“Huh!” sniggers the man. “Much less complimentary than looking at all that with round eyes to reflect on what lies behind it...”

“Everything has its time,” says a woman nearby, irritated. “What obliges you to stay here, if you’re disgusted?”

“Hey, old chap,” says a soft voice in the ear of the man, as the file-past is completed and the idlers drift away, “there’s something more interesting than your bomb...”

The worker starts. The man who has just spoken to him is an elegant tourist, clean-shaven, thin-faced, with cold blue eyes behind large round spectacles. He smiles.

“Come over here and listen,” the voice goes on, cautiously. He draws him away. “You don’t seem to like the rich very much.”

“No, not much. When one knows what poverty and injustice are...but what does it have to do with you? Why are you whispering in my ear?”

“Do you know the A.I.A.?”[40]

---

[40] This acronym was associated during Arnyvelde’s youth with the Association Internationale Antimilitariste, an organization whose French branch was founded in 1902 by three leading anarchists; the organization functioned as a major rallying point for French anarchists, maintained under intense

"Why are you asking me that?"

"Probably because I'm in it."

The man shakes his head. "Need to see. Me, I'm saying nothing. One doesn't know who one's talking to."

"Perhaps you've heart mention of Lemart?"

"What!"

"You see. That's me. Come. I have a proposition for you."

2. François Mirard

"Listen, old chap," says Mirard to the chauffeur, "I might as well let you go. I'm getting stiff in your old crock. I'd go faster on foot. Continue with my luggage. You'll get there eventually. Give the trunks directly to the domestics. You only have to say that they're Monsieur Mirard's. I'm expected."

"Mirard..."

"Yes, not everyone can be called Pasteur. My name is on the trunks."

"There's still a way to go..."

"Eight or nine kilometers, I know. Ah! My knapsack, damn it!"

Mirard picks up a knapsack from between his feet, buckles it on to his back standing in the auto, and then gets out and pays the driver. The latter hands him a card: *Sallez, taxicab, Thonon.* "If you need me when you leave…"

"Not soon, I expect."

François Mirard, head of the Physical Chemistry Laboratory at the Sorbonne. A tall fellow with burning eyes in a bony and tormented face that had led him to be called Baudelaire by his comrades at the Normale. With his coarse cloth suit, hunt-

---

police surveillance. It faded away before the Great War—notionally, at least—and a slightly different interpretation of the initials is subsequently indicated in the plot.

ing gaiters with multiple buckles, hiking boots, knapsack, he resembles the tourists of the time of Bertall or Gustave Doré.[41]

"You can't go wrong," says the chauffeur. "Straight ahead, go through Saint-Jean d'Aulph, and keep straight on to Vranges, where you leave the main road to turn left toward Ontriond. There's even a short cut—ask."

"I know. I did all that when I was twenty. And anyway, it'll be sufficient for me to follow the crowd."

Hoisting his knapsack up with a shrug of the shoulders, he sets forth with a long stride, obliged to follow a sinuous route, in a cloud of dust, through cars honking their horns furiously, hay-carts whose drivers are swearing, caravans and small trucks. An old peasant is trying to guide his frightened livestock through the crowd, a big fellow in a Basque beret leading an admirable goat with white fur hanging down to its hooves and horns in a triple spiral with milky opaline transparencies.

Incredible! Mirard thinks.

He evokes his excursions as a student on vacation, a certain pedestrian expedition from Grenoble to Thonon with a group of comrades...the impressive silence of this same road snaking between the serene mountains, scarcely troubled, at hour-long intervals, by the passage of some rattling automobile or some indigenous cart.

As the newspapers everywhere, diverted by the adventure, have kept the public up to date with the arrivals of illustrious or sensational suitors at the Palais Gioia, curiosity has grown, and in a thousand forms, the lure of lucre has exercised its attraction.

Incredible, in truth: Bohemians coming to set up, on the approaches of that curiosity, their displays of sweetmeats and their lotteries, releasing their children there as good luck charms; peasants finding better profits selling their fruits and

---

[41] The notable nineteenth-century illustrators Charles d'Arnoux (1820-1888), better known as the cartoonist "Bertall," and Gustave Doré (1832-1883).

flowers to passers-by than taking them to town, improvised lemonade sellers carrying barrels in their wheelbarrows; traveling circuses with their twenty automobile wagons, burlesque carousels with their strings of wooden animals, masts and motors, open-air theater performers or athletes heading for Ontriond to set up for an evening; fire-eaters, sword-swallowers, jugglers and fiddlers, calculating that they might be let into the palace for an hour and that the messieurs and ladies might recognize talent and merit...what receipts might fall into the extended hat of an artist that has just applauded by demoiselles with dowries of twenty-five million, a Vernail, and a hereditary prince!

Thus, the road from Thonon to Ontriond is animated by an extraordinary and baroque circulation, augmented by the ordinary traffic of agriculturalists, livestock, commercial vehicles and large tourist limousines, all cursing the slowness imposed on them by the most unexpected encumbrances. And along within them, echoing the merchants followed by slaves who unrolled carpets, displayed vessels, opened caskets of balms before Caesar or Basileus, come jewelers, antiquaries, dealers in rare flowers, exotic birds, counting on, if not seducing the rich Contessa, at least tempting the munificence of the suitors...

François Mirard marches lightly, treading that metamorphosed route and amusing himself with the revelation of the thousand faces. Suddenly, a kind of wave of silence passes along the innumerable procession. By some miracle, autos, pedestrians, carts and livestock move aside, leaving a broad furrow along the road. In the distance, under the bright sun, a swarm of reflections glimmers in which multicolored patches of delightful violence float and dance...

François Mirard has leapt on to a heap of stones.

Dazzled and laughing, it is there that he witnesses the unusual and marvelous cortege of Amarjit Singh, *en route* for the camp-site in Arlans. And when the last Hindus have passed, and the tumultuous crowd has reformed, he resumes walking with the same light tread, and his face continues laughing, with a gleam of tranquil and ostentatious challenge in his gaze.

3. Cf. La Fontaine XI: 16[42]

"You can call me Monsieur le Baron. I'm a papal baron…anyway, I have the papers. Baron Lemart. My landlady is the most incorrigible bigot in the canton, known and revered as such. Big hotels, boarding houses and villas are very bad when one wants to avoid informers. My old lady is rich and only lodges me. No police register. I was recommended to her by a Comte—a real one—with whom I play bridge in a club in Paris. Don't ever be astonished by what I say. I have a heap of names, professions and social situations. Quiet street, eh? I have a nice room with Jesus above my bed and Our Lady on my dressing-table. At a café, the difference in our dress would be noticed. You're coming to install an electric light on a table where I write at night. That goes with your costume. Promise the old lady politely not to disturb a speck of dust on the curtains or the cornices. Swear that you've respected cobwebs since your tenderest childhood. Come in, my good man."

Having opened a wooden door with a knocker, Lemart lets his companion pass. They go along a corridor with bric-à-brac furniture and faded tapestries ornamented with daguerrotypes, and go up a staircase on which an old lady appears, dressed in a moiré silk dress with jade trimmings, coifed in a frilly aubergine silk bonnet.

Having explained the presence of the workman, Lemart takes him into his room.

"Sit down. I mentioned something more interesting than a bomb. That would be to marry one of the girls and make the A.I.A. a profit of twenty-five million."

"You're mad."

---

[42] Volume XI of La Fontaine's *Fables* only contains nine fables.

"Not often. I weighed you up on the road. You've let yourself lapse into bad manners, and you talk like your smock, but you're better than that. You haven't always been a worker?"

"No."

"What's your name?"

"You amaze me. Détrêt, Bernard Détrêt. I had an education. My father was a printer in the Rue Saint-Maur. He was a local councilor. I've always had ideas of liberty and justice. It's stupid. There are some who let the world turn and don't do anything."

"What use has your education been to you?"

"To torment me more than the next man, because I liked reading and I understood. I should have been able to take over my old man's business. At eighteen I made a fool of myself over a girl. Nothing much—a wristwatch from a pawnshop. The old bandit didn't want to know. Police, threats of prison. My dad heard about it. I cited the old communards…their ideas, their liberty…it didn't go far. As soon as the gendarme passes the door…flat on the belly before the law and property. In brief, it ended with an impulsive decision. I joined the colonial. Literally. I've actually seen mates in narrow defiles, under the pretext of being attacked, cut the throats of negresses and fuck them before they were cold. Then there was the war. New school of law and civilization. Here I am. I don't recoil before good work. Only you're going a bit far."

"Sit down at that table. Here's a pen and paper. I'm going to dictate you a letter to the Comtesse d'Aldezza."

"To the…"

"You know how to spell? If you're stuck on a word, ask me. *Madame...*"

"What's this funny business?"

"You'll understand as you write. If you don't like it, you can tear it up. *Madame...*"

Lemart paces back and forth.

"*I've made a plan to throw a bomb into your magnificent palace. One arrives one night through the Bois d'Arlans. One climbs over the wall and in is inside. Passing along the lakeside, I go as far as the hall. I have what's need to reckon with your dogs. That's the ABC. Although bombs are out of fashion, pyrotechnics*...that's p, y..."

"I know."

"*...has made incessant progress. A flat machine, which can be dissimulated...*"

"Two *l*s?"

"One...*inside a jacket pocket can be powerful enough to cause a catastrophe of the first order.*"

"Is that true?"

"No idea...it ought to be possible. She won't know.... *of the first order...but I've reflected...*"

"Ah! So much the better..."

"*But I've reflected. Rather than be an enemy who will deliver his blow by night in a mask, it is more appropriate for me to act in broad daylight, with my anarchist faith visible to all eyes...!*

"Good! But that leads to what?"

"We're getting there. *Your palace, the enormous dowries of our daughters, those who are soliciting...*"

"What?"

"Soliciting—requesting, inquiring... *Those dowries, fortunate and powerful themselves in this world, by the blind hazard of birth or the execrable iniquity of the social system...everything that is yours, surrounding you and touching you, appears to me as the most flagrant of scandals, the most complete outrage to all the gehennas of this world. To the fight against these outrages I have devoted my life. I am one of those madmen who believe in the salvation of humankind by the destruction of injustice, and first of all by the destruction of those who represent it, enjoy it and eternalize it.* New paragraph. *The bomb...*"

"The bomb?"

"*...with which I have just threatened to confront you is my pretention to attempt, in my turn, the joust of which your daughters are the prizes. The Maharajah lately arrived and* *the others, are fighting with their money, their science, their worldly or industrial status. I shall have for wealth and science two terrifying and indestructible verities: that of human being, entirely naked, and that of justice.*"

"Entirely naked?"

"Symbolically. *Who can tell whether one of your daughters might not be conquered by those sublime verities, whose intercessor I am. Then, I shall doubtless employ the dowry to the ends of liberation, which I shall have made my wife adopt as her own.*"

"A bit bold!"

"*You have proclaimed that the joust is open to all. I await your response in order to present myself at the palace.* Sign it and put your address."

Détrêt puts down the pen violently. "Not that! I don't know what you expect. With a flick of the wrist she'll get the letter to the prosecutor or the commissaire. They'll pick me up like two sous' worth of birdseed."

"After the last sentence, add: *It is permissible, Madame, for you to give my letter to the police. That will be because your challenge to men is not what it appears to be—which is to say, an appeal without restriction, prejudice or dread.* Then sign it legibly and put your address."

"Just a minute. I repeat my question. Why all this? Let's admit that I'm summoned. I won't be capable of pulling it off."

"But yes. You're representing yourself honestly as an anarchist, the roughness of your language is permitted. In the face of those florid potentates, padded and pampered by all the complaisance of destiny, you're the one who has frayed his own path the hard way. What you know you've got from books, from life, from ordeals, like the man of the earliest ages, armed with a spear or a flint, conquering his nourishment against the wild beasts. And what you know, what you've found, they can't make out that they aren't truths. Admitting that they jeer at you a little—behind your back, you know how to make sure that they won't dare do it to your face—it won't be of any importance. You'll still be, in the final analysis, the bearer of those truths, which you've just declared terrible and indestructible."

"Which I've just declared…"

"In any case, we'll remain in daily contact. Every evening you'll report back to me, and I'll arm you for the following day. And when I judge that the moment has come, your place solidly assured, then..."

"What?"

"Then you'll talk to the Comtesse about me, you'll prepare for my entrance on to the stage…"

"We're getting there. I don't understand, but I'm beginning to. What role am I playing in this?"

"We are, indeed, getting there. It's limpid and irresistible. There's no hope, for me any more than for you, or anyone whatsoever, of competing by ordinary means with suitors of the caliber of those who are in the ranks. Are you a boxing champion, a hereditary prince, a factor owner whose name is displayed on every street-corner all over the world? And yet—twenty-five million would be nice to get your hands on, eh? You might well have them. Me too.

"First point: are you, are we, capable of pleasing, of seducing, one of the daughters? Of course. But the thing is to get to them, and, in view of the competition, not in a banal fashion. I've furnished you with an entry: the letter. It distinguishes you. You're no longer the common run of mortals. You arrive there with a personality that's trenchant, even compared with a Maharajah or a Vernail. You're interesting. That's the first point—the first big point.

"The second is to pull it off, as you put it. As for you, I'll take care of that, if you follow my lessons meekly. As for me, once inside, I'll take care of myself. Only it's a matter of getting in, of entering with a label that catches the eye. For two months I've been kicking my heels in Thonon, looking for the pretext. When you're there, when I have you, thanks to me, solidly in place, you'll talk about me to the Contessa. You'll reveal the existence of the A.I.A. to her, and the fact that I'm a top man in it. That thousands of men, ready for anything, united in a mysterious international association, have me for their leader…you'll construct my character, you'll put an aureole upon it...I'll deliver the patter about that occult and formidable power...

"Do you understand now? And, one pushing the other, it's fifty thousand bills that are at the end…with which to play, one day, on equal terms with the Vernails, the Maharajahs, and any of the other vampires who coagulate in their strongboxes the blood and the happiness of men. You've understood…? You've understood? Sign the latter."

4. Small Talk

Sitting carelessly on pink sand as fine as salt, or sprawling in white rattan armchairs with massive contours, the Contessa's guests are nibbling pastries and sipping iced drinks through draws. An ancient oak, one of the splendors of the park, which was once a forest, covers the group formed around Madame d'Aldezza and Samion, Herbert, Inukai Ozaki and little Prince Constantine, with a vast shadow that undulates to the slow rhythm of the foliage. A little to one side, Béron the boxer, a young man with a bright face and the jaw of a carnivore, its chatting with Klutzkil, the Polish painter, whose works, resolutely forsaking any representation of visible forms, arouse the ire of some and excite others at every independent exhibition. Fastened to the boxer's wrist by a steel chain, sleeping at Béron's feet, is the lion cub that the champion, by virtue of one of those caprices that amuse the newspapers, bought from a menagerie at the Neuilly fair. Making an effort to maintain a correct attitude, the boxer yawns behind his hand and, confiding a furious expression to Klutzkil, murmurs: "I'm bored, my dear painter!"

"I can't believe," says Herbert, "that a woman can bring to the study of magic the passionate persistence, the harsh penetration—in sum, the experimental will—of which a man is capable. She would deviate immediately into the mystical, spiritism or theosophy."

Samion is clad in a black velvet dress, only ornamented by a heavy necklace of green amber. Her head, whose chestnut-colored hair is curled into shells over the ears, rests on her bare arm, supported on the arm of the chair. Her knee is swaying gently, allowing a foot shod in a shoe whose green matches the amber of her necklace to protrude outside the dress.

She protests at Herbert's words, citing Gottfried Keller, who made mention of a young Italian noblewoman of the sixteenth century who competed with the alchemist Cornelius Agrippa. She invokes the example of Madame Blavatsky.

"Your magic," says Inukai, "is so far away from our modern sensibility!"

"In form, true," says Herbert. "It has resonances in the most recent metaphysics. That of Bergson often has parallels with it. Several of the latest postulates of biology and physics are anticipated in certain mystical charades of the Kabbalah. And then…what do you mean by modern sensibility? Is it exclusive of eternal problems?"

"To read your avant-garde litterateurs…," advances Constantino.

"Oh, them!" exclaimed Herbert. "They seem to have adopted the mission of repudiating the exaltation that leads to obsession with great problems. But do they have that obsession? The times are so sated with their observation. Emotion, works, have a direct grasp of immediate events and characters. Mind and sensibility model themselves on the innumerable frequency of phenomena, and phenomena alone. The style paints adventures, places and passions as seen from the window of an express train; the phraseology crepitates as if the ink were emerging from a Leyden jar!"

"The same old story!" sniggers Klutzkil.

"If you mix in, I'm lost!" implores Béron, in a low voice. "They're boring me to death and I don't understand a word they're saying. For two pins, I'd clear out. If we weren't on the lookout for the Maharajah I'd have made myself scarce as soon as I saw that today's demoiselle is Samion. Say, Kutzkil, I'm going irritate my wild beast on the sly. I'm going for a walk. Come with me—don't leave me on my own; I'm capable of not coming back."

"Hey! Your beast, Monsieur Béron!" exclaims Constantino, seeing the lion cub stand up and shake itself, growling.

"I ask your permission to take a short walk," says Béron. "This poor animal can't interest himself in your profundities. Keep me company, Monsieur Klutzil?"

As soon as they are some distance away he says: "Oof! I can't stand that Samion. She must feel the same about me too."

"Curious! You like Marden, and she's absolutely Samion, but for the hair..."

"And the manners! And…everything. Samion has chestnut eyes, Marden hazel..."

"You see the colors through your sentiments..."

"But, my dear chap, it's not admissible!"

"It will end up being. All of us—Vernail, Inukai, Stani—are virtually certain that it's fundamentally a matter of wigs, and that they're all one. But which of us is going to say to the Contessa: 'You're making fun of us'?"

"Obviously."

"Besides which, we wouldn't have the last word. She'll reply: 'Prove it.'

"'But Madame, in addition to the…uncanny resemblance of your five daughters, the strongest presumption is the system to which you subject us of only showing us one at a time.'

"'That's a rule of the game,' she'll say—she's perfectly entitled. 'Each of you, confronted by each of them, will soon fix his inclination, and would have no opportunity to manifest himself under several aspects…the facets that testify to the versatility of a man of value...' Vernail would go to Mercerelle, for example, and only to Mercerelle, Béron to Marden and only to Marden..."

"So what? That's what I'm doing."

"Precisely. You're taking a big risk..."

"Don't understand. If she loves me…?"

"It's clever, or even better—I think the idea's marvelous—if that really is the Contessa's goal, it's up to us to measure up to it. The Contessa brings out one of her daughters every day, without our knowing in advance which one it will be. Up to us to clear it up. And the person who'll seduce Marden will appear ridiculous to Samion, I assume…"

"Understood! What if I were to throw in the towel? It's too complicated for me."

"Immediately, that would be incorrect, the Contessa having asked us to witness the arrival of the Maharajah. On the other hand—I'm extrapolating the hypothesis—whoever pleases Mercerelle, and also pleases Gioia, Marden, Samion..."

"Stop! Stop! What connection is there between dear Marden, exuberant and straightforward, and that professor in velvet…?"

"Do as you like, champion! After all, you're a rival."

"You don't like Marden?"

"No, I'd rather go to Gioia. But if Marden, Gioia and the others... Bonjour, Monsieur Vernail, you were the only one lacking."

"Haroun-al-Raschid hasn't arrived yet?"

"No."

The three men head back toward the oak.

"I need to ask Ozaki about the plans for a little airplane," said Vernail. "I'll have it put together and brought here—to Thonon, to be exact—and to avoid the encumbrances of the usual route, I'll risk the grand tour via Annemasse, Taninges and Les Gets. Splendid stroll, anyway. My regards, Madame; Bonjour, Mademoiselle Samion."

He shakes hands and takes out his watch.

"It's half past five. His Highness left shortly before me. I don't think, in view of the traffic jam and the sped of the elephant that he'll get here for another hour. Unless the traffic, astounded by the cortege..."

The galloping hoofbeats of cavalry hammer the air, drawing near. A domestic appears.

"Madame la Comtesse, there's a troop of horse before the Palais. A cavalier dressed all in red with a curved saber in his hand is asking to be received by Madame la Comtesse.

"We're going to have some amusement," said Madame d'Aldezza. "Have him come in."

One of the Maharajah's officers arrives in the pathway on horseback. A few paces away, he dismounts and advances, bridle in hand. He bows profoundly, and in sufficiently fluent French, says that His Highness the Maharajah of Ezrapur, on his way to the Bois d'Arlans, will go past the Palais in a few minutes, and would like to pay his respects to Madame d'Aldezza.

5. A Duel of Carbuncles

In the center of the arc of the circle designed by the officers on the road in front of the wide open gate, the elephants, dromedaries and servants are in compact formation. In the driveway, a short distance from the perron where the guests of the Palais are gathered, the royal elephant is surrounded by Hindus in damask kaftans. Having descended the ebony and ivory stepladder, Amarjit, his arm on Narasa's nape, is moving slowly toward the perron.

"There's only one girl," he murmurs.

A furtive smile on the faces of the two sparkling men. Having reached the perron, the maharajah lets go of Narasa's neck. The prince and his companion bow solemnly before the Contessa.

"To think," Vernail whispers to Inukai, marveling and mocking, "that we were playing poker yesterday evening..."

But Amarjit, after having bowed and introduced Narasa, waits stiffly, his eyes haughtily looking past the human beings who are contemplating him, and whom Madame d'Altezza names as her guests.

"Prince," says the Contessa, "Monsieur Vernail, the great manufacturer, whose renown has doubtless reached your people, and whose engines awaken echoes in your ancient temples as they pass by."

Vernail is about to extend his hand. Amarjit inclines his head and says, gravely: "Unforeseeable destiny, Monsieur Vernail, leads us to our goal more rapidly and more surely than any carriage, even fitted with one of your engines."

Vernail is momentarily astounded by the pompous tone and unexpectedness of the statement. "Highness...Highness," he replies, in a tone no less grave, "that is true. Nevertheless, before the unforeseeable goal, the possessors of my vehicles can, by themselves, attain with ease and promptitude all the visible goals they please. That dispenses a few victories and joys to them, which add some pleasure to the irrevocable itinerary."

The members of the audience smile. The Maharajah has not blinked.

"Monsieur Inukai Ozaki," says the Contessa. "Utilizing a mechanism invented by a member of the Académie des Science, Monsieur..."

"Monsieur Rateau," says Inukai. "It's a kind of turbo-compressor."[43]

"I once knew a Monsieur Rateau," interrupts Amarjit, still impassive. "He had a long white beard and a pink face that many adolescents would have envied. First he wrote articles about the demoiselles of the Conservatoire, and then became a political reporter."

"It can't be the same one," says the Contessa. "The apparatus, placed in an aircraft that is under construction, ought to

[43] Turbines designed by Auguste Rateau (1863-1930) were already in use prior to the Great War, but he continued to produce new models thereafter. He was elected to the Academy in 1919.

permit Monsieur Ozaki, if his research is successful, to climb beyond twenty thousand meters."[44]

"Monsieur," says Amarjit, "the earth shrinks as you climb. Was it not Flaubert who wrote in the *Tentation* the sublime sentence: 'God is magnified by the ascension of thought.' Thought is the only useful aircraft, for the only altitudes that are worth reaching."

"Highness," Inukai replies, "do you mean that thought ought to suffice in itself, searching and finding its impetus within, and the only altitude to which it ought is that at which it will attain God by means of its own contemplation?"

"Yes, Monsieur," says the Maharajah. "And all the rest is impotent pride and deceptive vanity."

"However Highness, I believe I remember that in the *Tentation*, it's the Devil who pronounces that remark that you cited, and at the very moment that he is serving Saint Antoine as an aircraft. Whatever its point of elevation, thought remains static there, considering the same subjects and the same God, if nothing comes to excite, sustain and nourish its flight. A new and more elevated vision of the earth will add to our knowledge of the world. That knowledge is, precisely, the spur, the support and the nourishment of thought, by which means it grows incessantly by multiplying them, its possession and its consciousness of God."

Amarjit caresses his beard silently and turns his gaze, as if expecting a further introduction.

"His Highness Constantino d'Ornania," says the Contessa.

"Prince," says the Maharajah, "you will be a king—but what is the point of inheriting a crown and reigning over a population of men, if one is not first sovereign of oneself and the innumerable population of one's sentiments?"

"Also a Prince," says Stani, his chubby cheeks reddening and his melancholy gaze burning, "I shall not rein. The crown

[44] In our history that altitude was first reached in a fixed-wing aircraft in 1951.

prepared for me by my birth appeared to me both so heavy by virtue of the unmerited powers and privileges that it confers, and such a small thing by comparison with veritable royalty, that I renounced that crown to the profit of my brother Boris, I am only a man, humbly amazed by all that he has to learn, and perpetually full of admiration for the merits of a host of men of common birth."

"I did not know that," says Amarjit, untroubled, turning majestically to Stani's neighbor.

"Monsieur Klutzkil, who, with his brush, claims to be endowing the world with new images and recreating our vision of the universe."

"What's the point?" says the Maharajah. "The universe such as we see it is merely an illusion. Redesigning it under a new aspect will merely add one more illusion. To change the robe of the eternal Maia does not bring us a single inch closer to the essential reality, which is behind all appearances and which alone ought to attract and seduce us."

"Highness," replied Klutzkil, "your eternal Maia is a universe for the usage of prehistoric humans. The flowers, the trees and the people we still see are old and obsolete representations, possible for beings who had no other means of perceiving than their eyes, their nose, their mouth and their fingers, Endowed with the power of creation, painting is not photography. In a time when science, by means of its apparatus, reveals to me a more intimate and more complex constitution of things, the images of the universe that I attempt, while knowing them to be illusory, have the particularity of wanting to be in rapport and in harmony with my perceptions of the humans of these times. The antenna, the airplane, film, railways, the microscope, the telescope, electrolysis…as many new senses with which science enriches me. Your Maia was the imposition of the rudimentary human senses; mine will be the voluntary creation of the imagination, served by more subtle senses."

Amarjit remains indecisive for a moment. Then he makes the huge emerald of his necklace dance between his hands, and turns toward Herbert.

"Seigneur," says Samion, softly, "do you have the intention of continuing to teach us, one after another, a course in ethics?"

The Maharajah's face lights up with a jovial smile. "Indeed no, Mademoiselle. "Forgive me, and only see in that attitude an influence of the décor that I bring with me. In a smoking-jacket, I'm the simplest fellow in the world. Aren't I, Vernail? As for you, Mademoiselle, if you hadn't interrupted me, I would have stopped at you, for all ethics is signified and resolved in the grace of your face. Messieurs," he adds, extending his hands to Béron and Herbert, "you owe to Mademoiselle the avoidance of my apothegms, but I shall be deprived of your ripostes. To judge by those I drew from these messieurs, I have lost flavorsome lessons thereby."

"Monsieur Lesielt," said the Contessa. "Monsieur Béron."

"I watched the match in which you won your title so superbly, Monsieur Béron, and my bravos were not the least sonorous. If it pleases you, during your sojourn, to do a little training, there are two or three giants in my retinue that I'll gladly lend you."

Narasa says a few rapid words in Hindu to the Maharajah. The latter smiles broadly and silently. "Monsieur Béron, my secretary is asking me whether you'll accept his challenge?"

Béron, no less than the other members of the audience, looks in amazement at the young man in the golden turban, whose brocade robe emphasizes his delicacy, and whose amber-tinted neck with a quadruple necklace of sapphires has an altogether feminine finesse.

"We'll talk about it again," says Amarjit. "I hope that I shall have the great honor of welcoming you all to my encampment tomorrow, and also that a few trinkets that ornament it, and which I had brought from Ezrapur, will help you to tolerate the presence of the host."

Dusk is falling. Things are turning gray. The Maharajah seems to be ready to depart.

"Night is falling," says the Comtesse, "and it would not be to the advantage of the magic you have brought us to let shadows blacken the marvelous stones and tarnish the gold of the draperies." To Samion, she says: "Go and ask for all the torrents of our private sunlight."

Samion goes away. She comes back almost immediately. Before she has passed the threshold of the hall, an explosion of electric light springs from the fronton of the Palais, from between the crowns of the trees, from false ivy climbing the trunks and from globes suspended from garlands of foliage running along the pathways. At the dazzling eruption, from the emeralds circling the maharajah's neck to those circling the ankles of the royal elephant and those on its breastplate, from the diamonds of the plumes to the gemstones of the saddlecloths, to the brocade of the kaftans, gleams respond by myriads in scintillations, sheets and cascades.

Admiration holds everyone silent, emotion hastening their respiration.

"There are moments," Herbert murmurs," when it is well worth keeping the image of Maia, Klutzkil!"

"Prince," says Vernail, "what sage sentences and what virtues the eloquence of such dazzlements obtain! If I were a Maharajah, I would leave without dread to such rare sumptuousness the joy of all victories over everything and every man."

"And every woman, Monsieur Vermail?" asks Samion, ironically.

At that moment, passing through the dromedaries, the elephants and the Hindus, a man with a knapsack on his back, and covered with dust, appears at the gate and comes through. He stops for a moment, and contemplates the unusual spectacle, bathed with light himself. Then he advances, arrives at the foot of the perron, and says in a full and joyful voice: "Madame d'Aldezza, I salute you. I am Mirard."

The Contessa goes to him, takes him by the hand and leads him to her guests.

"I was expecting you, Monsieur Mirard. I have had a large and brightly-lit laboratory fitted out for you in a corner of the park. All miracles will be permitted to you there. This is Samion, one of my daughters."

After having bowed and taken the extended hands, Mirard says: "Miracles are rare, Madame, and often without brilliance for a person not rigorously knowledgeable in the pure sciences. A needle or a wire, for instance, which trembles by a millionth of a millimeter in the presence of a radiant body, might perhaps be an immense result for us, almost one of those so-called miracles. Agree, however, that it would not be at all dazzling...but all this is beautiful," he adds, contemplating the cortege. His voice is calm, simple, with a certain discreet malice. "In truth, who among us, in our poor Occident, could compete with such a rain of carbuncles? However, I shall try something..."

He takes off his knapsack slowly and places it on the ground. He unbuckles it, and takes out a few little bottles filled with white powders, which he puts in his pockets, and then a tube of glass thirty centimeters long

"Would it be possible, Madame, to turn down the electric illumination slightly?"

Samion goes to give an order. In the intrigued silence, Mirard, followed mechanically by the gazes of the audience, goes with his tube of glass to one of the nearby trees ornamented with lamps disposed among the ivy. He detaches two bulbs and fixes the two extremities of his tube in the empty sockets.

While he proceeds with this installation, the electricity decreases everywhere, in the lamps of all dimensions. The brilliance of the royal cortege has paled. A rather spacious and particularly somber zone extends around the vicinity of the tree, of which the mysterious tube is the center. Mirard advances into the zone and suddenly, like a geyser, as if an unexpected firework were fulgurating, he becomes flamboyant. From the toes of his hiking boots to his cloth cap, all of his garments, his hands and his face light with adorable gleams, profound radiance, as bright and velvety as those of the purest stained-glass windows under the most ardent sunlight. Streaming with that moving blaze, which jumps, floats and creeps in accordance with his gestures, he takes the little bottles of powder from his pockets. But the salts they contain, white under raw light, have been transmuted into incandescent masses of rubies, sapphires and topazes.

Mirard opens the bottles, takes pinches of powder in his fingertips, and throws them around his surroundings. A tuft of grass begins to shine with a more violent glare than the lord of Ezapur's plume; a flap of Narasa's blue robe suddenly sparkles with a dust of rubies, the trails of which Herbert receives on his sleeves; Samion's arm is constellated with topazes.

Mirard speaks, in his tranquil voice.

"This is a little amusement due to the property of fluorescence that certain substances have. That tube, in which the current I have caused to pass through it encounters the vapors of rare earths, is a mechanism of my manufacture, akin to the screen known as Wood's glass,[45] which has the property of only letting the ultra-violet part of the spectrum pass through—which is to say that, by absorbing all the surrounding visible light, it only allows the ambient bodies to be struck by ultra-violet light, which is a radiation invisible to our eyes."

He interrupts himself. "Highness, give me your hand, open..."

He drops a small heap of one of the powders into the palm.

---

[45] "Wood's glass," a barium-sodium-silicate glass incorporating nickel oxide, invented in 1903 by the American physicist Robert William Wood (1868-1955), blocks most of the visible part of the light spectrum, but is transparent to infra-red and ultra-violet wavelengths.

"...And permit me to add that tiny emerald mountain to the jewels with which the profigal Orient has covered you."

In the Maharajah's hand, a rutilant green aggregate scintillates, the fires of which divide into threads, grains and steams of emeralds as the hand moves.

"Fluorescence," Mirard continues, "is the property that certain bodies have of emanating a visible light particular to them as they receive invisible infra-red or ultra-violet rays. I shall take the opportunity another time to tell you, if it amuses you, how that property, due to atomic perturbations, allows us to glimpse the secret of the very structure of the universe. As for these powders, the one that changes into sapphires is osculine, obtained from the honest horse-chestnut; the one that causes topazes to flourish is uranine... They're petty powders. In the laboratory that you have offered me, Madame, I think I shall be able to find others that will permit me even rarer games."

He emerges from the shadow zone. Everyone returns to the perron.

"That's shown him—the Rajah," murmurs Béron to Klutzkil. "You've all possessed him properly. It only remains for me to administer a knockout punch to his young man."

III

1. A Man Among Men

Peignoir of lilac cretonne, white hair drawn into two thin bangs whose ends flutter over the shoulder-blades, the old lady, after knocking gently without having received any reply, carefully places the tray containing the chocolate on the side-table, goes to open the shutters, and sees Lemart sitting on the bed, finishing telling a rosary. She moves the bowl and the bread and butter, and approaches the small beside table, muffling her movements and her footfalls.

"Bonjour, my dear Madame," says Lemart, after having placed the rosary underneath his bolster.

"Bonjour, my dear Monsieur Lemart. Did you have a good journey?"

"Yes, thank you. Would you like to take that little white box from the mantelpiece? It's for you."

"You're too kind. Truly, may I open it? Oh, my Lord, Monsieur Lemaet!"

She takes out of the decorated cardboard box a missal bound in ivory with gold inlay.

"Shortly before catching my train yesterday, as I was passing the Rue Saint-Sulpice, I had the pleasure of thinking of you."

"I'm sure that you disturbed your occupations deliberately…you shouldn't have…how happy I am, Monsieur Lemart!"

"Has anyone called for me?"

"There's a gentleman in the dining room who has been waiting for half an hour for you to wake up."

"Did he tell you his name?"

"Monsieur Détrêt."

"Would you ask him to come up?"

She goes out. Lemart rubs his eyes, picks up his round spectacles from the little table and fits them to his nose. His eyes blink momentarily, and then his gaze becomes steady. Détrêt comes in.

"Bonjour, Monsieur le Baron."

"Bonjout, Détrêt."

The old lady leaves them.

"What's happened, Baron?"

"I have what I wanted. The wait in Thonon had dried me out, as I told you. Your clothes, your viaticum, the game that we're going to play…it was necessary to get the money together. We won't have any shortage for a while. You?"

"Me…not bad. I had to make my own way. You're a joker. You were supposed to advise me every day, but the very day I go out there, you hop it."

"You've been received at the d'Aldezzas?"

"Every day since since you went to see your bankers five days ago."

"My strategy is excellent. I waited before going, to see whether you received a response. You got one. It became serious; we needed money. So I kitted you out and hup! A good dog thrown into the water doesn't need to be a master swimmer."

"If you like. Result: I feel that I'm in a bizarre state, all my ideas coming apart."

"Because of the Palais?"

"Because of the people I've seen there."

"Start at the beginning."

"So, I was dressed for the part, like a man who works with his hands but can make himself neat when necessary. Auto. Thirty-five bullets, sixty both ways. The Palais: gold, marble, furniture genre Maple, Poiret, in sum, all there is of the most eccentric. The drawing room…oh, my poor friend! The slightest trinket in there represents enough for a worker's family to live on for ten years. 'Monsieur is expected,' says the flunkey.

"Between ourselves, I was direly troubled. The Comtesse arrives. Silk dress, beautiful hair, still blonde, frank face. She holds out her hand in a comradely fashion. 'Sit down.' Not at all intimidated by the fake threat that was in your letter. 'You did well to write to me. You were missing from our collection. At least…are you a true anarchist?'

"Might as well make the point immediately. I explain that I'm part of the A.I.A.—the international anarchist association. 'Anarchists have an association, then?' she remarks. She doesn't insist.

"Until then everything was going smoothly. At that moment, a young woman comes into the drawing room. 'Is this Monsieur the Anarchist? Bonjour Monsieur!'

"'May I introduce Marden,' says the Comtesse. Oh, Baron...!"

"What?"

"A gaze! Which goes through you, right behind the forehead…a kind of red blouse over a pair of breasts pointed to burst the silk..."

"Aha!" says Lemart, calmly, with a brief flutter of the eyelids.

"A grip like a fellow's hand and a skin…in my hand...like spoonful of strawberries on the tongue. A slut, with her rouge, her tits, her blazing eyes, which would be something to see at the head of a fine mob! But I tell you this…do I still want the Big Dance?"

"What?"

"I tell you that I'm a little up the creek without a paddle."

"Amorous?"

"Worse! I'm getting there. She sits down, crosses her knees…legs! In stockings the color of a cockchafer and fawn boots up to the calf with tops you could cut your finger on...

"'And toward what is your anarchism directed, Monsieur Décrêt?" she asks me.

"'What do you mean, toward what?'

"'What is your goal?'

"'But Mademoiselle, to remake the world…'

"She doesn't let me finish. 'Remake the world? You'll fit in very well here. Every one of us is pursuing the same goal.

Come. I'll introduce you to your rivals. We were waiting for you.'

"Now we're in the park. She takes me to a fellow who's holding a horse, as pretty as anything, not big, black, strutting like a cockerel. The fellow turns round. It's the Maharajah, in a jacket like you or me. No more of the other day's carnival.

"'Monsieur Décrêt, anarchist. His Highness Amarjit, Maharajah.'

"He holds out his hand. 'Delighted, Monsieur. You must give me recipes for plaguing the English…'"

"Get a move on."

"All right, I'll pass over the details. This is the gist of what I've seen and learned during my five days: all my theories smashed to pulp."

"Because?"

"Because I've been with men with no resemblance to what I've always believed. Strapping fellows, real men. Liberated. Not one disturbed by my quality of anarchist. On the contrary. I'm a little boy compared with them."

Lemart pats the coverlet of his bed.

"Not good, that. Explain."

"Note that I'm not disputing how they arrived at their situation. One can't away from that. Inequality of birth, luck, nerve, brigandage…I admit that. I'm talking about them as they revealed themselves before me. I repeat: they're men. The demoiselle of the first day was telling the truth. All of them have the same goal that we do: to remake the world. But instead of doing so with hatred of society and by destruction, it's by utilizing the world such as it is, and making it better by means of new constructions."

"I've already read that in the announcement of the distribution of prizes. They're going a little quickly."

"Possible. Vernail said to me: 'Personally, I'm working to make a broadly open world, a humanity sufficiently mobile to interconnect, freely to escape the ignorance of the village, suburbs and frontiers. I shall arrive at manufacturing vehicles so powerful, in such numbers, at prices so affordable, that thanks to them, on the numerous roads they will oblige governments to create, the relationships and exchanges of peoples…'"

"Wonderful! And did he also say that they would change human rapacity and filthiness?"

"I was capable of making that retort to him on my own, as to the Japanese Ozaki. The latter said to me: 'Risk one's life to throw a bomb? I'd rather risk mine climbing so far above the earth that I'll be able to bring back to human beings, I come down again, inconceivable velocities in new spaces.'"

"Same tall tales. What do you expect..."

"There's more. Alongside Vernail and Ozaki there's Mirard. He said: 'With highways open on the earth and in the sky, it will be necessary to change the moral condition of peoples and individuals. In my laboratory, I approach and track the natural laws from which one can extract a more exact conception of the universe, and hence more intelligent and harmonious theories of life...'"

"As if the discoveries of scientists could influence in any way the old passions and the venom of the human beast. Have Curie and the wireless diminished rapes of young women, the clientele of claques or suicides at Monte Carlo?"

"Wait. There's also a painter out there, Klutzkil..."

"As you wish!"

"Always joking. He claims to be preparing images of beauty for humans for the pleasures of which they will be capable thanks to Vernail and Ozaki's new routes and Mirard's laws."

Lemart smiles compassionately. "I'm waiting for the Maharajah."

"Exactly. He says that such noble examples have opened his eyes since he's been at the Palais, and that while the others accomplish their tasks, he wants to work on rousing the whole of India to make it a young republic, which will offer the world a land of joy under the most beautiful sun and in the most prodigious nature."

"Bloody fool!"

"The Maharajah?"

"You!"

"Thanks."

"Have you had the idea of looking at them from the right angle, while they spin webs from above to catch the daughters, and soften the brain in order to reach a higher octave than one another, the high C of the great air of the ideal? Translation: delight, at all costs. You've only been an opportunity, a pretext for ritornellos. Blessed bread! The marriages made, the daughters in the bed, the money in the bank, they'll take a closer look at the costs and returns of cars, pleasures in painting and twenty thousand leagues in the sky!

"Of all those at the d'Aldezzas' there isn't one who isn't pursuing the most egoistically interested goal. I understand that the demoiselles are desirable…of course!...who are trying not to offer themselves as ready-made whores served in silk, bodies petrified and embalmed by luxury, perfumes, rare cuisine and aristocratic sports! Let's pass on. The serious matter is the money. Good for the painter; colors and frames are costly. Good for the scientist…the poverty of laboratories! Good for the aviator! As for Vernail, the Mahamachinist, that's something else. Vernail, rolling in money, has no need of the dowry…but one only has to consider for a moment what the man is.

"You presume that he must blush with modesty when the newspapers call him the Napoléon of the motor, at fifty francs a line. And all that drum-beating...his luminous advertisements on the clouds! From the horn of plenty to which two true princes, an illustrious scientist, an artist, an impudent aviator and others of the same caliber have come, Vernail is drawing glorification! Talk about publicity! The entire world is interested in the story. A sentimental triumph coming to crown his other triumphs! Not bad, for the name, for the firm.

"There remains the Indian. And the pride! People like him who live in luxury can't have any ambitions left but the satisfactions of pride. All their claptrap, my poor friend, is fireworks! The belly, the check-book, the vanity—that's what it's necessary to see, to hear, and instead of listen to them like a plate of noodles, cry out to them: 'You don't give a damn about remaking the world, you bunch of bluffers! What you want is to sink your teeth into the cheese or get yourself out a difficult situation!'"

"Have you finished?"

"You're not convinced?"

"You've forgotten two of them: a young man and Stani, the other highness. The one named Leciel or Leciette—a child of the rich, that's understood—began by asking me what powder I was going to use to make a bomb that could fit into a jacket pocket and could demolish a palace like the one we were in."

"A trifle indiscreet!"

"I replied that I'd explain it to him when we knew one another a little better."

"Not bad."

"And to do what?" I added, laughing a little. "'One never knows what might happen,' he said. 'If one had to deal with too many men of your kind one day, one could use it to get rid of them wholesale...'

"'Don't understand.'

"'You're only at the primitive stage of the idea. Fellows like you, too elementary, spoil things by deflecting minds away from the only fecund means of obtaining the veritable anarchy. I know a bomb much more efficacious than yours, but much more difficult to compose. It takes up much less room than one that can be hidden in a pocket. It lodges in a tiny corner of the brain. It's the will.'"

"What!"

"He took me by the arm and took me for a stroll in the park. Then he started calling me *tu* right away. Yes, you're going to say again that I'm a plate of noodles, Baron. I'd have liked you to be there. 'You want to remake the world? Have you tried, to begin with, to remake yourself? Under what massive daylight do you know it, that world? Doubtless under the same leaden daylight beneath which you go yourself. Have you tested a few of your bombs on some of the scourges within you: the acceptance of ready-made ideas, including that of anarchism; idleness before the problems of being, those of instinct, the passions, the mind?'

"'Haven't had the means,' I said. 'You can talk—the son of a paymaster general.'

"Of course. And he replied..."

"'Nothing to do with it. It requires the expense of thirty books and the rest is meditation and the desire for experience.'

"I tried to mock. 'What has that given you?'

"'Precisely what you're looking for: the destruction of the world and its recreation.'

"'That's a bit strong! Necessary to explain. No more capitalists, no more prisons, hovel, hospitals...'

"'Yes, but that's of no importance. That's happening in another world, on another planet, which you no longer inhabit.'

"He laid it out plainly. He told me that he had repassed internally through all the stages of humanity, in order to arrive at living on his new planet; that he had liberated within him the instincts and the passions, had provoked them, to see them act from the height of his consciousness, that he'd toyed at his whim with hunger, fatigue, dolor, his senses, his heart..."

"You bought it?"

"He said to me: 'Do you have a pin?' I had one. 'Does it prick?' I went: 'Ow!'—he'd stuck it in the back of his hand. 'Put it in me anywhere you like.' I stick it in his cheek—a long way. He didn't blink. It bled, though. And after that, he looked me in the eyes in such a funny way that I felt ill at ease."

"Good. I see. We'll look at that one more closely. And the prince?"

"Oh, the prince... This is for you to understand why I've been turned upside down since I've been out there. If you've seen more accurately then me for the others, there's still two to whom your arguments don't stick. The prince? A lamb, a child, who said to me: 'Like you, I too am seeking a world where there will be justice and true happiness, a happiness that will not be made for some with so many tears of the others. That world doesn't exist, and it's necessary to make it. I'm ashamed of my fortune. I'd like to employ it to create a corner on the earth where one could attempt a sketch of such a world. If my dream seduces one of the d'Aldezzas, we'll leave, she and I, to realize an island of peace.' What would you have said to that prince, who held my hands and called me Brother?"

"I wouldn't have said anything at all." Lemart leaps from the bed. "I'm going to get dressed. You're not embarrassing me. I think we're going to have to play a tight game out there. We shall. Will you soon be in a position to get me in?"

"They're sympathetic toward me. I'll begin to talk about you whenever you wish. Look out!"

In picking up a garment, Lemart has allowed a thick wad of banknotes to fall from an inside pocket on to the carpet.

"I told you that my trip to my bankers was rewarding," says Lemart, calmly picking up the wad and going to a cupboard. "We'll be comfortable now, for a while."

He places the packet of cash behind a stack of linen.

"With regard to banknotes, a good story. While you were in Paris, Vernail was burgled."

"In Suresnes?"

"Here. His replenished wallet. Three nights ago. A hotel rat at the Splendid."

"No!"

"You didn't read the papers during your trip?"

"Didn't have time."

The ace, the king of rats, Damore, Zamore…arrived at the hotel under the name of the Marquis de Bera...Berna…that's not important. Slipped away early in the morning. No trace. Uproar by Vernail, who shook up the devil and his retinue from Thonon to Paris. Wireless to his good friend the Prefect. They've sent an inspector, another ace, in his genre, it seems. Levêque, Dolbêque…I don't have a memory for names."

"Delvêque."

"Why are you laughing?"

"A memory. Was there much in the wallet?"

"Twenty thousand, Vernail told us."

"A packet of cigarettes. He'll have others sent. Let's get back to interesting matters. Tell me a little about the demoiselles d'Aldezza."

"Yes. What's that?"

He has spotted a singular object in Lemart's hands: a fleecy tuft of black hairs that Lemart has taken out of one of his pockets and which he compresses between his fingers as he goes to the cupboard.

"Nothing. A beard. I use it sometimes when traveling. Tell me about the demoiselles..."

2. Boxing

Vernail and Klutzkil are walking along the edge of the lake, heading for the Arlans camp-site.

"Aren't they wicked?" says Vernail. "Their games surpass coquetry. I'll bet you four sous that it won't be Marden who watches the fight. It is, however, made for her more than for any of the others, who don't give a damn about it. Secondly, she knows that it would give Béron great pleasure to triumph in front of her. But does she feel anything whatsoever for Béron? And toward which of us is any of the other four leaning? Do you have any clue, yourself? I thought for a moment that Mercerelle had a fancy for the factory owner, the fellow with the stomach...but the demoiselle needs her sisters to admire me too. Very convenient! Each one is ingenious in mocking whatever the others admire. I'm looking out for the day when Marden will ask Mirard to use a skipping rope. Samion has already interviewed Béron on the subject of Averroes. A jolly mess. Instead to taking each of us for our superiorities...what do they hope to get from that salmagundi of qualities? My head's spinning. I'm no further forward than on day one. Yes, as an artist, you have the illusion. You'll tell me that Gioia...so much the better, my lad. Doesn't alter the fact that there are times when I'm sorely tempted to chuck it in."

"No further forward than you. Like you, tempted ten times a day to leave, for the same reasons as you. For the same reason as you, I stay."

"What?"

"The only serious one, the only one that can hold us, no cleverer than the comrades."

"Pinched, you too?"

"And exasperated to be. A smile from that admirable mouth, and there I am, lassoed, capable of making smiles with the other four until the moment I see her again, striving to rediscover Gioia in her sisters..."

"I know! She appears, you go to her…she speaks... Pffft!"

"We're like four-year-old children. From the very first day I'd have put my hand in the fire to swear that there's only one of them..."

"Of course!"

"And you still think so?"

"The hussies!"

"Between the two of us, have you already, a little closer…?"

"Mercerelle, Mercerelle! I took her to a regional fête…gaiety, projects, confidence…a raspberry wood on the roadside, on the way back. We stop. We go into the trees. After a quarter of an hour..."

"Did you have the leisure to look at her?"

A memory mists Vernail's eyes. "Yes."

"And the next day, under different hair, did you see the same Mercerelle?"

"The same."

"You held out your hands to her, still slightly tremulous?"

"Yes."

"It's really her."

"Really her."

"The same eyes, the same suntan on the nape of the neck, which was so abandoned yesterday. 'What is it?' she says. 'I'm Vénersise…or Samion…or Marden...' It's not true, your fibers cry. And yet it is true, your ears affirm…and your intelligence, even though it's lucid. It's really someone else: attitudes, sentiments, judgments..."

"I wasn't born yesterday. I've rolled and played hard. I've had to put on a lot of characters adapted to events. But there's always the fundamental character that subsists."

"If there's only one of them, she's…five!"

"No means of separating them!"

"I've thought of one…not cheap psychology…externally. Embracing Gioia, marking her, biting her…one would be able to see the next day..."

"Unrealizable boorishness."

"Unrealizable."

A silence.

"I've had thoughts of that sort…," said Vernail.

Not far away, through the trees terminating the park, are the pines of Arlans and the multicolored tents of the camp-site.

"Amarjit has submitted to the rules like the rest. One daughter at a time."

"But he's paying court indistinctly to all of them."

"I believe that he doesn't displease Gioia, my friend," says Vernail.

"That's quite possible. But I've seen Mercerelle listening to him with a singular interest."

"Eh? What do you expect me to do about it!" Vernail gets carried away. "Fair play!"

They look at one another, smile, and then shake their heads.

Beyond the limits of the park, in the pines, another two men are walking, also heading for the camp-site.

"I don't trust that one," says Vernail. "Lisielt, who isn't paying court to anyone. Too calm. Still waters. What fish swim there? As for the other, the newcomer..."

"Dangerous, that Baron of the Anarchist Pope? A trifle feuilletonesque. Do you believe in the A.I.A.?"

"In its existence, perhaps. In its action, no. Interests are too entangled, since the war, the social magma too complex."

The four men come together.

"Your prognostics, Messieurs?" says Lemart. "It seems that the first flick in round one...but Monsieur Lesielt claims..."

"Have you observed Narasa's eyes?" Herbert asks.

They pass the first tents. They reach a clearing and find Amarjit and a few officers sitting on brocade cushions nibbling Asian confectionery, with the Contessa and Mercerelle, her smooth black hair drawn back toward the nape, clad in a white dress striped with Rumanian embroideries, Détrêt and Stani. Béron, draped in an ample gray grown is smoking a cigarette and chatting to the Ornanian.

"And above all, no snaps! Suppose one of them got around—people would laugh. Béron in a fighting stance facing that demoiselle..."

Enveloped in a mantle of green silk, decorated with silver lamé and fastened at the hip by an amethyst brooch, Narasa, wearing a small green turban, is sitting to one side on a cushion, his legs folded beneath him, sheathed in trousers of the same silk as the mantle and tightened at the ankle by silver rings. Immobile and grave, he seems to be meditating, his gaze fixed.

"The world's isn't so wicked," says Stani. "People would see right away that it was an amusing photograph, a Béron on vacation."

"The world is very wicked—ours is, at any rate."

"You're crotchety."

"A little. This match is ridiculous. I accepted it out of politeness."

"And Marden isn't even here!" says Klutzkil.

"Who asked me to do it!"

"We were only waiting for you, Messieurs," says Amarjit. "Ozaki and Monsieur Mirard have sent their apologies. Their labors are absorbing them... Béron? Narasa?"

Two Hindus appear, carrying boxing gloves. As one of them approaches Narasa, the latter emerges from this dream and says a few words to him.

"Narasa would like to fight with bare fists," says Amarjit. "Do you accept, Béron?"

The champion smiles broadly. "Not important, Highness. I don't think Monsieur Narasa will do me any great harm. It's up to him. It's scarcely probable that he'll lay a hand on me."

"As for you..."

"It would be prudent, for the sake of his delicate anatomy, for me to be gloved." He extends his wrists to the Hindu. Meanwhile, Narasa stands up, unfastens the mantle, lets it fall, and advances into the grassy space.

"You're not afraid to allow that lovely individual to be hit?" the Contessa asks Amarjit.

Amarjit smiles.

Barefoot, his torso naked above the fluid silk dressing his legs, Narasa exposes his hybrid slenderness. The breast is that of a man, smooth, with two coral dots set against the amber-tinted mat skin; the soft parabola of the waist, the pulpy sinuosities of the flesh of the hips at every movement, are girlish; so are the fragile neck, with is nonchalant inflexions, and the slender feet, whose opaline toenails gleam through the lattice-work of the grass. His visage strangely calm, Narasa looks at all the members of the audience in turn, his green eyes shining with the hard, cold glitter of jade.

Béron waits for him, naked in his evident Occidental nudity, graceful and massive at the same time, only girdled by white shorts, his feet in leather boots that surpass the padding of his socks.

Scarcely are the combatants face to face, ready for the task, than the members of the audience see the Hindu's thin arm extend and the first strike the champion in the middle of his chest. Béron, surprised, steps back—but very rapidly, mocking again and smiling, he advances toward Narasa. His leather stumps strike, but only encounter empty air. Meanwhile, a further blow lands in his face. He laughs and become excited, covers his chest and his face with the coming and going of one folded arm, while the other, describing fulgurant ellipses, tries to punish the oriental.

Narasa's fists seem a host, flying, cutting through the air in a hundred places, striking Béron on the face, the shoulders and the epigastrum, forcing him to break away, breathless more with amazement than defeat.

Amarjit has risen to his feet, his face broad with laughter; his officers, their black beards quivering with joviality, look at the audience.

Herbert has approached Stani. "Take a picture, quickly!"

"Béron doesn't want…," Stani ventures.

"Béron will bless you, I swear!"

Docile to this imperative affirmation, Stani aims his Kodak.

Then Herbert goes to Mercerelle, who has also risen to her feet, her face amused, with a grave gleam in the gaze that does not accord well with that gaiety.

"Give me your hand, Mercerelle," Herbert murmurs. "Close your eyes for a moment, suspend all thought within you, all image of that combat, and listen to me..."

He speaks rapidly, articulating every word rigorously. "You know the adventure of the European in India…the levitation of a fakir in the middle of a crowd of spectators... Everyone, including the European, saw the man rise up vertically above the ground, remain in mid-air momentarily, and slowly descend again. Everyone was certain of the miracle. The European had taken a photograph. On developing the photograph, the traveler observed that the fakir had not moved. Squeeze my hand hard, and look again."

"Is it possible?" murmurs Mercerelle, her entire body shaken by a laugh that made Herbert's hand dance in hers.

Is it possible? She now sees a burlesque Béron fighting against an imaginary assault; Narasa, his legs folded, is sitting on his heels, his hands clutching his feet, and he has the same fixed gaze that he had a little while ago, turned toward an indeterminate point in space.

Meanwhile, Béron totters. But Mercerelle can no longer see the combat; she only has eyes for the motionless magician with the amber flesh.

Suddenly, Béron collapses.

Applause rings out, mingled with a rumor of amazement and commiseration. Mercerelle and Herbert sees Narasa stand up, placidly.

"Would you like me to challenge the Hindu in my turn?" Herbert asks. "I believe I know how to drop him without difficulty. It would only require one punch…but not against a mirage, this time!"

Mercerelle turns her head toward him, sharply. "No, I beg you..."

"Why not?" asks Herbert, astonished.

A fugitive blush stains Mercerelle's cheeks. "It wouldn't give me pleasure..."

3. Swimming

"Hoo!"

Amarjit, Narasa and Gioia arrive at the gallop of three small black horses, having gone through the gate and about to pass over the lawns. At Narasa's cry, the animals stop dead. Gioia, rather rudely projected toward the neck by the abruptness of the halt, straightens up briskly and leaps to the ground, but Amarjit is already before her and the trajectory of the young woman's arm ends in the Maharajah's hand.

"A little more surprise than Marden…," says Amarjit.

"I didn't think that, being so fast, Jahal would be so docile."

"Only to Narasa's command."

Domestics have come to take the horses. Amarjit and Narasa hand them their riding crops, Along with hers, Gioia gives them her jacket and felt hat. She is dressed in gray culottes, her legs gartered by leggings, with a chemisette of white silk tightened at the waist by a broad deerskin belt. Against the gilded flesh of her throat and the ivory sheen of her blouse, the beads of an opal necklace tell their changing gleams.

"Are the messieurs here?" she asks.

"Yes, Mademoiselle."

Gioia and her companions go around the building toward the lake. All the guests of the Palais have arrived, except for Béron, Détrêt and Stani, who have deserted.

Stani's pictures, which proved to the champion that the encounter was indisputably outside the rules, and that he had been knocked out by a fakir, had completed the boxer's disillusionment. It was one motive more for him to renounce an overly complex enterprise, in which he had only engaged in believing, summarily, in his glory and the opinion that the newspapers, the crowds in the stadia and innumerable easy lays had given him of himself.

Stani, after the match in the clearing, had decided that the Contessa's commensals were too strong for him, endowed with prestiges too rare for him to attempt to compete. Doubtless Vénerise was moved by the honesty of his soul, and his humanitarian dream, but also saw, he realized, that he was too candid, too childishly dazzled. He had gone, taking Détrêt, who had also become anxious and timid, with him; and the anarchist and the prince, like two children in a novel by Boussenard making a tour of the geographical world,[46] had gone to explore the human atlas and steep themselves in the verities of the species.

Amarjit had presented the Contessinas with a boat modeled on the excursion boats of the Palace of Ezrapur. For several evenings they had been meeting at the lake at tea time,

[46] Louis Boussenard, a prolific writer of Vernian romances, published *Le tour du monde d'un gamin de Paris* [A Parisian street-urchin goes around the world] in 1880, and subsequently added half a dozen sequels.

assembling on the vessel with the light, sinuous roof reminiscent of the roof of a pagoda, the hull plated with ivory and gold metalwork, and carpets passing over the edge trailing their silk in the russet water.

Anyone who wished took the oars, and someone else the tiller, or the vessel floated gently at the whim of the nonchalant water. Around the low tables laden with pastries, beverages and rare cigarettes, and the piles of cushions propitious to sumptuous repose, there was the voluptuous quietude of the body that releases the slightest resources of the mind.

There, everyone takes pleasure in shining.

Vernail, Mirard, Ozaki and Klutzkil arrive there, still feverish with the numerous thoughts of the day's work. Every exaltation momentarily gained in labor is immediately framed within the general gaiety and effervescence, adding another jewel to the subtle crown with which such a generous assembly ornaments the hour. The order and the singularity of the guests, and the sum of the powers and the talents that each of them represents, generate the most luxurious diversity of discussion.

Furthermore the presence of one of the Contessinas unleashes in each of them a vivacity of sentiments that stimulates his faculties. Each of them, in spite of the material evidence to which his reason must be submissive—the brutal difference of hair color, styles of dress and those, more subtle, of attitudes and mannerisms—suspects in his heart that the present young woman is uniquely the one that she says she is, sensing confusedly that she is perhaps also, beneath the artifice of appearances, one of the other four, or even all four of them. The memory immediately awakens of affinities and antagonisms, which, at other moments have declared themselves between him and the one that is here today and is perhaps also the one who was here yesterday, giving birth to a need for revenge against the deceiver at the same time as the hope of assuring his advantages over the elect.

The strange uncertainty that is troubling all the suitors' nerves obliges them to multiply their personality, to force them perpetually to overreach their specific eminence, apt to lose all glamour next to the one, or ones, whose character seems most distinct from theirs. Thus, Vernail and Ozaki, whom art leaves indifferent, are constrained to play a role in the esthetic controversies raised by Klutzkil, and the latter is obliged to carve out some prestige through the figures and gestures of Vernail, in which, torrentially, steel is founded, roads are opened and the factories and banks of five continents swarm. Meanwhile, Mirard throws into the party the treasures, the games, the burning and moving perspectives of science, in which the description of an atom imposes cosmogonic obsessions on thought.

To the estimates of all the jousters, in an atmosphere to singularly entangled, the interlacements of amorous vanity, science, art and technology design the most unexpected arabesques, sometimes composing, in a sort of grandiose panorama, an unreal and transcendent depiction of the world. Amarjit, abdicating the fatalistic morality of his race, enthusiastically claims his part of the demiurge, colors the possibilities raised with all the splendors of his heavens, and causes to stream therein all the perfumes and all the gems of the Thousand-and-One Nights.

Even Lemart does not hesitate to barter his violent restauration of the planet against the ideal upheaval that the marvelous effigy causes to sparkle.

"And who could measure," he says, "the effects of the irresistible power of action of the men who are here, having consented to a recasting of the world, enormous as the goal might seem and—after so many others!—so utopian. A single and imperious will to attain runs behind all our various activities! A will extending all the way to the limit of the real…only taking into account the tirades with which you once overturned dear Décrêt..."

"Tirades?" says Vernail. "What do you mean?"

"The day when he repeated to me the proud responses with which you had greeted his quality as an anarchist... The world refounded thanks to highways opened on the ground and in the sky, by you, Vernail, and you, Ozaki; morality recreated by your discoveries, Mirard; the images of a new Pleasure designed by Klutzkil..."

"I remember," says Mirard. "You're right. All that, in combination, formed a rather eloquent program..."

"Why not admit it? So eloquent that it appeared to me then to be pure verbalism. I thought that it was, as good people say, too beautiful to be honest."

"Eh! What does that mean?" says Vernail.

"What? That it was truly too idealistic, disinterested. To look squarely at the reality, your situation, your magnificence efforts are the consequence of both your temperament and your faculties, of an ensemble of successes, acquired speeds, but also—let's face it!—of your desire for grandeur or enjoyment…in brief, and principally, of a will, conscious or not, to self-aggrandizement..."

"Not at all!" interrupted Klutzkil, imperiously. "The truth of men like us, behind contingencies, is all effusion, the overflow of love, not the aggrandizement but the streaming of the personality, an irreducible need to give of oneself, to radiate what we believe, rightly or wrongly, to be our sun, our genius. Glory, money, pleasure, all of what you imply by aggrandizement, even health, is surplus...the moons of the solar sytem turn around it or don't, or don't even exist…the sun doesn't care. It exists, it burns; that is its law, its irreducible fatality, as I said."

"Good, good," says Lemart. "In any case, let's get back to saying that each of you, streaming his sun…whether to warm himself or to warm the universe, know that, in expressing the noble designs that Détrêt reported back to me, they included a fraction of mirage, of exaggeration..."

"Which is to say," Vernail cuts in, "that between our powers, whatever they may be, our sincere desires and changing the world there's the enormous entanglement of the real…and there is, damn it…

"No, Vernail!" exclaims Klutzkil. "To all that you can say, no matter how sage or well-founded, I have something to oppose that will sweep away your reasons and your sagacity, just as, in moments of faith, a simple frown of the Spirit sends the Letter to all the devils. Our grandiloquence on the day when Décrêt…I admit that it was verbalism, as Lemart says? What was it, fundamentally? A temporary overexcitement? Certainly. A desire to dazzle the anarchist? Agreed. But what more? The milieu, the atmosphere, one of the Contessinas, who was listening to us, judging us, perhaps admiring us…yes indeed! Those thoughts that we had, would we even have brought them forth without her exciting, creative presence? It's that presence that inspired them, and which obliges the words that it engendered to return to us, heavy with all their possibility."

"Well, so what?" says Vernail, rudely

"Well," continues Klutzkil, with the same vehemence. "Don't you see that all the parts of the miracle were born of that feminine influence? The miracle of our coming together, which permitted, by juxtaposing our riches, the discovery of the elements of a creation, so beautiful that that apostle of bombs was ready to give up his saltpeter in order to ally himself with us, the forces of love and construction! The miracle of our coming together and the paroxysm in which we're incessantly held by the presence of one of the Contessinas... With the result that our declamations, with which Lemart is lashing us today, take on a meaning here, where an appeal to amour resuscitated the mythological epics, as real, as solemn and as vital as that of the words that Jason had to pronounce in summoning the fifty companions of the *Argo*.

"Pardon me," says Herbert, abruptly. "If there's a miracle, it will be in our actions. For the moment, it's the eloquence that's continuing, and that overexcitement you mentioned. Personally, I'm asking myself more coldly whether it isn't bringing us all down to the same level, and the strange creation that's being envisaged here, being made, as Klutzkil says, depends..."

He interrupted himself. Gioia was listening to him with a little smile at the corners of her lips, as if prepared for some attack, doubtless accustomed to the young man's hostility.

Having hesitated momentarily and seen that smile. Herbert resumes: "All of you, Gioia, Samion, Marden…all of you…are so subtle, intelligent and liberated from ordinary rituals, even those of gallantry, even those of amour, that you doubtless put grandeur in itself above no matter what good deed willed and decided by anything other than its own beauty. The conquest of the Golden Fleece was a goal sufficient for Jason and his companions in adventure. It was a bonus that the hero encountered Medea."

"Let's grant that," says Gioia, amiable. "So?"

"Permit me…," says Klutzkil.

Gioia has nonchalantly unfastened her opal necklace and has started toying with the beads; then, while Herbert was talking, she has allowed it to snake over the floral pattern of the carpet overhanging the edge of the boat.

"No," says Herbert, "I won't permit. You've said, Klutzkil, that genius is a sun, whose only law is that of existing and burning. Whoever has received that prerogative, the heaviest and most splendid of treasures, doesn't have the right, or the power, to reduce it to the seduction of a woman, even one as exquisite as the Aldezzas. Whoever is the custodian of that holy Ark doesn't have the right, or the power, to veil it under a skirt. I don't permit, to be precise, the men you are here, if they consent to Lemart's dream, to shrink their genius to an amorous maneuver, or to lie to themselves, to the verity of their grandeur, in subordinating it to other influences than their enterprise itself and the effusion therein of their genius. The work or the action is sufficient in itself to the builders. Outside of that, all the rest, as you've said, Klutzkil, is surplus..."

"My necklace!" Gioia exclaims.

Bending over the water, she looks down, and the most prompt, leaning over like her, see the heavy item of jewelry sinking. Ozaki, who is holding the oars, holds them rigid in order to immobilize the boat at the location of the fall. Everyone suddenly has an expression simultaneously so surprised, saddened and perplexed that Gioia, who is looking at her companions with a confused pout, bursts out laughing; then, the confusion returning, and her face becoming grave, she says: "I had it..."

A silence, full of embarrassment and irresolution.

"I'll go look for it!"

In the same instant, her wrists on the edge of the vessel, so rapidly that so one is able to stop her, she swings herself over the side, hurls herself into the water and disappears with a great gilded splash.

Disarray among all the men. They look at one another, with a nervous and stupid laugh.

"Gioia!" cried Klutzkil.

"Gioia!" cries Mirard.

And all of them, Herbert alone smiling disdainfully, have the same indefinable expression of disturbance. And if Vernail, suddenly haggard, murmurs, his lips tremulous, loud enough for everyone to hear: "What if it were Mercerelle!" there is on the lips, in the eyes, and in the clenched fists of all the others, a similar legible anguish. What if it were Vénerise! What if it were Marden!

No more than another second has passed. Klutzkil has leapt overboard and dived in his turn. Lemart has followed him. A burlesque spectacle. Vernail, Mirard, Amarjit and Ozaki dive in then, along with Narasa, as if attached to Amarjit's movements. But although Ozaki, having dived skillfully and with a savant agility reaches Gioia at the moment the young woman returns to the surface, and Lemart, emerging from the water not far from the shore, seeing Gioia safe, swims toward it...it is otherwise for the scientist, the manufacturer and Narasa, who are struggling, thrashing their arms incoherently and desperately. Then Lemart occupies himself with Vernail, Klutzkil going to Mirard and Amarjit to Narasa. Their gesticulations having drawn the three imperiled men close to the bank, it is toward the shore that the Maharajah, the painter and the anarchist head.

Gioia, laughing at Ozaki and refusing his aid, clutches the boat at the same time as him, hoists herself up and falls on to the cushions. She sees Herbert, motionless, contemplating the whole scene impassively.

"Of course!" she says.

"It's absurd," he says.

"Indeed!" mocked Gioia. She wipes her eyes, blurred by droplets running from her hair. "In any case, my dear friend..."

"It's absurd, young woman," Herbert repeats, "to put so many lives at risk for a necklace, and the necklace itself, for a game!"

"A game," she says, "that shows me several things…and that your coolness and your will are precious friends of a prudence..."

Ozaki has embarked in his turn. Also rubbing the water from his eyes with his hands, he looks at Herbert rather severely.

"In fact, my dear Monsieur...."

"I'd be sorry," Herbert told him, "if you were to suppose me a poor swimmer." He seizes the edge of the boat, allows himself to fall gently into the water, and disappears.

Gioia emits a slight snigger. At that moment, not far from the shore, she perceives Amarjit supporting Narasa. His head tipped back on the Maharajah's shoulder, his eyes closed, the secretary is extremely pale. An anxiety abruptly draws Gioia's features taut.

"You're shivering," says Ozaki, seeing that change of expression. "We need to go inside right away..." He picks up the oars. "Monsieur Lesielt will be easily able to reach the bank on his own...."

His hands have begun to ply the oars mechanically, but his eyes, which have become burning, are glued to the young woman, whose fluid blouse, plastered by the water, delivers her breasts as if naked.

Herbert reappears, and grips the boat with one hand; in the other, he holds up the necklace.

"You see, Ozaki," he says, "it wasn't very difficult." He throws the opals at Gioia's feet. "There's your plaything, Mademoiselle."

Gioia is still gazing toward the bank. Amarjit has reached it. Aided by Lemart, he lays Narasa down on the grass.

"Row quickly, Ozaki," says Gioia, adding, by way of explanation: "It's true that I'm a little cold."

4. Magic

Through the glaucous light of the pines, Narasa, drawing away from the camp-site, heads for the clearing where he defeated Béron. Clad in a light costume of white flannel, with a delicate chemise of broad silk mesh open at the chest, shod in white deerskin sandals cut into thin straps, he walks unhurriedly, his feet gliding silkily over the pink needles of the pasts.

Having reached the clearing he finds it deserted, throws his jacket at the foot of a tress, sits down, then lights a cigarette and waits.

Also slowly, at the pace of two horses, one of which is Jahal, Herbert and Samion come into the Bois d'Arlans by an opposite path, heading straight for the clearing.

"You're as impatient as a child one is taking to see a fairy play for the first time, Samion. However, I'll be surprised if Narasa opens any doors to you that we haven't already passed through, and if you learn anything that we haven't approached in checking on Khunrath, Guaita, Sinnett, the first Sédir, Annie Besant..."[47]

---

[47] The references are to the Paracelsian physician Heinrich Khunrath (1560-1605), the Parisian lifestyle fantasists Stanislas de Guaita (1861-1897) and "Paul Sédir" (Yvon Le Loup,

"My impatience isn't for new arcana, and if there's any magic it will be in hearing Narasa talk personally about the things that I'd like to know. You've had the opportunity to have him to yourself as often as you like, but I can only talk to him in fragments in the midst of disparate gatherings."

"As much as I like? Amarjit doesn't like to let him go far. Fortunately, as Narasa judges me to be on a plan of knowledge worthy of his, we've been able to say a great deal in a few words."

"The jealous amity of Amarjit is justified by Narasa's psychic value. To have a magus for a secretary is worth one pampering him. That explains the rescue from the bath the other day..."

Herbert shakes his head.

"I criticized Gioia...," says Samion.

"There's a coldness between us since that little joke."

"She holds it against you."

"For having seen clearly."

"Clearly?"

"For having, as is appropriate, put genius above amour—or, more exactly, the amour that is genius above...the other..."

"She showed you immediately how amour number one comports itself, as soon as a skirt...amour number two...throws itself into the water."

"It was because of that nasty experiment that I wanted to give her a lesson. A nasty experiment that consisted of imposing on the weak point of individuals who are otherwise great."

"A weak point...their love for Gioia?"

"No, but that region of their love that makes them consent to this...sportive manner of showing themselves as lovers."

"If you had loved Gioia you would have jumped into the water at the same time as them."

1871-1926), and the theosophists Alfred Sinnett (1840-1921) and Annie Besant (1847-1933).

"An impracticable conditional. The lucidity that prevented me from doing as they did is what prevents me from loving Gioia…as they do."

"You don't love any of us."

"I don't know. Since I've been here, many minutes have passed in which I've felt—cerebrally—that if I had my heart of old, I would have experienced the most passionate enthusiasms."

"For?"

"For a host of attitudes of each of you, aspects of your beauty and your ardor for life…and also for the existence, the actions and certain words of a Mirard, a Vernail. Isn't that curious, Samion? I see something, I know that I could be violently aroused by it, and, as if in the presence of iron within me, my reason, or, more precisely, the tyrannical entity that my will has become, intervenes and leaves me cold, albeit abstractly admiring."

"That makes you a redoubtable observer, emotion troubling neither your eyes nor your ears. I don't know whether, in your presence, I dare ask Narasa the subtle questions, the confessions of a sort, that the questions we're going to touch on will incite..."

"I'll leave you."

"Oh! No!"

"I don't understand."

Without making any response, Samion gives Jahal a slight touch of the whip.

"It's neither timidity nor prejudice, nor petty feminine modesty," Herbert persists.

"Certainly not. Let's say spiritual modesty. I fear appearing ignorant, and I need your help."

"I've always seen you confess your ignorance forthrightly. Amusing to define the true sentiment that might retain a d'Aldezza from going alone wherever she pleases."

"But it's quite definite. I've just told you."

Herbert makes no reply.

"What time is it?" asks Samion.

"Ten to four."

"He'll be there at four. Let's accelerate." She raises her riding-crop.

"In order to be early?"

She maintains her pace.

"You don't think it curious," she resumes, "that a man so young should have acquired such a knowledge of the Occult?"

"That science isn't a question of time. It's a question of intensity of research…in the ascent."

"Until now I'd imagine fakirs as old men whose beards could be wrapped around them three times."

"He isn't a fakir. We've all applied that term to him by tacit convenience. He's a yogi. A bizarre story, which I extracted from him in the course of our conversations. The son of an engineer, he was a dutiful boarder at a college in Nepal. A Hindu-American sect unearthed him there after a sighting by one of its members, who designated the child as being the location of the reincarnation of some god or other, similarly Hindu-American. He was taken from the astounded father, a pedigree of twenty million years of anterior lives was discovered in him, and he was prepared for his divine destiny. Initiation—and serious. Before the god could be incarnated, rumors worried the father, who tried to reclaim his son. Tribunals, scandals; the rumor reached Amarjit, who took an interest in the young man, appeased the sect members, coaxed the father and took Narasa into his service."

"I can understand the attachment all the better if the mage is also a god."

"All reservations regarding the divinity."

"Do you believe in reincarnation?"

"Paramnesia often gives the key to certain memories…in other cases, the imagination…or the deregulated exaltation of credulity..."

"What astonishes me slightly," Samion interrupted, "is that after having passed through such a baroque adventure and the severe stages of Yoga, Narasa has retained that grace..."

"Add that coquetry. Have you noticed his ankle? I'm talking about the days when he dresses like everyone else."

"Noticed...to tell the truth…"

"He wears a little gold chain there."

"An oriental..."

They have arrived in the clearing, perceiving Narasa, who stands up. They dismount. Samon goes to the Hindu while Herbert attaches the horses to a tree. All three sit down casually on the grass.

"When I attempted…," Samion began, after the initial banalities, "…you'll be indulgent, Narasa, to the naiveties of which I might give evidence…when I attempted some discipline of the will and the means of fixation of thought, I thought about Buddhist mantras and the syllable which is pronounced by those who do so with a redoubtable solemnity..."

"Aum?" says Narana.

"Yes. And I thought that the interminable repetition of the mysterious lines in which that syllable had no other value than that of a method of numbing the mind... The goal to attain—the most difficult of all—being no longer to think about anything, to obtain silence, absolute if possible, in the disorderly train into which thoughts, images and conscious sensations and drawn…in sum, to reach a state, either of naked receptivity in which nothing will disturb the arrival of…forces, communication with…let's say the divine…to be able to form, in the field rendered perfectly virginal, a certain unique thought in which will then converge all the voluntary powers of concentration, of compaction..."

"The *Solve Coagula* of the Occidental Hermeticists," says Herbert.[48]

"Mademoiselle…," Narasa begins.

"Let's understand one another. What I mean is that there isn't any particular power, in and of itself, in the word *Aum*, nor in the mantras. Proffering them won't awake in the invisi-

[48] The motto of the alchemists is usually cited as *Solve et Coagula* [Dissolve and Coagulate].

ble…in a world exterior to ours…any unknown permanent entities attached to it. If it awakens anything, it's in us that it happens, exclusively. In the same way, if one sustains that reeling off the litanies will awaken the Lord, the Virgin or the Angels in a celestial abode where they're permanently resident..."

"You don't believe in Angels, Mademoiselle?"

"I've attained the esotericism of religions," says Samion. "In any case, I find at least as admirable as the symbolism of various paradises, the forces that we can raise or create in ourselves by exaltation, meditation or will, and which produce delights one attributes to paradise or confers the powers one expects from saints..."

Narasa looks at Herbert.

"It is possible, Mademoiselle, that the very sacred Aum and the mantras draw their power from the quality or the nature of our effusion, more than from a virtue that is proper to them and exterior to us. But it is the manipulation, the science, of that effusion which is the true mystery. What you call the discipline, the fixation of the will is nothing without certain…mystical conditions"

"And physical," says Samion. "I know."

Almost imperceptibly, Narasa smiles—the same haughty smile that Herbert had when Gioia first revealed to him that Samion had studied magic.

"Mercerelle," Samion continues, as if she has not seen the smile, "described your attitude on the day of the boxing match to me. Your hands were clutching your bare feet. I don't know what role the circuit of fluids plays in the play of forces that serve to condense and project the astral image…but that attitude creates by itself a current of forces. I've tried it, you know."

Briskly, she straightens up, falls back on her folded legs and extends her slender hands over her riding-boots. Thus seated, she gazes at the Hindu, her eyes suddenly wide and staring, her smile defying the gravity of her gaze.

"That's not entirely it, Mademoiselle," says Narasa, smiling in his turn.

In his turn, he adopts the attitude that he had during the combat.

"Oh! The bracelet! Samion exclaims, pleased.

In Narana's movement, the trouser-leg has lifted up, uncovering one of the ankles circled by a slender gold chain, shining softly on the brown flesh through a peacock green stocking.

"Amarjit likes to see that…thread on my foot," says the Hindu, sardonically.

"You ankle is as slender as a girl's, Narana," says Samion.

She amuses herself, having placed her fingers around Narana's ankle, in transferring them to her own.

"Indeed," she says. "And that silk, too, is finer than mine."

Narasa, with a certain preciosity, brushes the young woman's stocking.

"Yes," he says. "I'll give you a pair of these stockings, if you like, which Amarjit had woven for me in Jasgraun.

"I accept!" ripostes Samion, blushing slightly. "They're stockings? That's true elegance. Agree, Herbert, that the loftiest superiorities of human being don't prevent him dragging a perfidious petty ridicule into its transcendent prerogatives…if one thinks about the burlesque, utterly unesthetic thing that is a sock!"

"Take me for a dandy," says Narana, "but I share your opinion, Mademoiselle, and I would not dare take a step if I were wearing what you have just named..."

"In general," says Herbert, "the masculine leg, its rugged muscles, accords poorly…but here we are talking about garments like three shopgirls, O serious Samion, and far from Yoga..."

Samion smiles, her eyes on Narana's amber tinted hand, which is distractedly rustling the silk around the gold chain on his ankle.

"Well," she said, "there is one point on which I'd like Narana to be kind enough to fill me in. It's the subordination of all the physiological arcana to a preliminary mystical state. I'm not convinced by that at all. There are cases in which it's the physiological discoveries, the sensations that they provoke in the seekers, which lead them to reflection, to mystical meditation Do you count for nothing, my dear yogi, the prodigies of respiratory initiation?" Suddenly she said: "Oh! I'd like..."

She taps her boot with her riding crop. An indefinable hint of embarrassment insinuates itself into her grave and placid tone. "Show us how you were breathing, at the moment of the image in the match. I imagine that you were holding your breath, immobile and tight..."

"Give me your hand," says Narana

He places Samion's fingers on his breast and closes his eyes—but Samion utters a little cry.

"What do you have on your breast? A talisman?"

"A simple pebble, rather pretty..."

He undoes a button of his chemise, parts the cloth and shows a marvelous sapphire, carved in a plaque, held in an imperceptible circle of platinum and suspended by a thread of the same metal.

But Samion does not say anything. A blush rises to her face. It is not the jewel that she is looking at.

"Mercerelle," she says, suddenly cheerful and mocking, with the same reticence that she had in her voice just now, "was very impressed during the match by your nudity, my dear!"

Herbert also looks at that breast, and then his eyes go to Samion.

"Show Samion that strange and perfect torso," Herbert says. "She'll be better able to follow the savant palpitations of your breath..."

"I'm very impressed myself," Narasa simpers. "But truly, Mademoiselle Samion, isn't it a trifle ridiculous...we're talking esthetics. It's necessary for you not to look at me for a moment, I beg you, if you want me to obey."

He tugs delicately at the fine chemise, while Samion turns away, lightly fustigating the pink pine-needles at her feet. Motionless, Herbert as soon as the silk is on the ground, gazes for an instant at the exquisite naked bust before saying to Samion: "Cuckoo!"

Samion turns round. Before that nudity, her ruddy forehead has grown pale, and the riding crop is trembling slightly in the tensed hand.

A nearby sound of cracking branches breaks the strange silence that has fallen. A man is coming along one of the paths, whipping the branches that impede his progress with his cane. He approaches the clearing, comes into it, sees the group and comes toward them with a slightly astonished smile that immediately becomes cordial.

"Here's Amarjit," says Narasa, placidly. "Bonjour, Seigneur."

"Where are your sketch-pads?" says the Maharajah to Herbert and Samion. "Bonjour, Mademoiselle, bonjour Lesielt. I'm talking a walk. You're working in the open air? You've chosen a wretched model..."

5. Extraction

Vénerise, in the vast studio above the hall. At the foot of the keyboard of the organ, on the white woolen carpet that covers the entire floor, sheets of music have fallen in disorder. To the engravings, the moldings and the fresco images ornamenting the other walls, the organ, projecting from one of the panels, which it occupies entirely, adds a decorative beauty, austere in being monumental, gracious with its long shiny pipes.

Vénerise, her heavy blonde hair falling in two bangs over her shoulders, is dressed in a royal blue woolen tunic and sitting in the Turkish fashion on the carpet, in front of an immense crystal bowl. She is gazing—and the depths of her gaze seem to be lost elsewhere—at the frolicking of strange copper-colored fish with white fins, as diaphanous as vapor, like long scarves unrolling and undulating in indolent twists.

In the hollow of a bed of furs, its red fur staining the blondeness of the heaped skins with a narrow and languorous flame, the squirrel Illi is asleep. A bell rings lightly, which wakes it up abruptly and caused it to run to Vénerise and leap on to the young woman's knees.

"What is it?" she said, in a loud voice, without budging.

A little bulb lights up in one of the panels, above a thin black disk almost dissimulated between two engravings. A voice says: "His Highness is asking to be received by Mademoiselle."

"Show him in," says Vénerise.

The bulb goes out. A few moments later the studio door opens and a chambermaid lets Amarjit in.

He kisses Vénerise's hand and says: "Bonjour, Illi." Then he sits down on a nearby stool and, without any preamble, says: "Charming Vénerise, I've come to bid you adieu. My camp-site is being dismantled, since yesterday evening. In two hours, the Bois d'Arlans will have recovered its wild and melancholy integrity. I'm leaving for Jasgraun. Riots have broken out in my province at the same time as several others. We have a certain Granghi out there whose insurrectionist propaganda is preparing the same annoyances for England as Nana Sahib caused in '57. I shall see on the spot whether there is any possibility therein of taking a step toward the Republic of which we've dreamed. But far from here, will I still have the faith?

"Charming Vénerise, I'm leaving. I'm moved by the emotion that the news is designing on your face. There's nothing else for me to do but go. However, in the few instants that remain to me, great things might be accomplished. I would have come yesterday evening, but it's Mercerelle who would have received me. Just now, I dispatched an emissary to discover whether you would be at the Palais today. Thank heaven it was you, for it's to you that I want to say those great things."

Vénerise has pushed away the squirrel, which has gone back to the furs to sleep. She remains seated on the carpet. Her hands folded over her knees. "I'm listening," she says.

"Before then, answer me... Certain delicate subjects, among those that one ought to resolve without speech…demand to be tackled head on on the threshold of such an abrupt and grave separation. Among your sisters, has one of them allowed you to divine, in my regard, sentiments such that I might hope, if requesting her hand in marriage, to be welcomed?"

"Do you love one of us, then?"

"Yes. And her acquiescence with be the most delightful glory for me. And that one is you, Vénerise, do you not know that? But you are so closely linked with one another that if Marden or Gioia, Samion or Mercerelle had confessed to you her inclination for me, you might perhaps reject me, in order not to sadden Mercerelle or Marden, Samion or Gioia."

"That's possible," said Vénerise, "but wouldn't it be necessary, principally, that I should love you, Amarjit?"

"One evening, not long ago, you listened to me tell you the story of Shah Jehan the Magnificent, and describe to you the fabulous gardens of Shalimar. And you took account of the fact that exaltation that gripped me did not only come from the story of Shah Jehan. Then, was it my exaltation that overtook you, or was it another sentiment that I believed I read in you, as you let yourself go to a thousand adorable dreams? Projects of gardens more beautiful than the jewel of Kashmir elevated your enthusiastic and wonderstruck voice. I said to you: 'Come and preside over their creation, Maharani of Ezrapur!' And although you did not reply, your eyes were so full of enchanted visions that I thought, even so, that I could see your response therein. Would you like to tell me now whether I was mistaken, that evening?"

"Go with you…to India?"

"And become Princess of Ezrapur."

"We've deviated slightly. I haven't answered the question that you asked me first, with regard to my sisters. If I loved you, Seigneur, and I said yes to you, none of my sisters would be jealous. Each of them takes in your many perfections, and on other points, prefers you to some of our other friends..."

"Speak..."

"Marden has an infinite admiration for your skill and grace on horseback…but is aggravated by your tendency to an overconfident arrogance. Doubtless my sister must understand that it's the natural consequence of your high status, but in the end, as regards her own dilection, she would prefer you to be…a slightly simpler man. And I believe that you would have gained her graces earlier...by not hesitating, when you allied yourself with the company..."

She stops, and shakes her head with a semblance of confusion.

"Speak, dear Vénerise. This is an hour when I can hear anything. What rarer fortune is there than an opportunity to know oneself better by contact with true frankness..."

"The confession costs me, Amarjit, because it will leave you with a slightly vivid image of my sister. To call things by their name...she would doubtless not have detested it if, one of these days when you were out together, you had abdicated all your pomp, seized her wrists and proved to her lips that the lips of a Maharajah are also those of a man..."

Amarjit smiles, his eyes half-closed.

"It was," he says, "precisely by being a little too…forward that Marden did not please me. Although I appreciate her audacity, her ease, her beautiful vitality…the spontaneity of a young free animal…to make her my wife and the sovereign of Ezrapur, those qualities would not have failed to frighten me somewhat..."

"For Mercerelle, if it is more particularly the seigneur, the master of men, that attracts her, if she is pleased to imagine you issuing sovereign decrees, being able to organize the life, the mores and the esthetic of your estates...she regrets that all your fine powers are limited to your Ezrapur, and, it is necessary to add in passing, limited beyond you—until further notice—by the caprice of England..."

"My dear!" says Amarjit.

"Mercerelle's sympathies go to the princes...more precisely, to the conquerors of the present, men whose power is exercised in genuinely unlimited domains—Vernail, Klutzkil and Ozaki, for example. Mirard, at this moment or tomorrow, might overturn in an instant all the habitual ways of the world, and find himself at the head, not of a province of enormous Asia, but of the science, the art and the means of evolution of humanity entire..."

"Truly, Mademoiselle...," says Amarjit, piqued. He smiles. "If it were your sister who were expressing to me what you have said, I would respond that the empires of Messieurs Klutzkil, Mirard, Ozaki and Vernail, are nevertheless a trifle more unstable than mine. Those charming men might well be the princes you say, *if*...there is a serious little *if* in the test-tubes of one, in the industrial designs, the aircraft and the brushes of the others. My treasures, my palace, my forests, my people represent a thinner parcel of the vast world then the Possible of those messieurs...but that parcel is made of solid diamond, marble, earth..."

"We're talking about Mercerelle. The possible of the adventurers of science, art, space and industry tempt her more than your royalty established within its frontiers, and your treasures, numerous thought they are, whose limits will always be fixed by statistics. Every tomorrow that those men have before them is full of unknowns and incommensurables.

"As for Gioia, a gourmand of light, whether of fêtes, nature or intellect, she was immediately conquered by your unparalleled science of sumptuousness. And certainly, with you, she would have wanted all the splendors of India to blossom in never-extinguished magnificence. What debauches, Amarjit, what god-caparisoned beasts, ceremonies and corteges she would have imagined! But alas, my dear Seigneur, she would soon have wearied of them. Gioia, raised in the love of more modern beauties, would quickly have sent for artists, scientists and engineers from Europe and sought with them to make use of your Thousand-and-One Nights for actions closer to our numerous sensibility and our new needs..."

"Let's not talk any more about Gioia. Perhaps I would have liked to make her queen of that sumptuousness, and perhaps eventually succeeded in calming within her the vain demons of novelty by means of the dazzle of our millenary splendors...but since the excessive caprice of the necklace thrown in the water, her nature has seemed to me to be incompatible with the minimum of gravity required of a Maharani..."

"You're astonishing! The proof of that bath wasn't much more puerile or terrible than those that Greek princesses imposed on their suitors."

"But we're no longer in those legendary times of proofs...puerile indeed, my dear Vénerise. And those princesses offered poor tournaments compared to the subtle victories proposed to us here!"

"There remains Samion. She loved the wisdom and amplitude of your thought, but she would have liked you to be more universal, less attached to the philosophy of your race. She judges you too certain and not anxious enough..."

"But I've never thought that Samion might be my wife! If it's true that I'm certain—thank heaven!—what would I do with a presence perpetually occupied in shaking the tree of certitude, wanting to graft *but*s and *why*s on to every branch..."

"If, the poor fruits pruned and the branches grafted, the tree were to take on a new life...and might even become a different tree...."

"Of certainty?"

"Yes."

"We would be dead, Samion and I, before the first buds opened on such a tree. Now with you...or, rather, with the Vénerise in which I believed...for your manner of speaking today on behalf of your sisters troubles the image that I had formed somewhat..."

"What image, Amarjit? That of a sweet and deferential spouse?"

"Voluptuous in poetry and dreams, sufficiently not to love, like Samion, the reasoning before which every ideal and the most beautiful dream are reducing to limping...more serious than Gioia, more tender than Mercerelle and more…feminine than Marden."

"A worthy Oriental spouse."

"Which is to say..."

"It's true, Amarjot, that I am the woman you think…but to some extent, with respect to certain of the points that separates from them, the sister of each of my dissimilar sisters..."

"Ought I to understand that in order to please you, it would be necessary for me to be simultaneously a mystic, an inveterate reasoner, tender, brutal, smitten with all metaphysics and the most realistic of realizers…?" He stands up. "I love you, Vénerise. If you're laughing at me, let's conclude this conversation. Behind your tender and pensive eyes something might perhaps be hidden something even more cruel and more foreign to me than I divined with regard to your sisters. And yet…in the bright flame in your eyes, I would have passionately modeled, little by little, the image of man that I believe to be…the image that you would have wanted..."

"My dear Seigneur," says Vénerise, getting to her feet in her turn and going to lie down next to Illi, whom she caresses, "think how much this conversation, and the announcement of your departure, might have surprised me. I'd like to reflect on everything that we've just said. If you love me, may I request a little constancy? Go, and come back when the troubles have calmed down. Let's write to one another. I don't want you to go away sad, or discouraged."

"Ought I then to hope…?"

"This departure...what an annoyance for us all. So many pleasant hours spent in the camp... My dear Seigneur, it will be necessary to leave us some of the things that have delighted us. They would remind me of you every day."

"Oh! Certainly! Choose! It will be my greatest pleasure..."

"First of all, it's necessary to leave the lovely Jahal to Marden."

"On condition that she lends him to you occasionally."

"To Gioia the carpet of purple silk with gold lamé, on which your secretary was seated on the day of the combat."

"It's hers."

"With regard to Narasa..."

As if Vénerise's caressing hand had suddenly hurt him, Illi escapes from her and goes to hide under a divan.

"I'm sure that Samion would have an infinite pleasure…he's initiating her, in that...those doctrines of Yoga, as you know... You'll find him again when you return. It's necessary to leave Narasa for Samion."

Amarjit's face becomes suddenly impassive. "That's curious," he says. "Samion isn't the only one of you who's interested in Narasa."

"Oh?" says Vénerise. "You think so? Perhaps Marden…because of the horseback rides?"

"And Gioia, and also Mercerelle. I've seen them looking at my little secretary in a strange way on several occasions. And you…"

"I find him genteel. I love his eyes."

"I'm desolate. I can't leave Narasa here."

"Oh! Samion will be desolate too. Let's not talk about it anymore..."

She gets up, takes a small brioche from a tea-tray and goes to crumble it into the crystal bowl.

"All the same," she says, "What I find curious, in my turn, is that you depend so much on this Narasa. A prince like you doesn't have a private secretary. There must be state secrets between the two of you..."

"No, Mademoiselle," says Amarjit, with a hint of embarrassment in the voice that he tries to make light.

"They must be very droll, those stories of the court…except that I don't understand how a separation of a few months...a few weeks..."

"Dear Vénerise... Accept instead, you and your sisters, all the beautiful fabrics in my camp, my horses, the gold vessels from which you have done me the honor of sampling my pastries... I would like to go to Ontriond without any luggage… But I can't leave without Narasa, who is as precious to me as air and daylight..." Amarjit is upright. "Permit me to take my leave of you. I'll come back this evening to make my adieux to Madame your mother."

"With Narasa?" says Vénerise, in a tone that strives to be mischievous.

"Alas, no. Narasa left yesterday for Marseilles, to prepare for our embarkation."

"Gone!" says Vénerise.

"Mademoiselle…"

"That's unpleasant!" she says, harshly.

"I wasn't mistaken," says the Maharajah. "It's very singular that young women like you, so different, so demanding, find yourselves all five in accord, in the same sentiment, for the same man."

"It's even more singular that, having offered me your love and a throne, you refuse me immediately thereafter the single thing that pleases me: Narasa."

"Unfortunately, he pleases me too, and for precisely the same..." He interrupts himself abruptly. "Adieu, Vénerise."

He heads for the door. Vénerise remains immobile.

"Adieu, Vénerise," Amarjit repeats.

"If I had become your wife," says Vénerise, without turning round, "what would you have done with Narasa?"

"There is in each of us," Amarjit responds, gravely, "a great number of sentiments, and each of us has a life appropriate to his plane. From the obscure region where the instincts stir to the seventh region that is Atma, that of the spirit, those sentiments correspond, with increasing subtlety, to the elevation of the planes. My love for you blossoms in the harmonious summits of my being. All other things would have agitated beneath it. From the height of our embraces, we would have contemplated Narasa together, like one of those beautiful greyhounds that the ancient kings possessed, which they caressed distractedly..."

"Go away," says Vénerise. "Never come back here. I will give your excuses to my mother. Go rejoin your greyhound."

IV

1. Marden Nervous

Before the Lac d'Ontriond and its surroundings had become the property of Madame d'Aldezza, several peasant chalets had stood to the west of the lake, on the grassy slopes that are the ultimate foothills of the peak of Ansaux. The architect of the Palais had demolished the majority of those huts made of stones and plants, and built the laboratory in which Mirard had been installed on the site of one of them, situated high on the slope overlooking the lake. It was a construction glazed on three sides, the fourth being of stone, backed up to the hill by two small projecting wings. One contained an electrical generator and the other served as a darkroom.

Marden, rapping on the glass, causes the scientist, bent over a set of test-tubes, to raise his head. Mirard salutes her, with a distracted smile. She opens the door and comes in.

"I'm not disturbing you, Professor?"

"Yes, Mademoiselle. Sit down quietly in a corner. I'll be with you in a moment."

He continues to observe the battles of the liquids in the slender glass tubes, going back and forth between his experimental table and a blackboard, on which he scribbles formulae.

"Lesielt and Kluzkil are in the darkroom," he says, without raising his eyes from his flasks. "If it tempts you to watch their amusements...Klutzil is conducting trials in fluorescent painting with my powders. It's new, and quite pretty."

"Thanks. It's you I came to see."

"Delighted." He continues his manipulation of test-tubes tranquilly.

Sitting on a corner of the table, Marden mechanically picks up glass bulbs and rods, and makes them sparkle with reflected light. One rod slips from her fingers and breaks on the floor.

"Zut!"

Mirard turns his head. "It's not important."

"So much the better. Say, Professor, I came to talk to you about an excursion…"

"Oh?" says Mirard, his mind elsewhere.

"Tomorrow. Ascension of Aylserine and return via Orgins. Depart early in the morning. All available men. You're taking Vénerise. I'm the one who planned the excursion. Not dangerous, but hard. The girl needs a distraction, gross physical fatigue that puts the thinking machine to sleep. She's chagrined. The rest of us are trying to shake her out of it a little."

"That's very kind of you," says Mirard, who has only heard the last few words.

"That's all I had to tell you, Professor. Tomorrow morning, five o'clock, at the foot of the perron, knapsack on your back, alpenstock, sturdy boots. *Au revoir*. Work well."

"What?" Irritated, Mirard puts down a test-tube that he was holding up. "I wasn't listening properly. I beg your pardon. An excursion, tomorrow? Impossible."

"It's your impossible that's impossible."

"Very sorry." He picks up an earthenware receptacle, shakes the liquid contained therein, goes to put it in a little electric furnace, looks at his watch and marks the time on the blackboard.

"There! Now…bonjour, Mademoiselle. Come in, please. Sit down. What's happening?"

"Mirard, we're going to cheer up Vénerise, who has been depressed since Amarjit's departure. We're counting on you as much as on us."

"The delicate sweet thing loved that bejeweled excellence? I'm astonished. Not you?"

"Of course not…but he knew beautiful Indian poems, and perhaps he appeared seductive to Vénerise for reasons that the rest of us didn't perceive."

“Right. So?”

“So, sadness, and this excursion tomorrow.”

“My absence won’t be any handicap. On the contrary. I’m a poor alpinist. My ascensions are internal. Send Vénerise to me. I’ll take her with me to peaks so high that the thinking machine will have vertigo…those that you desire for her are no more fatiguing…and from which she’ll see her Maharajah the size of a pin-head.”

“Certainly, Professor. But that will be for another day. I’m convinced that each of you will be able to distract her brilliantly. Tomorrow it’s the turn of muscles, lungs, stupidity...”

“Look,” says Mirard, who is not really listening and looking at his watch frequently, “I have here, in that furnace, cooking at twelve hundred degrees, a mixture from which I expect colors…the true term would be light...that I can honestly call absolutely new…and of an intensity of brightness surpassing anything known. I’ve thought of something for the day that Ozaki attempts his ascension. If my solution succeeds, by coating his apparatus…by night, the aircraft will be visible at twenty thousand meters, like a large star among the stars, an unknown comet or…to the bewilderment of astronomers…a second moon. You see, what I have here...”

“Professor…,” says Marden.

Mirard takes out his watch.

“The first difficulty is finding substances capable of fluorescence. Sometimes a simple meadow plant, thoroughly crushed, delivers suitable solutes…and then, a sufficient quantity of rare earths, lucinium, gallium, whose vapors...”

“Oh! Your cravat!” says Marden. “Wait there.”

She leaps from the table, goes to Mirard and reties the two loose ends of the ribbon.

“You’re very kind,” says Mirard, lifting his chin mechanically. “I don’t notice…I’m boring you with my rare earths.”

“No, but it’s rather to Samion that it’s necessary...”

“Hmm… Samion irritates me.”

“No!”

"That is to say, she wants to know too much...persecutes me with questions. I'm not a college professor, there are rudiments I've completely forgotten. A liking for science is insufficient to replace, at a stroke, years of study and experiments."

"Poor Samion. And yet...in sum, you came here in the hope of dazzling one of us. Who could be closer to you, which of us, better than Samion, could be a companion capable of taking up residence on your peaks?"

"My dear, they're frightfully individual! A short visit from time to time...like the one we were talking about for Vénerise, fine—but taking up residence! It would be very ingrate for anyone who hasn't climbed them—if not built them!—stone by stone."

"Which of us, other than Samion, could love you worthily...I mean, in the sole manner in which you're lovable."

"Which is?"

"In the water, you lose your footing. On land, you admit to being a poor alpinist..."

"Eh? what does that mean?"

"It means that you lack certain physical qualities that are the basis of beautiful joys, of which you're deprived, and of which your wife would be deprived if, because she loves them, she wants to share them with you."

"I'd give her many others."

"Undoubtedly, instead of the pleasures of love that a young and beautiful woman might expect, your vapors of...lucinium...with an untied cravat...and trousers—look, professor!—that are hooked on the top of the boot."

"That's silly! I certainly think that the woman who will be my wife wouldn't pay attention to such trivia."

He adjusts his trousers disdainfully.

"None of us here is careless of those trivia!"

"I love one of you. I'll take responsibility, when the time comes, for being as beautiful—yes, Mademoiselle, and of the rarest of beauties—for her scarcely to think about looking at my cravat or the tops of my boots."

"Impossible! No matter how beautiful and great a man might be, we also want him to be elegant, a good swimmer and a good climber, capable of holding our intelligence in sufficient esteem to admit us into the most secret of his science, capable..."

"I love Gioia."

"That's an odd choice!"

"I love Gioia," says Mirard, gravely. "Your scarecrows don't frighten me. In spite of her caprices, the childishness of the necklace, Gioia is, for me, the image of all the elevated thoughts that inhabit me, all the luminous perspectives that my experiments and hypotheses cause to sparkle before me. Whatever discovery I make, whatever glory falls to me, the visage of Gioia offers me the perfect living symbol of it. I'm not, as you seem to believe, an old bear closed to everything that isn't his lab or his formulae. I'm extremely sensitive to beauty."

"On condition that it incarnates your lab and your formulae, Professor, and magnifies them! That's what you mean. And what—on the part of Gioia, if you please!—would make her love you?"

"Gioia would love me for the radiance, as a whole, of my work. Everything else would become miserable detail, dust—the cravat, the boots, the catastrophe of not being a mountaineer or a swimmer, or a warbler of barcaroles—before the world's homage to my work! She would be the wife of the man who had seized by the throat—with lucinium, Mademoiselle, and a few other...vapors—radiance, the true name of the force that is the architecture of atoms and suns!"

"Honor to you among men, Mirard! Gioia would be able to venerate your scientific grandeur. But Gioia's arms would also like to embrace the body of that grandeur; Gioia's mouth would like the homage of the world to blossom in the kisses of the hero's mouth. Gioia's mind would perhaps succeed in climbing voluptuously the interior peaks of your glory, but that wouldn't prevent Gioia's legs from wanting to bound on mountain slopes, and receive the caress of the waves, or her nostrils from burning in the wind of the road on which an auto would be able to bear the triumphant hero…as boldly as his genius bears his research."

"Thanks for the speech. If that's what Gioia wants, she can go to the devil…or the convent. We'll find her there in forty years, and the phoenix that she'll have searched for among men will have been replaced by a cat or a parrot. Look, Mademoiselle, let me work, I beg you. I'll explain myself another time to Gioia herself…"

He takes out his watch. "My mixture! It'll be overdone!"

He runs to the electric furnace, opens it, and seizes the earthenware vessel with a long spatula."

"Spoiled, damn it! I beg you, I beg you, don't play such tricks again!"

He places the vessel on the table. "Damn and double damn!"

The door of the room opens. Herbert and Klutzkil appear.

"What's wrong?" says Klutzkil. "Bonjour, Mademoiselle. What a racket! What's broken, Mirard?"

"It's…ask Mademoiselle! It's these spoiled children running in seven league boots toward the most confirmed bachelor! That we can all pack our bags, because we've believed in vain that we're somewhat interesting individuals, because Vernail isn't able to swim the channel or you, Klutzkil, climb Mont Blanc while playing the flute. Your trousers, Lesielt…isn't the crease slightly crooked..?"

"The great Mirard," said Marden in a mordant tone, "thinks it exorbitant that we desire in the man who will love us that he not be one-dimensional, and that, being rare among all men in one respect, he should also be in his other resources. So be it, and too bad! And thus we'll be old maids, if the complete man doesn't exist!"

"I don't think that Marden is wrong," said Herbert.

"And even if she were right ten thousand times over," said Mirard, getting carried away, "what connection would it have with reality? Can a jockey have time to study music, paining and metaphysics? To get to the point where I am, I've spent years and years cloistered in passionate attention. Let us remake the earth, humankind, the tyranny of art, science and sport! In the meantime, Mesdemoiselles d'Aldezza can burn candles to Saint Catherine! Mademoiselle, Messieurs, excuse me, but I'd like to try to repair the setback that has massacred my preparation..."

His hands trembling slightly, he returns to his test-tubes.

"Let's leave the professor," says Herbert. "He's in a state…unconducive to the serene taming of atoms..."

Marden, her hands in her belt, goes to the door, whistling between her teeth.

"Permit me to return to my hole," says Klutzkil. "I haven't finished. Your vocal outbursts interrupted me."

"Do, do," replies Mirard, already busy with his liquids.

"Until this evening, Mirard," says Herbert

Marden has her hand on the doorknob

"I'll go with you, Marden. I have something to say to you."

They are outside. The young woman is still whistling.

"You were a little sharp...."

Marden shrugs her shoulders. "I don't care. I've had enough. Let them all pack their bags, if they want."

"You wouldn't be any further forward," says Herbert, tranquilly.

"There isn't only Mirard, Vernail and the rest of you in the world!"

"Perhaps your sisters don't share your opinion."

"Yes, I think so. Otherwise, their choice would be made."

"Neither you nor your sisters will find anyone better than those who are here."

"What pretention! I admire you! Maman receives avalanches of letters every day. The tournament is still open, my dear! It hasn't ceased to be. The agitation we stirred up hasn't calmed down because we've reduced our intimates to the little group you form. When we go out in an auto, we're neither deaf nor blind. There isn't a single tourist, no matter how far away he comes from, who isn't devoured with curiosity to get into the Palais, to see us at close range! We only have to make a gesture...hold a few receptions. Béron, Stani, Détrêt and Amarjit have gone...a few more departures...carefully awaited, be sure of it, and..."

"And everyone stopped and discouraged by your present devotees would rush forward! What you've just said entails its own response. Those who weigh up the fact that a Vernail, a Mirard or a Klutzkil couldn't succeed, that a Maharajah or a Prince of Ornania have failed, would hesitate before venturing themselves...or would be vain fools who would only make you burst out laughing. And those who overcame that legitimate timidity would retreat more rapidly than the few stubborn individuals that we are before the excessively strange disciplines here—principally, the one that only allows us to see each of you for one day...which is enough to disorientate the best, and to give you a false and diminished image of the best..."

"It's the opposite that ought to occur!"

"Vernail has offered I don't know how many times to take Mercerelle away for a few days. He would have taken her to his factories, to the milieux in which he is a king. There, he would truly have shown himself to her as one of the giants whom she dreams of loving and inspiring..."

"And beyond that? And afterwards? Soon, that which is in Mercerelle of Gioia, of Samion, of Vénerise would experience with that giant the same disappointment that Mirard caused me just now: the lack of diversity..."

"Childishness! You've touched there upon the error that is drawing you all into an expectation that probably has no issue. Superior beings succeed in containing and expressing all diversities and all grandeurs in forms and states different from those in which one is accustomed to consider those same grandeurs. It's only necessary to be able to transpose. Are not a working drawing emerged from Vernsail's hands, which can be translated into a thousand living monuments of steel, or a decision that he can make with a word and which might transfigure a fragment of the planet, things that connect with the most ardent artistic tremors that stir Gioia? Aren't they more massive, but also as elevated and fecund as one of the metaphysical speculations that impassion Samion? Vernail manipulating one of his engines is—with a different elegance—more elegant than the finest dancer who pleases you, Marden..."

"Literature! Why did you say that I was right just now? That's not what I meant in speaking about a truly complete man?"

"Something like all men in one?"

"A man who can want a woman who contains all women."

Herbert stops abruptly. "What woman are you talking about?"

Marden does not reply, and kicks a few pebbles with the toe of her shoe.

"Who are you talking about?" Herbert repeats.

"But…each of us…who, by virtue of the reflection within her of each of her sisters, succeeds in representing that diversity, that multiplicity..."

Herbert remains silent for a few seconds in his turn. Then he said: "When you left Mirard I asked to accompany you because I had something to say to you. Did you know that Narasa hasn't left?"

2. Bacchus

They are going down the narrow path that leads from the laboratory to the Palais. Marden's excitement falls like a red flower cut by a stroke of a cane, but her face does not allow any sentiment to appear, and it is in an almost indifferent voice that she says: "Oh? Vénerise thought he was in Marseilles, if not already embarked."

"Amarjit was lying to Vénerise. There wasn't the slightest riot in his estates. Our Maharajah is tranquilly continuing at Evian the holiday he commenced at Thonon."

"Why…how…who told you that?"

"I discovered it myself, when, having business in Evian yesterday, I met the exceedingly pretty secretary there. We chatted. I filled in some details, and learned something rather piquant."

"Perhaps..." Marden hesitates. "It might be better not to tell it to Vénerise. May I know?"

They have arrived at the intersection of the descending path with the one that goes around the lake.

"Don't go back right away," says Herbert. "Let's talk a little walk."

They head toward Arlans.

"It's slightly complicated," the young man continues. "Since one afternoon when Amarjiit came upon us unexpectedly—Samion and I—with the young mage, almost naked..."

"Samion told me…."

"Good. It appears that the Rajah's imagination went to work. A certain number of clues pushed him to imagine that all of you…including you, Marden…had a strange inclination for his page."

"With regard to me, I beg you to believe…it's possible that Vénerise..."

"Shall I go on? A double sentiment awoke in Amarjit. Injured pride at seeing you prefer his secretary…and secondly, the fear of losing...it's not easy to say..."

"Don't say it. Amarjit took responsibility for making Vénerise understand that horror."

"A horror...what severity!"

Marden stops, surprised. She remains silent, and looks at Herbert apprehensively.

"On what basis are you judging? You were reproaching Mirard just now for only being a man of one thing. Here you are, in regard to another man, faced with a…sentimental singularity, which, in itself, is perhaps an enrichment of the personality. You turn away. Why?"

"Are you mocking me?" she asks, nonplussed.

"No. The diversity that you demand in an individual, I assume to be in all domains, and that you don't limit it to the intellectual..."

"What are you trying to say? None of us poses as a schoolgirl. But we're young women. There are…abominable things. I've never claimed... The diversity that we seek is an individual, beyond his specific genius, is the most numerous power to embrace the beauties, the joys of life...."

"Beauties, joys…where is the top, and the bottom? What is it that limits them, beyond the labels stuck on by morality, schools, fashions? *Omnia munda mundis...*"[49]

"That's what you claim, Herbert? Where is this preaching going? And this defense of Amarjit?"

"I don't care about Amarjit. I abandon him to you. He's only a pretext to catch you in flagrant illogicality. It's your unworthy severity that I'm criticizing. Let commonplace individuals apply their dense verdicts to the sentiments and actions that touch prejudice, but not you, who claim…for yourselves, naturally, and from those who love you…the most numerous resources. Is it not indispensable to whoever seeks such exaltation that he has the greatest possible and precise consciousness of his own resources—and, of course, his own limitations. And how can one acquire such a consciousness of oneself if one does not set out to go, without preliminary judgment, to anything that might be an element of that consciousness? The will to know—there, that's something better, more human, than St. Paul's *omnia munda mundis*. It's before that will that there's no longer anything ugly or base..."

"All right. But what is the objective of that knowledge?"

"The greatest blossoming of the individual in his entirety, in all domains and all his veritable resources."

"And the objective of that blossoming?"

"What Klutzkil once called radiance…the most magnificent gift, the gift of the vastest self to the world, the supreme

[49] To the pure all things are pure. The quotation is from one of the epistles credited to St. Paul.

joy, the supreme law for anyone who has understood the magnificent gift that the world is for us."

"We're strangely distant from a rather paltry point of departure. In parentheses, for a man with a dead heart, you've maintained a rather keen idealism…"

"Ephemeral gymnastics and the oratory of an old self, which circumstances have awakened and the self of today will immediately hang on the wall of ancestral portraits! What I'm saying to you corresponds to the proud and beautiful concepts that I once had…but of which the man that I have become experiences neither the warmth nor the enchantment..."

"I would like," Marden says, "to get back to your encounter yesterday and know—if you were told—the why of that comedy of riots and adieux played for Vénerise."

"Amarjit wanted to bring the situation to a head, to know frankly where all of you stood in his regard...and the measure of your penchant for the secretary. He had sincere hopes of Vénerise, and would have confessed the subterfuge of the farewell if she had agreed to be his wife. Before your sister's pretentions he saw clearly that nothing remained for him but to leave—not only because he had nothing to hope for in his own regard, but in order to remove his cherished rival from redoubtable worshipers."

"That's all, is it?"

"That's all."

"They're at Evian?"

"At the Imperial."

Marden makes an ambiguous movement.

"Are you going to tell Vénerise?" Herbert asks.

"I don't know."

"Isn't it to be feared that Vénerise…more sharply afflicted than we can suppose, might immediately invent no matter what pretext, leap into an auto and join Narasa?"

"To be feared? Fear what? Vénerise is free. Fear? For whom?"

"For her."

"I don't understand."

“Fear what? Of being hooked. A catch that would not go well with the beautiful diversity in which all of you take such a legitimate pride.”

“I don’t understand, if, by a sort of election among her diversity, better than a harmonious convergence of all her resources, it’s in what...in what you call being hooked, that Vénerise finds her joy.”

Herbert laughs silently.

“And then,” says Marden, irritated, “it only concerns her.”

“Her joy!” he says, as if he had not heard. “In any case, not the joy we were talking about a little while ago. Not the joy to which young women as rare and ambitious as you can and ought, more than anything else, to demand! It’s a matter of a young fellow whose equivocal charm has excited a few nervous fibers of one of you. Consequence: the vibration of those few networks risks ending in the captation of the entire being and all the resources of the excited demoiselle...or to put it another way, reducing to the most ordinary, the most usually human proportions, the astonishing character that you have to generously lent to Vénerise...and to each of you. No connection with the joy of radiance of which we were speaking.”

The young woman resumes whistling as she had done in Mirard’s laboratory. A singular attitude—she seems simultaneously disposed to put an abrupt end to the conversation with some brutal remark, while something in her, more distant from that impatience, is attentive.

“What does Vénerise have to fear, you asked? Being captured. The proof? It’s that is she were truly conscious of all her resources, Narasa escaping her, *pfft!*—would be simply a question of leaping into an auto. Would she not have...would you not have, *you* meaning all of you...the means to throw a thousand and one joys over one disappointment, whatever it might be? For such young women, any objective missed or destroyed must be immediately…let's say, like La Pisanella,[50] killed on a mountain of flowers; the death is not perceived, which gives way to that immense litter of corollas and perfumes..."

"Literature!"

"Solid and living reality! If not, you're decidedly not what you say you are, and it wasn't worth the trouble of enraging Mirard. Corollas and perfumes, that infinity of objectives that life and the world extend to your faculties and your appetites. So many objectives that—is it not so?—you judge all men lamentably narrow if, fixed on one alone, they forbid themselves the multitude of others. Mirard, Vernail, giants, so be it, but in the fashion of the Cyclops. A single eye, poor fellows—for you others, who gaze and desire though each of your cells as if by as many eyes, eh? Literature! Before a little corner of desire, a shady caprice of the flesh, literature, smoke in the wind that all the recourses of which each of you is overflowing, as rich as her and…how did you put it?...with the reflection each of the others at her disposal..."

They have reached the extremity of the lake. From the circular path that they are following, a narrower path branches off, which leads to the enclosure of the Palais and the Bois d'Arlans. They take it. At the far end, against the wall of high brambles in the arc of a circle that closes the property, a stone statue detaches its grandiose and svelte mass. It is a replica of the Bacchus of the Uffizi, the young god with the crown of vine leaves, his arm raising a cup, one leg flexed in the thrust of the dance.

Herbert, in mid-discourse, pays no particular attention to the work of art, seen many times before during walks in the park, but Marden has stopped. An unaccustomed gravity widens her bold and willful eyes.

---

[50] The prostitute in Gabrièle D'Annunzio's play *La Pisanella, o la morte profumata* [La Pisanella; or, The Perfumed Death] (1913).

"Herbert," she says, "that statue once stood in the hall of our father's house. My father was a man who devoted his genius and his fortune to the cult of joy…to a joy of unlimited blossoming…quite similar to the one of which you speak... A frightful accident interrupted him, and caused the enterprise that he had undertaken to collapse, but he had retained his marvelous idea in his mutilated body... After his death, Maman wanted the image with which he had illustrated his certainty to continue its symbolism for us and color our destiny..."

She hesitates continually, gripped by an emotion that she is no longer attempting to dominate.

"To come together…and with all of our resources extinguish Vénerise's pain... Of course! And to appeal to her to find within herself a thousand consolations of which were capable! And we've begun ourselves…this excursion tomorrow, proposed a little while ago to Mirard…but now the task is all the more difficult, since Narasa is still here and it's not only a memory that it's necessary to combat. But you're right. Vénerise will be able to…and not go."

"More difficult, eh?" says Herbert. "In that case, let's go back to our first suggestion. Let Vénerise, on the contrary, go to Narasa. It's necessary for her to welcome the proof that's offered to her. Let her go to Narasa, to see whether he is really capable of the embrace of the innumerable that is really permissible to you, and which you demand of your suitors…to see whether she really has the will to radiance, the will to all the superior events and which permits one, while savoring all of them, not to be limited to any one of them, to traverse them all and rediscover oneself liberated, in the expectation, after them and beyond them, always, of further sources of knowledge and aggrandizement...

"Let her welcome that proof as an opportunity to measure what she believes herself to be against what she is. Let her know whether she is like anyone else, whether she has surrendered herself completely, a slave like all women—and all men—to one of the faces of the innumerable. But if, having savored the moment, she finds that she is her own mistress, and completely free before the following minute and all the minutes of the possible, then she will know, and you will know, through her, that you truly are what it is necessary to be, in order to dare to hope for the innumerable companion—or to create him..."

3. - 200°

On the resurfaced road that departs from Lurzine and stops, unfinished, after a few kilometers, in the direction of the Col de Bloux, Gioia has left the auto at the foot of the stony path that takes climbers to the Grandforts. Having climbed up a hundred meters, she has turned on to a spacious plateau to the right of the road. There, around what was once a small farm, and which Ozaki has made his residence and his workshop, several large rudimentary wooden hangars stand, constructed for the aviator. The growl of turbines escapes therefrom. At the extremity of the plateau is the monoplane. Its body is a vast cylindrical cabin whose forward section, above the propeller, frames a large bulbous window composed of two superimposed sheets of glass several centimeters apart. On the top of the cabin is a bell-shaped porthole, presently tilted back.

In the cabin, still clad in her brown auto coat open over a white dress, coifed with a cashmere beret enclosing the blonde hair and cut short is a glittering curve at the nape, Gioia, sitting in a narrow leather armchair fixed to the floor, listens gravely to Ozaki's explanations.

"If I'm too technical," he says, "stop me. The propeller is variable in diameter. Here is the variation control, which, by means of rods connected to the axle of the motor, activates the mechanism place in the hub of the propeller. That hub is rendered watertight by a pressure-seal. Above all, it's necessary to protect the organs from the enormous changes of pressure that we're going to encounter. The cabin for the passengers and all the machinery is also sealed—no influence inside if the atmosphere outside. The visibility of the pilot, and that of the passengers remains intact by virtue of the void between the two glass sheets of the forward window and the porthole. That will prevent the formation of ice, which is produced by direct contact with the air at fifty to seventy degrees below zero, on the glass of the cabin, where a mean temperature of twenty degrees will be maintained. I'm not boring you?"

"What! When I think that it's because of this that you're going to become a new Columbus!"

"I think, at the heights that the turbocompressor, the form and resistance to pressure of my apparatus will permit me to reach, my eight hundred horsepower should permit me to attain a velocity of a thousand kilometers an hour—which is to say, a means of going from Paris to Buenos Aires between breakfast and lunch, traversing the three thousand kilometers of the Atlantic ocean that separate Dakar from Penambuco in three hours."

"Marvelous."

"Shall we continue the proprietor's tour? Here, this little orifice in the wall permits the escape of vitiated air. As for the wall of the cabin, it's a special sheet metal stiffened by profiled rivets, and its resistance extends all the way to that 272 degrees below zero at which I've tested it. An experiment of luxury, however, since the stratosphere, in which we'll be traveling, doesn't get below minus fifty-five or thereabouts."

"What is the stratosphere?"

"The region of the atmosphere that commences at a height of about eleven thousand meters...."

"You've experimented at 272 degrees below zero! Is that attainable?"

"Yes, with liquid helium. Would you like to have an idea of what the world would be like at two hundred degrees below zero? Let's get out of the aircraft and come with me to my den..."

Gioia stands up. Ozaki sets up a small iron ladder toward the ceiling of the cabin, goes out through the open porthole, equilibrates himself and holds his hand out to Gioia.

"How many could your airplane carry?" she asks, as she climbs up.

"Four. The pilot, the mechanic and two passengers. For a start, that's pretty good. If everything goes well, I'll see about a larger model…and even construct it..."

They traverse the plateau.

"For the first excursion, however," Ozaki continues, "I fear that I'll be alone. No mechanic wants to risk it. If I don't break my neck I'll find a hundred. In the meantime, I'll have to shift for myself. I can do it. The mechanic wouldn't be doing much more than keeping watch on all the manometers, barometers, barographs..."

They have reached the hangars. Workmen stop what they are doing to look at Gioia. Whispers run around. Ozaki opens the door to his office: a sober room; trestle tables and drawings.

"I'm obliged to take you through my bedroom..."

An iron bed, the strict minimum of furniture, a single image on the wall: a large photograph. Gioia strives to pass it discreetly, curious nevertheless regarding the female individual she distinguishes there.

Ozaki senses that curiosity. He blushes

"I believe you recognize the young woman on the wall."

"It's me," says Gioia, drawing closer. "But I don't know that photo."

Ozaki blushes a little more deeply, and attempts to adopt a casual tone. "Stani took it, during an excursion on horseback."

"Oh, yes! One of the thousand he took of us. But his Kodak was a small apparatus."

"I asked him for the negative. Finding it delightful, I had it enlarged. It pleases you, doesn't it?" he added, timidly.

"Yes. It's the riding costume I was wearing the day of the terrible drowning."

Ozaki looks away, and says, in a slightly muffled voice. "Yes. Shall we go on?"

Beyond the bedroom is a narrow lumber-room where there are trestles, planks and a few items of laboratory equipment. Ozaki opens a door and turns a commutator. A spiral staircase appears. He precedes Gioia. They go down.

"I fitted out this cellar following almost exact the indications of the scientist Louis Lecarme, who recounted one day in *Le Figaro* a visit that he made in Peru to one of his friends, the director of the Lima Observatory. That astronomer, an eminent physicist, had also installed a liquid air factory in his cellar……"

Gioia penetrates into a little room that receives exterior light through portholes of thick glass. Ozaki seals the room by puling toward him a door armored like that of a strong-room, supported by a strong rubber armature.

"These tubes, whose walls, as you can see, are completely coated, have winglets, and form a radiator. A current of liquefied gas can circulate therein, which will produce a progressive cooling of the entire room and its contents. As we're going to be part of the contents, and the refrigeration can soon reach minus two hundred degrees, we're going to put on appropriate diving-suits. They'll permit us to breathe and see clearly, and are made of a material that supports changes of pressure valiantly. You're not afraid?"

"Should I be afraid?"

Ozaki smiles and hands the young woman the pieces of one of two voluminous vestments that he has taken from an alcove in the room, similar to the suits worn by deep-sea divers, save for the footwear, which is of the same substance as the body of the apparatus.

"Am I stupid!" said Ozaki, embarrassed. "I didn't think about your dress..."

"Bah!" She has already tucked her skirt between her legs and, rolling it up to the knees, begins to insert herself into the trousers of the diving suit. Ozaki looks away.

"Why are you turning away, Ozaki? Are you afraid of my legs?"

He looks at her, and strives to smile. In his turn, he puts on the trousers, but awkwardly. It seems that his eyes dare not linger on Gioia's gestures and her revealed leg, gilded beneath the snowy weave of her stocking—but the spectacle causing his anguish is soon over."

"Do as I do," he says.

He passes his head and arms through the cassock that forms the upper part of the vestment. Then he takes a small air battery and installs it on Gioia's back, and then a helmet of glass and metal, equipped with a tube oscillating in the air.

"An acoustic wire that will keep us in communication.

He fits the helmet over Gioia's head, connects the tubes of the battery, and, the young woman dressed, equips himself in his turn, indicating by means of signs a few complementary arrangements.

"Can you hear me, Gioia?" says his voice, from one helmet to the other.

"Quite clearly."

"Off we go, then…"

He puts the radiators in circulation. A few moments later, a mist invades the room and is deposited as frost on the tubes and walls.

"First phenomenon," says Ozaki. "It's the water vapor in the atmosphere condensing. He points to a series of glass tubes on a table. "No thermometer can function at the cold whether we're going, even an electric resistance thermometer. Its via these test-tubes that we'll know the temperature. Each of them contains an acid or a gas whose freezing point is known. Look, here's the cyanide taken. We're at minus thirty-four. A slight chill, of no interest... The nitric acid…forty-seven now. The chloroform...seventy. That's nothing yet... Chlorine…102."

"We're a hundred degrees below?"

"Yes. Don't you feel anything?"

"Nothing."

"A hundred degrees is still very little... The alcohol…we're at minus 130... The nitrogen dioxide…167. It's becoming serious. Imagine the world, and us with it, suddenly transported into a space where the cold reigns that we're attaining now. This is what comes of it, better than with hypothesis, with the aid of Wells and Renard. Take one of those flowers, Gioia.

At the corner of the table is a crystal vase contains roses. The water is a solid black, but the flowers have conserved their form and color. Scarcely has Gioia touched them than the vase and the flowers are reduced to powder. She withdraws her hand swiftly. Ozaki's laughter sounds in her helmet.

"Difficult for Don José to conserve the flower that was thrown to him for long at this temperature.[51] But at minus 167 degrees, would sentimentality be that which ornaments comic operas? If we were to symbolize Carmen by quicksilver, we would find her strangely stable at this temperature..."

He picks up a thermometer and breaks it, extracting the rigid column of mercury from the tube.

"If one loses one's pen at the pole..."

He picks up a slate and scribbles figures with the mercury wand, which has become a pencil.

"Let's be honest," he goes on. "The fragility of flowers proves nothing if the heaviest and most elastic of metals is a friable as they are."

He bends down and picks up a lead pipe, which he raises to chest height and then drops. The pipe shatters into a thousand fragments, like crystal.

Delighted, Ozaki sketches the bow of a street conjurer.

"Amusing physical games. Korrigans gamboling in the vicinity of a fairy palace. We're going to penetrate into a more curious region..."

The temperature is still dropping. The air in the little room is transformed into an increasingly think mist. A kind of rain falling from half the height of the cellar begins to accumulate on the floor in blue-tinted puddles.

"The oxygen," says Ozaki.

The rain intensifies; the mist becomes even denser.

---

[51] In Act II of Bizet's *Carmen* (1875).

"We're approaching 195. Soon, the nitrogen..."

At that moment, blue sparks begin to spring between the electric wires that run from the corners of the room. The argon lamps explode, and arcs of immeasurable length are established between the sockets, of molten metal falling into the liquid oxygen in droplets that burn instantaneously, launching showers of sparks. A thick fog of liquefied air invades the glass of the portholes.

In a darkness the color of soot, where no object can any longer be distinguished except in staccato fashion, as if dancing in the wan reflections of the entangled explosions of electric lightning flashes and showers of sparks, there is a kind of intermittent howl of light around the diving suits. It seems to Gioia that the fluids are gradually penetrating the diving suit, flowing through it in lukewarm waves, and all piercing her with a thousand exquisite pinpricks.

Meanwhile, she looks at Ozaki, whose serene but dilated eyes the crepitating fires are licking, paining and sculpting chaotically with vermilion, blue and violent shocks through the curved glass of the helmet. Upright, in the massive vestment that can only be perceived in places at the eccentric hazard of the fulgurations, he contemplates the apocalypse. With an ample gesture, the lord of the forces he has released, he turns to Gioia and the pride that armed his gaze an instant before immediately becomes adoring admiration.

Gioia too is the prey of the unleashed light, and in the globe of glass, her eyes are voluptuous and her face proud to receive the fiery hosts. Between Gioia and Ozaki, the marvelous moment is established, as hard and splendid as a column of gold.

Abruptly, a strange dolor takes possession of the young woman, a sensation of burning and the tearing apart of all her fibers. She shivers, and totters.

Before she has even cried out, Ozaki, who has also trembled violently, bounds to the handle of the radiator, cuts off the current, and goes to open the portholes. The external air irrupts inwards, the mist clears, and daylight invades the little room. Nothing remains of the enchantment but the dust of flowers, metal and crystal on the floor.

"Just in time!" he says, having promptly unscrewed the air-tubes from Gioia's helmet and lifted off her helmet and his own. "How do you feel?"

"Perfectly well, now. There was only one slightly brutal shock…"

"I failed in my duty. We had attained the limit of the impermeability of the diving-suits, and were at risk, in another two or three seconds, of being electrocuted. The truth is that, knowing that limit, I hadn't yet pushed the experiment so far. And on looking at you...oh, Gioia, how beautiful you were! Proof that scientific work adapts poorly to any intrusive excitement..."

"I was looking at you, too, Ozaki—and you were handsome."

"In such a firework display, anyone would take on a grandiose aspect."

They have taken off the diving suits. Ozaki opens the armored door of the cellar and they both go up the little spiral stairway.

"Herbert was right," said Gioia, "sustaining a few days ago to one or other of us that at a certain altitude, all values dissolve. The one that you've just reached…is it only by science that limited it? What a symphony you constructed with the fire! And Marden would have exulted before the tamer of lightning-bolts!"

"You'd see me red with vanity," said Ozaki, laughing, "if this redoubt weren't so poorly lit."

They have reached the lumber-room that precedes the bedroom. Ozaki closes the door to the cellar. They go into the bedroom. Gioia stops.

"I fear…," she says, with a certain hesitation, "you said something just now…that doesn't augur well for a request that I have to make to you, and for which I came."

She sits down negligently on the bed. "When will you be ready…for the great ascension?"

"Soon. The last trials have been satisfactory."

"Three weeks? A Fortnight?"

"A week, if the weather is favorable. A week today. I'm waiting for a certain preparation from Mirard. Why? I hope you'll give me the pleasure of watching my departure..."

"Yes, yes, but…you're truly going to travel alone."

"Indeed."

"I have a companion to offer you."

"Admirable! A man who isn't afraid of a possible plunge of twenty thousand meters? A man with sufficient composure, whatever happens, to keep watch on my little swarm of dials?"

"Yes—except that it isn't a man, but a woman."

Ozaki starts. His voice becomes chilly. "You?"

"No."

He maintains silence for a moment, as if to collect himself, after an excessively violent shock."

"This isn't serious. I can only take a mercenary, ready to risk everything for a payment in proportion to the risk, or an equal tempted by the exploit."

She braces herself on the little bed, her head against the wall, one hand nonchalantly on the metal, crossing her legs and swinging them in the air; the stretched fabric of her dress emphasizes the young harmonies of her breasts and her legs.

"It's very serious, Ozaki."

He takes a chair. "Pardon me. I'm disturbed. Partly by the strange thing that you seem to want to ask me…more because I'm looking at you and to see you like this…don't you know that I love you passionately?"

"Be good, my little Prometheus. It's not a matter of me for the moment... Or, rather, it's a matter of granting me…this strange request..."

"If I succeed once, yes…perhaps. But I'd have to be insane, criminal, to associate with a danger full of unknowns…"

"You've just declared, with fewer adjectives, that you're ready to take a mercenary or an equal…"

"Which is to say..."

"Why should a woman—and know immediately that it's one of us—not be the equal of those among whom you'd find…that equal?"

"I know your intransigent feminine pride. And that you that you'll respond that you won't shake like a plum-tree to make all the ripe fruit fall…to be eaten? I prefer to respond simply that I refuse."

"The thing is," says Gioia, in a perfectly calm voice, amusing herself by using her free hand to roll a large pearl suspended around her neck, which is nesting in her cleavage, over her breast. Ozaki, suppressing his desire, does not take his eyes off that hand. "The thing is, my friend that it's Vénerise that you'll be taking. Can you imagine, in addition to the attraction that the ascent toward the ether, higher than anyone have ever dared to go, offers to her dreamy imagination, and in addition to the pride that she'll experience in, as you said, being part of your exploit…can you imagine…my God this is complicated..."

"Whatever it is, I repeat categorically, Gioia, that I refuse."

"But he's impolite, that Ozaki, to interrupt at the moment when one is having the most difficulty finding one's words!" Laughing, Gioia leans a little farther back on the bed. "Can you imagine that Vénerise is on the threshold…let's say of a proof, or the…psychological order, which she judges so grave…that she prefers…in sum, that she would like, first, to precede it with another proof, which only demands simple courage..."

"I'm listening to you in amazement."

"Perhaps one day I'll clarify the mystery for you... Having proved to herself, by confronting that danger, full of unknowns...but exclusively physical unknowns...the measure of her strength—I'll say that again, her courage—then she'll be able to dare the other proof..."

"More redoubtable, if I understand you correctly, than one that might end with her young beauty horribly crushed on the ground?"

Gioia lets go of the pearl, straightens up, sits on the bed and looks hard at Ozaki.

"Yes."

He shakes his head.

"I refuse. In all conscience, I can't make myself the accomplice of what I suppose to be a sentimental crisis…I won't permit myself anything beyond that word…and which, sharp as it might be, has, thank God, other means of being cured."

Gioia smiles scornfully. "It's sorted out like that in a good many romances. A ribbon, a jewel, a doll, even…and the girl is sprightly again, tears all gone, heart returned…"

"I don't mean..."

"A male crisis, yes, that counts! Suppose, for instance, that I go away now and make sure that you never see me again…"

"Gioia!"

"In fact, what would you do?"

He has become very pale.

"You too have your jewel, your doll…but it won't prevent you from taking off in your apparatus in a week's time…"

"How do I know?" he says, with a sudden distress and brutal irritation. "Why throw my two passions face to face, like two enemies, one of whom is in excess? And are they two? I believe that it's for you, to be worthy of you, that I'm going to attempt the victory for which I've labored for so many years..."

"Why would you come here if not to combine your victory with the conquest of Gioia d'Aldezza? But the first, you wanted before even knowing me!"

"What does that signify? Now that I do know you, my work and my love are inseparably confused."

He gets to his feet and paces back and forth.

"I won't take Vénerise. You've suddenly mixed me up, madly, in an adventure that's absolutely foreign to me. How can a woman of your intelligence provoke such a baroque situation? Only one thing is possible…plausible...at the very least, only one idea, of that order, could have made you come. That too would have rendered me desperate. But it would have an appearance of sense. It would have been…that you would ask me to take you. You're making my mind wander! But in sum, you would thus have remained until the moment of realization…that which you have been to me, that which you have become in the preparation of this moment…the blood, the heart of my work, the amour of my amour…and if my work had crashed to the ground, well, everything of me would have died with it!"

"Everything…which is to say, me included."

He plants himself directly in front of her, and says, curtly: "Yes."

An ironic "Thanks" is sketched on Gioia's lips, but immediately repressed. She dies not reply immediately. She is very grave, her gaze distant within her. She attempts to dissimulate that gravity.

"Another than you wouldn't have accepted my crushing so easily—another for whom I am, as for you, the goal, the heart..."

"And who, if I fall, will continue to hope for their adorable recompense..."

Silence on Gioia's part.

He resumes his pacing back and forth, in a fever that makes his voice burning, and the words collide.

"It's a dolorous thought that has often gone through me. After me, if I fall..? But until this moment, my faith responded to me by rejecting the incisive interrogation: I shall not fall! Into the interstices of that faith, other thoughts slid. To take her…in order that she should not be another's, if... In order that she should finally be conquered, if I triumph..."

"Where have you got the idea, Ozaki," she said, slowly, "that your triumph would necessarily have that consequence?"

He sits down again facing Gioia.

"I told you that my mind was wandering. You've led me to express sentiments that can be killed by exposing them to the light of day. The phrase I've just pronounced was glimmering in the profoundest depths of my being, in that fragile—but so powerful!—region where dreams float like light on water…all those cherished things…unformulated…which consciousness grasps with as many precautions as the dawn opening petals...."

He extends his hands toward Gioia. She does not take her own away. He takes them, squeezes them.

"And now, you have…no, you haven't said anything that has killed the fragile and powerful hope...but only asked…where have I formed it? Well, in my love, in my pride, in my desire, in the florescence, the conflagration of all my living, audacious…victorious forces. Gioia! Don't speak. Let me burn my hands on yours with a voluptuousness as marvelous as if it were...all of the possession..."

He is on his knees before the bed; he puts his forehead and his whole face on Gioia's hands. His lips pause, trembling and hesitant, suddenly pressing against the ardent palms.

Gioia disengages herself, and in the same curt tone that Ozaki had used a little while before, she says: "I agree to go up with you."

He stands up, moves aside, touches his forehead with a distracted movement. "No…no..it's sufficient for me that you said it."

Gioia is standing up, facing him, entirely self-controlled, calm and precise.

"I'll depart with you. A week today, did you say? That's good. That's not all, however. I don't want, by accompanying you, to conclude the adventure for the others who have thrown themselves into it. Nor do I want, if I come back alive, to conclude for myself the hope of many of my dreams. Perhaps you will be that man. I haven't yet exhausted the exigencies of the dream. I can't say any more to you. It's therefore necessary…"

The visage, until that moment a trifle severe, relaxes, smiles, becomes cheerful and malicious again.

"…That you accept, my dear Ozaki, that I offer—or, rather, that we offer—the proof of that ascension to each of our suitors. The one who accepts…will be the desired mechanic. It can't be so difficult to watch the manometers and shout out figures to you. As for me…well Ozaki, it will be necessary not to look at me too often. Twenty thousand meters of altitude in a sheet metal shell must be less docile to tame than two hundred degrees in a cellar..."

4. Encounters

"A night on the railway can render the cleverest minds a trifle muddy. I'll dot the *i*s. In any case, this evening, La Darlys will repeat the lesson. But you'll have time to think about it between here and Thonon. It's a blow to take. I'm supposing a client whose demanding mysticism—in brief, the sugar, the fondant, that of the amour in which one keeps a close eye of the fellow who's in front of you, with eyes that are gazing through him at his double in heaven, in the ideal—in a word, the other side of the ceiling."

"Like this?"

"Not bad. But you've got a fluttering eyelid. La Darlys will get you to rehearse in front of a mirror. Good. With that..."

Evian. Five o'clock. The terrace of the casino. At a table in front of two doors, Lemart and a tall young woman, too blonde, red waxed cloth hat, gray mantle, red scarf, and a visage in which the night spent in the carriage, hidden on the cheeks beneath ocher powder, allows its effect to be glimpsed in the corners of the eyes.

"With that…if you want it to pay off, of course, and to have another go; otherwise the client will let go, leave you the same tip he leaves the chambermaid and won't come back…so, you're all sighs, and it's still his portrait in the heavens that you're contemplating, while your hands play the butterfly on the hair..."

"Understood."

"A quarter of an hour later…the others are occupied…there's one who wants the girl. Good. You pick up the hair. La Darlys will furnish you with the wig. You put on the riding outfit or the tennis kit. The horsey one is more demanding because of the boots."

"I've got a pair in my trunk, shined, all that's required to satisfy..."

"Nothing at all. Special pairs that have been specially made to copy the real ones, those from out there. You'll be furnished with those too. You treat the client like a little boy who's just been forgotten in the drawing room..."

"I know the work…"

"The difficult thing is passing from the state of mind of the first to that of the second, or one of the other three…"

"The old man that had me first found that I had dispositions for the theater, and if I'd stayed with him…but one's stupid. The concierge's son, a rugby forward, and as if he's been born yesterday!"

"Your train's in half an hour. You can tell me about your childhood later. I'll continue the march-past. A third starveling…Hang on!" The voice becomes muffled, imperious. "Get up without hurrying. Get out. Go wait for the train at the station. La Darlys will finish the job. *A bientôt*."

"It's because of the girl who just came in?"

"Yes. Take a good look as you go. That's one of them…one of the real ones…from out there..."

"Impossible!"

"Go. *Au revoir*."

The blonde woman shakes his hand, and goes. Lemart takes a banknote from his pocket, puts it on the table, and gets up. At that moment, the new arrival, who is advancing slowly toward the empty tables on the edge of the terrace next to the lake, looking at the customers, perceives him.

Broad sweep of Lemart's hat, ornamented with a smile of astonishment and pleasure; an instant of feigned uncertainty as to whether he ought to limit himself to the sweep of the hat. The same uncertainty, not feigned, in the smile that replies to him. Resolutely, Lemart goes toward the newcomer.

"Bonjour, charming Mercerelle."

At that name, people at nearby tables raise their heads.

"Bonjour, Lemart."

Noticing the curiosity around her, she moves faster as she advances further.

"I dare not ask you whether I'm indiscreet," says Lemart. "Doubtless you have some rendezvous. I saw you searching..."

"A gaze of simple amusement. I wasn't looking for anyone. I had the auto stop in order to take a cup of tea by the lake." She seems to reflect, and comes to a rapid decision. "You're alone? Would you care to keep me company?"

"Delighted."

"I'm not disturbing you?"

"I came to meet a comrade—a young actress who's performing in the vicinity."

"The blonde woman that went past me?"

"Mademoiselle…Gramant…of the Odéon. One of my friends, the Comte d'Aranches, protected her during her final examinations at the Conservatoire."

"Oh?" says Mercerelle, perfectly indifferent.

They go to a free table.

"I'd like to be as close as possible to the quay," she says. "I'd be curious to see, if hazard permits, the landing of the boat in which our old friend Amarjit makes a little excursion every day, it appears. The pleasure of being on his path and observing his face when he recognizes me..."

"Indeed. Did he not take his leave in a rather extraordinary fashion?"

"He gave Vénerise the pretext of troubles in Ezrapur requiring an immediate departure. A rather impertinent story. But you..."

They sit down. Lemart orders the tea.

"I anticipate your reproaches. It's some time since anyone has seen me. I only got back yesterday…" He is playing negligently with one of his gloves, and lowers his voice: "Are you aware of the strikes that have just broken out in various places…among the post office employees in France, the employees of the banks in Madrid, on the railways in London…?"

"Vernail keeps us up to date better than the newspapers. I believe I've heard him mention it."

"Establish the connection between those strikes and my absence," he says, in a casual but circumspect voice. "That's why I couldn't write to you, and counted on justifying myself orally."

They are served.

"I'd be delighted to have news of the Palais," says Lemart, pouring the tea.

"Klutzkil in a frightful state because the Independents don't want his masterpiece...he oscillates between quitting us, extracting himself from the delights of our Capua, injurious to his art, and his love for Gioia, which retains him. Not to be touched with tongs, the painter, absolutely unseated. Vernail riveted to the preparation of a bolide that he's entering in the Central circuit. Mirard plunged, or as good as, in the barrels of liquid with which he's beginning to have the terrace of the Palais and Ozaki's aircraft painted..."

"Why are you smiling?"

"Was I smiling?"

"There was a certain mockery in your voice."

"Oh...Ozaki checking his helicopter and buckling his helmet: Lesielt going from one to another, idling and taking an interest..."

"Ozaki's ready?"

"He's taking off in four days. Monday the sixteenth at nine a.m., to be precise."

"A great morning for him, and perhaps for the world..."

"For Gioia too. He's taking her."

"Surely not!"

"Yes."

"What madness!"

"At any rate, she's showing more pluck than a lot of men."

"That's undeniable. But insane..."

"We arranged between us—you wanted to know why I was smiling?—to ask our friends which of them wants to accompany Gioia."

Brief involuntary grimace on Lemart's part. "And?"

Mercerelle takes a small case from one of her pockets, takes out a cigarette and lights it. "Something very curious happened."

"They all offered?"

"No. All of them, except Lesielt, who hasn't been asked, refused."

"That doesn't astonish me. It's their assent that would have been curious."

"Come, come..."

"All of those men have a superlative idea of their duty toward themselves, the first of which is not to risk their life, which is sacred, avowed to a goal superior to that which is in their common humanity..."

"Their desire, or their love for us, is part of that common humanity?"

"Let's understand one another, Mercerelle."

"I understand you very well. That manner of seeing, which is exactly theirs, gives rise to scenes of a very successful drama."

"I imagine them!"

"And identical. At first they begged Gioia not to go up. Inexplicable impulse...tragic childishness…a crime to risk a beauty—body and intelligence—so useful to the magnificence of the world…and to the excitation of genius…that of the messieurs in question, of course. The best of all..."

"There was a better one?"

"That was the moment when all the reasons…reason itself…was exhausted. The drama reached the major spheres. It isn't fear of dying, they said, but of that vain death exclusive of our mission. Ask me, Vernail cried, seeing me resolute in supporting Gioia..."

"Ah! You too..."

“Of course. And what a sensational pretext to measure my gallant’s amour! He was at my feet, that strong man, taking hold of my hands, my knees. ‘Ask me to pilot my own bolide on the Circuit, let me tempt death in one of my own ventures...in order that a catastrophe would leave you, and the world, with an image of me linked to my work!’”

“You don’t find that marvelous?”

Mercerelle blows on the ash of her cigarette, chasing away a little that has fallen on her skirt.

“All the same, do you know that you all have a fine talent for cruelty…?”

She smiles, enigmatically.

“By the way, why hasn’t Lesielt been asked? It would have been amusing to see that professor of will...”

“Perhaps he would have accepted. He’s eccentric enough. His self-possession, although we admire it, irritates us. The cold perspicacity that he has, and which sometimes goes further that one believes that one knows about oneself... Admit that what he calls Gioia’s childishness has quite serious reasons…but how embarrassing and curious you are!”

He reflects momentarily. “And me? Why wasn’t I offered…?”

“Doubtless because you weren’t there and we had no news of you. Are you saying that you’ll go up?”

“As a matter of acrobatics it’s not overly tempting. But the opportunity would have tempted me to show you all, better than I have so far, the man that I am. I won’t hide it from you that I’d prefer, like those messieurs, if it’s a matter of risking my life, to gamble it on my veritable personality, at the head of a fine crowd of insurgents. But in the meantime...”

Mercerelle is not listening. For some moments she has been staring intently at a growing dot on the lake.

“It’s Monday the sixteenth at nine,” she says, distractedly, as if she were talking about a game of tennis. Her eyes are riveted to a motor boat arriving rapidly, at the prow of which floats a crimson flame on which the image of an ivory chariot pulled by two tigers stands out.

"By the way, Lemart…would you like to do me a favor?" She is speaking lightly, without looking at him. "Obviously, we're going to exchange a few words with Amarjit…I have a commission to make to Narasa, on the part of one of us."

The boat reaches the dock. A Hindu servant gets to his feet. Amarjit leans on his shoulder and reaches the steps. Narasa follows him.

"…And I'd prefer it if Amarjit didn't hear what I have to transmit to his secretary."

"Entirely ready," says Lemart.

"I'll take a cigarette. At that moment..."

The two men approach. The Maharajah comes alongside the first tables of the edge and goes to traverse them. He sees Mercerelle. She looks straight at him, with a mocking laugh.

"Mercerelle d'Aldezza," says Amarjit to Narasa. Slightly constrained, he comes toward her. "What a happy surprise."

"Indeed," says Mercerelle. "What are you doing here? We all thought you were in Jasgraun, or nearly..."

"As I was about to leave Thonon I received a message from the British government asking me to wait..."

"Sit down, Amajit..."

The three men shake hands. Amarjit and Narasa sit down.

"And you, Narasa…who had departed for Marseilles?"

"I've come back, Mademoiselle."

"And you haven't informed us of all these events, Amarjot?"

"They're so recent.…"

He orders iced drinks.

"We'll be very amused this evening," Mercerelle goes on, "when I tell…but you'll repair your negligence, I hope!"

"Don't doubt it…however…the situation is delicate, you see…at any moment, a telegram..."

While he strings the phrases together Mercerelle observes Narasa surreptitiously. An almost imperceptible contraction is agitating one corner of his lips, as if a secret tension of his entire being were terminating there and betraying itself. Lemart has caught the indication at a glance.

"In truth, Highness," he says, "I can't help thinking about all our grandiose discussions in those charming hours on the pagoda-like boat..."

"Grandiose is the word," says Amarjit courteously.

"But how far it is from that…to envisaging that England..."

Mercerelle has taken out her cigarette case.

"What do you mean?" asked Amarjit, haughtily.

"The perpetual intervention of that England is something that is so…it goes without saying that I can't compare the impenitent revolutionary that I am... However..."

Mercerelle has held out her cigarette case to Narasa and lit a cigarette that he has just taken for him..

"One of my sisters has things to say to you...grave things…a rendezvous, one to one, for her..."

He does not blink. He simpers. "Yes. Where?"

"Say."

"The Imperial, three o'clock. Amar takes his siesta. What day?"

"Tuesday the seventeenth."

"Why so long?"

She plunges her eyes into his eyes of jade. "Because."

She has seized a straw, ripped off its paper envelope and planted it in Narasa's glass.

"That Lemart!" she says, laughing nervously "brings politics into places where life is so good, where one ought to think only of breathing in the moment. Is he still trying to evangelize you, Amarjit? Leave your republics…Narasa and I are contemplating the lake. Who can worry about telegrams from England before this sunset?"

5. Lurzine—Quebec—Ontriond

"Nineteen thousand eight hundred. The time, Lesielt?"

"Half past eight."

"Soon be dark. Impossible to prolong the day much longer."

"A fine game of hide-and-seek, Captain! Five or six times when the horizon swallows the sun and your winged finger goes to snatch it from the depths of the gorge!"

"But it's finished. The digestion of space is more rapid, after all, than my winged finger."

"You talk about nineteen thousand eight hundred meters like characters in Scudéry,[52] Messieurs," said Gioia. "My turn. I'm Atalanta. The sun was the first of the golden apples that the Hippomenean sky has thrown before me to slow me down. I'm not about to let myself get caught."

"Look out for the second one, which will the moon," says Ozaki. "It's ripening quickly. Look east."

"I still won't give in. We'll continue to run, Ozaki, in order that I can return before dawn."

The terrible command of the d'Aldezzas, at these height! But my promise will be kept, or there'll be a catastrophe. I only fear one now!"

"Where are we at this moment?"

"Somewhere over the Atlantic, about forty latitude and longitude, between Washington and Lisbon. Without your command and my promise, Gioia, we'd have continued in a straight line after refueling in Quebec. By now we'd be over the Philippines or Tokyo."

"You'll return there when you like. What a welcome. Japan will be your long-distance flight now. You'll find your statue on landing."

"Thanks."

"Sunk, Pegasus!" says Herbert. "The nag just flew over Hellas. A fly on a drop..."

"Of Greece?"

"Such a leaden pun must have augmented the weight of the aircraft. Pay attention, Ozaki!"

---

[52] Madeleine de Scudéry (1607-1701) wrote exceedingly long novels mostly consisting of interminable conversations.

"What speed, in revolutions of the compressor?"

Herbert rapidly scanned a series of large labels fixed above the manometers.

"Revolutions…thirty thousand."

"Perfect."

"My labeling system is good. Anyway, since this morning I've begun to get used to it. I know almost all your dials now."

"Honor to your ingenuity, Herbert," says Gioia. "That was very well and very quickly done this morning."

"Paper, a pot of glue, a pen. Not sorcery."

"All right—but allow one to admire the phlegmatic presence of mind with which, to substitute for an initiation as a mechanic, you stuck up your papers a moment after the…rather impromptu…invitation."

"It would certainly have been better to give me a little advance warning. But what an idea, between the two of us, initially to have preferred Lemart..."

"Do you believe his excuse?"

"Murky character. To be honest, I'm inclined never to believe anything he says."

"The strikes are real, though."

"But is it real that he had anything to do with them?"

"*Retained Paris movement electricians*. His telegram arrives as he was awaited outside the aircraft. Admitting that Lemart invented a role in the strikes recounted by the newspapers, that one wasn't known this morning."

"Easy, when we return to establish the existence or not," says Ozaki. "Light, please."

Herbert lowers a handle. The cabin lights up. In front of Ozaki, beneath the porthole, a bulb lights up the barograph, the compass and the indicators of speed. In the sky, darkness has fallen.

"Obscurity on earth as in heaven. The panorama passes to the interior."

"Let's agree that the one offered to us by the exterior…save for the glorious sensation of height for height..."

"You were disappointed," says Ozaki. "I foresaw that. Having gone up several times to ten thousand prepared me for that disappointment. Already, at ten thousand, the world appears as nothing more than a kind of gigantic route-map, odiously flat. You've seen Paris…as big as a sheet of letter-paper…the minuscule patches of towns, forests, the threads of rivers, railways... Except for the little bit of Canada and lunch in Quebec, your impressions of the voyage will be meager. By the way, in a few minutes, Lesielt, you can plug in Mirard's tubes."

A wire hangs down from the ceiling of the cabin, linked to two external items of apparatus, one fixed on top and the other underneath the hull.

"Here's the contact. At your orders, Captain."

"If the coating produces the anticipated glare, it won't fail to startle anyone who's sailing underneath us at the moment."

"Have you experimented?"

"On a reduced scale, in Mirard's darkroom. A light veritably as dazzling as the sun..."

"On a surface as extensive as the aircraft…don't you fear being dazzled yourself?"

"Bah! You can switch it off. Too bad for the experiment. If all goes well, as soon as the fireworks start, we'll be announced by wireless. The strolling transatlantics will know that the comet is inhabited, and by whom."

"*Vox clamantis in coelo…*,"[53] says Herbert.

"Plug in."

Herbert establishes the contact.

An immense light springs forth, enveloping the porthole in an unsustainable reverberation. Ozaki utters a howl of pain, and puts his hands over his eyes, letting go of the controls. A moment's suspension, the aircraft veers, assumes a vertical

---

[53] A voice crying out in the heavens. The usual reference, from the Vulgate version of *Isaiah* 40:3 has *deserto* [wilderness] intead of *coelo*.

position, and falls. Herbert has not had time to grab the wire. Gioia and he roll on the floor, cling on to parts of the engine, pull themselves half-upright and look at one another, the color of death.

The aircraft falls. The torn air resists, covering the throb of the propeller with a whistle that soon swells to become a kind of skewed roar. Metallic cracking sounds. The sheet metal undulates, buckles. The wings howl. Fulgurant, their thoughts seem dislocated, snatched from one millionth of a second to the next.

Gioia, her hands clutching the bars that surround the engine, has closed her eyes; her body is no more than a tremor, the teeth chattering, but the swooning consciousness tries to stiffen itself. In a murmur decomposed by the innumerable trepidation of her nerves, she groans a name, unintelligibly...

Meanwhile, Herbert, clinging to the ladder that leads to Ozaki's seat, has brought himself upright. Hanging on, tottering, he goes to the electric wire that he has just connected, tears it away, and the light that made the porthole and incandescent helmet is extinguished.

"Ozaki!" he cries. "Open your eyes! Your controls! Your controls!"

The other hears. He opens his eyes, the eyelids fluttering madly. He seizes the controls. He speaks, as if to himself.

"Ten thousand...gently…there…my fine wings...gently..."

The fall mutates into a slow, velvety glide; the metallic clamors due away; it seems that the aircraft is designing an ill-tempered ellipse in the reconquered element. Then, reconquered in its turn, it meekly resumes its course.

"We're safe, Gioia," says Herbert. The strange fellow has recovered all his calm of mind, in spite of the fact that he is trembling from head to toe. He goes to the young woman, detaches her hands from their support, draws her to one of the seats and sits her down. "Safe…it's over…isn't it, Ozaki?"

The latter does not reply. Herbert climbs a rung and looks at him.

"Yes," says Ozaki, his changed voice a trifle hoarse. "Look at the barograph. A fall of ten thousand five hundred meters. We're now at nine thousand. The engine can no longer give more than three hundred an hour. The return will take a long time...." An immense pride causes his lips to tremble. "She held, eh, the bird!"

He inclines his head toward the cabin. He sees Gioia, who is slowly coming round. Herbert, having returned to her, has knelt down and is squeezing her hands gently.

Without a word, Ozaki turns to the compass, and then his eyes are fixed on their route through space, seeming to plunge into his thoughts.

The hours are strung out, monotonously.

Gioia, exhausted, has fallen asleep. Herbert, sitting beside her, who has taken one of her hands in the gesture of a protective friend, is becoming drowsy in his turn. Ozaki only sees them thus at the moment when, breaking off his meditation, he says: "The Palais."

They wake up. A gray morning twilight. In the distance, on the ground, a dazzling patch is shining, with the same solar light that wounded the aviator, but whose radiation is paling with the increasing daylight. It is the terrace of the Palais.

"Here we are," signals Ozaki, via the wireless.

The loudspeaker installed on one of the walls of the hall releases the news to a composite group asleep in the armchairs and on the divans. Vernail, woken up, utters a cry that caused Klutzkil to straighten up with a start, and extracts the others from their torpor.

The intimacy of the Palais has been invaded, that night, by a certain number of strangers, whom the Contessa could not refuse the opportunity to witness the outcome of the flight and a victory qualified as historic in advance. Closeted in her room, frightfully anxious about an adventure that she could not prevent, she has asked Vernail and Klutzilk to be kind enough to welcome the visitors. There is an official representative of the Aéro-Club, a delegate from the Japanese embassy, a reporter from the Radia agency and a few other journalists who, on holiday in the region, came running, tempted by the prospect of a good story.

Until a late hour the conversation was brilliant as the regular guests strove to dispel their anxiety and the others to stay awake. A Parisian journalist led the game, pouring over the company a deluge of stories featuring interviews with negro kings, a lunch with the philosopher Bergson, saturnalias at the Lido, a football game with Maurice Maeterlinck...

The inexhaustible glibness has permitted a reporter from the Madrid *Libéral*—who also offered the excuse that he does not speak French fluently, although he understands it well enough—to remain silent. He is a courteous man of about thirty, thin, with a short black beard, a slender moustache and gold-rimmed spectacles. The Spaniard presented himself at the Palais the previous evening, attracted, he said, by the extraordinary lighting of the terrace, which he perceived from a distance while descending the Aylserine, where he had been on excursion. As he detailed his titles, Vernail has asked himself: *Where the devil have I heard that voice before?*...but his business affairs and amicable relations were so numerous!

In the pale early light there is a rush toward the park. The aerial voice from afar has preceded the aircraft. The sky is still empty and mute. Very agitated, Vernail goes up to the Contessa's floor and shouts the news personally.

Klutzkil sees Mirard, his eyelids swollen with insomnia, sitting on a bench. The scientist has spent the night in an extreme feverishness. He came into the hall for a few seconds, listened to the conversation without hearing it, and then went back to the park and stayed there, his eyes turned indefatigably toward the sky.

"They're arriving!" Klutzkil shouts to him.

"Now that it's daylight!" says the chemist, bitterly. "How do you know?" he asks, peevishly.

"Ozaki, by wireless, a moment ago."

"If my lighting had succeeded, I'd have seen them in the far distance, before sunrise…what can have happened?"

A dot in the west. Clamors. Spirals of the monoplane in the vast circle of the mountains. The landing. The race toward the apparatus—and the men stop momentarily to let Madame d'Aldezza pass.

Through the open porthole Ozaki emerges from the plane and lets himself down to the ground. They are about to run toward him, but there he is, as if a stranger to the crowd, seizing the wings, striking the surface, palpating the metalwork and caressing the sides tenderly, going from the axle of the propeller, surrounding it with his arms, and finally taking the propeller itself in his arms and covering it with kisses.

He raises his head, perceives the assembly of nonplussed spectators. "A fall of ten thousand five hundred meters, Messieurs!"

They surround him.

Meanwhile, Herbert has come through the porthole in his turn and, sitting on the edge of the opening, extends his hand to Gioia. That latter has appeared, pale but smiling and proud, and sits down facing Herbert, waiting for him to pull out the descent-ladder.

They are at the foot of the aircraft.

"Bad girl! Bad!" says the Contessa, feverishly embracing her daughter.

Then she stands aside in order to allow those she assumes to be as bewildered with gladness as herself to approach Gioia.

But the group formed by Gioia and her mother, with Herbert a little behind them, remains isolated. Some distance away, there is a swarm of men around the aviator, gesticulations and rumors, cut through by the thunderous voices of Vernsail: "We'll form a partnership. The earth and the sky!" Mirard: "So my tubes didn't..." the representative of the Aéro-Club, brandishing the barograph that he has detached from the aircraft: "Nine thousand eight hundred!" and the delegate from the Japanese embassy, holding Ozaki in his arms for an accolade: "The entire nation..."

V

1. Nocturne

A sob stifling in the pillow that the arms are kneading; a young semi-naked body, moist, contracting through the disordered sheets... The sob mutates into laughter of rage and distress... The laughing woman sits up in the bed, her face in her palms, her dilated and staring eyes plunging into the darkness of the room, filling with images...

A silky noise, almost imperceptible, in the lock. The key turns with a soft and precise slowness, as if gripped from without, inside the very lock.

The door opens, without a creak. A blade of exterior air comes to strike the naked shoulder of the girl on the bed. Torn from her thoughts she gazes at the door, stupefied, promptly extends her arm toward a commutator. A hand grips her arm. An indistinct form crosses the threshold and closes the door. Simultaneously contained and imperative, a voice says: "Don't cry out. Don't switch on the light. I have all kinds of things to tell you. You won't regret having listened."

"Let go of my arm. Who's there? What do you want?"

"I'll let go of this admirable arm if you promise to be good. You'll thank me for the darkness. There are truths so rude that they can only be given and received under cover. I'm bringing you those truths and enveloping them in darkness for you. You wouldn't hear them to the end in bright light. That would be a pity; they're very interesting, Mademoiselle...Mademoiselle...?"

The intruder has not let go of the arm.

"Curious. It was Vénerise with the long hair who came into this room, but you have Marden's short hair..."

Instinctively, with her free arm, she draws the sheet over her bare breasts.

"I recognize the voice. How dare you…how can you see me in the dark?"

"A gift I have..."

"What do you want with me?"

"Vénerise, or Marden, or another…the one whose arm I'm holding must already know that Vénerise didn't find anyone at the Imperial. Flown, the Hindus! Two days ago. Far away, the adored!"

A brutal shake of the arm, which frees itself. A leap toward the commutator.

"Not very brave for a d'Aldezza, this fear of the truth..."

Light. Lemart, his expression mocking, is beside the bed.

"On the contrary. It's the darkness I'm refusing. What do you have to say to me, and why this breaking and entering?"

Curt and rapid, the hands have passed over the face, effaced the confessions therefrom, tidied the hair and hoisted the chemise over the shoulder.

"Breaking and entering? That of your door. A very small matter compared with the other, that of your secret. For that one, I had an accomplice. Mercerelle, last Thursday at Evian. Better, five accomplices. Before Mercerelle, there were the confidences of all your eyes and your mannerisms, the day on the boat, that of the boxing match, twenty others... Let's pass on. Why the breaking and entering of the door? I told you. A delicate choice of terrain favorable for the florescence of certain truths. It's only the appearance of the procedure that's incorrect. Go to the heart of the procedure itself. It's that of a friend—your best, your true friend."

Motionless, she seems to have collected herself completely. She listens.

"I chose tonight, when I could catch you red-handed…in humanity. A poor girl, deceived, squeezing the debris of a broken dream desperately in her pillow. A picture. A d'Aldezza! But it's very useful that I surprise you thus, for your own good."

He advances into the room, picks up a chair, brings it close to the bed, and, still standing, says: "Do you want to hear me out? Or are you counting, as anyone else in your place would do, on calling for help at a given moment? Tell me whether I should sit down?"

"Sit down, Lemart. I'll hear you out. A veritable friend is a nice thing to have...."

"Bridle dropped, you're heading…all five of you…along a path terminated by a precipice. Several times now you've been able to glimpse the precipice…but you continue to run. The concept that you've formed of man, and of woman…by implication, you…has no relation to reality. The reality is your pillow and these sheets in chaos. The reality is me."

She smiles scornfully.

"Yesterday evening, when the aircraft landed, Gioia had a right to expect that her adorers would race toward her. It was his apparatus that Ozaki adored, Mirard only cared about his tubes..."

"How did you see that?"

"There were journalists there. I'd have been annoyed if the editor-in-chief of the Madrid *Libéral* had chanced to be one of them. He'd have been very astonished to discover a collaborator in me..."

"You weren't in Paris, then, for some strike..."

"The strikes had to do without me, as the *Libéral* had to do without my report. I haven't left the Savoy for a month.

"You agreed to accompany Gioia... The telegram..."

"A courtesy, in order not to delay the departure. The least of obligations. I had better things to do than risk breaking my neck."

"Ah! Good…the reality you claim to represent is that of the coward who sent the telegram."

"That of a wise man, in the circumstances. Too wise to yield to the whim of an eccentric and ingenuous virgin."

"The others found nobler excuses."

"I've told you that this evening, I'm the reality. You're talking about oratory conflagrations. The other day, before Mercerelle, I too indicated that I would more willingly die at the head of a revolution than in Ozaki's monoplane. That was for the eurhythmia of the conversation. It harmonized with the epic declarations of Vernail and Mirard. In fact, I was setting out to increase my prestige in your eyes. I was ready for it, even though the game had been a trifle hastily contrived. Your sister was much more preoccupied with a boat that was arriving than the flight to which she was inviting me...but I changed my mind completely when I heard what Mercerelle said to the young man. There was another way of increasing my prestige."

"You astonish me."

"I chose it. That's my visit this evening. It's to hang up in the carnival cloakroom that attire that you've forced your lovers to don, and the costumes you've put on yourself."

He advanced his chair slightly.

"They're going along with it. They'll conscientiously play to the end the singular drama into which you've drawn them. In coming here, they were ready for all proofs, save for those that touch their work. It's in their work that they counted on excelling in your eyes, triumphing, and all the rest was nothing to them but details. They saw you, fell in love. Spontaneously, sincerely, they've linked their love with their work. Your beauty, your graces, tour quality had what was required to symbolize, in their eyes, their ideal, their principal reason for living.

"It's at this point that a subtle duality is formed, in which poetry is confused with the real. Was their amour addressed to the objective woman or the symbolic woman? They didn't ask themselves the question. They weren't conscious of that duality. It's at the moment when they perceive it that the drama will unravel. They'll sort it out by sacrificing you. For such men, the great affair is their work, it's their mission. And what is their work, their mission if it isn't, in the final analysis, themselves in their highest expression?

"Superlative egotism, fatality of their powerful individuality, they only exist for themselves, in their work, in the exaltation of their superior self. Thus, in verity, it's themselves that they adore through you. That's a plot-twist which, although unconscious, is nevertheless a form of the eternal mode that makes woman the slave of man. But here it passes on to a plane so abstract that the enslavement can't be sensed either by the slave or the enslaver. The livery is an idol's robe.

"Now, beneath the livery thrown over you by your adorers, there was a pre-existent will equal to theirs, an ideal…an idea! It was you who set out to model their individuality, to subordinate their work to that idea... You demanded from them exploits that they were incapable of accomplishing, and which, above all, didn't interest them, with regard to their true, vital goals.

"The multiplicity of your pretentions disconcerted them, threw them off balance…let's say the word, stunned them. But their pride and their passion have prevented them, thus far, from seeing that it was on their sacrosanct grounds that your demands were playing. Now, they're going to see it. The drama is ripe. It's Ozaki's escapade that drew the curtain. Tomorrow, Ozaki and Mirard, suddenly embarrassed before Gioia, will become conscious that they immediately preferred to her, one of them his airplane and the other his fluorescence. Klutzil and Vernail, criticized by all of you for their negligence—which the return of the voyagers, safe and sound, no longer legitimates—will be led, in defending themselves, to see clearly what they would have staked in the adventure.

"The scales fall from the eyes, the duality bursts forth. Those women, symbols of their work, to whom Ozaki and Mirard instinctively preferred their work, who would not hesitate to ask Vernail and Klutzil to risk their work…are now revealed as foreign to the work, and those of the image that had been formed of them; they're no longer the same, they're no longer anything but women...

"Well, in spite of their passion, in spite of your beauty, your graces, your quality, the love of a creator for a woman in herself will yield to the love of their work...which is to say, the love of their ideal self. That's the reality, with regard to them. They'll go away. You've played an impossible game. You've expected from those men an impossibility multiplied by five..."

"So what?" she demands, impassively.

"It doesn't matter to you whether they go away because you don't love them. And you can't love them because of the idea with which you disguise reality, because of that quest for the impossible, which encumbers you. I'll pass on to you. Something must explain that quest, that superhuman chimera. It must be that you're a…that the five of you are a superhuman creature. The response is in that twisted pillow."

She looks at him with an immense disdain.

"You've taken a false path."

"No," he says, with a perfect assurance. "Oh, I admit that you're strong enough to get over a sentimental disappointment. I admit that the picture is only one page in a sumptuous album…of your sensibility. But it's sufficient to clarify your verity. The verity that the woman behind your chimera has a heart, and senses. She's human. She's not impossible to satisfy. Behind your chimera, there's something that isn't chimerical. It's the complexity, the number of your pretentions, of your desires.

"That's justified. Your wealth immediately heaped you with everything that is, for the majority, the goal of all pretentions and all desires. Does the world have what's necessary to match the excess of your appetite? What spoils everything is that you wanted to find that correspondence in a man, or through a man. The influence on girls, however intelligent, of the eternal seesaw of love stories and operas.

"It's the beloved man that you're waiting for, the great prism that renews and multiplies the world, so many treasures of which you had at your fingertips so young. Only, before, loving him, it's necessary for you to find a man, provided with the power of respiration, and of...how shall I put it…total prehension of the world. A dilemma that bars the route to amour. That man, who would be all men, doesn't exist There's a simple means of living in accordance with your verity.

That's to sample the totality of the world…in the world itself: it's to find all men…in all men."

"That's the crown of what you have to tell me? I could have attained that perspective on my own. It's permissible for you to submit it to my sisters. For myself, I thank you. I'll be happy if you would go."

"Your sisters? In talking to you, isn't it as if I were talking to all of them? It goes without saying that my singular is a plural. Unless it's your plural, which..."

He tapped the arm of the chair in which I was sitting.

"The perspective that I've indicated to you is far from concluding what I have to say. That would be infantile. You have indeed no need of me to think that the only way of living that suits you, and where you will fatally end up, which is to live as what is nowadays known as a bacheloress. But you do need me in order to realize that life. You're completely ignorant; you only know one face of the world, rich girl as you are: the face of visible beauties, ready roasted. Now, the world is truly exciting and splendid, and it's necessary to take its delights and juices for yourself by breaking the shell of appearances with your fingers, biting the fruit with your teeth to the core, and illuminating with your own light the diamonds hidden in its cellars. You need a guide, a solid and worldly wise companion. Without him, you'll go astray, poor girl; it will be your pretty fingers that the shell breaks, the flesh of the fruit will poison you, the darkness would stifle you. I will be that guide. You will quickly discover the extent to which I can be a man of adventure, lion and fox, vulture and mole, having excavated his life from day to day, every day growing his talons, his claws…his wings, capable inexhaustibly of extracting you from lassitudes, errors, checks, by always offering you, inexhaustibly, something more, something else."

"And where will that take me?"

"First of all, to know. Always penetrating existence more profoundly, but truly, and its countless faces."

She laughed. "To know! There's an infinitive that has already sounded in my ears, not long ago. And then? Afterwards?"

"To experience, to live, by every pulsation of your arteries—to find, in sum, even when you have had enough pulsations before each of your desires, the route, and its possession to the end."

"And then?"

"What 'and then?'"

"The goal of this knowledge, this insatiable satiation?"

"A goal? Ha ha! On earth? On this big bubble on which all of us, minuscule bubbles, dance in all the winds, under the fallacious tethers of morals, ideals, rhetorics! The goal is to *be*, fully, through all one's pores, to *be* with all one's forces, one's warmth, one's springs…until the bubble bursts."

"That's all?"

"But..."

"Your epic concludes with the bursting of the bubble?"

"Yes. What do you want to make me say?" He is troubled. "I'm a Christian. I have above that…absolutely personal ideas. This isn't exactly the time to discuss theology. We'll talk about it again, if..."

"If we ever find an opportunity to talk again."

"I'm tranquil. You'll find the opportunity, because it can't be otherwise. Unless, of course, you change body and soul and scratch out the hunger for the innumerable in the arms of a simple worthy husband."

She has extended herself in the bed, the sheet pulled up and listened to him with her head cued in her hand, her arm angled, looking straight at Lemart.

"You've interested me. Your proposal is very clear. Something is less clear. What does having you for a guide signify, exactly. Is it having you for a lover?"

He smiles

"And if you were my lover, either because you are the man that you declared just now to be chimerical, or because you force yourself between me and…all the men..."

He is still smiling.

"You project becomes murkier as I try to comprehend it. You don't love me. Your proposal includes everything that one might wish, except, certainly a declaration of love! On the other hand, since you're capable of being my guide, it must be that you know yourself, because you've experienced all those...impassioning...faces of the world. If that's so, what have they brought you? What need do you have of me?"

"It's quite true that I haven't mentioned love to you. That's because it's of no importance. Perhaps I love you. Have no doubt that there are for me—and for you—things that are much more interesting. Otherwise, how could I be discussing so calmly, before that naked shoulder that ought to be burning my mouth with thirst, and that marvelous body, which the sheet protects less than it...betrays? Have no fear. That which you bring me in taking me for your guide? Well, first of all, and principally, your millions."

She does not blink. "I believe that the moment has come to call for help. As anyone would do in my place...as you put it so well, in order to put me in advance of the uniformity of everyone else. I'd rather continue to be a being apart. It's droll. My millions?"

"I don't have a sou. The few banknotes that permitted me to put on a front here are as good as exhausted. We can skip the tirade about money, can't we? You must have heard it ten thousand times...and been close to enough artists and men of all qualities to know that there's no connection between the wealth of banknotes and that of genius. Admit that I have genius. That's what I want to barter, to put at your service, against one of the forms of your wealth—the grossest, your money.

"Thus far, I've had to accomplish exploits in order to dress decently and aliment the body of my genius, expending resources therein that could have been magnificently employed in the masterpiece of which I'm capable: enjoyment. Let's be fair. It's in the course of those exploits that I've been able both to measure my faculties and brush past the innumerable doors that I want to open to you. You understand now? Brush past. Most of the time, I've been obliged to remain on the threshold and look through the keyhole. Your money gives me—gives us—the keys.

"You asked me if I knew…yes. If I've experienced…no. It's my knowledge that needs your millions. You have need of my knowledge. The affair of money regulated, that material bases, leveled, there we are before one another, equal, with our true treasures: our intelligence, our avidity for enjoyment, our science of living. For the moment, of the two of us, it's me who's rich, from the latter point of view."

While he was speaking she has moved slightly—as if, by virtue of listening attentively, she has not noticed the nonchalant gesture of her leg, which, on bending slightly, has pulled the sheet down, uncovering her upper body. She has adjusted her arm on the pillow and the chemise has slipped down from the other shoulder. Her breast is bare, a lily-white globe, fresh life hard with sap.

"That's all you want from me?" she asks, gravely.

The eyes caught by that breast have blinked; a blush reddens the forehead. But immediately, the voice, rude and acrostic: "Yes, that's all… for the moment. Oh, you want to play with the strong! Naïve girl! You've thrown down a challenge to a man. Well, behold a man. Contemplate him. Do you think that my brain, with its proud light, its pullulation of will, is going to allow itself to be sucked in like that by your bare breast. Not worth the trouble of lifting the sheet. I'm not afraid. To yield at this moment to that which is tugging at my arms, my teeth, and hurl myself upon you? At the risk of your screams, of being caught, seized, or obliged to jump out of the window! Or worse…not to see in you, afterwards, anything but a woman like other women?

"Both of us want something that surpasses incalculably one hour, whatever it might be. We want life…all of life...all its hours, in which there are a hundred thousand adventures, a hundred thousand sensualities, in themselves, other than those of which two people, whoever they are, can be the field and the goal for one another. Let's go, together, to that life. I'll only be your cicerone. As for the desire I might have for you. I'm too well aware of something…far more ardent and vertiginous than slaking a bestial hunger like a beast.

"To hold you for an instant in my arms, physically? First, I want to hold you a thousand times in the arms of my desire alone, incessantly retained and stimulated. I want to make immense and terrible the hour when my desire has attained the point at which it's no longer that of the beast, but that of the entire being, which will have become desire... I want to prepare myself to make, in every hour that you live, an image of me rise up superior to the hour, whatever it might be...in order that you will be able, when the day comes, not only to yield, but also burn for me with the same flame... That in the margins of our alliance."

Stiffening himself, he recovers his calmness, his mocking tone.

"Let's leave that. We have time. I've told you that you know nothing, or only know one face, of the world into which I'm inviting you. Look…I'll give you an opportunity to reflect on what I've just told you. You, who are looking for a man, do you know what men are? While you dream of the coming of a hero…in the shadow of your virgin's chimera, do you suspect...do you know that something exists..."

He is entirely at ease, and sits squarely in the chair.

"Have you ever heard mention of the Petit Palais Gioia?"

2. The Petit Palais Gioia

I

Ten o'clock in the evening. Madame Juana enters the room where La Darlys is in the process of making up her accounts.

"Guite, there's a pullet here who wants to talk to you. Well dressed. An odd one—I can't tell whether she's come to be a lady or to offer herself one."

"Send her in."

Madame Juana goes out and comes back, followed by Mercerelle in a gray outfit and a little gray velvet hat."

"Bonjour, Madame," says La Darlys. Sit down. May I know what brings me the honor..."

Madame Juana has remained standing, against the door.

"I desire to talk privately."

"Leave us, Madame Juana." When the door is closed, she said: "I'm listening, Madame."

"I got the address of your house from one of my friends…in Paris..."

"Madame is from Paris?"

"Yes. I'd like to ask you to answer one question."

"My God, Madame, that depends somewhat on what brings you here," said La Darlys, reserved.

A silence.

"Madame," says Mercerelle, embarrassed, "I need your reply. "If it's such as I've been led to suppose, my intention would be to solicit you…under certain conditions…to engage..."

"My child, my experience isn't easily deceived. You have a distinguished air, a candid face in spite of your determined eyes, which permit me to think that you're not…an habituée. Speak to me with an open heart. This is the confessional. I'll never hear anything worse that I've heard before…and that's no small claim..."

"I absolutely need to know, first, whether it's true that you kept a house in Paris of the same kind as this one, and that one day you had the idea of coming to set one up in Thonon, but of a very special kind. You knew that among the usual coming and going of tourists, there was, this year, a certain agitation because of a Palais…a challenge.., of which the newspapers have talked..."

"That's true."

"Your idea…which you have realized…was to offer…discreetly…to those tourists piqued by the kind of legend formed around that Palais and who…did not feel sufficiently audacious to attempt to approach the five demoiselles…to offer them…as a substitute, a makeshift…the word doesn't matter...a kind of parody of the excessively difficult adventure."

"You're very well informed. I don't see any inconvenience in replying that that's exactly right...and that it was a fine idea, of which I have no reason to complain. That said..."

"I have a situation of fairly considerable fortune. I can dispose of a sum that we'll decide…even a large one…to thank you for having ceded to my request. You've discerned well. I'm not…an habituée. I'm a woman of letters, seeking to do first-hand research. Your idea is so original! You, I suppose, have counted on…how shall I put it?...the mediocrity of the greater number…their refusal to risk their petty male pride before young women above the average…a timidity that does not prevent them, of course, from crossing your threshold…because they were certain of finding here I don't know what...images…of those young women…before whom they could, with little effort, give themselves I don't know what gross illusion of victory…or, to put it better, a kind of revenge for their lack of audacity…"

"I see that Madame is not just anyone with regard to intelligence…there's only one small point to pick you up on. Lack of audacity? That's possible. But mediocrity...I've had gentlemen here, not only in terms of situation, but men of value. But you mentioned a sum..."

"Yes, yes…so my psychology is in default. It isn't only men of a rather ordinary quality who come. However, you admit…you find your profit in it, but you're not a dupe…you admit that it's an extremely gross caricature..."

"You're not taking the vice into account. Many are attracted by the originality of…my specialty. I don't gather here just any women. Take note that each of them is capable of putting themselves in the skin of the five genres required by the clientele..."

"But how have you been able to…style these women?"

"I can't say that I do it alone. I've been aided by a friend. But those are our little business matters. To get back to the price that you'll put..."

"Which you'll fix. The vice, yes...but is it possible to believe that certain men…for example…among your clients, there might have been the same ones who have been able to approach the real young women…those who are…received at the Palais…?"

La Darlys sank back in her armchair and sniffed, with a whistle.

"Oho! You're asking me strange things, my girl. I don't have much time to give you. You've arrived in the middle of working hours. All those bells you hear aren't the handbells of a children's choir, you know. It would be better if you got straight to the point. No need to put on kid gloves with Madame Darlys. It won't go beyond the two of us. Go on, I'll help you. The story about studying mores won't wash. The more I look at you, the more accurately I see. It's a personal matter. You want to know if someone in whom you're interested makes a little detour here now and again. But my poor dear, even if you offered me fifty thousand francs, I couldn't tell you, firstly, because I don't know the sames of all these gentlemen, and secondly, because a stitched mouth on that matter is the holiest of holies of the profession. Is that it? I've hit the bull's-eye? There you go. I'm sorry. It'll be necessary for you to go home empty-handed."

She has risen to her feet to conclude the conversation. Mercerelle has risen to her feet too, slightly pale but resolute.

"You said: fifty thousand francs."

"A manner of speaking. I could as easily have said a million."

"What if I really gave you fifty thousand francs?"

"What?" She has been gripped. She shrugs her shoulders. "You're not serious. Fifty thousand...to know a name?"

"No. To lend yourself to a comedy."

Someone knocks.

"What?" shouts La Darlys, angrily.

"It's me."

She goes to open the door to Madame Juana. "I'm busy with Madame. Take care of it on your own until we've finished—and don't let anyone disturb us. You aren't in difficulties, are you? Go."

She closes the door again.

"What's your comedy?" she asks, bluntly.

"Someone who revealed the existence of your house to me has offered, for certain reasons, to bring me to see what happens here. I reflected. I'd like to do something better than follow him and merely to see. I want to take the place of one of your…demoiselles, one evening when you've arranged for the men I'll identify to you to be here. It wouldn't astonish me at all if you already knew them."

Vague gesture on the part of La Darlys.

"I'm Mercerelle d'Aldezza."

La Darlys recoiled toward her little desk.

"One of the five…real ones. You'll inform them…you ought not to be embarrassed by these things…that you've been able to discover a demoiselle, an…habituée…who resembles in an astonishing fashion the daughters of the Palais d'Ontriond... You don't have portraits of us, then, as you didn't recognize me? That's marvelous! And the men are content!"

"No portraits, no," stammers La Darlys. "But indications of their mannerisms, the height, the genre...that's sufficed thus far. The men...ah, well..." She has lost all composure. "One of the true ones from the Palais!" She sits down, shaking her head. Gradually, she pulls herself together. Her eyelid creases, as if carefully closing over a sterling thought.

"Listen, Mademoiselle…in principle, for money, anything can be done. Except, you have to take account…if there were a row, consequences…in sum, if it were known that I'd lent a hand to it. There could...yes, via your messieurs, or friends of your messieurs... I'd be sunk in the business. I'd no longer be able to plant my cabbages, as they say…"

She has resumed smiling, wheedling, with a contained agitation that makes her voice slightly hoarse.

"Sit down then…planting my cabbages…one often wonders how one will end up…whether, at the end of business, one will have a little put by…enough to go plant one's cabbages in a small patch of one's own…around a little house…also one's own. But nowadays, carpenters, stone and cement.... Fifty thousand francs...has the air of being quite a sum…before an architect's drawings, it's three times nothing. You must know, you who live in a Palais and who have enough besides to bring…twenty-five million to your…it is really is twenty-five million…?

"Madame, if it's no longer anything but a question of money, I'll accept the figure you quote. I'll bring it to you on the evening that the comedy I'm paying for is played."

"Good, good…girls as rich as that, naturally...juggling with hundreds of thousands, on a whim... I can't absolutely refuse…but my child...I mean, Mademoiselle..." La Darlys flounders in the perspective of a deluge of gold, and suddenly softens. "Supposing that you discover what you want so much to discover…it wouldn't prove anything. They're bizarre, men. I can talk. Places like ours, they correspond to the funny little ideas that wander through their heads…but in the street, or when they're back home, they don't think about it anymore…they're worthy fathers of families…husbands who adore their wives. You can't know. I'm quite sure that the messieurs you want to bring here…are like all the rest. Think about it! Beautiful as you are! What connection is there with the poor girls I employ…?"

"Madame," says Mercerelle, "would you like us to choose the evening right away..."

II

"Excuse me," says Madame Juana, passing in front of Mercerelle to reach a kettle heating up on the kitchen stove.

"Madame Darlys warned you that it's a little narrow. The house is small. There's no other place to put these ladies..."

"Madame will be better off with us than waiting all alone moldering in a room," says Liliane. "She's right. It isn't boring. Nina does our cards for us and Gaby tells us stories of when she was a rep in the lace trade."

"Samion!" shouts La Darlys, opening the kitchen door, A thin blonde girl stands up and begins to tug at her hair while looking at herself in a dirty mirror hanging on the wall to the right of the stove. "How are things, Madame Christiane?" she asks Mercerelle. "Aren't these ladies very genteel?"

"Pardon me," says Juana, passing in front of Mercerelle again with her kettle and leaving the room. "Funny idea," she says to La Darlys in the corridor, "to have stuck your Christiane in with them. She's doing what she can to be amiable and put herself on their level, but it's obvious that she's on tenterhooks. Not her place. She's a princess, your spoilsport?"

"She's the one who wanted to wait with the girls. It interests her. It's teaching her. She's a woman of letters..."

"It's not polite, Guite, to keep secrets from me. It's the first time. I don't buy your woman of letters. It's for studying mores that she's reserved the big drawing room and the rooms around it? If you think that's convenient. I only have two rooms to receive the customers..."

"Are you going to pester me about that all night? I've told you a hundred times that I have superior reasons for keeping my mouth shut. She opens the door again. "Hey, Samion!"

"Here, Madame Darlys."

The blonde girl has covered her hair with a brunette wig, finishes arranging it, and follows La Darlys.

"Fortunately for the rest of us," says Liliane to Mercerelle, "they don't ask for her that often, Samion—she's the only one we can't do. Necessary to do too much fine talking. It's true that she can't do the others like us. She was a schoolteacher in her day, before falling into the game. She did her business in the workers' quarters. She was lucky that

Madame Darlys opened a house like this. It's got her back on her feet. The money's good."

"They don't ask for her often?" says Mercerelle.

"No—you understand. All the same, all those who come here…it's to surround the thing with a little spice, to amuse themselves with their imagination before…getting down to it…the Samion genre is the least sought after, because it reposes on fine enough conversation…to say the word, on intelligence. It's hard work, for a woman, to appear, and even to be, more capable, more learned that the one she's with. Because the client's pleasure, the more knowledgeable the woman is, is to say: keep talking…with one eye he's watching her talk, and with the other...he's looking at the bed. He knows full well that he'll have the last word."

"They don't come much for Samion," says Nina, "because intelligence is the least of the funds that one thinks of carrying on one's person in places like this…meaning to offense, Mesdames."

"None taken," says Gaby. "You can't pay your rent with intelligence. What good would it be to us?"

"Doesn't alter the fact," Nina insists, "that one likes someone better who talks well."

"Not my opinion. Those who talk best are always the most complicated…to put it another way, the most demanding…or to put it another, for the same money as the others, it's more work."

"Madame Juana opens the door. "Mercerelle!"

Mercerelle shivers. Gaby rises to her feet tranquilly and turns to a wardrobe fixed to the wall behind her, in which dresses are hanging, and takes a white wood box with black hinges from among the hats and boots on the shelf. She sits down, opens the box on her knees and takes out a hand mirror. She touches up her make-up, sticks a beauty-sort a little above the mouth, and pulls faces into the mirror, then adjusts her dress, puts the box back and goes to join Juana.

"Work in the same genre as Samion, but less difficult," says Nina. "Also necessary to be able to chat, but above all, to know how to be sarcastic, flirty, hold the client while he tells you that he invented the wire for cutting butter or can carry the Eiffel Tower on his shoulders. That's right?"

"It's funny," says Liliane, "all the time you've been there, I've been wondering where I've seen you before. That's reminded me. It was one afternoon when I was drinking at the casino in Evian with the Marquis, a friend of Madame Darlys—the afternoon when I arrived here. We crossed paths. I had a red hat and scarf…"

"Do you think so?" says Mercerelle. A surge of blood tightens her throat.

"Talk about a type, the one I was with! He said to me: Take a look at that one…she's a real one, from the Palais!"

"Oh" Very droll!" says Mercerelle, laughing falsely. "I'd like to be," she adds, "but I can't explain it. Your Marquis must have wanted to give himself the air of having relations. I've never set foot in Evian. It appears that it's..."

"A trifle pricey for hotels," says Nina.

"Madame Darlys has a friend who's a Marquis?" asks Mercerelle.

"That's a title he gives himself…Marquis of Bite-my-Finger. If he's anything, he's more like a king—the king of pimps. He's the one who unearthed us all or sent his pimps to propose we come here. It pays well. We don't have any complaints, anyway, do we, Nina?"

"No complaints. It's all a matter of playing the right part…"

"Vénerise…come on, Liliane or Nina?" calls Madame Juana, opening the kitchen door."

"It's Nina's turn," says Liliane.

"Not too soon to get rid of the rust," says Nina, getting up and going to a large cupboard. From a pile of fabrics, balls of wool and boxes of powder she selects a blonde wig with long bangs, puts it on over her short hair and fluffs it up in front of the mirror.

Mercerelle looks at her, her heart stirred by commiseration, distress and a frightful desire to burst out laughing. As

Nina heads for the door, La Darlys appears, moves Madame Juana to one side and, in a slightly strangled voice, says: "Madame Christiane, if you please. I have to say a few words to you..."

Mercerelle stands up. In the narrow passage between the stove, the women's chairs at the wall covered in dresses she takes a deep breath, clenches her fingers against her palms, and goes out into the corridor.

"The messieurs are there, Mademoiselle," whispers La Darlys.

III

Klutzkil had arrived first. "What's this about a double?" he asked La Darlys. "Where did you find her? Do you have photos of the young women, then?"

"You're very curious, my lad. If you knew all the tricks of the trade, perhaps you'd be in my place…and me in yours," she replied, laughing coarsely. "What I can tell you is that the pullet is a dancer at the Châtelet, and that someone who has an interest in my house encountered her absolutely by chance one evening recently hanging around in Montmartre. The affair was arranged, although it cost me dear—but there's nothing I wouldn't do for your pleasure... Go into that room and wait quietly. She's only just arrived and she's finishing getting ready.

"Look through the keyhole from time to time; the room opens into the big drawing-room. When you see her come in you'll have time to study her in detail. If it's no go, call me, and you can leave as you came. No one's more accommodating than me... If it suits, you have only to open the door, go into the drawing room and introduce yourself. The child knows what it's about. I'll leave you. Good luck. Would you like me to bring you some pictures to pass the time?"

Essentially similar, the welcome of Vernail, Ozaki and Herbert, put into the neighboring rooms opening on to the drawing room to wait. A slightly complicated situation with

Mirard. He was entering the strange house for the first time, having been completely ignorant of its existence until then. The others—Vernail via his secretaries and acquaintances at the Splendid, Ozaki from remarks let slip by his aides and mechanics, and Klutzil via comrades he has encountered—have known for a long time. There was no tourist in Thonon, Evian, Chamonix or Annecy who was not soon informed and tempted by hints dropped by hotel employees and chauffeurs...

Vernail, Klutzkil, Ozaki...had curiosity or salacity already pushed them, before this evening, to take a look? Had nausea or an enormous burst of laugher before the caricaturish simulacrum immediately caused them to retrace their steps? This evening, they were there, attracted by a letter simultaneously mysterious and precise. They were there, agitated by a troubled and stormy wait, pacing back and forth, each in the room where they had been enclosed by La Darlys, leaning over periodically toward the keyhole.

"Please go in, Madame Christiane," says La Darlys, opening the door to the corridor and standing aside to let Mercerelle pass. "Wait here for a moment."

She withdraws.

Mercerelle is clad in a gray two-piece or rather ordinary cloth. No other adornment than a pink coral saltire. Black shoes with very high heels and a rhinestone buckle. Her hair is cut short, like Marden's, but is blonde this evening—the blonde of Gioa's and Vénerise's hair.

She sits down in an armchair and opens a handbag, from which she first takes out a little mirror, looks at herself, smoothes her eyebrows, and then a small file with which she begins to file her fingernails. An oppressive silence around her, which a bell interrupts, but which closes in again immediately. She whistles a foxtrot, replaces the mirror and the nail-file in the handbag, leans back in the armchair tilting her head back, closes her eyes, stretches, and then crosses her legs. She reaches down to adjust one of her shoes, raising the foot slightly toward her idle hand in order to do so, uncovering her legs, serpents of jet. She remains thus momentarily, and then resumes her languid pose, as if ready to fall asleep.

Then all the doors open brutally at the same time. The men appear and see one another. Similar, their stupor and confusion, such that they go pale, and then blush as they try to sketch an incoherent smile. They make a movement of retreat, and stop, transfixed by Mercerelle's explosive and lacerating laughter. She beats the arms of her chair with her hands and leans back.

"Behold the lovers," she says. Hilarity punctuates the syllables.

"Messieurs...," It is Vernail who breaks the silence. "No need to look at one another like malefactors, or kids caught with the jam-pot. Let's see, what..."

His larynx congested, Klutzkil speaks. "Yes, what...we're not schoolboys. It's not the first time we've trodden the parquet of a bordello."

Mirard cuts in, awkwardly: "My God, Messieurs...I assume you've received a letter similar to the one I received. It revealed the existence of the house to me...as it did to you, I suppose...the finest of buffooneries...not to the honor of our unpleasant humanity. Except that inside that buffoonery, a means has been found of slipping a creature..." He looks at Mercerelle. "It's marvelous, Mademoiselle. You're a very pretty girl..."

"Yes," says Vernail, recovering a little aplomb. "It's amazing..."

Ozaki has not unsealed his lips. He is standing to one side with his arms folded, very pale.

Herbert is observing, waiting, his hands in his pockets.

"Come on," says Klutzkil, abruptly. "Let's go. What are we doing? Mademoiselle must take us for madmen."

"Yes indeed!" says Mercerelle. "The least mad is the one who's asking what you're doing. I'd welcome a drink."

"That voice!" says Ozaki.

"You're a dancer at the Châtelet?" Klutzkil asks.

"So it's said." She goes on the attack. "So it's really true that I resemble these famous heiresses? Not ordinary! Delighted that it enables me to make your acquaintance. You seem like very nice people. Listen, then: perhaps I'm a sister of theirs. Maman never told me the name of my father, nor whether he had a round or pointed nose."

They listen, prey to a turbulence of sentiments, horribly uncertain, full of suspicion.

"If it's to look at me that you're here…that's not very wicked. Is it just for that that I had to travel all night? If we could at least have a drink…you permit?"

She gets up, rings. La Darlys appears.

"Champagne, if you please."

Vernail and Klutzkil fall upon the brothel-keeper, their disturbance exploding.

"What is this mess? You knew full well that there were several of us..."

"Pardon, pardon," she says, solidly braced. "How could I know that you'd all come in together? It's unprecedented! The first one comes in, the others, on seeing someone, close their doors and sit quietly…to wait their turn, eh!" she snaps. "You know how it is!"

Vernail shrugs his shoulders furiously.

"As you saw us arrive…you should have warned us. We'd have left..."

"Of course! Well! You've seen the clientele refuse before, have you?"

"Leave Madame Darlys alone," says Mercerelle. "A lot of bother to have the champagne brought.!"

"I'll send it up," says La Darlys. She goes out.

"Well, lads," says Mercerelle, "it's finished, eh? No more fuss between you and with the boss. Sit down. So you know one another, then?"

"It's true that the resemblance is incredible!" says Herbert.

"They have a slimmer neck," says Vernail, extremely ill at ease. "Pardon me, my girl..."

"She has a little of all of them," says Klutzkil, "and at first glance...one could…be taken in…but the ensemble…the breeding…"

Someone knocks and comes in: a maid carrying six glasses and several bottles of champagne on a tray.

"Who's going to pop the cork? Relax. If you're as awkward before the heiresses, I can understand why they're in no hurry to throw their arms around your neck..."

"Mademoiselle," says Ozaki, his voice jerky and his chin trembling, "Give us the pleasure of not talking about...the persons you resemble…if you please."

"Oh! He doesn't seem very comfortable, your comrade," says Mercerelle.

Klutzkil has seized a bottle and is beginning to remove the seal.

"You, at least, know the life. You know, m'sieu…," she looks at Ozaki, swinging her leg, "…If my conversation displeases you, you only have to leave. I'm not keeping you, you know."

The cork pops. Klutzkil fills the six glasses. Mercerelle hands one to Ozaki.

"All the same, drink a glass before you go..."

Ozaki takes the glass an empties it in a single draught.

"…And *au revoir*!"

"*Ça va*, isn't it?" says the aviator, brutally.

Mercerelle drinks. She sets down her glass. "He hasn't gone? That's funny. I certainly don't have the intelligence or the education of...the ones I'm forbidden to mention…but I can see that you're all tiptoeing around. If it's only to see me that you've come, it seems to me that there'll come a time when there won't be any more embarrassment. Come on, Messieurs, I'm a good girl. I wasn't asked to come from Paris to recite *The Ant and the Grasshopper*. I'll tell you what's bothering you..."

"Not too bad, this champagne!" says Vernail, magnifying his voice, attempting an authority that will make the girl understand that she is penetrating into impossible terrain.

"The champagne," says Mirard, "is very good…but I've never understood why it's preferred to so many other wines. There are Burgundies as light, but with a taste that's…much more personal..."

"What's bothering you," Mercerelle goes on, serenely, "is that you came here to screw me, which you all have too much desire to do to decide to leave, and you're waiting to see how it will turn out, and who'll be the last one left..."

A very brief silence descends like a leaden cope over all the men. Vernail tilts, with a coarse laugh: "If that were the case, you'd have made a bad blunder, for a girl who's expecting her tip. Except, kid, I think..." The voice thickens.

"I don't know what these messieurs' sentiments are," says Herbert. "For my part, I can assure them, and you, of the purity of my intentions. I carry around a perpetual curiosity, ready to cross the threshold of a bordello as readily as that of a museum. I'd already been to this house one evening, the attractions of which had been incessantly whispered to me by the porter at the Splendid and the groom at the Café de Luc. I came, I saw…and I left as politely as possible, distressed by the opinion I formed of bipeds, my brethren, that such an ugly farce could have been prolonged for more than an hour and, even worse, could prosper! My presence here this evening corresponds to a similar curiosity. The promise of an unusual resemblance had what was necessary to intrigue me, without seeking any further. That said, I would gladly have left immediately, in spite of the desire to screw with which Mademoiselle credits me, if I had not been retained by something...extremely interesting, which it was impossible to formulate thus far without the risk of stupidly spoiling…an idea—oh, extremely tenuous—that crossed my mind as soon as I came into this drawing room, and which needs to…be solidified. To your health, Mademoiselle…?"

He pours himself a drink and raised his glass.

"The speech-maker of the band! You must be a député...or a journalist. Mademoiselle who? Christiane. I thought that La Darlys had told you my name."

"Your idea…formulate it anyway, old chap," says Vernail, embarrassed.

"It doesn't concern any of you, but rather Mademoiselle."

"Very flattering!" says Mercerelle, anxiously.

"Me," says Mirard, "I'll be frank...and more human than our friend. I admire him for seeing himself so clearly. In coming here, my sentiments were less clear than his…and they still are. I believe that deep down in me, there was a need…oh, I'm not very proud of it…if the person was as similar as I had been told…to…oh, damn! I'm getting bogged down in my desire for frankness. Also, this adventure of finding oneself face to face! But in confessing my petty villainy, I imagine that I'm rehabilitating myself, and that I'm also rehabilitating you…because all of us here, poor fellows are under the spell of the hussies…adorable, agreed, damn it, but…impossible!...that we're all here, possessed by the same obscure desire to avenge ourselves on a form that resembles theirs…for that pride, that iron will, inserted between them and our desire...or love…to hold the image, without the mind…momentarily subdued..."

"Yes," says Vernail. "I admit it."

"Let's give that need any name you like," says Klutzkil. "I confess."

"So what?" Ozaki suddenly cries, advancing, white-faced and striking the table with his fist. "What is it going to lead to, your confession? Are you going to turn around now? And we're all going to throw a veil over that dirtiness that should have remained buried in our deepest depths? What if we hadn't been taken by surprise, eh? We would have taken it! Me, I'm staying. I've having the girl. You resemble her too closely, my dear," he says, going to her and rudely putting his hand on her shoulder. "I'm going to free myself on her from an insupportable confusion. You, the curious, here's something to note down. The other day, I adored my aircraft, our descent; I was drunk with all sorts of intoxications, and my amour was among those intoxications. I remember very well that I said crazy things while embracing my victory, and Gioia's name was in my phrases...and in the meantime, I didn't even look at the real Gioia, who was there, two paces away. Eh! Clarify that! It's her that was in my idea, in my soul, her at whom I can continue to gaze with my eyes upraised, that I'll preserve, keep pure, while throwing her double as a bone to my desire!"

"Not stupid at all, what you're saying there!" exclaims Klutzkil, standing in front of Ozaki. "A false possession, but a fine lie, the calming illusion of having embraced, subdued the terrible desired body... The flesh satisfied and the mind that keeps intact the one who exalts the spirit, fusing with the dream that emerges from the work. To me, the image!"

"To me!" growls Vernail. "Your tirades have cleared away the marmalade in which Vernail was stuck. Of course! The beast has risen all the way to the brain. It's the true Vernail finding himself free again, the sated beast!"

"You aren't going to fight!" says Mirard. "You're frightening to behold. I give up! Thank God, I have goals as real and magnificent in themselves to efface this entire history within me, commenced like a dream, but which is turning into a base nightmare! Messieurs!"

Ozaki has not let go of Mercerelle's shoulder. Klutzkil has put his hand on the other shoulder and Vernail has seized her hands. Abruptly, Mercerelle frees herself from them, and takes shelter behind the armchair where she was sitting. She is trembling, and yet she confronts them, her taut expression becoming mocking and challenging.

"You're free, Mirard!" cries Vernail. "Me, I'm not letting go. You decide, then, girl. Is it the money? I'll make the highest bid."

"She won't have to decide. She'll obey. I'll carry her away.

Klutzkil has leapt upon her, and passed his arm around her torso, but Ozaki and Vernail take hold of Klutzkil's arms and part them, pushing the painter back violently and finding themselves face to face, teeth clenched, hands open, the entire body avid for combat...

Ozaki's fingers fall on Vernail's wrists. Mirard tries to separate them. "The men that you are! It's a whore..." And Klutzkil advances once again upon Mercerelle.

"Herbert! Your radiance, which is at the terminus of everything!"

She has shouted that.

"Aha! I suspected as much!" says Herbert, while, fulgurant, he goes to shove Klutzkil away, overturning the armchair between Mercerelle and the three men at grips, draws the young woman away, and runs with her to one of the rooms, the door of which he slams and, putting all his weight on the batten, turns the key.

IV

Yellow wallpaper strewn with green and red flowers, fake Oriental carpet, fake bearskin at the foot of the pitch-pine bed, a chair and a Louis XV armchair, a dressing table. On the wall, two crude copies of eighteenth-century libertine engravings.

Mercerelle has her back to the bed. They listen. A hubbub, footsteps fading away, a door slamming.

"Which of you is beneath that hair, which isn't any of you?"

She is calm. She is no longer trembling.

"Perhaps a sixth…," she says.

"Who shouts the words that I spoke one day to Marden?"

"Perhaps Marden herself."

Tranquil, her hands at the nape of her neck, she lifts up a blonde wing, lets it fall to the ground, and appears with Marden's tawny hair.

Herbert is not unduly astonished.

"You might well say *perhaps*. What did you come here to do?"

"It would be wrong of you to play the censor, you who told me to go toward everything with the desire for knowledge...before which nothing is base or ugly. I was told about this house. I wanted to see."

"To see what? Those men surrendered to their instincts? Driven to reveal themselves to themselves, at the same time as to you, in their naked desire? What have you learned from that? In what way does their attitude diminish their true being, which will remain beyond this moment of chaos? Why has the seeker of grandeur been so ingenious in setting this trap to precipitate the greatest into the worst opportunity for baseness? The modern Atalanta is no more than a Circe!"

"Naturally, when you talk about their grandeur, it's only a matter for you of their grandeur limited to their work? For me, it's also a matter of the grandeur of their love. What I learned this evening goes much further than what you call a moment of chaos. If they loved us as we really are, not through a mirage that they've created, their love, just now, would have quivered with disgust...or adoration. They would have brought their entire being into play. It's only their naked desire that rushed savagely on the physical image of those whose minds hold them in check. What have I learned? I've verified that what they called their need for vengeance, or the pretext of safeguarding the ideal woman, is their impotence before the other means they had of attaining the same physical end...which was to conquer the original. Entirely!"

"You've rendered that conquest impossible during the months they've been striving to do so."

A silence.

"You shouted my name. It came from memory. You couldn't have known that name, in the role that you'd taken on. They'll reflect on that. They'll guess the truth, confusedly. If they divine it entirely, they'll never dare to reappear."

"Bon voyage!"

"You're sacrificing them very lightly. Still in the name of the same dream, which nothing has educated!"

"Still!"

"And here you are now before a desert, into which only a miracle can bring the man of the dream."

"What tells you that it's now one man that I'm waiting for, and that, if it's necessary to renounce sharing my multitude with a single individual, I'm not ready to share it with the corresponding multitude? I, who want all of life, have only lived thus far under one of its aspects. It was only from that matrix that I envisaged the possession of the world, with my beloved companion. Does the impossibility of finding that companion prevent the world from existing? I've commenced the great voyage this evening. I'll depart alone. This evening, I've gone through the first portal of the world, under its strangest and most frightening sign: that of the naked desire of man. Was I afraid? I stayed with the whores for several hours. For several hours, I've been breathing the air of this house, where male desire oozes from the walls, grates and rages in all those ringing bells… Am I trembling? Where is the top? Where is the bottom? Beyond the labels stuck on by morals…eh? It's time to remember your sermons! For anyone who bears within themselves the will to knowledge, to blossoming? There's no man for me? There'll be men, there'll be life, and that will to radiance. Why should I be afraid? Fear! Look…what tells you that this very evening, I'm not ready to surrender to the one man who has revealed himself to be different from the voracious, who sensed the trap set for love..."

He shivers. A sudden amazement on that face, still assured.

"...Who has snatched me away from them? I'm ready, I tell you! Savant, armed with the rules of the game. I've done what was necessary, in order to know myself… strong enough, now, not to be a slave of any of the instants of the innumerable, of a stature to find myself entirely free before the following minute. The proof? This evening, I'm Madame Christiane. After leaving here. I'll find myself a d'Aldezza again, awaiting a new adventure among the hundred thousand adventures and the hundred thousand sensualities—in themselves!—of the world. Amusement, the rule of the game, is to savor to the full this evening's personality, the moment, the décor, the atmosphere! So let's see whether there's a limit to the liberty I'm carrying in my baggage, a point at which the fear will slip in that I'm determined not to carry away! I'm Madame Christiane, and you're the passer-by who comes to me with his desire..."

He takes a step back.

"Throw yourself upon me! Knock me down! But perhaps you're a timid client…or one of those complicated one's that one of the women mentioned...what would please you, my friend? Feeling my arms, by breast, my loins...it's not every day that one runs across a girl made like me! What a strange man, who can remain inert! However, he's the only one capable of understanding me…I'm fully conscious, Herbert. I'm amusing myself. And I'm beginning to understand the destiny that I've decided lucidly. It's true that I'm offering myself to you. Of the two of us, it's you who are afraid. Be bolder, my friend, and take advantage of the windfall!"

She takes off her jade top, throws away her coral necklace, brutally unfastens the white muslin blouse; now her shoulders are bare, her naked cleavage protruding from the silk chemise.

"I am, in fact, afraid…," says Herbert."

He is livid.

"…But not the fear, none of the fears, that you can imagine. I've understood you perfectly, and what a cold determination there is behind your present excitement. I'm afraid because I don't love you, afraid of soling that body, and perhaps the soul, by revealing sexual intercourse to you in an embrace devoid of love."

She has pushed down the shoulder-straps of her chemise. Her torso is naked.

He stammers: "You're beautiful. You're terrible. There's more than enough to throw oneself upon you, in fact. I could give in to the blood that's hammering in my temples…I could, for an instant let everything go that isn't the particle of me…in which the will is contained…clear…hard…like a ball of diamond…in that instant, it would be accomplished. The desire into which that proffered flesh throws me...oh, how it collides with the crumb of will, how it hates it! But it's holding firm."

He is standing very close to her. He seizes her arms.

"I'm a wretch. I've played with amour; this is my punishment. My heart can no longer find, of its own accord, the sincere effusion that would permit and sanctify the embrace. In the name of the love that ought to rise toward you in all its glory, I refuse this loveless intercourse."

He steps back.

"Get dressed. You're going home..."

He falls into the armchair. He puts his head in his hands.

She does not say a word. She picks up the blouse and the necklace. She gets dressed. He watches her dress. Nervous tics are shaking him. She goes to the door. He sighs hoarsely. She stops momentarily. He does not make a move toward her. His eyes hard, he watches her leave. The door closes. He gazes at the door with the same hard eyes.

3. The Next Day

I

She finishes dressing slowly. She is very late getting up. A light knock at her door and a clear voice: "It's me...."

"Come in, Maman."

The Contessa is holding opened letters in her hand.

"I came before. You were asleep. You came back very late last night. May I ask where you went?"

"No, Maman."

"I never question you. I have enough confidence in you always to wait for the moment when you choose to open your heart to me Recounting something in progress often risks stopping it or deflecting it. At my age, I'm fatally driven to advice—which is to say, to intervening in spontaneity, which has its own laws, and which is worth as much as my sagacity..."

"What solemnity, Maman!"

"Perhaps, however, the moment has come when you're too troubled to make a resolution yourself. I thought that one day, you'd come running to me, radiant, crying: 'This is the one I love!'"

A shrug of the shoulders.

"...I was watching the phases of your discovery in your face. Not very easy, though, to recognize you there in your enthusiasms and you decrescendos. I didn't want to influence you in any preference..."

She makes a little click with her lips.

"Bang."

She hands her the letter.

"I can imagine who sent these letters, Maman, and what they contain."

"Early this morning, Mirard's laboratory assistant began to dismantle the laboratory. Ozaki, Vernail and Klutzkil have been called away in a thunderclap, without remission, one by the embassy, another for his circuit, the third by his art-dealer. What a coincidence! It's not astonishing?"

"No, Maman."

"Something has happened, then?"

"Yes."

"Very serious?"

"It depends..."

"At the end of which, you're devoid of suitors. After so much fuss! I don't count Lesielt or the Baron Lemart. You'd surprise me by declaring that one of those two pleases you. Lesielt's always seemed to me to be a very curious case...marvelous lucidity, self-composure...a little too cold for my taste...and yours, I suppose. As for the Baron, that's another matter. The police are looking for him."

"Why?"

"You ask me *why* so tranquilly, when I tell you that the police are after one of your cavaliers? Why...oh, very complicated. In any case, not for his ideas...for violations of the common law. I received a visit from an inspector yesterday.

With the greatest politeness, I must admit, he told me that he'd hesitated as long as possible to suspect my guests, not wanting to admit that a redoubtable bandit has slipped in among them. But a long story…I don't remember exactly. He's found Détrêt, our anarchist…and little Stani... In the final analysis, our Lemart is his bandit..."

"Maman, I have a head and a heart full of things to tell you…I'm less irresolute at this moment than you think…and first of all…I don't want Lemart to be caught..."

II

She has sent away her hairdresser, and without finishing dressing she had thrown her white dalmatic over her shoulders and slipped her bare feet into silver mules. "Let's go into the park. I need fresh air, light."

They have gone downstairs. The Contessa has taken her daughter's arm, squeezing it gently against her own.

"I'm going to tell you, Maman..."

The mother senses both a child stifled by a great chagrin ready to burst into sobs and an Amazon stiffened in a determined will, on the threshold of an hour that contains her life.

They go toward the ancient oak whose shadow is velvety. A man who has rushed through the gate advances into the path they are traversing, catches them up, bows to the Contessa with a jerky gesture, and looks at the young woman with sparkling eyes.

"I need to talk to you. Allow me to speak to you for a moment."

Herbert. His attire is negligent, his shoes covered in dust. His pale face reveals a lack of sleep. His gaze seems immeasurably magnified and ablaze.

The young woman takes a step back. Then she holds herself still, mute, her face icy.

Herbert is before her, mute in his turn, simultaneously imploring and trepidating, in the excitement emphasized by his eyes.

The Contessa tries to read her daughter's expression in response to the young man's feverish attitude. Then, anxiously, she says: "Do you have reasons for not hearing him? Doubtless it's the...coincidence continuing. Would you like him to return after you've spoken to me...or do you want to wait to tell me what you want to tell me..."

"It's necessary to hear me," says Herbert. "I stand before you with the scepter that your challenge required."

A hard and acrostic smile on the young woman's lips. "It's too late," she says.

"Oh!" says the Contessa. "Things have reached that point, then!"

Outburst of dolorous laughter from Herbert.

"I beg you," he says. "I've come to you illuminated by a prodigious adventure. If my clothing is a trifle deranged, it because it was a struggle like that between Jacob and the angel. It's absolutely necessary that she hears what I have to say, Madame."

"Yes," says the Contessa. She takes a step in the direction of the Palais. The young woman makes as if to follow her. Swiftly, Herbert takes her hands, and in an infinitely soft and imperative voice, he says: "No."

She stops. No change in the firm expression.

They are alone.

"It was in a flash of lightning, immediately after your departure, that I understood. The combat that I had been obliged to sustain against my desire has revealed to me that I'm still capable of desire. The emotion born in me before what appeared to me to be a sacrilege has revealed to me that I'm still capable of emotion. Is it not tragic, or an enormous joke? What was it that, in the name of my emotion, aroused all the forces of my will against my desire? The certitude I had that emotion and desire had dried up within me!"

He takes a breath. He discerns that she is attentive, behind the closed expression.

"Afterwards, I left and went straight ahead, with the bewildered hope of seeing it clearly. As I attempted to put some order into the tumult of my thoughts, the stages of my life rose up before me…but this time bathed in the emotion that had not quit me since our duel. It was in that fever that my memory passed before me the immense minute in which I had once conceived what my work was to be, the minute of inspiration like those divine dazzlements that are forever striking mystics…the vision of a new world, of which joy would be the axis...

"At the evocation of that moment of yore, I suddenly realized that I was neither as wretched as I had told you, nor as desperate as I had believed. A hymn, a felicity, rose up within me, which I sensed without yet daring to make it precise in my consciousness...

"The emotion rediscovered that night was that which I had once forbidden myself, at the time of the necessary experiment, at the time when I had resolved to be nothing but a will to knowledge, and that all my actions, my desires, my effusions were to be nothing to me but documents. Last night, before the marvelous offering, the flood of desire, the storm of emotion, had resuscitated my heart, habit had maintained it before you, in its shroud…but the flood pursued its course, revivifying the desert terrains, the storm continued, sweeping away the mists…and I found myself suddenly intoxicated, stupefied, in the same way as the inspired day of yore…and the richest of men...but with, in addition, the experiments accomplished, all the powers attained with my will in the course of the journey!

"Everything that I had acquired, my emotion animates, setting my consciousness on fire, passion circulating in all the accumulated knowledge. The innumerable joy, in the name of which, you remember, I made a few remarks to you that moved you, while they were only for me the icy reflections of a former self…the innumerable joy become a permissible and living reality, streaming with juice and light. I've become conscious that I no longer have any need of that will, a cold vigil that administered my research, since I'm no longer searching, having found..."

He takes another breath. His excitement is such that it transposes his features, in the gaze of the listener.

"I had found love. My science of joy made my will a will to love. The sentiment of what I knew, of what I could do, became in me a song of love that kept time with my solitary tread, ringing like the tread of a king in the silence of the highway. And I thought, and I was sure, that you would understand the miracle that has brought me back to you, with the scepter.

"The will to love, is to go straight to the excellence of everything that is; it is to know how to extract the adorable that is in everything. Joy is to breathe, to live in a perpetual florescence of pretexts, goals and festivals of love. It's the joy of the poet. And the poet is the only one who corresponds to your dream: the only one who can not only be all men, but all the minutes and all the particles of creation, and the only one who can thus respond to your innumerable question. And you are the only one, you who have so numerously wanted love and have dared to combine it, the only one who will be able, with me, to savor, various as they are, all the perfections that I discover, at the same time as you will be, for me, perpetually to be reconquered, the image of perpetually insatiable and unsatisfied desire...

She cuts in, simultaneously mocking and bitter: "An image! They too pronounced that word..."

"But this time, no longer a determined election, but all of the elected life!"

The Contessa appears on the terrace of the hall, seeking the two young people with her gaze, hesitant to rejoin them

"I have something to ask your mother," he says. "Come." She follows him, perhaps curious, perhaps carried away in the surge of enthusiasm.

"Madame," says Herbert, mounting the stone steps and bowing ceremoniously. "I have the honor of asking you for the hand of your five daughters."

III

"Monsieur le Baron! Excuse me..."

It is about four o'clock in the afternoon. At the moment when the hired car stops outside the gate of the Palais and the chauffeur gets out to ring, a modestly-dressed thickset man with a dense black beard, who has been walking up and down in the road, approaches the vehicle.

"What is it?" Lemart demands.

"You're Monsieur le Baron Lemart. I had your description. I didn't know where to find you. I beg your pardon…a commission to make to you on the part of your friend Décrêt."

"Décrêt? Oh, yes…well, I'm busy. If you'd care to wait until I come out…"

"It's very urgent, Monsieur le Baron. It would be better if you knew before going in."

"Bizarre. What does he want with me, Décrêt?"

"To warn you..." The man lowers his voice. "He's been discovered by the famous Delvêque. Listen…I can't talk about in front of the chauffeur."

"Delvêque? Don't know him," says Lemart, haughtily. "But…quickly..."

He gets out.

"See to your business and wait for a moment," he says to the driver. "Well?"

"If I may, in brief…," the man begins. "Can you imagine that Delvêque, of the secret police, was on the track of a man named Dal Morre, the hotel rat…you don't know him? No, you can't know him, Monsieur le Baron. So, this Delvêque came all the way to Thonon, following an idea he had. He went back empty-handed. He came back again, with regard to a robbery…nothing again, but he stayed. Chatting here and there, as is his métier, his attention was caught by the people who were visiting the lady who lives here... Détrêt, a worker, an anarchist…that struck him. He investigated. Good. A flunkey told him that this Détrêt had brought a friend with him, a Baron…you, that is. Delvêque has been trying to talk to you for some time, but there was no mean of getting hold of you. And to come here, to the lady's house, without being sure..."

"What would he have to say to me, this Delbêque?"

"...vêque. I'm getting there, Monsieur le Baron. So, this Détrêt had left her abruptly, with a prince, a true one...."

"I know all that. You're wasting my time. Get to the point."

"I'm there. My Delvêque set about searching for my Détrêt. These cops have means of getting information. In brief, he found the address. The fellow was living in a lodging-house with the prince. Funny chaps, those two."

"Pardon me, but who are you?"

"A mate of Détrêt's I told you. I made his acquaintance in the lodging-house, and became a comrade because of the funny life he was leading with the prince. Me, I like eccentrics. It's not money he lacks, that Détrêt. The prince's, of course. Détrêt was taking the prince around all the lousy places he knew, and the other was taking him to concerts, museums...they said it was a pact to teach one another the sides of life they wouldn't have been able to get to know by themselves. In brief, to thread the needle, Delvêque, having found Détrêt, as you can imagine, didn't have to work too hard to get him to talk. The cop disguises himself, because it appears that those men know one another. He disguises himself as a worthy man, a man of my sort, it appears, with a bushy beard, a bowler hat..."

Lemaet scans the road rapidly. To his right is a gorge, at the far end of which, beneath a tunnel of debris, the Gravance runs, to his left the rocky buttresses of the Ansaux.

"....He talks to him," the man continues, "about the A.I.A. You're in it, Monsieur le Baron?"

"The ideas of the A.I.A. have interested me. But why are you pestering me, old chap, with your stories?"

"I need to transmit to you the information that Détrêt let slip, to be sure that it was you, before getting to the end. The A.I.A...different names...a false beard...one morning, when a wad of bills fell out of your pocket, the day after Monsieur Vernail had been burgled by a marquis…fake… Marquis Le-Mart. That's singular, isn't it? Delvêque knew enough..."

With the last syllables he has taken a slender iron chain from his pocket, thrown it over Lemart's wrist and twisted.

"Need for equilibrium in life, Monsieur le Baron. While some shave off their beards, others let them grow..." With his free hand he takes off the fake beard and reveals Delvêque.

Lemart has remained silent and impassive, meditating.

"You ought to take that off me," he says, because of the chauffeur. I have something to tell you."

"The chauffeur? I'll requisition him to take us back to Thonon. Thank you for having thought of the auro."

"Just a minute. Hide the toy while I talk to you…"

"You talk too much. I have a memory. You can tell me about it on the way."

"Good. You're going to get your fingers rapped. I'm on the brink of marrying one of the daughters. Do you think that she'll let me go down, given that? It's rotten public relations."

"You're scraping the barrel. I thought you were richer in imagination. It's the Maman who asked me to wait here, in anticipation of your coming."

"I thought you were richer in psychology. The mother and the daughter are two different matters."

"I don't have to get into all that," says Delvêque, abruptly. "Go!"

"Will you give me one second, before making the worst blunder of your life?"

"Go on."

"Stand this side so the driver doesn't see the metal wire. You'll understand. One of the girls adores me, I've come to ask for her hand, and if the mother says no, we'll hop it together. It's settled. Once married, it's the big haul, entry everywhere, all the high-ups in a rush to wipe out my dossier. I'll ask my friend the minister to give you a promotion. Think about it. If you take me, it won't change anything on my side.

The girl knows who I am. I'll be released, and it'll be you going to the druggist to get your fingers bandaged."

"Is that all? Let's go."

He tugs the handcuffs. Lemart loses a little of his calmness. His voice becomes humbler and grave.

"I'll make you another proposition. I'm not bluffing, Delvêque. I swear to you on the head of my mother, the old woman in Barcelona, on the Christ in whom I believe, that if you give me a quarter of an hour of liberty, I'll come right back here of my own accord, as I am at this moment, and I'll put my own hand in the wire."

"You've got a nerve! Do you take me for a sugar-plum?"

"I take you for a man capable of understanding, and who has a little heart under his cop's jacket. There are matters of sentiment between me and the girl. Extremely grave, for her as well. I can't be taken without seeing her. Here, Delvêque, listen. I've got a rosary in my breast pocket. I won't get it out myself, you'd mistrust my hand. Unbutton me, open the chemise. You see it? I haven't prepared that for you. Eh? If I'd anticipated you, I'd have come more discreetly. That rosary is the only thing in the world that's sacred to me. You know very well that there are worse for whom that's true. That's my case, Delvêque. I'll leave it to you as a pledge. May I die damned if I don't prefer to be in prison all my life than abandon it. While you hold it, it's as if you held me with something surer than this little chain...as if you held me hooked with something more important than the heart..."

"I'll admit that it's not a bluff, but even if God himself demanded it, I wouldn't let you go."

"Another thing. Don't let me go. Let the chauffer go look for her. Let him go to say that Monsieur le Baron Lemart is on the road, that he can't come in, and that he absolutely begs Mademoiselle d'Aldezza to come to the gate."

"Ha ha! You think..."

"She'll come. She's an extraordinary girl. If she comes, you'll begin to comprehend that there's something there. You'll take the wristlet off for five minutes, and walk a few paces. I'll make up something to explain your presence. Do you have your gun?"

"It goes without saying."

"Hold it in your pocket. If I make a single move that seems out of place, shoot."

"I know that you're a rogue in a hundred thousand, but you're shaking me."

"Shoot. Without warning. Bang."

"And I never miss. Driver!"

The man has been working on his headlights, completely indifferent to the singular conversation.

"Go into the Palais, have Mademoiselle d'Aldezza told that Monsieur le Baron Lemart is asking for her at the gate, and that it's impossible for him to come in."

The man takes vague note of the chain linking Delvêque's hand to Lemart's wrist. He leaves to run the errand.

"If he runs across the Maman, you're done for," says Delvêque.

"No one can get in the way of the daughter's will."

"I've thought of something. If the two of you leap into the auto and speed off, leaving me flat, I'll shoot."

"No need. If we get into the auto, you'll be with us

"You'll make me do what you want…you're a villain!"

"I beg your pardon for the trick in the carriage at Creil. It was necessary. You're a good man. Whatever happens, I'll remember today. May Christ watch over you, Delvêque."

"Save your tall stories and let's see."

An interval of silence.

"Look."

In the driveway, behind the chauffeur, a tall young woman with tawny hair and the red tunic.

"Damn! Quite a morsel! She's one of those with the twenty-five millions?"

"The only one. There is only one."

"What?"

"Will you take off the bracelet?"

"There…"

Delvêque frees the hand and takes out his revolver.

"…And here!"

Lemart goes toward the Palais, stops at the gate.

Delvêque remains some distance away, his hands behind his back."

She comes out. Mechanically, Delvêque raises his hat.

"Bonjour, Marden," said Lemart. And, curtly: "Are we going?"

"What do you want? The driver mentioned a chain. Who's that man over there?"

"An inspector of the Sûreté. I'm caught. If I make the slightest suspicious movement, he'll take out the loaded revolver he's holding behind his back."

"Charming. What do you want with me?"

"This. The policeman's astounded that you came to my call. We leave in that vehicle. He comes with us. You attest that you're ready to marry me. That's not true, but it saves us. That way, I can settle things with him. When we arrive at Thonon, you go to wait for me at an address I'll give you."

"At Madame Darlys?"

"There's no longer anyone there. No, elsewhere."

"Not bad, all that. Unfortunately, you've arrived too late. This morning, I might have gone with you."

"Oh. And now?"

"Now, I wanted to see right through you. That's why I've come. But our relationship ends here."

"You're an ingrate, child. You owe me your liberty. You might help me regain mine."

"I don't understand."

"It's thanks to me that you set foot in real life. What isn't very polite is to have gone there without telling me. I soon heard all about it. Big upheaval at the Petit Palais. La Darlys gone, the girls buckling their suitcases, Juana in a panic. It's you that's responsible for all that. On clearing up their statements, I understood that you'd blinded La Darlys with banknotes. She flew the coop this morning, fearful of the consequences of yesterday…and perhaps also of having to split the money. In brief, she's gone, leaving Juana a few thousand francs to sort everything out…but that doesn't concern you. What concerns you is that I congratulate you, and I congratulate me, on your debut. The life that I offered you, you've bitten into. I'm up to date with what you've done. You've had your first man. *En route* for the next."

"Your cynicism appeared to me to be picturesque, the night when you surprised me, not knowing which way to turn. Until this morning, events favored you. But another tempter arrived this morning. He's a man who resembles you in that he too is capable of the masterpiece that you signified by the word enjoyment—only he changed the word into that of love. Perhaps the actions are the same, but what there is behind them…is different."

A flash in Lemart's eyes.

"Good. Me too. There's something…very great behind all my actions, behind what you call my cynicism. You remember that you asked me whether what led me ended with the bursting of the bubble, and didn't go beyond it? I replied to you that I was a Christian. I'm guided by an enormous, gigantic thought…almost too enormous to be spoken…"

The voice trembles slightly, becomes muted.

"To accumulate in me, on me, like the ram of Israel, the most frightful burden of the sins of men, all of that by which they betray the law of love and fraternity, soiling the pure and naïve felicity of being that the Creator dispensed to them: to throw myself at every opportunity in which the evidence would splash me and inscribe upon me of mud, laxity, vice and injustice, in order to present myself before the Master who gave himself once for the salvation of humankind and cry to him: 'Your sacrifice was in vain! I am the evidence! *Ecce homo*, Lord! Everything has to begin again!'"

Laughter of the young woman.

"No."

"Why are you laughing?" he says, somberly.

"Because I don't believe you. Because that thought, even if it's sincere, is an excuse that you've thrown over your instincts."

"You're wrong. Do you know why the policeman allowed me to talk to you? Because I offered him, when swearing to go back to him, the rosary that I never take off, as a pledge of my word. That proves to you that I believe."

"It might prove that you're lying to yourself."

"I was right to say that my thought is too great..."

"Possibly. I prefer the one this morning's tempter brought."

He sniggers. "The poet?"

"Yes."

"Ah, my child! I suspected as much. What big things you've made me say for so little! You're not of a stature to parade yourself through all of life, as I thought for a moment. There are your horizons, buckled with the first kiss, once and for all. You don't tempt me anymore. I prefer prison. One gets out of there."

He strikes a pose. He takes a step toward Delvêque, and then turns back to her. "It's stupid. I would have got you out of that. All is not lost. You're still under the influence of your first man. You've got caught by his ideas. It's the banal mirage of a moment. You're worth more than that. Life goes on, beyond last night's pleasure. I'd have a lot more pleasures to pass before your eyes and into your heart."

"Him too—and now I'm going to him. We have nothing more to say to one another."

"Yes—I have to tell you...that if you're abandoning me, I'm abandoning you."

"Which means?"

"That if the act you committed last night has no importance for the liberated young woman, it resumes its gravity for the ordinary one. In the times of Emile Augier[54] what you

---

[54] The works of dramatist and Academician Emile Augier (1820-1889) won him a reputation as a censorious moralist.

did was called dishonor. It's still called that for a good part of the world in which you move and will continue to live."

"So what?"

"So what?"

"So, the lax Lemart releases the story..."

"I haven't yet encountered this...is this blackmail?"

"Words! It's a buoy that I'm grasping in the shipwreck."

"I don't know what you've been told. Don't get carried away either by the hope of scandal or the victory of believing me a poor enslaved girl. I'm a virgin, Lemart."

Delvêque is pacing back and forth, drawing a little further away from the point where he had stood, avoiding getting too close to the dialogue, but giving visible evidence of his impatience.

Lemart has remained silent momentarily. He has lowered his head. Thoughts whirling in his head suddenly turn his face pale, cause his shoulders to droop.

"Listen," he says, in a stifled voice. "I only have a moment. I beg your pardon. Forget the dirty threat. I'll get out. Prison isn't eternal..." His voice hastens, becoming indistinct at times. "Until now, I've been pulling all my strings. There's something true…something truer than all that. In spite of what I've said to you, all the ignoble things I've proposed, you sense deep down that I'm an intelligence...a force. The night when I came, we talked about my desire… I juggled with my desire, that night, before your bare breast, your body under the sheet…like someone who believed himself already victorious. And now you've changed your mind, and I'm caught. But your breast, your body…I can't juggle any longer. I have them engraved, burning, within me. In playing the juggler, I'm going to writhe with rage and thirst on thinking about them…out there. I..."

Drop of sweat form on his brow.

"I won't be able to support that rage. One doesn't forget such a vision. It might even be better to settle it right away, between his revolver…and your body..."

He groans.

"At least give me your hand."

She is afraid.

"Nothing but you hand. I tell you..."

She makes an effort and holds out her hand. He grabs it furiously, draws her body toward him; his eyes are bulging, his face crimson.

She screams: "Lemart!"

She struggles. At the same time, the chauffeur makes a move toward them to intervene. Lemart hooks his arm around the young woman's head, pushing her toward the auto, he pulls violently at the nape of the neck to bend it toward him, reaching out with his swollen lips. He offers his back to Delvêque.

The latter fires.

4. Denis Aury

"It was one evening," says Herbert, "in a late-night cabaret, when I suddenly had the acuity of impression that makes your eyes blink when the hour, the lights, the noise of the jazz, the odors and the coming and going of the drinkers hits you…the sensation of multiplicity that must to have aided me, when I met you, to divine the secret of the Palais Gioia...."

The studio. Penumbra over the blonde clarity of the lamp set on the table where the tea is served. The Contessa is smoking and watching the fluid swirls turn silver as they pass through the circle of light. Herbert is half-lying on the white carpet, his head on the knees of the young woman sitting next to the organ. The latter, with one hand, gently caress the young man's hair. One elbow on the keyboard, her chin in the palm of the hand, she is listening, but her gaze is not entirely in the present moment.

"The jazz-man, at the same time as he was tapping his drum, shaking his little bells, blowing into his little trumpet, and nothing from head to toe but one enraged contortion, had, just for a second, at the moment when one of the dancers was going passed him, a flutter of the eyelids, tender and melancholy, amazing in the face of that unhinged clown...

"I glimpsed in the face of a maître-d'hôtel, while he was inclining devoutly before a couple of new arrivals, a frightful rictus of cruelty as a waiter jostled him slightly; and scanning the frenetic audience with my eyes, I saw, or thought I saw, on faces here and there, a thousand triggered revelations that clashed incredibly with the ensemble of attitudes: a rapid passage of deep sadnesses, maternal thoughts in eyes scintillating with champagne, laughter and sensual deceptions; a hint of mischief, as fresh as a schoolgirl's in a frightful face plastered with make-up...

"My discovery would have been perfectly puerile without the nervous excitation of the moment and the intensity that can be obtained, by reaction, by a thought of a philosophical order catching you in such a milieu... In sum, ephemeral as they were, all those sentiments I glimpsed were at that moment passing through a being as real as the being that person avowed... If one of those hidden sentiments had been exteriorized, it was the same form as the visible being that it would have taken. A poor, tender and sad man would have abruptly appeared between two appearances of the epileptic puppet, a murderous maître-d'hôtel would have thrown himself on the awkward waiter between two appearances of that same maître-d'hôtel smiling at the clients...

"My imagination, escaping the ambience, evoked, experienced that hope of revelation in a similar slowing down of the psychological film, that quasi-simultaneity of different selves in the same individual, but in other beings than the individuals in the cabaret, where the multiplicity was embryonic, or, rather, reduced to a narrow and banal duality...

"I thought about beings richer in sensibility an knowledge, those that agitate incessantly and simultaneously a host of sensations, sentiments, desires...which is to say, as many selves as existent as their visible being, as many beings that are only manifest in a furtive, uncertain life, and to which consciousness merely makes a little fraternal gesture in passing...

"How eternally wretched the real being suddenly appeared, who contains in himself such a crowd, perpetually generated and renewed by all the batteries of the physical and spiritual organism, by the acquisition of muscles, senses, thought—a host of which every element, being the creature itself, could have become so concretely, but which has to be content only to be in a larval state, vanishing as quickly as it is awakened!

"For that dearth, of course, there are a thousand excellent reasons! The tyranny of actuality, the material impossibility of transporting oneself immediately to the place or the object of desire, social, moral, worldly obligation to be a certain being corresponding to a function, a milieu... But in the end, it was nevertheless the case that every individual above the average was, at the same time as a incessantly gushing source of possibilities of which the real being only used one or two drops, a frightful necropolis of stillborn beings, unaccomplished events and unattempted actions.

"I conceived then that the strange misery in question, the perpetual astriction or decapitation of a multitude of individuals within us, however inevitable it might be, could at least be tempered. I conceived—I didn't know you then!—an individual rich enough to float over the greatest possible quantity of material obstacles, free enough to break the greatest possible number of moral and social walls, and conscious enough of his multitude to attempt to realize the greatest number of his beings..."

"And passionately animated," says the Contessa, "by the will to joy. For what use would that richness, liberty and consciousness be if the person who possesses it isn't moved by an enthusiasm and a goal that give life and a meaning to his multitudes? My child was born and she has been brought up under the sign of that will, and it's that which inspired in her the idea, under her various appearances, of demanding of love a richness made of the same multitudes that she was conscious of bringing to love.

"The secret of the challenge was not only to recognize, under the wigs, the play of make-up and perfect science with which she incarnated her personalities...if the will to joy comes from her father, that art, my friend, must be from me, who was an actress...the secret was not only to recognize the unique Gioia through the five sisters. That discovery was only a point of departure. The veritable secret, for the man who claimed that beautiful demoiselle, was that he should bring out or reveal in himself an equal diversity, equally capable of being realized.

"The whole enterprise was very adventurous, and would have lapsed into I don't know what ridicule or catastrophe...and I wouldn't have lent myself to it...if the blood had not been running in my child's veins of the most extraordinary man: Denis Aury, who fled as a child from the house of a frightfully miserly father, recreated himself, by a succession of wonderments at the contact of the modern world, and formed an absolutely original conception of the joy of living.

"Having become rich on his father's death, he surrounded himself with all those who could extract from the world or add to it beauty and the means of happiness—artists, scientists, explorers. With them he attempted to metamorphose the village in which he was born. He thought of reconstructing human being by removing therefrom all the elementary coercions, and giving it all the forces restricted until then by material cares, exalting motives to turn toward joy and love.

"One night, an airplane crash made a horrible human wreck of him. Enclosed in every part by metal bonds and corsets, he kept his ideal intact for a long time. And like the Bacchus that he had placed in his house, he raised the cup, elevated that idea above the darkness into which his suffering was gradually dragging him. I had been the dazzling companion of his rise and his reign. When he began to buckle he did not want to me to be the companion of his diminution. Without a guide, mutilated myself in the merciful love that I wanted to give him and he refused, I fell—and I dragged him down with me—into abyssal depths...

"On feverish night, he smashed the statue and began to die. He became a poor delirious man, repossessed by flashes of the exaltation of joy that he had tried to elevate over the world. It was in one of those moments of resurrection, it was of one of those supreme effluvia, that Gioia was born..."

SF & FANTASY

Adolphe Alhaiza. *Cybele*
Alphonse Allais. *The Adventures of Captain Cap*
Henri Allorge. *The Great Cataclysm*
Guy d'Armen. *Doc Ardan: The City of Gold and Lepers*
G.-J. Arnaud. *The Ice Company*
Charles Asselineau. *The Double Life*
Henri Austruy. *The Eupantophone; The Olotelepan; The Petitpaon Era*
Barillet-Lagargousse. *The Final War*
Cyprien Bérard. *The Vampire Lord Ruthwen*
S. Henry Berthoud. *Martyrs of Science*
Aloysius Bertrand. *Gaspard de la Nuit*
Richard Bessière. *The Gardens of the Apocalypse; The Masters of Silence*
Albert Bleunard. *Ever Smaller*
Félix Bodin. *The Novel of the Future*
Louis Boussenard. *Monsieur Synthesis*
Alphonse Brown. *City of Glass; The Conquest of the Air*
Émile Calvet. *In a Thousand Years*
André Caroff. *The Terror of Madame Atomos; Miss Atomos; The Return of Madame Atomos; The Mistake of Madame Atomos; The Monsters of Madame Atomos; The Revenge of Madame Atomos; The Resurrection of Madame Atomos; The Mark of Madame Atomos; The Spheres of Madame Atomos; The Wrath of Madame Atomos* (w/M. & Sylvie Stéphan)
Félicien Champsaur. *The Human Arrow; Ouha, King of the Apes; Pharaoh's Wife; Homo-Deus; Nora, The Ape-Woman*
Didier de Chousy. *Ignis*
Jules Clarétie. *Obsession*
Michel Corday. *The Eternal Flame*
André Couvreur. *The Necessary Evil; Caresco, Superman; The Exploits of Professor Tornada* (3 vols.)
Camille Debans. *The Misfortunes of John Bull*
Captain Danrit. *Undersea Odyssey*
C. I. Defontenay. *Star (Psi Cassiopeia)*
Charles Derennes. *The People of the Pole*
Chevalier de Béthune. *The World of Mercury*
Georges Dodds (anthologist). *The Missing Link*

Charles Dodeman. *The Silent Bomb*
Harry Dickson. *The Heir of Dracula; Harry Dickson vs. The Spider*
Jules Dornay. *Lord Ruthven Begins*
Alfred Driou. *The Adventures of a Parisian Aeronaut*
Sâr Dubnotal *vs. Jack the Ripper*
Odette Dulac. *The War of the Sexes*
Alexandre Dumas. *The Return of Lord Ruthven*
Renée Dunan. *Baal; The Ultimate Pleasure*
J.-C. Dunyach. *The Night Orchid; The Thieves of Silence*
Henri Duvernois. *The Man Who Found Himself*
Achille Eyraud. *Voyage to Venus*
Henri Falk. *The Age of Lead*
Paul Féval. *Anne of the Isles; Knightshade; Revenants; Vampire City; The Vampire Countess; The Wandering Jew's Daughter*
Paul Féval, *fils. Felifax, the Tiger-Man*
Charles de Fieux. *Lamékis*
Louis Forest. *Someone is Stealing Children in Paris*
Arnould Galopin. *Doctor Omega*; *Doctor Omega and the Shadowmen* (anthology)
Judith Gautier. *Isoline and the Serpent-Flower*
H. Gayar. *The Marvelous Adventures of Serge Myrandhal on Mars*
G.L. Gick. *Harry Dickson and the Werewolf of Rutherford Grange*
Delphine de Girardin. *Balzac's Cane*
Léon Gozlan. *The Vampire of the Val-de-Grâce*
Jules Gros. *The Fossil Man*
Edmond Haraucourt. *Illusions of Immortality; Daah, the First Human*
Nathalie Henneberg. *The Green Gods*
Eugène Hennebert. *The Enchanted City*
Jules Hoche. *The Maker of Men and His Formula*
V. Hugo, P. Foucher & P. Meurice. *The Hunchback of Notre-Dame*
Romain d'Huissier. *Hexagon: Dark Matter*
Jules Janin. *The Magnetized Corpse*
Michel Jeury. *Chronolysis*
Gustave Kahn. *The Tale of Gold and Silence*
Gérard Klein. *The Mote in Time's Eye*
Fernand Kolney. *Love in 5000 Years*
Paul Lacroix. *Danse Macabre*
Louis-Guillaume de La Follie. *The Unpretentious Philosopher*
Jean de La Hire. *Enter the Nyctalope; The Nyctalope on Mars; The Nyctalope vs. Lucifer; The Nyctalope Steps In; Night of the Nyctalope; Return of the Nyctalope; The Fiery Wheel*

Etienne-Léon de Lamothe-Langon. *The Virgin Vampire*
André Laurie. *Spiridon*
Gabriel de Lautrec. *The Vengeance of the Oval Portrait*
Alain le Drimeur. *The Future City*
Georges Le Faure & Henri de Graffigny. *The Extraordinary Adventures of a Russian Scientist Across the Solar System* (2 vols.)
Gustave Le Rouge. *The Mysterious Doctor Cornelius* (3 vols.); *The Vampires of Mars; The Dominion of the World* (w/Gustave Guitton) (4 vols.)
Jules Lermina. *Mysteryville; Panic in Paris; To-Ho and the Gold Destroyers; The Secret of Zippelius; The Battle of Strasbourg*
André Lichtenberger. *The Centaurs; The Children of the Crab*
Listonai. *The Philosophical Voyager*
Jean-Marc & Randy Lofficier. *Edgar Allan Poe on Mars; The Katrina Protocol; Pacifica; Robonocchio; Return of the Nyctalope;* (anthologists) *Tales of the Shadowmen 1-11; The Vampire Almanac* (2 vols.)
Xavier Mauméjean. *The League of Heroes*
Joseph Méry. *The Tower of Destiny*
Hippolyte Mettais. *The Year 5865; Paris Before the Deluge*
Louise Michel. *The Human Microbes; The New World*
Tony Moilin. *Paris in the Year 2000*
José Moselli. *Illa's End*
John-Antoine Nau. *Enemy Force*
Marie Nizet. *Captain Vampire*
C. Nodier, A. Beraud & Toussaint-Merle. *Frankenstein*
Henri de Parville. *An Inhabitant of the Planet Mars*
Gaston de Pawlowski. *Journey to the Land of the 4th Dimension*
Georges Pellerin. *The World in 2000 Years*
Ernest Pérochon. *The Frenetic People*
Pierre Pelot. *The Child Who Walked on the Sky*
J. Polidori, C. Nodier, E. Scribe. *Lord Ruthven the Vampire*
P.-A. Ponson du Terrail. *The Vampire and the Devil's Son; The Immortal Woman*
Georges Price. *The Missing Men of the Sirius*
Edgar Quinet. *Ahasuerus; The Enchanter Merlin*
Henri de Régnier. *A Surfeit of Mirrors*
Maurice Renard. *The Blue Peril; Doctor Lerne; The Doctored Man; A Man Among the Microbes; The Master of Light*
Jean Richepin. *The Wing; The Crazy Corner*

Albert Robida. *The Adventures of Saturnin Farandoul; The Clock of the Centuries; Chalet in the Sky; The Electric Life; The Engineer Von Satanas*
J.-H. Rosny Aîné. *Helgvor of the Blue River; The Givreuse Enigma; The Mysterious Force; The Navigators of Space; Vamireh; The World of the Variants; The Young Vampire*
Marcel Rouff. *Journey to the Inverted World*
Léonie Rouzade. *The World Turned Upside Down*
Han Ryner. *The Superhumans; The Human Ant*
Pierre de Selenes: *An Unknown World*
Angelo de Sorr. *The Vampires of London*
Brian Stableford. *The New Faust at the Tragicomique;The Empire of the Necromancers (The Shadow of Frankenstein; Frankenstein and the Vampire Countess; Frankenstein in London); Sherlock Holmes & The Vampires of Eternity; The Stones of Camelot; The Wayward Muse.* (anthologist) *News from the Moon; The Germans on Venus; The Supreme Progress; The World Above the World; Nemoville; Investigations of the Future; The Conqueror of Death; The Revolt of the Machines; The Man With the Blue Face*
Jacques Spitz. *The Eye of Purgatory*
Kurt Steiner. *Ortog*
Eugène Thébault. *Radio-Terror*
C.-F. Tiphaigne de La Roche. *Amilec*
Simon Tyssot de Patot. *The Strange Voyages of Jacques Massé and Pierre de Mésange*
Louis Ulbach. *Prince Bonifacio*
Théo Varlet. *The Golden Rock. The Xenobiotic Invasion; The Castaways of Eros; Timeslip Troopers* (w/André Blandin); *The Martian Epic* (w/Octave Joncquel)
Pierre Véron. *The Merchants of Health*
Paul Vibert. *The Mysterious Fluid*
Villiers de l'Isle-Adam. *The Scaffold; The Vampire Soul*
Gaston de Wailly. *The Murderer of the World*
Philippe Ward. *Artahe ; The Song of Montségur* (w/Sylvie Miller) *Manhattan Ghost* (w/Mickael Laguerre)

MYSTERIES & THRILLERS

M. Allain & P. Souvestre. *The Daughter of Fantômas*
A. Anicet-Bourgeois, Lucien Dabril. *Rocambole*

A. Bernède. *Belphegor*; *Judex* (w/Louis Feuillade); *The Return of Judex* (w/Louis Feuillade); *The Shadow of Judex*
A. Bisson & G. Livet. *Nick Carter vs. Fantômas*
V. Darlay & H. de Gorsse. *Arsène Lupin vs. Sherlock Holmes: The Stage Play*
Séamas Duffy. *Sherlock Holmes in Paris*
Paul Féval. *Gentlemen of the Night; John Devil; The Black Coats ('Salem Street; The Invisible Weapon; The Parisian Jungle; The Companions of the Treasure; Heart of Steel; The Cadet Gang; The Sword-Swallower)*
Émile Gaboriau. *Monsieur Lecoq*
Goron & Émile Gautier. *Spawn of the Penitentiary*
Paul d'Ivoi. *Around the World on Five Sous* (w/Henri Chabrillat)
Rick Lai. *Shadows of the Opera: Retribution in Blood; Sisters of the Shadows: The Curse of Cagliostro*
Steve Leadley. *Sherlock Holmes: The Circle of Blood*
Maurice Leblanc. *Arsène Lupin vs. Countess Cagliostro; Arsène Lupin vs. Sherlock Holmes (The Blonde Phantom; The Hollow Needle); The Many Faces of Arsène Lupin; The Island of the Thirty Coffin; 813*
Gaston Leroux. *Chéri-Bibi; The Phantom of the Opera; Rouletabille & the Mystery of the Yellow Room; Rouletabille at Krupp's*
Richard Marsh. *The Complete Adventures of Judith Lee*
William Patrick Maynard. *The Terror of Fu Manchu; The Destiny of Fu Manchu*
Frank J. Morlok. *Sherlock Holmes: The Grand Horizontals; Sherlock Holmes vs Jack the Ripper*
Jean Petithuguenin. *The Adventures of Ethel King*
Antonin Reschal. *The Adventures of Miss Boston*
Frank Schildiner. *The Quest of Frankenstein*
P. de Wattyne & Y. Walter. *Sherlock Holmes vs. Fantômas*
David White. *Fantômas in America*
Pierre Yrondy. *The Adventures of Thérèse Arnaud*

Victor Margueritte. *The Bacheloress; The Companion; The Couple*

SCREENPLAYS

Mike Baron. *The Iron Triangle*
Emma Bull & Will Shetterly. *Nightspeeder; War for the Oaks*
Gerry Conway & Roy Thomas. *Doc Dynamo*

Steve Englehart. *Majorca*
James Hudnall. *The Devastator*
Jean-Marc & Randy Lofficier. *Royal Flush*
J.-M. & R. Lofficier & Marc Agapit. *Despair*
J.-M. & R. Lofficier & Joël Houssin. *City*
Andrew Paquette. *Peripheral Vision*
Robert L. Robinson, Jr. *Judex*
R. Thomas, J. Hendler & L. Sprague de Camp. *Rivers of Time*

NON-FICTION

Stephen R. Bissette. *Blur 1-5. Green Mountain Cinema 1; Teen Angels*
Win Scott Eckert. *Crossovers* (2 vols.)
Jean-Marc & Randy Lofficier. *Shadowmen* (2 vols.)
Randy Lofficier. *Over Here*

ART BOOKS

Jean-Pierre Normand. *Science Fiction Illustrations*
Raven Okeefe. *Raven's L'il Critters; Rave's Faves*
Randy Lofficier & Raven Okeefe. *If Your Possum Go Daylight...*
Daniele Serra. *Illusions*
Randy Lofficier. *Over Here*

HEXAGON COMICS

Franco Frescura & Luciano Bernasconi. *Wampus*
Franco Frescura & Giorgio Trevisan. *CLASH*
L. Bernasconi, J.-M. Lofficier & Juan Roncagliolo. *Phenix*
Claude Legrand, J.-M. Lofficier & L. Bernasconi. *Kabur*
Franco Oneta. *Zembla*
L. Buffolente, Lofficier & J.-J. Dzialowski. *Strangers: Homicron*
Danilo Grossi. *Strangers: Jaydee*
Claude Legrand & Luciano Bernasconi. *Strangers: Starlock*
Thierry Mornet & Juan Roncagliolo. *Guardian of the Republic*
J.-M. Lofficier & others. *Strangers 0: Omens & Origins*
J.-M. Lofficier, M. Garcia, F. Blanco & J. Pima. *Strangers 1: Strangers in a Strange Land*

CPSIA information can be obtained
at www.ICGtesting.com
Printed in the USA
LVOW07s1529301117
558159LV00001B/6/P